A Terrible Mistake

The Murder of Frank Olson and the CIA's Secret Cold War Experiments

H.P. Albarelli, Jr.

Published by:
Trine Day LLC
PO Box 577
Walterville, OR 97489
1-800-556-2012
www.TrineDay.com
publisher@TrineDay.net

Library of Congress Control Number: 2009934693

Albarelli, H.P., Jr.
A Terrible Mistake: The Murder of Frank Olson and the CIA's Secret Cold
War Experiments—1st ed.
p. cm.   (acid-free paper)
Includes references and index.
(ISBN-13) 978-0-9777953-7-6 (ISBN-10) 0-9777953-7-3
1. Olson, Frank Rudolph, 1910-1953. 2. Olson, Frank Rudolph, 1910-1953–
Death. 3. United States–History 20th century. 4. Human experimentation in
psychology–United States–Moral and ethical aspects–Case studies. 5. Human
experimentation in psychology–United States–Psychological aspects–Case
studies. 6. Psychotropic drugs–Research–United States. 7. LSD drug 8. Psychological warfare–United States–History–20th century 9. Behavior modification–Research–United States. 10. United States–Central Intelligence Agency.
11. Intelligence agents–United States–Biographies. 12. Social control. 1. Title

First Edition
10 9 8 7 6 5 4 3 2 1

Printed in the USA
Distribution to the Trade by:
Independent Publishers Group (IPG)
814 North Franklin Street
Chicago, Illinois 60610
312.337.0747 / www.ipgbook.com

PUBLISHER'S FOREWORD

Because something is happening here
But you don't know what it is
Do you, Mister Jones?
—Bob Dylan

The week after high school graduation, I "ran-away" from home. It was 1967, and I was 17 and had barely made the pomp walk, not because of grades, but hair. Late in my senior year my "Modern Problems" teacher kicked me out of his class. I thought, "Great ... don't have to come to school till third period." Soon I was in the principal's office watching my mother cry. I wasn't going to be allowed to graduate because my hair was over my ears. I cut my hair.

A few days after tossing the tassel, I wrote a note to the folks, said I was taking off for some time on my own, and hitchhiked down to Southern California to see an old grade school buddy.

Whoa, what a culture shock, small-town Oregon versus Los Angeles. Now, I had been in the big city before as a visitor, but never to run with the locals. My friend's school was still in session, so I went along with him for several days, celebrated his graduation, and went out on the town. California kids were wild, betting hundreds of dollars on street races in their cars, sneaking into strip clubs and on to private beaches, drinking and carousing, heck they even had their own drunk tank at their high school's graduation dance.

My folks had contacted my friend's parents before I even got there — it was decided I was simply taking a "vacation." After a week or so, it was time to start heading home. *Light My Fire* by the Doors was all over the radio, and the DJs were talking about an event, with a bunch of bands, up the road. I said goodbye to my friend and stuck out my thumb.

There's something happening here
What it is ain't exactly clear
—Buffalo Springfield

I had stumbled upon the Monterey International Pop Music Festival. My friend had jokingly told me about some of his old drinking buddies who wore nothing but white sheets and hung out at an esoteric bookstore. I didn't visit, but Monterey more than introduced me to a new phenomenon then booming through my generation.

By the time I got to the Monterey County Fairgrounds, I was broke and hungry, and began searching the ground for a dime to buy an orange or an apple (the cheapest food I could see for sale). My eyes spied a white envelope, I picked it up, written on the envelope was "Jones," inside was a ticket to get into the arena, and in I went. Blues Project started the show, Mammas & Papas closed the night, with Hendrix, Joplin, the Who, the Grateful Dead, and others sprinkled in between.

It may have been the music, or maybe the fact that I never found that dime, no matter, I got a "contact" high. Something was definitely happening here ... LSD. Published reports have Augustus Owsley Stanley III giving out 14,000 tabs, free.

And they thought it couldn't happen here
They knew it couldn't happen here
They were so sure it couldn't happen here
But ...
—Mothers of Invention

A Terrible Mistake, presents the hidden history of government activity with LSD, and of other covert initiatives that were coordinated by a small secretive cadre. Their actions have affected many, many people ... dramatically. "They" even lost lives — some cry "murder!" — and covered up the deeds. Bureaucracies are like that.

In the Machiavellian hubris of our day, power is dealt from the shadows, laying waste to our Constitution, while tricks and games enthrall an increasingly scratching populace. People are forced to the ground, allowed only to raise their heads to squabble on cue. Ours is a debased dysfunctional Republic, where our people are obese, our prisons are full, our schoolchildren do with less (some even homeless), our coins have slugs in them, our wars fought more and more by mercenaries, and our free press isn't — all while asking our children and those yet to be born ... to foot the bill.

Is this just the way of the world? Or are we seeing consequences from dark actions taken by a few — in secret, beyond supervision and reproach?

My father, a repentent "spook," in a 1979 interview, said: "It's a far more constructive experience to work for the church than to work for the Central Intelligence Agency. When you work for the CIA, the end justifies the means."

LSD was seen as a means to an end. Operations Bluebird, MKULTRA and all the other secret projects were seen as means to an end. The shattered and dead people were means to an end. The lies, secrecy and cover-ups were means to an end. Have we arrived at the "ends" desired?

TrineDay is amazed and pleased to be publishing *A Terrible Mistake*, a work while examining the veiled forecasted ends, exposes many of the wayward shoddy means, and *at last* — through the author's perseverance plus a little kismet — puts to rest an old official lie with the simple, mundane ... truth.

Oh, what's going on
What's going on
Ya, what's going on
Ah, what's going on
—Marvin Gaye

Onwards to the utmost of futures,
Peace,
Kris Millegan
Publisher
TrineDay
September 22, 2009

Where else could a red-blooded American boy lie, kill, cheat, steal, rape, and pillage with the sanction and blessing of the All-Highest?"

— George Hunter White

This book is for my children, Damien, Nicole, and David, and for Samantha, and for their children, who have yet to come into this sad and glorious world.

I'm interested in what happens in history, what history hides, what gets left out, and what is forgotten.

— Henry Bromell, *Little America*

History is on our heels, following us like our shadows, like death.

— Marc Auge, *Non-Places: An Introduction to an Anthropology of Supermodernity*

Even in this world more things exist without our knowledge than with it and the order in creation which you see is that which you have put there, like a string in a maze, so that you shall not lose your way. For existence has its own order and that no man's mind can compass, that mind itself being but a fact among others..

— Cormac McCarthy, *Blood Meridian*

The moon, silent and fatal, Hecate with her sidelong and wandering glances, griffins, lemurs, bloody hydras, hybrid monsters, fatal divinities of the night doze in the depths of the gorge and in the abysses of shadow.

— Gustave Moreau, 1897

Dr. Olson
Killed In
Hotel Plunge

Bacteriologist At
Camp Detrick Had
Been Here Ten Years;
Had College Degrees

Dr. Frank R. Olson, 42, of Old Braddock, a bacteriologist at Camp Detrick, fell or jumped to his death early today from a tenth floor room at Hotel Statler in New York City, the Associated Press reported.

Olson, according to the AP dispatch, was in New York with a friend, Robert Vern Lashbrook, a Defense Department chemist, to see a doctor. They had planned to return home today. However, early this morning Lashbrook was awakened to see his companion crash through window, shade and glass. Olson's underwear-clad body struck a fourth floor ledge and then landed on the side-walk.

A former captain with the Army Chemical Corps, Olson had been despondent over ill health, friends here stated. He had resided here with his wife since 1943, and he was well-known locally. All the children were born here.

He received B.S. and Ph.D. degrees from the University of Wisconsin and worked for a while at Lafayette, Ind. Survivors include his wife, Mr. [sic] Alice Wicks Olson; three children, Eric, 9; Lisa, 7, and Nils, 5; his mother , Mrs. Olaf Nelson, Hurley, Wis.; one brother, John H. Olson, Mt. Clemens, Mich., and a sister, Mrs. Hilda Anderson, Ironwood, Mich., one niece and one nephew.

-The News, Frederick, MD,
Saturday, November 28,1953

Dr. Frank Olson, 42, Bacteriologist, Dies In Hotel Plunge

Army Chemical Corps Expert Held in High Esteem by Colleagues

Dr. Frank R. Olson, 42, an Army Chemical Corps bacteriologist from Old Braddock, Md., fell or jumped to his death early today from a New York hotel room.

According to police, Dr. Olson, who worked at the biological laboratories at Camp Dietrich [sic], Md., arrived in New York Tuesday to see a doctor. He had been ill for several months and had become despondent. A colleague, Robert Van [sic] Lashbrook, accompanied Him. They planned to return home today.

Early this morning, however, Mr. Lashbrook awoke to see Dr. Olson crash through a window in their 10th floor room at the Hotel Statler, the Associated Press reported. Dr. Olson's body struck a fourth-floor ledge and fell to the sidewalk.

A Camp Dietrich [sic] spokesman said that Dr. Olson had been suffering from a severe case of ulcers, but had remained at work until Tuesday. He said that the bacteriologist , who had been at Camp Dietrich [sic] for several years, had been in "high esteem both personally and professionally" Surviving Dr. Olson are Mrs. Olson and three children.

-**The Evening Star,
Washington, D.C.,
November 28,1953**

Scientist Killed In Hotel Plunge

Frank Olson, forty-two, a bacteriologist for the Defense Department in Washington, was killed early yesterday in a plunge from a tenth-story room at the Hotel Statler, Seventh Ave. and 33rd St., police reported. Detective John Ward said he was identified by Robert Vern Lashbrook, thirty-five, a Defense Department chemist, who was sharing a room at the hotel with him. Mr. Olson's address was given as Route 5, Frederick, Md. Police said he has a wife and three children. Mr. Lashbrook was quoted by officers as saying he accompanied him here because Mr. Olson wanted to see doctors about a depressed state. Mr. Lashbrook told police they had been here since Nov. 24 and planned to return to Washington today. Detective Ward quoted Dr. Harold Abramson of 133 E. 58th St., as saying he had three visits from Mr. Olson in the last few days and that he was suffer-from a severe psychosis.

-*New York Herald Tribune*,
November 29, 1953

Introduction

I know something about obsessions.

Sinister Forces was an obsession that lasted more than twenty-five years as I researched, investigated, and interviewed for a book that turned into three volumes and more than a thousand pages, and even then only scratched the surface of the dark side of American history.

So, when I met Hank Albarelli for the first time in Florida some years ago I recognized a fellow traveler. Hank's obsession with the Frank Olson story has led him on a wild and often dangerous ride through the haunted American landscape of the 1950s and beyond. It examines some of the most nefarious aspects of the American intelligence community during the bleak atmosphere of the Cold War, and in doing so raises serious and so-far unanswered questions about the ethics of our mind control, behavior control and psychological warfare policies. No one who looks into this particular abyss comes away from the experience unaffected by it.

I don't want to give away the story that Hank has uncovered, or any of the juicy details or important discoveries that will change the way you look at this case. You need to read this book carefully, cover to cover, to understand the enormity of what transpired that autumn evening in midtown Manhattan. The number of interconnected links between people, places and events is astounding. Familiar names like Dick Cheney and Donald Rumsfeld turn up, as well as Warren Burger and Rudolph Giuliani, Howard Hughes and Robert Maheu; less familiar names like John Rousselot - an American congressman and John Bircher accused of being involved in the assassination plot against President Kennedy - also make an appearance. A walk through Hank Albarelli's masterful presentation of the Frank Olson case is like a tour of American political and cultural life during the last sixty years or more ... and, at the same time, it is a descent into a very particular hell. (Is there such a thing as *negative* nostalgia?)

Here we read of the CIA's interest in the occult, in Edgar Cayce, UFOs, parapsychology, and in the strange visions of the Book of Ezekiel ... I am not making this up.

Here we read of so many other victims of the mind control programs that we are forced to accept that Frank Olson represents only the tip of a satanic iceberg. Innocent people were falling like flies all over America in the 1950s, like the textile plant workers in New Hampshire who were infected with anthrax without their knowledge because their mill was doing work on the side in chemical and biological weapons research. Or the detective in Houston, Texas who committed "suicide" by shooting himself in the heart ... twice.

If anyone has any doubts that Congress should investigate cases of torture and human rights abuses allegedly carried out by members of the intelligence community during the Iraq conflict, one only needs to review the Frank Olson case. Our failure to fully investigate this scientist's death in 1953 contributed to further and ongoing abuses throughout the 1950s and 1960s. The very people – Cheney and Rumsfeld – who defended the CIA's actions in those cases when news of the CIA and military programs were exposed in 1975 are defending them again now, decades later, in a different guise and a different arena. In those days, it was MKULTRA, MKNAOMI, MKOFTEN, MKCHICKWIT, and of course Operations BLUEBIRD and ARTICHOKE. These are legendary names today; the stuff of pulp fiction and celluloid fantasy. But real people were drugged in those programs without their knowledge or consent. Men. Women. Children. Prisoners. Psychopaths. Prostitutes. Foreigners. Many of them were never the same again. Some went insane. Some died as a result.

And no one was held accountable.

Today we have Abu Ghraib, extraordinary rendition, waterboarding. Our excuse today – as it was then – is national security. Hank Albarelli very helpfully reminds us of what Bella Abzug – the New York Congresswoman in the funny hats that the right wing loved to hate – said during the 1975 investigation of the CIA's mind control programs::

> You cannot be strong outside if you are weak inside. You have to de- fend your own principles in order to be able to fight for acceptance of your principles in other places in the world....
> The question of the protection of our liberties and our freedom is the basis upon which this country remains strong.

That was in 1975. Nearly thirty-five years ago. What Hank Albarelli reminds us in this invaluable record of a "terrible mistake" is that we have yet to learn from those terrible mistakes

Or, more likely, not enough of us really care.

Hank Albarelli cares. And his concern is our gain. Part mystery story, part history, thoroughly documented and completely compelling, *A Terrible Mistake* is required reading for anyone interested in the lengths we have gone, to defend the nation against all enemies (foreign, domestic, and the purely imaginary) .. and, incredibly, against our own loyal and patriotic citizens.

Peter Levenda
2009

ACKNOWLEDGMENTS

Books like this one do not happen without the sincere aid and abetment of a good number of people. Here I must give thanks for the invaluable support these people provided me. First and foremost, researching and writing this book would not have been possible without Kathleen Rose McDonald, who never once flinched or hesitated when the skies grew darkest and the nights seemed endless. For that, and much more, I am forever grateful. Thank you, my daughter, Nicole Albarelli, who understood from the very start what this book is really about. Thank you, my sons, Damien Albarelli and David Albarelli, who provided more support than they can imagine by simply believing and being there every time I needed them.

My father, H.P. Albarelli, Sr., who perhaps understands the story of Frank Olson better than anyone I know, and my mother, Mary Nancy O'Neill, were also present, as always, without any doubts or concerns. A very special thanks goes to my mother who taught me something that I'll always hold high: her understanding of humankind and equality. While writing this book, I encountered numerous— indeed, far too many— instances of human subjects separated out for government-sponsored experiments only because they were African-Americans. When I interviewed some of the people responsible for this, I was consistently told that I didn't understand "how it was in the 1950s and 1960s," and that I didn't appreciate how people thought then and how they conformed to the times. These people, and their excuses, are wrong. I do, and did, understand, because my mother went out of her way, often at serious costs to our family, to have her children know that every human being is essential and has the same value, and that color and race are artificial constructs fashioned by petty men who need to dominate others.

My very special, heartfelt appreciation goes to Tammy Jean Ryea for attempting to keep me alive spiritually, to the extent possible, for always being there to help, and for being truly a lifelong friend. Tammy's amazing daughter, Samantha Eagles Ryea, offered absolute, unaffected joy and the world's most beautiful smile. I suspect she will become a fearless world traveler, great artist, and fine writer herself one day.

A million thanks go to Laura McDonald, who dug up a virtual gold mine on Jean-Pierre Lafitte.

My sincerest thanks and gratitude to Kris Milligan, my publisher, who was solidly there every step of the way, always understanding, patient, and ready to help. I dare say there is not another publisher like Kris anywhere in this world.

Margot White, my editor, with astounding skills and expertise took nearly one thousand, single spaced pages and turned them into a far better read than I ever imagined. Margot's wide range of experience in law, medicine, and human rights was invaluable to this book.

To Amber Lauren Smith, an extraordinary writer, who looked at many of my drafted pages early on; special gratitude and appreciation to Cali for putting up with a lot of negligence and impatience, but still being this man's best friend and always protecting me without personal concern. Thanks to my faithful readers Sylvana Lane, Keese Lane, Leah Soon Gardner, Daniel Gardner, and Kate Albarelli. I must give a very special shout-out to Paul Centellas, whose stars will soon dominate the constellations. Laura Ovitt also deserves my gratitude for sharing some very kind words.

As always, my very humble appreciation to my mentors, Robert Moore Williams, Richard Greene, Gladys Colburn, Howard Heflin, and Steve Tesich for pointing me in the proper directions and for seeing qualities in me others had not noticed. Richard Greene took the time to pry open a world for me I never knew existed.

David Kairys, Esq. was helpful and kind beyond the call of duty. If I were ever to need expert legal assistance I can think of no better lawyer anywhere than David.

William Hayward, producer of the seminal film, *Easy Rider*, who shared with me his less than pleasurable experiences with Dr. Lawrence Kubie, thus helping me catch a glimpse of what makes the mind of a "psychiatric icon" work. Bill and I corresponded extensively about Kubie, and I was tremendously saddened when I learned that Bill's boyhood demons had once again taken hold of him causing him to kill himself on March 9, 2008. I know that Bill very much wanted to read this book, and I would like to think that he still will.

A special thanks to Senator Gary Hart for his most helpful answers to my questions about his search for assassin QJ/WIN. Dr. Alan A. Block and his wife, Sharon Weaver, were very helpful and most kind. I will always fondly remember their warm hospitality.

Others who were most helpful are Eric Wicks Olson for tolerating my cynicism, providing me with a small mountain of emails, and answering my pesky questions over a period of five years; Paul Wolf, Washington, D.C. attorney extraordinaire; Daniel Brandt of Namebase.com, a superb repository of invaluable information; Peter Dale Scott; Jim Hougan; John F. Kelly; and Eddie Becker, all for hacking away a thick and heavy jungle of concealing vines.

I sincerely thank Belinda Blauer for her kindness and assistance with obtaining documents concerning her father's needless and painful death.

Dr. Daniel Winkler, at Harvard University, was always there to assist and to provide honest feedback and answers, as was Dr. Marjorie Senechal at Smith College.

Thanks to Ed Regis for expert assistance with biological warfare research and intros to several hard to locate people; Gary Hunt, Editor, *Magical Past-Times*, for expert information on magician John Mulholland; Mike Edwards for an excellent article and information on Mulholland; Uri Geller for insightful information on Henry Puharich; Stephen Endicott for expertise on the Korean War and biological warfare; investigative reporter Paul Avery for his insights into George Hunter White; Robert King, an extraordinary photojournalist, who unselfishly shared information about Garland Williams; Suzie Halewood, who was more than patient with me; Terry Sanderlin for bringing his brother Rex to my attention; Jack O'Connell, for writing the kind of novels that make reading a true pleasure, complete adventure, and escape from the crush of everydayism; Harry Huge, Esq. Eric Olson's attorney, and Richard A Medway, Esq. of Powell, Goldstein, Frazer & Murphy, LLP; and Allison Scopelliti, who made life easy when it should not have been; David Landsberg, a breath of fresh air in Justice's fouled corridor; psychologist Jeff Kaye for some very kind comments, and for standing up for what is right; and Corey Copeland for corresponding about Dr. H.E. Himwich.

A very special thanks to J.P. Mahoney, Brennan Mahoney, and David Cromer, better friends than a man could wish for. J.P., from the distance of Kansas, many, many moons ago, convinced me that good writing for the mind could be like fine music to the ears. One of these days soon, Cromer, I'm going to join you on that island paradise. Thanks to Linda Zurit, for her friendship, wit and eternal wisdom; Dr. Kitty McGinnis for attempting to take care of my inner-self; David Boys, life's perpetual drummer and all around cool fellow; Lucien Conien for figuratively yanking shrapnel from my wounds and shoving me back into awareness; John Marks for paving the way and sharing needed information; Albertine White for tolerating me as well as her husband, George; Rachael Wagner of the Perham Foundation; "Phen" Lafitte for her most kind assistance, hospitality, and patience; Rene Lafitte for her honesty and help with understanding an obscure man and his history; Roscoe Winterbottom for staying in there like a ghost who wisely chooses his entrances and exits; Marcel Martin; C.M. Mondolini; Dr. John Beresford; Dr. Jean Delay; Owsley Agustus Stanley; Al Haney; Janet Phelan and Dr. Aimee Phelan, who kindly pointed the way to Pierre Lafitte's New Hampshire location; and Sidney Gottlieb's attorney Tom Wilson, all of whom helped immensely. Very special thanks to writers Linda Hunt and Peter Levenda. Linda helped me tremendously with documents that seemed impossible to obtain, and her book on Project Paperclip is an expertly researched modern classic. Peter's *Sinister Forces* volumes go a long way toward explaining the hidden and major powers behind so much that we fail to see and fathom.

Very sincere thanks are in order to former private investigator and superb writer Sally Denton, who many years ago in Washington, D.C. and Denver, Colorado taught me the value of digging deeper and deeper and looking for the *complete* story; to writer and Fox Television reporter James Rosen for asking E. Howard Hunt my questions; to writer Len Colodny, who knows better than most who *they* are; to the CIA's Kathryn I. Dyer and Lee Strickland for their patient assistance and for aiding in my baptism by fire into the convoluted FOIA process; to Armond Pastore, for planting the first seeds leading toward solving the case, and for his friendship, honesty, hospitality, and terrific homemade bread. I miss him dearly.

My most sincere thanks to Dr. Sidney Gottlieb for always taking my calls and speaking truthfully. Dr. Gottlieb, despite all the unkind things written about him, was nothing less than a kind and respectful man to me; my thanks to Richard Helms for taking the time to clarify and explain certain important matters to me; Robert V. Lashbrook, for helping more than he ever thought he did; Hazel Ruwet for speaking with me; Arthur Vidich for his sincere words and honesty; the Gerald Ford Presidential Library; Cormac McCarthy for reinventing masculine reality; and masterful musicians Joey Fehrenbach, Moby, Teddy Thompson, Buddy Guy, Radiohead, Thom Yorke, Boz Scaggs, Pilot Speed, Lifehouse, Matthew Ryan, Dave Seaman, Nick Warren, Faithless, Dido, and Paul Lewis for providing the soundtrack for this book.

Thanks are in order for Katharine Higgon, Kings College Archives, London, UK; Daniel Brandt of Name Base; the National Security Archives, George Washington University; David Presswell, the type of fellow all television producers should be; Bill Curtis at A&E television; Courtney Bullock at NBC in New York for understanding what no one else did, and for providing me with assistance never expected; Spring Grove Psychiatric Hospital in Catonsville, Maryland for giving up its archives and artifacts; to writers Christopher Simpson and Edward Hooper for their excellent research and indispensable books.

I would be remiss not to thank Nolan Albarelli for his service to his country and his letters from Iraq; my brothers Michael and Dean, and my sisters Nancy and Beth for offering shelter from the storm; and, of course, Michael Heflin Albarelli and his beautiful wife and daughter, Masha and Alexandra.

Polly Armstrong at Stanford University; Manhattan Assistant District Attorneys Steve Saracco and Dan Bibb; Owen Winkle, for admitting that only the truth survives the test of time; the staff at the National Archives in Washington, D.C. and Maryland; the National Security Archives, George Washington University; Dr. Michael Neve; and two honest, caring, good, decent and understanding men who must remain unnamed, but not by any means unrecognized for opening the Way to the Truth.

In Richford, Vermont, where I holed up to write this book, I thank David and Reba Ryea, and Richard and Prudy Ryea and their fine family, all wonderful folks and the salt of the earth; Jim Backhaus, my occasional co-pilot; Joe

Pollender, world's most decent man; Ronald West, the nation's best fiddler; and Bill Wright, Steve Sheperd, Doug Kidder, Jane Kidder, Mark Marston, Yvonne Combs, a woman who genuinely cares about small town Vermont, Marion and Doug Paul, Richard and Diane McAllister, Rick Longe, James Longe, Alfred and Carolyn Gendron, Jim Guilmette, David Derby and Hilary Hardy, and Orsene Hogan, all of whom wear the hearty tradition of New England perseverance like rightful badges of honor; to Mary Robinson for always asking how the book was going; to Brian and Patty Lariviere for kindly keeping a close eye on my house and files while I was away; to Gene and Kathy Pynduss for being good neighbors; and to Helena Murray, Diane Gates, Tammy Cox, Brenda Lamb, Lou and Arn Byam, and Catherine Harkness.

My gratitude to Jen Huppert, Justin Walters, Dr. Katherine Ramsland, and my terrific *World Net Daily* editor Ron Strom for being the first to recognize the complexities of the Olson story; to John Sugg, former editor at Tampa's *Weekly Planet*, for being the second; and to Crime Magazine editor Pat O'Connor for being the third.

Jacob Yager and Jason Edwards, we love you, deeply miss you both, and wish every day that you both were here with us.

My heartfelt appreciation goes to Polly Crandlemire, who always kept the door open to me, no matter how foul my mood; with a very special 'thank you' to her husband and my good friend, Dick Crandlemire, for reading every page of this book multiple times with eyes well-trained by years with the federal government in Maine, Vermont, Florida, Laos, and Thailand, and for providing the kind of editorial feedback that made it a far better read.

Thanks to Samantha's Squeaky, the ultimate cool cat, who never fails to sense whatever needs sensing; and to the late Jonathan Wind, a great photographer, who died far too young. My deeply felt thanks and love go to Bruce and Kellie Maitland and their daughter and son, Brianna and Waylon, and Waylon's beautiful wife, and to Maura Murray, wherever she is, and to Maura's saintly father Fred. Unfortunately, the Maitlands and Fred know all too well that there is little justice in the world. Despite concerns far more important than mine, the Maitlands always asked how the book was going and were there to help; to Greg Overacker, world's best private detective, a rock amidst a sea of pebbles; and all the wonderful and beautiful ladies at Richford's Pinnacle Peddler, especially Christine Cooper, Paulette Legault, Sue Nutting, Katie St. Pierre, Claudette Garrow, Lynn Broderick, and Carolyn Smith, for keeping me supplied with the finest food and bake goods in all of New England. Lastly, I know I've forgotten some people and for that I ask their sincere forgiveness. *Salus populi suprema lex.*

Deep Creek Lake & New York City Timeline

WEDNESDAY, NOVEMBER 18, 1953 —
— Deep Creek Lake conference begins in evening.

THURSDAY, NOVEMBER 19 —
— Around 7:30 P.M., Frank Olson is drugged with LSD at the Deep Creek Lake meeting.

FRIDAY, NOVEMBER 20 — 9:00 A.M.
— Olson leaves Deep Creek Lake for Camp Detrick; he arrives home around 5:00 P.M.

SATURDAY-SUNDAY, NOVEMBER 21-22 —
— Olson is at home with his wife and family.

MONDAY, NOVEMBER 23 —
7:30 A.M. Olson is waiting for Ruwet in Ruwet's Camp Detrick office.

TUESDAY, NOVEMBER 24 —
7:30 A.M. — Olson is again in Ruwet's office at Camp Detrick.
8:45 A.M. — Ruwet calls Robert Lashbrook.
9:30 A.M. — Olson returns home to speak with Alice Olson.
Midday — On the way to CIA headquarters, Ruwet, John Malinowski, Olson and his wife stop at Hot Shoppe in Bethesda, Maryland for lunch.
1:00 P.M. — Olson and his wife arrive at CIA headquarters in Washington, D.C.
2:30 P.M. — Olson, Ruwet, and Lashbrook board flight for New York City
5:00 P.M. — in New York City, Olson meets with Dr. Harold Abramson at 133 East 58th Street.
6:30 P.M.— Olson, Ruwet and Lashbrook go to Statler Hotel and check-in.
10:30 P.M. — Dr. Abramson visits Olson's room at Statler Hotel.
12:00 midnight — Dr. Abramson leaves Olson's room.

WEDNESDAY, NOVEMBER 25 —
10:30 A.M. — Olson, Ruwet, and Lashbrook have breakfast.
1:00 P.M. — Ruwet and Olson accompany Lashbrook "on an official visit" most likely to the Bedford Street safe house.
4:00 P.M. — Visit is cut short and Ruwet, Olson, and Lashbrook go to Dr. Abramson's office for 4:00 P.M. appointment. Lashbrook and Ruwet leave Olson with Abramson.
5:00 P.M. — Lashbrook and Ruwet return to pick Olson up at Abramson's office.

7:00 P.M. – Ruwet, Lashbrook, and Olson have dinner together.

8:30 P.M. – Ruwet, Lashbrook, and Olson go to Broadway show.

– Ruwet and Olson leave show at intermission and walk back to Statler Hotel.

10:30 P.M. – Ruwet and Olson arrive at Statler Hotel.

11:15 P.M. – Lashbrook returns to Statler Hotel.

THURSDAY, NOVEMBER 26 –

5:30 A.M. – Ruwet awakens at 5:30 to find Olson not in the room they share.

5:35 A.M. – Ruwet wakes Lashbrook in adjoining room.

6:00 A.M. – Ruwet and Lashbrook find Olson in Statler Hotel lobby.

6:30 A.M. (approximately) – Ruwet, Lashbrook, and Olson check out of hotel and go by taxi to LaGuardia airport for 7:30 A.M. flight to Washington, D.C.

8:30 A.M. – Ruwet, Lashbrook, and Olson arrive in Washington.

8:45 A.M. – Lashbrook takes a taxi to his home; John Malinowski picks up Ruwet and Olson at airport and drives them into D.C.

9:20 A.M. – Olson asks Malinowski to stop the car so he can speak with Ruwet.

9:30 A.M. – Ruwet calls Lashbrook at home.

10:30 A.M. – Ruwet and Malinowski drop Olson off at Lashbrook's apartment at 1833 New Hampshire Ave., N.W., D.C. and then continue on to Frederick, Maryland.

11:30 A.M. – Dr. Sidney Gottlieb arrives at Lashbrook's apartment.

12:00 noon – Gottlieb drives Lashbrook and Olson to Washington airport.

2:00 P.M. – Olson and Lashbrook arrive back in New York City and go by taxi from LaGuardia airport to Dr. Abramson's residence at 47 New Street, Huntington, Long Island, arriving there at about 4:00 P.M.

4:00 P.M. – Abramson meets with Olson for about 45 minutes and then with Lashbrook and Olson together for about 15 minutes.

5:20 P.M. (approx.) – Abramson takes Lashbrook and Olson to the nearby Anchorage Guest House, Cold Spring Harbor, where the two men check in for the night.

7:00 P.M. – Olson and Lashbrook have Thanksgiving dinner at a local restaurant.

FRIDAY, NOVEMBER 27 –

8:15 A.M. – Dr. Harold Abramson meets Lashbrook and Olson at guesthouse and drives them to his New York City office.

– All three men meet in Abramson's office for about 2 hours.

1:30 P.M. (approx.) – Lashbrook and Olson return to Statler Hotel, check-in, and are given Room 1018A.

4:00 P.M. – Olson and Lashbrook have martinis in the hotel cocktail lounge.

6:00 P.M. – Olson and Lashbrook have dinner in the hotel's main dining room.

10:00 P.M. – Olson calls his wife a little before 10:00 P.M.

10:00 P.M. – Olson and Lashbrook return to Room 1018A.

10:00 P.M. (shortly after) – Lashbrook calls Ruwet.

11:00 P.M. – Lashbrook and Olson watch television until 11:00 P.M. and then retire for the night.

SATURDAY, NOVEMBER 28 –

2:25 a.m. – Lashbrook wakes at the sound of a loud crashing noise. Olson falls from hotel window and is dead five minutes later.

2:45 A.M. – Ruwet receives a telephone call from Gottlieb informing him that Olson is dead.

TABLE of CONTENTS

Prologue

In all chaos there is a cosmos, in all disorder a secret order.
— Carl Jung

It's a poor sort of memory that only works backwards.
— Lewis Carroll

It is February 16, 2000, a cold, gray morning in Manhattan. I'm sitting in a large, nondescript office, at the head of an old conference table that looks like it came from a government surplus warehouse. Stuck to the breast pocket of my suit jacket is an orange badge that reads: "Visitor Pass, District Attorney's Office, County of New York." I'm in the domain of the doyen of American district attorneys, Robert M. Morgenthau. Three windows on the far side of the room, overlooking the street below, are covered by Venetian blinds, despite the fact that the room's overhead lights are dim and half of them are either turned off or burned out.

Two other men are seated at the conference table a few empty chairs away from me. They are shuffling the files they have before them. The shorter of the two, with dark, closely cropped hair and wearing a gray suit, a crisp white shirt and nondescript tie, asks me again if I want more coffee. My cup is nearly full, so I thank him and say, "No, I'm fine, really."

The other man is much taller and more muscular than his partner. Nodding toward the room's open door, he says, "He'll be here any second. I passed him out in the hallway on my way in."

As if on cue, moments later, a light-haired man in a rumpled white shirt and tie, enters the room, balancing a styrofoam cup of coffee on top of a small stack of file folders, apologizing as he takes the chair closest to me.

The dark haired man, Assistant District Attorney Steve Saracco, introduces the light-haired man as "Warren," a detective assigned to the Frank Olson case. The detective offers his hand in greeting. "I'm glad you decided to come up," he says.

"Well," says Saracco, "I guess we can get started now." He looks at me and nods, "Maybe the best way to proceed is for you to tell us who killed Olson and why."

"That's getting right to the point," I say, thinking Saracco is every bit the tough former Marine he was described to be. "You don't want any background information, just the facts and nothing but the facts?" I ask.

Saracco sounds like the character Jack Webb on the popular television show, *Dragnet*. This is the first time we have met in person. Over the past six months I've spoken to him weekly on the telephone. Now, after nearly a month of trying to agree to dates and times, I've traveled to New York to meet with Saracco and his Cold Case Unit partner, Dan Bibb, also an Assistant District Attorney.

"Sounds good," Saracco says.

I name the two men who killed Frank Rudolph Olson on November 28, 1953, just two miles away from where we are all seated now on the sixth floor of One Hogan Place.

The room is silent for a few seconds, and then Bibb slowly speaks, "I've never heard either one of those names. How do they fit into all of this?"

"Is it okay to give some background now?" I ask.

"Sounds like we need it," the detective replies quietly.

I'm not at all sure where to begin. I take a deep breath, a sip of coffee, and start by explaining how I first became interested in the long and strange case of Frank Olson's death.

I skip the real beginning of my interest, which took place in a Catonsville, Maryland fast food restaurant, long since closed. I had taken my eight-year old daughter, Nicole, there after school. We were enjoying our soft drinks and a large order of French fries, when she conspiratorially leaned across the table toward me and whispered, "Dad, don't look now, but we're the only normal people in this place."

Nicole was right. Much to her dismay, I had looked around. Only four other tables and a booth were occupied at that mid-afternoon hour, but there was no question that the occupants were decidedly peculiar characters. One bearded, older man seated closest to us was carefully constructing some sort of tower out of straws, sugar packets, napkins, and plastic eating utensils. A lone woman, perhaps in her mid-seventies, seated at a table near the man, was carrying on an animated, serious, discussion with the empty chair across from her, which she addressed as "Norman." At the table next to her, a middle-age woman sat stiffly, unblinking, staring straight ahead. She held her hands out in front of her with her palms turned upward as if in offering. At a nearby booth, two men appeared to be playing cards, but when I looked more closely I saw that their game was nonsensical. Neither man spoke to the other or looked at each other. Periodically, one of the men would slap his hand down on the table and recite a string of numbers.

"Weird, huh," said Nicole.

"Yes," I said, perplexed and not at all sure how to account for the bizarre tableau before us.

My neighbor, a mathematics teacher at the local high school, solved the mystery for us a few days later. As newcomers to Catonsville, we were unaware that just a few miles from our new home was Spring Grove Mental Hospital, a State-operated facility and the nation's second oldest psychiatric hospital, founded in 1797 "for the reception and care of lunatics."

"During the fifties and sixties they did a lot of stuff here with LSD and other drugs," my neighbor explained.

"Stuff?"

"Experiments, crazy things. A lot of the test subjects still live around here. The Roy Rogers restaurant is a sort of gathering place for them."

I had read about the early government-sponsored experiments with LSD, but had thought little more about the incident or Spring Grove Hospital until about six months later. On that day, June 3, 1994, I read on the front page of the Metro section of the *Washington Post* that the body of biochemist Dr. Frank Olson, buried for forty years in nearby Frederick, Maryland, had been exhumed. Olson's two surviving sons had assembled a team of forensic scientists to examine the body. Eric and Nils Olson were questioning the cause of their father's death. They suspected it had resulted from foul play and not suicide, as had been claimed in 1953 by a Manhattan medical examiner. Their suspicions, according to the *Washington Post* article, seemed to rest on shaky ground, but the story reminded me that there had been an earlier, sensational story about Frank Olson's LSD-fueled suicide that had been in all the major papers for weeks in the summer of 1975.

I recalled from those earlier stories that, for reasons I could not remember, Olson had been dosed with LSD by the CIA and then, about a week later, had jumped from a high window in a New York City hotel. Now, for reasons that were again unclear, Frank Olson's name was once more in the news. That sunny day in 1994 as I sat with the newspaper spread out on the kitchen table, I wondered if there could be any link between the CIA and whatever had happened with LSD at Spring Grove Hospital. Very doubtful, I thought, but you never know. I was nearly forty-six years old and was becoming increasingly aware that truth was far stranger than fiction in our world.

After all, I reminded myself, hadn't President Richard Nixon, or one of his White House henchmen, conspired to dose a number of reporters and media figures, including Jack Anderson and Brit Hume, with LSD? Hadn't a CIA physician instructed either G. Gordon Liddy or E. Howard Hunt how to swab the drug onto an automobile's steering wheel? Hadn't someone plotted to do something similar to Daniel Ellsberg after he revealed the Pentagon Papers?

What, if any, were the links between those stories and Frank Olson, I wondered. Hadn't the CIA also plotted not only to have Fidel Castro assassinated, but also to poison him with exotic chemicals brewed at the very place where Frank Olson worked, Camp Detrick? What, exactly, had been Dr. Olson's job at that facility?

In a manner of speaking, I was hooked on the mystery of the Olson case then and there. Why hadn't anyone looked into all these bizarre stories that seemed to turn on LSD and to be somehow related? What was the common denominator? What was the CIA's role in the steady march of LSD across the nation in the 1960s and 1970s? How many people besides Frank Olson had been unwittingly dosed with LSD? Had anyone else died as a result? What possibly would motivate our federal government to commit such acts?

I knew a little bit about Washington, D.C. and how the government worked. I had spent a few years of my youth in the nation's capital, and had later worked for the federal government at several levels. When I was a boy, my father had worked for the Armed Forces Institute of Pathology, situated on the National Mall, just a stone's throw from the CIA's cluster of buildings near the Reflecting Pool. I would sometimes wait for my father to come out from his laboratory, while gazing in fascination at the many visible, and hidden, wonders of the older buildings along the Mall. My father was quite familiar with Camp Detrick and with what they did there in the 1950s. At times, he would even receive tissue samples for analysis from Camp Detrick and Edgewood Arsenal.

One of my father's high school classmates in Vermont had been future CIA director Bill Colby, whose own father had commanded Fort Ethan Allen, an Army installation not far from my father's and my hometown of Burlington. This seemingly simple coincidence was, in retrospect, just one of many strange coincidences that would highlight my investigation into Frank Olson's death. For example, during my third interview with Armond Pastore – the night manager at the New York hotel on the night of Olson's fatal fall – in his home in Sun City, Florida, we had taken a break from several hours of discussion to enjoy some of Armond's delicious homemade bread. Sitting at his cluttered kitchen table, he told me about his first days as an enlistee in the U.S. Army. Armond and his best friend had left Brooklyn to sign up for the war so they could fight the Nazis in Europe. The two young men, barely sixteen years old, had been sent to Fort Ethan Allen, outside Burlington. While there, Armond told me, his friend, Jimmy, had fallen in love with a local girl, whom he eventually married after the war.

"What was Jimmy's last name?" I asked.

"Fercenia," said Armond. "Jimmy Fercenia. He married a girl whose name was Gina."

"Gina Albarelli," I said, in amazement. "Gina is my father's sister; she's my aunt."

About three months later, during one of the earliest of countless conversations with Eric Olson, he asked me where I happened to be calling from.

Indian Rocks Beach, Florida, I told him. We had moved there about three years earlier from Catonsville, Maryland.

"Sounds familiar," said Eric. He told me that he and his family had come to Indian Rocks Beach about two months after his father had died. He had been nine-years old at the time. His maternal grandfather had been the minister of the small beach town's Presbyterian Church.

About six months after this, a close friend reminded me that, during the mid-1970s, we had once visited Deep Creek Lake, Maryland, the site of Frank Olson's LSD dosing by the CIA. We had stayed in an old stone cabin near the lake, the very same cabin where Olson and Dr. Sidney Gottlieb had stayed. Maybe some of Olson's energy remained behind and has infected you, laughed my friend. Maybe, I thought. Either that, or for most of my life I had been on a collision course with the Olson story.

Another coincidence occurred in Key West, Florida, in 1995, a few weeks after I had begun seriously digging into the facts of the Olson case. By chance, I met two retired, former government employees on vacation. The two men were fishing, and they invited me to join them. Although I dislike fishing, I surprised myself and accepted. This serendipitous encounter led to a seven-year dialogue about Frank Olson and the CIA. Both men, and several of their friends, had known Frank Olson well. And, it turned out, they had known others closely involved in the case, including Vincent Ruwet, John Schwab, Sidney Gottlieb, and Robert Lashbrook. Promised complete confidentiality as sources, they were extremely helpful to me.

A couple of years after this encounter, however, the District Attorney's office in Manhattan wanted to communicate with the two men and asked my help. When I refused to identify them, Saracco and Bibb had threatened me with arrest for obstruction of justice.

I had no intention of ever revealing the identities of the men. I had given them my word as an investigative reporter, and eventually Robert Morgenthau's office realized I was not going to relent. But that didn't stop them from coming at me from other directions.

One morning Saracco called me and said he had spoken to the CIA about the issue. "What if we did this?" he suggested. My ears perked up at the word "we."

"What if you gave us the two names and we simply verified their employment with the CIA."

Simply?

"Are you serious?" I asked.

"Completely," came the answer.

"Steve," I said, "how is that any different from my breaking my word to these men? How is that not a betrayal?"

Silence.

I had never spoken with or met anyone in the New York District Attorney's office out of choice. Early on in my research, a highly respected criminologist had warned me that journalists and prosecutors are not always a good mix. "They want what you have," he had advised, "and they won't stop at anything

5

to get it." There was that, and also the fact that I did not want to become a part of the story I was writing. The story was convoluted enough without mixing myself into it.

Eric Olson had asked me to have a discussion with Morgenthau's office, and despite serious reservations, I agreed out of respect for Eric. I had made it clear that I would never betray any of my sources, but that I would share any vital information that I could. Everybody had agreed that would be fine, but it wasn't fine for long.

Weekly telephone calls from Morgenthau's office and their requests for additional information became distracting, not because they took too much time, but because I knew that one thing would always lead to another. When Saracco called one morning and said he wanted to bring me to Manhattan for a couple of days, I foolishly thought that might be the end of it. When I checked into the hotel on the edge of Soho that Morgenthau's office had booked for me, I was given the key card to Room 1017. Frank Olson's fateful room had been numbered 1018A.

Eventually, at my request, the two sources I had met in Key West sent Saracco and Bibb a letter. The letter had been preceded about a week earlier by a package of items the two had also sent to Saracco. The items were ones that only certain government employees could have had. One of the items was a handwritten note by one of Olson's killers, dated 1953. The note was addressed to the head of the Federal Bureau of Narcotics at the time. It was written in French, in elegant handwriting, on a Statler Hotel, New York note card. Another of the items was a security identification card for a certain foreign country, issued after World War II. And then there was an Italian lira note that had been issued by the U.S. military occupation in Italy during the late 1940s, bearing James Jesus Angleton's signature. The last item was a photograph taken in Marseilles, France of one of Frank Olson's killers.

The letter that followed these items, as readers shall learn, spoke of Olson's death and revealed who had killed him, and why. Some of the terms used were oblique and cryptic, but the message and its import were abundantly clear.

Before the two sources mailed their letter, I told Steve Saracco it was being sent to him with the expectation that it would not be shown to Eric or Nils Olson or their attorney. My two sources had specifically requested this. They assumed that more information would be requested, and that the specifics about using particular information should be discussed in detail beforehand – and that it would be. Saracco quickly agreed to this, in writing. Despite this, as Eric Olson later told me, Saracco had allowed him and his brother Nils to read the letter.

Said Eric, "Steve broke his promise to you only because he was about to break a bigger one: namely, his commitment to prosecute a murder."

I found Eric's remark less than comforting. I had suspected all along that nobody would ever be prosecuted for Frank Olson's death, but had remained silent on the issue. My research into the case had produced a keen awareness of the motivations of many of the players. Trying to do the right thing, for me, had become unduly complicated. As predicted, "they want what you have." Inches became feet, feet yards, yards miles, and so on. For all the reasons that will become clear to readers, the story had become almost too complex and too convoluted to manage; it had also frequently come too close to home for many of the parties involved. The story of Frank Olson's death had become far more than the story of an ill-advised LSD drugging and subsequent suicide; it had also become much more than a simple tale of murder to silence a witness. The real story was turning out to be far more complicated and was appearing more and more to revolve around a long-secret, Government-sponsored covert operation that nobody wanted to recall or to speak about. The stakes had turned out to be higher than anticipated. For me, figuring out who was on which side, if any, or who was motivated by seeking the truth as opposed to covering the truth, or by monetary gain or self-aggrandizement, was becoming increasingly difficult.

My only motivation in researching Frank Olson's death had been to discover the truth behind it and nothing more. Where the search might lead, or where it would eventually end up, was not something I could manipulate or control for my own convenience. Most of all, without the ability to guard the identities of my sources there would be no discovery of the truth. I was ready at any given moment to go to jail to protect my sources, and to keep my word, and it remained a constant struggle for me to stay on the sidelines as an observer and a journalist. My son, Damien, asked me at the time, "If a man can't be trusted to keep his word, what good is he?" What good, indeed?

If Frank Olson could speak to us from beyond the grave, I have no doubt he would object to having become a patron saint for today's conspiracy obsessed world. Through his bizarre and untimely demise, Frank Olson has become an American archetype, a dark icon symbolizing the chambers of horrors known as psychological and biological warfare. He was also an unfortunate man who suffered the ultimate bad trip and failed to live to tell about it.

None of this is to say that Olson was not the victim of some malevolent government plot seemingly lifted straight out of an *X-Files* episode. Indeed, as this book will reveal, and document, he was just such a victim. It is also true, however, that Olson was an unassuming and somewhat innocuous man, a true disciple, a patriot of sorts reflective of his times, a "company man," if you will. Olson was not the kind of person who courted danger or intrigue. He was a simple man who found pleasure in his work and in his family. At home, he delighted in entertaining his wife and three children, and at work, he would don his white lab coat and pass the hours developing new and exotic ways to kill people — people who were considered to be the enemies of a way of life that had survived two world wars, at a horrendous human cost.

A highly trained biochemist and specialist in the airborne delivery of lethal microorganisms, Olson worked at the highly secured, ultra-secret Camp Detrick in Frederick, Maryland. Today, the installation, now called Fort Detrick, is to biological warfare what Transylvania is to the legend of Count Dracula.

Yet, despite his unusual profession, had Olson not plunged to his death in such bizarre circumstances, and had he not been connected with particular institutions and agencies, he most likely would have remained completely unknown outside his family and friends; just another anonymous government scientist. He would have remained nameless like the thousands of mostly nameless others who had the great misfortune of being experimented upon by a government that had lost sight of any semblance of morality or respect for human life. But, as readers shall see, fate had other plans for Frank Olson.

Today, remnants of Frank Olson's legacy are scattered everywhere about our cultural landscape. The story of his strange death has taken up permanent residence in the modern codex of conspiracy legend and lore. Olson was the subject of a lengthy poem, *CIA in Wonderland,* by the widely published David Clewell. The epic poem is available on the Internet, capturing Olson's demise with the stark refrain, "Frank Olson is flying, and it's a long way down." A punk rock band has adopted the name MKULTRA, in mock homage to the covert program under which Olson labored. In the popular film, *Conspiracy Theory*, the same program is cited by Mel Gibson's character as the cause of his bizarre and manic behavior, alleged to be not unlike Olson's behavior after being dosed with LSD. In Norman Mailer's fictionalized magnum opus on the CIA, *Harlot's Ghost*, Olson becomes the nameless, but ultimate, "VICTIM." Best selling crime writer, Elmore Leonard, portrays the near absurdity of Olson's alleged suicide in his thriller, *Be Cool*: "The guy went through the window. A closed window. Shattered the glass going through it and screamed all the way down to the pavement."

Even the eloquent junkie and Beat writer, William S. Burroughs, who in his own LSD-induced haze put a bullet through his wife's head, weighs in with his own spin on Olson's death in his collected essays, *The Adding Machine*. In more recent years, Olson's saga has become a major chapter in two collections of America's premier conspiracy stories — *The Rough Guide to Conspiracy Theories* and *The 80 Greatest Conspiracies of All Time*. Olson's twisted story was also the focus of an opera staged in New York City, the three-part *Defenestration Opera*. It was a side remark in the excellent film, *The Good Shepherd*, and can be identified as a sidebar item in countless television melodramas.

Hardly a factual book chronicling the CIA has been published in the past thirty years that does not contain some mention, or note of suspicion, about Olson's fatal fall. His mysterious death has been the featured subject of numerous televised documentaries on CBS, NBC, ABC, CNN, TBN, The Discovery Channel, A&E Investigative Reports, *Unsolved Mysteries, Sightings*, and a slew of foreign features produced in England, Israel, Japan, and Germany.

Worldwide, Frank Olson's death has become a touchstone for the fear of shadow government, and a focal point for justified paranoia about mad scientists running amok among innocent, unsuspecting populations.

Ironically, despite this intense and widespread attention to Olson's story, the only real result has been a stark underscoring of the complexities and unexplained mysteries surrounding his death. Once, out of near total frustration, Eric Olson said to me, "Jesus, it's like a nightmare that never stops. It just keeps replaying itself over and over again, and there's never anything new. Nothing."

In a very real sense, there is a terrible nothingness to the media's endless repetition of Frank Olson's story, not only because it is usually intended as entertainment, but also because, like Hollywood's perpetual replay and exploitation of all forms of violence, it numbs us to the horrible deeds our government has perpetrated. And, still, we are left with the question: Did Frank Olson jump or fall through a shaded, closed window, or worse yet, was he pushed or thrown? And if so, why, and by whom?

Writing this book has been a circuitous task. That task, which spanned over ten years, was convoluted and torturous at times. It was also, as already noted, strangely serendipitous at times, often lending credence to claims that coincidence is not a random occurrence, but sometimes deliberate in some way. Some of the coincidences encountered along the way, as noted above, were startling and eerie, striking close to home. At other times, peculiar things occurred that made me think that I had not chosen my subject but instead the subject had chosen me. People often ask writers how and why they pick their subjects. They never ask if perhaps their subjects picked them.

One of the more striking coincidences occurred about seven months into my research of Olson's death. I had gone through a particularly grueling two-week period that had produced little to no satisfying or usable information, and I was emerging from a long series of dead end interviews and telephone contacts. It felt as if the information flow, once seen as promising, was slowing to a grinding halt; people were clamming up, as if they'd received serious warnings. Then, at the start of what looked as if it would be another dismal week, I received a call from a friend.

He asked me if I remembered a woman with whom we had worked during the late 1970s in Washington, D.C. Sure, I said. What makes you ask? Well, said my friend, I ran into her a few days ago and she asked about you. That's nice, I replied, thinking there was something about this woman that I needed to recall that might be very important. It dawned on me hours later.

The woman, whose name I can not mention in this book, had formerly been married to a CIA official who had worked under Dr. Sidney Gottlieb at the Agency's Technical Services Staff. I recalled speaking to her over fifteen years earlier about a horrific experience she had had in the mid-1950s. I also remembered that I had obtained, through a Freedom of Information request, several Department of Justice letters and memoranda that cryptically referred to a woman who had had a very similar experience. Now, reading once again, I realized that the DOJ documents were about the woman I knew and had worked with.

I telephoned her and, as a result, everything related to my research for this book changed. The information floodgates once again opened. And, again, the unknown force that had been guiding my pursuit of the story – some writers refer to it as "the research angel" – delivered yet another coincidence that reinforced my commitment to the Olson case. (The story of the woman, whom I call Sally Hartman, is contained in Appendix One of this book. It is one of the most horrific and egregious accounts of attempted government mind control on record.)

The story of Frank Olson's death, which includes the history of the CIA's Cold War experiments, is a very complex one. It is impossible to relate without invoking and involving a vast array of names, organizations, places and facts. In the course of writing this book I garnered, reviewed and studied over 100,000 pages of government documents. Sometimes the process was hard-fought, the result of numerous Freedom of Information requests and persistent appeals. Despite this, it is insufficient to recount occurrences and incidents relying solely upon CIA or other government documents. This is primarily because inevitably someone will charge, "You can't trust anything the CIA says or writes." Or, "Everyone knows the government lies all the time to the people." While that may sometimes be the case, with respect to the story of Frank Olson, ironically, the key files concerning his death that were released by the Agency were never intended for public scrutiny.

In addition, I have attempted diligently to verify each and every fact presented in this book. When I distrusted documents, or found them questionable or less than credible, I did not rely on them. Apart from CIA files, a fair amount of information that has been published about Frank Olson's death is less than reliable and some is simply untrue. Much of this information is the result of incessant retellings of certain presumed "facts" surrounding Olson's story, and some of it is the result of sheer fabrication or invention.

I have made every effort to avoid repeating unreliable information and, when I do so out of necessity, I explain why certain accounts and claims are false.

Without doubt, Frank Olson's death is often characterized as the result of a "conspiracy." In many cases, the term "conspiracy theory" is used simply to dissuade the public from questioning an official account of some important historic event and/or to discredit those who do so. In fact, "conspiracy" is a legal term; it has an accepted statutory definition. It may surprise readers to learn that a "conspiracy" is actually a fairly simple and bare bones series of actions. Very little is required to meet the standard, legal definition of conspiracy. One such definition* is, as follows:

Conspiracy is a separate offense, by which someone conspires or agrees with someone else to do something which, if actually carried out, would amount to another Federal crime or offense. It is an agreement or a kind of partnership for criminal purposes in which each member becomes the agent or partner of every other member. It is not necessary to prove that the criminal plan actually was accomplished or that the conspirator was involved in all stages of the planning or knew all of the details involved. The main elements that need to be proven are a voluntary agreement to participate and some overt act by one of the conspirators in furtherance of the criminal plan. If a person has an understanding of the unlawful nature of a plan and knowingly and willfully joins in that plan on one occasion, that is sufficient to convict him for conspiracy even though he had not participated before and even though he played only a minor part. A conspiracy may exist when the parties use legal means to accomplish an illegal result, or to use illegal means to achieve something that in itself is lawful.

Wheel and chain conspiracies are two types of conspiracies described in prosecuting offenders. A chain conspiracy involves parties linked together in a linear fashion. Typical drug or firearm smuggling organizations are chain conspiracies. It may consist of a series of drug deals, from manufacturer to the street dealer. In a wheel conspiracy, the ringleader is the "hub" and subsidiary parties are the "spokes." It is generally easier for prosecution to prove that a "chain" constituted a single conspiracy than it is to prove that a "wheel" was a single organization.

The goal of this book is not to engage in semantics about the term "conspiracy," but to identify and follow through on the probative questions: What, exactly, happened to Frank Olson? Why did it happen? Who was responsible?

For me, Frank Olson's story and the story of the CIA's Cold War experiments are in large part a reflection of a time in American history when nothing appeared as it was, when dark and sinister forces were at work behind a façade of peaceful and carefree times. It is, as Santayana warned, important to understand history so that we do not repeat it or, if we see that we are repeating it, to expose it for what it is, once again.

In the fall of 2000, during one particular week, I was spending about eight hours a day in a windowless room, methodically going through the infamous and copious MKULTRA files at the National Security Archives in Washington, D.C. Seated across the table from me was an attractive young woman who was looking through the same boxes of files.

After a day pondering this "coincidence," my curiosity got the better of me and I asked the woman the reason for her interest in MKULTRA. She replied that she was a CIA attorney, researching background for a civil suit that had been filed against the Agency. I inquired "by whom?" but she refused to identify the source of the lawsuit. When she asked the source of my interest, I explained

I was researching a book on the death of Frank Olson. She expressed no curiosity about this, and only remarked, "I guess it's pretty coincidental that we're here at the same time."

That night, in my room at a Dupont Circle Hotel in Washington, D.C. where I was staying, I received a telephone call around 10:00 P.M. The caller was another CIA attorney, someone with whom I had spoken a week earlier on the telephone.

"There's something on television that you might want to see," he said, telling me which channel to tune in.

"How did you know I was here?" I asked him.

"You told me, didn't you?"

"Not that I recall."

I knew I had not given him the name of the hotel I was staying in because at the time I had spoken with him, I hadn't yet booked my reservation.

"No, I'm sure you did. Anyway, watch the show."

I hung up and turned my attention to the television. The show was a documentary entitled, "The CIA and Assassination." It made no mention of Frank Olson or his death.

H.P. Albarelli, Jr.
Richford, Vermont
May 2009

*Conspiracy Law & Legal Definition: http.//definitions.uslegal.com/conspiracy.

BOOK ONE
1953-1956

1

November 28, 1953
New York City, 2:30 A.M.

The techniques employed will vary according to whether the subject is unaware of his danger, aware but unguarded, or guarded. The most efficient accident, in simple assassination, is a fall of 75 feet or more onto a hard surface. Elevator shafts, stairwells, unscreened windows and bridges will serve.
— CIA Assassination Manual, 1952

We'll name them as they jump out of windows.
— U.S. Rep. Karl E. Mundt, 1948

A doorman rounding the corner of 33rd Street and Seventh Avenue was the first person to spot him. The doorman, who has long since disappeared, had slipped away from his post at the Statler Hotel for a quick drink at the nearby Little Penn tavern. Returning, he was about fifty yards away from the hotel's main entrance when a shape came into his line of vision, something falling from high above the sidewalk. He stopped and looked on in disbelief. It was a man.

Later, the doorman would tell Armond Pastore, the hotel's night manager, "It was like the guy was diving, his hands out in front of him, but then his body twisted and he was coming down feet first, his arms grabbing at the air above him." The falling man struck a temporary wooden partition that shielded work underway on the hotel's facade, the impact producing a sickening thud. He bounced off the plywood wall, landing hard on the sidewalk.

In 1975, and later in 1994, Pastore, whose full name is Armando Diaz Pershing Foch Pastore, was asked by every major television network in the United States to recall Frank Olson's death. In summer 1994, he was flown to New York to assist a team of forensic investigators who were reconstructing Olson's fall. Film crews and producers from Germany, England, Australia, and Japan have interviewed him. Reporters from the *New York Times* and *Washington Post*, and countless other newspapers, have knocked on his door. Pastore, an intelligent, good-natured man who would rather talk about his "amazing grandchildren," clearly enjoys the attention but his recollections remain steadfast and he never attempts to embellish his account or comment on anything he can't recall.

Nearly forty-five years after Olson's fall, Pastore told the author, "I can never forget it. Those scenes play over and over in my head. They haunt me like some ghost looking for a proper resolution." Sitting in the living room of his modest Florida home, Pastore recounted what happened:

"It was late, about 2:30 in the morning, and the doorman came running in all excited. I think his first name was Jimmy. For the life of me, I can't remember his last name. I think it was Davis or Doyle, or something like that. He didn't work there all that long. He was what we called a 'druggo' back then. You know, a guy with some bad habits, a junky. Anyway, he comes running in yelling, 'We got a jumper, we got a jumper.' I told him to calm down and asked him where. He pointed toward the front doors and said, 'Out front, on the sidewalk.' I shouted to the desk clerk to call security and the police and then I ran outside."

Pastore found a group of five or six people standing over a middle-aged man. Several other people were hurrying across the street from Pennsylvania Station. The man was lying on his back, one arm outstretched, fingers extended as if he was reaching for something. His legs were close together, twisted to the side. He was wearing only a white, sleeveless undershirt and white undershorts.

"I knelt beside him," Pastore says, "thinking about what best to do. He looked up at me and tried to speak, but only blood came from his mouth. I told him, It's okay, buddy, we've called for help."

The man's pale green eyes searched Pastore's face. "There was blood running from his eyes, nose, and ears," Pastore recalls. "I saw a large section of shattered bone sticking out of his left arm, and there were a few pieces of broken glass around his body."

"Just hold on. You'll be okay," Pastore reassured the man, immediately feeling a twinge of guilt. "I knew he wasn't going to make it." Pastore felt the cold of the concrete sidewalk in his knees. He told the doorman, now standing several feet away, to go and get a blanket for the man.

Pastore wondered what was taking the ambulance so long, and the jumper attempted to speak again. The effort caused grotesque red bubbles to form around his mouth. Pastore remembers, "I took my handkerchief and carefully wiped the froth away from his face. Then I asked him, 'Can you tell me your name?' but he didn't answer."

Pastore saw a priest from nearby St. Thomas' Church hurrying across 7th Avenue toward the scene, holding a folded stole and Bible. "There were two uniformed police officers a few yards behind him," Pastore recalls.

The doorman returned and handed Pastore a folded wool blanket. "When I began to cover his legs and torso," Pastore says, "I noticed a large splinter of tan wood protruding from his chest." The man groaned; his eyes momentarily focused on something above Pastore. The two policemen were standing over them now. One of the officers squatted next to Pastore and said sotto voce, "Jumper?"

"I guess," Pastore answered.

Rising to his feet the officer ordered the small group of gawkers to move further away. The priest knelt next to the man, opposite Pastore, and began to administer the last rites. Several blocks away, Pastore heard the sound of an approaching siren.

Pastore says the man looked at him imploringly, again trying to speak. "His right hand clutched my arm and he raised his head slightly, his lips moving. His eyes were wide with desperation. He wanted to tell me something, I leaned down closer to listen, but he took a deep breath and died."

Pastore recounts that he then went back inside the hotel to talk with the front desk personnel and the hotel's security man on duty that night. "I knew the guy had to have come from somewhere out of the hotel, but I had no idea where. The Statler is a big place. We had about 2,200 rooms and over 1,000 employees. It was like a small city operating twenty-four hours a day. Somebody had to know something."

He asked the front desk employees if anyone had called down from a room to report a jumper or anything unusual. There had been no calls. He asked the hotel's security man if he'd checked to see if the rooftop doors were locked. He had and they were.

"Did you check all the windows?" Pastore asked.

"Best I could. It's pretty dark out there," the man replied.

Pastore says, "I was dissatisfied with the information I was getting, so I went back outside."

The ambulance had left only minutes before and the street was nearly deserted. The two uniformed police officers stood near the spot where the man had lain, talking to a man in a trench coat. Pastore crossed 7th Avenue and stood on the curb in front of Pennsylvania Station. He began systematically scanning the Statler's front façade, looking for an opened window or anything unusual. He started with the rooftop and top level, the nineteenth floor, carefully working his way across and down, window by window, floor by floor, until he reached the street. He saw nothing that appeared unusual.

The guy had to come from somewhere, Pastore told himself. "Every time I focused on a window I thought of the guy's eyes, the look on his face. I'd seen that look before, in Italy and France during the war, on the faces of guys that knew life was over for them. It's a look you don't forget."

Pastore repeated this process and still saw nothing. "I was just about to give up when I saw something move near a window. I concentrated on the spot and then after a few seconds I saw it move again."

"It was the shade," Pastore explains. "It was the window's drawn shade catching in the breeze. Somehow it had been pulled way down and was hanging outside the window."

He stared intently at the shade for a moment and then began to count the number of windows directly above it, and then the adjoining windows toward the west end of the building. Double-checking, he counted again. "It was room 1018A," Pastore states.

Crossing 7th Avenue again, Pastore told the two police officers he thought he knew which room the man came from. "I gave them the number, and told them I was going to go up and check the room. They said they'd be right up."

Re-entering the hotel, he went to the cashier's desk and asked to see the registration card for room 1018A. There were two names on the card, Robert Lashbrook and Frank R. Olson. Lashbrook had listed his home address only as Washington, D.C. No street name, no telephone number. Olson's home address was written as RFD 5, Frederick, Maryland. Again no telephone number. They had registered only about ten hours before, on November 27.

Pastore then summoned the hotel's security man to accompany him to the tenth floor. "Bring your pass keys," he told the man.

They took the elevator in the main lobby. As they ascended, the security man asked, "You don't really think the other guy's still in the room, do you?"

"I told him I didn't know what to think," Pastore says.

The elevator doors slid open and the two moved silently down the thick carpeted hallway. Given the lateness of the hour, the hotel's public areas were deserted; no sound came from any of the rooms they passed. They stopped at Room 1018A. Pastore leaned close to its door and listened for a moment. There was no sound on the other side. He gripped the doorknob and attempted to twist it open. It was locked.

"There's not going to be anyone in there," the security man said, handing him the passkey.

Pastore says, "I slid the key into the lock and then I thought, what the hell am I doing? The other guy could be in there. I thought, anybody could be in there. Who knows what we could be walking into? So I said to my security man, 'Let's wait for the police to come up.'

"The whole time we waited we didn't hear a sound come from the other side of the door," Pastore says. "Then, after about twenty minutes or so, down the hall, we heard the elevator's bell sound, and when the doors opened the two policemen from out on the street stepped out." As they approached, talking to one another, Pastore raised a finger to his lips to hush the men.

The older of the two officers pointed toward the room's door and asked quietly, "Somebody in there?"

"I'm not sure," Pastore answered.

Pastore stepped further away from the door and explained in a low voice that it was locked and that the registration card showed two men had checked into the room. The older officer asked, "Did one of these guys call down to the desk?"

"No," Pastore answered, "there were no calls to the desk."

"The officer's eyebrows went up with that," Pastore recalls, "He nodded toward the door again and told me, 'Open it. We'll go in first,' and then he and his partner pulled out their revolvers."

Pastore unlocked the door and stepped aside as the officers pushed it open and moved cautiously into the room, revolvers in hand. After a moment, Pastore warily followed them in. The room was dark except for the light spilling in from the hallway and the partial glow that came from the room's nearly closed bathroom door. One of the officers pushed the door open with his foot.

Pastore saw the man at the same moment as the officers. He was seated on the bathroom's commode. "It was the oddest sight," Pastore recalls, "the guy just sitting there. He was holding his head in his hands as if lost in thought. There was a pair of socks and an undershirt hanging over the shower rod." The officers stepped closer and one of them demanded, "What's going on here? What happened?"

"The guy looked up and slowly said, 'I woke up when I heard a sound. I'm not sure what happened,'" Pastore says.

Pastore stood at the center of the room looking about. Because he had to step around them, he noticed that the covers from the bed closest to the room's single window were mostly on the floor as though flung off in a single sweeping motion.

"The window was smashed out completely," Pastore recounts. "I mean it was gone. There were just a few small slivers of glass left sticking out of the frame. I didn't see any glass on the radiator beneath the window, or on the carpeted floor or the windowsill."

"You didn't see the guy go out the window?" one of the officers asked the man.

"No. I just heard a noise and then I woke up."

"Sir, please stand up slowly," ordered the elder officer. "And let's see some identification."

Pastore says the man calmly stood and walked to the nightstand where he picked up a wallet, which he opened and handed over. "The guy was tall and slim," Pastore recalls. "He had sort of light colored hair and was wearing glasses. There was nothing distinctive about him that I can remember. You know, a pretty ordinary guy, except there was this strange calmness about him."

Both officers examined the wallet; the younger one writing something down on a small pad of paper. "I could see what appeared to be an official looking identification card with some sort of government seal on it," Pastore says.

"The man that went out the window, what is his name?" the younger officer asked.

"Olson. Frank Olson," the man replied.

As the one officer questioned the man, Pastore recalls watching the older officer, whose name he later learned was Joseph Guastefeste, begin to search the room. Guastefeste opened dresser and nightstand drawers, looked into the bathroom's medicine cabinet, under the bed. Out of the room's single closet, Guastefeste lifted a small suitcase and set it on one of the beds. Pastore says, "He tried to open its metal latches but it was locked. He asked the man to open it and the guy took a small key from his pocket and unlocked the suitcase."

"And you say you didn't see Mr. Olson go out the window?" the questioning policeman continued.

"No, I didn't," the man said.

Pastore, now standing at the room's door, watched the officer with the suitcase remove a crumpled, folded sheet of paper from one of its side pockets. The officer unfolded it, studied it for a moment and then refolded it, slipping it into the side pocket of his tunic.

"Is there a reason you stayed in the room, Mr. Lashbrook?" the younger officer asked.

The man shrugged and said, "What could I do?"

"You didn't think of going down to check on Mr. Olson?"

"I looked out the window. I saw him lying there. There were people running from the station," Lashbrook replied. "What could I have done? I could see that he had help. I thought it best to wait here."

Pastore shakes his head in disgust. "Can you believe it?" he asks. "The guy's friend, or co-worker, or whatever, is lying down there bleeding on the sidewalk and he doesn't even go down to see how he is. I mean, what kind of animal reacts like that?"

After all these years it is revealing of the sort of man that Pastore is to see him get so worked up recounting a story he has told hundreds of times. "When I was there, on the sidewalk with Olson, trying to help him, I felt so helpless... and then to think the whole time I'm down there this Lashbrook guy is looking down on us." Pastore shakes his head again. "I don't know."

"I'll tell you this, too," Pastore says after a moment. "In all my years in the hotel business, I never encountered a case where someone got up in the middle of the night, ran across a dark room in his underwear, avoiding two beds, and dove through a closed window with the shade and curtains drawn. I mean, how the hell do you do that?" Pastore, who has nearly three decades experience working in some of Manhattan's finest hotels, pauses again to reflect. "Christ, even when they tossed Kid Twist out the window they opened the damn thing first."

He is referring to Abe Reles, a lisping psychopath who specialized in death by strangulation for the syndicate's infamous Murder, Inc. Reles, whose nickname was Kid Twist, made the fatal mistake of talking to New York prosecutors about "lord high executioner" Albert Anastasia, a close associate of legendary crime bosses Charles "Lucky" Luciano, Meyer Lansky, and Santo Trafficante Jr. On November 12, 1941, Reles' lifeless body was found beneath a sixth-floor window of the Half Moon Hotel on Brooklyn's Coney Island. The Brooklyn District Attorney had placed Reles in the hotel under 24-hour protective custody, guarded in a way "that would have made the crown jewels safe in Jesse James' parlor," as an assistant district attorney would later write.

Pastore also mentions the fatal fall of Laurence Duggan that occurred five years before Olson's death in 1948. He says he can't remember specifically what was said but recalls that one of the officers in Olson's room made a remark to his colleague about Duggan's suicide.

"It happened not far from the Statler," Pastore recalls. "I remembered the minute the cop mentioned it. Duggan had been some sort of government official who was supposed to have been cozy with the Commies. I think the cop said something about Olson's fall looking like Duggan's."

Later that night, unbeknownst to Pastore, investigating detectives at the 14th Police Precinct would also be considering Duggan's death. Detectives there would speculate in their written report about the possibility that Olson and Lashbrook were "involved in some committee hearing," as they were "aware that Sen. McCarthy's Committee was in town around this time" and "the case of Duggan of the State Department came to mind."

Laurence Duggan was killed in a fall from a sixteenth floor window in the midtown Manhattan building that housed the Institute of International Education, which he headed. The incident occurred on December 20, 1948 and was marked by several unusual circumstances not the least of which, as investigators in the Manhattan District Attorney's office would discover decades later, were a number of odd similarities between his and Olson's death. Only a few days before his fall, Duggan, who had been the chief of the Latin American Division at the State Department in Washington from 1934 to 1944, and then a diplomatic adviser to the United Nations Relief and Rehabilitation Administration, had been vigorously questioned by the FBI about secret contacts he maintained with Soviet intelligence agents while he worked for the State Department. The FBI also wanted to know about his relationship with another department employee, notorious accused spy Alger Hiss, who was about to go on trial. Two days after Duggan's death, Congressman Karl Mundt, a Republican from South Dakota who headed the House un-American Activities Committee, sarcastically commented, "We'll name them as they jump out of windows."

Says Pastore, "They ruled Duggan's death a suicide, too, even though he had an overcoat and one galosh on when he fell. I mean, who takes off a galosh and then decides to jump out the window?"

Pastore takes a drink of water and goes back to his account of Frank Olson's death. "The officer conducting the room search went back to the closet. He reached in and lifted out a hanger holding a pair of dark dress slacks. 'Are these yours?' he asked Lashbrook."

"They belong to Olson," Lashbrook answered.

The officer slipped the pants from the hanger and, holding them by the waistband, began going through the pockets. After a moment he looked up at Lashbrook and said, "Would you happen to know where Mr. Olson's wallet is?"

"No, I don't," Lashbrook said, "I think that he might have lost it a couple nights ago."

Pastore says the officers looked at one another. "It was one of those moments, if you know what I mean," Pastore says. "Then one of the officers handed Lashbrook his billfold back and told him to get dressed. 'You're going to have to come with us to the station house,' the officer told him."

Lashbrook moved to the room's closet and took a white dress shirt from a hanger and slipped it on. As he was buttoning the shirt, the telephone on the nightstand between the twin beds began to ring.

"Do you mind if I answer that?" he asked.

"Go ahead," said one of the officers.

Lashbrook picked up the receiver and said, "Yes?" After a pause he said, "We seem to have a bad connection. Could you speak up some?" There was another short pause and then he said, "Well, I appreciate that, but the police are here just now so I'll have to get back to you."

He hung up, finished buttoning his shirt, leaving it open at the collar, slipped on a suit jacket, and lifted an overcoat from another hanger.

Pastore followed the police and Lashbrook out of the room, pulling the door shut. The security man was leaning against the hallway wall smoking a cigarette.

"You ask me," the man said, "that was one cool cucumber."

Minutes later, Pastore explains, he was back on the hotel's main floor, standing in the doorway to the switchboard room. On the way down from the tenth floor he had decided to check for himself with the hotel's operators about what calls had been placed for room 1018A.

"I asked the operator if there had been any calls made from the room after 2:00 A.M. She told me she had placed one call," Pastore says. "You have to understand," he explains, "that back then, in the Fifties, if you were a hotel guest you didn't make your own calls like it's done today. Then, you had to call the hotel's switchboard, give her the number you wanted, and she would place the call for you and get your party on the line.

"Sometimes, when it was slow," Pastore recalls, "the operator would stay on the line after the call was placed and listen in. Anyway, that night, not long after Olson went out the window, she said that there had been one call made from the room to a Dr. Harold Abramson. I think it was to South Oaks Hospital out on Long Island. She told me that when a man answered, the caller said, 'Well, he's gone,' and then the other man said, 'Well, that's too bad.' That was it, nothing else was said. Then the guy hung up."

About forty-five minutes later, Pastore says he was at the hotel's front desk writing his incident report on the events concerning room 1018A. "I happened to look up and I saw Lashbrook enter the hotel through the front doors. He walked across the lobby to the elevators, passing only several feet from where I was standing, but never turned to look at me. I watched him wait for the elevator doors to open. I couldn't believe he was back already. Unbelievable. He wasn't gone for more than an hour. I mean, it takes longer than that to get a damn parking ticket fixed."

Later that morning, riding the Long Island Rail Road to his home in Mineola, Pastore says he thought about everything that had happened. *I'll never be able to get this out of my head*, he told himself. Now decades later, he says, "Olson's eyes, the way he looked up at me, trying to tell me something, with only blood coming out of his mouth. That sight has haunted me forever. What the hell did he want to say? I mean, what the hell happened in that room?"

2

November 28, 1953
Washington, D.C., 5:40 A.M.

At the same hour that Armond Pastore was riding the railroad home from the Statler Hotel in New York, four CIA officials gathered in a small, 2-story office building in Washington, D.C. The two-story structure, called Quarters Eye and situated in the area known as the National Mall was one of several non-descript buildings near the Lincoln Memorial and Reflecting Pool. Hastily constructed during World War II, the buildings had been intended as temporary military housing that would be dismantled after the war. But the fledgling intelligence agency, less than ten years old, was growing by leaps and bounds; space was needed desperately.

Three of the CIA officials had been summoned by pre-dawn telephone calls from on-duty security officer Bernard F. Doran, former wartime security agent with the Manhattan Project in Los Alamos, New Mexico, who had joined the CIA's staff in 1951. Earlier that morning, around 4:30 A.M., Doran had received a phone call from Dr. Sidney Gottlieb, chief of the CIA's Chemical Branch. Gottlieb told Doran that there had been "an incident in a hotel in New York City, involving a death." Gottlieb explained that Robert Lashbrook, assistant chief of the Chemical Branch, had been in the hotel when the incident occurred and that New York City detectives were now investigating. Lashbrook was awaiting instructions, Gottlieb said.

Immediately after speaking with Gottlieb, Doran – according to the report he wrote later that same day – telephoned his superior, Col. Sheffield Edwards, director of the CIA's Office of Security. OS, as the security office was called, had the responsibility to protect Agency personnel and facilities from compromising situations and unauthorized penetration. OS also performed other, more surreptitious tasks. Its agents were widely regarded as experts in carrying out "black bag" and "clean up" jobs, and were infamous for less sophisticated "hard knuckle" operations.

Doran told Col. Edwards that a civilian employee from the Army's biological warfare center at Camp Detrick, Maryland had died after diving through a window at the Statler Hotel in New York City, and that detectives from New York's 14th Precinct were on the scene. Doran also told Edwards that the dead man was Dr. Frank Olson, who had been working on a top secret, eyes-only project for the CIA, overseen by Gottlieb and Lashbrook.

Col. Sheffield Edwards, a former wartime Office of Strategic Services intelligence officer, instructed Doran to call Dr. Gottlieb back, and then to telephone Gottlieb's superior, Dr. Willis Gibbons, chief of the Agency's Technical Services Staff (TSS) of which the Chemical Branch was a part. Edwards instructed Doran to tell the two men to meet him as soon as possible in Gottlieb's Washington office in the Quarters Eye building.

Edwards arrived at the Quarters Eye office around 5:40 A.M.; Gottlieb, Gibbons, and Doran were waiting for him. Gottlieb was talking on the telephone with Lashbrook, who had just called from a pay station in the Statler Hotel. Edwards instructed Gottlieb to tell Lashbrook to move to another room at the hotel and to wait there for further instructions.

Gibbons, a former executive with Bell Laboratories and the U.S. Rubber Co. who had recently become head of TSS, then gave Edwards a thorough briefing on the situation. Gottlieb helped by explaining that Lashbrook had been with Frank Olson in New York City "on two occasions during the last week." Gibbons told Edwards that Olson "was taking psychiatric treatment" for "severe depression" from Dr. Harold A. Abramson in New York. Col. Vincent Ruwet, at Gottlieb's suggestion, had made the arrangements for Olson to go to New York, they explained, because Ruwet, was the officer in charge of Camp Detrick's Special Operations Division where Olson was assigned.

Edwards asked why Dr. Abramson had been selected to treat Olson. Gottlieb replied that it was "due to the fact that [Abramson] is a cleared consultant of both this Agency and the U.S. Army Chemical Corps, and that the sensitive nature of [Olson's] work, part of which he was performing for TSS, made this appear desirable." Abramson, Gottlieb explained, had been under contract with TSS's Chemical Division since 1952 to conduct experiments with LSD. Dr. Gibbons added that Olson "had been treated five or six times during the last week by Dr. Abramson," and explained that Olson and Lashbrook had "returned to the Washington area for Thanksgiving but went back to New York for further consultation with Abramson."

Said Gibbons, "Yesterday, Abramson decided that Olson should be placed in a sanatorium for treatment for a period and arrangements had been made with the Chestnut Lodge Hospital near Rockville, Maryland."

Added Gottlieb, "Olson said that he was willing to take this treatment, but last night after he and Lashbrook checked into the Statler Hotel for the night, Lashbrook woke up to the sound of a crash and found that Olson had dived through the window, blind, glass and all."

In a memorandum signed by Col. Edwards that same day and stamped "Eyes Only," the CIA security chief wrote that he then "questioned Dr. Gibbons and Dr. Gottlieb at some length on certain matters that had occurred prior to this incident." Those matters (judging from what Edwards wrote concerning

Gibbons' and Gottlieb's explanations) revolved around a meeting of three CIA-TSS officials — including Gottlieb, Lashbrook, and an unnamed third person — with a group of seven scientists from the Special Operations Division at Camp Detrick, with which the CIA maintained a top-secret relationship. The meeting began on Wednesday, November 18, 1953. It took place in a two-story log and stone house overlooking Deep Creek Lake, a remote, heavily wooded area of Western Maryland. Wrote Edwards, "It appears that the purpose of this liaison and connection was to discuss and work on matters of mutual interest in the sensitive and covert fields."

Gottlieb told Edwards that after the entire group had assembled on Thursday, November 19, "it was decided to experiment with the drug LSD, and for the members present to administer the drug to themselves to ascertain the effect a clandestine application would have on a meeting or conference." Gottlieb elaborated, saying that "a very small dose" of LSD was placed in a bottle of Cointreau and that "all present except two of the persons had a drink thereof." Wrote Edwards in his report: "This included Gottlieb and the Commanding Officer of Special Operations, [Col. Vincent Ruwet]. Olsen [sic] also was included in the group."

The LSD, Gottlieb continued, had a definite effect on the group, to the point where "they were boisterous and laughing" and eventually were "unable to continue the meeting or engage in sensible conversations." The group turned in around 1:00 A.M., Gottlieb said, but many of the Special Operations personnel, including Olson, "complained of wakefulness during the night."

The next morning, Friday, November 20, Gottlieb said he drove home, as did Olson. Then, on Tuesday, November 24, Col. Ruwet telephoned Gottlieb at his Quarters Eye office and reported that Olson "appeared mentally depressed." Gottlieb then suggested that Lashbrook take Olson to New York to be treated by Dr. Abramson.

It wasn't necessary for either Gottlieb or Gibbons to provide Edwards with background details about LSD or the CIA's drug experiments. Edwards was more than familiar with the Agency's use of psychochemicals. Since 1950, under the ultra-secret Bluebird Project, the CIA had been secretly experimenting with the use of drugs — including heroin, opium, mescaline and LSD — on unwitting subjects. From its inception, as readers shall learn in greater detail, the tightly compartmentalized project was Col. Sheffield Edwards' baby. Indeed, Edwards had selected the code-name "Bluebird" after an attendee at an early planning session made an offhand remark about creating a non-lethal arsenal for "making subjects sing like birds." Throughout its first year of operation, Edwards chaired all Bluebird Project meetings, some of which were held in early 1950 in New York and Montreal.

A scant three dozen documents, merely outlining the Bluebird Project, have survived the many purges of CIA records over the past half-century. One memorandum, dated February 10, 1951, provides a telling glimpse of Bluebird's dimensions: "Bluebird Teams are to include persons qualified in medicine, hypnosis, psychological interrogation, the use of the electroencephalograph, electric shock and the polygraph." Another document, dated May 4, 1951, poses the following challenges to Bluebird Teams:

> Can we make an unwilling subject talk; Can we prevent our own agents who fall into enemy hands from disclosing information vital to us; Can a man be made to commit acts useful to us under post-hypnotic suggestion; Can we condition our own people so they will not be subject to post-hypnotic suggestion."

Another May 1951 memorandum chillingly poses the question: "Can a person under hypnosis be forced to commit murder?"

Following his briefing on November 28, Col. Edwards instructed Gottlieb to call Lashbrook back and to tell him that a special security officer from the Agency would call on him at the Statler Hotel around 8:00 A.M. "to assist and follow any further dealings or interviews with the police." Edwards then telephoned the special security agent and ordered him to go immediately to the Statler Hotel. Meanwhile, Gottlieb called Lashbrook, now in Room 488 of the Statler, and alerted him to the fact that the special agent was on his way.

Finished with these details, Edwards asked Gottlieb if anyone had contacted Olson's wife about her husband's death. "I spoke with Vincent Ruwet at about 2:45 this morning and asked him to go to Olson's house," Gottlieb replied. "He's probably there right now.

3

November 28, 1953
Frederick, Maryland, 6:25 A.M.

Fifty-five miles southwest of Washington, D.C. in Frederick, Maryland, Alice Olson was up early on this Saturday morning after a mostly sleepless night, filled with worry about her husband. There was much to do before Frank arrived home. Already Alice had placed the leftover turkey in the oven to warm with a fresh batch of stuffing. She had washed and peeled nearly five pounds of potatoes and rolled out two piecrusts. Then she set out three bowls for hot cereal and began to heat a pan full of milk. Alice poured herself another cup of coffee and sat at the kitchen table.

The children were still asleep, but she knew that at any minute one, or all three, would be awake. Daddy will be home today, she had told them the night before after Frank called. They had been so excited they didn't want to go to bed. With the combined anticipation of the imminent arrival of their father and, in a few short weeks, of Santa Claus, they had already put the Christmas tree up and the children were beside themselves with delight. Eric, nine years old, had fallen asleep on the living room floor next to the tree, after she had put the younger Lisa and Nils to bed. Alice had carried the sleeping Eric to his bed.

Despite the last four stressful days without Frank at home, especially for Thanksgiving, Alice felt fresh and alert today. The past week had been a trying one. The worst week of my life, she thought, absently-mindedly running a fingertip around the rim of her cup. But now Frank would be home sometime before noon and she looked forward to a worry-free weekend.

When Frank called yesterday he sounded so much better than when he had left on Tuesday. That last day, riding with him to Washington, D.C., had frightened her tremendously. She had never seen Frank act like that. In the Hot Shoppe in Bethesda, where they stopped for lunch, Frank had stunned her when he pushed his plate away and said, "I can't eat this food, it's poisoned."

It had all begun a few days earlier when he had come home from work, a week ago Friday. He had been away for three days at another one of the seemingly endless series of meetings he attended. Often he would have to travel across the country, and frequently overseas. This time, however, he hadn't gone far, attending a two-night session held at a remote group of cabins at Deep

Creek Lake, Maryland, only about sixty miles from Frederick. The morning Frank left, Alice had seen the directions to something called "Deep Creek Rendezvous" resting on top of the kitchen table.

Vin Ruwet, Frank's division chief and a family friend, had driven up to their house to pick Frank up. Vin blew his horn, and Frank kissed her goodbye as she handed him his coat.

"I'll see you in a couple of days," he said. "Tell the kids to be good and that I love them." Alice had waved to Frank and Vin as they drove off.

Then Frank came home two days later, on Friday, around dinnertime, and the whole world changed. That was when it started, Alice thought.

Whatever *it* was.

She sensed something was wrong the moment he walked in the door. There was a stiffness in the way he kissed her hello and held her. Like he was doing something mechanical, devoid of any meaning or affection. His eyes betrayed him right away. It was as if he wasn't focused on anything, like something more important had a hold over him.

At the dinner table that evening Frank didn't have a word to say. She asked him how things had gone with his trip and he mumbled, "fine." As always, the children had a thousand things to tell their father, but she could see he wasn't really paying attention to them. It was as if Frank had brought something home with him, something invisible that seemed to be consuming any semblance of normalcy. He had no interest in eating; he just shifted his food around his plate. She had prepared apple pie, his favorite dessert, but after taking a small bite he left the rest uneaten.

Alice finally said, "It's a shame the adults in this family have stopped communicating." And for a moment the old Frank, the Frank of less than three days ago, looked up at her, smiled, and said apologetically, "We'll talk later after we get the children to bed."

But they never did.

Later that night, after the children had gone to sleep and the house was quiet, Alice remembered how she came into the living room and Frank was sitting on the couch, staring into space.

"What is it?" she had asked him. "What's wrong?"

"You don't need to know," he said.

"What is wrong, Frank?" she insisted.

Frank stared down at his hands and then said, "I've made a terrible mistake."

"What?" she asked. "What could possibly be that terrible? You're here, you're fine, you're with us, what is it?"

But Frank only said again, "I've made a terrible mistake." And then again, "I've made an awful mistake."

They lit the fireplace and sat on the couch together looking at the flames. Frank reached out and took her hand tightly in his. They sat silently like this for nearly an hour and then he said, "I'm going to have to resign Monday morning."

"What on earth are you talking about?" Alice asked. "Please tell me."

But Frank wouldn't say. For nearly the whole weekend, he had remained sullen, and by Sunday afternoon Alice decided it might be good to get him out of the house. She suggested they load the kids into the car and drive into downtown Frederick to see a movie. The only film playing was Irving Pichel's *Martin Luther* starring Niall MacGinniss. The movie was depressing and the children fidgeted the entire time. Frank stared glumly at the screen and when the film ended he didn't say a word.

On Monday morning, two hours after leaving for work, Frank called home and said that everything was going to be okay. "I talked to Vin," he told Alice. "He said that I didn't make a mistake. Everything is fine. I'm not going to resign." Frank sounded relieved. And just like that things seemed normal again.

But it did not last long.

The next day, Tuesday, before noon, Frank had unexpectedly returned home. A colleague of Frank's from Camp Detrick, Dr. Joseph Stubbs, was with him. Frank had walked into the house and announced to Alice, "I've consented to psychiatric care. I've agreed to go and see a doctor."

Alice, astounded by the statement, remembered that she wasn't sure what to say with Dr. Stubbs there in the kitchen. When she hesitated, Frank said, "Joe wanted to come home with me because he thought I might do you bodily harm."

Bodily harm?

Did she hear him correctly? She remembered standing at the kitchen sink when Frank said that and feeling her legs begin to buckle.

"What are you saying?" she asked, stunned.

"I'm sorry, it's just that they're afraid that I might hurt you."

Alice gripped the back of a chair and moved unsteadily to sit at the kitchen table across from Frank's colleague.

"It's going to be all right," Dr. Stubbs said.

All right? Alice remembered thinking. *No, it's not all right. It's not all right at all. I don't understand any of this.*

Dr. Stubbs and Frank went into the living room and talked for about half an hour and made a telephone call. Alice sat at the table the whole time not knowing what to do or think. When they came back into the room, Frank said that they wanted him to return right away to Camp Detrick, where they were making arrangements for him to see a psychiatrist.

"A psychiatrist?" Alice asked. "Why?"

"I'm not sure," Frank said. "It's what they think is best."

"They? Who are they?" Alice asked.

"Don't worry, it's going to be all right," Frank said.

"I want to go. I want to ride with you," Alice blurted, startling herself with the impulsiveness of the demand.

Frank looked at Dr. Stubbs, who shrugged and said, "I'll call Ruwet."

"No, I'll call him," Alice said. When Vin answered, she told him why she was calling and he told her to come back to his office with Frank. Ruwet said they could all ride together to Washington where, he explained, Frank was going to receive some assistance.

After meeting up with Ruwet at his office, Frank and Alice rode with him to his Frederick home where he changed from his officer's uniform into civilian clothes. Then, the three of them were picked up by an unmarked military vehicle driven by another of Frank's colleagues, John Malinowski.

As soon as they were in the car, Frank became very nervous. "Where are we going?" he asked Ruwet.

"To Washington, D.C. and then on by air to New York," replied Ruwet.

"New York? Why New York?" Alice asked.

"So Frank can get the medical attention he needs," Ruwet explained.

"How long are you going to be there?" Alice asked Frank.

"Not long," Frank said.

"How long?" she insisted. "Thanksgiving is Thursday," she reminded him.

"I'll be home for Thanksgiving, don't worry," Frank said, "I promise."

But she did worry.

At the Hot Shoppe, where they stopped for lunch en route to Washington, Frank acted even more nervous than before. He appeared scared when he looked about the restaurant with suspicion and when his food came he pushed it away, saying it was poisoned.

"You have to eat something," she urged.

"You don't understand," Frank said, "they can put anything they want in my food."

"Who are 'they'?" Alice asked.

"Forget it," Frank said.

In Washington, D.C. they drove past the Treasury Department and the White House and then, after a few more blocks, parked next to what appeared to be a military building near the Reflecting Pool. Ruwet told Frank and Alice to wait in the car, and then he entered the building. Alice held Frank's hand and made him promise to be home for Thanksgiving. I promise, Frank said. Minutes later Ruwet came back outside. Frank squeezed her hand as he slid out of the car and said, "I'll see you in couple of days." Alice watched as Frank and Ruwet walked into the building. And that was the last time Alice saw Frank.

Two days later, while Alice was busy preparing Thanksgiving dinner for Frank and the children, Ruwet had come by the house alone. He told her that Frank had been only an hour away in a car heading home, but had abruptly decided to go back to New York because he was concerned he might do something wrong in front of the children.

Do something wrong? What? Why hadn't he called? It just wasn't Frank. All week she had tried to shake from her mind images of a man she didn't know. Frank had acted so strangely. *What was happening to him?*

But then yesterday on the telephone, the first time she had spoken to him in three days, there were no traces of this stranger. Frank sounded so much better, so much more himself.

"Don't worry," he had told her. "Everything is fine. Tell the kids I miss them a whole lot and that I'll see them tomorrow." That was Friday.

Alice was shaken from her thoughts by the sound of a car outside. She moved from the table to look out the kitchen window. The early morning sky was winter gray and a light snow was falling. There was a dark military sedan sitting in the driveway with the engine still running, spewing clouds of exhaust across her front lawn. Behind the steering column she saw Vin Ruwet. Seated next to him was her family's physician, Dr. John Schoolman.

Alice's first thought was, *Goodness, what are they doing here so early and on a Saturday?* And then she thought, *Oh God, no. No, no.* Her hands clutched at the edges of her apron as she stared out the window.

Outside, Vincent Ruwet turned the car's engine off and sat considering the small brick house while he tried to think of what he was going to say. Four days earlier, Ruwet and Frank Olson had shared a room in New York's Statler Hotel. Robert Lashbrook had been in the adjoining room. In just a few more days, Ruwet would recount in writing his time in Manhattan with Olson:

On the first day there, Frank was acting very nervous and said, "Vince, I need to talk to you alone."

Ruwet asked Robert Lashbrook, "Bob, could you give us a few minutes."

When Lashbrook went into the room adjoining theirs, Frank demanded, "Tell me what's going on."

" Going on...?"

"What's behind all of this? I need to know."

"Frank, calm down."

"You're supposed to be my friend, Vin."

"I am your friend."

"Then let me go," Olson demanded. "Let me simply disappear."

Vincent Ruwet looked up from his thoughts and saw Alice Olson standing in the window gazing back at him. He glanced across the seat at Dr. Schoolman and reached down and opened the car door.

Years later, Alice Olson said she felt she "had been kicked in the stomach." Her chest grew tight and she felt nauseous. Her knees slowly gave way and she sank to the living room floor, sobbing.

Ruwet gently lifted her to her feet and helped her into an easy chair. He motioned Dr. Schoolman toward the kitchen and mouthed the word *water*. Alice was crying and he offered her his handkerchief.

After a moment, she said, "Tell me what happened?"

"There was some sort of accident," Ruwet informed her.

"What kind of accident?" she asked wiping away the tears streaming down her face.

"I'm not sure. I think he fell...or jumped, out of a window."

"Jumped?" Alice said, confounded.

"Or fell. Yes."

"But how? What happened?"

"I'm not sure. I'll try to find out."

"I should have gone with him," she sobbed. "I should have gone up there with him."

After Ruwet and the doctor departed, promising to return soon to help her make the proper arrangements, Alice sat in her living room replete with its decorated Christmas tree and brightly wrapped gifts, and cried. For a brief moment she thought she had only imagined Ruwet's visit and that the day was really about to begin as hoped. She thought of Frank telling her that he had made a terrible mistake. She thought of the ominous banks of fog rolling in across their front lawn. She thought of Frank calling the night before and telling her he loved her and that he'd be home soon. She thought of Ruwet's words about Frank either falling or jumping out of a window.

A terrible mistake...fell or jumped. A terrible mistake.

Alice heard a sound and looked up to see their son, Eric, standing at the room's entryway. "Why are you crying, Mommy?" the boy asked. She held out her arms and said, "Come here," picking the boy up and holding him tight. Looking out of the room's large picture window, through the clustered, leafless saplings and maple trees of her backyard, she could barely make out the gray fence of Camp Detrick in the distance.

4

Frank Olson and Camp Detrick

Frank Olson was among the very first scientists to be hired to work at Camp Detrick. He was hand picked by Dr. Ira L. Baldwin, Detrick's newly appointed scientific director. Baldwin, an agricultural bacteriologist, had been Olson's thesis advisor in 1938 at the University of Wisconsin, and he had been very impressed with Frank's talents. Frank, pursuing his Ph.D. in biochemistry, had exhibited the kind of mature enthusiasm and unrelenting work ethic that any shrewd employer would want. It was only natural, four years later, after Baldwin was hired to oversee and staff Camp Detrick's fledgling research program, that he thought of Olson.

Frank Rudolph Olson was born on July 17, 1910 in the small town of Hurley in Iron County, Wisconsin. His parents, Andrew and Fredericka Johnson Olson, had immigrated to the United States from Sweden in 1890. Frank was the youngest of three children born to the couple. Andrew supported his family by harvesting and selling ice for the Chequamegon Ice Company. From sunup to sundown, he would use hand saws of varying lengths to cut large frozen blocks from the area's many snow covered, wind-swept lakes. He would haul the blocks of ice to the company's two-story icehouse by horse-drawn wagons equipped with snow-skids. There, the blocks would be stacked, sometimes twenty feet high, insulated with hay, and then sold. During the warmer months business was brisk; but the work, back breaking and dangerous, was mostly performed in sub-zero temperatures. Andrew Olson, however, who had worked as a zinc miner in Wisconsin, welcomed being outdoors in the fresh air.

After school, young Frank Olson, from the age of ten until he left home for college, often worked alongside his father on the frozen, snowy lakes. At night he would come home with cheeks rosy-red and hands so stiff from the cold that he had to soak them in warm water before sitting down to dinner. Sometimes, while doing his homework after dinner, young Frank would fall asleep at the kitchen table. In grade school, he was an excellent student, with a talent for science, and at Hurley's Lincoln High School, from 1923 to 1927, he concentrated on the Latin and Scientific Course. There, his grades were consistently excellent and by junior year, Frank had developed a real passion for chemistry.

In May 1927, Frank was accepted at the University of Wisconsin in Madison and began his studies in chemistry there the following month. About a year earlier, after reading a magazine article about German chemist and Nobel Prize winner, Fritz Haber, Frank had told his parents that he wanted to become a chemist. He would later tell some of his colleagues that he admired Haber's relentless spirit and perseverance. Interestingly, Haber was deeply involved in the development of the poison gases used by Germany during World War I. Haber's wife, Clara, also a chemist, vehemently opposed his work in chemical warfare and she committed suicide by shooting herself in the heart following an argument with Haber over the subject. Sadly, Haber's son, Hermann, also would later commit suicide because of his shame over his father's chemical warfare work.

In college, Frank was an outgoing student. He pledged to a fraternity, joined the local Masonic Lodge and, to help defray expenses, enrolled in the University's Reserve Officers' Training Program. Majoring in chemistry, he approached each of his laboratory challenges with zest and a strong sense of self-assuredness. According to one of his professors, Elizabeth McCoy, "What Frank lacked in learning he made up for in sheer determination." His grades were often nearly perfect, but records reveal that he failed miserably in military science.

Frank returned home to Hurley in June 1931 after receiving his undergraduate degree. He attempted to find work, but jobs were scarce. The nation was still caught in the Depression, and small towns like Hurley would be the last to recover. Frank's father had passed away in May 1929, so Frank moved in with his mother, Fredericka. He did what he could to earn money – cutting firewood, delivering groceries, doing odd jobs – but finding full time work was a job in itself. He soon became bored and restless, and sorely missed campus life and his interaction with numerous classmates.

After nearly two years in Hurley, Frank decided to return to the University of Wisconsin in the fall of 1934 to study for an advanced degree in chemistry. He rented a small bedroom from an older couple living near the university, enrolled in classes part-time and took a job working nights in a creamery.

Alice Smith Wicks met Frank at the University of Wisconsin, where she was an undergraduate majoring in home economics. The tall, attractive, dark-haired minister's daughter from Rhinelander, Wisconsin had admired the intense, blond-haired doctoral student for several months before they happened to meet at a social function. The two hit it off right from the start. Alice was surprised to learn that Frank had grown up only about eighty miles north of Rhinelander. And she discovered that, despite his intensity, he had a fun loving side, making her laugh and feel happy whenever she was with him.

Alice came more and more to enjoy her time with Frank, but she was in no hurry to get married or to become a housewife and mother. She took her college studies seriously, and wanted to do something in the business world after graduating.

In July 1938, one month after receiving his Ph.D. in biochemistry, Frank accepted a position as an assistant researcher in the Botany and Agronomy Department at Purdue University's Agricultural Experimental Station in West Lafayette, Indiana. His starting salary was $1,980 a year. Tired of living in tight quarters, he rented a house for $45 dollars a month, sharing it with three other bachelors employed at Purdue. Years later, he described his work at Purdue as "The study of the effect of mineral fertilizers on symbiotic and non-symbiotic nitrogen fixation and the effect of fertilizers and crop rotation on the vitamin contents of cereals."

Following her graduation, Alice took an entry-level management position with a department store in Chicago. She was entirely on her own and relished the amenities of urban life. Alice enjoyed White Sox baseball games at Comiskey Park and became a dedicated jazz aficionado, frequenting Singer's Rendezvous on Superior Avenue and the northside's Aragon Ballroom. But, back home in Wisconsin, Alice's mother, Hattie, died suddenly, so Alice felt compelled to return to Rhinelander to help her father raise her twelve-year-old sister, Virginia. Family members say that Alice was "very, very close" to her father, Charles Wicks, and that giving up her independence "was of little consequence when she was able to fill her mother's role."

Alice wrote to Frank weekly from Rhinelander and, when she was able, traveled to Indiana to visit him. Frank, deeply in love, wanted more than ever to marry Alice and had asked her several times, but she didn't feel ready yet. "Let's wait a little longer," she told him. Then, her father unexpectedly remarried and Alice finally said 'yes' to Frank. They were married on September 7, 1940.

The couple moved into a small, one-bedroom apartment on West Lafayette's Sheetz Street, not far from Frank's work, and they quickly became friends with many of the other couples connected with Purdue. Alice would later say, "Life in Indiana was easy and enjoyable. We had a lot of friends and would get together with them often to go to the movies or to play bridge. Frank loved his job and really enjoyed working in a university atmosphere." Despite the peacefulness of Indiana, however, the threat of war was spreading worldwide. Already, Japan had invaded China, and Germany had invaded Poland, Denmark, Norway and France. In late summer 1940, the German blitzkrieg against Britain began, and in June 1941, Germany invaded the Soviet Union, yanking the Soviets into alliance with the United Kingdom. In December 1941, Japan attacked the United States at Pearl Harbor, and four days later Hitler declared war on the United States.

Years earlier, in May 1933, after completing his Army officer's training requirements at Wisconsin, Frank had entered the Reserve Officers' Corps as a second lieutenant. Now, on March 20, 1942, the Army was calling him to active duty. Frank was granted a leave of absence from his job and two weeks later he was in uniform.

Frank and Alice Olson were in Texas on the day after Christmas, 1942, when Ira Baldwin, Frank's former thesis advisor, telephoned and asked Frank to come to work at Edgewood Arsenal in Maryland. Frank was now an Army first lieutenant stationed at Fort Hood, fifty miles southwest of Waco, Texas. Baldwin, hired just three days earlier by General W.C. Kabrick of the Army's Chemical

Warfare Service, was aggressively recruiting scientists. His mandate from General Kabrick had been plain and simple: "Get me the best you can find and get them fast." Baldwin was given an astounding initial budget of $6,000,000. "If you need more, let me know," said Kabrick.

"If I said, 'I want that man,' Baldwin later recalled , "unless the Manhattan Project said they needed him, I got him."

Frank Olson didn't have to think twice about Baldwin's offer. He told Alice to start packing their bags, they were moving to Maryland. Frank's orders, as Baldwin promised, arrived three days later. "Frank told me, 'They're starting a new program, but I can't tell you anything about it,'" Alice later recalled. "He was excited and frightened at the same time about going." Alice was pregnant with their first child when she and Frank moved across the country. Eric Wicks Olson would be born shortly after Alice and Frank arrived in Maryland. A little over a year-and-a-half later, Eric's sister, Lisa, was born, and the youngest Olson child, Nils, was born about three years later.

Frank and Alice moved into a cramped two-bedroom apartment in Frederick, Maryland. Frank was whisked off almost immediately to work on classified projects within the confines of Edgewood Arsenal, eighty-three miles east of Frederick, in Gunpowder, Maryland. His starting salary was $4,600; his job title was Temporary Research Assistant, with a thirty-day assignment that was changed to full-time after about forty days. It would still be two months before anyone considered using nearby Detrick Field in the nation's burgeoning biological warfare program. Declassified Pentagon records reveal that when Olson reported for duty at Edgewood's Army Chemical Center on December 31, 1942, he was assigned to the Technical Division, pending transfer to Camp Detrick.

Not a great deal is known about Frank's work at Edgewood, except that three of the people he first encountered were Lt. Col. Arvo T. Thompson (called "Tommy"), Capt. Frank M. Shertz, and Major Harold A. Abramson. The Technical Division consisted of only five members, including Thompson and Shertz. It was charged with identifying potential work sites and lab facilities, developing plans for expanded research programs, and maintaining contacts with British scientists who worked at England's Porton Down facility on projects of mutual interest. According to former colleagues of Olson, he and Tommy Thompson got along especially well, maintaining their friendship through their days together at Camp Detrick, until Thompson's unexpected suicide in May 1951.

Harold Alexander Abramson, a highly trained, forty-two year old Columbia University trained physician and psychiatrist, was a medical officer in Edgewood's Technical Division, assigned to the Office of the Chief. According to the few scant Army documents that survived his death in 1953, Olson was assigned in early February 1943 to work under Major Abramson on a classified project involving chemotherapeutic aerosols.

The project, partially funded by the Josiah Macy, Jr. Foundation of New York, originated out of the concern on the part of military medical authorities that the Germans and Japanese would use poison gas against American troops. From hard experience the Army knew that, in addition to producing large numbers of immediate casualties, gas attacks also caused casualties from secondary infections like pneumonia and bronchitis. Toxic gas inhalation has much the same effect on the mucous membrane as an attack of influenza: an impairment of natural resistance to infection.

Prior to being assigned to war duty at Edgewood Arsenal, Dr. Abramson had been conducting extensive allergy research at Columbia University and Mt. Sinai Hospital in New York. In the course of this research, he had developed an efficient method of reducing the size of aerosol droplets so that an aerosol mist could pass through the smallest bronchial tube into the lungs. Using the technology derived from this research, Major Abramson conceived the idea that aerosols might be used in the treatment of victims of toxic gaseous agents and to protect the respiratory tract and lungs against secondary infection.

Major Abramson, assisted by First Lieutenant Frank Olson and several other Edgewood scientists, began his search for the proper aerosol using a solution of sodium hypochlorite. Also assisting was Dr. Vernon Bryson of the Long Island Biological Association. Still operational today, the association is a private research group founded in 1924 by a number of wealthy entrepreneurs, including J.P. Morgan and William K. Vanderbilt. The group has organizational ties to the controversial eugenics research conducted by Charles Davenport's Cold Spring Harbor Department of Eugenics. During World War II, Vannevar Bush, head of the Office of Scientific Research and Development, strongly supported the association's work.

With help from Dr. Bryson and the Air Force's Office of the Air Surgeon, Abramson and Olson traveled to Mitchell Field on Long Island where they used a barracks for experiments. According to the Long Island Biological Association of Cold Spring Harbor, men housed in the barracks "suffered no discomfort from sleeping in air saturated with sodium hypochlorite, but their rifles and other metal equipment were corroded."

Major Abramson persisted, conducting a number of experiments at Edgewood and on Long Island through which it was discovered that the lungs absorbed penicillin aerosol. Dr. Bryson volunteered to test the inhalation on himself, with no ill effects. After additional experiments, it was "found that enough penicillin was absorbed from the inhaled aerosol to be carried in high concentration through the blood stream." On the basis of these experiments, the Surgeon General set the standardization of nebulizers to be used by Army medical personnel for aerosol inhalation therapy.

In addition to Olson's travel with Dr. Abramson to Long Island in 1943, the two men also ventured into New York City for a series of meetings with OSS officials. As readers shall learn in far greater detail, these meetings revolved around experiments the wartime intelligence service was conducting with various formulations of 'truth' drugs.

Following the war's end, in October 1946, Dr. Abramson was awarded the prestigious Legion of Merit by General Alden H. Waitt, Chief of the Army's Chemical Corps, for "vital contributions to war efforts." Here it is pertinent to point out that much of Abramson's aerosol research at Edgewood, and later at the Cold Spring Harbor Biological Laboratories, was funded by the Josiah Macy Jr. Foundation, a private New York-based group that would soon become instrumental in the CIA's and Abramson's experiments with LSD.

While Frank logged long hours at Edgewood, Alice was left with the job of setting up house in a small three-room apartment the couple had rented in Baltimore. In late March 1943, Alice secured a much roomier apartment in Frederick on East 15th Street where they lived for about three years. Eventually, after Frank had been transferred to Camp Detrick, they were able to afford a small three-bedroom house on a quiet, wooded lot called Old Braddock Heights, only about a mile from Camp Detrick.

Meanwhile, Frederick was a long commute from Edgewood, and Frank was able to come home only occasionally on weekends, for a day or two at the most. At first, Alice found Maryland very different from Wisconsin and Indiana. People in Frederick kept to themselves and were harder to meet and to get to know. In the early 1940s, Frederick was a tight-knit agricultural community, its ethos primarily one of hard work and minding-your-own-business, with little time for play or socializing. Said Alice, "You have to be born here or live here a generation to be considered a Fredricktonian."

But Alice, like Frank, moved with a self-confidence that tended to overlook obstacles, and soon she formed strong friendships with many of "the Detrick wives." These women very much admired and looked up to her. She was a bit older than most of them, smart, college educated, understood things instinctively, and she wasn't afraid to speak her mind. Former friends recalled Alice's "infectious smile and hearty laugh"; several said that Alice was "always the one that other women would go to in times of trouble." Like all of the women, Alice was proud that her husband had been selected for work at Camp Detrick, despite knowing almost nothing about the nature of that work. Years after Frank's death, she told writer Jeanne McDermott, "Just as we speculated about the atom bomb project—you have friends who are physics majors and they all go to Los Alamos—we knew when we came here; all the wives said they must be working on germ warfare. For young couples trying to establish a life together, it didn't help in sharing."

One item that Frank did share with Alice was a copy of a Chemical Corps Medical Treatment and Death form on which he made his wife the emergency contact. The signed, one-page form reads: "In the event of death, I authorize the Commanding Officer at Camp Detrick, Maryland to make arrangements for and conduct the processing of my remains and to place them in a sealed casket which shall not thereafter be opened." Below that the form stated: "I authorize post-mortem examination of my remains to be made exclusively by proper Army representatives in their discretion."

In the early 1940s, Camp Detrick was to biological warfare what Transylvania is to the legend of Count Dracula. Like the bloodthirsty count's residence, Detrick was a place steeped in intrigue and dark, frightening rumors. Situated on over 1,000 acres of pristine real estate, the site had humble beginnings in 1929 as a small, seldom-used emergency landing field for military aircraft. Called the Frederick Municipal Airport after the bucolic town it bordered, the field had only one hangar and was operated by a lone employee. The site was renamed Detrick Field in honor of squadron flight surgeon, Capt. Frederick L. Detrick, a graduate of the Rockefeller Institute in New York and a faculty member at nearby Johns Hopkins University in Baltimore.

The decision to locate the nation's biological warfare center at Detrick Field was made in the early years of World War II. President Franklin D. Roosevelt had become increasingly disturbed over mounting intelligence reports that Germany and Japan were stockpiling poison gas. There were also reports that Russia, Britain, and Canada were far ahead of the United States in biological weapons research. In early 1942, following the intense work of a number of high-level and blue-ribbon study groups, Roosevelt ordered the War Department — precursor to the Department of Defense — to take whatever measures were necessary to bring the United States up to speed with Axis and Allied powers.

In response, the War Department created the War Research Service (WRS), and installed George Wilhelm Merck as its director. Merck was a natural for the job, as he was already a high-ranking consultant to the War Department on biological warfare. He was also head of Merck & Co., one of the oldest and largest pharmaceutical companies in the world. The firm had its beginnings in the late-1600s in Darmstadt, Germany as the E. Merck chemical factory. In 1891, George Merck, George Wilhelm's father, left Germany to establish Merck & Co, in New York City. His son, George Wilhelm Merck, born in West Orange, New Jersey and a Harvard graduate, had assumed control of the company in 1925. The younger Merck dynamically guided the company to become the largest full-line producer and distributor of pharmaceuticals in the world. Merck & Co. has since been responsible for countless innovations in the drug industry, including many in the controversial areas of enthnogenic products and shamanic inebriants.

In 1914, Merck's German operation was the first company worldwide to synthesize and patent methylene dioxymethamphetamine, or MDMA. As readers shall see, MDMA, a semi-synthetic psychoactive drug popularly known today as Ecstasy, was tested in the early-1950s under the codename EA-1475 at the Army's Edgewood Arsenal.

Appointed WRS director by Secretary of War Henry Stimson in 1942, George Merck promptly hired Dr. Edwin B. Fred as chief of research and development. An agricultural bacteriologist and former president of the Society of American Bacteriologists, Dr. Fred was dean of the University of Wisconsin Graduate School and, later, president of the University. While at Wisconsin, Frank

Olson had been one of Dr. Fred's best students. Dr. Fred was also a colleague of Dr. Ira Baldwin, who in 1942 was chairman of Wisconsin's Department of Bacteriology.

Merck also recruited John Phillips Marquand to be Director of WRS's Division of Biological Warfare Information and Intelligence. Merck had known Marquand from their student days at Harvard. He had become a well-known satirical novelist and had no experience in the world of intelligence gathering or bureaucracy when Merck hired him. Marquand displayed his naïveté when he made it his first priority to consolidate, under WRS's auspices, the flow of germ warfare intelligence from the Army, FBI, Federal Bureau of Narcotics, Office of Strategic Services, and Office of Naval Intelligence. Marquand's effort failed quickly and miserably.

George W. Merck, however, was no neophyte in biological warfare. Previously, he had served as a high-ranking consultant to a top-secret group called the WBC Committee. The WBC committee had been formed in the fall of 1941, two months before the attack on Pearl Harbor, when Secretary of War Henry L. Stimson asked Frank B. Jewett, president of the National Academy of Sciences, to appoint a working group to make a complete survey of the biological warfare capacities of other nations. Wrote Stimson to Jewett, "Because of the danger that might confront this country from potential enemies employing what may be broadly described as biological weapons, it seems advisable that investigations be initiated to survey the present situation and the future possibilities."

Jewett turned to his good friend Dr. Edwin B. Fred at the University of Wisconsin to identify who would be best for the group. Fred picked Merck; Dr. Ira Baldwin; Thomas Bourne Turner, chair of the Department of Bacteriology at Johns Hopkins University; Thomas Rivers, director of the Rockefeller Hospital in New York; William Hay Taliaferro of the University of Chicago; and Louis O. Kunkel of the Rockefeller Institute. Merck chaired the group, which was named the War Bureau of Consultants, or, as it was commonly referred to, the WBC Committee. Acting as military liaison to the committee were Maj. Arvo Thompson and Lt. Col. James H. Defandorf from Edgewood Arsenal.

Starkly illustrating the enemy dangers that preoccupied the Secretary of War were a series of incidents that had occurred two years earlier in

New York. The first incident occurred on February 3, 1939. Dr. Ryoichi Naito, an assistant to Dr. Shiro Ishii — head of Japan's secret germ warfare program — visited the Manhattan offices of the Rockefeller Institute for Medical Research and asked for samples of the yellow fever virus strain stored there for use in vaccinations. The Institute refused the request, but Dr. Naito repeatedly returned, harrassing Rockefeller Institute scientists with questions about the virus.

During one of Naito's uninvited visits, scientists were stunned to hear him brag that he had recently spent eighteen months at the Robert Koch Institute in Berlin. At the time, the Koch Institute, a renowned research facility, was a hub for Nazi biological research.

According to declassified military intelligence documents, several days later, after Naito had apparently gone away, a well-dressed man approached a Rockefeller Institute laboratory technician on the street a few blocks away from the Institute. The man, who declined to identify himself and spoke with an unidentified foreign accent, informed the technician that he worked for a famous scientist who needed samples of an extremely virulent yellow fever strain that was held by the Institute.

The technician suggested he speak with the Institute's director, but the man said that wouldn't work because of professional jealousies. Then the man blurted, "I'm willing to pay you $1,000 for your help."

When the technician declined the offer, the man said, "What if I were to give you $1,000 now and $2,000 more on delivery?"

Again, the technician, whose annual salary was less than half of what was being offered, nervously declined, telling the man that yellow fever cultures were kept under tight security. Unfazed, the man suggested that the technician extract the virus from one of the Institute's caged primates. After this and other options were rejected, the man angrily walked away, never to be seen again.

Six months later, a highly respected Japanese bacteriologist, Dr. Yonetsugi Miyagawa, sent a letter to Dr. Wilbur Sawyer, director of the Rockefeller Institute, requesting samples of the virus. Sawyer refused and immediately notified authorities. As readers shall see, the motives behind the incidents were more horrible than anyone could have imagined.

On February 17, 1942, the WBC Committee sent Secretary Stimson its massive printed survey of the world's existing biological warfare capabilities. The document numbered over 1,000 pages, with an additional 230-pages thick appendixes. Given this substantial evidence, the committee concluded that biological warfare was a distinct possibility and that it posed a real threat to national security. The WBC urged that steps be taken immediately to formulate defensive and offensive measures to protect the nation against its use. The report stated:

> The value of biological warfare will be a debatable question until it has been clearly proven or disproven [sic] by experiences. The wide assumption is that any method which appears to offer advantages to a nation at war will be vigorously employed by that nation. There is but one logical course to pursue, namely, to study the possibilities of such warfare from every angle, make every preparation for reducing its effectiveness, and thereby reduce the likelihood of its use.

Acting on the findings of the WBC Committee report, Secretary Stimson recommended that President Franklin Roosevelt create a civilian agency to be charged with the task of devising specific strategies for defensive and retaliatory biological warfare. Recommending that such responsibilities be placed under a civilian agency caused a fair amount of consternation and disciplined dissent among high-ranking War Department officers. However, Stimson successfully argued that he was doing everything possible not to alarm the public or alert the press, and assured the military that any actual biological warfare programs set into motion would fall under their control.

Consequently, on May 15, 1942, Roosevelt authorized Stimson to establish the War Research Service (WRS). It was located within the innocuous Federal Security Agency, precursor to the U.S. Department of Health and Human Services. Named as WRS director was George W. Merck. Due to the military's concerns over control, WRS's responsibilities were essentially advisory in nature. Dr. Edwin Fred continued on with WRS as a consultant and helped Merck smoothly guide the new group's recommendations through a maze of federal entities, not the least of which were the Army's Chemical Warfare Service, the U.S. Public Health Service, the Army's G-2 intelligence corps, the Office of Naval Intelligence (ONI), the FBI, and the Office of Strategic Services.

WRS was also responsible for initiating biowarfare research projects in universities and in private facilities, with the strict proviso that these civilian organizations were to be "limited to carry out such projects as were assigned to the Chemical Warfare Service by WRS."

Initially, Merck had felt strongly that by solely marshalling the diverse civilian research resources of American universities and private institutions, WRS could surpass all other nations in developing biological programs and weaponry. However, Merck quickly found that this predominantly civilian approach was rife with problems, not least of which were coordinating programs, establishing and maintaining strict security and secrecy, and dealing with the military's fierce objection to not having complete control over WRS. Realizing that he didn't have the political muscle to lock horns with the War Department, Merck swiftly surrendered virtually all WRS authority to the Army's Chemical Warfare Center at Edgewood.

The Edgewood Chemical Warfare Center is situated sixty miles northwest of Washington, D.C. on 10,000 acres of wooded land jutting nearly eight miles into the Chesapeake Bay. Today, the land is enclosed by high, electrified fencing and patrolled around-the-clock by a force of 600 armed, land and air security personnel. Large signs posted everywhere warn that the "Use of Deadly Force Is Authorized" against trespassers. The War Department had purchased the Edgewood site in 1917 and it was originally called Gunpowder Neck Reservation. In 1918 the center's name was changed to Edgewood Arsenal. Edgewood bears the distinction of being the site of the nation's first human experiments with deadly warfare gases.

In 1915, in Langemarck, Belgium, the Germans had used poisonous liquid chlorine against Allied troops. The attack, which killed over five thousand soldiers and left nearly ten thousand others seriously wounded, marked the beginnings of modern chemical warfare. Survivors of the attack recounted men everywhere dropping to the ground clutching their throats in horrendous pain, followed by severe vomiting and diarrhea. Field surgeons dubbed the affliction "air hunger." Medics described eerie battlefield scenes: piles of bodies with grotesquely contorted faces, strange bluish clouds floating above the trench tops, and enemy troops moving freely about dressed in what appeared to be deep sea divers' suits with large, windowed metal helmets.

Stunned by the attack, the United States had responded by creating its own Chemical Warfare Service (CWS) at the newly acquired Edgewood site. In September 1920, the Army established a chemical warfare school at Edgewood and began papering major U.S. cities and train stations with recruiting posters glorifying the reasons why Americans should enlist in the effort. A few months later, CWS constructed a prototype gas chamber at Edgewood. At first, rabbits, goats, horses and donkeys were herded through the chamber and then volunteer enlisted men were used in experiments to discover antidotes to lethal gases. This would be the first of many Edgewood experiments using human subjects.

In December 1942, after Dr. Ira Baldwin was hired as WRS scientific director, the Chemical Warfare Service decided that far more space was needed for their biological warfare operations. Edgewood Arsenal had grown to become the largest chemical weapons facility ever assembled worldwide. Edgewood maintained a staff of 1,200 researchers working on more than 4,000 potentially poisonous substances. One account of the center read:

> The entire arsenal had cost around $40 million, and within its walls were two hundred and eighteen manufacturing buildings, seventy-nine other permanent structures, twenty-eight miles of railway, fifteen miles of roadway, and eleven miles of high tension electrical transmission lines. Its factories were capable of producing over two hundred thousand chemical bombs and shells per day.

But, as huge as the Edgewood site was, it simply wasn't suitable for what the Army had in mind for its biological warfare operations. In January 1943, the Chemical Warfare Service instructed WRS to begin looking for a new location.

In March 1943, following an intensive search, Baldwin and Merck recommended Detrick Field in Frederick, Maryland as an ideal site. However, about eight months earlier the airstrip had been quietly taken over by the OSS. They were using it as a base for covert training operations; OSS had no intention of letting go of the property. Baldwin contacted OSS Special Operations Branch Commander, William Vanderbilt, former governor of Rhode Island, but Vanderbilt rebuffed Baldwin's overtures. Repeated phone calls to Vanderbilt, some answered by a young aide named James Jesus Angleton, were unsuccessful. Finally, Merck told Baldwin that he would contact Stanley P. Lovell, a friend who also happened to be OSS Director of Research and Development.

Lovell, who readers will again encounter as a serious player in the cover-up of Frank Olson's death, was instrumental in getting the OSS to relinquish its hold on Detrick Field. As revealed in a March 24, 1943 letter written by Brigadier

General Alden H. Waitt, head of the Army's Chemical Warfare Service, to Lovell:

> You will be interested to know that we have acquired Detrich [sic] Field and are going ahead rapidly with the project. I feel that you were responsible in a large measure for our being able to take it over. I know that OSS released the field at considerable sacrifice. We appreciate your help and the willingness of Commander Vanderbilt to cooperate with us.

Waitt's letter doesn't mention that Merck and Baldwin had considered moving WRS's biological operations to two other locations, also being utilized by the OSS. One was a complex of factories, presumably vacant, owned by the Bata Shoe Company near Aberdeen, Maryland and being used by OSS for counter-insurgency training. The other was Deep Creek Lake, a remote, heavily wooded site in Maryland that the OSS was using for paramilitary training.

Merck found the Frederick site particularly attractive because of its rural remoteness but convenient proximity to Washington, D.C., the War Department, and Edgewood Arsenal. Baldwin was especially pleased with the location because its agricultural surroundings reminded him of his home state of Wisconsin and were ideal for maintaining the hundreds of animals that would be needed for experiments. Detrick Field was renamed Camp Detrick in early April 1943. According to Fort Detrick's former (and aptly named) public affairs officer, Norman M. Covert, the relocation of biowarfare experiments to Frederick was "cloaked in the deepest wartime secrecy, matched only by the Manhattan Project." Military historian Lt. Col. Richard M. Clendenin wrote in the late 1960s:

> Reasons for the stringent security were twofold, not only to prevent the enemy from learning that work was being done in BW [biological warfare], but also to keep the public and even the Armed Forces themselves from becoming unduly alarmed over the possibility of BW.

Naturally, the townspeople of Frederick were a little bit curious about the tremendous amount of activity at the once quiet airfield. With round-the-clock construction underway and a security force of about 200 uniformed and plainclothes agents, rumors became rampant that the acreage was being refashioned for use as a large new airfield for bombers. When it became obvious that no hangers or additional runways were being constructed, however, and when convoys filled with German POWs were seen rumbling down Frederick's main streets, townspeople speculated that the site was being used for mass exterminations. But when townspeople saw that the German POWs were being used as laborers, they guessed that the field was being converted into an internment camp for German Americans from nearby Baltimore. When truckloads of caged rabbits, mice, goats, guinea pigs, and monkeys were hauled in, rumors circulated about experiments with futuristic death ray weapons.

Only when the post office and railroad began delivering crates filled with laboratory and medical equipment to the site did some of the area's more astute citizens realize that perhaps something wholly different was afoot at the camp. Once-classified reports by a joint team of OSS and Army Counter Intelligence Corps (CIC) agents reveal that onsite security may not have been as tight as believed. According to one CIC official, writing in early 1944:

> It is this agent's opinion that anybody who really wanted to find out that bacteriological warfare activities are being conducted at Camp Detrick could easily do so by studying the backgrounds of the technical civilian employees employed there and by analyzing the type of material purchased by the post procurement in Frederick and the types of material which is [sic] shipped into Frederick by Railway Express.

On May 6, 1943, Frank Olson was transferred from Edgewood Arsenal to Camp Detrick. When Frank reported for duty, military work crews were still stringing barbwire for the elaborate security fences that surrounded the camp's perimeter. The more difficult work of digging postholes and mixing and pouring concrete was left to Nazi POWs trucked in from nearby Camp Ritchie and Fort George Meade. Army guards toting Thompson submachine guns shadowed the Germans everywhere. Inside the vast compound, construction workers labored 24-hours a day finishing over 100 research buildings.

Prior to his transfer, Frank had been thoroughly briefed that the work he was about to undertake would be unlike anything ever attempted in the United States. The relentless emphasis on secrecy within Camp Detrick's gates and walls was continually underscored. Scientists were routinely reminded to be on the alert for potential enemy spies and saboteurs. Posters everywhere warned about "careless talk" and "loose lips."

A few weeks after their arrival in Maryland, Alice showed Frank letters she had received from friends back in Wisconsin and Indiana. The letters told of FBI and War Department investigators who had come around asking questions about Frank. Was he a loyal American? Did he have any friends from other countries? Was there anything about his life or past that was odd or disjointed? Was his wife a good American? One of Alice's friends wrote: "What on God's good earth is Frank working on back there?" It was frightening and exciting to be the center of such attention. Alice knew from Frank's guarded comments that whatever he was doing within the confines of Edgewood Arsenal and Camp Detrick, it was very important to the war effort.

In 1988, asked by a CIA attorney what she knew about Frank's work at Edgewood and Camp Detrick, Alice said:

> I knew he was a biochemist, and I knew they were working in aerosols, that masks were involved, crops were involved. I knew nothing except what I could speculate from the fact that he was a biochemist and I knew

the people—where their degrees came from, what departments they were in, like agronomy which would be crops, that sort of thing. But I knew nothing of his work.

Another thing that Alice knew, but rarely spoke about, were the dangers that Frank's work sometimes presented. In 1976, she would remark to a friend that one Saturday in mid-November 1948, Frank came home late from work badly shaken and limping, with his right leg heavily bandaged. He told Alice he had been working on a special project at the Free Flight Tunnel at Langley Air Force Base in Virginia, when the cuff on the right leg of the loose fitting work whites he was wearing became caught in a bolt on a motor generator. The engaged machine yanked his trousers further into itself, ripping them, and pulling his leg into contact with the whirling parts of the generator. The quick thinking of a colleague, Lee Buchanan, managed to free him from the machine, but not before he suffered severe contusions to his lower right leg and ankle. Alice was aghast when Frank showed her his injured leg, which in places was swollen to nearly twice its normal size and horribly discolored by purple, gray and black bruises.

FBI and Army security reports on Frank Olson from 1943 through 1945 reveal little more than that he was well regarded among his friends, neighbors, and colleagues. Mario Gianeinzio, who had attended Lincoln High School with Olson and who was now a teacher there, told Army investigators that Olson was "a man of exceptionally good character and morals." Gianeinzio said that he recommended Olson for any "position of trust and confidence."

Ida Jackson, a self-described "housewife" in Frank's hometown of Hurley, told Army Counter Intelligence Corps investigator David E. Kelly that she had known the Olson family for over thirty years. "Frank has a good reputation in this community," Ida said. "He had the courage to go and become a well educated man and now he serves his country well as a scientist."

William H. Peterson, a professor of biochemistry at the University of Wisconsin-Madison, told investigators that he had known Olson for about twelve years. Said Peterson, "I would classify Olson as having good mentality, but not outstanding. He's an excellent man on applied work, but not outstanding on theoretical work." Added Peterson, "Frank has a diplomatic way of dealing with people" and "he is a man of absolute loyalty to the United States."

Another professor at Wisconsin, Elizabeth McCoy, said that she first met Olson when he came to the school "as a crude Northwoods boy from Hurley" but that he "developed into a keen chemist." McCoy, who in 1942 served as a consultant to the WBC Committee, highly recommended Olson "as a good American citizen."

Former WRS research director and then-University of Wisconsin president, Dr. Edwin B. Fred, told Army investigators that Olson was "a resourceful type of man" who worked his way through college by operating "a local milk route." Said Dr. Fred, "Olson never has much trouble getting his ideas across

49

to others." Fred highly recommended Olson "for any position of trust with the government."

Mrs. Sigfreid M. Hauge, a former West Lafayette neighbor of the Olsons, told Army investigators, "Frank and his wife both enjoyed a good reputation and were well-liked. I considered him to be most pleasant and the possessor of a good personality. Both he and his wife were frank, honest persons."

But not all was well with Frank, and soon the reports on his performance would become less than flattering. Within months of his arrival at Edgewood Arsenal, Frank complained of stomach pains that had sporadically flared up in the past. At times, it was so severe he was unable to work. In Frank's estimation, by late-1943 the problem had become debilitating.

According to a once-classified FBI report, Olson appeared before an Army Retiring Board on November 26, 1943 at Walter Reed General Hospital in Washington, D.C., and presented the case that, due to his stomach ailment, he was no longer fit for active duty. The Board agreed that he was "incapacitated by reason of Duodenum, ulcer of, chronic, cause undetermined" and that he should be released from active duty with the Army, but it also decided that Olson's incapacity "was not incurred in line of duty" and therefore he was "not entitled to retirement pay benefits."

Frank was dissatisfied with the Board's assessment. On January 8, 1944 he appealed his case, contending "that his disability did not exist prior to his entry into active service." He asked that the Board amend its report "to show his disability as having been incurred in line of duty." As evidence supporting this, he submitted a recent letter solicited from a physician who had seen him in January 1942, two months prior to his reporting for active duty. The letter certified that before he had gone on active duty he "showed no evidence of having an ulcer."

Olson's appeal was denied. On February 2, 1944, the Secretary of War's Separation Board notified him that it had carefully considered his case and determined that "no new or additional information" had been presented that the Retiring Board had not already reviewed. The Retiring Board's decision was sustained.

Undeterred, Frank appealed again. This time, on May 14, 1945, the Secretary of War's Disability Review Board took up the case. The FBI report reads, "On May 28, 1945, [Olson] was certified to the Administration of Veteran's Affairs as being entitled to Retirement Pay Benefits in the amount of $172. 50 per month." Veterans Administration records issued on June 21, 1944 to Olson read: "The monthly payment pursuant to this award will continue during the period in which you are 30% degree disabled."

According to military records, Olson was officially given an honorable discharge from the Army on April 18, 1944 at the rank of captain. After less than two years of active duty he was once again a civilian, but little else changed in his life. He was asked to stay on at Camp Detrick and continue his work as a biochemist.

From 1945 through 1948, Olson's personnel file reveals nothing unusual. Routine security checks with former classmates, neighbors, and colleagues continued to produce glowing comments and recommendations. None of the security checks performed by the Army and FBI during this time make any mention of Olson's ulcer condition.

However, it appears that towards the end of 1949, problems began to develop with civilian employee Frank Olson. In October of that year the Army's Counter Intelligence Corps (CIC) conducted a routine security check on all the scientific personnel who had visited the Chemical Corps' Dugway Proving Ground in Utah, or who had worked on Operation Harness, a less than successful experimental program involving teams of American, British, and Canadian microbiologists who sprayed virulent agents like anthrax, brucellosis and tularemia over the Bahamas, Antigua and New Hebrides.

CIC agent Fred Berry wrote in a report headed "SECURITY COMPROMISE" that several of Olson's supervisors complained that he "plays internal politics, is a detrimental influence on morale, [and] divulged information to associates who should not have received it...[and] does not follow orders and has had numerous altercations" with military police.

Then, during a subsequent routine FBI security check, Dr. Morris Guggenheim, assistant chief of Camp Detrick's medical branch, told FBI Special Agent John J. Grogan that he was only "casually associated" with Olson, but nonetheless he felt compelled to say he thought that Olson "is conceited, talks too much and is not particularly reliable from a technical standpoint."

Dr. Leslie A. Chambers, Camp Detrick's Biological Division chief and Olson's superior from early 1946 through late 1949, was harsher in his assessment of Olson. Chambers told agent Grogan that Olson "had an aggressive personality and did not care what he said." Chambers additionally said that Olson "was unsettled and tactless, almost to the point of indiscretion." Complained Chambers, contrary to what his superiors Col. Vincent Ruwet and Dr. John Schwab would say several years later, Olson "usually overindulged in alcohol on occasion at dances or stag affairs at the Officers' Club." Wrote agent Grogan in his report, "Dr. Chambers felt that [Olson] had a detrimental influence on the morale of the personnel at Camp Detrick. He does not believe [Olson] would divulge information of a confidential nature to unauthorized persons, but stated that [Olson] has informed associates of information which [Chambers] thought [Olson] should have kept to himself."

Dr. Chambers was not the only Camp Detrick official who had serious concerns about Olson. According to Grogan's report, Dr. J.L. Roberts, a bacteriologist, said he had known Olson since 1934 when both men attended the University of Wisconsin, shared an apartment, and briefly worked toether at Purdue University after that. Dr. Roberts echoed Chambers in stating that Olson was "extremely tactless" and that on occasion would be "under the influence of alcohol to the extent of near exhilaration."

51

Dr. Roberts also maintained that Olson was "inclined to be quick tempered" and was "violently opposed to control of scientific information by the military or otherwise, and opposed supervision of his work in any form." Roberts added that Olson "had difficulties with the Military Police on Camp Detrick by refusing to show his pass while entering or leaving or by exceeding the speed limits." Dr. Roberts also told Army investigator Gregg S. Bertram: "I don't believe that Olson is engaged in any militant activity against military supervision of research at Detrick, but, like other professional research men on the post, he opposes it, and does not hesitate to so state to anyone present regardless of their authority." Dr. Roberts also told Army investigators it was his understanding that Olson didn't intend to remain at Camp Detrick very long, "as he stated to me in confidence that he wishes to engage in business for himself, manufacturing chemicals for use in scientific research." Explained Roberts, "He has had this ambition for many years and undoubtedly will be discontented until he attains his goal." But, like Dr. Chambers, Roberts told investigators he believed Olson "is satisfactory with regard to honesty and loyalty," and that he knew Olson "had made no breaches of security."

Interestingly, Roberts also told special agent Bertram that, "while working with Olson at Purdue University, he [Roberts] recalls occasions when Olson had expressed sympathies toward Germany in preference to England, prior to the time the United States entered the war." However, Roberts told Agent Grogan that "at the time, Olson thought Russia had the lowest way of life, and hated Communists." According to Grogan, "Dr. Roberts stated that Olson never expressed any sympathies against the United States and [Roberts] does not believe he had any feelings toward the philosophy of Nazism."

Despite this harsh criticism from his fellow workers and supervisors, Olson's overall personnel assessment and security reviews were graded well and recommended his continued employment at Camp Detrick. Maj. Phillips D. Thayer, Chief of the Chemical Corps' Intelligence and Security Division in 1948 and 1949, deemed that Olson's security investigation "discloses no derogatory information."

Here it should be emphasized that the primary purpose of the investigations was to determine that Olson was loyal to his country, had the appropriate level of character and integrity, and was not a security risk. This point is underscored by a report written a few days after Olson's death by Army security agent, J.W. Corey. His report states:

The 1947-1948 CIC [Counter Intelligence Corps] investigation [of Frank R. Olson] consisted of appropriate checks and interviews. Sixteen of the eighteen interviews conducted were favorable. Two, with colleagues at Camp Detrick, contained slightly unfavorable information, which, however, did not reflect on SUBJECT's loyalty, character, or integrity. SUBJECT was considered by the two men to be tactless. One thought him qualified as a chemist but not outstanding, and thought that he drank too much. The other indicated that SUBJECT was openly resentful of supervision, either military or civilian, but that this was a fairly common quality among scientists. Both felt that SUBJECT had not as yet decided on exactly what he wanted his life's work to be.

That Frank did not get along with everyone he came in contact with was well established among his colleagues at Camp Detrick. Said former colleague and friend Donald Falconer, "Frank could be really temperamental sometimes, and he wasn't always diplomatic with people. But he wasn't the only person like that." Said Henry Eigelsbach, "You get a lot of highly intelligent scientists together in close quarters and stressful situations and there's bound to be occasional conflict. Frank was not the most diplomatic or tolerant person out of everyone at Detrick, but he was never offensive toward me. I enjoyed his humor." Perhaps Dr. J.L Roberts, Frank's former Wisconsin university classmate, put it most bluntly when he remarked to Army investigators, "I must admit, [Frank Olson] has made many enemies which will probably in later life affect his career."

One scientist with whom Olson clashed was Dr. Henry Karl Puharich, later known as Andrija Puharich, the man who introduced the controversial Israeli psychic Uri Geller to the world. Puharich, who passed away in 1995 under circumstances never resolved – but not connected to Frank Olson – was an Army officer in the early 1950s. During that time, Puharich was in and out of Edgewood Arsenal and Camp Detrick, meeting with various high-ranking officers and officials, primarily from the Pentagon, CIA, and Naval Intelligence. The purpose of the meetings was Puharich's relentless attempt to convince the military and Intelligence agencies to take the potentials of parapsychology seriously.

In February 1953, Puharich gave a lecture on extrasensory perception to the Pentagon's Advisory Group on Psychological Warfare and Unconventional Warfare. A few months later, he was asked to give a similar presentation to the Air Force Aviation School in San Antonio, Texas.

In November 1953, ten days before Frank Olson's death, Puharich was invited to the Pentagon to meet with CIA officials and psychological warfare experts. The group was interested in funding his research into extrasensory perception, but made it clear that funds would have to go through a university that would act as what Puharich termed "a blind." He agreed to the proposal but nothing happened for several months, until his commanding officer, Col. Norman W. Elton, at Edgewood Arsenal, asked if he would consider doing another lecture on extrasensory perception before a select group from Edgewood, Camp Detrick, and the CIA. The request set off a discussion on the subject between the two men, during which Elton voiced some skepticism. Puharich responded by expressing his opinion that "extrasensory perception was a reality, and that it could be proven in people with exceptional talent."

Puharich later recounted in his book *The Sacred Mushroom: Key to the Door of Eternity*, "I pointed out that there was also evidence to the effect that the talent was widely diffused throughout a normal population, and that it was probable that everyone has some of it sporadically."

"Well, if this is true," Elton persisted, perhaps revealing his true agenda for bringing up the subject, "isn't it possible to find some drug that will bring out this latent ability, so that normal people could turn this thing on and off at will?"

"It would be nice to have such a drug," Puharich replied, "because then the research problems of parapsychology would be half solved. You see, the main problem in extrasensory-perception research is that we never know, even in a person of great talent, when this mysterious faculty will manifest itself. So we just sit around like a fisherman in a boat who puts his hand in the water every once in a while, hoping that a fish will swim into his grasp. There have been some reports of primitive peoples using such drugs extracted from plants, but I have never heard of one that worked when tested in the laboratory."

"Well," Elton replied, "if you ever find a drug that works, let me know, because this kind of thing would solve a lot of the problems connected with Intelligence."

On this note, Puharich abruptly ends the account of his conversation with Col. Elton in the book and has no more to say about the Army's interest in drugs. He then plunges headfirst into an account of communication he claims to have had with an ancient Egyptian who lived over four thousand years ago. According to Puharich, the Egyptian, Ra Ho Tep, told him of a long lost ritual involving sacred mushrooms "and its astonishing effects upon human consciousness," and guided Puharich and his colleagues to the discovery of an extremely rare species of *amanita muscaria* growing in the woods of Maine.

Recently uncovered document fragments from the mostly destroyed MKUL-TRA collection reveal that Puharich had far more contact and interaction with the CIA and Army concerning drug experimentation than he indicates in any of his books. Indeed, it appears that Puharich participated in a number of secret experiments with *amanita muscaria*, the species of psychoactive mushrooms mentioned in his book. The experiments took place at prisons for men in New Jersey and Maryland, as well as at the Spring Grove Mental Hospital in Catonsville, Maryland. Also involved in these experiments was Dr. Amedeo Marrazzi.

Worth noting, is that Col. Norman W. Elton, according to declassified Army documents, oversaw the "use of volunteers in research in defense against chemical warfare," including "the exposure of individuals to the hazards of toxic chemicals." These chemicals being "standard or candidate CW agents or they may be standard or candidate therapeutic agents."

In a later 1953 presentation at Edgewood Arsenal that perhaps presaged the subsequent development of remote viewing, Puharich predicted the day "in the not too distant future when a select cadre of soldiers will possess the ability to telepathically accomplish critical intelligence tasks, and may well hold the mental abilities to observe and counteract enemy movements and tactics."

That Puharich favored and was quite open-minded toward matters esoteric was not disputed by anyone, much less Puharich himself. His claims in the early 1950s ranged from the existence of extraterrestrial entities on earth to man's ability to communicate with higher intelligences that dwarfed human intellectual capacities.

Frank Olson scoffed at such claims, perhaps more out of fear of the unknown than from objective knowledge to the contrary. One day in mid-1952 he made a less than flattering remark to Puharich who was a guest at a Chemical Corps Biological Division briefing on hallucinogenic plants. Puharich, more than capable of countering any form of derision or skepticism, quickly challenged Olson to a debate. The ensuing conversation rapidly evolved into an embarrassing incident for Olson. Puharich called Olson a "frightened schoolboy who had not yet managed to overcome his fear of the dark." Olson's retorts were far less sophisticated and the argument would likely have degenerated into fisticuffs had not the Chemical Corps' medical director and Puharich's friend, Col. Norman Elton, intervened and put a stop to it.

Here it is most interesting to note that during Frank Olson's last week in New York City with Robert Lashbrook and Vincent Ruwet, Lashbrook would take the time to hand-deliver a CIA travel check to renowned stage magician John Mulholland. The check was for Mulholland's trip that same week to Chicago to meet with Puharich and a close associate, an officer in the Army's Psychological Warfare Office. The meeting would cover a number of subjects, including hypnotism, in which Puharich was intensely interested. Just six months earlier, he had attended a demonstration of hypnosis and sleight-of-hand practices staged at the Statler Hotel for CIA and selected Federal Narcotics officials. Mulholland, the magician, had also attended the Statler event. Reportedly, Mulholland remained skeptical about hypnosis throughout his life and never incorporated hypnosis into his stage shows. It was revealed years later, in fact, that at the 1953 Chicago gathering magician Mulholland had become "so frightened of something that Puharich did" that he abruptly left the meeting, aborted his Chicago stay and immediately flew back to New York.

In the postwar years 1946 and 1947, Olson spent a fair amount of time working closely with bacteriologist Dr. Theodor Rosebury on a highly technical, two-hundred-and-twenty page monograph entitled "Experimental Air-Borne Infection." Olson was one of eleven co-authors of the publication, which credited an additional sixteen assisting writers, all of whom were Camp Detrick employees. Another of the publication's co-authors was First Lt. Norman G. Cournoyer, whom readers will meet again later in this book.

The monograph reported the results of a scientific investigation conducted at Camp Detrick between December 1943 and October 1945. Specifically, the "assigned task" was to design and construct a special chamber "for the study of air-borne clouds of highly infective agents under conditions of safety to the operating personnel and others, and in a manner such as to elicit reproducible, quantitative data on information of small laboratory animals by the inhalation route."

Dr. Rosebury first became seriously involved in biological warfare in early 1942, when he teamed up with fellow Columbia University bacteriologist, Dr. Elvin A. Kabat and authored a 40,000-word paper designed "to scare Washington officials about the dangers of bacterial warfare." Its title was: "Bacterial Warfare: A Critical Analysis of the Available Agents, Their Possible Military Applications, and the Means for Protection Against Them."

The paper served its intended purpose, perhaps much more so than the two scientists ever imagined. It was immediately classified TOP SECRET by the National Research Council and the Pentagon. Despite their unhappiness at the authors' moral reservations regarding the development and use of biological weapons, top-ranking Pentagon and Chemical Corps officials reached out with undue haste to recruit Drs. Rosebury and Kabat into the fold. Both men officially joined the staff at Edgewood Arsenal, and then Camp Detrick; Rosebury as a full-time division chief, Kabat as a consulting researcher.

Most germane to later parts of this book is Rosebury and Kabat's recommendation in their bacterial warfare paper that the best "delivery systems" for biological agents were airplanes. "The airplane," the two wrote, "is clearly the most useful means for the dissemination of infective agents." The paper went on to emphasize that small, low-flying airplanes were ideal for delivery of certain biological agents "against assembled ground troops or civilian populations."

Frank Olson greatly admired dark-haired, good-natured Rosebury. Described by Columbia University's alumni group as "truly a Renaissance man," Rosebury was a talented cabinetmaker, musician, dancer, writer, and public speaker, as well as a voracious reader who made a habit of keeping himself finely tuned to current events and world politics. Often, during breaks from working on the monograph, Frank would ask Rosebury's opinion about a wide variety of subjects unrelated to work at Camp Detrick. In many ways, Rosebury, who was six years older than Frank, assumed the role of mentor to Olson. It was in this context that Olson would eventually begin asking questions about dentistry, a field Rosebury soon realized was of more than passing interest to Olson.

Dr. Rosebury was well equipped to answer Frank's questions. Before coming to Camp Detrick, he had graduated from the University of Pennsylvania School of Dental Medicine. Shortly thereafter, in 1928, Rosebury joined Columbia University's Department of Bacteriology, concentrating initially on researching "the biochemical and nutritional aspects of dental caries." In 1938, he traveled to Alaska where he studied the diets of Eskimos in relation to their rate of tooth decay. He discovered that, contrary to conventional beliefs at the time, an important cause of dental caries was not "mushy, refined foods, but certain hard, compact, carbohydrate-rich foods" which became lodged in the crevices of teeth and remained as breeding grounds for bacteria. Today, Theodor Rose-bury is considered the "grandfather of modern oral microbiology."

Olson was fascinated by the way Rosebury could make any discussion about teeth and dental care an intriguing experience. Rosebury once told Frank to pay more attention to his own dental needs, and Frank promised to do so. Soon after, Frank announced to Alice that he was seriously considering a change of occupation to retrain himself as a dentist. Olson's colleague, Dr. Henry Eigels-bach, recalled that during the last two years before his death, Olson "spoke fairly often about leaving government work, and of his interest in going back to school and becoming a dentist." Eric Olson would tell the author in 2001 that in the 1970s, his mother had remarked several times that his father was intending "to retrain himself as a dentist," and it is interesting to note that today Frank Olson's youngest son, Nils, is a well-respected dentist practicing in Frederick, Maryland.

When Rosebury resigned his post at Camp Detrick after the war and re-turned to teaching at Columbia's College of Physicians and Surgeons, Olson was sorely disappointed. In 1949, Rosebury published his book, *Peace or Pes-tilence: Biological Warfare and How to Avoid It*. The book caused a flurry of controversy at Camp Detrick because its author dared question the use of microbiology for warfare. The book also caught the attention of the FBI. A December 7, 1950 FBI memorandum to J. Edgar Hoover reads:

> The book *'Peace or Pestilence'* is a source of considerable controversy among the employees at Camp Detrick, Maryland, and [two names redact-ed] share the opinion that it should never have been written, inasmuch as it exposes the experiments being conducted in biological warfare by the United States. It goes into considerable detail concerning them and also indicates the location of Camp Detrick and to some extent indicates the number and caliber of the personnel involved.

The remaining two pages of the memo are almost completely redacted, but there are indications that it primarily concerned Camp Detrick and Special Operations Division (SOD) personnel.

As can be imagined, the FBI's scrutiny of Theodor Rosebury was bound to have repercussions for Frank Olson. Already under watchful eyes because of his less than glowing performance reviews and his occasional altercations with military police, Olson was questioned several times by the FBI about his rela-tionship with Rosebury. Former colleague Ben Wilson would later comment, "I think Olson's hot headedness was tempered by the experience. Some of those FBI agents could be pretty grueling with people...tough, really tough. I think they shook him up. At first it may have been a novelty, the attention, I mean, but then it had its effects."

Coincidentally — or perhaps not —, around the same time that Frank Olson joined the SOD, the FBI decided it had to have a formal liaison with Camp

Detrick, specifically its Special Operations Division. A heavily redacted January 5, 1950 memorandum to J. Edgar Hoover from the Bureau's special agent in charge of Baltimore reads:

> [C]oncerning the designation of an Agent of this Office to maintain liaison with representatives of the Army's Biological Warfare Center at Camp Detrick, Maryland, the liaison relationship to be initiated upon receipt of advice from the Bureau concerning the final arrangements being made by the Intelligence Division of the Department of the Army with the U.S. Army Chemical Corps.

The memo goes on to state that direct contact had already been established with SOD chief John Schwab, and that Schwab was knowledgeable about the FBI's interest in Camp Detrick, indicating that Schwab himself, or possibly Lt. Col. Vincent Ruwet, could have been the SOD agent designated to be FBI liaison agent. Equally possible is that both men were FBI liaison agents; the Bureau's document states that an "alternate liaison" had also been selected. The memo continues:

> During the interview with [redacted name of Camp Detrick liaison agent], it was ascertained that the Special Operations Division operates directly under Major Harold J. Isbell, CMLC. At the present time, there are twelve persons employed in the Special Operations Division at Camp Detrick, although plans are being made to increase the personnel and expand the operations of this Division. A new building, which is to house the offices and laboratory of [SOD], is under construction and should be completed by August, 1950.

Further pointing toward Schwab and Ruwet as FBI liaison agents is that other Bureau documents from the 1950s clearly reveal that the FBI was well aware of a highly secret experiment in the works that involved a select team of SOD scientists infiltrating the Pentagon complex, where approximately 30,000 people worked, to contaminate the building's air conditioning system with a stimulant.

Other SOD projects that were revealed to the FBI by its liaison agent included "a possible [SOD] field group at an Atomic Energy installation," perhaps the Oak Ridge Laboratory. Significantly, the document citing these projects concludes with the recommendation that "this matter should be more thoroughly discussed with Dr. Schwab from a scientific point of view." The reference to Dr. Schwab is quite possibly an unintentional oversight by FBI censors, given that all other names of Camp Detrick personnel are redacted in all other documents.

There is no indication or any hint in the FBI's records concerning SOD that the Bureau knew anything about the CIA's relationship with the division. Indeed, FBI documents from the same time period concerning its surveillance of Camp Detrick activities reveal that, on behalf of the Advisory Committee to the Secretary of National Defense on Biological Warfare, the Bureau conducted thorough background checks on all the various members of the Advisory Committee. Among these appointed members was Robert Prather Joyce, who, according to the FBI, was then employed at the U.S. Department of State as a policy planner. Joyce, according to his background investigation, had been a former OSS and Central Intelligence Group employee, having worked in Bern, Switzerland at the same time as Allen Dulles and James Kronthal, who readers shall soon learn more about. FBI records also reveal that Joyce worked in the U.S. Embassy in Cuba and was "on a friendly basis with" writer Ernest Hemingway, who sometimes lived in Cuba. According to the FBI's file, Hemingway served "as an informant" to the Embassy. What the FBI did not seem to know was that Joyce was still very much a CIA official and that his State Department office was only a cover.

Throughout the years 1947-1949, Frank Olson devoted the bulk of his time to laboratory work within the confines of Camp Detrick. His work focused primarily on assessing and improving protective masks and clothing. His title changed in mid-1947 from Research Biochemist to Senior Research Biochemist, Personnel Protection Branch, Chemical Corps. After Rosebury had returned to the world of academia and writing books, Frank grew bored and restless and, as he remarked to Alice and a number of colleagues, he was thinking about looking for a new challenge.

Then, one Saturday evening in late July 1950, John Schwab and his wife were playing canasta with Frank and Alice Olson when the subject of the recently formed Special Operations Division came up. Frank remarked to Schwab that certain quarters of the post were buzzing with rumors about creation of the division, but that details were scarce.

After a moment, Schwab said, "Well, right now there's only about ten of us in the division. I really can't tell you much about [the division's] plans other than to say they're cutting edge."

"Security's tight," Frank commented.

"Tighter than tight."

"Well, I bet it will be exciting work."

"You could find out for yourself," said Schwab, "if you decide to join the division."

"Are you serious?" Olson asked, excitedly.

"We'd love to have you with us, Frank."

Within a few weeks, Frank Olson became a member of the elite Special Operations Division.

5

Special Operations Division Camp Detrick, 1950-1953

Frank Olson officially transferred from the Physical Defense Division of the Chemical Corps to the newly formed Special Operations Division in early September 1950. At the time, his annual salary remained at $8,000, but within six months it was increased to $8,920. He was excited about moving into work that would be less rote and that allowed for travel to places other than drab Chemical Corps installations.

In less than a year, Frank was named SOD Chief, Plans and Operations Branch. His job description read:

> Plans, directs and coordinates the programs of the Division with other divisions of the Agency and other agencies conducting work of a similar or related nature. Collects and evaluates data, foreign and domestic, relative to activity of interest to the division with particular emphasis on the medico-biological aspects. Maintains active liaison with other agencies for the mutual exchange of technical and operational data.

Olson first met Dr. Sidney Gottlieb, along with Gottlieb's TSS superiors, Willis Gibbons and Eardley Hazell, at a one-day conference on the offensive uses of psychochemicals held at Edgewood Arsenal. Gottlieb later said that he found Olson to be a "personable, good natured fellow with a winning smile." Frank again encountered Gottlieb, accompanied by Robert Lashbrook, at SOD's Detrick laboratories in early 1952. At the time, Lashbrook, less than a year after receiving his PhD in chemistry from Stanford University, had been formally appointed the TSS Chemical Division's liaison to SOD, requiring frequent visits to the facility.

Beginning in April 1951, CIA and SOD personnel made quarterly retreats to one of several isolated locations, where they would spend about three days together discussing project progress and future plans. These rendezvous, as they were called, took place at various locations: Lost River, West Virginia; Maryland's Eastern Shore, near the town of Easton; and Deep Creek Lake, Maryland, not far from the presidential retreat at Camp David. (After Olson's death, the meetings continued, although they increased in frequency for several years, and a new meeting site just outside Front Royal, Virginia was added to the list.)

Gottlieb, Lashbrook, and Olson, along with SOD chief Dr. John Schwab, came together again in 1952 at another Chemical Corps conference, this one dedicated to the subject of "the use of psychochemicals as a new concept of warfare." Also attending the gathering were Dr. David B. Dill, Chemical Corps, Medical Division; Dr. John P. Clay, an Army physician working on special projects in France and Switzerland; Dr. Sidney Gottlieb from the CIA; and Stanley Lovell, a special consultant to both SOD and the CIA, and former research director of the OSS.

The conference was lead by Dr. L. Wilson Greene, Chemical Corps Scientific Director, the man largely responsible, along with Stanley Lovell, for the creation of Camp Detrick's Special Operations Division. Dr. Greene, a civilian, was a strong advocate of the use of mind-altering drugs, including mescaline and LSD, covertly and in battlefield situations. Sidney Gottlieb found Greene's thoughts most impressive and worthy of pursuit. Much later, Gottlieb would admit:

> I was fascinated by the ideas Greene was advancing. He was convinced that it was possible to actually win a battle or larger engagement without killing anyone or destroying any property. While I found this to be a novel approach to war, I was somewhat skeptical about it, but I was intrigued by the potential applications of psychochemicals to much smaller conflicts and situations. There I saw tremendous promise.

Indeed, Dr. Greene was dedicated to the notion that wars could be won without any bloodshed or property destruction. "I'm convinced that it is possible, through the techniques of psychochemical warfare, to conquer an enemy without the wholesale killing of his people or destroying his property," enticed Greene in his introductory remarks at the conference.

Greene explained to the conference attendees that he had developed his concept of psychochemical warfare from intensive research and an original idea suggested by Dr. Alsoph H. Corwin, a chemistry professor at Johns Hopkins University. Corwin, after earning his doctorate at Harvard, worked as a research scientist for the National Defense Research Committee during World War II and throughout the 1950s under various contracts with the Army Chemical Corps and Office of Naval Research. He is noted for having developed a chemical method for restoring corroded antiquities, a process that helped decipher the Dead Sea Scrolls. In 1947, Corwin wrote a letter to the Chemical Corps Technical Command proposing that the Corps seriously consider "the potentialities of enzymes as toxicological warfare agents." Corwin detailed the effects of enzymes on vital bodily functions, and described how certain drugs and poisons could interfere with them; he included a list of specific substances that would produce "morbid interferences."

Especially worth considering, wrote Corwin, was the "spectacular possibility" of "producing mass hallucinations and uncontrolled hysteria by intoxication" through the use of drugs. While the known list of drugs producing severe hallucinations did not seem to indicate any substance known to be "sufficiently active to be useful in chemical warfare," Corwin suggested that:

> An intensive search in this field would uncover substances capable of destroying necessary vitamins in such a manner as to bring on hallucinations or other abnormal mental phenomena and at the same time capable of causing those actions in much lower concentrations than any of the drugs now available for the purpose.

When Corwin's letter came to the attention of Dr. Greene, he was instantly hooked on the proposed concept and, after contacting Corwin, Greene quickly took up the search for suitable drugs. Within a few weeks Greene had developed a list of nearly 1000 chemical compounds and drugs "known to cause mental disorders in man." According to Greene, additional study revealed that "the endocrine or ductless glands appear to be the most vulnerable organs of the body for psychochemical attack." Greene's next task, after further consultation with Army biochemists and biologists expert in aerosol delivery mechanisms, was to identify ideal chemical agents that, "airborne in aerosol or vapor form, could be absorbed into the blood stream through the breathing apparatus and be carried by the blood to the endocrine gland we wish to affect." The purpose for this research was clear:

> By upsetting the gland function, by either reducing or accelerating its activity, the supply of the gland products (hormones) is interfered with and, in certain instances, abnormal mental conditions result." Dr. Greene's consultations found that the "thyroid gland is especially interesting in this connection because some mental disorders are attributed to thyroid deficiency.

In an earlier preliminary report on the subject, Dr. Greene had identified some of the targets under consideration:

> It would seem that the populations of the great land masses of Russia, Siberia, and Mongolia would be particularly susceptible to any chemical which affects the thyroid. These people are known to exhibit a high degree of thyroid deficiency because of the lack of iodine in the drinking water in that part of the world. There is some evidence that there is a higher percentage of mental abnormality (by Western standards) among those people than in areas where the thyroid is known to be generally normal.

Dr. Greene's presentation about the potential uses of psychochemicals in warfare caused a real stir among conference attendees, generating animated discussion concerning the benefits of tactical and strategic uses of such drugs.

Attendees became even more excited when Dr. Greene shared top-secret information with them about a very recent and "incredible discovery" of a previously unknown drug that "causes hallucinations and suicidal tendencies in man." The drug was quite effective and powerful in "extremely small amounts," Greene explained, with symptoms amounting to a cornucopia of disorders. They included "uneasiness, vertigo, restlessness, difficulty of concentration, sight disturbance, a feeling of suffocation, hysteria, unsteady and uncertain movements of the arms and legs, and hallucinations." Hallucinations ranged from the simple to the more complex, Dr. Green said. His preliminary report quoted a researcher's description: "Flickering, glimmering, glittering, scintillating, rapid and slow blotting of colors, sparks, whirling, traveling small dots, light flashes and sheet lightning."

Attendees asked, what is this amazing drug?

"It is a derivative of ergot," Dr. Greene replied, "called lysergic acid diethylamide." Researchers in the Swiss laboratory where it had been discovered referred to it as "LSD-25," he said.

Dr. Greene's own excitement about the incredible drug was more than evident and he implied to attendees that LSD-25 could well be that much sought after magical psychochemical that would transform modern warfare. Greene, as readers shall soon learn, was already smitten with the potentialities of LSD through top-secret information being generated from the very heart of activities around the drug's development. Greene was especially taken with LSD-25 because research demonstrated that the drug produced mental abnormalities in all four of the categories already identified as being of military significance and therefore desirable: "Epilepsy, manic-depressive psychoses, psychoneuroses and toxic psychoses."

Attendees asked, do we have access to this drug?

"At the moment, no," Dr. Greene said. "But, we will shortly."

Has any thought been given as to how best to deploy this drug? inquired one attendee.

"Preliminary research shows that the drug is ideally suited for both tactical and strategic situations," Dr. Greene said. "It also appears well suited for sabotage uses."

Attendees queried, how would it best be delivered in strategic situations?

"Dissemination from a bomb, perhaps," explained Greene. "Or from a generating device in the form of a colorless and odorless vapor or faint dust."

"Like a crop dusting operation?" asked one attendee.

"Yes," Greene replied. "Air currents could carry the colorless cloud over the enemy's position or population concentration, catching people completely unaware. In targeted urban areas, the cloud from multiple bombs or generating devices would blanket the densest portion. Advance troops infiltrated into the area could signal from the ground when the appropriate time had arrived."

And in sabotage situations?

"Saboteurs and intelligence operatives could release psychochemicals from hand-operated generators," Greene explained. "These might be used against groups of a few hundred people situated together or against small groups of a dozen or less." Dr. Greene said that active consideration was being given to developing hand generators and delivery devices similar in size and composition to an eyeglasses case or fountain pen.

Dr. Greene then remarked that the discussion about "generating devices provided a good opportunity" to briefly mention a couple of the more exciting projects that were currently underway with SOD. Both projects involved aerosols, Frank Olson's area of expertise. The first project, Greene explained, was focused on "a grouping of extremely toxic chemical warfare agents that are of such volatility that, as I'm sure Dr. Olson could better explain than I, they can be disseminated only as aerosols." Greene elaborated:

> Little is known of the physical characteristics of chemical agents upon which the production of satisfactory aerosols depends, or the possibility of modifying these characteristics to attain the most effective toxic aerosols. This information is essential for the development of these weapons, and we are pleased to have Drs. Schwab and Olson with us today to answer any questions anyone may have after, during our break.

The second project, Greene explained, concerned aerosol cloud travel:

> Because so many existing toxic agents are most effective as small solid particles widely disseminated in air, current work is concentrated on the travel of aerosol clouds over various types of terrain. Upcoming field projects will focus on long distance cloud travel and the behavior of aerosols when released over populated areas, small and large.

At the conclusion of the conference, Dr. Greene looked again at John Schwab and Frank Olson and remarked that the next several years would "surely be exciting ones" for the Chemical Corps and SOD, in light of their new partnership with the CIA which "promises to pursue the great potential value of psychochemicals as related to multiple levels of warfare."

We have no information about how Olson or Schwab reacted to Greene's LSD presentation. However, given the fact that research employing the drug would begin all out within a few months at Camp Detrick, it seems that SOD scientists were as exhilarated as Dr. Greene at the prospect of waging war with toxic, psychoactive drugs. It is highly doubtful that either Olson or Schwab ever anticipated at the time that they themselves would fall victim to the effects of LSD.

Camp Detrick's SOD had not emerged in its entirety right from the drawing board, but instead evolved over time from the Special Projects Division, established just after the decision to build Camp Detrick in April 1943. The Special Projects Division (SPD) was set up within the Office of the Chief, Chemical

Warfare Service, to carry out particularly sensitive projects initiated by the War Research Service, and to oversee the crème de la crème of defensive and offensive biological warfare experiments for various federal agencies, or those contracted out to universities and private laboratories throughout the country.

Within eight months of its creation, SPD had evolved into a massive bureaucracy with nearly 4,000 employees. SPD maintained close liaison with the Medical, Ordnance, and Intelligence Departments of the Army and Navy, the Army Air Force, the U.S. Public Health Service, the U.S. Department of Agriculture, and the British and Canadian governments' biological warfare organizations.

In essence, SPD became so far-reaching and grandiose in design that within about eighteen months the name Special Projects Division simply vanished as far as employees, media, and locals were concerned; "Camp Detrick" encompassed everything. By late 1947, however, the need for organizational restructuring, consolidation and compartmentalization again emerged, particularly for highly secret special projects. Significantly, in 1948, the Committee on Biological Warfare recommended to Secretary of Defense James Forrestal the development of biological agents as covert and paramilitary weapons. The Army's various secret operational units (which later would evolve into the elite Special Forces Command) were especially attracted to the recommendation to consolidate.

In 1950 Forrestal quickly approved the creation of Camp Detrick's Special Operations Division. Forrestal's approval was accelerated by the recommendations of the Ad Hoc Committee on Chemical and Biological Warfare – called the Stevenson Committee, after its chairman, Karl P. Stevenson, president of Arthur D. Little, Inc. The Committee on CBW also included, among others, the CIA's Dr. Willis A Gibbons. As readers will recall, Gibbons was not only research director for U.S. Rubber Company, but more importantly, he was chief of the CIA's Technical Services Section.

The CIA happened to come along, within a few months of SOD's creation (and of Dr. Gibbons' hiring), with a laundry list that mirrored some of the projects already underway or planned by SOD. The consolidation of chemical and biological warfare projects within the new Special Operations Division greatly benefited the administrators of SOD and enabled their burgeoning budget.

At any rate, towards the end of 1950, almost three years before DCI Allen Dulles would approve the MKULTRA Program, the CIA established an "informal agreement" with SOD to pursue projects that the Agency requested. Funding for projects for 1950-51 was nearly $500,000, and project funding (excluding personnel and some equipment and supply costs) escalated to a high of $675,000 by the mid-1960s. CIA funding was tracked and managed under the cryptonym MKNAOMI. Confidential sources informed the author in 1999 that this cryptonym was named after Dr. Harold Abramson's assistant, Naomi Busner. According to CIA reports from 1975, this agreement was formalized through "a charter contained in a 1952 Memorandum of Understanding between the CIA and Army's Chief Chemical Corps Officer."

Sidney Gottlieb would reveal decades later:

> CIA envisioned Detrick's SO Division as a creation very much like the earlier Division 19. It was similarly compartmentalized, with the strict military security on top of ours. Needless layers of interplay and approvals were eliminated. Little to nothing was reduced to writing, except essential reports. The right hand never knew what the left was doing, unless we wanted it otherwise. It worked nicely; things were accomplished expeditiously.

Division 19 had been a highly secret operation tucked away within the National Defense Research Committee's Office of Scientific Research and Development. Established on June 28, 1941 by Roosevelt's Executive Order, Division 19 was run by Dr. H. Marshall Chadwell, who readers have already met in his capacity as head of the CIA's Office of Scientific Intelligence. Most of the documents concerning the work of the Division 19 are still classified and may well never be released for public scrutiny. However, a few declassified files exist and although they are sketchy, they do reveal the scope and, sometimes, the specifics of certain Division 19 projects.

One project was Operation Skatole. Skatole is an organic compound having a strong odor, found naturally in feces, beets, and coal. It is used as a fixent in the manufacturing of perfume. Also indelicately and unofficially referred to as Operation Stinky, the project involved solving "the problem of producing a vivid blend of skatole, sulfur compounds, and organic acids, dispersed in a carrier that shall provide a consistency easy to use and yet a substance difficult to remove from skin and clothing." In other words, the objective was to devise a product that approximated the foulest of fecal odors. According to a December 1943 letter, Dr. Chadwell met with a group of the nation's finest corporate chemical engineers and posed the odorous challenge to them. A subsequent letter to Chadwell from one corporate executive began with this observation:

> Fecal odors are variable, depending probably on the diet and on the state of health...but we are confident that we shall soon have the desirable compound at hand.

Concurrent with Division 19's Operation Skatole was a closely related OSS project dubbed Project "Who? Me?" Stanley Lovell, who oversaw research and development for the OSS, explains in his 1963 book, *Of Spies & Stratagems*, that Division 19's "skatole compound, a liquid which duplicated the revolting odor of a very loose bowel movement," was placed in "collapsible tubes" that were secretly "distributed to children in [the] Japanese-occupied cities [of Shanghai, Canton and Peiping]. Continued Lovell, "When a Japanese officer, preferably of high rank, came walking down the crowded sidewalk, the little Chinese boys and girls would slip up behind him and squirt a shot of 'Who? Me?' at his trouser seat." (One can't help but think that Chadwell and Lovell could have saved a significant amount of time and money had they simply consulted a Vermont farmer.)

Other Division 19 programs were devoid of any humorous elements and were far more lethal. Many were taken over by SOD and the CIA during the fury of the Cold War, including the CIA's cautious alliance with the Mafia, as well as with the OSS's highly classified assassination programs. The latter were recast by the CIA as "executive action," "health alteration" and "incapacitation" programs. Well before the CIA was conceived, at the height of World War II, Division 19, through the OSS, began the systematic recruitment of underworld figures that were most adept at "close-in killing methods."

In addition to recruiting Mafia hit men, the OSS operated an "assassination and elimination" training program at Camp X near Oshawa, Ontario, in Canada. George Hunter White, who trained at the facility with a number of Federal Narcotics agents on loan to the OSS, dubbed it "the school for mayhem and murder." White also took advanced training at another OSS school quite close to Deep Creek Lake, Maryland, about a year prior to his first impromptu assassination on a crowded street in New Delhi, India.

Given the cornucopia of lethal weapons and innovative equipment that Division 19 came up with for the OSS—including silent pistols, signet rings containing L-pill Zyankalium ("L" for lethal), and poison dart pens— one can easily see how the division served as a model for the CIA's Technical Services Section.

Details about the actual mechanics of the OSS assassination programs are scant, but we are able to catch a glimpse through the recollections of former government-paid "professional killer" Michael Milan. Milan, a nom-de-plume to protect his true identity after he entered the entertainment industry, reveals in a tell-all book, *The Squad*, that he was recruited by the OSS on the recommendation of Manhattan's Republican boss, Sam Koenig. As Milan put it, he was hired to be a "triggerman to work military bases on the East Coast." Born and raised in Manhattan's Lower East Side, Milan was trained by a mobster named August "Little Augie" Del Grazio. Milan was "running the skim" for Meyer Lansky and Benny Siegel and claims that he committed a number of assassinations under the direction of Office of Naval Intelligence Capt. Roscoe McCall. (McCall, as some readers may be aware, was part of the effort to get Mafia drug lord Charles "Lucky" Luciano to assist the Navy and OSS with Operation HUSKY, the invasion of Sicily. McCall's collaboration with "Lucky" also involved "setting his people up in the OSS to police the New York waterfront.")

Milan, meanwhile, maintains that he later brought his lethal skills to a band of professional assassins called "The Squad" that was operated surreptitiously by FBI director J. Edgar Hoover. Milan writes that "The Squad" also sometimes "found itself working for the CIA," despite the fact that Hoover "hated Allen Dulles" and called him a "Harvard pantywaist." (Dulles attended Princeton, not Harvard.) In ensuing chapters of this book, readers shall learn far more about the CIA's assassination programs.

Without doubt, a good many of the projects usually considered to have originated with the CIA were already underway within Camp Detrick or the Chemical Corps well before the agency had formalized its contract with SOD scientists.

One such project was the notorious Shellfish Poisoning Project, code named the SS Project. Long attributed to the CIA's TSS, the project was first undertaken in July 1944 by a research team at the George Williams Hooper Foundation, University of California, under the direction of Swiss born toxicologist Dr. Hermann Sommer. The work of Sommer's team was primarily to collect large amounts of paralytic shellfish poison (*Gonyaulax catenella*), to be used in chemical studies under the direction of Dr. Byron Riegel at Northwestern University. Supplementing the collection of the California team were shellfish poisons sent from the California Public Health Laboratory and the U.S. Food and Drug Administration.

Other lesser known SOD projects undertaken prior to the formalization of a relationship with the CIA involved testing the effects of salmonella poisoning, botulinum toxin sprays, kala-azar (a parasitic disease), lymphogranuloma inguinal (a herpes-like virus), yaws and, perhaps most ominous of all, developing "the ability to induce cancer through covert means."

Additional SOD projects, still classified more than fifty years later, involved testing "various pharmaceutical products of interest in the research and development stage" at a number of American drug manufacturing firms. Some of this drug testing, according to former Camp Detrick scientists, was conducted in Haiti and British Guyana. As one former SOD researcher explained:

> Why Haiti? Why Guyana? Simple. There were no laws or rules pertaining to what we were doing. The companies knew this. Nobody of any consequence paid attention. The people used in the experiments were of no consequence to anyone. Families, relatives were no problem.

The former SOD scientist identified other locations where similar SOD projects were undertaken:

> Central Africa, the Belgium Congo back then. We obviously did work in Europe, in England and France. There was some done in Morocco, some in Iraq and neighboring countries, Viet Nam, a couple of projects in Canada. Not all of this involved product testing; some was in follow-up to things we learned through captured German and Japanese scientists and files.

Near the end of World War II, several Camp Detrick bacteriologists, soon-to-be assigned to SOD, were among the scientific and intelligence gathering teams sent to France, Germany and Japan to assess Nazi and Japanese biological warfare capacities. Additionally, in November 1943, Maj. Gen. Leslie Groves, head of the Manhattan Project — America's top-secret atom bomb program — selected Lt. Col. Boris T. Pash to head up a special project. Col. Pash, then chief of the Counterintelligence Branch of the Western Defense Command, was in charge of security for the Manhattan Project. Groves chose Pash to lead a secret investigation not only of Germany's nuclear capacities, but also the biological warfare activities of the Nazis. The investigation was dubbed the Alsos Mission, and Pash was given about forty talented enlisted personnel with varied scientific credentials to accomplish the task. None, however, were from Camp Detrick.

Pash, a former Hollywood High School teacher who had helped direct the controversial wartime internment of Japanese-American citizens, was a tubby, no-nonsense man who took up his Alsos assignment with zest. His team's subsequent report on Germany's biological warfare program was quietly issued in September 1945 to a small and select review team at Camp Detrick that included Frank Olson, Arvo Thompson, and Gerald Yonetz. The report revealed that Germany's program "had been conducted by third-rate personnel whose principal efforts had been directed to defensive measures against the Allied use of biological agents, and specifically against the many acts of sabotage against the German Army by guerilla fighters in Poland and Russia."

Quite pertinent to the remainder of our story are Boris Pash's career moves after his Alsos duties were concluded. While his published resume states only that he held a number of high profile military positions and was once detailed to the CIA, it is the hidden parts that are most intriguing. From 1948 through 1953, and most likely later, Pash was assigned to the CIA, where he was placed in charge of a group called PB/7, an innocuous name for an assassination bureau composed of at least five former OSS hit men of the same stripe as Michael Milan. As revealed in Congressional hearings, Pash's division's charter read in part: "PB/7 will be responsible for assassinations, kidnappings, and such other functions as from time to time may be given it."

Pash's other functions, as uncovered by Allen Dulles biographer Leonard Mosley, included participation in the CIA's ironically named Health Alteration Committee, of which Pash was a member, along with the CIA's Richard Bissell and Sheffield Edwards. The Health Alteration Committee was responsible for targeting individuals — including leaders of foreign countries — for severe incapacitation or assassination with special weapons, drugs, exotic poisons, induced diseases, and other means.

The Health Alteration Committee, which interfaced often with SOD scientists on many of its projects, and may survive to this day in another incarnation, operated from about 1952 to about 1968. In 1953, it authorized the LSD dosing of a high-ranking elected official in the Philippines. In 1963, the committee approved sending Iraqi leader Abel Karim Kassem an expensive monogrammed handkerchief that had been dipped into a lethal poison concocted by SOD to kill anyone who used it.

Some scientists at the time the Alsos report was issued, particularly those with the CIA and Camp Detrick, felt that Pash's report downplayed Nazi biological warfare advancements in order to give greater play to the Third Reich's nuclear activities. SOD microbiologist Ben Wilson later said, "If the German microbiologists were so 'third-rate', why did the country go to such lengths to recruit so many of them to come over here to work after the war?" Gerald Yonetz said in 1999, "The findings of Pash and Goudsmit's [Samuel Goudsmit, a physicist was scientific head of Alsos; Pash was the military head of it] team, which I think included Carlo Henze and Jesse Hofer, both good men, but not bacteriologists, were not entirely accurate." According to Yonetz:

> We found out later that the Nazis were more advanced on certain things than anyone thought. Henze, who was then head of the Sandoz Foundation, later admitted this, I believe.... But on the Japanese disease filled balloons and the horrible doings in Pingfan and other places, which Pash's guys didn't look into, we got that more than right because it was our people doing the investigating.

Yonetz's reference to balloons was specific to a series of events in 1945, when the Japanese released nearly two hundred high-altitude balloons, which were carried by winds to the western United States. Some of the hydrogen-filled balloons, over 33 feet in diameter and capable of carrying payloads over 300 pounds, were discovered "to contain incendiaries." American intelligence officers believed the balloons were test runs for "subsequent employment as biological agent carriers." In May 1945, according to Chemical Corps reports, "five women and children in Oregon were killed while tampering with a charge fixed to one of the grounded balloons."

The gruesome horrors of Japan's biological warfare programs were exemplified by the activities of Lt. General Shiro Ishii's Unit 731, where ghastly germ warfare experiments and live vivisection of human beings were discovered to have been going on for years. These experiments are well documented today. It was Camp Detrick personnel, including to a minor extent Frank Olson, that played a role in uncovering Unit 731's atrocities, but not before alarm bells had gone off throughout Chemical Corps headquarters when it was learned the Russians had captured several Japanese scientists from Ishii's unit. The Russians curtly informed U.S. military leaders that Unit 731 had conducted an overwhelming number of grisly biological experiments using human subjects. Eventually, some researchers would claim that these human subjects included American POWs.

At this time, the United States was holding a good number of Ishii's top scientists, but had not yet captured General Ishii himself. One week after Japan surrendered in September 1945, Lt. Colonel Murray Sanders was dispatched from Camp Detrick to Japan to investigate Unit 731's activities and to interrogate as many of its scientists as possible. Sanders, who traveled by ship, knew nothing about the unit's horrific human experiments that involved Russians, Chinese, Koreans, and Manchurian POWs, as well as petty criminals, spies, and anyone else that Ishii deemed "inferior."

In Japan, Sanders was greeted dockside by Dr. Ryoichi Naito, the physician who, unbeknownst to Sanders, had been dispatched to New York by Ishii years earlier, in 1939, to get samples of yellow fever virus from the Rockefeller Institute. Sanders was unaware that, as a scientist, Naito had been part and parcel of Ishii's wartime activities. And now Naito had been assigned to serve as Sanders' interpreter. The American did not speak Japanese and therefore had to rely heavily on Naito during interrogations. As translator, Naito was in a perfect position to manipulate questioning and to mislead Sander's investigation.

Sanders devoted nearly nine weeks to interrogating several of Unit 731's top germ warfare scientists. He learned nothing about any experiments involving human subjects. Just before returning to Camp Detrick, Sanders began feeling ill. Back at the installation he was diagnosed with tuberculosis, which left him incapacitated for two years.

In January 1946, when Camp Detrick's Lt. Colonel Arvo Thompson arrived in Japan to pick up where Sanders had left off, he was under the impression that Shiro Ishii was dead. Two months earlier, an announcement had been made in the Japanese press that Ishii had been assassinated and that his unidentified killer had escaped. Fortunately, a few disbelieving American Counter Intelligence Corps agents were skeptical, thinking the reports were a ruse, and they continued the hunt for Ishii. Soon their efforts paid off, and the general was found alive and well, living in the lap of luxury on his family's estate.

Thompson was given immediate access to Ishii and he wasted no time. Beginning on January 22, he commenced daily interrogation sessions with the general, pressing hard for details about Japan's biological warfare capacities. But the United States still had no idea of the immense size of Japan's germ warfare program. When it had become amply apparent to Ishii in 1945 that Japan's defeat was imminent, General Ishii had ordered his officers and troops to dismantle, destroy, and burn to ashes all evidence of Unit 731's existence. Critical files and documents were secreted away and buried in remote locations across Japan. Without this background material, even though Thompson relentlessly pressed for details, Ishii was able to grossly misrepresent the scale of his research, saying that his operation was quite small and limited in scope, and that he only used a few small farm animals as test subjects.

No other animals? Thompson pressed. No humans, no prisoners of war?

Absolutely not, insisted Ishii, feigning indignation.

What about the many reports that your unit did use humans?

Rumors, Ishii scoffed. Not true, completely false.

No large, complex, well-equipped laboratories? No cadres of highly trained scientists?

I wish, replied the general.

Soon Ishii was dangling carrots before his captors, hinting that he could perhaps produce far more information if he and his officers were granted immunity from prosecution as war criminals. Ishii knew very well that his record of human experimentation would make Nazi activities in the same areas look like child's play.

After four weeks of interrogations, Thompson returned to Camp Detrick with a wealth of information despite Ishii's lies. But still there was no evidence of human experimentation. The wily Ishii had skillfully avoided the subject at every turn in his interrogation, always sidestepping Thompson's pointed questions by offering little gems of information he knew would divert the Americans' attention away from his legacy of atrocities. Thompson understood the general was being evasive and withholding a great deal; back at Camp Detrick he would tell close colleagues he trusted Ishii as far as he could spit.

Nonetheless, Camp Detrick's Chemical Corps officers forwarded some of Thompson's detailed notes to Frank Olson because the notes concerned Japanese protective clothing and gear used by Ishii's operatives at Unit 731. Olson was asked to carefully analyze the Japanese equipment and compare it with equipment being used by the Chemical Corps.

Eventually, Ishii was granted his demand for immunity by his American captors, well before the world became aware of his experiments:

> ... that ranged from gruesome to horrific: Ishii's researchers injected tetanus into the heels of prisoners; left naked men outdoors in 40 degrees below zero until their limbs froze solid as rock; fed them typhus contaminated tomatoes; placed prisoners in glass rooms and sprayed them with anthrax, cholera, typhoid, plague-infected fleas, and other diseases to calculate the minimal lethal dose; contaminated chocolate, bread, tooth powder, milk, cream, and butter with anthrax spores; tied prisoners to a stake and then exploded germ bombs overhead, while soldiers wearing protective gear timed their deaths with stopwatches; infected women with syphilis, impregnated them and, after the child's birth, vivisected both; drained blood from humans and replaced it with horse and monkey blood in order to create artificial blood; dissected persons alive.

Estimates show that Ishii's unit treated at least 3,000 people like this; possibly even double that number. In all written documents, the unit routinely referred to its human subjects as "monkeys."

In 1987, Murray Sanders told writer Jeanne McDermott that he thought General Shiro Ishii had been brought to Camp Detrick to lecture on his human experiments, sometime after 1947. Other former Camp Detrick scientists have also reported that Ishii came to the installation, but none would go on record or admit to having attended his lectures. And in 1951, Tommy Thompson reportedly picked up a gun and blew his own brains out all over a Tokyo hotel room.

Within a few short weeks of his SOD appointment, Frank Olson's growing restlessness was abated by a rigid travel schedule. Earlier, in 1949 and 1950, according to former colleague Gerald Yonetz, Olson had "gotten the travel bug" and a "yen to visit other places" following trips to California and Antigua. Old photographs published in 2002 in a German publication reveal a smiling Olson standing in his bathing suit at surf's edge in Antigua's Half Moon Bay. Olson had traveled to the Caribbean in 1949 to take part in Operation Harness, a massive experiment conducted by the Americans, British, and Canadians, in which several thousand animals were killed. The animals were sprayed with deadly anthrax, brucellosis and tularemia while floating offshore in containers resting in dinghies. Records reveal that about 1,000 sheep transported to the area had to be killed before the experiment began because they were found "unsuitable," and that nearly 500 rhesus monkeys were slaughtered on arrival because they were sick with pneumonia.

Olson's role in the experiment was to oversee the effectiveness of the protective suits worn by most of the bacteriologists. Many of them suffered from extreme heat exhaustion and dehydration because the suits were so heavy. According to recent reports in the West Indian press, nobody ever calculated "how many Antiguans, Bahamians and Hebrideans died or were made seriously ill" as a result of the experiment, "because the British government still isn't saying."

In September 1950, Olson ventured to Oakland, California where other Camp Detrick and Navy scientists conducted secret experiments with *Serratia marcescens*, an allegedly harmless bacterium simulate for anthrax. The purpose of the experiments was to determine how vulnerable an American city would be to an enemy biological warfare attack.

Olson was present for the tests in order to ensure that appropriate protective clothing and gear were in safe, operational condition and properly stored and used. He watched as the simulated germs were loaded onto the USS ACM-13, a navy minelayer docked at Treasure Island in San Francisco Bay. After the ship glided under the Golden Gate Bridge to a position about two miles off the coast of San Francisco, it sailed up and down the coast for the next six days "spewing out three-mile lines" of bacterium mixed with "separate clouds of fluorescent particles...composed of zinc cadmium sulfide, a chemical compound that glowed in the ultraviolet." One can only imagine watching through an ultraviolet light at the time and seeing the luminous particles rain down on San Francisco like shimmering, magical fairy dust.

In 1987, writer Jeanne McDermott revealed, "on the seventh and last day of the tests, the ACM-13 left harbor, headed offshore two miles and cruised along the coast." At dusk, the scientists onboard began releasing thick clouds of *Serratia, each* about "five miles long and 200 feet thick." The clouds "rose above the ship, gliding across the water to San Francisco and from there across the bay into Berkeley, Alameda, Richmond, Oakland, and San Leandro."

For the most part, Camp Detrick scientists determined the experiments to be quite successful. Camp Detrick's official report on the tests, according to writer Ed Regis, stated that traces of bacteria simulate "were found as far away as twenty-three miles inland." Continued the report:

Nearly every one of the 800,000 people in San Francisco exposed to the cloud at normal breathing rate (ten liters per minute) inhaled 5000 or more fluorescent particles.

One of those 800,000 people exposed to the mock attack was Edward Nevin III. Nevin, an Irish immigrant who worked for Pacific Gas and Electric in San Francisco and raised seven children, died on November 1, 1950. His physician listed the cause of death as "bacterial endocarditis, secondary to *Serratia marcescens.*" At the same time as Nevin's death, ten other patients were diagnosed with the same bacterium. Doctors were completely baffled by what they considered an extremely unusual outbreak. Then, twenty-six years later, in December 1976, Nevin's grandson, Edward J. Nevin III, picked up a newspaper while waiting for a train and read an exposé about Camp Detrick's 1950 mock germ warfare attack on San Francisco.

Declassified Navy files reveal that while Frank Olson was in San Francisco in September 1950, he and John McNulty, a Navy officer attached to Camp Detrick, also participated in Operation Greenhouse, a secret Navy-sponsored nuclear test which involved "NRDL [Naval Defense Radiological Laboratory] fall-out collectors," and "biological warfare trials." By some accounts, these trials were conducted part and parcel with the vulnerability experiments. States one October 1950 report on the fall-out tests:

> During the tests, the Health Physics Branch experimented with the fall-out collectors designed for the 6.4 program of Operation GREENHOUSE to gain experience and determine differences between greased and non-greased plates. During these BW trials, large quantities of fluorescent particles (zinc sulfide) were released as aerosols from a destroyer operating off-shore west of San Francisco.

At first glance, Olson's presence at fall-out testing seems out of place, given his duties at Camp Detrick. However, in 2001 the author discovered that on January 17, 1950 Olson had been granted an Atomic Energy Commission (AEC) Q clearance allowing him access to secret and restricted AEC data and projects. The clearance was renewed on April 13 of the same year, and was cancelled by the Chemical Corps' intelligence division within twenty-four hours of Olson's death.

Readers may wonder at this point if perhaps Olson's AEC involvement was related to the claims made by Camp Detrick security officials that Olson had cancer at the time of his death. The answer to this, at present, remains unclear; however, the subject of the CIA's involvement with radiological warfare in the 1950s has almost completely escaped scrutiny, despite hard evidence of deep CIA participation, some of which may have involved Olson and several of the Agency's TSS scientists.

Former colleague Henry Eigelsbach recalled that Olson "very much enjoyed his infrequent [pre-SOD] trips overseas" and "to other installations around the United States," including journeys to Dugway Proving Ground in Utah and Fort McClellan in Arkansas. In the 1950s, Dugway was a chemical, biological and radiological testing facility almost 2,000 square miles in size and employing nearly 900 people. Fort McClellan, near the Appalachian Mountains, was a former World War II POW camp for German and Italian soldiers. In 1947, the Chemical Corps took over Fort McClellan for use as an "educational" facility teaching, among other things, how to use LSD and BZ for offensive purposes. (BZ is a psychoactive drug like LSD, but far more powerful.)

In 1945 and 1946, Olson made several trips to the isolated terrain of Granite Peak in Utah's Salt Lake Desert. The 250-square mile area, thirty-five miles from Dugway, was used for tests with "living biological agents, munitions, and aerosol cloud production and performance." Within a two-year period, over 10,000 "test animals" were killed in experiments at the site, where about 160 Army and Navy personnel worked. For unexplained reasons, the site, which cost $1,376,000 to construct in 1944, was closed in late 1946 and "turned over to Dugway Proving Ground for surveillance." Olson's duties in Utah were described as "working with protective devices, including clothing and masks, and measures."

On at least five occasions spread out over 1951, 1952 and early 1953, Frank Olson journeyed by military aircraft to Fort Terry on Plum Island, off Long Island, New York. The 840-acre island, purchased by the U.S. War Department in 1901, is only about 135 miles from New York City. In 1951, the Army's Chemical Corps selected Plum Island as a non-animal research and development site, so as to sidestep federal laws banning experiments involving certain highly infectious animal diseases within the continental United States. After spending millions on the Plum Island facility and arousing stiff opposition from nearby mainland residents, the United States Department of Agriculture took the island over from the Army Chemical Corps in 1954.

Joining Olson on at least two of his Plum Island trips was Lt. Col. Oliver Fellowes, a special assistant to George Merck and former vaccine researcher for pharmaceutical giant Merck, Sharpe and Dohme. Lt. Col. Fellowes worked with virus's at Camp Detrick, often freeze-drying large quantities to be tested in the field. In a 1986 interview, Fellowes recalled:

> We dried the virus in bulk. Then we sometimes mixed the powder with feathers and, though I never discovered where the tests were carried out, I know the mixture was to be delivered in the same way as leaflets were dropped over enemy territory, in leaflet bombs. The system worked particularly well with swine fever. The pigs simply ate the feathers and died.

In mid-1952, Fellowes left his post at Camp Detrick for two years and worked full-time on Plum Island setting up animal laboratories there.

Olson's task on Plum Island was to "review the installation of ventilation-system security and safety." Overall security at Plum Island was intended to be "even tighter than that at Camp Detrick." Indeed, Olson's colleague, Don Falconer said in 1999:

> Frank remarked a couple of times that he was really put to the test working at Fort Terry. Just getting to the island was a difficult task and, once there, security was relentless. There were guards everywhere constantly patrolling the shores and perimeter. Frank, I think like everyone who worked there, hated the weather and the boredom. He only went there when he had to.

Said another of Olson's colleagues, Dr. Gerald Yonetz, "The commitment to security on Plum Island was beyond extreme, and it was warranted. It would have been disastrous if certain things had gone wrong there. Absolutely disastrous."

Refusing to provide any details, several former Camp Detrick researchers have stated that the Army Chemical Corps' involvement in Plum Island's work was "far more extensive and intensive than thought," extending well beyond 1954, when the U.S. Department of Agriculture took the island over. Also very much involved throughout the 1950s, and perhaps later, was the CIA, acting through a number of its Camp Detrick surrogates. Additionally, the years 1952 through 1955 saw what many at Camp Detrick considered "an aggressive move by the CIA" to infiltrate as many covert Agency scientists as possible into the ranks of Camp Detrick's and Edgewood Arsenal's various research divisions. Said Dr. Henry Eigelsbach, "We heard reports all the time that one person or another working with us was actually a CIA employee, but we were never sure." Camp Detrick's former spokesman and historian Norman Covert said:

> There were CIA people who infiltrated the [Camp Detrick] laboratories. They did their own work, and we know now what they did with LSD and other psycho-illnesses. They had their own little cells there— they worked on their own, and I suspect that a very small circle of people knew that.

Dr. Seymour Silver, former scientific director at Edgewood Arsenal, told investigative author Linda Hunt in 1990:

> Do you know what a 'self-sustained, off-the-shelf operation' means? Well, the CIA was running one in my lab. They were testing psychochemicals and running experiments in my lab, using my people, and weren't telling me. They were spying on us. I said, 'You go spy on the enemy, not on us.'

Said another Edgewood Arsenal scientist who asked not to be identified:

> In the mid-1950s and 1960s, it got crazy. There were CIA guys all over the place at Edgewood and Detrick, passing as simple civilian or enlisted personnel. You had to take extra care with anything you said because of these guys trying to score Brownie points by passing info back to the Agency.

It is generally believed that the virulent African swine fever virus used by the CIA against Cuba's swine population in 1971 was from Plum Island's stock. Former Camp Detrick researchers, speaking under terms of anonymity, have stated that sealed vials containing the virus "were transported by CIA employees from Plum Island to Fort Gulick" in Panama, where writer Jeanne McDermott reported the vials were handed off to "an anti-Castro group" who transported them by trawler "and put [them] ashore near the U.S. Navy base in Guantanamo Bay." McDermott writes, "Six weeks later, African swine fever, a debilitating hog disease, broke out for the first time in the Western hemisphere, killing five hundred thousand pigs on the island." Said one former Camp Detrick researcher:

> I don't think it's any great secret where that swine fever virus came from. We brought it to Camp Terry [Plum Island] in 1953 or 1954 from East Africa, and a few years later the CIA's boys took it from there to God only knows where.

As readers shall learn, this was but one of many biological attacks, as well as assassination attempts, spearheaded by SOD and CIA against Cuba and Fidel Castro.

Also assisting Olson and his colleagues in their Plum Island activities were Drs. William Arthur Hagen and Erich Traub. Dr. Hagen, a key advocate for the creation of the Plum Island experimental station, was dean of the Cornell University veterinary school in Ithaca, New York and a renowned authority on *Bacillus anthracis* (anthrax). In a small laboratory at Cornell in 1943, Hagen fashioned what writer Michael Christopher Carroll deemed "the most virulent, concentrated brand of anthrax on Earth." In his masterful 2004 book about Plum Island, *Lab 257*, Carroll revealed that in 1956 Hagen "bequeathed to [Plum Island] twelve vials of 'N' [anthrax], enough to kill about a million people."

Dr. Traub, whose collaboration with the Plum Island facilities was performed exclusively at Camp Detrick and Edgewood Arsenal until late-1955, was a former Nazi who had overseen biological warfare for the Reich Research Institute in Germany during the war. Traub, who worked directly under Reichsfuhrer Heinrich Himmler, specialized in viral and bacteriological diseases and was assisted by Anna Burger, who was also brought to the United States after the war to work with the Navy's biological warfare program. Traub, who was seriously considered for the position of Director at Plum Island, also worked at the Naval Medical Research Institute in Bethesda, Maryland, the United States Department of Agriculture research laboratories, also in Maryland, and the Armed Forces Institute of Pathology in Washington, D.C. Before World War II, Dr. Traub had been awarded a fellowship at the Rockefeller Institute in Princeton, New Jersey and while he was there, he frequently attended pro-Hitler rallies at the American Nazi Movement's Camp Siegfried on Long Island.

Meanwhile, Frank Olson's work continued to involve frequent travel. Among his notable foreign destinations, which we know from the various entry and exit stamps in his passport, were Africa, France, Germany, England, and Norway. Within the United States, Olson traveled to Arizona, San Francisco, Mississippi, and New Hampshire.

In Africa, Olson traveled twice to Spanish Morocco, where all that is known is that he had "something to do involving the leather tanning trade there." There are reports that Olson also spent time in the Belgian Congo, but these are unconfirmed. However, it is clear that several other SOD researchers did spend time there from 1951 through 1954, and later.

We also know that Olson journeyed at least once to Tanzania. Olson's colleague at Camp Detrick, Dr. Henry Eigelsbach, told the author in August 2002, "I believe that Frank went there in 1951 or 1952, only because the Military Air Transport System provided return transportation from the UK via a stop in Africa. Our group, with one exception, yours truly, returned in this interesting, exotic way." Added Eigelsbach, "I still had at least two more weeks of laboratory work to accomplish on Tularemia vaccine research and returned later."

Other former Camp Detrick scientists recounted that "sometimes work-related trips were taken to Africa" but none of the scientists would specify where or why. From scant declassified records and interviews, it is evident that on at least a half-dozen occasions, SOD researchers requested that their British counterparts at the Porton Down Micro-Biological Research Establishment in England perform field experiments in Africa. Occasionally, SOD scientists acted as "observers" of these tests. Lt. Col. Oliver Fellowes recalled in his 1986 interview that field experiments conducted by the British with rinderpest in Kenya involved over 10,000 animals. Rinderpest is an extremely virulent, highly infectious cattle disease known as "cattle plague."

In England, as expected, Olson, often accompanied by other Camp Detrick scientists, went to the Porton Down facilities where, as readers will learn far more about, British army officials and physicians were conducting their own experiments with LSD, LAE (a drug similar to LSD but much less potent), as well as other psychoactive drugs.

In Norway, former Camp Detrick officials, speaking anonymously, have reported that Olson's trips "may have been connected to work connected to the testing of psychoactive drugs" by "government-sponsored physicians there, on people in Oslo mental institutions, including children who were classified as disenfranchised war babies." Some reports out of Norway in the past five years centered on Dr. Carl Wilhelm Sem-Jacobsen, a former captain in the OSS, who held contracts with the Pentagon and CIA. Recently, other reports out of Norway and the UK seem to confirm these experiments, but this writer was unable to find any evidence that Olson was involved in them.

In Germany, it has been reported by several confidential sources, including two former CIA officials who worked occasionally in Germany at the time, that in the late summer of 1953 Olson had brief dealings with legendary CIA official William King Harvey. Reportedly, Olson first met Harvey when both men, along with TSS staffer Peter Karlow, attended a hastily convened Artichoke Committee meeting held at a safe house on the outskirts of Frankfurt. Harvey, a former FBI agent who had been forced out of the Bureau in 1947 for alleged misconduct, was the CIA's newly appointed station chief in Berlin. Harvey's soon-to-be wife, Clara Grace Follick, was also a CIA employee, who at the time worked as a special assistant to General Lucien K. Truscott, the CIA's director of operations in Germany. Follick, best known by her initials CG, also helped oversee and manage the CIA's several safe houses and a secret makeshift prison in Germany, answering to John McMahon, a young and trusted aide to Truscott. More than likely, McMahon was also present at the Artichoke meeting.

Olson initially had been dispatched from Camp Detrick to England, and then Germany, as part of a three-man team charged with interviewing two German scientists, under consideration for transport to the United States. They were believed to be experts in the areas of protective clothing and masks. While in the American Zone in Berlin, Olson was notified to attend the Frankfurt meeting.

At the meeting, which appears to have spanned about two hours, the plans for the CIA's European Artichoke Teams were discussed in detail. William King Harvey was quite knowledgeable about Artichoke techniques and objectives, having had first hand experience with Artichoke's predecessor, Project Bluebird. In 1950, he had traveled from his stateside desk to Pullach, a town on the outskirts of Munich, to participate in the interrogation of an Austrian Count suspected of being a double agent for the Russians. Harvey had been accompanied on the trip by a Bluebird team equipped with ample truth inducing drugs, including sodium pentothal.

Also discussed at the Frankfurt meeting was a strange 1949 occurrence referred to in some CIA files as "the Berlin Poison Case." In the late 1940s, postwar Berlin was extremely chaotic and dangerous. The CIA's chief of clandestine operations, Frank Wisner, a Southern bred aristocrat, Wall Street lawyer, and fierce anti-communist, had flooded Germany's capital with hundreds of spies and double agents, most of them systematically picked off by the Soviets before they were even able to scuff their shoes.

Judging from all available CIA files, the poison case grew out of an incident taking place in one of two safe houses in Berlin. One of the safe houses was operated by the CIA; the other may have been operated by British intelligence. According to one brief account of the case, dated May 5, 1953, seven Soviet defectors were being held in the houses, and at some point in time all seven were "given an unknown poison by a Soviet agent who escaped." The defectors were promptly taken to a nearby hospital, where they were treated by at least one toxicologist and a neurologist. All seven survived.

But soon after the incident, a woman who apparently had, along with her husband, also been among those held in one of the safe houses, in an unidentified capacity, "began getting symptoms" from a mysterious illness and "died (recently apparently)." The account goes on to read:

Examination at [redacted] clinic identified sickness as multiple sclerosis. The autopsy contradicted the analysis but failed to identify the illness, which caused partial dissolution of brain tissues. Now [redacted] husband, [redacted], is developing similar symptoms. Request is made to locate the seven defectors and find out what has happened to them.

On May 14, 1953, following the Frankfurt meeting attended by Olson, a secret cable was sent to DCI Allen Dulles. The cable, obviously revealing Dulles' interest in the poisoning incident, read: "At present, investigating case histories defectors and due past interrogatory information [redacted], desire further check story [redacted] medical examinations. Please advise names doctors attending [redacted] for our investigation."

Ten days after this cable was sent, a stateside Artichoke Conference meeting, chaired by Security Office chief, Sheffield Edwards, was convened in Washington at CIA headquarters. Again, the "Berlin Poison Case" appeared high on the agenda. Edwards voiced his dissatisfaction about overseas Agency personnel dragging their feet in responding to information requests, complaining "there was a great deal of difficulty in getting factual information quickly from all sources."

Other writers have alleged that while in Germany, Olson witnessed what have been termed "terminal experiments" being conducted by either American Army or CIA officials on former Nazi SS officers. While there is some scant circumstantial evidence that Olson may have witnessed the interrogation of a suspected Eastern European double agent, this author has not been able to unearth evidence documenting that Olson witnessed any experiments involving former Nazis. This subject, as well as Olson's other travels within Europe, will be covered in greater detail later in this book.

In Mississippi, Olson made one visit, along with several other researchers, including Dr. Gerald Yonetz, to Horn Island, ten miles off the coast of the small town of Pascagoula, Mississippi. Horn Island was selected by the Chemical Corps in 1953 to be used as an experimental site, but the 2,000-acre sea bound site was reportedly never used as intended, allegedly because Army engineers miscalculated the prevailing winds which blew eight months out of the year toward the mainland's populated areas. Despite this, over the past 40 years, some Mississippi residents have maintained that experiments were conducted by the Army on Horn Island, in the mid-to-late 1950s, using a drug far more powerful than LSD, perhaps BZ, an extremely potent nerve gas that profoundly affects mental functions. The Army did experiment with BZ elsewhere, including Vietnam, where, despite Pentagon denials, it was used offensively. BZ continues to be stockpiled in huge amounts at Edgewood Arsenal to the present day.

Interestingly, in October 1973, two men, who had been fishing from a pier on the Pascagoula River, reported seeing a large oval-shaped craft that was making a buzzing sound. As they stared at the machine, a hatchway opened and three very strange, ghostlike entities emerged and floated toward them. The entities wore no clothing and, according to the men, they appeared "like large legs" with wrinkled skin and conical noses and ears. The entities took the two men into their oval craft where they performed medical examinations on them. About 40 minutes later, both men found themselves back on their fishing pier. The incident has become a major milestone in America's UFO legacy: The Pascagoula Incident. The account the two men provided about their abduction has never been disproved or adequately explained.

Olson's New Hampshire trips took place in the first quarter of 1953, according to Yonetz, who says he accompanied Olson at least once to a large woolen mill in the state. Yonetz said that he did not recall the exact location or the purpose of the trip, but thought it had something to do with "hides or leather hides, like that." Said Yonetz, "He [Olson] had done some things with hides previously in the Middle East somewhere... I don't remember the particulars." The New Hampshire trip was most likely to the Arms Mill in Manchester. Readers shall learn more about this mill in a later chapter.

Over the past decade there has been a fair amount of media speculation, primarily on the Internet, about Olson's possible travel to Korea during the 1950s and his possible involvement with the alleged use of biological weapons by the United States against the North Koreans. The evidence is highly circumstantial; no report has surfaced containing any proof that Olson traveled to Korea or worked on any programs directly related to the Korean War. Every one of Olson's former Camp Detrick colleagues interviewed for this book, except one, said they had no knowledge of his travel to Korea or of his involvement with the war there. Two of his former colleagues pointed out that Olson was in Europe during many of the significant events in Korea.

Norman Cournoyer, who worked with Olson at Camp Detrick prior to the outbreak of the Korean War, has made at least one vague statement to the media implying that Olson may have had something to do with Korea and that it is possible he knew something about the use of biological weapons there, but as readers shall see, this writer found numerous flaws in Cournoyer's statements. More importantly, when this writer interviewed Cournoyer and asked specifically about his supposed statements concerning Olson and Korea, Cournoyer, clearly uncomfortable with the question, first denied making them, and then said that he had been "manipulated some and misquoted."

Not surprisingly, as SOD's projects expanded into highly sensitive areas, so too did the scrutiny the division was under from the FBI and CIC. Files from both organizations reveal that during the years 1952 and 1953, contacts between covert informants at Camp Detrick and Edgewood Arsenal and FBI and CIA agents became more frequent and specific. The FBI was especially concerned about the possibilities of enemy penetration into either of the installations,

81

and about the accidental mishandling of any of the lethal substances the SOD scientists were using in their various projects. The CIC was constantly worried that "the researcher ranks" at Camp Detrick could become infiltrated by enemy scientists. Read one document:

> The growing number of researchers from different national backgrounds, or from other countries, is cause for concern. Security officers must be ever vigilant that all proper and required measures are followed faithfully in screening these researchers before they are allowed to access any work areas or projects that could result in compromising, or worse, situations.

An FBI document from early 1953 reads: "The reporting lines between the Bureau's liaison agents within Detrick's Special Operations Division have become more effective and timely over the past several months." However, the document continues:

> While this development is seen as good, there remain some central concerns about the lack of security and safeguards within certain laboratories connected to the division. The accidental or intentional release of closely guarded information and materials is paramount with the expansion of [SOD's] projects.

Accidents among the SOD researchers were not uncommon but most, due to an extremely high level of safety consciousness and precautions, were of a relatively minor nature. There were exceptions, however. In 1951, about the same time that CIA-funded work at Detrick was intensifying, Olson and a number of his colleagues – including Drs. Ben Wilson and Joseph Stubbs – discovered, after the fact, that forty-six year old civilian microbiologist William A. Boyles had become fatally infected with anthrax. When Boyles had become ill, Army physicians initially diagnosed it as a bad cold. Attempting to recuperate at home, his condition worsened and he developed a high fever. Army doctors still failed to become concerned and they denied Boyles' wife's request that he be admitted to Camp Detrick's hospital. With his temperature soaring dangerously, Boyles consulted a private physician who took him to the nearby public hospital in Frederick.

As soon as the military physicians were consulted, they realized their mistake. Boyles was rushed within hours to the Detrick hospital where he was quarantined. But it was too late, and Boyles lapsed into a coma and died. Detrick officials moved quickly, falsifying Boyles' death certificate and issuing a press release stating that Boyles had passed away as a result of pneumonia. Boyles' family was not informed that he had contracted anthrax, but were told that his pneumonia may have been related to his work and therefore his wife was eligible for a small amount of federal compensation, which she began receiving soon after her husband's death.

Within about two weeks of Boyles' death, an attending physician leaked news about its true cause to other Detrick scientists, provoking a minor uproar over the internal secrecy, as well as the diagnostic laxness of Army physicians and their initial refusal to admit Boyles to the Detrick hospital.

Decades later, Alice Olson would comment that Frank never told her any details about Boyles' death but that she clearly knew Frank had been disturbed by it. "Frank went to the funeral," Alice told writer Jeanne McDermott in 1987. "I said, what did he die of? Frank said pneumonia. I said, you liar. I knew if he hadn't died of a classified disease Frank would not have gone. But the precautions were incredible...the men were always getting shots."

According to Col. Murray Sanders, some Camp Detrick researchers were cavalier in their attitudes toward the installations' strict safety requirements, and apparently Olson fit this bill on occasion. Dr. Gerald Yonetz recalled:

> Frank could be pretty impatient with all the safeguards and layers of precautions. He was result driven and didn't like to be held up any. He was especially irritated by the routines at the gates with the MPs. You had to show your badge regardless... Frank felt this was ridiculous...it caused some problems once in a while.

Sanders observed that sometimes the hazards of biological warfare work were simply too great, despite the safety measures taken, recalling that when researchers began working with brucellosis and tularemia, entire groups would fall ill. On occasion, buildings had to be shut down, sealed off, and decontaminated. In later years seriously contaminated buildings would have to be permanently sealed off.

Chemical Corps historian Richard M. Clendenin wrote in a 1968 chronicle of Camp Detrick that in the early 1950s, one zealous researcher approached scientific director Dr. Ira Baldwin and complained that safety regulations interfered with his work and that he was willing to work without them at any personal risk. From writer John Bryden we learn that this was British scientist Dr. David Henderson, on loan to Camp Detrick. Baldwin's reply to Henderson was:

> Well, David, you know really, I'm not worried about whether you get killed or not. If you do, we'll feel sorry and go to the funeral, and we'll come home and go to work again. But if we get organisms out into the air and Farmer Jones's cows over here get anthrax and they die, we'll have a congressional investigation and that will shut up the whole post. So, I really am not as much interested in you as I am in this question of protecting the community.

In 1968, then-retired Frederick County Health Commissioner, Dr. Forbes H. Burgess, told investigative journalist Seymour Hersh that he had encountered several strange cases that Detrick officials told him "not to report" because they wanted them "kept out of the papers because it was the plague and we didn't want to alarm anyone." Dr. Burgess also claimed there were cases of meningitis, anthrax, and typhoid fever at Camp Detrick.

Hersh reported that on October 18, 1953, only a month before Olson's death, a twenty-four year old civilian employee, Ralph W. Elbert, died of an undisclosed illness in Camp Detrick's hospital. Over the past several decades some writers have speculated that Elbert's work was somehow connected to SOD activities, but this has never been confirmed.

Murray Sanders states there were "casualties in the workshop" from the very start of things. Former Olson colleague Ben Wilson, a civilian scientist at Camp Detrick, observed, "It was a typical start-up situation whereby confusion and disorganization were not at all uncommon." Wilson said, "The Army was trying to accomplish too much too quickly with too little hard knowledge and without any well defined objectives." In Wilson's view:

> The career military people in charge didn't always understand what we were dealing with or the tremendous dangers that some of our work posed, but they pushed for results nonetheless, creating situations where tragic mistakes were bound to occur.

"We had some deaths at around that time," Sanders recalled. Once, after he returned from a trip to Washington, Sanders found the building housing the brucellosis experiments closed and sealed shut. On another occasion, a researcher, who had been one of Sanders' former students at Columbia University, became seriously infected with a lab virus and almost died. The researcher was Gifford Pinchott III, the son of the Governor of Pennsylvania.

Human deaths were not always accidental at Camp Detrick. Sometimes they came intentionally and unexpectedly. In May 1951, Frank was greatly upset to learn that Tommy Thompson had checked into a hotel in Japan and put a gun to his head, killing himself. The suicide didn't seem to make any sense to Olson or any of his colleagues. Frank told Alice that he simply could not imagine why Tommy would take his own life and that he thought it strange that the Detrick higher-ups had so little to say about the death. Alice agreed, and for several days many of the Detrick wives whispered about what a terrible thing it was for a man as handsome and engaging as Thompson to have died in such a way. There were rumors, perhaps inevitably, suggesting murder due to secrets that Thompson had uncovered while interrogating Shiro Ishii. There were also stories about blackmail resulting from other matters concerning Ishii's interrogation, as well as about Thompson being despondent because he allegedly had cancer, but nothing was ever confirmed. Oddly, a number of publications, including several released by the military, have misreported the year of Thompson's death, moving it back anywhere from two to four years.

Over the past several decades, there have been stories of other Camp Detrick scientists who reportedly committed suicide, but public information officers at the installation stated they had no figures concerning these. But, as readers shall learn, Frank Olson was not the only person who attended the fateful November 1953 gathering at Deep Creek Lake and who reportedly killed himself.

Often overlooked in the chronicles of Camp Detrick are the countless deaths suffered by the hordes of research animals—monkeys, rabbits, pigs, guinea pigs, goats, sheep, horses, burros, and cows— brought there for experimental purposes. Eric Olson recounts that his mother mentioned on a number of occasions how Frank would come home at times morose and depressed about having had to use one or another of SOD's favored simians in a terminal experiment. On one occasion, Alice recalled to Eric, Frank had come home looking especially glum and told her "all the monkeys died." Writer Ed Regis wrote in his book, *The Biology of Doom*, that Camp Detrick's "anthrax trials alone consumed more than 2,000 rhesus monkeys."

Judging from partial CIA records for 1953 and 1954, SOD researchers transported over 500 rhesus monkeys into its laboratories during one eight month period. Eventually, a CIA-front company, the Amazon Natural Drug Company, operated in part by a former Federal Bureau of Narcotics official, Garland Williams, transported many of the monkeys from South America to Camp Detrick.

Recalled former Olson colleague, Dr. Henry Eigelsbach:

> It was unavoidable not to become attached to some of the animals, especially the monkeys. You're there almost constantly with them, and you begin to notice them, to look into their eyes, to see how they behave and react to you. You grow fond of them, as any normal person would. Frequently, it was no different than having to put the family pet to sleep. It was sad like that.

6

November 28, 1953
Statler Hotel, Room 488
New York City

The special agent dispatched by security chief Sheffield Edwards to the Statler Hotel to assist Robert Lashbrook has been identified in CIA documents only as "Agent James McC." In 1999, a former CIA official, speaking on the condition of anonymity, told the author that this was James W. McCord, Jr. The name will be familiar to readers who recall McCord's June 1972 arrest for breaking into the Watergate headquarters of the Democratic National Committee. Less well known is McCord's involvement in a prior, unsuccessful burglary attempt in May 1972 by fellow-Watergate cohorts, E. Howard Hunt and Gordon Liddy. This earlier one had targeted the offices, and safe, of Las Vegas newspaperman Herman Milton Greenspun.

Called "Hank" by his friends, Greenspun was the editor and owner of the *Las Vegas Sun*. Brooklyn-born, Jewish, and a fierce Zionist, the dashing, blue-eyed Greenspun was an old-school, firebrand newsman. Fearless, he had no qualms about rubbing elbows or locking horns with mobsters like Meyer Lansky, Bugsy Siegel, and Johnny Rosselli; multi-millionaires like Howard Hughes; narco-lawmen like George Hunter White; or politicians like Senators Estes Kefauver and Joe McCarthy. McCarthy frequently maligned Greenspun by calling him "Greenscum." During a 1952 Las Vegas radio show, McCarthy drunkenly charged Greenspun with being an "ex-Communist." Greenspun, who just happened to be in the audience, jumped from his seat and challenged a quickly retreating McCarthy to back his charge with facts.

The reported target of the 1972 break-in to Greenspun's offices was a locked safe containing a treasure trove of information on specific, high-profile individuals, including politicians, law enforcement officials, confidential informants and presidential candidates. As we shall learn later, one of these individuals was a mysterious and extremely elusive former CIA contract employee who had been in the Statler Hotel on the night of Frank Olson's death.

The CIA's Office of Security hired James McCord, Jr. in 1951. Previously, the dark-haired, ruggedly handsome, University of Texas graduate had been employed as a special agent for the FBI in Washington, New York, and California. Former lawmen who knew McCord say he "was a sterling professional, always focused and deadly serious about his work." A former CIA official who worked with McCord said, "He was a no-nonsense kind of guy. He got the job done no matter what the problems."

Like many agents wooed away from the FBI by the CIA in the early 1950s, McCord was recruited because of his sharply honed investigative skills and his expertise in counterespionage tactics. In the 1940s, he had been part of a highly classified FBI intelligence operation, the details of which are still under lock and key. The operation involved key Soviet agents, Jacob Golos and Col. Boris Bykov, whose covert networks included American spies Laurence Duggan, Maurice Halperin, Whitaker Chambers, and Elizabeth Bentley. Frequently during this operation, McCord came into contact with fellow FBI man, William King Harvey, who handled the Bentley case for the Bureau, and then went on to become a CIA official. Harvey, whom readers shall learn more about, became a CIA employee several years before McCord, after having been forced out of the Bureau by director J. Edgar Hoover.

McCord's first assignment from the CIA was to conduct background investigations of Agency employees to discover anything in their pasts that could prove damaging or embarrassing to the Agency. This was a particularly important job in the early 1950s, when Senator Joseph McCarthy was aggressively targeting CIA vulnerabilities. With ample exposure to the complexities and dimensions of espionage, McCord considered that there was some validity to McCarthy's claims of CIA infiltration by Communist agents.

By mid-1953, McCarthy was at the peak of his political powers and was particularly prone to make serious allegations about the CIA, Army, and State Department, whenever and wherever he could. McCarthy's staff had been digging into the CIA's dirty laundry for months; their findings convinced McCarthy that Soviet operatives had burrowed into virtually every section of the agency. Meanwhile, newly appointed CIA director Allen Dulles had been informed that McCarthy was about to launch a massive investigation into the intelligence agency. McCarthy had alerted his chief counsel, Roy Cohn, to get prepared.

A duly concerned Dulles moved to counteract McCarthy's anticipated assault by assigning a number of his most talented staff at CIA to work full-time on McCarthy-related issues. McCord was among those assigned, and for a brief while, he worked closely with veteran CIA official and fledgling Inspector General, Lyman B. Kirkpatrick. Dulles had asked Kirkpatrick in April, 1953 to make it his "personal responsibility to handle the McCarthy problem for him and to act as his immediate assistant in his efforts to protect the Agency from McCarthy's attack."

According to the CIA's Public Information Office, McCord, in his first years of service, worked out of the Agency's Manhattan field office with the title, Domestic Field Investigator for the Office of Security. Subsequently, in the summer of 1953, he would be transferred to Washington, D.C., where he was assigned to the Security Research Staff (SRS), an Office of Security branch, directed by retired Brigadier General Paul F. Gaynor. In this position, McCord would be in and out of New York and Washington on assignment. The SRS was primarily responsible for detecting foreign attempts to penetrate the CIA, interrogating defectors and suspected spies, and operating several 'behavior modification' programs that were part of the CIA's top-secret Bluebird and Artichoke Projects, which predated Project MKULTRA.

Shortly after McCord had been hired in 1951, the CIA organized a series of high-level meetings with the Army, Air Force, Navy, and FBI. The purpose of the meetings was to explore the formation of an interagency task force to coordinate the myriad of mind control projects underway within various government departments and agencies. The upshot of one of these meetings, held on April 2, 1951 and attended by Gaynor and Sheffield Edwards, was the FBI announcing that it no longer had any interest in participating in the joint activity. Reportedly, the Bureau's decision to withdraw was spurred in part by J. Edgar Hoover's anger at the CIA for hiring away so many of his agents, including McCord and William Harvey, as well as James O'Connell and Robert Cunningham — two additional CIA security officials who later worked on the Frank Olson incident.

Meanwhile, throughout the early 1950s, SRS director Paul Gaynor was one of the CIA's staunchest advocates for developing a wide array of behavior manipulation tools and programs. Gaynor was especially interested in the use of psychochemicals during interrogations. He would often dispatch key staff members like Bruce Solie, Morse Allen, and McCord, to various parts of the country to discretely investigate studies reporting better ways to "control individuals." McCord and Allen, a former Naval intelligence officer, had known each other since 1942 when the two were tracking down suspected subversives in New York. (Solie, in January 1954, would be closely involved in the CIA's cover-up of the Frank Olson incident. And, as we shall soon see, Morse Allen would also work on the Olson case and produce an intriguing report about his death.)

According to his typed report, stamped "SECRET" and dated five days later, James McCord knocked on the door of Room 488 at New York's Statler Hotel around 7:50 A.M. on November 28th, only about five hours after Frank Olson had died.

Lashbrook opened the door and after McCord identified himself, the no-nonsense security agent immediately began interviewing Lashbrook about events leading up to Olson's fatal plunge. Prior to traveling to New York, McCord had quickly reviewed Lashbrook's personnel file, finding that Lashbrook had been hired by the CIA in September 1952, and been quickly promoted to deputy chief of TSS's Chemical Branch about six months later. McCord consulted Agency employees about Lashbrook; they described him as "a serious young man, studious in nature, with unquestionable loyalties to his country," a "brilliant chemist," and "a hard worker, not shy about burning the midnight oil." McCord began his interview by asking Lashbrook to explain how long he had known Frank Olson, why he had traveled to New York with him, what the two had done while there, whom they had seen and to whom they had spoken, who had seen them, and who had spoken to them.

The facts, just the facts, all the facts, and nothing more. Most Americans, just beginning their addiction to the moving picture boxes sprouting up in living rooms everywhere, thought that *Dragnet's* Sgt. Joe Friday had refined the art of retrieving facts to a science, but McCord had been around long before him. Damage control. There could be no effective damage control without all the facts. It was all very standard procedure for the former FBI agent, who was more than adequately skilled in establishing the foundation for the main focus of his questions: What happened to Frank Olson? Why did he dive through a closed window to fall over 100 feet to his death on the sidewalk below?

Lashbrook's first statement to McCord would become a serious point of contention and controversy forty years later, when this author first noticed it in the record and queried a number of people, and the CIA, about it. Lashbrook had reportedly prefaced his answers by telling McCord that Olson "was a biochemist and *Agency employee assigned to a project at Camp Dietrick* [sic]." [Italics added by author. This statement and subsequent controversy will be treated fully in a later section of this book.]

Lashbrook also told McCord that Olson had been suffering mental health problems for "about a year," and that he and Olson's superior at Camp Detrick, Lt. Col. Vincent Ruwet, had brought Olson to New York so that Olson could see Dr. Harold Abramson for psychiatric treatment. Olson's specific afflictions were "persecutions, delusions and guilt feelings," explained Lashbrook. His delusions and feelings "were not in areas related to his work," Lashbrook insisted, but instead came from his receiving government disability pay for ulcers that he believed he did not really have and "therefore believed he was cheating the government."

Apparently, judging by the contents of McCord's report, Lashbrook had said nothing about any meeting or experiment at Deep Creek Lake in Maryland the previous week. However, given that Olson had been working on top-secret CIA-funded projects and that security concerns about Olson's knowledge of these projects was paramount, it is likely that McCord, to some extent, would have been briefed about the nature of Olson's activities before being dispatched by the Office of Security.

Lashbrook explained that during Olson's last session with Dr. Abramson, on November 27, the physician had recommended that Olson go to a psychiatric hospital, Chestnut Lodge in Rockville, Maryland. McCord was already aware that this was an exclusive, private psychiatric facility that the CIA used for in-house employees and other 'sensitive' cases. Lashbrook told McCord that Abramson had telephoned Chestnut Lodge to make arrangements for Olson, "accompanied by Lashbrook," to be admitted around noon the next day, November 28. Olson was to be placed in the care of Dr. John P. Fort, a psychologist and a noted expert in treating people with schizophrenia. Lashbrook explained that after this last session with Abramson, he and Olson had returned to the Statler Hotel for the night. They were given room 1018A on the tenth floor. Wrote McCord in his subsequent report:

> They watched television for a while and then the two went to the hotel cocktail lounge where each had two martinis. They later had dinner in the hotel's main dining room. Lashbrook stated that no other alcoholic beverages were consumed by either of them. Lashbrook stated that at this time, [Olson] appeared cheerful and in a considerably better mood. Shortly before 10:00 P.M., [Olson] telephoned his wife. [Lashbrook] stated that [Olson] appeared reluctant to discuss his condition with his wife. Lashbrook added that [Olson's] wife had had psychiatric care early this year.
>
> At about 10:00 P.M., [Olson] and Lashbrook returned to their room. They had Room 1018A, which contained twin beds. Lashbrook stated that shortly after 10:00 P.M., he called Colonel Ruwet, who agreed to meet them at the plane's arrival in Washington at about 9:30 A.M., November 28, 1953. Lashbrook and [Olson] watched television in their room until about 11:00 P.M. Lashbrook stated that [Olson] remarked that he felt more relaxed than he had for a long time. Both then went to bed and Lashbrook fell asleep. Lashbrook stated that, recalling that [Olson] had 'disappeared' the day before, he, Lashbrook, took the bed nearest the door.
>
> Lashbrook stated that he was unable to fix the time definitely [sic] but that [at] about 2:30 A.M. he heard a loud crash of glass. He said [Olson] had jumped through the window shade and the glass and landed on the sidewalk of Seventh Avenue, across the street from Pennsylvania Station.

Lashbrook went on to explain that after he looked out the shattered window and saw Olson lying on the sidewalk, he had immediately telephoned Dr. Sidney Gottlieb at his home in Virginia to tell him "what had happened." Next, he had "reported the incident to the hotel telephone operator" and then telephoned Dr. Abramson, who had told him he "wanted to be kept out of the thing completely."

Shortly after speaking with Dr. Abramson, Lashbrook said, "some uniformed police officers and hotel employees came to his room." He explained that "the uniformed police made a search of the room and found no papers belonging to [Olson], with one exception." The exception was a letter to Olson from the Veterans Administration concerning a lapsed insurance policy. Lashbrook told McCord the letter was now in his suitcase. He explained that "on Thursday night, the 26th, Olson had thrown the letter into a waste paper basket" and Lashbrook had later retrieved it. How, or when, Olson obtained this letter has never been explained, and McCord throws no light on the issue.

Lashbrook said that while the police were still in the room, "Dr. Abramson called back and indicated that he had changed his mind about wanting to be 'left out completely,' and would assist." According to McCord's report:

> Lashbrook stated that no one exhibited any curiosity about this call. He stated that he observed that during the first call to Dr. Abramson the doctor's voice was loud and clear. During the second call, he could not hear the doctor very well and speculated on the possibility of a tapped wire.

McCord did not elaborate on this either.

Lashbrook told McCord that after the officers searched the room, they had taken him to the police station at 138 West 30th Street, where two detectives from the 14th Detective Squad had questioned him. Before the interview began, Lashbrook said, one of the detectives asked him "to turn out his pockets."

Lashbrook told McCord that in his pockets were several airline tickets from his recent trips, as well as some hotel bills, and "a receipt on plain white paper for $115 dated 25 November 1953 and signed by John Mulholland." The receipt was for an "advance for travel to Chicago," said Lashbrook. (Readers will recall that Mulholland, whose real name was John Wickize, was a prominent New York magician who had participated in a seminar on hypnosis in Chicago the week before Olson's death, for which the CIA had picked up the tab. As readers will learn, it turns out that Mulholland was at the time under contract to the CIA to write a manual on "the art of deception" and "to perform other operational support activities as needed.")

Also in his pocket, Lashbrook told McCord, were three additional items: a post card with Colonel Ruwet's home address and telephone number in Frederick, Maryland; a slip of paper with Dr. Abramson's office and home addresses and telephone numbers on it; and another slip of paper bearing the address of Chestnut Lodge Hospital in Rockville, Maryland.

In addition to these items, Lashbrook said he had a slip of paper in his pocket with the name of Federal Narcotics Bureau official George Hunter White — as well as White's CIA alias, Morgan Hall — and the addresses of White's apartment in New York, as well as the safe house he operated for the CIA in Greenwich Village. [It is important to note here that a large section of McCord's report pertaining to George Hunter White remains completely redacted. A 1999 request from the author to the CIA to declassify the report was refused.]

Lashbrook said that after the detectives completed their examination of the contents of his pockets, they had asked him why he had "been somewhat uncooperative when questioned by the police in his room at the hotel." Lashbrook had explained "that because of the nature of [Olson's] illness" he had

91

been reluctant to discuss the subject while hotel employees were in the room. "[Lashbrook] indicated to the detectives that he came to New York with [Olson] to see Dr. Abramson and that [Olson] was seeing Dr. Abramson because of mental illness," McCord wrote.

According to McCord's report, Lashbrook said the detectives had then asked to see his wallet and that they had examined his identification credentials, which consisted of four security pass cards, one each to the Adjutant's General's Office (AGO), the Department of Defense, the U.S. Army Chemical Center, and the Central Intelligence Agency. One of the detectives asked him to verify the address of his Washington, D.C. home, an apartment near Dupont Circle. Lashbrook complied and told the detectives he "shared his apartment" with a person named Edwin Spoehel. The detectives apparently had expressed no curiosity about his credentials or his roommate, and handed Lashbrook his wallet back.

McCord describes the final segment of Lashbrook's session with the NYPD, as follows:

> At the conclusion of the interview by the detectives, all papers were returned to Lashbrook and they assured him that there would be no publicity emanating from the Police Department regarding the incident. They requested that between the hours of 9:00 A.M. and 12:00 noon on 28 November 1953, Lashbrook identify [Olson's] body at the Morgue, Bellevue Hospital, 29th Street and First Avenue, New York City. They further indicated that there would not be any further need to question him.

McCord notes that he finished debriefing Lashbrook around 9:30 A.M. on the 28th and advised Lashbrook that he would meet with him again later that day at the Statler Hotel after Lashbrook returned from officially identifying Olson's body at the Bellevue morgue. McCord's report contains no explanation as to why he did not accompany Lashbrook to the morgue, but as readers shall see, it is believed that McCord, together with at least two FBI agents, took advantage of Lashbrook's absence to conduct further investigations, particularly to search all the rooms near and adjacent to Room 1018A.

Lashbrook returned from the morgue, according to McCord's resumed report, around 12:30 P.M. and told the agent he had "made the official identification of [Olson's] body and that funeral arrangements would be made by Colonel Ruwet or [Olson's] wife." The two remained together in Room 488 for the next four hours while Lashbrook made a series of telephone calls. McCord observed that, "other than exhibiting fatigue," Lashbrook "appeared completely composed." After one of his calls, Lashbrook told McCord that his superior, Dr. Sidney Gottlieb, had instructed him to meet with Dr. Abramson at 9:15 that evening "to obtain a report" from Abramson, which he was to hand carry back to Washington.

According to McCord's report, he and Lashbrook left the Statler at 6:00 P.M. and crossed the street to Pennsylvania Station where they met another CIA Security Office agent who had been dispatched from Washington to relieve McCord. [The CIA has identified this agent only as "Agent Walter P.T., Jr." His complete name has never been revealed and the Agency declined the author's request for the name. Agent Walter's objectives are not explained in his two-page report detailing his time with Lashbrook, nor do we have any explanation as to why the CIA chose to have McCord relieved at this time. It appears that Agent Walter's assignment was simply to accompany and observe Lashbrook through the conclusions of his stay in New York, but this is conjecture on the part of this author.]

With a little over four hours remaining before his scheduled appointment with Dr. Abramson, Lashbrook suggested to agent Walter that they take a walk and go to a movie. According to Walter's report, the two men walked to the Criterion Theater, on the corner of 44th Street and Broadway. There they watched *Cease Fire*, a 3-D war movie directed by Owen Crumb and filmed a year earlier in Korea, during the fighting. The film featured actual American soldiers in all the lead roles. (One of the soldiers was killed in battle just hours after his movie death had been filmed.)

After the movie, the two men had dinner four blocks away at McGinnis's Restaurant on West 48th, and then they walked to Dr. Abramson's office at 133 East 58th Street, a stately, turn of the century, three-story brick building. The office was on the building's top floor in Room 310. Lashbrook introduced agent Walter to Dr. Abramson "without the use of the agent's name and indicated that he was a friend accompanying him in an advisory capacity."

Then, curiously, according to Walter's report, Lashbrook asked him to "wait in the reception room while he spoke to Dr. Abramson." However, agent Walter stated, even after Lashbrook and Abramson had closed the door, he was able to overhear a portion of their conversation. What Walter heard, as recorded in his report, is quite intriguing, but Walter offers no comments on it:

> Upon closing the door, Dr. Abramson and Lashbrook started a discussion relating to security. Dr. Abramson was heard to comment to Lashbrook that he was worried about him. Lashbrook then stated that he thought it would be best if he dictated to Dr. Abramson. Prior to his dictation, they listened to portions of a conversation that had been recorded. Although names were not mentioned, it is believed that the recording represented an interview between a physician or psychiatrist and [Frank Olson]. This related to Lashbrook's observations of [Olson's] behavior prior to [Olson's] demise. Lashbrook told Dr. Abramson that [Olson] had told him that as far back as March 1953 [Olson's] wife had suggested that [he] see a doctor because of his depressed condition. Lashbrook further stated that it was his impression that [Olson] had delusions and was suffering from guilt and persecution complexes. Lashbrook mentioned that [Olson] thought

he was stealing money from the government. Lashbrook also indicated to Dr. Abramson that [Olson] had told him that he thought the agency group was putting benzedrine in his coffee to keep him awake. Toward the close of his dictation, Lashbrook indicated that he had had dinner at the hotel with [Olson] at which time [Olson] had said to him, 'I haven't felt better for a long time.' Several times during Lashbrook's dictation, the dictation was interrupted and he and Dr. Abramson listened to portions of the tape recording.

At this point in his eavesdropping, agent Walter alleges that he heard Lashbrook and Dr. Abramson leave the room closest to the outside door, where he was standing, and enter another room. Soon it became obvious that both men were having a drink together while continuing their discussion. Wrote Walter:

> Dr. Abramson was heard to remark to Lashbrook that he was 'worried as to whether or not the deal was in jeopardy' and that he thought 'that the operation was dangerous and that the whole deal should be reanalyzed.'

Moments later, Lashbrook rejoined Walter in the waiting room and the two departed Abramson's office. On the street outside, they hailed a taxi and returned to Pennsylvania Station where Lashbrook boarded the midnight train back to Washington.

7

November 30, 1953
CIA, Washington, D.C., 3:30 P.M.

Lyman B. Kirkpatrick, Jr. had been CIA Inspector General for only eight months at the time of Frank Olson's death, but he was far from being a stranger to his CIA surroundings. Kirkpatrick, nicknamed "Kirk" by his colleagues, had worked for the Agency since its inception in 1947 as the Central Intelligence Group. Before that he had been an OSS officer, joining that organization in early 1942, when it was in its infancy and called the Office of the Coordinator of Information. In December 1942, as a member of the OSS Secret Intelligence Branch, Kirkpatrick made his first of many indelible stamps on espionage history when, much to the amazement of OSS London chief David Bruce, he was able to secure a much-wanted transcript of a top secret session of Britain's Parliament. Kirkpatrick was quickly promoted to the rank of major and given command of the OSS intelligence unit at Headquarters, Twelfth Army Group. After that he became intelligence-briefing officer for legendary General Omar Bradley, who went on to be the first chairman of the Joint Chiefs of Staff. It would not be an exaggeration to say that Kirkpatrick cut his teeth on the craft of intelligence. Or perhaps it was the craft that cut its teeth on Kirkpatrick.

Once considered heir apparent to the top CIA post, Kirkpatrick had served the Agency in a number of high-ranking positions, including those of Deputy Assistant Director of Special Operations and Deputy Assistant Director of Operations. On December 13, 1950, CIA director General Walter Bedell Smith made Kirkpatrick his Executive Assistant. Official Agency historian, Ludwell Lee Montague, described Kirkpatrick's position as "the nexus between the Director and Deputy Director on the one hand, and the specialized Deputies and Assistant Director on the other." During many of their private conversations together, Smith made it clear to Kirkpatrick that his assistance was invaluable and that should Smith depart the director's post, Kirk would be his successor. So sure was Kirkpatrick of the promise, he would tell recruits, "I'm going to be director here some day." But life didn't always deal a fair hand, even when one played by the rules.

Kirkpatrick well understood what he was now up against as Inspector General (IG), a contentious and thankless job that granted him supervisory authority over programs and activities that were never meant to be known or scrutinized by anyone beyond their originators. Kirkpatrick was aware of the loathing he aroused within the Agency. People in the operational branches regarded him with disdain and did everything possible to avoid his presence. Frank Wisner's contempt for him was unconcealed. Wisner, the CIA's Deputy Director of Plans, had gone so far as to convince DCI Dulles to appoint a separate internal inspector for his myriad clandestine operations. Wisner's dark fiefdom was declared off limits to Kirkpatrick. Within days of Kirkpatrick's appointment as IG, once-close colleagues like Richard Helms began finding ways to be unavailable when he came around or requested a meeting. The fledgling IG knew that this bureaucratic shunning came with the territory, but nonetheless it was difficult to accept. This difficulty was compounded by the fact that Kirkpatrick was permanently confined to a wheelchair.

In July 1952, shortly after traveling through Southeast Asia on CIA business, Kirkpatrick had fallen critically ill. For two weeks he lay in a Washington, D.C. hospital, paralyzed, with only his mind functioning normally.

"I was aware of an iron lung outside the door," recalled Kirkpatrick years later, "but, thankfully, the nerves controlling my chest muscles stayed in working order so it was not needed." But his next few weeks in Walter Reed General Hospital, where he was subsequently transferred, were hell. The following five months at the Institute of Physical Medicine and Rehabilitation at the New York University Medical Center were not much better. Doctor's were baffled by his symptoms. After days of tests and consultations, they decided that he had somehow contracted poliomyelitis while in Bangkok. Spinal taps showed small traces of the disease, doctors told him. They said that most likely he would never again be able to sit upright. But he defied their predictions.

After being discharged from the Institute, and over his physicians' strong objections, Kirkpatrick insisted on returning to work. On March 27, 1953 he wheeled himself into an empty office in the CIA's Administration Building, just a few doors away from Dulles's office. Thirty-seven years old, the once muscular, six-foot-five bulk of health and virility was now emaciated and pale, unable to make it through a normal work day without napping at his desk for an hour. Despite his legs now rendered useless and his right arm completely flaccid, he never gave any hint that he thought these shortcomings could impede his job performance. Compensating for his disability would become an art form and second nature. For example, to shake hands, an obligatory gesture in his position, he would pick up his right arm with his left hand and awkwardly extend it forward.

Meanwhile, much had changed at the CIA during his absence. Before his illness, Kirkpatrick had been Executive Assistant to DCI General Walter Bedell Smith, as well as Chief of Operations overseeing all of the Agency's integrated clandestine activities. Kirkpatrick had enjoyed an excellent working relationship with Smith. Called "Beetle" by his friends, Smith had visited Kirkpatrick often in the hospital. During one visit Smith, in his customary blunt fashion, had told him, "Don't worry about the fact that your legs won't work; all I care about is your brains."

But now Smith was gone. He had been replaced on January 24, 1953, when newly elected President Dwight Eisenhower tagged Allen Dulles to be his DCI. Smith resigned on February 9, three days after the Senate confirmed his appointment to be Under Secretary of State. Dulles' previous job, CIA Deputy Director for Plans, had been given to Frank Wisner, a Wall Street lawyer from Mississippi who had been a Naval intelligence officer assigned to the OSS in Rumania and Germany. Wisner had also previously headed the Office of Policy Coordination, a covert action component of the CIA.

There were other changes, as well. Richard Helms, a former OSS officer, had been Kirkpatrick's deputy; Helms was now in Kirkpatrick's old job as Chief of Operations. Unbeknownst to Kirkpatrick, Helms had been officially confirmed in the position in January 1953. Kirkpatrick later wrote that he had resented "the fact that nobody from Washington had the courage to come and tell me that this had been done."

Amid all the bureaucratic shuffling, reshuffling and jockeying for power, things had become chaotic. Complicating matters, Senator Joseph McCarthy had declared war on the CIA, launching the first of several all out attacks. McCarthy proclaimed to the nation that the Agency was riddled with more than one hundred communists and that he was going to ferret out each and every one.

One morning, after Kirkpatrick had been sitting in his new office for several days with nothing to do, Dulles strolled in and asked him if he would be willing to become the agency's Inspector General. Happy to be back at work and bored out of his skull, Kirkpatrick answered that while he had "hoped to return to my old job," he would be happy to do whatever the director wanted. Dulles, less than fond of internal strife, had no interest in seeing matters revert back to any semblance of days past, and so Inspector General it was.

The IG's position was a relatively new one at CIA, having been created by DCI Smith. Stuart Hedden, a fifty-two year old New York lawyer and investment banker with no inhibitions about speaking his mind, had served as the Agency's first IG from 1951 through to Smith's resignation. At the time of Hedden's appointment, Smith made it clear to the CIA's staff that the IG's requests "for information were to be treated as requests from the DCI himself, and that Hedden was privileged to short-circuit the chain of command in seeking information." Despite this unequivocal directive, and others like it, Hedden had frequently clashed with the clandestine services chiefs. Even the CIA's official historian wrote, "There was notable animosity in the personal relationship between Hedden and Wisner, the DDP."

When Kirkpatrick was appointed IG, Hedden pulled him aside and advised he "insist that Allen [Dulles] agree that you are responsible only to him" and that Dulles also grant him unfettered access to all CIA sections and offices. Hedden's advice was forthright and sincere, but it would be years before Kirkpatrick even came close to Hedden's recommended levels of authority. Much later, Kirkpatrick recalled, "It took nearly two years before we finally were able to establish the work of the Inspector General on a sound basis in the Agency."

In April 1953, well before the Olson case came along, Kirkpatrick received his first serious assignment from the DCI. Dulles wanted the fledgling IG to take the lead on fending off attacks from rabid Commie-hunter, Sen. Joseph McCarthy. Kirkpatrick recalls that Dulles made it clear he was to "make it my personal responsibility to handle the McCarthy problem for him and to act as his immediate assistant in his effort to protect the Agency from McCarthy's attacks," which McCarthy was unleashing every chance he could. Dulles told his IG he wanted him to work closely with Security Office chief Sheffield Edwards to ensure that no "McCarthyites" infiltrated the Agency. Moreover, Dulles wanted Kirkpatrick to make sure that no CIA employees were blackmailed or convinced to give McCarthy or any of his many persuasive investigators any information, negative or positive, without explicit authorization from the DCI. Dulles was adamant about keeping McCarthy away from the CIA; before an assembly of 600 CIA employees, Dulles emphatically stated that he would "fire anyone who goes to McCarthy without my personal authorization."

In his memoirs, published in 1968, Kirkpatrick recalls that the "McCarthy Underground" practiced many "unsavory methods of operation," including "a not very subtle form of blackmail," whereby targeted CIA employees "would be contacted by telephone and told that it was known that they drank too much, or were having an 'affair,' and that the caller would make no issue of this if they would come around and tell everything they knew about the Agency." Within days of being given the McCarthy assignment, Kirkpatrick became widely and unofficially known as the "McCarthy Case Officer."

As part of his McCarthy assignment, Kirkpatrick was expected to collaborate closely with the FBI, which was no easy task. In the early 1950s Bureau director J. Edgar Hoover's disdain for the CIA was no secret. He had ordered his agents not to cooperate with the Agency without express permission from his office. It did not help that most Bureau agents considered CIA agents to be ivy league elitists who had no real world experience, much less calloused hands. "They were mostly rich boys, trust fund snobs, who thought they were God's answer to all the world's ills, acting like a bunch of modern day self-appointed Knights Templar," said one former FBI official. At the conclusion of World War II, Hoover had skillfully and manipulatively convinced President Truman that any continuation of the OSS would result in the creation of an "American Gestapo," and the Bureau director thought he had carte blanche to police both domestic and international matters. When the CIA finally emerged, Hoover had been less than pleased but bound and determined to battle the agency for turf he considered his own. There was also the matter of Bureau agents who defected to the CIA. Following William Harvey's joining the Agency, Hoover lowered the boom, declaring, "No more."

Kirkpatrick knew he was stepping into a minefield against which neither he nor his job was well fortified. Earlier in 1951, before Kirkpatrick's illness, the CIA, through Sheffield Edwards, had invited the FBI to join its interdepartmental Artichoke Committee that had been set up to coordinate 'behavior control' projects, including experiments with psychoactive drugs. Hoover, however, had sent a loud and clear message that the Bureau would have nothing to do with it. (The Army, Navy, and Air Force, on the other hand, had all come on board for Artichoke.) When Hoover, shortly thereafter, heard that Federal Bureau of Narcotics agent George White – whom Hoover detested because of White's excellent press contacts and love of publicity – was working closely with the CIA in New York, he ordered the Mid-Atlantic and New England FBI offices to steer clear of White and the Agency.

The CIA's strong presence in New York City especially irritated Hoover, who keenly knew that dominant influence in New York was essential to establishing a stalwart intelligence organization, one with tight connections to every important international private and public entity. Hoover would become incensed whenever he learned, always after the fact, that the CIA's Domestic Operations Division was attempting to recruit foreign diplomats posted to the UN to serve as informants or double agents.

As DCI Smith's assistant, Kirkpatrick had learned through experience that Hoover was not one to retreat. For example, when DCI Smith had insisted that Kirkpatrick try to get the CIA a seat on Hoover's Interdepartmental Intelligence Committee, Kirkpatrick had bent over backwards. After Hoover had flatly rejected Smith's requests three times, Kirkpatrick arranged a one-on-one between the DCI and the FBI director. Still, Hoover held fast, saying that he, personally, would decide which meetings might be of interest to the Agency, and that the CIA could attend such meetings only at Hoover's discretion. This enraged Smith.

Without doubt, Kirkpatrick's work as IG was daunting, extremely time-consuming and now, with new and hotter brush fires to extinguish every day, there was also this – the Olson affair. Early on November 30, 1953, Dulles had summoned Kirkpatrick to his office and dropped what Dulles called "the matter of Frank Olson" in Kirkpatrick's lap. Find out what happened and give me a report on it, the DCI instructed. Work closely with Larry Houston, Dulles said.

Larry Houston, whom Kirkpatrick knew well, was the Agency's General Counsel, a job in many ways diametrically opposed to Kirkpatrick's objectives as IG. Lawrence R. Houston, a Harvard and University of Virginia Law School graduate, had worked for the OSS as a deputy chief of mission in Cairo, Egypt. After the war, he accepted an appointment as general counsel of the Central Intelligence Group created by President Truman's 1946 executive order. Houston helped draft the National Security Act of 1947, creating the CIA, and then served as its general counsel from 1947 to June 1973, an unusually long tenure.

The facts that Dulles provided to Kirkpatrick that day about Olson's death were few and vague, but provocative. Some time, two days ago, in New York City, Olson, a biochemist assigned to CIA projects at Camp Detrick, had jumped out of a closed hotel window to his death, Dulles said. An Agency employee had taken Olson to New York after he had participated in "an experiment" conducted several days earlier. Dulles explained that the experiment might have involved a new drug that the Agency was interested in. This drug was called LSD, short for lysergic acid diethylamide. Dulles explained that it appeared as if the drug, a potent hallucinogen, had possibly provoked Olson's suicide. The DCI went on to explain that he felt it imperative Olson's widow begin receiving federal employee death benefits soon, and that everything possible be done to prevent any controversy concerning Olson's death, or embarrassment to the CIA. The public attention already being drawn to the Agency by McCarthy's attacks was more than anyone wanted to contend with. Nobody needed the media or enemies of the CIA to pounce upon what was generally regarded as a messy suicide, Dulles said.

Years later, Kirkpatrick would remark that it had occurred to him to ask Dulles why he had been chosen for the Olson case instead of Frank Wisner's own Inspector General, Winfield Scott, but he had thought better of it. Scott clearly had jurisdiction over the programs related to Olson's work, but for some reason, Dulles had chosen Kirkpatrick to investigate the case. Kirkpatrick knew very well that if Wisner's division wanted to keep anything secret about the Olson incident, there would be little Kirkpatrick could do about it. The glacial wall of obfuscation erected by Wisner would always stand in his way. "I simply welcomed the fact that I had been given something to do," recalled Kirkpatrick.

Since becoming IG, Kirkpatrick had realized that the ever-crafty Dulles was doing everything possible to shield certain activities from scrutiny. The Agency's clandestine operations and counter-intelligence units had been off-limits to Kirkpatrick and so he would have to be especially careful with the Olson inquiry. Kirkpatrick knew it would take time for him to grow into his position and for the Agency to grow comfortable with him in it. For now his main goal was simply to hold onto his job. Over the coming years, Kirkpatrick would carry out the IG position with a diverse mix of skills. One day he was the "bastard at the family reunion," Kirkpatrick said in a 1978 interview, the next "I was chaplain and conscience" of the Agency. "You can't have a nice IG," he added. "You have to be a son of a bitch."

Apparently, many within the CIA shared Kirkpatrick's sentiments. In 1986, Richard Bissell, a high ranking agency official who clearly had a large ax to grind with Kirkpatrick, said, "Wisner hated [Kirkpatrick]. Allen [Dulles] ended up hating him. Kirkpatrick is a funny person. He is very bright, well informed, articulate, but he would knife anybody in the back for not much more than twenty-five cents worth of advantage."

Kirkpatrick began his investigation into Olson's death on the morning of December 1 by dispatching his aide to interview Sidney Gottlieb's and Robert Lashbrook's immediate superior, TSS Research Director Willis A. Gibbons. Gibbons, as readers may recall, was a former associate director of research and development for the U.S. Rubber Co. who had been with the CIA for only about two years, but he was an old hand in biological warfare matters. From 1949 through 1951, he had been a member of the Ad Hoc Committee on Biological Warfare, or the Stevenson Committee, as it was known, created by Secretary of Defense James Forrestal. With Gibbons' active participation, the Committee had concluded that the United States was "not prepared for biological warfare" and strongly recommended the country aggressively research and develop "offensive potentialities" as quickly as possible.

Kirkpatrick's aide began his interview of Gibbons by asking what type of work Olson had done for CIA. "Eyes Only," Gibbons explained, meaning that Olson's work had the highest security classifications. Gibbons explained that Olson had been assigned to the Special Operations Division at Camp Detrick for the past few years. SOD, it will be recalled, was the rigidly compartmentalized group dedicated to offensive biological warfare projects for paramilitary and covert operations. SOD also served as an adjunct facility for CIA research and development. Security was extremely tight. Of CIA personnel, only Drs. Sidney Gottlieb, Robert Lashbrook, and Henry Bortner were cleared to enter SOD premises, Gibbons said. The only other person who had access to SOD that Gibbons was aware of was Stanley Lovell. Lovell, a New England industrialist and erstwhile chemist, was a high-ranking consultant to the CIA who had been instrumental in organizing SOD. He now served as liaison between the CIA and Camp Detrick.

Kirkpatrick surely recognized Lovell's name from his years with the OSS. Stanley Platt Lovell had been OSS Director of Scientific Research and Development. A chemist by training, he owned and operated the Lovell Chemical Co. in Watertown, Massachusetts. Kirkpatrick also knew that Lovell had a reputation for being extremely devious. In 1943, a minor controversy had arisen out of Lovell's use of Federal Narcotics Bureau agents assigned to OSS, including George Hunter White. The incident had involved the unwitting administration of truth drugs to a group of American atom bomb scientists at a Manhattan hotel – a situation, Kirkpatrick would later recall, not completely dissimilar to "the matter of Frank Olson." Lovell and White, as readers shall learn, were instrumental in the OSS's development of truth drug, and the two men maintained a close and lifelong friendship.

Gibbons explained to Kirkpatrick's aide that although the bulk of Camp Detrick personnel worked on biological weapons of mass destruction, SOD concentrated on those that could be used against individuals and small groups. SOD also specialized in identifying lethal plants and infectious diseases that could be employed covertly to kill or incapacitate people. Diseases like yellow fever, Rift Valley fever, tularemia, and encephalitis, Gibbons explained. Plants like the unpredictable *claviceps purpurea*, which is actually an ergot fungus, and the deadly curare from South America, which causes death by asphyxiation, by first causing the skeletal muscles to relax and then eventually become completely paralyzed.

While his aide was interviewing Gibbons, Kirkpatrick had reviewed a smattering of files provided by TSS Chemical Division director, Dr. Sidney Gottlieb. Gottlieb had personally brought the documents to Kirkpatrick's office, and the IG noted that Gottlieb had seemed somewhat nervous when he first arrived. Gottlieb was young, thirty-four years old, not long on the job and still trying to adjust to the rigors of intelligence work and its byzantine bureaucratic structures. Through CIA personnel records and consultations with Agency officials, Kirkpatrick had learned all that he could about Gottlieb.

Gottlieb was born on August 3, 1918 in New York. Much to the dismay of his parents, he had two clubbed feet. Doctors did everything possible to correct the problem, but at the time knowledge about treating congenital defects was limited. For his first twelve years, young Sidney was forced to wear special metal braces on his legs. Other youngsters viciously harassed him, and by the time he was seven years old he had developed a serious stuttering problem. Rid of his braces as he entered his teens, Gottlieb wore special built-up shoes for several more years. His right foot was never fully corrected, and for many years he had to use slightly altered footwear. Attending elementary and high school in the Bronx, Gottlieb was an outstanding student who displayed a natural bent for the sciences. After high school, he completed nearly two years at City College of New York before transferring to Arkansas Polytechnic College. Arkansas was followed by the University of Wisconsin in Madison, from which he graduated magna cum laude in 1940 with a Bachelor of Science in agriculture.

At Wisconsin, Gottlieb had attended classes taught by Dr. Ira Baldwin, who would become Camp Detrick's first director of scientific research in 1942. After Wisconsin, and at the urging of his brother, Gottlieb continued his education, earning a doctorate in organic chemistry from California Institute of Technology in 1943. That same year he, like Frank Olson, married the daughter of a minister.

Upon receiving his Ph.D., Gottlieb immediately attempted to enlist in the Army, but was rejected because of his deformed right foot. Desperately, he tried to enlist in other military branches, but repeatedly was turned away. "I wanted to do my share in the war effort," he said years later. "I felt I had a duty to serve yet I couldn't convince anyone that I would not be hampered in my performance." Bitterly disappointed, in the fall of 1943 Gottlieb took a job with the U.S. Department of Agriculture in Washington, D.C. There he performed basic research on organic soil matter and its chemical structure. In 1945, he transferred to the U.S. Food and Drug Administration, where he spent two years developing analytical techniques for determining the presence and amounts of various drugs in the human body. He became an expert in this area of applied science, and was frequently called upon to testify for the government in court cases. "I enjoyed my FDA time," he said, "but the work became mostly repetitive and sometimes pretty monotonous. I needed more of a challenge."

In 1948, Gottlieb left the FDA and went to work for the National Research Council, also in Washington, D.C. There he worked on a number of projects involving plant diseases and fungicides. "I was exposed to some interesting work concerning ergot alkaloids as vasoconstrictors and hallucinogens," Gottlieb later recalled. He switched jobs again in late 1949, when he was recruited to be a research associate at the University of Maryland, where he concentrated on how fungi metabolized in the skeletal portion of plant cells known as lignin. In January 1951, an official with the Hercules Chemical Company recruited him to join the CIA. Gottlieb officially started work for the Agency on July 13, 1951, and his first supervisor was a former Hercules Chemical employee. Gottlieb could not recall the name of either Hercules official. Within weeks, Gottlieb was elevated to chief of the TSS Chemical Branch.

Each file handed over by Gottlieb had been stamped in bold red ink: *SECRET*. Also on many documents was the program cryptonym: *MKULTRA*. Kirkpatrick was somewhat familiar with the program and knew that it operated under the utmost secrecy. His questions to Gottlieb about MKULTRA were met initially by silence, followed by Gottlieb's hesitant suggestion that answers would best be obtained from Dr. Gibbons. Kirkpatrick noticed that Gottlieb's stutter began to reveal itself. He was also aware that Gottlieb had been born Jewish without any social pedigree, which made him an odd fit at an agency notorious for preferentially hiring wealthy WASP males. Gottlieb told co-workers that despite having been born Jewish, he was an agnostic who found spiritual comfort in his voracious readings of ancient Eastern religions. Above his desk he kept a typed quote from the Quran which read: *"Until when They come, it will be asked of them: Did you reject my Words while you had no full knowledge of them? Or what was it that you did?"*

Kirkpatrick well understood that while Gottlieb was an oddity of sorts, he enjoyed particular favor with CIA director Allen Dulles. Like Gottlieb, Dulles had been born with a clubfoot and both men had been ridiculed as youngsters for 'bearing the cloven hoof of the devil.' It was a strong but never mentioned bond between them. Kirkpatrick knew that Gottlieb and his wife Margaret lived with their three children on a small farm in Virginia where they raised goats. Gottlieb was well known around the agency for proselytizing about the benefits of drinking goat's milk. In the early 1950s, many Agency men considered Gottlieb a "free thinker," but nobody questioned his brilliance.

After questioning Gottlieb, Kirkpatrick arranged a meeting with security chief Sheffield Edwards. Perhaps his old friend could throw some light on the Olson matter before he met with Gibbons, Kirkpatrick thought. He and Edwards had served together as OSS officers in Europe during the war, enjoying some memorable moments in France. But Edwards, head of the Office of Security, was of little help. Yes, he knew about the TSS experiments. No, he did not know the full range of TSS activities, Edwards told him.

"And this drug called LSD," Kirkpatrick asked, "what can you tell me about it?"

"It's best that you speak with Wisner or Helms about that," Edwards said.

"Can you tell me anything about it?"

"We've been aware of it for a while. Chadwell's group is doing a full blown study but it won't be available for another year or so."

"Anything else?"

Edwards thought a moment and said, "We think the Russians may have it also, or something similar. Helms thinks they may have dosed George Kennan with the drug last year. He's convinced it was the only reason Kennan would have acted the way he did."

Kirkpatrick knew that Edwards was referring to George F. Kennan, the American Ambassador to Russia at the time. Earlier, on February 19, 1952, Kennan had made some remarks during a press conference at Templehof airport in Berlin that created deep agitation with the Soviets. The ambassador, who later claimed he thought he was speaking off the record, had angrily told a reporter that life in the US Embassy in Moscow was comparable to what he had experienced while confined to a German internment camp in 1941-42.

"Anything else you can tell me about this drug?" Kirkpatrick persisted.

"You'll have to discuss that with Wisner and Helms. Dulles knows all about it," Edwards said judiciously. Kirkpatrick would later recall that Edwards uncharacteristically revealed some nervousness when he spoke with him. Edwards, like Gottlieb, had had a stuttering problem in his youth, and to compensate, according to Kirkpatrick, he "spoke in a slow and distinctive manner."

After reviewing his aide's interview with Gibbons, Kirkpatrick decided to re-interview the TSS chief himself. His first question for Gibbons was, "Who has quantities of LSD besides the Agency?" Gibbons ticked off a short list that began with George White at the Narcotics Bureau. Said Gibbons, "He has some. I'm not sure of how much. White's an expert with Kefauver's committee, and a close friend of Halley. He has good access to criminal types."

Kirkpatrick awkwardly jotted down a few notes with his left hand. He wrote the names George White, Estes Kefauver, and Rudolph Halley, placing a question mark next to Halley's name. As with Lovell, Kirkpatrick knew White from his days with the OSS and Army intelligence. Gibbons did not elaborate on White's relationship with the Agency. Kirkpatrick was also aware that Halley, a former U.S. District Attorney in New York, had been chief counsel for Senator

Kefauver's Crime Committee, which had recently held nationally televised hearings. Halley had also been president of the New York City Council.

Gibbons explained that Dr. Harold Abramson also had a supply of LSD. Abramson was affiliated with several medical institutions in New York, Gibbons said. "His subjects are all abnormal," he added. Kirkpatrick asked if any other physicians in New York had LSD and Gibbons replied there might be a few other doctors, but he was not sure.

Who else has it? Kirkpatrick asked.

The Agency's TSS Chemical Division, as well as at least two other sections of clandestine services, and both the Office of Scientific Intelligence and Office of Security worked with the substance. (One can only guess at Kirkpatrick's surprise, and perhaps anger, on learning the Security Office was experimenting with LSD, given the results of his meeting with Sheffield Edwards, the head of it.) All of these Agency branches, Gibbons explained, besides conducting their own experiments, provided grants-in-aid for research with the drug through various cutout organizations to conceal their more expansive activities. It wasn't uncommon for some funds to pass through several cutout groups before reaching the intended destination. Many universities across the country, which were conducting CIA research, were unaware about where their funding originated. The system could be labyrinthine, Gibbons said, but he knew, for example, that Dr. Robert Hyde at the Boston Psychopathic Hospital and Dr. Harris Isbell at a Federal prison in Lexington, Kentucky were running experiments for the Agency.

"I think Isbell and Abramson have been at it the longest," Gibbons remarked, adding that a physician at the University of Illinois in Chicago, Dr. Carl Pfeiffer, also had a quantity of LSD. Gibbons explained that Pfeiffer conducted experiments at a reformatory in Bordertown, New Jersey and at the federal prison in Atlanta, Georgia. There are a few researchers who are attempting to discover what parts of the body LSD works on, through radioactive experiments, Gibbons said, but he would have to get their names for Kirkpatrick.

"Does anyone outside the United States have the drug?" Kirkpatrick asked.

"Yes," replied Gibbons, "at least two places have it. There's some at the Naval Air Station in Atsugi, Japan and some at the Agency's field station in Manila." Gibbons said nothing about the Manila station having already used the drug to dose a local elected official there, nor is it clear that he knew about the incident.

Gibbons said that there was no LSD kept in Europe that he knew about. "I know Bill Harvey in Germany has recently expressed an interest," Gibbons said, "but nothing has been provided yet." Bill Harvey was head of the CIA's base in Berlin. People called him "the Pear" behind his back, because of his ill maintained physique. Kirkpatrick was well aware that Harvey was a colorful and controversial character. Harvey had been an FBI agent before coming to the CIA. Forced out of the Bureau after having earned the wrath of J. Edgar

Hoover, he had been recruited by the agency's highly secret Office of Special Operations. Once, in 1951, Kirkpatrick and DCI Smith had attended a stormy meeting with Hoover, during which the cantankerous FBI chief went on a rampage, complaining about the CIA's hiring of Harvey.

Kirkpatrick jotted down a few more notes and then inquired about the source of the CIA's LSD. Gibbons told him he was not clear on the mechanics of acquisition. "It's an experimental drug," Gibbons said, "not under Federal control." He thought it came from two pharmaceutical companies. One was in Basle, Switzerland, called Sandoz. The other was Eli Lilly and Company in Indianapolis, Indiana. "We may also get it from other sources," Gibbons said, adding, "Lilly has been trying to make it for some time now."

Kirkpatrick may have found this last statement contradictory and perplexing, but the record reveals no indication that he said anything.

Have any of the CIA's people had experience with the drug? he asked.

"Gottlieb, Lashbrook, Cooper, Hughes, and Al Ulmer have all had it," Gibbons said. "Wisner, Helms, Barnes, and Roosevelt all know about it."

Who at the Deep Creek Lake meeting was given LSD? Kirkpatrick asked.

"Everyone, as far as I know," Gibbons said, "except for Malinowski, who doesn't drink, and one other SOD scientist who has a heart condition."

"Were Gottlieb and Lashbrook given LSD?"

"No, not them."

"Hughes? He was with CIA group there?"

"Allan Hughes. He's assigned to TSS from the military. I doubt that he was given the drug."

"And its effects on people?" Kirkpatrick asked.

"OSI knows the most about that, I would assume," Gibbons said. "Dr. Chadwell [OSI chief] has a massive study underway that we've consulted on."

"What can you tell me about Frank Olson?" Kirkpatrick asked.

"He's had a history of mental disturbances that predate the experiment," Gibbons replied. "It's my understanding that last summer he told his wife he was upset. She suggested he see a doctor. She has also been seeing a psychiatrist." He went on, "Olson had problems with being division chief because he thought he couldn't handle the job. He asked to be fired, and then wanted to resign. Dr. Abramson said he'd been delusional for months. Abramson came to the conclusion that Olson should enter a sanitarium."

There is nothing in Kirkpatrick's file to indicate his reaction to or thoughts about his December 1st interview with Gibbons. Years later, Kirkpatrick would say that the CIA had a very good in-house psychiatric staff, leading one to think he may have questioned in his own mind why Olson had been taken to Abramson and not treated by a CIA physician. Said Kirkpatrick in 1967, "often the strain of the secrecy involved in the work of the Agency became overpowering and caused emotional disturbances. For this reason the organization wisely always kept a good psychiatric staff."

Finished with his interviews of CIA in-house personnel, Kirkpatrick turned his attention to the detailed statements taken from those people who had been directly involved in Olson's trip to New York - Vincent Ruwet and Robert Lashbrook.

Judging from Lt. Col. Vincent Ruwet's observations of Frank Olson, he, of all the men who attended the Deep Creek Lake gathering, knew Olson best, even though their association had only begun in July 1951. This was when Ruwet first reported to Camp Detrick to serve as Assistant to the SOD chief. At the time, Olson was SOD branch chief of planning and training. About a year later, Ruwet was promoted, as was his superior, Dr. John Schwab, SOD chief. According to Ruwet's statement, he and Schwab had "prevailed upon" Olson to become Acting Chief of SOD. Ruwet states that Olson had agreed to "this reluctantly since he said that he was adverse to taking on administrative-type work and preferred closer touch with the laboratory bench."

Olson lasted only six months in the new position. In March, 1953, according to Ruwet, Olson "was removed at his own request" as SOD chief and returned to his former position. At the same time, Lt. Col. Michael R. DeCarlo was appointed Chief of SOD, but within two months he was promoted, and Ruwet returned to the position.

Ruwet described Frank and Alice Olson as being "extremely popular persons" among Camp Detrick's staff and families. Ruwet's wife would tell the author in 1999 that she and her husband socialized frequently with the Olsons, often going to each other's homes for dinner parties and to play cards, or to travel into downtown Frederick to watch films at the cinema. "We enjoyed their company a lot," said Mabel Ruwet. "They cared a great deal for each other, and they were fun to be around. We always looked forward to spending time with them."

Frank was "almost an extrovert," Ruwet wrote in his report. He "liked a practical joke, but did not carry it to excess." He was a "life of the party type," Ruwet added, but always caring of others. "He was the first one on hand to assist anyone who might have troubles, either professional or personal."

Ruwet ranked Olson's professional ability as "outstanding," basing this on almost daily interaction with Olson for over two years. In his statement, Ruwet elaborated:

> During the period prior to the experiment my opinion of his state of mind was that I noticed nothing which would lead me to believe that he was of unsound mind. He had the normal family worries. Occasionally he had trouble with his ulcers but was always reluctant to discuss personal troubles with anyone.

In the first of his few scant references to Olson's drug dosing, Ruwet seemed deliberately concise: "The experiment took place Thursday, November 19th,

1953 in the evening." He then quickly moves forward in time and writes, "I saw Dr. Olson on Friday morning. We had breakfast and he appeared to be agitated and at the time I did not consider this to be abnormal under the circumstances." Ruwet does not explain why he drew this conclusion, or what the "circumstances" were, nor does he provide any details about the experiment, or anything else, that occurred at Deep Creek Lake.

According to Ruwet's account, after breakfast, Olson had "asked if I would object if he rode back to 'home-station' with Mr. Champlin," to which Ruwet agreed. Ruwet did not explain, but Champlin was Dr. Everett Champlin, also a scientist from SOD who attended the Deep Creek Lake meeting and had been dosed with LSD there.

Ruwet did not see Olson again until the following Monday morning, November 23 when, according to Ruwet:

> I came to work about 7:30, and Dr. Olson was waiting for me in his office. He appeared to be agitated and asked me if I should fire him or should he quit. I was taken a-back by this and asked him what was wrong. He stated that, in his opinion, he had messed up the experiment and did not do well at the meetings.

Ruwet explained that he had talked to Olson for about thirty minutes, telling him he had "the wrong impression," that he had "done well in the meetings, and that his participation in the experiment was above reproach." Olson seemed relieved with this, Ruwet recounted, but over the remainder of the day he "appeared to have some difficulty in concentrating." Again, Ruwet offers nothing about the "experiment" or any information about why Olson thought he had "messed up."

The next morning, November 24th, however, Olson was waiting again for Ruwet in his office. Ruwet observed that this time Olson was "greatly agitated and, in his own words, 'all mixed up.'" He told Ruwet that he thought himself "incompetent" and that "he had done something wrong." Ruwet describes their conversation:

> He could not say exactly what he thought he had done wrong. He made reference to the fact that he thought he should not have been retired for physical reasons but when this was pushed he shifted to the fact that he felt incompetent to the type of work he was doing— when this was pushed he seemed to look for something else which he had done wrong.

Ruwet recounts that he then spent about an hour going back and forth with Olson before "it became apparent to me that Dr. Olson needed psychiatric attention." He explains, "I continued the discussion but in such a way as to attempt to get him to suggest that he needed some help. This he did, finally." Ruwet then abruptly adds he was not the only person speaking with Olson at the time, and that a Dr. Stubbs was present and that he and Stubbs agreed Olson needed help. Nowhere does Ruwet indicate who Dr. Stubbs is or when or why he came into the conversation. The author has identified Stubbs as Dr. Joseph James Stubbs, a SOD biochemist, about whom readers will learn more. Called Jim by his friends, Stubbs had also been present at the Deep Creek Lake meeting, but reportedly was not dosed with LSD because he had a heart condition.

After getting Olson to agree he needed help, Ruwet's report says he told Olson that he was going to telephone Robert Lashbrook at the CIA and arrange for someone to help him. Ruwet does not explain why he came up with this seemingly impromptu offer nor does he explain why Olson could not receive proper medical attention at the Camp Detrick hospital, which was staffed with several capable physicians. Ruwet writes only that Olson agreed to the call and "said that he would go home at once and discuss the situation with his wife, which he did." However, never before revealed, except here and earlier in this book, Olson did *not* go home alone, making this part of the story all the more puzzling. Dr. Stubbs accompanied him home. According to a never before published deposition taken from Alice Olson in 1988, she said: "The next morning [Frank] came into the house and said, 'I've consented to psychiatric care,' and, 'Jim Stubbs wanted to come home with me because he thought I might do you bodily harm.'"

Ruwet called Robert Lashbrook after Olson and Stubbs left his office. He wrote that he "briefed Lashbrook on the situation," telling the CIA official he thought Olson "was in serious trouble and needed immediate professional attention." In turn, Lashbrook "said he understood and would take immediate action." Ruwet's report states that within minutes of his hanging up with Lashbrook, he received a phone call from Alice Olson, asking if she could accompany Frank on the ride to see Lashbrook in Washington, to which Ruwet agreed. Nowhere is it explicitly stated, but apparently, either Olson or Dr. Stubbs had informed her that her husband was going to see Lashbrook.

Minutes later, Ruwet writes, Lashbrook called him back and asked what time Olson was expected to arrive in Washington "since he had arranged for an appointment in New York with a psychiatrist and that he would obtain air reservations for us to go to New York." Five minutes later, Ruwet states, Frank and Alice Olson arrived at his office, apparently without Dr. Stubbs. At this point, Ruwet told Alice that Frank was going to be taken to New York because he "had to see a physician who had equal security clearance so he could talk freely." From Ruwet's office, the three then went to Ruwet's home where he "changed from uniform to civilian clothes," and then John Malinowski, another SOD scientist, picked them up and drove the three to Washington.

John C. Malinowski— who also attended the Deep Creek Lake meeting, but was not dosed with LSD because he did not drink alcohol— was developing aerosol devices intended for use in the covert delivery of lethal biological agents such as anthrax. In 1960 and 1961, Malinowski helped head up a special SOD project, classified *EYES ONLY*, at the request of the CIA. It produced several-dozen gelatin capsules, each containing a lethal dose of botulism. In 1961, the capsules were passed from SOD to Robert Maheu, a former FBI agent and then CIA contractor, who in turn gave them to Mafia legend John Rosselli. Rosselli was supposed to use them for the assassination of Fidel Castro and his brother Raoul. Later, in 1966, Malinowski participated in a top secret simulated biological attack on the New York City subway system.

Ruwet's report states that on the ride to Washington, Olson was "greatly agitated, and, in his own words, 'all mixed up.'" Ruwet recounts that the group stopped for lunch at a Hot Shoppe restaurant in Bethesda, Maryland, just outside the Capitol. There Olson became "highly suspicious" of the food and drink served. Alice Olson would later say in her 1988 deposition that Frank suddenly pushed his plate away saying, "I can't eat this, it's poisoned."

Once the group arrived at the CIA buildings on the Mall, Ruwet recounts, he went in alone to speak with Lashbrook, leaving Frank and Alice in the vehicle with Malinowski. "I found out later," Ruwet writes, "that Olson had asked Mr. Malinowski to leave the car so that he could talk to his wife, which was done." There are no details provided by Ruwet about what Frank and Alice spoke about. In Alice Olson's 1988 deposition, she does not mention the incident and says hesitantly: "[Malinowski] took us to— as I recall the barracks on the Mall were there, and I think this probably— I believe— I was so confused and so worried at this point I was just sitting in the car being taken. I think we went to the Mall and let Frank out. I kissed him goodbye and Malinowski drove me home, and that was the last I ever saw [Frank alive]."

Ruwet returned to the vehicle about fifteen minutes later "and suggested to Mr. Malinowski and Mrs. Olson that they leave us there and that we would get to the airport with Dr. Lashbrook, who was going with us." Ruwet, Olson and Lashbrook flew out of Washington National airport around 2:30 P.M., arriving at New York's LaGuardia airport around 5:00 P.M. on Tuesday, November 24. Ruwet reports that, on the plane, Olson said, "he had the feeling that someone was out to get him."

In New York, the three men traveled by taxi to the office of Dr. Harold A. Abramson, which was located in a brick townhouse at 133 East 58th Street. Ruwet writes nothing about Dr. Abramson's background nor does he acknowledge any awareness that Olson was already well acquainted with Abramson, having worked closely with him during World War II. Decades later, Sidney Gottlieb would testify in a civil court case related to another alleged CIA drug dosing, that Abramson had been selected to treat Olson because he had gone through the arduous CIA security clearance process and also because at the time he was "one of the few experts on LSD in the United States." Indeed, as readers shall learn much more about, Dr. Abramson had been conducting experiments with LSD in New York for at least a year prior to Frank Olson's arrival at his door.

Lashbrook and Ruwet left Olson with Abramson for about an hour, at the doctor's request. When they returned, Abramson suggested they go to a hotel, at which point Lashbrook said he had already made reservations for them at the Statler Hotel. Abramson said he would join them at the Statler "about 10:30 P.M. with some sedatives" and also suggested that they all have a "highball" once they got to the hotel, wrote Ruwet. Olson drank one martini, Ruwet recounted, but refused a second one. At dinner, "[Olson] ate very little; still appeared to be very suspicious of Dr. Lashbrook and myself."

Following drinks and dinner after registering at the Statler, the three men went to their rooms. Olson and Ruwet were sharing a room, with Lashbrook staying in the adjoining room. The three gathered in the shared room to wait for Abramson's arrival, but Olson asked Lashbrook to leave him and Ruwet alone so they could speak privately.

According to Ruwet's account, after Lashbrook had gone into the adjoining room, Olson anxiously asked Ruwet, "What's behind all this? Give me the low-down. What are they trying to do with me? Are they checking me for security?"

Ruwet said he did his best "to reassure [Olson] and tried to show him wherein factually he was imagining these difficulties."

Dr. Abramson arrived that evening around 10:30 P.M. carrying a "bottle of bourbon and some Nembutal for Dr. Olson," Ruwet recalled without comment, despite the fact that this rather dubious prescription seemed less than ideal for a person in Olson's alleged condition. (Nembutal is a barbiturate used to slow down the nervous system and help people sleep. It was also used for hypnotic purposes. Many physicians consider it dangerous to mix the drug with alcohol.)

Lashbrook re-joined Ruwet, Abramson and Olson and the four of them continued drinking until about midnight, at which time Abramson departed, but not before suggesting Olson take a Nembutal capsule so he could sleep. Ruwet reports that Abramson instructed Olson to take a second Nembutal if he had any difficulty sleeping.

The next morning, Wednesday, November 25th, Ruwet states, the three men had breakfast and then he and Olson accompanied Lashbrook, at his suggestion, "on an official visit which he had to make." Ruwet does not say where or what the visit was, but only that it was cut short because Olson "became highly suspicious and mixed up." The three then went to Abramson's office for Olson's 4:00 P.M. appointment.

Ruwet and Lashbrook again left Olson with Abramson, returning an hour later to pick him up to return to the Statler Hotel. Before the three left for the hotel, Abramson advised Ruwet and Lashbrook that Olson should return for another appointment on Tuesday, December 1. This date was selected because Olson had informed the doctor that he planned to return home the next day for Thanksgiving holiday with his family. Ruwet asked Abramson if the doctor wanted him to return with Olson or if Frank should come alone. Abramson replied it was entirely up to Olson. There was no question about Lashbrook returning with Olson.

That evening, Ruwet recounts, he, Olson and Lashbrook had dinner and then went to a performance of the Rogers and Hammerstein musical, *Me and Juliet*, at the Majestic Theater on West 44th Street. During the performance, Ruwet states, "Olson appeared to get upset during the first act and at intermission he was highly agitated and stated that people were outside waiting to arrest him on his departure from the show." Ruwet responded to this by trying to reassure Olson that he "personally would guarantee him that he will be with his family for Thanksgiving."

"I don't believe you," Olson fired back.

"Well, you have to," Ruwet replied. "I give you my word of honor."

"I don't believe you," Olson said again.

"Look, Frank, we already have plane reservations to go home tomorrow."

"That means nothing."

Ruwet then suggested, "Maybe you don't want to see the rest of the show. Do you want to leave and talk?"

"Yes," replied Olson.

The two walked back to the Statler Hotel, leaving Lashbrook, who, Ruwet said, wanted to stay for the second act. Ruwet provides no account whatsoever about what he and Olson talked about from this time until about 11:30 P.M., when Lashbrook joined them at the hotel.

The next morning, Thanksgiving Day, at 5:30 A.M., Ruwet awoke to see that Olson was not in his bed or in the room. Ruwet immediately woke Lashbrook up in the adjoining room and the two dressed quickly and rushed downstairs to search for Olson. Why there was such sudden alarm about Olson's absence is not explained. When the elevator doors opened on the hotel lobby area, Ruwet and Lashbrook spotted Olson sitting in a chair with his hat and overcoat on.

"Where did you go?" Ruwet asked Olson.

"I was walking around for a while," was the reply.

"But, why?" asked Ruwet.

"I'm not sure," said Olson. "But I got rid of my identification cards and wallet."

"Why did you do that?"

"Because you told me to, Vince. You were with me."

"I wasn't with you, Frank."

"Oh," Olson said. "Yes, I guess that's right, I must have been dreaming."

Despite this odd behavior from Olson, Ruwet provides no explanation, and the three checked out of the hotel and caught their flight to Washington. At Washington National airport, John Malinowski picked up Olson and Ruwet; Lashbrook took a taxi to his apartment near Dupont Circle.

Halfway out of Washington, on Wisconsin Avenue, Ruwet states, Olson asked Malinowski to stop the car.

"What's wrong?" Ruwet asked.

"I would just like to talk things over," Olson said.

Ruwet complied and Malinowski pulled into a Howard Johnson's parking lot near the old Bethesda-Chevy Chase Woodward & Lothrop department store. Olson asked Malinowski to leave the car so he could speak privately. After Malinowski stepped outside, Olson told Ruwet "he couldn't go back to Frederick since he was so mixed up. He was ashamed to meet his wife and family."

"What do you want to do?" Ruwet asked.

"Just let me go," Olson replied. "Let me go off by myself."

"I can't do that."

"Well, then," Olson said, "turn me over to the police. They're looking for me anyway."

Ruwet recounted they then "discussed this at considerable length," but provides no details of that conversation, other than to say that he convinced Olson the "police did not want him." Ruwet recounts that he then suggested that perhaps Olson "would like to go back to New York to see Dr. Abramson." Olson agreed to this. Ruwet then telephoned Lashbrook at his apartment from a Howard Johnson's pay phone. Lashbrook told Ruwet to bring Olson "to his apartment immediately."

Once there, Ruwet and Lashbrook decided that Olson should return to New York right away. Lashbrook then telephoned Sidney Gottlieb at home in Virginia. Gottlieb said he would come to Lashbrook's apartment at 1855 New Hampshire Ave. as soon as possible. Ruwet provides no reason for the urgency of these seemingly unnecessary and hasty decisions, but he says that he felt Alice Olson "was entitled to know what the situation was and because she was expecting [Frank] for Thanksgiving dinner I should proceed to Frederick to brief Mrs. Olson."

At the time Ruwet departed for Frederick, he describes Olson's condition as "the worst that I had seen him, since the experiment took place," implying, but never explaining, that Olson's condition during the experiment was far worse than he had indicated earlier in his report. Ruwet then writes, "This was the last time I saw Dr. Olson." But, as he notes, he did speak to Olson on the following night, Friday, November 27. Around 10:30 P.M., Friday night, Ruwet recounts, Lashbrook telephoned him from New York to inform him "that reservations had been made for Dr. Olson at Chestnut Lodge" asylum in Rockville, Maryland and that he and Olson had plane reservations "for the following morning" to return to Washington.

[Readers shall learn more about Chestnut Lodge, but should know at this point that the asylum, or sanitarium as it was sometimes called, was a facility that had been approved by the CIA Security Office for use, about eighteen months prior to Olson's referral.]

Lashbrook suggested in the Friday night phone call that Ruwet meet their plane at the airport the next day, which Ruwet agreed to do. Ruwet then jokingly asked Lashbrook "if Dr. Olson was still speaking to me." Lashbrook asked Olson the same question and Frank was overheard to reply, "Why, yes, let me have the phone." Ruwet states that Olson sounded "quite relaxed" on the phone and told Ruwet that he had agreed to go to Chestnut Lodge.

Ruwet then told Olson he would see him the following morning, Saturday, at the airport and Frank replied, "You don't have to do that, I'm sure you have work to do around the house." Ruwet said, "Think nothing of it, I'll be there to meet you."

"Fine," said Olson, "I'll see you in the morning."

Ruwet concludes his observations by writing, "At approximately 2:45 A.M., Sat. Nov. 28th, 1953, I received a call from Dr. Gottlieb with a message that Dr. Olson had died."

Kirkpatrick then turned his attention to Dr. Robert Lashbrook's observations, which cover much the same ground as Ruwet's and generally agree with his account, but provide additional details about Olson's final hours in New York after he had left Ruwet in Washington and returned with Lashbrook to New York on Thanksgiving.

Lashbrook writes that after Ruwet departed his Dupont Circle apartment to meet with Alice Olson, Sidney Gottlieb, who had arrived from Virginia, drove him and Olson back to the Washington airport where they boarded a plane for New York, leaving Gottlieb behind. From New York's LaGuardia Airport they took a taxi to Dr. Abramson's Huntington, Long Island office, arriving there at about 4:00 P.M. Abramson was a psychiatric research consultant at the nearby State Hospital in Central Islip, as well as at South Oaks Psychiatric Hospital. Lashbrook writes, "Dr. Olson was alone with [Abramson] about one hour, followed by about 20 minutes with Dr. Olson and me [with Abramson]." Following this, Lashbrook recounts, Abramson "obtained local lodging for us [at the Anchorage Guest House in Cold Spring Harbor], and Olson and I then went to a local restaurant for a Thanksgiving dinner, after which we went to bed." Lashbrook explains nothing about the twenty minutes he and Olson spent together with Abramson.

Over dinner and later at the guesthouse, Lashbrook recounts, Olson told him that "he felt he had cheated the Government in connection with his retirement from the Army [due to his disability], and that he should be punished for this." Lashbrook notes in his statement he was not familiar with the details of what Olson was referring to, but that both Ruwet and Dr. Abramson had indicated to him that they could "see nothing dishonest or morally questionable in connection with [Olson's] retirement." Lashbrook goes on to state that Olson then claimed that:

> ...everyone, including me, was in a plot to 'get' him; he said I and the others knew the master plan for the plot, and he wanted to know what it was. He said he had failed in his job, that he was so disgraced he could not face returning to his family. He said he felt he was guilty of security

violations because he felt he, on occasion, had exceeded his interpretation of the need-to-know principle.

While one could easily imagine Frank Olson delivering these thoughts and feelings in an animated and emotional manner, Lashbrook states, "Except in certain well defined areas he spoke intelligently and rationally and he acted in a socially acceptable manner."

According to Lashbrook's account, Thursday night was uneventful. The next morning, Friday, Lashbrook and Olson were picked up by Dr. Abramson at the guesthouse and the three rode together into New York City to Abramson's East 58th Street office. "There we had a conference during which the physician told Dr. Olson that hospitalization would be in his best interests," Lashbrook writes.

Lashbrook adds, "After a while Dr. Olson agreed," indicating that initially Olson was less than receptive to Abramson's recommendation. Lashbrook states that Olson "preferred some place near his home and friends," so following "a discussion and telephone conference with [Dr. Gottlieb], a private hospital near Washington was selected. [Abramson] made arrangements with the hospital, but they had to prepare [Olson's] room and could not take Dr. Olson until the following day (Saturday)." Lashbrook added, "Dr. Olson agreed he would be a voluntary patient" and parenthetically wrote: "([I]t was agreed he would not be formally committed)."

The hospital, as noted in Ruwet's report, was Chestnut Lodge in Rockville, Maryland, a private psychiatric facility founded in 1910 as Chestnut Lodge Insane Asylum. At the time of Frank Olson's proposed admittance to the facility, it was widely known for pioneering in the intensive psychodynamic-psychotherapeutic treatment of serious mental illness, including schizophrenia and multiple personality disorders. Among its staff were many notable physicians, including Frieda Fromme-Reichman, Harry Stack Sullivan and David Rioch.

People who lived near the facility, however, often complained of "constant screaming and moaning" coming from some of its twenty buildings. Local teens in the area called its gothic-looking main building "the House of Horrors," "Psychoville," and then later "Hannibal's House."

Despite Olson's request that a hospital near his home be selected, Chestnut Lodge was primarily chosen because, by 1953, it had a history of use by the CIA and many, if not most, of its physicians had security clearances from the Agency. One former CIA official said, "Throughout the 1950s, Agency employees in need of psychiatric care, that I was aware of, either went to Chestnut Lodge or Sheppard Pratt Hospital in Baltimore."

After Olson agreed to voluntary commitment to Chestnut Lodge, Lashbrook reports that he attempted to obtain plane reservations "for a return to Washington that day," but that no seats were available. After making reservations for Saturday morning, he and Olson returned to the Statler Hotel, checked in once again, and were given room 1018A. [Room 1018A was actually on the hotel's

13th floor but was designated as such because three lower floors were used for special functions.] Lashbrook observed at this time:

> Dr. Olson appeared no longer particularly depressed, and almost the Dr. Olson I knew prior to the experiment, although he still maintained the various misconceptions I have mentioned before.

Lashbrook recounts that once they had settled into room 1018A, Olson "washed out his dirty clothing." While Olson did this, Lashbrook called Ruwet to let him know what "the course of action" was. He wrote that Olson also talked to Ruwet "in a cheerful" manner. Lashbrook then states that Olson telephoned his wife, noting that, "this was the first time he felt he dared speak to her.

Olson's call to Alice is verified in her testimony before a Congressional Committee in 1975. Alice testified at that time:

> I talked to [my husband] on Friday night [November 27, 1953] just after Colonel Ruwet had talked to him, and it was a fine discussion— everything was 'we will see you tomorrow'— it was not goodbye. That was the one thing that consoled me [through all the years], was that I knew that this could not have been an intentional act [of suicide], because he did not call up to say goodbye— it was 'I will see you tomorrow.'

On Olson's alleged suicide, Lashbrook succinctly states:

> Sometime around 02:30 Saturday morning I was awakened by a loud noise. Dr. Olson had crashed through the closed window blind and the closed window and he fell to his death from the window of our room on the tenth floor of the Statler Hotel.

In his observations of Olson as a scientist and person, Lashbrook remarked that he first met Olson in early 1952. This would have been, according to CIA files, less than a year after the CIA had hired Lashbrook. Lashbrook first encountered Olson as part of his TSS duties, when he would meet monthly with SOD scientists to monitor their work on CIA projects. In addition to this, Lashbrook stated that he also had "attended three 2-day conferences which were held in isolated locations" to discuss SOD progress on CIA projects, at which Olson had been present. Lashbrook wrote, "Prior to the experiment, Dr. Olson was a competent scientist with an excellent command of his field...that performed his duties in a superior manner" and was "highly regarded by his colleagues, both as a scientist and as a friend."

There is no evidence to be found that indicates Inspector General Lyman Kirkpatrick ever interviewed Robert Lashbrook about his role in Olson's death or in the experiment that preceded it and seems strongly connected to it. Assuming Kirkpatrick reviewed Lashbrook's background, he would have found that the tall, sandy-haired, mild-mannered chemist had only recently joined the CIA, in September 1951, shortly after receiving his PhD. in chemistry from Stanford University. Born in Los Angeles in 1918, Lashbrook attended South Pasadena High School and then went on to Redlands University, also in California, where he majored in chemistry, and to the University of Arizona, where he received a master's degree in chemistry. During World War II, he served in the South Pacific with the 15th and 17th Air Force Weather Squadrons. He retired from the Air Force Reserve as a lieutenant colonel. While studying for his doctorate, and briefly afterwards, he worked for the Schuckl Company, a food processing plant in Sunnyvale, California, where, in September 1951, the CIA recruited him.

In early 1952, after TSS was reorganized into divisions and the agency began hiring significantly more people, Lashbrook was named Deputy Chief of the Chemical Branch. As readers shall learn, in 1952 and 1953, Lashbrook took LSD "about a half-dozen times" in TSS experiments in which CIA scientists acted as their "own guinea pigs."

Drs. John L. Schwab and Sidney Gottlieb — the only others asked to submit statements about Olson's death — agreed with Lashbrook and Ruwet on Olson's character and professionalism. By 1953, Dr. John Schwab, a biochemist, had achieved living legend status at Camp Detrick after overseeing a 1949 'vulnerability test' of the Pentagon building. The test involved sending into the complex two 3-man teams pretending to be air-quality workers. The teams sprayed billons of Serratia marcescens microbes into the building's air conditioning intake valves proving that security was not effective and that, had the teams been enemy forces using anthrax, they would have wiped out at least half the nation's military top brass.

Schwab recalled that in May 1943, he and Olson, who were both then commissioned Army officers, had worked together on a "classified research project" at Camp Detrick. Apparently, this was the same project with which Dr. Harold Abramson had been involved. Schwab said they worked on the project for about a year, but states that he "was not in close contact [with Olson] professionally or socially" during this time. Schwab does not reveal what his role was in the project, but he does say that "Olson's work" was "mainly in the field of aerobiology" and that Olson remained in this field through to November 1953. States Schwab, "Dr. Olson was considered an authority in the field of aerobiology, a science which had developed considerably during the years 1943 to 1953 at Camp Detrick." Observed Schwab, from late-1945 through to Olson's death, he and his wife had "numerous social contacts" with Frank and Alice Olson. He described Frank as "always extremely cheerful" and "more than willing to help anyone in distress." Wrote Schwab, "Olson was a family man, taking great interest in his home and the activities of his family. He imbedded in the minds of his children the need of religion in life, making sure that they attended their Sunday school regularly and would also encourage his friends' children to attend with them."

Schwab, who attended the Deep Creek Lake meeting and was reportedly dosed with LSD there, makes only one scant reference to the meeting and the so-called experiment. He writes, "I had no personal contacts with Dr. Olson after the experiment." Interestingly, Schwab then states, "I had first learned on Monday, November 23rd, 1953 from Lt. Col. Vincent Ruwet that Dr. Olson *had been exposed and was showing symptoms of reaction.*" [Italics added.] Schwab does not explain what he means by his use of the word "exposed," and we are left to assume that perhaps the term "showing symptoms of reaction" is a reference to Olson's reaction to LSD. Schwab concludes his statement by writing that he was notified at 3:00 A.M. Saturday, November 28 that Olson "had leaped from the Statler Hotel," and that at 6:00 A.M. he received "confirmation that the leap was fatal."

Dr. Sidney Gottlieb's statement was only eight short paragraphs long. He wrote very little that the other three men had not already stated, except for some curious personal comments. He wrote, for example, that out of mostly scientific conversations with Olson, "a fairly close personal relationship had also developed" between them. Gottlieb recounted that he and Olson had met together, either at Camp Detrick or the CIA, a total of "thirteen or fourteen" times over a two-year period. On these occasions, Gottlieb stated, "the principle topic of conversation was official business," but a "minor part of the various conversations I had with him concerned personal matters unrelated to our scientific or official relationship."

Gottlieb elaborated further:

> During this period Dr. Olson seemed to me to be a very effective research scientist, in excellent command of his field of experimentation and very devoted to the successful execution of his duties. He seemed to me a stable individual, not particularly given to making snap judgments and able to get along very well among his colleagues. It was made known to me on several occasions, through incidental remarks made by either himself or his colleagues, that he had been suffering from recurring trouble with a duodenal ulcer. I had no occasion to observe any instance when this interfered with his work.

Gottlieb did not specify what Olson's "field of experimentation" was. On the Deep Creek Lake experiment, Gottlieb stated simply:

> Up to the time of the experiment, I observed nothing in Dr. Olson's behavior or actions which was different from that described above. On November 20, the day after the experiment, I had occasion to observe Dr. Olson for about two hours in the morning, between 7 A.M. and 9 A.M. Aside from some evidence of fatigue, I observed nothing unusual in his actions, conversation, or general behavior.

Gottlieb states that he next saw Olson on Tuesday, November 24, just prior to Olson's departure for New York with Ruwet and Lashbrook. Gottlieb observed that Olson "seemed to me to be confused in certain areas of his thinking, particularly as regarded his feelings on incompetence in relation to his job and to the futility of trying to help him."

Gottlieb states that his next contact with Olson was on Thursday, November 26, in Lashbrook's apartment. Over a period of about one hour, he observed that Olson "seemed more disturbed and agitated than he had been the previous Tuesday. He talked in a clear manner, but his thoughts were confused. He again talked about his incompetence in his work, the hopelessness of anybody helping him, and the fact that the best thing to do was to abandon him and not bother about him."

Concluded Gottlieb, who wrote nothing about events surrounding Olson's death, "It seemed to me that he was very mentally disturbed at this time."

8

December 2, 1953
New York City, 14th Police Precinct

O n December 2, the day before he submitted his case report on Olson
to Sheffield Edwards, CIA security agent James McCord went to New
York's 14th Police Precinct to meet with James Ward and David Mullee,
the two detectives who were investigating Frank Olson's death and had questioned Robert Lashbrook. The reason for McCord's visit, while not explicitly
stated in his report, appears to have been to discuss Olson's death with the two
detectives and to view their written police reports and any evidence the detectives may have found.

The surviving police report on Olson's death, obtained by the author from
the New York City District Attorney's Office, contains a number of provocative
items which, as readers shall see, would come into focus decades later, in 1994,
when legendary New York District Attorney Robert M. Morgenthau surprised
many observers by reopening the investigation into Olson's fatal fall.

Among the most intriguing aspects of the existing police report is that it
quotes from an earlier police report submitted by uniformed officer Joseph
Guastefeste. The existing report quotes Guastefeste's report in which he states,
"in view of the facts set forth it is requested that the case remain active." This
provocative quote is also extremely frustrating because no copy of Guastefeste's
report exists. According to the New York City Police Department, the Guastefeste report must have been misfiled after Detectives Ward and Mullee assumed
responsibility for the case, or it was lost or destroyed. In any case, it has never
been found.

A second curious element in the police report appears in the "supplementary
investigation report" completed by detectives Ward and Mullee, which states that
Olson and Lashbrook "registered in Room 1018A on November 26, 1953." The
detective's report makes no mention of the return trip to Washington, D.C. made
by Ruwet, Lashbrook and Olson on that same day, Thanksgiving. The detectives'
report states: "[O]n the morning of November 26, 1953, Lashbrook, with the deceased, returned to New York City and registered in the Staler Hotel." Certainly,
this part of the report does not agree with Lashbrook's account to McCord -
that he, Lashbrook, and Olson returned to New York from Washington, traveled

to Long Island to see Dr. Abramson and spent the night in a guesthouse there, checking back into the Statler the following afternoon, Friday, November 27.

Was this a simple mistake or do these discrepancies exist for some other reason? What actually happened?

Also intriguing is that the detectives' report states: "Due to the importance of the positions held by the deceased and Lashbrook with the U.S. Government, the facts in this case were related to FBI agent George Dalen (by telephone)." However, the report contains nothing more about the call to Dalen.

Finally, the report file includes a typed, unsigned, letter dated December 1, 1953. The letter was addressed to Detective Ward and it would appear to be from Olson's wife, Alice, but it has no signature. The letter requests that "all personal effects of Dr. Frank R. Olson be sent to Lt. Col. Vincent L. Ruwet, 1004 Rosemont Ave., Frederick, MD." The letter's next line reads: "I understand that the effects contain a recent letter from the Veterans Administration regarding insurance which is of particular importance." The report contains nothing more about this letter.

When special agent McCord entered the 14th Police Precinct detective squad room around 5:30 P.M., December 2, we do not know how McCord identified himself to the detectives, but his subsequent report reveals that the detectives expressed no reservations about sharing information with him. (We are left to assume that McCord introduced himself as either a CIA or Department of Defense investigator.)

When he arrived at the Precinct, McCord found that David Mullee "had reported to duty on the evening shift a little earlier than Detective Ward." Waiting for Detective Ward to arrive, McCord queried Mullee about the reports on Olson's death. Mullee explained that on November 30, the case had been officially closed after being ruled a suicide as a result of Olson's jumping from the Statler Hotel window. However, before closing the case, Mullee acknowledged, he and Ward were initially "very suspicious" that Lashbrook and Olson were "engaged in some homosexual affair and also were mulling over in their minds" the possibility that the case had actually been what Mullee termed a "homocide." McCord's report also reveals that Mullee told him that he and Ward considered the possibility that Olson and Lashbrook "were involved in some committee hearing for they were aware that Sen. McCarthy's Committee was in town around this time." Mullee said that in considering the McCarthy hearings, he and Ward also recalled the 1948 death of former State Department official Laurence Duggan. Like the investigation into Olson's death, the police inquiry into Duggan's fall had been closed within hours with the finding that Duggan had "either jumped or accidentally fell through an opened window."

At the time of his death, Duggan had been forty-three years of age, married, and the father of four children. Many of Duggan's friends had expressed serious doubts about his having killed himself Christmas week without leaving any explanation to his family. Close friends, notably Sumner Wells, a former State Department undersecretary and ambassador to Cuba, were quick to point out that Duggan had been in high spirits and was looking forward to working on many projects. Duggan's wife and brother told reporters that he had been bothered by ulcers for several years, but that the problem had been greatly improving. New York's Police Commissioner, Arthur W. Wallander, reported that there were "no signs of foul play or violence" in Duggan's office and that there had been "no witnesses to the incident."

Within five hours of Duggan's death, Congressman Karl Mundt, acting chair of the House Un-American Activities Committee, and California Congressman Richard M. Nixon, a ranking member of the committee, suddenly called a press conference where they made a stunning announcement: less than two weeks before his fatal fall, they said, Duggan had been named in a closed subcommittee hearing, along with five other State Department officials, as possibly being a spy. The following day, Washington reporters asked Mundt who the other five officials were, and Mundt replied, "We'll name them as they jump out of windows." Later that day, reporters learned that Duggan had been questioned by an FBI agent on December 10, ten days before his death.

Moreover, a few days before Duggan's death, the man who reportedly had revealed Duggan's name to the subcommittee told the *New York Herald Tribune* that Duggan's death "might have been another Masaryk affair;... the technique of pushing people out of a window was tried on Masaryk with success." "Masaryk" was Jan Masaryk, former Foreign Minister of Czechoslovakia, who had fallen to his death (nine months before Duggan) from the window of a government building in Prague. (According to some historians, the "traditional method" in Czechoslovakia of assassinating politicians is throwing them out windows, a practice called 'defenestration.')

As a result of their suspicions regarding Olson's death, Detective Mullee said he and Detective Ward had called the local office of the FBI and asked special agent Edward A. McShane, Jr. to "see whether or not they knew anything about either Lashbrook or [Olson]." McShane, at the time a thirty-eight year veteran with the FBI, told the detectives that he knew nothing about either man but said that he would check with other Bureau agents. Before hanging up, however, McShane remarked that Olson's death also brought to mind the "odd suicide of Forrestal."

Former Secretary of Defense James Vincent Forrestal died on May 22, 1949, after falling from the sixteenth floor of the U.S. Naval Hospital in Bethesda, Maryland. Forrestal's broken, bloodied body was found clad in pajamas and a bathrobe. The bathrobe cord was wound tightly around his neck. He had been hospitalized due to "operational fatigue" attributed to "excessive work." His death was ruled a suicide, but for many people, including members of Forrestal's family, the matter remained far from resolved. Forrestal's brother, Henry, told reporters at the time of the death that he "believed that someone threw my brother out the window" and that he considered it quite strange that his brother died "just a few hours before I was to take him home." Additionally, Forrestal's spiritual advisor, Monsignor Maurice Sheehy, told reporters that an unidentified Navy warrant officer at the hospital had told him that Forrestal "didn't kill himself."

Meanwhile, McCord's report about Olson's death makes no mention of the fact that McCord knew McShane or that he had worked with him and for the FBI in the past. Further, there is no indication in the report that he disclosed anything to Mullee or Ward about these connections. However, FBI documents uncovered in 1999, as well as interviews with former FBI agents, reveal that McCord and McShane did subsequently discuss not only Duggan's and Forrestal's deaths, but also the strange deaths of CIA official James Speyer Kronthal, State Department employee John C. Montgomery, and CIA security analyst Frederick E. Crockett. [Readers shall soon learn more about Kronthal's death, which occurred only months before Olson's.] The deaths of Montgomery and Crockett had been "officially" closed, but now came to mind.

James Montgomery, an associate of Kronthal's and ostensibly head of the U.S. State Department's Finnish desk, but actually a CIA employee, had been found dead on January 24, 1953 in his Washington, D.C. home, apparently strangled. His nude body was found with a bathrobe cord around his neck. Montgomery's death was ruled a suicide by D.C. police, but U.S. Congressman Fred E. Busbey of Illinois had called for a full House investigation into the death. Busbey told the *Washington Post* six-days after Montgomery died, "There are stories being bruited about that the police have been told not to talk." (Busbey's fellow House members declined to take up the investigation.)

Just seven days after Kronthal's death, Frederick E. Crockett, a CIA security analyst with whom McCord was familiar, had been discovered on April 8, 1953, in a semi-conscious state in his gas filled D.C. apartment on Wisconsin Avenue. Police had ruled Crockett's condition an "attempted suicide," and the CIA told reporters at the time that "there was no reason to believe" that Crockett's attempt had anything to do with Kronthal's death. (Crockett survived the incident and lived until January 17, 1978.)

When Detective James Ward arrived at the Precinct on December 2 to be interviewed by James McCord, he essentially reiterated what Mullee had said and complained that getting information from Lashbrook had been "like pulling teeth." Ward said that he and Mullee had first obtained Dr. Abramson's name not from Lashbrook but "from the hotel operator who apparently intercepted Lashbrook's call" to Abramson. Ward added that he "could not believe anything could be so secretive that Lashbrook would have been justified in being so uncooperative." It was primarily for this reason that Ward and Mullee had contacted the FBI, Ward explained. Ward said FBI agent McShane "was equally unbelieving and had expressed the opinion that he did not know of any government work so confidential as to justify a lack of cooperation with police officials."

McCord asked if the FBI was still interested in the case and, according to his report, Ward replied that "he believed they were doing further checking into the background of Lashbrook."

In response to McCord's final question about any publicity the incident had generated or reporters who might have been interested in the case, the detectives told McCord that some reporters had expressed curiosity about the case but that, because of an ongoing newspaper strike, "none of the more important" papers "have been published since the incident occurred." McCord's report concludes, "Detectives Ward and Mullee were fully cooperative and advised that they would be willing to give further help if it were desired."

* * * * *

On the same day McCord was meeting with Detectives Mullee and Ward, two additional special agents from the CIA's Security Office were also in New York gathering materials on Frank Olson's death. One of these agents, identified only as "Agent John D.P.," visited the New York City Department of Health, Bureau of Records and Statistics, where he obtained a Certificate of Death for Frank Rudolph Olson. The document, signed by Assistant Medical Examiner Dominick DiMaio, stated that an autopsy on Olson's body had revealed that death had been caused "by multiple fractures, shock and hemorrhage" due to his "jumping or falling from a 10th floor window."

Elsewhere in New York, the second agent, identified only as "Agent Jeremiah J.M.," was busy conducting what appears to have been a background investigation of Dr. Harold Abramson. According to Jeremiah's report, the agent visited the New York Public Library where, in the 1952 "Who's Important in Medicine," 2nd. Edition, he found a lengthy entry for "Harold Alexander Abramson" that detailed the highlights of his career. Most notable was that Abramson, who had obtained his MD from Columbia University in 1923, and had been a National Research Council Fellow at Berlin's Kaiser Wilhelm Institute for Physical Chemistry and Electrochemistry in 1926-27, had also, during World War II, in 1942-43, initiated and directed penicillin aerosol therapy for lungs for the Technical Division of the Chemical War Service, a predecessor of Camp Detrick. Agent Jeremiah also noted that during World War II, Abramson had been awarded the Legion of Merit, given to members of the Armed Forces for exceptionally outstanding service to the United States. According to the Medical Directory of New York State, "Dr. Abramson's practice is limited to Immunology and Allergy." It made no mention of training or credentials in Psychiatry.

That Dr. Abramson was not a practicing psychiatrist apparently was of some concern to the CIA's Office of Security. A subsequent report by agent Jeremiah to Sheffield Edwards, dated December 4, 1953, elaborated on this issue in great detail. The report also revealed that Abramson's relationship with the CIA was far broader than previously surmised, and raised additional mysteries of its own.

The two page document begins with reference to yet another case report, Number 74150; the Olson case was Number 73317. Case Number 74150 had also involved Dr. Abramson, who had been interviewed by an unidentified Security Office agent on May 22, 1953. According to agent Jeremiah, that earlier report had "indicated that [Abramson] was an allergist," but had "further indicated that [he] was engaged in psychiatric research testing the efficacy of a new drug under a grant by some foundation in Washington, D.C."

Agent Jeremiah's report then points out that according to the earlier report, "Dr. Margaret W. Ferguson, a psychiatrist, had been hired by Dr. Abramson for work on this research project and that in the process of the earlier Office of Security investigation Dr. Ferguson had stated "that Dr. Abramson is an allergist who is in charge of a series of psychiatric experiments." Agent Jeremiah's report does not reveal what triggered the earlier case involving Dr. Abramson, but a May 2000 interview with Dr. Ferguson by the author sheds some light on the subject.

Dr. Ferguson, in her mid-eighties and bed-ridden at the time of the interview, vividly recalled her work with Abramson, an experience she remembered as "not at all enjoyable or scientifically rewarding for me." Dr. Ferguson, who had come to the United States from Glasgow, Scotland in 1940 to attend medical school, said that she "encountered Dr. Gottlieb several times in Abramson's office, as well as Dr. Lashbrook." She explained that Lashbrook may have "visited Abramson more often" but she remembered Gottlieb more clearly because "he always went out of his way to be flattering." She elaborated, "He was quite a ladies man, quite handsome, but always most respectful. I knew he was with some sort of secret service but didn't know who he really worked for." Dr. Ferguson explained that she had been displeased with her work with Abramson because it did not comport with her desire to practice psychiatry in the conventional sense.

Dr. Ferguson: My job was to essentially oversee loose knit experiments that were conducted on university students and allergy patients at the time.
Albarelli: *Experiments?*
Ferguson: With hallucinogenics, mostly LSD.
Albarelli: *In what form was the LSD?*
Ferguson: Liquid. We spent a lot of time trying to determine the proper dosage.
Albarelli: *Do you recall the dose ranges considered?*
Ferguson: I think we began low ... at about fifty or sixty micrograms and then moved upwards to about one hundred and higher. I don't think we ever exceeded about one hundred and fifty. It may have been a bit less.
Albarelli: *Were there any problems?*
Ferguson: Many. A good many; too many to suit me. We ran experiments on students out of an old, unused space in Mount Sinai Hospital. We

did some experiments out on Long Island where [Abramson] had another office. Once there was a student who came back over the weekend from a Friday experiment. He was shaking, terribly frightened and vomiting. I wasn't sure what to do, so I called Dr. Abramson at home. He told me to tell the boy to come in on Monday. I couldn't do that. I took care of him myself."

Albarelli: *Did you ever meet Frank Olson?*

Ferguson: I'm not sure. I think I did. I think he came in more than once; more than just that week, but a lot of people came to see Dr. Abramson. Other doctors. I remember Dr. Max Fink... Dr. Hoch, and Dr. Hyde from Massachusetts. There were a lot of doctors from the military that came to see him... uniformed men sometimes. Dr. Fink did a lot with electric shock treatments. I found much of that distasteful in the extreme. I also did a fair amount of work with Dr. Murray Jarvik, you might be familiar with his name, and I did... I worked on LSD studies with [Dr.] Harris Isbell and [Dr.] Conan Kornetsky around that time. Kornetsky was delightful.

At the time that Dr. Olson died, in October 1953, I was transitioning out of Abramson's office into a new job. I was quite happy to get away. Dr. Pelican had replaced me. He was there then...at the time Olson died."

Albarelli: *Do you recall his first name?*

Ferguson: I think it was Edward, I'm not sure... it was a long time ago.

Albarelli: *Is his name spelled the same as the bird, or another way?*

Ferguson: I'm not sure. You really need to find Dr. Pelican. He could tell you a lot. He would know.

9

December 2, 1953
CIA Headquarters, Washington, D.C.

A massive mahogany desk anchors the center of the room; a matching credenza is cluttered with books, mementos, and framed photographs; an enormous world map is suspended on the wall above it. This is the office, the inner sanctum, if you will, of the Director of Central Intelligence (DCI), Allen Welsh Dulles. Behind the desk, the Director sits with pen in hand, hunched over a blank sheet of white paper. Clenched between his teeth is a briar pipe that has long since gone out. The DCI is busy drawing up a checklist of items that must be attended to by the Agency's Inspector General Lyman Kirkpatrick for his investigation into Frank Olson's death.

Kirkpatrick is due in Dulles's office within the hour to discuss with the DCI and his deputy director the Olson case. Earlier that day, Kirkpatrick called to report on his meeting with Deputy Director of Plans Frank Wisner, who oversaw TSS. According to the IG, neither Wisner nor Richard Helms had known anything about the plan to conduct an experiment at the Deep Creek Lake meeting back in November. Kirkpatrick also reported, however, that during a meeting last May with TSS, Helms had deemed LSD to be "dynamite" and said that he wanted to be advised at all times when the drug was intended for use, and that Wisner also had subsequently issued a directive to TSS that no LSD should be used experimentally without his permission.

Dulles begins by writing:

(1) Get reports from (a) Abramson (b) White/Chadwell (c) Lashbrook.

Dulles hesitates, then continues:

(2) Contact Col. Ruette [sic: Dulles meant to write Ruwet] *re compensation claim and through him keep in touch with wife (Gibbons).*

He sits back in his chair, thinks for a moment, then continues:

(3) Cabell will talk with Bullene (Gen).

Cabell is General Charles Pearre Cabell, the CIA's deputy director, a four-star Air Force general from Dallas, Texas who had been head of Air Force Intelligence. Dulles himself had selected the less-than-curious and imaginative Cabell for that position. Now, Dulles thinks Cabell would be the best choice to deal with Army Chemical Corps commander Major General Egbert F. Bullene, the man responsible for overseeing work at Camp Detrick.

The DCI considers his list for a moment, and adds:

(4) Impound all LSD in our possession and stop all tests under our direct control (4a) ascertain location

(5) Consider effects on outside experiment under our grants-in-aid when reports in under (1) above

(6) Gibbons to find out if any correspondence re use of LSD

(7) Keep track of all the unwitting participants through Ruwet

(8) Larry Houston, Sheff Edwards talk with Gottlieb and bring Abramson to Washington after report received

(9) Review Agency policy, draft new information

(10) Look over reports on use of LSD.

He considers the list once more and, now satisfied it's complete, sets the paper on a corner of his desk where Kirkpatrick can easily reach it.

Dulles leans back and reaches across his desk for a stick match to fire his pipe. As he draws deeply on the pipe, a cascade of thoughts concerning personal and Agency affairs, all of which seem to demand his immediate and undivided attention, distract him. Dulles thrives on the chaos of directing the nation's intelligence matters, but there are times when it can be difficult to fathom the order of things. Recently he had written down something his wife, Clover, had told him that psychologist, and next door neighbor, Dr. Carl Jung had said: "In all chaos there is a cosmos; in all disorder a secret order."

Dulles liked that. The common person knows next to nothing about the real order, the secret order, of the world. Dulles, like many in the CIA in its early years, was a product of wealth and privilege; he had attended the finest private schools, rubbed elbows and knocked heads with only his ilk, and understood well that social status virtually opened any door, and even created some doors where none existed. Pulling the world's strings, deciding what was best for the world's common stock, was better left to his class. Convention and tradition were their touchstones; they had little tolerance for things esoteric or for people that disrupted the status quo. If there was a secret order in the cosmos, he was surely part of it; indeed he was at its center, along with a select few others.

Clover, on the other hand, was different. She was quite taken with Jung's thoughts and beliefs, and Allen, while essentially considering her psychoanalytic pursuits mostly nonsense, was quite content to indulge them so long as it kept her occupied and away from his private affairs. Indeed, it was Dulles' affair with Jung enthusiast Mary Bancroft that led to Clover's attraction to things Jungian to begin with. And, the DCI thinks, Jung is good for Clover, about that there is no doubt. Dulles is not at all sure that Clover could have kept herself together as well as she did after their son, Allen Macy Dulles, had been seriously wounded in that god-forsaken place so far away, without Jung's consolation.

Sonny, as young Allen was affectionately called, had been "a brilliant, high-strung, solitary boy" with "an almost pretty face, with long curly brown hair and blue eyes, but he was slight and unathletic." Throughout his youth, he had been desperate for his father's attention, yet he spent much of his time with his mother, or, when Clover was often away, in the care of family servants. Sonny was close to his older sister, Toddy, a manic-depressive who experienced what the family discreetly called "episodes." In Sonny's early teens, Clover hired a man to tutor him in sports and to act essentially as a role model, but the effort was short-lived after the man seduced Toddy and briefly ran away with her to California.

After graduating from Princeton in only three years, Sonny attended Balliol College, Oxford, where he received a degree in history, but much to the dismay of his parents, he enlisted in the Marine Corps in 1950, when the Korean War began. Upon completion of his basic training, his uncle, John Foster Dulles, then managing partner of high-powered Wall Street law firm Sullivan and Cromwell, finagled a cushy stateside desk job for Sonny. But twenty-two year old Sonny would not have it, and he promptly volunteered for duty in Korea.

Shortly after the November 1952, election of Dwight Eisenhower as president, on November 14, second lieutenant Dulles, assigned to the First Marine Division, was shot in the leg and wrist while commanding a rifle platoon that came under heavy sniper fire. The next day, following treatment in a field hospital, Sonny was back on the line with his troops. This time he wasn't so lucky. He was struck in the head by fragments from an 81-mm mortar shell. Part of his brain was obliterated and a chunk of metal was lodged in what remained. His company's executive officer told his parents, "I was there when they brought him in. He kept trying to get off the stretcher and go back. Some of his men were crying. I've never really known anyone like him."

Allen Dulles was stunned by the news from Korea. Sonny lived, but would never be the same. Colonel Albert R. Haney, a 36-year old intelligence officer who ran guerrilla operations in Korea, arranged to have young Allen evacuated to a naval hospital in Japan. Clover had broken off her studies with Jung in Zurich to rush to Sonny's bedside. Sonny had made a remarkable physical recovery, but upon regaining consciousness he was unable to recognize his mother. He had brain surgery at the Yokosuka naval hospital and after that remained unconscious for several days. When he came to, his father was there at his bedside, but Sonny seemed confused at the sight of him. Doctors told the elder Dulles that there were still shell fragments lodged deeply in Sonny's brain and that it was doubtful he would ever completely recover.

Physically fit, Sonny was flown home on February 25, 1953 to a room at Bethesda Naval Hospital. At this point, he could recognize and converse with his parents, and, at times, was almost his old self, smiling, joking, curious about world events; but then Sonny's face would go blank suddenly, and for hours on end he would stare off into space. Other times, he was irrationally afraid, hands shaking, and he would break down in despair, crying or shouting at those around him. Occasionally he acted on his unknown fears, became uncontrollable, sometimes violent, and had to be restrained. The day following Sonny's flight from Japan into Washington's Andrews Air Force Base, Allen Dulles had been driven to Capitol Hill to be confirmed as director of the CIA.

Now, Dulles has been nearly nine months in the DCI's office. Meanwhile, Sonny is convalescing in his mother's care, but his mental condition is unimproved. His bouts of fear and erratic behavior are becoming more frequent and often Clover is overwhelmed in caring for him. At Dulles' suggestion a full time male nurse, meeting the necessary and rigid security requirements, has been brought in. The DCI has not yet even imagined it, but eventually Sonny, following a brief stay at Chestnut Lodge Hospital in Maryland, will have to be sent away for full-time care to an exclusive sanitarium in Germany on Lake Constance, within eyesight of the Swiss border. But for now, Dulles is convinced that through the marvels of modern science Sonny's mind can be healed; his mental faculties restored so he might better enjoy his remaining days.

Dr. Harold G. Wolff, a world-renowned neurologist and expert on migraine headaches and general pain, was treating Sonny. He was the central cause of Dulles' optimism and conviction; the DCI had the utmost confidence in Dr. Wolff's skills. Within weeks of Wolff's initiating care of young Allen, the elder Dulles and the physician became good friends. Indeed, the DCI was about to ask Dr. Wolff the following week if he, and one of his close colleagues at Cornell University, Dr. Lawrence Hinkle, would undertake a major study of brainwashing for the CIA. The Agency was willing to pay handsomely for the study. Dulles would be anxious for Wolff's acceptance, which came promptly.

Dr. Wolff, a painfully thin, intense man, who some accused of having an "overpowering personality"— his obituary in 1962 noted: "He had little time for causal amenities..."— was a Harvard educated physician. Upon graduation he had spent two years at the Phipps Clinic at Johns Hopkins University under the direction of Adolph Meyer, and a year in Russia with Ivan Pavlov. In 1932, after Cornell opened its new medical center at New York Hospital, Wolff joined the faculty as chief of the Neurology Division.

Thoughts of Sonny were not the only distractions preoccupying Dulles when the "Olson affair," as it had quickly come to be known, first landed on his desk. Additionally, pressing matters in Guatemala, Iran, and stateside were also weighing heavily on him. When Dulles first summoned Lyman Kirkpatrick to his office, the Inspector General had to wait nearly an hour for Dulles to complete an unscheduled meeting on Guatemala with Colonel Albert Haney.

Haney, who passed away in Florida in 1998, at age 83, had begun an illustrious military intelligence career in 1941, after attending Northwestern University and Boston College. During World War II, then Lieutenant Haney was stationed in Panama where he headed a fifteen-member team of Counter Intelligence Corps (CIC) special agents charged with counterespionage and sabotage to protect the Panama Canal. Here Haney, who insisted his men call him "The Chief," came into frequent contact with OSS and FBI agents who also operated throughout Central and South America. Once, in British Honduras, he wrongly arrested a notorious rumrunner suspected of covertly assisting Nazi submarine refueling operations, earning himself a sound tongue-lashing from then OSS officer George Hunter White.

In October 1953, Allen Dulles and Frank Wisner, the Agency's clandestine service chief and Dulles' former law partner, were actively casting about for an ideal man to command a paramilitary group to overthrow "Communist-leaning" Jacobo Arbenez in Guatemala on behalf of United Fruit, some of whose land Arbenz had appropriated. When Haney's name was suggested, based on his work organizing guerilla forces in Korea, Dulles also immediately recalled Haney's speedy assistance in securing Sonny's evacuation to a military hospital in Japan. The search ended, and Haney was summoned from his post as CIA station chief in Korea to come to Washington. Briefed in late-October by Dulles and Wisner, Haney promptly accepted responsibility for directing field operations for what was now less-than-modestly called Operation Success.

Besides organizing a coup in Guatemala, Dulles was also preoccupied with activities against nationalists in Iran. In late March 1953, a little over two months after Eisenhower's inauguration, Dulles had approved sending $1 million to the CIA station in Tehran for use "in any way that would bring about the fall of [Mohammad] Mossadegh," Iran's Prime Minister who had nationalized British oil concessions in Iran. Dulles' brother, John Foster, now Secretary of State under Eisenhower, considered Mossadegh a "madman" and became a "most enthusiastic cheerleader" for CIA's Operation Ajax, the plan to oust Mossadegh. By November 1953, with Mossadegh overthrown, the Dulles brothers were doing all they possibly could to fortify Iran's newly imposed leader, Shah Mohammad Reza Pahlavi. Indeed, Operation Ajax's speedy success accomplished much in cementing CIA covert action, including murder, as a favored means for rapid regime change.

Germany, especially its capital Berlin, was also a constant contender for Dulles's attention. Now divided into four occupational sectors commanded by the French, Soviets, British, and Americans, the city was a contentious cauldron of tensions, intrigue and danger. In response, the Agency had set up a wide network of safe houses to deal with informants, defectors, and double and triple agents, and by late 1952, was employing Artichoke techniques - the use of drugs for interrogation — on many of these people.

Earlier, in 1945 when Dulles had been with the OSS, he had selected the U.S. intelligence headquarters building in the Zehlendorf district of Berlin. Dulles had soon departed Berlin for work stateside, and Richard Helms had inherited the task of organizing clandestine affairs in Berlin. But Helms, too, would soon leave for Washington, and by 1952 intelligence operations — requiring coordination among the CIA, Army, Air Force, and Navy — were so chaotic in Berlin that then Agency assistant director of special operations, Lyman Kirkpatrick, was asked to analyze matters. Kirk found it all to be a bigger mess than imagined and thought effective coordination might be impossible. By 1953, American intelligence operatives were referring to Berlin as "Kidnap Central" and "Kidnap City." It was becoming commonplace for operatives to be snatched from their homes and off street corners, then tortured by East German and Soviet agents. Many such abductions were preludes to political assassinations that became commonplace.

There was also the matter of James Kronthal's recent death, which surely must have been on Dulles' mind after he was notified about Frank Olson. Like Olson, Kronthal was only forty-two years old when he died. Dulles used to call him 'Jimmy' and had considered Kronthal his protégé and a member of his family. Dulles often remarked to those close to him that Kronthal reminded him of Sonny because of his sensitive and retiring ways.

James Speyer Kronthal was born into wealth and privilege on August 21, 1912. He had attended the exclusive Lincoln School in New York with Nelson Rockefeller and then went on to complete his studies in economics, history, and art history at Yale, Harvard, and the University of Paris. Kronthal, who spoke French and German fluently, was small-framed and slight, weighing just 130 pounds and standing five feet, six inches tall. While in college in the United States, he had worked for the investment-banking firm, Speyer & Co., where his father, Leon Kronthal, was a partner. By the age of 29, James had become an assistant professor of art history at Harvard, but he left this position in June 1941 to join the U.S. Army. Ten months later, in April 1942, he became an intelligence officer in the OSS at the rank of captain where he became an experienced intelligence analyst and was soon promoted to chief, OSS Section D, where he supervised the "evaluation processing and intelligence direction of materials on the Near-Middle East and Southeastern Europe."

After being discharged from the Army, Kronthal was hired by the CIA (then called the Central Intelligence Group), on May 5, 1947. His first assignment was to succeed Allen Dulles as Chief of Station in Bern, Switzerland on the recommendation of Richard Helms, then director of the Agency's covert operations arm, the Office of Special Operations. Helms wrote that Kronthal "is a top flight intelligence officer who commands respect from his subordinates more through demonstrated knowledge and IQ than through personal warmth and affability. He is rather retiring as a person but this does not affect his leadership or firmness of purpose." When Kronthal's Bern tour ended he was temporarily assigned as a training instructor with wide travel privileges in the CIA Quasi Military Training Division in Washington, D.C. As a cover for his sensitive work he was given an office and cover employment with the State Department. Eight months before Frank Olson's death, shortly before noon on March 31, 1953, the personnel director at the State Department received a telephone call from CIA security chief Col. Sheffield Edwards. Edwards said that he was calling to inform the director that James Kronthal had been found dead at his Georgetown residence that same day around 10:30 A.M. Edwards explained that "an empty vial had been found by the body and the presumption was that [Kronthal] had taken poison." The CIA was working closely with the D.C. Metropolitan Police, advised Edwards, and as soon as "the autopsy was performed and the body released someone from the CIA would be in touch again." Almost as an afterthought, Edwards wrote that a "personal note left for an acquaintance" had been found near the body, but that no mention was made of this to Kronthal's family when they were notified of his death "since it presumably has no bearing on his family relationship."

The next day, April 1, Matthew Baird — CIA Director of Training and Kronthal's superior — filed a personnel form on Kronthal with the agency's main records office; it reads, "termination by death." According to the form, Kronthal had only two days earlier been promoted to CIA deputy director of training, a promotion he had eagerly sought.

Also on April 1, the *Washington Post* reported on its front page that Kronthal, an "important administrative officer in the hush-hush Central Intelligence Agency," had been found dead in his white-brick home in the exclusive Georgetown neighborhood where he lived alone. According to the article, two officials from the CIA's Office of Security, Gould Cassal and McGregor Gray, had discovered Kronthal's fully clothed body on a day bed in his second floor bedroom. The two men had reportedly been dispatched to Kronthal's home after he had failed to report to his cover-office at the State Department and a telephone call to his home had gone unanswered. D.C. police investigators told the newspaper that Kronthal's maid, Mrs. Lavinia Thomas, had arrived at his home as usual at 8:30 A.M., and found a brief note from Kronthal asking her not to disturb him because he wanted to sleep late.

Homicide detective Lawrence Harnett, who maintained a close and cooperative relationship with the CIA, told the *Washington Post* that police had found a handwritten letter "to a male friend," indicating Kronthal was "mentally upset because of pressure connected with work." Also found, said Hartnett, was "an empty vial" on the bedroom floor. The newspaper noted that an autopsy performed that day indicated Kronthal had died between 10 P.M. and midnight on Tuesday, March 31.

Kronthal's actual cause of death was not revealed in the article, or later, and Washington, D.C. coroner, Dr. A. Magruder MacDonald, never released his findings from the chemical analysis done on Kronthal's body, nor on the substances in the vial found near it. Dr. MacDonald listed the cause of death only as "apparent suicide." Kronthal's body was promptly shipped to New York, home of his parents. Frank E. Campbell Undertakers, the same firm that would process Frank Olson's remains months later, handled the body in New York.

Never revealed until decades later was that on the evening Kronthal died, he had had dinner with Allen Dulles at Dulles' Georgetown home. The two men

133

dined alone while, unbeknownst to Kronthal, two of Sheffield Edwards' security officers listened in on their conversation from an adjoining room. In 1989, a book published by three respected intelligence community observers laid out the grim details of that dinner and Kronthal's subsequent death. The book revealed that Kronthal was a homosexual and pedophile who had been seriously compromised and blackmailed by the Nazis during World War II, and then later by the Russians. Kronthal had become a double agent in the late-1930s, after the Gestapo discovered and exploited his sexual proclivity for young boys. Later, the Soviets uncovered the Nazi's files on Kronthal and, in 1947, after he had taken his new post in Bern, they orchestrated a situation where he was secretly filmed with young Chinese boys in highly compromising positions.

A subsequent book, published in 2001 by Joseph J. Trento, reveals more about Kronthal's pathetic story. Trento, a former investigative reporter who worked for Jack Anderson, wrote that it was CIA security chief Sheffield Edwards who had first alerted Dulles to problems with Kronthal. Trento recounted a meeting that took place between Dulles, Edwards, and General Lucien Truscott, President Eisenhower's intelligence advisor. At the meeting, Edwards bluntly told Dulles, "Sir, six of the men you have brought over from OSS into the CIA are serious security risks." Truscott added that all six were homosexuals and therefore Eisenhower was extremely concerned that Sen. Joseph McCarthy, then in the middle of a serious attack on the CIA and Army, would discover information about the six. Dulles asked for the names and was stunned to see Kronthal's among them. When Edwards handed Dulles the Security Office's assembled file on Kronthal, Dulles had been shocked and deeply hurt. He had never suspected that the brilliant young man whom he had regarded as his protégé could be a traitor.

Following the meeting with Edwards and Truscott, Dulles invited Kronthal to dinner at his home, during which, according to retired CIA official Robert Crowley, Kronthal saw a side of Dulles he never knew existed. Allen then gave a sad speech about how personal compulsions destroy careers, wrote Trento. Meanwhile Edwards' security officers listened in from an adjoining room. It would actually be another two years before Dulles knew the full extent of Kronthal's treachery and the damage done. Around midnight, Kronthal said good-bye to Dulles and walked home, followed by the two security officers. Said Crowley to Trento:

> Allen probably had a special potion prepared that he gave Kronthal should the pressure become too much. Dr. Sidney Gottlieb and the medical people produced all kinds of poisons that a normal postmortem could not detect.

Dulles is pulled away from his thoughts by a call from his secretary that Kirkpatrick is waiting to see him. He tells her to send Kirkpatrick in. Moments later his door swings open and the IG wheel's himself into the room. Dulles stands by way of greeting and motions his Inspector General closer to the desk.

After a few minutes of small talk, Cabell joins the meeting and Dulles tells the two men that he has drawn up a list of tasks he thinks are important in the Olson case. Kirkpatrick spends a little less than an hour with Dulles and Cabell, but apart from an eight-word notation in his desk calendar —"Meeting with DCI and DDCI on Olson case"— there is no other record of the meeting, nor any known reports about what was discussed.

Following Kirkpatrick's departure, Dulles' thoughts wander to this drug, this stuff called LSD, this amazing substance that Helms would soon classify as "dynamite." The memorandum requesting his formal approval for conducting experiments with LSD had been put before him earlier in April 1953, and in untypical fashion he had hesitated for ten days before signing off on the program. The requesting document reads:

> We intend to investigate the development of a chemical material which causes a reversible non-toxic aberrant mental state the specific nature of which can be reasonably well predicted for each individual. This material could potentially aid in discrediting individuals, eliciting information, and implementing suggestions and other forms of mental control.

In addition to the material, LSD, the request also stated that MKULTRA would concern itself "with research and development of biological and radiological materials capable of employment in clandestine operations to control human behavior."

Who knew what this drug could really do, Dulles thought, in considering his approval. Who really understood LSD's full effects? Dulles knew that, at the time he had given his formal approval, extensive experimentation with LSD and other hallucinogens had already been underway with CIA support for nearly two years under the auspices of Projects Bluebird, Artichoke, and MKNAOMI at Camp Detrick.

Now months later, Dulles also knew that the drug had already been used in a number of situations overseas. In Manila, one of the first field stations to request use of LSD, agency operatives had expertly slipped a dose of about 90 micrograms into a glass of water consumed by Philippines president, Elpidio Quirino, shortly before he was to make a public address. It will make him appear unstable, perhaps even out of his mind, the DCI had been told. Not the qualities the general populace looks for in its leader. Dulles may have also been aware that narcotics agent George White was widely whispered to have slipped the drug to columnist Drew Pearson while the two were in a Havana nightclub in early 1953, and, at about the same time, to a political opponent of New York City Council president Rudolph Halley.

Agency Director of Operations Richard Helms and Director of Plans Frank Wisner had briefed Dulles over a period of several days on the need for Project

MKULTRA and the "covert chemical, biological, and radiological materials for use in clandestine operations." Said Helms years later:

> All of this [LSD activity and drug experiments] started back in the very early Fifties, when, you will recall, we were just coming out of the Korean War and there was deep concern over the issue of brainwashing. As a matter of fact, a man named [Edward] Hunter had written a book entitled *Brainwashing in Red China*, and "brainwashing" was a literal translation of the Chinese words, and we wondered what it was all about. Did they use sodium pentothal or drugs of one kind or another? We had learned that something called LSD had been discovered in Switzerland by a scientist named Hoffman. It was tasteless, odorless, and colorless and taken in small quantities, created a kind of schizophrenia.... We felt that it was our responsibility not to lag behind the Russians or the Chinese in this field, and the only way to find out what the risks were was to test things such as LSD and other drugs that could be used to control human behavior.

On April 13, 1953, the same day that he gave his approval to Project MKULTRA, Dulles sent a memorandum to the Agency's Deputy Director for Administration.

As "contemplated by TSS and discussed with me," Dulles wrote:

> [MKULTRA] consists of ultra-sensitive work. . . . The nature of the research and the security considerations involved preclude handling the projects by means of the usual contractual agreements.

Additionally, directed Dulles, Agency administrators were to pay all MKULTRA costs and invoices without the required normal financial documentation and with only the signed authorization of Dr. Sidney Gottlieb and Dr. Willis Gibbons. TSS would retain all financial documents in its own files, stated Dulles, and would "endeavor wherever possible to obtain documentary support of invoices, such as cancelled checks, receipted bills, etc., and these will remain in TSS files."

Apparently, Helms and Wisner had made a strong impression on Dulles through their briefings. On April 10, just three days before he approved MKULTRA, Dulles made a major policy speech in Hot Springs, Virginia to the national Alumni Conference of Princeton University, Sonny's alma mater. Dulles focused exclusively on what he termed "Brain Warfare," or the "battle for men's minds" provoked by "the international tensions" called the Cold War. Said Dulles, no doubt with Sonny in mind:

> The human mind is the most delicate of all instruments. It is so finely adjusted, so susceptible to the impact of outside influences, that it is proving a malleable tool in the hands of sinister men. The Soviets are now using brain perversion techniques as one of their main weapons in prosecuting

the cold war. Some of these techniques are so subtle and so abhorrent to our way of life that we have recoiled from facing up to them.

Dulles went on and poetically recited a long litany of evil Soviet practices, including the domination of huge land masses and populations, using "powerful jamming equipment" to "eliminate the reception of foreign radio messages," a "Government approved" media, persecution of and mass purges of racial minority groups, religious intolerance, and a concentrated program of "brain-conditioning" directed at turning human beings "into humble confessors of crimes they never committed or [to] make them the mouthpiece for Soviet propaganda." Dulles seemed most concerned with "brain-conditioning" and Soviet efforts to develop "new techniques" that employed Russian "science and ingenuity" in the "study of mental reactions and in the nefarious art of breaking down the human mind."

Most alarming, Dulles declared, was that the Communists were now applying brainwashing techniques "to American prisoners in Korea." It "was not beyond the range of possibility," he warned, "that considerable numbers of our own boys there might be so indoctrinated as to be induced, temporarily at least, to renounce country and family." The United States would do all possible to combat Communist oppression, Dulles said, but it was "handicapped" in doing so because there were "few survivors" of Soviet brainwashing, "and we have no human guinea pigs ourselves on which to try out these extraordinary techniques."

One can only imagine how uncomfortable it might have been for Dulles to be questioned about having "no guinea pigs" in light of the fact that CIA programs he had approved months earlier were aggressively experimenting on human beings with an array of mind control and behavior modification techniques far surpassing anything the Soviets were accused of.

10

December 4, 1953
CIA Headquarters, Washington, D.C.

As expected, Dr. Harold Abramson arrived at Lyman Kirkpatrick's office at a little past noon on December 4th. Sidney Gottlieb had come by the day before to advise Kirkpatrick of Abramson's impending visit. Gottlieb asked Kirkpatrick if he wanted him personally to escort Abramson to the IG's office. Kirkpatrick said not to bother, and told Gottlieb he would make arrangements through CIA General Counsel Houston to meet Abramson.

After Gottlieb left, Kirkpatrick once again reviewed a Security Office report on Dr. Abramson. The two page, single-spaced document revealed that some months earlier, on May 22, 1953, Abramson had been interviewed by the CIA in relation to his conduct of "psychiatric research testing [of] the efficacy of a new drug." The document also indicated "that Dr. Margaret W. Ferguson, a psychiatrist, had been hired by Dr. Abramson for work on this research project." (As we shall see, the CIA, under its MKULTRA program, funded this project.)

The report went on to state, "Dr. Abramson limits his practice to allergy and immunology," and noted he was a member of the American Psychosomatic Society and a member of the editorial board of Psychosomatic Medicine. The reporting security investigator stated that on the day before he issued his findings, he had contacted an official of the New York State Division of Professional Law Enforcement who "advised that any licensed physician may practice psychiatry without additional licensing." The official stated, however, "it is usual for physicians who practice psychiatry to have some extra formal training in the field and to be certified by some organization such as the American Psychiatric Association or the American Board of Medical Specialists."

Lastly, the agent referenced Abramson's practice of medicine since 1925 and the fact that the doctor had received his M.D. in 1923 from Columbia University. He also noted that Abramson had studied physical and electro-chemistry in Germany at the Kaiser Wilhelm Institute, had been an instructor in medicine at Johns Hopkins University in 1928-29, and had taught biochemistry at Harvard in 1929 through 1931. Abramson was currently an assistant professor of physiology at Columbia University, as well as Associate Physician and Chief of Allergy

Clinic at Mt. Sinai Hospital in New York City, which the investigating agent noted was one of the nation's "best hospitals."

Before arriving at Kirkpatrick's office, Abramson had spent a little over two hours with Houston, providing a verbal report of his "observations on Frank Olson." Houston had telephoned Abramson a few days earlier, in New York, to say he needed a detailed written report in order for Olson's wife to file a claim for death benefits with the Federal Bureau of Employees' Compensation.

A secretary had hand delivered a transcribed copy of Abramson's report, dated December 4, 1953 to Kirkpatrick minutes before the doctor himself walked through his door. Kirkpatrick had only had time to scan the four-page document, but judging from his notated file copy, a number of sections appear to have caught his eye, perhaps arousing his suspicions about what had really happened in Room 1018A at the Statler Hotel.

Kirkpatrick underscored several lines on the first page of Abramson's report. In reference to his initial consultation with Frank Olson on Tuesday, November 24, Abramson had written:

> I attempted to confirm what I had heard, that an experiment had been performed <u>especially to trap him</u> the preceding week, but he emphasized that his present problem did not lie in that area and that his problem was his own ability to live up to his own concept of what his performance of his duties should be and his inability to attain the perfections necessitated by the needs of his work.

Kirkpatrick underscored the words *"especially to trap him."* Trap him? What did Abramson mean by this? Two paragraphs later, Abramson had written:

> The next day Mr. Olson spent an hour with me, in which he again appeared agitated. There was repeated discussion of his concern with the quality of his work, his guilt on being retired from the Army for an ulcer, and <u>his release of classified information.</u>

Kirkpatrick underlined the last five words of the last sentence. *"...his release of classified information."* What did this mean? What information was released? And to whom was it released? And how was it released?

Unfortunately, there are no known written records indicating that Kirkpatrick asked Abramson about this, or that he learned anything from Abramson about any of these curious references. Apparently his one meeting with Abramson did not generate any subsequent written report by Kirkpatrick.

Curiously, about ten weeks later, Abramson sent a second written report on Frank Olson, this one to Sidney Gottlieb. This one-page report was addressed to one of Gottlieb's pseudonyms, Sherman C. Grifford, and mailed to a TSS front operation in Washington, D.C., Chemrophyl Associates. The report, for reasons unknown, refers to Olson as "John Q. Smith."

This time around, Abramson wrote: "I was called in consultation to see John Q. Smith about ten days after Mr. Smith had received 70 micrograms, by mouth, in a highly protected situation." (Abramson does not identify specifically what the 70 micrograms consisted of.) His report continues:

It appeared that Mr. Smith had profound guilt feelings because he had been retired as an officer during the last war and was drawing a pension. His intense feelings of guilt resulted from receiving government money to which he felt that he was not entitled. These feelings were not eliminated by his realistic understanding that he had appeared before a retirement board. A strong feeling of inadequacy dominated his present work.... In several hours of interviewing, for a period of two days, his agitation could not be directly linked with a psychotic state, until he said that his sleeplessness had been caused by the FBI, who had surreptitiously been placing amphetamine or caffeine in his food at night to keep him awake.

These feelings of having drugs being placed in his food had been present for at least five months before he had received his therapeutic dose of 70 micrograms. He also disclosed that he had shown bizarre behavior for nine months before so that his wife thought he needed medical attention. This led to an outpouring of an intense desire on his part to be punished by the authorities for his past conduct of taking money fraudulently from the government following his retirement by an Army board.

Concluded Abramson's report:

Information subsequently received revealed that he had discussed suicide frequently during the previous year and, to the best of my information, had been talked out of suicide twice. In my opinion, Mr. Smith had been suffering from some type of depressive psychosis which, although reluctantly recognized by his family and friends, had not received adequate medical care.

It is my opinion, also, in view of my experience with various ambulatory types of subjects, that this dosage could hardly have had any significant role in the course of events which followed.

Here it should be noted that Abramson's "John Q. Smith" report contradicts his earlier statement made the day after Olson's death, November 29, 1953. In that statement Abramson recounted that Olson said "that for some weeks the CIA group had been putting something like Benzedrine in his coffee." Additionally, as readers will see, weeks later, in May 1954 Dr. Abramson again stated that Olson's death was not related to any drug, including LSD, that he was given and that there were extenuating circumstances to his death. He did not elaborate on what those circumstances were.

11

December 18, 1953
CIA Headquarters, Washington, D.C.

Lyman Kirkpatrick hand delivered his final report on Frank Olson's death to Allen Dulles on December 18, just two-and-one-half weeks after being assigned to review the case. Attached to his concise two-page cover memo were nearly twenty-five pages of case-related documents. Kirkpatrick's memo to Dulles began with a most intriguing paragraph:

> A review of these [attached] files plus our conversations with Dr. Abramson, the psychiatrist involved in the case, and Dr. H. Marshall Chadwell, [Assistant Director, CIA Office of Scientific Intelligence], who received a full description of the case from Stanley Lovell, indicates certain matters that should be attended to before the case is closed. It further should be noted that on 17 December, some 23 days after the event, Dr. Gibbons and Col. Drum came to [me] to report that Dr. Gibbons had just learned that Col. Drum knew of the experiment in advance and had given his approval to Dr. Gottlieb to conduct it on an unwitting basis.

As provocative as this paragraph is, the remainder of Kirkpatrick's memo, and its attachments, provide no explanation regarding "*the full description of the case*" that Chadwell obtained from Lovell, nor is there any elaboration anywhere in the report on the "*certain matters that should be attended to before the case is closed.*" Chadwell, as earlier mentioned in this book, oversaw the CIA's Office of Scientific Intelligence. During World War II, he had been director of Division 19, a highly secret unit of the U.S. National Defense Research Committee (NDRC) that devised covert weapons and sabotage devises. In this position Chadwell would often come into contact with Lovell, who was research and development director of the OSS's dirty tricks department. Indeed, when Lovell was first recruited into the war effort, he had to pass muster with top ranking NRDC officials Dr. Vannevar Bush and Chadwell. Following the end of the war and before joining the CIA's staff, Chadwell had worked for the Rockefeller Foundation in New York and the U.S. Atomic Energy Commission (AEC). He also worked closely with Dr. Caryl P. Haskins, a pioneer in radiation genetics and biophysics, while with the AEC and CIA.

As readers may begin to appreciate, Dr. Chadwell's role in the CIA's drug research and its related operational programs, while wholly escaping any scrutiny in reportage on these subjects, exceeded the involvement of most Agency officials from other branches.

The paragraph concerning Dr. Chadwell and Lovell becomes all the more puzzling when one considers an equally provocative note that is contained in the attachments to the report. The note, drafted by Dr. Chadwell himself and dated December 14, 1953, contains highlights of a conversation between Dr. Chadwell and Dr. Gibbons on that same day. The typed note reads:

> Lovell has not heard anything from Gibbons.
> Lovell reported that Quarles and George Merck were about to kill the Schwab activity at Detrick as "un-American." Is it necessary to take action at a high place.
> Lovell knew of Frank R. Olson. No inhibitions. Baring of inner man. Suicidal tendencies. Offensive usefulness? [Chadwell]told [Sheffield] Edwards Saturday AM, the 12th.

The note was carbon copied to a single name: "*McMahon*." This was John N. McMahon, who readers have already met in his capacity as a trusted CIA aide to General Truscott in Germany. McMahon went to work for the CIA in 1951 after graduating from Holy Cross College in Massachusetts. Following a six-month indoctrination period, he spent the next eight years overseas. The CIA refused to tell the author where McMahon had been stationed, but former agency officials confirmed it was Europe, specifically Germany, as we have seen, and possibly later France, where McMahon was involved in "technical and scientific matters." He returned to the United States in 1959 to work on the U-2 spy plane program and in 1965 was named director of the Office of Special Projects. He went on to become chief of TSS in 1974 and then eventually Deputy Director of Operations and Deputy Director of Central Intelligence.

Kirkpatrick's report does not explain why McMahon was copied on Chadwell's note, nor does it contain any other reference to McMahon. However, it appears highly likely that it was because of Olson's participation in the investigation of the "Berlin Poison Case."

Kirkpatrick's report raised a number of issues in its conclusions. On the use and effects of LSD on Olson, he stated that even though Olson was given only "one-seventh the amount of the drug" that had been proven, through "extensive Agency and private practice" tests, to produce no lasting "ill effects," it was "apparent that there is a strong possibility that the drug was a trigger mechanism precipitating Olsen's [sic] suicide."

Kirkpatrick wrote that although Dr. Sidney Gottlieb knew "all of the individuals who received the drug," nonetheless, "he obviously was not aware of their medical records." Kirkpatrick based his conclusion not on any interview with Gottlieb, but apparently on the sole fact that Dr. Gibbons had informed Kirkpatrick that "only one individual was excluded from the experiment, because of a heart condition." Pointed out Kirkpatrick, "Gottlieb was not aware that over a period of five years Olsen [sic] had apparently had a suicidal tendency." Again, judging from the record, Kirkpatrick based this statement solely on information provided by Dr. Gibbons, despite the fact that none of the people closest to Olson who were interviewed had said anything about Olson having suicidal tendencies.

Lastly, Kirkpatrick concluded: "Although there is an Artichoke Committee on which TSS, OSI and Security sit, this committee was never advised or consulted about this experiment." Kirkpatrick knew full well that "using employees of another agency could seriously jeopardize our relationship with that and all other agencies should this become known." In light of the November 19, 1953 Artichoke Committee meeting that took place concurrently with the Deep Creek Lake gathering, it was unlikely the Committee had not known about it.

Kirkpatrick's recommendations to Dulles were surprisingly few, brief and tame. They were:

(a) There should be immediately established a high-level intra-Agency board which should review all TSS experiments and give approval in advance to any in which human beings are involved, and to all others involving matters of policy or large amounts of money.
(b) The Deputy Chief TSS [Col. James Drum] should be reprimanded for his poor judgment shown in this instance and consideration should be given as to whether this individual should continue in his present position.
(c) Chief TSS [Dr. Willis Gibbons] should be admonished to exercise tighter supervision and control over the use of this drug and should render periodic reports to [Richard Helms] over its use and the result.

TSS Research Chairman Luis deFlorez was upset and angry about Kirkpatrick's recommendations. Both he and Gibbons had strongly protested against any reprimands being issued against anyone. Gibbons, according to Kirkpatrick's diary, had come to his office on December 1 "to make a strong plea that no disciplinary action be taken on the Olson case." Two days later, Kirkpatrick's diary notes, "DeFlorez came in to say that he thought any reprimands in the Olson case would be unfortunate." Kirkpatrick told deFlorez he would take his request under consideration, but when deFlorez learned the Inspector General had not withdrawn his recommendations to the DCI, he sat down and wrote his own memorandum to Dulles, which he himself hand delivered through assistant DCI Charles Cabell. Stated deFlorez:

I feel that a formal reprimand in this case would be an injustice, since reprimands are applicable to those guilty of negligence, disloyalty, or willful

acts detrimental to an organization, rather than to those involved in difficult circumstances caused by mischance or factors beyond our control. In
this case, I believe that both men concerned acted in good faith and with
the desire to advance their work. Whether they lacked the foresight or wisdom to grasp all the possibilities that might occur is, of course, debatable.

DeFlorez then drew on his navy experience and, as an alternative to reprimand-
ing Gottlieb and Drum, recommended, "If such action were taken in the tradition
of the sea, where the commander is automatically at fault in case of failure, then
it would be in order to apply the reprimand to both Dr. Gibbons and myself."

The same day deFlorez delivered his letter to Dulles through Cabell, it was
returned to deFlorez bearing a handwritten note from Cabell succinctly reading: "Your request acceded to." That same day, February 10, Cabell handed
his secretary three typed letters bearing the signature of Allen W. Dulles with
accompanying handwritten instructions to "Hand carry to Gibbons, Drum,
Gottlieb. Have them note having read and return to Kirkpatrick for Eyes Only
file. These are not reprimands and no personnel file notations being made."

The letter to Dr. Gibbons contained two short paragraphs. In the first,
Dulles advised Gibbons, "I consider the unwitting application of LSD in an
experiment with which you are familiar to be an indication of bad judgment on
the part of [Drum] and [Gottlieb]."

Dulles then informed Gibbons that he had instructed CIA Deputy Director
of Plans, Frank Wisner, "to constitute a review board composed of the appropriate officials from within the Agency periodically to review TSS research and
experiments."

Dulles' letter to Col. Drum also cited "poor judgment" in another respect;
Drum's staff had apparently agreed that when they intended to use "a drug on
a group of subjects not entirely witting that such an experiment was to be made
on themselves." Dulles then advised Drum "that in the position of responsibility which you hold you are expected to exercise greater judgment than was
indicated in this case."

The letter to Gottlieb consisted of a single paragraph in which Dulles faulted
the Chemical Division chief for not "apparently" giving "sufficient emphasis
to the necessity for medical collaboration and for proper consideration to the
rights of the individuals to whom it was being administered." Wrote Dulles,
"This is to inform you that it is my opinion that you exercised poor judgment
in this case."

Chemical Division assistant chief Robert Lashbrook received no letter from
Dulles, nor did Kirkpatrick recommend he be issued one, despite that, as we
shall learn, it was Lashbrook who administered the LSD to Olson.

Remarkably, none of the letters make any reference to Olson by name.

Decades later, both Gottlieb and Lashbrook would remark separately that
they could not recall ever seeing any of the three letters. Over twenty years later,

144

in 1975, it would be revealed, when copies were released, that the letters had been painstakingly drafted and re-drafted at least six times before Dulles signed his name to them.

On December 9, 1953, about a week before Kirkpatrick issued his report and recommendations, CIA General Counsel Lawrence Houston drafted a memorandum for the record on the Olson case. His memo was one paragraph long. He had "compiled and reviewed all the information available to the Agency relating to the death of Dr. Frank Olson," he wrote, concluding, as follows:

> It is my conclusion that the death of Dr. Olson is the result of circumstances arising out of an experiment undertaken in the course of his official duties for the U.S. Government and that there is, therefore, a direct causal connection between that experiment and his death. I have been authorized by the Deputy Director of Central Intelligence to state that this is the official position of the Central Intelligence Agency.

On January 4, 1954, Houston rendered his findings to IG Kirkpatrick in the form of a two-page memorandum. Houston led off by alerting Kirkpatrick, "[T]his case is closed so far as [my office] is concerned," with the possible exception that the Agency may be called on to help with Olson's "lapsed life insurance policy" with the Veterans Administration, adding, "but I trust any such help will be in the form of advice rather than action." As to the case itself, Houston said his comments "are fairly simple" and that there was "no dispute as to the facts." He explained:

> All agree on how the experiment was carried out and on the succeeding events as they relate to Dr. Olson. The implications are in dispute. It is, of course, perfectly possible that the suicide grew out of a pre-existing state which was not affected by the experiment. However, we have taken the position officially that the experiment at least "triggered" the suicide, and, as all the facts tend to support this conclusion, we should accept it as final. In any case this has been the position from the start of Dr. Gottlieb and Dr. Lashbrook, yet these two, supported by Gibbons, are insistent that it is practically impossible for this drug to have any harmful after effects. These two positions are, to me, completely inconsistent.
> If the drug 'triggered' the suicide, ergo the trigger itself is inherently dangerous under certain circumstances. Therefore, I am not happy with what seems to me a very casual attitude on the part of TSS representatives to the way this experiment was conducted and to their remarks that this is just one of the risks running with scientific experimentation. I do not eliminate the need for taking risks, but I do believe, especially when human health or life is at stake, that at least the prudent reasonable measures which can be taken to minimize the risk must be taken and failure to do so is culpable negligence. The actions of the various individuals concerned

when the effects of the experiment on Dr. Olson became manifest also revealed the failure to observe normal and reasonable precautions. The offices of the Agency charged with the responsibility for matters of this sort, particularly the Security office and the Medical Staff, were not informed, although we were informed that the TSS representatives were clearly concerned over the security aspects and actually referred Dr. Olson to Dr. Abramson for medical treatment.

As a result, a death occurred which might have been prevented, and the Agency as a whole, and particularly the Director, were caught completely by surprise in a most embarrassing manner.

It seems we can conclude from Houston's well reasoned final remarks on the case that more extensive conversations and interviews took place concerning the actual nature of the "experiment" than Kirkpatrick's written reports indicate. Yet we know little, if anything, about what those conversations and interviews might have found. Additionally, it seems that there was some concern, unexplained, about Olson's lapsed insurance policy, yet we don't know why. Was there more significance to this policy having lapsed than would normally be the case? Why did Olson allow this policy to lapse? Why was there correspondence to this effect taken to New York or found in New York? Why was there such concern to retrieve a letter about the policy?

Decades later, in 1978, Kirkpatrick would insist that, given the circumstances, he considered his Olson report to be quite strong in its recommendations. "The DDP [Deputy Directorate of Plans] hierarchy opposed it," he said. "And I didn't have the authority to follow-up...at the time I was still trying to determine what the tolerable limits were of what I could do and still keep my job." Former colleagues, who knew him well, say Kirkpatrick regretted "not being more inquisitive and forceful" on the Olson case. "He knew they were pulling the wool over his eyes," but "[he] didn't have the juice to burrow deeper into the facts and get the full story. He had to bide his time and then get them back in spades with the Bay of Pigs report." Kirkpatrick himself said of that report, which we shall learn more about, "[Dulles and Cabell] were both exceedingly shocked and upset, irritated and annoyed and mad and everything else about it."

12

December 28, 1953
CIA Headquarters, Washington, D.C.

One month after Frank Olson plunged to his death, CIA security director Col. Sheffield Edwards instructed Robert Cunningham, the Agency's Cover Branch chief, to set up employment backstopping for Robert Lashbrook. Backstopping is the process by which the CIA creates a viable, fully documented employment alias for an employee. Col. Edwards explained that Camp Detrick officials had alerted his office that Alice Olson was about to file an insurance claim for double indemnity; the company holding the policy would very likely launch a complete investigation into Frank Olson's death.

"We can't have Lashbrook's Agency connection known to anyone," said Edwards. Damage control. Lashbrook had provided a fair amount of information about himself and also about Olson to two detectives at New York City's 14th Police Precinct. The detectives, Edwards explained, had not only examined Lashbrook's AGO (Adjutant General's Office) card, CIA identification, and Camp Detrick pass, but had also eyeballed highly sensitive materials related to CIA consultants John Mulholland and George Hunter White, as well as a CIA safe house in Greenwich Village. Information concerning other CIA connected individuals involved in Eyes Only projects was also seen by the New York police.

Security agent James McCord had assured Edwards that the detectives, James Ward and David Mullee, as well as Detective John Scaffardi, who had also worked the Olson case, would cooperate with the CIA in any way needed. Edwards had initially been very concerned about the crime scene report filed by patrolman Joseph Guastefeste, the uniformed police officer in charge. Guastefeste had formally requested that "the case remain active" for further investigation "in view of the facts set forth." Put a lid on this, Edwards had instructed McCord, trusting that his special agent's years of experience and contacts in Manhattan would work the desired magic.

Which they did. Ward and Mullee closed the case. Olson's death was ruled a suicide, and the supplemental police report identified Lashbrook only as "a consultant chemist" with the War Department's Defense Bureau. Detective Ward had even been so helpful as to tell McCord that a few reporters had been sniffing around the precinct house trying to get more details about Olson's death, but that McCord could count on him and Mullee to handle things properly. However, the detectives had played it safe and forwarded details of the case to the FBI's New York field office, speaking directly with special agent George Dalen. But, of course, McCord, a former FBI agent, knew Dalen, and Edwards was confident that McCord would manage Dalen.

Edwards was now able to turn his attention to creating the right cover for Lashbrook. Cover chief Cunningham, meanwhile, had already begun the process. Cunningham had spoken with Lashbrook just two days after Olson's death and had asked Lashbrook what backstopping he thought would best fit the story he had told the New York detectives. At the time, Lashbrook asked that he be backstopped to the Department of the Army, G-4, Research and Development section, the Army's logistical and facilities support division.

"Put me under section chiefs Col. Bjarne Furuholmen and Lt. Col. Jackson Lawrence," Lashbrook had requested, adding that he had already talked the matter over with his superior, Sidney Gottlieb. "Don't backstop me to Camp Detrick," Lashbrook had urged. "That may only draw attention to our work there."

Initially, this sounded fine to Cunningham. But then another security agent in Edwards' office raised the concern that backstopping Lashbrook to G-4 would only arouse more curiosity about the Olson story, especially from other G-4 employees, who knew nothing about the Olson incident, but who would surely become curious if they heard more about the case.

While Edwards did not consider this a serious concern, he told Cunningham, "Let's make things simple and easy. Assign Lashbrook's employment backstopping to the Chemical Corps' Commanding General."

His rationale was that the Chemical Corps' Commanding General, Major General B.J. Bullene, was "already fully compliant of the facts of the Olson case." In addition, so too was Col. Vincent Ruwet who was a Chemical Corps commanding officer at Camp Detrick, as was Major Max Etkin, Camp Detrick's security chief.

"All three of these men are fully compliant of the facts," reasoned Edwards, "and they're all cleared by this office for top-secret liaison with the Agency. If anyone comes around asking questions they'll know how to handle it and won't have to second guess anything."

Cunningham agreed with Edwards' logic, but pointed out that TSS chiefs Willis Gibbons and Sidney Gottlieb both seemed strongly in favor of Lashbrook's own preference for the Army's G-4 division. Cunningham explained that he thought Gibbons and Gottlieb were more comfortable with G-4 because of any possible resentment and blowback that might surface from Olson's Chemical Corps colleagues. ("Blowback" is a CIA term and metaphor for the unintended consequences of CIA actions kept secret from the public at large.)

"Well, run the Chemical Corps option by them and see if it flies, otherwise go ahead with G-4," Edwards advised. "The last thing I want is a chain of less than committed participants in this thing." As Cunningham was leaving, Edwards added, "Regardless of where his backstopping occurs, I want to be notified immediately about anyone contacted as a result of any insurance investigation or any other inquiry."

A little over three weeks later, Cunningham reported in writing to Edwards about the construction of Lashbrook's cover employment. First, Cunningham had met with Gottlieb regarding TSS's "position on utilizing Camp Detrick [Chemical Corps]." As expected, Gottlieb still favored using G-4's division through Col. Furuholmen. Cunningham had relented. He, Gottlieb and Lashbrook had met with Col. Furuholmen and his deputy, Lt. Col. Lawrence, at the Pentagon where Cunningham had laid out to the officers the proposed cover arrangements for Lashbrook. Officers Furuholmen and Lawrence, noted Cunningham in his report, had both been top-secret cleared by the CIA in October 1953.

Furuholmen agreed to the backstopping; it was decided that Lashbrook would be listed as a G-4 consultant who had been serving in that capacity for nearly three years.

Cunningham explained that the two officers both clearly understood that as a result of having "been a witness to a suicide in New York City" during November 1953, it was extremely important that Lashbrook and the CIA "never be connected in any way to the incident." Cunningham concluded his report: "No further action is anticipated in this case and it is being considered as closed in this Division."

13

January 12, 1954
CIA Headquarters, Washington, D.C.

DCI Dulles and Deputy Director Cabell had just been briefed on the final stages of the investigation into Frank Olson's death when an intriguing letter was handed to Allen Dulles for his approval. Written by TSS chief Willis Gibbons, the letter concerned the "Availability of LSD from the Sandoz Company, Basel, Switzerland." The letter was attached to a report on a meeting between a Sandoz official and an unidentified CIA official. The meeting had been arranged by Dr. H. Marshall Chadwell, CIA chief of the Office of Scientific Intelligence who had known the Sandoz official for a number of years.

Dated September 4, 1953, the report described in detail an "extraordinary change" in attitude on the part of Sandoz officials toward their work with LSD. In 1952, the report stated, Sandoz had assigned over 200 laboratory researchers to investigate LSD and Sandoz had been delighted with the progress they had been making. But, this year "an extraordinarily different atmosphere prevailed." Sandoz officials no longer appeared interested in the drug. The CIA officer reported that he asked if Sandoz was "giving up their work" with LSD and LAE, a related drug. The Sandoz official's "answer was vague," but included the startling view that Sandoz needed "to get some agency to undertake a systematic study of [LSD]." The report continued:

> Perhaps he emphasized a little too much their willingness (eagerness) to have some official body in the United States take on study of these drugs. I couldn't help wondering if he wanted to get it plainly on the record that they had made these [drugs] available to the West, least traffic with Russia look bad at some future date and in some future world situation.

The report's author considered it "incredible" and "unbelievable" that Sandoz had lost interest in its work with LSD and speculated that perhaps the company "had become alarmed at the ethical and moral problems involved," which he thought "improbable," or that the company had experienced "serious accidents," which the author also viewed as "improbable." The report then describes in some detail what transpired next:

A luncheon was arranged for me [where a number of Sandoz officials] were present. During an absence from the table of [name redacted], I said to [name redacted], apparently an official of the company, 'I hope you are not abandoning your interest in the ergot derivatives.' 'No,' he said, '*but we are burned children.*'

Then he mentioned a considerable quantity of unfavorable publicity, which he said had stemmed 'from the [redacted] press.' He said he did not know who had been responsible for it. He remarked that this publicity had commented on possible political and military uses of the agents.

The final section of the report concludes with several intriguing observations:

A follow-up should be made on the present illness of [a Sandoz scientist, name redacted]. I picked up a hint that it is mental. I also picked up the suggestion that it was related to his experimental work. This raises the question of whether frequent self-experimentation with ergot derivatives could be responsible. This is of enough importance to justify investigation, I think. [Lastly,] I have reason to believe that the Sandoz Company has on hand about 20 pounds of LSD. This is a fantastically large amount. This should be checked. If true, one can make interesting speculation as to why they made so much so early in the trials of this agent.

The letter drafted by Willis Gibbons and handed to DCI Dulles on January 12, 1954 had been attached to the September 4 report quoted above concerning the availability of ergot-based LSD from the Sandoz company.

As it happened, two CIA officials had traveled to Sandoz headquarters in Switzerland from December 7 through December 18, 1953. They were told that a "report that Sandoz held a stock of 10 kilograms of [LSD] is denied by company officials" and that instead, Sandoz laboratories "have produced approximately 40 grams" of LSD in all; specifically, "that of the last batch of 20 grams, 10 were shipped to the U.S. [for CIA use] and 10 remain in stock."

Additionally, Sandoz had assured the CIA officials that no LSD had been given or sold to the Soviet Union or any country "behind the Iron Curtain," and Sandoz did "not believe the material is being, or could be, produced behind the Iron Curtain today." Further, Sandoz officials agreed to keep the CIA timely informed on all future production of LSD and on any inquiry about the drug from any other country or individual. Lastly, as a result of this December trip, Sandoz had agreed to supply the CIA with about one hundred grams of LSD per week for the next two years plus.

The CIA placed an extremely high priority on securing a steady supply of LSD and in keeping the drug out of the hands of the Russians or any of its allies. Evidence for this level of importance is that copies of Gibbon's letter and its attachments were circulated secretly to several high level State Department officials, including Under Secretary of State and former CIA director, Gen. Bedell

Smith, as well as Lampton Berry, Deputy Operations Coordinator at the State Department, and Frances E. Willis, U.S. Ambassador to Switzerland at the time.

Here it is quite worthwhile to look at yet another CIA report concerning a December 8, 1953 meeting between a confidential Agency informant and a U.S. representative of the Sandoz company. (Neither man is identified by name in the partially redacted report; however, former CIA officials, speaking anonymously, identify the informant as Dr. Harold Abramson.)

According to the report, the two men had dinner at a New York City restaurant during which the Sandoz representative "drank a fair amount of bourbon and led the conversation." Observed the informant: "He had a curious and tiresome tendency to lard all that he has to say to me with flattery.... I do not know what the point of this flattery was; probably nothing more than the fact that [he] is a rather small individual who has made his way in the world by getting on well with people. Perhaps this is how he accomplishes it."

Niceties aside, the informant then relates the gist of his observations. The Sandoz representative brought up a particular subject matter so persistently, wrote the informant, that "I could not help wondering just what his motives were." About a year earlier, he noted, the same Sandoz representative had "brought up the same matter in very much the same persistent way. So far no ready explanation has occurred to me for this persistence other than that he is keenly interested in the matter."

The Sandoz man had evidently blurted, "The Pont Saint Esprit 'secret' is that it was not the bread at all."

The man was referring to a peculiar illness outbreak in 1951 in the small French village, Pont St. Esprit. There, in late summer of that year, hundreds of villagers had suddenly fallen ill, many wildly hallucinating and behaving in bizarre ways. After a great deal of debate, scientists were called in to investigate the situation. The scientists, including at least two prominent Sandoz researchers, had concluded that the villagers had suffered ergot poisoning that originated in a shipment of contaminated baked bread they had received the same day of the outbreak.

"For weeks the French tied up our laboratories with analyses of bread," said the man, but it turned out they had been wrong. "It was not grain ergot, it was a diethylamide-like compound."

"If the material wasn't in the bread then how did it get into the people?"

"I think the whole business was an experiment," the man replied.

"An experiment?"

"Maybe by the French government," said the man. Then, according to the report, he began to talk about LSD, saying Sandoz was "still very much interested" in the drug. Adding, "One small reason I'm here in the U.S. is to dispose of our LSD. If war breaks out our LSD will disappear."

Interesting to note is that the CIA was hardly content to have only Sandoz as a supply source for LSD. On February 3, 1953, about ten months before the trip to Sandoz, TSS chemical division deputy chief Robert Lashbrook had written a memorandum for the record stating:

> Since the unusual properties of ergot and, more importantly, Lysergic Acid have been known to ARTICHOKE for some time, the development of this chemical has been of intense interest.... For matters of record, apparently chemists of the Eli Lilly Company working for [TSS] have in the past few weeks succeeded in breaking the secret formula held by Sandoz for the manufacture of Lysergic Acid and have manufactured for this Agency a large quantity of Lysergic Acid which is available for our experimentation. This work is a closely guarded [TSS] secret and should not be mentioned generally.

Four months later, on June 1, 1953, Lashbrook forwarded an approval request to Sidney Gottlieb, Willis Gibbons and TSS research chairman Admiral Luis deFlorez for Project MKULTRA, Subproject 6. The purpose of Subproject 6, which was approved by all three men the next day, was to develop "a reliable source of lysergic acid derivatives [LSD] within the U.S. as opposed to our present complete dependence upon Swiss sources, and, in addition, it aims to extend the isolation and testing program of the hypnotic natural products from the Rivea species of plants."

Lashbrook's request emphasized that the only processor of ergot in the United States of any significance was Eli Lilly and Company of Indiana, and therefore the CIA would be paying the company the amount of $5,000, so that the Agency could take "full advantage of both [Eli Lilly's] long experience in this field and the large stock of materials which it has available."

On October 26, 1954, TSS Chief Willis Gibbons sent another memorandum to Allen Dulles, via Deputy Director of Plans, Frank Wisner. The memo concerned a "newly discovered synthesis by Eli Lilly and Company." Gibbons was clearly excited about the company now being able to supply the Agency with synthesized LSD. It was only a matter of months, he apprised Dulles, before Lilly could deliver the drug "in tonnage quantities." He continued, "LSD can now be produced in quantity and recent technical developments make it possible to disseminate solids in an effective manner" to the Army's Chemical Warfare Corps. Explained the TSS chief:

> Most of the significant information currently available on the disabling effects of LSD on humans has been obtained from the research activities supported during the past three years by the Chemical Division of TSS, under the direction of Dr. Sidney Gottlieb. TSS is continuing its research effort toward developing a capability for covert use of this material, and the availability of LSD in large quantities will not affect our program. However, we feel it is highly advisable that certain components of the Department of Defense be advised of both the new synthesis at Lilly and

153

our data on the effects of this material on human beings. TSS therefore intends to appraise the Chemical Corps and the Air Force of this information, through previously established scientific channels.

Also on that day, the Commanding Officer at the Army Chemical Corps in Maryland had been given important news by two of his top scientists who had just returned from a visit to Eli Lilly's research Laboratories in Indianapolis, Indiana. Eli Lilly, the two scientists had been assured, could now furnish the Chemical Corps with 100-200 grams of LSD, and that the company "had agreed to furnish gratis small samples of the various synthetic lysergic acid" recently developed. The two scientists also noted that Lilly was setting up a group for the study of LSD "via the electroencephalographic techniques using deep penetrating micro electrodes." The scientists underscored the past problems of ergot supply in manufacturing LSD, due to market speculators and research demands, and applauded Lilly's development of synthetic products that eliminated these problems. The Chemical Corps could now go full steam ahead with LSD experiments.

Despite the recommendations stemming from the Olson investigation, no LSD under the CIA's control was ever impounded by the Agency, nor did the CIA do anything to slow or halt its LSD experimentation, or that of its subcontractors, following Frank Olson's death. If anything, Olson's death seemed to accelerate the CIA's LSD activities.

14

February 18, 1954
U.S. Department of Justice
Washington, D.C.

On a chilly morning one month after the CIA officially closed its investigation into Frank Olson's death, CIA General Council Lawrence Houston left his office and walked several blocks to the U.S. Department of Justice, where he was to meet with Deputy Attorney General William P. Rogers. Attorney Houston had spoken with Rogers by telephone several days earlier about a pressing matter that needed prompt attention and, following that conversation, Rogers had suggested Houston come to his office.

Houston hand-carried what he subsequently described as "the complete investigation, with conclusions and recommendations on a case which indicated a variety of violations of criminal statutes relating to the handling of official funds." He elaborated, as follows:

> This case arose during the review of a highly complex clandestine operation. The information was developed by the Inspection and Review Staff, Deputy Director (Plans), and even in its completed form would be unintelligible to a person not thoroughly familiar with the Agency and its operations due to the use of pseudonyms and cover companies and to various circumstances arising out of operational considerations.

During his meeting with Rogers on February 18, Houston pointed out that one of the individuals involved in the case "was almost certainly guilty of violations of criminal statutes," but that the CIA "had been able to devise no charge under which he could be prosecuted which would not require revelation of highly classified information." Rogers, a former New York assistant district attorney who would go on to become U.S. Attorney General and then Secretary of State, asked several questions about the individual.

According to Houston, Rogers told him "that under the circumstances he saw no purpose in referring the matter to the Department of Justice as [the CIA was] as well, or, in light of the peculiar circumstances, perhaps better equipped to pass on the possibilities of prosecution." He did advise Houston that if the CIA "could come to a firm determination in this respect," [the Agency] should make the record of that determination as clear as possible and retain it in [CIA] files." Cautioned Rogers:

> If, however, any information arising out of [CIA] investigations revealed the possibilities of prosecution, then [the Agency] would have an obligation to bring the pertinent facts to the attention of the Department of Justice.

Houston readily agreed, "that any doubt should be resolved in favor of referring the matter [to the Justice Department]." Rogers then advised Houston to have the CIA "follow through carefully on any such case" and said that, if necessary, such cases should be reduced to "a formal exchange of letters, but that he "saw no reason why present practices could not be continued without formal documentation."

On February 23, Houston, clearly pleased with the newly consummated understanding between CIA and the Department of Justice, which now allowed the Agency to determine on its own when to report violations of criminal activities by CIA personnel, sent a memorandum to Allen Dulles detailing his meeting with Rogers and their subsequent agreement. Houston prefaced his memo with the following two introductory paragraphs.

> From time to time information is developed within the Agency indicating the actual or probable violation of criminal statutes. Normally all such information would be turned over to the Department of Justice for investigation and decision as to prosecution. Occasionally, however, the apparent criminal activities are involved in highly classified and complex covert operations. Under these circumstances investigation by outside agency could not hope for success without revealing to that agency the full scope of the covert operation involved as well as this Agency's authorities and manner of handling the operation. Even then, the investigation could not succeed without the full assistance of all interested branches of this Agency. In addition, if investigation developed a prima-facie case of a criminal violation, in many cases it would be readily apparent that prosecution would be impossible without revealing highly classified matters to public scrutiny.
>
> The law is well settled that a criminal prosecution cannot proceed in camera or on production of only part of the information. The Government must be willing to expose its entire information if it desires to prosecute. In those cases involving covert operations, therefore, there appears to be a balancing of interest between the duty to enforce the law which is in the proper jurisdiction of the Department of Justice and the Director's responsibility for protecting intelligence sources and methods. This is further affected by physical considerations.

On March 1, 1954, after learning that the understanding between CIA and the Department of Justice met with Dulles' approval, Houston sent a copy of his understanding "of our conversation regarding the investigation of possible criminal activities" arising out of CIA operations to Deputy Attorney General Rogers. Wrote Houston in his brief cover memo: "If you find no objection to this statement, please return and we will retain it in our files for future guidance." Rogers returned the unaltered copy of the statement the same week and it was placed in the General Counsel's files marked *SECRET, EYES ONLY,* never to see the light of public scrutiny for another twenty years.

15

January 19, 1954
CIA Headquarters, Washington, D.C.

A little over a month after Lyman Kirkpatrick issued his findings on Frank Olson's death, Robert Lashbrook received a telephone call from the Pentagon. Major Thomas Walsh, a high-level Army Chemical Corps security officer, was calling to ask if Lashbrook was aware that the widow of a patient who had died in a New York hospital was suing the Chemical Corps.

According to a top-secret CIA Security Office memorandum written days later, Lashbrook replied that he wasn't, but then asked Walsh if the lawsuit he was referring to had grown out of an incident which had occurred a little over a year earlier at the New York State Psychiatric Institute.

Yes, that was the incident, answered Walsh, adding that any assistance the CIA could provide "in any way to hush the thing up" would be greatly appreciated. Lashbrook told Walsh he would get back to him, and then he went to see his superior, Dr. Sidney Gottlieb.

The following day, Gottlieb and Lashbrook met with CIA security chief Sheffield Edwards and briefed him on the incident, which had resulted from a series of Chemical Corps "experiments involving the injection of mescaline derivatives into patients" at New York State Psychiatric Institute (NYSPI), a hospital affiliated with Columbia University. Gottlieb explained to Edwards that Lashbrook was aware of both the experiments and the patient's death after having been "advised about them" by Dr. Amedeo S. Marrazzi. Marrazzi, director of the Clinical Research Division, Army Chemical and Biological Corps, also worked closely with the Special Operations Division (SOD) at Camp Detrick. It was Marrazzi's division, in partnership with SOD, which had been covertly providing NYSPI with approximately $1,000,000 for the experiments. Gottlieb further explained that the CIA "had no funds involved" in the specific experiment which had resulted in the patient's death. However, Gottlieb added, Marrazzi's division had been keeping the CIA closely informed about its "various activities along these lines" and in late February 1953, about a month after the patient's death, the CIA had invested $65,000 in the experiments.

The day after his meeting with Edwards, Gottlieb telephoned Major Walsh at the Pentagon and advised him, per instructions from Edwards, that the CIA "did not want the Agency's name mentioned in connection" with the New York State Psychiatric Institute case. Major Walsh assured Gottlieb that the CIA would not in any way be mentioned and that he would keep the Agency informed in the event of any undue publicity. Additionally, as reflected in the subsequent CIA Security Office memorandum, Walsh assured Gottlieb "that the lawyer" for the widow suing the Chemical Corps "was a military man, (presumably a reserve officer) and had been advised the case involved military connections. The lawyer stated he would give the case no publicity."

Harold Blauer died on January 8, 1953, at the age of forty-two, at the New York State Psychiatric Institute, a place where people went for special care and help. The son of Jewish immigrants, Blauer, a professional tennis player who five years earlier had been ranked fourteenth-best in the United States, was suffering from depression due to a failed marriage. Harold had known his wife Amy since childhood and they had been married for seventeen years before separating. When Amy flew to Mexico to obtain the divorce, Harold had fallen into a state of depression. He felt that divorce was tantamount to failure, and he was deeply concerned about the wellbeing of his two daughters. As his depression deepened, Harold was unable to sleep or eat. He lost all interest in work and grew increasingly despondent. His personal physician recommended he go to New York's Bellevue Hospital for psychiatric evaluation and help.

Blauer had agreed. He took time off from his job as tennis pro at the exclusive Hudson River Club in New York, and voluntarily checked himself into the hospital. After five weeks in Bellevue, Blauer was responding well to treatment and his doctors were encouraged. Anticipating that he would be able to go home soon, they had him moved to the New York State Psychiatric Institute on December 5, 1953, where he was quickly given the diagnosis "pseudo-neurotic schizophrenic."

By this time, Amy had returned from Mexico. She was quite concerned about Harold and had been visiting him in the hospital almost every day. Indeed, to many friends and family members, the couple appeared as if they were on the verge of reconciliation.

The New York State Psychiatric Institute is a highly respected facility with many distinguished physicians on staff. It was founded in 1896 after New York State legislation placed all "chronically insane" individuals under the protection and care of the state. Today, NYSPI's website boldly proclaims, "Proud of its long and accomplished history, the New York State Psychiatric Institute continues to work at the leading edge of today's discoveries in mental health." Unknown to Harold and Amy Blauer in 1953, the NYSPI was conducting aggressive psychopharmacology experiments on patients without their consent.

In 1950 and 1951, Camp Detrick's ultra-secret Special Operations Division had entered into at least two multi-year contracts with the NYSPI for the "psychological investigation of potential chemical warfare agents on human beings."

According to once secret files, SOD was especially interested in obtaining "new technical data...which would provide a firmer basis for the utilization of psychochemical agents both for offensive use as sabotage weapons and for protection against them." Stated the contract for the experiment in which Harold Blauer died:

> The [NYSPI] will conduct studies of psychochemical agents on human beings to determine clinical effects on psychological behavior, including controls on normal human subjects necessary to evaluate the more profound changes expected in the behavior of psychiatrically liable subjects.

Under the terms of the top-secret contract, SOD "would supply certain chemical derivatives" to NYSPI for experiments on unwitting patients, and NYSPI would communicate its findings to SOD in quarterly reports. The Army selected NYSPI because its research division had accumulated considerable experience, beginning in 1944, with experiments using a wide variety of hallucinogenic drugs, including LSD. In 1945, as readers will see in greater detail, the OSS and Federal Bureau of Narcotics had conducted extensive experiments with "truth drugs" at the Institute. Also influencing the choice of NYSPI was that its psychiatrists' willingness to experiment with psycho-chemicals met with the strong approval of research physician, Dr. Harold A. Abramson, who had long held a number of top-secret contracts with the Army's Chemical Corps and the Office of Naval Intelligence, as well as with the CIA.

The director of the Institute's experimental psychiatry division was Dr. Paul H. Hoch. Born in Budapest in 1902, Hoch attended medical school in Hungary and Germany. In the late 1920s, he studied psychiatry and neurology at the renowned Burgholzli Psychiatric University and Mental Hospital in Zurich. There Hoch studied under Dr. Eugene Bleuler, a Swiss psychiatrist whose seminal work on psychoanalysis and schizophrenia strongly influenced his close associate Carl Jung. While in Zurich, Hoch met another young physician named Ewen Cameron who would go on to achieve far greater notoriety with his own CIA-funded experiments.

Dr. Hoch came to the United States sometime around 1933 and quickly taught himself English by reading newspapers and listening to the radio in his Fifth Avenue hotel room. Soon after his arrival, he began working at Manhattan State Hospital and in 1934, with the assistance of young lawyer John Foster Dulles, he was granted a full immigration visa and obtained his New York medical license. In 1942 at the advent of the war, Hoch was Chief Medical Officer for war neuroses with the United States Public Health Service in New Jersey and New York City. In this capacity, he first encountered Dr. Harold Abramson, who was assigned to the Office of the Chief, Chemical Warfare Service. [It has been suggested that Hoch also met Frank Olson at this time, but while it seems possible, and is well established that Abramson, as well as George Hunter White, were well acquainted with Olson in the early 1940s, the author has been unable to find any confirmation that Hoch knew Olson prior to 1951.] During his wartime service, Hoch again encountered Dr. Cameron, a Scot who had just become a U.S. citizen. Cameron joined the American war effort and worked with the American Psychiatric Association's military mobilization committee supporting a team of psychologists who were drawing up psychological profiles of major Nazi leaders, including Hitler.

Hoch joined the NYSPI staff in 1948. Shortly thereafter, following his appointment as the facility's Principal Research Scientist in Psychiatry, he began actively promoting the controversial work of Dr. Franz J. Kallmann, a German who served as the Institute's Associate Research Medical Geneticist. Kallmann's mentor before coming to the United States had been Dr. Ernst Rudin, chief geneticist at the Nazi-supported Kaiser Wilhelm Institute of Psychiatric Research in Berlin. Many historians credit Rudin — an enthusiastic proponent of "race hygiene" and forced sterilization of those deemed mentally "unfit" — with helping author the diabolical genetic rationale for mass extermination by the Nazis of hundreds of thousands of people during the Third Reich. In the mid-1930s, Kallmann, while working with Rudin at the then Rockefeller Foundation-funded Kaiser Wilhelm Institute, argued for the sterilization of even the healthy relatives of schizophrenics in order to eliminate all defective genes. Ironically, Kallmann was hired at the Rockefeller-funded New York State Psychiatric Institute after he had been forced to flee Nazi Germany because he was Jewish and married to a Lutheran, in clear violation of Nazi law against the marriage of non-Aryans to Aryans.

The day before Harold Blauer was to be discharged from NYSPI and return home, he was given an injection of a highly potent experimental mescaline derivative code-named EA-1298 by the Army's Chemical Corps. The drug had been concocted in the laboratories of Camp Detrick's SOD which, since October 1952, had been under the direction of Dr. Frank Olson. NYSPI records reveal that Blauer attempted to refuse the injection because four previous injections of the drug had made him extremely uncomfortable and frightened. Notes made by Dr. James P. Cattell, NYSPI senior research psychiatrist and the physician who injected Blauer with the fatal dose, as well as the previous four injections, reveal that Blauer was "very apprehensive" about receiving the fifth injection and that "considerable persuasion [was] required" to make him accept. Additionally, Cattell's notes reveal that before the fourth injection, Blauer told the doctor he did not want to receive any additional shots, but that his protests were ignored.

There is no evidence that Blauer gave written consent for the experimental injections; however, written consent was not required in the early 1950s. There is no doubt that Blauer had no idea he was being used as a guinea pig in an experiment to develop offensive chemical warfare agents. Clearly the injections given to Blauer were not intended in any way to serve any diagnostic or therapeutic purposes, but instead were intended to advance the Army's chemical warfare objectives and perhaps knowledge of how certain chemicals might affect mental patients.

Here it should be noted that in May 1951, Dr. Hoch and Dr. Cattell delivered a paper on the effects of mescaline and LSD before the American Psychiatric Association. "The administration of mescaline," they wrote, "produces an acute reversible psychosis that consists of diverse psychological phenomena usually occurring in a clear setting of consciousness." Hoch and Cattell neglected to mention that the Army Chemical Corps underwrote their experiments, but they did explain that the experiments involved "fifty-nine patients," all "suffering from schizophrenia." Observed the two doctors, "Anxiety increase was the most frequent emotional change...under the drug. Many patients displayed hostility, [and] paranoid manifestations were very frequent."

When Dr. Cattell and attending nurses persisted in telling Blauer he needed the fifth injection, Blauer insisted that he did not. "Besides, the last shot made me feel terrible for a week," he argued. Indeed, Institute records reveal that the fourth injection had caused Blauer great distress. "Two hours after receiving it he was trembling uncontrollably. He lay in bed for nearly two days shaking and moving his head back and forth. "I'm in awful shape," he told his nurse. "I feel as if something is inside my head. I don't know if I can stand it."

Blauer continued to protest as nurses readied him for the fifth injection. Under the protocol Dr. Hoch designed for the experiments, the fifth injection of 450 mg of EA-1298 which Blauer received was sixteen times greater than his previous injections. "I'm fine now," Blauer told Cattell. "I'm going home tomorrow, I don't need to be given anything." Despite this, the fifth injection was administered. Within seconds, Blauer became highly agitated. He began sweating profusely, his arms and legs flailing wildly. Attendants were summoned to restrain him. Within three minutes of the injection his body stiffened grotesquely, as though he had been electrically shocked. Thick froth poured from his mouth, covering his chin and throat. Approximately thirty minutes later he began convulsing and then lapsed into a coma. Doctors pounded on his chest, administered artificial respiration and oxygen, and injected him with glucose and sodium amyl. Blauer died one hour later.

At the same time that Blauer reacted to his injection, another patient across the hall from him was given the same drug, slightly milder in strength. Her reaction was so violent that the administering nurse stopped the injection when it was only one-third complete. Still, the woman began screaming and flailing wildly about her bed. Later the woman said, "I've been in hell. Why did they put me in hell? They were supposed to make me feel good. I've never felt this bad before; I feel terrible."

The New York deputy medical examiner, Dominick DiMaio, the same official who months later would determine that Frank Olson's death was a suicide, ruled that Blauer's death was due to a therapeutic drug administered by

Institute physicians that "aggravated a previously undetected heart problem" which "triggered a fatal coronary."

Two days after Blauer's death, Chemical Corps chief Col. Milward W. Bayliss dispatched Dr. Amedeo Marrazzi to New York to investigate the facts surrounding Blauer's death and to submit a report to his military superiors. Marrazzi, the son of Italian immigrants whose father was a New York building contractor, had received his M.D. from New York University College of Medicine, working his way through as a taxi driver and part-time teacher. He was recruited in 1948 to the Army Chemical Corps Medical Laboratory at Edgewood, Maryland to experiment with nerve gases that the Nazis had developed during World War II. In 1951, Marrazzi had been promoted to chief of the Chemical Corps Clinical Research Division.

Dr. Marrazzi's report on the NYSPI incident stated that, regardless of Blauer's death, the results of the experiments "thus far were very useful for the Army's purposes." So useful were they, in Marrazzi's view, that he recommended increasing funding for the NYSPI experiments by $120,000. While in New York, Marrazzi went to the medical examiner's office and met with deputy examiner DiMaio, with whom he was well acquainted. According to Chemical Corps documents, Marrazzi asked DiMaio to place all the Blauer records in a confidential file in the medical examiner's office, instructing DiMaio that the information was not to be disclosed to anyone. So stringent was this that when Blauer's personal physician requested his patient's records, he was told that "he was to stay out of the matter and that others would be taking care of the case from that point on."

On the same day that Dr. Marrazzi had arrived in New York, the Institute's chief researcher, Dr. Hoch, asked Camp Detrick's SOD if he could dissect Blauer's brain so he could better study the effects of EA-1298 on human tissue. SOD approved Hoch's request, and instructed him to maintain absolute secrecy about SOD's involvement. Before Hoch had begun the autopsy, however, SOD withdrew its approval because of mounting concerns about liability. Hoch complied without objection.

Amy Blauer was informed of her ex-husband's death within about an hour of its occurrence. She was told that Harold had died as a result of a heart attack triggered by the injection of a therapeutic drug. She was told nothing about any experiment or about any involvement of chemical warfare agents being tested by the Army at NYSPI. Troubled by how little information she was being given, Amy contacted her family's attorneys and asked them to look into the matter. Amy's attorneys, contemplating a possible lawsuit, requested all available information from NYSPI about Blauer's treatment and death. They were given a thin file that contained nothing about any experiments, the drugs involved, or the Army.

On April 2, 1953, Amy's attorneys filed a complaint in the New York Court of Claims against the State of New York, alleging that Blauer's death was caused by NYSPI negligence. David Marcus, then Assistant Attorney General of the State of New York, was assigned to defend the case. Marcus, who had been told of the Army's involvement with Blauer's death, agreed to keep that involvement a secret, and on several occasions he postponed the examination of witnesses at the direction of the Army. Besides being told that secrecy was required for national security, Marcus was told that:

> [Any] adverse publicity would make it extremely difficult for the Army to place similar contracts for chemical studies in the future if the public were to become aware of such experiments.

Marcus, at the prompting of government attorneys, decided to pressure Amy Blauer to settle her claim quickly without going to court. In January of 1954, the Assistant Chief of Staff of the Army's Intelligence Division verbally agreed to pay one-third of any out-of-court settlement if the Army's role was not disclosed. Marcus sought and received the collusion of Dr. Newton Bigelow, the New York State Commissioner of Mental Hygiene, in keeping the Army's involvement a secret. Over the ensuing months, the Army made sure all documents pertaining to the Chemical Corps and SOD in NYSPI files were taken out of the state of New York and turned over to Dr. Marrazzi, who placed them in a secure safe in his Chemical Corps office. It appears that on at least one occasion agents of the Federal Narcotics Bureau, who were acting in concert with SOD and CIA, hand carried some of these documents to Washington, D.C.

In late June 1954, attorneys at the U.S. Department of Justice in Washington, D.C. became involved in the cover-up of Blauer's death. In early July, federal attorneys informed Marcus that if it became necessary to go to trial, which should be avoided at all costs, Amy Blauer could be told that the "source of the chemical [given to her ex-husband] was an Army Medical Officer of the Army Medical Authority or the Army Chemical Center Medical Laboratory." Justice Department Civil Division attorney George S. Leonard stressed to Marcus that if the source of the compound had to be revealed, it should be attributed to the Army Medical Corps, not to the Chemical Corps. Leonard also stressed that the contracts between NYSPI and the Army were not to be revealed under any circumstances. Additionally, according to New York State Attorney General office documents, Leonard "forcibly informed Mr. Marcus that the pre-trial procedures and any further proceedings should be limited to the medical aspects of the case." Other Justice Department attorneys told Marcus that, if need be, NYSPI doctors should state in court "that mescaline derivatives had been coming into general use for the diagnosis and therapy of mental patients," a claim that had no basis in fact.

In July, after Assistant Attorney General Marcus returned to New York from his meetings with Justice Department attorneys, he bargained hard with Amy Blauer's lawyers for a settlement. Marcus told Amy's lawyers that it was the

State's firm contention that nobody had been negligent in Blauer's death and that he had died of a heart attack and not an injection. However, Marcus said, in the interest of avoiding the expense and adverse publicity of a trial, New York State would be willing to settle the case for $15,000.

In making this offer, Marcus did not inform Amy's attorneys that the United States, through the Justice Department and the Army Intelligence Division, would be paying half the agreed upon amount. By letter dated April 27, 1955, then Assistant U.S. Attorney General Warren E. Burger — soon to be a Justice of the U.S. Supreme Court — informed Marcus that a payment of $7,500 would be made to the State of New York as soon as administrative arrangements were made.

New York law required that a Court of Claims judge approve settlements against the State and that the court make a *prima facie* case showing that the State was negligent. Unexpectedly, the Court of Claims judge handling the Blauer case refused to approve the $15,000 settlement figure. Marcus and government attorneys then raised the settlement offer to $18,000. The Claims Court judge, following a brief hearing, approved the new figure. Marcus then had Amy Blauer sign a release precluding another lawsuit against the State of New York related to the case and releasing the "...organization, group, government body or agency, which furnished the drugs" injected into her ex-husband. After all was said and done, Amy Blauer and her two daughters received about $10,000 and still didn't learn a thing about the true facts surrounding Harold Blauer's death or about any involvement on the part of the Army and U.S. government. But, as readers shall learn, the mystery of Harold Blauer's death was far from being a settled matter.

Incredibly, about a year after Harold Blauer died, and less than two months after Frank Olson's death, according to notations made in 1954 by federal narcotics agent and CIA consultant George Hunter White, an extraordinary gathering took place at a CIA-funded safe house in New York in March of that year. In attendance, in addition to George Hunter White were Dr. Paul Hoch, Dr. Harold Abramson, Dr. Max Rinkel, and Dr. Edward W. Pelikan, an assistant to Abramson. They met to discuss on-going LSD experiments being funded by both SOD and CIA. According to a report drafted by White, the meeting continued the next day at the Hotel Dennis in Atlantic City, New Jersey. White's notations on the meeting reveal single-word references to the "Statler" and "Olson," indicating that some sort of discussion about the events of November 28, 1953 had taken place. Several additional meetings took place in New York that included Robert Lashbrook and Sidney Gottlieb.

Beginning two weeks after this series of meetings and lasting for nearly eighteen months, experiments using LSD were conducted at least several times a month at the New York safe house. Around this same time, Dr. Hoch and a number of colleagues formed a private corporation, the Research Foundation of Mental Hygiene, which was promptly awarded several six-figure contracts by the Army Chemical Corps. Also at the same time, Dr. Marrazzi renewed the contracts with NYSPI for further drug experiments on human subjects, often using other hallucinogenic drugs besides mescaline, including harmaline and bufotenine, sometimes combined with electroshock therapy, insulin comas, and lobotomies.

Later, in February 1954, Drs. Marrazzi, Hoch, Abramson and Dr. Maurice Seevers from the University of Michigan met again in New York to plan a series of psycho-chemical conferences to be held at the Chemical Corps' Medical Laboratories' offices in Maryland. At this meeting it was decided that Marrazzi would both chair and coordinate the conference and that the first gathering would be held in early May. Notes from the planning meeting reveal that the group engaged in considerable discussion about the merits of:

> ... structuring a formal program involving the administration of small doses of LSD-25 as a way of screening personnel, especially those in sensitive positions, for anxiety proneness and more importantly for the effects of anxiety on their conduct, judgment, ability to make decisions, execute tasks and maintain security.

A 44-page report on the First Psychochemical Conference, held on May 12, 1954, listed its presenting participants: in addition to Drs. Marrazzi, Hoch, Abramson and Seevers, were Dr. Carney Landis, NYSPI; Dr. E. Ross Hart, Neurology Branch, Chemical Corps; Dr. Frank Fremont-Smith, Medical Director of the Josiah Macy Jr. Foundation; Dr. Carl Schmidt, University of Pennsylvania; and Dr. Jacob Finesinger, University of Maryland Psychiatric Institute.

Marrazzi opened the one-day conference by telling participants that presentations and discussions would focus exclusively on "contract reports on psycho-chemical aspects of warfare." He explained:

> It is perfectly obvious that a military objective is to produce incapacitation and, although not the most dramatic form of incapacitation, certainly one of the most telling is the derangement of coordination, in other words, mental incapacitation with the whole train of events which it involves and the drain it places upon the military resources of a great number of people. Obviously such an objective might be accomplished in large groups or small groups or even in single individuals.

Marrazzi elaborated further that the current interest of the Chemical Corps "is in the larger group" and in order to achieve that end the Army Medical Laboratories and Chemical and Radiological Laboratories had "surveyed compounds known to have mental effects, starting out with very familiar ones." Commented Marrazzi, "We were aided in that brief survey by a number of consultants, including Dr. Seevers on one occasion, and we finally selected those of immediate interest though not exclusively these few: the mescaline series, the lysergic acid diethylamide and the marijuana series." Marrazzi said that work on these drugs thus far would have been difficult without the strong support and assistance from Dr. L. Wilson Greene, Scientific Director of Chemical and Radiological Laboratories, and the Chemical Corps' Dr. C.L. Butler and Dr. B. Witten. (Readers will learn more about this conference in Book Two.)

Handwritten notes on the conference report obtained by this author indicate that several of the day's formal presentations, specifically those lead by Drs. Hoch, Landis, and Abramson, involved off-the-record discussions about the deaths of Harold Blauer and Frank Olson. The same notations reveal that Dr. Abramson informed participants that Olson's death was not related to his having been given LSD and that there were extenuating circumstances involved, which apparently he did not explain.

As readers may rightly conclude, clearly NYSPI, the Chemical Corps and SOD thought the cases of Harold Blauer and Frank Olson were closed and that nobody would ever learn the real story behind their horrible deaths. But, as readers shall see, they were wrong.

16

March 1954
Indian Rocks Beach, Florida

Several weeks after Frank Olson's death, Charles and Ina Wicks suggested to their daughter, Alice Olson, that she pack a few bags and come to Florida with her three children for a visit. "They'll love it here and it would do them a world of good to get away," Charles told Alice. Ina, Alice's stepmother, said, "It would be good for you, too."

Since Frank's death, Alice had been feeling as though she were sleepwalking through life. Hardly a night passed when she didn't wake up expecting to find her husband lying beside her. Awake, she would agonize about what had caused Frank to do something so irrational as jumping through a closed hotel window. The man she had known and loved would never have left her and their children alone, devastated and guilt-ridden. When she did manage to sleep, Alice had horrible nightmares during which she saw Frank lying on the New York sidewalk bleeding and mangled. During the day, everywhere she looked she saw something that reminded her of him. She felt as if she were "in a daze" throughout the weeks following Frank's death, she later recounted.

Alice never viewed her husband's body. After his corpse had been shipped back to Maryland, she inquired about his missing personal effects. Where were Frank's wallet, identification credentials and other personal items? she asked. Gone, she was informed. Gone where, Alice asked. For unexplained reasons, Frank had thrown the items away while wandering the streets of New York one night, she was told. Thrown away? Why, she asked. It isn't clear why, she was told. When she inquired about funeral arrangements, she was informed that because Frank's face and body had been so disfigured from his fall and subsequent autopsy, it would be impossible to have an open casket service. For Alice, Frank's funeral was a surreal experience. The church for Frank's service was overflowing with mourners. Nearly all of Camp Detrick's SOD scientists, officers, and civilian employees, many accompanied by their spouses, were in attendance. The next day, Alice would tell her friend, Agnes Tanner, whose husband, Herbert, was a SOD chemist, that among those who stopped to wish her well were two men who were complete strangers.

"That was Bob Lashbrook and his boss," Agnes told her. "I don't know what the boss's name is, but they're both nice young men. As a matter of fact, Bob was just at our house a few nights ago for dinner." Then Alice's friend lowered her voice and said, conspiratorially, "They both work for the CIA, you know." It was then that Alice remembered Lashbrook's name as the man Frank had gone to see in Washington, D.C. at one of the buildings near the Tidal Basin.

A few days after Frank was buried, Robert Lashbrook and his boss, Sidney Gottlieb, came by the Olson's home to express their condolences. Alice made coffee for the two CIA visitors, and they all sat awkwardly in her living room. Both men were "very sympathetic," Alice would later say.

Lashbrook told her, "I really don't know why Frank did it, but I'd be glad to tell you anything I know about what happened."

Gottlieb said they would give her any information she wanted to know about what Frank "was like in his last days and hours."

Alice recalled that she "was shaking so badly I could hardly pour coffee for them or hold a cup." It would be another twenty-five years before Alice saw or spoke with Lashbrook or Gottlieb again.

In the days following Frank's death, Col. Vincent Ruwet and Dr. John Schwab from Camp Detrick had been especially helpful to Alice. Ruwet helped Camp Detrick commander Lt. Col. Michael DeCarlo put together a special memorial service for Frank, held the first week of January 1954. Nearly all of Frank's colleagues and friends attended the service and many of them fondly recollected Frank's days at Camp Detrick. DeCarlo told the assembly, "We will all miss Frank greatly...There are times when it's hard to fathom life."

A few days after the memorial service, the Women's and Homemaker's Club that Alice helped organize held a small gathering with her closest friends in attendance. Over coffee, tea and cake the women did their best to help Alice feel better. When she got ready to go home, Agnes Tanner drew her aside and said that when things were less confusing and Alice was feeling better, she would like to speak with her about the Deep Creek Lake meeting Frank and her husband Herbert had attended. Alice said she would like that, but time never seemed to allow the two women to get together.

Meanwhile, Ruwet and Schwab visited Alice frequently. Ruwet stopped by several times a week. She didn't know how she would have managed without him. Confused, exhausted, numb with grief, lost about what to say to her bewildered children, Alice felt there was simply too much to do and she had little inclination to do it.

Alice knew nothing about events that had transpired behind the scenes following Frank's death.

No doubt Alice would have been greatly surprised to know that Lt. Col. Ruwet had conducted a thorough search of her home. Alice had been at the funeral parlor when Ruwet and an officer from Camp Detrick's Intelligence Division methodically combed through her home, opening drawers and searching shelves and rummaging through closets. According to an Army "security report" dated December 1, 1953, Ruwet's search had "disclosed no classified material."

The report indicates the immediate concerns of its author, Army security agent J.W. Corey. After meeting with Major Paul Walsh of Camp Detrick's Intelligence Division, Corey itemized the security concerns, as follows:

> Missing at present is Olson's identification badge and possibly two AGO cards. Olson is assumed to have had the two cards by virtue of his service as an Army officer and his travels in Europe as a civilian for the Chemical Corps. The missing badge carries Olson's picture and division and is constructed in a manner as to be difficult to alter. The badge permitted Olson access to the post in general and to his own division, but Major Max Etkin, Camp Detrick, Security Office, Intelligence Division is positive that a person resembling Olson could not gain access to the Special Operations Division by use of the badge.

Alice would have been even more astonished to see agent Corey's next paragraph:

> Olson received a disability pension for duodenal ulcers and also suffered from heart trouble. He was faced with the necessity of spending six months in a hospital, and was by nature so nervous that he would not have been able to spend such a long time immobilized. Etkin believes that Olson committed suicide because he was also suffering from cancer, although there has been no definite indication of cancer. (Note: If an autopsy was conducted, cancer would have been noted.) At the time of his death, Olson was being examined for a "classified" disease. This is the normal procedure for any employee of Special Operations Division— when they become sick, they are examined to discover whether or not they are suffering from any of the diseases with which they come in contact.

Corey's report fails to identify Olson's alleged "disease," but it can be safely assumed that Corey was simply copying what he had found on Olson's death benefits forms. Security agent Corey also does not explain, beyond noting Olson's nervousness, why he concluded that Olson "would not have been able to spend" six months "immobilized."

The weather had been perfect during the week that Alice and her children visited Indian Rocks Beach, Florida. It was the beginning of March, the days were warm but not yet humid, and after the sun set each evening cool, soothing breezes blew in off the Gulf waters across the small, idyllic barrier island. Charles Wicks had been right, his grandchildren loved the change of climate and scenery. Nine year-old Eric, the oldest child, was in nonstop motion from morning to night. His younger sister and brother, Lisa and Nils, followed him everywhere.

Alice often sat on the beach, watching the children play. She and Ina had great fun building sandcastles for seven year-old Lisa to stomp on, but Ina could see that Alice was deeply troubled by her husband's death. Alice was easily distracted and would lose her train of thought; sometimes her sentences would trail off without completion. At any given time during the day, Ina would notice Alice quietly crying.

One evening, after the children had fallen asleep, Charles asked Alice if she had learned any more about Frank's death. No, she hadn't, she said. Things had been too chaotic for her and the children, trying to get by without Frank. His superior at Camp Detrick, Col. Vincent Ruwet, had helped her maneuver through all the bureaucratic red tape and fill out the many forms necessary for her to collect federal employee's compensation benefits.

"What about VA benefits?" Charles asked.

"I didn't apply for those."

"Why not?"

"I'm not sure. Vin and John Schwab said there most likely would be a problem with them."

"Alice, why had Frank gone to New York," Ina asked, hesitantly.

"To see a psychiatrist," Alice said quietly.

"But why?" Charles asked. "What was wrong with him?"

Alice started to cry and said she wasn't sure. Just prior to going to New York, Frank had been away for three days at a scientific gathering, she explained. The meeting had been held at a remote location in western Maryland called Deep Creek Lake. Alice had seen the mimeographed driving instructions to the location. Frank had left them behind on the kitchen table the morning he had departed for the meeting, she explained. Curious, Alice had scanned the cover sheet headed "Deep Creek Rendezvous." It read in part, "Two story, fairly new, stone cabin 30 feet from lake; 40 yards on a slope from Highway 219." And then, in keeping with Camp Detrick's extreme security, the two-page document instructed: "Camouflage: Winter meeting of script writers, editors, authors, lecturers, sports magazines. Remove CD [Camp Detrick] decals from cars."

Alice recalled that the second page had listed the names of all the participants expected at the meeting. In addition to Frank's name, there was *Vin Ruwet, John Schwab, Joe Stubbs, Herbert Tanner*, and *Lt. Col. Everett E. Champlin*. Also listed, in a separate column, were the names of the two men who had come to her house after Frank's death, *Sidney Gottlieb* and *Robert Lashbrook*, and two additional names she had not recognized, *Allan Hughes* and *H. Bortner*. Frank's colleague, John Malinowski, whom everyone called "Mal," was the name indicated as having drawn up the directions for the meeting.

Everything was fine the morning Frank departed, Alice explained, but when he returned home on a Friday afternoon, something was extremely wrong. He looked haggard, there were dark circles under his eyes and his clothes looked disheveled, as though he'd slept in them. He was uncharacteristically distant and uncommunicative. Later that evening, after the children had gone to bed, Frank told Alice he had made "a terrible mistake." Alice recounted how Frank had said it several times, yet each time she had asked what his mistake had been, he only promised to tell her later.

"Did he tell you later?" Charles asked.

"No," Alice said. "Things got too confusing after that. He said he wanted to resign and get a new job. I didn't know what to think at that point."

"He wanted to resign?" Charles Wicks said, surprised. He knew his son-in-law had recently been promoted to Director of Plans and Assessments for Camp Detrick's ultra-secret Special Operations Division, and he had seemed pleased with his work.

Alice explained that when Frank had gone to work the following week he had attempted to resign on two separate occasions. During his second attempt, Frank's superior, Col. Ruwet, had told him he thought he needed psychiatric treatment. It was then that arrangements had been made to take Frank to New York, Alice told her parents.

"But why New York City?" her father inquired, puzzled. "Why not the hospital right there at Detrick? Or somewhere closer, like Johns Hopkins in Baltimore or Walter Reed Hospital in Washington, D.C.?"

"I'm not sure," Alice said. "I think because Vin Ruwet thought it would be best for someone in New York to see him. Someone security cleared who could talk candidly with him."

Charles Wicks said he thought that recommending psychiatric care for someone who only wanted to leave his job sounded extreme. Were there any other signs that Frank was disturbed, he asked. Alice said that, besides his uncharacteristic mood and worry about having made "a terrible mistake," there had been only one other thing that had caused her concern.

Alice described the episode that had occurred when Frank was driven to Washington, D.C., to take the flight to New York and Alice had ridden with him. They had stopped to have lunch at a Hot Shoppe in Silver Spring, Maryland on the outskirts of the Capital. When the waitress brought his food, Frank had shocked Alice by pushing the plate away saying, "I can't eat this, it's poisoned." Alice said she had asked Frank what on earth he was talking about and he replied that she wouldn't understand. A half-hour later he and Col. Ruwet had departed for New York.

"It was the last time I ever saw Frank," Alice said quietly.

"Col. Ruwet was there when he died?" Wicks asked.

"No," Alice said, "he came home before that. On Thanksgiving day, for the holiday."

"Why didn't Frank come home with him?"

"He did," Alice said. "But on the way home from the airport with Vin he decided to go back to New York."

"But why?" Wicks asked.

Alice looked down at her hands folded in her lap. There was a long pause before she answered.

"Because he was afraid he might do or say something irrational in front of the children."

"He said *what*? Why would he say that?"

"It's what Vin told me. I don't know why."

"But why would Frank be concerned about that?"

"I don't know, Pop. I really don't. I've thought about it so much... but I don't know why."

Alice did not say anything to Ina and Charles about what had happened the day Frank had unexpectedly returned home from work in the middle of the morning to tell her he was going to New York, that he had agreed to psychiatric care there; that Joe Stubbs had come home with him because, as Frank had told her, "he thought I might do you bodily harm." Alice could not bring herself to say that to anyone. It was beyond comprehension.

There followed a long silence. Charles Wicks was unsure what to say. Alice broke the long silence, telling Ina and Charles that it had been wonderful for her and the children to come to Florida to visit. Alice said she wished Frank had lived long enough to come with them. "Frank and I talked a lot about visiting," she said. "I'm sure he would have loved it here."

Alice didn't know it at the time, but Frank had often traveled to the Sunshine State, always in secret, never for rest and relaxation purposes. Frank had journeyed to Florida in special military aircraft, traveling from secret sites located in Utah and Texas, and from Carroll Island, Maryland. As chief of SOD's Planning, Training and Intelligence section, he had helped oversee a global quest to locate, collect and catalog samples of every natural and organically grown plant with lethal or hallucinogenic properties. The search, which involved Drs. William Mosher and James Moore, both from the University of Delaware, had begun in Florida and surrounding states, and quickly expanded to cover virtually every region of the globe. Heading up the search had been Dr. Friedrich Wilhelm Hoffmann, a highly trained, multi-lingual biochemist and former Nazi scientist who, in 1949, had been secretly smuggled out of Germany into the United States to work with SOD on the development of nerve gases, tabun and sarin. In 1990, Dr. Moore told investigative journalist Linda Hunt, "We were all paid by the CIA."

Around the same time that Olson died, Dr. Hoffmann, who was dubbed "Chief of Agents" at Edgewood Arsenal, began aggressive research into developing defoliants. Assisted by a large cadre of Camp Detrick biochemists, Hoffmann's research led to the creation of the notorious dioxin-laden Agent Orange, which wreaked havoc and devastation on American troops in Vietnam, as well as on the Vietnamese.

Here it is interesting to note that Dr. Frederick Hoffmann's global drug quest evolved into the CIA-created and controlled Amazon Natural Drug Co., or ANDCO as it was commonly known. Joseph Caldwell King, the CIA's former Western Hemisphere chief, who had been a major participant in the Agency's early assassination programs, oversaw the operation of ANDCO. Closely assisting King with ANDCO business was Garland Williams, the former head of the Federal Narcotics Bureau's New York branch and a former officer with the Army's Counter Intelligence Corps, who became deeply involved in the interrogation of Korean POWs. Readers shall learn much more about Williams, who was very close to George Hunter White.

Rev. Wicks, who was in his early seventies when Alice and her children visited, did not know what to make of the account that Alice provided to Ina and him that week in Florida. In his many years as a minister, someone to whom people confided their innermost thoughts and troubling experiences, he had heard few stories as perplexing as this one. He thought back now to some of the conversations he had had with his son-in-law during visits to the Olson's home.

It was the summer of 1951, during a visit to Frederick, Maryland to see Alice and Frank and their grandchildren, when Charles and Frank had had a long conversation about events in Germany and in the Communist-controlled section of that country. Frank, who had never left North America during World War II, had already traveled to Germany twice and had been shocked at what he had seen. Eastern Europe was chaotic in the early 1950s. The war had left large areas completely devastated. Whole towns and cities had been leveled to piles of rubble. In Düsseldorf alone, Frank said, nearly ninety-five percent of the houses had been destroyed. Seven million Germans had perished in the war and two million more had been left physically disabled.

Frank had told Charles that homeless families were everywhere, with nothing to eat and no shelter. In Berlin, in the first two years following the war, over 50,000 people had died, from starvation, hypothermia, and disease. Eleven million German soldiers were held as POWs immediately after the war. In Eastern Europe, thirty-five million people were displaced from their homes. Children by the thousands died of starvation.

"I've never seen anything like it," Frank told Charles. "The pain and suffering was unbelievable. Everywhere I saw people who reminded me of my parents, and children that looked like my own."

Frank explained that following the Potsdam Conference in summer 1945, Germany had been divided into four zones of occupation. Traveling inside the former Greater Reich was an exercise in treachery. Fortified checkpoints and barricades heavily guarded by American, Russian, French, or British troops were everywhere. Traveling within and throughout the zones were countless intelligence agents, counter-intelligence agents, double and triple agents, paramilitary bands, collaborators, informers, defectors, and fugitive war criminals. It was commonplace for any of these people to be snatched off the streets, interrogated, beaten, raped, tortured and murdered. Assassination in public places, work sites and homes was elevated to an art form. The brutal and bizarre became mere backdrops for reality. In East Germany thousands were arrested for speaking out against or questioning the newly installed Communist government. Many would never be heard from or seen again. Maintaining one's sense of morality, patriotism and purpose was difficult in such an environment regardless of which side you were on.

Some Americans could not take the pandemonium, Frank said. He told Charles about an American named George Shaw Wheeler who had defected. In April 1950, Wheeler and his wife Eleanor asked the Czechoslovak Communist government to grant them asylum. Wheeler, at the time, had been working for the Department of Defense (then the War Department) in the American zone of Germany. His job was directing the activities of the Army's De-Nazification Branch, closely related to Project Paperclip. After their defection, Wheeler held a press conference to explain that the central motive for their crossing over was their indignation over what he termed a "typical gangster plot" by American authorities in their "brutal and unlawful" treatment of Czechoslovak citizens and others. Wheeler claimed he was "ashamed" of the activities of the Army's Counter Intelligence Corps, the CIA, and of those American journalists who looked the other way and covered up illegal acts committed by Americans.

Wheeler also claimed that he was "disgusted" with high-ranking Army officials who constantly intervened to protect Nazis that they were interested in sending to America for work there.

Frank had not told his father-in-law he had met Wheeler in late-winter 1950, as part of one of his early SOD assignments: interviewing and assessing a number of former Nazi biochemists for possible work at Edgewood Arsenal in Maryland.

When Alice and her children left Indian Rocks Beach for home, Ina Wicks told her oldest grandchild, Eric, "You have some big shoes to fill at home," and that he "had to take special care of his sister and brother." Ina took Alice's hand and said, "You're going to have to be extra strong now."

Back home in Maryland, Alice Olson did her best to get on with life without Frank. But coping with his death became increasingly difficult. For a few months, Alice's spirits were greatly lifted when she began receiving the amorous attentions of a local man. Friends noticed a lively sparkle returning to Alice's eyes and that she was smiling and laughing again, but then things went all wrong; the man was accused of taking immoral liberties with minors. Following this, Alice sank even deeper into depression. Some people who knew her well say she was overcome with self-doubt and confusion about Frank's sudden and strange death. For solace Alice turned to alcohol, and within a few years she had become heavily addicted. Alice's world slowly began to fall apart, and for the next twenty years, apart from the occasional inquisitive question from one of her children about their vanished father, or an angry outburst from Alice in response, Frank Olson's death was rarely spoken about.

17

June 9, 1954
CIA Headquarters, Washington, D.C.

S ecurity Research Staff chief Paul Gaynor leans back in his chair to read a memorandum he has just received from Morse Allen of his staff. In December 1950, forty-three year old Allen had been assigned to head Project Bluebird, and then to direct Bluebird's successor, Project Artichoke, until that project became largely overshadowed by Sidney Gottlieb's MKULTRA program. The memorandum Paul Gaynor is about to read is stamped *SECRET* and the subject is "*PROJECT MKULTRA*." It reads:

Sometime during the fall of 1953, Mr. Sidney Gottlieb made a tour of the Far East for reasons unknown, but undoubtedly in connection with official business of TSS. According to [redacted] and according to other sources [redacted], GOTTLIEB gave out samples of psychogenic drugs and ran some tests on various people out there using this drug. It is not definitely certain that it was LSD nor do we know the details Mr. GOTTLIEB used in describing the chemical but this appears to be the likely chemical. GOTTLIEB also is reported to have given some of the chemical to some of our staff officers in the [redacted] with the idea that the staff officer would place the chemical in the drinking water to be used by a speaker at a political rally in the [redacted]. Results unknown.

Why GOTTLIEB gave out the chemicals or what he said in connection with them or the exact days these chemicals were distributed and to whom are unclear. Mr. [redacted] and Mr. [redacted] are interested in all information along this line and [redacted] should be questioned in detail concerning this.

It has been reported that chemicals, pills or ampoules, having a psychogenic effect have been passed around to some of our people in [redacted] and whether these were handed out by GOTTLIEB or other TSS people is unknown. It is [redacted and unreadable]. [Redacted], who recently returned from Germany, said he heard of staff officers who had been given the chemicals and used them on subjects during interrogations. No specific information. He should check for further information. It is also reported that [redacted] refused to interrogate, on the polygraph, a subject who was being held captive, and was given a chemical (possibly one referred to above) and in this connection he was supported in his refusal by [redacted]. However, this said incident occurred after Craig's [unknown person] absence. [Redacted] was reported to have told [redacted] to run the cases regardless [redacted]'s views and opinions in the matter. Since it is well established that subjects under effect of drugs are not suitable polygraph material, this point is of [unreadable word] interest. This matter should be checked out with [redacted] and [redacted]. [Redacted] has no information on the above.

[Redacted] recently received information that the [redacted] have been working for TSS secretly on a project known as MKULTRA at the [redacted] apparently doing testing work on drugs and drugs in combination with hypnosis. Details are lacking.

Back in 1943, OSS was attempting to study drugs which might be useful in the interrogation of prisoners of war. Connected with the experiments was one Major George H. White, an Army officer and probably a G-2 man. White conducted experiments particularly using Marijuana, and made some reports on these which we have in our files under DRUGS-OSS Research. White apparently left OSS, date unknown, but it appears that White or some one else by the name of White has currently been picked up by TSS and is engaged in doing secret work on drugs at an apartment in New York City which TSS has hired for White. According to our information, this apartment is well equipped, including two-way mirrors, and White gives to visitors the various chemicals, which he apparently is testing for TSS. However, we have received some information that White may have given "aphrodisiacs" to people for personal reasons. We are also informed that any effort to tamper with this project MKULTRA is not permitted and it is under this MKULTRA project that White is now working.

There is some reason to believe that GOTTLIEB and probably this White were present at the experimentation which resulted in the death of an Army officer by suicide sometime around Thanksgiving Day in New York City. This Army officer allegedly jumped out a window to his death after taking LSD. Our information clearly reflects that GOTTLIEB was in on the experiment; however, the writer has seen no proof of this. It is not known, however, as to whether or not this experimental situation, which led to the death of the Army officer, occurred prior to or after GOTTLIEB's visit to the Orient, and this question is one that must be resolved.

Having finished reading the memorandum, Gaynor places it on his desk and puzzles over the document's closing question. Nothing in all his years working for the CIA leads him to imagine that over forty years later a Manhattan assistant district attorney would seriously contemplate the same question.

18

November 23, 1956
Camp Detrick, Maryland

Agnes Tanner was worried sick. Her husband, Herbert, had been ill for three years now, and in the last few months things had gotten worse. Herbert had had his first seizure in December 1953, about two weeks after he had come home from a scientific meeting held at Deep Creek Lake, Maryland. Agnes knew Herbert had gone there because he had remarked a couple days before leaving for the meeting that some consultants to SOD had selected the secluded site, a favorite spot Herbert and Agnes enjoyed visiting at least once or twice a year. Herbert referred to Deep Creek Lake as their "hideaway spot," and Agnes loved going there so that Herbert could get away from the pressures of work at Camp Detrick and she could have him all to herself.

"It's going to seem strange going there without you, Boss," Herbert had said. *Boss.* That was Herbert's affectionate nickname for Agnes. A lot of people at Camp Detrick called Herbert "Herb," but Agnes never did. To her he was always Herbert. At times, she would refer to him as Dr. Herbert. And now Dr. Herbert's mysterious illness, which had plagued him for years, was worsening.

"You have to go see somebody," Agnes had pleaded with Herbert when he first fell ill. "You can't go on like this."

"It'll be okay, Boss. Don't you worry any, I'll be fine."

It always went like that; Herbert would just brush things off. Would not discuss what was wrong with him. When he had his second seizure, more prolonged than the first, she had asked, "At least tell me what you think is causing this. What's wrong?"

"I can't tell you," said Herbert.

"But why?"

"I just can't tell you. That's all. Please, don't ask me again."

Agnes was accustomed to the secrecy surrounding Herbert's work, but this was different. Much different. This was her husband's life that might be at stake.

Agnes remembered Herbert's first seizure. They had gone Christmas shopping in Washington for the day and they were driving out of the city on the way home. Herbert was at the wheel and suddenly he pulled off the road into a filling station. He sat back in his seat and groaned, his body jerking. Agnes was beside herself with fear.

"What is it, Herbert? What's wrong?"

Herbert groaned again and muttered something.

"What?"

"Where are we? What is this place?"

Agnes threw her door open and ran around the car to the driver's side. She opened Herbert's door and carefully helped him slide across the seat to the passenger's side. He slumped against the door and stared glassy eyed down at the floor. She took the wheel and a few miles down the road Herbert had come out of whatever had taken hold of him.

Before she could talk him into seeing a doctor, it had happened again a week later. As they were sitting down to dinner, Herbert fell from his chair onto the floor and lay there, semi conscious for nearly five minutes. It happened a third time, ten days later, as Herbert was preparing to go to bed.

Herbert Tanner had never had a seizure in his life before December 1953. Agnes became more insistent that he see a doctor and he finally relented, but he refused to go to the Detrick hospital for fear that people he worked with would find out he was ill. He went to a private physician in Washington, D.C. When Herbert came home from his doctor's visit he told her everything was going to be fine. The doctor had given him some medication. Agnes was greatly relieved, but the medicine seemed to have no effect and the seizures happened again and again.

After Herbert had begun having seizures, he had been unable to sleep for more than two or three hours at a time. He would get up in the middle of the night and pace the floor, back and forth, back and forth, sometimes for an hour or longer. Pacing, he talked to himself, often saying, "I can't find the answers. I can't find the answers anymore."

Beginning with Herbert's fifth seizure, his performance at work became seriously affected. He had lost his power of concentration, grew tired easily and would often momentarily forget what he was doing or where he was.

One night after dinner, two years into Herbert's illness, Agnes asked, "Did something happen the time you went to Deep Creek Lake?"

Herbert was quiet for a while, and then said, "Why are you asking that?"

"I'm not sure, just a feeling. I guess it's because that's the time I connect everything with... and I saw Alice Olson the other day in the grocery store, and I remembered that was right before Frank died."

"Nothing happened there," Herbert said. "Nothing at all."

But clearly something had happened somewhere, and something was seriously wrong with Herbert.

Agnes wondered about the young man who had come home with Herbert one evening and had stayed for dinner. His name was Robert Lashbrook. Perhaps he knew something about what was wrong with her husband; it had been obvious from the way Lashbrook talked that he was quite familiar with Herbert's work and SOD. Agnes had heard from some of the other Detrick wives that the CIA had several men working closely with SOD, and she was sure Lashbrook was one of them. He had come to their house only a few weeks after Herbert had gone to the Deep Creek Lake meeting; in fact, it had been only a week after Frank Olson had died in New York. Herbert had called him Bob, and Agnes found him to be a delightful conservationist. Agnes cooked seasoned steak that night, one of her many specialties that Herbert loved. While Herbert and Bob talked, Agnes overheard Bob make reference to the Deep Creek Lake meeting. After Lashbrook left that evening, Herbert mentioned that Bob had not wanted to eat at the Detrick Officer's Club because he hadn't wanted anyone to see him.

"Goodness, why not?" Agnes had asked.

Herbert waved her question off. "I don't know," he said.

Agnes knew better than to ask again. Herbert would never say anything more on the subject. It was not at all uncommon for Dr. Herbert to go away for meetings and to tell her nothing whatsoever about them. Agnes knew that most of his work was top-secret and that he could never discuss it with anyone outside SOD. But still there were lots of social gatherings that included all of Herbert's colleagues, and Agnes couldn't help but hear bits and pieces of gossip. Agnes, years later, recalled what it was like:

> There were parties on weekends, big parties, with loads of people blowing off steam and acting silly, but work was never discussed at these gatherings. Never by the men, but we wives would talk and without fail things would come out. Over time you could piece a lot together, if you tried.... After Frank Olson died a lot of us women did our best to help Alice out of her doldrums. She felt somehow that it was her fault that Frank had died the way that he did. She wrapped herself up in guilt and wouldn't hear that she had no blame about anything. Over the months I heard lots of things about how Frank died. Things that didn't fit with the story we had all been told. Joe Stubbs, who I think knew more than he let on, couldn't make sense of Frank's death. Eventually, we all knew that somehow the Deep Creek Lake meeting was part of it... We knew that other Detrick men had been at the meeting and that they too had problems after. There was talk that John Malinowski and Everett Champlin had serious problems... Herbert told me to ignore the gossip. He always refused to talk about it, but I could see that just the mention of the Deep Creek Lake meeting caused him to turn away and to withdraw into himself.

Dr. Herbert Tanner, with a PhD in physical chemistry from Stanford University, is considered by many to have been one of the founding fathers of Camp Detrick. He first came to Camp Detrick in April 1943, about two weeks before Frank Olson arrived. Herbert had happily left behind a well-paid job at Dupont Chemical in Delaware to do his share in the war effort. After the war, he stayed on to do more than his share. He loved the work and felt he was making a difference in the world. By the late-1940s, Herbert was chief of Detrick's Munitions Division, responsible for countless innovations in the program. He and Dr. Harold W. Batchelor, who had come from Kansas State University, were instrumental in designing a huge, bombproof cloud chamber for testing aerosol particles. The chamber, which weighed over 130 tons, was dubbed the 8-Ball.

In late-1954 and 1955, Tanner would assist Batchelor in reviewing a huge amount of biological data Batchelor had gathered in Germany from former Nazi scientists recruited through Project Paperclip. In 1950, along with Frank Olson, Joe Stubbs, Ben Wilson and others, Herbert joined Detrick's Special Operations Division. Tanner became chief of SOD's Device Branch at the same time that Ben Wilson was appointed head of SOD's Agent Branch. Frank Olson worked very closely with both groups. Wilson's Agent Branch was responsible for selecting out of the world's most infectious microorganisms those best suiting the CIA's objectives with its Projects Bluebird, Artichoke and MKULTRA, as well as Camp Detrick's MKNAOMI program run in concert with the CIA's TSS branch. Tanner's Device Branch would design and produce the delivery systems for the infectious agents selected by Wilson's shop. Over the years the Device Branch produced such items as cigarette lighters that sprayed deadly germs, and shoe heels that released lethal poisons. Its list of biological items would put James Bond's suppliers to shame.

In November 1956 Herbert was told by personnel officers at Fort Detrick (Camp Detrick had been renamed by then) that they were "strongly advising" him to retire. Herbert Tanner was only sixty-two years old, had hardly ever taken a day off in over twenty years, and now his days of doing the work he loved were over. Later he was briefly rehired by Fort Detrick to work in the Safety Division, but Herbert knew it was "make-work," and it was outside his field.

Herbert Tanner continued to have seizures and eventually he suffered a severe stroke in 1961. Shortly thereafter, he died.

Agnes felt that her world collapsed when Herbert passed away. She was lost without him. One day about a year after his death, Agnes drove from Frederick to Deep Creek Lake. It was late fall, a grey, dreary day. As if on cue, it began to rain just as she stepped from her car. She could not shake the feeling that something had happened here when Herbert had attended that November meeting years before. Another fourteen years would pass before Agnes Tanner learned anything about what had occurred at Deep Creek Lake and what had happened to her husband.

BOOK TWO
From Brainwashing to LSD

Introduction

Contrary to what TSS chief Dr. Willis Gibbons told Inspector General Lyman Kirkpatrick, and contrary to what Kirkpatrick wrote in his report to DCI Allen Dulles concerning Frank Olson's death, the CIA never impounded any LSD, much less called a halt to experiments with the drug. In fact, as numerous declassified CIA documents reveal, CIA-sponsored projects using LSD and other psychochemicals actually accelerated after Olson died. Indeed, on December 17, 1953, about two weeks after Olson's death, TSS Chemical Branch chief Sidney Gottlieb and his deputy Robert Lashbrook traveled together from CIA headquarters to New York City specifically for this purpose. In New York, Gottlieb and Lashbrook met with George Hunter White, Federal Narcotics Bureau agent, at the CIA's Greenwich Village safe house. There, at 81 Bedford Street, according to White's date book notations, a CIA "tech squad" upgraded the sound recording and observation equipment in the CIA-funded house.

Five days later, Gottlieb was back in Washington, D.C. and telephoned White with official approval of a "trial run" to test the new installations at the Bedford Street location. During subsequent weeks, several additional "LSD tests" were conducted on unidentified and unwitting subjects at the Greenwich Village safe house.

Several additional CIA documents vividly illustrate the Agency's acceleration of LSD experimentation. One such document is a memorandum, written three-and-a-half months after Olson's death, to CIA director Allen Dulles, deputy director Charles P. Cabell, and Directorate of Plans chief Frank Wisner. The memorandum's lead sentence states:

> Our studies of unconventional warfare have included for some time the potential agent Lysergic Acid Diethylamide (LSD), which appears to be better adapted than known drugs to both interrogation of prisoners and use against troops or civilians.

Attached to the memorandum was a preliminary study that urged further investigation and aggressive pursuit of the "intelligence implications of LSD." Seven months later, following the in-house release of a more detailed study of LSD, Frank Wisner and Dr. Willis Gibbons enthusiastically informed DCI Dulles that the Indiana-based pharmaceutical firm Eli Lilly and Company "has developed a practicable commercial total synthesis of LSD using readily available raw materials" making it entirely possible "that in a matter of months LSD could be available in tonnage quantities." In Frank Wisner's words:

> Most of the significant information currently available on the disabling effects of LSD on humans has been obtained from the research activities supported during the past three years by the Chemical Division of TSS under the direction of Dr. Sidney Gottlieb. TSS is continuing its research effort toward developing a capability for covert use of this material and the availability of LSD in large quantities will not affect our program. However, we feel it is highly advisable that certain components of the Department of Defense be advised of both the new synthesis at Lilly and our data on the effects of this material on human beings.

The conclusion is inescapable: If anything, Frank Olson's death invigorated an already aggressive program researching LSD's offensive and defensive potentialities. What was the CIA attempting to do with LSD and other psychochemicals? What were the Agency's objectives in experimenting so widely with the drug? What relationship did the Korean War have to the CIA's relentless researching of LSD? What role did the U.S. military play in the covert development and use of LSD? What impact did the CIA's projects Bluebird and ARTICHOKE have on the creation of MKULTRA? To answer these questions one has to go back to the late 1940s and early 1950s and examine the genesis of the CIA's interest in interrogation techniques, brainwashing, and behavior modification.

1

Brainwashing

At the time that all this took place, we felt the country was in crisis. We were just at the hottest part of the Cold War. We felt an aggressive attack by the Soviet Union could not be ruled out, and I will only make the analogy, that, you know, in a wartime situation, things are done that you would never do in some other situation. People get killed. People kill other people. And their justification for it is that their land is threatened, and it was for that kind of reason that we felt it was justified to do this, and we tried to find a mechanism that existed in the drug world that seemed to be a good mechanism to do this.
— Dr. Sidney Gottlieb, September 22, 1995

It is a truism that no nation can expect to survive unless it knows the nature of its enemy and unless it maintains the moral tone as well as the armed strength necessary to defend itself against him. We Americans have had available to us for a quarter of a century a long stream of testimonials starting at least as early as the Moscow trials of 1936, which reveal to us the new methods that Communists use to manipulate the minds of human beings— a technique called variously indoctrination, brainwashing, thought reform, and other things. Call it what you will, it is the total psychological weapon by means which, equally with its sputniks and armed might, Soviet Russia firmly expects to conquer the rest of the world.
— Eugene Kinkead, 1959

Nobody did more to advance interest and alarm about brainwashing than Edward Hunter.
— CIA official John Gittinger, 1979

E dward Hunter did not want anyone to know he was working for the CIA. Under the terms of his securizzzzty and employment agreement with the Agency he was to appear to be a self-supporting, independent writer and journalist. As far as his readers were concerned, he had no hidden agenda, no biases, and no affiliation to anything or anyone other than pursuit of the truth. That his preferred topic was "brainwashing" appeared to be nothing more than the result of his extensive travels throughout Asia and professional time spent in Singapore, Hong Kong, and Tokyo. His career as a foreign correspondent had begun in 1927, and he had served as a reporter and editor for the Hankow *Herald* and the Peiping *Leader*. Somewhere along the way, he developed a keen interest in psychological warfare as practiced by the Japanese and the Chinese. Also along the way, like many journalists of his day, he joined the CIA as an undercover operative.

Like other journalists, Hunter often approached life behind a shield of skepticism; he was cynical but deliberate in his choice of subjects. He wrote with authority and command, making it difficult to tell, even today, when his writing morphs from the truth into the party line, the puffed up CIA propaganda he was directed to put before the public and for which the CIA was paying him.

Hunter's books and articles were intended to serve as bellwethers on the increasingly sophisticated and expanded use by governments of psychological warfare, or "brainwashing," as he preferred to call it. The cover of his widely read book, *Brainwashing*, bore the bold come-on, "The True and Terrible Story of Men Who Suffered and Defied the Most Diabolical Red Torture."

Like many CIA operatives in the Agency's early days, Hunter was no neophyte to his assigned duties. When World War II broke out, he had joined the OSS as a propaganda specialist, and when OSS was disbanded he went into the Strategic Services Unit, the federal intelligence agency formed by Executive Order immediately after World War II. SSU had been created from the Secret Intelligence and Counterintelligence branches of the OSS. Said Hunter in 1978, shortly before his death:

> Everyone was worried and upset that SSU was going to be a sort of peacetime American Gestapo. SSU reported to the Secretary of the Army, but the guys who were pushing hard for the CIA...Kirkpatrick, Wisner, Dulles...they were pretty unhappy about this, but in the end they all got what they wanted.

When the CIA was created in 1947, Hunter, without missing a beat, left SSU and became an Agency employee. Asked thirty years later for the official date, he said he was not sure, but "it was right around the time the Korean War was beginning."

Long before his intelligence work, Hunter had been a reporter at the *Newark Ledger* in New Jersey and then moved on and up to the *Chicago Tribune*'s Paris office. After Paris he began covering events in Japan and China for various news services from about 1925 until the time of the Japanese detachment of Manchukuo to China. He also extensively covered the Second Italo-Abyssinian War between Italy and Ethiopia in 1935-36. About this time, Hunter developed a strong interest in psychological warfare methods and the use of propaganda, and, on his own, began intensively researching both subjects. Recounted Hunter in the late 1950s:

In Indochina, I covered the trials of some of the terrorists who had engaged in such propaganda warfare pressures as rolling a hand grenade down the aisle of a children's cinema when a Walt Disney movie was being shown. Those on trial spoke the same language, with the same expressions and the same explanations, as I had heard from Red China, and had read in the diaries kept by the guerrillas in Malaya. A set of Soviet Chinese textbooks were smuggled out of China for me. They were being used in every school from Dairen in Manchuria to Canton in the south. I came across the same teachings as I heard in the interviews, read in the diaries, and listened to at the trials. One day I interviewed secretly a young man who had come out of Red China on a mission. I had known his family. During the interview, he used the phrase 'his nao' or 'wash brain.' I immediately stopped him, asking what he meant. He laughed and said, 'Oh, that's nothing; it's only something we say when close relatives or friends get together.' When somebody said something the Peiping Government wouldn't like, a relative or friend was liable to say to him, 'Watch out, you'll get your brains washed.' That was the first time I heard the word 'brainwashing.' I was the first to use the word in writing in any language, and the first to use it in a speech in any language except for that small group of Chinese. That and its connotation, against this background that I have been weaving ever since I started in journalism, especially during the years since the civil war in China became acute, was like a streak of lightning, clarifying the pattern of which I had already discerned its shadows. Brainwashing was the new procedure, built up out of all earlier processes of persuasion, using the Pavlovian approach to make people react in a way determined by a central authority, exactly as bees in a hive.

Years later, in an interview, Hunter claims, "When I first heard about brainwashing, I wrote a memo to the [CIA], but nobody was really interested. It took a while for things to catch on... but about this same time the Pentagon developed an interest all on their own...I assume because of what was happening in Korea."

Hunter maintained in the same interview that the CIA "had nothing to do with the publication of his first book, *Brainwashing in Red China*, published in 1951, about eighteen months after he went to work for the Agency. "I did my own work on brainwashing," Hunter said. "The Agency didn't tell me what to write or when to write it. I was my own man, not always an organizational man, but loyal and honest to the last."

In 1958, testifying as a "writer and foreign journalist" before the House Un-American Activities Committee — which was completely unaware of his CIA ties at the time — Hunter told them:

I remember when I was a young man, every personnel department was looking for leadership qualities. What was sought was a man's capacity as an individual to achieve new things. Today that is not even considered by personnel departments in their employment policies. They ask, instead, if the man 'gets along' with everybody. *They do not ask what is his individuality; they ask how he conforms.* When we raise a young man to believe at all costs he must get on with everyone, we have put him into a state of mind that almost guarantees, if he falls into the hands of the enemy, such as the Communists, that he will react as he had been raised, to try 'to get on,' because he must not be 'antisocial.' *Being 'antisocial' has become the cardinal sin in our society. We have to again go back to characteristics of ours which made us, as individuals, say that what is right is right, and whether or not it is antisocial makes no difference.* The young man who broadcast for the Red Chinese was simply 'getting along' as he had been taught to do by our educators. [Italics original.]

The "young man" Hunter was referring to was one of an allegedly large group of American POWs who either "collaborated with the enemy" or "defected" after captivity to North Korea. [The number of apparent "collaborators" was said to be "large," but the actual number who opted not to repatriate was 21. M] According to Hunter, "unlike other wars the United States had fought, a relatively high percentage of American troops defected to the enemy side after being captured." The reason for this, in Hunter's view, was "brainwashing." Reports of intensive interviews conducted later with some of these POWs, led some American psychologists to conclude that sleep-deprivation, torture, and other psychological manipulations aimed at controlling the minds of POWs had effectively broken their "autonomy as individuals" and "allegiance to country," rendering them "puppets acting at the will of their Communist masters." People in the United States were said to be flabbergasted and alarmed that American troops had apparently defected in large numbers. Countless articles about this new phenomenon appeared in newspapers across America, exacerbating the belief that something dreadful was occurring. After the word "brainwashing" first appeared in articles in the *Miami Daily News* and *New Leader* in September and October 1950, suddenly hardly a day went by without a major news story devoted to the subject.

Eventually, as with any germ of thought that saturates the collective consciousness of the American public, Hollywood and book publishers would latch on to "brainwashing" as a means of entertainment and making money. In quick succession, three feature films — *The Manchurian Candidate, Telefon,* and *The Ipcress File* — hit big screens nationwide. (Amazingly, Hollywood has continued to this day to craft films around themes of brainwashing, including movies marketed to children, best exemplified by the 2004 release, *The Spongebob Squarepants Movie,* within which the beloved Plankton controls the minds of the citizens of Bikini Bottom, forcing them to do his work.)

Recently completed "authoritative" studies of the numbers of U.S. personnel captured or interned during the Korean War provide the total of 7,245

American POWs. Of this number, an astounding 2,806 died in captivity, mainly due to starvation and disease, with some beaten to death or shot, a mortality rate of forty-three percent; 4,418 were returned to U.S. military control, and 21 refused repatriation.

The number of American soldiers who refused repatriation was extremely low (about one-half of one percent of American POWs in Korea). The number is further dwarfed when compared to the numbers of defectors from previous wars. Indeed, a strong argument can be made that the more significant number was the total number of American POWs who died in captivity: 2,730, or 38%.

Moreover, the panic over brainwashing seems overblown, indeed deliberately manufactured and spread. Looking back, it appears remarkable that the American government, as well as numerous social scientists and psychologists, reacted as they did, quickly assuming the veracity of claims about brainwashing in the absence of facts or evidence, while seeming oblivious to the far greater phenomenon of mass manipulation by the Nazi propaganda machine. In reality, captured American troops in Korea were not brainwashed, but instead were subjected to extremely intense programs of education and re-education by their Chinese captors.

Meanwhile, brainwashing, as a practice or technique with the primary intent to influence, persuade, and indoctrinate was not unfamiliar to the United States and its institutions. The American techniques for consumer advertising and mass marketing had already taken on many of the principle characteristics of brainwashing. In many ways, the word 'brainwashing' arrived in the Western world's lexicon at a fortuitous time in the Cold War when words were needed to fuel, shape and structure attitudes about Communism. In the political arena, McCarthyism can be viewed, in many ways, as a means of brainwashing American citizens about the dangers from "reds" who were said to have infiltrated the U.S. government.

Writer Raymond B. Lech described what he learned about the experience of American POWs in Korea in this way:

> The most common term used to describe what went on is *brainwashing*, although the communists did not wash any brains. Rather, they were intent on filling them. 'From daybreak in the morning until approximately two hours after darkness,' recalled Maj. Milford Stanley, 'we were subjected to continuous indoctrination, reading and discussing Marxism and other communist propaganda defacing the United States and United Nations.'

Were American POWs brainwashed in Korea as is today widely believed in the United States? Perhaps a 1956 U.S. Department of the Army publication best answers this question:

> In Korea, American prisoners of war were subjected to group indoctrination, not 'brainwashing.' Many POWs were put in solitary confinement

for various reasons, such as punishment for infractions of camp rules. However, this type of isolation was not used in conjunction with any 'brainwashing' process. The exhaustive efforts of several Government agencies failed to reveal even one conclusively documented case of the actual 'brainwashing' of an American prisoner of war in Korea.

Like Edward Hunter, Albert D. Biderman was a seminal figure in the Cold War's brainwashing programs. Biderman, a traditional academician, was a Senior Research Associate in Social Psychology at the Bureau of Social Science Research and a principle scientific investigator for the United States Air Force's probe into "the stresses associated with interrogation and captivity." Throughout the early 1950s, and beyond, the CIA, as well as the various military intelligence services, indirectly funded much of Biderman's work. Over the years he worked with a virtual who's-who of prominent CIA grantees and sub-contractors, many of them fellow academics.

Immediately following World War II, and early in his professional career, Biderman was recruited to participate in what he later termed "a global program of interrogation of German scientists on the results of Nazi research, as well as other matters." The program, which was soon dubbed Project Paperclip, eventually resulted in bringing hundreds of German scientists, many of them "former" Nazi party members and former SS officers, to America to work with the United States military and the defense industries. Biderman for a time worked alongside researchers from Camp Detrick and Edgewood Arsenal, as well as with notorious future MKULTRA subcontractor, Dr. D. Ewen Cameron. Cameron, a psychiatrist with McGill University's Rockefeller-funded Allan Memorial Institute in Montreal, had traveled to Germany in November 1945 with a team of Allied psychologists to examine and interrogate Nazi Rudolph Hess and other Nazi war criminals awaiting trial at Nuremberg.

One of the Germans interrogated by Biderman was Frederick W. Williams, who, after being recruited by an early incarnation of the CIA, was let go because of his rabid, uncontrollable anti-communist sentiments. For a short while, after Williams was hired by the Americans, Biderman worked under him "on surveying occupied Germany." Later, in 1951, Biderman went to work for the Air Force's Human Resource Research Institute at Maxwell airbase in Alabama. Here, he spent his time on a number of projects, some still classified, and he had his first contact with the CIA front, Society for the Investigation of Human Ecology (later shortened to Human Ecology Society).

Biderman, in 1978, said that he had known that the Society was funded by the CIA, but that initially he had been informed only that the group was operated under an endowment through "headache and pain expert" Dr. Harold G. Wolff, professor of medicine at Cornell University and soon-to-be president of the American Neurological Association, who specialized in migraines, among other things. Biderman's first project for the Air Force's Research Institute and the Human Ecology Society was Operation REPAIR. It was a top secret program to study the effects of brainwashing and other forms of stress on American POWs held in Korea. The project was overseen by Lieutenant Colonel James L. Monroe, a physician and Air Force officer who would later head the Human Ecology Fund. Monroe was also a high-ranking officer in the Pentagon's Prisoner of War Office. He supervised Biderman's work and, beginning about 1956, was assigned by TSS official John Gittinger to personally oversee the horrendous "psychic driving" and coma "therapy" experiments of Dr. D. Ewen Cameron at McGill.

Biderman's first contact with the Human Ecology Society came when he "was invited to a meeting about sharing mostly classified information I had gathered for the Research Institute concerning what was happening to people interned in China." At the meeting, Biderman met Dr. Lawrence Hinkle, John Gittinger, and Lt. Col. Monroe. During the six years Biderman worked for the Air Force's Research Institute, he received at least one large grant from Drs. Wolff and Hinkle to research and write extensively about POW's in Korea; the work was funded by the MKULTRA project.

TSS psychologist John Gittinger, together with Drs. Wolff and Hinkle, had helped organize the Society for the Investigation of Human Ecology in 1952. In 1983, Gittinger was deposed in a lawsuit filed against the CIA for harm done by Dr. Cameron's experiments at McGill University. Gittinger's deposition is revealing:

> Gittinger: It was during 1954 that the Society for the Investigation of Human Ecology was organized and augmented. It was done with the idea...it has been the idea all the way along in relationship to this to be a research organization. Dr. Wolff was involved in this because he was a very...a very famous neurologist. And when I first met them that year [in 1954, when Gittinger was hospitalized for a serious back injury at Cornell Hospital, and was assigned at the same time by the CIA to work on brainwashing projects with Drs. Wolff and he, Wolff, was the doctor for Allen Dulles' son who was very ill up in that area, and a very close friend of Dulles, who was DCI and quite eager to have Dr. Wolff participate in any way that he professionally felt that he should.
>
> In connection with the work that they were doing there, they began to realize that they needed to kind of expand a bit, so the Society was formed under Dr. Wolff's aegis. He selected what was the original Board of Directors, which I believe are printed in the first and only record of the Society, the public record for the Society... I was largely responsible for beginning to set up a certain amount of work...and was charged with the responsibility of trying to get people, recruit people, who would be the responsible people there.
>
> Question: *Who were these people?*
> Gittinger: I had met Jim Monroe, Colonel Jim Monroe, who at that time was part of the time on active duty with the Air Force but more

often than not was not. And I recruited him to become the director of the Society.

Question: *Others?*

Gittinger: I also talked to Walter Pasternak, who was a neighbor of mine, talked him into coming to the Society because our idea... was to work the whole area of behavioral sciences. And by the behavioral sciences I mean things like psychology, psychiatry, social anthropology, and sociology, and so forth. This organization was set up totally under the Agency [CIA].... At about the same time, I had been asked to come back to Washington and set up the Behavioral Activity Branch in the Chemical Division of TSS. And myself, and a fellow named Robert Goodnow, were the Behavioral Activities Branch.... The reason we were in the Chemical Division was because there was a great deal of interest in trying to develop methods and techniques of understanding better interrogation techniques and techniques used by the Soviets and Chinese... This was at the time, at the beginning of all these problems connected to brainwashing. And consequently we were urging the Human Ecology Society to do anything they could in finding out what various people were working on in the areas of influencing human behavior, interrogation, and brainwashing... This was around the time the... Society looked at the work of Biderman, who worked with the Society... and the work... of others.

Now, at about this period of time, I saw this article... this article Psychic Driving, which appeared in The American Journal of Psychiatry in 1956... it was by Dr. [D. Ewen] Cameron, and I became interested in Cameron... in his work...

Question: *Did you know [as stated in his application for funds to the CIA's Human Ecology Society] that Cameron was going to use LSD in his work?*

Gittinger: I did not know that... I had no reason to have been interested in whether he was going to use LSD or not.

Question: *Did you or didn't you read [Cameron's] application?*

Gittinger: I undoubtedly read the application, sir. I do not remember it at all...

Question: *Do you mean after the Olson death, you wouldn't have noticed the sentence that says, "We propose to use LSD-25 and other similar agents as a means of breaking down the ongoing pattern of behavior"? Do you mean that didn't mean anything to you?*

Gittinger: Well, not in the context of the way you put it, sir. I didn't have anything to do with Dr. Olson's death, and that's the only thing that I knew of in relationship to this, that work was being done in Canada on LSD, in Saskatchewan. They were working on schizophrenics but we were not...and we, I suppose I should say I was not...I was not interested in LSD research, period. This was not my expertise and not anything that I had... and we certainly would not have been interested in LSD research under

the aegis of the Human Ecology Society because this was not particularly
what they would do. And if you go back and read originally when we
began to do it, [Cameron] was not talking about drugs at all. We were not
interested in it because [Cameron] was using drugs [in his work]... that I
can say categorically.

Question: *Did you do anything to have the Society tell him that he
shouldn't use LSD?*

Gittinger: Absolutely not.

Question: *You can't remember a sentence about LSD after a man died
from having the Agency give him LSD?*

Gittinger: Well, I didn't know that.

Question: *In 1957 you didn't know that Olson had died from LSD?*

Gittinger: I did not.

Question: *Look, friend, you and I are both pretty close to our Mak-
er and let me tell you that I think you have done something terrible,
but lying about it today you ought to think about.*

Another prominent name in the annals of military and CIA research on brainwashing is Dr. Robert J. Lifton. Lifton, whom readers will meet again in the final
chapters of this book, served from 1951 to 1953 as an Air Force psychiatrist in
Japan and Korea. On his last military assignment, which may have extended into
1954, Lifton returned from the United States to Korea as part of Project REPAIR
to interview, along with other Air Force and Army psychiatrists, American troops
returning from North Korea, where they had been POWs held by the Chinese
Communists. The understanding was, as Lifton once said, that the POWs "had
been put through a process that we later came to call 'thought reform.'"

Among the project's other interviewers were CIA psychologist John Gittinger and Dr. James L. Monroe. After the Korean War ended, Lifton, who has
steadfastly claimed that he never worked for the CIA, spent eighteen months in
Hong Kong researching Chinese 'brainwashing" techniques. In 1961, the fruits
of his research were published in the book, *Thought Reform and the Psychology of Totalism: A study of Brainwashing in China*. ("Totalism," a word first
coined by Lifton, is his term for the characteristics of ideological movements
and organizations that desire total control over human behavior and thought.)
Lifton's book is a meticulously detailed account of the experiences of fifteen
Chinese citizens and twenty-five Westerners who underwent attempts at 'brainwashing' by the Communist Chinese government. Lifton says that his study
began "as a psychiatric evaluation of Chinese Communist 'thought reform,' or
'brainwashing,'" and that it "is based upon research which I conducted in Hong
Kong in 1954-55." Lifton's *Thought Reform* is considered an essential work for
understanding the techniques aimed at 'mind control.' [Lifton chose the term
"thought reform" because he had not found evidence of a permanent change
in thinking and beliefs, as suggested by the term, "brainwashing."]

Following his work in Hong Kong, Dr. Lifton, collaborated closely with his mentor Erik Homburger Erikson, a prominent psychologist who had fled Nazi Germany for the United States. Together with noted MIT historian Bruce Mazlish, Lifton organized a group to apply psychology and psychoanalysis to the study of history. Called the Wellfleet Psychiatry Group, after the Massachusetts town where Lifton lived and the group met, the three men focused mainly on psychological motivations for war, terrorism, and genocide in recent history.

As a result of the publication of Lifton's *Thought Reform* and his book on Vietnam veterans, *Home From the War,* his name became widely known and well regarded. He was often called to testify in high-profile court cases as an expert witness on 'brainwashing.' Not the least of these cases was the trial of Patty Hearst. Lifton testified as a defense witness in the 1976 trial, arguing that the group that kidnapped Hearst, the Symbionese Liberation Army, had employed techniques similar to those he wrote about in *Thought Reform.* Also testifying on Hearst's behalf were two MKULTRA subcontractors, Dr. Louis Jolyson West – an associate of Gittinger's who once killed an elephant with LSD administered as part of a CIA experiment – and Dr. Martin Orne, a Harvard University professor who experimentally hypnotized and tested Harvard students and sent their scores to Gittinger at the CIA for analysis. Lifton's colleague and good friend, Dr. Margaret Singer, also testified at the Hearst trial. Singer, in 1953, was a staff psychologist at Walter Reed Army Institute of Research in Washington, D.C., where she specialized in studying returned Korean War POWs. In this position, she frequently came in contact with Albert Biderman. After she left the Walter Reed Institute, Singer established herself as an authority on cults, or "new religions," and "their real or alleged malfeasances."

POW Confessions of Biological Warfare in Korea

Greatly exacerbating the raging public fervor and concern in the 1950s about the brainwashing of American troops were the "confessions" of a number of Air Force pilots who "confessed" that they had dropped biological bombs on North Korea. In early May 1951, North Korea's Minister of Foreign Affairs, Pak Hen Yen, charged that the United States was dropping biological bombs containing the small pox virus on his country. Months later, he claimed also that bacteria carrying insects had been spread by U.S. aircraft across sections of North Korea. In early March 1952, Zhou En-Lai, China's Minister of Foreign Affairs, indignantly charged that a number of American Air Force pilots shot down by the North Koreans would be treated as war criminals because they were dropping biological bombs. Days later, the Soviets brought similar charges against the United States before the United Nations General Assembly. On March 26, 1952, Zhou En-Lai sent an urgent telegram to the Secretariat of the United Nations in which he charged that U.S. Air Force aircraft flew over 400 sorties during which they spread large quantities of germ-infected insects over North Korea.

In May 1952, North Korean radio announced that two American pilots from the 3rd Bomber Wing had confessed to dropping bacteriological bombs on North Korea in January 1952. Lieutenant Kenneth Enoch and Lieutenant John Quinn had been shot down on January 13 near Anju. Their North Korean interrogators demanded that they confess to dropping biological bombs, and when the two refused, they were placed in solitary confinement for weeks, and tortured. After two months, Enoch broke. He later explained that, faced with horrible physical and mental pain, insanity, death, or a "ridiculous confession," he had chosen the latter. Quinn also eventually broke and both pilots were filmed reading their confessions concerning use of biological weapons. In all, eventually thirty-six American pilots signed confessions to using germ warfare.

The confessions captured worldwide attention, and convinced many that the charges against the United States were true. Many nations expressed their shock and condemnation over America's assumed acts. By summer 1952, biological warfare was a heated issue everywhere, resulting in large protests in several countries. Matters intensified after additional downed American pilots confessed to the use of biological weapons and the media worldwide had a field day with the confessions, never mentioning the much larger numbers of American pilots who were being severely tortured to make similar confessions, and who never did so.

An authoritative book on the U.S. Air Force during the Korean War, published in 2000, by military historian John R. Bruning, states: "Recent revelations by historians working in the archives of former Eastern Bloc countries reveal conclusively that the accusations against the USAF were a construct of communist propaganda. In fact, North Korea's secret police actually infected at least two North Korean prisoners with cholera to further give evidence of America's germ warfare campaign.... Although epidemics ravaged North Korea during the war, no hard evidence was ever found that linked the United States to them."

Other experts on the subject disagree strenuously with Bruning. Stephen Endicott and Edward Hagerman, authors of the book, *The United States and Biological Warfare*, have been consistent critics of those that discount allegations of germ warfare use in Korea, and argue that there is ample circumstantial evidence that biological weapons were used by the United States. Endicott and Hagerman were the first foreigners to be given access to classified documents in the Chinese Central Archives, documents that substantiate the claims of Zhou-En-Lai. The two were also able to interview multiple Chinese scientists who actually investigated, at the time of their occurrence, the outbreaks resulting from alleged germ warfare. The two authors also claim that American pilots only retracted their confessions because they were threatened with court martial and other harm. Especially troubling are Endicott and Hagerman's claims that they read "interviews with American spies (Chinese defectors) who had been parachuted in to check on the effects of biological warfare," and a large quantity of documents and reports generated by Chinese medical teams that painstakingly investigated the various outbreaks in North Korea, as well as "reports of false alarms."

Yet, the fact remains that nobody to date has definitively proven or disproven the charges of biological warfare. Says Endicott:

> Secrecy still surrounds this period, raising doubts about whether the United States was sincere in finally ratifying an international protocol against biological warfare in 1972.... The need for less concealment remains. Greater knowledge and historical perspective can help the public and policy makers join together to prevent what happened in the heat of the early Cold War from happening again.

Former Camp Detrick scientists, who would have been the very people responsible for developing and producing the biological weapons allegedly used in North Korea, were interviewed for this book. Not surprisingly, those who were willing to talk about it categorically deny that biological weapons were used during the Korean War. Said Gerald Yonetz:

> It's no secret that we developed and tested [such] weapons...we did, the Canadians did, the Japanese did, the Russians, the French, the British... you name them, they developed them, but we didn't use them in Korea. At least, not that I know of, and I was in a pretty good position to have known.

Henry Eigelsbach, one of Camp Detrick's infectious diseases experts, said, "I'm sure [biological weapons] weren't employed. A lot of what was claimed that we used wasn't even ready for tactical use. We were working at refining for use most of these weapons long after the war."

In fairness, it should be pointed out that other former Camp Detrick scientists flatly refused even to discuss the issue or to answer any questions concerning biological warfare in Korea. Said one scientist, who had been close to Frank Olson and declined to be identified for this book, "It's ancient history one way or another. Who really cares at this point in time?"

In recent years, Robert Jay Lifton, now eighty-three years old, has been a strong critic of the current "War on Terrorism." He has stated, despite his view that terrorism itself is an increasingly serious threat due to the proliferation of nuclear, chemical, and biological weapons and totalist ideologies, that the war is misguided and is a dangerous attempt to "destroy all vulnerability." Recent media reports have revealed that at Guantanamo Bay, Cuba, where U.S. Army interrogators, as of this writing, have been holding – in some cases for years — a large number of alleged terrorists, without charges or due process, the interrogation trainers employed a particular demonstration chart that is of interest. It is a chart showing various "coercive management techniques" for use on Guantanamo Bay prisoners. These euphemistically named "management techniques" included "sleep deprivation," "prolonged constraint," and "exposure."

Incredibly, the chart, according to journalist Scott Shane, "had been copied verbatim from a 1959 Air Force study of Chinese [interrogation] techniques used during the Korean War to obtain confessions, many of them false, from American prisoners."

Moreover, the chart being used at Guantanamo had originally been extracted from a 1957 article written by Albert D. Biderman (misidentified by Shane as "Alfred"). Asked for comment on the origins of the chart, U.S. Senator Carl Levin, a Democrat from Michigan and chairman of the Senate Armed Services Committee, said that "every American would be shocked" to know where the training chart came from. "What makes this document doubly stunning is that these were techniques to get false confessions," said Levin. "People say we need intelligence, and we do. But we don't need false intelligence."

Remarkably, Biderman's chart, exactly as employed by military trainers, can be found posted on several anti-cult sites on the Internet, where it has been available for at least the past twenty years. The torture methods illustrated in Biderman's "Chart of Coercion" are apparently used by some cults to control their members.

In 1963, a decade beyond the end of the Korean War, Biderman published *March to Calumny: The Truth About American POW's in Korea.* The book is a remarkable, fully documented, portrayal that goes sharply against the hysteria and fear infecting America in the 1950s concerning its so-called "traitor" soldiers and "American collaborators." Those misguided perceptions, coupled with the even greater fear of Communist domination, as amply fueled by McCarthyism, were exploited with tremendous media support to create and sustain the CIA's reactionary BLUEBIRD, ARTICHOKE, and MKULTRA programs. TIME magazine's review of Biderman's book summarized its conclusions, as follows:

> Americans indulged in some profound breast beating when they heard that G.I. prisoners in Korea had been brainwashed into collaborating on a massive scale with the enemy. Once again, Jeremiah's were able to wail that Americans had gone soft from too much good living. But all this emotion was uselessly expended, according to Albert Biderman, a sociologist with long experience in military affairs. Impressively marshalling facts and figures, Biderman argues that U.S. prisoners in Korea behaved as well as prisoners generally have any time anywhere.

Biderman's book lays out in fine detail the torments and horrors American troops experienced in captivity in Korea. A number of sections of his book are revealing, especially those concerning torture. An earlier book by Eugene Kinkead, *In Every War But One,* published in 1959, had outraged Biderman because it contained statements "denying that torture was used against the American prisoners in Korea." Kinkead's book defined "what was and was not torture" according to Army sources he had consulted. Wrote Kinkead:

... The Army defines torture as the application of pain so extreme that it causes a man to faint or lose control of his will. The bastinado, the iron maiden, the rack, water dropping unceasingly on the head, bamboo splinters stuck under the fingernails and ignited—these are forms of torture.

The Army does not consider prisoners being made to stand in water, being improperly clad, being kicked, slapped or kept in cramped quarters as torture. These things are uncomfortable, and they do cause stress. But it is stress of the same general order as a combat soldier undergoes, and a prisoner must be able to endure such stress just as the combat soldier must endure gunfire and close-quarter lunges of the enemy on the battlefield.

Torture of a severe and brutal nature was administered against Americans, Biderman countered, laying out in graphic and horrific detail numerous documented accounts of such acts. Eight years after the Korean War had ended, Biderman, along with Herbert Zimmer, an associate professor of psychology at Georgetown University in Washington, D.C., who had worked closely with Biderman at the Air Force's Office of Scientific Research, edited and published a book entitled, *The Manipulation of Human Behavior*. Briefly, the book is a thorough examination of how to interfere with human physiology and psychology in order to manipulate human behavior, be it through the use of hallucinogenic drugs, hypnosis, physiologic and sensory deprivation, or environmental stimulation. Biderman and Zimmer's book uses the word "torture" on only one page, but the contents describe, in graphic and lurid detail, a cornucopia of "control techniques" that any layperson would shudder to think about and undoubtedly would consider torture. Biderman and Zimmer's introduction to the book speaks for itself and enticingly portends what is to follow:

> This book represents a critical examination of some of the conjectures about the application of scientific knowledge to the manipulation of human behavior. The problem is explored within a particular frame of reference: the interrogation of an unwilling subject.... 'Can man really be made to behave contrary to his profoundest beliefs and his conscious self-interests?'.... *Several scientists have reported on the possible application of scientific knowledge that might be made by the most callous interrogator or power. The results of their thinking are available here for anyone to use, including the unscrupulous.*

With the groundwork thus laid, the book expounds eagerly the findings of eight "distinguished" scientists, each of them "chosen because of his previous work in the particular specialty that is the subject of his paper." Most germane to the subject of this book is that nearly all of these scientists had also found their way into the CIA's MKULTRA mind control program years earlier.

THE LONG FORGOTTEN VOGELER INCIDENT

Events in other parts of the world, besides Korea, also acted to significantly pique the CIA's interest in interrogation techniques and brainwashing. At the start of the 1950s, a fledging CIA was confronted with an onslaught of reports about Soviet, Chinese and North Korean torture and psychological manipulation activities. American intelligence agents, foreign collaborators, informers and others engaged in a fierce ideological struggle with Communism were routinely being snatched from distant sidewalks and taken to secluded, remote locations and prisons where they were subjected to prolonged interrogation that often featured the administration of torture and mind-altering drugs.

Mostly forgotten today, but a prime example, is the case of American Robert Vogeler, who was arrested for espionage in Communist Hungary, imprisoned, and tortured. Vogeler, an International Telephone and Telegraph (ITT) executive with close ties to U.S. intelligence, was snatched from an automobile by two machine-gun toting Hungarian State Department border guards on November 18, 1949. Stripped of his passport and all personal effects, Volgeler was beaten, accused of being a spy, drugged and then interrogated for sixty-five hours straight. He was then taken to a tiny, windowless prison cell adjoining a room where other prisoners were tortured every night.

Vogeler later wrote, "Their screams were obviously calculated to drive me to distraction." After several days of this, he was told by a special interrogator, "Before I've finished, we'll know everything there is to know about you."

Replied Vogeler, "I've already told you the truth."

"Not the truth I want to hear," replied the interrogator. "If Mindszenty told me what I wanted him to tell me, so will you.... Even if Jesus Christ were sitting in your chair, He'd tell me everything I wanted Him to."

Eventually, Soviet inquisitors broke Vogeler; American intelligence officials claimed that behavior modification and psychochemical agents were used in the process. On February 21, 1950, the Budapest Criminal Court sentenced Vogeler to fifteen years in prison. Seventeen months later he was released. Two of Vogeler's colleagues, Hungarian citizens arrested at the same time, were far less fortunate. Imre Geiger and Zoltan Rado were hung on May 8, 1950.

Declassified, "EYES ONLY" CIA and Naval Intelligence documents from June 1950 reveal that both intelligence agencies were especially interested in the "major implications in terms of medical research and interrogation techniques" of Vogeler's treatment while imprisoned. Reads one memorandum from R.H. Hillenkoetter, Director of Central Intelligence, to Naval Intelligence Director, Rear Admiral Carl F. Espe, "Field representatives of this Agency were advised that in the event of Mr. Robert Vogeler's release from prison in Hungary, they are to give every assistance to his expeditious movement to the United States without interrogation in the field." Hillenkoetter justified this directive by explaining:

You are probably aware of the fact that this Agency has conducted a considerable amount of experimentation along the lines [believed to have been carried out on Vogeler by Russian interrogators]. The matter is naturally one of priority operational interest to this Agency.

The "considerable amount of experimentation" the CIA director referred to was an intense, covert program operated by the CIA in tandem with Naval Intelligence, aimed at "identifying and testing the effectiveness of suspected Soviet Russian, or satellite countries, activity in the areas of physical, psychological, mechanical and medical interrogation techniques." Initially code-named Project Pelican, and then Operation Boomer, and finally Project Bluebird, the CIA's ever-expanding experimentation program, as we have seen, had its genesis in the wartime "truth drug" activities of the Office of Strategic Services, precursor to the CIA.

Early CIA Interrogation and Brainwashing Concerns

A February 24, 1949 memorandum written to security research chief Paul Gaynor by an unnamed official reveals the Agency's first moves toward establishing an in-house interrogation program. The memo, citing a January 1949 article published in a weekly British Roman Catholic newspaper called the *Tablet*, claimed that Hungarian Communist secret police had made extensive use of a "will-destroying" drug called "actedron" on political prisoners in Soviet-occupied countries and that they were planning to use the drug on Cardinal Josef Mindszenty. The Cardinal had been arrested the day after Christmas, and on January 19, 1949, it was announced that he had "confessed" to having committed "high treason" as an "imperialist agent" of Britain and the United States. When he was placed on trial, an event that drew worldwide news coverage, Mindszenty appeared as if he were drugged and was reciting rehearsed lines.

According to the memorandum, the CIA had discovered that "actedron" was "a trade name for the drug we know as Benzedrine (or amphetamine sulfate)." The memo elaborates with enthusiasm:

Although no trace of the use of Benzedrine for interrogation purposes in the Unites States can be found, it has been the contention of this office for some time that the drug has strong possibilities for the extraction of information during interrogation. The drug, Benzedrine, administered in sufficiently large doses, acts as a strong stimulant and makes the subject over-confident, undiscriminating and somewhat lacking in inhibitions (provided the subject is allowed no physical outlet for his newly acquired energy other than conversation). It is during this period that it is felt that a great deal of information could be elicited which ordinarily would not be obtained.

The memo informed Gaynor that the case of Cardinal Mindszenty illustrated the relevance of Benzedrine:

[C]ertain admissions of guilt were consistently made over a period of days which would indicate that a condition existed during which the Cardinal was continually under the influence of some unknown force, and not merely for a period of a few hours as would be the case with the utilization of the 'Benzedrine depression' phase. The production of this [phase] could be caused to recur periodically but the subject would first have to be given new doses of the drug, which would produce acceleration before the desired depression. If this were the case, the Cardinal's testimony would be inconsistent because of the opposite mental state, which would be present during the two different psychological phases. For this reason, it is felt that some additional technique was used on Cardinal Mindszenty in conjunction with, or independent of, the administering of the drug, Benzedrine....

Moreover, the memo advised:

It would appear that each CIA employee exposed to the possible use of those techniques, because of overseas assignments, should be well informed as to his degree of susceptibility to the various procedures and as to how he might recognize the attempted use of the process.... For these reasons, and others, this branch recommends that the Agency move as quickly as possible to establish a more formalized interrogation research effort.

In June 1949 the director of the CIA's Office of Scientific Intelligence, Dr. Willard F. Machle, embarked on a special tour of Western Europe to personally review and assess field investigations into Soviet interrogation techniques. Dr. Machle, a strong-willed former medical researcher at the Kettering Laboratory in Cincinnati, was the former director of the U.S. Army's Armored Medical Research Laboratory. Accompanying Machle on his trip were several officials from the CIA's Security Branch and recently formed Interrogation Research Section.

A partially redacted September 26, 1949 memorandum to CIA Security Chief, Sheffield Edwards, reveals specifics about the objectives and activities of Dr. Machle's two-month tour abroad:

The main objective of this trip was to discover whether the Russians or Russian controlled countries are or have in the past been utilizing interrogation and espionage techniques which involve the use of drugs and hypnosis.... During the trip, the Polygraph (lie detector) was used in sixteen different cases during which [several words redacted] were processed. In four different cases, suspected Communist agents were processed by drugs and the establishing of the state of hypnosis for interrogation purposes. (It was interesting to note that Polygraph tests could be run and the hypnotic state could be established and maintained through the use of an interpreter.)

Concludes the memo's author (an official in the Interrogation Research Section whose name is blacked out):

> From the contacts made throughout this trip, it can be said with a great deal of certainty that the Russians [and certain of their allies] are utilizing drug interrogation to a considerable extent and are utilizing hypnosis in special and important instances. These instances seem to involve the trial preparation procedure used in several extremely important espionage trials. As far as can be ascertained from the limited approach made, it would seem that the Russians are not, at this time, utilizing hypnosis operationally in their espionage set up. It is, although, interesting to note that the Russians definitely do possess the know-how of such operations, should they care to utilize these techniques.

The memo's author then recommends "that steps be taken to create facilities for the susceptibility testing and briefing of certain classes of individuals going overseas. It is further recommended that security validation teams be established for use overseas and that specialists be trained in the use of drugs and operational hypnosis." Warns the writer:

> It must be remembered that when the effects of the drug wear off, it is probable that the subject will be completely unaware of the fact that he talked freely and was possibly indiscreet. For this reason, it is desirable wherever possible to associate the use of the drug with liquor, in order that this effect will not arouse suspicion. Nevertheless, it should also be remembered that the subject subsequently may be expected to feel remorse, embarrassment or alarm over things he knows he has said. Extreme reactions in such event could be: a) flight; b) suicide; or c) personal danger for the operator. It is possible that reactions of this type might outweigh the benefits which might be gained by the use of the drug.

A 1951 *"EYES ONLY"* memorandum to CIA director Walter Smith, reveals in considerable detail the Agency's mounting concerns about the interrogation techniques used on Robert Volgeler:

> Reports of the Vogeler trial in February 1950 contain statements of use of persuasive techniques in obtaining Vogeler's testimony– *'On at least two occasions during testimony, Vogeler forgot his lines in such a way as to indicate clearly he had memorized his testimony word for word, as if playing a part in a play.'* Some of his statements are cited with the conclusion that *'It appears from all foregoing that Vogeler, acting under compulsion of an unknown nature, has been induced to memorize, recite prepared confession.'* It was observed that '*...fellow defendants...are presumably confessing under same compulsion he is.'*

A press summary of the Vogeler trial reported: '*One aspect of the present trial that is unique...is the personality of one of the defendants, Vogeler. His is an unusually strong character; he is a man of firm convictions and great self-confidence. He has powerful friends and sufficient intelligence to realize the limitations of his protagonists. What forces can the opposition muster, which will make a strong man cooperate during the public performance and apologize humbly for the 'sins' he has committed? There appears to be no evidence that actual torture has been employed...<u>Drugs</u> may be partially responsible for his cooperation. He appeared to be fatigued, his voice was subdued, his usual emotional mode of expression was replaced by a dull monotone...<u>Hypnosis</u> is sometimes believed to be responsible for the docile attitude of the accused... <u>Fatigue</u> is applicable in the present case because Vogeler appeared to be exhausted... The most logical explanation for his conduct appears to be a combination of all of the above over a long enough period of time to break even such a will as Vogeler's... If such a man can be influenced to give false testimony, it can be anticipated that all individuals who are given the "treatment" will acknowledge equally fantastic stories.*' [Underlining in the original.]

A follow-up report by the CIA's Security Research Service reveals that the Agency was indeed digging deeply into its Eastern European sources for additional information about interrogation techniques. The findings included the following assessment:

According to 1950 reports based on the consensus of a large colony of Russian refugee intellectuals, the Ministry of State Safety of the USSR is the one department that can set up its own scientific research institute. The central problem for all Soviet physiologists appears to be pathology— 'in particular a study of the conduction and nature of the disorders of man by means of various external stimulations.' These problems have been studied by the All-Soviet Institute of Experimental Medicine, and a string of affiliated branches, of which the Institute of Judicial Experimental Medicine was one.

Here was in progress the most inhuman experiences of prisoners. Here, not only the various ways of psychological influence were studied, but also the high-scale physiological experiences: resistance of the organism to various methods of external influence; developed theories of conditioned reflexes and the influence of conditioned stimulation on the nervous system and mind of man...

The scientific research institutes of Pavlov and Orbelli have worked '*on a method of shattering the human mind which was based on the behavior of Soviet war-prisoners.*' The task of Soviet physiologists *has been 'to tear down the nervous system.... Soviet physiology is described as on the road to treatment and stimulation of pathological processes, including the ability 'to repair the nervous system at will.'*

The report, which caused considerable alarm within the CIA, stated that captured Nazi documents made it clear that as early as 1935 the Germans believed that the Russians were using drugs on prisoners. "In 1946 a botanist was interrogated who had been sent to study the Nikita botanical gardens during the German occupation of Crimea in 1943," reads the report:

> He stated that these gardens were devoted to raising the sub-tropical plants for their speech-inducing effects. Extensive crossbreeding experiments had been done in Nikita Gardens and its sub-division at Bakchisarai using such plants as *Bambusa, Euphorbia, Juniperus Sabina, Solanacae* and *Peganum Harmala*. The Germans learned that extract of *Peganum Harmala* plus extract of *Anabasis Affula*, a plant only found in Tashkent, produced a speech-inducing drug, which the Russians called Harmalin. It was found that 'a human being given Harmalin will repeat exactly what's been suggested to him, after effect wears off. However, the interrogation where he repeats must be by same person who established original rapport when subject was under Harmalin.'

Additional captured Nazi documents, covered in the report, identified a prominent biochemist, who had once worked for I.G. Farben, the German chemical and pharmaceutical company that manufactured the gases used to kill millions of concentration camp prisoners. This biochemist had confirmed, after apprehension in 1947, Germany's strong interest in developing speech-inducing drugs. "The Germans learned of the effects of *Anabasis Aphylla* through interrogation of Russian prisoners of war," reads the report, "who revealed that this plant was frequently used by the Russian police during their investigations." The report also revealed that the Russians could extract alcoholic preparations from *Anabasis* plants that were used to cause an intoxicating state in subjects, inducing them to talk freely, and also making them more susceptible to hypnosis and post-hypnotic suggestion.

As alarming and abhorrent as the techniques and experiments carried out by the Germans and Russians were, as outlined in the CIA's reports, this would not be a deterrent to the Agency to move aggressively forward to replicate and surpass the efforts of their predecessors. American POWs recently returned from Korea, along with many other unwitting individuals, would soon find themselves facing an all-new set of horrors in their homeland.

2

Bluebird

Subject lost all ability to stand or walk and was carried to his own bedroom. Subsequently, he in turn was irrational then apparently felt that he was dying as he asked for his crucifix, crossed himself numerous times, prayed aloud and made gestures of a religious nature.
— CIA Project Bluebird Report, 1951

They're locking them up today, they're throwing away the key, I wonder who it will be tomorrow, you or me?
— Arthur Lee

April 18, 1951, CIA Headquarters, Washington, D.C.

On April 18, 1951, Dr. H. Marshall Chadwell, former deputy manager of the New York office of the Atomic Energy Commission and now CIA deputy director for Scientific Intelligence, delivered a copy of a revised Project Bluebird plan to the office of Allen Dulles, less than three months into his job as the Agency's Deputy Director for Plans. Dulles was out of his office, so Chadwell left a message recommending that Dulles present the BLUEBIRD plan to representatives on the Agency's Intelligence Advisory Committee from the Navy, Army, Air Force and FBI "with a solicitation for their assistance and their designation of an individual in each of the organizations for us to work with." Recommended Chadwell, "If you present [the plan] to the IAC meeting rather than handling it individually [I suggest] that other offices and Department of State and AEC representatives be dismissed before you discuss this subject."

Dr. Chadwell's personal delivery of instructions and recommendations about Project Bluebird provides a glimpse of the extremely high level of secrecy that surrounded the project and all of its yet-to-come operational permutations. A July 25, 1950 memorandum reads:

All matters and materials related to BLUEBIRD should be marked EYES ONLY and not, under any circumstances or for any reasons, be circulated among or shared with any persons outside those on the attached approved list.... It is understood that under no circumstances is the special project to be discussed with any persons other than those especially cleared.

The code name BLUEBIRD had resulted from a comment made at a 1950 planning committee meeting of the Office of Special Operations (OSO) – that the objective of improved interrogation techniques was to get a subject "to sing like a bluebird." Simply put, the initial objectives of BLUEBIRD were to devise the most effective means possible for obtaining specific information from unwilling subjects. The project focused almost exclusively on situations deemed "Special Interrogations" or "SI" in which the quick and complete "inducing of full disclosure" was paramount.

At BLUEBIRD's inception, CIA officials made it clear that no method of obtaining information was taboo from consideration. Documents from the project's earliest meetings reveal a laundry list of methods, including the use of "ego-depressant" drugs like heroin and morphine; polygraph; electro-shock therapy; the use of "mechanical aids"; lobotomies; hypnotism; fatigue; isolation; sensory deprivation; and torture.

In November 1950, the OSO committee proposed expanding BLUEBIRD by separating it into five essential areas: "the establishment of training of up to four additional teams besides the two currently in use; adopting formal operational methods for the functioning and control of all teams; an expanded research and development program; better coordination of all drug research that was currently underway government wide; and improved intelligence over the gathering and estimating of foreign interrogation capabilities." The committee further proposed a specific composition for interrogation teams because "experience to date has shown that an interrogation team operates most effectively with the following trained personnel:

(1) Medical doctor, trained in SI;
(2) SI interrogator with language abilities, which were of extreme importance;
(3) Polygraph operator, also with foreign language abilities;
(4) Interpreter;
(5) and a technician trained in polygraph, communications and photography.

The proposal added that "I&SS (Intelligence & Security Services, precursor to the Office of Security) will recruit a medical doctor to complete the medical complement of the three teams.... Training will cover all aspects of BLUEBIRD activity and will include special information and techniques developed in the course of the operational research program." The BLUEBIRD committee's expansion proposal concluded rather exuberantly:

> After the research programs have been developed, it is recommended that BLUEBIRD conduct experiments and develop techniques to determine the possibilities and practicability of positive use of SI on willing and unwilling subjects for operational purposes. Positive use of SI would be for

the purpose of operational control of individuals to perform specific tasks under post hypnotic suggestion and, in addition, would cover research in training fields and defensive conditioning against application of SI by un-friendly elements. This field, if it is found that the application of SI is pos-sible and practicable, offers unlimited opportunities to operating offices.

Without doubt, Project BLUEBIRD laid the foundation for all of the CIA psychological manipulation and mind control programs still to come.

Meanwhile, two additional, and significant, steps were taken to put BLUEBIRD into operation. In 1949, Frank Wisner, Office of Policy Coordination assistant director, created a scientific steering committee to conduct a complete inven-tory of all chemical and biological weapons then in existence, including those employed by the Nazis and Japanese during World War II. Based on that in-ventory, Wisner instructed the committee to come up with "ideas in the areas of chemical, biological and radiological warfare" and "if a concept is deemed workable the Committee will recommend competent scientists or engineers to supply detailed information to round out any such plans." Wisner said the committee would work closely with selected personnel from the Joint Chiefs of Staff, Camp Detrick, military intelligence, and the CIA's Division A.

The second step involved a two-month overseas mission in late summer, 1949, by a CIA team under polygraph expert Morse Allen from the Secu-rity Office. Allen's mission "was to discover whether the Russians or Russian controlled countries are or have in the past been utilizing interrogation and espionage techniques which involve the use of drugs and hypnosis." Allen met with high-ranking American occupation officials in Germany, Poland and Hungary, as well as numerous informants and "returning Prisoners of War at border points... Several hundred of these returning POW's were interrogated in hopes of discovering the use of drugs or hypnotism techniques on them." Allen reported after his return, "During the trip, the Polygraph (lie detector) was used in sixteen different cases... In four different cases, suspected Communist agents were processed by drugs and the establishment of the state of hypnosis for inter-rogation purposes." Allen drew several conclusions from his trip:

From the contacts made throughout this trip, it can be said with a great deal of certainty that the Russians and several Russian dominated coun-tries are utilizing drug interrogation to a considerable extent, and are utilizing hypnosis in special and important instances. Those instances seem to involve the trial preparation procedure used in several extremely important espionage trials. As far as can be ascertained from the limited approach made, it would seem that the Russians are not, at this time, utilizing hypnosis operationally in their espionage set up. It is, although, interesting to note that the Russians definitely do possess the know-how of such operations, should they care to utilize these techniques.

It is recommended that steps be taken to create facilities for the susceptibility testing and briefing of certain classes of individuals going overseas.
It is further recommended that security validation teams be established
for use overseas and that specialists be trained in the use of drugs and
operational hypnosis.

The day after Allen submitted his trip report, he sent CIA security chief Sheffield Edwards a detailed proposal for what he termed "security validation
teams." According to Allen, these would be multi-function groups of 2-4 agents
highly-trained in general interrogation techniques — use of the polygraph, drug
administration, hypnosis - as well as basic medical skills. The teams would be
limited to carrying out "the ultimate polygraph screening of all CIA personnel;
the processing of any loyalty cases which might arise from time to time; [and]
more detailed screening of special security categories," such as government
departments and agencies, including the Atomic Energy Commission, the Pentagon, and the State Department. Teams would be located in Washington, D.C.,
Detroit, and California; overseas they would operate in Germany, France, and
England. The CIA's Security Office would direct all teams, but close cooperation from the Agency's Office of Scientific Intelligence, Special Operations, and
Technical Services was expected.

On October 11, 1949, Allen sent yet another proposal to Edwards for an
additional, enormous survey of interrogation methods. This one would encom-
pass a vast literature search, and more:

> The review would include all articles in periodicals and books written by
> specialists on such subjects as general interrogation, psychological interro-
> gation, the use of the polygraph, truth serum and hypnosis.... The research
> of sections of police departments and criminology laboratories might all
> prove to be very beneficial.... Liaison with professional hypnotists could
> contribute many pointers, which might be applied to certain phases of
> our problems.... *This research would [also] involve the volunteering of
> subjects for actual laboratory experiments.*

The specific "problems" referred to, and for which BLUEBIRD administrators
sought solutions, as well as human subjects, included the following:

> Can we create by post-hypnotic control, an action contrary to a person's
> basic moral principles?
> Could we seize a subject and, in the space of an hour or two, by post-
> hypnotic control have him crash an airplane, wreck a train, etc?
> Can we make an unwilling subject talk?
> Can we prevent our own agents who fall into enemy hands from disclos-
> ing information vital to us?
> Can a man be made to commit acts useful to us under post-hypnotic
> suggestion?

Is there an accurate test we can use to see if a man is under post-hypnotic authority?

Can we condition our own people so they will not be subject to post-hypnotic suggestion?

Edwards promptly responded to Allen's proposal, suggesting that he boil down his voluminous collection of interrogation literature to a pilot project aimed at testing the best and most promising techniques in the field.

The proposed field test excited Allen who had all along envisioned a far wider role for the "validation teams" than just clearing government employees. Morse Allen had wanted the teams to be used for aggressive interrogation of both domestic and foreign subjects, using state-of-the-art drugs, hypnosis and whatever means possible. On April 20, Rear Admiral Roscoe Henry Hillenkoet-ter, then-CIA director, approved "TOP SECRET PROJECT BLUEBIRD, to be implemented by security chief Edwards."

On May 9, Sheffield Edwards and Morse Allen met with Dr. H. Marshall Chadwell, the CIA's chief of scientific intelligence (OSI), to discuss how OSI "might lend support to Project BLUEBIRD, [and on] the covert collection of information from the U.S. Government sources." The three agreed that Chadwell's office would arrange to have Army intelligence agents comb "through the Nuremberg Trials papers looking for information on drugs, narco-analysis, and special interrogation techniques" used by the Nazis, before and during World War II. The search would focus primarily on information regarding "speech inducing drugs, narco-analysis and hypnotism." It was agreed that as soon as the desired information had been collected, Chadwell, Edwards, and Allen would launch "initial trial BLUEBIRD projects in the field within the next few weeks."

Following the decision in June to reconstitute the BLUEBIRD teams to include medical doctors, psychiatrists, or psychologists, Edwards requested approval, "EYES ONLY," from the DCI to send the first BLUEBIRD team to Germany for a two week period in July and August:

> This will be the first project of the BLUEBIRD team, and the captain of the team must be allowed considerable latitude by your operating officials [in the field]. The project will serve as a training and research project in addition to its operational significance.... The team to be sent is the basic team which has just been completed by the addition of a doctor-psychiatrist.

According to several written reports, the results of BLUEBIRD's interrogation sessions overseas were mixed; some sessions produced "no remarkable results" and others produced "detailed and significant information." One report for a 1951 session reads ominously: "other detailed information was obtained but because of subject's physical condition this interrogation was concluded rapidly and before all the desired information could be secured." A medical report completed by the BLUEBIRD physician on this team reads:

> The Subject complained upon the first day of having been ill since early morning... He said he had been sick in his stomach, and that he had vomited. I went over him carefully, and found that although he had slight abdominal tenderness, he was not seriously, acutely ill. His heart action was good, his blood pressure within normal limits, and his lungs were free from any acute inflammation....
>
> In approximately two hours from the time the medication was administered, the Subject became sufficiently conscious to prohibit the safe utilization of [redacted drug name] at that time.... It became apparent toward the end of the third interrogation that Subject's physical condition had suffered a considerable deterioration. Subject's pulse, while not alarming, showed some fluttering and was generally weaker, Subject's respiration became labored and painful, Subject became completely irrational and disoriented and ultimately Subject lost all ability to stand or walk and was carried in a semi-conscious condition to his bedroom. Subsequently, he in turn was irrational, then apparently felt that he was dying as he asked for his crucifix, crossed himself numerous times, prayed aloud and made gestures of a religious nature.

Detailed BLUEBIRD reports, such as the one above, were circulated only to carefully selected individuals. Those persons "who have been briefed on BLUE-BIRD" included, by 1951: William King Harvey, J.H. Alberti, James Angleton, H. M. Chadwell, Cuyler Clark, H.H. Cooper, Robert H. Cunningham, E.H. Cushing, James H. Drum, Allen Dulles, John Earman, Sheffield Edwards, Richard Helms, Lyman B. Kirkpatrick, Frank Wisner, Dr. William Webster.

In October 1950, concurrently with implementation of BLUEBIRD, the CIA's chief of ultra-secret Staff D — which then included Richard Helms and James Angleton — requested that security director Edwards immediately contact former OSS officers who "experimented during 1945 and early 1946 with a drug known under the cryptonym 'SUGAR.'" The Staff D chief explained that "a few selected" former OSS agents now with the CIA's Office of Special Operations (OSO) had used "SUGAR" with "some success" in an interrogation.

Meanwhile, Stanley Lovell, former head of R&D for the OSS and now a special consultant to both the CIA and Camp Detrick, was also claiming success using "SUGAR" in interrogation. Lovell, described by historian Troy Thomas as a "devious little nihilist," had written in 1942:

> As was to be expected, the project [of developing a truth drug] was considered fantastic by the realists, unethical by the moralists, and downright ludicrous by the physicians.

Stanley Lovell urged the Agency to locate George Hunter White, a former OSS officer "with considerable experience with Project SUGAR." On November 4, 1950, the Agency's security chief wrote to the chief of Staff D:

> Unfortunately, the files of OSO fail to reflect full details concerning the nature, characteristics, use and effectiveness of this substance [SUGAR]. It is known, however, that the substance was originally furnished to OSS by the Narcotics Bureau of the Treasury Department. George Hunter White, formerly with OSS and now believed to be stationed with the Narcotics Bureau either in Chicago or San Francisco, should be in possession of additional details concerning this matter.... As you are well aware, this Office is, of course, most interested in anything which can be developed concerning the possibility of oral administration, *particularly surreptitious oral administration,* of such substances in connection with BLUEBIRD matters. [Emphasis added.]

Six months later, in June of 1951, TSS deputy chief Colonel James H. Drum told Dr. Sidney Gottlieb that George White was supervisory agent at the New York City branch of the Federal Narcotics Bureau, and that Gottlieb should contact him there. Gottlieb was told to learn as much as possible about Division 19's "truth drug" project as administered operationally by George White's secret OSS team. Division 19 was the combined OSS and National Defense Research Committee unit that worked on special weapons projects. Drum also told Gottlieb that OSO was especially interested in what had happened with the "truth drug" interrogation of a gangster named August Del Grazio shortly after the war.

Drum also briefed Gottlieb about a committee of scientists that had been set up to investigate the interrogation of prisoners of war through the use of drugs. The request for the scientists' committee originated with Military Intelligence Service chief General George V. Strong, who had asked the National Defense Research Council to devise an effective way to use drugs to interrogate captured German U-boat officers for information about German submarine movements. OSS scientists had informed Strong that it would not be easy to identify drugs useful in interrogation, and that efforts conducted earlier in November and December of 1941 had proven less than successful.

Those efforts had been spurred by a proposal submitted to the Office of the Coordinator of Information (COI), precursor to OSS, by Arthur Upham Pope, an archaeologist and expert in Persian art and culture in the 1930s and 40s. Pope was chairman of the Committee for National Morale, a patriotic confederation of social scientists, anthropologists, psychiatrists and psychologists that included Dr. Henry A. Murray, Dr. Harold Abramson, Gordon Allport, Clyde Kluckhohn, Ruth Benedict, and then husband and wife Gregory Bateson and Margaret Mead. Scientists affiliated with Pope's committee met with COI researchers, who were interested in the "truth drug" proposal and were most curious about the potential of scopolamine. Scopolamine, a chemical variant of atropine, is a multi-purpose alkaloid derived from *solanaceae* plants such as henbane, deadly nightshade, datura, belladonna and mandrake. The drug had long been one that found its way into myths and folklore: in Norse legends it was used to summon powerful gods; Shakespeare's witches stirred steaming pots of nightshade; Machiavelli penned a comedy about Mandrake; American comic book characters donned *noms de plume* derived from the plants; and Carlos Castaneda's Don Juan made ample use of the drug.

Morale Committee scientists, including Drs. Murray, Kubie and Harold Abramson, had previously conducted a thorough review of available literature on scopolamine and had found that a Texas obstetrician, Dr. Robert E. House, observed in 1916, while delivering babies, that mothers given scopolamine (often combined with chloroform) as a sedative sometimes became talkative and would reveal things they would not ordinarily discuss. Dr. House, as early as 1897, suggested the potential of scopolamine as a truth drug while observing its effects in treating persons addicted to cocaine and morphine. He realized that the drug might be useful in the interrogation of criminal suspects and, after a few quick experiments conducted in a Dallas prison, he enthusiastically made public announcements about his "remarkable discovery."

In 1931, after a series of sensational public demonstrations, House emphatically asserted that, under the influence of scopolamine, "a person could not lie" and that the drug "could distinguish the innocent from the guilty." However, about a year later, other less enthusiastic and more discerning scientists found that House's conclusions and claims were a bit shaky, but little publicity was given to these counter-claims.

The COI researchers believed that by combining morphine with scopolamine, a "state of twilight sleep" could be induced in subjects and that under such a spell they would talk freely about matters they normally would not discuss. Both groups of scientists agreed to cooperate on testing the scopolamine-morphine mixture. Initially, the project showed promise, but experiments conducted on mental patients at St. Elizabeth's Hospital in Washington, D.C. and on inmates at the Maryland House of Corrections proved disastrous. Some subjects slipped into comas, or they hallucinated to the point of losing touch with reality. When one subject nearly died of heart failure, the research with scopolamine was finally abandoned.

Despite these ongoing problems, the National Defense Research Council, working closely with OSS through Division 19, assembled the requested group of scientists: Drs. John Whitehorn of Johns Hopkins University; Winfred Overholser Sr., superintendent of St. Elizabeth's Hospital in Washington, D.C.; Roger Adams, National Defense Research Council; Watson W. Eldridge, also of St. Elizabeth's Hospital; Lawrence Kubie, a prominent psychiatrist and psychoanalyst with the New York Neurological Institute at Columbia University; and Edward Stricker of the University of Pennsylvania, among others. The group worked in secret, first under the auspices of MIS and then, beginning in January, 1943, under OSS, reporting only to Stanley Lovell, who reported to OSS director William "Wild Bill" Donovan.

When OSS initially took the project over from the MIS, Donovan, with urgings from Division 19 chief Chadwell, had instructed Lovell to consult closely with Dr. Roger Adams, an organic chemist from the University of Illinois who worked with NDRC. Educated at Harvard and the Kaiser Wilhelm Institute in Germany, Adams was best known for his research on organic arsenic compounds, local anesthetics, stereochemistry and gossypol. Adams was especially interested in research with marihuana. During World War I, Adams had served as a major in the Chemical Warfare Service in Washington, D.C. where he developed gases for use on the battlefield. When World War II began, Adams returned to the NDRC's Division B to develop bombs, fuels, tactical gases, and chemical weapons. Prior to the Second World War, Adams wrote numerous, widely circulated papers on dangerous drugs and marihuana, and was frequently a consultant to the Federal Bureau of Narcotics.

According to Narcotics Bureau files, in 1941, Adams and Dr. Walter Siegfried Loewe of the University of Utah produced "by chemical modification, two highly active tetrahydrocannabinols," as well as "a synthesized tetrahydrocannabinol." (Tetrahydrocannabinol is the active chemical in cannabis and one of the oldest hallucinogenic drugs known.)

Shortly before Frank Olson's death, scientists at Camp Detrick and Edgewood Arsenal had begun spending the $1.5 million allocated for extensive classified research with Dr. Loewe's THC, or synthetic marihuana. The central purpose of the research, according to Army records, was to explore the potential of marihuana to create "hypnotic like states," among other things. (It has often been remarked, only the federal government would see the wisdom of spending substantial sums of money to study something that countless Beat poets, writers and jazz musicians at the time could have explained for free.)

At his first meeting with the selected group of scientists, Stanley Lovell emphasized the urgent need to move forward expeditiously with the truth drug project, because military planners were clamoring for better intelligence on Nazi U-boat maneuvers in the North Atlantic, and captured German submarine officers were proving to be less than forthcoming with details. Also of great concern, Lovell explained, were the beliefs of Pentagon officials that the Russians had already developed an effective truth drug, and that the Germans were using such a drug in their interrogation of American prisoners, as well as concentration camp inmates. Lovell later noted, "Despite the Geneva Convention with its limitations on questioning captives, the prisoner-of-war officers wanted to try it." Additionally, according to Lovell, OSS recruiters and trainers wanted a drug that could effectively "help screen out of our groups any German spies or sympathizers."

Lovell and his chief assistant, Allen Abrams, described exactly what they wanted:

(1) It must be administered without the subject's knowledge.
(2) It must induce a talkative mood and, if possible, a full exposure of the truth, as the subject knew the truth.
(3) It must not be habit-forming or physiologically harmful; and
(4) It must leave no remembrance or suspicion of any kind.

Following this, Abrams called an initial briefing for the two ranking members of Division 19, Drs. Chadwell and W.C. Lothrop. Lovell then paid a personal visit to the head of the Federal Bureau of Narcotics, Harry Anslinger, and requested that one of the bureau's top "dope busters," George Hunter White, be assigned to work with the OSS on the "truth drug" program. Anslinger was more than happy to comply, and soon he ended up re-assigning nearly a dozen narcotics officers to the ranks of OSS.

In White's case, the reassignment was relatively easy, because months earlier the former drug agent had taken temporary leave from the FBN and enlisted in the OSS. Lovell now gave White the task of overseeing the delicate "truth drug" experiments, pending a decision by Lovell's scientists about the best drug for use. Years later, Lovell wrote, "There never was any officer in American uniform like Major White. He was . . .the most deadly and dedicated public servant I've ever met."

After weeks of trial and error, it was the Adams-Loewe synthetic compound derived from marihuana that the OSS decided was its most promising drug. According to a 1945 OSS report by Assistant chief Abrams, the drug in its liquid form had to "be ingested in order to be effective." The report explains, "This can be done either by eating, as in candy or food, or by inhalation, by means of a cigarette. It has been found that the cigarette method generally gives a quicker effect."

And this is where Col. Drum's 1951 briefing for Sidney Gottlieb left off. Drum explained to Gottlieb that it was the Adams-Loewe concoction that had been dubbed "SUGAR," and that details about its actual use and effectiveness were still unknown for the most part. Therefore, it was considered imperative to interview George White who would, it was hoped, be able to fill in the missing gaps.

Apparently, Drum and Gottlieb were unaware that White had already met months earlier in New York with then CIA consultant and future DCI Allen Dulles to discuss the old OSS truth drug project. Like it or not, Dulles thought, despite the doubts of some, biological warfare was a reality that had to be reckoned with. According to Gottlieb's recollection years later:

When I was hired by CIA in the summer of 1951, projects BLUEBIRD and ARTICHOKE, to a large extent, were already off the drawing boards and well into the operational phases. The decisions to pursue certain substances for interrogation, and other uses, had been made about a year before I came on. I'm not saying this to evade responsibility; what I'm merely doing is stating a fact. People may draw whatever conclusions they want, I still take responsibility for my role in the projects. At any rate, I contacted George White in New York [and] after OSO staff reviewed some Division 19 research and development reports. They found certain projects intriguing and wanted to know a lot more.

Sometime in early 1952, maybe it was February or March, I was asked to contact White. He and I first met in Washington in my office. Then, after a day or two, I drove up to Boston with him. He was working on an interesting narcotics case around there that he thought I might enjoy experiencing up close, as they say. Riding up together, we had a chance to really discuss matters of interest to OSO. Most of what we talked about was his work with the Division 19 truth drug program and other, related matters....

George ... was always armed to the teeth with all sorts of weapons; he could be gruff and loutish, vulgar even, but then turn urbane to a point of eloquence.

Gottlieb and White had driven together to New Haven, Connecticut, where White was working a narcotics investigation involving a fifty-year old business-man and millionaire who, White explained, "owned two Cadillacs, a supermar-ket, a few bars and a tremendous amount of real estate." Narcotics agents in New York had been tipped off that the businessman was connected to a New York crime family and that he was operating a heroin ring that made bulk de-liveries up and down the East Coast, as well as dealing heavily in firearms and counterfeit jewelry. Working undercover for White in New Haven was a man whom White introduced to Gottlieb as Louis LaChapelle, also-known-as Jean Labadie. White described him as a "special employee" for the Narcotics Bureau.

From New Haven, White and Gottlieb had returned to New York City where they had met with Dr. Harold Abramson at his Columbia University laboratory to discuss his experiments with LSD and other hallucinogenic drugs.

At his Narcotics Bureau office, George White had shown Gottlieb a three-page document marked *SECRET* and dated June 2, 1943. Titled "Report on TD." It listed the original Truth Drug committee, chaired by Dr. Winfred Overholser, professor of psychiatry at George Washington University. Besides Drs. Whitehorn, Stricker, Kubie, and Eldridge, the committee also included E.P. Coffy, Director of FBI Laboratories; Harry Anslinger, Commissioner of Narcotics, U.S. Treasury Department; Admiral Charles S. Stephenson of the Navy Bureau of Medicine and Surgery; Colonel R.D. Halloran of the Surgeon General's Office; and Lt. Colonel R.E. Looker of the Army's MIS. From OSS were George White and Dr. James Alexander Hamilton. The document revealed the following:

Exhaustive review of all relevant pharmacological literature narrowed the field to a half dozen drugs. Preliminary experiments found attention of some variety of cannabis as the drug of choice. Three varieties of cannabis were studied: cannabinol from Indian Charis, tetrahydrocannabinol acetate derived from the above, and synthetic cannabinol. Of these, the [Adams-Loewe] acetate derivative was found to be preferable. Various routes of administration were explored: oral administration, burning in smokeless charcoal, spraying, and inhalation in cigarettes. Of these, inhalation in cigarettes is the only route which can be recommended at the present time. Standard cigarettes may be loaded with .02 grams of Loewe's acetate. The drug is introduced into the cigarette with a 1/4cc tuberculin syringe and a specially prepared #22, 1 1/2 hypodermic needle.

White's 1943 Report on TD expounded on the effects of cannabis:

With some reservations, the effect of tetrahydrocannabinol acetate may be said to resemble that of alcohol. Small amounts produce relaxation and a feeling of well-being. Moderate amounts produce elation, loquacity, euphoria, and irresponsible behavior. Large amounts produce stupor and lethargy. There is no regular amnesia for events which transpire during the period in which the drug is effective, although memory for details may be blurred.... The tendency toward talkativeness and elation is probably more marked than in alcoholic intoxication.

Then would you say in your estimation that the drug is less than ideal? Gottlieb queried.

White replied yes, and said he was sure a better drug might be available somewhere, but that the committee overseeing the OSS project really had little time to research everything that was out there. On this issue, the 1943 report stated:

Tetrahydrocannabinol acetate is *not a perfect 'truth drug' in the sense that its administration is followed immediately and automatically by the revelation of all the secrets which the subject wishes to keep to himself.* Indeed, a careful evaluation of the psychological mechanism involved leads to *the conclusion that such a goal is beyond reasonable expectation from any drug.* However, the drug does produce a psychological state of relaxation, talkativeness, and irresponsibility, which might be extremely useful to a skilled interrogator. However, no experiment can be expected to duplicate the situation which occurs when enemy prisoners are interrogated, and the final proof of the drug must wait on field testing. [Emphasis added.]

What can you tell me specifically about the experimental sessions and field tests? Gottlieb asked. White explained he had not been present at every session, but he had observed what he thought were the more significant field sessions.

218

The very first experiments using mescaline were conducted in a Philadelphia hospital in January 1943. Three OSS officers volunteered for the experiment, Col. Ainsworth Blogg and two noncommissioned officers, identified in reports only as "Wagner and Kessler." The experiment was a dismal failure. None of the three men had given up any information, nor had they ever come close to reaching what observing scientists considered "a proper state of relaxation."

The next experiments had taken place at New York's Belmont Plaza Hotel and at Dr. Lawrence Kubie's Neurological Institute where Kubie had administered *cannabis indica* to subjects, with unsatisfactory results. During follow-up experiments at Kubie's Institute using the Adams-Loewe mixture, one subject experienced such bad after effects that he had required hospitalization for over eight weeks at the Walter Reed Hospital in Washington, D.C. Prior to using the drug on enemy POWs, White recounted, he and OSS psychologist, Dr. James Hamilton, had conducted a series of experiments during 1943 at selected hotels in New York (including the Pennsylvania Hotel, the Belmont Plaza, the Roosevelt Hotel, and the Hotel Des Artistes; and in Washington, D.C at the Manger-Annapolis Hotel. In these hotel-based experiments, they used primarily Army recruits as subjects.

The gothic-faced Hotel Des Artistes, located at 1 West 67th Street, had been selected because it was also being used by the OSS as a "finishing school" for wartime agents. Within several weeks, New York's now gone Alamac Hotel would also be used at least once before the CIA and U.S. Army began using it as a temporary housing site for former Nazi officials brought into the United States. The first experiment, overseen by White, again at New York's Belmont Plaza Hotel, took place in September 1943. The subjects were six Army enlisted personnel from Edgewood Arsenal in Maryland. The experiment lasted three days and involved both George White and Dr. Hamilton, as well as Dr. Allen Abrams, OSS research and development deputy chief. On the second day, they were joined by Chemical Corps officers Dr. Harold Abramson and Capt. Frank Olson.

According to a 1943 letter by White to another FBN agent, Abramson and Olson had attended the session because they were interested in pursuing "aerosol delivery possibilities with Loewe's acetate."

Also observing the effectiveness of these interrogation-drug sessions were OSS officers Charles Siragusa and Ulias C. Amoss. [As readers shall learn more about, Siragusa and Amoss had come to New York for a meeting regarding what White referred to as the "Mafia Plan,"an OSS assassination program.]

Within weeks, White and Hamilton would also conduct drug-interrogation experiments using other OSS officers, as well as unwitting Atomic Energy Commission scientists in Washington, D.C. and in San Francisco. The surreptitious experiments had the assistance of legendary CIA operative Edward Lansdale, then working for both MIS and OSS.

On November 24, 1943, White, Lovell, and Abrams met at the Pentagon with General George Strong to thoroughly brief him and his staff on the results of the truth drug program thus far. White's presentation revealed that experiments had been conducted on patients at Johns Hopkins University in Baltimore and St. Elizabeth's Hospital in Washington. The following day, White and Hamilton were back in New York at the Hotel Roosevelt conducting another round of experiments. About a week later, about thirty army officers suspected by Counterintelligence Corps agents of being Communists were interrogated, with five officers admitting to their Communist affiliations.

Were the enlisted men volunteers in the experiments? Gottlieb asked.

In a fashion, White replied.

What do you mean by that?

White explained that most of the personnel recruited for these experiments had been told that OSS was conducting trials of a new drug that might cure shell shock. However, they were not informed about anything connected to interrogation use, because of concerns that the information would compromise the experiments.

Gottlieb had asked White about the experiments on enemy POWs. White had explained that there had not been that many experiments. The most significant had involved a captured Nazi U-boat commander who was being held at a POW camp in Virginia where high-ranking German commanders were taken for interrogation. OSS had tested the drug on POW's there and at Fort Holabird in South Baltimore, Maryland. There are written reports about it somewhere, White said, but as he recalled, this one U-boat commander, the sole survivor of his submarine's sinking, had been singled out for truth drug interrogation because of his obvious knowledge of German naval maneuvers.

According to a 1945 OSS truth drug report that later turned up in White's files, the German officer was invited to the camp's officer's club "for a few social drinks, which was more or less customary." The German officer, after a few drinks, "would talk freely on most all matters," but:

> [I]t could be seen that while he would talk freely on most all matters, he was well aware of the fact that an attempt might be made to obtain information from him. The opportunity was found to give him a cigarette [that] had been loaded, and after approximately half an hour had passed from the first administration, one of the company, in a round-about and innocent manner, lead up to the question of maximum depth of the submarine [that this officer commanded].

The report describes what happened after the U-boat commander was given cannabis:

> [The German,] definitely under the effects of the drug, was still wary and indicated he would not give information on this point. Some time later, after two more cigarettes had been consumed, the talk was led around to morale, and he freely conversed about the general lowering of morale

220

of German submarine personnel. *However, no information was ever obtained concerning maximum depth.* [Emphasis added.]

Was the drug tested on anyone besides enlisted personnel and POW's? Gottlieb asked.

One person, White said, a criminal type.

Was his name Del Grazio? Gottlieb asked, following Colonel Drum's request.

Yes, August Del Grazio, White said. Everyone called him "Little Augie." Way back he was "Augie the Wop." He passed away just last April in Lenox Hill Hospital, White added. I visited him the week he died.

You knew him well? Gottlieb inquired.

Better than most people thought, White explained, with the wink of an eye. White said he often would frequent Little Augie's saloon on St. Marks Place. He and Del Grazio would also get together at each other's homes on a regular basis. Del Grazio was not your ordinary run of the mill criminal, said White. He had been around; he knew the ropes, had traveled widely, and was well read, very reserved and always well dressed.

White had first met Del Grazio in 1938 when the dapper gangster was in business with an opium dealer named Jacob Weinstein. Both men, White explained, not only dealt opium but also occasionally enjoyed the drug's pleasures. Del Grazio had made a great deal of money during Prohibition, and after its repeal had fluidly moved into narcotics, particularly opium. In the 1930s, he had journeyed to Istanbul, where he began to purchase large amounts of raw opium from local farmers for processing in France. But Del Grazio quickly realized that his business could prove far more lucrative if he set up his own opium processing factory in Turkey. During World War II, however, two brothers, Elie and George Eliopoulos, who operated arguably the world's largest opium ring at the time, forced Turkish officials to expel Del Grazio from Turkey. Subsequently, when the Eliopoulos brothers discovered that Del Grazio had fled to Berlin, they arranged to have him arrested by the Gestapo and thrown into Dachau concentration camp. After about a year, Del Grazio bought his way out of Dachau and returned to New York, a changed man due to the horrors he witnessed while imprisoned.

It was at this time that White had first encountered Del Grazio after a drug bust for which no evidence was found on Del Grazio and he was released. After this, White and Del Grazio became friends. They would meet periodically, sometimes playing chess in White's Forest Hills apartment. Over time, Del Grazio became a confidential informer to White. Years later, George would estimate that he and Del Grazio had met together on thirty or forty occasions.

Did you test the truth drug on him? Gottlieb asked.

Like I said, White replied, Augie was no babe in the woods. It would have been pretty difficult, if not impossible, to try to slip something like that past him. Let's just say that after he had his epiphany in Germany he was pretty cooperative on certain matters.

So the reports about the truth drug and Del Grazio were exaggerated? Gottlieb asked. *You're saying he was actually an informer without the drug?*

You could say that, White shrugged. He told Gottlieb more about his relationship with Del Grazio.

One day in 1943, Del Grazio had come by White's apartment, as he often did. The two men had drinks and began discussing the war and events in Italy, where Del Grazio still had family. At the time, the Allied armies were still five months away from landing on the south coast of Sicily to begin their take over of the island. Del Grazio told White that Meyer Lansky's attorney, George Wolf, was interested in getting Lucky Luciano released from prison in exchange for his assistance with the anticipated Allied invasion of Sicily. Luciano's contacts in Sicily, where he was born, would be invaluable to the U.S., Augie remarked.

White said he did not doubt that for a moment, but that nobody with OSS, including himself, would touch such a proposal.

Well, it doesn't really matter a whole lot, replied Del Grazio, because there are things happening on other fronts to accomplish the deal, things involving some very powerful people.

Del Grazio was close to criminal mastermind Meyer Lansky, the two having grown up together in New York's Lower East Side, and Lansky was very close to Lucky Luciano. When Luciano had been sentenced in 1936 to serve thirty-to-fifty years in prison for operating "the largest organized prostitution ring in America," Meyer Lansky had made a solemn promise to get him out long before his term was up.

By "powerful people" you mean Lansky? White had asked Del Grazio.

And others, like Lucky's lawyer, Moses Polakoff, and certain others, came the reply.

White knew Del Grazio well enough to know that pushing the subject would not help, so he dropped it at the time.

The subject did not come up again between White and Del Grazio until early 1946, when White had read in Walter Winchell's newspaper column that "Luciano was in Cuba and was being considered for the Congressional Medal of Honor because of his services rendered to the Allied forces in connection with the invasion of Italy."

You didn't know that Luciano had been released? Gottlieb asked.

I knew that, of course. We all did, White responded. What I didn't know was that Luciano was in Cuba at the time, and that he was being considered for a medal. I thought that was ludicrous. I was shocked to learn Luciano was in Cuba, readily accessible to his criminal associates in New York and Miami, not to mention Lansky, who owns half of Cuba. I assumed that maybe Augie had done something, or that Wolf or Lansky or all of them had done something to get Luciano out, but that no way did Luciano help with the invasion of Italy, and no way in hell was he going to stay in Cuba if I could help it.

The day before Gottlieb left New York, he and White met at the Narcotics Bureau office where White introduced Gottlieb to agents Arthur Giuliani and Vance Newman. Also present was "special employee" LaChapelle, who was known at FBN by his real name, Pierre Lafitte. As readers shall soon learn, Giuliani, Newman and Lafitte would, within a year, play prominent roles in the CIA's drug experiments at their Greenwich Village safe house in New York.

Back in Washington, Gottlieb reported his findings to Colonel Drum and Willis Gibbons. Drum asked if he thought the OSS cannabis drug was worth pursuing as part of the Agency's programs. Based on all that he had learned, Gottlieb said, no, he did not think the cannabis-based substance was worth further investigation; there were better options out there worth pursuing. But, he added, George White might be able to help with certain matters related to field experimentation. Gottlieb reported that White would like to help in any way he could, adding that his easy access to unsavory criminal types could be of tremendous assistance.

Gibbons told Gottlieb he would take the matter under consideration and discuss the suggestion with Richard Helms and Frank Wisner. It is not clear if Col. Drum was aware at that time that George White had already been vetted for Project BLUEBIRD by James Angleton. Angleton had met with White at least twice already in Washington, and once in New York. Gottlieb would say decades later that he was unaware of Angleton's recruitment of White. "It didn't surprise me to learn later that it had occurred," said Gottlieb, adding:

> It was still early in my career, but I was coming to keenly understand that things were not always what they seemed to be, and that nobody ever took one course of action when others were available. Initially, it was confusing, but over time one learned that there was a duality to intelligence work that always had to be taken into account.

By early summer 1951, Project BLUEBIRD administrators had further refined their interrogation research to focus exclusively on "special interrogation and hypnotism techniques" applied to "war and specific Agency problems." The problems were listed with startling specificity:

- Can we 'condition,' by post-hypnotic suggestion, Agency employees (or persons of interest to this agency) to prevent them from giving information to any unauthorized source or for committing any act on behalf of a foreign or domestic enemy?
- Can we, in a matter of an hour, two hours, one day, etc., induce a hypnotized condition in an unwilling subject to such an extent that he will perform an act for our benefit?
- Could we seize a subject and in the space of an hour or two by post-hypnotic control have him crash an airplane, wreck a train, etc.?

•Can we [long and short range] through post-hypnotic control induce a subject to commit violence against another individual, or induce a subject to murder another individual or group of individuals?

•Can we through post-hypnotic control create a condition whereby a subject would forget any such induced act after the subject is brought out of his 'conditioned' state?

Obviously, the CIA was especially interested in hypnosis as both an offensive as well as defensive weapon. In February 1951, BLUEBIRD team members led by Morse Allen received "special private instructions" in hypnosis techniques from an expert whose name has been redacted in all CIA documents concerning the sessions. Allen reported several days later that the training went extremely well, but noted, "No exact estimate of the course's value can be determined *until actual results have been obtained upon subjects.*" [Emphasis added.] Allen continued:

Certain fundamental questions were specifically answered in the course of the instruction and are regarded as being of extreme importance in BLUE-BIRD work. The questions are set out in question and answer form below:

Question: *What percent of subjects can be subjected successfully to hypnosis techniques?*

Answer: 85% to 95%.

Question: *Can a person under hypnosis commit an act against his religious or moral scruples or against his training or upbringing?*

Answer: Yes. Anything could be done by a person under hypnosis, including murder.

Question: *Can a person under hypnosis be forced to commit suicide?*

Answer: Yes, this can de accomplished indirectly and it can be done directly.

On August 8, 1951, H. Marshall Chadwell, following a conference with a group of military representatives, requested that for security reasons the Office of Security designate a new code name as soon as possible for Project BLUEBIRD. As Chadwell put it, "BLUEBIRD was chosen to cover a particular field operation. The word has been in use for quite some time and is known to several persons no longer connected with the project." Eight days later, Sheffield Edwards notified Chadwell that the new name was "ARTICHOKE."

3

Artichoke

The disposal of the Subject is not immediately contemplated but explor-atory investigations and discussions have been initiated. According to the Subject's own confession...he had twice enlisted and deserted from the [redacted] in 1948 and 1949. Fingerprints, photographs, and details of his confession in this connection have been forwarded to [redacted] for verification. In the event these allegations are found to be true, that the [redacted] are willing to have custody of Subject, and providing that the penalty to be imposed is substantial, AIS [Army Intelligence and Security] may turn over Subject to the [redacted]. If this avenue of disposal does not materialize, AIS shall in any event attempt to provide disposal in terms of the most severe measures feasible so as to insure it from further compromise by Subject.
— CIA Memorandum, Request for ARTICHOKE Use, 1
November 1951

Sidney Gottlieb took LSD for the first time in late 1951, about a year after being hired by the CIA. Guiding him on his maiden voyage into reaches unknown was Dr. Harold Abramson. This first session took place in New York City. Asked about why he felt compelled to experience the drug firsthand and how it affected him, Gottlieb later said:

It made no sense to use the drug on others without having first experi-enced it myself.... I discussed the merits of self-administration with Col. Drum on a number of occasions. He eventually agreed.

We then took it... I can specifically remember two places. The first time was in the presence of Dr. Abramson in New York City, the second time was in a hotel room in Washington, D.C. In D.C. there was also a physician present. I don't remember his name. I think it was another one of our consultants.

What was the initial dosage you took?

I can only give you the approximate dosage. It was approximately one hundred micrograms, taken mixed into a glass of water.

Were there others who self-administered the drug that first time with you?

Yes, Dr. [Henry] Bornter. Later on, after he was hired, Bob Lashbrook took part in those early self-administered experiments.

Do you recall how LSD made you feel?

It was a long time ago, but, yes, I do remember some things. I felt nothing for about thirty or forty minutes. Then I had an odd sensation in my mid section... my chest felt as if it expanded some... I felt that time altered, but I'm not sure I can explain that to you.... Then I had a feeling... a feeling of out-of-bodyness, also very difficult to describe. It was as if I was in some kind of translucent wrapping that enveloped my entire being, like an aura enclosed my body. I felt very good, focused, centered. My thinking, my thought process, was clear yet different; there was a fluidity to it that was unusual...and a feeling of complete euphoria took hold of me for several hours, subsiding slowly as the drug wore off.

How many times did you take LSD?

I don't recall an exact number of times. Between 1952 and 1955, perhaps a dozen or more times... perhaps upwards of two dozen times or more.

Any regrets having taken LSD?

None whatsoever, I consider the overall experience to have been very beneficial.

And again, the motivation for this self-experimentation was what?

To experience the drug first-hand, to experience its subjective effects... I felt if we were going to administer the drug to others that it only made sense to experience the drug first-hand, to establish subjective measures, so to speak. These were the early days of ARTICHOKE and MKULTRA... when there was considerable thinking that LSD could be put to effective uses.

ARTICHOKE. Various reports bandied about on the Internet claim that Project ARTICHOKE was named after Allen Dulles' favorite vegetable. This seems unlikely given that all formal program cryptonyms were selected from a list drawn up at the time by Paul Gaynor's staff in the Agency's Security Research Service (SRS) of the Office of Security. One account from a former intelligence official is that the ARTICHOKE label was drawn from a 1951 newspaper account concerning Ciro Terranova, a ruthless criminal who was commonly referred to as the "Artichoke King" because he terrorized vegetable merchants in New York, where in the 1930s he cornered the artichoke market. "It was tongue-in-cheek, like a lot of the cryptonyms selected," said the official.

Nonetheless, ARTICHOKE marked a real acceleration of Project BLUE-BIRD, and a programmatic expansion into areas previously not imagined by the CIA. Perhaps SRS chief Paul Gaynor best captured the core purpose of ARTICHOKE when, in 1952, he posed the project's ultimate question to the CIA's Medical Office chief:

Can we get control of an individual to the point where he will do our bidding against his will and even against such fundamental laws of nature [like] self-preservation?

Initially, ARTICHOKE was the responsibility of the Agency's Office of Security, with former BLUEBIRD director Morse Allen assigned to oversee day-to-day matters. Allen eagerly took on the job, but immediately ran headlong into jurisdictional battles with the Agency's Office of Scientific Intelligence (OSI). In late 1951, OSI managed to gain control of ARTICHOKE, but by September 30, 1952 the Security Office was back in the driver's seat. Frank Wisner formalized the transfer of responsibility in a memorandum stating that all "the various offices concerned" had agreed that "over-all responsibility for Project ARTICHOKE should be transferred from the Office of Scientific Intelligence to the Assistant Director for Security," Sheffield Edwards. Wisner added, however, without explanation, that "responsibility for the foreign scientific aspects of the subject covered by Project ARTICHOKE" would "remain in the Office of Scientific Intelligence." Inter-departmental squabbling continued, however.

According to a 1952 CIA report on the jurisdictional battles, there was "a glaring lack of cooperation among the various intra-Agency groups, fostered by petty jealousies and personality differences that result in the retardation of the enhancing and advancing of the Agency as a body." When the decision was made that Security would regain control, Allen promised he would "call upon the research and support facilities" of TSS, if necessary, but nowhere is there any indication that he did so. According to Sidney Gottlieb, "We were never called on to do anything that I can recall, other than to attend review meetings and to report on our own programs, but our hands were full with other matters, so I'm sure we were greatly relieved they didn't."

During the time ARTICHOKE's lines of authority were in dispute, incoming Scientific Intelligence chief Marshall Chadwell and the Agency's Medical Division were nonetheless contracting with individuals from a number of federal agencies. An April 7, 1953 memorandum from Chadwell and the Medical Division Chief states that people with specific skills for special ARTICHOKE projects had been recruited from the U.S. Department of Agriculture, the Food and Drug Administration, the Department of Health, Education, and Welfare, and the National Institutes of Health. In addition to tapping talent pools at federal agencies, ARTICHOKE officials attempted to forge collaborative lines with Army, Navy, and Air Force intelligence, and with the FBI. All three military branches had already embarked on their own research into interrogation and narco-hypnosis (the Navy was readying its "Pelican Teams" to conduct intensive interrogation), but all three agreed to send representatives to ARTICHOKE conferences on a regular basis.

Only FBI director, J. Edgar Hoover, rejected the Agency's overtures and refused to allow his employees to participate.

A 9-page November 1951 memorandum to Frank Wisner and Richard Helms from Morse Allen reads like an instruction manual for "the uses of ARTICHOKE and special requirements necessary for ARTICHOKE in the field." The document also clearly laid the groundwork for the safe house activities conducted by George White and Pierre Lafitte in New York beginning in 1952, even though at the time, White's activities fell under Project MKULTRA. It reads:

> Artichoke techniques should only be used as a last resort or when all other means have failed in a particular problem or series of problems...or when a subject is completely recalcitrant or particularly stubborn.

But the document also suggests that "the same techniques "could successfully be used immediately upon the development of a case as a starting point for obtaining information," or "at any given point in the development of a case." With stunning precision, the document clarifies that ARTICHOKE experiments would be:

> ... best operated in a hospital or in a hospital-type area, [but in] the event hospital-type facilities could not be procured, it would then be best to carry out ARTICHOKE operations in a safe house or safe area, but not in a military prison, concentration camp, barracks, or similar area....
>
> For technical reasons, it is best to have two adjoining rooms with a bath also adjoining or very close by. The best possible type of room to carry out the actual Artichoke activities is a room in which there is a bed or studio couch or cot, and if possible, this room should be fairly large size since a crowded room might produce confusion and hinder the development of the Artichoke technique. The adjoining room mentioned above is essential for the setting up of technical equipment, i.e. recording devices, transformers, etc. This room, of course, is also essential as an observation room and listening post for persons interested in the case to make notes or prepare questions as the interrogation develops....
>
> The bathroom is essential [if the] Artichoke doctor in handling the case needs water for various purposes, [and because] occasionally the Artichoke technique produces nausea, vomiting, or other conditions which make bathroom facilities essential....
>
> [It] is essential that all [Artichoke teams] have all possible information concerning the subject, [including a] full, detailed physical description of the subject or subjects to be examined, including age, medical history, psychiatric history, any known physical weaknesses or peculiarities. Is he alcoholic, drug addict, etc.? [Teams should also know] exactly what is the present condition of the subject, i.e. has he been in prison or confinement? If so, for how long? Has he been in solitary confinement? Has he had standard prison fare? Has he been well-fed or has he been on restricted diet? Has he been subject to any third-degree treatment? Has

he been subject to exhaustive interrogation in the immediate past? Has he been threatened with physical injury or worse? Has he ever escaped detention before? Should he be considered dangerous?

Under the heading, "Special Points Concerning Artichoke Techniques," the document advises:

The ideal situation in regard to the use of Artichoke would be to create a complete and perfect amnesia in every subject.... It should always be remembered that some individuals do not respond in any way to chemical treatment or psychological attack. Some pass into a complete state of coma without reaching a twilight zone (talking zone)....

Every effort should be made never to identify members of the Artichoke team by their true names in the presence of or in the hearing of the subject. Artichoke team members will use fictitious names in carrying out the Artichoke techniques....

A room that is more or less soundproof is better than a room where there are distracting sounds and disturbances.... The observation room should be kept as quiet as possible....

It should also be noted that nausea or violent reactions are not normal reactions, but are only set forth [herein] to call attention to certain possibilities that *may* occur...

As a rule, individuals subjected to Artichoke techniques will be entirely co-operative, passive, and lethargic.

By the first quarter of 1952, the CIA had assembled four ARTICHOKE teams, placing one each in Japan, Korea, Germany and France. Several additional teams were in training by February 1953. Each team consisted of three people committed to a four-to-six month renewable term, and respectively designated "research specialist," "medical officer," and "security technician."

Beginning as early as March 1952, field requests for ARTICHOKE teams arrived at CIA headquarters on a regular basis. For example, a March 17 cable reads: "Request permission give Artichoke to [name redacted] while team in France. [Redacted] have failed break subject though convinced he [redacted]."

Results of ARTICHOKE interrogations also began arriving at CIA. For example, a June 12 cable from Germany reports:

Artichoke team examined subject...results positive. Team considers case most successful in their experience...Actual questioning covered 1 hour period on 9 June...Since subject experienced complete amnesia after first treatment further testing was decided against.

And CIA headquarters sent instructions to the field regarding ARTICHOKE teams on the way, as in this terse August 9 cable to Korea from CIA:

Desire send Artichoke team from 18 August to 9 September to test important new technique. Desire minimum 10 subjects. Will brief senior officials types of subjects desired. Technique does not, *not* require disposal problem after application.

An August 19 cable from CIA headquarters to an unknown location reads: "Artichoke team will probably work vicinity 19 August to 7 September...can be used on any subject. No additional disposal problem."

Not all ARTICHOKE teams were dispatched to locations out of the country. Some were deployed domestically to two CIA safe houses, one in a Washington, D.C. row house, just blocks away from the State Department on K Street, and another on Maryland's Eastern Shore, a large farm bordering the idyllic and secluded town of Easton. Both of these safe houses were expensively equipped with large two-way mirrors, sound recording equipment, numerous concealed and remote-controlled microphones, and motion picture taking equipment.

In addition to outfitting the safe house with state-of-the-art technical equipment, the CIA also, on occasion, employed a number of high-priced call girls for what it termed "operational activities to be conducted in the safe houses." (Contrary to countless published reports, there is no evidence that George White used prostitutes in his New York safe house. As readers shall see, the situation was different later on with regard to his San Francisco safe houses.)

As would be revealed in documents that first became public in 1975 when the "facts" surrounding Frank Olson's death were released, Project ARTICHOKE quickly fell under the informal control and coordination of a group referred to as the ARTICHOKE Committee, established in April 1952 by then-CIA director Bedell Smith. The Committee's role was deliberately defined as "informal" because, as was often the case in the Agency's byzantine hierarchy, a formal ARTICHOKE Conference – consisting of CIA department and section heads – oversaw both the project and the Committee.

Frank Olson, now a Camp Detrick civilian employee assigned to CIA contract work with SOD, was appointed to the ARTICHOKE Committee in May 1952. Olson's role on the Committee is described in documents produced in 1975 by the presidential-appointed Rockefeller Commission, which readers will learn far more about. According to the documents:

> [Olson was] concerned initially with drugs that would assist in interrogation, but the concept expanded to include drugs that would serve as a defense against hostile application to Agency employees as well as drugs that would afford some control when administered to an individual.

Chief among these drugs, stated the Commission, were sodium amytal, sodium pentothal and LSD.

Surviving minutes from nearly a dozen ARTICHOKE Committee meetings show that the committee's work mostly focused on ARTICHOKE team recruitment and project enhancement, and that the committee functioned in a routine and congenial fashion. However, not everything was always peachy keen with the group. A handwritten note by one CIA official on the committee reveals what might have been strong dissent among committee members. That dissent could just as easily have been expressed against some of today's "war on terror" practices. The note reads:

> What in God's name are we proposing here? Does it not strike anyone but a few that these projects may be immoral and unethical, and that they may fly in the face of international laws? What really are we attempting to accomplish? Where does respect for life and human dignity come into play?

The unidentified writer was reacting to a proposal concerning "the possibilities of inducing subjects to go against their will and personal belief's and commit acts such as murder." Another note, scribbled by someone with the initials "JG" on a proposal drafted month's later, reads: "Where does this stuff end? The sheer madness of some of these ideas is getting difficult to swallow."

ARTICHOKE Conference meetings regularly delved into consideration of immoral practices. At one of its earliest meetings, in December 1951, the six-member group discussed at length how to use a "standard electric-shock machine" to produce "normal shock effects" including convulsions and eventually amnesia, "following a series of shock treatments." An unnamed college professor, who was also identified as a psychiatrist, appeared before the conference and explained that through the use of a Reiter electric-shock machine he "could guarantee amnesia for certain periods of time and particularly he could guarantee amnesia from any knowledge of use of the convulsive shock." According to conference minutes, the professor explained that electric-shock machines set at producing " lower current type of shock" would have the "effect of making a man talk." Said the professor:

> However, the use of this type of shock is prohibited because it produces in the individual excruciating pain, yet there is no question in my mind that any individual threatened with such pain applied through the machine would quite willingly give up information.

Apparently, the conference felt no compulsions to terminate the discussion not did they seem concerned with any prohibitions, given that the meetings minutes reveal that they were most interested in the electric-shock machines effectiveness for "third-degree methods" whereby subjects would complain, as the professor described, "that their heads were on fire." One conference member asked if an electric-shock machine could be employed to induce a "groggy condition in a subject," followed by an attempt to apply hypnosis to the subject. The professor replied that he knew of no such effort, but he eagerly agreed to make just such an attempt "in the near future." Another conference member remarked that it was his opinion that through the application of electric shock "an individual could gradually be reduced to a vegetable level."

Another conference five weeks later, took up the subject of lobotomies. A lobotomy is a radical form of psychosurgery in which the prefrontal cortex of the brain is cut into or destroyed. American neurologist and psychiatrist Dr. Walter Freeman performed the first prefrontal lobotomy in the United States in 1936. Within a few years, Freeman had refined the procedure to drilling holes in a subject's scalp. Later, in 1945, he devised what is termed "transorbital lobotomy," involving using an icepick-type device under the eyelid and against the top of the eye-socket and then using a small hammer to drive the device through the bone and into the brain. Perhaps the nation's most infamous lobotomy case was Rosemary Kennedy, JFK's sister, upon whom Freeman himself performed the procedure with disastrous results that left the young woman in an infantile and incontinent state for the remainder of her life.

ARTICHOKE officials were most curious to know if lobotomy-type procedures on enemy subjects could help elicit information and permanently erase memories. Sheffield Edwards and Morse Allen met with a number of experts to explore and discuss the possibilities with lobotomy, including doing a complete review of the work of Dr. James C. Poppen of the Lahey Clinic at the Boston Psychopathic Hospital. During the late-1940s, Poppen and others at the clinic performed over three hundred lobotomies. ARTICHOKE officials also explored the work of Dr. Lothar B. Kalinowsky and Dr. John E. Scarff at the Neurological Institute at Columbia University in New York, as well as work with electric shock therapy at the same facility.

On the afternoon of January 29, 1952, Sidney Gottlieb met with Morse Allen, from the Agency's Office of Intelligence and Security, a little known and deliberately obscured branch of the Security Research office. Accompanying Allen was a prominent Washington, D.C. psychiatrist, Dr. John Cavanagh, a deep cover member of one of the CIA's very first ARTICHOKE teams and one who had already made over twenty trips overseas for the Agency. Allen and the psychiatrist had come to Gottlieb's cramped office to review the state-of-the-art ARTICHOKE activities within the Office of Technical Services (OTS), as TSS was now known. Gottlieb explained that while OTS was but one of many sections within the ARTICHOKE Conference, OTS under Willis Gibbons was totally committed to ARTICHOKE activities.

Morse Allen was a forty-two year old expert in the use of the polygraph and a former State Department official whose task had been to root out suspected communists from government employment. In his State Department work, Allen frequently collaborated with CIA agents James McCord and William Harvey when both were also with the FBI, as well as with narcotics agent George Hunter White.

Allen asked Gottlieb to brief the Washington psychiatrist on OTS's work with "this miraculous new drug everyone was talking about, LSD-25." The

Security Office must be kept up to speed on any and all developments with the drug, Allen stressed. Gottlieb would later recall:

> I had been cautioned about sharing too much with Morse Allen without clearance from [Richard] Helms through Willis Gibbons or Col. Drum.... It's important to know that I was not on the ARTICHOKE team, in the ARTICHOKE group that the Office of Security or Security Research ran. My knowledge of ARTICHOKE teams stems from my attendance at conferences or meetings at which I represented technical services. ARTICHOKE and technical services were, in nearly every sense of the word, separate. They had separate purposes, separate supervision, not all the time in synch with one another... The Church Committee blurred the lines between all these programs, MKULTRA, ARTICHOKE, Bluebird, QKHILLTOP, Chemical Corps, NAOMI, SHADE, all of them became one and I was... I didn't have any problem with answering for them all, but I didn't... I didn't oversee all these projects. Let's leave it at that.

Gottlieb told Allen and the psychiatrist it was crucial that "the name LSD was not used anywhere" and that OTS staff, without exception, "referred to LSD by an applied nonsense name." Gottlieb explained that OTS was very encouraged by recent experiments conducted in New York and Michigan with LSD. "The drug is quite capable of producing extremely strong mental disturbances when used in small amounts," Gottlieb remarked, according to a briefing document written the same day by the psychiatrist. "An amount placed on the head of a pin produces effects lasting up to forty-eight hours," Gottlieb told the two. "Experiments on a controlled basis are on-going but there is still much work remaining."

Allen, known for his impatience with physicians and researchers, asked, "What about its powers to produce amnesia? What can you tell me about that?"

"Nothing encouraging," replied Gottlieb. "The drug impacts recall ability to a certain extent but not fully."

"Is there any other drug that can be used in combination with LSD that would produce amnesia?" asked the psychiatrist.

Gottlieb said he seriously doubted it, but OTS had been conducting research in which meretran, an analeptic stimulant, was mixed with LSD. The effects of mixing the two drugs heightened LSD's effects.

"Does it promote amnesia in any way?" Allen asked.

"No," replied Gottlieb. "It keeps the subject charged and awake. In the application of LSD, it's an added pressure mechanism in keeping subjects awake."

Who was overseeing the research? Allen asked.

Gottlieb, mindful of Gibbons' cautions, sidestepped the question by responding that his deputy director, Bob Lashbrook, would have to get back to Allen with that information. Subsequent memos revealed that it had been Dr.

Harold E. Himwich and Dr. Carl Pfeiffer who were conducting the experiments with meretran. Both physicians were among the very first to be retained as consultants by the CIA in the early 1950s. Dr. Himwich, Gottlieb repeatedly stated throughout his post-CIA years, along with L. Wilson Greene, had been instrumental in drawing Gottlieb's attention to the existence of LSD. Himwich, who died in 1975, had focused on the causes of schizophrenia and helped found, with his wife Williamina (a doctor who worked at Edgewood Arsenal) the Thudichum Research Laboratory at Galesburg State Research Hospital in Illinois. It was also at Galesburg where Himwich conducted many of his experiments for the CIA.

Dr. Carl Pfeiffer, who was awarded multiple CIA contracts over the years, concentrated his early work on "drug-induced psychotic states in human males." His earliest undertakings for the Agency commenced in 1951 at the New Jersey Reformatory at Bordentown. Here he experimented upon twenty young male inmates between the ages of twenty-one and thirty, giving each LSD and amphetamines to test the ability of the drugs to induce psychosis. Later, at the Atlanta Federal Penitentiary, he used sixteen inmates, inducing psychotic states with LSD. Pfeiffer's Agency work lasted through to at least 1960.

Gottlieb met again with Allen and several other SRS employees in October 1954 to provide a detailed verbal report on OTS research activities related to ARTICHOKE and QKHILLTOP, another project overseen by Allen. Launched in 1954, QKHILLTOP's central purpose was to carefully study Chinese Communist brainwashing techniques and to incorporate the best of these techniques into Project ARTICHOKE. Much of the QKHILLTOP research was conducted at the Cornell University Medical School Human Ecology Study Program. Within less than a year, Gottlieb's MKULTRA project would fund the offshoot of QKHILLTOP, the Society for the Investigation of Human Ecology (later shortened to the Human Ecology Fund).

Morse Allen's report on Gottlieb's projects provides us with one of the most in-depth looks at OTS activities at the time. Gottlieb told Allen that

> [OTS's] main sections of research fell into eight categories, the most important being:
> Clinical Evaluation of Chemicals (especially LSD) on Humans; Hypnosis training;
> Studies of Chemicals on Totally Unwitting Subjects;
> Special Problems Involving how to Bring the Chemicals to Unwitting Subjects; and
> Physiological Studies.

At the start of his report, Gottlieb explained that Dr. Harold Abramson of Columbia University and Mount Sinai Hospital "is carrying out a series of experiments for OTS with a group of [subjects] at the Mount Sinai Hospital, using LSD primarily." Gottlieb said that to date "Abramson has carried out two hundred interviews on sixty subjects using standard subjective-type tests and tests aimed at psycho-motor responses." Gottlieb further explained that Dr. Harris Isbell and Dr. Victor Vogel were experimenting on imprisoned drug addicts at the United States Public Health Service's Addiction Research Center in Lexington, Kentucky to measure "the chronic toxicity and tolerance of LSD." Isbell and Vogel had secured "two complete wards" of prisoners for their experiments, some of which involved dosing subjects with LSD daily for 30 days straight or longer. "Of particular interest," Allen wrote, "is the fact that, according to Dr. Gottlieb, Isbell has found that a tolerance to LSD is reached after twelve hours and hence, LSD could only be successfully and profitably used once in every four days."

Gottlieb at this time also informed Morse Allen about Dr. Carl Pfeiffer, recently of Emory University, who was "studying the effects of flicker and epileptic type seizures produced by chemicals with flicker or sound." Gottlieb said that Pfeiffer previously "had done very advanced work along these lines" and that he still "had access to all that work." Allen noted that while most of OTS's research seemed focused on LSD, there were additional projects involving "the plant known as kava-kava" and "on the so-called Jamaica dogwood (eritrina)," and "on piule, ormosia, the Mexican mushroom, panaelous, and rivea chorimoosia, a form of piule."

Allen also recorded Gottlieb's report on the collaboration between OTS and the Eli Lilly Company which had "succeeded in making a total synthesis of LSD," and that another private drug house was "trying to synthesize hyacine (scopolamine)." Allen wrote, "Dr. Gottlieb stated he regarded this as important since it is known that scopolamine is one of the few chemicals which produces amnesia fairly regularly, and amnesia is of interest not only to OTS but to other components of the Agency."

On hypnosis, Gottlieb stated OTS was no longer attempting to use hypnosis in operational work but "was doing studies in recall via hypnosis and also was attempting to find out if hypnosis could be used to improve memory." Gottlieb said OTS hoped to eventually use several expert consultants to perform advanced work in experimental hypnosis.

On the subject of chemical experiments with unwitting subjects, Gottlieb explained that Narcotics Bureau agent George White had been set up in a safe house apartment in New York for more than a year and was successfully using LSD on unwitting subjects. Gottlieb then noted that OTS was financing a considerable amount of research through the Army's Chemical Corps at Camp Detrick. He said that while scientists there "were, generally speaking, interested in the production of diseases as biological and chemical weapons for warfare use, there were nonetheless certain areas of extreme interest to OTS, particularly in connection with covert activities." Allen noted that Gottlieb "cautioned all present that the nature of this work was so sensitive that further discussion was unwarranted and requested no notes be made in this connection."

Lastly, Gottlieb told Allen's group that delivery of chemicals to subjects "was one of the more complex and difficult problems OTS was forced to study." He explained that John Mulholland, a famous stage magician and sleight-of-hand expert based in New York, "was now on the OTS payroll and that Mulholland had "written a manual on simple ways to bring chemicals to bear on a subject." Gottlieb said OTS "was studying techniques for common use such as distraction of attention, all kinds of useful gadgets and small items that would squirt solutions into a person's drink without their knowledge."

At this point in his meeting with Gottlieb, Allen asked him, as Chief of Technical Services, to provide updates on OTS's LSD activities. When Allen and Gottlieb had met previously, on January 29, 1953, they had discussed how OTS could assist ARTICHOKE, and Gottlieb had "indicated a complete willingness to work in close harmony with Security, the Medical Staff, and all others in furtherance of ARTICHOKE." According to Allen's report, Gottlieb now explained that under OTS contracts with numerous outside researchers:

> very advanced work was being conducted with the drug [and]... the results to date were very encouraging, so much so that [OTS] did not wish to call to attention any Agency interests concerning LSD and, hence, plan to use the nonsense name 'SERUNIM' rather than make reference to LSD.

Allen's report quotes Gottlieb in some detail, as follows:

> ...[I]n many ways, LSD, because of the infinitely small amounts necessary to produce a narcotic effect, the drug is regarded as a 'very interesting and potentially effective agent for our use *if it could be properly developed.*' [Italics original.]
>
> [He] pointed out that LSD is quite capable of producing very strong mental derangement when used in amounts so small as to be unseeable [sic] and incapable of being tasted or smelled.
>
> Dr. Gottlieb also stated that by careful control, LSD can be made definitely non-toxic and with the extremely important advantage that the individual taking the LSD is completely normal on the following day.

Allen then asked Gottlieb if he thought LSD could induce amnesia and Gottlieb responded, "LSD would *not* produce amnesia but because of the totally disorienting effect of the chemical, the individual taking it has little accurate memory of what went on." Allen's report then states that Gottlieb cautioned Allen about relying too much on the potentialities of LSD, and told the ARTICHOKE director that he felt it was unwise to mention anything about OTS's work with LSD at ARTICHOKE meetings.

That Allen was so curious about LSD and that ARTICHOKE administrators were conducting their own independent experiments with LSD and other drugs was upsetting to Gottlieb, given that the universe of knowledgeable LSD researchers was so limited. It did not seem smart to have such a limited field of experts being approached from separate and uncoordinated branches of the CIA. Gottlieb would later remark:

> It was as if there was a stampede for knowledge about LSD, to explore all of its possibilities, and the various Agency branches and offices were tripping over one another in the process. They were also often at cross-purposes with their views on how the drug could be used and in what situations. ARTICHOKE staff wanted the drug out of the labs and into the field for operational use, defensively and offensively. Our approach within [OTS] was more cautious and studied.

Also worth noting is that following their LSD discussion, Allen briefed Gottlieb on the fact that a group of ARTICHOKE consultants had recently traveled to Mexico, Latin America, and the Caribbean. According to Allen, the ARTICHOKE people had shipped large amounts of exotic plant materials back to the Agency in an effort to stockpile, catalog, and use in ongoing experiments. The goal was to identify new substances that could be employed for interrogation and "information retrieval," as well as for more extreme activities, like surreptitious murders. Thus far, Allen explained, over fifty plant samples had been brought back to CIA headquarters, including several forms of datura, jatropha, and *erythyina indica*, all potent and sometimes lethally poisonous, ethno-botanical substances. At the time, the Agency's Security Office, as well as its covert operation branches, were pressing hard to find both substances and delivery techniques that could be employed to disable and/or kill silently and without detection.

About four weeks later, Allen again met with Gottlieb and expressed further interest in LSD, asking specifically about using the drug as an inducement "in getting selected individuals to commit acts of substantial sabotage or acts of violence, including murder." Allen was especially interested in the possibilities of using LSD and other drugs, perhaps in combination with hypnosis, to induce extreme violence and, although he never mentioned the words "assassination" or state sponsored murder, these intentions seemed quite obvious to Gottlieb. Allen had remarked at the time that his interest in this subject had been prompted by a series of "public kidnappings" and "secret police-sponsored murders" that had occurred recently in divided, chaotic Berlin.

At the same time that ARTICHOKE administrators were seriously contemplating the assassination possibilities of drugs and hypnotism, Sidney Gottlieb had been meeting regularly with narcotics agent George White whom he had requested the CIA recruit as a paid consultant. The request was slowly working its way through proper channels. Meanwhile, Gottlieb explained, it would be fine for White to conduct some activities informally. In March 1952, Gottlieb handed White several ampoules of LSD — without any elaborate explanation to what precisely the liquid drug was — asking that the narcotics officer discretely experiment with the drug. White assured Gottlieb that he would put the drug to good use as he had a number of planned interrogation sessions scheduled soon.

In April 1952, responding to pressure from both Stanley Lovell and Gottlieb, Col. Drum (Gottlieb's superior) authorized George White's paid consultant role. At the same time, Drum instructed Gottlieb, as chemical branch chief, to draw up a work plan specific to White's location in New York for approval. Drum told Gottlieb that White's services would not be appropriate for participation on any of the Artichoke teams currently being composed, but that James Angleton and Frank Wisner considered the Manhattan safe house ideal for continued drug experimentation similar to what was being practiced at the Foggy Bottom location. Drum also informed Gottlieb that Angleton and Wisner were interested in possibly retaining the services of White's elusive "special employee" Pierre Lafitte. (Gottlieb did not know it at the time, but Angleton had had several meetings on his own with White.) Drum instructed Gottlieb to initiate Lafitte's background check and make arrangements for him to meet with Wisner, Angleton and other OSO representatives in Washington.

Gottlieb telephoned George White the first week of May, and on May 9, they met in Hartford, Connecticut. Also present was Lafitte who had been working under cover with White on a case involving heroin, gun running, and counterfeiting. In Hartford, White and Lafitte met with Gottlieb in his hotel room to discuss the possibility of the CIA employing Lafitte's services for 'special projects,' and then they discussed LSD for the first time. To Gottlieb's surprise, White announced that he was quite knowledgeable about LSD and had already had several discussions about it with Stanley Lovell and James Angleton, as well as Dr. Harris Isbell, Dr. Abraham Wikler, and Dr. Victor Vogel — three doctors on staff at the federal prison hospital in Lexington, Kentucky.

White had known all three physicians for about seven years. He had known Angleton—upon whom the lead character played by Matt Damon in the film *The Good Shepherd* was based—for at least nine years. White and Angleton had met many times during World War II in Rome, Italy, where OSS officer Angleton had risen to chief of X-2, the counterintelligence arm of the OSS.

White now told Gottlieb that his awareness of LSD also came from the FBN's observations of Alfred Hubbard, whom White described as "a real opportunist" who was "making a small fortune peddling" guided LSD sessions as a means to new levels of awareness. Hubbard, commonly called "the Johnny Appleseed of LSD," was born in Kentucky at the turn of the century and did hard time as a youthful offender. He later became an OSS officer during World War II. Hubbard once remarked, "I never owned a pair of shoes until I was twelve." He took LSD for the first of countless times in 1951, and reportedly a short while later attempted to convince FBI director J. Edgar Hoover to try the drug. Throughout the 1950s, Hubbard received large shipments of LSD directly from Sandoz in Switzerland, with Agency approval. One 1955 letter from the Sandoz company to "Dr. Alfred Hubbard" (he was not a physician or medical doctor) reveals that in June of that year, Hubbard purchased "43 boxes of L.S.D., 25 ampoules per box." Hubbard was instrumental in pioneering LSD as a drug for the treatment of alcoholism, and was responsible for turning writer Aldous Huxley on to the drug. Timothy Leary also once credited Hubbard for drawing his serious attention to LSD and other psychedelics.

Gottlieb later recounted, "White and I discussed Hubbard at length.... I wasn't familiar with Hubbard at the time, but White seemed to know a fair amount about him." White explained to Gottlieb that, according to Federal Narcotics Bureau files, Hubbard had a tremendous supply of LSD, which he had purchased directly from Sandoz in Switzerland. Charles Siragusa, FBN Rome office head, had informed White that Hubbard had enough LSD to produce in excess of "over one-thousand LSD experiences." Gottlieb would later say that he had "serious doubts" upon first hearing this, but that after checking with Agency officials he learned that, if anything, Hubbard "most likely had more LSD than the amount described by White."

On June 5, 1952 Gottlieb telephoned White in New York and informed him that Willis Gibbons had made arrangements for Pierre Lafitte to meet with OSO officials about several sensitive projects on June 23. In the meantime, however, Gottlieb and White met on June 9 in Hartford, Connecticut, where White was working a narcotics case, and Gottlieb proposed that he "become a CIA consultant." White noted in his diary, "I agree."

Meanwhile, Pierre Lafitte was meeting in Boston and New York with a CIA official identified only as "McClain." On the evening of June 23, Lafitte's wife, Rene, telephoned White at home to let him know that Pierre was being held overnight in D.C. for further meetings with Sheffield Edwards, Frank Wisner and Richard Helms. The next day, Lafitte was back in Connecticut where White met up with him and they drove to Boston for a two-day CIA training session led by Robert Lashbrook.

In September, Gottlieb flew to New York to lead another two-day training session for FBN agent Arthur Giuliani and Pierre Lafitte. The training took place at the elegant Hotel Roosevelt on Madison Avenue at 45th Street where Lafitte had been working undercover as a bell captain, thanks to George White. In this position, Lafitte had easy access to all of the hotel's guests and its 1,000 rooms.

For this 'training,' Gottlieb brought about two dozen small ampoules of LSD for White. Gottlieb explained to him that each container held enough for one dose per individual. Although at the time White's status as a formal consultant still awaited final approval from FBN head Harry Anslinger, nonetheless Col. Drum had informed Gottlieb that the delay was only a formality and that White's training and work could begin anytime. Before Gottlieb returned to Washington, he instructed White to secure a suitable safe house in the city, preferably in the area of Greenwich Village. They discussed the technical requirements over dinner. White's diary reveals that the day following his dinner with Gottlieb, after briefing Harry Anslinger, he began looking for potential safe house sites. He also did not delay using the LSD ampoules Gottlieb had left with him.

Two days later, Gottlieb telephoned White to tell him that he had set up a November 19 appointment for him at CIA headquarters with Dr. Willard Machle, assistant director in the Office of Scientific Intelligence. Machle was a physician, toxicology expert, and former Director of the Army Medical Research Laboratory who had headed OSI before being replaced by Chadwell. Now Machle wanted to meet with White to review arrangements for White to share with OSI the results of certain experiments that had a bearing on ARTI-CHOKE objectives. Gottlieb told White that he and TSS chief Willis Gibbons would sit in on the meeting.

Three weeks following Gottlieb's September visit, James Angleton and Gottlieb met with George White in New York about progress with the search for a safe house and they also discussed several projects for Lafitte. Gottlieb and Angleton informed White that a well-known New York-based magician, John Mulholland, would begin training classes at the Hotel Roosevelt on the first of November. Mulholland had been retained by the CIA to write a manual on "sleight of hand" techniques and to teach the skills to carefully selected agents.

That evening White, Lafitte, Angleton and Gottlieb had dinner with Dr. Harold Abramson, and were joined by Robert Lashbrook, Col. Drum and Willis Gibbons, who had flown up from Washington. Over dinner, Gibbons explained that White and Lafitte would jointly run experiments with drugs — including LSD and LEA, a less potent form of LSD — provided by the CIA through Dr. Abramson, and that monthly reports would be submitted to the Agency either through the Washington mail-drop or to Robert Lashbrook when he was in New York on one of his regular visits.

According to White's date book and letters, Angleton returned on November 27 to have Thanksgiving dinner with George and his wife, Albertine, at their apartment. The next evening, while Albertine was at work, White and Angleton drank gin and tonics laced with LSD. White recounted later that he had a "delayed reaction" and that Angleton had a "pleasurable experience." White wrote that Angleton "after really coming under the effects of the drug" talked him into taking a taxi to Chinatown, where the two were to have dinner. There, White recalled, with plates of food before them, they commenced to "laughing about something I can't remember now" and "never got around to eating a bite."

About a week later, on December 5, Sidney Gottlieb was stunned to learn from Robert Lashbrook that George White had been thrown in jail. Gottlieb later recounted, "My first thought was that it had something to do with the LSD he'd been given, but then Bob told me that George had been jailed for contempt of court. I don't remember the details, but it was a relief to hear them." Lashbrook told him that White had been jailed for refusing to reveal the name of an informer in a federal grand jury investigation against a notorious gangster, Thomas "Three Fingers" Luchese. White had told U.S. Attorney, Myles J. Lane, that he would give the name only if all members of Lane's staff were to leave the jury room.

The informer is Lafitte? Gottlieb asked.

Yes, replied Lashbrook.

Lashbrook explained that Federal Judge David Edelstein had ordered White to give up the name and that White justified his refusal by citing the murder of Eugene Giannini two months earlier.

White told Edelstein, in his no-nonsense, blunt style, "There's no way under the sun that I'm going to give this informer up."

"And your reason for not complying with my order?" the judge asked.

White cited the murder of Eugene Giannini, another of his informers, and former dope peddler and henchman to Lucky Luciano. "Look what happened to him when his name got out," said White. "He got two bullets to the head, your honor."

Judge Edelstein ordered White to jail. He told White, "This is not a punitive sentence; it is a coercive sentence. You hold the key to the lock."

But Edelstein was not wholly correct. Attorney and City Council President, Rudolph Halley, White's close friend, held a key of his own. Halley quickly called Anslinger in Washington, apprising him of the situation. What should I do? asked Halley.

Get him out, Anslinger said. Whatever it takes. Tell White he can talk with or without Lane's people in the room, but use an alias for Lafitte in any testimony about him, and make sure he isn't called before the grand jury.

An hour later, Halley and White walked out of the jailhouse to a throng of anxious reporters.

"What about this informer?" asked a reporter.

Halley draped his arm around White's shoulders and said, "White's statement to me is that this man will be killed, just as Gene Giannini was killed, if his name becomes public."

"Will he give up the name if forced?" asked another reporter.

"An informant's life and blood should not be on Mr. White's conscious," said Halley, solemnly. "I hope that the U.S. Attorney will have Mr. White questioned through proper channels. In my five years before this court, I have never seen a federal agent forced to reveal the name of an informer. Mr. White has been before this jury day after day, not for them to get evidence— but to get something on Mr. White."

"Where's White now?" Gottlieb asked Lashbrook.

"Here at the hotel, upstairs with Lafitte. We have a training session tonight," Lashbrook replied.

In 1998, Gottlieb recalled that according to George White and Pierre Lafitte, Gene Giannini had been the subject of one of their most successful LSD interrogation experiments:

> George conducted a good number of experiments on people he encountered in his professional work, criminals, narcotics dealers, gangsters... He told me a number of times that the sessions yield a fair amount of useful information, some very useful information. I think Giannini fell into the 'very useful' group. Beyond that I don't know that I ever knew anything about Giannini or any of the other criminal types that George dealt with. It was not a world I frequented.

Gottlieb also vaguely remembered that Lafitte [under the name Martin] had worked as a bell captain at the Hotel Roosevelt in 1952, but that he, Gottlieb, was not aware that Lafitte had also worked part-time as bell captain at the Statler Hotel as of August or September 1953.

Perhaps the best-written account of what occurred with Giannini comes from Pulitzer Prize winning reporter Ed Reid. Reid, who began his illustrious writing career in 1935 with the Brooklyn *Eagle* newspaper, and went on to receive the coveted George Polk Memorial Award and the Page One Award of the New York Newspaper Guild, was a close friend of George White's, as he was with New York City Council president and attorney Rudolph Halley, and a number of the CIA officials who worked with White. On numerous occasions, White, sometimes accompanied by Robert Lashbrook and/or Gottlieb, lunched with Reid in New York.

Reid, whose tough, fast-talking, cigarette dangling newsman depicted in so many film noir movies of his day, had witnessed Giannini's interrogation on the night of April 8, 1952. White and Lafitte had driven Giannini from Idlewild Airport to White's Greenwich Village apartment. As Reid wrote in 1953:

> Giannini, glass in his hand, looked around and smiled. He leaned back and talked and talked and talked. He talked about the syndicate in Manhattan, about its friends in high places, in political clubs, in the halls of Justice, in the United States Attorney's office in the Federal Building on Foley Square. He gave names, dates, places—such as Tommy Brown, John Ormento, Joey Rao, Eddie Coco, Louis 'King' Dioguardio, Saro Mogavero, Vinny Mauro, Johnny the Bug, Joe Stracci, Socks Lanza, Charlie Albero, Joe Biondo, Sam Accardi, Gyp the Gap and Jerry the Lug. He talked.

Five months later somebody murdered Giannini. On September 20, his body was found in East Harlem face down in the gutter with two bullets holes in his head. Within days, two of Giannini's closest associates in New York were also killed. No one has ever been arrested for any of the murders. All three slain men had provided George White and Pierre Lafitte considerable information about illicit drug dealing and mob connections. All three had been subjects in White's early LSD experiments, the results of which presumably benefited the CIA's Project ARTICHOKE. The files on all three murders have long since been lost or misplaced by New York crime officials. Were these early subjects disposed of gangland style because they were a threat or liability to someone? As far-fetched as it may seem, the "disposal problem" would soon become a primary concern of Project ARTICHOKE officials.

A rapid succession of intra-Agency memos from early 1951 reveals that the "disposal" of ARTICHOKE subjects who had been held for security or interrogation purposes was considered of paramount importance. A memorandum dated March 7, 1951 discusses the subject in detail and defines the concern succinctly:

> PROBLEM: To dispose of blown agents, exploited defectors and defecting trainees who have sensitive knowledge of our operation as makes it necessary to hold them in maximum custody until either (a) operations have progressed to a point where their knowledge is no longer highly sensitive or (2) the knowledge that they possess in general will be of no use to the enemy.

A second memo written the same day, March 7, by another Agency branch also expresses concerns with the "disposal" issue and expounds on what is meant by that term:

> The definition of 'disposal,' in brief, was understood to mean the providing of a facility to keep the 'disposed' person in security until his knowledge of operations is no longer of value to the enemy.

But the task of creating a 'holding' facility was judged to be "a very difficult and expensive mechanism." According to a third memo:

> The idea of isolation of these people in any one place or in a number of places [is] difficult, in that sooner or later they would rebel and cause complex problems.

What do we do with these subjects, agonized CIA operations administrators? Do we eventually release them and risk exposure and compromise at some future time? Do we hold them indefinitely in isolated compounds set up just for such purposes? Or do we "actually permanently dispose of them," as one memorandum put it. (Little did the CIA know the issue would resonate over fifty years later with the nation's war on terrorism.) Neither college textbooks nor business manuals nor legal tomes offered hints or guidance about such problems. But perhaps science did.

In mid-March, security chief Sheffield Edwards, following consultation with Scientific Intelligence chief H. Marshall Chadwell and Morse Allen, came up with what he thought was an ideal solution: amnesia-inducing drugs. Proposed Edwards:

It is [my] desire that OSI investigate some method of treating such people in a way that would cause semi-permanent amnesia for a period of approximately one year.

After a flurry of meetings within the various clandestine branches, a recommendation emerged: funds would be made available "to initiate the synthesis of, and clinical tests with, compounds suitable for inducing amnesia." A "well-qualified" physician, unidentified in declassified documents, was selected for the work and a deadline of December 31, 1951 was set for coming up with the ideal drug.

Eight months later, on November 1, 1951, CIA headquarters received a request from overseas for "authorization for the use of Artichoke" on a subject whose name is still classified, but is thought to have been an East German double-agent being held in a Frankfurt safe house for interrogation. The three-page request makes no mention of the possible use of amnesia-inducing drugs but it is highly revelatory of certain objectives behind the use of "the ARTICHOKE technique." The memorandum discusses the subject being interrogated and states that, following intensive interrogation, possibly including torture, he "has changed to a relatively more cooperative attitude and he has begun to furnish considerably more information." The memo continues in stunning detail, and with intriguing elements redacted, as follows:

Nevertheless the extent of truth and completeness of this information cannot yet be determined. The field as well as Headquarters has agreed that the procedure of interrogation and treatment indicated above [this being a redacted section of about five typed lines that most likely described the types of torture used] should be continued and that the ARTICHOKE Technique should be applied at the conclusion of the debriefing sessions....

I&SS [CIA's Inspection and Security Section] will be notified when appropriate conditions materialize for briefing and dispatch of ARTICHOKE team. The ARTICHOKE operators have asserted that Subject's cooperation is not required for successful application of ARTICHOKE....

The disposal of Subject is not immediately contemplated but exploratory investigations and discussions have been initiated. According to Subject's own confession to [redacted] he had twice enlisted and deserted from the [redacted] in 1948 and 1949. Fingerprints, photographs, and details of his confession in this connection have been forwarded to [redacted] for verification. In the event that these allegations are found to be true, that the [redacted] are willing to have custody of Subject, and providing that the penalty to be imposed is substantial, [Army Intelligence and Security] may turn over Subject to the [redacted]. If this avenue of disposal does not materialize, AIS shall in any event attempt to provide disposal in terms of the most severe measures feasible so as to insure it from further compromise by Subject.

In January 1954, an ARTICHOKE Team traveled from Washington, D.C. to Germany. In a safe house outside Frankfurt, they faced what a subsequent report deemed "a hypothetical problem, namely: Can an individual of [redacted] descent be made to perform an act of attempted assassination involuntarily under the influence of ARTICHOKE?" The same report laid out the "essential elements of the problem" as follows:

> As a 'trigger mechanism' for a bigger project, it was proposed that an individual of [redacted] descent, approximately 35 years old, well educated, proficient in English and well established socially and politically in the [redacted] Government be induced under ARTICHOKE to perform an act, involuntarily, of attempted assassination against a prominent [redacted] politician or if necessary, against an American official.
>
> The SUBJECT was formerly in [redacted] employ but has since terminated and is now employed with the [redacted] Government. According to all available information, the SUBJECT would offer no further cooperation with [redacted]. Access to the SUBJECT would be extremely limited, probably limited to a single social meeting. Because the SUBJECT is a heavy drinker, it was proposed that the individual could be surreptitiously drugged through the medium of an alcoholic cocktail at a social party, ARTICHOKE applied and the SUBJECT induced to perform the act of attempted assassination at some later date.
>
> All the above was to be accomplished at one involuntary uncontrolled social meeting. After the act of attempted assassination was performed, it was assumed that the SUBJECT would be taken into custody by the [redacted] Government and thereby 'disposed of.' Other than personal reassurances by [redacted] means of security involving the project, techniques, personnel and disposal of the SUBJECT were not indicated. Whether the proposed act of assassination was carried out or not by the SUBJECT was of no great significance in relation to the overall project.

On September 8, 1952 Gottlieb telephoned White and asked him to pick him up at the airport in New York the next day, explaining he was coming to attend a one-day conference. "I expect to have some good news for you when I arrive," Gottlieb said. The next day, White made a notation in his diary: "Gottlieb visits for conference. Says 'clearance' is ok for CIA & that consultant status is being processed." On the ride into Manhattan, Gottlieb handed White a vial of LSD. White's diary entry for the next day, September 10, reads: "Met Lafitte— give him vial for trial re Gottlieb." The next day's entry reads, "Call Gottlieb re Janey test— Lafitte." The following day, September 12, an entry reads: "Call Gottlieb re Janey test & several reports of Lafitte." "Janey" was one of several code words White employed over the years for LSD. What happened with the "vial for trial" is a stunning, never before revealed example of political foul play and dirty trickery.

On December 19, 1952 Sidney Gottlieb telephoned George White from CIA headquarters to tell him that his Agency consultant's contract had finally passed its last hurdle. White would officially go onto the CIA's payroll on January 1, 1953. Gottlieb asked White if he had selected an alias yet. White responded that he had decided on the name "Morgan Hall," an alias he had employed recently in a number of undercover operations in New England. Set up a bank account at New York's National City Bank under that alias, Gottlieb instructed, put me on the account as a co-signer under the name "Sherman R. Grifford," and begin forwarding all written information to Bob Lashbrook at a Washington postal box address he had given White earlier.

"Merry Christmas, George," said Gottlieb.

Nineteen-fifty-three was a banner year for the CIA's ARTICHOKE activities. At a January 12 Artichoke Committee gathering Willis Gibbons reported that OTS staff were working hard to identify additional scientists to conduct LSD experiments, ideally at colleges, universities or private laboratories around the country. Gibbons remarked that OTS had high expectation for the drug but due to its unpredictable nature, there would need to be extensive controlled experiments with human subjects. To date, Gibbons reported, OTS had identified nearly fifty universities and colleges that appeared well suited to such experiments and that fieldwork related to security clearances was well underway at eighteen of the campuses. At the same meeting, Morse Allen reported that efforts to recruit staff positions for the Tokyo-based ARTICHOKE team were progressing on schedule, as well.

In mid-February, Allen chaired an ARTICHOKE Conference with Paul Gaynor's staff to discuss recent developments with hypnosis experiments and the on-going search for additional personnel skilled in the art of hypnosis. Allen reviewed the results of three meetings held in the past month with hypnotists in New York and on the West Coast. H. Marshall Chadwell announced that OSI's ARTICHOKE work was advancing well ahead of schedule and that there were now two ARTICHOKE Teams assigned to work in West Germany and that plans for a third were only awaiting the addition of another psychiatrist and trained hypnotist. Chadwell reported on meetings between OSI and OTS staff with New York stage magician John Mulholland, remarking that the meetings had produced several additional possible candidates for hypnotists to be employed both domestically and overseas. Chadwell reminded conference attendees that Mulholland would be in Washington the same month to lead training sessions in the art of deception. (Readers shall soon learn more about Mulholland.)

Paul Gaynor informed the group that according to information from contacts in Great Britain, the USSR was training its own ARTICHOKE-like teams. Gaynor said that several reports focused on so-called Soviet "Confession Gangs" that were trained in highly sophisticated interrogation using sounds and lights, and that a Swedish psychiatrist with expertise in sensory deprivation and fatigue had trained some of these teams. Gaynor said Soviet teams were reportedly using a wide variety of drugs in interrogation, with some sessions lasting as long as twenty-six days.

At the same meeting, Sidney Gottlieb and Robert Lashbrook reported that work with Camp Detrick's SOD was progressing well. Lashbrook explained that OTS staff scientists were working closely with SOD's Dr. Herbert Tanner, Dr. Grayson Hoffman, and Dr. Ben Wilson on designing devices for the surreptitious delivery of small but lethal amounts of toxic agents, and that Frank Olson, John Malinowski, and Allen Knott were consulting with Dr. Harold Abramson about portable protective gear that could be easily carried and would protect field operatives from exposure to toxic substances used by hostile forces. Gottlieb reported that he was "very pleased" with SOD work and cooperative activities being carried out with the Office of Naval Research. Gottlieb also reported on OTS work with British scientists attached to the Science Intelligence Service at Porton Down Biological Centre in England. He mentioned that Centre scientists, in consultation with SOD researchers, were experimenting with LSD and other hallucinogenic drugs on "volunteer enlisted personnel" at Porton Down.

At another February Artichoke Committee meeting, notes reveal that there was considerable discussion about interrogation methods employed by French troops in Indochina. According to H. Marshall Chadwell, CIA operatives in Europe and Asia reported that French physicians had been flown into Vietnam for interrogations that were "particularly effective but frequently amounted to little more than medieval-style torture sessions." Paul Gaynor updated the group on continuing efforts to explore the potential of electro-shock for "Special Interrogation," stating that additional consultations with "noted experts in the field" had taken place over the previous two months.

The meeting, as well as a follow-up gathering held a few days later, also dealt with what conference members referred to as the "Explosive" case, a moniker given to an individual who was closely aligned with Project ARTICHOKE and who worked for a "division" that, according to conference minutes, was "preparing to turn him loose" because of perceived temperamental and psychological problems. Apparently, when issues and stability concerns first arose about "Explosive," his drinks were surreptitiously dosed with at least two drugs to no obvious effects. One former intelligence official interviewed for this book, and speaking on terms of anonymity, has maintained that "Explosive" was Frank Olson of Camp Detrick's Special Operations Division. Another former official maintains, however, that "Explosive" was a Russian double agent. Available documents fail to identity this person with certainty. Requests to the CIA to provide un-redacted copies of several documents that could positively identify "Explosive" have failed. In all, three Freedom of Information requests concerning "Explosive" were submitted to the Agency's Public Information Office.

They were all ignored, lost, or set aside. Interesting to note is that two days after the April 16 meeting, Frank Olson and Dr. Joseph J. Stubbs were given a party at Camp Detrick honoring the two men for their ten years with the Chemical Corps.

An Artichoke Committee meeting was convened on November 19, 1953, the same day Frank Olson and some of his SOD colleagues shared LSD-laced drinks at the Deep Creek Lake lodge with several of Sidney Gottlieb's staff. The single-page agenda led off with a detailed discussion of LSD and then moved to reports on ARTICHOKE team activities which were occurring now almost weekly. Dr. Henry Bortner, a chemist with the Office of Technical Services, had been excused from the Deep Creek Lake meeting so that he could represent OTS at the ARTICHOKE meeting. Bortner, after conveying Gottlieb's regrets for not being in attendance, briefed the group on the initial list of twelve sub-projects that had thus far been approved for the yet to be christened MKULTRA program. Bortner would tell Gottlieb the following week that Morse Allen had been uncharacteristically quiet and seemingly disinterested in the sub-projects.

Sheffield Edwards had inquired, in particular, if George White was involved in Subproject number 3. Bortner introduced it as a Federal Bureau of Narcotics project. Edwards asked if George White was involved with it and Bortner confirmed that White was, in fact, leading Subproject 3 — unwitting drug experiments on some of the more unsavory members of New York's underworld. Edwards seemed satisfied with this. Bortner also reported that MKULTRA Subproject 3 also involved White's former OSS "truth drug" colleague, Dr. James A. Hamilton. Hamilton, now at Stanford University Medical School, had been contracted to study the "possible synergistic action of drugs which may be appropriate for use in abolishing consciousness." At the meeting's conclusion, Edwards told the assembly he and Paul Gaynor were extremely pleased with ARTICHOKE's advances over the past year and that they were looking forward to making equal headway in the coming year.

But Gaynor may have not been entirely pleased. Gaynor's handpicked ARTICHOKE director, Morse Allen, was engaged in a power struggle with Sidney Gottlieb for control of the project. Allen had earlier told Gaynor he had reliable reports that Gottlieb's OTS, with strong support from Wisner and Helms, was devising its own mind control program to be conducted apart from OS and OSI. Allen was upset about the extent of bureaucratic infighting within plain sight of DCI Dulles and DDCI Cabell, but Gaynor dissuaded Allen from complaining too loudly or going to the top with his unhappiness. Gaynor's advice was good, and it turned out well for Morse Allen to have heeded it. Despite the fact that OTS would soon launch its own "mind control" program, MKULTRA, Allen would retain leadership of Project ARTICHOKE for at least a decade longer. (Contrary to many publications and written accounts, ARTICHOKE was not replaced by MKULTRA and the two projects continued to run concurrently, at least until 1958, if not longer.)

On July 20, 1954, ARTICHOKE director Morse Allen was alarmed to learn that a group of unidentified researchers attending a Washington, D.C. scientific conference were discussing the use of LSD for interrogations. The CIA's Security office had made sure that a number of the Agency's own scientists – operating undercover in various universities and private groups – were attending the event. One of them reported that a foreign scientist had "made the statement that experimentally LSD had been used in interrogation and had proved remarkably successful." The scientist elaborated that:

> [About] 100 gamma of LSD was given to a [redacted country name] officer who had been instructed not to reveal a significant military secret.... [Nonetheless] after the LSD was given to the officer, under interrogation, he gave all the details of the secret which was recorded and after the effects of the LSD had worn off, the officer had no knowledge of revealing the information [and] did not believe that he had revealed anything.

Where did this story originate? asked the startled Agency officials. Was this hearsay? Was this misunderstood information based on another incident? Who was this officer? How can we learn more? Who has the details and further information? Stated a brief Agency report on the account:

> This information is extremely important because it is the first actual reported use of LSD in successful interrogation along intelligence lines although there is some information along criminal lines coming out of Germany. The facts, however, and details are at the present writing very limited.

As provocative and intriguing as this account is, we are left without any additional knowledge of any further developments.

In a 1995 deposition, Sidney Gottlieb was asked, "Who was Morse Allen?"

"To the best of my remembrance, he was a member of something called the Security Research Staff," Gottlieb replied, somewhat vaguely. "And he was in the technical branch in the Office of Intelligence and Security of the CIA."

"Did [Allen] have anything to do with the MKULTRA program?"

"Nothing except in the sense that MKULTRA matters were discussed at meetings with the ARTICHOKE people present."

"So he was a BLUEBIRD/ARTICHOKE person?"

"Well, the word BLUEBIRD, I don't even remember in the transition, in the sequence of events where these things got names. I don't remember what BLUEBIRD was... But [Morse Allen] was an ARTICHOKE person, yes."

"Were BLUEBIRD and ARTICHOKE teams sent overseas?"

"Not that I recall or know of. I have no specific ARTICHOKE knowledge. That was not my responsibility... I was not on the ARTICHOKE team, in the

ARTICHOKE group that the Office of Security ran. My knowledge of ARTI-CHOKE stems only from meetings at which I was at, at which ARTICHOKE representatives were also at."

In follow-up, Gottlieb was later asked, "In countless places it has been written explicitly or implicitly that you were deeply involved in the two projects, BLUEBIRD and ARTICHOKE, with some even claiming that you directed ARTICHOKE. Is that true?"

"The short answer is no. I wasn't involved in BLUEBIRD at all. Frankly, I don't recall the program except vaguely, primarily because I was hired about a year or two after the project began. ARTICHOKE is confusing to fathom due to all of its permutations and cross agency involvement, but I didn't direct the project. In fact, ARTICHOKE continued well into the term of MKULTRA, but I couldn't really tell you much about its activities at that time. It was operated by another branch entirely, [Office of Security] or the [Security Research Staff], and things were very compartmentalized then."

"Was Frank Olson or Camp Detrick involved in Project ARTICHOKE?"

"Not that I'm aware of. I believe he [Olson] was under the relationship... under the program known as MKNAOMI. That was begun... that relationship was already in place when I came to CIA, but I oversaw the program beginning sometime in late 1952, I think."

"Did BLUEBIRD or ARTICHOKE deal with Camp Detrick personnel?"

"Not that I know... I doubt it. But I don't know the specifics of ARTI-CHOKE. I can only answer for MKULTRA. That was mine."

4

Magic, Hypnosis, and High Strangeness

The magician [Mulholland] and George White had at least three or four meetings, maybe more.
— Sidney Gottlieb, 1997

There are few subjects about which so little generally is known as that of the art of deception.
— John Mulholland, 1953

Send all written reports to Granger Research Company. Call us collect in the event of anything of concern or out of the ordinary.
Use only those names on the Granger stationary when corresponding with us by wire, telephone, or written letters.
— Sidney Gottlieb to John Mulholland, 1954

The subject was persuaded, under hypnosis, to stab her co-worker with a pair of scissors.
— Morse Allen, CIA-SRS, 1953

In June 1953, federal narcotics agents George White, Vance Newman, and Arthur Giuliani, and Narcotics Bureau special employee Pierre Lafitte, crossed Manhattan from FBN headquarters to the Statler Hotel on West 34th Street and Seventh Avenue. In a third floor Statler conference room, they met CIA officers Sidney Gottlieb, Robert Lashbrook, Henry Bortner, and Ray Treichler (a TSS chemist and newly appointed liaison to Camp Detrick's SOD), and also John Mulholland, one of the nation's most renowned magicians. The reason for the gathering was that Mulholland had been retained by the Agency weeks earlier to teach trickery and sleight-of-hand to selected agents. Mulholland's initial contract with the CIA's TSS states:

> Mr. Mulholland will broaden the scope [of his work under MKULTRA subproject 4] to include services in connection with consultation, inclusive of training in CD/TSS {Chemical Division/TSS] selected areas.

These expanded services will also include travel and operations supplies, including those necessitated by training sessions.

According to Dr. Sidney Gottlieb, John Mulholland's entry into the world of clandestine affairs came about, as follows:

> We were casting about for a trustworthy person expert in magic, someone who knew sleight-of-hand well and who was well-grounded, that was professional and was skeptical of the more bizarre trends in magic, someone who could interface well with our people and the narcotics officials working with us.... We interviewed a number of people around the country, finding nobody really satisfactory, and then Dr. S.L. Quimby at Columbia, who was already working with the Agency on another project, suggested to Bortner [TSS Chemical Division employee] we speak with Mulholland. Dr. Quimby knew that Mulholland had performed before a number of American troops on USO tours and was pretty patriotic... And, to make a long story short, we eventually contracted with Mulholland.

Who was Dr. S.L. Quimby?
A former Naval commander, I think... and a physicist at Columbia University....Very well known, as a matter of fact. He was a friend with [Dr.] Harris Isbell, another Agency contractor, and [Dr.] Harold Abramson.

Did Quimby work for the CIA as a contractor?
I think... I believe that he did. I think he's already been identified, sometime in the Seventies' hearings, in that role.

What did he do for the Agency?
I don't recall specifically what he did... something related to his field of study, I'm sure.

Can you be more specific on Dr. Quimby?
I don't really recall all that much about him.

Did Dr. Quimby have anything to do with John Mulholland?
He may have, possibly. I think it was possible that they knew one another.

What do you recall about stage magician Mulholland?
It was so long ago...not much, unfortunately. I liked him. He was easy to work with... He was well to do, I think, or seemed to be. A folksy looking fellow, tall, very tall, always well dressed.... We knew that his real name wasn't Mulholland. We knew there was a dispute over that before I interviewed him in New York. I attended one of his shows before that. I don't recall his real name any longer.

Gottlieb did not mention that the CIA's Security Office, in the person of Paul Gaynor, and perhaps also Morse Allen, had raised a number of concerns about Mulholland in the process of clearing the magician for Agency contractual work. Chief among Gaynor's concerns were Mulholland's "sexual proclivities" and his long-standing relationship with his personal assistant Dorothy Wolf. As noted earlier in this book, SRS chief Gaynor was expert in identifying and exploiting certain idiosyncrasies of targeted individuals. Mulholland had employed Ms. Wolf for about seven years before he married Pauline Nell Pierce, yet he had never ended his romantic entanglement with Wolf. Indeed, Mulholland's love for Wolf was so sincere and steadfast that he informed his wife-to-be that his relationship with Ms. Wolf would not end and that Pauline would have to accept it if they were to be married. According to Mulholland biographer Ben Robinson, Pauline Mulholland once remarked, "Johnny was so much a man, one woman's love would not satisfy him."

Despite Gaynor's concerns, Mulholland was finally approved for work with the Agency. Robert Lashbrook hand delivered Mulholland's security oath to him in New York for his signature on November 14, 1953. This was almost two years after Professor S.L. Quimby had first suggested Mulholland for hire in early 1952. Gottlieb had first met Mulholland in mid-November 1952, and then in early February 1953, briefed him on the specifics of what TSS wanted the magician to do for the CIA. Understandably, Gottlieb had grown impatient with the security clearance process. In fact, Gottlieb had gone so far as to speak personally to Dulles about Mulholland. Also significant is the fact that Mulholland was extremely well connected with circles of power: the Rockefeller family, including Nelson, had been boosters of Mulholland; Mulholland's wife Pauline was related to Barbara Bush, George H.W. Bush's wife; and Pauline was a distant cousin of former U.S. President Franklin Pierce. Pauline herself came from a very wealthy family, and her father, Arthur J. Pierce, was a Brigadier General in the U.S. Army.

On April 13, 1953, before Mulholland's security clearance had gone through, Gottlieb telephoned him in New York to discuss the magician's initial scope-of-work. Gottlieb wanted Mulholland to train selected TSS personnel to be able to understand and perform basic sleight-of-hand trickery. For this training, Mulholland was to develop detailed written descriptions and instructions for making and using simple mechanical aids. TSS personnel needed to know how to use such aids in virtually any setting, under any conditions. As Gottlieb explained:

> In a very real sense, we would like to fashion each of our selected employees and other persons with firm basics in trickery, so that detection does not occur.

Following additional discussions, Gottlieb instructed Mulholland to deliver to him as soon as possible a written proposal for an operations manual that would detail how certain magic tricks could be employed in clandestine operations.

Mulholland was quick to the task, and within two weeks he mailed Gottlieb an outline of his manual, which would emphasize instructions for covert techniques for the undetectable administration of materials in "solid, liquid or gaseous form." Moreover, Mulholland assured the Agency, "No manipulation will be suggested that requires training of muscles not normally used, nor any necessitating long practice." Weeks later, Mulholland submitted his revised outline emphasizing "tricks with pills, liquids, and loose solids,"specifically pointing out that instructions would deal with "pills one-quarter the size of an aspirin tablet."

Along with his outline, Mulholland submitted an estimated budget of $3,000 for six months' work, with vouchers to be sent monthly or biweekly as his work commenced. Gottlieb telephoned Mulholland the first week of May and instructed the magician to address his biweekly invoices to "Sherman C. Grifford" – Gottlieb's pseudonym – at the post office box of Chemrophyl Associates, Southern Station, Washington, D.C. Within days, and using Chemrophyl stationary, Mulholland sent written confirmation of Gottlieb's instructions. (We do not know whether Mulholland noticed the type fonts used on the letterhead that slyly employed an "I" at the end of ChemrophyI, instead of an "l," allowing anyone with a discerning eye to identify the acronym "CIA.")

On May 5, Gottlieb, writing on ChemrophyI stationary signed "Sherman C. Grifford," informed Mulholland: "The project outlined in your letter of April 20 has been approved by us, and you are hereby authorized to spend up to $3,000 in the next six months in the execution of this work." Gottlieb enclosed a check for $150 to cover Mulholland's latest invoice submitted. In closing, he wrote: "A very crowded schedule of travel makes it necessary for us to delay until June 8th our next visit with you. An effective alternative to this would be for you to come down to Washington on May 13, 14, or 15 to discuss the current status of the work. Is that possible?"

Mulholland plunged head first into writing the sleight-of-hand manual, working eight-to-ten hours a day, constantly revising. He put aside distractions and canceled other commitments, including magic lessons for a long roster of eager students. He even suspended production of *The Sphinx*, a magazine devoted to the magical arts, that he published and co-edited with Dr. S.L. Quimby. Quimby, as can easily be imagined, was most understanding of the publication's suspension.

Gottlieb and Mulholland met with Robert Lashbrook and Ray Treichler at TSS's Quarters Eye offices in D.C. during the third week of May. Treichler had just returned from a meeting in New Jersey with Sandoz Company officials. Besides serving as liaison to Detrick's SOD, Treichler was the liaison between TSS and the nation's major pharmaceutical companies, although they may have believed he was a U.S. Army Chemical Corps official. At the May meeting, the group discussed Mulholland's forthcoming manual, now titled *Some Operational Applications of the Art of Deception*, and Gottlieb requested that

Mulholland schedule the first training sessions in New York for TSS officials and a few carefully selected Federal Bureau of Narcotics agents who were working closely with the CIA. Gottlieb told Mulholland that FBN supervisor George Hunter White, whose New York office was not far from Mulholland's, would contact him shortly to arrange training dates. Lashbrook informed Mulholland that he would arrange a lunch for him to meet George White the following week in New York. Treichler told Lashbrook that he would try to join them for lunch.

George White's date book for the following week reveals that he had dinner with Mulholland and Lashbrook, and on the same evening, he had been notified by FBN special employee Pierre Lafitte that a CIA-funded safe house had been established in Chicago. Within a few weeks, the first of about six sleight-of-hand training sessions took place at New York's Statler Hotel.

In July, Gottlieb met again with Mulholland to arrange his next assignments for the CIA, some of which would require travel. Mulholland agreed to the additional work. Early in August Gottlieb notified the Agency's financial office that he was establishing an additional MKULTRA subproject under Mulholland's name, and expanding the provisions set out in MKULTRA Subproject 4 "to include an allowance for travel for Mr. Mulholland and for operational supplies used in the course of this project." Explained Gottlieb, "Certain portions of subproject 4 require experimental verification by Mr. Mulholland. The item for operational supplies is intended to provide for the purchase of supplies used to test or verify ideas."

About six months after Frank Olson's death, Lashbrook notified Mulholland that he was to hold onto all written reports and invoices for TSS and any other documentation that he would normally mail, until otherwise notified. Lashbrook explained that he would personally pick up the magician's reports and vouchers and would hand-deliver any checks made out to Mulholland. TSS was, Lashbrook explained, indefinitely suspending use of its Chemrophyl Associates, Washington, D.C. post office box, although there would very likely be one soon in New York. The New York box apparently never materialized, however. Weeks later, Gottlieb informed Mulholland that all future reports, invoices, and correspondence were to be sent to a new Washington, D.C. post office box, this one registered in the name of "Granger Research Company." Unlike the Chemrophyl stationary, which bore only the name "Sherman Grifford," the Granger stationary listed three names: Samuel A. Granger, President (Gottlieb); Robert V. Wittstock, Vice president (Lashbrook); and Ralph J. Labaugh (Treichler).

By mid-1955, Mulholland's work and travel related to the occult or parapsychology intensified considerably. Around the same time, Mulholland's generally concise, professionally written communications with Gottlieb and Lashbrook assumed a more relaxed style, often referring cryptically to "the girls," "the women," and "the women in Maine." Magician and Mulholland biographer Ben Robinson speculates, without elaboration, that it "is likely that these people were psychic test subjects who attempted to read maps while blindfolded at a distance." Robinson adds: "Possibly he [Mulholland] was referring to the prostitutes employed by the Agency for the development of their new drugs. Both operations existed simultaneously."

Robinson is only partially correct. References to "the girls" began to show up also in George White's date book at the same time, and it is certain that White had nothing to do with psychic experimentation. White had, however, recruited three young women to assist with the LSD experiments he was conducting in the Bedford-Barrows Street safe house. None of these women were prostitutes, however. Two were aspiring actresses whom White had first encountered through his wife, Albertine, and the third was married to a close friend of the Whites. Interesting to note is that all three women had been dosed with LSD, one unwittingly and the other two knowingly. While it is possible that Mulholland used these women for physic experiments, it would appear doubtful since White makes no mention of it anywhere. Moreover, sources close to White, and highly knowledgeable about Mulholland's work for the CIA, report that the magician's "girls" were actually several young women that Mulholland had recruited through his secretary-mistress Dorothy Wolf. He recruited them not only for physic tests, but also to secretly dose CIA-targeted individuals with LSD and other drugs. The targeted individuals were located in Maine, New Hampshire, Illinois, and Connecticut, as well as other states.

Some of this clandestine work was directed at Henry (Andrija) Puharich and possibly also some of his associates. Since February 1952, TSS officials had been intrigued with Puharich's claims about telepathy and clairvoyance, especially in connection with a device Puharich employed called a Faraday Cage, essentially a copper-lined box that Puharich claimed "increased the abilities of a psychic by a thousand fold." Puharich described the cage as a "shield from electromagnetic radio waves, allowing only extremely low frequency (ELF) magnetic waves to get through." On several occasions Puharich had asserted to CIA scientists: "There isn't a psychic warfare operation or research laboratory in the world that does not make use of the [Faraday] Cage." Robert Lashbrook went so far as to hand write a letter to Mulholland expressing, at length, TSS's views on the value of using the cage. Wrote Lashbrook, "As far as we can tell, the group does not indicate why the cage should work.... Good luck, John. Don't take any wooden nickels."

Gottlieb and Lashbrook, both of whom may have been in over their heads on the subjects of telepathy and psychics, were acutely aware that U.S. Army officers at the Pentagon and in Army intelligence were especially interested in the Faraday Cage. The two TSS men had no intention of being left in the proverbial dust by the Army on any potentially significant scientific development. The U.S. intelligence community and military use Faraday cages, or Faraday shields as they are sometimes called, extensively. Many CIA and NSA buildings are enclosed within Faraday cages, intended to act as a Tempest shield (eavesdropping protection), and also as mitigation against electromagnetic pulse. Additionally, intelligence agencies employ portable cages to shield passports, credentials, documents, and credit cards from electronic interference.

In 1963, for reasons unknown, Mulholland decided to reveal his true name — John Wickizer. Born in Chicago in 1896, he had become enthralled by magic at the age of five when his mother, Irene May Wickizer, took him to a performance by the great magician Harry Kellar. A few years later, mother and son relocated to New York City, where Mulholland quickly sought out the Society of American Magicians. Within a short period of time, the young boy was effectively an apprentice to Kellar. Later, he became the protégé of renowned magician, John William Sargent. At the age of 15, Mulholland gave his first professional show and, according to his biography, "from that day forward was a professional magician."

Besides his stage act, Mulholland also worked as a "manual training instructor" at New York's Horace Mann School, sold books door-to-door, and even took a few classes at New York City College, although he never earned a degree. In 1925, Mulholland embarked on a world tour, accompanied by his mother, Irene. On tour, he not only performed, but also sought out other conjurers who helped him hone his magic skills. During the 1930s, Mulholland performed and studied in Greece, Japan, Korea, Manchuria, China, Java, Malay, Siam, Burma, India and other countries. In 1932, after returning to New York, Mulholland married Pauline Pierce and laid to rest the "mama's boy" rumors that had plagued him.

By the time the CIA approached Mulholland in 1952, he was one of America's most famous stage magicians, as well as a prolific writer, having authored about a dozen books. He was also an avid reader, with over four thousand books in his library on magic. In addition, Mulholland became editor of *The Sphinx*, a magazine devoted entirely to the magical arts and magicians. He co-edited the magazine with amateur magician and Columbia University professor of physics, Dr. Shirley L. Quimby. Quimby had maintained a long association and friendship with Mulholland based on their shared passion for magic. Beginning as early as 1929, Professor Quimby often assisted Mulholland with his stage acts. At a June, 1929 convention of the American Society of Magicians in Manhattan, it was reported that "Mulholland was invisibly assisted by Dr. Shirley L. Quimby, apparatus expert," in the performance of a particularly difficult and challenging trick that greatly impressed fellow magicians.

Professor Quimby was also a close associate of CIA contractors Dr. Harris Isbell, Dr. Paul Hoch, and Dr. Harold Abramson, as well as several other physicians and university-based scientists who covertly worked for the Agency and the U.S. military. Several entries in George White's diaries reveal that Quimby attended at least two highly secret gatherings in the Georgetown neighborhood of Washington, D.C., along with several other noted American scientists, including noted geneticist and cancer researcher Dr. Robert S. Goodenow, who also met at least twice with John Mulholland, and Clark B. Millikan, a professor at the California Institute of Technology and a highly respected aerospace researcher. It is suspected that Goodenow may have consulted with the CIA and Mulholland to help devise a special pin-prick type device to be used to covertly induce diseases in targeted individuals.

Secret CIA files reveal that Quimby participated in LSD experiments conducted by Dr. Isbell at the U.S. Public Health Service Hospital in Lexington, Kentucky. The same files also reveal that Quimby had helped transport illegal drugs confiscated by the Narcotics Bureau (marihuana, hashish and heroin) to Naval storage yards outside New York City, and from there to the CIA for possible use in experiments, or for other purposes.

From 1954 through 1957, and possibly later, Professor Quimby – a former wartime Navy lieutenant commander – was a key player in an EYES ONLY secret program called Project HKDECOY. Little is known about the project other than that it was TOP SECRET and initially involved the development of "protective gear and other materials and products," as well as "delivery mechanisms" for clandestine intelligence agents. Former Camp Detrick researchers say that HKDECOY "grew out of a pilot project overseen by SOD administrators Frank Olson and Col. Everett Champlin." (Readers may recall that Champlin was also in attendance at the infamous Deep Creek Lake meeting during which Olson, as well as Champlin, and others, were dosed with LSD.) From 1954 through 1955, HKDECOY operated undercover within the Office of Naval Intelligence as "a theoretical study project" aimed at developing "special tools and models."

In early 1956, CIA-TSS administrators Gottlieb and Henry Bortner, in consultation with Professor Quimby, decided that the ONR cover was no longer secure enough to conceal the planned projects. Therefore, it was recommended and approved that HKDECOY would be moved under the cover of MKULTRA. Among the projects specifically planned were *human experiments of a type not easily justifiable on medical-therapeutic grounds.*

Readers may be more familiar with the Quimby surname because Professor Quimby was married to Dr. Edith Hinkley Quimby, also a physicist and a world- renowned pioneer in radiology. She, like her husband, was a professor at Columbia University where she had established a research laboratory. Edith Quimby is widely noted for her work in measuring the penetration of radiation, thus enabling physicians to calibrate the exact dose of radiation and to control its side effects. Former intelligence officials say that Edith Quimby, like her husband, maintained project-related ties to both the CIA and ONR.

Sidney Gottlieb recalled years later that he "first spoke with Mulholland on the telephone, after Dr. [Shirley] Quimby assured me that he could be trusted." Gottlieb further recounted:

> That conversation was confined to the possibility of his providing training in sleight-of-hand. He knew nothing about LSD or any other drugs,

and there was no reason for any of that to be shared with him. After an exchange of letters and more calls, I met with him in Connecticut at his home. We discussed the Agency in general and specifically TSS needs related to his skills. He was happy to become a contractor with us; he seemed to really relish the work, and he had a good grasp on what was needed despite that I could not always be as specific as might have helped more. We socialized on a number of occasions and we were joined sometimes by Bob [Lashbrook] and George White. George had a parrot at the time that he talked to Mulholland about. He was trying to teach the parrot to do some unusual things, but I don't recall what. I don't know that Mulholland was any help with the bird.

Robert Lashbrook apparently benefited from his participation in Mulholland's sleight-of-hand training. According to his testimony in a 1986 deposition, when asked how Frank Olson and others were slipped LSD at the Deep Creek Lake lodge, Lashbrook flippantly responded: "There were two Cointreau bottles... One in your left lapel, one in your right lapel."

Question: *How were the people [at Deep Creek Lake] to be given LSD chosen?*
Lashbrook: Okay. There was one of the people at Detrick that was specifically excluded because of a medical problem. And I did not know about the medical problem. I think it would have had to have come from Ruwet. I did not take it. I do not believe Sidney [Gottlieb] took it, because we felt that there must be people on hand who would be able to do something if anything was required to be done. So not everyone took it, no.
Question: *Well, if the man with the medical problem reached for the Cointreau bottle, what would you do, pull it away? You knew there was LSD in the Cointreau bottle.*
Lashbrook: There were two Cointreau bottles.
Question: *You shifted them around so only the people—*
Lashbrook: Sure.
Question: *—who you wanted to have it, had it?*
Lashbrook: (*Witness nods his head up and down.*)
Question: *Is that right?*
Lashbrook: One in your left lapel, one in your right lapel. Yes, of course.
Question: *Was that meant as a joke?*
Lashbrook: Okay.
Question: *I don't think it's very funny when somebody dies as a result of something you did. You may think it's funny, but I don't.*
Now. What do you mean, in your lapels? Where were these two bottles you are talking about?
Lashbrook: Okay. As I recall, the after-dinner drink was served to the individuals. There was no provision made for anyone to go back for a second portion of the after-dinner drink, which contained LSD, because

the amount in each dose was— yeah -- in each drink was purposely small, and there was certainly concern— or wanted to make sure that no one got an excessive amount. So the bottle, which contained LSD, was very carefully controlled.

Question: *Who controlled it?*

Lashbrook: As I recall, I did. And it was very careful how much was taken out of that particular bottle, yes.

Question: *How did you choose Olson to receive the bottle?*

Lashbrook: I guess because he was there.

Question: *Did everybody get it? I thought you said everybody didn't get it?*

Lashbrook: Except those who were specifically excluded for some specific reason.

Question: *How many were specifically excluded for some specific reason?*

Lashbrook: At least one person from Detrick, and I don't recall how many, but I think at least two people from our group.

Contrary to published accounts, Mulholland's work for the CIA did not end with his trickery manual or with his consultation concerning hypnotists. CIA documents reveal that the popular magician continued to work covertly for the Agency at least through the end of 1957, and, as we shall soon see, some of this work was quite intriguing. However, at this juncture, it is important to point out that there is no evidence whatsoever that John Mulholland knew anything about Frank Olson's death, nor that he was involved in any way. Nor is there evidence to support allegations that Olson, accompanied by Lashbrook and Ruwet, visited Mulholland while the three were in New York in November 1953.

It is noteworthy, however, that Mulholland flew to Chicago a few days after Olson's death, and about three weeks later, he had sent Gottlieb and Lashbrook a highly critical report he had written on paranormal researcher Andrija Puharich entitled *A New Type of Experiment in Parapsychology*. (Readers would be justified in questioning Mulholland's credentials in psychology and parapsychology. Like many magicians of his day, he had no medical education or advanced science training, and there is little evidence that he understood the basics of psychology. The fact that TSS officials assigned him to evaluate scientific projects that were clearly beyond his knowledge seems odd.)

As readers have seen, a receipt for Mulholland's flight to Chicago was found in Robert Lashbrook's pocket when Lashbrook had been searched by the New York police following the death of Frank Olson. The ticket shows that Mulholland departed New York on December 3, 1953 on United Airlines. (The fact that Lashbrook, trained not to carry such documentation on his person, still had such a receipt in his pocket may indicate that he was still flustered, shaken, or distracted by Olson's death.) In Chicago, Mulholland spent two days meeting with Puharich, as well as with Clark Thorp, a chemist, and a man named Kenneth Miller, both of whom were from the Armour Research Foundation.

Puharich was working with Thorp and Miller under contract. Joining Mulholland in Chicago for the meeting were Lashbrook and Hank Bortner, also a chemist, from the CIA.

The Armour Research Foundation is a research and funding institute attached to the Illinois Institute of Technology that conducts extensive scientific research for the U.S. Army, Navy and Air Force, including the Army's Chemical Corps. Much of this research is classified and concerns radio frequency interference reduction, as well as other projects. Armour continues to be an active Department of Defense contractor.

Dr. Clark E. Thorp was the manager and chairman of Armour's Department of Chemistry and Chemical Engineering in the 1950s. Thorp is considered the "Father of Modern Ozone Research," primarily because of his expertise concerning Ozone toxicity and its effects on humans. Scientists say that it was Dr. Thorp's work that "led the way to clearing Ozone as a potential pollutant." It is unclear who Kenneth Miller was, but, at the time, there were at least two Kenneth Miller's working for the CIA.

Mulholland biographer Robinson writes that the magician's Armour "assignment was to assess the value of research by Thorp and company," but this seems hard to imagine given Mulholland's lack of scientific training in any of Armour's undertakings. Robinson claims that Mulholland "respectfully submitted" a "very detailed two-page report" to Gottlieb stating that "*The Literature Survay* [*sic*] *on Thought Transference* [was] most Pollyanish in [its] make-up." (One cannot help but think that Gottlieb and Lashbrook were using, and indulging, Mulholland for something other than scientific expertise—which he clearly lacked – and tapping his real skills for devious purposes. A handwritten, cryptic note from Lashbrook to Gottlieb in 1955 fails to illuminate much of the story: "Mr. Mulholland again discounts the bulk of what he witnessed, nonetheless every objective was achieved." Robinson, in his biography, provides no hint whatsoever of the specific research Mulholland was evaluating at Armour so it is very difficult to ascertain what he was really doing in Chicago. It is abundantly clear from Robinson's book that Mulholland detested Puharich, but here it is important to note that the CIA and the Army never wrote Puharich off, or discounted his work, but they did closely monitor his work.

Mulholland may have had a decided bias against Andrija Puharich, but he appears to have been much more open-minded toward psychic Eileen Garrett. Robinson writes that the magician obliquely admitted that Garrett "was never caught cheating throughout her career." Perhaps Mulholland would not have been so charitable in his judgments had he known that Garrett was quite close to Puharich. In two of his books and several of his published articles, Puharich writes extensively about the January 22, 1952 telepathy experiment that involved Mrs. Eileen Garrett and that was especially intriguing to the CIA.

Mrs. Garrett's role in the experiment was as the "receiver" of telepathy. The "sender" was Loren Wedlock, an acquaintance of Puharich's about whom we know nothing. She sat outside the Faraday cage, observing Garrett through a transparent mesh. The purpose of the experiment, according to Puharich, was to have Garrett, via a trance-induced personality named Abdul Latif, carry on a conversation with Wedlock, the "sender" in which Garrett/Latif would "guess the moment when an electrical charge of ten seconds duration was placed upon the walls of the Faraday cage." Garrett went into a self-induced trance, and, relates Puharich, thereafter "the conversation was carried on between her alleged control personality, Abdul Latif, and Mr. Wedlock." Through an indicator placed in front of him, Wedlock could tell when the electrical charge occurred. Confounding matters, Wedlock had a conversation with Garrett/Latif about "the use of vocal sounds in increasing telepathy." Puharich writes, "Abdul Latif obliged by giving certain vowels, demonstrating the sound production, and describing the effect this sound was to have." To demonstrate, Garrett/Latif "produced the sound E, and emitted a head-splitting version of this particular vowel." The experiment went on for about thirty minutes, during which three electrical charges of ten seconds duration each were placed upon the walls of the cage. Mrs. Garrett correctly identified two of the charges, which Puharich claimed was "an unusually good demonstration of telepathy."

When the experiment ended, Garrett went to her room to rest, and then reappeared an hour later, saying that as soon as she had awakened from her trance she had suffered severe abdominal cramps for about a half hour, "followed by three watery stools in rapid succession." Following this apparent unpleasantness, Garrett said that she experienced an unusual feeling of exhilaration and relaxed with a feeling of "unusual mental acuity" coupled with "traveling" clairvoyance. By this, Puharich says, "she meant that she had the distinct impression of literally looking in upon friends in New York City, Washington, D.C., London, and Southern France."

Puharich was fascinated by Garrett's feelings of unpleasantness and clairvoyance, but for unexpected reasons. Checking her blood pressure, he found it "to be twenty-five points lower than normal." Moreover, her skin was flushed, her pupils were pinpoint narrow, and her eyes were shining brightly. All of these manifestations, said Puharich, were "the general symptoms of parasympathetic activation." Puharich followed up immediately by running additional experiments with Garrett. The first experiment placed her back in the Faraday cage but with no electrical charges made. Puharich said he "thought it would be a better test of [Garrett's] sensitivity of the moment to eliminate the electrical charges, and see whether she would be deluded into making calls of targeting that were not there." Over a period of thirty minutes Garrett did not make one call, commenting aloud that she had no sensation of any electrical charges.

After a twenty-minute break, Garrett was subjected to another experiment, this one with six electrical charges made over the course of thirty minutes. She called all six correctly, and Puharich concluded that when "the parasympathic nervous system is activated there is an increased amount of acetylcholine released into the nervous system." Puharich described this activation as "being a state of cholinergia."

Later, in 1955, Puharich recalled the Garrett experiments after he had given another of his telepathic subjects, Harry Stone, some of the highly potent mushroom *Amanita muscaria*. Stone described the effects of the mushroom to Puharich, who thought it remarkably similar to Garrett's feeling of 'traveling clairvoyance.' "That is," said Puharich, "he seemed to be able, in his mind, to see through walls, and to distant scenes and places. The *Amanita muscaria* induces cholinergia in an individual due to the presence of the drug muscarine, which is one of the very potent cholinergic drugs." Puharich ran a series of highly successful experiments with Stone using *Amanita muscaria* and other drugs that especially captured the interest of the CIA. These experiments eventually blossomed into its controversial remote viewing programs involving a wide array of targets, including convicted murderer and egomaniac Ira Einhorn. Einhorn, who had once been close friends with Puharich and had written the introduction to the 1962 edition of his book, *Beyond Telepathy*, claimed in the 1990s, while on the lam for murder in Europe, that Puharich's CIA-sponsored drug research in 1953 and 1954 was linked to Frank Olson's death.

OTHER AGENCY MAGICAL PURSUITS

The CIA did not confine its magical pursuits to Mulholland's sleight-of-hand deception training. For a while, before such projects were transferred away from the purview of Morse Allen's SRS to Gottlieb's TSS, the Agency delved deeper into the black arts. Amazingly, this aspect of CIA activities has nearly completely escaped any public scrutiny until now. What we know is sketchy but most intriguing. Says former CIA-TSS official Edward Bensinger:

> For a while it became pretty bizarre. We were looking into all sorts of strange matters, meeting with some pretty kooky characters, but a few were interesting... scary, but interesting. I saw some demonstrations that were unbelievable.... For some of us the task was uncomfortable and crazy. We had had little to no exposure to these sorts of things apart from Hollywood movies. It was unsettling, to say the least.

One hint of the depth of research is found in the introduction to the CIA's assassination manual, which will be covered in greater detail in an upcoming chapter. A 1952 draft version of the manual describes a man named Hasan-Dan-Sabah who used the drug hashish to "induce motivation in his followers, who were assigned to carry out political and other murders, usually at the cost of their lives." Hasan-Dan-Sabah's credo with his closest initiates and most skilled assassins was: "Nothing is true, everything is permitted." States the CIA's manual, "Assassination is a term thought to be derived from 'Hashish,' a drug

263

similar to marijuana." It is certainly intriguing, for a number of reasons, that the Agency included this reference in its assassination manual. First and foremost is the nexus among Hasan-Dan-Sabah (also known as The Old Man of the Mountain), Hassan-I-Sabbah, an Iranian born in 1056 near modern-day Tehran, and the Knights Templar, a legendary group that nearly all of the CIA's founders and earliest employees openly admired and sought to emulate.

Respected writer and former *Newsweek* editor, Evan Thomas, writes in his masterful book, *The Very Best Men*, that William Colby, an OSS officer who later became DCI, "credited [Frank] Wisner [the former OSS officer who founded the CIA] with creating the atmosphere of an order of Knights Templars, to save Western freedom from Communist darkness." Other prominent early CIA officials strove to perform "work worthy the Knights Templar" and to belong to a "cultish crusade." Frequently, the Agency characterized itself as "the good guys versus the evil empire." Several heavily redacted CIA documents reveal a keen interest in the Ark of the Covenant, Solomon's Temple, and the "peculiar apparatus reportedly witnessed by Ezekiel." 'Ezekiel's Vision' is a biblical passage extremely important to Jewish mystics. It has also long been a source of fascination and mystery to many in the UFO community. Biblical passages about the "rock at Horeb" led the CIA to investigate the science of dousing to locate "concealed springs and water" and "other hidden sources of valuable natural resources." One document reads, in part:

> These subjects without doubt appear strange and extreme, but one cannot easily escape the reality of their effects and impacts. Exploration of a thorough nature is wise, and may well prove beneficial in a number of areas. Thusly, concerns about appearances, or ill comments, should be put aside, but caution should be exerted at every step.

Another document speaks of "the need to be ever vigilant in our pursuits" and the "need to verify whether these claims are real or are embellishments that have taken on a life of their own over the decades." One fragment outlined the possible use of cats as couriers because they "are highly magnetized animals" and could be utilized for the covert delivery of unidentified items.

For some time, TSS researchers were especially interested in the work of psychic Edgar Cayce. According to one document, in the early 1960s, consultants acting covertly were employed to spend time at the Association for Research and Enlightenment, housed in Cayce's Virginia Beach, Virginia headquarters. Related to these esoteric and occult explorations is another CIA-requested task for Mulholland: "an examination and explanation of certain of the Masonic designs and architectural features incorporated into the Federal City." Among those listed for examination were "the Capitol complex, the zodiacs of the Library of Congress, Meridian Hill Park, and the recently [1952] installed Mellon Fountain."

As already touched upon elsewhere in this book, the work of Dr. J.B. Rhine at Duke University's Parapsychology Laboratory in North Carolina was of special interest to the CIA's Security Research staff. One former CIA official has reported that the writings of Martin Ebon on parapsychology and the paranormal were likewise of special interest to the Agency, and that many of Ebon's books originated in studies conducted by the CIA's SRS and TSS branches. Ebon wrote over twenty-five books on subjects such as life after death, communication with the dead, ghosts, and exotic ESP. Born in 1917 in Hamburg, Germany, he emigrated to the United States in 1938 and worked as managing editor of the Foreign Language Division of the Overseas News Agency. During World War II, Ebon joined the staff of the U.S. Office of War Information where he became an expert on the Soviet Union. After the war, he became closely aligned with the Parapsychology Foundation in New York, and was executive editor of the *International Journal of Parapsychology*.

An examination of Ebon's extensive writings reveals that he was nearly always at the forefront of paranormal studies, and that often his writings paralleled the secret research of the CIA. Ebon has written authoritatively about Faraday cages, ESP, telepathy, bio-energy, hypnosis, remote viewing (well before it became all the rage), electromagnetic waves, and out-of-body experiences. In one of his books he revealed details of a three-year CIA program designed to make "a serious effort" to advance ESP research "in the direction of reliable application to the practical problems of intelligence."

Lastly, perhaps the most controversial of Mulholland's consultations for the CIA was his inquiry into the phenomenon of UFO's. That the CIA had any early interest in UFO's may surprise some people, but in December 1952, Dr. H. Marshall Chadwell, CIA chief of scientific intelligence, sent a memorandum to then-DCI Walter Bedell Smith warning that:

[U]nexplained objects at great altitudes and traveling at high speeds in the vicinity of major U.S. defense installations are of such nature that they are not attributable to natural phenomena or known types of aerial vehicles.

Earlier in September of that year, Chadwell had expressed his concern to Smith that the Soviets might be attempting to manufacture a UFO-type incident to confuse the U.S. military and the Air Warning System and perhaps mount an attack because "a fair share of our population is mentally conditioned to the acceptance of the incredible." It seems that Chadwell really did not know what to think about unexplained objects in the sky.

Of course, no story that is inclusive of the occult and high strangeness can be complete without some reference to UFO's. Sometime in 1956 and again in early 1957, Sidney Gottlieb asked magician John Mulholland to examine the ever-expanding number of UFO sightings and to render his opinion. Gottlieb, most likely acting on behalf of someone at a higher level within the CIA, perhaps knew that Mulholland had a firm bias against the possibility of unexplained aerial phenomena. In 1952, Mulholland had written a somewhat narrow minded article for *Popular Mechanics* claiming that all UFO's were pie plates controlled by strings. Upon reading the piece, a number of credible scientists, as well as Pentagon officials still alarmed by unexplained UFO sightings, privately wished that the entire matter were as simple as Mulholland put it. But for the Army and CIA, as is well documented today, it was not that simple.

In early 1956, the Agency asked Mulholland to "discretely investigate events surrounding an unidentified-aerial object and related phenomenon [sic] witnessed in the skies and on the ground in Kentucky." The incident, one well-known today in UFO annals, occurred near Kelly, Kentucky. There, on August 21 and 22, 1955, at a small farm owned by the Sutton family, eight adults and three children experienced an extremely frightening encounter with unexplained entities. The incident began with the sighting of a large saucer-shaped object flying over the farm emitting a multi-colored trail. A neighbor, Mr. Taylor, who had been visiting the family at the time, first saw the saucer. When he told the family about what he had seen they laughed at him, suggesting he had seen a falling star. Shortly thereafter, however, the family dog erupted in violent barking and then uncharacteristically cowered under the porch. Taylor and one of the Sutton men ventured cautiously outside to see why the dog was barking. As they stepped from the porch they spotted a strange glowing object approaching across a field. Within seconds, they realized that the object was an iridescent creature about three feet tall, with a round, oversized head.

Taylor and Sutton ran back into the house, seized a shotgun and a .22 rifle and watched the entity slowly approach the house. When it was within twenty feet of the house, they opened fire and the entity disappeared into the darkness. Minutes later, either the same entity or another just like it appeared at a side window looking in at the terrified family. Again, the two men opened fire, blasting through glass and screen; the entity did an acrobatic back-flip and vanished like the first. Certain that they had killed or wounded whatever it was, the two men and several other family members ventured outside—only to see another entity reach down from the porch roof above and touch one of the men on the head with a talon-like hand.

Everyone outside and inside the house screamed. Within minutes, several entities were surrounding the farmhouse. The men shot one that was sitting on a tree branch near a window, but it simply floated to the ground and then disappeared. The family later told police that the entities "moved in a strange way" as if their "legs were stiff" and when they moved or ran "only their hips moved" with their "long arms almost dragging on the ground."

The frightened family at this point piled into cars and drove to the nearby police station, about 15 minutes away by car, returning with several officers to search the place. However, the entities were nowhere to be seen. Several local officers, state police, and a photographer interviewed the petrified family and recorded their accounts. The police found a strange luminous patch of earth where one of the entities had reportedly fallen to the ground. But when the entities failed to reappear, police and others eventually left the Sutton farm.

After the police left, the entities returned to the farmhouse, peering into its windows at the family huddled together in fright. The next morning the police returned, as did a number of reporters from Kentucky radio stations and newspapers, as well as from neighboring Indiana and Tennessee. The reporters and local radio personnel pestered the family with incessant questions mixed with mockery. The publicity drove the family to exhaustion and reached the point where they refused to cooperate or speak with anyone. The Sutton family became the target of snide remarks and ridicule from local townspeople, even though highly respected ufologists took them seriously.

The police found that the family seemed to be quite truthful about what they claimed they had seen, and there was no evidence at all that anyone had been drinking or doing anything else to effect their mental states.

The Kelly, Kentucky case remains on the books as unsolved and unexplained. Surviving family members and their relatives continue to stand by their story. They have never attempted to make a penny from what happened to them, despite numerous offers from various media people. American tabloids relish the Kentucky incident and often cite it when reporting on similar occurrences.

Unfortunately, there are no known documents that reveal Mulholland's investigation, findings or any report by him on the Kentucky incident.

In 1997, former TSS chief Gottlieb, asked about UFO's said: "They were out of my reach of knowledge. I found the subject fascinating, as do a lot of people... That something is there, and that people see something, is unquestioned. I think, for me, it's best to leave it like that."

Did the CIA leave it like that?

"I assume not, no."

Asked about the Kelly, Kentucky incident, Gottlieb said he could not recall ever hearing anything about it.

From Agency financial documents, it is evident that Mulholland traveled in 1957, via Houston, to Lubbock, Texas and Alamogordo, New Mexico. TSS official Robert Lashbrook joined Mulholland on part of this jaunt, possibly also visiting his good friend and former Washington, D.C. roommate, Dr. Edwin Spoehel, who was then assigned to White Sands Proving grounds in New Mexico. Several months before their trip, on June 4, an unidentified aerial object had been sighted in Alamogordo over Holloman Air Force Base, causing alarm among security officials at the base and at nearby White Sands Proving Grounds, a highly sensitive weapons testing installation. At about 12:30 A.M., a large blue and green colored, round object had slowly approached the base from the Sierra Blanca area to the north and west. When the object was over the base, it performed odd aerial maneuvers, swinging back and forth in the sky. Stunned military officials observed the object from the ground for about fifteen minutes. Then it moved off toward the White Sands area, where it eventually disappeared.

Possibly related to this incident was another one that occurred in Levelland, Texas (near Lubbock) in early November, weeks before Mulholland visited the area. There, on November 2, around 10:50 P.M., police received a frantic report from two men whose truck had broken down just at the moment they witnessed a large object, about two hundred feet long, approach them. Within minutes, local police were inundated with additional calls from frightened people who reported seeing the same object. Around midnight, one particular caller who had been driving alone on the highway about ten miles north of Levelland, reported seeing a huge object sitting in the middle of the road. His car's engine and electrical system simply died, and he had watched the object from inside his car for several minutes before it silently rose from the road and vanished in the night sky. About five minutes later, a college student, also driving alone, experienced a similar engine breakdown just as a large blue and green object landed about twenty-five yards away from him. Over the next hour, similar calls continued to come in to perplexed local police. Around 1:20 A.M., two patrolmen, about four miles outside of Levelland, witnessed the highway ahead of them light up as if it were mid-day and a huge object, glowing blue and green, passed over the highway in front of them. In all, police received over fifteen calls from people who claimed to have seen strange aerial objects that night.

HYPNOTISM AND THE CIA

In 1945, a small novel was published which told the story of a group of diabolical Germans who secretly hypnotized selected Allied personnel in order to carry out a series of actions harmful to the United States and Britain. The novel's hero, Johnny Evans, must save the day and the Free World, but not before his love interest and the book's heroine is captured by a mad German scientist who strips her and brutally beats her in an attempt to force her to betray love and country. "*She did not faint until they had beaten her, with their fists and a rubber hose, and mostly on her body, for several minutes...*"

The novel, *Death of the Mind*, was co-authored by G.H. "George" Estabrooks who included the following curious and intriguing introductory note aimed, perhaps, at certain careful readers:

> This is a work of fiction and, as such, deals with imaginary persons and incidents.... It is also true that the authors have inserted no scientific theories for the purposes of fiction and have described no hypnotic phenomena which have not been observed during known experiments.

Among those careful readers, as might be expected, were certain officials at the CIA.

George Hoban Estabrooks was a professor of psychology and chairman of the Department of Psychology at Colgate University in New York. He had been a Rhodes scholar and completed his Ph.D. at Harvard University in 1926. Most people who came into close contact with Estabrooks considered him to be brilliant but overly egotistical when it came to his claims about hypnotism: "I can hypnotize a man, without his knowledge or consent, into committing treason against the United States." Besides hypnotism, Estabrooks was very interested in telepathy and early in his career he worked with Walter Franklin Prince and Gardner Murphy, who established the Boston Society of Psychical Research. In 1942, when Estabrooks bragged that he could turn any man into a traitor through hypnosis, the War Department quickly took notice and summoned the professor to a meeting at the Pentagon.

Asked one general, "What was the likelihood that the Japanese would employ hypnosis against the United States?"

Replied Estabrooks, "Two hundred trained foreign operators working in the United States could develop a uniquely dangerous army of hypnotically controlled Sixth Columnists."

"You're kidding," said another general.

"No, I'm not," Estabrooks shot back, "Besides, are you willing to take the chance?"

Apparently, the Pentagon was not willing to chance it, as evidenced by an article of Estabrooks that appeared in 1971 in *Science Digest*. In it, Estabrooks reveals his work in hypnosis:

> One of the most fascinating but dangerous applications of hypnosis is its use in military intelligence. This is a field with which I am familiar through formulating guidelines for the techniques used by the United States in two world wars.... The 'hypnotic courier'...provides a unique solution [to communication in war]. I was involved in preparing many subjects for this work during World War II.

Decades earlier, in 1939, Estabrooks and Milton H. Erickson, another prominent American hypnotist who also performed contract work for the CIA, had conducted an experiment for the FBI, which Erickson later recalled in fascinating detail:

> At the end of an hour they asked me to awaken Tommy, to bring him out of the trance, talk awhile, then put him back into the trance, and reorient him to that first trance. They had a program of exact movements, and they asked me...to have him visualize the entire procedure. Tommy gave a blow-by-blow account of the first hour, including the exact time in which so-and-so uncrossed his legs, when he re-crossed them, when he shifted his hat over to one side, when he lit the other fellow's cigarette, when the other fellow lit his cigarettes.

As with many of the CIA's early activities, the Agency's interest in applying hypnosis to intelligence work originated with the OSS during World War II. At the time, OSS and British intelligence mounted a concerted effort, still largely unexamined, to use hypnotists and hypnotism in the war effort. One of the more detailed glimpses into these efforts comes from OSS research director Stanley Lovell. During the war, Lovell had anxiously inquired of "two of the most famous psychiatrists in the country" about the possibility of hypnotizing "a German prisoner-of-war" and then smuggling "him into Berlin or Berchtesgaden where he would assassinate Hitler in that posthypnotic state, being under a compulsion that might not be denied."

The psychiatrists whom Lovell had consulted were Dr. Lawrence Kubie, who had assisted George White with the OSS truth drug experiments, and brothers Karl and William Menninger. None of the three shared Lovell's enthusiasm.

"There is no evidence," the Menningers said, according to Lovell, "that supports posthypnotic acts, especially when the individual's mores and morals produce the slightest conflict within him. A man to whom murder is repugnant and immoral cannot be made to override that personal tabu."

Kubie took a slightly different tack, pointing out, "If your German prisoner-of-war has adequate and logical reason to kill Hitler, Heydrich or anyone else, you don't need hypnotism to incite or motivate him. If he hasn't, I am skeptical that it will accomplish anything."

Days later, Lovell recounts, he was summoned to OSS deputy director Col G. Edward Buxton's office to meet a hypnotist "who alleged he was a master of post-hypnotic suggestion."

Unfortunately, other than providing us with a mostly silly account of what may or may not have occurred in Buxton's office, Lovell provides nothing else about OSS use of hypnosis, despite the fact that numerous, completely unsupported claims have been made over the past decades about the OSS's use of posthypnotic couriers and assassins.

The CIA's interest in hypnotism developed from Morse Allen's fascination with the subject. Commencing in early 1951, Allen, who had only had about four-months part-time study and training in hypnosis, convinced the Agency to cover the cost of his participation in a four-day course given by a well-known stage hypnotist in New York. According to Sidney Gottlieb:

> The origins of CIA interest in hypnotism began before I arrived at the Agency with [Morse] Allen and others in SRS who recognized the practice as a possible means for eliciting information. Apparently there was earlier interest in the subject with the OSS, but I'm unaware of the details or extent of that. Morse Allen, as I understand it, became deeply involved in conducting hypnosis experiments at headquarters and elsewhere.... I recall only one meeting with a hypnotist named {Milton] Erickson in New York around 1952 or 1953... The interest in magic, besides what had been reviewed in captured German documents at the war's end, was initiated by TSS's MKULTRA or perhaps a little earlier than that program was begun. Initially our interest was in slight-of-hand practices, in the art of surreptitious delivery or removal. Those that were trained became pretty

good at it. In some ways, the training was a welcomed relief from more serious matters.

With the advent of ARTICHOKE, Morse Allen was easily able to incorporate hypnotism into many aspects of the program, including hiring hypnosis consultants Estabrooks and Erickson, among others. He also recruited a cadre of volunteer Agency support staff, all of whom — given the tenor of the times — were women. They were used in an intensive series of hypnosis experiments, most of them conducted in CIA-owned buildings and Washington, D.C. hotel rooms. The experiments grew increasingly complex, as well as dangerous. Some 'secretaries' were hypnotized to engage in sexual acts with complete strangers whom they would be induced to approach in Washington, D.C. bars and restaurants. One particularly appalling experiment is reported by researcher John Marks:

> On February 19, 1954, Morse Allen simulated the ultimate experiment in hypnosis: the creation of a 'Manchurian Candidate,' or programmed assassin. Allen's 'victim' was a secretary whom he put into a deep trance and told to keep sleeping until he ordered otherwise. He then hypnotized a second secretary and told her that if she could not wake up her friend, 'her rage would be so great that she would not hesitate to kill.' Allen left a pistol nearby, which the secretary had no way of knowing was unloaded. Even though she had earlier expressed a fear of firearms of any kind, she picked up the gun and 'shot' her sleeping friend. After Allen brought the 'killer' out of her trance, she had apparent amnesia for the event, denying she would ever shoot anyone.

In July 1954, SRS Chief Paul Gaynor and Morse Allen met to discuss a proposal from Estabrooks involving the "idea of [the Agency utilizing] couriers that had been hypnotized." According to several CIA documents about the meeting, Allen informed Gaynor that the idea "is not new and I am absolutely certain that Estabrooks did not invent the idea." When Gaynor questioned the viability of the concept, Allen explained, "We [CIA] ourselves have carried out much more complex problems than this and in a general sense I agree that it is feasible." However, continued Allen, "There is no proof whatsoever that the hypnosis cannot be broken by another competent hypnotist."

Gaynor also inquired about what he termed the "third-degree" problem, meaning what would occur if a courier was subjected to third-degree interrogation tactics or given drugs. "We don't know at this point in time," answered Allen, "but we expect to have answers to this issue soon as a result of planned experiments that are soon to be carried out."

Gaynor also questioned Allen at length about the likelihood of SRS being able to definitively determine whether or not an individual could be "made to commit murder" under hypnosis. Again, Allen responded that Agency experiments, already underway, had thus far shown "promising results" and that the "long ago raised problems of moral inhibitions blocking hypnosis" did not seem to be "that great a problem at all." When Gaynor asked when an "actual demonstration" could be enacted, Allen replied, "there have already been a number of successful tests with [name redacted, but believed to be Milton H. Erickson] that showed religious and moral inhibitions were not problematic." Allen explained that one subject, an Agency employee, had been induced to "commit harm to fellow employees on a number of occasions... resulting in physical violence."

Before Gaynor and Allen concluded their meeting, the two also discussed the use of "hypnotized individuals as counteragents," which Allen again said was "not new" and "has been discussed many times." Added Allen, "We hope to demonstrate this through field tests we are working on at present."

Regarding Estabrooks's proposal, Allen said he was prepared to meet with the hypnotist, together with Gaynor, but he was concerned that the "things Estabrooks is proposing, he [Estabrooks] has never carried out in any fashion except in laboratory-type experiments."

Four months after Frank Olson's death, on March 22, 1954, four CIA officials, along with twelve volunteer subjects, assembled in a suite on the tenth floor of the Statler Hotel, only a few doors away from room 1018A where Olson had gone through the window. The purpose of the gathering was to demonstrate the power of hypnosis to influence people to do something they ordinarily would not do. A hand-drawn, printed diagram used for the exercise depicted a hotel room very similar to the one in which Olson and Lashbrook had stayed the night of Olson's death. It is unknown for what purpose the diagram was used.

An intriguing 1958 CIA document written by Robert Lashbrook reveals that MKULTRA's pursuit of the use and benefits of hypnosis extended at least until that year, with much of the work performed under the cover of the Human Ecology Fund. The document recounts that Lashbrook visited an MKULTRA subcontractor to close out a project involving "30 cases called for in the original design, [but only] 18 have been completed." We are not told what the "cases" were about. At the end of his meeting, Lashbrook writes, the lead person on the project "gave me his usual long involved talk on the difficulties he had encountered which account for the delays." Then, writes Lashbrook: "He also talked at some length about his 'experiments' with hypnosis, some aspects of which are mildly hair-raising."

5

April 10, 1953, Hot Springs, Virginia

T he day was cloudy, gray, and drizzling rain, perhaps fitting for a major address on such a solemn subject. The program for the event had read: "Remarks by the Honorable Allen Welch Dulles on the Horrors of Brain Warfare." The gathering was the National Alumni Conference of the Graduate Council of Princeton University. DCI Allen Dulles had traveled 200 miles by military aircraft to the town of Hot Springs, Virginia to deliver his address. Reading between the lines of his speech, in retrospect, it is amply apparent that its words were little more than a summary of the CIA's central concerns and a harbinger of Agency programs soon to follow. Said Dulles:

> In the past few years we have become accustomed to hearing much about the battle for men's minds—the war of ideologies—and indeed our government has been driven by the international tension we call the "cold war" to take positive steps to recognize psychological warfare and to play an active role in it. I wonder, however, whether we clearly perceive the full magnitude of the problem, whether we realize how sinister the battle for men's minds has become in Soviet hands. We might call it, in its new form, "brain warfare." ...If we are to counter this kind of warfare we must understand the techniques the Soviet is adopting to control men's minds.... Some of these techniques are so subtle and so abhorrent to our way of life that we have recoiled from facing up to them.
>
> ...Except for official use, foreign publications have been almost wholly eliminated from the Soviet Union. For a long period, the official publication "Amerika" was tolerated on the theory that its circulation was so limited that it did no harm. That has now been stopped. Of course, nothing is published in the Soviet Union that is not Government approved.
>
> If, by chance, Soviet artists, scientists, doctors, or technicians deviate from the official line they are quickly forced to recant or are purged. To be different is a crime. These days it seems a bit dangerous even to be a doctor in the Soviet Union. Racial minority groups within the Soviet Union which once enjoyed their own individual cultures, have been largely eliminated by mass purges or forced migrations to "safe" areas. The persecution of Jews and their prospective elimination was one of the latest evidences of this phase of the Soviet campaign.... During the past few years, in particular, the people of the Soviet Union and of the Satellites have been

given one theme song about the Western democracies and especially the United States; namely, that we are the enemy of the Soviet people, that we are plotting their downfall and attempting their encirclement. We are portrayed as the protagonists of atomic and bacteriological warfare, and our government is said to be dominated by the most vicious campaign of hatred that any country has ever attempted against another. It is a campaign intended to condition the minds of the Russian people so that their leaders could embark on any type of aggressive action against the free world. Unfortunately, it is a campaign that is making steady progress under conditions where no dissenting voice is allowed to interrupt the hate tirade, even though the crescendo may be toned down during "peace offensives."

The second phase of the brain-conditioning program of the Soviet's is directed against the individual, case by case. Here they take the selected human beings who they wish to destroy and turn them into humble confessors of crimes they never committed or make them the mouthpiece for Soviet propaganda. Here new techniques wash the brain clean of the thoughts and mental processes of the past and, possibly through the use of some "lie serum," create new brain processes and thoughts which the victim, parrot like, repeats. The development of these new techniques has been under way in the Soviet Union for a long time. We first had some inkling of what they were doing during the notorious purge trials of the late 1930's. Then we saw hardened old Bolsheviks, veterans of many revolutions, who became like docile children in the hands of the Soviet prosecutor, Vishinshy. With alacrity and seeming enthusiasm, they confessed to all manner of extraordinary crimes against the Soviet State, and hastened to invite the death sentence. How far these confessions were truth and how far they were fiction remains today a mystery; but certainly the men who made these confessions had gone through a mental metamorphosis when they appeared before the State prosecutor.

...After the war, Soviet science and ingenuity made rapid strides in the study of mental reactions and in the nefarious art of breaking down the human mind. Possibly the case that most startled the West was that involving the confession of Cardinal Mindszenty, in Hungary. Here, a man of proven courage and outstanding intellect was brought to a point of publicly confessing actions which those who knew this outstanding character could not possibly have attributed to him. More recently, in Czechoslovakia, we have had the trial of Slansky, Clementis and their associates who had fallen into disfavor with Moscow. Here, again, we had hardened products of the Communist system. The only trouble with Slansky & Co. was that Moscow wanted someone else to have their jobs, so they up and confessed to these crimes and misdemeanors against the Communist State which would assure their removal from the scene.

There is one interesting feature about this type of trial; it is the length of time between arrest and confession. It is rarely less than six months.

This is not because "Communist justice" cannot move rapidly when it wants to. In fact, few things can be more rapid. But in cases where detailed confessions in open court are desired, there must be a considerable period — probably a minimum of around three months— to properly indoctrinate the intended victims. Mere written confessions could be much more quickly extracted by torture.

What does the indoctrination consist of?

We, in the West, are somewhat handicapped in getting all the details. There are few survivors, and we have no human guinea pigs ourselves on which to try out these extraordinary techniques. The Soviets have their political prisoners, their slave camp inmates and finally, and most tragic of all, our own countrymen whom they held as prisoners.

We now have, however, some evidence on which to base a judgement.

A few have escaped from the ordeal of brain-washing to tell their story. One of the first was Michael Shipkov, a young Bulgarian officer educated at Robert College in Istanbul. He served for a time with the American Mission in Bulgaria following the end of the war. In 1949, he was arrested by the Bulgarian Communists, subjected to the brain-washing technique, miraculously managed to escape, reported on his experiences to the American authorities and then, in attempting to escape from Bulgaria, was tragically caught and liquidated.

The techniques employed in the case of Shipkov were somewhat crude given the pattern of the later, more refined methods. One element stands out in all the known cases. It is endless interrogation by teams of brutal interrogators while the victim is being deprived of sleep. In the earlier days, as in the Shipkov case, some minor tortures were employed, Shipkov was forced to stand in an awkward position without being allowed to move during interrogation. Only a short time was required to "break" him as all that was required of him by the Communists was a signed confession....

During and after the late war, the Soviets made extensive efforts to reindoctrinate German and Japanese prisoners of war. Many of these have not even yet been repatriated. Those that have been released have been sent back to their homeland as missionaries for the Communist faith. Recently, there has been a new development in Soviet procedures, which takes on, for us, an even more alarming significance. The Communists are now applying the brain-washing techniques to American prisoners in Korea and it is not beyond the range of possibility that considerable numbers of our own boys there might be so indoctrinated as to be induced, temporarily at least, to renounce country and family.

The Communists have recently been showing a film portraying young American aviators who publicly make spurious "confessions" of participation in the use of germ warfare against North Korea. We have a copy of this film and I saw a showing the other day. Here American boys— their identity is beyond doubt— stand up before the members of an international investigatory group of Communists from Western

Europe and the Satellites and make open confessions, fake from beginning to end, giving the details of the alleged dropping of bombs with bacteriological ingredients on North Korean targets. They describe their indoctrination in bacteriological warfare, give all the details of their missions, their flight schedules, where they claim to have dropped the germ bombs, and other details. As far as one can judge from the film, these pseudo confessions are voluntary. There is little prompting from the Communist interrogations.

More recently, the Chinese Communist radio broadcast what they claimed was the recorded voice of a Colonel and Major of the United States Marine Corps, captured last July, giving, in the greatest detail, fictitious information regarding preparations for bacteriological warfare in Korea. Since then, these alleged confessions have been introduced by the Communists into the proceedings at the United Nations.

These statements bear the usual hallmarks of Soviet imposed fabrications— for example, the humiliation and repentance of the individual at having engaged in such activities. Again, as in the case of the Soviet trials, there is a period of some six months between the date of capture and the alleged confessions: adequate time to allow for the elaborate planning by the Communists of what the confession should contain, the drafting of the "scenario," as it were, and the—roughly— two to three months needed for the indoctrination of the patient.

The only factor that prevents the Communists from employing these procedures on a mass scale is the problem of manpower for the task and the shortage of trained interrogators. Presumably there are schools in which interrogators are trained in the techniques of brain-washing. However, to deal with a hundred victims at a time would require the services of four or five times as many trained interrogators over a protracted period. Each man has a team assigned to him and each case is individually prepared.

I have talked with the one man who has gone through the brain-washing process, an eminent American missionary in China. He had the unique experience of going through the treatment and then of being released and given his freedom. This is very unusual under Soviet practice. This man described how he had been subjected for seventy-five days to the monotony of interrogation, mostly during the night hours, by relays of brutal questioners, deprived of sleep and subjected to the effect of bright lighting during the period of his questioning. As far as he knew, no drugs were used, but of course they might have been used without his knowing it. In this case, no direct physical torture was applied.

After many days of this interrogation his mind was broken down, and he went into court and gave what he now recognizes to be completely false testimony against one of his fellow missionaries, asserting with confidence that this other missionary had a concealed radio with which he was communicating with "the enemy." He gave this testimony with vigor and with what, at the time, was apparent complete confidence in its truth.

The information on which I have based these remarks is none of it secret; it is all available to any student who wishes to study this form of warfare which is now being practiced against us. It seemed to me useful to gather some of the facts together so that we can be alerted to the danger and are not misled or troubled by these fictitious confessions— whether from Communists victimized by other Communists or by our own people who fall into Communist hands.

After Dulles had returned to Agency headquarters, CIA staffers would go out of their way to congratulate the DCI on his fine address and to thank him for drawing the attention to what they viewed as perhaps the most important issue of the times confronting the United States. DCI Dulles was so flattered that he instructed the Agency's public relations office to print additional copies of his speech and to deliver them to every Agency employee, as well as to each senator and congressman on Capitol Hill. On May 8, the magazine *U.S. News and World Report* excerpted Dulles' speech under the bold heading, "Brain Warfare: Russia's Secret Weapon."

On April 13, three days after returning from Hot Springs to Washington, D.C., DCI Dulles approved the Agency's MKULTRA program, exempting it from all normal CIA financial and administrative control due to its "ultra-sensitive work."

6

MKULTRA

Does the CIA project office approve of these immoral and inhuman tests?
— CIA official, May 20, 1955

APRIL 2, 1954, CIA HEADQUARTERS, WASHINGTON, D.C.

Sidney Gottlieb's telephone in his Quarters Eye office rang around 9:35 a.m. on April 2, 1954. As was his habit, Gottlieb answered his own calls. George White was calling from New York. Gottlieb listened attentively as the narcotics agent explained that he had been summoned the previous day to appear before a special New York State investigative commission. Headed by NY State Investigations Commissioner William B. Herlands, the commission had been created months earlier to investigate allegations that New York Governor Thomas Dewey had secretly accepted a $375,000 payment from notorious gangster Charles "Lucky" Luciano in return for granting him parole on February 2, 1946.

The Luciano affair, sometimes referred to as Operation Underworld, is one of the strangest and least understood events in the history of the United States intelligence community. The only certainty is that Commissioner Herlands subpoenaed a bevy of Mafia dons, as well as officials from the Manhattan District Attorney's office and the Office of Naval Intelligence, in an effort to get to the bottom of the allegations against Dewey. The voluminous transcripts and documents generated by Herlands' investigation make it abundantly clear that the US Navy had a chummy wartime relationship with the Mafia. Moreover, they reveal that Secretary of the Navy, James Forrestal — soon to become Secretary of Defense — had been a secret advisor to Dewey in his run against Harry Truman for the presidency in 1948. A year later, Forrestal would "commit suicide" at the Bethesda Naval Hospital in Maryland in a manner similar to Frank Olson.

Before hanging up with Gottlieb, White told him he would be hand delivering a detailed report on Herlands' investigation to the Chemical Branch chief, but had wanted to warn the Agency that the commission's inquiry was dangerously close to discovering OSS "truth drug" experiments. Gottlieb thanked White for his call and immediately informed his superior, Dr. Willis Gibbons, about White's current predicament. Later Gottlieb would recount:

I remember telling Dr. Gibbons I was becoming increasingly concerned that George was becoming a bull in a china shop. There seemed to be some new unexpected development every week.... Gibbons told me a few days later that Dulles was aware of what Herlands was doing and to keep on top of White, but not to worry about things. I assumed this meant that someone had contacted Herlands, but I didn't know who or how. I knew that Dulles was fond of White, and assumed that the DCI had dealt with the matter himself since it was my understanding that his brother, John Foster, knew Herlands. After this incident, things calmed down a lot on the White front. Maybe the entire affair shook him up more than it did me.

Asked if he knew that George White was dosing many of his friends and acquaintances with CIA-supplied LSD at this time, Gottlieb replied, "No, I didn't know that, but I can't say, in retrospect, that I'm surprised." White's 1953 and 1954 date book entries reveal that he drugged at least seven unwitting people for no apparent reason other than to see the effects of LSD on unsuspecting people. One woman drugged by White during a dinner party at his home had required brief hospitalization. Another woman, a friend of his wife, suffered long-term effects from the drug and subsequently required psychiatric treatment for over thirty-five years. A young aspiring actress who lived in the same apartment building as the Whites was drugged in 1954 and hours later had found herself on the roof of the building, contemplating jumping to escape the monsters trying to drive her mad.

White delivered his promised written account of the Herlands' matter to Gottlieb the following week. In it White explained that on the evening of March 31, he had received a telephone call from Deputy Commissioner of Narcotics, George Cunningham in Washington. Cunningham told White that he was to meet with William Herlands, New York State Commissioner of Investigations, the next day because Herlands needed White's assistance. Cunningham said he did not know the nature of it. The next morning, White had gone to Herlands' office at 270 Broadway where Herlands had greeted him warmly and introduced him to his chief investigator, Capt. William Graffnecker, a retired New York City police detective.

At this meeting, White reported, Herlands had explained to him that he was investigating the circumstances surrounding the Luciano parole and that because White, in 1951, had given testimony concerning Luciano before a Senate Crime Committee headed by US Senator Estes Kefauver, Herlands needed White's assistance.

White told Herlands, "I'd be pleased to afford whatever assistance I can."

To which Herlands replied, "Good. Give me a minute to get a court stenographer in here."

When the stenographer came in, Herlands asked White to raise his right hand so that he could be properly sworn in to give testimony. Herlands then promptly began to question White, who was taken aback by the suddenness of Herlands' actions, but nonetheless sat ready to answer whatever questions he was asked. Herlands began by saying that he wanted to know all of the details surrounding White's conversation with August Del Grazio in 1943, when the gangster first brought up the subject of Luciano's possible parole. White complied and recounted the same information he had provided to Sidney Gottlieb in New York City in 1952. About twenty minutes into his questioning, Herlands asked White if Del Grazio had told him that he had been sent by underworld attorney George Wolf or "by any named underworld character?"

White replied, "I don't believe so. I am trying to strain my recollection on that and I will add something in just a moment that might shed some light on the subject."

Herlands impatiently shot back, "Suppose you do it now, because we are interested in getting the complete light on the whole picture."

White leaned forward in his chair and replied, "This is a very delicate matter and I would like this to be off the record."

The transcript of White's questioning at this point reads: "COMMISSION-ER HERLANDS: Off the record."

The transcript resumes with Herlands stating on the record: "Mr. White, you have just told me off the record about some experiment with a drug, the results of which are still presently not fully determined."

White replies, "Right, and which are still highly classified."

The transcript continues:

> Herlands: *In view of the fact that you say that the drug is still highly classified in its use—*
> White: And the experimentation with it.
> Herlands: *—and the experimentation with it, we won't go into details of it except in that you say you have a memorandum—*
> White: Of subsequent conversations.
> Herlands: *—of subsequent conversations by and with Del Grazio while he was under the influence of this drug, is that right?*
> White: That's right.
> Herlands: *This drug was in the nature of a truth serum?*
> White: I wouldn't say what the nature of the drug is.
> Herlands: *Is the purpose of the drug to induce—*
> White: I'm not going to discuss that.

During a lunch meeting in Washington with Gottlieb a few days after his deposition with Commissioner Herlands, White handed over his written report of the session, as well as several additional reports that detailed Bedford Street safe house activities with subjects under the influence of LSD. Gottlieb, according to White's date book, advised that he and Lafitte "slow down" their experiments while the "Herlands quiz" was still fresh. The Agency was seriously contemplating opening additional safe houses in Chicago, Detroit, Washington, D.C., and San Francisco, Gottlieb explained, inquiring if White might be interested in relocating to the City by the Bay. White responded that he and his wife would very much like to go to the West Coast. Gottlieb told White he had already discussed the relocation possibility with Anslinger and that his response had been favorable. Give us a few months to work things out, Gottlieb said. Years later, Gottlieb would reflect on these events:

> I don't remember a lot about what precipitated the move to San Francisco. Certainly, there were concerns that [the Agency was] pushing things, exposure wise, by remaining in New York. By that point in time a lot of people knew about the Village safe house...people with law enforcement, with the Narcotics Bureau, FBI, some military officials, some press people that White was close with, politicians, and criminal types that White had taken there.... Helms had real concerns about the program and possible exposure... and, of course, George's perceived recklessness was a factor. Bob [Lashbrook] had become uneasy, somewhat leery of working with George by this time... Even then, in the mid-1950s, San Francisco was seen as a looser environment, a place less uptight about certain matters.

Safe house activities were only put "on hold" briefly. Within a few days of their Washington meeting, Gottlieb called White and said that the Herlands Commission had been "taken care of" and everything could go back to normal.

George White's status as a special CIA consultant was unaffected by the 1954 Herlands investigation, and perhaps because it had been upgraded the previous year, in July 1953. At that time, White had been formally assigned by the Federal Narcotics Bureau to the Agency for a three-month period beginning August 1, for $3,500 on a reimbursable basis. Narcotics Bureau Commissioner Harry Anslinger had telephoned Sidney Gottlieb on July 20 to complain that White was already spending a considerable amount of his work time on CIA matters, and "because of political factors attendant to the change-over of administrations, he desires to have a plausible reason for White's absence."

"What do you need?" Gottlieb asked.

"A confidential memorandum stating that the CIA will carry White on its books for defined dates and a commitment for reimbursement to the Narcotics Bureau," Anslinger replied.

"I'll have the budget office send that right away," Gottlieb promised.

"How long is it likely that the Agency will need White?" Anslinger asked. Gottlieb replied that he was not sure, but the term would run at least two years or longer.

Sidney Gottlieb had traveled to New York in May 1953 to review plans with White and to have a personal look at the Bedford Street safe house, now fully equipped with a large two-way mirror, hidden microphones, and an expensive movie camera set up behind the mirror. Gottlieb approved of everything and he handed White several hundred dollars in cash, telling him to open an account at National City Bank under White's CIA-granted alias, "Morgan Hall," and Gottlieb's domestic alias, "Sherman C. Grifford." A few days later, White sent a letter to Gottlieb that read in part:

> The bank was a little sticky about opening an account in the absence of references from another bank, and also found it hard to understand how Morgan Hall got by all these years without a bank account.... What with suspicious banks, landlords, utility companies, etc., you will understand that creating the Jekyll-Hyde personality in the form of Morgan Hall is taking a little doing.

Years later, Gottlieb would tell Congressional investigators that, in addition to himself, the person who dealt with White's New York MKULTRA project was Gottlieb's deputy, Robert Lashbrook, whose alias in New York was "Richard Lansing." White's date book entries for 1952 through 1954 reveal that, in addition to Gottlieb's numerous telephone conferences and regular meetings in Washington, D.C. with White, Gottlieb had met with White in New York on six occasions. Lashbrook, during the same period, visited White a total of seven times.

During this time, Gottlieb instructed White to address and send all mail intended for the CIA to "Richard Lansing" or "Sherman Grifford" at the Washington, D.C. post office box registered to Chemrophyl Associates, the bogus front company established by CIA officials to handle MKULTRA-related matters. The company, which maintained a small clerical staff, also oversaw MKNAOMI operations from 1953 through to at least 1959, but its primary function was to oversee the burgeoning number of MKULTRA subprojects being funded through TSS's Chemical Branch.

Project MKULTRA had been formally approved by DCI Allen Dulles on April 13, 1953, after Richard Helms, the Agency's director of operations, had strongly advised him to create a program for the research and development of "covert biological and chemical materials... thus enabling us to defend ourselves against a foe who might not be as restrained in the use of these techniques as we are." Dulles, also on Helms' recommendation, exempted MKULTRA from normal CIA administrative and financial controls and record keeping. Prior to approving MKULTRA, the Agency, under the codename MKDELTA, had already embarked on some research in the development and use of biological and chemical weapons. The name MKDELTA, however, was not retired and it continued to be used to track the operational use of MKULTRA techniques and weapons. Nearly all MKDELTA files, along with those of MKULTRA, were destroyed in 1973. One CIA official described MKDELTA's bureaucratic routing function as follows:

> MKDELTA was an action indicator which would automatically flag any request containing it, put it in a prominent place, to the attention of the

approval mechanism for this, which I believe was the Deputy Director of Operations.

Over the past fifty years there has been much speculation about the meaning of the digraph "MK." Some writers have maintained that it signifies "mind control" or, oddly, that it designates the initials of a prominent pharmaceutical house that supplied the CIA with drugs. Former CIA officials speaking under the terms of anonymity have stated that "MK" were the initials of an administrative secretary whose initials appeared on many Agency documents. "OS [Office of Security] selected them as the digraph for domestic TSS projects," said one official. "It was common to do this." Indeed, MKNAOMI was named after Dr. Harold Abramson's secretary in 1952 and 1953, whose first name was Naomi.

Also, contrary to popular belief and numerous publications and articles, the MKULTRA series of projects–there were 144 in all–did not replace Project ARTICHOKE. Instead, the two projects operated concurrently. In 1998 Sidney Gottlieb described the relationship between the two projects, as stated earlier:

> [TSS], represented either by myself or Bob Lashbrook, would routinely do MKULTRA briefings at Artichoke Conferences at least until about 1958 or perhaps later. I'm not sure when Artichoke was phased out or replaced but it never was placed under the MKULTRA umbrella or folded in as a subproject.

MKULTRA's contract for Subproject 2 was issued in May 1953 to Dr. James A. Hamilton, George White's former partner in the OSS 'truth drug' trials. Hamilton, a highly respected Stanford University psychiatrist, initially received $4,650 for what the CIA termed "the study of possible synergistic action of drugs which may be appropriate for use in abolishing consciousness." Hamilton's project, which was renewed repeatedly until 1960, called for the "allocation of $1,000 for animal experiments," and "to study methods for the administration of drugs without the knowledge of [human] patients." This phase of the project called for the "preparation of a manual" for the CIA encompassing "a survey of methods which have been used by criminals for surreptitious administration of drugs." As might be assumed, this survey drew heavily on the experiments under surveillance at the Bedford Street safe house set up by White. Hamilton, during his OSS days, had established himself as a strategic and creative thinker who maintained personal and professional associations with many powerful individuals, including Allen Dulles and "Wild Bill" Donovan. During the war, Hamilton had devised an elaborate scheme known as the 'Hamilton Plan' – a strategy to widely mobilize anti-Hitler opposition throughout Germany and Europe through the use of rumors and psychological manipulation.

James Hamilton was the first person to propose to Donovan that the OSS recruit and train a team of sophisticated prostitute-assassins who would use their seductive charms and skills to gain access to targeted Nazi generals and officers. Hamilton was also the first to propose that the OSS establish a psychological assessment unit, modeled after Britain's War Office Selection Board, to identify and eliminate OSS recruits who could not measure up to the agency's strict requirements and demands. Hamilton's assessment unit also resulted in Harvard's Dr. Harry Murray developing his aggressive and harsh techniques for determining agents' abilities to lie, hold liquor, and stand up under pressure, among other traits.

From the earliest years of the OSS, Dr. James Hamilton, often acting in concert with Stanley Lovell, had been directly involved in its research and development of biological weapons of mass destruction. Indeed, recently declassified top-secret OSS documents reveal that Hamilton may well have been largely responsible, along with Lovell, for pushing the Army's Chemical Warfare Corps into its deadliest biological weapons research. Hamilton also maintained close friendships with controversial anthropologist Margaret Mead and New York-based 'psychiatrist' Dr. Harold Abramson. Mead, who worked for the OSS during the war and subsequently was awarded a million dollar grant from the Office of Naval Research, as well as financial assistance from the CIA, often called on Hamilton for advice and assistance. Hamilton frequently visited Abramson when he was in New York assisting George White with activities at the Bedford Street safe house.

At times, White, on instructions from Gottlieb, would supply Hamilton with LSD for the physician's research. White in turn would sometimes receive his supply of the drug from a Boston-based research psychiatrist, Dr. Max Rinkel, who is credited with first bringing LSD to the United Sates in 1949. Rinkel, who fled Germany when Hitler came to power, would often hand-carry LSD to New York for White, as well as for Drs. Paul Hoch and Harold Abramson.

CIA documents reveal that when White's safe house experiments required a drug other than LSD – such as heroin, morphine, or cocaine – he would obtain supplies from huge stockpiles of confiscated narcotics kept at an army warehouse just outside New York City, in New Jersey. Recently declassified Bureau of Narcotics documents reveal that, in addition to White and the CIA drawing down this supply, the National Naval Medical Research Institute in Bethesda, Maryland also utilized it. In 1951, the Institute received three hundred and thirty ounces of marijuana "to be used for research purposes." A month later it received twenty-five grams of heroin to be used at the Bethesda facility.

DR. HAROLD ABRAMSON & MKULTRA

MKULTRA Subproject 7 contracted with Dr. Harold A. Abramson, the physician who "treated" Frank Olson. The mandate of Subproject 7 was broad-based and open-ended, encompassing "the conduct of experiments with LSD and other hallucinogenics." Prior to the creation of the MKULTRA program, Dr. Abramson had received CIA funds for LSD experiments through the

Office of Naval Intelligence. Subproject 7, over a six-year period, evolved into Subprojects 23, 27, and 40.

Abramson's initial funding from TSS for MKULTRA work was $45,650 ($364,000 in 2008 dollars); it included secretarial costs of $6,500 and consulting fees of $22,500 for a psychologist, psychiatrist, and neurophysiologist. An additional $4,500 was allocated to stipends for "volunteer" experiment subjects, and $3,500 for tape recorders and photography equipment.

According to one 1956 TSS memorandum, "during the period 3 July 1953 to 3 July 1955, Dr. Abramson furnished a total of $76,420.00 [in MKULTRA funding] to New York's Mount Sinai Hospital for a portion of the work on an approved MKULTRA activity (subprojects 7 and 23)."

While working at Mount Sinai Hospital, Abramson also served as research director for the South Oaks Psychiatric Hospital in Amityville, Long Island. South Oaks had been founded in 1881 as the Amityville Insane Asylum. In May 1965, about two years after his MKULTRA contract had ended and his experiments resumed under MKSEARCH, Abramson convened a group of forty-five psychiatric investigators, including nine from foreign countries, at South Oaks Hospital. The purpose of the gathering "was to exchange information and discuss problems regarding the use of a remarkable drug that has been the focus of research in psychiatry for more than twenty years."

Of particular interest to the psychiatrists gathered at South Oaks asylum were the discussions of LSD and children. The group favorably reviewed the work of Dr. Lauretta Bender, a child neuropsychiatrist best known for creating the Bender-Gestalt Test, who had treated fourteen schizophrenic children, between the ages of 6 and 11 years old, with 100 mcg of LSD "daily for six weeks," reportedly "without any side effects, toxic reactions, or regressive behavior." It is not known if the CIA directly funded Bender's experiments, but it is amply clear that the Agency closely monitored her work with LSD. Apparently Bender had no ethical qualms about such experiments on children.

Abramson later noted in a paper he wrote on children and LSD that in addition to LSD, Bender also included the drug psilocybin in experiments on "six pairs of matched, pre-puberty, schizophrenic boys." Besides Bender's work, the South Oaks group also considered the LSD experiments of Dr. Alfred M. Freedman, of New York Medical College, with "12 autistic, schizophrenic children who were attending a day school."

It is unknown if any follow-up studies were done on any of these children, nor what the ultimate purpose of the drug experiments might have been in terms of any therapeutic benefit since none was mentioned. Nor is anything known about the extent to which the children's parents were aware of the drugs being given to their children or of the risks involved. The academic articles extolling these experiments make no mention of existing codes of medical ethics, all of which were clearly violated.

By all accounts, Abramson enjoyed turning his friends on to LSD as much as George White did. Former colleagues of Abramson's recall LSD sorties held at his Long Island home. Said one former colleague, who declined to be identified, "These LSD parties were held well before the hippie stuff of the 1960s and 70s, but were just as wild and crazy, right along with all the sex and what have you." Said another, "You'd be very, very surprised at who attended some of these events, but I'm not the type to kiss and tell."

It is interesting to note that, despite it becoming widely known in the mid-1970s that Abramson worked for the CIA, the Agency steadfastly refused to provide details of his involvement in MKULTRA and has instructed its employees, past and present, to refrain from discussing anything whatsoever about Abramson in relation to MKULTRA.

One exception occurred during a 1986 deposition, however, in which Robert Lashbrook was asked about Dr. Abramson and Frank Olson:

> Question: *What did you decide to do [with Frank Olson] after it was determined he was not 'acting right.'*
> Lashbrook: The conclusion was to take him up to New York to see Dr. Abramson.
> Question: *Dr. Abramson, he's an allergist, isn't he?*
> Lashbrook: It has been alleged that he is. He was a psychiatrist too. He was in the psychiatry business. To begin with, we felt that the best person for Frank Olson to see would be someone who was familiar with LSD, since it appeared that that might have some effect on his situation. We had only about two psychiatrists who knew something about LSD who were immediately available on the East Coast. Dr. Abramson was one of them. Gottlieb talked on the telephone with both of them, and it turned out that Dr. Abramson was in the best position to help us.
> Question: *Why did you need somebody who was in the CIA to save a fellow's life?*
> Lashbrook: Why did they?
> Question: *Why did you or Gottlieb feel that you needed a CIA doctor to do it?*
> Lashbrook: I think we probably felt it would be desirable to have someone who knew something about LSD. That was a very limited number of people, as I say, about two who were in the psychiatry business.
> Question: *Two were in the CIA, or two in the country?*
> Lashbrook: Two that we knew of on the East Coast. Neither one was in the CIA.
> Question: *Well, Dr. Abramson was witting of the CIA connections of all you people, wasn't he?*
> Lashbrook: Yes. And there was one other psychiatrist in the same position.
> Question: *Why couldn't you go to a psychiatrist outside of the CIA?*
> Lashbrook: Why?
> Question: *Why didn't you, since you could have gotten an expert?*
> Lashbrook: Inside the CIA?

Question: *Outside the CIA.*

Lashbrook: Yes.

Question: *You are denying that Dr. Abramson was an allergist, I take it.*

Lashbrook: Well, he was certainly in the psychiatry business. Whether you call him an allergist or a dogcatcher, he was in the— he was classified as a psychiatrist.

Question: *All right. You took him up to Abramson. Then what happened?*

Lashbrook: Abramson talked to him.

Question: *Then what happened?*

Lashbrook: I guess we came back to Washington, D.C.

Question: *Then what happened?*

Lashbrook: Then I went with Frank back up to New York.

Question: *Why did you go back up to New York?*

Lashbrook: Because it was decided that maybe he should talk to Abramson more.

Question: *Who decided that?*

Lashbrook: I believe it was Sid [Gottlieb] talking on the phone with Abramson.

Question: *So then what happened? You and Olson went to see Abramson a second time?*

Lashbrook: Right.

Question: *Then what happened there?*

Lashbrook: When we were through, we were ready to come back to Washington, D. C., only we couldn't get a reservation on the airplane. And so there was a question whether we'd go to the airport and just wait see if we could get on standby or stay in New York City until the following morning when we could get a reservation. And I think I was reluctant to go to the airport on standby. I wasn't— I was sure Frank would be all right, but it would be very crowded, very boring. I was a little hesitant. So we decided to stay overnight in New York.

Question: *Where did you stay?*

Lashbrook: I think it was the Statler Hotel.

Question: *What happened that night?*

Lashbrook: Well, he jumped out the window.

Question: *Where were you when he jumped out the window?*

Lashbrook: In bed.

Question: *Did you know he had gotten out of bed?*

Lashbrook: No.

Question: *You didn't hear him get out of bed?*

Lashbrook: No.

Question: *What did you do when he jumped out the window? What floor were you on?*

Lashbrook: I think it was the thirteenth floor, although I don't know they had a thirteenth floor. It was very high.

Question: *What did you do when he jumped out the window?*

Lashbrook: Ran to the window and looked out the window.

Question: *Then what did you do?*

Lashbrook: Well, what did I do? Well, I could see that Frank was out the window on the sidewalk and people rushing over to him. What did I do? I got on the phone and I called, as I recall, I called down to the desk. I called Sid Gottlieb, and I called Dr. Abramson.

Question: *And then what happened?*

Lashbrook: I figured I better wait in the room, wait for the police.

Question: *Police come to the room?*

Lashbrook: Yes.

Question: *What did you tell them?*

Lashbrook: What could I tell them?

Question: *What did you tell them?*

Lashbrook: He jumped out the window.

Question: *Did you tell them he was an Army man that had taken LSD?*

Lashbrook: I'm sure I told them he was an Army man.

Question: *Isn't it a fact that a cover story was made up for the police, that everybody lied, you and the others, lied to the police and made up a cover story that wasn't true at all?*

Lashbrook: That's not quite correct.

Question: *What exactly happened?*

Lashbrook: I did not—wasn't -- I did not tell the police that he had taken LSD. That would have been very stupid to have done so. To begin with, no one knew the name LSD at that time. Beyond that, it didn't really matter. He had jumped out the window.

Question: *Well, didn't the CIA want to cover up the fact that he had jumped out the window?*

Lashbrook: No. It was public knowledge. It was in the newspaper.

Question: *But wasn't it covered up that that resulted from the LSD he had been given? Wasn't that covered up until it came out about twenty-two years later in the President's Commission report?*

Lashbrook: It was not revealed for the simple reason that the CIA did not wish to indicate an interest in LSD, yes. This does not imply any evil motives whatsoever.

The Occult Side Of MKULTRA

On the esoteric side again, one MKULTRA project, funded in 1957 through the Human Ecology Fund, perhaps had its genesis in the earlier work of the Ahnenerbe, a Nazi 'think tank' founded in 1935 by SS head Heinrich Himmler and focused on the occult. The MKULTRA program funded drug experiments conducted by Aleister Crowley, a controversial, and some would say depraved, practitioner of the 'black arts,' and considered a 'high priest' of occultism. The World War II 'truth drug' research conducted by Stanley Lovell's OSS department had briefly examined Crowley's experiments with drugs, but had discarded them because OSS scientists found Crowley "simply too difficult to fathom."

Nonetheless the CIA took a second look. Here it is worth noting that Crowley, according to writer Richard B. Spence, was a lifelong intelligence operative for the British government. Respected occult historian Kenneth Grant informs us that Crowley, who passed away in 1947, was introduced to the use of drugs by another occultist, Allan Bennett. Crowley apparently enjoyed the effects of drugs upon himself, as years later, in Paris in the 1920s, he was experimenting with mescaline, and in the late 1930s was introduced to the wonders of peyote by Aldous Huxley. Compounding matters was Crowley's longtime addiction to heroin, which had allegedly first been prescribed for treatment of his severe "spasmodic asthma." Like Crowley, Bennett also suffered from chronic asthma, which he treated with self-prescribed "opium, morphine, cocaine, and chloroform, in a cycle." Apart from this, what seemed to attract the CIA's scientific attention was Crowley's use of drugs such as datura, called the "juice of the Vedic Soma," and a hallucinogen sometimes called "Raziel's Sapphire" that was used by Native Americans in Florida. Crowley variously combined these drugs with sexual practices and wrote of his experiences in lurid detail.

Apparently, this tied into safe house experiments that George White, Dr. James Hamilton, and John Gittinger were conducting, first in New York and then in San Francisco. Gittinger would say years later:

> Yes, we were interested in the combination of certain drugs with sex acts... we looked at the various pleasure positions used by prostitutes and others...this well before anything like the Kama Sutra had become widely popular. Some of the women, the professionals, we used were very adept at these practices.

It is not known what precisely Gittinger meant by "professionals," either prostitutes or Agency-employed sex agents, which several former Agency officials admit were first used by the OSS and then by the CIA. Said Gittinger in a 1987 interview:

> For a while we employed several prostitutes for project-related work in the safe houses. They would lure clients in for the purposes of drawing information from them while they were preoccupied or distracted.

This would have fit neatly with Crowley's practice of "sexual magick" and drugs. Grant writes that Crowley "used them [drugs] all in his search for the mysterious elixir potent to unseal the gates of the invisible world. He also wished to compare the states of consciousness induced by their use with those resulting from madness, obsession and mystical exaltation."

Liz Evans, a former aspiring actress and sometime prostitute ("to pay the rent and make ends meet") who knew George White well when she lived in San Francisco, recalls that White and Gittinger were "more than a little fascinated with the tricks of the trade, if you know what I mean." Evans recounts that she met with Gittinger several times for "long interviews" and then carried out "about five or six assignments" at White's request. She says she had "no idea the CIA was involved in any of this stuff" until the mid-1970s, "after George died and a lot of articles came out in the San Francisco papers about his work."

Evans, who recalls very little about her specific assignments, makes it clear that she was "paid to practice my womanly charms" and that on more than two occasions, White had directed her to escort foreign dignitaries to particular events. She says, "I'm sure George filmed parts of those encounters if he could have. A lot of the times there were guys with George who had movie cameras and sound equipment." Asked if she ever traveled outside the United States at White's request, Evans recalls that she went "to Mexico and another place near there," where she met White, but she could not recall any details. "We met some other people there...it was a long time ago." Asked if White or anyone associated with him had ever hypnotized her, Evans says, "We used to play these crazy games at that, hypnosis and like that, yes, I think I was hypnotized once by a friend of George's." She does not remember who it was or where.

Evans remembers that White "three or four times at his house" dosed people with LSD "just for fun." She recalls, "He gave it to me once and I hated every minute of it. I told him if he ever did it again that would be the last time he did it to anyone."

Evans also recalls that White, or "someone who worked with him... sometime around 1959 or 1960," dosed "a really pretty, blond-haired waitress at [San Francisco's] Black Sheep bar." Says Evans, "her name was Ruth [Kelley] and George wanted her to take part in things, but she had no interest, so he, or someone he told to, dosed her with LSD." Kelley, who also performed as a singer at the bar, was dosed during one of her singing performances in 1960, according to CIA documents. Evans says, as CIA documents confirm, "She nearly flipped out during her set, but somehow managed to hold on. After she finished, she ran outside and got a cab to take her to the hospital. A few days later she was okay."

Another fascinating SIHE (Society for the Investigation of Human Ecology) project, funded through MKULTRA, involved "analysis and assessment" of Dr. Carl Jung's "phylogenetic unconscious," later called the "collective unconscious." The CIA appeared especially interested in "the autochthonous revival of ancient myths and signs" in the minds of individuals unaware of and uneducated about such ideas and theories. Again, it appears that the drugs LSD and mescaline were somehow linked to the project, but how, specifically, is not revealed in the scant materials documenting the project. Nor are we given any hints as to which university (other than that it was a "university") or researchers were involved.

From comments made by TSS psychologist John Gittinger in a deposition and unpublished interview, we are able to glean that the Agency's MKULTRA project secretly funded the LSD research of Danish neurologist Einar Geert-Jorgensen in Denmark. Amazingly, Geert-Jorgensen, during one five –year period at Frederiksberg Hospital, administered LSD to over 250 mental patients without their consent and, apparently, without damage to Geert-Jorgensen's career. According to investigative journalist Alex Frank Larsen:

> [Geert-Jorgensen's experiments]... spun out of control when many of the patients, some of whom had been given their 'medicine' forcefully and were left unattended in basement cells, were overcome with upsurges from their troubled subconscious....[One patient] reacted by stabbing her boyfriend to death, some committed suicide in the wake of the treatment, and many remained stricken and haunted for years, some permanently addled.

MKULTRA And Ken Kesey's Acid Tests

On the less tragic side, a talkative Gittinger also revealed that he and at least two other CIA researchers from TSS's Chemical Division had attended, as "curious observers," Ken Kesey's "Trips Festival" in La Honda, California and an "Acid Test" at San Francisco's Longshoremen's Hall. The "Trips Festival," held in 1966, featured what Gittinger called "an oddball mix of music, merriment, and bizarre behavior." The Festival had been conceived by Stewart Brand (of Whole Earth catalog fame), Zack Stewart, Ramon Sender (both of the Tape Music Center and Ann Halprin Dance Company), and Ken Babbs of Kesey's Merry Pranksters. Music for the event was provided by Big Brother and the Holding Company, featuring then-unknown Janis Joplin. LSD was liberally distributed by the legendary San Francisco outlaw chemist Owsley Stanley. Stanley described the event:

> It was completely out of control...Back in those days, we were really rough with [LSD]. A large dosage was really rough. It would be a hell of a jolt for a guy in his late thirties to suddenly come face-to-face with the universe that way.

A few weeks later, Gittinger's two TSS colleagues attended one of the earliest "Acid Tests" held outside of San Francisco. The "test" (really a psychedelic party) featured huge bowls of LSD-spiked punch. Nobody had any idea how much of the drug had been added to the mixture of fruit juice and soda. Music was provided by a group called the Warlocks, soon to become the Grateful Dead. Author Ken Kesey (*One Flew Over the Cuckoo's Nest*) described these events:

I've tried to think of the real origins of this phenomenon, which I consider myself to be a large part of. One of the people it goes back to, of whom you may not have heard, is George Stern. He was an activist and poet and he did 'happenings.' He and Michael McClure and Allen Ginsberg would do these things in San Francisco. When I first saw them, I thought, 'This is the new edge of the way entertainment's going to be done.'

Recalled CIA man Gittinger:

Once, after these LSD parties became more commonplace, [Alfred] Hubbard and some doctor, I can't remember his name, tried to attend one event. It was crazy from the start. These two bald-headed, portly guys in dark suits walking into the middle of all this madness. You can imagine that the paranoia count went through the roof as they tried to mingle with the crowd and people began melting away from them. I don't think they were there for more than ten minutes before they headed out the door. At least when we went to these things we made an effort to blend in with things.

CANCER AND MKULTRA

The MKULTRA program also explored cancer and experimented with various techniques for "inducing cancer." One 1954 document concerns research into methylcholanthrene, a chemical compound that the CIA claimed "is now recognized as probably the most potent known carcinogen in the production of tumors of various types." The document continues:

If this hydrocarbon can be produced in the laboratory by chemical transformation of normal constituents of the human organism, it is possible that the substance may arise in the body through a process of abnormal metabolism—and initiate cancer.

Another related CIA document outlines a project to evaluate methods of manipulating carcinogenic variables, including stress:

The research to be undertaken during the 12 months period will be devoted to an analysis of the neural and endocrine mechanism of stress and the chemical agents that influence it.... Chemical agents that have been found active and within a suitable toxicity range will be subjected to clinical screening on appropriate patients, the initial screening being carried out as heretofore on advanced cancer patients. The amount of money devoted to chemical synthesis will be much reduced and chemical compounds available from various sources as well as those synthesized in the project will be screened. As heretofore any agents which prove of interest in cancer will be subjected to further evaluation both on transplanted animal tumors and on cancer patients. This cancer phase of the project will be considered a by-product of the major objectives, which will be directed to the problem of stress.

MKULTRA & RADIATION EXPERIMENTS

When DCI Allen Dulles approved the creation of the MKULTRA Program in April 1953, his memorandum stated that the program was organized into: "Two Extremely Sensitive Research Programs." The first was listed as, "(a) Covert studies of biological and chemical warfare." The second program was redacted from all documents released publicly, and the Agency still refuses to release the documents in uncensored form. However, from several confidential sources close to the CIA, we are informed that the second program was, "(b) Covert Studies of Radiation Warfare." Wrote CIA officer Richard Helms of the second MKULTRA program:

> In *all* cases dealing with field (b) [radiation warfare], it is mandatory that any connection with the Agency should be known only to an absolute minimum number of people who have been cleared for this purpose. In *no* case should any manufacturer or supplier be aware of Government interest.

For nearly four decades the CIA has maintained that its MKULTRA program did not conduct any projects related to radiation. This, however, is not true, according to information provided to investigative journalist and writer John Kelly by Dr. Sidney Gottlieb.

In 1958, Dr. Wallace Lane Chan, who would later become a special assistant to the Deputy Surgeon General of the U.S. Public Health Service, working under MKULTRA subproject 86, launched research aimed at: "Establishing and substantiating the 'bona fides' of agent and/or staff personnel through techniques and methods other than interrogation." In other words, Dr. Chan wanted the CIA to have the means to know whether a covert agent extracted from another country is their agent and not a 'replica' agent produced by training and plastic surgery.

To insure that agents were not replaced with 'replica' agents, Chan proposed that CIA agents be made radioactive before being dispatched to their assignments.

"Radioisotopes, with predetermined half lives, can be selectively implanted and/or injected," wrote Dr. Chan.

Dr. Sidney Gottlieb confirmed to Kelly that "Wally Chan" worked under him and that "we were working in that field" of covert, radioactive markers. When Kelly asked the former TSS chief whether Subproject 86 experimented with humans, Gottlieb said, "My general remembrance is 'yes', they tried them on humans."

Related to MKULTRA Subproject 86 was Subproject 140 operated by a contemporary of Dr. Chan's at Stanford Medical School, Dr. James A. Hamilton, already encountered by readers in this chapter as the contractor on MKULTRA Subproject 2. Subproject 140 focused on "assessment and feasibility studies on covert marking systems." A March 30, 1965 report written by Hamilton to the CIA reads:

> We are now conducting a new series of experiments on 100 prisoner-subjects [at Vacaville prison in California], in which radioactive iodine uptake of the thyroid are T-4 uptake of red cells, and several other measures which we have developed, are being related to previously-studied variables.

Said Gottlieb on the purpose of injecting prisoners with radioactive iodine, "It was the same one [as the Chan project]. It was the general objective of seeing whether we could put [in] a covert marker of some kind. And the reason for the radioactive iodine is that it's so commonly used in thyroid research."

As underscored by writer Kelly, radioisotopes can be harmful:

> Any dosage of radiation carries with it a risk of cancer and a myriad of other harmful effects. As early as 1946, Dr. Joseph G. Hamilton [no relation to Dr. James A. Hamilton], the godfather of radiological warfare, wrote that radioisotopes 'produce internal radiation of the very sensitive bone marrow and even rather trivial amounts can produce lethal effects.'

In addition to MKULTRA, the Agency's ARTICHOKE program, operated by the Security Office, considered radioisotopes or tracers as a means to determine whether a certain drug or chemical would effect parts of the brain the CIA wanted to zap. As one ARTICHOKE researcher wrote with stunning precision in 1954:

> The use of certain type liquids and solids which can be traced in their passage through the human body is well known. We have been advised that either at the Massachusetts General Hospital or in one of the Harvard units that there was a very advanced unit being developed for the tracing of radioactive material throughout the human body and particularly in the brain.... We have received information from competent people that almost any element can be made 'active' in some way or other and its passage throughout the body and to the brain can be observed.... Along these lines, several of our most important consultants have constantly urged exploration of the tracer techniques as a method of advanced ARTICHOKE studies.

The same researcher recommended the use of tracers to find a drug, which would produce a "chemical lobotomy," that could be triggered by direct radiation of the brain, as follows:

> A non-toxic drug may be found by radioactive-tracer techniques that will be attracted to such an area (of the brain), and so produce a taming that

can last for some time....*Ultrasonics* or some other *radiating* energy may be developed to give a physical stimulus to such an area without injury.

Lastly, the ARTICHOKE researcher recommended that the amygdaloid nucleus area of the brain be studied. He wrote:

> At present, this brain center can be specifically stimulated by a current passed through wires inserted through the brain by operation. Such a procedure is obviously useless to this project; but ultrasonics or other means of radiant energy may yet be improved or modified so that a 'cross-fire' (as with X-rays) arrangement could be focused on a selected small region in the brain without affecting the surrounding areas. The Amygdaloid nucleus is interesting because it has been stimulated in humans producing fear or anger. Monkeys' amygdaloids have been removed; producing tameness. Temporary inhibition of this region (possibly of others) should tame humans.

At the same time that ARTICHOKE researchers were considering the use of radiation and ultrasonics, the CIA was sponsoring research conducted by Dr. Charles Geschickter, in conjunction with the National Institutes of Health, under which monkeys were exposed to radiation in the form of radar in hopes of developing a technique to secretly render a human unconscious.

In their aggressive pursuit of such techniques, CIA officials met with Dr. Webb Haymaker at the Armed Forces Institute of Pathology in Washington, D.C. to discuss the use of radiation to affect "emotional centers of the brain or elsewhere in the nervous system." According to journalist Kelly, Dr. Haymaker "was unnerved by the CIA's proposal," and the CIA later noted in its own report on the meeting that Haymaker "would not care to be consulted again in this matter." However, Dr. Haymaker apparently had a change of heart or was able to put aside his discomfort at some point. As Kelly observed, Haymaker "subsequently conducted human radioactive experiments" and in "one such experiment, a 43-year old comatose man received eight injections to the brain of radioactive tritiated thymidine over a six-month period with the last injection being given four hours before he died."

Dr. Haymaker subsequently co-authored a book with former Nazi scientist Dr. Hubertus Strughold who had carried out grisly and inhumane experiments at Dachau concentration camp.

Other CIA contractors and employees who were involved in radiological warfare projects included Boris T. Pash, former director of the Alsos Mission, the postwar Allied mission to locate, intern and evaluate the knowledge of Germany's atomic scientists. Pash presented a proposal to the CIA in January 1950 calling for "the formulation of doctrine and policy, the evolving of operational techniques, the making of plans, and the preparation of projects for the conduct of Biological, Chemical and Radiological operations." A few months after Pash submitted his proposal, CIA assistant director for Office of Policy Coordination (OPC) Frank Wisner wrote, "OPC is at present engaged in covert unconventional activity on a limited scale," including "biological, chemical, and radiological warfare."

By 1954, Wisner was proposing that the CIA grant "consideration...to the development of a radiological weapon which, it is hoped, would make profitable use of substantial quantities of radioactive waste materials—which now constitute a considerable disposal problem—to neutralize or interdict enemy activity in localized areas for relatively short periods without simultaneously causing substantial loss of life and the destruction of property."

One 1954 CIA proposal for the development of radioactive warfare recommended its use in Vietnam on behalf of the French:

> The potential of [a radioactive weapon] is obvious not only in military terms of overrunning selected resistance points at a minimum loss in casualties to the attacking force and in the preservation of the physical assets in the area (which both our military forces and the local civilian population could use to good advantage) but also form the important humanitarian and psychological standpoint of waging war without causing the wide-spread destruction of life and property attendant upon the use of lethal weapons of whatever kind. It would also appear that such a weapon might be used to advantage defensively in fighting delaying actions or in such battles as the one at Dien Bien Phu, where a protective ring might have been thrown around the town to prevent the attacking forces from approaching beyond a certain perimeter.

MKULTRA AND HUMAN ECOLOGY

On October 26, 1954, Sidney Gottlieb, accompanied by TSS staffers Robert Lashbrook and Henry Bortner, traveled from Washington, D.C. to New York City to participate in a daylong meeting at the Statler Hotel. Morse Allen of the Agency's Security Research Service had requested the meeting. Also in attendance were Dr. Paul Hoch, Dr. Harold Abramson, Dr. Edward Pelikan, and several representatives from Camp Detrick's SOD, including Col. Vincent Ruwet and Dr. John Schwab. Allen had called the meeting so that Gottlieb and his TSS subordinates could present the details of their burgeoning MKULTRA program in order to "comprehensively assess its usefulness to SRS's Project QKHILLTOP."

Very little is known about Project QKHILLTOP other than that it was initiated sometime in 1954 and, about a year later, the project recruited Dr. Harold Wolff, the physician who treated the war injuries of Allen Dulles's son. Wolff had also been physician to the Shah of Iran, Mohammad Reza Pahlavi, and also to his popular rival, Iranian Prime Minister Mohammed Mossadeq (overthrown by the CIA's Operation Ajax in 1953, to reinstate the Shah). Wolff, according to former intelligence officials, was essentially rewarded for his treatment of Sonny Dulles by receiving a multi-year CIA contract to study the brainwashing techniques of the Soviet and Communist China, as well as the interrogation techniques of both, including interrogation with drugs.

Overseeing QKHILLTOP was the CIA's front group, the Society for the Investigation of Human Ecology (SIHE). The Society, MKULTRA Subproject 48, was physically located at 123 East 78th Street in New York City, adjacent to Cornell University's Human Ecology Study Program (Cornell University Medical School Annex). CIA documents state that SIHE's principle purposes were to act as "a reasonable and efficient cutout for funding MKULTRA subproject 48 projects; and "to provide a mechanism for exploiting the human ecology research program in other areas *outside* Cornell University." [Italics in original.] In other words, to serve as a cutout for other selected MKULTRA projects.

SIHE's initial corporate officers were Dr. Harold Wolff and Dr. Lawrence E. Hinkle, CIA employees Phyllis B. Sheridan, Helen Goodell, and Dr. Joseph C. Hinsey, Dean of the Cornell Medical School. The number of officers soon expanded to include Dr. Adolf A. Berle, Jr., Dr. Carl R. Rogers, and Dr. John C. Whitehorn. As some readers may be aware, Berle, a close friend of DCI Dulles, was a former Assistant Secretary of State and U.S. Ambassador to Brazil. Rogers, a noted psychiatrist, was a founder of the 'humanistic' approach to psychology, and a Nobel Prize nominee. Whitehorn, a widely respected biochemist and a psychiatrist, was a former president of the American Psychiatric Association. Others closely associated with SIHE were Dr. Samuel Lyerly, the group's research director, Dr. Robert Goodnow, Preston Abbott, Edgar Shein, Dr. Robert L. Williams, David Rhodes, and TSS's Ray Treichler.

QKHILLTOP continued until 1963, and, contrary to other reports, was always operated independently from TSS's MKULTRA. Almost all of QKHILLTOP's files were destroyed in 1973 at the direction of then DCI Richard Helms.

In a fascinating civil suit deposition taken in 1983, former CIA staff agent, psychologist, and TSS employee John Gittinger provided illuminating details about Project QKHILLTOP and TSS activities. Gittinger, who joined the CIA staff in February 1951 and interviewed Sidney Gottlieb for his first Agency job, explained that QKHILLTOP created the CIA-controlled Society for the Investigation of Human Ecology to serve as a conduit and cover for CIA projects and funding. Gittinger revealed that the idea for the Society was conceived in a meeting between Allen Dulles, Dr. Harold Wolff, Dr. Lawrence Hinkle, and Dr. Adolf Berle. Dulles wanted the Society to be the cover for the CIA's aggressive investigation of all facets of the human mind, and also to concentrate on enhancing intelligence-gathering techniques, including the analysis of handwriting and body-positioning (today, body language).

People who knew Allen Dulles well, including Gittinger, said that when Dulles had lived for a while in Switzerland next door to psychologist Dr. Carl Jung, he had become enthralled with handwriting analysis through his many conversations with Jung. When Dulles became DCI, one of his first initiatives was to create a handwriting analysis branch under the auspices of TSS. At a March 1957 Human Ecology Board of Directors meeting it was proposed and approved that the Society would also vigorously explore handwriting analysis.

Gittinger also explained in his deposition that, while he served as chief of TSS's Behavioral Activities Branch, all TSS Chemical Division employees, as well as other CIA operatives, were required to attend a training course entitled "Defensive Pharmacology." The course was operated by Butler Medical Center, a CIA facility in Providence, Rhode Island. As part of the training, each employee had to ingest one hundred micrograms of LSD. Medically supervising those who had taken LSD were two course instructors, "a Chinese and German doctor," whose names Gittinger said he could not recall. He did recall, however, the name of the physician who primarily oversaw the course, Dr. Conan Kornetsky. Kornetsky, at the time of this writing, is a distinguished professor at Boston University School of Medicine.

About a year after George White left New York to open a CIA-funded safe house in San Francisco, Gittinger embarked on yet another curious investigation under the auspices of the Human Ecology Fund: an eighteen-month project focused on the "sexual habits and proclivities of Chinese males." Explained Gittinger, "We were interested in the sexual life of certain of the Chinese because it was something we had very little information on." In 1957 and 1958, Gittinger had White, and his Narcotics Bureau assistant, Ira Feldman, recruit prostitutes who reportedly had "extensive experience" with Chinese males. For several months, Gittinger traveled to California to interview the prostitutes. In 1987, Gittinger said:

> Through the help of Morgan Hall [George White's alias] we got three prostitutes who specialized in Chinese males, and I interviewed them on their attitude...and something about the way Chinese males behaved.... Morgan Hall told me a great deal about...he had a very, very interesting life, and had a great deal of experience in terms of interrogation and eliciting of information, both directly and indirectly.... We attempted to systematically keep track...to know about the sexual habits and the like of all...of the various ethnic and racial groups we were concerned about or interested in... this kind of information was very useful at times.

DR. ROBERT HYDE & LSD

Dr. Robert W. Hyde told people in Bakersfield, Vermont, where he had been born in 1910, that no matter how much he loved the Green Mountain State, its hardy folk and its white winters, he would have to leave the state "if I really wanted to spread my wings and soar to those heights I knew I could reach." After graduating from the University of Vermont medical school, Hyde went to Boston in search of his chance to soar. In 1949, he became assistant superintendant of Boston Psychopathic Hospital (today, the Massachusetts Mental Health Center), where he did indeed soar to heights he never knew existed, on the wings of LSD.

Hyde's story and his connection to the CIA has been for the most part overlooked in the annals of LSD. Largely overshadowed by the immense ego, self-promotion and inflated saga of Sandoz Pharmaceutical's Albert Hofmann, Hyde made incalculable contributions to the CIA's pursuit of the "miraculous drug" known as LSD.

Bob Hyde's friends will tell you, without exception, that if anyone had the audacity to ingest an unknown drug purely out of curiosity, it was Hyde. The son of a widely loved and respected Vermont general practitioner who taught young Bob a tremendous amount of useful information about physiology. Hyde, within months of his arrival in Boston was regarded as an "amazing and fearless researcher" who had an almost "pathological obsession with discovering more about medicine." Said one of Hyde's former colleagues, "As a kid, Bob trudged through the snow in northern Vermont, carrying his father's black bag from house to house, helping where he could and watching, and listening, as his father treated people. Bob had that unique mix of country common sense combined with advanced schooling and a worldliness drawn from exposure to other places. He was comfortable in his skin and in any given situation. He wanted to make a difference and he had no patience with people that didn't share his convictions."

Hyde attended medical school at the University of Vermont in Burlington, graduating in 1935. While a student he participated in the school's Reserve Officer Training Corps, graduated as a second lieutenant, and went to work as an intern at the Marine Hospital in New Orleans. Ten years later, Hyde moved to Massachusetts to work for the Boston Psychopathic Hospital. Assisting Hyde was Dr. Max Rinkel, a German émigré and neuropsychiatrist who had fled Hitler in 1936.

As a result of research by Alston Chase, we know today that Hyde recruited Harvard University students, possibly including notorious Unabomber Theodore Kaczynski, for a series of CIA-funded LSD experiments that spanned at least two years. Chase reveals that in the spring of 1954, Hyde paid a group of six Harvard seniors $15 an hour to participate in an experiment using a drug they had never heard of, "lysergic acid." The drug might produce an "altered state," they were told as each was offered "a little vial of a clear, colorless, and odorless liquid, which they were told to drink."

Chase writes that each student reacted differently to the LSD. One student "had a bad trip and tore a telephone off the wall. But none can remember doing it." Everyone remembered that "some became paranoid, but can't remember who." One student told Chase that he became "mildly schizophrenic." Others were scared. None were told that the CIA had sponsored the experiments.

In the late 1960s, Bob Hyde returned to Vermont where he set up a small private psychiatric practice and became director of research at the Vermont State Mental Hospital in Waterbury, a small town close to the world famous Stowe ski area. According to one of his former patients, Hyde's work with LSD continued at the Waterbury facility, which had received CIA funds for experiments through at least two Agency conduits, the Human Ecology Fund and the Geschickter Fund for Medical Research. The projects under these funds were monitored by TSS psychologist John Gittinger, who had first met Hyde at Boston Psychopathic, where he and TSS biochemists Henry Bortner and John Glavin had supervised the LSD experiments.

In 1997, Karen Wetmore, a Vermont woman who had been a patient at Waterbury, brought a lawsuit against the State of Vermont claiming that she had been unwittingly used as a subject in drug experiments approved by Dr. Hyde. Wetmore, who had been a patient at the Vermont facility throughout her teens and early twenties, further charged that Hyde had experimented on other Vermont State Hospital patients.

Wetmore's attorney, Alan George, had an extremely difficult time obtaining documents from officials in Vermont, a state with less than a stellar reputation for public access and freedom of information, but eventually he was able to obtain evidence linking the State Hospital to the CIA, its front organizations and its money conduits. One report revealed that the Waterbury facility had taken federal funds to experiment on schizophrenics with "antipsychotic drugs, including tri-fluoperazine," (an antipsychotic more commonly known as Stelazine), a drug that was of interest to the CIA during the 1950s. The results of the study were disturbing: "It's like old times. It's bedlam...[with patients] constantly pacing back and forth like animals." One former Waterbury employee who worked on the project attests:

> There were some incredibly crazy things done under that project. For the life of me, I could not make sense out of anything. If you asked or questioned what was going on, physicians said, 'Don't worry yourself, just do it.'

Vermont investigative journalist Louis Porter, who assiduously pursued Wetmore's story, wrote in a 2008 article that Dr. Milton Greenblatt was one of the primary consultants working on the study. Greenblatt worked closely with Dr. Hyde at the Massachusetts Mental Health Center, formerly Boston Psychopathic. Greenblatt was quoted in a 1994 newspaper article about the CIA's LSD experiments: "You must remember that the protection of patients was evolving in those decades. We need to be fair about judging the past from current criteria." Greenblatt, who seemed quite skilled at manufacturing excuses and casting blame on the context of the times, also claimed disingenuously that the LSD experiments he and Hyde conducted were undertaken "before researchers knew much about the intense psychotic reactions and flashbacks that haunt some LSD-takers for years." Apparently, the physicians had not read reports of previous LSD experiments. Greenblatt could not recall how many patients were given LSD under his direction, but he said, "as far as I know none had adverse reactions." Not so for the staff members given LSD, however. "There was one fellow, an occupational therapist, who was made quite psychotic, and it took him a while to recover," said Greenblatt.

Karen Wetmore settled with the State of Vermont after the case became a detriment to her health. She suffered two heart attacks during the pre-trial proceedings and could take no more of the stress and aggravation caused by Vermont's bureaucratic bumbling and delay tactics. Wetmore's attorney reluctantly agreed to the undisclosed settlement (said to be very small). "I thought we had a pretty solid suit, frankly," he said. State of Vermont officials declined to speak about the case.

In 1981, when Sidney Gottlieb was asked to describe Dr. Hyde's experiments, he said he was unable to recall specifics, but claimed the subjects had been "volunteers":

> I can only describe the general, the most general description of [them]. They were associated with Harvard University and [Hyde and his associates] over a period of several years did a series of experiments on voluntary Harvard University students, and on some volunteer staff members of Boston Psychopathic Hospital and they did some work on patients at the hospital investigating the psychotherapeutic possibilities of LSD. That's all I can recall.

Queried further about CIA or MKULTRA funding of any other organizations in the Green Mountain State, Gottlieb said, "I recall some work, perhaps some related to SI [special interrogations] at the university up there. It may have been funded through one of the cover groups, Macy or Human Ecology... I'm just not sure."

PRODUCING A MODEL PSYCHOSIS

One of the most guarded and least documented of the early MKULTRA projects was Subproject 9, first undertaken at Emory University in Atlanta and the University of Illinois. Among TSS officials, Subproject 9, which evolved over a five-year period into Subprojects 26, 28, and 47, was commonly referred to "the Atlanta project" or "the bullpen project." Overseen by Dr. Carl C. Pfeiffer, the project on paper involved "the use of various sternutatory [chemical substance that produces sneezing and other effects] agents on normal and schizophrenic human subjects." In fact, it was far more complex, indeed frightening; it involved intentionally producing psychotic states with LSD. Documents concerning Pfeiffer's work at Atlanta Federal Penitentiary reveal that:

> ...[his experiments] produced a model psychosis characterized by visual and auditory hallucinations.... Hallucinations last for three days and are

characterized by repeated waves of depersonalization, visual hallucinations, and feelings of unreality.

According to a detailed and "complete" listing of MKULTRA projects, composed in 1976 by CIA attorney A.R. Cinquegrana, Pfeiffer was assisted in his experiments by Dr. Andrew Lasslo of the University of Tennessee, and by toxicologist Dr. Edward Pelikan, who was working closely with Dr. Harold Abramson at the time of Frank Olson's death.

Marvin Williams, imprisoned in the Atlanta penitentiary throughout the 1950s and early 1960s, participated in Dr. Pfeiffer's experiments and later recalled what it was like:

> I didn't know what I was getting into. I just wanted the little extra money for personal things, like soap and cigarettes, and the few benefits that went along with volunteering. I knew nothing about LSD or any hallucinogenic drug. If I'd known, I would have never in a million years jumped on board.
>
> I thought, like most of the other guys, that it was a straight out drug test. You know, to see how strong or weak, or good or bad, the drug was. But that's not what happened with us, at least not with me and the others I knew. The tests went on for weeks; we kept getting handed a glass of what looked like water... drink it, they said, and then blam, I don't know what. The roof and the sky exploded. Crazy things happened. I mean really crazy, like not real, but happening. It was like I was in a jungle someplace with wild animals all around me; all these crazy beasts trying to kill me and... Never again, man, never again.

Williams begins to cry and shakes his head, recalling the experience:

> I'm not a smart guy. I didn't have much school or learning. I didn't know what was going on. A lot of us became pretty crazy, you know, like insane. We had to be locked up alone for days, and even then the energy...the anger was everywhere inside you, overwhelming, like explosive.

In a 1981 deposition, Sidney Gottlieb spoke about Pfeiffer's Atlanta experiments. He claimed that Pfeiffer's work was in "an ultra sensitive area" subject to "easy misinterpretation and misunderstanding," but he admitted that it "involved inducing psychotic states" through the use of LSD and other drugs. Gottlieb recalled that Pfeiffer's "psychotic states" work had begun in 1951 at the University of Illinois, where he headed the Pharmacology Department, and that it continued until "1958 or so," and was "picked up by other physicians in the early 1960s."

Gottlieb added:

> *"We learned a lot from the Atlanta experiments. The Agency learned that a person's psyche could be very disturbed by those means."*

Additionally, in an October 1954 presentation to Morse Allen and his staff who were exploring TSS activities relevant to their Projects ARTICHOKE and QKHILLTOP, Gottlieb stated that Pfeiffer was studying the effects of "flicker and epileptic type seizures produced by chemicals with flicker or sound." Gottlieb said the work was of "a very advanced nature" and that TSS was in "constant communication" with those doing the work.

Another researcher who was conducting experiments similar to Pfeiffer was Dr. Harold E. Himwich, a brilliant psychiatrist whom Gottlieb greatly admired. Gottlieb is on record remarking twice that Himwich "greatly influenced the work of the TSS Chemical Branch." Himwich, according to Gottlieb, "conducted [work similar to Pfeiffer] at a mental hospital in Illinois, I think it was in Kankakee, one of the Illinois State mental hospitals." Gottlieb was referring to Galesburg State Hospital in Illinois where Himwich, in 1951, established the Thudichum Research Laboratory. "Dr. Himwich was interested among other things, in the psychotherapeutic effects on mental patients of LSD," said Gottlieb. "A good portion of his work involved human experimentation."

During the time Pfeiffer was conducting experiments in Atlanta some of the more infamous inmates were Francois Spirito, considered the "father of modern heroin trafficking" and about whom readers shall learn far more, and also Joe Valachi, infamous Mafia stool-pigeon. Another inmate and Pfeiffer experimental subject was Antoine D'Agostino, also a heroin dealer, who was declared insane while in prison after he suddenly claimed he was having religious visions and was being visited regularly in his cell by the Virgin Mary.

Former Atlanta penitentiary inmate, Marvin Williams, recalls that concurrent with Pfeiffer's drug experiments, "The level of violence went up with the level of paranoia that was everywhere; causing the acting out of some incredibly crazy stuff was an everyday occurrence [at the prison]." Said Williams:

> It was like they wanted us to be out of control. The more guys acted in unpredictable ways the happier the doctors seemed to be...like they were getting what they wanted and everything was cool, but for us it was like being in hell where everyone wanted to kill you, do horrible things to you.

While in Atlanta prison in 1962, Joe Valachi became deeply suspicious of people around him, claiming they were "trying to slip stuff in my food and drinks." Worried that "something was going to happen," Valachi requested solitary confinement. Once there, he refused to eat and only drank small amounts of water. Then on the morning of June 22, 1962, after being forced out of isolation, he picked up a piece of pipe and viciously murdered inmate John Joseph Saupp, a man he did not know. Said Valachi to the guards that seized him after the attack and to the prison's warden: "I was in a fog...I just went crazy. You can't understand how I felt. I don't know if I was coming or going."

Forty-eight hours later, prison consulting psychiatrist, Dr. Harry R. Lipton, would find his neuropsychiatric examination of Valachi perplexing. Wrote

Lipton: "No hallucinatory experience or suicidal tendencies could be elicited....Whether his ideas in reference to having been 'called' or branded a 'rat' were delusions or had an actual basis in fact, this examination could not determine.... At the present time he is considered not psychotic." But, concluded Dr. Lipton, Valachi seemed to be suffering from a "paranoid state" characterized by "delusions of persecution." Said one prison official days after the incident, "I get the feeling that Valachi will never come out with a full account of the whole story."

It is unknown if Dr. Lipton was aware that since 1951, and through to the time of Valachi's convoluted saga, the Atlanta Penitentiary had been the site of secret CIA-funded experiments centered on deliberately, intentionally creating "drug-induced psychotic states in human males" through the use of LSD and a highly-experimental drug called MER-16, which produced "a model psychosis characterized by visual and auditory hallucinations" which often lasted for upwards of "three days and are characterized by repeated waves of depersonalization, visual hallucinations, and feelings of unreality."

Fascinating to note here is that three days after he killed Saupp, when he learned that the U.S. Attorney in Atlanta was preparing to seek the death penalty against him, Valachi managed to make contact with George White's special assistant Pierre Lafitte, who in turn contacted Robert Morgenthau, then U.S. Attorney for the Southern District of New York. Lafitte told Morgenthau that Valachi was "ready to spill the beans" on the Mafia and the DA arranged for Valachi to plead to a lesser charge of murder in the second degree.

PRESIDENT NIXON & LSD ATTACK

In recalling the overall MKULTRA program, Gottlieb summarized:

> Things advanced very smoothly at the beginning of the project, but as the sub-projects began to multiply, so too did the task of keeping on top of everything. Eventually we were managing over one hundred and forty [sub-projects], not including those at Human Ecology that we were also responsible for.

Gottlieb explained that by 1956, three years into MKULTRA, the Human Ecology Fund had become a central funding conduit for MKULTRA projects:

> I don't recall the specific number [of MKULTRA] sub-projects under Human Ecology. It may have been about ten initially and then, by 1956 or 1957, another fifteen or twenty.

With that much money coming into Cornell University where SIHE's financial transactions were managed, some employees in the school's accounting department began "raising issues and asking questions" about the source of the funding, Gottlieb recalled, "so in 1957 we made the decision to have [SIHE] break away from Cornell and become wholly independent. That made everyone happier all the way around." Gottlieb added an historic note:

> It was fortuitous that LSD was winding down [in the research community] by the early 1960s because Sandoz was becoming increasingly concerned about liability issues and was having serious second thoughts about the drug's therapeutic values.

Some of Sandoz' concerns may have been prompted by the fact that the company had expended considerable resources toward developing and refining LSD and had received little in the way of compensation or profits back from the many physicians who paid very little for ample research amounts.

In May 1962, the American Psychiatric Association, by contrast, took a very different tack, concluding that LSD was a unique drug "capable of inducing in a patient the single most powerful emotional experience of his life" and should be "used selectively" and ideally only after the physician took "it himself before administering it to patients."

Sandoz, meanwhile, continued to express mild concerns. The pharmaceutical giant mailed out letters to its widely dispersed research community stating that the company was "faced with a considerable moral and practical problem in relation to the use and possible abuse of Delysid [LSD's marketing name]." For the most part, only a small group of physicians were willing to first try the drug themselves, not to mention risk their careers by engaging in egregiously unethical experiments.

"But," said Gottlieb, "we weren't ready to walk away from the drug... other governments, like the Soviets, were still aggressively researching the covert merits of LSD." Insisted Gottlieb, "There were many unreported instances where use of the drug caused serious concerns. In the early 1970s, CIA was constantly warning the White House that attempts to dose the President and his staff were being made."

In September 1977, in a closed hearing, Gottlieb told a group of U.S. Senators that during one of President Nixon's trips overseas in 1972 "members of his staff were drugged," and "displayed signs of disoriented behavior."

Senator Edward Kennedy incredulously asked Gottlieb, "Members of the Presidential party?"

Gottlieb replied, "Yes. And specifically it included the President's physician himself and some of his associates. There were...you know, inappropriate tears and crying, I remember, was part of this manifested behavior."

"I'm interested in this," said Kennedy, "since you first raised it, the specific circumstances which you raised here, which I think has extraordinarily grave implications."

Replied Gottlieb, "My remembrance is that they decided it was an 'indeterminable' thing, that long after the incident they could not, at least unequivocally, conclude that this behavior was due to some covert drugging."

Gottlieb was reluctant to go into detail about the incident. He told Kennedy he was not sure of the exact dates, saying that "maybe it was in 1971 or 1972." When reporters attempted to question him further about rumors of the incident he declined comment. President Nixon's physician during the years involved, Dr. Walter T. Kasch, refused to answer any questions.

Gottlieb later said the incident alone justified "all of CIA's concerns, suspicions, and fears about Soviet use of psychochemicals. If we hadn't had our own research program we would have never known what was happening."

The incident involving Nixon's staff occurred in May of 1972, Gottlieb claimed. Nixon was in Moscow for a summit conference with the Russians. "As I recall," said Gottlieb, "at the moment President Nixon was signing an important agreement with the Soviets, at least two or three members of his staff were stricken with the effects of their drugging by Soviet agents. One of the men in the President's party was especially affected." The man, who Gottlieb declined to identify, had actually stayed in the Kremlin, along with others, with Nixon. At one point, the drugged man begged the Secret Service to have him flown back to the United States. "I can't stay here any longer," he said, "I'm losing my mind. I'm falling apart, I'm falling apart." For months after the man had returned to Washington, D.C., he acted so bizarre that he was sent twice for psychiatric observation. His first observation session and analysis took place at Sheppard Pratt Hospital in Baltimore, where physicians concluded that he may have been given LSD or BZ in a time released form. His second session took place during a stay at the private psychiatric retreat in Maryland, Chestnut Lodge, where he was examined by Dr. Robert Fort, the same physician who had been assigned in November 1953 to see Frank Olson.

Another member of Nixon's summit party was also strangely affected long after the trip. This man, a White House staffer, had actually been apprehended by Soviet security and intelligence agents outside the Kremlin where he had wandered late one night. There, on Moscow's streets, he had walked aimlessly about, asking people where he could find Rasputin and "what time did the pharmacies open." The man had also reportedly thrown his passport away, telling Soviet agents that it contained "tracking devices inside."

Said Gottlieb, "We kept a close eye on these men for a number of years after they were drugged. We were concerned about their well being."

Gottlieb was reluctant to go into any detail about some of the more notorious MKULTRA projects such as the horrible LSD and psychic-driving experiments conducted by Dr. D. Ewen Cameron at McGill University in Montreal. Cameron's work resulted in long, drawn out lawsuits filed by nine of his victims. Gottlieb's final words to the author on MKULTRA were:

> I no longer expect anyone to understand or to appreciate what we were trying to achieve with the project. Did we make mistakes? Of course, we did. But we also learned a great deal; we also garnered a tremendous amount of knowledge and know-how.

In 1964, MKULTRA became MKSEARCH, with all active sub-projects carried over. The next year, the Human Ecology Fund was dissolved. According to the CIA, no files from MKSEARCH are available because most, if not all, were destroyed in 1973 along with most MKULTRA records. MKNAOMI, the joint CIA-SOD Camp Detrick project, operated until 1970. Former SOD researchers say that some MKNAOMI files were maintained, but nobody, including anyone at the CIA or Army, will disclose where they are.

MKSEARCH projects were, in many ways, just as gruesome and inhumane as those of MKULTRA. CIA Deputy Director for Intelligence Ray Clines recalled in a 1977 interview that in 1964 he traveled from CIA headquarters to a laboratory at University of California-Los Angeles where he was shown a group of sad-eyed, shaking chimpanzees who had had the tops of their heads removed so that a tangle of electrodes could be plugged into their brains. Clines listened attentively as proud UCLA researchers explained how they were able to control the chimps from afar.

Other former CIA-funded researchers admit, anonymously, that the UCLA experiments were replicated at several other research institutions and that they were intended to eventually lead to the ability to control human subjects remotely to do anything controllers desired. Did any of these researchers ever get to the point where they experimented upon human subjects? Says one scientist, who had been employed at a facility outside Washington, D.C.:

> We did [use human subjects]. In the late-1960s a couple researchers reached that point. We didn't use normal subjects, however...we couldn't get the approval, but we did use mental patients. I understand that other CIA-funded researchers did some sort of similar experiments on foreign POWs outside this country...I don't have any specifics on those tests.

Another former CIA clandestine operations official, Charles Yothers, said in a 1977 interview, that while he was in Saigon during the 1960s the "backside" of Monkey Mountain in Da Nang "was a denied area" because it was used for brainwashing North Vietnamese POWs "into supporting the overthrow of their government." Yothers would not provide details of the "brainwashing."

In late January 1963, Marine Corps Major General V.H. Krulak wrote a top secret memorandum to Secretary of Defense Robert S. McNamara regarding "the special prisoner interrogation project" authorized by McNamara for use in Vietnam. That project, employing techniques developed under Project ARTI-CHOKE, according to Krulak, was overseen by a "U.S. ARMY project officer," who "is most knowledgeable, having been in the program from its inception" and also had "a deep technical background and much practical experience, and was in charge of the actual use of the techniques against hostile individuals in Europe." Krulak reported that the use of these techniques in Vietnam held "great promise for assisting in the production of timely tactical intelligence, with little difficulty and little risk of exposure."

Krulak told McNamara that certain of the interrogation techniques would only be used "in the case of high level prisoners or those who are believed to possess broad strategic or political knowledge," but that this was problematic to American interrogators because there "simply were not enough prisoners of this type captured to influence the action, even if they told all they knew."

However, one particular technique showed special promise, wrote Krulak. He stated:

> There are many promising—and far more secure—opportunities for employing the technique in the field. A case in point is Plei Mrong, a Montagnard training center set up by U.S. Army Special Forces in pure Viet Cong territory, 25 miles from the Cambodian border. The center sustained, and repulsed after many casualties, an attack by a force of several hundred hard core Viet Cong. Several prisoners were taken and were vigorously interrogated by our people. A few broke down and disclosed valuable information on personalities and the location of Viet Cong sanctuaries on the infiltration route from Laos. It is the view of the Army project officer that surreption [sic] on the spot use of the interrogation technique would have broadened greatly this valuable intelligence break-through, and on a most secure basis, since the subjects were too simple, too ignorant, to have any idea of what was going on.

7

June 23, 1954
Federal Narcotics Prison Farm
Lexington, Kentucky

In all probability, this type of behavior is to be expected with patients of this type. Perhaps the drug will break down some of the barriers.
— Dr. Harris Isbell, August 3, 1953

Riding in the back seat of a taxicab through the front gates and onto the grounds of the farm, Sidney Gottlieb's attention was caught right away by the dairy cows grazing on an expansive, lush meadow. Gottlieb leaned toward the window to get a better look at the animals. At least 50 black-and-white cows lazed about, heads down into grass. Just beyond the meadow loomed the prison farm's huge main building with its stately Art Deco façade and multi-storied central tower. Beyond that, Gottlieb could see the enormous barn that housed the cows.

Close to the barn were a group of inmates (farm administrators favored calling them "patients," despite the fact that they were forcibly confined to the facility) tending a large tomato patch. The idyllic tableau offered an impression of pastoral serenity. Three months earlier, on the first of what would become half a dozen visits, Gottlieb had asked Dr. Harris Isbell, the Farm's research director, if working on the farm afforded the patients any positive benefits toward curing their addiction. Isbell had surprised him by responding that, no, for the most part, it did not.

"Many of our patients are from urban areas," Isbell had explained. "They don't care much for agricultural work or to be around animals." After a moment, Isbell had added, "Besides, the ones taking part in our experiments don't have the time."

During that first visit in July 1953, Gottlieb had been told that the Farm was a 'working' part of the United States Public Health Service's Addiction Hospital. Situated on 1,200 acres outside Lexington, Kentucky, the huge brick and stone complex had been built for a whopping $4 million price tag and had opened in 1935. Run jointly by the U.S. Bureau of Prisons and the Public Health Service, the Narcotics Farm, or "Narco," as it was referred to locally, treated thousands of patients, mostly heroin addicts. Among its predominantly unknown patients were a number of distinguished individuals: writer William S. Burroughs; his son William, Jr., also a writer; actor Peter Lorre; Barnet Ross, a boxer, war hero, gun runner, and close friend of Jack Ruby; and jazz greats Chet Baker, Sonny Rollins, Elvin Jones, Sonny Stitt, and Joe Guy. In 1964, a band composed of former farm inmates entertained the nation with music on Johnny Carson's *The Tonight Show*.

As part of its overall program, the facility maintained its Addiction Research Center (ARC). Made fully operational in 1936, the Center focused its work on investigating why certain people became addicted to drugs and others did not, and trying to find medical cures for addiction. Dr. Isbell was passionate about the Center's work. A tall man with thinning, dark hair combed back on his head, and wearing horn-rimmed glasses, Isbell was nearly forty-five years old when he first met Sidney Gottlieb. He was considered an expert on addiction problems and was often called upon to lecture and testify before medical groups and Congress. Isbell was especially proud of ARC's accomplishments. Much of ARC's work involved using inmates, or patients, as guinea pigs. As some readers may be aware, in America throughout the 1930s to the 1960s, while it was not technically illegal to use human subjects in medical research, the ethics and morality of the practice were rightfully called into question. The Tuskegee syphilis experiments were underway throughout these decades and they were later called unquestionably unethical during this era, regardless of the US Public Health Service turning a blind eye. The provisions of the 1947 Nuremberg Code would have been known to physicians and scientists during the 1950s and 1960s. The government's experiments were also in violation of several U.S. court decisions in the 40s, 50s, and 60s that had established the requirement of consent for established, non-experimental medical procedures. Although some court decisions may have been outside these states' jurisdictions, nonetheless, there was recognition of the basic requirement of consent for medical interventions. There was not a lower standard for non-beneficial, experimental procedures.

In 1975, it would be revealed that ARC experimented with nearly eight hundred drugs on human subjects. It was often claimed that the subjects did not seem to have suffered lasting harm. The notion of "harm" in medical ethics, however, is not confined to evidence of physical injury; it is, rather, the overall harm caused by treating such people as 'less than' human, as disposable, exploitable, 'not normal,' of no significant value. This is harm, regardless of any lasting physical or mental damage from the drugs. It is, therefore, unquestionable that these people were harmed. The general framework is, briefly that certain groups of human research participants–such as children, prisoners, individuals with questionable capacity to consent, students, or employees of the institution conducting the research–are considered to be either relatively or absolutely incapable of protecting their own interests. It is, therefore, by definition, unethical and harmful to experiment on them. These principles had been established since Nuremberg, regardless of what the United States was doing.

Well before the CIA had taken an interest in ARC, the Center had developed a close working relationship with the Federal Bureau of Narcotics. Supervisory agents George White, Charles Siragusa, Vance Newman, Arthur Giuliani, and other bureau officials frequently visited the facility and were close friends with many of its physicians, including Dr. Isbell and facility director Dr. Victor H. Vogel. White and Siragusa especially enjoyed having dinner with the Farm's director, followed by endless rounds of drinks at one of Vogel's favorite restaurants in nearby Louisville's Brown Hotel. Giuliani would take advantage of the trips to the Farm and attempt to interview, and sometimes interrogate, any patients he could identify who might have useful information on the Mafia, his specialty at the bureau.

During the Second World War, the OSS had secretly conducted a number of experiments in conjunction with Kentucky's ARC, some of which involved outside physicians Drs. Lawrence Kubie, Roger Adams, Robert C. Tyron, and Harold Abramson. It is thought that because of FBN Commissioner Harry Anslinger's close relationship with Dr. Vogel — as well as George White's involvement with the OSS 'truth drug' program — that the Lexington facility was chosen as one of many test sites.

In the late 1940s and early 1950s, ARC, with Dr. Harris Isbell overseeing, also conducted experiments for the Office of Naval Research (ONR). ARC's secret relationship with ONR ran at least through the late 1950s and frequently included research physicians from the University of Kentucky, which received funding for experiments from the Geschickter Fund for Medical Research, a CIA front. In the early 1950s, ARC experiments for the Navy focused on the study of codeine substitutes, as well as the ongoing experiments with 'truth drugs' in interrogation.

Throughout April to September 1953, in addition to Gottlieb, four other research scientists from Camp Detrick's SOD visited the Kentucky facility. They included Col. Vincent Ruwet and Frank Olson.

According to former SOD and FBN officials, Olson accompanied Ruwet on the trip so that he could review and study the "protective measures" taken by ARC in their fledgling experiments with LSD. One former SOD researcher, speaking on condition of anonymity, revealed that SOD's Olson, Ruwet, and Dr. Benjamin Wilson, returned to Kentucky in September 1953 to observe portions of Isbell's LSD experiments.

In a July 24, 1953 memorandum to a TSS Liaison and Security Officer, Gottlieb wrote that one of the primary objectives of his earliest ARC visit "was to inform National Institutes of Health and U.S. Public Health Service officials, in a secure manner, of our interest in and support of the research program of Dr. Harris Isbell." Gottlieb also stated that he informed the Director of the

National Institutes of Health, Dr. William H. Sebrell, Jr., "of the defensive aspects of the Agency's interest in Dr. Isbell's program and of our financial support of it." In his memorandum, Gottlieb never mentioned any specifics about the "program" but, as readers shall see, other documents make it quite clear that he was referring to Isbell's experiments with LSD. In regards to Sebrell, Gottlieb stated, "No details of the research program were divulged, but Dr. Sebrell approved highly of our general aims and indicated that he would afford us full support and protection."

Apparently, there were a few wrinkles in the CIA's budding relationship with ARC, not least of which was the competing interest of a "Dr. Chapman," believed to be Dr. Kenneth W. Chapman, who also worked at the Narcotics Farm. According to Gottlieb's memorandum, he had met with the Security Chief of the U.S. Department of Health, Education, and Welfare in Washington, D.C. to discuss Dr. Chapman's research. The HEW official told Gottlieb that he had already spoken with Chapman, who informed him that since "his personal interests lay along other lines" he "would prefer not to become involved in any way" with the CIA sponsored experiments at ARC.

According to CIA documents, an April 9, 1953 letter from Isbell to CIA Technical Services chief Willis Gibbons had alerted the Agency that ARC would be continuing its research on LSD and that the center was going to contact the Sandoz Company to ask if it could "obtain a reasonably large quantity of the drug." Isbell told Gibbons that ARC was planning to conduct "a study of the mental and other pharmacological effects produced by the chronic administration of the diethyl-amide of lysergic acid." Isbell's letter had prompted Gottlieb's initial visit to ARC.

Isbell's LSD project moved forward quickly and on August 3, 1953, he wrote to CIA Chemical Division Chief Gottlieb:

> I feel sure you will be interested to learn that we were able to begin our experiments with LSD-25 during the month of July. We obtained 5 subjects who agreed to take the drug chronically [sic]. All of these were negro male patients and all of them physically were in very excellent shape.... Arrangements have been made with the Sandoz Company to obtain a supply of the drug.

Despite the fact that black patients accounted for only about thirty percent of the Farm's patients at that time, all of Isbell's experimental subjects were African Americans. Writer Marjorie Senechal, whose father, Dr. Abraham Wikler, was an ARC physician and who grew up on the grounds of the farm, states:

> In Narco's first years, the vast majority of the patients were white, fewer than a tenth were black and the rest were Chinese, Hispanic, and other minorities. After the war, as blacks migrated from the south to northern cities, the percentage of black patients climbed to thirty.

Isbell's letter reflects his apparent bafflement regarding the social and racial disparities experienced by the black men:

> The behavior of the patients in our ward has been disappointingly quiet. All five men have been extremely quiet, agreeable and polite with each other, the psychiatric aides and the doctors. They definitely are more reserved than we expected, and we have a distinct feeling that they are somewhat afraid, most especially of the physicians involved. We have made a strenuous effort to break through this barrier but have succeeded only partially. The relationship with the psychiatric aides, who actually will be the key observers, is becoming somewhat more free and easy, but the degree of rapport obtained so far is not nearly so great as we expect with white subjects. Reserve and lack of rapport with the physicians are as great as initially. In all probability, this type of behavior is to be expected with patients of this type. Perhaps the drug will break down some of the barriers.

In early October 1953, Isbell sent Gottlieb another report, this one a quarterly report covering the months July 1 through September 30, 1953. The report stated that after "six patients, all negro, male former addicts, volunteered for the experiments" he had undertaken a preliminary test, during which LSD was "given daily" to the men. Nowhere in his report did Isbell mention that in order to induce his "volunteer" to participate in the experiments, he had promised them drugs of their choice, including morphine and heroin. In 1975, former Farm patients would appear before a U.S. Senate committee to talk about this practice. Said one, Edward M. Flowers, "My whole reason for going into the program was to get drugs." This could hardly be considered "voluntary" participation. Isbell's report continues:

> Initially, doses of 20 to 40 micrograms were administered [to each patient] and the dose was increased each day. Very few effects were observed until the dose had been increased to 100 micrograms.... It was, therefore, felt that patients might have developed tolerance during the preliminary period.
> ....For this reason it was necessary to obtain data on the effect of single isolated doses which were spaced at least three days apart... the [dose] range extending from 90 to <u>300</u> micrograms." [*Underlining original.*]

Isbell described the physical effects created by these doses, including dilation of pupils, blood pressure elevations, increased tendon reflexes, and tremors of large muscle groups. Regarding the effects of LSD on the mental status of these subjects, Isbell wrote:

> The mental effects of LSD-25 were very striking and varied from person to person... [They] included anxiety, a feeling of unreality... feelings of electric shocks on the skin, tingling sensations, choking... [Changes in]

patient's body image [with] the patient's hands and feet appearing to grow, or decrease, in size. Marked changes in visual perception were reported. These included blurring of vision, abnormal coloration of familiar objects (hands turning purple, green, etc), flickering shadows, dancing dots of light, and spinning circles of color. Frequently, inanimate objects were distorted and changed in size. Occasionally, patients reported seeing visions consisting of rapidly changing fantastic scenes which resembled 'Walt Disney movies.'

In early 1954, following Frank Olson's death, narcotics agent George White convened a meeting in New Jersey that included Dr. Harris Isbell, Col. Ruwet, and Dr. Paul Hoch, Dr. Harold Abramson, and Dr. E.W. Pelikan to discuss ARC's projects and other LSD experiments.

Dr. Isbell's LSD experiments continued throughout 1954. Early that year, on March 5, Dr. Henry Bortner notified Isbell that he had requested Dr. Harold Abramson to send him "a vial of Sandoz BOL-148." Explained Bortner: "As you will see from the enclosed information on this material, it has a dual interest from my point of view: as a narcotic and as an antidote for LSD-25." Bortner asked Isbell, "If you found it convenient, I would like for you to test its narcotic effect in some of your patients. There won't be enough material to do any extensive work, but essentially I am interested in confirming the Swiss report." On another subject, Bortner concluded: "I talked to Dr. [Shirley] Quimby last week with regard to your trip to Atlantic City and he agreed to send you a letter authorizing the travel [related to CIA Project HKDECOY]. He will also be ready to accept the proposal for next year in the near future." (See Book Two, Chapter 4 for more on Dr. Quimby and Project HKDECOY.)

It is unclear if the CIA incorporated ARC's experiments into its MKULTRA program. None of the surviving CIA documents regarding Isbell's work mention the program, as was standard practice in all other MKULTRA subprojects. Several subsequent Department of Defense documents, however, refer to the Navy's involvement with ARC as falling under the CIA's Project MKPILOT. It is also possible that MKULTRA Subproject 36, which involved at least one Camp Detrick SOD scientist, also involved Dr. Isbell. Details of this Subproject are few; all we know for certain is that the CIA granted $3,000 to the National Institutes of Health for a highly secret project that involved several Army Rangers surreptitiously boarding a foreign freighter for the purpose of interrogating a foreign national, using hypnosis and drugs, including LSD.

In mid-July 1954, Dr. Isbell reported to TSS officials, "Our experiments on tolerance to LSD-25 have been proceeding well, although I continue to be somewhat surprised by the results, which to me are the most amazing demonstration of drug tolerance I have ever seen." Isbell elaborated:

I have had 7 patients who have now been taking the drug for more than 42 days... All 7 are quite tolerant to both the physiological and mental effects of the drug. We have attempted to break through this tolerance by administering double, triple, and quadruple doses.

Two days later, TSS deputy chief Robert Lashbrook traveled to Kentucky to meet with Isbell and toxicologist Dr. E.W. Pelikan. Interestingly, after Frank Olson's death, Pelikan had left his work with Dr. Harold Abramson and joined the ARC staff. Lashbrook hand carried to the Kentucky facility 100 milligrams of LSD, 1 gram of cocaine, and an ounce of potassium tellurite. Potassium tellurite, used together with agar — a gelatinous product taken from red algae —, is used as a medium for growth of some bacteria.

Regarding these materials and purposes, Lashbrook wrote, somewhat cryptically:

Ed [Pelikan] will get busy with i.v. animal tests on the tellurite and will use the other materials in the Armour project. Dr. Isbell couldn't undertake any studies with the tellurite because of the nature of his situation.

(Details of the "Armour project" are unknown, but as readers shall learn, Gottlieb was quite active at the same time with projects involving the Armour Research Foundation of Chicago.) Lashbrook also noted, without explanation, that Dr. Pelikan had informed him that a 5-10 milliliter i.m. dose of colloidal sulfur would produce "excruciating pain for 8 to 10 hours" and that it was "not detectable with X-ray, and is available commercially."

Isbell followed up his July report with another on September 15, stating that he was pleased with the results of his experiments regarding tolerance to LSD. "Once tolerance to LSD has been well developed," he wrote, "it requires four to five times the dose to which the patient is tolerant to restore the LSD-reaction to its original intensity." However, he noted, "Tolerance to LSD is lost in three days following discontinuation of the drug." At the end of his five-page report, primarily concerned with his search for antidotes to LSD, Dr. Isbell stated that he intended to aggressively continue his LSD research "following my return from Europe," indicating that perhaps he, like other CIA subcontractors, was also performing work overseas for the Agency.

CIA records reveal that Robert Lashbrook visited the Narcotics Farm again on December 29, 1955 to meet with Isbell. It is not clear if Dr. Pelikan was still at the facility at this time. Lashbrook's visit concerned Isbell's experiments with bufotenine and Rivea seeds, which the CIA wanted Isbell to test on farm patients. Bufotenine is a highly toxic chemical in the venom and eggs of several species of poisonous toads. It has also been detected in the urine of schizophrenic subjects. First discovered in 1934, bufotenine is considered by many scientists to be a naturally occurring psychedelic, or psychotomimetic, drug. Sandoz's Albert Hofmann synthesized the drug in 1955.

Although it is unclear whether Isbell and Lashbrook knew that earlier experiments with bufotenine elsewhere had proven disastrous, it is likely they were aware of this. Two months earlier, on October 12, the first test with intravenously injected bufotenine, sponsored by NIH, had been conducted on four prisoners at the Ohio State Penitentiary. All of the men's faces turned purple, they hallucinated for a short time, vomited and experienced sharp chest pains. (Three years earlier at the same Ohio prison, nearly four hundred inmates had been injected with live human cancer cells in an experiment sponsored in part by NIH.)

Around the same time as the Ohio prison experiment, another bufotenine experiment was carried out on mental patients, conducted about the same time as the Ohio prison experiment, this one at Dr. Harold Abramson's State Hospital in Central Islip, New York. (Two years earlier, Frank Olson and Robert Lashbrook had visited Abramson at his Islip facility that fateful week in New York.) In Abramson's Islip experiment, patients injected with bufotenine not only developed plum-colored faces, some had gone into shock and nearly died. One woman had screamed, "I'm dying, I'm dying. Why are you killing me like this?"

In 1952, following consultations with NIH scientists, Camp Detrick's SOD had begun initial research and animal experiments with bufotenine-like substances, but that had been sidelined by a priority placed on LSD near the end of the year. SOD's Dr. Gerald Yonetz recounts, "There was a long, long list of drugs, including stuff like bufotenine, henbane, atropine, you name it. But somebody high up the ladder became enthralled with LSD and for a while everything else took a back seat."

Rivea corymbosa seeds are a species of morning glory that contain an alkaloid similar to one found in LSD. The seeds and plants are indigenous to Latin America, Mexico and Peru. They are used as vision-inducers, in rituals, and as cures for certain illnesses. The seeds provided to ARC came from the National Institutes of Health's Dr. Seymour Kety and Dr. Joseph Cochin.

Lashbrook wrote that in earlier NIH tests on dogs and cats, the "chief reactions [to Rivea seeds] seemed to be sedation with catatonia and analgesia without producing sleep, dilation of pupils, and anorexia." He noted, "There seemed to be a wide margin between effective and lethal dose and effects were obtained with amounts of the order of 50 seeds per dog, indicating a relatively high potency."

Before Lashbrook departed the Kentucky Farm, he informed Isbell that he would provide ARC with LSD from the Eli Lilly Company for testing as soon as Dr. Carl Pfeiffer had finished his own experiments with the drug. Readers may recall that the CIA had earlier contracted with Eli Lilly & Company of Indianapolis to manufacture LSD domestically so that the CIA would not have to rely on Sandoz, a foreign company, for their supplies.

On August 24, 1956, Sidney Gottlieb made what is believed to be his last trip to Lexington to visit Dr. Isbell. Gottlieb stayed at the Farm for about three days. His discussions with the ARC director were wide ranging and concerned several intriguing subjects, including Charas — handmade hashish found in India, Nepal, and Pakistan - as well as other, psychosis producing drugs, including an unidentified "French compound." They also reportedly discussed the hypnosis of Farm patients in order to measure the effects of LSD on suggestibility. The two also discussed "the problem of [finding a suitable] anti-interrogation" drug. One possibility considered was Nalline, the trade name for a narcotic antagonist that counteracts the effects of narcotics. Gottlieb and Isbell also reviewed the Farm's upcoming experiments with a substance identified only as K-302 and also with a "crude preparation of fungus."

In 1958, the Farm experimented on patients - again, African-American patients — with both K-302 and the mysterious fungus and determined that both could induce psychoses similar to LSD reactions.

From a recently surfaced letter we know that Dr. Isbell also conducted experiments on African-American inmates using Ibogaine hydrochloride. Ibogaine is a naturally occurring psychoactive compound first used, long ago, in African rites. The November 29, 1956 letter was addressed to Dr. Jack Graeme and Dr. H.R. Snyder, both research physicians with Ciba Pharmaceutical Products, Inc. of New Jersey, a company that later merged with Sandoz. Isbell informed the two that Ibogaine "definitely is an hallucinogenic material and that further exploration will show that the Ibogaine psychosis will have both resemblances and differences to the LSD psychosis."

Isbell was confident of this because he had experimented on eight subjects, whom he described as "all adult, Negro male former morphine addicts." Isbell explained that he had given the men multiple doses of the compound ranging from 50 mg to 300 mg. Some of the men, wrote Isbell, "had marked reactions," others "severe reactions." Isbell concluded that he was anxious to conduct further experiments, and asked Dr. Graeme, "Could you supply enough [Ibogaine] for about 15 men, estimated about 250 mg for each man?"

CIA funding to ARC and Dr. Isbell, most of which passed through the Office of Naval Research for security reasons, appears to have ended sometime in 1962, but funding from the CIA front, Geschickter Fund, continued until at least 1965.

8

Assassination

...[I]f you needed somebody to carry out a murder, I guess you had a man who might be prepared to carry it out.
— Richard Helms, 1976

In retrospect, it might be said that the [1949] letter to General Donovan can be considered the template for many of the Agency's assassination programs that followed.
— Richard Helms, 1979

Assassination was a matter of keeping up with the Joneses. Every other power practiced, and as far as I know still practices, assassination, if need be.
— Former CIA Director of Special Operation

There is no easy answer to the question of assassination.
— Richard Helms, 2002

In 1952, according to declassified TOP SECRET Camp Detrick records, SOD officials purchased every nonfiction publication available on the U.S. market that concerned the subject of assassination. High on the list were multiple copies of *The Assassins* by Robert J. Donovan. On its cover jacket, Donovan's book promises to be the "authentic and extraordinary story, told here completely for the first time, of those men who have hoped to alter the course of history by murdering the President of the United States— and in three cases have succeeded."

Also revealing are SOD financial records, submitted to the CIA for approval as part of the MKNAOMI project. The records list multiple items purchased in pursuit of a highly sophisticated cornucopia of chemical, biological, and other substances and products for silent, covert killing. MKNAOMI's purchases included:

various knives ranging from 2-inch blades to 16-inch blades;
silencers and suppressors for handguns and rifles;

rat poison;
boxes of multiple syringes;
special needle points;
articles on gout;
car tail pipes;
auto repair clamps;
Ungar units;
(unidentified) drugs for "X" project;
contact cement;
super Anahist;
small spools of piano wire;
chemicals for the "disposal" of guard dogs;
blow-guns and dart guns;
thin nylon rope;

And the list goes on and on. According to one former SOD scientist, speaking anonymously:

> Under the terms of our relationship with CIA it was required that some of us become, to whatever extent possible, experts on the historical antecedents of assassination. I'm not sure why this was mandated, there were never any group discussions on the subject, but I suppose it made sense. I myself was pretty surprised by the historical depths of chemical use in assassination. It was fascinating to learn that lethal venoms were used to surreptitiously kill dignitaries and emperors, that the Greeks poisoned wells and drinking water with black hellebore roots, that the Spartans employed toxic smoke to kill their enemies, and that during the Middle Ages diseased bodies were actually catapulted long distances into enemy ranks.

Former SOD scientist Dr. Gerald Yonetz contributed his recollections, at length:

> The CIA was always looking for ways of killing people or to make them sick.... They had various categories ranging from making someone slightly sick to very sick to terminally ill. On the lethal front they categorized substances ranging from slow kill to quick kill and a good many in between. They had [chemical] agents for all these. The list was expansive.
>
> Nothing was conventional by the day's standards, except for maybe the dart gun [SOD] developed. It was noisy but deadly. The CIA was originally using phonograph needles as darts but these weren't at all stable in flight. Our Detrick shop worked up better projectiles, what we called *flechettes*, that were small and highly effective. When we tested them at Aberdeen they traveled so fast through the air that the photo lab there was unable to capture any image....
>
> We had periodic meetings with the CIA to discuss the how-to's of killing people. Frank Olson was there at these retreats... if they weren't in

Deep Creek they were either held at Lost River or Berkeley Springs, [West Virginia]... The dart gun we developed eventually evolved into a flechettes-firing rifle that was tested for the Army in the Sixties. I don't think they worked very well; I know the CIA had no interest in them back then.

It is doubtful that any country has made the effort the United States did in the 1950s to assemble and analyze every known substance that could kill a person relatively easily, quickly and surreptitiously. By mid-1953, SOD researchers had developed a list of nearly 150 lethal substances that it had tested extensively, killing thousands of animals in the process. The SOD inventory includes many familiar disease-causing substances — *Salmonella typhimurium*; *Botulinum toxin*; *Staph EntB*; shellfish poison; *Bacillus anthracis* (anthrax); and *Variola virus* (smallpox) — as well as less familiar ones — *toxiferine*; *microcystis seruginosa* toxin; *Pasteurella tularensis* (tularemia); *Coccidioides immitis* (valley fever); and *Bungarus Candidus* venom. Clearly, by the early 1950s, state-sponsored killing had been elevated to an art form and a science. Assassination, however, had even deeper roots than these SOD activities.

Some SOD scientists, in their studies of state-sponsored killing, no doubt, understood that assassination is as old as mankind itself. Examples abound from Biblical times, as well as from histories of the ancient Roman, Greek, and Persian empires. Assassination is the currency of much political history and classical literature, and in many cultures today it is still regarded as a standard *modus operandi* in circles of power.

In the United States, however, assassination has always been regarded officially as an aberrant practice. Nonetheless, it is widely known that the nation's intelligence community has, for the past half-century or longer, maintained well-trained, active assassination teams or hit squads.

The practice of assassination as an operational arm of the U.S. intelligence community— apart from those roving, marauding, murderous guerilla bands that functioned during the Civil War with sanctioning from military leaders— was first formally proposed to Major General William J. Donovan, head of the OSS, in November 1949.

At that time, former OSS director and then CIA consultant, General William Donovan received a letter from a friend to whom he had issued a challenge several months earlier. The letter's author — whose name is redacted in the copy provided by the CIA — greets "Dear Bill" and apologizes for taking so long to get back to Donovan with his "thoughts on the problem which you raised when I saw you last." The author then gets right to the task at hand, setting out "the means that I think might be most efficacious." Beginning with the intended outcomes, the author is stunningly specific:

> You will recall that I mentioned that the local circumstance under which a given means might be used might suggest the technique to be used in

that case. I think that gross divisions in presenting this subject might be (1) bodies left with no hope of the cause of death being determined by the most complete autopsy and chemical examination, (2) bodies left in such circumstances as to simulate accidental death, (3) bodies left in such circumstances as to simulate suicidal death, and (4) bodies left with residua that simulate those caused by natural diseases.

Continuing his dispassionate survey, the writer proceeds to elaborate various detailed protocols for disguising, concealing or avoiding trace evidence of cause of death, enabling undetected assassination:

I believe that there are two chemical substances which would be most useful in that they would leave no characteristic pathologic findings, and the quantities needed could easily be transported to the places where they were to be used. One of these, sodium fluoacetate, when ingested in sufficient quantities to cause death does not cause characteristic pathologic lesions nor does it increase the amount of fluorine in the body to such a degree that it can be detected by quantitative methods. The other chemical substance which I have in mind is tetraethyl lead which, as you know, could be dropped on the skin in very small quantities, producing no local lesion, and after a quick death no specific pathologic evidence of the tetraethyl lead would be present.

If an individual could be placed into a relatively tightly sealed small room with a block of CO_2 ice, it is highly probable that his death would result and that there would be no chances of the circumstances being detected. It is highly probable, though, that there would be a period of hyperactivity in the course of such a death.

Another possibility would be the exposure of the entire individual to X-ray. When the whole body is exposed, a relatively small amount of radiation is sufficient to produce effects that would lead to death within a few weeks, and it is highly probable that sporadic deaths of this kind would be considered as due to blood dyscrasias.

If it were possible to subject the individual to a cold environment, he would freeze to death when his body temperature reached 70 degrees, and there is no anatomic lesion that is diagnostic in such cases.

There are other techniques which I believe should be mentioned since they require no special equipment besides a strong arm to smother the victim with a pillow or to strangle him with a wide piece of cloth, such as a bath towel. In such cases, there is no specific anatomic change to indicate the cause of death, though there may be serosal petechiae and marked visceral congestion which would suggest strangulation along with some other possibilities.

A shorter, second letter to "Bill," dated three months later and presumed written as follow up to the first, reads:

Due to work pressures here I haven't had adequate time to pursue your questions regarding visceral congestion and strangulation. Assembly and review of available literature, which I am presently accomplishing for you, best answer the other issue you raised related to simulated suicide. *I agree with your assumption that falls from high places are simplest to carry out and most effective.... [The] treatment of coffee or a drink before-hand, thus allowing others to participate in the scenario as described, is encouraged. In the proper settings, simulated suicide is foolproof.* [Emphasis added.]

Obviously, Donovan was no stranger to the art of murder. Indeed, in his role as OSS director he had received a detailed report in 1943 from high-ranking OSS officer and Harvard anthropologist, Carlton S. Coon, advocating adoption of political assassination as an instrument of state policy and the formalization of an ultra-elite assassination bureau. Coon rationalized that "the world is now too small and too tight to permit a continuation of the process of trial and error.... A mistake made in one quarter will of necessity spread rapidly all over the world, for all our apples are now in one barrel, and if one rots the lot is destroyed." Coon proposed a scheme not unlike what one would expect from a place somewhere between George W. Bush's Pentagon neoconservatives and an omnipotent clan of X-Men:

> ...we cannot be sure that the clear and objective scholars who study the existing social systems and draw blueprints for a society to suit our tech-nology will always be heard, or that their plans will be put into operation. We can almost be sure that this will not be the case. Therefore some other power, some third class of individuals aside from the leaders and the scholars must exist, and this third class must have the task of thwarting mistakes, diagnosing areas of political world disequilibrium, and nipping the causes of potential disturbances in the bud. There must be a body of men whose task it is to throw out the rotten apples as soon as the first spots of decay appear. A body of this nature must exist undercover. It must either be a power unto itself, or be given the broadest discretionary powers by the highest human authorities.

According to Gen. Donovan's biographer, Anthony Cave Brown, to whom Coon graciously gave a copy of his assassination corps proposal long missing from OSS archives, Donovan perhaps "gauged it imprudent and undesirable" to create the assassination corps. However, there is ample circumstantial evidence that the OSS, with or without its director's official sanction, created it nonetheless.

First, there is Major Coon's own experience with assassination, which ap-parently well exceeded the bounds of academic mutterings. Coon was very likely involved in the murder of French Admiral Jean-Francois Darlan, a Nazi-collaborator, in Algiers on Christmas Eve 1942. Second, the OSS maintained a secret training center, modeled on the SOE's Camp X, a "school for mayhem and murder," as one notable American attendee dubbed it, that taught such esoteric skills as "silent killing" and "close-in fighting." (Readers shall learn more about Camp X in this book's section on George Hunter White.) Lastly, there was Coon's association with a number of notorious Corsicans during and after the Darlan assassination. In 1943, Coon traveled to Corsica to formally cement these associations.

Underscoring these facts is the OSS's official War Report, as well as other declassified OSS documents, which reveal the agency's deep concerns, at one point, that it was "recruiting Mafiosi and, on a smaller scale, hit men from the ranks of Murder, Inc. and the Philadelphia 'Purple Gang.'" According to the report: "The [OSS Operational Group] consisted of tough little boys from New York and Chicago, with a few live hoods mixed in.... Their one desire was to get over to the old country and start throwing knives." The report adds that by 1945 "there were several murders" and that "these guys were considered to be so dangerous" that the Allied High Command ordered them "confined to a castle near Spezia."

Like the OSS, the U.S. Army also maintained more than a passing interest in assassination, especially given the chaotic situation in Berlin and Eastern Europe at the end of the war. Thus, the Army, primarily through its Counter Intelligence Corps, made concerted efforts to recruit from its existing ranks any servicemen who had been imprisoned for murder or other violent crimes.

From 1949 through 1951, the fledging CIA studied assassination techniques even more aggressively. A particularly blunt Agency memorandum reads:

> Let's get into the technology of assassination, figure most effective ways to kill— like Empress Agrippina —do you want your people to be able to get out of the room? Do you want it traced?

Empress Agrippina was the wife of Roman Emperor Claudius, whom she wanted to murder so that her son Nero could attain the throne. Claudius had a fondness for eating mushrooms, and the Empress decided to poison him by mixing lethal mushrooms in with those he most favored eating. Among the Empress's concerns, according to Gordon and Valentina Wasson, was that the poison she employed could not be "sudden and instantaneous in its operation, lest the desperate achievement should be discovered." Or, as the CIA's memorandum casually expressed it, the Empress "had to have time to get out of the room before Claudius keeled over." So she chose the deadly *Amanita phalloides* mushroom, which the Wasson's wrote was an excellent choice:

> The victim would not give away the game by abnormal indispositions at the meal, but when the seizure came he would be so severely stricken that thereafter he would no longer be in command of his own affairs.

Suffice it to say, Nero took the throne.

Who Was QJ/WIN?

In his 1985 novel, *The Double Man*, former U.S. Senator Gary Hart, co-writing with fellow senator and future Secretary of Defense, William Cohen, tells of an intriguing character referred to only by his CIA-given codename, QJ/WIN. Described as an "agent" with the Agency's assassination program, Hart's protagonist, Tom Chandler, a U.S. Senator himself, frantically spends half the novel trying to locate the elusive, enigmatic QJ/WIN. Chandler's quest is complicated by interactions among a worldwide conspiracy led by a renegade KGB colonel, a war funded with Mafia drug money, and high-level CIA infiltration and deception. The conspiracy is complex and riddled with false turns. Naturally, only QJ/WIN holds the key to saving the United States from impending doom.

"How much does [QJ/WIN] know?" Senator Chandler demands of a 'Deep Throat' type called Memory.

"He knows everything," is the cryptic reply.

By "everything" Memory means that QJ/WIN holds the proverbial key to unlocking the core mysteries of virtually all of the Twentieth Century's paramount conspiracy theories. "If there was a connection between executive action and Kennedy, he undoubtedly knows it," intones Memory.

Hart's QJ/WIN is also the pivot of knowledge about the CIA's ZR/RIFLE operation, initially aimed at killing Fidel Castro, among others. And if that is not enough, Memory also informs Chandler that QJ/WIN is a repository of information about "the drugs" that liberally and illicitly pour into the United States and are somehow connected to the CIA's assassination program and its marriage-of-necessity with the Mafia.

Senator Hart's book bears the obligatory disclaimer that "some portions of this novel deal with occurrences and actual events... but the depiction of KGB and CIA operations within the Soviet Union and the United States is fiction and should not be construed as being factual— or even probable."

Hart's disclaimer with regard to QJ/WIN is misleading, considering that the mysterious agent did exist and that his CIA code-name was in fact QJ/WIN. Most significantly, in July, 1975, about nine years before he wrote his novel, Senator Hart traveled to Holland to secretly meet with the real QJ/WIN and to question him about his involvement with the CIA's assassination program, including attempts to kill Castro, and about the murder of President John F. Kennedy.

Like his novel's protagonist, Hart was intrigued by QJ/WIN, a man often referred to in intelligence circles as the "assassin's assassin." Senator Hart journeyed to Holland from Moscow, where he had unrelated official business. Before leaving Washington for Moscow, Hart had asked CIA director William Colby to arrange the secret meeting for him with QJ/WIN in Europe. DCI Colby agreed to the request and told Hart that he had no idea where QJ/WIN was, but that he would have an Agency official locate him as soon as possible.

In Moscow, Hart was handed a handwritten, unsigned note from another CIA official letting the senator know that QJ/WIN would meet with him in Amsterdam, where Hart had a scheduled layover on his return flight to the United States. Hours later, Hart sat in an Amsterdam cafe anxiously awaiting the arrival of QJ/WIN, but the enigmatic assassin never arrived, and Senator Hart returned home disappointed.

The codename QJ/WIN first appeared publicly in 1975, when it was revealed during a U.S. Senate Select Committee hearing investigating the CIA and its various assassination programs. The codename QJ/WIN was said to be that of the first recruited assassin in the Agency's "Executive Action" program, as its assassination program was euphemistically termed. The committee pieced together various aspects of the identity and work history of QJ/WIN, including that his background apparently involved dealings with, or working for, the OSS, and that by the early 1950s he was considered a highly skilled intelligence operative with impeccable skills in the arts of deception, disguise, evasion, and overall counter-intelligence work. By the late-1950s, QJ/WIN was well known and widely respected for his unique array of attributes both domestically and overseas. High-level, hardened CIA officials respected the man, and when a difficult task, like the murder of the Congo's Patrice Lumumba, arose in November 1969, the Agency dispatched QJ/WIN for the job. The sheer gravity of designating and dispatching a man halfway around the world to kill a high-profile foreign leader should not be underestimated. Had QJ/WIN been caught at his bloody task, the United States might have had serious questions and issues to confront.

From the 1975 Senate Committee's findings we also know that QJ/WIN was a man who had performed work for the Federal Bureau of Narcotics, and perhaps other federal agencies, and that QJ/WIN himself was "of criminal background." One astute writer, Stephen Rivele, has pointed out that this is a curious phrase, "of criminal background." OJ/WIN is not said to be a "criminal" himself, but that his "background" is one of a criminal nature.

The 1975 Senate Committee also informs us that when the CIA, in the fall of 1963, attempted to recruit assassins for its Executive Action program, no reliable, experienced, professional killers were keen to step forward to murder foreign leaders. Not only were they seriously concerned that they, as the assassins, would be hunted down after the fact, but also that it was extremely likely they, too, would meet untimely deaths either at the hands of the hunters, or local law enforcement, or even their handlers. The Senate Committee's findings strongly implied that QJ/WIN knew — probably through his "criminal background" dealings — Santo Trafficante, Jr., Johnny Rosselli, Paul Mondolini, and Francois Spirito, as well as other known drug traffickers. When former DCI Richard Helms was asked about QJ/WIN, he replied that "if you needed somebody to carry out murder, I guess you had a man who might be prepared to carry it out."

Another important fact revealed in the Committee report and often over-looked in QJ/WIN's spotty history, is that QJ/WIN was hired not only to be an assassin but also, and primarily, to "recruit" and direct assassins. In other words, QJ/WIN was a sort of 'commander of assassins,' thus the term "the assassin's assassin." As one 1962 CIA financial document distilled his role, in part:

> QJ/WIN is under written contract as a principle agent, with the primary task of spotting agent candidates. QJ/WIN was first contacted in [*here two lines are redacted, but partial words appear to be 'Ellis Island,' 'New York' and 'Anslinger'*] in connection with an illegal narcotics operation into the United States. For a period of a year and a half, he was contacted sporadically by Luxembourg, on behalf of the Bureau of Narcotics. Files of the Bureau reflect an excellent performance by QJ/WIN. In October 1960, [*page ends here and does not continue*].

An addendum to the same document reveals that QJ/WIN was paid by the CIA for about twenty-eight months at the rate of about $750 a month, plus travel and operating expenses of about $300 every six months, as well as being given a car and food allowance. (Readers may want to note that $750 in 1960 has the same buying power as $5,400 in 2009.)

Had it not been for an unlikely source – the handwritten notes of CIA officer William K. Harvey – this is all we would know about QJ/WIN. It turns out that Harvey's notes, on close examination, are a wealth of information about our elusive "assassin's assassin" and also about the CIA's thought process and intentions concerning assassination. Harvey wrote his random jottings primarily because he was brought in to oversee the ongoing Agency assassination plots against Fidel Castro (see below). Harvey's notes are here reproduced [italics added by author]:

> 1) Legal, ethical-moral, operational problems; political; non-attributability.
> 2) Our own experience (Bangkok) (& effect on DDP) and experiences w/KGB (Crossup, Bandera group, Khokhlov—require most professional, proven operationally competent, ruthless, stable, CE-experienced ops officer (few available), able to conduct patient search & w/ guts to pull back if instinct or knowledge tells him he should, and w/ known high regard for operational security, assessment...
> 3) Maximum security: (highest not secure enough) & within KUBARK [CIA] only (e.g. *how much does [Charles] Siragusa need to know?*) Limitation on number code clerks for enciphering and deciphering. No approach to other Govt. Agencies.
>   a. Within [CIA], one focal point for control, search, training, case offering, etc. DDP authority in this focal point mandatory. DCI officially advised?

b. Max security cable commo for innocuous cables only; no restrictions on travel; possibility of one-man overseas (Europe) control base with own (non-Station) commo—word-of-mouth & no bashfulness re trips.

c. (Every operation to be rigidly case-officered. No silk-shirt PA's [principle assets]. No PA's except for search or intermediaries....

d. No approach to officials of foreign governments. (Non-attributability; no American citizen or American resident for direct action. Possibly for approach to foreign elements.) No criminal who tainted by use by another American agency. Use of case officers who can pass as foreigners—and limited official references. No chain of connection permitting blackmail. Avoid discussion with foreign officials until all possibility of search through.

e. No approach to any agent who ever [worked for] a U.S. Govt. agency. Training by opposition would reveal.

f. Use of <u>already</u> tested assets (e.g. QJ/WIN—probably in the search.

g. Stand-by list of [CIA staff people] who can pass as foreigners.

h. Pretext: Kutube/D [FI/D] search; this established (e.g. Rome).

i. No discussion in CIA stations.

j. No team until ready to go, if at all.

4) Blackmail

a. No American citizens or residents or people who ever obtained U.S. visas.

b. No chain of knowledgeable staffers. Strictly person-to-person; single ops.

c. No meeting any candidate in home territory.

d. Exclude organized criminals, e.g. Sicilians, criminals, those with arrest records, those w/ instability of purpose as criminals.

e. Staffers involved—selection.

5) Cover: planning should include provision for blaming Soviets or Czechs in case of blow... organization criminals, those with record of arrests, those who have been engaged in several types of crimes. <u>Corsicans recommended</u>. Sicilians could lead to Mafia.

6) Testing on nominees essential: re following directions, security, blackmail.

7) Former resistance personnel a possibility. Period of testing, surveillance, etc. for each selection. All CIA personnel should have some CE experience.

8) Use <u>nobody</u> who has never dealt w/ criminals; otherwise will not be aware of pitfalls or consider factors such as freedom to travel, wanted lists, etc.

9) Should have phony 201 [personnel file] in RI [CIA records center] to backstop this. All documents therein forged and backdated. Should look like CE file.

10) Possible use of defectors for these actions.

Silverthrone and stable in... What limits on team or individuals selected? No 'team' until ready to go. Danger of standbys. Keeping of files.

According to William Harvey's biographer, Bayard Stockton, in 1962, QJ/WIN "was about to go on trial in Europe on smuggling charges." No details are given as to the nature of the charges or to the identity of the item(s) being smuggled. Around the same time, perhaps as late as 1964, QJ/WIN and his wife were living in Cologne, Germany, where he may have been operating a small business, either a restaurant or shop. On June 17, 1963, Harvey wrote a memorandum to the chief, FI [Foreign Intelligence] Staff, stating that, "the original justification for employing QJ/WIN no longer existed."

Eight months later, on February 14, 1964, the CIA issued a dispatch stating that QJ/WIN "has been terminated." The dispatch elaborates:

> Renzeny [CIA station chief] told [QJ/WIN] on 21 April that the operation in which he was to play a role had been shelved and therefore his contract, which ran out on 29 February, was not renewed. He was reassured that this action did not result from anything he had done and his past cooperation was appreciated. It was mentioned as conceivable that the operation might have been off and running had he been able to establish his cover last year. QJ/WIN accepted the reason for termination and said he would always be available if he could be of any assistance. In discussing his future, Renzeny suggested, now that he has received all the necessary authorizations for doing business in Germany, he seriously consider going ahead with the venture in Cologne. QJ/WIN said he would discuss this with his wife...
>
> Since January 1962... QJ/WIN's only assignment has been to establish cover. This requirement was confirmed by [written and formal directive] of 28 may 1962 and during [redacted words] discussions in headquarters in July 1962. 27 months and some $18,000 later he is still not in place, although [redacted name] made an issue of this with him in August 1963. Whether he ever really intended to commit himself to this assignment remains a question....
>
> QJ/WIN's personal history reflects major instability and the habit of hedging his bets is undoubtedly part of his character. This does not imply a security breach. There is nothing to indicate that he has discussed his KUBARK [CIA] relationship with anyone, except perhaps, his wife. Rabney is known to QJWIN by true name. Renzeny used the name "Pierre" with him, but it is assumed that he has identified Renzeny's true name.

It would also later be revealed that, according to QJ/WIN's CIA personnel file, he had testified at the trial of French Marshal Philippe Petain. Petain, a World War I hero, had been voted Head of State after the French defeat in June 1940, but Petain had surrendered to the Nazis, transforming his government into little more than a puppet dictatorship headquartered in the resort town of Vichy. In August 1945, Petain was tried for collaboration and treason. He was convicted and sentenced to death, but Provisional Government president Charles de Gaulle commuted his sentence to life imprisonment. Petain died in prison in 1951 at the age of ninety-five. QJ/WIN would later quip that Petain was "perhaps the least of the terrible traitors, but punishment was nonetheless merited."

THE "TERRIBLE CONSTANT" OF HEROIN

Writer Stephen J. Rivele, who has gone farther than most in attempting to identify QJ/WIN, states that, "a terrible constant "emerges in the quest to identify QJ/WIN and "that is heroin." Rivele, as will be shown in Book Three, is correct. Heroin was always either a driving force or at the margins of many of the CIA's postwar covert operations, along with a huge cast of unsavory characters and drug traffickers who were always at the beck-and-call of the Agency. Writes Rivele:

> At the *very least*, the CIA has not scrupled to do business with the traffickers of heroin, offering protection and support in return for their collaboration in covert activities. All of this was done, of course, in the name of national security. [Italics original.]

Over the past five decades a tremendous amount of information has been published documenting the CIA's close involvement with international heroin traffickers and cartels. Placed within the broader context of organized crime in general, historian Alan A. Block has termed this relationship "a modern marriage of convenience." Block writes that organized crime "has been and continues to be inextricably linked to international political movements and to that segment of the American political establishment known as the espionage community or perhaps more aptly, the transnational political police." Block chooses as his best example the World War II collaboration between the Mafia and the Office of Naval Intelligence to use "professional criminals from the New York metropolitan area in a special and highly secret project" that was not exposed until 1977. It was Operation Underworld, the alliance between mobsters — like Meyer Lansky, Lucky Luciano, and Frank Costello — and the Navy to safeguard American harbors and ports and to assist in the American invasion of Sicily.

After World War II ended, the Mafia continued to benefit significantly from this collaboration. The wartime alliance produced a culture in which organized crime, drug dealers, hit men and the American intelligence community remained uneasily in bed with one another. As Block describes it:

> For organized crime researchers, the major point to reflect upon is the indisputable fact that certain organized crime figures and syndicates are deeply embedded in transnational political movements and the transnational political police. And the recognition... that organized crime and municipalities are inextricably linked must not obscure the profound

329

impact of organized crime on foreign affairs, the world of 'high' politics. It may very well be the case that certain political assassinations or other intelligence moves may be done not in the interests of foreign policy carried out by hired goons and thugs, but rather in the interests of drug smugglers and international gamblers, carried out by their clients in the intelligence services.

Historian Alfred W. McCoy was perhaps the first to pin down the CIA's early and close alliance with foreign drug traffickers. McCoy describes his troubling discoveries:

> To an average American who witnesses the dismal spectacle of the narcotics traffic at the street level, it must seem inconceivable that the government could be implicated in the international drug trade. Unfortunately, American diplomats and CIA agents have been involved in the narcotics traffic at three levels: (1) coincidental complicity by allying with groups actively engaged in the drug traffic; (2) support of the traffic by covering up for known heroin traffickers and condoning their involvement; and (3) active engagement in the transport of opium and heroin.
>
> It is ironic, to say the least, that America's heroin plague is of its own making.... In effect, American drug policy has been crippled by a contradiction between DEA attempts to arrest major traffickers and CIA protection for many of the world's drug lords.... The CIA's protected covert action assets have included Marseille's Corsican criminals, national Chinese opium warlords, the Thai military's opium overlord, Laotian heroin merchants, Afghan heroin manufacturers, and Pakistan's leading drug lords.

Peter Dale Scott, the historian who gave us the term "deep politics"—the process of politics "at levels usually not acknowledged or reported and indeed repressed and denied"— writes eloquently about the "terrible constant":

> Dishonesty, manipulation, and even self-deception are widespread in our nominal democracy. So little of what really goes on is acknowledged that the notion of deep politics as earlier defined, 'political practices and arrangements that are usually repressed rather than acknowledged,' needs to be defined more fully....
>
> The CIA and other agencies appear to have collaborated closely with the Federal Bureau of Narcotics in [the] operational use of drug traffickers. [The] CIA helped establish important institutional support for the traffic in postwar Sicily, on the Marseille waterfront, and throughout Southeast Asia....
>
> The inevitable result of this use of drug traffickers was a nationally protected drug traffic, in which many key traffickers, because of their government connections, were not prosecuted.

COL. BORIS T. PASH AND ASSASSINATION

Prior to being called up for duty in World War II, Boris Pash was a physical education teacher at Hollywood High School in California. Had the war never happened, most likely Pash's only claim to fame would have been his 'discovery' of actress Lana Turner, one of his students. It was Pash who first drew the attention of a top talent scout to high school student Turner.

Pash, who attended divinity school, graduated from seminary in 1917. During the Russian Revolution, Boris sided with the White Russians and in 1920, after marrying, he returned to the United States with his wife and son. Pash earned his undergraduate degree in physical education in Massachusetts and, later, his Master's degree from the University of Southern California in Los Angeles. When World War II began, Pash was teaching at Hollywood High School. Having participated in ROTC during college, Pash was called up for active duty in 1940. As Chief of the Counter Intelligence Division, he was first assigned to the Army 9th Corps and later to the headquarters of the Western Defense Command.

Pash's first intelligence job was overseeing security on the ultra top-secret Manhattan Project in Los Alamos, New Mexico where he dogged physicist Robert Oppenheimer, later contributing to Oppenheimer's destruction. Pash was particularly heavily involved in the internment of Japanese-Americans and their families during World War II. In the internment camps, Japanese-American citizens were stripped of their basic civil liberties, and forced into inhumane, heavily fortified concentration camps in California, Arizona, and other states.

In 1981, Pash appeared before a hearing of the Commission on Wartime Relocation and Internment of Civilians where he shocked those present by stating that the camps that held Japanese-Americans "were not concentration camps" despite their being surrounded by barbed-wire and armed guards, because the inmates "could go to work in the fields" each day.

During the final months of World War II, the U.S. raced the Soviets to capture all documents pertaining to Nazi and Japanese chemical and biological warfare research, as well as the scientists who might be of value to the United States. This effort was spearheaded by what has been described as "a murderous intelligence operation" launched in 1943 to capture key German scientists, particularly those involved in nuclear research. Formally dubbed the Alsos Mission, the operation was conceived by Dr. Vannevar Bush, director of the U.S. Office of Scientific Research and Development, Maj. Gen. George V. Strong, chief of Army intelligence, and Maj. Gen. Leslie R. Groves, head of the U.S. atomic bomb project at Los Alamos. Groves selected Lt. Col. Pash to be military head of the mission. (Physicist Samuel Goudsmit was added as scientific director when Pash proved unable to identify or evaluate the scientific significance of documents recovered from Italian laboratories by the Alsos mission in 1944.)

At its start, the Alsos Mission focused on finding Nazi nuclear scientists, but was expanded near the war's end to include the capture, and eventual recruitment, of Germany's top biological and chemical weapons researchers. Alsos agents, for example, were especially interested in finding Nazi anthrax expert and SS major general, Dr. Walter P. Schreiber, but in 1945 Soviet troops, with the same objectives, had spirited Schreiber away. In 1948, Schreiber inexplicably turned up in West Berlin, claiming that he had escaped. Remarkably, despite being wanted for war crimes and strongly suspected of being a double agent for the Russians, Schreiber was hired by the U.S. Army's Counter Intelligence Corps. Linda Hunt reveals in her classic book, *Secret Agenda*, that Schreiber was employed at Camp King, a large POW interrogation center in Oberusal, Germany.

In the first quarter of 1951, a team of three scientists from Camp Detrick, who were attached to a CIA-funded special operations unit, traveled to Germany to interview Schreiber and other captured scientists. The team included Dr. Frank Olson, then Special Operations Division branch chief for planning and intelligence activities. Its mandate was to learn all that it could about a Nazi SS project that had entailed using "psychochemical drugs" on concentration camp inmates. Schreiber and SS Col. Wolfram Sievers, director of the Ahnenerbe's Institute for Scientific Research (Himmler's think tank for study of the occult), had been in charge of the project, which ran from 1942 to November 1943. (Sievers was hung in 1948, after being tried and convicted for war crimes at Nuremberg.)

Col. Boris Pash and his Alsos Mission colleagues considered Schreiber to be one of their greatest catches. Many U.S. officials, however, were greatly upset when the *New York Times* reported on October 7, 1951 that Schreiber was in Texas working for the U.S. Air Force. The article made no mention of the fact that Schreiber was wanted for war crimes. Former Nuremberg prosecutors and several Jewish groups were outraged to learn of Schreiber's presence in the U.S. and complained loudly to the White House. Nothing was done about it. In February 1952 the *New York Times* reported increasing pressure to take action against Schreiber because he had performed "medical experiments on unwilling concentration camp victims."

When Schreiber's employment contract with the Air Force and Army expired, the CIA blocked efforts to send him back to Germany and, in May 1952, they arranged his relocation to Buenos Aires, where he was given a job by the Argentine government as an expert consultant on "diseases and epidemics." Several Fort Detrick researchers, who declined to be identified, have maintained that Schreiber, on at least two occasions, lectured at the Frederick, Maryland facility. (Readers shall learn more about the use of captured Nazi scientists and scientific information in the next chapter.)

In November 1975, former CIA official E. Howard Hunt, convicted of participating in the Watergate break-in, told a newspaper reporter that "in 1954 or 1955," he had learned that "the CIA had a small unit set up to arrange for the assassination of suspected double-agents and similar low-ranking foreign officials."

Reporter John M. Crewdson recounted his extraordinary interview with Hunt in a special article in the *New York Times*. Hunt was then at the federal correctional institution at Eglin Air Force Base in Florida, where he was serving an eight-year sentence for his role in the Watergate break-in. Hunt told Crewdson that he recalled being informed by his CIA superiors in the mid-1950s that Boris T. Pash, an agency official, was then in charge of an assassination unit.

Crewdson reported that, "during the period in question, he [Hunt] was staff officer assigned to the CIA's Balkans division, and that on one occasion he and his colleagues had encountered 'very substantial problems' with 'an organization that the Agency was maintaining in West Germany.'" According to Hunt, the problem concerned an Albanian within the organization "who probably was a penetration." ("Penetration" is the CIA term for an agent suspected of, or discovered to be, working for a hostile intelligence group.) Hunt explained to Crewdson:

> It was decided to 'neutralize' the man in such a way that the other side would not know that we were aware of his activities, and of course assassination was the obvious answer.

Hunt said he had inquired at the time about arranging for such an assassination and "I was told that we had that capability," and "that the guy to see about this sort of thing was Colonel Pash." Hunt described Pash as "a mysterious figure" around the Agency who "was kind of a joke" among other CIA officials. Added Hunt, "It was a wary joke, though. Nobody really knew what he was doing."

At any rate, Hunt, at the direction of his superiors, spoke with Pash, telling the colonel, "Look, we have this problem here, is this something you guys can handle?"

According to Hunt, Pash had replied that he was not sure, and he seemed shocked that Hunt had approached him. Hunt claimed that he never heard back from Pash, adding derisively that Pash's sole purpose with Program Branch 7 seemed to be "drawing his salary and drinking coffee."

During Crewdson's interview of Hunt in 1975, the topic of assassination had come up because, at that time, a Senate Select Committee, the Church Committee, was investigating the CIA's involvement in assassination of foreign leaders. Reporter Crewdson queried the Committee about Col. Pash, but was told that "no reference to Pash had been included by the CIA in the information on the Agency's assassination plots," and that the CIA had no comment on Pash or whether he had ever worked for the Agency.

However, the Church Committee investigating CIA activities did interview Boris Pash about his CIA assignments. The resulting report reveals that Pash was assigned to the CIA from March 3, 1949 to January 3, 1952, and that he continued well beyond that date to work on "several CIA projects," none of which are identified. In the early years of the Agency, Pash formally served as Chief of Program Branch 7, commonly referred to as PB/7. The branch was initially a "special operations" unit within the Office of Policy Coordination, precursor to the CIA itself. OPC was organized into seven branches that handled covert actions, PB/7 being one of them. "According to Colonel Pash," states the CIA's report, "PB/7 was responsible for 'such activities, which the other six branches didn't specifically have.'" Despite Pash's ambiguity, he admitted that although PB/7 "was not operational," it was involved in the "planning of special operations," such as encouraging defections from Communist countries, and "contingency planning for the deaths of foreign leaders such as Stalin."

The former Director of Operations Planning for OPC, however, was questioned by the committee and, as evident in the Church Committee's report, he did not agree with Pash's vague assertions. As the former director in charge of supervising the programs of all seven OPC branches, he was able to be a bit more specific. PB/7, he said, "was responsible for assassinations and kidnapping as well as other 'special operations.'"

The director, who is not identified by name, clearly reported for a time to Allen Dulles, and testified that in 1949 he had consulted with Frank Wisner, the director of OPC. Wisner "agreed that Pash should have jurisdiction over assassinations." According to the testimony of the Director of Operations Planning:

> Kidnapping was also part of PB/7's 'catch-all function,'.... .Kidnapping of personages behind the Iron Curtain...if they were not in sympathy with the regime, and could be spirited out of the country by our people for their own safety; or kidnapping of people whose interests were inimical to ours.... [Assassination] was a matter of keeping up with the Jones [sic]. Every other power practiced, and as far as I know still practices, assassination if need be. So, reluctantly, we took that into account.

Despite Pash's testimony that he had no recollection of ever being asked to undertake any assassination planning, his former PB/7 Deputy Chief testified that he had "a clear recollection that the written charter of 'special operations' stated: 'PB/7 will be responsible for assassinations, kidnapping, and such functions as from time to time may be given it...by higher authority.'" The former deputy stated, moreover, that he "construed the charter's reference to 'higher authority' to include the State Department, Defense Department, National Security Council, and the President of the United States."

By contrast, Pash offered the excuse that he "may have glanced over" the charter language and claims to have thought:

> Well, this is typical OSS approach to things...to them using words like that is maybe a common thing...I think they felt big in talking that way...There were some very good men in OSS, some dedicated men...But also there were a lot of entrepreneurs and adventurers... So when CIA was formed a lot of these people with these wild ideas and wild approaches were there.

So, of course, when you say you're in charge of 'all other activities'... these fellows might have ideas [such as] ...'it's easier to kill a guy than to worry about trailing him.'

LT. COL. LUCIEN CONEIN AND ASSASSINATION

After QJ/WIN and Boris Pash, Lt. Col. Lucien Conein may be ranked as another of the more intriguing people involved in the practice of state-sponsored murder. Conein, according to CIA and FBI files, was "a former member of the Corsican Brotherhood," a shadowy, secret group of unknown membership that finances its operations through drug trafficking and contract assassinations, and which reportedly still operates worldwide today. People familiar with the Corsican Brotherhood say that it "makes the Mafia look like the Kiwanis Club" and that " the entire concept and practice of 'omerta' originated with the Corsicans." Said Conein of the Corsicans:

> When the Sicilians put out a contract, it's usually limited to the continental United States, or maybe Canada or Mexico. But with the Corsicans, it's international. They'll go anywhere. There's an old Corsican proverb: 'If you want revenge and you act in twenty years, you're acting in haste.'

Born in Paris, France, Conein was sent to the United States by his mother when he was only five years old. He was raised in Kansas City by his French aunt, a World War I bride. His aunt assured that he retained his French citizenship, and in 1939, when World War II began, Conein hitchhiked to Chicago and went to the French consulate where he enlisted in the French army. "I didn't have hardly any money," he later explained, "but I wanted to see France and Europe and to kill Nazis in the process." Following the German takeover of France, Conein helped deliver weapons to the French Resistance forces and trained civilian fighters in the arts of sabotage and killing. While in France, Conein gained the nickname "Black Luigi."

After the war, Conein returned to Chicago, where he joined the U.S. Army and was assigned to the OSS because of his fluency in French. (It is possible that around this time, he met fellow OSS recruit, E. Howard Hunt.) Later, the OSS transferred Conein to the Pacific theatre of operations where he led commando raids against Japanese-held bases in North Vietnam.

In 1947, Conein joined the CIA at the rank of Lieutenant Colonel, which allowed him to use his military standing to conceal his Agency employment. In his early Agency years, he worked in at least five countries in both Europe and Southeast Asia performing "sensitive tasks," according to CIA files on Conein, which largely remain closed to public access. In 1951, the chief of espionage in West Germany recruited Conein to establish a base of operations in Nuremberg. The central purpose of the base was to recruit and dispatch covert agents into Warsaw Pact countries to identify and eliminate troublesome East German and Soviet agents. The operation was mildly successful but lost a large number of personnel, who were murdered, imprisoned, or simply vanished.

About eighteen months into his Nuremberg assignment, Conein was transferred to work for William King Harvey, chief of the CIA's Berlin station. His duties in Berlin are mostly unknown, but former intelligence officers say that he "served as a link between Harvey and the military, which was operating a number of safe houses throughout West Germany. Said one former official:

> Lucien [Conein] helped with certain human exports out of Germany to the U.S., and served as liaison frequently to delegations from [Camp] Detrick and Edgewood [Arsenal] that arrived to do interviews or assessments on any prospective German scientists that somebody back home thought would be worthwhile to ship back.
>
> Did he come into contact with Frank Olson or others from Special Operations? It's pretty likely, but that contact would not have been significant in any way. Olson wasn't high enough up on the ladder; he was a foot soldier, so to speak, and Lucian mostly played with the big boys.

In 1954, Conein was dispatched to work with General Edward Lansdale in Southeast Asia. His work primarily entailed mounting covert operations against the government of Ho Chi Minh in North Vietnam. By 1959, Conein was working closely with future DCI William Colby, then CIA station chief in Saigon. In 1967, Colby would launch perhaps the largest assassination program ever mounted by the CIA, the Phoenix Program, which systematically murdered, kidnapped, and tortured hundreds, if not thousands, of Vietnamese people. Many, if not all, of the extreme interrogation and torture methods, such as water-boarding, used by the Army and CIA today originated with or were refined by the Phoenix Program.

Conein, under Colby in Vietnam, worked closely with local tribesmen, the Montagnards, and ran commando raids into Laos and North Vietnam. Conein was also closely involved in the violent overthrow and assassination of Ngo Dinh Diem, president of South Vietnam.

Conein's name first surfaced publicly after he had left Vietnam for the United States – he was said to have played a role in the assassination of John F. Kennedy. Several credible writers have advanced the argument that Conein was closely linked to former OSS officers, E. Howard Hunt and Mitchell Werbell, III, two men also strongly suspected of playing roles in Kennedy's death.

Around this same time, Conein was joined in the United States by a character introduced earlier and about whom readers will soon learn far more, Jean-Pierre Lafitte. Conein had known Lafitte since his wartime days in France, and had later used Lafitte for at least one sensitive mission in Vietnam. The two men shared in common not only their French heritage, but also a mysterious connection to the Corsican Brotherhood. Lafitte had years earlier been awarded a special Corsican Brotherhood medallion bearing the Brotherhood's coat-of-arms and the Napoleonic Imperial Eagle. Lafitte would later claim that Conein had been awarded the same honor at about the same time. Also like Conein, Lafitte was fluent in French and Vietnamese.

Pierre Lafitte — a pseudonym he used in the United States for at least twenty years prior to 1960 — was expert in many so-called black-operations, including breaking-and-entering, covert surveillance, disguises, and impersonation. According to Gerald Patrick Hemming, a former soldier-of-fortune and CIA contractor who knew Conein well, "Lafitte, who we jokingly called 'Powerful Pierre' after some cartoon character, was a master at all, except killing." Explained Hemming, "He was French, or at least I think he was, and didn't care much for blood. Fine food, wine, and money were his things. Maybe not in that order, but that's what he enjoyed most in life." According to Conein, Lafitte had been in Vietnam at the time of Diem's death and had "assisted in important ways, but never in any way related to actual murder." In 1962, Conein would put CIA officer William King Harvey in touch with Lafitte, who was at the time involved in a number of shady business enterprises and shuttling back and forth between Germany, Luxembourg, South Africa, and the United States.

In November 1973, Conein was asked to work for the Drug Enforcement Administration (reportedly, he was approached by E. Howard Hunt, then a 'special employee' in the Nixon White House). Conein naturally thought of his friend, Lafitte, who had worked extremely closely with George Hunter White, Charles Siragusa, Vance Newman, and other FBN agents in New York, Boston, Houston, Chicago, California and overseas. Lafitte, who knew virtually every major drug trafficker in the world, including the entire cast of the infamous French Connection case, now gave his friend Conein a crash course in the machinations of international drug trafficking.

Thanks to Lafitte, Conein quickly progressed from consultant to director of the DEA's newly formed Special Operations and Field Support Division. His responsibilities were "to create worldwide intelligence networks, both inside and outside the United States, and to identify and ultimately stop the work of the many significant drug traffickers." According to the *Washington Post*, some of Conein's activities were "so sensitive that they required approval of [Secretary of State] Henry Kissinger's {Foreign Advisory] Committee." According to handwritten notes by the CIA's William King Harvey — who was himself deeply enmeshed in operating Agency assassination projects at the time — Conein was assembling special "hit-squads" composed of former CIA contractors and veterans of the Bay of Pigs invasion to target and assassinate foreign drug traffickers.

According to author and investigative reporter Henrik Kruger, "a DEA official told *Washington Post* reporter George Crile: 'When you get right down to it, Conein was organizing an assassination program.'"

In 1976, investigators for the Church Committee, mentioned earlier, told newspaper reporters off-the-record that Conein "had recruited twelve retired CIA men, not previously known to Conien, to perform assassinations and special interrogations on drug traffickers." A subsequent *Washington Post* article stated that Conein, who died in 1998, "appears to have stretched so far the boundaries of legality that they were undertaken in total secrecy."

ATTEMPTS TO ASSASSINATE CASTRO

Nowhere in the annals of the CIA did their desire, intensity, and dedication to assassinating a foreign leader reveal itself more blatantly than in their attempts to murder Cuba's president Fidel Castro. This long-running CIA effort at killing, combined with the collaborative efforts of Camp Detrick's SOD — using technology and toxins developed by Frank Olson and his fellow researchers — is a remarkable story. In 1967, uncharacteristically, the CIA made a concerted in-house effort to reconstruct the Agency's involvement in plans to assassinate Castro. The "SECRET, EYES ONLY" report describes the challenges of that reconstruction:

> Because of the extreme sensitivity of the operations being discussed or attempted, as a matter of principle no official records were kept of planning, of approvals, or of implementation.

In fact, the planned attempts to murder Castro were so numerous that the report categorizes them into nine specific headings and time frames.

It appears that the earliest schemes to kill Castro, as well as his brother, Raoul, and chief aide, Che Guevara, were devised between March and August 1960. One plan was to use an SOD-produced aerosol spray containing a chemical "that produces reactions similar to those of LSD." According to the CIA's report, this scheme was set aside because TSS scientists believed "the chemical could not be relied upon to be effective." Another scheme, also subsequently discarded, involved bombarding Castro, Raoul, and Che with "psychic energizers" to drive the men insane or to suicide. Little is known about these so-called energizers except that the concept originated with a small team of university-based parapsychologists in cooperation with Dr. Henry Puharich.

Yet another plot, one that pre-dated the Bay of Pigs, involved giving Castro a box of his favorite cigars laced with a lethal toxin and some LSD-type substance out of Camp Detrick. According to Jake Esterline, head of the CIA's Cuban Task Force before the Bay of Pigs fiasco, the cigars were never given to Castro because the Agency had not been able to identify a reliable and trustworthy person to deliver them. Sidney Gottlieb recalled the cigar plot distinctly when asked about it, but said the plan never went beyond the talking stage.

In one of the more absurd efforts to destabilize Castro, SOD scientists proposed using thallium salts, a compound used by women as a depilatory. The salts were intended to cause Castro's trademark beard to fall out — the idea being that this would somehow emasculate him in front of his shocked countrymen. SOD scientists labored long and hard to perfect the compound, denuding countless poor animals – including cats, dogs, monkeys, and several sheep - in the process. Former SOD scientist Gerald Yonetz said, "It was a pretty silly project. The thinking was that SOD would test it on all types of hair. That's why the sheep were used, to try to replicate the hair of certain racial types as opposed to others. The results were disastrous sometimes." The tests on animals revealed that too much of the salts produced paralysis, brain damage and even death, but that did not deter SOD or CIA scientists who chalked the extra effect up to "unanticipated benefits." The scheme fell through when nobody could figure out how to administer the salts to Castro.

The Agency's first "seriously-pursued" plan to kill Castro was hatched in August 1960. The CIA's reconstruction dubbed this the "Gambling Syndicate Phase," a term considered preferable to the word "Mafia." Given the cast of characters involved, however, the term "Mafia" was more accurate. This particular plan eventually included a number of people whom readers will meet repeatedly throughout the remainder of this book - people who had played a significant role in Frank Olson's death seven years earlier.

In late summer 1960, the CIA's Deputy Director for Plans, Richard Bissell, asked Office of Security chief Sheffield Edwards to contact Mafia members who owned Cuba's numerous gambling hotels and casinos. Bissell thought that the various Mafioso already familiar with the island could most easily get close to Castro. Gottlieb later said that in one meeting about this plan, it was proposed that a man named William Alexander Morgan be used for the job. Morgan was an American mercenary and sometime CIA operative in Cuba with access to Castro, but it had been reported that "Morgan was under heavy surveillance at the time and was about to be arrested any day."

Another covert operative considered for the Castro assassination plot was Jean-Pierre Lafitte, then traveling back and forth between the United States and Cuba. Laffite had mysterious dealings on the island with enigmatic John Maples Spiritto, believed to be a pseudonym for a Corsican who had come to the United States in 1951. Spiritto had been proposed by the CIA's Western Hemisphere Division chief J.C. King to replace the rebellious, hard-to-control William Morgan in the plot to murder Castro.

According to Cuba's intelligence service, Spiritto had performed "special services" for the Federal Bureau of Narcotics in the 1950s in New York City and for the CIA in Mexico and South America. Spiritto had occasionally come into contact with Boris Pash, who, according to Church Committee reports, also performed "special functions" for the CIA in Latin and South America.

William Morgan reportedly "flew off the handle" when Spiritto informed him that he was being replaced as the Agency's leading choice to kill Castro. After Spiritto threatened to expose some of Morgan's financial dealings to the Agency, Morgan calmed down and agreed to assist Spiritto. By way of assistance, Morgan introduced Spiritto to Frank Sturgis and Rex Sanderlin, two more American soldiers-of-fortune who had soured on Castro and wanted him removed from power. (Sturgis would later be arrested in the infamous Watergate break-in, and Sanderlin would die mysteriously in Cuba in the early 1960s.)

Despite J.C. King's high level of confidence in Spiritto, the former FBN special employee made graves mistakes in attempting to carry out the assassination. Ignoring the training he had received from Jean-Pierre Lafitte, Spiritto failed to keep a low profile on the island and, instead, engaged in risky, high visibility escapades, at one point accidentally killing a rebel soldier in a barroom brawl. A sadly disappointed King relieved Spiritto of his duties.

Bissell later insisted that it had not been his idea to use the Mafia, and that it had come from J.C. King. King, not surprisingly, denied that the idea was his and told several Agency officials that the Mafia idea had originated in a conversation among Office of Security employee James O'Connell and narcotics agents George Hunter White and Charles Siragusa.

At any rate, Sheffield Edwards quickly contacted Robert Maheu, a private investigator and former FBI agent who had worked with security officer James McCord when he was also an FBI agent. Edwards asked Maheu if he had any Mafia contacts in Cuba. Maheu, who had performed "sensitive" contract work for the CIA for years, had excellent contacts among the underworld, not the least of which was dapper mobster Johnny Rosselli, then living in Los Angeles, where Maheu had an office. Edwards and Maheu agreed that Rosselli would be ideal for the Castro assassination job and that Maheu should meet with him as soon as possible. Maheu said that he would contact Rosselli, but that he was concerned about being involved in a job whose objective was to kill Castro. According to the CIA's report, "Maheu was authorized to tell Rosselli that his 'clients' [whom he was instructed not to identify] were willing to pay $150,000 for Castro's removal."

OS chief Edwards named security officer James "Big Jim" O'Connell as his lead person in overseeing the operation, and assigned him to keep an eye on Maheu. O'Connell, a former FBI special agent, was then Chief, Operational Support Division for the CIA's Office of Security under Edwards. Like Maheu, O'Connell had worked in New York for the Bureau and is reported to have been closely involved in the Agency's cover-up of Frank Olson's death.

O'Connell and Maheu met Rosselli in New York City on September 14, 1960 and Maheu made his pitch to Rosselli. Rosselli, who had been around the block numerous times, so to speak, was nonetheless reluctant to become involved in the assassination of Castro.

"Look, I don't like the guy any more than you guys do," Rosselli said, "but to put a hit on the head of another country... that's big league, real big league."

Maheu told Rosselli he would make it worth his while and that Castro's death was necessary for the safety of America. Rosselli finally agreed to introduce Maheu to "a guy I know who might help."

Said Rosselli, "This guy, his name is Sam Gold, he can arrange to put you in contact with the people in Cuba who might do the job."

340

Maheu and O'Connell thanked Rosselli profusely and, according to the CIA's report, Rosselli told them "he had no interest in being paid for his participation in the job and believed that Sam Gold would feel the same way."

Rosselli shook hands with the two, saying, "People might think we're hoods but that doesn't mean we aren't patriotic."

The CIA report quotes a memorandum for the record prepared by Sheffield Edwards on May 14, 1962 that states: "No monies were ever paid to Rosselli and Giancana ['Sam Gold' was actually Chicago Mafia head Sam 'Momo' Giancana.]"

Edwards meanwhile informed Bissell that he had made contact with a private investigator, Maheu, who in turn had contacts with mobsters in Cuba that might offer assistance in getting close to Castro.

Days later, Bissell and Edwards reported up the chain of command to DCI Allen Dulles and DDCI Charles Cabell on the plan to assassinate Castro. The CIA's report reads: "Edwards recalls that Mr. Dulles merely nodded, presumably in understanding and approval. Certainly there was no opposition."

O'Connell and Maheu met with Rosselli again on September 25 in Miami at the Fontainebleau Hotel, where, without O'Connell present, he introduced Maheu to "Sam Gold." Gold told Maheu that he had a man, whom he identified only as "Joe," who "could serve as a courier to Cuba and make arrangements there." O'Connell observed Gold from afar, but he soon learned that "Gold" was Giancana and that "Joe the Courier" was Florida Mafia chief Santo Trafficante, Jr., who owned a number of thriving gambling operations in Cuba. Castro had not yet permanently closed the American-held casinos and hotels in Cuba, and, according to the CIA report, Trafficante "was making regular trips between Miami and Havana" on Mafia business.

Well before Rosselli, Giancana, and Trafficante entered the overall scheme to kill Castro, the CIA's TSS branch, under the direction of Cornelius Van Schaack Roosevelt (a grandson of president Theodore Roosevelt), had been preparing technically for the job. In concert with Fort Detrick's SOD and TSS's Chemical Branch, TSS had assembled an arsenal of toxic weapons to be used against Castro. According to the CIA report:

> TSS chief Roosevelt remembers that four possible approaches were considered: (1) something highly toxic, such as shellfish poison to be administered with a pin (which Roosevelt said was what was supplied to [U-2 pilot] Gary Powers; (2) bacterial material in liquid form; (3) bacterial treatment of a cigarette or cigar; and (4) a handkerchief treated with bacteria.

Apparently, the CIA had initially thought that the best way to kill Castro using the Mafia was in the "typical, gangland-style killing in which Castro could be gunned down." Giancana, however, had been flatly opposed to the use of guns and mockingly told Maheu that "only a fool" would take on such a task that would surely result in death for the assassin.

341

Giancana reportedly said that he would prefer that some sort of lethal pill or drug be placed in Castro's food or drink. At least, this is what the CIA's report claims he said, thus implying that the Mafia had come up with the surreptitious dosing scheme despite the fact that TSS staff and federal narcotics agents had been training for years in the deceptive art of dosing unwitting subjects. They had, at the very least, the direct experience of having successfully done this to Frank Olson and others at Deep Creek Lake in 1953.

At any rate, Trafficante eventually told Maheu and O'Connell that his "inside guy" in Cuba was Juan Orta, then head of Castro's Office of the Prime Minister. Trafficante explained that Orta had been receiving substantial kickbacks from gambling operations for years, but now that Castro was in power he had lost that income stream and badly needed money to maintain his lavish lifestyle.

In February, Bissell assigned legendary CIA officer and former FBI agent, William King Harvey, to oversee the Castro operation.

One former Agency official who knew Harvey says this "was an obvious choice for Bissell to make at the time" because of Harvey's extensive experience in post-war Germany, where "he routinely dealt with sticky and wet situations" — meaning kidnappings and assassinations. Said this same official: "Agents, ours and theirs, were going down all the time [in Germany]. It wasn't unusual to lose two or three guys in one month, sometimes one week. Half of them we would never see again; we had no clue what happened to them." Harvey's notes on his recruitment, quoted in the CIA's report, reveal that Bissell called the Agency's assassination plan the "Executive Action Capability" meaning, in Bissell's view, a *general standby capability to carry out assassination when required.* [Emphasis added.]

One of Harvey's first official acts was to approach Dr. Edward Gunn, the Agency's Chief of Operations in its Medical Services branch. Gunn, according to the CIA report, said that Harvey "wanted him to consult with Sidney Gottlieb" on whether toxins and chemicals could be effectively used to kill Castro. Harvey was upset because more than half the substances so far considered for use had proven ineffective. Apparently, Gottlieb came through for Gunn because in March 1961 Rosselli passed a packet of lethal pills to Trafficante. Trafficante promptly handed the pills off to Orta, but Orta backed out, telling Trafficante he could not go through with the plan. At least, this is what the CIA's report asserts. Other, non-Agency reports over the past several decades have considered it highly likely that Trafficante was playing both sides against the middle and was dealing with not only the CIA but also with Castro, to whom he was personally reporting back to on each and every step of the scheme. (In a 2007 interview, Castro said he knew Orta was a "traitor" at the time, but made no mention of Trafficante.)

Harvey was less than happy that Orta had backed out, but Rosselli said that Trafficante knew at least two other contacts in Cuba who would move things forward. One was Tony Varona, a doctor who headed a Cuban anti-Castro group and who had family ties to the owner of the largest casino in Cuba.

According to the CIA report, "the Executive Action program [as placed under Harvey] came to be known as ZR/RIFLE." Its principle asset, as we know from above, was QJ/WIN, who was recruited earlier by Jean-Pierre Lafitte [known primarily as "Pierre"] for use in the planned assassination of Lumumba in the Congo. That operation was to be run by Agency official Justin O'Connell, who reportedly "made a survey of the scene, [and] decided he wanted no part of an assassination attempt, and asked to be released— which Bissell granted."

In early April 1962, Harvey asked Edwards to put him in touch with Rosselli. After getting the approval of Helms, Edwards did so, and on April 8, Harvey and O'Connell met with Rosselli in New York City. O'Connell recalls that Maheu also joined them. The four men met at the Elk Room in the Savoy Plaza Hotel and then went to an after hours nightclub where actress and mob moll to Giancana, Phyllis McGuire, newspaper columnist Dorothy Killgallen, and Liberace, were enjoying a late night performance by singer Rosemary Clooney (actor George Clooney's late aunt).

Harvey went to Miami on April 21, having stashed in his car's glove compartment a packet of lethal pills manufactured at Fort Detrick. It is difficult to avoid formulating a vivid image of Harvey the Pear, gonzo-like, without a care in the world, driving down the highway on his way to sun, sand, and God knows what else, with visions of assassination in his head. In Miami, Rosselli told Harvey over dinner at Joe's Stone Crab that Trafficante was out of the picture now; after Castro had closed the last of the casinos in Cuba, Trafficante no longer had access to the island. However, Rosselli said, not to worry, he had a man who could handle the job better than any other. The man's name was "Maceo." It is not known whether Harvey, at this point, knew that "Maceo" was "Frank Maceo," another of Pierre Lafitte's many aliases. That Harvey did, within a few days, realize it was Lafitte is certain; the two were seen having dinner and drinks several times during the last week of April.

By this time, Harvey had contacted JMWAVE station chief Ted Shackley to procure crates of handguns, rifles, machine guns, small bombs, grenades, and electronics equipment. JMWAVE was the codename for the CIA's secret intelligence gathering operation in Miami. Shackley, called the "Blond Ghost," was to deliver the supplies to a man named Tony Varona, the Cuban, anti-communist doctor (mentioned earlier) who was close to Trafficante. The crates of weapons were piled into a rented U-Haul truck for delivery that day, by prior arrangement. Although the CIA report claims that Shackley and Lafitte both handled the keys to the truck, there is no indication where the weapons were taken or to whom they were delivered.

The following month, Lafitte called Rosselli in Los Angeles to report that he was in Cuba and that the lethal pills were with him, but Varona's "inside man" was nowhere to be seen. Lafitte called Rosselli again the next day to report that "things are getting a little hot around here, and I think I'm coming back to the States soon." When Lafitte returned to Los Angles he told Rosselli "I've had enough of Cuba for a long time to come." Rosselli tried to convince Lafitte to consider returning to the island after a few weeks, but Lafitte replied, "Are you kidding? Johnny, they're lining people up over there and shooting them down like clay pigeons. And they do not care if you're an American or not."

In February 1963, following the Cuban Missile Crisis, Harvey met Rosselli in Los Angeles to inform him that the "operation [to assassinate Castro] would be closed off." Why he could not have telephoned Rosselli to say this is unclear. In June 1963, Rosselli flew to Washington, D.C. to meet with Harvey, who was leaving for an extended assignment in Rome the following week. On his first evening in D.C., Rosselli joined Harvey and his wife for dinner at a well-known restaurant. During the meal, Harvey was called away by a waiter who told him that he had an important telephone call. On the phone was Sam Papich, a longtime FBI agent, who had known Harvey from his days with the Bureau.

"Do you know who you're eating with?" Papich asked.

"You mean besides my wife?" asked Harvey.

"Yes."

"Yes, I do," said Harvey.

"Are you crazy?"

"No, I'm not, Sam," said Harvey. "Is there a point to any of this?"

"Yeah, there is," said Papich. "Right now you're being observed by the FBI."

"Christ," said Harvey, "I thought you were going to tell me something that was going to ruin a great meal."

The CIA's efforts to kill Castro continued unabated for at least two more years, playing out like a *Commedia dell'arte* production complete with masked buffoons. Whatever could go wrong inevitably went wrong. In January 1963, even while former OSS officer, attorney and Nazi war crimes prosecutor James B. Donovan was presumably negotiating in good faith with Castro for the release of the Bay of Pigs prisoners, the CIA's TSS had prepared a skin diving suit as a gift for Castro. The suit, said Sidney Gottlieb, had been "heavily dusted inside with the Madura foot fungus." The fungus produced a painful, disabling, and chronic skin disease composed of small subcutaneous, boil-like growths filled with putrid pus. Amputation was not an uncommon consequence of the disease. To insure "that things would work," Gottlieb explained, the suit's "breathing apparatus" was contaminated with *tubercle bacilli*.

Gottlieb said he had no knowledge about what happened to the suit or the breathing apparatus after TSS officials handed them off to others in the Agency.

Later in 1963, the Agency explored a scheme of doing away with Castro "by means of an explosives-rigged sea shell." States the CIA report, [One Agency official even went out] "and bought two books on *Caribbean Mollusca*." Apparently, the books lacked instructions for making the shells explode, and the plan was soon scrapped. Another plan involved securing "a midget submarine loaded with explosives." This too was scrapped. Agency officials also considered using Black leaf 40, a common insecticide that contains deadly nicotine sulphate. The CIA's Dr. Edward Gunn spent hours developing a delivery device, and on November 22, 1963 at a meeting in Paris, France, the device was handed over to a would-be assassin. Reads the CIA report: "It is likely that at the very moment President Kennedy was shot, a CIA officer was meeting with a Cuban agent in Paris and giving him an assassination device for use against Castro."

"CLOCKWORK ORANGE" ASSASSINS

In the summer of 1975, British clinical psychologist and writer Peter Watson attended a NATO-sponsored conference on stress and anxiety in Oslo, Norway. Watson sat in on a lecture about 'symbolic modeling' given by Dr. Thomas Narut from the U.S. Naval Hospital at its southern NATO headquarters in Naples, Italy. Symbolic modeling, according to Watson, is a "process whereby anxious people could be taught to cope with certain stresses by watching others (usually on film) cope with these stresses." During his prepared remarks, Narut strayed from his script and made a few comments that made Watson sit up straight in his chair and listen all the more attentively. Narut remarked that such coping techniques were being employed with "combat readiness units" to "train people to cope with the stress of killing."

Intrigued by Narut's presentation, Watson and another psychologist approached the Navy physician after his talk, wanting to ask him questions about the types of military units he was referring to. Dr. Narut, according to Watson, "said that he was referring to two types of combat readiness units: the ordinary commando unit, and also to naval men inserted into embassies abroad, under cover, ready to kill." Dr. Narut told the two psychologists "that men were being sought from military prisons to act as assassins in overseas embassies."

After Watson and his colleague, Dr. Alfred Zitani, concluded their questions and Narut departed, Zitani turned to Watson and asked, "Does that guy realize what he just said?"

Watson met again with Dr. Narut for a longer interview during which he took detailed notes. He wrote:

> Several years ago Dr. Narut completed his doctoral thesis on whether certain films could provoke anxiety and whether forcing a man to do tasks irrelevant to the film while watching it might help him to cope with the anxieties the film provoked. Narut's naval work, however, appeared to involve establishing how to induce servicemen who might not be naturally inclined to kill to do so under certain conditions.

Dr. Narut told Watson that the method "was to screen films specifically designed to show people being killed or injured in violent ways. By being

345

acclimatized through these films, the men were supposed eventually to become able to disassociate their emotions from such a situation." Dr. Narut also added that U.S. naval psychologists specially selected men for these commando tasks from submarine crews, paratroops, and some were convicted murderers from military prisons.

Narut further explained to Watson that the process had three phases. First was *selection* which involved looking for men "who had shown themselves capable of killing" in premeditated ways. Dr. Narut said the best killers were men with "passive-aggressive personalities" and men with "a lot of drive" who are well disciplined, not nervous, and "who periodically experience bursts of explosive energy when they can literally kill without remorse." Second was *stress reduction training*, which involved taking selected trainees to special wards in Navy hospitals and to the Naval Neuropsychiatric Laboratory Center in San Diego, California. Here the men were "given a special type of '*Clockwork Orange*' training aimed at reducing and eliminating any qualms they had about killing. In this pursuit, the men were shown "a series of gruesome films, which get progressively more horrific." The men were forced to watch every frame of the films and to avoid their looking away they were fitted into head harnesses with devices that kept their eyelids always open. Said Dr. Narut:

> One of the best films shows an African youth being crudely circumcised by fellow members of his tribe. No anesthetic is used and the knife is obviously blunt. When the film is over the trainee is asked irrelevant questions such as, 'What was the motif on the handle of the knife?'

The third phase was *dehumanization of the enemy*. This was aimed at getting the men "to think of the potential enemies" they will have to kill "as inferior forms of life." Narut told Watson that the films used "are biased to present the enemy as less than human" and that "the stupidity of local customs is ridiculed, [and that] local personalities are presented as evil demigods rather than as legitimate figures." Narut said the entire process took a few weeks, and that its most recent usage had been "towards the end of 1973—at the time of the Yom Kippur War."

After Watson wrote an article for London's *Sunday Times* about Dr. Narut's remarks, several American journalists attempted to interview the doctor. Contacted at home by one writer, an irritated Narut said, "I can't say a word about the conference. I have nothing at all to add to things," and he hung up. Other reporters who tried to reach Narut were less successful and were told that he was no longer employed at the Naples naval facility; one reporter was told that the facility had "nobody with the name Narut on staff." Within days, Navy and Pentagon officials emphatically denied everything that Dr. Narut had said. Eventually, one persistent journalist was informed off the record that the Navy "kept elite units of trained assassins at secret locations across the world," and that the overall designation for some of the units was Project Pelican. "The project is a matter of national security," said one Navy official in the Pentagon. Not long after Watson's article appeared, a psychologist at the San Diego Neuropsychiatric Center contacted him to say that the films indeed existed and that they were loaned out to other facilities.

Readers who are adventure film aficionados may recall that in the 1980s and 1990s several American action films using specific details from Dr. Narut's revelations were released for worldwide distribution. Just two examples are *Universal Soldier* and *La Femme Nikita*. At the time the films were released, a number of reviewers faulted them for creating "fantastic... and unbelievable situations that surpassed the absurd."

Twenty years ago, investigative journalist John Kelly – whom the CIA considers its nemesis and whom it has on occasion aggressively attempted to silence, wrote:

> The CIA is defined by assassination. After Frank Olson died at the hands of the CIA, no one expressed contrition or moral concern. On the contrary, they didn't even want to give each other slaps on the wrist for fear it would hinder 'the spirit of initiative and enthusiasm so necessary in our work.'

Kelly puts it more succinctly than anyone before or since. Indeed, in 2000, when then- prominent Harvard essayist and human rights activist, Michael Ignatieff, wrote an article about Frank Olson for the *New York Times* Sunday magazine, what most readers did not know, according to Ignatieff, is that the story was originally intended for the highly revered *The New Yorker* magazine. Midway through writing his article, Ignatieff was contacted by an editor at *The New Yorker* who told him that the magazine had lost interest in the story because "everyone knows that the CIA kills people." One might easily argue that America, in the first years of the twenty-first century, has lost its moral standing in the world because attitudes like this one have numbed the national psyche.

In 1951, the CIA generated a document entitled "A Study of Assassination." Since its declassification in the spring of 1997, the document has come to be known as "the Assassination Manual." [See *Appendix Three* of this book.] The manual was initially drafted for use in Latin America, and had some relevance for the CIA's 1954 overthrow of president Jacobo Arbenz Guzman in Guatemala, as well as the assassination of fifty-eight targeted Guatemalans. However, a cursory look at the document quickly reveals that it was intended for much wider use. On page six of the twenty-paged document, for example, under the heading "Accidents," the manual instructs readers:

> The most efficient accident, in simple assassination, is a fall of 75 feet or more onto a hard surface. Elevator shafts, stairwells, unscreened windows, and bridges will serve. Bridge falls into water are not reliable. In simple

cases a private meeting with the subject may be arranged at a properly cased location. The act may be executed by sudden, vigorous grasping of the ankles, tipping the subject over the edge. If the assassin immediately sets up an outcry, playing the 'horrified witness,' no alibi or surreptitious withdrawal is necessary. In chase cases it will usually be necessary to stun or drug the subject before dropping him. Care is required to insure that no wound or condition not attributable to the fall is discernible after death.

Falls into the sea or swiftly flowing rivers may suffice if the subject cannot swim. It will be more reliable if the assassin can arrange to attempt rescue, as he can thus be sure of the subject's death and at the same time establish a workable alibi.

If the subject's personal habits make it feasible, alcohol may be used [*two words redacted*] to prepare him for a contrived accident of any kind.

Falls before trains or subway cars are usually effective, but require exact timing and can seldom be free from unexpected observation.

Decades later, a Manhattan assistant district attorney, investigating the death of Frank Olson, would state that the manual's defenestration section is, "A perfect recipe for murder under the right situation. It's tailor made for Olson's fall."

9

LSD & Pont-St.-Esprit

It wasn't as if we were Nazis and said, 'If we ask for consent we lose our subjects'; it was that we were so ethically insensitive that it never occurred to us that you ought to level with people that they were in an experiment.

— Louis Lasagna, 1994

It is a multiple eyed monster
it is hidden in all its elephants and selves
it hummeth in the electric typewriter
it is electricity connected to itself.

— Allen Ginsberg, "Lysergic Acid"

In the year 1500, a Dutch painter named Hieronymus Bosch set his brush to canvas and produced one of the world's most intriguing works of art. Entitled *The Temptation of St. Anthony*, the triptych is today considered a masterpiece rich in enigmatic symbolism. Viewed at its most basic level, the painting is replete with evil entities, demons in clerical garb, and grotesquely and lewdly endowed figures. Men appear with the elongated snouts of rodents, nude women display grotesque sexuality, and everywhere there are Cathar, alchemical, and astrological symbols. Strange aerial craft and bird-like ships loom in a dark, fiery sky. In the distance a town burns, while demonic infants float in muddy lakes curdled by the flames. Three oddly clad men assist St. Anthony, obviously in a state of distress, across a small bridge. Overall, the painting exudes an atmosphere of doom and utter pandemonium.

Centuries later, in the heyday of psychedelic America, mass produced prints of Bosch's *Temptation*, along with his *Garden of Earthly Delights*, would grace college dorm rooms and apartment walls everywhere, because of the alleged power of Bosch's images to trigger or enhance hallucinations. Depending on their focus and state of mind, onlookers could believe themselves to be prancing across Elysian Fields or trapped in the horrors of a perpetual nightmare.

Bosch's subject, St. Anthony of Egypt, was said to possess miraculous powers. In the year 231 A.D., Anthony rejected society and retired to a life of solitude and meditation in the desert. When he was fifty years old, he built a monastery and organized an ascetic order of monks, who taught people that prayer and the Sign of the Cross repelled the Devil. Anthony's order, over time, evolved into a group well known for their ability and skills at treating people afflicted with ergotism – poisoning from the alkaloids of ergotamine-ergocristine fungus – which produces a state very similar to that produced by LSD ingestion. In the Middle Ages, ergotism was called *ignis sacer* ("holy fire"), or "Saint Anthony's Fire," named after the monastic order founded by Anthony. It is doubtful that Anthony ever imagined that his name would someday be strongly associated with LSD-fueled psychedelic journeys.

Pont-St.-Esprit, Provence, France, August 16, 1951

Behold the town. Situated on the Rhone River, founded in the 5th century, is the town of Pont-St.-Esprit in the Languedoc-Roussillion region of southern France. It is 1951, yet if any visitor were to gaze about, he or she would see few, if any, trappings of modernity. Indeed, any visitor would easily feel they had been transported back at least a thousand years in time. Observed one visitor in 1951, "the area surrounding the town has lain for centuries comparatively untouched by the convulsions that have rent the remainder of the world, as is witnessed by the numerous Roman and mediaeval buildings that still remain intact.... It is a place where, so one might imagine, 'nothing ever happened here.'"

August 16, 1951 had begun as yet another uneventful day in the idyllic town until two hours before noon, when a young farmer stumbled through the front door of Dr. Jean Vieu. The man, who lived nearby, was babbling incoherently and waving his arms about as if he was being attacked by a swarm of bees. No sooner had Dr. Vieu managed to calm the man then a second neighbor appeared at his door. This man, too, was ranting nonsensically and seemed to be in the grip of wild hallucinations. It took Vieu and two assistants nearly an hour to convince the man that the snakes he claimed were slithering about his insides were not consuming him.

Five minutes later, a third man, also acting bizarrely, arrived at the doctor's door. Soon, and for the remainder of the day, the bewildered doctor was inundated by a stream of strangely, often wildly, disoriented townspeople. By nightfall, he was doing his best to treat nearly 75 delirious patients, 22 of whom had to be sheltered in a barn because the local hospital was overflowing with stricken victims. Doctors were summoned from surrounding areas and they, too, were baffled by what was happening.

Many patients had to be forcibly tied to their beds. When nurses ran out of rope they used horse harnesses. Some patients managed to break free of their restraints and ran screaming through the streets. An eleven-year-old boy threw his mother to the ground and tried to strangle her. A local politician stripped off his clothes and merrily danced naked in the town square. An elderly man ran about yelling, "My belly is full of snails. They are burning me to death! I am in the water." When he finally sat down, he said, "I am now sending out radio messages everywhere. Get me an X-ray, get me the X-ray, and you can see."

One young man in his early twenties had become so violent that he had to be subdued by three ambulance attendants. Even the attendants could not restrain the man, who viciously fought them, and two more came to their assistance. With considerable effort, the five men were able to put the crazed young victim into a strait jacket. But as they tried to fasten it, the young man suddenly pushed the attendants away, ripped the jacket from his body, and tore the thick canvas down the middle into two pieces.

Eventually the young man was tied down with thick leather straps, in a prone position on his back, onto a cot in a local jail cell. Within minutes, however, he had loosened one strap and chewed the others to pieces with such a frenzy and intensity that some of his teeth fell out of his bloody mouth. When he finally managed to break loose, he screamed that monsters were attacking him and he seized the metal bars of his cell, frantically trying to escape. With superhuman strength, he was able to bend them slightly, before he was again restrained.

Another young lad of about twelve years of age ran about the town screaming that dead people were rising up out of the ground at a nearby cemetery. "They're coming to eat us, they're coming to eat us alive," warned the frantic boy. A young woman in her late teens tore off her dress and went about in her underwear, mimicking the sounds of farm animals. Another woman went from door to door announcing that the Second Coming was at hand, shouting, "The Son of God will be here at any moment, repent now while there is still time!" A five-year-old girl told her mother, "Tigers are going to eat us all. They're going to rip us to pieces!" The girl pointed to the ceiling of her room and cried, "Blood is dripping down on everything. Can't you stop the blood?"

Dogs and cats were not immune to the outbreak and were also behaving oddly. Several animals dropped dead. One dog sat in the town square and howled at the sun for nearly an hour before someone hauled it away.

A police officer, called to the scene, remarked later that there had been no sexual acts, rapes, or molestations committed during the incident. This, despite the fact that many people seemed possessed by an odd euphoria, and went about profusely professing love for the world and all its inhabitants. As one Paris reporter described the town's bizarre outbreak:

> It is neither Shakespeare nor Edgar Poe. It is, alas, the sad reality all around Pont-St.-Esprit and its environs, where terrifying scenes of hallucinations are taking place. They are scenes taken straight out of the Middle Ages, scenes of horror and pathos, full of sinister shadows. The doctors are beside themselves with work; the rumors are wild and contradictory; fear hangs over the town everywhere. No one knows when it will end.

With every passing hour, rumors and speculation ran rampant about the cause of the spontaneous outbreak of insanity. Some townspeople claimed that the local gendarme had poisoned the town's water supply. A story circulated that a mad man was running amok pouring poison into food and water. Another claimed that a defrocked priest had placed a horrendous curse on the town and was performing Black Masses that were resulting in the spreading madness. Satan himself was said to have been released from the depths of Hell on to earth. Other, more pragmatic rumors were also circulating. Perhaps on the morning of the outbreak, that low-flying unmarked aircraft had sprayed the town with an unknown substance. Or, it could have been those well-dressed foreign strangers who had passed through the town the day before who had perhaps performed diabolical deeds in their wake. Maybe some soldiers bearing strange insignia had silently swept through the town's outskirts the night before, releasing colored vapors from odd, hand-held devices.

By August 18, fifty homes in the town were being used as emergency wards; over 250 people had fallen victim to the mysterious malady. Thirty-two people had been carted off to an insane asylum on the outskirts of Marseilles, and four people were dead, three men and one woman. The fatal cases were poorly documented. Local doctor Albert Gabbi and two colleagues examined the dead and concluded: "Three of these people were old and in bad health. The woman had hyperthyroidism. One of the men was only 25 years old and had been in good health previously." Gabbi reported that all four people "died in muscular spasm and in a state of cardiovascular collapse. The blood urea was raised to 150 mg. per 100 ml. The woman showed at her death a moist gangrene of the toes."

Children, according to Gabbi's group, developed disorders more quickly than adults. "In two cases," Gabbi stated, "we observed epileptiform convulsions, controlled by barbiturates." The doctors summarized their findings as best they could:

> An interesting feature of some cases was that the delirium was the first serious sign to be noted; it then appeared very late— between 10 to 12 days after the first onset of the poisoning. It is difficult to know just how many people presented with only slight disorders— disturbances of digestion and sleep— but it was about 150. A pregnant woman was seen with frank hemorrhages, and several women menstruated prematurely. Now that we have gathered the documents together, 15 days after the poison was taken, it is still too soon to give a definite balance sheet. Nevertheless, we can foresee the complete disappearance of the vascular disorders, but we cannot say what the effect will be on the minds of some of the patients, in particular on the minds of alcoholics who fell victim to the poison.

PONT-ST.-ESPRIT AFTERMATH

In the late-1960s, American writer and investigative journalist John G. Fuller, an associate of Dr. Henry Andrija Puharich, began researching the Pont-St.-Esprit outbreak. Fuller, who often published in the *Saturday Review*, had first learned of the incident years earlier, when he had read a small news article in the *New York Times*, datelined Paris, August 28, 1951. He was intrigued by the article and knew "that here was a medical mystery story of fascinating interest and intense drama." He clipped the article out of the paper, filed it away, and quickly forgot about it.

Six years later, Fuller wrote an article for the *Saturday Review* on the work of Dr. J.B. Rhine and Dr. Karlis Osis in the field of parapsychology. Drs. Rhine and Osis were both prominent scientists at Duke University in North Carolina, who spearheaded experimental research in the field of parapsychology. Perhaps unbeknownst to Fuller, and to anyone outside of a very tight circle at the time, the research being done by Rhine and Osis was partially funded by the U.S. Army, the U.S. Office of Naval Research, and the CIA.

Several months after Fuller's article on Rhine and Osis had been published, Dr. Osis telephoned the journalist to ask if he would be interested in "exploring a new and revolutionary step in the probing of the deepest workings of the human mind." Fuller jumped at the opportunity and met with Osis a few days later at his office in the Parapsychology Foundation at 29 West 57th Street in New York — coincidentally, a five-minute walk from the Statler Hotel. At that time, Osis, was exploring issues related to the question of an afterlife by experiments involving psychophysiological measurements and observations. He was working with a highly gifted subject, and investigating multiple reports of deathbed visions by the physicians and nurses present in the subject's room. The work of Dr. Osis connects in myriad ways to the multidimensional story of Frank Olson.

Karlis Osis was born in Riga, Latvia in 1917. The tall, thin, intensely handsome man was one of the first psychologists in the world to have obtained a doctoral degree with a thesis on ESP, extra sensory perception. After graduating from the University of Munich in 1950, he was hired as a research associate for the Parapsychology Laboratory at Duke University from 1951 to 1957. There he was a colleague of Dr. Rhine, although he frequently traveled to New York City to confer with other research psychologists, physicians and colleagues who shared his varied interests. Among those whom Osis met in New York were Dr. Harold Abramson and magician John Mulholland. Osis was especially interested in certain facets of magic, and his association with Mulholland focused primarily on vanishing objects and dematerialization. Mulholland and Osis also shared a deep fascination with apparitions and poltergeist phenomena, which they discussed extensively.

Former intelligence community sources who knew Osis, and who spoke only under conditions of anonymity, report that Osis met with Drs. Sidney Gottlieb and Robert Lashbrook on several occasions in New York, and that Osis traveled to CIA headquarters in Washington, D.C. on at least two occasions. Gottlieb, when interviewed by this author, would say only that he was familiar with Osis's "passionate work" and that he had "deep respect for him." Asked if the CIA might have been interested in Dr. Osis's research with animals, namely with the reactions of cats and dogs to the unseen and to certain other phenomena, Gottlieb replied, "At one time, the Agency was drawn to the subject."

When writer John Fuller met with Dr. Osis in New York in 1957, Osis launched into a lengthy discourse about the work of the Sandoz Company and its discovery of the extremely powerful drug LSD, which Osis described as having "created strange and unpredictable reactions on those volunteers who have tried it." Osis told the intrigued Fuller that at the time "small samples of the drug were being circulated to serious and competent researchers" and that "the general public know nothing about its properties, or for the most part, that it even existed."

Said Osis, "For that matter, no journalists have yet been invited to write about the drug, but if you are interested you could be the first, if you want."

Fuller was both very interested and flattered, but Osis had not yet finished. He explained to Fuller that if he so desired he could experience the wonder of LSD firsthand by taking a dose in the presence of a competent physician and psychologist. Fuller later identified the psychologist as Dr. Harold Abramson and said that Dr. Osis also told him about the LSD experiments of Dr. Paul Hoch at New York State Psychiatric Institute.

Recalled Fuller, "Dr. Osis explained that it would involve an entire day in the office, beginning at nine o'clock in the morning, and extending straight through until evening."

Osis also warned Fuller that the drug could produce unpleasant or frightening reactions. Still intrigued, but cautious, Fuller said he would seriously consider the psychologist's offer.

The next morning, Fuller called Osis and declined the extended opportunity. The writer was in the middle of several pressing writing projects and had a stage play soon opening its pre-Broadway tour. Fuller explained that he could not handle any added stress or unpredictability in his life. Dr. Osis thanked Fuller for his consideration and that appears to have been the last contact he had with Fuller.

Later that same day, however, Fuller remembered the news clipping he had filed away years earlier. Wasn't ergot also the base of this new and powerful drug that Dr. Osis had talked about? He asked himself. He dug through his files and found the clipping about the Pont-St.-Esprit incident. Once again reading the brief article's mention of wildly hallucinating townspeople, Fuller felt better about having turned Osis down; once again he filed away the clipping and forgot about the strange event that had occurred in France.

About nine years later, in 1966, Fuller was giving a lecture in a quaint New England town hall about the contents of his recently published book, *The Interrupted Journey*. The book was a meticulously researched and reconstructed account of the still controversial UFO-alien abduction of a married couple, Betty and Barney Hill. The strange incident had taken place on September 19 and 20, 1961, one mile south of Indian Head, New Hampshire. The Hill abduction case is believed to be one of the first that occurred in the United States. It is also one of the best documented and most perplexing of a long line of such

cases. Throughout the years there has been a tremendous amount of speculation and theorizing about what happened to the Hills, as well as occasional
references to the irrelevant fact that the couple was of mixed race (Barney was
an African-American). At various times, stories have circulated about possible
involvement by Air Force, Army, and CIA intelligence officials as part of the
MKULTRA and MKNAOMI programs.

When Fuller paused midway in his question and answer session, a man in
the rear of the hall shouted, "This stuff seems right out of some crazy science
fiction book, Mr. Fuller. You sure that couple wasn't taking some of that LSD
stuff?" Of course, by the mid-1960s, LSD was widely known by the public at
large, and frequently used by the counter-culture and others in America. Fuller
brushed the question off with a brief reply that the Hill's had never experimented with any drug.

Returning home two days later, Fuller once again pulled out his tattered file
containing the Pont-St.-Esprit article. This time he did not put it away until his
book about that incident had been completed. *The Day of St. Anthony's Fire*
was published in 1968.

The British edition of Fuller's book, published in 1969, was reviewed by
Griffith Edwards who observed:

> The official explanation [of the outbreak] was of flour having been con-
> taminated by an organic mercury fungicide, but much of the evidence
> points to a variety of ergot poisoning. The similarity of the symptoms to
> those of LSD effects is startling.

Edwards essentially summarized Fuller's own conclusions. At the end of his
book Fuller quoted one of the many physician-experts with whom he had consulted: "There is one and only one cause of the tragedy: Some form of ergot,
and that form has logically got to be akin to LSD."

Much overlooked in Fuller's book is a brief section noting the presence
of Sandoz Company researcher Dr. Albert Hofmann in Pont-St.-Esprit during
the summer of 1951. Hofmann himself has briefly, and parenthetically, mentioned the French outbreak in his own book, *LSD: My Problem Child*, first
published in 1979, but for some reason, he does not mention that he was in
the town of Pont-St.-Esprit in the days immediately following the outbreak.
Hofmann's account is not only parenthetical, but of questionable accuracy:
"[The mass poisoning in the southern France city of Pont-St.-Esprit in the
year 1951, which many have attributed to ergot-containing bread, actually
had nothing to do with ergotism. It rather involved poisoning by an organic
mercury compound that was utilized for disinfecting seeds.]" Elsewhere, Hofmann again peculiarly downplays or evades the truth about the etiology of
Pont-St.-Esprit's days of madness. In an eloquently written chapter of Gordon
Wasson's classic, *The Road to Eleusis*, Hofmann provides an overview of the
"storied past" of ergot of rye, but totally overlooks Pont-St.-Esprit.

Fuller informs his readers that in August 1951, after Hofmann and his superior Dr. Arthur Stoll learned of the Pont-St.-Esprit outbreak, they were "alarmed because the psychogenic symptoms were identical to those of LSD-25, and the two of them were sitting on top of the knowledge that the possible explanation for *ergotisme historique* might lie partially in the discovery of the new drug." Fuller, who interviewed Hofmann and Stoll, wrote that the two physicians "lost no time getting in touch with Professor [Gaston] Giraud at the University of Montpellier, and within days a meeting was held with many of the doctors involved in the Pont-St.-Esprit case." Professor Giraud was a lead scientific investigator into the incident.

At this meeting, Hofmann and Stoll "revealed their new studies to [the assembled doctors], and compared the results to those of *le pain maudit* ['the damned bread']." Fuller continues:

They reviewed all the facts together: how the ergot forms on rye grain, then ferments under certain conditions of humidity, liberating several alkaloids of ergot. LSD-25, it was noted, was one of the alkaloids produced by the fermentation of ergot.

> Hofmann pulled no punches when he talked to the doctors gathered at Montpellier. He described the discovery of the new drug as 'appalling, frightful, and shocking.' He told them that, regrettably, if it were improperly used and distributed, it might bring more destruction than the atomic bomb. Highlighting the psychogenic effects of LSD-25 and historical ergotism, which were strikingly similar, he condensed them into two main categories: (1) Magical and enchanting hallucinations of colors, in the nature of Ali Baba's cave; (2) Atrocious hallucinations, including changes in distances, or with the ceiling descending and the walls closing in on the victim. The new discovery did not produce direct erotic symptoms, as hashish and other drugs often did....
>
> The doctors at the meeting agreed that mercury poisoning was not evident in any manner, especially because of the persistent lack of kidney or liver damage.... The evidence was stronger now than it had ever been. Ergotism, especially in the light of the traces of ergot found in the analyses at the Marseilles laboratories, was unquestionably the probable cause of the rare outbreak.

Fuller's book would not mark the end of his intersection with the fringes of Frank Olson's story. Once again, fate would draw him even further into Olson's saga, but not for another seven years.

John Fuller was not the first writer to have been intrigued by the Pont-St.-Esprit incident. In January 1952, several months after the outbreak, British physician, lawyer, and Member of Parliament, Dr. Donald McIntosh Johnson visited the French town. There, Dr. Johnson, who happened to be a strong opponent of the use of marihuana and hashish, met for several days with Dr. Jean Vieu. Later, Johnson wrote a short book about what he learned. He specifically noted that Dr. Vieu's reports "made no mention of any burning sensations in the limbs, or sensation of 'fire', in any of his patients," and that all those affected experienced "a euphoria, which then transformed itself into a nervous depression with anxiety and delusions of persecution." John was one such case of delusion that Dr. Vieu shared with him:

> Of particular interest is the sorry case of Monsieur Pache of the Route Ba-gnoles. Today, Monsieur Pache goes round Pont Saint Esprit with a limp resulting from a broken leg, which he acquired through jumping from an upstairs window. Monsieur Pache, it appears, made his spectacular jump because, gripped with intense panic, he felt himself 'enclosed' and was impelled to make his escape.

Johnson had devoted much of his medical career to studying the physi-ological and mental effects of hashish and marihuana on humans. He was especially interested in the euphoric effects of the drugs as well as their alleged enhancement of creativity. He had poured over the classic treatise by Jean-Joseph Moreau de Tours, *Hashish and Mental Alienation*, written in 1845. Like Moreau de Tours, Johnson firmly believed there existed a nexus between marihuana and certain forms of mental illness.

Relying heavily on a September 1951 British medical journal article that maintained the Pont-St.-Esprit outbreak was caused by something other than bread ergot, Dr. Johnson, through his own study, drew the same conclusion. In reaching this point, he noted, "I was informed that experiments had been made at the Sandoz Laboratories at Basle in which similar psychological symptoms, but lasting only a few hours, had been produced by the injection of a large dose of ergot, but no record of these seems to have been published."

Dr. Johnson decided that some form of Indian hemp had caused the out-break. He wrote, "In fact, Indian hemp is— with perhaps the exception of the synthetic drugs, Benzedrine and dexedrine, which must, out of the nature of the case, be ruled out— the only known drug which could have caused these symptoms.... The case for Indian hemp being the cause of the sickness at Pont Saint Esprit goes beyond mere conjecture. It is very strong indeed."

Of course, today all authorities on psychoactive drugs discount Dr. John-son's conclusion, but these same authorities remain divided on the actual cause. Unfortunately, Johnson, a trusting soul, failed to probe more deeply into the reports he had heard about recent drug experiments at Sandoz Laboratories.

Nor could Dr. Johnson, or other medical authorities, have known that at the time of the Pont-St.-Esprit outbreak, a group of Camp Detrick scientists just happened to be visiting France. The evidence is in Frank Olson's passport, as well as the passports of other SOD scientists. Nor was Johnson aware that Sandoz and CIA officials were engaged in discrete, ongoing discussions about the "secret of Pont-St.-Esprit."

In 1975, Dr. D.V. Siva Sankar wrote:

> The history of LSD-25 is recent, even though ergot itself dates back to Christ. Ergot, the central ingredient of LSD, is a fungus of rye bread, although it is also found in other small number of plants of the gramineae family. (The gramineae, or 'grass,' family of plants is comprised of over 10,000 species, and is the most ecologically and economically important of all plant families.) Ergot of rye, purple-brown protrusions from the ears of rye, is scientifically called *Secale cornutum*, yet has many localized nicknames such as 'horned rye,' 'spurred rye,' and 'tollkorn' (German for "mad grain"). Ergot is produced by a parasitic fungus, and is defined in French dictionaries as '*petit ongle pointu derriere le pied du coq*,' or in English, 'small pointed talon behind the cock's foot.'

As Dr. Sankar said, ergot has been around since Christ, and may well pre-date Christ. Biblical accounts of famines in Egypt and Israel are, today, believed to have been caused by the fungal infection of crops. In the Middle Ages, during particularly rainy summers, whole harvests of rye were ruined by ergot fungus. When farmers and bakers, because of ignorance or starvation, went ahead and produced bread from infected flour, people's hands and feet became grotesquely gangrenous. The affliction came to be called "Anthony's Fire" or "Ardents disease" because fingers and toes appeared as if they had been charred. People struck by the disease also hallucinated, acted bizarrely, and some went mad. Women suffered spontaneous abortions. Since about 1835, midwives have used ergot extractions to slow and stop childbirth hemorrhages. As early as 1582, midwives were using ergot to precipitate childbirth, claims German physician Dr. Adam Lonitzer.

Dr. Jean Thuillier, a noted French psychiatrist and pharmacologist, observed, "The mental illnesses seen in the Middle Ages caused by ergotism did not arise from a hallucinogenic property of the fungus, but from massive doses of alkaloid vasoconstrictors, and no doubt also from hysterical reactions provoked by the alarming appearance of the gangrenous limbs."

Dr. Thuillier recounts his numerous contacts and work with virtually all of the earliest notable LSD researchers. He states, for example, that in 1951 Sandoz liberally supplied Dr. Paul Hoch at New York State Psychiatric Institute with LSD that was soon given the trade name Delysid; and that one of Thuillier's colleagues, identified only as "Bernard P.," who routinely prescribed LSD to patients, committed suicide after his own self-experimentation. Observed Thuillier, "[Whatever] effects his underlying mental state had on this act, it is certain that LSD had an influence in this drama and that it precipitated it."

Especially significant in the history of LSD and psychotropic drugs is the work of Gordon Wasson and his wife Valentina Pavlovna. The couple traveled the globe in search of exotic and rare psychoactive mushrooms, and they were the first scientists to use the term 'ethnomycology.' Over a forty year period, the two collected and catalogued the "food of the Gods." In 1977, Wasson commented that throughout his many excursions to Mexico from 1952 through 1962, "I didn't send a single sample to an American mycologist. I didn't get a penny, not a single grant from any government source. I'm perfectly sure of that."

There is no reason to doubt Wasson, but what he did not know at the time of his excursions was that the United States government was closely monitoring every one of his trips and that each and every one of his collected samples found their way back from Mexico to CIA-funded laboratories. Wasson also sent his samples to Albert Hofmann at Sandoz Labs in Switzerland. Hofmann, according to Wasson, "was doing the key work synthesizing the active ingredients" of the samples. What Wasson again did not realize was that the fruits of all of his and Hofmann's labors were being plucked from the vine by the U.S. Army and CIA, both of whom, since at least 1948, had covert operatives working in the Sandoz laboratories.

Wasson also was unaware of CIA penetration into a number of his Mexico excursions. In 1956, Dr. James Moore of the University of Delaware, under secret contract with the CIA's TSS, traveled to the Oaxaca section of Mexico to collect rivea corymbosa samples. Moore, according to Wasson, was collaborating with an Argentine-based mycologist, Dr. Rolf Singer, a Bavarian-born Jew who had fled Nazi Germany in 1933 for Czechoslovakia. Eventually, he traveled to the United States where he secured a job doing research at Harvard University, and in 1948, he left the U.S. to go to Argentina to study hallucinogenic mushrooms.

Wasson, in a 1977 interview, implied that Singer had some sort of ties to the CIA through Moore, but the specifics are unclear and it must be stated here that Wasson reportedly did not care much for Singer and considered his work "rushed" and often "borrowed" from others. Wasson only traveled once with Moore, in 1956, and the experience was horrible, he said. Said Wasson: "he was an awful ass... He expected to have a water closet in Mexico. It was laughable."

Wasson also reported that he had once been approached by either the CIA or FBI. "I'm not sure which," he said. They wanted him "to do work for the government." He turned them down, saying he thought the effort "patriotic," but did not want his work being classified secret. "I wanted to publish all my findings," he explained.

In the same interview, Wasson said that Albert Hofmann "worked in some way with the CIA" and that Hofmann's "discoveries were imparted in whole by Sandoz to the U.S. government. Sandoz wanted to be on the right side of things." Hofmann's connection to the CIA has never been officially confirmed by the CIA, which maintains a policy of not commenting on or revealing information on foreign citizens who find their way into its employment. Former Agency officials have commented anonymously that several Sandoz scientists and officials, including Hofmann, maintained a close relationship with the CIA, but the "Agency never fully trusted the Swiss" and "always held a dual insurance policy with Sandoz" by vetting and placing covert employees within the firm's laboratories and administration.

In the same 1977 interview Wasson spoke of the Frank Olson case. "What they did to that man... the government. I couldn't believe that anyone would be so crazy as to do what was done to him with LSD," he said.

In October 1960 a rather enigmatic figure suddenly appears in the story of LSD who would be described later in so many different ways as to remain something of a mystery. His name was Michael Hollingshead. At the time he first appears in the LSD saga, he was apparently an executive secretary at a British public relations firm operating in New York City. At the suggestion of a British physician and friend, Dr. John Beresford, Hollingshead, wrote to Sandoz Laboratories in Basle requesting a supply of LSD. Beresford had suggested that Hollingshead tell Sandoz the drug was for "bone-marrow research." About two weeks later, a package arrived postmarked from Switzerland containing pure LSD and an invoice for $285 for "approximately one gram of lot number H-00047, the "H" for Hofmann, as in Albert Hofmann.

According to Hollingshead, he and Beresford diluted the LSD, mixing it with baker's sugar to the point where they had a thick pudding-like paste that they scooped into a large mayonnaise jar. Later, it was estimated the jar contained about 5,000 spoonfuls of LSD, each spoonful containing a little more than a 200 milligram dose. Altogether, one gram was considered enough for 10,000 doses of LSD.

After filling the mayonnaise jar, Hollingshead licked clean a sheet of wax paper that held the residue of the psychedelic mixture. About thirty-five minutes later, Hollingshead climbed to his rooftop in Greenwich Village and, for nearly fifteen hours, stared at stars, sky, city lights, buildings, streets and people while his mind traveled around the world and back several times. Hollingshead would later say that his initial mental journey was beyond description, word defying. Beresford estimated the wax paper held the equivalent of about five very heavy doses of LSD.

Hollingshead was so taken with the drug that he contacted writer Aldous Huxley to learn more about it. Huxley, who had taken LSD a number of times with Alfred "Johnny Appleseed of LSD" Hubbard and others, referred Hollingshead to Timothy Leary at Harvard University. A spellbound Leary listened as Hollingshead extolled his LSD experience. Leary was at first skeptical, but was soon won over by observing the effects of LSD on some of his friends. Within weeks, Leary was eagerly ingesting a heaping spoonful of LSD concoction from Hollingshead's magic mayonnaise jar. According to his own account, Leary's first "trip" lasted five days and the world would never be the same again. (Hollingshead subsequently published his memoirs under the modest title, *The Man Who Turned on the World*.)

In the early 1960s, especially 1962 and 1963, LSD exploded across the American landscape. Every important national publication took note of the sensational new drug. News articles focused on activities at Harvard University and on expat communities in Mexico, where renegade researchers relocated. Harvard professor Timothy Leary jumped on the psychedelic wave and rode it into America's hungry soul. He wrote to Sandoz Pharmaceutical's New Jersey office requesting a supply of psilocybin, a potent drug derived from mushrooms. Sandoz promptly shipped a large amount of the drug to Leary, with a cover letter stating that the company "was only too happy to assist Harvard research" and was "interested in sponsoring work in this area..." Sandoz asked Leary to "please send us a report of the results" (on psilocybin).

Of course, Timothy Leary had no inkling that a carbon copy of the Sandoz letter was forwarded to the CIA's Robert Lashbrook.

The CIA was less than pleased about the activities of Professors Timothy Leary and Richard Alpert at Harvard University. The two scientists had drawn far too much attention to the drug. Uncontrolled street supplies of LSD were showing up everywhere. Agency analysts predicted that soon LSD – "acid" as it was now called – would flood the youth and counter-culture markets. Said Sidney Gottlieb in 1997, "It was not a good development, in my view. LSD's not a recreational drug; it's not meant to be taken causally or for reasons to have fun."

In a 1986 deposition, Robert Lashbrook scoffed at the activities of Leary and Alpert, saying, "There was a group of psychologists at Harvard who I think were responsible for LSD becoming a popular drug. We had nothing to do with them."

Lashbrook was then queried about Henry K. Beecher, distinguished Harvard scientist (about whom readers will soon learn more).

Question: *"Well, didn't Professor Beecher report to the CIA that a Swiss doctor had suffered a severe depression after taking LSD and killed himself three weeks later?"*

Lashbrook: I think there was a Beecher. Okay, I think there was a Dr. Beecher who had some contact with the CIA. There were rumors to the effect that someone at Sandoz— that's what you're talking about.

Question: *A Swiss doctor. It's in the Church [U.S. Senate Select] Committee report.*

Lashbrook: Okay. There were rumors that someone at Sandoz Company, which is in Switzerland, had taken LSD and, as I recall, had jumped off a building and had killed himself. We sent a person to Sandoz Corporation to try to verify this story. Sandoz Corporation definitely denied it. So there was a rumor, and possibly the source was Beecher. I don't know. But the Sandoz Corporation, in our inquiry, denied it.

Question: *So the Church Committee report is correct?*

Lashbrook: On the basis of what our information was from the Sandoz Company. And the Sandoz Company ought to have known. I don't know why the Sandoz Company would have covered it up.

Question: *Had you heard of any other deaths or injuries in experiments with LSD or other hallucinogenic drugs?*
Lashbrook: No.
Question: *You never heard that Harold Blauer died on January 8, 1953 after receiving an injection of a mescaline derivative in an experiment sponsored by the Army? You never heard that?*
Lashbrook: I don't think so, but you said mescaline, which is not LSD.

THE UNITED STATES ARMY AND LSD: EARLY YEARS

In November 1948, L. Wilson Greene, Scientific Director of the Army's Chemical and Radiological Laboratories at Edgewood Arsenal, Maryland received a communication marked TOP SECRET from Dr. John P. Clay, a high-level Army consultant to the Chemical Division at the European Command Center in Heidelberg, Germany. Clay's purpose was to alert Greene to the existence of a "powerful hallucinatory agent" that had been "recently discovered" by scientists at the Sandoz pharmaceutical company in Basle, Switzerland. Experiments "are actively underway on abnormal subjects at Swiss institutions," Clay reported, "and results appear very promising." Clay's dispatch concluded:

> The synthesized substance is called LysergSaure-Diathylamid [lysergic acid diethylamide]. Its laboratory code is LSD-25. Will monitor and report on all future activities and studies.

Clay, a chemist, added that his information regarding the powerful drug had come surreptitiously from "a closely-held source inside the Sandoz Laboratories."
About three-weeks later, Dr. Clay — a descendant of John Clay, one of the original Virginia settlers in 1613, and of statesman Henry Clay — reported once again to Greene about the "important work being performed by Dr. W.A. Stoll at Sandoz laboratories." Clay elaborated admiringly on Stoll's work:

> Stoll was the first researcher to systematically investigate the psychological phenomena of LSD-25. He, through a series of experiments with normal and abnormal subjects, reported disturbances in perception that led to hallucinations, acceleration of thinking, and slight dimming of consciousness, but without a lessening of judgment.
>
> In his experiments, Stoll also found that [LSD] was outstanding in producing a clear-cut blunting of the affect and suspiciousness that were often seen in schizophrenic patients....
>
> Dr. Albert Hofmann, a Swiss chemist at Sandoz Laboratories, first synthesized [LSD] in 1938, but did not discover its hallucinogenic effects until April 1943, after he accidentally exposed himself to a small quantity of the drug. Overall, Hofmann reported having an amazing and beautiful experience.

Dr. Clay concluded his communication by stating that he would continue to "closely monitor all future studies at Sandoz Laboratories that could be beneficial to psychological warfare themes." Stated Clay, "Our agent on the inside has well proven his agility and scientific worth without compromising his delicate position." About a year later, Clay again reported on the activities of Dr. Stoll:

> Dr. Stoll's investigation of LSD-25 continues intensely... he has lectured about what he and Sandoz Laboratories term, 'The New Hallucinatory Agent' before the Swiss Society of Psychiatry and the Association of Physicians in Zurich.

Clay expressed concern that public acclaim regarding the discovery LSD-25 and its promotion as "this major breakthrough in clinical treatment of mental patients" would draw the interest of physicians and nations that could interfere with the interests of the Army and United States. "The compound is very expensive to produce," Clay wrote, "but this, of course, will not deter other nations which want the drug for purposes other than treatment." Recommended Clay, "We should act quickly to gain the needed amount of this drug as quickly as possible and to do whatever is necessary to keep it out of the hands of undesirables." Clay noted that LSD had been slow to capture the serious attention of the American medical community, and pointed out that it was the work underway on LSD's non-therapeutic use that deserved the Army's attention.

Army reports written months later reflect Clay's advice and offer substantiating observations from experiments at St. Louis State Hospital, Washington University Medical School in St. Louis, Missouri. There, physicians had reported "that LSD-25 was a drug that induced a controlled toxic state within the nervous system and that it re-activated anxiety and fear with apparently just enough euphoria to permit recall of provoking experiences."

Not long afterwards, physicians at Ypsilanti State Hospital in Michigan, according to Army files, reported that although their experiments led "to the conclusion that LSD appeared to be a substance for therapeutic investigation in the treatment of psychoses," nonetheless:

> At the same time period another aspect of LSD effects was becoming apparent. Specifically, could this or other similar drugs be administered by U.S. officials in order to gain information of national security impact, and what could be done to protect our officials against such an event?

Of special concern to the Army were reports that the Russians were far ahead of the U.S. in their research and development of chemical warfare agents. Similarly, the CIA was alarmed at reports that radio stations behind the Iron Curtain were urging listeners to "collect ergot because considerable quantities were needed." Equally troublesome were reports that the Soviets employed over 100,000 scientists in their chemical warfare service and that remarkable advancements were being made with mind-altering drugs. As readers have already seen, the Korean War served to skyrocket alarm, after countless reports came in alleging the 'brainwashing' of American POWs through the use of hallucinogens and other drugs.

In addition to the work being performed in Ypsilanti and St. Louis, physicians at Spring Grove Mental Hospital in Baltimore, Maryland were documenting case after case of the successful use of LSD in treating alcoholics and "in surfacing repressed material in the minds of patients, permitting transference of vital information to psychiatrists." At the same time, doctors in England and Canada were claiming similar results and were marveling at the varied uses of LSD which, they said, included treatment of frigidity, sexual aberrations, and severe schizophrenia.

Several hospitals even employed LSD as an alternative medicine in treating the pain of terminal patients. Serious medical researchers with their ears to the ground were hard pressed not to hear about and become curious about LSD. Military scientists were no exception, although their interests were drawn primarily to the potential powers of the drug to surface repressed and vital information during interrogations, and perhaps to offer a "humane and alternative weapon system" to immobilize and temporarily incapacitate whole nations in lieu of mass destruction or atomic annihilation.

By late 1950 and early 1951, Army scientists were discretely dispatched from Edgewood Arsenal and Camp Detrick to witness first-hand what was occurring experimentally with LSD and other hallucinogens. As we have seen, several of Camp Detrick's SOD researchers and biochemists, including Frank Olson, Vincent Ruwet, and Gerald Yonetz, visited the nearby Spring Grove facility to observe LSD's effects for themselves.

Based on the reports of these Army observers, the Pentagon and Chemical Corps made a concerted effort in 1951 to collect and consolidate all records of LSD experiments and bring them under what it dubbed the Ad Hoc Committee on Psychochemicals. The voluminous data was eventually brought within a more formal structure called the Ad Hoc Group on Psychochemical Agents, in June 1955. Heading this group was renowned neurologist Dr. Harold G. Wolff. It will be recalled that Wolff, at the end of 1953, just days after Frank Olson's death, had been handpicked by CIA director Allen Dulles to head a study of brainwashing, including the use of psychochemicals in such efforts. The 1955 Ad Hoc Group's central mission was to fully explore and research the military's potential offensive and defensive uses of LSD.

The Ad Hoc Group, or Wolff Committee, as it was commonly called, began its task by reviewing over one hundred scientific reports on LSD that had been identified by Edgewood and Camp Detrick researchers. Within eight months, Wolff's Committee issued a series of strong recommendations that LSD, and other hallucinogens, be aggressively pursued by both the Pentagon and CIA. Of course, as readers are now well aware, the CIA was already doing just that, as was the Army.

Among the few concerns and reservations expressed by Wolff's group was the issue of using human subjects, which had first been raised in early 1953 by the Chemical Corps' Advisory Council. Earlier, in the fall of 1952, the Council had reported to the Secretary of Defense that researchers had arrived at the point beyond which essential results "could not be obtained unless human volunteers were utilized." Therefore, the Council recommended that the Secretary of Defense establish a policy that would officially endorse the use of human subjects in classified drug research. The Council further recommended that although the Nuremberg Code of 1947 would be cited as the principle guidelines for the Army's experiments, it urged that three articles of the Code be modified.

The first of these suggested modifications concerned Article One of the Code which requires, *"The voluntary consent of the human subject is absolutely essential."* This would be changed to require "the volunteer's consent to be in writing and his signature witnessed."

The second modification concerned Article Five of the Code, which states: *"No experiment should be conducted where there is an a priori reason to believe that death or disabling injury will occur; except, perhaps, in those experiments where the experimental physicians also serve as subjects."* It was recommended that this be modified by deleting the final phrase, "except, perhaps, in those experiments where the experimental physicians also serve as subjects."

Finally, the Council suggested that an additional rule be added which would "prohibit the use of prisoners of war as volunteer subjects." The Council was silent on the subject of forcibly using POWs in experiments.

Following receipt of the Council's recommendations, Secretary of Defense Charles Erwin Wilson issued a policy memorandum governing the use of human subjects for all of the service branches. The policy directive, commonly called the "Wilson Memorandum" and marked "TOP SECRET" on each of its three pages, authorized the Army, Navy, and Air Force "to use human volunteers in experimental research conducted with the development of defenses of all types against atomic, biological and/or chemical warfare agents." It provided specific guidance for the use of human subjects, which included the rules set forth in the Nuremberg Code, as modified by the Advisory Council's recommendations.

Wilson's policy required that whenever an experiment "was proposed pursuant to the memorandum that the nature and purpose of the proposed experiment shall be submitted for approval of the service Secretary and required that the service Secretary approve, in writing, the proposed experiment and the persons to be in charge of the experiment, and require the service Secretary to inform the Secretary of Defense of each approved research proposal."

The seeming sincerity of the Wilson Memorandum, sadly, was diluted and rendered largely ineffective when it was transmitted to the various services, service sectors, and Chemical Corps. Some sectors and divisions of the Corps apparently never received a copy of the policy at all. Others were given verbal notice of the existence of the policy, but abbreviated and never followed up. Some service branches simply continued to operate as if the policy did not exist.

The CIA, for its part, sat in on at least two of the Advisory Council's meetings, and was well aware of the policy's existence, but never noted the directive in any of its project memoranda, and operated its joint projects with the service branches without any attention to the directive's guidelines. Indeed, one Agency memorandum, written months after the Wilson directive, recommended the use of prisoners of war, as well as Federal prison inmates, for experiments with LSD, mescaline, morphine, and scopolamine, without any allowance for subject notification or 'voluntary consent' — something of an oxymoron in any case, under the circumstances.

According to Army reports, two months after the Wilson Memorandum was issued, in May 1953, the Army Staff presented the Secretary of the Army, Robert Ten Broek Stevens, former chairman of J.P. Stevens textile company, with a "proposed directive to implement the Wilson Memorandum." Reads one report: "Although [Secretary Stevens] agreed in principle with the proposed instructions to the field, he rejected the initial proposal because it was restricted to biological agent research rather than chemical, biological, and radiological agents and because he believed that the "TOP SECRET" classification should be downgraded in order to make the instructions more readily available to subordinate elements that would be conducting the research."

About a month later, on June 30, the first guidelines for Army Staff were released. They included the rules set out in the Wilson Memorandum and also directed that no human subject research be conducted without the specific written approval of the Secretary of the Army.

Over the next five years, according to Army documents, approval was sought from the Army Secretary for at least six human subject experiments, including the use of LSD and lethal nerve agents. Meanwhile, none of the joint experiments sponsored or funded by the CIA were submitted for written approval. In fact, no evidence of *any* approvals for any joint projects, including those for which funds were channeled through CIA front organizations or private institutions, could be found.

THE TWO FACES OF DR. HENRY BEECHER

Dr. Henry K. Beecher was a Harvard-trained anesthesiologist and consultant to both the CIA and the Army who made over forty trips overseas for the CIA alone. In September 1952, Beecher reported to the Agency's TSS branch on what he called "ego-depressant drugs," thus updating Sidney Gottlieb's staff on LSD experiments in Europe. Following World War II, Beecher had closely studied captured Nazi files concerning experiments at the notorious Dachau and Mauthausen concentration camps. In 1951 and 1952, Beecher met several times with SOD administrators Frank Olson and Vincent Ruwet in France and Germany to consult with the two about a top secret SOD operation known as Project Span. In August 1952, he journeyed to Europe to meet with as many foreign researchers as possible. His objective had been to see what advances had been made with known 'truth drugs,' but it was LSD that captivated Beecher's attention almost from the start of his trip.

Regarding the extraordinary potency of LSD, Beecher described the amounts being worked with as:

> [dosages] so small that one can calculate that the water supply of a large city could be disastrously and undetectably (until too late) contaminated with quantities apparently readily available.... It should not be a difficult trick to sink a small container of [LSD] near the main outlet of water storage reservoirs, and the container arranged to 'excrete' a steady flow of the material over a period of many hours or days.
>
> ....If the concept of contaminating a city's water supply seems or in actual fact is found to be far fetched (that is by no means certain), there is still the possibility of contaminating, say, the water supply of a bomber base, or more easily still, that of a battleship.

Beecher, perhaps thinking how to best conceal any such act of contamination, then states:

> For centuries in Europe, outbreaks of 'The Dancing Madness' have been variously attributed to mass hysteria, to ergot poisoning, and so on. Within the year [sic: it was the previous year, 1951], such an outbreak occurred in France. This was attributed to the use of infected grain. There is some reason to believe that *the grain involved came by mistake from an area in France where ergot production for experimental purposes is being carried on.* [Italics added by author.]

The Agency's consultant then smoothly returns to his proposal of contaminating a battleship with LSD as a way to test the effect of group dynamics on LSD's properties. "Our own current work," Beecher observes, suggests that:

> ....[LSD]will produce hysteria (unaccountable laughing, anxiety, etc.). *While our studies so far have been carried out in isolated individuals, one at a time, it is well known that hysteria is compounded when several vulnerable individuals are together. LSD can produce a temporary state of severe imbalance, hysteria, and insanity. It requires little imagination to realize what the consequence might be if a battleship's crew were so affected.* [Italics added.]

367

Apparently, Beecher's suggestion to dose the entire crew of a battleship went beyond hypothetical musings because he then states:

> While biological warfare is outside of my field of competence, I understand that a chief problem is to get toxins in sufficient concentration in contact with a significant number of people. The use of lysergic acid derivatives indicated above may well be an exception to this limitation. The matter urgently requires further study. Conceivably this might be an unusually merciful agent of warfare: temporarily nullifying the individual's effectiveness, but not permanently damaging him. I have outlined the above points in a somewhat dogmatic way to make the point clear. Needless to say, much more work needs to be done. We need to know, for example, if ordinary chlorination of the water will oxidize the lysergic acid derivatives. Evidently the heat required to bake bread does not. What are the effects of air, light, etc. Are there antidotes, etc.? In the doses we have been using, about a gamma per kilogram of body weight, the maximum effect is attained in about two hours after ingestion by mouth, and the duration of effectiveness is about six hours. We need to know the effects of large doses, of prolonged administration of small doses and so on, to mention a few matters for study.

There are no known written follow-up reports by Beecher concerning further developments of his schemes for dosing public water reservoirs or entire battleships with LSD. It is known, however, that Dr. Beecher's activities throughout the 1950s occasionally put him in contact with Drs. Harris Isbell, Abraham Wikler, Harold Abramson, Paul Hoch, and several SOD and Edgewood Arsenal researchers, including John Schwab. In addition, according to the date books and diary entries of narcotics agent George White, Dr. Beecher attended at least one of the CIA's physician gatherings at the Statler and Belmont hotels in New York City.

Controversy about Beecher's undercover activities extend even to the CIA's Bedford Street safe house in Greenwich Village. The speculation stems from a March 15, 1952 letter from Beecher to one of his colleagues, a renowned neurologist and founder of biological psychiatry in the United States, Dr. Stanley Cobb. The letter has provoked some speculation that both Beecher and Cobb were somehow involved with, or knowledgeable about, George White's Bedford Street safe house experiments because the letter mentions "Bedford" and "pharmacological lobotomies." However, it is more likely that the brief letter referred to government-sponsored experiments at a Veteran's Hospital in Bedford, Massachusetts. Speculation exists also, primarily on the Internet, concerning Beecher's relationship with Drs. Seymour Kety and Nathaniel Kleitman. Also worth noting, but seemingly never before noticed, is that Beecher was in France during the Pont-St.-Esprit outbreak and at the time of the seemingly random LSD dosing of a young American in a Paris café, about which readers will learn more.

In a July 1978 interview with investigators for John Marks' seminal book, *The Search for the Manchurian Candidate*, Dr. John M. Von Felsinger, a colleague of Beecher's, candidly revealed, in response to questions about his work and Beecher's with LSD, that "a good deal of the human testing on new psychoactive drugs was done in Haiti."

Asked the interviewer, "Why Haiti?"

Von Felsinger replied, "Because there aren't any [testing] guidelines there." He also said that, besides the work in Haiti by American researchers, "a number of American-based drug houses were interested in screening a whole series of psychedelic drugs [in Haiti]." He added, "There was a mad scramble on at that time [mid-1950s] to develop psychoactive drugs... It was difficult and expensive to screen them on human subjects with restrictions and that sort of thing... At the time the whole idea was discovering drugs that could be used to influence human behavior."

"What types of subjects were used in Haiti?" asked the interviewer.

"I was down there for a slightly different purpose...but I'm sure they used populations that we couldn't. They could use hospital people, prison people, people off the street."

Evidently, Von Felsinger was unaware of the domestic population groups from which the CIA selected its subjects.

Von Felsinger told the interviewer that in addition to his own and Beecher's research with psychoactive drugs for the CIA and Army, Dr. Nathan Kline "at the Rockland State Hospital in New York" was performing experiments supported by the CIA and Army and that the drugs, like his and Beecher's LSD, had been provided primarily by the CIA. Rockland State Hospital was a notoriously cruel facility that had been shockingly, but accurately, portrayed in the 1948 award-winning film, *The Snake Pit*, starring Olivia de Havilland. After the film was released to appalled audiences, state of New York officials, including Dr. Paul Hoch, decided that Rockland needed a public relations "overhaul." Included in the makeover was a research component directed by Dr. Nathan Kline, a flamboyant, widely respected psychiatrist. Kline had once seriously proposed placing lithium, a mood stabilizer used for treatment of bipolar disorder, in the nation's drinking water. Von Felsinger also said that the drug research had included heroin that "came from the Federal Bureau of Narcotics."

Dr. Beecher's covert relationship with the CIA and Army is also well worth noting in light of Beecher's controversial and contradictory reputation on the issue of reforming the treatment of human subjects in medical experiments. His reputation as an ethics proponent stemmed from a medical journal article he wrote in 1966 detailing twenty-two cases of experimental studies conducted in the United States where the subjects were not informed that they were participating in experiments unrelated to their medical care. Historian David Healy writes: "The impact of the article was immense. The [National Institutes of Health] and the [Federal Drug Administration] were forced to design consent forms and institute ethical review boards. A series of Senate hearings on these and related issues demonstrated that the medical attitude was that doctors should decide what patients were told." It was widely assumed that Beecher was a proponent of informed consent. The reality was otherwise; some of Beecher's closest colleagues sharply criticized his use of subjects. Said Louis Lasagna, his research assistant at Harvard, in 1994 before a Presidential Commission:

> It wasn't that we were Nazis and said, 'If we ask for consent we lose our subjects'; it was that we were so ethically insensitive that it never occurred to us that you ought to level with people that they were in an experiment.

Found among Dr. Beecher's papers after his death was a ditty of a poem that read in part:

> A shy little snail from Toulouse,
> Who was normally quite recluse,
> Went out on the town,
> And acted the clown,
> Singing out 'LSD's my excuse'....
>
> A snail was made wildly to wave,
> When in mescaline he did lave,
> As he did ingest,
> He got manic depressed,
> And the cure sent him into the grave.

About the same time that Henry Beecher was poring over captured Nazi documents, Edgewood Arsenal scientific director, Dr. L. Wilson Greene, was developing his own thesis that LSD could well be a major advance toward 'non-violent war.' A significant step in reaching this conclusion was Dr. Greene's review of a massive amount of Nazi files and documents, many of which have never seen the light of day in America. Greene would later recount that, prior to his discussions with Dr. Alsoph Corwin at Johns Hopkins University, he first discovered the characteristics of psychochemicals during a routine scientific staff meeting in 1946 at Edgewood. A team of Chemical Corps physicians, including several from Camp Detrick, had just returned from Germany to report their findings and observations on the interrogation of captured Nazi scientists at Nuremburg's Landsberg Prison. One of the physicians "remarked that he had been surprised to learn that the Germans [had] conducted what appeared to be elaborate human experiments [on concentration camp prisoners] using hallucinogenic drugs... including mescaline and various compounds drawn from ergot."

Greene was intrigued with the report and became fascinated with the possibility of employing mind-altering drugs as a more 'humane' weapon of war. He spoke with members of the Chemical Corps team and learned that OSS and Office of Naval Intelligence officials, under the auspices of the U.S. Naval Technical Mission, had produced a number of studies, including one top-secret report detailing Nazi experiments, entitled *German Aviation Medical Experiments at the Dachau Concentration Camp*. After reviewing nearly three hundred pages of the report, Greene was disappointed to find fewer than two pages devoted to Nazi drug experiments. However, he noticed several unexplained references to an intriguing research institute called *Das Ahnenerbe*, apparently operated by Reichsfuhrer Heinrich Himmler's dreaded SS, which at least one writer deemed "the new Knights Templar, defending the Nazi 'faithful.'" It appeared that *Das Ahnenerbe* was the organization responsible for ordering and conducting the horrific drug experiments at Dachau and other locations.

L. Wilson Greene doggedly pursued the subject and, after subsequent meetings with Army G-2 intelligence officers and further review of a large cache of captured documents, he was able to learn a great deal more about the activities of the *Ahnenerbe*.

In short, Himmler — along with occultist Hermann Wirth and race-obsessed Richard Walter Darre, had founded the Ahnenerbe in 1935. It was set up as a Nazi think tank and 'research' institute dedicated to anything under the sun that could be seen as promoting the anthropological and cultural history and 'superiority' of the so-called Aryan race. The Ahnenerbe's founding papers state that its primary objective was "to promote the science of ancient intellectual history." Its guiding thought, as enunciated by Himmler, was: "A *Volk* lives happily in the present and the future as long as it is aware of its past and the greatness of its ancestors."

The Ahnenerbe operated a vast number of branches and over thirty programs, including 'folk' research, religious history, astronomy, geophysics, biology, botany, expeditions, cave studies, natural history, and plant genetics and preparations. In April 1945, American troops stumbled across a massive cache of Ahnenerbe files hidden in a dark, dank cave called Kleines Teufelslock (the Little Devil's Hole) near the Bavarian village of Pottenstein. For the next four years, American intelligence officials closely studied the captured documents, eventually sending many to the Army's Edgewood Arsenal and Camp Detrick.

Greene was amazed to read that Ahnenerbe-funded expeditions had spent months in the jungles of South America and the mountains of Tibet in search of exotic, hallucinogenic substances and plants. Documents revealed that numerous samples had been collected and returned to Germany from one extensive trip to Amazonia, South America's Amazon rainforest. Another excursion to Tibet and the forbidden city of Lhasa was able to amass huge amounts of mind-altering substances. Ahnenerbe teams also trekked the mystical Himalayas where they collected every plant specimen that caught their fancy.

Within weeks of launching his research, Dr. Greene came across documents that threw more light on the Ahnenerbe-funded mescaline experiments. Year's later, in 1961, French writer, Christian Bernadac, would use the same files to account for the horrors of Dachau. Bernadac reveals that the Ahnenerbe performed extensive experiments at Dachau and other camps with "a Mexican plant, a tiny thornless cactus, peyotl, [combining] the required properties and potentialities" and another Mexican plant that he said was "*Sinicuichi* [an auditory hallucinogenic], which robbed those who assimilated it of their memory." Bernadac speaks of progenitors of peyote and mescaline, citing the Huichol Indians of Mexico and an obscure early-1900s New York cult leader, Joseph Rave, who replaced the communion wafer with a "drink of light" comprised of mescaline. Also extolled were brothers Julian and Aldous Huxley who tripped repeatedly on mescaline and LSD. Bernadac then reveals that eight Dachau inmates were selected for drug experiments, conducted by SS physician Col. Kurt Plotter. In vivid detail, Bernadac, who interviewed one of the former inmates, Arthur Haulot, writes that Col. Plotter handed Haulot a glass of cognac laced with mescaline. Haulot recounted that nothing happened for the next two hours.

"Then I began to be aware of the effects of the poison," Haulot said. "I saw an extraordinary, an incredibly colored vision. The visions kept on coming. They started to come quite quickly until I felt that my head was entirely filled with these creations. For me these visions assumed geometric forms, shifting from rhomboids to undulating curves. Each of them arose from a source, a central point of very profound violet out of which they pulsed with a rhythm that I felt as music, taking on both the subtlest and the richest of colors."

After a while, Plotter walked over to Haulot and asked, "Listen to me, carefully. Do you think that with a man in your condition, it would be possible to get him to say things that he doesn't want to admit?"

Haulot recalled, "It took a great deal of effort for me to understand his question, and I answered very decidedly that it wouldn't be possible."

About an hour later, Plotter asked the same question. "At that time," Haulot said, "I was dominated by the visions which kept growing richer and more vividly colored all the time, so that the fact of being forced to return to reality, and particularly to open my eyes and reason, seemed to me to be an agony beyond any comparison with all that I had suffered until then in three years of life in the concentration camp."

With effort, Haulot answered, "Yes, everything," and then he added: "Ask me if I killed my father and my mother, I'd say yes, just to get you to leave me in peace." Plotter laughed and left the room.

Soon after reading about the Dachau mescaline experiments, Greene's attention turned to the powerful drug about which he had been alerted months earlier through top-secret Army reports from Europe. Right away, Greene later said, he "was struck by the physical proximity of the laboratory doing the most to refine ergot and the camp where most of the mescaline experimentation was performed." The Sandoz Laboratories in Basle, Switzerland were only about four hundred kilometers, or 248 miles, away from Dachau. Greene went back to his recently received reports from Army intelligence and refreshed himself with the account of "what we thought was then the mostly-by-chance discovery of LSD-25 in 1942 or 1943 by Hofmann at Sandoz."

> [The] company's site in Basle was separated from Germany by the Rhine River...and Basle's economic backbone was comprised of the corporate trinity of Sandoz, Hoffman-LaRoche, Ciba-Geigy, all large pharmaceutical firms.

Greene learned that Hofmann had actually worked under the direction of the highly respected physician Arthur Stoll, founder and director of Sandoz's aggressive drug research program. During World War I, Stoll had been an associate in Berlin to world famous chemist and Nobel Laureate, Dr. Richard Willstatter. Around the same time Hofmann was hired by Sandoz, according to Greene's findings, Stoll's laboratory was diligently working on ways to isolate and prepare in pure form "the intact active principles of medicinal plants whose active principles are unstable or whose potency is subject to variation." This objective was particularly attractive to Hofmann because of his deep interest in the development of natural chemical products. Said Greene, "Stoll's laboratory was concentrating its efforts on such plants as foxglove, Mediterranean squill, and ergot."

Beginning in 1946 through to mid-1949, Greene recounted, "after three Sandoz researchers volunteered to self-administer LSD-25 in order to confirm, and possibly replicate, Hofmann's 'wondrous experience' with the drug to a very skeptical Arthur Stoll," Stoll's son, [Dr. Werner A. Stoll, a psychiatrist at the Bleuler Clinic in Zurich], undertook a number of human experiments on about twenty [it was twenty-two] people at the University of Zurich." Greene found that documentation concerning these experiments was scant, and recalled what he later termed "troubling rumors or gossip" that the experiments, or related tests, resulted in "at least one death, possibly more," involving one "unwitting mental patient," "the suicide of one nurse," and "the death in Geneva of a woman physician who had been depressed" and had taken LSD-25 and became more depressed, "killing herself three weeks later."

In August 1949, as we have seen in chapter 5 of Book One, Dr. Greene published his report advancing psychochemical warfare as "a new concept of war."

10

August 30, 1955
CIA Headquarters, Washington, D.C.

Beginning in June 1954, six months after Frank Olson's death, the CIA's Office of Scientific Intelligence, at the formal request of OSI chief Dr. H. Marshall Chadwell, embarked on what it termed "a thorough and comprehensive evaluation of the significance of current knowledge about LSD-25, and related drugs." Continued Chadwell's request: "Knowledge of the unconventional, as well as the therapeutic, use to which this most unusual drug might be put, both offensively as well as defensively, is of considerable strategic significance. The broad objective of [the requested study] therefore is to review, analyze, and evaluate biochemical and pharmacological research on LSD-25 and other psychogenic drugs."

The broad-based and intensive research undertaken for these OSI objectives, following extensive consultations between OSI researchers and TSS Chemical Branch, Office of Security, and Camp Detrick SOD scientists, was officially closed on February 1, 1955. The OSI report on LSD was formally released seven months later, on August 30, to a limited number of CIA officials. The report's primary conclusions are framed by this introductory statement:

> LSD-25 is the most potent psychochemical agent available at the present time. Trace quantities of LSD-25 create serious mental confusion of the manic and schizophrenic type and render the mind temporarily susceptible to suggestion.

The report continues: "Since the effect of the drug is temporary, in contrast to the fatal nerve agents, there are important strategic advantages for its use in certain operations." [The next five lines are blacked-out.] The report observes that "because LSD is colorless, odorless, and tasteless," it could possibly "be used clandestinely for the contamination of food and water."

On the value of LSD-25 for interrogations, OSI officials were apparently concerned that there was still "insufficient data to confirm or deny LSD usefulness for eliciting statements from subjects under its influence." The implication is that experiments conducted thus far had produced mixed results. The report makes no mention of Frank Olson or his death, but it does provide details of a startlingly similar case, as follows:

> *Past experience has shown that LSD-25 produces such an over-*
> *whelming emotional and intellectural upheaval in the individual*
> *that any experiments with this substance must be very rigidly con-*
> *trolled. Once, in a Swiss mental hospital, a practical joker sneaked*
> *a few granules of LSD-25 into a staff nurse's coffee. The frantic girl,*
> *apparently driven to believe that she had become schizophrenic,*
> *leaped to her death from the hospital rooftop.* [Italics added.]

The next segment of the report is inaccessible; the title is completely blacked-out, as is its first long paragraph. However, its second paragraph is partially visible and makes clear the topic:

> The epidemic in Pont-St.-Esprit, France, during 1952 [sic] where the entire
> population of the town was believed to have been infected by bread from
> ergot-bearing rye, is typical. The hallucinations, the general detached hys-
> teria, and temporary mental impairment of the victims is [sic] typical of
> reactions to ergot.

This outbreak occurred in 1951; it is odd that OSI researchers miswrote the date. Use of the word "typical" suggests that other outbreaks occurred and were studied. It is impossible to know if they are mentioned here because the next two lengthy paragraphs are blacked-out entirely.

Following its section on Pont-St.-Esprit, the CIA's report devotes special attention to the cultivation and availability of ergot in other countries, especially those in the Soviet bloc. The report emphasizes the fact that naturally occurring ergot "is considered of commercial value in Bulgaria, Czechoslovakia, Eastern Germany, Hungary, Poland, and Rumania, despite the fact that "the ergot of eastern European origin has a lower alkaloid content than most western European varieties."

Clearly, the Cold War race to manufacture and stockpile ergot (to the extent possible without deterioration) was on. In East Germany, the Agency found ergot "is now cultivated in the Plant Research Institute of the Academy of Science, Gatersleben. The Institute undertook the cultivation as a result of a 1951 failure to obtain ergot of sufficient potency to meet the pharmaceutical standard of East Germany." Moreover, the CIA learned:

> Large-scale field experiments involving inoculation procedures were car-
> ried out in 1952 and 1953; and the constancy of alkaloid content of
> various indigenous strains as well as Hungarian, Portuguese, and Finnish
> strains was recently reported after an extensive and well-documented sur-
> vey by the Plant Research Institute.

Remarkably, in Poland, states the report, people were being encouraged by radio to collect ergot and send it to "the provincial ergot buying officer" because "considerable quantities of raw, unprocessed ergot are needed in a certain chemical process."

In the Soviet Union, of particular interest to the CIA, the Ministry of Plant Protection and the Ministry of Agriculture oversaw ergot cultivation and collection. The section on Russia states, "In recent years no Russian grown ergot has appeared in foreign markets," despite the fact that ergot had grown naturally in the rye fields of Russia for decades, and had not diminished.

During World War II, according to the report, the Sandoz firm in Switzerland, finding that it was "unable to obtain supplies of ergot because of the exigencies of war," started to grow its own. Switzerland was now (1955) "the main world producer of finished ergot preparations." Nonetheless, the report reveals, Sandoz still purchased raw ergot on contract from other countries, including the United States. Also, warned the report, Sandoz was selling large supplies of ergot to the Soviet Union.

The report provides extensive details about the work of Sandoz Laboratories, and specifically Albert Hofmann. The descriptions are rather technical and seem likely to have originated from one or more sources very close to the company, and probably from inside. While a fair amount of this information is known today, in 1954 hardly any of it had been published or reported. The report states, with clinical precision:

> Medical interest [in LSD] was aroused when Dr. Hofmann of Sandoz, Ltd., Switzerland, suffered psychic disturbances while experimenting with LSD-25. Arthur Stoll of Sandoz, Ltd., and his co-workers are responsible for most of the knowledge of this powerful agent, as well as for its partial synthesis. W.A. Stoll studied extensively its psychological effects....
>
> In 1952, Stoll submitted 11 normal adults to the Rorschach test, these being under the influence of 30 grams of LSD-25, and repeated it at a later date without the LSD-25. A Rorschach syndrome was produced by the disinhibition of the thought processes with a decrease of precision and wealth of content. In spite of the small number of cases from which to judge, the changes do not seem to be accidental since the relevant factors become changed in a corresponding sense and lead to a logical conclusion.
>
> The clinical picture of LSD-25 intoxication, corresponding to the LSD-25 influenced Rorschach syndrome, is regarded as unspecific and as an instance of the exogenous reaction type. Both typical psycho-organic traits occur, as do others suggestive of schizophrenia.

By way of comparison, the report cites the reactions of "an artist" to LSD-25, who, at the time of the experience, was able "to sketch and then reproduce in vivid colors those bizarre fantasies of the human mind which seem to be somewhat commonplace to the schizophrenic." The artist reported:

> ....[F]or hours he inhabited a nightmare world in which he experienced the torments of hell and the ecstasies of heaven. Since there are no words in

the English language to convey the sensations, visions, illusions, hallucinations, colors, patterns and dimensions which his disordered mind revealed, he stated that he will never be able to describe

The report concludes with an especially revealing account of the CIA's aggressive efforts to replicate Sandoz's patented formula for LSD. States the report:

> The knowledge of the chemical structure of the ergot alkaloids which has been gained as a result of [Sandoz's] analysis and degradatics has also made it possible to attempt their chemical synthesis. Partial syntheses were accomplished by Stoll and coworkers, [Drs.] F.C. Uhle and W.A. Jacobs and others. In 1953-54, Uhle completed 11 of the 12 steps, which he considered necessary for the complete synthesis.
>
> *As indicated earlier, in September 1954, [Dr. Edmund] Kornfeld and other staff workers of the Eli Lilly Research Laboratories, Indianapolis, Indiana working with [Dr. Robert Burns] Woodward of the Converse Memorial Laboratory, Harvard University, completed the total synthesis of both lysergic acid and the ergot alkaloid ergonovine. These partial and total syntheses are of great significance for the manufacture of the known, naturally occurring active principles and closely related derivatives."* [Italics added.]

In layman's terms, the CIA, in concert with Eli Lilly pharmaceutical company and a Harvard University laboratory, had appropriated the Sandoz formula for LSD and now had the means to manufacture an endless supply of the drug.

11

December 20, 1957
San Francisco, California

I was working for Uncle Sam. I was doing more than you were doing, Buster.
— Ira "Ike" Feldman, FBN agent

If Ritchie's claims are indeed true, he has paid a terrible price in the name of national security.
— Judge Alex Kozinski, U.S. Circuit Court

Deputy United States Marshal Wayne Ritchie was feeling good. It was nearly Christmas and he was looking forward to having a few days off to enjoy time with his girlfriend. Tonight he was enjoying a holiday party with fellow federal employees at the United States Post Office Building in San Francisco.

Ritchie had already had a couple of bourbon and sodas. Like everyone else, he was in a relaxed, jovial mood. He laughed heartily at the jokes his colleagues were telling. He was well into his third drink when he began to notice an odd sensation in his chest. About ten minutes later he felt flushed, then hot and cold at the same time, and suddenly full of energy. The voices around him began to fade in and out. Sounds swirled around him; the colored lights on the small Christmas tree in the corner of the room were shape shifting into fantastic patterns, mesmerizing him. Ritchie was feeling increasingly strange and disoriented. He decided to go upstairs to his office to sit quietly and drink a glass of water.

In his office alone, Ritchie drifted into reflecting on the past ten years of his life. At the same time, his strange disorientation intensified. Ritchie, 30 years old at the time, had been in the Marines for five years and for a year, had been a guard at Alcatraz prison before becoming a U.S. Marshal. He described his feelings that night in his office: "I became depressed and was overcome with a sense that all my friends and acquaintances had turned against me."

Ritchie went outside for some fresh air. On the sidewalk, he felt "as if I was walking in a tunnel." He began to feel better, more euphoric, and he dropped in at several nearby bars and had a drink in each. At the last bar, he decided he needed to buy an airplane ticket for his girlfriend who had recently told him she wanted to visit New York City. Seemingly minutes later, he found himself in his apartment where he picked up his two service revolvers. He then drove to the Fillmore district's Shady Grove bar and with the guns in hand, he demanded that the bartender give him all of his cash. Ritchie later said he fully expected to be caught in the act and perhaps killed, thus putting an end to his mental anguish and mounting paranoia.

While the nervous bartender was pulling bills out of the cash register, a waitress managed to distract Ritchie long enough for one of the customers to hit him over the head, knocking him unconscious. When the police arrived on the scene, Ritchie politely and tearfully asked one of the officers to shoot him in the head and save the state of California the cost of dealing with him.

Days later, baffled by what he had done, Ritchie pleaded guilty to armed robbery and was given a suspended five-year sentence and fined $500. He was also forced to resign from the Marshal's Office. He remained severely depressed for years, and suffered disturbing flashbacks and nightmares related to the robbery. Once a confident, tough and happy man, Ritchie became a paranoid, suicidal introvert, lacking self-confidence and self-esteem. Every day was a struggle for him to maintain his sanity.

Forty-five years later, in March 1999, retired on social security after thirty-four years as a house painter, Ritchie was living with his wife in California when he read the obituary for Dr. Sidney Gottlieb in a San Francisco newspaper. Gottlieb's death notice mentioned the MKULTRA project and its unwitting drug dosing program, operated by George Hunter White out of the CIA's safe houses in New York and San Francisco.

Ritchie suspected that he had been dosed in 1957 with some sort of drug, perhaps LSD. He voiced his suspicions to his wife and friends and they encouraged him to do further research. One friend remarked that, according to his own recollection, White had operated more than one safe house in San Francisco. White's San Francisco safe houses had been in operation through 1964, often bringing prostitutes and confidential informants into their surreptitious experiments.

Ritchie discovered that White's papers, diaries, and date books had been donated posthumously to a small foundation in Sunnyvale, California, not far from where Ritchie now lived in San Jose. He arranged to visit the foundation where he was startled to read an entry in White's date book for December 20, 1957: "xmas party Fed. Bldg. Press Room." The former marshal read through more of White's papers and discovered that a special employee for the Federal Bureau of Narcotics had directly assisted White with his San Francisco activities. The employee, Ira Feldman, commonly called "Ike," had been hired by White in 1955, a few months after White had set up shop on the West Coast in the CIA-funded safe house. Located in San Francisco's Telegraph Hill neighborhood at

225 Chestnut Street, the building had a panoramic view of the Bay and was outfitted with state-of-the-art sound and listening equipment, hidden movie cameras, and two-way mirrors. Despite that he was a federal marshal, Ritchie had known nothing about the joint CIA-FBN operation in the 1950s. At the time, Ritchie had known only that White and Feldman worked for the Narcotics Bureau.

In October 1999, Ritchie, now 75 years old, filed a timely $12 million lawsuit against the CIA and the DEA (successor agency to the FBN), alleging that he had been dosed with LSD. Also named in his suit were CIA officer Robert V. Lashbrook and FBN special employee Ike Feldman. After denying the government's motion to dismiss the case and for a summary judgment, the district court for Northern California held a four-day bench trial.

During the trial's proceedings, Ritchie's attorney, Sidney Bender, relied heavily on the deposition testimony of Ike Feldman, who made a series of incriminating, contradictory, and outrageous statements about his role in the CIA's safe house and LSD drugging:

> **Attorney**: *Now, all these people that you personally drugged, you never did any follow-up on them, in the sense of telling them that you had drugged them, did you?*
> **Feldman**: Not all the people that I drugged. I drugged guys involved in about ten, twelve, period. I didn't do any follow-up, period, because it wasn't a very good thing to go and say, "How do you feel today?" You don't give them a tip. You just back away and let them worry, like this nitwit, Ritchie.
> **Attorney**: *When you say "let them worry," you mean let them have a head full of LSD and let—*
> **Feldman**: Let them have a full head, like what happened, like what happened with this nut when he got out and got drunk.
> **Attorney**: *Mr. Feldman, did you ever witness anybody slipping LSD to another person?*
> **Feldman**: Never did.
> **Attorney**: *Did you ever slip LSD to another person?*
> **Feldman**: Never did. Never did.
> **Attorney**: *And were there ever prostitutes that you gave LSD to, to give to other people?*
> **Feldman**: I imagine there were. I don't remember what they were doing off times.
> **Attorney**: *Didn't you have a great reputation as having a lot of whores?*
> **Feldman**: Whores, just like you, too. You are a whoremaster, too. I was working for Uncle Sam. I was doing more than you were doing, Buster.

Wayne Ritchie lost his case against the Government and CIA. In early 2006, the Ninth U.S. Circuit Court of Appeals ruled that Ritchie failed to prove that he had been drugged with LSD as part of the CIA's mind control operations. But the court expressed serious misgivings about its decision and said that it was "quite possible" that Ritchie was telling the truth and that the CIA had dosed him with LSD.

Said Judge Alex Kozinski, "This is a troubling case. If Ritchie's claims are indeed true, he has paid a terrible price in the name of national security."

One surprise witness who testified on Ritchie's behalf was psychiatrist Dr. James S. Ketchum. Ketchum, before testifying, interviewed Ritchie for six hours. Then he reviewed all of the case files, researched the effects of LSD, and concluded that the former federal marshal had been the victim of "a covertly administered dose of either LSD or an LSD-like substance."

Government and CIA attorneys, not the least happy with Ketchum's involvement in the case, argued that Ritchie was lying and had never been given LSD by anyone. They accused him of concocting his story in order to gain financial reward and publicity. One government lawyer said that Ritchie gleaned some of his story from the 1997 Mel Gibson film, *Conspiracy Theory*.

As Dr. Ketchum recounts:

> I spent two-and-a-half days on the witness stand, mostly answering questions from CIA lawyers. Ultimately the outcome was not favorable, unfortunately. The judge [there were three judges] didn't feel convinced, and neither did the Appeals court. The judge said, 'If you can explain this man's criminal behavior with LSD, then I suppose you could blame anyone's criminal behavior on LSD.' And this really wasn't very logical and didn't fit the facts, but that's how it ended up. It was a rather unhappy ending to an unhappy story.

Dr. Ketchum was very familiar with the effects of LSD and other hallucinogens. In 1961, the Army's Edgewood Arsenal had hired him as a research psychiatrist. Two years later he became chief of Edgewood's Psychopharmacology Branch. In 1966 he was acting chief of clinical research, and from 1968 to 1971, he was Chief of Clinical Research. Edgewood Arsenal, under Ketchum's guidance, conducted numerous experiments with LSD, BZ, and other powerful drugs. Ketchum described his work at Edgewood:

> When I arrived [at Edgewood Arsenal], the LSD program was just in its nascence. There had been some work done by others there with LSD, but they had never had a psychiatrist. And they'd run into a few problems that made them think they ought to have one. So I was given pretty much a free hand over the next few years to develop a program that would be safe and also provide the information that was being sought, not only about LSD but about drugs like BZ, and others....
>
> I watched a number of people—actually, more than a hundred—going through the experience of having BZ, which is a long-acting atropine type compound. It produces delirium if given in sufficient dose.

Half-a-milligram is sufficient in the case of BZ, as compared with about 10 milligrams of atropine....

People [under the effects of LSD] generally know that their [hallucinations] are not real, but produced by the drug. Whereas with BZ, the individual becomes delirious, and in that state is unable to distinguish fantasy from reality, and may see, for instance, strips of bacon along the edge of the floor.

Critics of the Army's LSD experiments at Edgewood Arsenal, which involved, according to military reports, thousands of subjects, many unwitting, claim that the program was disorganized and not known to be very safe. Follow-up studies performed by the Army revealed a large number of subjects with ongoing psychological problems stemming from having been given LSD, BZ, or other drugs. No long-term follow-up studies were ever conducted.

BOOK THREE
Secret History

1

August 1963
CIA Headquarters, Washington, D.C.

Lyman Kirkpatrick, replaced in 1961 by John S. Earman as the CIA's Inspector General, is now, in 1963, the Agency's Executive Director. Kirkpatrick is preparing for a trip overseas when he is summoned to the DDCI's office. The Agency's DDCI is now General Marshall Carter; its DCI is John Alex McCone, former chairman of the Atomic Energy Commission. Allen Dulles and Charles Cabell are gone, having been dismissed by President Kennedy because of the disastrous Bay of Pigs invasion of Cuba.

DDCI General Carter, a former special assistant to the Secretary of Defense, wants to speak to Kirkpatrick about a recently completed Inspector General report on TSS activities. As Kirkpatrick sits down with Carter, the general asks what Kirkpatrick knows about the MKULTRA program, its nearly 150 subprojects, and rumors about the death of an unnamed Army scientist somehow tied to the program.

Kirkpatrick's replacement, John Earman, who had previously worked alongside Boris Pash on Operation Bloodstone — a U.S. State Department program that recruited Soviet émigrés and Nazi collaborators to America — had been conducting a routine review of TSS programs when he came across several financial documents referring to "safe houses" in New York and San Francisco. What were these domestic safe houses used for? Earman had asked Sidney Gottlieb, who was now head of Technical Services Division (TSD), formerly the Technical Services Section.

They're apartments we rent, Gottlieb replied.

Used for what? Earman insisted.

Drug testing, Gottlieb said.

Drug testing on whom? Earman asked.

Gottlieb hesitated before answering. Testing on a broad range of people, he said, all of them unwitting.

American citizens? Earman pressed.

Yes, Dulles approved the program years ago, Gottlieb explained. It's all well documented in our files.

Earman had been stunned by Gottlieb's answers. He immediately went to Gottlieb's superior, Richard Helms, now head of the Directorate of Plans, Wisner's old job. Did the DCI know about these safe houses used for drug experiments? he asked. Helms said he was not sure, but he would be happy to bring McCone up to date on TSD matters.

Earman had completed his review of TSD in early August, issuing his written report on August 14. In its introduction, the report sounded an alarm:

> Research in the manipulation of human behavior is considered by many authorities in medicine and related fields to be professionally unethical; therefore, the reputations of professional participants in the MKULTRA program are, on occasion, in jeopardy. Some MKULTRA activities raise questions of legality implicit in the original charter.

Moreover, the new IG noted, "The MKULTRA charter [as issued April 3, 1963 by DCI Dulles] provides only a brief presentation of the rationale of the authorized activities." Earman's report continued:

> A final phase of the testing of MKULTRA products places the rights and interests of U.S. citizens in jeopardy. Public disclosure of some aspects of MKULTRA activity would induce serious adverse reaction in U.S. public opinion, as well as stimulate offensive and defensive action in this field on the part of foreign intelligence services.

Earman pointed out that Dulles's original charter approving MKULTRA "exempted it from audit," and that the program "was eventually stabilized at 20 percent of TSD's annual research and development budget," breaking out to about $1,000,000 per year "over the ten-year history of the program." Also, over the past ten-years, MKULTRA had branched out into many additional "avenues to the control of human behavior," including "radiation, electro-shock, various fields of psychology, psychiatry, sociology, and anthropology, graphology, harassment substances, and paramilitary devices and materials." Some of these added program areas "do not appear to have been sufficiently sensitive to warrant waiver of normal Agency procedures for authorization and control," Earman wrote, and there was ample reason for "redefinition of the scope of MKULTRA."

As to reviewing the program, Earman stated he was especially concerned that MKULTRA record keeping be protected from "approach to inspection." He observed, "There are just two individuals in TSD who have full substantive knowledge of the program and most of that knowledge is unrecorded." Of even greater concern to the IG was to promote MKULTRA's use of "unwitting subjects in normal life settings" for testing drugs. As Earman pointed out in his repor:

> It was noted earlier that the capabilities of MKULTRA substances to produce disabling or discrediting effects or to increase the effectiveness of

interrogation of hostile subjects cannot be established solely through testing on volunteer populations. Reaction and attribution patterns are clearly affected when the testing is conducted in an atmosphere of confidence under skilled medical supervision.

Consequently, Earman continued, TSD had "entered into an informal arrangement with certain cleared and willing individuals in the Bureau of Narcotics in 1955 which provided for the release of MKULTRA materials for such testing as those individuals deemed desirable and feasible." (Earman, either intentionally or unintentionally, seemed to ignore that TSD actually established its arrangement with the Narcotics Bureau earlier, in 1953.) Earman next provided details of the CIA's arrangement with the FBN:

> The initial arrangement obtained the services of a senior representative of the Bureau and one of his assistants on the West Coast. A parallel arrangement was established on the East Coast in 1961. [Again, Earman, has his dates wrong, either because he had been misinformed by TSD officials or he was attempting to obscure any focus on the years 1952 through 1954 in New York City.] The Director of the Bureau {Harry Anslinger] has been briefed on the activity, but the Deputy Chief, TSD [Robert Lashbrook], who has guided MKULTRA from its inception, is of the opinion that the former would disclaim all knowledge and responsibility in the event of compromise.
>
> The MKULTRA program director [Sidney Gottlieb] has, in fact, provided close supervision of the testing program from the beginning and makes periodic visits to the sites....
>
> The particular advantage of these arrangements with the Bureau of Narcotics officials has been that test subjects could be sought and cultivated within the setting of narcotics control. Some subjects have been informers or members of suspect criminal elements from whom the Bureau has obtained results of operational value through the tests. On the other hand, the effectiveness on individuals at all social levels, high and low, Native American and foreign, is of great significance and testing has been performed on a variety of individuals within these categories.

At this juncture, Earman moved to the heart of his concerns:

> A significant limitation on the effectiveness of such testing is the infeasibility of performing scientific observations of results. The Bureau agents are not qualified scientific observers. Their subjects are seldom accessible beyond the first hours of the test. The testing may be useful in perfecting delivery techniques, and in identifying surface characteristics of onset, reaction, attribution, and side-effect. In a number of instances, however, the test subject has become ill for hours or days, including hospitalization in at least one case, and the agent could only follow-up by guarded

inquiry after the test subject's return to normal life. Possible sickness and attendant economic loss are inherent contingent effects of the testing.

The MKULTRA program officer stated that the objectives of covert testing concern the field of toxicology rather than medicine; further, that the program is not intended to harm test individuals, and that the medical consultation and assistance is obtained when appropriate through separate MKULTRA arrangements. The risk of compromise of the program through correct diagnosis of an illness by an unwitting medical specialist is regularly considered and is stated to be a governing factor in the decision to conduct the given test. The Bureau officials also maintain close working relations with local police authorities, which could be utilized to protect the activity in critical situations.

There have been several discussions in the public press in recent months on the use of certain MKULTRA-type drugs to influence human behavior. Broadly speaking, these have argued that research knowledge of possible adverse effects of such substances on human beings is inadequate, that some applications have done serious harm, and that professional researchers in medicine and psychiatry are split on the ethics of performing such research. Increasing public attention to this subject is to be expected.

Following analysis of MKULTRA's control system, dubbed MKDELTA, and defined by the IG as "the cryptonym" or "indicator covering policy and procedure for the use of biochemicals in clandestine operations," Earman again focused on his primary concerns:

The final stage of covert testing of materials on unwitting subjects is clearly the most sensitive aspect of MKULTRA. No effective cover story appears to be available. TSD officials state that responsibility for covert testing is transferred to the Bureau of Narcotics. Yet they also predict that the Chief of the Bureau would disclaim any knowledge of the activity. Present practice is to maintain no records of the planning and approval of test programs. The principal responsibility for the propriety of such testing rests with the MKULTRA program director and the Deputy Chief of TSD [Gottlieb]. The handling of test subjects in the last analysis rests with the Narcotics agent, working alone. Suppression of knowledge of critical results from the top TSD and CIA management is an inherent risk in these operations.

Final phase testing of MKULTRA substances or devices on unwitting subjects is recognized to be an activity of genuine importance in the development of some but not all MKULTRA products. Termination of such testing would have some, but an essentially indeterminate, effect on the development of operational capability in this field.

Of more critical significance, however, is the risk of serious damage to the Agency in the event of compromise of the true nature of this activity. As now performed under Bureau of Narcotics auspices, non-Agency personnel are necessarily fully witting of the true nature and significance of their assignments, and of the sponsorship of CIA. Compromise of this information intentionally or unwittingly by these individuals at some time in the future is a hazard that cannot be ruled out.

A test subject may on some occasion in the future correctly attribute the cause of his reaction and secure independent professional medical assistance in identifying the exact nature of the substance employed, and by whom. An extreme reaction to a test substance could lead to a Bureau request for cooperation from local authorities in suppressing information of the situation. This would in turn broaden the circle of individuals who possessed at least circumstantial evidence of the nature of the activity.

Weighing possible benefits of such testing against the risks of compromise and of resulting damage to CIA has led the Inspector General to recommend termination of this phase of the MKULTRA program. Existing checks and balances on the working level management of such testing do not afford the senior command of CIA adequate protection against the high risks involved.

On November 29, 1963, ten years to the day after Frank Olson's fatal fall, another meeting was held in DDCI General Marshall Carter's office to discuss the MKULTRA program, in light of Earman's completed report. General Carter, who had replaced Cabell, was a West Point graduate who had attended the National War College as a representative of the State Department. He had also served in a U.S. embassy overseas before being appointed DDCI in March 1962. When DCI McCone reached out for Carter to join him in Washington, D.C., the general was head of the Army's Air Defense Command at Fort Bliss, Texas.

In addition to General Carter and Earman, several other key figures attended the November 29th meeting: Richard Helms, Lyman Kirkpatrick, Dr. Ray Treichler, now TSD Chemical Branch chief, and Sidney Gottlieb. A CIA memorandum summarized its purpose: "The main thrust of the discussion was the testing of certain drugs on unwitting U.S. citizens." According to the memo, Gottlieb opened the meeting with a "brief history of the MKULTRA program which was not in any way at variance with the IG report of August 1963 on this subject." Gottlieb and Treichler, knowing that Earman was concerned about the risks of exposure of the experiments, "argued for the continuation of unwitting testing, using the principal point that controlled testing cannot be depended upon for accurate results." Apparently, Gottlieb's argument was somewhat effective because Earman, Kirkpatrick, and Carter did not counter argue that unwitting testing was objectionable on this count. The three also accepted "the necessity for having a 'stable of drugs' on the shelf'" and for the need for "continued research and development of drugs– not only for possible operational use but also to give CIA insight on the state of the art in this field and in particular to alert us to what the opposition is or might be expected to do in the R&D and employment of drugs."

Treichler diplomatically stated that TSD was not in "disagreement" with Earman on any of his findings "with the exception of the unwitting testing problem." General Carter jumped in and made it clear that he "understood the necessity for research and development of all types of drugs, to include the testing." However, the unwitting testing conducted in the domestic safe houses also troubled the DDCI. What about conducting tests on unwitting foreign nationals instead, Carter suggested.

Well, we considered that, Treichler said, but ruled it out after discussions with several senior chiefs of stations. "They thought it was too dangerous, and the lack of controlled facilities would be a big problem."

IG Earman did not comment on this, but later wrote he thought Treichler's comment about "the lack of controlled facilities" was an odd remark given that the CIA had very little actual control over George White's safe houses. From his review of the rented apartments, Earman could clearly see that CIA officers at best were on site only a few times a month despite frequent, sometimes daily, use.

After further discussion, the group agreed that the MKULTRA charter, as originally approved by Dulles, would be modified to conform to some of Earman's recommendations, that procedures for unwitting experiments would be reviewed by the Agency's Medical Office and selected consultants, and that if Helms wanted a continuation of unwitting experiments on U.S. citizens "to operationally prove out these drugs," perhaps DCI McCone would have to be consulted directly for his decision.

A few days later, Helms met with McCone, and the following day he informed Earman that the Director had no problems with the continuation of unwitting experiments on anyone. Earman responded that he still had serious concerns about the issue. The next day, he wrote a memorandum to McCone, expressing his concerns and recommending that the domestic safe houses be closed and testing on U.S. citizens end. McCone put off making a decision, and a year later, DDP Helms wrote to McCone and Carter reminding them "that our testing program which deals with unwitting persons has been in a stand down status for over one year." Meanwhile, he warned, "I am sure you are aware of...indications during the past year of an apparent Soviet aggressiveness in the field of covertly administered chemicals which are, to say the least, inexplicable and disturbing... Our positive operational capability to use drugs is diminishing,

Owing to a lack of realistic testing, we are approaching the point where the operational target itself becomes the test subject. With decreasing knowledge of the state of the art, we are less capable of staying up with the Soviet advances in this field. This in turn results in a waning capability on our part to restrain others in the intelligence community (such as the Department of Defense) from pursuing operations in this area." Despite that the Agency had "become unable to devise a better method of pursuing such a program than the one we have with the Narcotics Bureau which has been completely secure for over eight years and we have no answer to the moral issue," Helms recommended that the CIA "resume the testing program immediately" and "stop living with the illusion of a capability which is becoming minimal."

Despite Helms's recommendation to resume testing, McCone postponed taking any action. Eventually TSD on its own closed the California safe houses in 1965, and the New York safe house in 1966. It is unclear if Earman, McCone, or anyone else outside TSD, ever learned about the Washington, D.C. safe house or the one in Chicago used on occasion by Pierre Lafitte. Some Agency officials later reported that there were always rumors about other domestic safe houses in various cities, including New Orleans, Kansas City, and Las Vegas, but no documentation about them has ever been released by the CIA.

A July 1954 TSS memorandum concerning the Washington safe house reveals some of the considerations that went into selecting such facilities. The memo reads in part:

> The house itself should be of the brownstone row-house type having a basic area of no less than three floors, or possibly four.... It should be of sufficiently strong construction to accommodate at least two or three of the standard drawer-type safes together in any given area.... The house itself must not have janitor service, no doorman and no secretarial service.... The matter of 24-hour protection was discussed and it was agreed that this would be important. In this connection, it was felt that if it could be arranged properly, [redacted name] would reside in the house in the apartment on the top floor. All present agreed that girls living in the house would not be a good idea and a suitable watchman who resided in was not sound.

Presumably, the reference to "girls" was to the high priced call girls who were routinely used in the activities conducted at the safe house.

2

Who Was George Hunter White?

This is not only the story of my life; it is the story of a way of life, a policeman's way of life. A particular kind and vintage of policeman; a federal narcotic agent of the era that precedes the immediate present.... Morals and vital truths you'll have to draw for yourself, as separate dividends. As a former newspaperman I know better than to set down more than the what, the who, and the where. And the me. I wouldn't have changed a minute of it.

— George Hunter White, 1970

I don't dislike criminals. I have a lot of friends who are murderers. When I used to hang around with gangster types, I had very good times in their company.

— George Hunter White, 1971

Were Elmore Leonard and John Le Carre ever to conspire together to create a fictional character, it is likely that such a person would closely resemble George Hunter White. Brash and crude, urbane and articulate, White was a jumble of contradictions, an American original drawn from the hardscrabble streets of the Fifties, a decade whose sinister underbelly is frequently overshadowed by its languid, carefree reputation. White was as relaxed in the presence of the world's most notorious heroin dealers as he was with the nation's highest ranking crime fighters. With ease, he hobnobbed with hoodlums and princes, with politicians and pimps, with millionaires and skid row kings, with district attorneys and stone cold killers. White embodied the term "legend in his own time." He was one of those who could invoke in others equal measures of genuine respect and unabashed fear. A short, muscular man with an infectious grin that could instantly give way to a cold, menacing glare, White was revered among his peers for his relentless cunning, political wiliness, and surprisingly quick physical agility. Never one to mince words, at times he could be brutally frank, and at others, as one former colleague observed, "George could charm the hide off from a rabid dog." Former OSS research and development chief, Stanley Lovell, in 1963 said:

> There was never any officer in American uniform like Major White. He was roly-poly, his shirt progressing in wide loops from neck to trousers,

with tension on the buttons that seemed more than bearable. Behind his innocent, round face with the disarming smile was the most deadly and dedicated public servant I've ever met.

White's multi-faceted career spanned an unprecedented era of historical divergence. His early years as a cub reporter, immigration and border agent, and Army officer, best exemplify his idealism, his overriding sense of justice, and his loyalty to small town American values. As he matured and settled into his dual roles as lauded federal narcotics agent and surreptitious CIA contractor, his sub rosa existence darkened beneath clouds of Cold War paranoia and deception that hung over America. The America of White's heyday, the Fifties, was far from today's America. Television had yet to put its stranglehold on the American culture and psyche; comic books, dime novels, and noir films defined the man's man and real masculinity. George White fit the image everyone wanted and aspired to. He would have been a role model for every red-blooded American boy who wanted to stand up for truth, justice, and the American way, and to kick the hell out of the Commies and the Mafia creeps in the process. White was a cop, maybe even the cop's cop, the quintessential crime and dope buster. And in the Fifties, as any kid who grew up in those days knows, cops were there to help, they were your friends, someone to run to when your parents could not help or were not there. Or, at least, that is what every adult said back then.

George White received his earliest indoctrination into the art of clandestine operations in 1942 at the ominously named Camp X. Located on the north shore of Lake Ontario, between the Canadian towns of Oshawa and Whitby, the camp was the first paramilitary training school in North America. Established in December 1941, just one day before the Japanese attacked Pearl Harbor, the 270-acre site was operated by Britain's ultra-secret Special Operations Executive. SOE had been formed as a branch of MI-6 in July 1940, after Winston Churchill instructed his military advisors to counter Nazi blitzkrieg victories and "set Europe ablaze." SOE's first order of business was to recruit and train hundreds of secret agents, who would be responsible for advancing sabotage, subversion, and organized resistance against Axis occupied areas. Camp X, also called Project J and STS-103, offered its carefully selected students a full curriculum in the techniques of guerrilla warfare, covert action, and assassination. In his diary entry for February 28, 1942, just three days after he had arrived there, White referred to the Ontario site as "the school of murder and mayhem."

Training at Camp X was extremely rigorous. Recruits were routinely roused well before dawn to perform several hours of strenuous physical exercise before they were allowed a Spartan morning meal consisting of little more than a glass of milk and a hard roll. Then it was on to a full day of classes with instructions on subjects like "Close Combat," "Small and Concealed Weapons," and "Silent Killing." The camp featured a number of extremely difficult "infiltration courses," one of which featured a large swamp dubbed "Lake Oshawa" by SOE instructors; for more substantial water exercises, the frigid waters of Lake Ontario were only twenty minutes away. Camp X's training ethos was kept simple; it revolved around the mantra, "Kill or be killed." Several times a week, trainees would participate in group jiu jitsu training, led by their chief instructor, British Major William Ewart Fairbairn, during which words were chanted, in cadence with martial movements, for hours on end. Said one former student years later, "It turned our values upside down and we wondered about making a world fit for terrorists."

White was among the first group of Americans to be sent to Camp X. At the rank of captain in the newly formed Office of Strategic Services, White had been hand picked for training at the facility, along with eight other OSS officers, including Philip Strong, Louis Cohen, and Kenneth Downs. On a snowy, gray, February morning, White and his companions stepped from the overnight train to Toronto into a waiting staff car that took them to the camp.

The OSS, first organized in 1941 by President Franklin Roosevelt and General William Donovan, was the nation's premiere intelligence agency, precursor to the CIA. Col. Garland H. Williams, of the OSS's Special Activities Division, had known White for several years, having been his supervisor and mentor at the Federal Bureau of Narcotics' New York office before the war. He had issued White's orders for the trip north to Camp X.

At five-feet-seven inches tall, White was a stubby but brawny young man. In school White had shunned conventional team sports in favor of aquatics, and he was an especially good free-style swimmer, winning many competitive events. Often, as a teenager, while visiting relatives near Sausalito's Stinson Beach, White would alarm his family by crashing into the cold surf and swimming several miles into shark-infested waters and treacherous currents. Throughout his life, White made it a near religious practice to take long, solo swims in whatever waters were available. He was heedless of hidden dangers. Before and after the war, he was well known among New York law enforcement officials for his impromptu swims in the dank waters of Manhattan's Hudson River. It was almost as if each watery excursion were an exercise in regeneration, a baptismal cleaning of sorts. By the time White reached his early twenties, his most distinguishing features were his disarming blue-eyes and broad, muscular, swimmer's shoulders, which one colleague described "like those of an ox."

Born in Los Angles on June 22, 1908, White had moved with his family to Alhambra, California, where his father was an official with Bank of America. An accomplished chess player, White's father was elected mayor of Alhambra on a reformist ticket. Most likely, young George inherited his enthusiasm for fighting crime and corruption from his father. As a student, White was above average and well known as someone "who would always stick up for the little guy" and never tolerate dishonesty. He was also known for having big plans for his life. In his later years, he recalled, "When I was a small boy, all the kids on my block wanted to be railroad engineers, policemen, firemen, lifeguards, soldiers, cowboys or spies. Well, I've never been a railroad engineer or cowboy, but I've managed all the rest."

White attended Oregon State College and then, in 1929, went to work as a newspaper reporter, first for the *San Francisco Bulletin* and then the *Los Angeles Evening Express*. One of his first assignments in LA was to help cover a story on mobster Jack Dragna. In the course of digging into background for the piece, he had occasion to meet a suave young hoodlum, recently arrived in LA from Boston, by the name of Johnny Rosselli (also known to local law enforcement officials by his real name, Filippo Sacco). Rosselli was doing his best to shed his Italian accent, and just beginning to run the high-life gauntlet with Hollywood molls, dolls, rising stars, fading and falling stars, and tough guys like Dragna. Throughout his dual FBN-CIA career, White's path and Rosselli's would cross frequently.

Soon after pursuing the Rosselli story, and while working on a series for the LA City News Service about gambling among Hollywood studio moguls, White realized that his prowess for infiltrating groups could be put to a more exciting and satisfying use. He attempted to join the notorious LA Narcotics Squad, but there were no openings. White is quoted as saying to squad director Captain Edward Chitwood, "Newspapering is all right, but it makes a bystander out of you. I want to get out on the field, where the game is going on." White quit journalism in 1931 when the Hearst conglomerate took over his Los Angeles employer. From 1932 to 1934, he worked in California for former Justice Department agent, Harold H. Dolley, a noted private detective and state law enforcement official. Dolley became White's early mentor and taught the twenty-two year old everything he knew about investigative work. Dolley was also responsible for having infamous West Coast "rope," or swindler, Iris Ford, privately tutor White in the intricacies of her trade. Following Dolley's sudden death in San Diego, White went to work for the U.S. Immigration Service's Border Patrol on August 30, 1934. In the final decade of his life, White described the Border Patrol as "a herding, harassing and alien-ejecting police force whose well-meaning but often short-tempered officers found it difficult to remember that their border-jumping subjects were human beings whose defections were not exactly heinous or vicious in nature."

White's first few months on border patrol were spent "ranch-checking, outwitting 'walk-arounds' at frontier roadblocks, and shaking down freight trains and hobo jungles." After seven months, given his investigative experience and ability to speak Spanish, he was assigned to the Patrol's Intelligence Unit, in Calexico, California. He worked undercover in several border towns and cities for nearly eighteen months, frequently coming in contact with federal narcotics agents, including Spencer Stafford, who was shot and killed by a corrupt, machine-gun toting local sheriff in 1935 in Post, Texas. It turns out that Stafford, and several other narcotics agents, had encouraged White to become a federal "dopebuster," and in late 1935, White took the entrance exam for employment with the Federal Narcotics Bureau. With assistance from a close friend of his father, U.S. Senator William Gibbs McAdoo, former Secretary of the Treasury under President Woodrow Wilson, White was hired in 1936. Thus began one of the most unique law enforcement and intelligence careers in U.S. history.

George White's rookie years with the Narcotics Bureau were shaky, at best. From the start, FBN director Harry Jacob Anslinger had serious reservations about his twenty-eight year old agent from California. Assigned initially to a series of rote jobs in the Midwest, White's performance was lackluster. The rookie found cities like St. Paul and Minneapolis dull and unsophisticated in sharp contrast to the more cosmopolitan West Coast areas he was accustomed to. In addition, the Bureau's preference for team operations came hard for the young agent who had acquired and honed his skills in solo fashion. White, by nature, was a loner who embraced responsibility and hard facts — qualities not always well received in any bureaucracy. He wanted to be on the field and in the game, yet he wanted to play by his own rules. Often, this conflict caused White to act indecisively. Early on, Anslinger mistakenly viewed White's hesitation as lack of initiative. In 1964, Anslinger wrote, "I was at first inclined to fire White for not displaying enough get-up-and-go." But Anslinger's attitude would change. Soon, he would come to keenly appreciate that in George White he had an agent who was nothing short of extraordinary.

After several months in the Midwest, White was given a temporary assignment in San Francisco. Excited about his return to home territory, the young agent was convinced his career was about to take off. He was wrong. In November 1936, only a week into an undercover assignment in the hardboiled Tenderloin district, White was taken for all his "buy" money by two street-wise con artists who promised him opium in return, and who then disappeared with the cash. White caught up with the men hours later at a wharf-side gin mill. When he confronted the two thugs with his badge and gun, one of the men grabbed White's weapon while the other knocked him to the floor. White pulled a small derringer from his pocket and shot one of the men, but the bullet bounced off the man's skull.

Anslinger was outraged by newspaper accounts of the incident and he banished White to an obscure assignment in Seattle, Washington, with a stern warning that his job was hanging by a thread. Unlike New York, Chicago, and Los Angeles, which were coveted duty sites for ambitious agents, Seattle was considered far off the path to promotion and glory. Nonetheless, when White arrived in the Emerald City in December 1936, he was determined to make the most of the assignment.

On December 12, after staking out a number of Skid Row locations, White observed a man selling opium out of the hollow rubber tip of a crutch he walked with. White quickly collared the man and offered him the choice of arrest or release in return for the identity of his supplier. The man gave up his supplier, Lum Soon Git, also known as Charlie Lum, a hatchet man, or assassin, with the infamous criminal wing of the Hip Sing Tong. White soon learned that Git, who had a long arrest record, was just a small-time middleman, but when White cornered the man and offered the same proposition as he had to the street dealer, Git shrewdly countered the offer with a proposal of his own: that he become a confidential informant in exchange for his freedom and "a few bucks thrown my way now and then." White was leery, but after interrogating the man at length he became convinced Lum could be an important asset for the FNB. White took the offer to his superior, J.B. Greeson, along with the enticing bait that Git had confided he could provide White access to a major West Coast dealer. White explained that he and Git had devised a plan whereby they would infiltrate the dealer's operation. Greeson, after consulting with Anslinger in Washington, D.C., reluctantly approved White's plan. We can only guess that perhaps Anslinger saw the scheme as a possible way to permanently shed his troublesome rookie. Given the dimensions of White's proposed operation, Anslinger and Greeson knew the plan was extremely risky. To date, no narcotics agent had been able to break through the wall of secrecy enclosing the Chinese syndicate.

Git was offering a major dealer named Chin Joo Hip, also known as the "King of Montana" and the "Old Man of Butte." Hip operated a labyrinthine narcotics, gambling, and prostitution empire out of Butte. Joo Hip's connections were far reaching and tied into major illicit concerns in Los Angeles, Chicago, Kansas City, Pittsburg, and New York. Lum Git informed White that Joo Hip's operation moved several hundred pounds of opium monthly across the United States. In early February 1937, White, under the pseudonym John Wilson, and Lum Git boarded a train bound for Montana.

Chin Joo Hip seemed to have stepped straight out of a Charlie Chan movie. Adorned in a long silken mandarin robe, and a drooping Fu Manchu mustache, the elderly man took White and Git to his home above the store. Here, White explained that he was acting as a go-between for a wealthy uncle on the West Coast who desired to purchase large amounts of opium and morphine. With great foresight, Git told the old man, "The world is changing rapidly and to rule out doing business with a man because of his race is to ignore markets of tremendous potential and wealth." But still Joo Hip was cautious, telling White and Lum that he could not sell anything directly to them. All of his drugs were obtained through a connection in New York that took his orders by coded wire, he explained, and then that connection would air mail the shipment under the guise of a legitimate mail-order business. Joo Hip's code word for morphine was "sugar," a pseudonym that White would occasionally employ fifteen years later for LSD.

White's dealings with Joo Hip soon took him and his informer Git to New York in hot pursuit of mail-order boss Jimmy Wong. Never having traveled east of the Mississippi before, White was enthralled with the added intrigue and bustle of New York. Operating out of a double room in the Times Square Hotel, with an adjoining room occupied by two FBN technical agents manning microphones and recording equipment, White brought a letter of introduction from Joo Hip, and was able to meet face-to-face with Wong. The young agent quickly learned that Wong's operation was far larger than previously thought, with outlets in nearly every major urban area on the East Coast.

Anslinger, duly impressed with the results of the investigation, assigned White several seasoned agents to assist in bringing Wong down. On November 19, 1937, after months of dealings and cross-country trips, the Narcotics Bureau moved on Wong. Over fifty people were arrested nationwide, with hundreds of pounds of drugs seized. George White's name and praises were sung in newspapers nationwide. Harry Anslinger called White to personally congratulate his new star agent and promote him to the Bureau's coveted Manhattan office, under the supervision of his top field agent, Garland Williams.

White's well-deserved new posting to the Big Apple fortuitously coincided with the heyday of organized crime in America. "The period is that of Luciano and Anastasia, Lepke and Costello and cement-garnished Hudson River interments for the abruptly deceased," as White once aptly described it. Within weeks, White was working closely with Garland Williams who had been promoted to district supervisor in New York in the mid-1930s and whose job it was to smash the many international drug cartels operating in the city. Historian John C. McWilliams tells us that Garland Williams "was likely the first agent to use dogs (German Shepherds and fox terriers) to sniff out drugs." White and Williams were racking up countless busts and, to Anslinger's pleasure, bringing glorious headlines for the FBN.

Then, World War II upset the enforcement bandwagon and both White and Williams were summoned to war-related duties. Williams, within a year, helped organize and became head of the Army's Counter Intelligence Corps. At about the same time, George White, at the request of FBN chief Harry Anslinger, joined the OSS.

White was sent to Camp X not only to be trained, but also to become a trainer himself, which he did when he was assigned in 1942 as Branch Chief of Schools and Training for the OSS Counter-Espionage Division in Washington, D.C. Subsequently, he became Deputy Chief of Counter-Espionage, or X-2, as it was commonly called. In his trainer role, White rotated among several secret sites, including Area B3, a 9,000-acre center hidden away in Maryland's Catoctin Mountain Park, a few miles from today's Camp David Presidential retreat. Another secret training site was known as Area A2, a 5,000-acre wooded site near Quantico, Virginia. "The Farm," located forty miles from Washington, D.C., was a third site. White's own training continued, as well. In May 1942, together with Garland Williams and Philip Strong, White took a brief break from his trainer's position to attend a six-week advanced commando and parachute school in Virginia.

Among White's first OSS students were several novice officers who would later become top CIA officials: Richard Helms, Frank Wisner, Jr., James Jesus Angelton, Lyman B. Kirkpatrick, Jr., Thomas Karmessines, and William Colby. Several other notable students were anthropologists Carlton S. Coon and Gregory Bateson, psychologist Dr. James A. Hamilton, future Federal Narcotics agent Howard Chappell, and Alfred M. Hubbard, an elusive and fascinating figure who arrived at OSS's Area B fresh from a stint in prison. Hubbard, as readers already know, would later become "the Johnny Appleseed of LSD." Michael Burke, who would also become a CIA employee and then a high profile executive who ran the New York Yankees and Madison Square Garden, was another of White's trainees in Maryland. In his 1984 memoir, *Outrageous Good Fortune*, Burke provides a telling glimpse into the OSS training regimen:

> All of us were in our twenties or early thirties, all a bit uncertain, masking edginess with silence, guarded because we had been individually admonished that our identity must be kept secret from every other student throughout the course....
>
> Classroom instructors taught us codes and ciphers, how to operate a W/T (wireless telegraphy) set, how to shadow a man or elude one tailing you, how to pick a lock, how to use a mini-camera. We were drilled in the cellular structure of an underground network, the correct use of couriers, cutouts, and letter drops. All the usual tradecraft.
>
> Outdoors, we were trained to strip, reassemble, and fire a .45 automatic pistol, a Thompson submachine gun, a Sten gun.... When we had mastered the guns, we moved on to simulated house-to-house fighting—day and night—blasting away at targets that popped up like ghosts in a fun house. We learned how to put together detonating caps, primer cord, and plastic explosives to blow up a bridge or a rail line; we learned close combat and knife fighting and wondered how much, if any, of this stuff we would ever use.

Without doubt, many OSS recruits were men cut from a different cloth than ordinary folks. They were men who were drawn to danger, who had little problem crossing moral lines, and who relished being part of an arcane group. R. Harris Smith, in his history of the OSS, quotes one of its officers as saying:

> We were working with an unusual type of individual. Many had natures that fed on danger and excitement. Their appetite for the unconventional and spectacular was far beyond the ordinary.

Dr. Henry Murray, OSS psychological warfare chief who later conducted secret CIA-funded experiments at Harvard in the 1950s, observed:

> The whole nature of the functions of OSS were particularly inviting to psychopathic characters; it involved sensation, intrigue, the idea of being a mysterious man with secret knowledge.

It was not long before George White's training skills were demanded at other and newer locations. The OSS training complex soon expanded to several additional locations in Maryland, including one that bordered Edgewood Arsenal, and another in Garret County, just a few miles away from Deep Creek Lake. There were others, including a converted estate in Fairfax, Virginia, and a West Coast commando center in San Clemente, California. In addition, several urban centers or "finishing schools" were established in New York City at 630 Fifth Avenue and at 55 West 42nd Street, with an adjunct branch in Long Island. Other "finishing schools," were operated in San Francisco and in the Hollywood section of Los Angeles. These schools focused primarily on imparting the skills of "urban terrorism," "partisan recruitment," and counterintelligence techniques. Here it is interesting to note, the OSS's location at 630 Fifth Avenue was the International Building in Rockefeller Center, which also served at that time as the headquarters of British intelligence in the United States.

Kermit Roosevelt, OSS chief historian, reveals in his declassified *War Report of the OSS*, that all OSS training "stressed from the beginning the importance of maintaining cover." Students at all its schools "were forbidden to disclose their real identities and lived under assumed names. At the same time, they were instructed to attempt to pierce the cover of their fellow students." Roosevelt explains:

> Intensive interrogation exercises of various types were carried on in attempts to force the student to break his assumed identity. In each of these the student was made familiar with the various techniques of interrogation and the importance of the most minute detail was stressed. The entire atmosphere at all training establishments was designed to prepare the trainees psychologically for the fact that the life of an agent is a constant and continuing gamble with detection.

In the same report, Roosevelt explained the basic concept of "compartmentalization" in intelligence matters, which he dubbed the "principle of insulation," as well as the need for, and functions of, "safe houses."

In his position as OSS training chief, Col. White demonstrated a pronounced flair for innovation. He designed several challenging field exercises that required individual students to develop their own cover stories, secure "appropriate cover credentials," and then attempt to penetrate a highly secured industrial establishment in one of four selected cities, Chicago, Baltimore, Pittsburgh, or Philadelphia. White's field exercises, in addition to providing training, served the added function of pointing up serious security weaknesses in the nation's defense plants.

White gained a reputation as a trainer extraordinaire. Enhancing that reputation was White's willingness to put his own special and lethal talents to practical use in the field. Charles Siragusa, one of White's OSS recruits whom he trained in both Maryland and New York, had also trained as a narcotics agent under

White's and Garland Williams' supervision in the FBN New York office. He would later describe White's teaching style:

> George had no patience with theory or textbook techniques. Everything he taught were things that he himself had actually performed in real situations. Sometimes the stuff he came up with was pretty damn scary.

Siragusa, a Sicilian-American who grew up in New York's notorious Lower East Side, fondly recalled OSS training in "jiu jitsu, dirty fighting, the handling of plastic explosives, and the use of other tools of sabotage." Ira "Ike" Feldman, who would work closely with White during the Cold War years, also appreciated White's skills for their practical value. "If he said something worked you could go to the bank with it," said Feldman. "George could kill a man a hundred different ways and still have some left over."

With his ever-widening reputation, it was only natural that White's skills would be in demand beyond the training centers. In April 1943, at the urging of his chief scientist, Stanley P. Lovell, General Donovan summoned White to his Washington, D.C. office, where he and Lovell gave him a thorough briefing on OSS efforts to develop a "truth drug."

Stanley Lovell was a wealthy Boston scientist and business executive in the chemical industry who had joined the war effort in early 1942 when he was recruited to the staff of the National Defense Research Committee. After meeting with NRDC directors Drs. Vannevar Bush and H. Marshall Chadwell, Lovell was granted a high-level security clearance and put to work as a science advisor with the Quartermaster Corps. Lovell quickly established himself as extremely talented and ingenious, given to devising unique and lethal inventions. In his 1970 study of the Donovan OSS years, Corey Ford referred to Lovell as "a sunny little nihilist" who took great delight in developing "diabolical devices."

During one of his first Quartermaster Corps assignments, Lovell's unusual talents were brought to the attention of William Donovan. Once again, Lovell was recruited, this time by Donovan himself, who brazenly informed Lovell at their first meeting that he had decided to make the Boston businessman "my Professor Moriarty," the name of Sherlock Holmes' nefarious nemesis. Lovell replied to the imposing Donovan, "Do I look to be as evil a character as Conan Doyle made him in his stories?" To which Donovan sharply retorted, "I don't give a damn how you look. I need every subtle device and every underhanded trick to use against the Germans and Japanese.... You will have to invent all of them, Lovell, because you're going to be my man."

One of Lovell's first official acts for OSS in his role as chief scientist in charge of research and development was to bring in George White, who was then assistant director of counter-espionage training. White, whom Lovell had not yet met, had been highly recommended by Dr. Lawrence S. Kubie, a neurophysiologist and psychoanalyst associated with New York Psychoanalytic Institute. Kubie had earlier collaborated with White on a series of highly unusual, unethical and secret drug experiments using penitentiary prisoners and mental patients in state operated facilities in New York and Baltimore. Kubie was a special psychiatric consultant to the U.S. Army's Chemical Corps and the Counterintelligence Corp (CIC) at Fort Holabird, where he was testing the effects of certain drugs on the ability of POWs "to withstand intense interrogation and not divulge vital information." During this time, he was in contact with Dr. Harold A. Abramson, also an OSS officer, whom he had known from Columbia University and the Rockefeller Institute, where Kubie served as a researcher and National Research Council fellow. Kubie was also a close associate of Dr. Frank Fremont Smith, medical director of the Josiah Macy Jr. Foundation, which would soon serve as a front for the CIA's psychochemical experiments on unwitting persons. In a 1965 letter to Stanley Lovell, Kubie would remark that he had been "deeply involved" in the Army's G-2 drug experiments "with Anslinger, Adams, and White."

White's special skills were also demanded outside the United States, in the theater of war. In late 1943, the OSS faced a perplexing problem in India where Allied shipping relied on the port of Calcutta. OSS personnel overseeing the port noticed that the heaviest air bombardments coincided with peak shipment schedules and they surmised that a spy somewhere within the shipyards must be communicating schedules to the Japanese. But, OSS agents had been unable to identify who it was. With port losses mounting, Donovan dispatched George White, now a lieutenant colonel, to Calcutta. Disguised as a longshoreman by day, White studiously observed the commercial and social patterns of the port. At night, he frequented the harbor's many bars and brothels, intent on learning all that he could about the area. After several weeks of this, White had identified the spy, and prepared to act. A few days later, at about noon, on a crowded, harbor side street, White reportedly stepped from a dim alleyway and confronted an elderly, white-haired Chinese man who was hobbling along with the aid of a large wooden crutch and crooning softly to himself. To the shock of onlookers, White seized the man by his neck, threw him to the ground, knelt on his chest and yanked a wig from his head, revealing a far younger man. White then shot the stunned man twice in the head and calmly rose and vanished into the crowd.

The cinematic-like account of White's violent dispatch of the spy has been repeated often in words and print, never losing its shock value. However, the actual event itself strays some distance away from the widely spread legend and the truth. Make no mistake, White was reasonably certain that he had identified the spy, and the man was a Chinese resident of Calcutta, but the disguise and crutch were pure invention, and the setting of the event mostly fiction. The more accurate version is that after weeks of investigation, White had become fairly certain that the spy was a Chinese bootmaker who operated a small shop in the city's commerce center. After days and nights of steadfast surveillance,

White secreted himself in the man's shop early one morning, having prearranged for his subordinate on the assignment, Army Sergeant Frank Welch, to enter the shop shortly after it opened. The plan was that Welch would attempt "to skillfully extract information" from the man while White observed from his hiding place. But the plan failed to come off as expected. The shopkeeper, while "undergoing" what White later termed "some sensitive interchange" with Welch, apparently felt threatened and pulled a "long and very sharp knife." Thinking Welch was about to be stabbed, White, again in his own terms, "interfered terminally" with his revolver.

According to Stanley Lovell's abbreviated account of the killing, White's actions "caused a British-American incident comparable to the Boston massacre in reverse." Wrote Lovell, "I never knew what happened, precisely, but it was the head of the Japanese spy system [whom White killed], and when the air raids stopped the British apparently decided to forgive the unforgivable." Lovell's certainty that the murdered man "was the head of the Japanese spy system" is intriguing, given that White himself would write decades later that he was "never able to find out for sure whether or not the man was actually and definitely a spy."

On July 12, 1945, after the war was over in Europe, Colonel George White flew from Europe to New York City for three days of merrymaking with Garland Williams and then met with Commissioner Anslinger in Washington to discuss White's return to narcotics work. Within weeks, White was discharged from the OSS and Army and headed for work as the Narcotics Bureau's branch chief in Chicago.

White was soon back in the thick of things, meeting with Santo Trafficante, Sr. in Miami on September 3, 1945. Head of a lucrative Havana-based gambling, narcotics, and prostitution empire, Trafficante, Sr. was a close associate of Meyer Lansky. The elder Trafficante, from his Tampa, Florida base, oversaw Lansky's expansive criminal and narcotics operations, as well as operating, with help from his son, Santo, Jr., a number of his own lucrative gambling casinos, hotels, and brothels in Cuba. (Santo, Jr., as readers shall learn, would go on in the 1960s to conspire with the CIA to assassinate Fidel Castro by using exotic poisons manufactured in the Camp Detrick laboratory that Frank Olson had toiled in seven years earlier.) White's meeting would be the first of many unexplained encounters with the Trafficante's over the next ten years.

Around the same time that he met with Trafficante, Sr., White made additional excursions to visit several other Mafia chieftains. While the reasons for these visits are not revealed in any FBN documents or in White's copious date book entries, it is certainly interesting to note that all of the mobsters he met with would soon become confidential informants for the CIA and participate in Agency-initiated assassination schemes.

Who Was Garland Williams?

Following his September 1945 meeting with Trafficante, White again met with Garland Williams, still on active duty with the Army, in New York. As noted, Williams had been White's supervisor and mentor in the Bureau's New York office. Williams' own career with the FBN had begun in 1926 when he worked under Anslinger for the U.S. Treasury Department's Division of Foreign Control, or, as it was popularly known, the Prohibition Unit. The unit's mission was to stem the flow of illegal alcohol into the U.S. from foreign ports. Anslinger later recounted that he had delivered a particularly critical assignment to Williams over the phone, reaching him in New Orleans, where Williams lived for a number of years. Anslinger had told him, "Here's your list of targets. I expect you to break every one of these gangs. Ask for whatever you need and we'll get it for you."

Anslinger's list featured a number of well-known, vicious mobsters, including Louis "Lepke" Buchalter, Albert Anastasia, and Jacob "Gurrah" Shapiro, all major players in the notorious 107th Street Gang. Buchalter and Shapiro have achieved near mythical status in crime annals as the twisted minds behind "Murder, Inc.," also known as the "Extermination Department." These two monikers described the nationwide crime syndicate that was responsible, throughout the 1940s and early 1950s, for killing over one thousand persons. One of the most widely recounted of these murders was that of Abe "Kid Twist" Reles. A teetotaling, lisping killer who specialized in stranglings for the syndicate, Reles agreed to testify against Buchalter and Anastasia, and was placed under protective custody in the "squealers suite" at the Half Moon Hotel in Coney Island, New York. On November 12, 1942, under the supposedly watchful eyes of at least five police officers, Reles "fell" from an opened sixth floor hotel window to his death. A few weeks earlier, he had told the Manhattan district attorney: "You don't know those bastards like I do. Anywhere in the world, they'll find me, if I was on the outside. Anywhere in the world. And they'd knock me off."

Also on Williams' list was August Del Grazio, a smooth-talking, Lower East Side operator, whom readers have already encountered, and who had strong ties to Lucky Luciano. "Little Augie," as Del Grazio was nicknamed (not to be confused with fellow gangsters "Little Augie" Orgen, "Little Augie" Carfano, or "Little Augie" Pisano), was a drug smuggler of large repute in the 1930s. He worked closely with notorious Greek narcotics dealers living in France, who specialized in purchasing large amounts of legally manufactured morphine and heroin from Paris and Berlin-based pharmaceutical firms for illegal exportation to the United States. Indeed, here it should be underscored that the vast majority of heroin and morphine shipments that entered the United States in the 1930s were obtained from legally operated pharmaceutical companies. In his brilliant study, *Space, Time and Organized Crime*, Dr. Alan A. Block, informs us:

At the beginning of this period, the illicit trade in refined narcotics depended to a large extent on diverting legally manufactured narcotics. Organized criminals were typically located at the tag end of the drug-manufacturing and marketing process.

During the 1930s and 1940s, the majority of legal drug factories and pharmaceutical houses were located in Germany, France, and Switzerland, including such companies as Merck, Hoffman La Roche, A.G., I.G. Farben, and Sandoz, all major suppliers of morphine, heroin, cocaine, and dilaudide. As Block describes it, "While legal shipments went out the front doors of these firms, countless crates of drugs earmarked for illicit trafficking were going out the back doors. It was a highly lucrative operation for many criminals at the time." It was also quite lucrative for the pharmaceutical companies.

Like subordinates George White and Charles Siragusa, Williams would gravitate from the world of pursuing gangsters and illegal drug traffickers to the world of deep intelligence. Williams' baptism into the clandestine world occurred in June 1940, when as a reserve officer at the rank of colonel, he was reactivated for wartime duty and made chief of the resurrected Corps of Intelligence Police (CIP), part of the Army's Military Intelligence Division. The CIP, forerunner to the Army's better known Counter Intelligence Corps, originated in 1917, and at its peak operated with 250 agents. Its mission was to serve as a secret domestic intelligence group that spied on German-Americans and infiltrated groups suspected of subversive activities. It especially targeted the activities of suspected "Reds," labor unions like the International Workers of the World, groups of Socialists, and some African-Americans, about whom it charged, "At the bottom of the negro unrest German influence is unquestionable."

The CIP also served as a special security group for the American Expeditionary Force in France. Col. Ralph H. Van Deman, who earned the title "Father of American Military Intelligence," had initially wanted to recruit CIP agents who possessed "outstanding personal character, military aptitude, fluent linguistic ability in French and German, social poise and diplomatic manner." Informed by veteran recruiters, "There ain't no such animal," Van Deman had to settle instead for more flexible standards. His initial group of recruits consisted of "a former felon, a French deserter, a pro-German, a mentally unbalanced individual," a Communist who had done hard time for "demonstrations against the property of John D. Rockefeller," several "morons," "a sharp Creole," a "very shrewd Hebrew," "a coterie of Harvard men," and "an Englishman, with all characteristics appended."

On October 25, 1917, just as this motley band set foot on French soil, U.S. Marines arrested them because of their suspicious appearance. Among the rag tag group was a French teenager from Louisiana (perhaps younger than sixteen, and his nationality remains in dispute) who would later work in New York under the name Jean-Pierre Lafitte, on assignments for George White and Garland Williams.

Following World War I, the CIP nearly slid into oblivion. In 1940, the outfit resurged with the outbreak of a new war in Europe, and the Army scrambled to staff it with qualified men. In late 1940, Garland Williams was detailed from the Narcotics Bureau to the CIP, the first of many FBN agents assigned to intelligence posts by Commissioner Harry Anslinger. Anslinger's stated objective was "better overall coordination of clandestine domestic activities between the Narcotics Bureau and military intelligence." Here it should be pointed out that Anslinger was no neophyte to the craft of intelligence. In 1918, during World War I, he had worked for a little-known secret intelligence office within the U.S. State Department and served as a spy within the entourage of Kaiser Wilhelm II. In 1921, according to his resume, he "directed undercover work in conjunction with the British Intelligence Service on the Bolshevik movement in Europe." Later, beginning in 1922, he served as American Consul in Germany, Venezuela, and the Bahamas.

Williams had trained for his CIP assignment at the FBI school in Quantico, Virginia, and subsequently had additional counterinsurgency schooling at a CIP center in Chicago. When Williams was promoted to head the CIP a year later, in 1941, he quickly established additional operational training centers at secluded military bases in and around Washington, D.C. These included Maryland's Fort Holabird, Fort Mead, Fort Belvoir, and Camp Ritchie, and Virginia's Fort Hunt. Situated less than forty miles away from what would soon become the Army's biological warfare center, Camp Detrick, Camp Ritchie specialized in training interpreters and POW interrogators. At the time, the majority of Army intelligence officers who spoke a foreign language were sent to Camp Ritchie.

With his strong undercover narcotics background, it is not surprising that Williams' overall training scheme for the CIP featured a number of exercises that centered on harbor and industrial security, particularly in New York City and Baltimore, at secretly selected office buildings and large hotels. Included in the latter were New York's Rockefeller Center, the Belmont Plaza Hotel, and the stately Pennsylvania Hotel (across from Penn Station), renamed after the war, the Statler Hotel.

Much of this activity occurred after Williams had become OSS Director of Special Training, again at Anslinger's request. At that time, all the training programs for military intelligence, the OSS, FBI, Secret Service, and FBN were carried out jointly. They sometimes involved FBN agents other than Williams, particularly Charles Siragusa and Jean-Pierre Lafitte.

In the early 1940's, Pierre Lafitte (he rarely used the name Jean, and was often referred to as "the Pirate" or "the Ghost") was enrolled by Williams for nearly six months at Camp Ritchie's Military Intelligence Training Center, located near today's Camp David. Lafitte had remained in Europe following World War I and, under a number of aliases, had worked at a variety of jobs, legal and illegal, ranging from sous chef to drug courier. It is doubtful that Williams had any clue that Lafitte had joined, and then deserted, the French Foreign Legion in the 1930s, and that he had participated in a number of criminal enterprises in Marseilles, France in the late 1930s.

At Camp Ritchie, Lafitte was considered an expert in "close quarter infiltration, disguise, and silent killing." He was also sought after because of his fluency in French, Italian, and German, having mastered the latter during his novice years with CIP in Europe during World War I. His multi-lingual talents surely must have assisted in possible interrogation situations. Following the end of World War II, Lafitte left his duties at Camp Ritchie and promptly headed to the intrigues of post-war Europe.

In Europe, Lafitte tried to reconnect with his former associate Francois Spirito, but Spirito had fled France after the war because he was wanted for, among other things, murder and collaboration with the Nazis. Lafitte was told that Spirito was actually hiding out in Boston, Massachusetts with his sister, who was married to a prominent physician.

Deciding to make the most of his time, Lafitte traveled to Paris in search of Spirito's associates, including another Frenchman and Nazi collaborator, Joseph Orsini. Orsini, it turned out, had also fled France for the United States, where he had established ties with major heroin suppliers. Lafitte decided to return to New York, however, without having consummated any drug dealings.

Returning to New York, Lafitte contacted Garland Williams, who had just returned to the Narcotics Bureau from war-torn Korea where he had served with the Army's 525th Military Intelligence Service Group that supervised POW interrogation teams in Korea. Earlier, at the end of World War II, Williams had headed a covert interrogation unit assigned to Heidelberg, Germany.

GEORGE WHITE AND THE CIA

On January 22, 1949, George White made national headlines again, after he kicked open the door to Room 203 of San Francisco's Mark Twain Hotel and arrested legendary jazz singer Billie Holiday for possession of opium. Holiday was in the Golden Gate City for a sold-out, month-long engagement at Joe Turner's renowned Café Society Uptown in the Fillmore district. Arrested at the same time with Holiday was her manager, John Levy, a brilliant jazz bassist and part owner of a New York nightclub.

White claimed that as he entered Holiday's room, accompanied by a San Francisco police detective, he saw the singer, clad in only a nightgown, run into the bathroom clutching a small dark bottle. Chasing across the room, he grabbed the singer just as she smashed the bottle on the open toilet bowl. He then dragged her back into the bedroom, where he ordered her and Levy to get dressed for a trip downtown to police headquarters for booking. There, the two posted $1,000 bail and were released pending trial. The next day a chemical analysis of glass fragments from the broken bottle revealed that it had contained opium.

Two weeks later, Holiday was indicted by a Grand Jury for violation of local drug laws. Levy, to everyone's surprise, was not indicted. White, who also claimed to be surprised, told reporters, "Levy to us is a nothing guy." In court, he elaborated on this, stating: "Levy was a minor pimp and opium user. I only wanted him as an informer. I thought he was a smart man who'd do anything he could to extricate himself from trouble...As pimps go, on a scale of ten, I'd give him possibly seven...I wouldn't have pegged him as a pimp if I hadn't known, any more than I could tag a high-class prostitute. No 'P' on his forehead."

In court, Holiday's attorney Jake Ehrlich made mince meat of the local District Attorney, and Holiday was found not guilty, but not before White and Ehrlich locked horns. Ehrlich claimed that the raid had been made with the assistance of a well-placed informer, implying that Holiday's manager, John Levy, was that informer.

White denied that any informer had been used in the case.

"Oh," shot back Ehrlich, "I know you are holy and righteous and never make a mistake."

White simply glared at the attorney.

It is fascinating to note that before Holiday went on trial, the blues singer had been sent to psychologist Dr. James A. Hamilton, White's former OSS truth drug confederate. Hamilton says that White referred Holiday to him because "he sort of felt from the other side that he would like to help." Explained Hamilton, "The reason for doing this kind of thing was that she was royalty, we thought— I thought, and I think George White thought. He did bust her, but why else would George get me, a really tough person to have? I can tell you why, because George is all cop, a cop with a tough exterior but with a heart of gold, so he got me, and this whole thing was done— not with his connivance, because he wouldn't connive, but putting me with Jake Ehrlich— that's as far as he could go as a cop to stack the case against himself. So that's what happened there."

On Holiday's confinement at Twin Pines, Hamilton said, "She felt that in order to get by in confinement she had to have ample quantities of booze, and as I remember she had a mixture of crème de menthe and brandy which amounted to nine ounces a day... She took command of that hospital. She set the hours that she would eat, and she had her drinks when she wanted them, fixed when she wanted them, I mean a psychiatric hospital cook doesn't usually act as a bartender."

From the moment he left the OSS in 1945, White had desperately wanted to continue his clandestine intelligence career as an employee for the just forming CIA, and he had made this known. But it was not to be. George was simply not a good fit for what he bitterly termed, "that gaggle of ivy-league, lawyer-types who wouldn't know a real spy if they tripped over one in broad daylight." When Sidney Gottlieb appeared with his proposal that White become a consultant to the TSS Chemical Branch, White considered the offer a godsend.

In 1952, while approval of White's MKULTRA consultant contract dragged on for several months past its expected date, he angrily complained to Garland Williams, "It was only last month that I got cleared. I then learned that a couple of crew-cut, pipe-smoking punks had either known me– or heard of me– during OSS days and had decided I was 'too rough' for their league and promptly blackballed me. It was only when my sponsors discovered the root of the trouble they were able to bypass the blockade. After all, fellas, I didn't go to Princeton."

White had earlier become especially perturbed in November 1952 when fellow narcotics agent and former Army Criminal Investigations Division officer, Henry L. Manfredi, was hired by the CIA to work in its Rome branch office. Especially grating was that White had been instrumental in establishing the office when he had been with the OSS, and he also resented the fact that Manfredi would go to work for the intelligence agency under the guise of being a Narcotics Bureau agent. Particularly revealing of Manfredi's true status was a letter discovered in the late-1980s by historian Dr. Alan A. Block. Written and signed in 1967 by Richard Helms, as director of "Secret Group One," the letter was addressed to the Secretary of the Treasury. Helms sought to bring to the Secretary's "personal attention the transfer of Mr. Henry L. Manfredi to a career position in Treasury's Bureau of Narcotics after more than fifteen years service in this Agency."

As it turned out, the fates eventually smiled upon White and he was rescued from his employment woes by freshman CIA official Dr. Sidney Gottlieb who recognized a sense of shared perspective with White. As Gottlieb described it,

> One of the first conversations we had revolved around his unhappiness with the Bureau and being rejected for regular CIA employment. I could relate to his bitterness because of my experience with being rejected for duty in the military, for reasons I was more than happy to overlook. It was the type of frustration that hit home.

Contrary to other published reports, White's first meeting with Gottlieb took place in Washington, D.C. in early May 1952, at a location that White termed in his date book "the CIA Quarters I building." That initial meeting had included both Gottlieb and his deputy, Robert Lashbrook. On May 27, White met in Boston with TSS chief Dr. Willis Gibbons and then again with Gottlieb on June 9 in New Haven, Connecticut, where White was wrapping up an especially difficult case. White had actually invited Gottlieb to come to New Haven to observe narcotics work up close. Gottlieb's flight into New York's Idlewild Airport on June 9 was met by Pierre Lafitte, White's "special employee" at the time.

On the drive to Connecticut, Gottlieb was intrigued to hear Lafitte tell about his involvement with the FBI's attempts to solve the January 1950 robbery of over $1.2 million from the headquarters of the Brinks armored car company in Boston, a heist that had dominated newspaper headlines nationwide for months. "He was a natural story teller," says Gottlieb, "able to make every detail come alive without invention...a fascinating person."

Gottlieb would discuss White's future with the CIA during his New Haven visit. Over dinner one night, White told Gottlieb and Lafitte about his work between 1950 and 1951 as special investigator assigned to the U.S. Senate Special Committee to Investigate Crime in Interstate Commerce, chaired by Senator Estes Kefauver, a Democrat from Tennessee and a close friend of Narcotics Commissioner Harry Anslinger. As soon as the committee was authorized, Anslinger had assigned two of his most trusted agents, White and Charles Siragusa, to be its sole investigators. They would be attempting to establish the reach of organized crime and the Mafia, whose very existence was, at the time, seriously questioned by some elected officials on Capitol Hill and beyond.

During dinner, Gottlieb listened as White expounded on the ever widening and multifarious criminal holdings of mob-mastermind Meyer Lansky. White recounted the results of his grueling work for Kefauver's Committee, "that showed that the reach and grip of organized crime on America was beyond what anyone imagined." Nonetheless, Kefauver's Crime Committee had left the impression that it was unable to prove that the Mafia existed and that it was a serious force in international drug trafficking. During the committee's many televised public hearings, no names of known French and Corsican traffickers had even been mentioned.

Months later, White was again meeting with Gottlieb and also Lashbrook in New York when he introduced them to the former high-profile chief counsel of the Kefauver Crime Committee, Rudolph Halley, a close friend of White's. Halley, a child protégé who graduated from Columbia Law School at the age of fourteen, was now running on the Liberal ticket against Robert Wagner to become mayor of New York. Halley's campaign cry had been: "Clean up New York, sweep out crime, gangsters and Tammany Hall." It has long been rumored among former intelligence operatives that White may have dosed at least one of Halley's political foes with LSD and, judging from White's date books and correspondence, it appears certain that he and Halley may have indulged in LSD together on at least one occasion.

In addition to being close friends with George White, Halley was also close with former OSS director William Donovan and CIA and Camp Detrick consultant Stanley Lovell.

At the start of the Kefauver Crime Commission's work, both White and Halley had met privately with an unknown gangster named Jack Ruby, who had been asked to give the committee information on the mob's operations in Chicago. Halley later informed Kefauver, "Ruby is a syndicate lieutenant who has been sent to Dallas to serve as a liaison for the Chicago mobsters," and that "Ruby was the payoff man for the Dallas Police Department."

Following their Connecticut and New York meetings, White and Gottlieb met again on October 20 in Washington, D.C. That meeting, according to White's diary, was to "prepare cigs." Without doubt, "cigs" refers to cigarettes laced with the marijuana extract devised by Lovell's OSS scientists. Judging from subsequent entries in White's diary, the "cigs" were used in experiments involving twelve unwitting subjects that Gottlieb surreptitiously observed.

Ten days after their "cigs" meeting, White returned again to Washington, D.C. to report on his work with Gottlieb to a gathering of CIA officials, including James Angleton, Stanley Lovell, Willis Gibbons, Robert Lashbrook, and Col. James Drum. As a result of this presentation, the assembled CIA officers issued a formal recommendation to begin testing LSD on unwitting persons in New York. Later the same day, White made a notation in his appointment book that reads, "Call Anslinger re CIA, etc."

White's first official act under contract with the CIA was to establish a safe house in New York City. On May 14, 1953 he wrote in his diary: "Call Gottlieb re Barrow St.— he says rent at $215." As we now understand, this was a relatively easy task to accomplish. White simply renewed the lease on the Greenwich Village apartment at 81 Bedford Street that the Narcotics Bureau and CIA had already been using for interrogations, such as Giannini's. With the CIA's money, White simply rented an adjacent apartment on Barrow Street that conveniently allowed both units to be surreptitiously connected by a two-way mirror and a concealed doorway. White quickly went about decorating the new unit with French posters and exotic curios from around the world. Commented CIA psychologist John Gittinger who worked closely with White, "George had a real fondness for collecting strange objects." An elusive French businessman owned the building where the two safe house apartments were located, and he would occasionally bring pornographic items from Europe as gifts for White's expanding collection.

It seems that White also had a number of friends in the pornographic publishing business, including one John Alexander Scott Coutts, or "John Willie" as he was most popularly known. Willie ran a small publishing domain that included the pulp magazine, *Bizarre*, published for ten years between 1946 to 1956, containing nude and bondage artwork, and he wrote a graphic novel, *The Adventures of Sweet Gwendoline*.

White was also a close friend of pornographic and lesbian pulp fiction writer Gil Fox, author of over one hundred lurid and provocative titles. George and Albertine White lived just a few blocks away from Gil and Patricia Fox, and the couples socialized on a regular basis during the 1950s. It was Gil who introduced George to the work of John Willie, and Patricia who baptized Albertine in the "pleasures" of spanking and other sexual aberrations. Fox would tell writer Douglas Valentine in 2002, "George was into high heels. That was his major fetish.... He was playing out his sexual fantasies too. One time [Patricia] and I went with him to see his hooker girlfriend at a hotel. She tied him up and strapped him to the bed and whipped his ass. She had high heels on."

Several weeks after this, on November 28, 1952, exactly a year before Frank Olson died, White dosed Gil and Patricia Fox with LSD. Fox recalled that it was snowing that night and that the snowflakes on Cornelius Street where they had stopped their car "were red and green and blue— a thousand beautiful colors, and we were dancing in the street."

On May 21, 1953, the CIA formally designated White's safe house as MKUL-TRA Subproject 3. An Agency memorandum-for-the-record reads:

> Subproject 3 will involve the realistic testing of certain research and development items of interest. During the course of research and development it is sometimes found that certain very necessary experiments or tests are not suited to ordinary laboratory conditions. At the same time, it would be difficult, if not impossible, to conduct these as operational field tests. This project is designed to provide facilities to fill this intermediate requirement.

The document continues, with stunning candor:

> Ostensibly, the apartment is rented to one Morgan Hall; this is an alias used by George White for a number of years. When White uses this alias he assumes the cover of an "artist" and a 'seaman.' White, of course, is interested in narcotics and reputed to have contacts in the underworld and among seaman who are in or on the fringes of the narcotics business... for one reason or another, he is able to get these people to his apartment at 81 Bedford Street where he tries to elicit information.
>
> From time to time White gives drugs to these unaware individuals through drinks, cigarettes, and perhaps food. After [interviewing such individuals], White advises TSS as to what drug was administered and gives his judgment as to success attained.
>
> White is aware of TSS interest in specific drugs. However, TSS does not supply White with drugs and does not suggest which, if any, drugs are to be given to specific individuals. Procurement and use are White's decisions. On one occasion [Sidney Gottlieb] Chief, Chemical Division did take some LSD from Dr. Harold Abramson to White; this White could have gotten from Abramson directly.

Around this time, White, who always tended toward over consumption, began to drink, and on occasion, to drink excessively. His wife, Albertine, out of concern for his health, suggested that he take up a hobby "in order to take his mind off the pressures of his work" and "as a much needed diversion to better spending the down time he had with his extensive travel." In 1951 through 1954, it was not uncommon for White to be gone from home for weeks on end, often to locations in Ecuador, Peru, Cuba, Mexico, and France. As a hobby, White took up leatherwork and apparently made belts, wallets, purses, and small tote bags. His diary, over several months, is riddled with references to his "leather work" and various "leather projects." On August 3, 1954, he gave Gottlieb a hand-tooled belt with brass buckle as a birthday gift. The same year he proudly presented Albertine with a "beautiful multi-pocketed purse that he had worked on for over six months." Interesting and humorous to note, is that some writers have misconstrued White's hobby and "leather" diary notations as references to another nefarious, sadomasochistic MKULTRA project undertaken for the CIA.

White, at this point in his career, was gaining a reputation for occasional hard drinking in his off duty hours. Lafitte would later say of White, "He could consume unbelievable amounts of gin, yet show no indication of intoxication or impairment. He was a friend like no other, always there, like the Rock of Gibraltar. But he could be obstinate, about that there was never any doubt. The only discernable sign of his drinking was his increased stubbornness, which could put any bull to disgrace."

A few years before his death in 1975, George White sat down at his desk in Stinson Beach, California to write his autobiography. He had drafted a preamble and outlined twenty-five chapters when he fell seriously ill. Several months later, he passed away from cirrhosis of the liver. White died several months before the first revelations about Frank Olson's death and MKULTRA, and before a Congressional Committee began searching for him for interviews. Nowhere in his outlined autobiography, or in any of its draft chapters, did White allude to the CIA or to his years as an Agency contractor. Nowhere in any of its nearly sixty pages is the CIA mentioned in any context.

413

Jean Martin, aka Jean-Pierre Lafitte

Unpublished, Untitled Manuscript, n.d.*

The two men sit side by side in straight-backed wooden chairs watching the couple in the opposite bedroom through a large two-way mirror. On the floor beside them rests an RCA reel-to-reel tape recorder, its twin spools slowly, silently, revolving. A few feet away from the recorder, angled so as to eliminate glare and to capture everything in the opposite room, is a Kodak movie camera mounted on a tripod. The camera's chassis emits a low whirling sound. Mounted on the wall to the left of the camera are several curious items. There is a large hand-carved ivory opium pipe, a tachi sword, an OSS Smatchet blade, and a Burmese spirit mask. Beneath these items, thumb tacked to the plaster, are a dozen or so black and white photographs of nude couples engaged in various sexual acts.

From a room somewhere behind the men drifts the faint strains of music and a woman's sad voice. 'Here is a fruit for the crows to pluck, for the rain to gather, for the wind to suck, for the sun to rot, for a tree to drop, here is a strange and bitter crop....' One of the seated men, who wears a hand tooled leather holster on his belt holding a Smith and Weston .38, shifts his husky weight in his chair and says quietly to his companion, "She gets more attractive every time I see her."

The other man nods and says in an accented voice, "Molto bello." Unlike his partner, he is slight in frame. His sable hair is combed straight back on his head, his eyes dark, set squarely on a handsome, swarthy face. "What a waste of sin," says the man with the gun. "Yes," the other man agrees. "It will hit any second now." The man with the gun reaches down beneath his chair and picks up a bottle of Gibson's gin. He takes a deep pull from it, glances at his wristwatch, and says, "He's a tough son of a bitch." "That he is," says his companion. "But, look he is slipping now." In the opposite room, a slim, light haired man dressed in a sleeveless white undershirt and dark dress slacks lies half reclined on an unmade bed watching a shapely brunette wearing only a lacy brassiere, matching panties, and a garter belt fastened to sheer stockings. She is standing before the mirror's other side, pouring two small glasses, which rest atop a dresser, half full of scotch. As the woman turns and approaches the bed holding the drinks, the reclining man says, "I don't know if I need that." "One more won't hurt," says the woman.

"That other one hit me like a load of bricks," the man says. "You're not tired, are you?"

"No, no... it's not that," the man says, trying to sit upright with difficulty.

The woman hands him one of the drinks and sits on the edge of the bed, running her free hand gently up and down the man's back. Upright now, the man takes a sip from the glass. He leans forward, sets the glass on a nightstand, and lies back heavily on the bed. He stares up at the ceiling for a moment, an astonished look on his face. "See," the woman says, smiling seductively. "Just what the doctor ordered, wasn't it."

"Jesus," the man says a dazed look now on his face. He moans and begins absently rubbing his forehead.

"What's the matter, sweetheart?"

"I'm not sure. I feel really strange."

The woman leans over the man and places her mouth close to his ear. Her lips purse and lightly touch his lobe. She says, "You're not going to go to sleep on me now, are you?" But the man does not hear her. His eyes are now closed and he is oblivious to his surroundings.

"Like I said, sweetheart, just what the doctor ordered," the woman says.

She sits considering the unconscious man for a moment, and then turns and stares smiling into the large mirror.

*The date of Lafitte's manuscript is uncertain. It is the author's understanding that it was written sometime in the early-to-mid 1970s.

3

Who Was Pierre Lafitte?

Lafitte often works hand in glove with the FBI, but even that organiza-tion doesn't know the true story of his astounding background.
— James Phelan, 1956

Question: Let me ask you about a man named Jean-Pierre Lafitte; you may have known him by the name Jean-Pierre Martin. Do you recall him?

Gottlieb: I'm very encouraged that you've asked me about him...very encouraged.
— Author's interview with Sidney Gottlieb, 1999

I never wanted nor sought out any publicity; I wasn't interested in the spotlight. I had seen early in my life what the spotlight could do to a person. I only wanted to have a good life. I wanted to enjoy life to the fullest, to live a complete and happy life. Maybe, compared to others, I went about it differently, but I have no regrets. I've enjoyed my life tremendously.
— Pierre Lafitte, 1974

After Olsen's [sic] 'fall' from the hotel window, [Pierre Lafitte] left New York for a few weeks. He traveled to Florida's Gulf Coast and there stayed in a small cottage provided by [Santo] Trafficante [Jr.]. It may have been the only time Papa relaxed in years, although we later learned that he might have been in Havana for some of that time.
— Phen Lafitte, 2001

On November 13, 1952, just after daybreak, Monsignor James Willett, the pastor of St. Joseph's Cathedral in Bardstown, Kentucky, entered the rear door of his church, a class Grecian design built of stone and brick in 1819. Willett was stunned to discover that the cathedral had been robbed. Missing from its walls were nine large, framed paintings, including a masterpiece, *The Flaying of St. Bartholomew*, believed to have been painted by famous Neapolitan artist Mattia Preti, also known as Il Calabrese. Within days, the cathedral's robbery made headlines across the nation. It was assumed that the priceless paintings had been transported across state lines and therefore the FBI entered the case. Following nearly five months of no reported leads or developments in their investigation, in April, 1953, FBI agents arrested three people in Chicago: Norton I. Kretske, an attorney, Joseph DePietro, a deputy bailiff for the Municipal Court of Chicago, and a man identified only as Gus Manoletti.

The case went to trial on October 1, 1953. The first witness called by the assistant United States attorney was Monsignor Willett. The government's next witness caused a stir in the courtroom and provoked loud objections from defense attorneys. The witness answered to the name "Jean-Pierre Lafitte," but when he approached the stand, everyone could see that he was the person they knew as Gus Manoletti.

Lafitte was a confident and well-spoken witness. Dark-haired, slim, well dressed, he spoke with a very heavy accent—some said it was French, others said Italian. Lafitte appeared to be either in his late forties or early fifties, said he lived in San Diego, California and that he had been employed for the past three years as a special investigator for the Federal Bureau of Narcotics. Before that, he testified, for thirteen years he had been employed overseas on "special missions for the United States government." As to the Bardstown Cathedral case, he explained, he had been specifically assigned by the FBI in November 1952 to locate the stolen paintings. He had posed as a buyer for the art world, he testified, and, after months of undercover work, had purchased the stolen goods for $35,000 from Kretske and DePietro. When those two were caught in the act of selling the paintings to Lafitte, all three men had been arrested. Lafitte had been placed in the same cell with Kretske and DePietro, in hopes of gaining more evidence against them. When the two men were released on bail, Lafitte was also turned loose.

Since Lafitte was the government's star witness, attorneys for the defendants made concerted efforts to find out more about his background. Under cross examination, Lafitte, speaking with an accent "that made it impossible to understand him at times," according to newspaper accounts, did admit that he resided in New Orleans and not California. However, when he was asked to provide specifics about his work for the federal government, prosecutors objected. The judge sustained their objections, agreeing that the information, due to public interest, and perhaps national security concerns, should not be disclosed.

Defense attorneys were angered and frustrated by the rulings, and even local and federal law enforcement officials present at the trial were overheard asking one another who Jean-Pierre Lafitte was, what exactly had he done prior to this case, and what else did he do for the government, including the Federal Bureau of Narcotics. "Your honor," pleaded one defense attorney, "how can we adequately represent our clients if we are not allowed to at least know who Mr. Lafitte is?"

Who was Jean Pierre Lafitte? While researching this book, hardly a week went by without the question being asked, often many times over. How had Lafitte so successfully and all but completely escaped any public attention or scrutiny, yet at the same time had led an unbelievably adventurous and dangerous life? How did a man, touted by some of the world's most discerning palates and food critics, escape any notice even from esoteric circles with gastronomic interests? How could such a man — hired by alleged CIA operative and JFK assassination suspect Clay Shaw, who praised him as "the best chef in New Orleans" — elude serious scrutiny? How could a man who had risked life and limb to single-handedly capture one of America's most wanted murderers, have virtually no crime fighting reputation whatsoever?

How could a man who had traveled to every continent and numerous countries, under no fewer than forty-five aliases — often for purposes of swindling millions or to assist the assassination of people in extremely high-profile positions — not be known at least in some of those small, tight-lipped circles? Who was this obscure, mysterious character who had so skillfully trekked across history without leaving so much as a finger or foot print? Some of the answers to these questions, and many more, would take years to discover.

In 1952 a number of federal agencies, including the FBI, Federal Bureau of Narcotics, and CIA, had widely planted the cover story that Lafitte had first arrived illegally in the United States that year, from Europe, and that he had been promptly arrested and imprisoned. However, the truth about how Jean Pierre Lafitte first set foot on American soil is far more fascinating.

The name "Lafitte" belonged to two brothers, Pierre and Jean, born in 19th century France. The brothers were notorious and celebrated for pirating Spanish, French, and British ships in the Gulf of Mexico, looting cargo holds of vast booty that they sold in New Orleans' open air markets and bazaars. The brothers operated a livery stable as a front, and also engaged heavily in the slave trade, selling some captives at a dollar a pound to legendary Jim Bowie. While their exact birth dates and causes of death are subjects of debate, it is well established that the Lafitte brothers were urbane, well-read, multi-lingual "beau brummels" who were very much involved in espionage, serving as double-agents for Spain and America.

Throughout his life, our Jean-Pierre Lafitte, who generally used only the name Pierre, would claim that he was a direct descendant of the Lafitte brothers. On several occasions he claimed he had been born in 1902 or 1907 in the United States, the illegitimate son of a Louisiana madam who ran a string of brothels and carried him from parish to parish on her hip, supported by the holstered pistol she always carried. Later, some people who claimed to know Lafitte would say he had been born in Corsica, while others reported that he was a native of Belgium. According to Lafitte himself, when he was about seven years old, his mother's Louisiana business holdings had gone sour and she had left the United States with him and gone to France, where, after several months in Paris, she settled in Marseilles.

In the early 1900s, Marseilles was a thriving center of commerce on the Mediterranean Sea. Already one of the oldest and most culturally diverse cities in Europe, it was also France's undisputed capital of crime. By the 1930s, huge quantities of raw opium, transported to Marseilles from Turkey through Munich, Basel, and Strasbourg, were being transformed into heroin. The best heroin in the world, the best heroin money could buy, was in Marseilles. And there were tremendous profits in dealing heroin, tremendous recurring profits. Many Corsicans migrated there from their island homes a little over one hundred miles southeast of the port city. By the late 1960s, over 600,000 Corsicans would populate Marseilles.

Less than a year after settling in Marseilles, Lafitte's mother vanished. Later, Pierre would tell people she had abandoned him after she had returned from a trip to Shanghai with Pierre in tow. However, from sketchy French accounts, it appears that she was murdered, although her body was never found. Less than sympathetic relatives, who thought they had inherited a prepubescent servant, took in homeless Pierre. Not surprisingly, Lafitte ran away within a year, after "taking all that I could and then some more." The young boy survived for three years living on the streets and working in some of the many restaurant kitchens that operated in the city. Lafitte described it years later:

> For me it was common sense to seek out such work. I never had to worry about where my next meal was coming from, and the kitchens were always warm, dry and safe. That I would learn a skill which would be useful later in life never crossed my mind, but that is how I came to know my way around a kitchen so well.

Lafitte developed a real culinary talent and by the age of fourteen, after he had secured permanent living quarters on the floor above a notorious seaman's tavern, he was routinely called upon to fill in for errant and truant chefs. During his non-working hours, he laboriously honed his skills at larceny and other illicit craft. In the process, he encountered other boys his age, nearly all of whom were equally busy on the wrong side of the law. Among his closest companions were Francois Spirito, who had come to Marseilles from Naples, and Corsicans Paul Bonaventure Carbone, Antoine D'Agostino, and Joseph Orsini, later Spirito's lieutenant. As readers will discover, by the 1930s, Spirito and Carbone ruled the Marseilles underworld; they operated an international heroin network that reached to French Indochina, Egypt, Turkey, Greece, Germany, Yugoslavia, and South America. According to Lafitte himself, during his pre-war years in Marseilles, he briefly fell under the tutelage of Jean Voyatzis, a major international drug smuggler and "the greatest importer of manufactured Chinese opium into Europe." Lafitte's world at that time also included illicit traffickers like Elie Eliopoulos and August Del Grazio.

Sometime between 1936 and 1937, Lafitte decided to return to America. French authorities say that it was because he was wanted for desertion from the French Foreign Legion, in addition to several arrests for smuggling, and opium and heroin trafficking. Reportedly, Lafitte deserted the Legion "at least six times." He denied it. By the time Lafitte departed Europe for America, according to his own account, he "could fluently speak five languages, get by with another two or three, and pass without question or any suspicion as a citizen of any of a dozen countries. However, I never thought of myself as an imposter. I was a master impersonator."

The late 1930s found Lafitte traveling back and forth between New York City, Montreal, Boston, Paris and Marseilles. In the early 1940s, in France, he reportedly had dealings with Henri Déricourt, double agent extraordinaire, who sold drugs and black market goods for Francois Spirito. Déricourt was an accomplished pilot who, from 1951 through to his disappearance in Laos in 1962, flew loads of gold and heroin out of Indochina for Air Opium, operated by drug kingpin Bonaventure "Rock" Francisci. According to FBI files, Lafitte maintained contact with Déricourt even after setting up shop in the United States.

During World War II, Lafitte had somehow been able to avoid the draft, but, nonetheless he participated in many highly dangerous OSS operations in Nazi-occupied France and Belgium. Before his death in 1975, George White, who for decades adhered strictly to the FBI-CIA cover story about Lafitte's first coming to the U.S. in 1952, would write to former colleague Garland Williams about "how absolutely amazing it is that every one and their brother has swallowed hook-line-and-sinker the myth of Lafitte's arrival here... if I didn't know that he'd been around since before they invented iced tea I'd probably believe it myself."

In all actuality, White had known Lafitte since at least 1948, after the narcotics agent traveled to Marseilles from Istanbul to meet with American vice-consul Bill Camp about the burgeoning number of heroin processing laboratories sprouting up in the port city. Also attending the meeting with Camp was French Surete Nationale Narcotics Squad Inspector Edmund Bailleul, who would come to the United States in 1953 to work closely on a major case with White. During White's one-week stay in Marseilles, Bailleul and another French agent took him to Manoir, a small cafe in the Old Quarter of Marseilles, where the three men met with confidential informer Lafitte to discuss the Surete's efforts to apprehend Dominique Albertini, an underling to Corsican drug kingpin Paul Mondolini.

White and Lafitte hit it off in grand style, spending hours together, drinking and discussing Lafitte's strong interest in returning to New York City to open a restaurant there. The gathering turned out to be the beginning of a long association.

Lafitte did eventually move to New York City in 1950, but his initial efforts to establish a restaurant there failed; he returned to France before the year was out, but within months he was back to try again in New York. Eventually his attempts paid off and he opened his first of two under-financed and ill-fated restaurants. Said George White, "If it had been only the food that insured his success, he would have had the best place in New York. But, Pierre, of all people, wasn't always gracious in his dealings with the unions, the bottom-feeders working for the City, and the mob collectors, who had to have a piece of everything." White later claimed that Lafitte and his silent backers "torched [both restaurants] for the insurance."

In 1951 White reached out for Lafitte's help when fugitive Frenchman Joseph Orsini was arrested in New York City for dealing heroin. Orsini, also wanted in France for collaboration with the Nazis, had known Lafitte from their days growing up together in Marseilles. Orsini had honed his drug trafficking skills in pre-war Europe under the tutelage of kingpin dealer Antoine D'Agostino. After the war, Orsini had escaped a death sentence in France for his Nazi collaboration, and he fled to South America, then made his way to North America in 1947, along with notorious Marseilles dealer Francois Spirito.

In October 1950, a confidential informant told his FBN handlers that two Frenchmen in New York City named Joe Dornay and Francois Merle were dealing large amounts of heroin being smuggled into the United States and Canada from France. The two Frenchmen, claimed the informant, had been operating between Montreal and New York for about ten months, never transporting or selling less than two-to-four kilos of heroin at a time. Narcotics agents began searching for Dornay and Merle, names they were completely unfamiliar with, and that they soon concluded were aliases. After four frustrating months, agents received a tip that Dornay was living with a girlfriend in a Lower East Side apartment. The tip proved correct and Dornay, along with his vivacious female companion, was arrested in March 1951. FBN agents, led by Arthur Giuliani, found several false passports in the apartment and, under questioning, Dornay admitted that his real name was Joseph Orsini and that he had been born in 1903 in Bastian, Corsica. The short, dark-skinned, sleepy-eyed, balding man with a pencil thin-mustache shook his head slowly and told agents, "I guess you got me."

In April, Orsini was transferred to Ellis Island pending deportation proceedings. When he was placed in a cell there, he was surprised to find that his cellmate was Pierre Lafitte, whom he had known off-and-on for twenty-five years. According to FBN reports released years later, Lafitte was being held for an unspecified minor crime and was soon to be released. However, other confidential Bureau reports reveal that Lafitte, who was working undercover for the FBN, had been placed in the cell only minutes before Orsini's arrival. Following the expected greetings and exchange of news, Orsini, who had not seen Lafitte since the end of the war, asked his friend if he was interested in making some money.

"In here?" asked Lafitte.

"No, no, not in here. On the outside, once you get out."

"Sure," replied Lafitte. "I have to eat like everyone else."

"I have a way for you to make some very serious money."

"How so?"

"So much it would make your eyes pop out."

"Look," said Lafitte, playing along, "you got my interest. Everyone likes money. I'm no different. So how do I make some 'very serious money?'"

"Narcotics."

Lafitte raised his eyebrows, feigning surprise, and slowly nodded his interest.

Orsini then told his old friend about the elaborate heroin network he had established, slipping from English to Italian to French, languages in which Lafitte was also fluent. Eventually, Orsini asked Lafitte if he would help handle his business after he was deported and until he could secrete his way back into the United States. Orsini made it amply clear that he would make it well worth the effort. Lafitte, of course, readily agreed, asking Orsini to tell him who he should make contact with once he was released.

"Go to my apartment and Marcelle will explain everything to you," Orsini said, referring to his girlfriend, Marcelle Demard Ansellem, who had not been arrested because Orsini had told the FBN that she knew nothing about his drug dealings. "She knows all that you need to know."

Orsini also explained how Lafitte could help him to return quickly to overseeing his North American drug network after his deportation. Lafitte, Orsini explained, would write a letter for Orsini's signature to a friend of Orsini's in Buenos Aires who would arrange for Orsini to enter Argentina. As Lafitte later reported, Orsini's girlfriend "Marcelle and I would take the papers to the Argentine Embassy in New York and arrange for Orsini to get a visa." Once Orsini was deported to Argentina, he would "quickly travel to Mexico, where, with the assistance of Santo Trafficante [Jr.], who maintained an elaborate network throughout South America, Cuba, and Mexico, he would set up shop so as to direct New York operations by remote control, so to speak." Lafitte would essentially take Orsini's place in New York and act as his mouthpiece, "representing his interests and seeing that the money kept flowing down to Mexico."

Orsini rested his hands on Lafitte's shoulders and said, "I'm going to need as much cash as possible, and quick, once you get out. I'm counting on you, my friend. I'm trusting you with my life."

"You're not making a mistake," replied the undercover agent. "I'll come through for you."

Lafitte was released on May 29. He met with Orsini's girlfriend the next day. Ansellem, who had already been informed that Lafitte was to be trusted during one of her jail visits to Orsini, briefed Lafitte about Orsini's vast and elaborate heroin operation, and the names and operations of his various partners. First there was Salvatore Shillitani, nicknamed Sally Shield. Orsini, according to FBN files, first met Shillitani in January 1949. At the time, Orsini was having trouble collecting on a large drug sale and, understanding that Shillitani possessed unique "retrieval skills," had asked him for help. Shillitani collected the owed amount, plus interest, and Orsini was so impressed that he offered Shillitani a piece of his ever-expanding business, which he operated with Francois Spirito, Antoine D'Agostino, Carmelo Sansone, and Angel Abadelejo. Shillitani accepted the lucrative offer and introduced Orsini to his occasional partner, Eugenio Giannini. Naturally, Shillitani had no clue that Giannini was also feeding information to narcotics agents White and Guiliani.

Within months, the expanded Orsini Group, as law enforcement officials later dubbed it, was running bulk heroin shipments from France and Italy to Montreal, where shipments would be broken down and run across the U.S. border at crossings in Rouses Point, New York and Richford, Vermont. The Group also sent unwitting people with cars to Europe on vacations, where the cars would be secretly loaded with drugs for transport back to the United States and Canada.

Marcelle Ansellem told Lafitte that before Orsini had been arrested he was able to conceal over $100,000 in cash and three kilos of heroin. She explained that she was in the process of converting the drugs into additional cash so that Orsini and Lafitte could increase their dealing volume substantially, but the deal she had set up would take a few more weeks. Lafitte told Ansellem that he had an associate in San Diego, California that could help a lot. "He wants two kilos of heroin now and he'll pay good money." Lafitte's San Diego "associate" was George White. Through the next several weeks, Lafitte managed a convoluted and highly sophisticated series of manipulations, deceptions and covert dealings that entailed convincing every level of Orsini's drug network of his, Lafitte's, legitimacy as a drug dealer. Two days after meeting Lafitte, Ansellem had introduced him to Salvatore Mezzasalma and Vincent Randazzo. Lafitte had already met Salvatore Shillitani. Observed Lafitte later, "You could see why Orsini was the leader. He itched on Ellis Island, and over on Manhattan Shillitani scratched."

White soon informed Lafitte that the time had come to try to set up a large heroin purchase between the Orsini Group and an FBN agent posing as a buyer. White had decided that because of the complexity of the case, a veteran narcotics agent "with nerves of steel" should be brought in from another city to act as the buyer. "It's too much of a chance to use any of our agents in New York or Boston," White reasoned. Neither Lafitte nor White have ever identified the agent brought in, but it has been revealed that "this agent had a marked characteristic: He walked with a limp." The agent assumed the name "Tony Rizzo," claimed he was from California, and that he limped because of a car accident two months earlier.

Lafitte expected the buy to be made from Shillitani, but White decided Randazzo would make a better mark. Said White, "Let's ease in through the side door first with Randazzo and let news of the buy pass on to Shillitani. It will put him at ease and then we can nail him, too."

When Randazzo met with Tony Rizzo, he immediately started grilling the agent. "Randazzo was as subtle as a whack on the head with a baseball bat," Lafitte later wrote. Randazzo asked Rizzo multiple pointed questions, and after Rizzo left their initial meeting satisfied that he had passed muster, Randazzo leaned toward Lafitte and said, "He's got a real bad limp, huh."

Lafitte's heart dropped. He instinctively knew that Randazzo had made Rizzo as a federal agent. Within minutes he telephoned White and said, "We have big trouble. Randazzo made our guy."

A few hours later, Shillitani called Lafitte. "I want to see you right away," he said. "I'll pick you up in twenty minutes."

Shillitani drove Lafitte to an apartment in the Bronx where Randazzo and two of his associates were waiting. Lafitte knew that the two were "professional killers." He later recalled, "These two guys relished murder like some guys liked hot dogs. One was expert with an icepick, the other with his bare hands, and the two were always hungry."

Randazzo got right to the point. "Your associate Tony Rizzo is a fed," he charged.

"This some kind of joke?" Lafitte responded. He turned to Shillitani. "What's with this guy, is he crazy or what?"

"Don't give us that bullshit," shouted Randazzo. "The guy is a federal agent. He's a veteran agent who has limped for years."

"You're wrong," Lafitte countered. "Tony may look like some other guy, but I've known him for fifteen years and he's no fed." Lafitte grabbed Randazzo's shirtfront and pulled him in close. "I'm telling you, he's no more a federal agent than I am. You got that?"

Amazingly, Randazzo began to waver. "Well, maybe I'm wrong, I don't know," he said. "Maybe they just look alike. Maybe I made a mistake."

Shillitani stepped in and told the two he had had enough. "Shake hands," he ordered, "and stop this stuff. We got business to do. We got a deal to make for Joe." He turned to Lafitte. "I've got you set up with Francois Spirito for some of the dope you need. He's all set to do business but is in Montreal for a couple weeks, meanwhile we can give you a few ounces of good stuff."

Later that day, Lafitte met with White. "That was a close call," he said. "You got that right," said White. "It's time to start thinking about wrapping this case up."

Lafitte later recounted, "We still wanted to get to the guy who had sold the heroin to Shillitani, so I reported back to Shillitani that we were displeased with the quality of the few ounces he had given me."

Shillitani told Lafitte, "I don't have anything to do with that," and he took him to see a low-level pusher named Joe Valachi.

Confronted, Valachi said, "It came to me as good stuff. What do you want me to do about it?"

"Nothing," said Lafitte. "It is good enough for now, but I want you to know you got to do better."

"Okay," Valachi said. "We'll make a better deal next time."

The next day Shillitani, over coffee, said to Lafitte, "I got something a guy like you can use."

"What's that?" Lafitte asked.

"How would you like a couple hundred grand in counterfeit?"

Lafitte recounted he "whistled and tried to pull myself together." He had not anticipated this development in the case.

"I don't know," he told Shillitani. "It would depend on some things."

"Like what?"

"Like the quality and the price."

"The quality is terrific," Shillitani grinned. "And the price, too. It's all in tens and twenties. Fantastic quality, the best there is. I can give you a sample along with a legal bill and you can't tell the difference."

Lafitte recalled, "He wasn't kidding. The quality was as good as anything coming off the presses in Washington, D.C. I told him I'd take the entire two hundred grand. Then I met with White, and then he and I met with his friend John Hanley." Hanley, a Secret Service agent, had formerly worked as a FBN agent and in that capacity had, along with fellow agent Crofton Hayes, interviewed Meyer Lansky in 1949 about Lucky Luciano's heroin activities. He was very pleased with the information put before him. He and White decided to make the ensuing case a joint operation between the Secret Service and FBN, with both agencies agreeing to take down the entire Orsini-Shillitani crew in one fell swoop.

On July 28, 1951, around 9:30 P.M., Lafitte met with Shillitani on a prearranged corner of Lexington Avenue, where Shillitani was to deliver the funny money. As darkness fell over the city, a three-block area surrounding the avenue was riddled with concealed Secret Service and narcotics agents. In all, over forty agents anxiously awaited Shillitani's arrival. When his Cadillac pulled up to the curb, Lafitte opened its rear door and climbed inside. Shillitani handed the undercover agent a cheap suitcase containing the money.

Lafitte later recalled, "I leaned back in the seat and began examining the money, thinking it had been almost two months to the day since we had begun our investigation and my nerves were screwed as tight as a banjo string. I was tired and greatly looking forward to ending my association with the likes of Sally and Orsini. Shillitani sat next to me, humming softly to himself. Out of the corner of my eye I saw an agent come out of the hotel and push his hat back on his head. In the rear-view mirror I saw men converging on the car. Shillitani wasn't watching. It wasn't until the door was yanked open that he looked up."

A little over an hour later, another team of ten FBN agents busted the remainder of Orsini's group. Orsini himself was soon sentenced to ten years imprisonment, but after serving seven years he was deported to France, where he was arrested on the Nazi collaboration charge. Without explanation, he was released two weeks later, and he promptly returned to dealing drugs.

Marcelle Ansellem was sentenced to two years. Shillitani and Randazzo received fifteen-year terms in prison. Shillitani's wife was never charged. It would be nearly four more years before Valachi would be arrested and sent to prison. When arrested, Francois Spirito claimed his name was Charles Henri Faccia, but agents quickly showed him "wanted" papers, including his photo, from France. He was sentenced to ten years in Atlanta Federal Penitentiary, but, as we shall see, was released after about two years.

In his written summary of the Orsini case, Lafitte recalled the case of Eugenio Giannini, who had been murdered "on an uptown street in New York." Said Lafitte, "The mob thought he might have blown the whistle on them. When I heard about Giannini, I knew how lucky I had been." Of course, Lafitte was being less than forthcoming about the slain pusher because he, along with George White, had had a direct hand in dosing Giannini with CIA-supplied LSD during one of the very first, pre-MKULTRA interrogations at Barrow Street. It would not be at all far fetched to speculate that perhaps Giannini had been deliberately betrayed by the FBN to the mob so that his murder would be insured and so that his being dosed with LSD would remain a tightly held secret. It is interesting that according to White's date book, Lafitte notified White of Giannini's murder only moments after it occurred. Also worth noting here is that for over a half-century, criminologists and historians have remained completely unaware of the remarkable role LSD played in several of the Mafia's most momentous occasions.

Many Americans may still recall the nationally televised testimony before the Senate Rackets Committee of Mafia turncoat Joe Valachi. His testimony dominated the airways in late September and early October 1963. Nobody, however, recalls Valachi's non-televised admissions to the FBI about Pierre Lafitte. While Valachi's story seems to differ in some ways from the conventional one, it is worth repeating in small part here.

Prior to his songbird act for the FBI and U.S. Senate—that some crime authorities claim was a well-concocted and coached performance based less on fact than on a law enforcement agenda—Valachi had murdered John Joseph Saupp in the Atlanta Federal Penitentiary yard.

When the U.S. Attorney in Atlanta sought the death penalty for the killing, Valachi managed, through a go-between, to get a message concerning his plight to the U.S. Attorney for the Southern District of New York at that time, Robert Morgenthau. The go-between, whose name has never before been revealed, was Pierre Lafitte. Valachi's message was that he was prepared to spill the beans on the Mafia. As readers will learn, the fact that Lafitte was the go-between to Robert Morgenthau would eventually play an important role in the subsequent investigation into Frank Olson's death.

With the spectacular conclusion of the Orsini case, Pierre Lafitte's undercover career went into overdrive. Nine months after Frank Olson died and Lafitte returned to New York from several secluded weeks in the Tampa, Florida area, Lafitte was hired by newspaper publisher Herman "Hank" Greenspun to go to Las Vegas and pose as a shady businessman named Louis Tabet. Upon his arrival, Lafitte checked into a swanky suite in the El Rancho Vegas, a gambling hotel, and began spreading the word that he had come to town to try to purchase Roxie's, an infamous and extremely popular brothel located in the Formyle section of Las Vegas. Roxie's was owned and operated by a former Los Angeles police officer, Edward Voight Clippinger, and his wife Roxie, who together oversaw a lucrative chain of bordellos dotting the West Coast and Nevada. Months before, Greenspun had written a sardonic editorial in his newspaper that ridiculed the local sheriff, a longtime nemesis to Greenspun and all of the competing Vegas brothels he relentlessly harassed and put out of business in his illicit course of protecting Roxie's.

The Las Vegas *Sun* editorial read: "After a short stakeout of only ten years, the sheriff's office amassed sufficient evidence to suspect that the Roxie was not on the list of the Automobile Association of America as one of the approved hotels." Greenspun then set aside his sarcasm and opened fire with both barrels. Sheriff Glen Jones held a "financial interest in Roxie's," and had been protecting the establishment from law enforcement authorities for years. Jones sued Greenspun and the *Sun* for libel and $1 million. Greenspun knew that Jones was very well connected to Nevada's political machine and was concerned that the courts would side with the sheriff. He also knew that Jones had been taking bribes and kickbacks for years, and he discussed the situation with his new investigative reporter, Ed Reid, the same Reid who had previously worked in New York for the *Brooklyn Eagle* and was well acquainted with George White and Pierre Lafitte. Reid recommended that his boss speak with White about hiring Lafitte to come to Las Vegas and entrap Jones in his illicit doings. "If anyone can nail this guy it's Pierre," Reid told Greenspun. "I'll get White on the phone for you."

In Las Vegas, Lafitte, posing as Tabet, quickly learned that Roxie's was taking in huge profits each month, or as Roxie, who was motivated to sell due to adverse publicity, boasted to him, "We have a real money machine."

"How much exactly do you take in a month?" Lafitte asked.

Roxie winked wryly. "Enough to keep things hunky dory."

"'Hunky dory' to me means a lot," Lafitte shot back. "Maybe more than it does to you."

The transcript of Lafitte's secretly recorded conversations tells the rest:

> Roxie: *February was a little slow. We did about $80,000.*
> Lafitte: Is that the total?
> Roxie: *It includes two thousand from the bar, one hundred from the cig machine, and eighteen hundred from the dormitory.*
> Lafitte: Pretty sweet operation.

> **Roxie:** *You've got to promise me one thing, though. Those girls... are devoted to me. I don't want to let them down. I expect the buyer to keep them on.*
> **Lafitte:** If they do their job okay, it's okay by me as long as the profits keep coming in. A whore's a whore, what's the difference.

Not surprisingly, George White came to Las Vegas for a few days while Lafitte was there. One can imagine that White could hardly stay away after Lafitte had telephoned him to report that Roxie's bordello was populated with more than two-dozen of what he termed "the most beautiful and sexiest dolls you've ever seen." But imagine is all we can do, as White did not detail the visit in his date book, as was routine with most of his travels. However, a letter to his friend, attorney Rudolph Halley, is somewhat revealing. "It has been said that temptation is often the handmaiden to a man's downfall," White wrote, "and while I am not disagreeing, given my recent trip to Las Vegas and Madame Clippinger's amorous joint, I will hardly cooperate in my own marriage's demise. Suffice it to say, my good friend, that had you been there with me, we together would share this belief." What may interest readers even more is that White brought a supply of LSD along with him to Sin City. Lafitte, years later, recalled:

> With George old habits die hard, and his practice of dispensing this crazy drug fostered by the CIA was not left behind in New York when he traveled to Las Vegas... One of Roxie's girls, the youngest and perhaps prettiest, nicknamed 'Sissy,' did not have the best of times under the influence— but George proved an expert travel guide through the netherworld of visions and horrors, and I suspect they both will recall the journey with joint trepidation and fondness for years to come.

Pertinent to underscore here is that Las Vegas and its eclectic cast of characters would soon play central roles in the mysterious doings of the CIA and its burgeoning alliance with organized crime. Neither Lafitte nor White were newcomers to Las Vegas, and both men were more than well acquainted with the city's seamy underside, especially the doings of eccentric millionaire Howard Hughes, his special assistant Robert Aimee Maheu, a former FBI agent and a CIA contractor, and underworld financier Meyer Lansky. Hughes, as has been widely reported, maintained a close and lucrative association with the CIA. The Agency contracted with many of Hughes' companies for specialized services, including leasing several of his private islands for anti-Castro bases. Writers Sally Denton and Roger Morris revealed in 2001 that at the time of his death Hughes was earning a staggering $1.7 million a day "from U.S. government contracts, mostly from the CIA."

While there is no evidence that Lafitte played any role in Hughes' doings, Lansky and Maheu's operations are a different story. Despite his unusual yet active undercover investigatory role with a number of federal agencies, Lafitte on occasion helped broker Lansky's international drug deals, and also worked on occasion for Maheu's private investigation firm, both in New York and Las

427

Vegas. Indeed, according to Lafitte himself, it was Maheu who "dropped my name" to editor Hank Greenspun for the case involving Sheriff Jones. Said Lafitte, "George [White] and Ed Reid didn't know where I was at the time, but Maheu did because I was on assignment for him." Lafitte would also reveal that on several occasions working for both Lansky and Maheu, "always under one alias or another," the job required assuming "front of the house" hotel jobs, such "as night porter, bellman, and even once on the Strip, front desk man."

On December 22, 1969, alarm bells went off at the CIA. TSS chief Sidney Gottlieb announced at a staff meeting that the FBI had arrested Lafitte in New Orleans, where he was working as manager-chef of the posh Plimsoll Club in the World Trade Mart. Unbelievable, came the incredulous response, how could that be? Doesn't he sometimes work for the FBI?

Find out what's going on, ordered Richard Helms, now director of the CIA. And make certain there are no photos of him in the newspapers or any magazines, instructed Helms.

Apparently, the Bureau had had little choice but to pick Lafitte up. Six years earlier he had swindled an unfortunate speculator named Ralph L. Loomis out of nearly $400,000. Ironically, the elaborate scheme, involving diamond mines in Africa, had originated out of an FBI sting operation, which the Bureau had called Lafitte in on to do undercover work. Lafitte had made investments under the alias Anthony Shillitani while in the Belgium Congo in 1960 on another deep-cover assignment for the CIA.

It is worth noting that Lafitte turned up in yet another tangle of major, historic proportions during the 1960s. Around the time of the JFK assassination, Lafitte worked for the Reily Coffee Company and then as a chef for the World Trade Mart, both in New Orleans. William B. Reily, an avid anti-Communist, owned the Reily Coffee Company and was closely connected to McCarthyite and rabid anti-Communist Edward Scannell Butler, who were both close to CIA assistant director Charles Cabell, CIA SRS chief Paul Gaynor, and Agency ARTICHOKE official Morse Allen. Readers may recall that alleged JFK assassin Lee Harvey Oswald also worked as a maintenance man for the Reily Coffee Company in the summer of 1963.

According to FBI documents, during its six-year "search" for Lafitte, the notorious agent had used dozens of aliases, including Louis Romano, Frank Maceo, Paul Maceo, Jean Martin, Peter Martin, John Martin, Jack Martin, Paul Martino, Paul Mertz, Jean Mondolini, Louis Hidell, Paul Jehan, Jean Jehan, Louis Mancuso, Jacques Montaine, Peter Orsini, and Louis Tabet. Within weeks of his arrest by the FBI in 1969, Pierre Lafitte was quietly released, and he quickly vanished for another five years.

In his later years, after retiring from the Narcotics Bureau, George White said of Pierre Lafitte:

I thought I had led a damn interesting life, but compared to Pierre my times were pretty tame. I've done it all, but he's done even more, and before some of it was ever done he invented it. He was what you would call a changeling. I don't mean master of disguises, I mean an actual chameleon, a man that had the ability to transform himself right in front of you. He could go from good to bad, from rich to poor, from royalty to commoner, from intellectual to simpleton, from hoodlum to police officer. He would disappear for months or years at a time and then he would show up, knock on your door, like only a day or two had passed. He mastered time as it affected him; it was as if time waited for him.

I liked him but I never trusted him because he was always in the game. He only loved and cared for his wife and children; everyone else was fair game in the scheme of things. He was the greatest imposter and confidence man that ever lived, not because he was a good actor but because he was a hundred different people in one.

But White was not completely trusting of Lafitte; in the draft of his autobiography, he wrote:

There's a side to Pierre that rarely reveals itself, but is always there. A dark, abysmal side, and once you become aware of it, it's almost impossible to be completely at ease with him.

James Phelan, who wrote for the *New York Times*, *The Saturday Evening Post*, and *Paris Match*, was one of the very few people, besides White and a couple others, who were able to get close to Lafitte. Here it should also be noted that Phelan, according to JFK assassination authorities Lisa Pease and James DiEugenio, occasionally served as an FBI informant himself, and perhaps also a CIA informant. Phelan was a good friend of Robert Maheu, a former FBI agent and CIA employee, and the CIA's go-to guy and go-between for assassination projects. At any rate, Phelan believed Lafitte was perhaps the most unique person he had ever encountered. "When I first heard of a man who called himself Pierre Lafitte," Phelan wrote, "my credulity was strained beyond the most elastic boundaries. Even after I met him, I had difficulty believing that he was even semi-real, or that he had done any of the things that he said he had done." Out of respect for Pierre's privacy, Phelan always described him in general, and sometimes deceptive, terms. "He was a short, bald man with cold blue eyes and a French or Italian accent." (Lafitte was not short, had a full head of hair, and had dark eyes and a French accent.) Phelan met Lafitte several months after his undercover Las Vegas work for Greenspun. Phelan explained that the *Sun* articles about the entire affair that ran in Greenspun's newspaper never mentioned Lafitte or his role in bringing down Sheriff Jones or any others. But as an investigative reporter, Phelan instinctively knew that despite the amazing story publicly revealed, there was more, far more, to it all. He met with Greenspun, and the feisty editor told him all about the missing Lafitte part. "The story was even more amazing than I had imagined," said Phelan. "I asked Greenspun, 'How do I get to talk with Lafitte?' He said, 'I have no idea where he is or how to reach him. He calls here once in a while to see how things are going. I can tell him you're interested in talking with him.'" Phelan said that he told Greenspun he would deeply appreciate that.

At least that is the story Phelan consistently told, and later wrote in his memoirs. But what Phelan did not say was that he was a good friend of George White. Indeed, he had written a number of popular men's adventure magazine articles about White's FBN exploits. Phelan knew White long before he had ever spoken to Greenspun, and he had met White, along with Lafitte, on several occasions well before the Las Vegas affair was ever conceived, but, of course, out of respect for both men, Phelan kept this to himself. His silence added to the mystery and intrigue that hung about the exploits of both men. After the Greenspun-Roxie case, Lafitte would visit Phelan at his California home. Phelan's wife, Amalie, a highly respected psychologist, recalled:

> It wasn't uncommon for Pierre to come by... but always unannounced, at anytime of the day or night. Jim didn't mind. He enjoyed his time with Pierre. They would sit for hours on end talking. Once, late, around midnight, I looked out the kitchen window and there was Pierre sitting on a bench in the back yard waiting for someone to notice him out there. That was Pierre— there one moment, gone the next.

Asked about Lafitte's mysterious lifestyle, Amalie said,

> There was no question that he lived a life of intrigue. Jim would get odd little post cards from him from places all over the world... There was a sense of danger always around him.... I asked Jim once if there was any reason to be concerned in having Pierre come around. Jim said, 'It's a good question. I don't imagine he goes anywhere without a shadow.'

Amalie and Jim's daughter, Janet, also remembers Lafitte. "I was pretty young, but yes, I remember him. He was very mysterious, always appearing out of nowhere to talk with my father. I couldn't help but be fascinated by him. He put off airs like a movie star. There was just something about him."

Said James Phelan of Lafitte,

> He used dozens of different names—and occupations—in dealing with mobsters around the country, and somehow kept his identities straight in his mind. Years later, he sent me a birthday card from the Belgium Congo—where he was engaged in God knows what. It had forty of his names—like Orsini, Monaco, Tabet, Shillitani—on it, but not the name Pierre Lafitte.

430

Phelan's Belgian Congo line was a crafty citation. What the investigative reporter did not mention was that Lafitte was in the Congo at the very same time that the CIA had slated Patrice Lumumba for assassination, a fact that surely did not escape Phelan's notice. Was Lafitte the never-identified CIA assassin WI/ROGUE? It appears likely that he could have been, or, at the very least, that he was quite close to QJ/WIN and WI/ROGUE.

Former FBN agent and high-ranking U.S. Treasury department official Malachi L. Harney made some studied observations of Lafitte in his little known book devoted to the subject of informers and law enforcement. Harney introduced Lafitte as a "most interesting character" and the "type of person sometimes of invaluable assistance to the law enforcement officer, who is an outsider, but must be in a compartment of his own. This is a sort of 'private eye' individual but a very special variety of that genus." Claimed Harney, conforming to the cover story put out by the FBN about Lafitte's beginnings with the Bureau, and embellishing some on his own with the Orsini case story: "As an indication of his versatility, this man, who never had any previous contact with the narcotic traffic [sic], was able, when released from [Ellis Island] under security bond, to make a case resulting in the disclosure of a ring importing seventeen kilograms of heroin monthly through the Port of New York, through connivance of crewmen of the French Lines, who were members of a Corsican smuggling mob. Cooperation of the Federal Bureau of Narcotics with the French police brought about the seizure of a large clandestine heroin conversion plant in the outskirts of Paris. In addition to its magnitude, this case was highly important for its timing and for its revelation as to the source of a flood of heroin into New York. Lafitte, with Narcotic's Bureau District Supervisor George H. White, went on from there to develop a case against a leading narcotic distributor in New England— a Mafia character who, as a sideline, had connections which enabled him to filch a steady supply of revolvers from a factory before the registry numbers of the weapons were recorded."

Harney then speculated: "Lafitte would have been a great detective in any organization, combining a tremendously keen mind with a histrionic ability which made him an undercover operator par excellence. Some of his motivation to assist the law is quite simple. He has been able to make a good living at it, when one considers the rewards for recovering property and similar emoluments. He had a special reason for coming to us, in that he was anxious to enlist some official sympathy on trying to clarify an obscure nationality status."

Harney does not explain this status not does he tell us how Lafitte's immigration status was ultimately resolved, but we do know that in 1957 Bernard Fensterwald, a former State Department employee who had just been hired by U.S. Senator Thomas C. Hennings, Jr., contacted the FBI at the direction of Senator Hennings to inquire about the Bureau's reaction to a request to Hennings to sponsor legislation to block the deportation of Lafitte. FBI official Louis B. Nichols responded: "I told Fensterwald that this, of course, was a matter for the Immigration Service and, on a purely personal and confidential basis, the Senator should be exceedingly cautious before he got out on a limb; that if he inquired into Lafitte's background he would find an extensive record; and that under no circumstances would the Bureau support Lafitte. I told him officially, of course, we could not take a position but that, personally, we would hate to see some friend embarrassed and he should be very cautious. Fensterwald stated that was enough for him." All of this, of course, significantly adds to the overall mystery that still to this day surrounds the man known as Pierre Lafitte.

That Lafitte was often in dicey, precarious, and intriguing, but critical situations, where his presence was carefully concealed and rarely noted, is perhaps the best testament to his extraordinary ability to remain invisible whenever he so chose, and also attests to the desire of those who employed him to keep his activities secret. When James Phelan revealed that Lafitte had spent time in the Belgium Congo nobody seemed to notice that it had been at the same time that Patrice Lumumba was killed. The fact that Lafitte was employed in New Orleans at the same place as Lee Harvey Oswald is beyond provocative; that he was all over the drug cases involving Eugene Giannini, Joe Valachi, and the legendary French Connection case tells of his extraordinary skills and deep connections; that he shadowed George White throughout New York after being vetted by the CIA relays much about what his objectives were; that a United States Senator would go to great lengths to protect him from law enforcement and deportation, and that the FBI cooperated in these efforts, all underscore his importance.

The fact that Pierre Lafitte was there at a Manhattan hotel with Frank Olson only a few months before Olson's death tells us a great deal about his being privy to the machinations of both the CIA and SOD.

Pierre Lafitte Continued...

As with George White, the year 1953 was a seminal one for Pierre Lafitte, with both men finding themselves in Cuba at the beginning of that year and again in 1954, 1955, and later. As was the case with White, we are uncertain what specifically took Lafitte to the island nation; however, some things are clear. Interviews with former associates of Lafitte reveal that he was well acquainted with Amleto Battisti y Lora, a wealthy Corsican who had come to Cuba via Uruguay. Battisti, a tall, slim man who shaved and waxed his head, was often referred to as a "Mafia kingpin" and "Mafia family head." He was a member of Cuba's House of Representatives, owned a bank in Havana, and operated Havana's luxurious Hotel Sevilla Biltmore, built in 1908 at a cost of millions and within which criminal mastermind Meyer Lansky held a silent partnership. Battisti, always cunning, extremely intelligent, and the quintessential ladies man, took special pride in regularly importing new groups of prostitutes from abroad "for the exclusive enjoyment" of his guests at his hotel, which he had taken over in 1939. He also operated at least two casinos in Cuba and several bolita gaming operations in Florida, in partnership with Santo Trafficante, Jr., the head of the Florida Mafia.

Lafitte had known and worked with Battisti in France, where the two had teamed up with Francois Spirito to operate an extensive white slavery and prostitution ring that extended from France to Egypt, and beyond. Few Americans in the 1950s had heard of Battisti. The few who had were mostly movie actors, entertainers and writers. In Cuba, Battisti was a hotelier to celebrities, hosting Frank Sinatra, George Raft, Robert Mitchum, Lana Turner, Ava Gardner, Enrico Caruso, Josephine Baker, Errol Flynn, Gloria Swanson, George Simenon, and Graham Greene.

Battisti was also very much involved in drug trafficking, with some law enforcement officials claiming he was a major dealer in heroin. Indeed, it was Battisti who convinced Lucky Luciano, following his deportation from the United States, that Cuba was the ideal location from which to establish his main heroin distribution route into North America. Cuban writer Enrique Cirules states that Battisti was head of one of several Mafia families headquartered in Cuba. Battisti was also quite close to Meyer Lansky, who maintained a home in Cuba. A 1958 U.S. Treasury Department special investigation report on Battisti stated: "Mr. Battisti, in the opinion of the undersigned, is capable of anything." Ironically, Battisti, who on occasion employed Lafitte in Cuba to carry out sensitive missions, once quipped, "[Pierre] is a little too untrustworthy to deal with, except for when the need arises, and unfortunately it does on occasion."

In addition to Battisti, in Cuba, Lafitte also dealt with Amedeo Barletta and Paul Damien Mondolini. Barletta, a Calabrian, was Mussolini's counsel and "administrator of Mussolini's family in the United States," and, according to the FBI, had been a wartime double agent planted by the Italians in Latin America. In 1942, the Bureau ordered his arrest in the Dominican Republic but he fled to Argentina, where he remained until the end of the war. Soon thereafter, he turned up in Havana as a representative for several large American automobile and pharmaceutical companies, including, according to writer Cirules, General Motors. Before the war, Barletta had been a General Motors sales manager in the Dominican Republic, where he clashed with dictator Rafael Trujillo, who charged that Barletta was plotting to assassinate him. Cirules also claims that Barletta, alongside Lansky and Battisti, headed a "Mafia family" and was involved in drug trafficking.

Paul Mondolini, aka Paul Marie Bejin, Jacques Desmarais, and Eduardo Dubian, was born in 1916 in Corsica. In wartime Marseilles, where he migrated at an early age, he worked, like many morally ambidextrous bandits, both for the Resistance and collaborated with the Germans during the Nazi occupation of France. Remarkably, later he had served as chief of police in Saigon, before he went on to gain worldwide notoriety when he took part in the 1949 robbery of the royal jewelry of the wife of the Ismailian prince Aga Kahn. Mondolini's association with Lafitte extended back to their days of drug running in Marseilles and Indochina for Francois Spirito and Paul Carbone. In Cuba, where he did not really establish himself until 1955, Mondolini, in partnership with Corsicans Antoine D'Agostino and Jean Baptiste Croce, who owned two nightclubs in Havana, became a major player in moving heroin via Cuba to Montreal. Interesting to note here is that Mondolini's prominent activities in Cuba coincided almost day-by-day with numerous trips to Cuba by CIA Inspector General Lyman B. Kirkpatrick. Readers will recall that Kirkpatrick, the official who conducted the CIA's investigation into Frank Olson's death, said in 1968 that his trips to Cuba were "an effort to help the [Cuban] government establish an effective organization to fight Communism," despite the fact that nobody, the CIA included, was convinced at the time that Castro "was an avowed Communist." Kirkpatrick would also say that during that period of time the CIA was flush with money. "There basically wasn't a limit," he said. "We got what we asked for." And nearly two thirds of the money went for covert operations.

British crime historian Charles Wighton significantly noted, in 1960, "The overseas section of the Corsican gang working in the closest collaboration with the American Mafia in Montreal, Havana, and Mexico City [is] run by [Antoine] D'Agostino and the notorious Paul Mondolini." Indeed, it was Mondolini, along with fellow Corsican Jean Jehan, who masterminded the infamous international heroin caper popularized by the hit film *The French Connection*. Worth noting here is that Jehan, according to CIA records produced in 1976, was thought to be the owner of the Bedford Street building in New York City where George White operated his CIA-funded safe house. Throughout his drug trafficking career, which extended well into the 1970s, the small-framed, impeccably dressed, multi-lingual Mondolini was considered one of the shrewdest and most intelligent dealers that the FBN had confronted.

In Cuba, Lafitte was also well acquainted with Santo Trafficante, Jr., whom he initially knew from his days in Tampa and St. Petersburg, Florida. Trafficante, beginning in 1955, spent a lot of time in Cuba looking after his numerous casino and hotel properties, including the Sans Souci, Havana's oldest gambling casino, the Hotel Deauville, the nightclub Capri, the Havana Hilton, and one of Havana's most popular casinos, the Tropicana. Trafficante was no stranger to Cuba. His father, Santo, Sr., born in Sicily and godfather of the Florida mob, had gambling and bolita operations there that pre-dated World War II and that Santo, Jr. had helped operate since the early 1940s.

Santo Trafficante, Jr., much like his close partner in crime Meyer Lansky, maintained an elusive yet steadfast relationship with the CIA. Some former government officials have observed that Trafficante's cautious alliance with the intelligence community was based "on a quid pro quo relationship whereby both sides prospered in their frequently similar objectives." Perhaps Trafficante's close relationship with Lansky insured his relative immunity from law enforcement and prosecution. (Santo, Jr. was never convicted of breaking any federal law.) As has been noted, Lansky's alliance with the CIA extended back to the days of the OSS and the long kept secret Operation Underworld.

In 1950, Lansky opened a major new heroin avenue between Turkey, Marseilles' processing labs, and America's ever-expanding demand for the drug. Chief among Lansky's suppliers were Paul Mondolini and Antoine D'Agostino. Often facilitating the reliable and uninterrupted flow of heroin to its ultimate sales points on America's streets was Pierre Lafitte, who played a brokering role in many of the larger shipments that were routed to Lansky's dealers. We can only assume that Lafitte's other life as an undercover federal informant and investigator significantly helped his darker deeds involving drug trafficking. According to Sally Denton and Roger Morris:

> As so often in his career, Lansky in his new French connection enjoyed the U.S. government as a de facto silent partner. He trafficked with the secret sanction, protection, and sometimes collaboration of the CIA, the FBN, and other Washington agencies. From its OSS roots during the war, the CIA was now in expedient alliance with organized crime against Communism's influence around the world. CIA stations in Turkey and elsewhere in the Middle East discouraged or even suppressed investigations of opium-growing or smuggling by local politicians, military, and other officials enlisted as allies or even intelligence assets against the Soviets. By the same rationale of national security, successive American administration's refused to confront the known collusion with drug traffickers of allied governments in France and North Africa. From the Mediterranean, the new heroin supply routes soon extended as well to Indochina, where U.S. intelligence and drug enforcement agencies first clashed among themselves and ultimately colluded, in what would become by the end of the sixties a vast new channel of the Syndicate's narcotic trade, with momentous consequences.

At the same time he was launching his French connection pipeline, Lansky decided to relocate from Florida to Havana, Cuba, where he thought he could more easily manage his drug trafficking because Cuba was far more accessible for the tight-knit group of Corsicans and Frenchmen that served him. (Many of these men were on the watch or wanted lists put out by the FBN and FBI at this time.)

It is significant to note here that Lafitte also knew the enigmatic John Maples Spirito (apparently no relation to Francois Spirito), one of the most mysterious characters in Cuba's revolutionary history, as well as Frank Sturgis, his long overlooked comrade-in-arms, Richard "Rex" Sanderlin, and soldiers of fortune William Alexander Morgan and Herman Marks. All four characters are listed in Lafitte's book outline on Cuba, with the introductory line: "Never was there a more brave and fascinating (some would argue foolhardy and opportunistic) band of men than those I encountered in Cuba during the budding revolution there."

Lastly, of significance, there was John Martino. Martino's name is found in a number of George White's address and date books and in Lafitte's notes concerning his trips to Florida and Cuba. Martino, a self-described small businessman in Miami, was virtually unknown until Castro's Revolutionary Guards arrested him on July 23, 1959 for illegally entering Cuba. Lafitte had known Martino for at least seven years prior to his arrest. From about 1950 through to 1959, Martino had maintained a close association with Santo Trafficante, Jr., to whom he supplied gambling and electronic equipment for Trafficante's Havana hotels and casinos. Beginning about 1955, Martino partnered with former CIC and CIA-TSS employee Allan Hughes in his Cuban electronics ventures. As readers may recall, Hughes was present at the fateful Deep Creek Lake meeting where Frank Olson was dosed with LSD.

In 2000, the author asked legendary soldier of fortune and CIA operative Jerry Hemming about Hughes.

> Author: *You met [Allan] Hughes in Cuba?*
> Hemming: Yeah, I sure did.
> Author: *This was when?*
> Hemming: Around 1958 or 1959, I think. A while ago.
> Author: *What do you recall about Hughes?*
> Hemming: Not a whole lot. He was there in Havana with Martino... They were working together on some sort of electronics deal. I'm sure the Agency was involved with it somehow... Hughes had been in the Army's CIC not long before this.
> Author: *Did you speak with him?*
> Hemming: No. Never had the chance to.
> Author: *Do you think Hughes was working for the CIA at the time?*
> Hemming: It wouldn't surprise me if he was. It was right before Sid Gottlieb's crew got busted and thrown in the slammer down there.
> Author: *Do you know what happened to Hughes?*
> Hemming: Nope. Don't have a clue. People came and went in those days.

Only recently has Martino been given the kind of attention he deserves vis-à-vis his activities in Cuba and the assassination of JFK. Noted historian David Kaiser writes that Martino was close to Santo Trafficante, Jr. and, prior to his arrest, had been hoping to open a brothel in Havana. Kaiser also reports that Trafficante was in contact with Frank Sturgis and William Morgan. Martino was imprisoned in Cuba's notorious La Canbana fortress, where his fellow prisoners eventually included Morgan, arrested and executed by firing squad for betraying Castro, and three CIA officials who had been arrested for attempting to either bug or bomb the Chinese embassy.

Lafitte, operating under the alias Jean Pierre Martin, visited Martino in prison on at least one occasion in 1961. This is known only because of a notation made by White: "Pierre to see Martino Cuba—call Rene." "Rene" was Lafitte's wife. A subsequent notation by White reads: "Siragusa re Martino Cuba." This pertains to former OSS official and FBN agent Charles Siragusa, who was approached by the CIA in 1960 about contacting American Mafia figures in Cuba, or elsewhere, to help the three CIA employees imprisoned with Martino to escape. It is thought that perhaps Siragusa contacted White and Lafitte for help with this.

According to a January 1978 report by investigative journalist Jack Anderson, Siragusa said that he had met with CIA-TSS officials in 1960 about "three Spanish-speaking CIA operatives [that] had been arrested while pulling a Watergate-style break-in at the Chinese Communist News Agency in Havana." The CIA authorized Siragusa "to spend up to $1 million to effect the rescue of the imprisoned agents." Interesting to note is that the three CIA operatives were employees of the Agency's Technical Services Division, at the time under the direction of Dr. Sidney Gottlieb. The three men, David Lemar Christ, Thornton J. Anderson, and Walter E. Szuminski, according to CIA records, were audio and electronic specialists highly-trained in bugging devices. According to former CIA officials, all three men had also worked closely with Allan Hughes, and according to Gottlieb, Hughes was assigned by the Air Force to the CIA. Gottlieb confirmed that the three men had entered Cuba using aliases and false identification papers issued by the Agency's Technical Services Division. Also interesting to note is that while the three were imprisoned in Cuba, Gottlieb's Technical Services shop gave serious consideration to secreting an unnamed, "former Air Force officer" who was an expert hypnotist, into their cells to allegedly either hypnotize them or to assassinate them before they could be interrogated. Knowledgeable, confidential sources say that this was Hughes. However, this is unverified, and the CIA declined to comment on the subject. Lastly, Gerry Hemming, who was briefly imprisoned with the three men, said, "They were all scared out of their minds. They knew that other Americans had been executed by Castro, and they were scared shitless they were going to be lined up at the wall and shot."

About this same time, in the summer of 1960, another CIA official approached Charles Siragusa. This was Vincent Thill, who had worked earlier in Berlin with William Harvey. According to testimony before a U.S. Senate committee in October 1977, Siragusa said that Thill requested his help in recruiting Mafia figures for the purposes of assembling an assassination team. Remarkably, Siragusa said that Thill promised that "each team member" would "be paid $1 million in fees and expenses" for each kill. Siragusa testified that he declined to assist Thill, but CIA documents have emerged that indicate otherwise.

A January 1961 Agency file reveals that Harold Meltzer, a close associate of Meyer Lansky's, was among those seriously considered for the CIA's assassination team. Meltzer had been arrested in the past by the Narcotics Bureau, and had cooperated with agents George White and Siragusa on an unidentified "project" in New York in 1956 and 1957. During this period, Meltzer also had business dealings with Pierre Lafitte in Los Angeles, where Meltzer lived and owned a sportswear company and several automobile dealerships. Lafitte and Meltzer operated and partly owned together, two restaurants at about the same time that Lafitte recruited Meltzer to invest in a diamond mine in South Africa.

4

Who Was Francois Spirito?

Francois Spirito: Well known international narcotic violator and member of one of the largest smuggling rings in France. FBI #837850A. Federal narcotics conviction in New York City in 1951.
— U.S. Treasury Department, Bureau of Narcotics, 1953

For me it was a far greater relief to be free from the [Atlanta] prison's terrible experiments than from mere confinement. Much was unbearable in that place.
— Francois Spirito, 1961

Less than three weeks after Frank Olson had died, a tall, dark-haired, slender man with the good looks of a French movie star, despite the dark circles under his eyes, walked into a Manhattan sandwich shop only blocks away from the Statler Hotel and ordered a cup of black coffee. Seconds after he had been served, an attractive woman appearing to be in her early thirties took the stool next to Spirito, even though several others were vacant. Spirito nodded politely at the woman and went back to his thoughts. When the counter waitress asked to take her order, the woman casually waved her away, and then swiveled toward Spirito.

"You look tired, Francois," she said, smiling.

Startled by the unknown woman addressing him by name, Spirito asked if he knew her.

"No," she answered, "you don't, and there really isn't any time for you to do so." She looked over her shoulder toward the shop's entrance and nodded.

Three plainclothes officers rushed into the shop. They seized Spirito by his arms, informing him they were Immigration and Naturalization Service agents and that he was under arrest for being in the United States illegally. Outside on the sidewalk were three Federal Narcotics agents.

"Illegal?" Spirito protested. "But, how can that be? You don't understand. I was only just released from prison here in your country weeks ago."

Five days later, Spirito was on his way back to France, courtesy of the United States government.

Francois Spirito, apart from being dubbed the Father of Modern Heroin Traffickers and the Grand King of the French Underworld, is today a man shrouded in mystery, legend, and broad based disinformation. A highly popular 1970 French film called *Borsalino* was loosely based on Spirito's criminal exploits. Starring heartthrobs Jean-Paul Belmondo and Alain Delon, the film made Spirito and his partner in crime, Paul Bonaventure Carbone, highly romantic and adventuresome figures—despite the fact that both men had been notorious wartime Nazi collaborators, assassins, black market kings, worldwide heroin traffickers, and white-slavery dons. Throughout the 1930s, Spirito took particular delight in his French media appellation, "The Al Capone of France."

Like many of France's notorious pre-World War II gangsters, Francois Spirito learned the ways of crime on the streets and alleyways of Marseilles. Details about his early years are riddled with uncertainty, thanks in large part to disinformation disseminated in the 1950s by the CIA and FBN. Some criminologists have written that Spirito was born in 1899 in Marseilles; others claim that he was born years later in Paris. Still others say that Spirito was a Corsican by birth and that his given name was Charles Henri Faccia. There are those who allege that he was born in Naples, Italy in 1901. All of these are false. His birth name was Lydio Spirito and he was born in 1898 in Sicily, the son of Dominick Spirito and Rosina DeNola. His family moved to Naples when he was four years old, and then migrated to Marseilles when he was about nine years old. There his father occasionally worked as a stevedore on the thriving Marseilles docks, and his mother sometimes worked as a maid. The family, which included two additional children, had little money and lived in a cramped flat with one bathroom and two bedrooms.

As a youngster, Lydio excelled in school but was quickly lured away from the classroom by the cornucopia of pleasures and intrigues offered up by the centuries old coastal city. When Lydio was thirteen years old and nearly six feet tall, he adopted the more French sounding name Francois and moved into his own squalid one-room flat. This he did to exert his independence and better practice his burgeoning criminal skills, having taken up with a gang of ruthless juveniles and street toughs who terrorized the small merchants and shopkeepers around the harbor. The gang had its makeshift headquarters in an abandoned hemp factory on Canebiere Avenue. By the time he was fourteen, Francois was notorious for burglarizing the fishing vessels and yachts that filled Marseilles harbor, and he moved into a larger three-room flat. As his roommate, he chose his girlfriend, a beautiful young woman named Suzanne Filleau. Suzanne, who was three years older than Francois, worked as a prostitute and was much sought after, but Spirito convinced her to give up her trade and keep house for him. Suzanne's pimp was a vicious thug named Antoine la Rocca who maintained a "stable" of nearly fifty prostitutes and also operated several well-known Marseilles brothels. He was outraged that a young upstart would have the nerve to steal away one of his high earners.

"Do you want me to kill him?" asked one of la Rocca's closest henchmen, Antoine D'Agostino, an Algerian-born youth with great ambitions, also still in his teens and close with the young, weasel faced Auguste Ricord, who would go on to become a major heroin dealer.

La Rocca thought a moment. His anger said that Spirito should pay with his life, but his shrewd intellect dictated that he could use such a fearless man in his burgeoning crime organization.

"No," he told D'Agostino. "Beat him to the point where he'll never think of crossing me again. Then bring him to me."

Fearing that he could not handle him alone, D'Agostino took two thugs along to teach Spirito his lesson. Hours later, bloodied and with several broken ribs, Spirito shook hands with la Rocca and agreed to join his outfit, but on condition that Suzanne would stay with him.

La Rocca had big plans for Spirito, most of which revolved around the dashing young man becoming a purveyor of white slaves and an armed robber. At the time, armed holdups were becoming a phenomenon in the United States, and la Rocca saw no reason why they could not be lucrative in France. Spirito had no problems with his new boss's plans, especially his dealings with young women, and he also soon found that he enjoyed robbing people at gunpoint. The money, split with la Rocca, was good, and he and Suzanne were able to move into an even larger, furnished flat. Suzanne wanted a family. Francois told her they should wait a year, but he had no real interest yet in having children.

Writes Derrick Goodman:

> And Francois (now rewarded with the underworld nickname 'Le Grand Lydro') knew that the first stepping stone in his career had been reached when la Rocca provided him with a convenient alibi one night when the coppers were on his tail. He rose swiftly in stature and became known as a man who never forgot a friend in need. He never forgot his enemies either, and there are several unsolved murders in the files of the Marseilles Police Judiciaire which carry the mention 'Spirito' followed by a large question mark.

Francois was enjoying life too much to settle down, and he had ambitions, most of which revolved around more money. He also knew that he was far smarter than la Rocca and that he could do far better without having to pay needless homage to a boss. When he first encountered Paul Carbone, a criminal who matched him in wits and courage, Francois jumped at the chance to team up with him.

By all authoritative accounts, Francois Spirito first encountered Paul Carbone, five years his senior, in 1913, in Alexandria, Egypt. Carbone was there working as a pimp, after he had been taken in by an older prostitute who provided him with the tutelage necessary to manage her carnal affairs. Prior to going to Alexandria, Carbone had dropped out of school at the age of nine and had devoted his time to providing for his widowed mother. The oldest of three sons, Paul spent his days filling sacks with sand collected along Corsica's coast, which he sold to local builders. When he was about fifteen, he decided he had had enough of the work, and he set off for Egypt. Spirito had just begun traveling regularly to Egypt, importing young French girls, white slaves, from Paris. White slavery was wide spread at the time. Says historian Derrick Goodman, "Let me put it this way: white-slavery [in France at the time] is to common prostitution what trigonometry is to simple mathematics."

Carbone, who had been in Alexandria for eighteen months, was just beginning to do well financially, sending home most of his wages to his mother. But his success drew the attention of three rival pimps who determined to do away with the upstart. The three snatched Carbone off the street, tied him up, blindfolded him, and took him out into the desert where they buried him up to his neck in sand, pouring a jar of honey over his head so as to attract hungry ants. The ants failed to appear, because there were none in that part of the Sahara, yet after three days of no water, blinding sun, and near freezing nights, Carbone was close to giving up the ghost. Miraculously, as he was slipping into unconsciousness, he looked up to see Francois Spirito smiling down at him. On the way back to Alexandria in a mule cart, Spirito told Carbone, who he had only met once or twice in passing, that he had overheard the pimps bragging in a bar about their deed and had decided he could not leave the Frenchman in such a precarious state. Thus, the two struck up what would be a life-long friendship and business partnership.

After spending about a week recuperating, Carbone, no longer thrilled about doing business in Egypt, talked Spirito into traveling with him to Shanghai, where the two spent about a year smuggling opium. At the start of World War I, the two adventurers returned to France, enlisted in the army and were sent off to North Africa. During the war, both Carbone and Spirito were awarded medals for bravery. After the war, the two headed to South America in search of their fortunes. Carbone told his trusty sidekick, "My destiny for too long has been tied to sand. I need to go to a place where there is none." In Peru, they resumed pimping, and soon were handling nearly twenty young women who worked exclusively for them. With a steady source of funds and time on their hands, the two devised a highly illegal but infallible way of winning at chemin-de-fer, a version of baccarat.

Flush with money, Spirito and Carbone returned to France and plied their gambling skills at nearby Monte Carlo where they significantly increased their illegal winnings at baccarat. With these earnings, they once again turned to the business of prostitution, this time establishing their own upscale brothel in Montmarte. At the time, all the brothels in Paris were controlled by an immensely obese Italian named Charles Codebo, famous for his slogan: "Five francs for five minutes: room, towel, and lady included." Carbone and Spirito moved quickly and "bought Codebo's partner out."

Then, as Carbone's longtime mistress, Germaine Germain, better known as Manouche, recounts,

> [Late] one evening, their wide-brimmed Borsalinos pulled down over their eyes, hands pushed down in their raincoat pockets, just as they had seen in so many American gangster movies, Carbone and Spirito visited Codebo. They informed him that they were now his partners in one-third of his business— and, for merely another third, would be glad to furnish him with the 'protection' he would be needing from now on.

With their new profits, Spirito and Carbone financed a chain of brothels throughout France, staffing them with young women from nearly every country in Europe and South America. The money poured in and the two men swiftly gained entry into the fledgling heroin market. Opium was dropping in popularity and heroin was rapidly becoming a drug much in demand. Entry into drug trafficking proved to be more difficult than entry into the sex trade for the two. Other players, major, well established traffickers, did not take kindly to the two upstarts from Marseilles, but by this time, Carbone and Spirito, through hard bought experience, had become adept at squaring off with opposing forces. Chief among their opposition was "the top-hat overlord of dope," Elias Eliopoulos, described by historian Dr. Alan A. Block as "a Greek (also allegedly a Jew) living in Paris... who [from 1928 through 1930] was under the protection of a Mr. Martin, called 'Zani,' of the Prefecture de Police." According to Block, "For his part Zani received information on other traffickers and, most importantly, 10,000 francs every month." Spirito, who offered Zani a greater monthly stipend flavored with subtle threats of exposure, displaced Eliopoulos's cozy arrangement. Eliopoulos, threatened with huge losses, fought back, but Zani by this time had tipped American authorities off about Eliopoulos's activities.

In 1952, crime journalist Will Oursler said of the Greek dealer: "He was the man who gave the modern underworld of drugs definitive shape." It would be Carbone and Spirito who would mold that shape into a sophisticated international business by establishing the first heroin-processing laboratory in France and establishing transnational smuggling routes into every major continent.

As the Carbone-Spirito empire expanded by leaps and bounds, the two decided on a division of labor: Carbone concentrated on keeping their brothels supplied with white slaves, while Spirito focused on their rapidly widening drug trade. Joining Spirito's activities at this time were former Corsican Shepherds, the Guerini brothers, Antoine, Barthelemy, Lucien, Francois, Pascal, and Pierre, all of whom would break away from Carbone and Spirito during the war, aligning themselves closely with the French Resistance. "At the end of 1930," Goodman says, "the Grand Lydro took a Messageries packet to Alexandria, which was then the centre of the Eastern Mediterranean drug supply centres. He was accompanied by two young Provençal ladies to attend to his corporal needs during the business trip."

Suzanne Filleau, meanwhile, had finally realized that Francois had no interest in a family and she had moved in with Antoine D'Agostino, who promised children right away.

During a stopover in Turkey, Spirito encountered August Del Grazio, who was in Istanbul to shepherd a large shipment of opium into New York City. The two traffickers took a liking to one another and, most likely, readily recognized the advantages their alliance could bring to their respective businesses. Spirito organized the supply points in several Middle Eastern countries, including Egypt, Turkey, and Afghanistan, for black, unprocessed opium, which was transported to Marseilles for processing into high-grade morphine and heroin.

Twice during the pre-war years, Spirito became bored with France and, longing for a change of scenery, he journeyed illegally to the United States, where his younger sister Angelina had lived since 1905. Both times he traveled with large shipments of opium. On his first visit, he was arrested in Boston for criminal trespass and illegal entry. On his second trip, in 1939, he was arrested for smuggling over fifty pounds of opium aboard the *SS Exeter*, but he was sent back to France and charges were quickly dropped because of his law enforcement connections.

According to FBN files, later that same year, Spirito encountered Pierre Lafitte after Lafitte had defected from a rival prostitution ring operating in Marseilles and offered his procurement skills to Spirito. Decades later, Lafitte would lament his involvement in the white slavery trade, a practice that thrived in the 1920s and 1930s throughout Europe (and that has experienced an alarming resurgence in the first part of the twenty-first century). Said Lafitte, "It was something I held no fondness for and that I deeply regret." Nonetheless, Spirito and Carbone, with Lafitte's help, rose to the top of the white slaver's heap. One of France's top policemen, Alfred Morain, noted in 1931 that white slavery and drug trafficking were "two special sections [that] presented especially complex problems." Morain described the many cases:

> ...[Y]oung [French] girls— minors —were genuinely deceived as to the fate which awaited them [after they] were taken abroad by means of false passports, were sold, in the literal sense of the term, money down, by their kidnapper, and were afterwards forced by the buyer to prostitute themselves for his profit.

It is interesting to note that Morain, in his discussion of drugs, observed that a good deal of the cocaine sold illegally in France by traffickers like Spirito "is most often imported from Germany," with one of the "most sought after brands being the 'Merck' of Darmstadt." Said Morain, "just after the War [World War I], it was often said that the Germans were using cocaine as a means of enfeebling the French race." Historian Alan A. Block has graphically demonstrated that, at this time, "tracking of the legitimate [European] drug trade" revealed "which drugs from which producers moved across the line into 'underground' markets." Block cites examples of large stocks of legal drugs diverted to illicit markets: in 1928, "France exported 346 kilos of morphine to the United States, what the U.S. Federal Narcotics Control Board reported were 'illicitly imported.'" Another example cited is, "In 1925 the Swiss pharmaceutical giant Sandoz exported over 1,300 kilos of morphine to a Japanese firm which had no record of the transaction... and [which law enforcement officials believed] passed into the illicit international traffic."

Paul Carbone's mistress, Manouche, recounts that Carbone, who was nicknamed "Blaze," typically wore "a wide-brimmed Borsalino hat, like Al Capone's, only black instead of Capone's famous white." At the same time, a friend informed Manouche:

> Carbone is the 'Emperor of Marseilles.' They don't do anything down there without consulting him first— and he does whatever he wants down there without consulting anybody. In short, he is a gangster. Top class. Not so long ago a cousin of his friend Spirito was in a boxing match. The cousin fights under the name of Kid Francis. You've heard of the bantamweight black boxer from New York, Panama Al Brown?

Manouche replied that she had, indeed, heard of him because writer Jean Cocteau, whom she knew well, managed Brown. Her friend explained that after Brown beat Kid Francis, Cocteau, who was widely believed to be Brown's lover, was beside himself with joy, jumping up and down, screaming. Outraged, Carbone had walked over and punched Cocteau in the face, knocking him out, and Spirito leaped into the ring with a pistol in hand, yelling, "I'm going to shoot the bloody nigger who's beat my Kid." At that moment, an American fight judge entered the ring to declare Brown the winner and Spirito brutally pistol-whipped the man. A full-scale riot broke out among the hundreds of fans in the hall, and it took the local police hours to restore order.

As might be expected, honest and aggressive law enforcement officials created problems for the competing brothel operators and drug traffickers. Carbone and Spirito determined they needed to form political alliances and allies. Carbone, with better connections than Spirito, contacted his younger brother, Jeannot, nicknamed "Scarface," who had been unsuccessfully tried in 1930 for the murder of a Senegalese pimp. Jeannot Carbone introduced his older brother to Simon Sabiani, Marseilles' Fascist deputy mayor, soon to be mayor. Sabiani was a World War I hero and a peculiar and outspoken politician who did nothing to conceal his alliance with Carbone and Spirito. He even boldly declared his friendship with the two, who were viewed by many lower-income French citizens as Robin Hood-type figures. Sabiani included them on campaign banners and posters. In return, Carbone and Spirito became Sabiani's muscle and brute force. They hurt people in Sabiani's opposition, and there are reports that they methodically murdered people who were viewed as problems to Sabiani's administration. The two also helped break worker strikes and carried out violence and mayhem in support of Sabiani's objectives.

Soon Spirito and Carbone had amassed a large, dedicated gang of thugs, all of whom were more than willing to use violence. Writes Alfred McCoy in his classic book, *The Politics of Heroin: CIA Complicity in the Global Drug Trade*:

> In February 1934... several days after an inflammatory speech by a Fascist army general, massive street demonstrations erupted on the Canebiere, Marseille's main boulevard. The thousands of leftist dockworkers and union members who took to the streets dominated this political confrontation until Carbone and Spirito's political shock force fired on the crowd with pistols. The national police intervened, the workers were driven from the streets, and the wounded were carted off to the hospital.

Alfred McCoy writes, "In Marseille, Carbone and Spirito were the vanguard of the right wing." The two also lived in the lap of luxury, traveling everywhere in chauffeur driven limousines, eating in the finest restaurants and drinking the best wines. They wore handmade silk and wool blend suits, owned several yachts moored in Bandol and at least five bars and restaurants as well as many real estate holdings in Paris and Marseilles. In Marseilles alone, they operated over twenty-five brothels, most of which were staffed with young Jewish women forced into prostitution.

When World War II arrived and the Nazis marched into France, matters became more violent. Carbone and Spirito's gang, with the blessings of the German authorities and agreement that the Nazis would turn a blind eye to their criminal activities, began attacking Jews in the streets, and vandalizing, looting and burning shops and businesses owned by Jews. At the height of the occupation, Spirito owned a bar on the Vieux-Port that was a favorite hangout for the Nazi's security forces, *Reichssicherheitshauptamt*, called the SS or "le Gestapo" by the locals. Even after their political clout began to wane, Spirito and Carbone were able to capitalize on the German occupation by collaborating with the Gestapo unit in Marseilles. Frequently that collaboration would have a high human cost. "On July 14, 1943," writes McCoy, "the Resistance showed its strength for the first time by machine-gunning the headquarters of a pro-German political organization in downtown Marseille (the PPF, whose regional director was the Fascist ex-mayor Simon Sabiani). The following afternoon Carbone and Spirito handed the Gestapo a complete list of all those involved."

During this time, Spirito and Carbone were launching their own vicious war against a rival drug trafficking gang. In efforts to do away with the competing group as quickly as possible, they imported to Marseilles over fifty Corsicans skilled at murder. Among this group of killers were the especially ambitious Jean-Paul Stefani and Ange Foata, two highly experienced assassins who are said to be the envy of many of the assassins that would soon be recruited by the CIA. Foata, within months of proving himself with numerous murders, was assigned to oversee a newly developed drug route to Western Europe via the Orient Express from Turkey and Yugoslavia.

Everything changed for Spirito when Carbone was killed in December 1943 by the French underground, when a sleeper rail car he was riding in was dynamited. Several tons of mangled steel cut one of his legs off at the knee. Legend has it that as he lay dying, he smoked a cigarette and sang songs to comfort the other injured passengers around him, but Manouche reports that he was taken to a nearby hospital still clutching his severed leg. When an attending priest asked him, "Do you believe in God, my son?" he replied, "That all depends." He died about an hour later, minutes before Spirito arrived at his bedside. His dying words, uttered to the priest, were, "That's life... c'est la vie."

Manouche writes that, after Carbone's death, Spirito continued to work "hand in glove with the Krauts" and that he most likely absconded with the 11 million francs in savings Carbone left behind, giving nothing to Carbone's wife, family or mistress.

According to FBN reports, in 1944, following the D-Day invasion, Spirito, accompanied by Sabiani, fled France to Spain. Shortly thereafter, both men were condemned to death *in absentia* by the French courts for their collaboration with the Nazis. From Spain, Spirito journeyed to South America and then moved on to North America, arriving in Montreal, at the age of forty-six years. There, Spirito quickly organized major heroin shipments, by automobile, to New York City, through several Canadian border portals located in Rouses Point, New York and Richford, Vermont. Spirito's trafficking partners in Canada included Eugenio Giannini, Jean David (aka Jean Legat), his old associate Antoine D'Agostino (alias Jean Sisco), now married to Suzanne Filleau, Dominick Venturi, Jean Venturi (Dominick's brother), and, according to some former law enforcement officials, Pierre Lafitte, who may have been operating under the alias Pierre Martin. When the loose knit group began to seriously penetrate the U.S. market with heroin sales, they aligned themselves with crime boss Gaetano Lucchese, who headed the first American Mafia family to move into heroin trafficking on an organized and grand scale.

Lafitte, years later, confirmed that he had been in Montreal at that time. He wrote, "I encountered Spirito only once or twice in Canada before we came together in New York at the Statler Hotel. That was in Montreal, with D'Agostino. I don't recall what, if anything, he said at the time. I would think it was about the Orsini deal. After New York, I never saw him again."

In October 1951, following Spirito's arrest and before his ten-year prison sentence for his part in the Orsini case, FBN Commissioner Harry Anslinger addressed a letter to the head of France's Criminal Police Commission, Marcel Sicot. Wrote Anslinger:

> On August 23, 1951 our agents arrested an individual hitherto known only as BIG FRANK, but subsequently identified as Francois Spirito, who was an associate of Orsini in his illegal activities and who is living with Maria

Castellani, who was mentioned in previous correspondence between us. Francois Spirito maintains that he is actually Charles Henri Faccia, born in Marseilles on June 10, 1899, son of Charles Faccia and Annaise Bianchetti.

This is contrary to statements made by Maria Castellini who stated that she was the widow of Charles Faccia, who died in Marseilles in February 1950. It is also contrary to information received by us from other sources, which indicates that this man is actually Francois Spirito, and that he is wanted for certain crimes committed in France. Questioning of Spirito and Maria Castellani apparently reveals wide differences in the stories told by each, indicating that the identity of Faccia has been assumed for the purposes of hiding his real identity.

A photograph and a Photostat copy of the fingerprint card of Francois Spirito alias Charles Henri Faccia are attached, and it is requested that efforts be made to learn the true identity of this individual.

Commissioner Sicot responded to Anslinger and verified that the man being held by the FBN was indeed Francois Spirito. On November 15, he again wrote Anslinger "to inform you that the extradition of Francois Spirito was requested by the French authorities following a warrant issued in absentia by the Court of Appeals of Chartres (Eure-et-Loir) on October 24, 1951, sentencing him to twenty years at hard labor and ten years of prohibited residence for theft of a particular nature." Continued Sicot:

> This conviction followed a warrant of arrest issued on February 3, 1947 by the Judge of Instruction at Dreux... You are informed that Mr. [Charles] Siragusa [FBN agent], in the course of a conference, which took place on this date at the International Bureau, has been informed of the above facts. Moreover, a certified copy of the Warrant of the Court of Assises in Chartres has been delivered to Mr. Siragusa. Finally, a letter of introduction was delivered to Mr. Siragusa; he will go to Marseilles in order to obtain a copy of the warrant of the Court of Justice at Marseilles, dated November 6, 1945 from the Procurer of the Republic in that city. There, documents will be transmitted to you by Mr. Siragusa, in order that they may be produced during the trial of Francois Spirito at New York.

It would be about two years before Francois Spirito would be released from Atlanta's Federal Penitentiary. The prison was a most notorious place at the time. Years before Spirito arrived there, Italian newspaperman and anti-Fascist Carlo Tresca had exposed the facility as a place riddled with corruption, where it was easy for inmates to purchase morphine and heroin. One inmate told Tresca that he had intentionally broken parole so that he could return to the prison to continue his dealing. "One more year," the man told Tresca, "and I'll have enough to live in peace to the end of my life."

In addition to rampant drug dealing within the Atlanta facility, it was selected in 1951 by the CIA and U.S. Army to be a secret site for the conduct of experiments involving drugs and their ability to produce psychotic behavior. Few specifics are known about these experiments other than the fact that they were eventually formally recorded in CIA documents as MKULTRA Subprojects 9, 28, and 47. Many of the CIA's prison experiments were continuations of OSS tests. Readers should note that FBN agent Charles Siragusa was very knowledgeable about them and was involved in many of the MKULTRA experiments, especially those conducted in New York City, Kentucky, and Atlanta. In 1999, Dr. Sidney Gottlieb said, "We learned a lot from the Atlanta experiments. The Agency learned that a person's psyche could be very disturbed by those means. From the earlier pre-Agency tests we found that violence was relatively easy to draw out."

After Spirito was returned to France in late 1953, he spent less than a year in custody, and he was released again. He then purchased an expensive restaurant and bar on the French Riviera. He occasionally traveled to the United States, Canada, and South America, and, by many accounts, continued to traffic in heroin. Strong rumors among law enforcement officials have persisted for years that Spirito was the untouchable financial arm of the infamous French Connection case, made popular by the film of the same name. Spirito died of natural causes in October 1967. According to French law enforcement authorities, he was never again arrested.

5

January 30, 1973
Warrenton, Virginia

A review of the files of the Identification Division, Federal Bureau of Investigation, Washington, D.C. as of August 21, 1975, revealed no criminal record relating to Dr. Sidney Gottlieb.
                              —FBI Memorandum, August 3, 1975

Sid [Gottlieb] did what any Agency employee would have done when ordered by the DCI. CIA isn't a Dick and Jane-like bureaucracy; here you do what your superior tells you to do. In the case of the destroyed files it wasn't like Sid had any choice. He did what Helms ordered, and then got hung out to dry for doing it.
                              — CIA official, March 13, 1999

Sidney Gottlieb had departed the CIA's headquarters building in Langley, Virginia early in the morning to drive to the Agency's Records Center in Warrenton, Virginia, about forty miles away. The day before, he had received an urgent telephone call from the chief of the Center. The chief had called to protest instructions to destroy a large number of boxes containing original files on the Agency's drug and biological warfare programs. Gottlieb thought it best to meet with the Records Center chief to explain things in person and to insure that the files were indeed destroyed. Gottlieb was tired, having just returned several days earlier from an exhausting trip overseas, but DCI Richard Helms had been adamant that all MKULTRA files be burned before they could possibly fall into the "wrong hands" and be misinterpreted or used to embarrass the CIA.

In mid- September 1975, the CIA, on the instructions of DCI William Colby, launched an internal investigation into the destruction of Agency records related to research and development of drugs and toxins. The investigation, quickly dubbed the "ULTRA probe" by Agency insiders, ran from September 17 to September 30, and, according to Agency documents, "was limited in scope to avoid interfering in any way with other ongoing investigations of this matter, including that of the FBI."

The official in charge of the internal investigation is unidentified in CIA documents, but the author has learned that he was assisted by former TSS psychologist John Gittinger and TSS operative Frank H. Laubinger. Readers will learn more about Laubinger in a later chapter of this book. Gittinger, as previously mentioned in an earlier chapter, was a psychologist hired in 1951 by the CIA to work in the TSS branch. Indeed, it was Gittinger who had interviewed Gottlieb before he was hired by the Agency. At the time of Gottlieb's death in 1999, Gittinger said, "Sidney Gottlieb was one of the most brilliant men I've ever known." Gittinger, considered a genius by many who worked with him, devised a fascinating method of personality testing and assessment used by the CIA, which eventually set up a proprietary company in Washington, D.C. run by Gittinger. The company, Psychological Assessment Associates, which operated branch offices in Europe and Asia, hired other scientists, including David Saunders of the Educational Testing Service, which prepares College Board Examinations. Both Drs. Harold Abramson and Robert Hyde made extensive use of Gittinger's research. Also quite intrigued by Gittinger's work were Drs. Harris Isbell and Abraham Wikler at the Lexington, Kentucky Narcotics Farm, who submitted the personality tests of resident addicts to Gittinger's company for scoring.

The lead investigator conducted the internal MKULTRA probe primarily by interviewing key CIA employees and focusing on four general areas:

(a) Destruction of files related to MKULTRA and the continued existence of any such files on paper;

(b) Destruction or continued existence of other files possibly related to drugs;

(c) The existing MKNAOMI records and the question of whether records related to the Agency's involvement in toxin programs have been destroyed; and

(d) The system for retiring records to Records Center and Archives, records retrieval, and records destruction.

Not surprisingly, no existing drug-related MKULTRA files were located. Initial interviews revealed that Dr. Sidney Gottlieb had been instructed by DCI Richard Helms to destroy all MKULTRA files in late January 1973. The actual destruction took place on January 30, over the strong protest of the chief of the Agency's Records Center. The Center's chief wrote a memorandum for the record stating: "Over my stated objections the MKULTRA files were destroyed by order of the DCI (Mr. Helms) shortly before his departure from office."

Later, in June 1973, Sidney Gottlieb had ordered his administrative assistant to remove all MKULTRA files from his office safe and to burn them. This took place shortly before Gottlieb retired from the CIA. It was believed that in Gottlieb's safe there had been at least four MKNAOMI folders containing information about Frank Olson and many of the SOD projects he had worked on, but those too were burned. The administrative assistant kept no record of what she had destroyed. She had been Gottlieb's assistant for only about six weeks before she was instructed to destroy the files. During three of those six weeks Gottlieb had been in Europe.

"I never thought for a moment to question my instructions," the assistant recalled to the investigator; "I did what I was told."

She also remembered, when asked, that she had destroyed a number of technical journals and printed papers written by Dr. Gottlieb, as well as some files that detailed highly sensitive personnel matters concerning people in TSS and SOD, and that some of those files were stamped SECRET SENSITIVE. She did not read or scan any of the files before destroying them.

The Agency's investigator reported that on September 29, 1975, he had had a discussion with Dr. Sayre Stevens, CIA deputy director of Science and Technology, about Stevens' own investigation of Project MKNAOMI and SOD records. Dr. Stevens told the investigator that he was "convinced that no papers or files were remaining from the two extant MKNAOMI files." He explained,

Gaps in the files are the result of a conscious policy on the part of TSS and SOD to keep very little paper on the project. This has been the practice from 1952 to 1970.

Stevens added:

All of the people formerly connected with MKNAOMI to whom I spoke asserted that the practice of keeping little or no record of the activity was standard operating procedure, regardless the activity or sub-project.

Gittinger asked about the SOD activities under MKNAOMI that had been conducted overseas in Europe and in Asia. Stevens explained that while activities were conducted in both areas, again, no records or files had been discovered documenting anything.

Additionally, Dr. Stevens contacted several Army officers at Fort Detrick and was informed that "no records on MKNAOMI or the Special Operations Division, Fort Detrick, can be located anywhere." Stevens surmised, "These records were destroyed when the BW/CW [biological warfare/chemical warfare] materials were destroyed at President Nixon's order." Stevens also speculated that Dr. Gottlieb's destruction of the contents of his safe's MKULTRA records included MKNAOMI files.

Of the voluminous MKULTRA files in the Warrenton Records Center that were destroyed, the investigator reported, "One box of this material dealt with environmental sampling for biological and chemical warfare manufacturing activity." He also speculated that MKNAOMI reports on activities in France and Germany were also destroyed. However, two MKNAOMI files remained, according to the investigator. "They contain Agency documents covering the period 5 May 1952 to 18 February 1970, as well as reports originated by Camp Detrick during the period 1960-1969." None of these documents made any mention of Frank Olson or his death.

Concurrent with the CIA's probe into the destroyed files, the FBI launched its own criminal investigation into "the destruction of Government Property." In late August 1975, FBI official J. B. Adams telephoned John Elliff, the task force director of a United States Senate Select Committee that was examining the CIA's MKULTRA program. According to FBI documents, the official advised Elliff "of our investigative interest in Dr. Sidney Gottlieb and of our desire that the Committee be aware of this investigative interest so that their activities would not adversely impact on the Bureau's investigation." Elliff quickly replied that he would make sure that the Committee's inquiry would not hamper the FBI's interest in Dr. Gottlieb. A few days later the FBI made a concerted effort to inform all of its special agents assigned to the MKULTRA case to make it clear to anyone interviewed that the Bureau's investigation "was initiated on August 1, 1975 at the direction of Assistant U.S. Attorney General Richard L. Thornburgh." Thornburgh's written directive to the Bureau reads in part:

> This Division's [Criminal Division] investigation of CIA activities in possible violation of Federal criminal statutes has disclosed that records of the CIA relative to drug testing conducted by the CIA were reportedly ordered destroyed in 1973 by Dr. Sidney Gottlieb, an official in the CIA's Directorate of Science and Technology. In 1973, Gottlieb retired and took up residence with his wife in India. A possible motive for the destruction is that Dr. Gottlieb may have continued such testing after 1963, the year the program was officially halted.

Thornburgh also wrote:

> It is requested that appropriate investigation be undertaken in the United States to include but not be limited to the interview of former supervisors and subordinates of Gottlieb to determine the detailed circumstances of his involvement in the drug testing program and the destruction of official records related thereof.

Attorney General Thornburgh directed that any reports stemming from the investigation "were to be classified SECRET since the CIA data appearing in these reports was so classified." The directive made no mention of former DCI Richard Helms, who had ordered Gottlieb to destroy the questioned files. At that time, Helms was serving as U.S. Ambassador to Iran in Tehran, a position he had held since 1973 after being fired as DCI by President Nixon.

On August 18, FBI director Clarence Kelley was notified by special AIRTEL message from the Bureau's Alexandria, Virginia office that the CIA's Inspector General, Donald F. Chamberlain "had learned that Sidney Gottlieb had returned to the Washington, D.C. area preparatory to testifying before the Senate Select Committee on Intelligence sometime in the near future." The message also disclosed that IG Chamberlain had informed the FBI, "Gottlieb has advised a representative of the CIA that he has retained an attorney, one Terry Lenzner of the law firm of Truitt, Fabrikant, Bucklin, and Lenzner, Washington, D.C., and has requested that any attempts to contact him be made through his attorney,

Mr. Lenzner." The last line of the message read: "CIA was unable to furnish Gottlieb's current local address."

Terry Falk Lenzner is a living legend among lawyers and politicians in Washington, D.C. In the late 1960s, fresh out of Harvard law school, Lenzner went to work as an assistant to Robert Morgenthau, then the U.S. Attorney in New York. After that, at the age of thirty, he was hired by the Nixon administration to run the legal services department of the Office of Economic Opportunity in Washington, D.C. At the same time that he was representing Sidney Gottlieb, he was deputy counsel for the Senate Watergate Committee. In 1981, Lenzner left work at one prestigious Washington, D.C. law firm to become a partner in another, that of Rogovin, Huge, & Lenzner. Readers will encounter attorneys Rogovin and Huge again in this book in their respective capacities representing the CIA and Frank Olson's son, Eric Olson.

A subsequent AIRTEL message to Bureau director Kelley, sent a few days later, advised that FBI investigators in the field had determined that "from the time that [CIA's] drug testing program was reportedly phased out in 1967 up until the time of Dr. Gottlieb's retirement from CIA in June, 1973, his superior had been Mr. Richard M. Helms, who is currently United States Ambassador to Iran in Tehran" and that Mr. Helms, then Director of Central Intelligence, had ordered Gottlieb to destroy all of the Agency's drug testing files." This information had been obtained from telephone interviews with two CIA officials, who were then located in London, England and Ottawa, Canada. The message then suggested, "The Bureau may wish to discuss with the Justice Department the advisability of pursuing this matter through investigation abroad."

A week later, the FBI notified attorney Terry Lenzner that they wanted to interview his client, Sidney Gottlieb, as to his "role in the reported destruction of CIA official drug testing records, and the basis he had, if any, for their destruction." At the same time, the Bureau issued a brief bio on Gottlieb that stated he had "entered [CIA] duty as a GS-14 on July 13, 1951." An attached report also stated that interviews with a high ranking former CIA official told FBI investigators, "He did not believe that Dr. Gottlieb would have destroyed MKULTRA records for any sinister or self-serving reasons." The former official also remarked, "As far as the overall MKULTRA Program was concerned, even though some interesting and valuable conclusions could have been drawn from the experiments, for all practical purposes it developed no confirmed application for operational use by American intelligence services nor did it confirm such use by opposition intelligence services."

Attorney Tony Lenzner quickly responded to the FBI's request to interview Gottlieb and said that he would have to consult with his client and could not state if Gottlieb would make himself available for an interview by Bureau agents. A few days later, Lenzner told Bureau agents that because Gottlieb was under "enormous pressure to testify before the United States Senate, I am unable to make Dr. Gottlieb available for interview in the foreseeable future." Lenzner said that he would contact Bureau agents when Gottlieb was available.

On October 14, still not having interviewed Gottlieb, FBI investigators were notified by FBI director Kelley that a Bureau Criminal Division attorney "had been informed of an article appearing in Washington, D.C. newspapers over the past weekend, indicating that Dr. Sidney Gottlieb had testified before the Senate Subcommittee to Investigate Intelligence Activities." Stated Kelley: "It was indicated [in the newspaper articles] that Dr. Gottlieb was granted immunity before testifying and that he testified concerning the destruction of records in this matter." Nonetheless, Kelley concluded, "Field office agents should conduct investigation to determine if Dr. Gottlieb will submit to interview since he has testified before the above committee."

What director Kelley did not state in his notification to field agents was that Bureau attorneys had vigorously attempted to block the granting of immunity to Gottlieb by the U.S. Senate committee. Read one Bureau legal document on the issue: "A memorandum has been sent to the Deputy Attorney General recommending the [Senate] Committee call specific co-workers of Dr. Gottlieb who could give information the Committee is seeking without resorting to a use of immunity grant for Dr. Gottlieb." It is not known whether or not FBI director Kelley had seen a Teletype message from Washington, D.C. field agents that stated:

> On September 23, 1975, Mr. Terry Lenzner, attorney for Dr. Sidney Gottlieb, advised that the Senate Subcommittee to Investigate Intelligence Activities, commonly referred to as Senator [Frank] Church's Committee, voted on September 23, 1975, to give Dr. Gottlieb use immunity regarding his, Gottlieb's, testimony before that committee. Mr. Lenzner stated there will be a brief court hearing in U.S. District Court, Washington, D.C., in order to provide Dr. Gottlieb with the use immunity referred to above, and that Dr. Gottlieb is scheduled to testify before Senator Church's committee in ten days. Mr. Lenzner advised his client would consent to an interview by representatives of the FBI, but said interview will have to take place after Dr. Gottlieb's appearance before Senator Church's committee. Mr. Lenzner stated that he would notify the FBI for a mutually agreeable time for the interview of Dr. Gottlieb after his appearance before Senator Church's committee.

Gottlieb's testimony before the Church Committee was extremely disappointing to everyone in attendance at the secret hearing held on Capitol Hill. Besides having been given immunity, Gottlieb appeared before the committee under the alias "Joseph Scheider," a name selected for him by Lenzner. (Some writers have incorrectly stated that he appeared as "Victor Scheider"; several other writers have erroneously reported that "Scheider" was Gottlieb's birth name. Gottlieb never used the name "Scheider" anywhere else.) At the time that he appeared, it was still assumed that all the MKULTRA and MKNAOMI records had been destroyed, and, without any written evidence to rely on, nobody on the committee, including its investigators and staff, had any real inkling of the scope or purposes of the Agency's drug and toxins program. Not surprisingly, Gottlieb was less than forthcoming about any of the details of the drug programs and answered most questions with the response that he could not recall specific program details. (On the CIA's assassination or so-called "Executive-Action" program, as readers have seen in Book One, the Committee was more fortunate and Gottlieb was considerably more talkative.)

Anticipating that Committee members would ask him why he had destroyed files in 1973, Gottlieb made the following statement:

> In late 1972 and early 1973, I began to systematically clean out and destroy files and papers which we felt were superfluous and not useful, relevant, or meaningful to my successors. In the case of the drug files, I specifically checked with my supervisor to obtain authorization and concurrence to destroy these files. My reasons for feeling that they should be destroyed were essentially threefold and had nothing to do with covering up illegal activities.
>
> There were three reasons that the files were destroyed. One, as with the other files which were destroyed in a continuing and important CIA program of files destruction to handle a burgeoning paper problem, there was constant pressure to retire files and to destroy those files which had no further use. Two, with my retirement and that of others connected with this work, and with the drug work over and inactive for several years, these files were of no constructive use to the Agency. They were the kind of sensitive files that were capable of being misunderstood by anyone not thoroughly familiar with their background. Three, the files contained the names of prominent scientists, researchers, and physicians who had collaborated with us and who had been assured that their relationship with CIA would be kept forever confidential. I felt that the careers and reputations of these people would be severely damaged or ruined, for instance, in today's climate of investigations, if their names and CIA connection were made public. I felt a special deep personal obligation to respect this assurance of confidentiality and to make as certain as I could that these particular CIA sources would never be revealed.

On January 14, 1976, the Department of Justice notified FBI director Kelley that two days earlier attorney Terry Lenzner advised both the department and a Special Agent of the FBI that he "would not make Dr. Gottlieb available to the FBI for interview." A week later, on January 21, FBI field agents investigating the destruction of Government property case were advised that "no further investigation should be conducted in this matter in view of Dr. Gottlieb's attorney not making him available for interview." A few days later, Bureau field agents were informed that Gottlieb had returned to India, but they were unable to verify the report.

BOOK FOUR
1975-1985

CIA MEMORANDUM TO THE INSPECTOR GENERAL, JULY 14, 1975

Recent media coverage of Agency testing of chemical substances on individuals brings to mind one incident which, as a result of the press exposure, might prompt a misinterpretation of a one-time Agency training program. It is reported here so that you will have it in file should the question be raised.

Over a period of five years or so, the writer headed a team of "indoctrinators" used in the"Enduring Enemy Detention" training program for sheep-dipped* personnel assigned to OSA [Office of Special Assistance]. The program was under the supervision of the Psychological Services Staff/OMS [Office of Medical Services]. During the conduct of the program, it was not unusual for a trainee to experience hallucinations, and in fact they had been pre-briefed on the possibility and given guidance on how to handle the situation—which several did most effectively.

One student, name not recalled but available in the writer's reports of the exercises hopefully still maintained somewhere in the Office of Security, during an exercise experienced hallucinations and had difficulty with handling the situation, in fact was near hysteria. In an in-situation discussion with him to assist him in confronting the situation, he broke out of the problem by stating that he believed he was being held in the basement of a mental hospital in Virginia and that a hallucination gas was being pumped into the room through the air conditioner. He could not be dissuaded of the belief, even when it was pointed out that others in the room were not so effected [sic]. In fact, he wondered aloud how we were able to filter out the gas. Of course, there was no gas, no drug, no chemical substance. However, on the presumption the student is no longer assigned to the Agency, this incident should be documented for reference should he ever come forward with his misunderstanding of what actually transpired.

Also for the record only: The writer served as a volunteer for an OMS "pill-taking" experiment, as one in a group of 20 or 30 as I recall. Later I learned that the pills I had been given were placebos, and that I was in the control group, rather than the group given the substance. I did not know this in advance, of course, and participated out of <u>trust</u> for the OMS official conducting the test.

---

*Sheep-dipped: A widely used intelligence agency practice of providing officials or operatives with new and false identity, military, and employment records, often to make it appear as if the person has resigned from his/her employer agency and taken a new position in the private or civilian sector.

1

July 14, 1975

Between the years 1947 to 1974, oversight of the CIA by the U.S. Congress was virtually non-existent. Capitol Hill's dominant attitude toward intelligence activities could be easily summarized as, "Don't ask, don't tell." Senator Frank Church of Idaho perhaps put it best in 1975, when he wryly remarked that the ethos of Congress's "so-called" watchdog committees was, "We don't watch the dog. We don't know what's going on, and furthermore, we don't want to know." In 1956, Massachusetts Senator Leverett Saltonstall, who ostensibly oversaw the CIA and whose brother was a high-ranking agency official said, "The difficulty in connection with asking questions and obtaining information is that we might obtain information which I personally would rather not have, unless it were essential for me as a member of Congress to have it."

Former New York Congressman Edward Koch provided a telling anecdote in 1974 when he described his attendance in January 1969 at a breakfast meeting for eighteen freshman Congressmen at the CIA's Virginia headquarters. Then CIA director Richard Helms greeted the group by saying, "Gentlemen, this is probably the only time you will ever have an opportunity to ask any questions of the CIA. So ask."

Koch raised his hand and said, "Mr. Helms, I really have two questions. How many people do you employ, and what is the size of your budget?"

Helms replied, "There are only two questions I can't answer, and those are the two."

Astounded, Koch said, "Mr. Helms, are you telling me, a Member of Congress, that I can't learn the size of your budget? After all, I vote on that budget. Somehow or other I ought to be able to see it."

Said Helms, "That is exactly what I am telling you. That budget item is buried under some other items and you will not know what it is. It is passed upon by a few Members of Congress and you will never know what it is."

"You mean," Koch asked, "it could be buried under Social Security?"

"We have not used that one yet," replied Helms, "but it is not a bad idea."

Retired Air Force Colonel L. Fletcher Prouty, who served as special liaison officer between the CIA and the Defense Department, writes that in 1955, when Senator Mike Mansfield attempted to pass a law establishing "a strong watchdog committee" to oversee the CIA, Senator Saltonstall led the opposition with the claim that no such committee was needed. Prouty, who became the model for "Mr. X" in Oliver Stone's controversial film *JFK*, writes further that Saltonstall and others in Congress knew precious little about the nation's intelligence community. Said Prouty,

> They knew how big the CIA was within the bounds of the 'real' or intelligence organization; but none of them knew about its tremendous global base capability, and what is much more important, none of them knew the intricacies of the Agency's supporting system that existed in the name of the Army Special Forces and the Air Force Air Supply and Communication Wings.

Had Congress ever displayed any curiosity about CIA activities during this time, it is unlikely anything would have been learned. The Agency, at best, felt little responsibility to the nation's elected representatives. Former CIA director Allen Dulles, who held the job during the tumultuous Cold War years from 1953 through 1961, once said he "felt obliged to tell the truth only to one person: the president." Dulles, who was prone "to fudge the truth," as he termed it, would on occasion be candid with a subcommittee chairman, "that is, if [he] wants to know." Or when convenient, as Dulles once quipped to his staff, "I'll just tell them a few war stories." Another former CIA director, William Colby, said:

> The old tradition was that you don't ask. It was a consensus that intelligence was apart from the rules...that was the reason we did step over the line a few times, largely because no one was watching. No one was there to say don't do this.

From the mid-1940s through the 1970s (and perhaps well beyond), the media frequently slept in the same bed as Congress and the CIA. Consequently, media oversight of intelligence activities was essentially nonexistent. On those rare occasions when reporters did cover something that involved the CIA, their stories were colored with shades generously provided by intelligence officials. Today, it is generally conceded that many reporters and newspaper columnists in the 1950s, and later, were more than chummy and cooperative with their friends in the intelligence community. In researching this book, several graphic examples of this were encountered, including instances where journalists actually produced stories that falsely presented "facts" so that CIA objectives could be better served. Two examples, quite germane to this book, were Edward Hunter and Pulitzer Prize winner Ed Reid.

As we have already seen in this book's section on brainwashing, Hunter, while a reporter for various newspapers, was also a covert propaganda specialist for the CIA. He is credited with having coined the word "brainwashing." Reid, who was a widely recognized crime reporter, was very likely privy to some of the concealed details of Frank Olson's death. Previously classified CIA documents reveal that Reid, a reporter for the *Brooklyn Eagle* and *Las Vegas Sun* newspapers at the time, had unprecedented access to one of the CIA's Manhattan safe houses, and on at least two occasions had actually observed unwitting individuals being dosed with LSD.

The traditionally passive attitudes toward non-existent CIA oversight began to change in 1972. The high-water mark of that change is usually considered to be the Watergate reporting of Bob Woodward and Carl Bernstein. However, today's tendency to trivialize and simplify history overshadows the significant work of writers like David Wise and Thomas B. Ross, newspaper columnist Jack Anderson, and investigative reporter Seymour M. Hersh, all of whom preceded the Watergate duo by over a decade. These earlier writers forged a trail through journalistic topography previously unexplored, blazing the way for future reporters. When Wise and Ross published their book *The Invisible Government*, the CIA actually considered buying every copy on the market, until Random House told the Agency it "would just print some more." Seymour Hersh's work was especially instrumental in the soon-to-explode story of an unknown biochemist named Frank Olson.

On December 22, 1974, the *New York Times* published the first in a series of articles by Hersh that exposed illegally conducted CIA activities. Wrote Hersh:

> The Central Intelligence Agency, directly violating its charter, conducted a massive, illegal, domestic intelligence operation during the Nixon Administration against the antiwar movement and other dissident groups in the United States, according to well-placed Government sources.

The illegal operations, according to Hersh, resulted in the CIA developing secret files on nearly ten thousand American citizens. Over the next few weeks, Hersh revealed other Agency abuses that included illegal telephone wiretaps and break-ins, infiltration of a wide assortment of ethnic and émigré groups, and secretly funded CIA media outlets and publishing houses. Hersh's litany of CIA wrongdoings shocked most Americans, who had known next-to-nothing about the nation's expansive intelligence community. The revelations caused many readers, for the first time in their lives, to seriously consider the complexities of government-sponsored covert actions, and to question their rationale.

Ironically, Hersh's best source for his series was the CIA itself. As former Senate investigator, Loch K. Johnson, points out, "A select few CIA insiders immediately recognized the Hersh disclosures as part of a highly secret compilation of questionable activities that had been gathered by CIA Director James Schlesinger." Schlesinger had been appointed director on February 2, 1973, after President Richard Nixon fired Richard Helms for not being more cooperative in matters related to Watergate.

Schlesinger, who had been a high-ranking defense analyst at the Rand Corporation and head of the Atomic Energy Commission before becoming DCI, had a solid reputation as a no-nonsense administrator. He made his mark on the CIA the moment that he entered his new Langley office and told the departing Helms, "This is a gentleman's club, and I am no gentleman." And then, as if to prove it, he informed Helm's administrative assistant of twenty years, "I won't be needing you any more." Said former Technical Services Division employee, W. Timothy Adams, "Schlesinger changed the orientation of the Agency. I think he moved too fast before he knew what was going on."

Schlesinger's secret compilation - the 'skeletons' list that found its way into Hersh's articles — had come about in early May 1973. At that time, he was informed by CIA General Counsel Lawrence Houston that a federal judge had learned that Watergate burglars, E. Howard Hunt, a "retired" CIA employee, and G. Gordon Liddy, a former FBI agent, had, in 1971, broken into the Los Angeles office of psychiatrist Dr. Lewis J. Fielding. Particularly upsetting to Schlesinger was the revelation that Hunt and Liddy had committed the break-in with substantial material assistance — in the form of disguises, false identity credentials, cameras, tape recorders, and film processing services — from the CIA's Technical Services Division and its Office of Security. For the break-in, Liddy had carried a razor-sharp, folded Browning knife because, as he later wrote, his "sterile (that is *nontraceable*) CIA 9-mm assassination piece" was too noisy. Hunt and Liddy were after Fielding's files on patient Daniel Ellsberg of "Pentagon Papers" fame, especially any that related to Ellsberg's reported "kinky sex habits" and "use of hallucinogenic drugs like mescaline and LSD."

The conventional story handed down over the years, and repeated in numerous books, is that Schlesinger flew into a rage at the news about Hunt and Liddy, and summoned William Colby, then CIA Deputy Director for Operations, to his office. Schlesinger — who had only been CIA director for three months, and who would depart within several days to become Secretary of Defense - allegedly told Colby that he would not stand for being blindsided by any more news about illegal CIA acts related to the still erupting Watergate scandal.

"I'll turn this goddamned place upside down and fire everyone, if necessary," Schlesinger shouted. Former Agency officials say that Colby spied an opportunity in Schlesinger's anger and quickly suggested that the director act decisively and wipe the CIA slate clean. On May 9, Schlesinger issued a directive, drafted by Colby, ordering "all the senior operating officials of this Agency to report to me immediately on any activities now going on, or that have gone on in the past, which might be construed to be outside the legislative charter of this Agency." Schlesinger also invited "every other person presently employed by the CIA to report to me on any such activities of which he has knowledge." And then lastly, he directed, "any CIA employee who believes that he has received instructions which in any way appear inconsistent with the CIA legislative charter shall inform the Director of Central Intelligence immediately." Two days later, Schlesinger departed the CIA to become Nixon's Secretary of Defense. Nixon, at the urging of Secretary of State Henry Kissinger, appointed Colby the Agency's new director.

Legendary CIA man, David Atlee Phillips, provided a glimpse of the reaction among Agency personnel to Schlesinger's directive when he wrote:

> Shortly after my return to Venezuela, an extraordinary instruction arrived in Caracas as well as in every other CIA station in the world. In Washington, it went to all CIA employees, from the most senior managers to the men who constructed wooden crates in the warehouses. Schlesinger wanted to be informed about instances now or in the past when CIA had engaged in activities which might be considered questionable. It was a tricky question to put to intelligent people who spent the better part of their adult lives in espionage and covert action, both illegal in every country of the world. The unusual survey made many of us ponder the fine line between acceptable and dubious illegalities.

The number of responses to Schlesinger's request, initially called "potential flaps," but soon dubbed the "Family Jewels" in the media, and "Skeletons" within the CIA, quickly grew to 693 typed pages, piled nearly three inches high. Included among the reports were one-paragraph accounts of the "use of a member of the Mafia [Johnny Rosselli] in an attempt to assassinate Fidel Castro"; multi-page reports of CIA technicians being used to conduct "audio surveillance" during the Democratic National Convention in 1968; reports that CIA officials participated in a police raid on an American citizen's home in Maryland during which the citizen was shot by police; memos revealing that CIA officials allowed U.S. Marshals who feared assassination by drug lords to use a CIA-operated safe house; and a detailed account of the Agency's domestic spying operation called CELOTEX II against columnist Jack Anderson and reporter Brit Hume.

Tucked away near the middle of the pile were several little-noticed documents that broadly outlined something called "Drug Testing Program." One brief memorandum summarized "research into behavioral drugs" and stated that tests had been conducted "on monkeys and mice" and "human volunteers." Another item, filed under the same heading, briefly referred to "at least two incidents" during which CIA-connected persons had been killed as a result of "drug experiments," but no names, dates or locations were noted.

On December 27, five days after Hersh's "massive spying" story hit newsstands, White House Deputy Chief of Staff, Richard Cheney, advised President Gerald Ford to establish an executive branch blue-ribbon commission to investigate possible illegal CIA activities. Cheney, who served in 1969-70 as a Special Assistant to Donald Rumsfeld, then director of the U.S. Office of Economic Opportunity, told Ford that he needed to act quickly to avoid the White House being "whipsawed by prolonged Congressional investigations" that were sure to come as a result of Hersh's revelations. Cheney advised that by appointing "a blue-ribbon investigative commission," the White House could seize the offensive, demonstrate leadership in troubled times, help reestablish public trust and faith in government, and perhaps circumvent "Congressional efforts to further encroach on the executive branch."

Cheney and Rumsfeld, along with the President's trusted counsel, Philip Buchen, further advised Ford that he needed to exercise caution in appointing commission members so to avoid charges of initiating a whitewash effort.

On January 4, 1975, Ford issued an Executive Order creating the "Commission on CIA Activities Within the United States." Ford's mandate to the Commission was "to ascertain and evaluate any facts relating to activities conducted within the United States by the Central Intelligence Agency that give rise to questions as to whether the Agency has exceeded its statutory authority." In a statement prepared for the media, Ford announced that the Commission "will immediately have the benefit of the report already furnished to me by Director W.E. Colby of the CIA." Almost as an afterthought, Ford added, "The Justice Department is, of course, also looking into such aspects of the matter as are within its jurisdiction." Mindful that Congress was organizing its own hearings, Ford concluded, "I am aware of current plans of various Committees of the Congress to hold hearings on matters similar to those which will be addressed by the Commission. Whether hearings are undertaken by existing oversight Committees, or should the Congress deem a joint House-Senate Committee to be the best approach to avoid a proliferation of hearings, it is my strong hope that the Committee consider the findings and recommendations of the Commission."

For reasons unexplained, Ford acted against the advice of his staff and selected Vice President Nelson Rockefeller as chairman of what quickly became known as the Rockefeller Commission. Rockefeller had, for decades, maintained extremely close ties to the intelligence community and was, therefore, viewed as an unlikely choice for a genuine "clean up." As early as December 1954 and extending through December 1955, Rockefeller had served as President Eisenhower's representative on the National Security Council's Operations Coordinating Board (OCB), which was very much involved with CIA clandestine operations. Gerald Colby and Charlotte Dennet write that Rockefeller acted as "Eisenhower's 'circuit breaker,' informing the president of CIA covert operations while protecting the president's 'plausible deniability' before Congress, since some operations ran afoul of American or international law." Former intelligence officer and historian, William R. Corson, wrote in 1977:

> A review of the major covert action projects approved during Rockefeller's tenure on the OCB reveals that he doubtless gained personal knowledge about many of the things he was later called upon in 1975 by President Ford to investigate.

Moreover, Rockefeller's knowledge and approval of drug experimentation and brainwashing research went far beyond his OCB experience. Still largely overlooked in the public record is the fact that the U.S. Department of Health,

Education and Welfare (HEW) undertook drug experiments sponsored by the CIA when Rockefeller was department undersecretary in 1953. Many of these experiments involved CIA funding and required Rockefeller's specific approval. Also, beginning in the early 1950s, the Rockefeller Foundation had been funding CIA-front groups like the Fund for Human Ecology, which was directly involved in CIA-supported behavior "modification" experiments. Beginning even earlier, in 1943, the Foundation had been funding a psychiatric research facility, the Allan Memorial Institute in Montreal, Canada, which soon became the site of some of the CIA's most notorious and horrific psychological experiments, conducted by Rockefeller-funded Dr. Ewen Cameron.

Other Commission members selected by Ford included: AFL-CIO chief Lane Kirkland; General Lyman L. Lemnitzer, former chairman of the Joint Chiefs of Staff; Erwin Griswold, former Harvard Law School dean; C. Douglas Dillon, former JFK treasury secretary; and John T. Connor, Chairman of the Board and CEO of Allied Chemical Corporation. They were, as historian Kathryn S. Olmsted underscored, "all privy to CIA secrets or noted for their strong support of governmental secrecy." Kirkland was a staunch supporter of CIA-funded labor activities in Latin America. Lemnitzer had a strong hand in planning the CIA's Cuban Bay of Pigs debacle. Griswold, in March 1972, argued before the Supreme Court that Army spying on citizens against the Vietnam War was not illegal. Dillon, chairman of the Rockefeller Foundation, had participated in discussions about the CIA's assassination of the Congo's Patrice Lumumba.

In sum, the Rockefeller Commission hardly appeared to be a group that would maintain any semblance of objectivity in its collective duties. Regardless, when the Commission's membership was announced at a news conference on January 6, Ron Nessen, White House press secretary, told reporters that all members of the Commission had been closely checked and "would not have been picked if they had any connections with the CIA which would hamper them." Nessen acknowledged only that Rockefeller himself had "some knowledge of how the CIA operated" through his service since 1969 on the President's Foreign Intelligence Advisory Board, established by President Kennedy after the Bay of Pigs fiasco.

For Commission executive director, Ford selected David W. Belin, former assistant counsel for the President's [Lyndon Johnson] Commission on the Assassination of President Kennedy, commonly called the Warren Commission. As a Congressman from Michigan, Ford himself had been a member of the Warren Commission and had been "impressed with Belin's professionalism and thoroughness." Belin was a highly regarded Des Moines, Iowa attorney who had, following his participation on the Warren Commission, authored two books on the JFK assassination. He was a staunch advocate of the lone-assassin theory and relentlessly argued that most Americans put credence in "sensational conspiracy theories" regarding Kennedy's assassination because of "irresponsible

465

critics who have deliberately and grossly misrepresented the record." Eight years before his strange death in 1999, Belin called Oliver Stone's film, *JFK*, "a big lie that would have made Adolf Hitler proud."

Little is known about the inner workings and activities of the Rockefeller Commission. The vast majority of the Commission's files remain classified, and will not be accessible to researchers, or to the public, for another twenty years. With an open-ended budget and a staff of eleven lawyers and fifteen support personnel, the Commission exercised its discretion to operate well away from any public and media scrutiny. The Commission defended this decision with the explanation:

> Because of the sensitivity of the CIA's intelligence and counterintelligence activities, and their critical relationship to national security, the Commission recognized that it must close its sessions to the public. But, as a consequence, it has felt all the more an obligation to conduct a diligent investigation, assuring the American people that all serious questions of legality and propriety within the area of responsibility assigned to the Commission have been carefully investigated and analyzed.

Despite this, public opinion polls taken at its inception revealed that most Americans expected that the Commission would produce "another cover-up."

One of the few facts known about the Commission's work is that one of its first agenda tasks was understandably a review of the CIA's "Family Jewels" documents. The scant and seemingly innocuous documents about drug testing originally submitted to Schlesinger in 1973 had expanded. They now included about twenty-five additional, detailed pages about the programs. Coincidentally, these new documents had been assembled just days after the formation of the Commission because the Department of Justice wanted to conduct its own, separate review of the "Family Jewels." A CIA memorandum dated January 13, 1975 describes a December 31, 1974 meeting at the Justice Department during which CIA director William Colby "briefed the Acting Attorney General Laurence Silberman on the Agency's 'skeletons' list." The memorandum states: "John Warner [CIA General Counsel] accompanied the Director to that meeting and also present was James A. Wilderotter, Associate Deputy Attorney General. The Acting Attorney General stated that, under the law, he would be required to look into certain of these matters. The Director assured him of cooperation."

Colby, in his 1978 memoirs, describes the meeting without mentioning the presence of Warner and Wilderotter. Colby writes that Acting Attorney General Silberman had phoned him and told him to come to his office because of concerns about Seymour Hersh's sensational, December 1974 articles. Said Silberman, "It looks like we have some further business to discuss." When Colby arrived at Silberman's office, Silberman waved copies of Hersh's articles at him. "What else have you boys got tucked up your sleeves?" asked Silberman. Colby recalled that in the course of his explanation about the drug experiments cited in the articles, he told Silberman about the "Family Jewels" list.

"That's very interesting," Silberman responded. "Tell me, did you turn that list over to the Justice Department?"

"No," Colby replied in a manner he described as "nonplused."

"You're a lawyer, Bill," Silberman said, ushering Colby into the proverbial woodshed. "You have had in your possession evidence of illegal actions. As a public servant, you're obliged to turn such evidence over to the proper authorities, in this case the Department of Justice. In withholding that evidence for a year and a half, Bill, you may have committed a crime yourself."

Colby writes that he was "shocked" by Silberman's words. "After a moment, when I had recovered a bit, I said, 'The thought that the "Jewels" should have been reported to Justice never crossed my mind. I reported the list to the chairmen of our appropriate congressional committees and issued the directives that corrected the situation. I thought that was sufficient.'"

"Well, maybe," Silberman replied. "But in any case you better let me have that list and I'll see what we should do about it."

Three days after Colby's meeting at the Justice Department, according to the January 13, 1975 CIA memorandum, Silberman called Colby again to request "cooperation from the Agency in the Department of Justice looking into these matters, to include a review of files." Silberman assured Colby that the Justice Department "would treat the information provided with due regard to sensitivities." According to the somewhat cryptic memo, Silberman "requested this task be performed in accordance with general guidelines of a similar ongoing review by Justice on certain matters." Silberman assured Colby that files could be reviewed at either the CIA or the Department of Justice, but "at no time would files be left with Justice until further discussions took place."

The first step in implementing this course of action took place at the Department of Justice on January 7, when CIA General Counsel Warner met with two teams of DOJ attorneys, one from the Civil Rights Division and one from the Criminal Division. At the meeting, Warner explained "the sensitivities and the problem of inadequate records in certain cases" and "made abundantly clear... that there would be difficulties in responding on a timely basis because of the on-going activities of the [Rockefeller Commission] and review by congressional committees."

On January 9, five Justice Department attorneys spent a full day at CIA headquarters reviewing the "Family Jewels." According to Warner, the CIA answered questions, and educated the attorneys "on Agency organization and functions." Warner said that the group was so befuddled by the Agency's Byzantine structure that he drew up an organization schematic for them to use in their review. After the meeting, Warner informed Colby that the DOJ attorneys planned to return the next day to start reviewing backup files for seven activities, including the "use of drugs for experiments in influencing human behavior." The interest of the attorneys in this activity had been especially piqued by one "Family Jewels" item that read:

> In January 1973, Dr. Sidney Gottlieb, advising that he was acting on instructions from DCI Richard Helms, ordered the destruction of all records associated with drug research and testing. On 31 January 1973, seven boxes of progress reports, from 1953 through 1967, were recalled from the archives and destroyed. In addition, twenty-five copies of a booklet entitled "*LSD-25: Some Un-Psychedelic Implications*" were destroyed.

One of the first documents given to the attorneys upon their return was a July 26, 1963 document entitled, "Report of Inspection of MKULTRA." The report had been compiled by CIA internal inspector John Vance for the Agency's Inspector General, John S. Earman Jr. (See Book Three, Chapter 1.) Known as "Jack" to his colleagues, Earman's tenure with the Agency extended back to 1948, when, along with Col. Boris T. Pash, he was the CIA's representative with the notorious Operation Bloodstone, the recruitment of Nazi military officers, engineers, and scientists for CIA operations.

The Justice attorneys had no idea what MKULTRA was. Upon inquiring, they were told that it was primarily a "tracking" name, or in CIA parlance, a cryptonym, used to identify "project activities that were concerned with the research and development of chemical, biological, and radiological materials capable of employment in clandestine operations to control human behavior." CIA officials explained that "MK" was a diagraph that signified a program that was primarily operated domestically, i.e., in the United States. "ULTRA" was the program's actual codename.

According to a cover memo attached to the report, Earman advised then CIA Director John A. McCone that "it was deemed advisable to prepare the report of the MKULTRA program in one copy only, in view of its unusual sensitivity." Earman also noted that MKULTRA had been authorized in 1953 by then-CIA Director Allen Dulles, and that "normal procedures for project approval, funding, and accounting were waived." Wrote Earman:

> The concepts involved in manipulating human behavior are found by many people both within and outside the Agency to be distasteful and unethical. There is considerable evidence that opposition intelligence services are active and highly proficient in this field. The experience of [the CIA's Technical Services Division] to date indicates that both the research and the employment of the materials are expensive and often unpredictable in results. Nevertheless, there have been major accomplishments both in research and operational employment.

What were those accomplishments? asked the Justice attorneys. After all these years, it's hard to say, replied the officials. Can we review the "research and operational employment" files that supported those accomplishments?

inquired the attorneys. That is a problem, CIA officials responded. Records for the MKULTRA program had been destroyed two years earlier. And, said the officials, as Earman's report noted, because normal procedures were waived for the program, "a substantial portion of the MKULTRA record appears to rest in the memories of the principle officers" responsible for the program and "is therefore almost certain to be lost with their departures." Were any of these officers still employed by the CIA or available for interviews? inquired the Justice attorneys. Virtually all were retired, dead, or unavailable, replied the officials, but let us see what we can do.

The DOJ attorneys were intrigued by several sections of Earman's report. Especially interesting was what was termed MKULTRA's "final phase of testing materials"– experiments that involved "their application to unwitting subjects in normal life settings." Stated the report:

> [The] capabilities of MKULTRA substances to produce disabling or discrediting effects, or to increase the effectiveness of interrogations of hostile subjects, cannot be established solely through testing on volunteer populations.

Because of this problem, the report explained:

> [the CIA's Technical Services Section] entered into an informal arrangement with certain cleared and witting individuals in the [Federal] Bureau of Narcotics in 1955 which provided for the release of MKULTRA materials for such testing as those individuals deemed desirable and feasible. The initial arrangement obtained the services of a senior representative of the Bureau and one of his assistants on the West Coast.

According to Inspector General Earman's report, the "particular advantage" of drug testing arrangements with the Federal Bureau of Narcotics "has been that test subjects could be sought and cultivated within the setting of narcotics control." The report further elaborated:

> Some subjects have been informers or members of suspect criminal elements, from which the Bureau has obtained results of operational value through the tests. On the other hand, the effectiveness of the substances on individuals at all social levels, high and low, native American and foreign, is of great significance and testing has been performed on a variety of individuals within these categories.

However, Earman noted, there were significant limitations to the drug experiments performed by the Narcotics Bureau, not the least of which was "the infeasibility of performing scientific observation of results." Earman, apparently assuming that scientific study was paramount, not to mention feasible, in these experiments, bluntly wrote:

469

The Bureau agents are not qualified scientific observers. Their subjects are seldom accessible beyond the first hours of the test. The testing may be useful in perfecting delivery techniques, and in identifying surface characteristics of onset, reaction, attribution, and side effect. In a number of instances, however, the test subject has become ill for hours or days, including hospitalization in at least one case, and the agent could only follow-up by guarded inquiry after the test subject's return to normal life.

In the final analysis, Earman was troubled by the relationship between the CIA and the Narcotics Bureau. First, Earman had been surprised to discover the safe house arrangement between the two agencies. Equally surprising to him was that it had originated in the mid-Fifties. Although Earman did not note this in his final report, initial drafts reveal that the Inspector General's staff had found it especially puzzling in light of their careful review of a 1957 report completed by Earman's predecessor, Lyman B. Kirkpatrick Jr. That review had found nothing in Kirkpatrick's report on TSS's drug program that indicated the existence of any arrangement with the Narcotics Bureau. Not surprisingly, Kirkpatrick's report had also not identified any problems with the program.

Kirkpatrick had written that TSS's use of psychochemicals, including LSD and mescaline, had produced "some concrete results." Kirkpatrick noted that "six specific products," including a refined version of LSD, had been developed for "operational use" by TSS. Three of the products "are discrediting and disabling materials which can be administered unwittingly and permit the exercise of a measure of control over the actions of the subject." Kirkpatrick further wrote that the three products had been used operationally on six different occasions "on a total of 33 subjects." The other three products developed by TSS were a "knockout material used to facilitate unconsciousness," an "alcohol extender which produces a degree of inebriation out of proportion to the amount of alcohol consumed," and "a stimulant similar to Benzedrine in effect but without its undesirable after-effects."

Kirkpatrick's report spoke approvingly of the issues of "conducting essential tests and experiments" to produce "the end product to operational use." Experiments "are generally conducted on animals" the report stated. TSS had engaged the "services and facilities" of the National Institute of Mental Health in conducting experiments on "its ape colony" to study the effects of LSD and knockout substances, but human experimentation had produced its "best results" in mental institutions and prisons, claimed the report. Extensive testing was taking place at the Federal Narcotics Addiction Hospital in Lexington, Kentucky, but, observed Kirkpatrick, "experiments conducted under controlled conditions and the results may be quite different from those obtained in the operational use of the material."

Concluded Kirkpatrick, "Much more testing must be conducted before the behavior program can be considered to have accomplished its objectives."

Kirkpatrick made no mention of Narcotics Bureau safe houses. Nor did he mention any unintended results, injuries or deaths, as a result of any experiments conducted or sponsored by the CIA.

Second, and of critical concern to Earman, was "the risk of serious damage to the Agency in the event of compromise of the true nature of this activity." Without ever specifically defining what he meant about the "true nature of this activity," Earman concluded that under the arrangement with the Narcotics Bureau "non-Agency personnel are necessarily fully witting of the project and significance of their arrangements, and of the sponsorship of the CIA." Wrote Earman, "Compromise of this information intentionally or unwittingly by these individuals at some time in the future is a hazard that cannot be ruled out." Earman also wrote that he was concerned about the possibility of a test subject correctly attributing "the cause of his reaction" and then seeking help from an "independent" professional to identify "the exact nature of the substance employed, and by whom." This potential problem, combined with the resultant broadening of "the circle of individuals who possessed at least circumstantial evidence of the nature of the activity, greatly concerned the Agency's Inspector General and led him to conclude that Federal Narcotics Bureau involvement in the CIA's drug experiments contained "high risks" to "the senior command of CIA." Therefore, Earman recommended "termination of this phase of the MKULTRA program."

Justice Department attorneys had a long list of questions after reading Earman's report. Not the least of these was, had the CIA acted on Earman's recommendation and terminated the involvement of the Narcotics Bureau in the program?

Yes, replied CIA officials, explaining that on June 9, 1964, almost a year after Earman turned in his report, CIA Deputy Director of Plans, Richard Helms, had reconstituted the MKULTRA Project and changed its name to Project MK-SEARCH. Officials told the Justice attorneys that day-to-day responsibility for MKSEARCH remained under the Deputy Director of the Agency's Technical Services Section and that all new projects had to be approved by DDP Helms. In addition to Helms signing off on MKSEARCH, officials explained, the program was also approved by Lawrence K. White, CIA Deputy Director of Support, Lyman B. Kirkpatrick, the CIA's then-Executive Director, and Marshall Sylvester Carter, Deputy Director of Central Intelligence.

But did that mean that the Narcotics Bureau's participation in the drug experiments was terminated? inquired the attorneys.

CIA officials said they weren't sure that had been the case, and that Helms' memorandum recommending the change made no mention of the Bureau. The officials produced several additional memoranda that detailed actions after Earman had submitted his report.

Who were the non-Agency individuals connected with the Narcotics Bureau's involvement in MKULTRA? the attorneys asked.

We aren't sure of the names, replied CIA officials, promising to try to find out.

What was the precursor project to MKULTRA and MKSEARCH called Project ARTICHOKE? asked the Justice Department attorneys.

That, too, was a problem, said the officials; most of the ARTICHOKE records had been destroyed along with MKULTRA files. But, as far as they could tell, explained the officials, ARTICHOKE was a project similar to MKULTRA, but operated apart from TSS and under the auspices of the Agency's Office of Security. ARTICHOKE, the officials said, had also briefly been under the control of the CIA's Office of Scientific Intelligence, but since mid-1952 had been back under the Security Office. The project occasionally shared scientific findings with other CIA branches, officials said.

The attorneys asked to see whatever ARTICHOKE records remained, especially those related to drug experiments.

CIA officials responded that it could take several days to locate and assemble any records. Within forty-eight hours the seemingly innocuous request opened a whole new can of worms at the CIA.

The first sign that something was amiss was the CIA's discovery of a note written by Dr. E.H. Cushing, a CIA scientific advisor and Assistant Chief Medical Director for Research and Educational Services for the Veterans Administration to Dr. H. Marshall Chadwell, Deputy Director of the CIA's Office of Scientific Intelligence. (Dr. Chadwell, a Harvard PhD in physical chemistry, had joined the CIA in 1950 after working in New York as an executive at the Rockefeller Foundation.) Cushing's brief note, dated October 23, 1953, read:

> I&SO [Inspection and Security Office, precursor to the Office of Security] has prepared a new set of 'by-laws' for the [ARTICHOKE] Committee, which will include approval of testing of drugs on volunteers among Agency personnel.

Next, the CIA discovered another note by Dr. Cushing. This one, dated October 29, 1953, referred to "a draft memoranda to be returned to the ARTICHOKE Committee, entitled 'Experimental Project Utilizing Trainee Volunteers.'" But searchers were unable to locate a copy of the draft memorandum.

Then searchers came across yet another note concerning a conversation between Dr. Chadwell and Dr. Willis Gibbons, Deputy Director of TSS. The startling note, dated December 14, 1953, was headed, "Conversation With Gibbons" and read:

> 1. Lovell has not heard anything from Gibbons.
> 2. Lovell reported that Quarles and George Merck were about to kill the Schwab activity at Detrick as 'un-American.' Is it necessary to take action at a high place?
> 3. Lovell knew of Frank R. Olson. No inhibitions. Baring of inner man. Suicidal tendencies. Offensive usefulness? HMC [Chadwell] told Shef Edwards Saturday A.M., the 12th.

472

The note was carbon-copied to someone identified only as "McMahon." It also bore three handwritten lines. The first two lines read: "Conv. 15 Dec. in HMC's office. No action on HMC's part unless requested." The third line read: "Gibbons & Quarles at cocktails."

CIA researchers were able to quickly identify all of the persons named in the December 14 note except for "Frank R. Olson." Who was Frank R. Olson? they asked.

What they soon discovered had them wishing they had never asked.

A hastily written January 29, 1975 CIA memorandum for the record, bearing many typographical mistakes, headed "SUBJECT: Frank R. Olson," reveals what the CIA research team initially learned about Olson. The document states, in part:

> Mr. Olson, who committed suicide on 28 November 1953, was a civilian employee of the U.S. Army Chemical Corps, then located at Camp Dietrich [sic]... Mr. Olson had been in New York City during the preceding week undergoing psychiatric treatment from a Mr. Harold Abramson. Mr. Olson had been accompanied by Robert Lashbrook, a TSS employee at the time. Mr. Lashbrook and Mr. Olson had a room at the Statler Hotel in New York City. At 0230 hours, Mr. Lashbrook was awakened by a crash and discovered that Mr. Olson had dived through the hotel window. After the incident, Mr. Lashbrook called Dr. Gottlieb and then called the hotel desk which, in turn, called the police.

The memo went on to relate that less than three hours after Olson's death, Bernard F. Doran, a CIA personnel security officer, convened a meeting at CIA headquarters with three individuals: his superior, Col. Sheffield Edwards, director of the CIA's Office of Security; Dr. Willis Gibbons, TSS director; and Dr. Sidney Gottlieb, TSS's Chemical Branch chief. At that meeting, Drs. Gibbons and Gottlieb told Col. Edwards that on "Wednesday and Thursday, 18 and 19 November 1953, a group of individuals from the Special Operations group at Camp Dietrich [sic] and from TSS" gathered "at a cabin at Deer Creek Lake [sic]." Gibbons and Gottlieb related that the gathering "had been kept on an 'EYES ONLY' basis, known only to a few persons in the Agency and at Camp Dietrich [sic], including Generals Bullene and Creary [sic] of the Army Chemical Corps." At the gathering, according to Dr. Gottlieb, on the evening of November 19:

> ... it was decided to experiment with the drug LSD and for the members present to administer the drug to themselves to ascertain the effect a clandestine application would have on a meeting or conversation.

Bullene is General Egbert F. Bullene. General William M. Creasy is misidentified as General "Creary." Bullene was commander of Edgewood Arsenal in Maryland. Creasy created a stir before Congress in 1957 when he came out in support of LSD as a weapon of war; he also was involved in the Harold Blauer case.]

Dr. Gottlieb now told Col. Edwards that a "very small dose" of LSD "was placed in a bottle of Cointreau and that all present, except two individuals, had a drink thereof." Mr. Olson was included in this group, Gottlieb explained, going on to say that the LSD "had a definite effect on the group to the point where they were boisterous and could not continue the meeting or engage in sensible conversation. Dr. Gottlieb stated that Mr. Olson, among others, complained of wakefulness during the night."

The January 29, 1975 memo continues:

> On Tuesday, 24 November 1953, the Commanding Officer of Special Operations, Camp Dietrich, Colonel Ruette [sic] called Dr. Gottlieb and stated that Mr. Olson appeared mentally depressed. Dr. Gottlieb then suggested that Mr. Lashbrook take Mr. Olson to New York City to be treated by Dr. Abramson.
>
> From that point there were a series of psychiatric treatments in New York City until 28 November, when it had been planned to place Olson in a sanitarium called Chestnut Hotel [sic], near Rockville, Maryland. Because Messrs. Lashbrook and Olson had not been able to make plane reservations, they stayed overnight at the Statler on 28 November, when the suicide occurred.

A follow-up CIA memorandum dated January 31, 1975 sought to clarify some of the hurried details provided in the earlier document. This memo had as its subject, "Project ARTICHOKE." It stated:

> In the review of file information in SRS [Office of Security Research Service] materials, one incident which occurred in November 1953 appears worthy of note. Although it was not clear from the file information whether or not the incident occurred under the auspices of Project ARTICHOKE, the incident did involve the use of LSD in an experimental exercise.
>
> One Frank OLSON, a civilian employee of the Department of the Army, committed suicide a week or so after having been administered LSD by an Agency representative. Details concerning this incident apparently will be reported in a separate memorandum, but it appears that the drug was administered to several unwitting subjects by a Dr. Gottlieb, at the time a branch chief in TSS (now OTS). On the day following the experiment, OLSON began to behave in a peculiar and erratic manner and was later placed under the care of a psychiatrist. A few days later, OLSON crashed through a window in a New York hotel, in an apparent suicide.

A subsequent memorandum, dated February 3, 1975, also designated "Project ARTICHOKE," provides additional details about how the information on Olson had been discovered. The memo reads:

> In the conduct of investigating Project ARTICHOKE, attempts were made to locate and review all available Office of Security information pertinent

to Project ARTICHOKE. The information base...was the materials found in old SRS files, specifically a box of materials provided out of retirement from WTC.

The reference box of materials also contained a file entitled 'LSD,' pertaining primarily to one Frank OLSON. Much of the information contained in the 'LSD' file appeared to be I.G. [Inspector General] file information. The Office of Security file on Frank OLSON was not reviewed, as the OLSON matter was to be handled separately by a different review.

On February 5, 1975 Donald F. Chamberlain, CIA Inspector General, sent a memorandum to DCI William Colby regarding: "CIA R&D and Testing of Behavioral Drugs." Attached to that memo was a "sterilized summary" of the CIA's drug testing projects that was to be shared with the Justice Department attorneys and the Rockefeller Commission. The summary blacked out (redacted) the names of people, places, and dates, and substituted in their place "identity," or "Iden" numbers. In the various drafts this document went through, Frank Olson's identity number varied from 9 to 17. The final summary concerning the Olson incident, officially approved "for release to authorities investigating the CIA," reads:

The predecessor organization of the Office of Technical Service was the focal point of the operational investigation of behavioral drugs, although none of the office's records on this activity are in existence, having been destroyed in January 1973. As noted above it [TSS] participated in the meetings of the so-called ARTICHOKE Committee. That office maintained liaison with personnel at Iden 6 [Camp Detrick], with who [sic] meetings were held once or twice a year to discuss questions involving behavioral drugs.

At one such meeting at Iden 7 [Deep Creek Lake] in Maryland, Iden 8 [18-19 November] 1953, with seven representatives from Iden 6 and three from CIA, eight of those present were administered LSD which had been introduced into a bottle of Cointreau. Although records of an inquiry by the Inspector General into the incident indicate that those present discussed testing on unwitting persons, and agreed in principle that such a program should be explored, none of them were advised until some 20 minutes after they drank the Cointreau that it had been treated with LSD. Of the two who did not take it, one did not drink alcohol beverages at all and the other refrained because of a heart condition.

One of the members of the group, a civilian employee of the Department of Army named Iden 9 [Dr. Frank R. Olson], had serious side effects. He was sent, at CIA expense, with an escort from CIA, to New York, where he received treatment from a psychiatrist, commencing Iden 10 [November 24].

While in New York for this treatment, he threw himself through a closed window in his room on the tenth floor of the Iden 11 [Statler

Hotel], falling to his death. CIA, in a document of Iden 12 [December 9, 1953], signed by its General Counsel, certified Iden 9's death resulted from 'circumstances arising out of an experiment undertaken in the course of his official duties for the United States Government.'

This was the official position of the Agency, established for the purpose of assuring that the survivors of Iden 9 received compensation from the BEC [Federal Bureau of Employee Compensation]. Iden 9 had experienced some instability and delusions prior to the incident, and it was judged that the drug served to trigger the act leading to his death. Reprimands were issued by the DCI to two CIA employees held responsible for the incident.

Five months after its formation, on June 6, 1975, the Rockefeller Commission hand delivered its final report to President Ford. The report consists of 251 pages, broken into nineteen chapters. The section dealing with Frank Olson comes under Chapter 16, "Domestic Activities of the Directorate of Science and Technology," which has as its first subsection, "The Testing of Behavior-Influencing Drugs on Unsuspecting Subjects Within the United States." The subsection states:

The [CIA's] drug program was part of a much larger CIA program to study possible means for controlling human behavior. Other studies explored the effects of radiation, electro-shock, psychology, psychiatry, sociology and harassment substances.

The primary purpose of the drug program was to counter the use of behavior-influencing drugs clandestinely administered by an enemy, although several operational uses outside the United States were also considered.

The report then notes that the Commission's investigation of the programs was hampered due to the fact that "only limited records of the testing conducted were available" because "all the records concerning the program were ordered destroyed in 1973." Also, notes the report, "all persons directly involved in the early phases of the program were either out of the country and not available for interview, or were deceased." The report further attests that in 1963 the CIA's Inspector General had questioned the "propriety of testing on unsuspecting subjects" after discovery of "a number of instances" in which tests subjects became "ill for hours or days," with actual details unavailable because "of the destruction of the records and the unavailability of witnesses."

The Rockefeller Commission report then recounts the fate of Frank Olson, as follows:

The Commission did learn, however, that on one occasion during the early phases of this program (in 1953), LSD was administered to an employee of the Department of the Army without his knowledge while he was attending a meeting with CIA personnel working on the drug project.

Prior to receiving the LSD, the subject had participated in discussions where the testing of such substances on unsuspecting subjects was agreed to in principle. However, this individual was not made aware that he had been given LSD until about 20 minutes after it had been administered. He developed serious side effects and was sent to New York with a CIA escort for psychiatric treatment. Several days after, he jumped from a tenth floor window of his room and died as a result.

The General Counsel [CIA] ruled that the death resulted from 'circumstances arising out of an experiment undertaken in the course of his official duties for the United States Government,' thus ensuring his survivors of receiving certain death benefits. Reprimands were issued by the Director of Central Intelligence to two [sic] CIA employees responsible for the incident.

2

June 11, 1975

On June 11, 1975, around noon, Eric Olson answered the telephone in his Cambridge, Massachusetts's apartment. On the other end was Greg Hayward, his sister Lisa's husband. Greg was calling from their home in Frederick, Maryland.

"Have you seen today's *Washington Post*?" Greg asked excitedly.

"No, why?" Eric said.

"There's a story in it that you need to read right away," Greg said. "It's about your father."

"My father?" Eric said, confused. "What about my father?"

"Go out and get a copy," Greg said. "Then call me back."

Eric ran several blocks down Harvard Street to the Out-of-Town News kiosk in Harvard Square and bought a copy of the newspaper. The story was on the front page, under the bold headline, "Suicide Revealed."

Its first sentence succinctly summarized: "A civilian employee of the Department of the Army unwittingly took LSD as part of a Central Intelligence Agency test, then jumped 10 floors to his death less than a week later."

The article stated that the unnamed man "was given the drug while attending a meeting with CIA personnel working on a test project that involved the administration of mind-bending drugs to unsuspecting Americans and the testing of new listening devices by eavesdropping on citizens who were unaware they were being overheard." The newspaper had learned of the incident from the Rockefeller Commission's report to President Gerald Ford, publicly released the day before.

The article stunned Eric.

"I stood there in the middle of the Square reading it," he said. "After two paragraphs, my hands were shaking. I thought, 'At long last, after all this time, some sort of news arrives.' Then I thought 'This is my father they are writing about. This 'civilian employee' drugged by the CIA with LSD, this man who fell from ten floors up, this must be my father."

Alice Olson would read the article later that same day. Earlier that morning she had left her Frederick, Maryland home to go to the hospital for a series of tests that her doctor had ordered, and she had missed several calls from her closest friend, Rena Dorrell. Rena's husband, Dr. William W. Dorrell, had also been a scientist at Fort Detrick. Alice's telephone was ringing when she returned home, exhausted. It was Rena again.

"Look at the front page of the *Washington Post*," Rena said. "You're not going to believe it."

Alice picked the paper up from the kitchen table, where she had tossed it earlier.

"I screamed and said, 'That's Frank,'" Alice later recalled. The following morning, Alice's doctor called to inform her that she had cancer.

The years following her husband's death had been less than kind to Alice Olson. Coping with Frank's absence became increasingly difficult. People who knew Alice well say that she was simply overcome with self-doubt and confusion about Frank's sudden death. For a brief period of time, not long after 1953, Alice had been able to put her confusion aside when she had begun dating a man whom she thought really cared for her. But life dealt her another cruel hand when she discovered that the man, a friend of the family during her days with Frank, was actually much more interested in her sons, one of whom he had molested while on a camping trip.

Devastated, Alice began to seek solace in the bottle. Soon she had become a severe alcoholic. And for years she stayed that way. Often, her father, Charles, and stepmother, Ina, would telephone from their home in Florida, only to find Alice incoherently drunk. "You have to get a hold of yourself," Charles told her. "If not for yourself, then at least for the children," Ina said sternly.

Having a mother in Alice's condition was hard on the Olson children. Frequently they would come home from school and find Alice in a stupor or passed out at the kitchen table. One Christmas Eve, she was arrested for driving while intoxicated and spent the night in jail. In 1967, Alice lost her job as a schoolteacher. She was in and out of rehabilitation programs.

"Sometimes she was a mean drunk," says Eric Olson. "For a long time, the subject of my father was strictly taboo in our house." Nils Olson recalls, "The most innocent of questions about my father would set her off. She would fly into a rage or burst into tears." Eric adds, "She would scream at us, 'you are never going to know what happened in that hotel room. Never.'"

And it went on like that for years until suddenly, in 1973, Alice experienced an epiphany of sorts. As if preparing for something of great importance to occur, she stopped drinking and, in her sobriety, began to diligently pick up and reassemble the shattered pieces of her life. It was almost as if she had a premonition that the events of 1975 were approaching.

The day after the *Washington Post* article appeared, Lisa Olson, now Lisa Olson Hayward, and her husband, Greg, drove from their Frederick, Maryland home to that of retired Army colonel Vincent L. Ruwet, a few miles away. Ruwet, besides being Frank Olson's commanding officer at Camp Detrick, had been a close friend of Frank and Alice. Ruwet and his wife, Hazel, had frequently socialized with the Olsons. Just days after Olson's death, Ruwet had testified in a sworn affidavit, "We became very friendly socially and I saw a great deal of him and his family, both at his home and they at my home." As readers have seen, it was Ruwet who had come to the Olson's home on the morning of November 28, 1953 to inform Alice that Frank was dead.

Minutes after reading the *Post* article on June 11, Greg Hayward, at Lisa's urgings, telephoned Ruwet to ask if he could confirm that the unnamed "civilian employee" was indeed Frank Olson. Hazel Ruwet answered the call and told Hayward that her husband wasn't home. Hayward explained why he was calling, and Mrs. Ruwet replied, "Vin wouldn't know anything about that."

Later that day, Hayward called back and found Ruwet home. The retired military man reluctantly confirmed that Frank Olson was the unnamed man. According to Eric Olson's account of the phone call, Ruwet told Hayward that he had "just come in from a meeting at the CIA where he had gotten authorization to provide precisely this information."

Remarkably, Ruwet also told Hayward that, in addition to Frank Olson, Ruwet, too, had been drugged at the same meeting, but when Hayward asked for details, Ruwet refused to say anything more.

After Greg hung up, Lisa anxiously asked, "What did he say?"

"It was your father," Greg said. "He knew. He knew about it all."

"All these years?" Lisa asked.

"All along," said Greg.

Lisa had known Greg since she was in grade school. Greg lived on the other side of the large open field across the road from the Olson's house. He and the Olson children rode the same school bus each morning. Greg's father had disappeared when he was a small boy, so there was an immediate bond between him and Lisa, who had been 7 years old when her father died. Greg's mother's second husband had worked at Fort Detrick, and then the Pentagon.

When Greg and Lisa arrived at Ruwet's home on June 12, they confronted him at his front door brandishing a copy of the *Washington Post*.

"You knew all about this," Lisa admonished. "For over twenty years, you knew all about this and said absolutely nothing."

"I couldn't say anything before," Ruwet said. "You have to understand that I was under orders of the strictest secrecy."

"You were my father's friend," countered Lisa.

"You don't understand," pleaded Ruwet.

"I understand," said Greg Hayward, who had served two tours in Vietnam as an Army Ranger. Now a practicing attorney in Frederick, he had soured on U.S. intervention into Southeast Asia. "I understand that what you did was flat out wrong," Hayward said.

"No," Ruwet argued, "I did my duty and you should know that."

When the couple scoffed at his protestations, Ruwet became defensive and tried to discourage them from going to the media with anything. Lisa grew angrier when Ruwet told them that they "would be making a terrible mistake" if they intended to seek redress from the CIA. "Wait before you do anything," Ruwet argued. "Let me talk to your mother. She'll understand."

Still angry, Lisa and Greg left, telling Ruwet that his deception was inexcusable and that they would pursue any means available to expose him and the CIA.

"You better call your friends at the CIA and warn them," Greg said out the car window before they drove off.

In the days following the June 11, 1975 Washington Post revelations about Frank Olson's death, the CIA refused to comment on the authenticity of the reports about the still-unidentified civilian scientist. Only after relentless hounding by the press did the CIA confirm the Rockefeller Commission's scant account, but at the same time the Agency denied having provided the Commission with any information about Olson or the incident.

"Please be advised that the CIA did not provide any document or any other written materials on this topic to the Rockefeller Commission," said Agency spokesman Charles E. Savige. Directly contradicting this statement was the Commission's claim to the media that its only information about Olson had come directly from the CIA. At the same time, unidentified sources had informed the *Washington Post* that "at least three other people" had been unwittingly dosed with LSD at the same meeting with Olson. When questioned about this by reporters, a Rockefeller Commission attorney oddly responded, "I really don't feel that I'm going to be in a position to make a comment unless something so outrageous comes out that I feel I have to, and at this point I haven't seen anything."

Meanwhile, the Olson family, overcome with the news, was trying its best to monitor press reports. They discussed securing an attorney to represent them and to ward off constant calls and contacts with the media. On June 19, following a family meeting in Alice Olson's living room, Eric Olson telephoned Harry Huge, an attorney and partner at the prestigious Washington, D.C. law firm, Arnold & Porter. Olson had first met Huge in 1973, in West Virginia. At the time, Huge was the lead attorney in a lawsuit against the Pittston Coal Company. The suit arose from the devastating flood that had crashed through West Virginia's Logan County on February 26, 1972, after a mammoth coal-waste dam had collapsed. Over 130 million gallons of water and one million tons of sludge swept through sixteen small mining communities bordering Buffalo Creek. Over 125 people,, many of them women and children, had been swept away in the torrent and killed. Over a thousand others had been injured, and nearly four thousand people were left homeless. An entire valley had been wiped out.

The Pittston Coal Company owned the dam and denied any responsibility for the disaster. In a remarkable story of relentless resolve and courage, 625 survivors joined together to sue the company for negligence, recklessness, property loss, and mental suffering. The firm Arnold & Porter agreed to handle the $64 million case on a contingency-fee basis, and within two months settled out-of-court for $13.5 million, with $8 million provided for "psychic impairment" claims, in recognition of the ongoing psychological impact on survivors. As part of the lawsuit, Huge retained the services of Dr. Robert Jay Lifton, whom we first met as a brainwashing consultant during the early 1950s. Lifton, a widely respected author and Harvard professor of psychiatry and psychology, was also considered an expert witness in assessing "the psychological effects of trauma" on the miners and their families.

At the time of the Buffalo Creek tragedy, Eric Olson, in graduate school at Harvard, was coincidentally collaborating with Lifton on a number of academic projects, including co-authorship of a book entitled, *Living and Dying*. The book, dedicated by Eric to his grandfather, Rev. Charles Hall Wicks, was described by the *New York Times* as an "eminently sane, accessible, succinct argument for a more open cultural relationship with death." The small volume contains a number of ironic passages, given that it was published a little less than a year before the Olson family learned the details of Frank Olson's death. Olson and Lifton, who liberally sprinkled the book with references to popular musicians like Jimi Hendrix, Janis Joplin, and Jim Morrison, wrote, "When a person takes his own life, not only does he demonstrate his own failure to master death anxiety; he reveals a social failure as well. The society has not managed to share with him its symbols of continuity. In committing suicide, a person makes a once-and-for-all total effort to master death anxiety. Paradoxically, suicide can be an attempt to assert symbolic integrity: it is a way of holding to certain principles, of actively defining one's life boundaries, and of affirming value."

In one of the book's more revealing parts dealing with the acceptability of death, Olson and Lifton wrote: "For a child gradually coming to believe that the death of a father is real, the largely unspoken process of mourning would be something like this: 'It's summer and Daddy is not here when I go swimming; it's fall and Daddy is not here when we eat Thanksgiving dinner; it's Christmas and Daddy is not here when we open the presents.'"

Praeger Press, an academic press that would later be revealed to have served as a CIA conduit for multiple propaganda titles backed by the Agency, published the Olson and Lifton book.

As might be expected, due to their close collaboration, Dr. Lifton asked Eric Olson to accompany him to West Virginia to help interview the surviving Buffalo Creek miners and their families and document their injuries. While there, Eric forged a lasting friendship with Harry Huge. "We met under some pretty grim and stressful conditions," Huge said in a 1999 interview. "Eric's and Dr. Lifton's work was quite significant." (Eric was unaware that at the time of his work on the flood, as would subsequently be revealed in the CIA "Family Jewels" disclosures, the CIA was covertly studying the psychological effects of this disaster.)

Now, several years later, Eric asked Huge if he would file a lawsuit against the CIA on behalf of his family. Huge, already well aware of the case through the publicity it was drawing, promptly agreed. But, within a few days, he informed the Olsons that he had to withdraw his services because he had learned that another attorney in his firm, Mitchell Rogovin, was representing the CIA as outside counsel in the looming Congressional hearings, thus presenting a conflict.

Eric quickly turned to David Rudovsky, a good friend who had recently opened a small, two-lawyer firm in Philadelphia. Eric had first met Rudovsky in 1968 when he had shared a house with him for two years while working on his Ph.D. in economics at the University of Pennsylvania. As an undergraduate, Eric had studied economics at Oberlin College in Ohio. In 1966-67, on an Oberlin Fellowship, Olson was teaching economics and English in India when he received word that he had been awarded a grant from the San Francisco-based Asia Foundation. The grant would allow Eric to stay another year in India to do research. But, just a few weeks before the grant was to take effect, the Asia Foundation suddenly ceased operations in India, after it was reported in the *New York Times* that the Foundation was heavily subsidized by the CIA. Allen Dulles reportedly conceived the foundation's covert role in 1954, when it was first formed as the non-profit Committee for a Free Asia. Here it is interesting to note that it was also the Asia Foundation that partially funded Dr. Robert Lifton's brainwashing research that he conducted in Hong Kong in 1954 and 1955.

About a year after returning to the United States, in the summer of 1968, Eric moved from Frederick, Maryland to Philadelphia to begin a Ph.D. program in economics at the University of Pennsylvania. Eric says, "This was before I gradually migrated into the field of psychology." In 1971, Rudovsky had joined forces with David Kairys, a graduate of Columbia University and University of Pennsylvania law schools, to form the law firm, Kairys and Rudovsky, which in 1975 became Kairys, Rudovsky, and Maguigan.

David Rudovsky and David Kairys were no neophytes to controversy and doing battle with the government. Since 1971, their firm had served as Philadelphia counsel for the National Emergency Civil Liberties Committee (NECLC), a citizen's group dedicated to defending civil liberties and to extending the guarantees of the Bill of Rights to all people, including the poorest and least powerful. NECLC was founded in 1951, when Sen. Joe McCarthy and Congress's House Un-American Activities Committee, spurred on by the Cold War, had mounted what the group termed "a harrowing assault on civil rights."

One of the many high profile cases handled by Kairys and Rudovsky in the early 1970s was called the case of the "Camden 28." The case stemmed from an August 1971 incident, indirectly tied to the earlier "Catonsville 9" case, involving the arrest of twenty-eight people charged with raiding the Camden, New Jersey draft board offices, located in Camden's post office, and destroying Selective Service records. Kairys and Rudovsky defended those charged and raised the unique and ultimately successful defense of "overreaching governmental activity." This novel defense was premised on the fact that a paid FBI informant had provided the plans and equipment necessary for entry into the draft board's offices. Said Kairys in a 1972 front-page story in the *New York Times* about the case, "This is not law enforcement; it is the FBI acting illegally as a political force." Kairys, the article reported, filed a motion that charged, "Without the actions, expertise, and material and moral support of the FBI informer, the conspiracy would have remained abandoned and the entry into the post office building and the destruction of draft board files, which the FBI sat and watched for over two hours, would never have happened." Ironically, it would be three years before the Olson case would come along, and another thirty years before Kairys and Rudovsky would learn that a government informer had also played a critical role in Frank Olson's death.

As fate would have it, Kairys and Rudovsky would handle two other cases that had uncanny connections to the subsequent Olson case. The first involved representation of the Institute for Policy Studies (IPS), a Washington, D.C. non-profit research and social change think tank. Beginning in 1968, and continuing through 1974, IPS was the target of a deluge of illegal government surveillance activities, including the burglary of its offices, telephone wiretaps, mail tampering, theft of documents, and infiltration by numerous paid informers. These activities were conducted by the FBI, CIA, the Office of Naval Intelligence, the Army's Counter Intelligence Corps, and the metropolitan D.C. police department. Through the efforts of Kairys, Rudovsky, and Holly Maguigan, the government conceded that it had "absolutely no evidence of any criminal activity on the part of IPS or any of its employees." When the IPS investigation was in its final years, its directors retained the services of Mitchell Rogovin, a Washington-based attorney with the firm Arnold & Porter, who had a widely known reputation for defending people and groups who were victims of civil liberties attacks and government abuse. In 1975, as readers shall see, Kairys and Rudovsky would face Rogovin on the opposing side of the CIA's table.

The second case involved Kairys and Rudovsky representing a prison inmate named Jerome Roach. While awaiting trial in Philadelphia's notorious Holmesburg Prison in 1973, Roach had agreed to take part in an experiment conducted by Wallace Laboratories with a medication identified only as W-2429. Four days into the experiment, Roach experienced "symptoms of physical illness including sore throat, sore joints, fever, nausea, and sores and rashes." Roach was sent to Philadelphia General Hospital, where he was kept for several weeks and then returned to Holmesburg. When he became sick again, he was denied adequate medical treatment. Subsequently, he retained Kairys and Rudovsky to represent him. Rudovsky sued the company that conducted the experiment, the prison system, and the city of Philadelphia for $400,000. As a result of his suit and related efforts, the state of Pennsylvania thereafter prohibited all such experiments in state and county prisons, and Roach was awarded compensation.

Later, it would be revealed that in addition to Holmesburg having been used for pharmaceutical company drug experiments, the prison had been used extensively by experimenters from the U.S. Army's Chemical Research and Development Laboratory at Edgewood Arsenal, and from Fort Detrick.

Around 1:00 in the morning, the day after the June 11, 1975 *Washington Post* story broke, Rudovsky received a telephone call from Eric Olson in Boston.

"Did you read that stuff in the papers?" Olson asked

"About the CIA and LSD?" Rudovsky replied.

"Yes," Olson said.

"Yeah, I read it," Rudovsky said.

"That's my father," Olson said.

Rudovsky later said in a 1999 interview, "And I [remembered] he had told me when we lived together his father had committed suicide, but I never really kind of followed up with it."

"Well, how the hell do you know that?" Rudovsky asked in 1975.

"All the facts fit," Olson replied, and then he recounted the highlights of the confrontation between Ruwet and the Haywards.

"God, that's just amazing, absolutely incredible," said Rudovsky.

David Kairys recalls Rudovsky telling him that they were going to represent the Olson family. "I had read the articles on the incident in the papers," Kairys says. "I knew right away it was an important case based on the Rockefeller Commission report and the CIA connections to Frank Olson's death. David [Rudovsky] said that he knew Eric and that we were being considered along with someone {Huge} at Arnold & Porter. David and I were both interested in doing the case. Then there was quickly a series of discussions with Eric, and soon Alice. We had several discussions about whether it was better or worse to have a connected firm do the case, but when the D.C. firm withdrew, it was our case."

On July 10, 1975, at the urgings of their new attorneys, Kairys and Rudovsky, the Olsons held a press conference in the tree-lined backyard of Alice's modest, two-story home in Frederick, Maryland, the same house that Frank Olson had proudly built in 1950. The day before the event, the family had granted *New York Times* journalist Seymour Hersh an exclusive interview.

Eric Olson says, "We selected Hersh for three reasons. First, Hersh deserved the story, because if it had not been for his reporting on domestic wrong-doing of the CIA there would have been no Rockefeller Commission." Secondly, Eric says his family thought it "could learn a lot" from Hersh in return. Third, says Eric, "My family understood that a front page story in the *New York Times* would guarantee the level and amount of serious attention the story deserved and required."

Hersh interviewed the Olsons at Alice's home. His first words to the startled family were, "This must be the most uncurious family in the United States. I can't believe you fell for that story twenty-two years ago."

Eric told Hersh that his family wanted "to get the story out, so our father's friends and colleagues— and also our friends —would know what the CIA has done." Alice told Hersh that she was "stunned" by the Rockefeller Commission revelations. "It never occurred to me that there could be foul play," she said. Alice said that the family planned "to sue the CIA for wrongful death."

The Olsons explained to Hersh that, following Lisa and Greg's confrontation with Vincent Ruwet on June 12, Alice had a private conversation with the retired military officer, during which Ruwet revealed that her husband had been dosed with LSD shortly after dinner one evening during a meeting of CIA and Camp Detrick Special Operations Division personnel. Alice reported that Ruwet had admitted to her that, in addition to Frank, "four special operations division scientists were told that they had been given lysergic acid diethylamide, and that their reactions would be observed." Alice added, "We do not know what occurred during the remainder of this meeting."

Ruwet, said the Olsons, had also told Alice on June 12, that Frank had been sent to New York City because he had shown "signs of imbalance at work the next week," and that the New York trip had been recommended by an unidentified colleague. Ruwet said Frank had been accompanied by a CIA employee to "see a psychiatrist, Dr. Harold A. Abramson, who held appropriate security clearances." Alice told Hersh that she had telephoned Abramson the day after her discussion with Ruwet and that she had asked Abramson specifically what he recalled about treating her husband. Alice told Hersh, "He told me that he remembered absolutely nothing about it."

"Surely, you must recall something," Alice had pressed.

But Abramson had repeated his denial to Alice. He claimed, "he didn't remember anything about it, but he did know that Dr. Olson was a 'very, very sick man.'" Abramson told Alice, "We were going to put him in Chestnut Lodge Mental Hospital because he was such a sick man."

Alice asked Abramson about any remaining files he had on her husband. "My files have been destroyed," he replied.

In his article that appeared the next day, Hersh wrote, "The Olson family also said that it would seek further facts about the role of Dr. Abramson, the New York psychiatrist who had 'several long sessions' with Mr. Olson." After interviewing the Olsons, Hersh had also telephoned Dr. Abramson at his New York office and asked him to comment, but Abramson "refused to discuss the issue." Abramson told Hersh, "I'll have to consult a lawyer because this is a serious matter. I'm being accused of something I did 22 years ago."

Hersh also contacted David Belin, executive director of the Rockefeller Commission, to inquire why the Commission had not contacted the Olsons.

Said Belin, "The staff didn't feel it was necessary to talk to the family. They didn't know what it would add— once we found out what had happened."

Wrote Hersh, "Mr. Belin further said that the CIA had explained that it could not tell the Olson family about the LSD testing because it 'wanted to get the family a pension.'"

All the major television networks and countless newspapers nationwide covered the Olson family's press conference. The narrow dirt road leading to the house was lined along both sides bumper-to-bumper with cars. Family, friends, and neighbors had to park on the main road about a quarter mile away and hike up the steep hill leading to Alice's house. The expansive open field across from the house was packed with cars and a dozen remote broadcast vans. Leslie Stahl of CBS scurried around interviewing people, while Gonzo journalist, Hunter S. Thompson, on assignment for *Rolling Stone*, politely knocked on Alice's front door asking to "use the facilities." Nils Olson said, "There was almost a carnival atmosphere to the entire event. I remember that it struck me as somewhat odd."

In a prophetic and powerful family statement, Alice Olson told the assembled media:

> We believe that Frank Olson's death has meaning only when it is placed in the context of a family story on the one hand and in the context of global CIA misconduct and immorality on the other. In telling our story we are concerned that neither the personal pain this family has experienced nor the moral and political outrage we feel be slighted. Only in this way can Frank Olson's death become part of American memory and serve the purpose of political and ethical reform so urgently needed in our society.
>
> We are one family whose history has been fundamentally altered by illegal CIA activity, the family of the only American so far identified as having died as a result of CIA treachery.... We intend to sue the Central Intelligence Agency for the wrongful death of Frank Olson. In doing so we hope the full story of Frank Olson's death will emerge. We hope that the CIA will be held publicly and punitively accountable for its actions. We hope that this legal process, painful as it will certainly be for this family, will lessen the chances that other families, other persons, will have to suffer such abuses.

In response to a flurry of questions from reporters, Eric Olson said, "I think that the CIA and any other agency has to become accountable for its actions."

Alice said that she and her children "will file a lawsuit against the CIA, perhaps within two weeks, asking several million dollars in damages." Looking pale and drawn, Alice explained, "I was convinced that my husband's death was not a deliberate or willful act. I felt that he must have plunged through that window in a state of panic brought on by I know not what. This was the impression I tried to convey to my children."

Eric picked up on his mother's words and told reporters, "We hope the full story may emerge as a result of our lawsuit." He said, "This LSD was given to five high-level scientists. We are asked now to believe that the CIA took an incredible risk with these scientists, and we don't know why."

Asked to elaborate, Eric replied, "I feel pretty confident there are a lot of things we still don't know... In this case there's another possibility. There may have been some intent... We have no reason to believe they wanted to kill my father, but it's possible."

Lisa Hayward told reporters that she found the role of Dr. Harold Abramson in her father's death to be particularly troubling. Lisa said that Abramson's account that her father "was very, very sick" made no sense, especially in light of the fact that he allowed Frank Olson to be "housed on the 10th floor of a hotel." Nils Olson remarked, "Dr. Abramson's treatment of my father deserves serious scrutiny."

Asked about her husband's behavior after his return from the still mysterious meeting between CIA and Camp Detrick personnel, Alice said that Frank had "not acted irrational or sick." She explained, "He came back to this house right after noon and he was very quiet, he was an entirely different person. I didn't know what had happened. I just knew that something was terribly wrong. The entire weekend he was very melancholy and talked about a mistake he had made. He said he was going to leave his job."

The day after the press conference, David Kairys received two unexpected telephone calls. The first was from a woman who identified herself as Beatrice Shelley. She was calling from her home in Flushing, New York to tell Kairys that she had some information that might be of interest to him.

On the night of Frank Olson's death, Beatrice and her husband had been staying at the Statler Hotel, in the room next to Olson's. This was non-adjoining room 1020A. The Shelley's were on their honeymoon. That night, she explained, they had gone out to the theatre. Beatrice told Kairys she thought they had returned to the Statler around midnight and that they were in their room for the remainder of the night. She said that they did not hear anything at all unusual that night, and remarked that her husband was a particularly light sleeper. Said Beatrice, "I'm really surprised he didn't hear something if a window was broken."

The morning after Olson's death, Mr. and Mrs. Shelley, knowing nothing about what had happened next door to them, had gone out shopping. When they returned to the hotel around noon, they found two men searching their room. Beatrice said that she noticed right away that they had "moved several things around quite a lot." She described the men as "FBI types," but said that they identified themselves as "working for the hotel." When the Shelleys asked the men what they were doing, they were told that a suicide had occurred in the room next to theirs the night before.

Kairys asked Beatrice if she had happened to see Olson's room that morning and she said no, but explained that she believed that her room, which she described as "small," was the same size and layout as Olson's. Beatrice ventured that she found it "hard to picture anyone running in her room" and going out the window because "they would have had to go from the bed to the door and then weave around the beds to get to the window."

Kairys asked Beatrice if it would be possible to speak to her husband about his recollections of that night and she said that she was now divorced and that her husband was mentally ill and in and out of institutions. "But," Beatrice said, "we still see each other and we've already talked about this on the phone." Three days later, she called Kairys back to say that she had spoken to her former husband. She said that he recalled that sometime during the night of Olson's death he had heard "noises in the hallway" outside their room and that he also remembered "a white vehicle with a red light pulling up to the curb outside the hotel." But, other than that, he remembered nothing more.

The second call to Kairys came from a Manhattan attorney named Neil S. Wolfram. Wolfram, who maintained a practice at 200 Park Avenue, told Kairys that he was an expert on the legal implications of drug experimentation. He explained that he was calling to suggest that Kairys and Rudovsky think about including an allegation of assault in their lawsuit, for the unwitting dosing of Olson with LSD. Wolfram also told Kairys that Dr. Harold Abramson "was probably associated with the Josiah Macy Jr. Foundation," which did drug related research for the government, possibly including work for the CIA and the Army. At the time, the lengthy and close alliance between the Macy Foundation and the CIA had not been publicly revealed and Kairys' efforts to pursue such links between the foundation, CIA, and Dr. Abramson met a stone wall. In addition, unfortunately, given the crush of other duties and responsibilities confronting the Olson's attorneys, there had been no real opportunity to fully explore Wolfram's leads. (It would be another three years before the publication of John Marks's seminal book, *The Search for the Manchurian Candidate*, exposing the Macy Foundation's link to the CIA.)

Six years after he telephoned Kairys, in 1981, Wolfram published a much overlooked, but very important book, *Psychiatric Research and the Politics of Law*. Wolfram's book is a brilliant and provocative examination of medical and academic experimenters motivated by what Wolfram states was "a desire to progress from 'clever contentions,' 'profound arguments,' 'brilliant hunches' and 'theories' to 'scientific methods' with 'experimental manipulations and verification' of 'facts' gathered by means of human investigations 'in the laboratory' resulting in 'observation and measurement.'" Wrote Wolfram:

> When the advisory power for involuntary commitment was transferred to the new specialty of psychiatry, the institutionalized victims were converts from warehoused objects to subjects for iatrogenic (an injury, illness, adverse condition in a patient by medical intervention) experiments intended to create physical disease or depersonalization, anxiety, tension,

fear, resentment, depression, elation, hostility or aggression, using illicit substances, nonmedicinal chemicals and mind altering somatic drugs.

Kairys also received a call from a New York attorney who said he had seen the July 10, 1975 *New York Times* story that mentioned Dr. Abramson. The attorney said that he had been Abramson's patient in 1959 after being referred by a general practitioner for an allergy problem. After a few visits, the attorney recounted, Abramson began treating him psychologically and suggested that the attorney take LSD. Abramson provided the attorney with literature on the new drug. The attorney told Kairys that he had researched LSD on his own and had spoken with a number of people about the drug. "I stopped seeing Abramson," said the attorney. "I thought he was crazier than me."

A few days after speaking with Neil Wolfram, Kairys received a call from Edward Tinsley Chase, a widely respected editor with New York-based G.P. Putnam publishers. Chase told Kairys that he had been closely following the story of Frank Olson, and that one of his authors, John Fuller, had also been following it. Chase was, in fact, calling on behalf of Fuller, whom readers have already encountered in this book's chapter on the strange outbreak at the French town of Pont-St.-Esprit.

Fuller, Chase explained, was fascinated with the Olson case and wanted the cooperation of the Olson family and their attorneys so that he could immediately begin investigating and researching a book about the death of Frank Olson. Chase assured Kairys that neither he, nor Putnam or writer Fuller had any connection, contract, or financial interest from any government agency, and that they would share all of their investigative findings with the Olson's and their attorneys. Kairys told Chase that he certainly thought the offer worth exploring, but when he presented it to Alice and Eric Olson, they had some reservations. In the ensuing weeks the proposal fell between the cracks, never to be discussed again.

Decades later, after Fuller had passed away, Chase would say that the writer's excitement about a possible Olson book centered on his considerable research and knowledge of the Pont-St.-Esprit outbreak, and that after his book, *The Day of Saint Anthony's Fire*, had been published, he increasingly believed that perhaps the outbreak had been deliberately caused. From his extensive research on Pont-St.-Esprit, Fuller knew that most medical experts who had studied the outbreak were convinced that its source "was most likely to be a derivative of ergot; of extremely concentrated power; able to produce bizarre and incredibly unique psychic symptoms." After the revelations concerning Frank Olson had become public, Fuller had become convinced that LSD had been the source of the bizarre outbreak at Pont-St.-Esprit.

A July 11 *Washington Post* article about the Olson's 1975 press conference revealed that the family "believed that [Frank Olson] was accompanied to New

York... by a CIA agent, Robert Lashbrook, and two [sic] of Olson's colleagues from the Special Operations Division at Fort Detrick." The Olsons declined to name the two colleagues, but *Post* reporter Bill Richards wrote that sources familiar with the incident had told him one of the colleagues "who went with Olson to New York was Vincent L. Ruwet.... then Olson's superior and now a bacteriologist for Micro Biology Associates in Bethesda, Maryland."

Richards' sources had also said that Ruwet had been "among those Special Operations researchers who were given LSD without their prior knowledge" at the meeting with the CIA. But, when Richards telephoned Ruwet, the retired officer refused to confirm or deny the report. Ruwet had told Richards that "he sought legal help from the Army today after learning that his name was connected with the LSD incident and that the Olson family was planning to sue the government over Olson's death."

Said Ruwet, "I'm seeking legal counsel for advice, not because I've done anything wrong. I believe I'm almost certain to be called either for the defense or for the government. I asked the Army to provide me with legal counsel as a retired officer. I'm not going to spend my hard-earned money on this."

Ruwet refused to provide Richards with any information about his or Olson's work with Camp Detrick's Special Operations Division, but other sources, Richards wrote, told him "that the CIA contract [with SOD] was so secret that members who were working on various aspects of it did not even discuss their work with each other." However, Richards reported, "One of the former researchers on the project said they were experimenting with, among other things, the production of a gas that could be laced with LSD to immobilize an enemy force."

In preparing his story, Richards had also interviewed former SOD scientist, Dr. Joseph J. Stubbs. For reasons unknown, Stubbs did not reveal to Richards that he had been present at the November 1953 Deep Creek Lake gathering at which Olson had been dosed. Nor did Stubbs mention his subsequent participation in Ruwet's discussions with Olson about Olson's preparations to travel to New York.

Oddly, Stubbs told Richards that, "a number of rumors surrounded [Olson's] New York trip." Said Stubbs,

> We were all shocked. I still can't believe that he committed suicide the way they said. It's like it's coming out of the blue now. I never heard anyone talk about LSD after Olson's death and I still think there's something odd about this. We were all baffled by it. We couldn't look back on any reason why he did it.

Seemingly, Dr. Stubbs was unaware that Olson had been dosed with LSD and incredibly perhaps, he had forgotten his presence the day Ruwet made the decision that Olson needed psychiatric attention.

The day after the Olson's press conference, the *New York Times* published a story by reporter Joseph B. Treaster that seemed aimed at removing more of the mystery out of Frank Olson's trip to New York, but added some confusion, as well. Published under the bold headline, "Detective Said Scientist Had 'Severe Psychosis,'" Treaster revealed that he had obtained a copy of the 1953 police report concerning Olson's death, the same report that was completed by Detective James W. Ward of Manhattan's 14th police precinct and that was discussed previously. Treaster, relying on the account provided to Det. Ward by Robert Lashbrook in 1953, stated that Olson "had come to New York on Nov. 24, 1953 with Col. Vincent Ruwet and checked into the Statler Hotel. Olson was examined twice by Dr. Harold Abramson, a physician who had offices at 133 E. 58th Street" and "Mr. Olson and Colonel Ruwet returned to Washington on the morning of Nov. 26."

"Then, on that same afternoon," Treaster wrote, Olson returned to New York, "accompanied this time by a man who identified himself as Robert Lashbrook." Lashbrook and Olson "again visited" Abramson and, according to the police interview of Lashbrook, Olson "was advised to enter a sanitarium as he was suffering from severe psychosis and delusions." Olson was to enter Chestnut Lodge in Rockville, Maryland "under the supervision of Dr. John Fort," Detective Ward had written. Ward's report also stated that after Lashbrook found that Olson was not in his bed, Lashbrook had said that he called the hotel operator and "at this time, learned that Olson had jumped out of the window."

Treaster wrote: "Detective Ward said that his report was based on information given him by Mr. Lashbrook but that he had verified the facts in interviews with Colonel Ruwet and Dr. Abramson."

Treaster also revealed that despite Detective Ward's finding that Olson's death was a suicide, the Manhattan Medical Examiner's Office had attributed the death to "multiple fractures, shock, and hemorrhages." According to sources, Treaster wrote, "no autopsy had been performed, but that an incision was made in the body, apparently in an attempt to learn whether Mr. Olson was intoxicated at the time of his fall."

Treaster, who had been informed that Detective Ward had since died, also attempted to reach Dr. Abramson for comment, but was informed by the doctor's secretary that Abramson had nothing to say about the Olson case. Treaster, however, reported that Abramson "had been one of the first Americans to study the effects of the powerful mind-altering drug LSD," beginning his research in 1951. In 1959, Treaster wrote, Abramson "told a scientific meeting on LSD that at the outset [of his research] many of his colleagues opposed his work with the drug, regarding him as 'a sort of psychiatric Dracula.'"

On July 12, 1975 *Washington Post* reporter Bill Richards called David Kairys and asked if the attorney would tell him about what communications the Olsons had had with the Rockefeller Commission and what information the Commission had shared with the family.

"We haven't received any information from the Rockefeller Commission," Kairys said.

"Have you spoken to anyone there?" Richards asked.

"We've tried to," Kairys said, "but they told us they had nothing more to share other than what was in their report to the president."

"Let me ask you," Richards persisted, "we've heard that there were others besides Frank Olson who were dosed with LSD at the same meeting. Do you know anything about that?"

"As a matter of fact, I do," Kairys answered. He then explained that just the day before, Alice Olson had given him a copy of a two-page memo from November 1953 that contained a "tentative list" of people who had attended the meeting in question.

"Does it say where the meeting took place?" Richards asked.

"Yes," said Kairys, "in Deep Creek Lake, Maryland. It's a secluded resort area about forty miles west of Fort Detrick."

Kairys explained to Richards that John "Mal" Malinowski, of Camp Detrick's Special Operations Division, had prepared the November 1953 list of attendees for the Deep Creek Lake meeting, termed a "rendezvous" in the memo. "Unfortunately, we learned earlier today that Malinowski is dead," Kairys said.

The list of names, Kairys told Richards, was divided into two columns. The left-side column read: "Lt. Col. Ruwet (driver), Dr. J. Schwab, Dr. J. Stubbs, Dr. F. Olson, Ben Wilson (driver), Dr. H. Tanner, [and] Mal, driver." The right-side column listed the names: "Dr. S. Gottlieb, Dr. R. Lashbrook, A. Hughes, [and] H. Bortner."

"Besides Olson, Ruwet, and Stubbs, do you know who any of these people are?" Richards asked.

"Schwab, Tanner, Wilson, and, of course, Malinowski were all Fort Detrick employees," Kairys said. "We've been told that Dr. Gottlieb was a CIA official, perhaps Lashbrook's superior. We think that Hughes and Bortner were also CIA employees, but we aren't sure."

After speaking with Kairys, Richards called James N. Roethe, whom he described in his subsequent article the next day as "the attorney in charge of the Rockefeller Commission's report on CIA experiments with LSD." Asked why the Commission had not communicated with the Olsons, Roethe said, "There hadn't been any reason to contact them." Richards then asked why the Commission's report did not reflect everything the Commission had learned about the CIA's use of LSD on unsuspecting persons.

"You obviously don't put everything in a report, every little detail," replied Roethe. "You put the main points in. I think that's been done, and I don't think it will do any good to get into these details."

Richards informed Roethe that he had learned that other scientists had been dosed with LSD at the Deep Creek Lake meeting. "Do you know who these people were?" he asked.

"I'm not about to give any names out," said Roethe. "I really don't feel that I'm going to be in a position to make a comment unless something so outrageous comes out that I feel I have to, and at this point I haven't seen anything."

Richards next called Rockefeller Commission executive director, David Belin, at his home in Des Moines, Iowa. Belin told Richards that he thought the Commission knew that the LSD was administered to a small group. Said Belin, "There certainly was no intent to imply that it was only administered to one, but it was only one person who had a very extreme reaction to it."

Richards asked Belin what he based this statement on and Belin said he would not go into the details of the incident.

"Do you know the names of the others who were dosed at the meeting?" Richards asked. Belin answered that he assumed that Roethe had the names.

Reporter Bill Richards then telephoned Eric Olson at his mother's Frederick home. Richards asked if the Olsons knew who the other scientists were that had been dosed at the Deep Creek Lake meeting. Eric asked Richards if he had spoken to Vincent Ruwet.

"He won't talk to reporters," Richards said.

"Ruwet didn't say who else had been dosed," Olson said, "but he did say that at least one person hadn't been given LSD because of a medical problem."

"Who would that have been?" Richards asked.

Eric said he wasn't sure, but he thought it was Dr. Stubbs. He had just learned from his mother, Alice, that Stubbs had a heart condition in 1953. The Olson's also assumed that Schwab and Tanner had also been dosed with LSD, Eric said. Because Ben Wilson was "not a high-level scientist," they thought he had not been dosed. Olson also told Richards that it was his understanding that Dr. Tanner "had passed away from natural causes several years ago," but that John Schwab was still alive.

Richards located John Schwab that same day, in Ohio, where the retired military man was living. Schwab confirmed that he had been Ruwet's and Olson's commanding officer in 1953 and that he had attended the Deep Creek Lake meeting.

"But," said Schwab, "I was not present when the LSD was administered." Schwab explained, "I had nothing to do with that part of the meeting. Very often at this type of meeting you have sub meetings in different parts of the place where the gathering is held."

It is important to point out that Richards was not aware at the time that the Deep Creek Lake lodge, called Railey's Cabin, where the meeting had taken place, consisted of one large room with a stone fireplace downstairs and four very small bedrooms and a single bathroom upstairs. Any "sub meetings" would have been difficult unless groups had gone outside.

Schwab also told Richards that despite the "official explanation" about Olson's death, he was aware that Olson had been given LSD. "I don't know exactly when I learned, but I could not tell the family," he said. "I was under restrictions at the time. When you're in this sort of business, that sometimes happens."

Schwab identified Sidney Gottlieb and Robert Lashbrook as CIA "contact or control points" with Camp Detrick's SOD. He said he could not recall anyone else being at the Deep Creek Lake meeting besides the two CIA men and Olson and Ruwet.

"What about Dr. Joseph Stubbs and Dr. Herbert Tanner?" Richards asked. Schwab replied that he only remembered those people he had already identified. Obviously, Schwab was not telling all that he knew.

Richards next called Dr. Stubbs at his home in Frederick, and asked him about his presence at the Deep Creek Lake meeting. Stubbs, who had been quite cooperative two days earlier, saying that he was "baffled" by Olson's death, now claimed, "I can't even recall having been at or near Deep Creek Lake. I just can't recall ever hearing anything about this. It's been 22 years, and I don't want to struggle to recall it now." Had someone warned Stubbs about saying more?

Richards called the CIA and asked if the agency would "confirm the place of the meeting, the names of those who attended, who among them worked for the CIA, and who gave the LSD to whom." A CIA spokesman told Richards: "We won't have anything to say about that. Obviously, anything we have to say will be said up on the Hill."

Bill Richards wasn't the only reporter busy digging into the Olson story. On July 12, 1975 *New York Times* reporter Joseph Treaster revealed that Dr. Dominick DiMaio, the acting chief of the Manhattan Medical Examiner's office, had decided because of new disclosures about Frank Olson's death, to reopen the case, "which was closed in 1953 without a definite finding." Remarkably, Dr. DiMaio had been the assistant medical examiner on duty the night Frank Olson's body had been brought in for examination. DiMaio told Treaster "that his office had no police powers, but that Manhattan District Attorney, Robert M. Morgenthau, said he had begun looking into the death to see whether he had jurisdiction and whether the statute of limitations had expired."

Treaster had spoken by telephone the previous day with David Kairys. Kairys told the reporter that the Olsons, based on Alice's conversation with Ruwet, "now believed that it was highly likely that Robert Lashbrook and another man who worked for the CIA whose name was Sidney Gottlieb" had administered the LSD to Frank Olson.

"You're saying that the man the CIA selected to escort Olson to New York for treatment was the same man that dosed him with the LSD?" Treaster asked Kairys.

"That is what we have been told," Kairys said. "Not only that, but also accompanying Olson, beside Lashbrook, was Vincent Ruwet."

"One of the other Camp Detrick scientists who Lashbrook also dosed with LSD?" asked Treaster.

Years later, Kairys would say, "I hadn't yet fully realized how absolutely outlandish everything sounded until Treaster and I discussed it and he responded like he did."

After speaking with Kairys, Treaster called the CIA and inquired about Lashbrook and Gottlieb, but the Agency "refused to confirm or deny" that either man was an employee and declined to say anything about the incident involving Frank Olson.

Dr. DiMaio told Treaster that he did not recognize the name Sidney Gottlieb, but he now said he had serious concerns about the statement Robert Lashbrook had given to the Medical Examiner's stenographer, Max Katzman, who was also on duty the night Olson died. DiMaio recalled that CIA officer Robert Lashbrook had "formally identified Olson's body" but, said DiMaio, Lashbrook had omitted "four big things" when asked for details about Olson's death. DiMaio said that records indicated that Lashbrook "never mentioned the man had taken LSD."

DiMaio also told Treaster that he was troubled by Seymour Hersh's story published two days earlier. The story revealed that Frank Olson's widow, shortly after her husband's death, had been informed that Lashbrook witnessed Olson "going at a full run toward the [hotel] window" and then "go through both the closed window and a drawn shade." That did not mesh at all with what Lashbrook had told the police and Medical Examiner's office: that he had awakened to the sound of breaking glass and found Olson's bed empty.

Moreover, DiMaio stated, he was displeased that Lashbrook had not been more forthcoming about Olson's treatment by Dr. Abramson. "He didn't tell us the man was under psychiatric treatment, and he didn't give us the name of the physician," said DiMaio. "In other words, we knew absolutely nothing.... He should have given that information to us— if not under questioning, then voluntarily." DiMaio said that in reviewing the record he found that Lashbrook, besides providing the Medical Examiner's office with a brief description of Olson— his age, marital status, occupation — said only that Olson "had been depressed for some time."

When Treaster had spoken with David Kairys, the reporter had questioned the attorney about Frank Olson's mental state in 1953. "What about Lashbrook's statement to the Medical Examiner and the footnote in the Rockefeller Commission's report that claimed that a few remaining CIA records indicated that Frank Olson may have had a history of emotional instability?" Treaster asked.

"I told him that by all accounts everyone, family and friends alike, all of his co-workers that we spoke with, told us that Olson was perfectly normal," Kairys told Treaster. "There was no evidence that I had seen that indicated he had any history of emotional instability. I also suggested to Treaster that he call Alice Olson and discuss the question with her."

Treaster called Alice Olson. As reflected in his subsequent article, Alice at that point had challenged Lashbrook's statement to the Medical Examiner's office. Treaster wrote: "She said that her husband had not exhibited any signs of depression" until after he had been given LSD. Prior to the CIA-SOD meeting, Alice said, her husband "never exhibited any emotional instability," nor had he ever visited a psychiatrist prior to going to New York to see Dr. Abramson.

The day after speaking with Treaster, Alice Olson received a letter in the mail from a man she had never heard of. The one-page, typed letter read:

> Dear Mrs. Olson:
> After reading the newspaper accounts on the tragic death of your husband, I felt compelled to write you.
> At the time of your husband's death, I was the assistant night manager at the Hotel Statler in New York. In fact, I was at your husband's side almost immediately after his fall. He attempted to speak but his words were unintelligible. A priest was summoned and he was given the last rites.
> Having been in the hotel business for the past 36 years and witnessing innumerable unfortunate incidents, your husband's death disturbed me greatly due to the most unusual circumstances of which you are now aware.
> If I can be of any assistance to you, please do not hesitate to call upon me.
> My heartfelt sympathy to you and your family.

The signature at the bottom of the letter read: Armond D. Pastore.

On July 14, 1975 the *Washington Post* reported that neither the New York police department nor the Medical Examiner's Office "has actively reopened an investigation" into Frank Olson's death. Dr. DiMaio was now saying "he lacked the investigatory powers to reopen an inquiry" and that he was "simply waiting for new information" from the police department.

"It's reopened to the extent that if anybody does anything we would hope they would bring it to our attention. I don't have any police powers to do otherwise," said DiMaio. Asked if he had at least attempted to speak with Dr. Harold Abramson, DiMaio said, "I'm sure Dr. Abramson will not talk, for obvious reasons."

The situation appeared to become wholly Kafka-esque when a spokesman for New York Police Commissioner, Michael J. Cobb, the same day said, "Our official position is that until we've been notified by the medical examiner's office that they've found anything different, we are not investigating."

Also commenting was Manhattan District Attorney Robert M. Morgenthau, who said that he had not begun investigating anything and, according to the *Post*, "said his staff was checking to see whether the district attorney's office had jurisdiction, and whether the statute of limitations on prosecuting had expired." Asked for comment on the day's developments, David Kairys said, "The way we understand it is that they had officially reopened the case."

Ten days after their press conference, on July 17, the Olsons sent written notice to the CIA that they intended to sue the Agency, pursuant to the Federal Tort Claims Act, for the wrongful death of Frank Olson. In a letter signed by Alice and her three children, the Olsons stated that, "the relief which we claim is as follows:

1. *A full and complete disclosure to the family of all of the details surrounding the circumstances which lead to the illegal administration of LSD and the resulting death of Dr. Olson. We do request appropriate assurance from the proper government official that such full and complete disclosure has been made. The family, mindful of the circumstances and the painful details that this disclosure may entail, reserves the right at its discretion to make some or all of the details public. The family will be glad to advise the CIA, if that becomes necessary, in a proper and dignified release of this material to the public.*
2. A statement from the appropriate government official and/or Department stating that such acts which led to the death of Dr. Olson were contrary to the rights of American citizens and to the Charter of the CIA. We also want assurance that appropriate steps have been taken, either by way of Executive Order or Directive, or appropriate CIA Rules and Regulations, which specifically forbid the kind of activity which resulted in the wrongful death of Dr. Olson; and
3. Monetary damages in the maximum amount of $10,000,000 (ten million dollars). (As you know, Section 2675 (b) of the Federal Tort Claims Act requires that the maximum amount of damages be set forth in any claim filed with the appropriate agency so as not to preclude any appropriate monetary recovery in United States District Court if legal action is required.

Concluded the letter, "We hope the sooner this matter is resolved the better. However, we are prepared, after living with this for over twenty-two years, to pursue our rights to their eventual conclusion, no matter how long this may take."

Also on July 17, 1975 the enigmatic Robert Lashbrook emerged from the shadows to speak with the *Washington Post* and *New York Times*. Acting on tips from unnamed sources, reporters found the fifty-seven year old former CIA official living in Ojai, California, an upscale community eighty miles north of Los Angeles. Lashbrook had left his Langley-based job with the CIA in 1963 for undisclosed reasons. In separate interviews years later, Lashbrook would say that he left the CIA because one of his three children "was having a lot of trouble with asthma... and I thought we just better find a new climate." After moving from Virginia to California, Lashbrook, who had a Ph.D. in chemistry from Stanford University, worked for the Ventura Division of Northrop Corp. and then began teaching science in an Ojai high school, the position he still occupied when *Washington Post* reporter Austin Scott reached him at home.

Lashbrook was surprisingly candid with Scott. He recalled many details about the Deep Creek Lake meeting at which LSD was given to "four top-level research scientists." Lashbrook recounted details about accompanying Frank Olson to New York to see Dr. Harold Abramson. And, Lashbrook said, he vividly recalled Olson's death.

"I woke up because there was a noise," Lashbrook told Scott. "I turned on the light and noticed Frank wasn't there. I saw the shade. It was one of those pull-type window shades and that was going around and around and the window was broken... And then I saw him down on the sidewalk below... There's a train station there, and a number of people were running from the train station to the sidewalk..."

"What did you do then?" Scott asked.

"As I recall," Lashbrook said, "I called the desk. I don't recall [what I said] except to inform them, and ask them to call someone... I put on my clothes and waited... I figured the police would arrive sooner or later."

"You didn't leave the room or go down to check on Olson?" Scott asked.

"No, I did not," Lashbrook said. "I stayed in the room... It was 10 floors up, a distance away. If I'd gone down, what could I have done, because as I say, I saw people running over where he was...I figured the police would be wanting to ask questions of me."

While he waited for the police to arrive, Lashbrook said he telephoned CIA employee Dr. Sidney Gottlieb "in Washington to inform him of Olson's death." Lashbrook declined to provide any information about Gottlieb, but did acknowledge that Gottlieb had also been present at the Deep Creek Lake meeting when Olson had been given LSD.

Lashbrook explained that he "was one of as many as four CIA employees" present at the meeting. He told both newspapers that the LSD was administered "on the first night" of the three-day "secret seminar" at Deep Creek Lake. The first day of the 1953 meeting, Wednesday, November 18, had begun with "a technical discussion that included the subject of LSD," Lashbrook said. In the evening, LSD was given to four Camp Detrick scientists.

"I think it was in an after-dinner liquor or something like that," Lashbrook recalled. He told reporter Scott that he did not want to discuss "whether the drug was put in the drinks before or after they were brought into the room" or who it was that decided "who should be given LSD."

"You see," Lashbrook said, "I don't really know a lot of things... I don't really know what I should say and what I shouldn't."

Lashbrook, however, did say that Olson acted "no different from anyone else" after being given LSD. "The general effect is some agitation, confusion. In general the effect is such it makes it difficult for a person to go to sleep at night, and as I recall, that went on. People jabbered away until late at night and early the next morning."

Lashbrook also recounted that the following week he learned that Olson was showing signs of being upset. "Somewhere, and I don't know exactly where, the decision was made that Dr. Abramson was probably in the best position to help out. He was familiar, he had done pioneering work with the material... I guess arrangements were made for Olson to see Dr. Abramson."

Asked if he saw any signs of "undue disturbance in Olson" on the night he died, Lashbrook said, "If I had, I would have stayed up all night with him. We had dinner at the hotel together. He seemed quite normal... just small talk. He didn't talk about anything that bothered me... What probably happened was that this sort of brought out something in the past that bothered him, and I never really was able to determine just exactly what this was." Lashbrook had told *New York Times* reporter Joseph Treaster that before Olson was given LSD, "as far as I know, he had been perfectly normal... Possibly LSD had brought up something in his past that was bothering him."

Lashbrook also told both newspapers that in the four weeks since the CIA's LSD experiments were first revealed in the Rockefeller Commission's report and ensuing news reports, no one had contacted him about the Olson incident, nor had the Rockefeller Commission ever contacted him before it wrote its report.

The day before reporter Scott had telephoned Lashbrook, he had been informed by the Olson family about the letter Alice Olson had received from Armond Pastore. After speaking with Lashbrook, Scott called Pastore at the Diplomat Motor Hotel in Ocean City, Maryland, where he was now manager.

Pastore disagreed with Lashbrook's account and told Scott that the night of Olson's death there had been no call to the hotel's desk from anyone regarding "a jumper." Explained Pastore in a hurried interview, "[The] doorman came to me and told me someone came out the window. He was lying on the sidewalk when I got there and he was still alive and trying to mumble something but I couldn't make it out. It was all garbled and I was trying to get his name. We got a priest, and he stopped mumbling before they got him in the ambulance."

Pastore recounted that after he determined what window Olson had come out of, "I went and checked at the desk and saw there were two people there. I went up and started to knock and then decided there might be trouble so I sent down for the police and waited... waited about one half-hour, and then I went in with the police. We opened the door and there was this fellow sitting in the bathroom with his head in his hands. He had on his under shorts or his pajamas. He wasn't dressed."

On July 18, 1975 New York City Police Commissioner, Michael J. Codd, announced that he had received a request from the Olson family for "a full-scale investigation" into the facts surrounding Frank Olson's death. Codd said he had ordered his detective bureau "to look at the whole matter as to just what may have been the totality of circumstances under which Mr. Olson died." That same day a detective bureau spokesman announced that the case had been assigned to Deputy Chief William J. Averill, the chief of detectives in Manhattan. According to the announcement, Averill had already initiated his review of the case.

That same day, Manhattan District Attorney Robert M. Morgenthau told reporters that the Olsons had also formally requested his office to investigate the case. Morgenthau said that no official decision had yet been made but that he was "looking into certain aspects" surrounding Olson's death. Asked what those aspects were and if they included Lashbrook's or the CIA's actions, Morgenthau refused to comment any further.

Four days later, Deputy Chief Averill told the Olson family that his pre-investigation was underway and that he was "reviewing police department records" and interviewing "prior and present" members of the department. Averill told Kairys and Rudovsky that he also "planned to interview everyone who had been involved in any way" in Olson's death and that "it was likely" he would send investigators to California to interview Robert Lashbrook and to Maryland to interview Vincent Ruwet. Asked about what cooperation he was receiving from the District Attorney's office, Averill said he "couldn't speak for that office and that questions should be directed to Mr. Morgenthau." When Averill was questioned about Morgenthau's earlier statement about determining whether "the statute of limitations had run out in the Olson case," Averill said, "If there's any suggestion of homicide — and I'm not saying there is — there's no statute of limitations."

Recalled David Kairys, "Over the next few days, and then few weeks, we remained optimistic that formal and aggressive investigations would go forward. We sent everything we had to the police department and district attorney's office, but nothing really occurred and eventually things just tapered off and people in New York stopped returning our phone calls."

On the same day the Lashbrook articles appeared, investigative journalist Nicholas M. Horrock revealed in the *New York Times* that unnamed sources that had worked for the Rockefeller Commission were beginning to speak out. Horrock wrote that these sources had informed him that Dr. Sidney Gottlieb, now identified as the director of the CIA's LSD testing program, had "destroyed the drug program's records in 1973 to hide the details of possibly illegal actions." According to Horrock's sources, Gottlieb destroyed at least "a total of 152 separate files" concerning CIA drug testing shortly after then agency director Richard Helms destroyed "other records."

Moreover, Horrock had also been informed by the same Rockefeller Commission sources that Gottlieb "was personally involved" in the experiment that ended with Frank Olson's death and that Gottlieb "also commanded" a covert drug testing program operated by the Federal Bureau of Narcotics on the East and West Coasts. According to other sources, Horrock wrote that Gottlieb had retired from the CIA a few months after Helms left in January 1973 and then worked as "a paid consultant to the Drug Enforcement Administration" (successor agency to the Federal Narcotics Bureau) before traveling to Africa and the Far East.

Horrock, citing "intelligence sources," also stated that Dr. Gottlieb enjoyed recounting an anecdote about an incident that occurred when he was "returning

501

to Washington aboard an airliner in the nineteen-fifties." After getting up to ask "the stewardess to prepare him a martini," he was returning to his seat when he encountered "a quiet, baldish, pipe smoking man" who asked him, "Is that LSD you're drinking?" Horrock wrote: "[The] well-informed passenger was Allen W. Dulles, the director of the CIA."

Over the next few days, leaks from former Rockefeller Commission employees continued, this time in the direction of the *Washington Post*. On July 20, Austin Scott revealed that several unnamed former employees had complained that, "the commission felt itself horribly rushed on many phases of its investigation."

Peter Clapper, who had handled the commission's public relations, talked to Scott on-the-record and said, "There was no effort to white wash in the Rockefeller report, but it was a hurry, hurry job." A former commission attorney who went unnamed told Scott "the LSD investigation was probably the most frustrating to work on, because the records had been destroyed." Another commission attorney who was quoted by name, Robert Olson, (no relation to Frank Olson) revealingly remarked, "There is apparently a conflict on the matter of who ordered destruction of the records. It was not a matter that we attempted to resolve." Attorney Olson explained that the CIA had given the commission two documents that said two different things on the subject: That Dr. Sidney Gottlieb had been "instructed" to destroy the drug testing files, and that Gottlieb "had initiated" destruction of the files.

Said attorney Olson defensively, "You're [the media] engaging in a lot of Monday morning moralizing... I think you're getting the public stirred up about the [CIA], making the agency appear to be a devilish institution." The attorney went on to say that people should take the "context of the times," including the Cold War and McCarthyism, into account.

And then, in a statement that must have offered little solace to the Olson family, he said, "I'm confident that the people who destroyed the records no doubt felt it would be embarrassing to the agency, or embarrassing to somebody, to have the whole subject come out."

With the Olson family tragedy now nationwide news, the Ford Administration realized it was confronting a monstrous public relations disaster. Many White House insiders argued that if the situation were left unchecked it could seriously jeopardize national security. Following a series of West Wing meetings, Alice Olson and her three children were invited to come to the White House to meet with President Ford. To the American public the invitation appeared impromptu and heartfelt, but examination of the political machinations behind the invitation reveals other motives.

A July 16 memo to President Ford, written by White House Counsel Roderick M. Hills, methodically dealt with what it deemed "the question of what considerations are relevant in deciding whether the President should meet with Mrs. Olson and her three children to express his sympathy on behalf of the

American people and his apology on behalf of the United States Government."
Hills cautioned at the start of his memorandum that the Olsons had hired
Rudovsky and Kairys to represent them and that the attorneys had already "in-
dicated the intention of the family to sue for several million dollars."

Hills, who within weeks would become chairman of the Securities and Exchange Commission, continued, "The fact the President expresses his own outrage at the circumstances of Dr. Olson's death could be some encouragement to
the family's determination to sue and could also raise their expectations as to the
amount of money they expect to receive in settlement of that law suit. It could
also affect the judge who tries the case and will have the authority to set damages." But Hills discounted this as a "conclusive factor" in determining whether
or not to meet with the Olsons, "given the circumstances of this incident."

Continued Hills:

> The intensity of the family's reaction and background of the lawyer they
> have hired do raise some possibility that they may react discourteously
> toward the President's invitation. This factor, however, we do not regard
> as material, since any such reaction would be more harmful to them than
> embarrassing to the President. However, it is conceivable that their lawyer
> may insist that he be present at such a meeting. We recommend that it be
> made clear that the lawyer not be invited.

Hills was referring to attorney David Kairys, whom he would soon telephone. Kairys, as readers have seen, had been lead counsel on the Camden 28
case and had greatly embarrassed and angered J. Edgar Hoover and Attorney
General John Mitchell when he obtained a signed affidavit and testimony at trial
from an FBI informer admitting to aiding and abetting a crime. The informer's
admissions had made the front pages of the nation's major newspapers.

The memo then turned to the substance of Hills' concerns: the Olson family's
anticipated lawsuit against the federal government. Citing an "initial memorandum" from the Civil Division of the Department of Justice, Hills explained, the
Division had the "opinion that any tort action against the United States by the
Olsons would be barred by the Federal Employees Compensation Act on the
ground that [Frank Olson] was injured 'in the course of his official duties' and,
therefore, the family is entitled to survivors' benefits and nothing more." However, Hills cautioned, further discussions with Justice's Civil Division "has led them
and me to conclude that the [FECA barring] defense is not conclusive because:

> (i) The bizarre circumstances of [Frank Olson's] death could well cause a
> court of law to determine as a matter of public policy that he did not die
> in the course of his official duties.
> (ii) *Dr. Olson's job is so sensitive that it is highly unlikely that we
> would submit relevant evidence to the court on the issue of his duties.*"
> [Italics added.]

503

The extraordinary memorandum from Hills to President Ford continued:

> The latter circumstance may mean, as a practical matter, we would have no defense against the Olson law suit. *In this connection, you should know that the CIA and the Counsel's office both strongly recommend that the evidence concerning [Frank Olson's] employment not be revealed in a civil suit.*" After this, Hills added, "You may wish to discuss this matter in more detail at this time. [Italics added.]
>
> If there is a trial, *it is apparent that the Olsons' lawyer will seek to explore all of the circumstances of Dr. Olson's employment as well as those concerning his death. It is not at all clear that we can keep such evidence from becoming relevant even if the government waives the defense of the Federal Employees Compensation Act. Thus, in the trial, it may become apparent that we are concealing evidence for national security reasons and any settlement or judgment reached thereafter would be perceived as money paid to cover-up the activities of the CIA.* [Italics added by author.]

Hills concluded his memorandum by recommending that President Ford invite the Olsons "to a meeting at the White House to receive from the President an expression of sympathy on behalf of the American people and an apology on behalf of the United States Government." Hills also recommended that "the Attorney General be authorized to attempt a negotiated settlement with attorneys for the Olson family" and that "the President, during his meeting with the Olson family, suggest that the Attorney General would be willing to discuss the matter generally with the Olson family attorneys."

While Special Counsel Hills was busy preparing the President to meet with the Olsons and deal with their lawsuit, other White House officials were carefully drawing up Ford's remarks for the meeting and the media.

A July 11, 1975 memorandum marked "SECRET" from Deputy Assistant Richard Cheney to Chief of Staff, Donald Rumsfeld, read: "Attached is a proposed brief statement for the President to use at his Press Conference" on what Cheney deemed, "the Olson matter/CIA suicide."

Cheney wrote, "At this point, we do not have enough information to be certain we know all the details of this incident. Furthermore, there are serious legal questions that will have to be resolved concerning the Government's responsibility, *the possibility of additional compensation, and the possibility that it might be necessary to disclose highly classified national security information in connection with any court suit, or legislative hearings on a private bill intended to provide additional compensation to the family.* Therefore, Marsh [John O. Marsh Jr., a Cabinet rank counselor to Ford who had been his National Security Advisor when Ford was Vice President], Hills and Cheney strongly recommend that the President limit his remarks to an expression of regret over this tragic event and a willingness to meet personally with Mrs. Olson and her children to offer an apology on behalf of the Government. Any discussion that goes beyond those issues raises questions which we are not yet in a position to answer." [Italics added.]

Since Cheney's July 11, 1975 memorandum was first revealed in the mid-1990s, a number of journalists and writers have sensationally claimed that it is evidence of "a cover-up" and that Cheney and Rumsfeld were privy to hidden information about Olson's death. Indeed, one brief look at the subject on the Internet will prove that this claim has entered the media stream as often-repeated truth.

Unfortunately, none of these claims are true. They exist only as evidence of yet another ill-researched legend that morphs into truth through repeated citation. To briefly explain, (this writer finds it unduly uncomfortable to defend Cheney and Rumsfeld in any regard), when Cheney warned about "the possibility that it might be necessary to disclose highly classified national security information," little to no information about Olson's job at Camp Detrick, as well as the work of SOD, the CIA's MKNAOMI, or MKULTRA had been released to the White House, Congress, the media or the public. It would still be another two weeks before the Olson family and their attorneys would receive the information about Frank Olson that has come to be called the "Colby Papers" or "Colby Documents." Nobody in the White House, with perhaps the exception of members of the National Security Council, in July 1975, knew anything about the CIA's and SOD's biological warfare and mind control research and experiments of the 1950s through the 1960s. In short, and ironically, what Cheney was warning about actually *did* begin to occur that same month, and continued to occur over the next two years, as exemplified by the subsequent Congressional investigations by the Kennedy and Church Committees.

Ironically, however, this does not mean that the White House, and perhaps members of the Rockefeller Commission, were not aware of certain facts about Olson's death that were never revealed to anyone outside a small circle that may have included Cheney and Rumsfeld. In other words, there was a cover-up in play, as subsequent chapters will evidence, but Cheney's July 11 memo itself was not evidence of it.

The other significant fact that was amply demonstrated by White House memos and internal communications was that at the very start of July 1975, White House officials and also Department of Justice officials had un-redacted copies of many, if not all, of the CIA documents that would later become known as the "Colby documents."

3

Friday, July 18, 1975, 7:35 p.m.
Philadelphia, Pennsylvania

David Kairys was entertaining friends in his Philadelphia home when his telephone rang. In the middle of telling a humorous story, Kairys excused himself and picked up the receiver. A man on the other end identified himself as Roderick Hills. He said he was calling from the White House in Washington, D.C. and that he was Counsel to the President.

Kairys hesitated momentarily, thinking that it was a friend playing a joke just days after the Frank Olson story had exploded nationwide.

"So I listened, not wanting to express doubts because I wasn't sure who it was," Kairys says. "The voice sounded like a pretty good White House counsel imitation if he wasn't the real thing, but I was also thinking it was a joke. Watergate was fresh at the time, and I remember thinking, and I think saying, something like, White House Counsel, wasn't that John Dean's last job."

Quickly it became apparent that the call was no joke. Hills said that he was calling on behalf of President Ford. "The President asked me to invite Mrs. Olson to a confidential meeting with him at the White House on Monday, July 21st."

"That's only three days away from now," Kairys said.

"Yes," said Hills. "The President would very much like to meet with Mrs. Olson on Monday."

Kairys, concerned about the timing and appearance of a meeting with Ford, asked Hills to explain the purpose of the meeting and what subjects might be discussed. Years later he told the author, "Such a meeting is usually done after the issues and claims are resolved. We had only announced days before that we intended to sue. We hadn't met with anyone. We'd had no discussions as of yet with anyone. I also didn't want the Olsons to get swooped up into some media show. But, I knew Alice particularly would want, and surely deserved, both a meeting with and an apology from the President."

Hills told Kairys that President Ford had no intention of discussing the Olson's legal claims with Alice. He explained that he had already personally handed the issue over to the Attorney General.

"President Ford feels strongly and personally about what has happened to the Olsons,' Hills said. "He is outraged and only wants to express sympathy and apologize."

Kairys said that he appreciated Hills' candor and asked if Hills literally meant that just Mrs. Olson was invited. "No," said Hills, "I meant to say that the whole family is invited."

"What do you mean by a 'confidential' meeting?" Kairys pressed. "Would there be any press conference or press coverage?"

Hills said there would be no press conference. But, he continued, there would be a statement released saying, very briefly, that there was a meeting, who was there, and what was discussed.

Kairys asked, "Does the statement have to be part of the visit?"

Hills answered, "We have an obligation to do it; it happens anytime someone meets with the President. The President doesn't want to be secret with the people." Hills added, "And there are people who constantly watch who comes and goes from the White House." Recalls Kairys, "He indicated that this was a necessary part of the visit and could not be dispensed with."

Kairys thanked Hills for the call and said that he would speak with Alice about the President's request and would get back to Hills as-soon-as-possible. Hills again emphasized that Monday was the day that Ford had selected and he gave Kairys his White House and home telephone numbers. "Feel free to call me at anytime," Hills said.

"Alice Olson was clearly moved by the White House invitation and wanted to go to see Ford, without question," David Kairys said later, "although she didn't object when I said I wanted to continue to negotiate the conditions under which the meeting occurred."

Negotiations, conducted day and night over the telephone with Hills, quickly resulted in a commitment from the White House that the Olson's attorneys would meet with U.S. Attorney General Edward Levi "to start a process that could resolve the family's claims" and "a pledge of full discovery of documents" including everything held by the CIA, Army, and other federal agencies on Frank Olson. As Kairys pointed out, "The documents were an absolute requirement." Kairys said that Hills also readily agreed to the family's request that the White House meeting be private, with no press coverage or television cameras. Kairys, however, did agree that a White House photographer could be present to take pictures, knowing that Alice would especially want them. Kairys was mindful of additional, substantive concerns about the implications of the meeting, however:

Nils, Lisa, and Greg generally went along with Alice's view of the meeting, agreeing with or deferring to her, but Eric was less moved by the idea of the meeting or an apology. Eric and I were skeptical of suicide and wanted to push on rather than settle, which involved some risk. The government had some substantial defenses if it came to an all-out legal fight, but we had some good answers for those defenses. It was hard to predict how it would come out. It was clear that what the government most wanted, apparently from the day Frank died, was to avoid a real investigation.

On July 21, the Olson family, including Greg Hayward, met in the Oval Office with President Ford. The meeting lasted approximately fifteen minutes. Ford warmly greeted the family and solemnly apologized for what had happened. He said to Alice Olson, "The disclosures about your husband are of great concern to me. I know that nothing could be done to totally make up for what has happened, but you have my deepest sympathy." Ford told the family that on behalf of the American people he was deeply sorry. Then the President departed from the advice his staff had given him and he informed the Olsons that he was ordering CIA director William Colby to meet with them that week and to provide them with all documents that related to Frank Olson's death that were in the CIA's possession.

After this the family stood nervously making small talk with the President, while the White House photographer moved about the room taking pictures. Eric Olson recounts that Alice let slip that she had been ill recently and that Ford said that he hoped it was "nothing serious." Characteristically, Alice said nothing about her cancer and replied that she was troubled by a bruised arm injured in a fall on ice the previous winter. Ford remarked that as a long-time Michigan resident he was well acquainted with cold winters. Everyone smiled at this and the photographer expertly captured the solemn event's only light-hearted moment.

Following the Olson's departure, White House press secretary, Ron Nessen, told reporters that the President had informed the family that "he would make available information on the case" and that Ford had requested that Attorney General Edward Levi meet with the Olson's attorneys "to discuss the claims they wish to assert against the CIA by reason of Dr. Olson's death." Nessen handed reporters copies of a brief statement written by the Olsons in which they thanked President Ford for supporting their efforts to "become fully informed about Frank Olson's death and to obtain a just resolution of this entire affair." The statement optimistically concluded:

> We hope that this will be part of a continuing effort to insure that the CIA is accountable for its actions and that people in all parts of the world are safe from abuses of power by American intelligence agencies.

4

July 24, 1974
CIA Headquarters, Langley, Virginia

Two days after the Olson's White House meeting, the *New York Times* reported, "President Ford has instructed the Central Intelligence Agency to make available to the family of Frank R. Olson 'all relevant materials and documents' concerning his death and the agency's LSD drug experiment in which he participated shortly before his death." The *Times* had learned of Ford's instructions to the CIA from a telephone interview the previous day with David Kairys. An ensuing phone call from the *Times* to the White House press office confirmed what the newspaper called "the unusual step." During the same call, a White House press officer said that a meeting between the Olsons and CIA director William Colby had been scheduled for the next day.

Eric, Nils, and Lisa Olson Hayward, accompanied by their two attorneys, met with Colby on July 24 in his seventh-floor office at the CIA's Langley, Virginia headquarters. The Olsons entered through the main lobby, replete with its huge inlaid emblem of an eagle, shield, and sixteen-point compass star. The sprawling 1,500,000 square-foot aboveground and subterranean complex, situated on nearly 260 acres of land, had been completed in November 1963, ten years after Frank Olson's death.

At the time the Langley building was officially opened, Colby had been working for the CIA since summer 1950, when the outbreak of the Korean War spurred his patriotic fervor and he joined the staff of the Office of Policy Coordination (OPC). OPC was the CIA's covert action arm overseen by Frank Wisner who, according to Colby, ran the group "in the atmosphere of an order of Knights Templar." During World War II, Colby had served as an officer in the Army. His extensive training in parachuting, counterespionage, sabotage and paramilitary operations made him a natural recruit for the OSS, which he joined in 1943. At the rank of major, Colby's OSS exploits were adventurous and varied; he served in France and England and commanded the Norwegian Special Operations Group.

A lean, aloof, distinguished looking man, Colby once described himself as "the traditional gray man, so inconspicuous that he can never catch the waiter's eye in a restaurant." Colby's father had been a career military man and talented journalist, his mother a deeply religious Irish Catholic. Colby grew up an Army brat, moving frequently, living on army bases from the humid South to frigid northern New York and Vermont, as well as in China and France. After three years of high school in Burlington, Vermont, the "longest period of settled life that I experienced in my youth," as Colby called it, he attended college at Princeton and graduated from Columbia law school. He was determined to become a labor attorney and joined the firm Donovan, Leisure, Newton, Lumbard, and Irvine, headed by William "Wild Bill" Donovan, former head of the OSS.

From 1968 to 1972, Colby's CIA career passed through its most controversial phase when he oversaw the notorious Phoenix Project (Phung Hoang Project) in Vietnam. Critics of the $80 million program, and they are legion, maintain that it was responsible for the torture and assassination of between 20,000 and 40,000 South Vietnamese citizens. Testifying before a congressional committee in 1972, Colby said, "I've defended [Phoenix] as a necessary element of war. The communists, curiously enough, say it was the most effective program ever used against them... The Phoenix, I always thought, was not all that effective. But if you have a secret mafia inside your population you better find out who they are, and that was what Phoenix was all about, to identify who they were."

In his memoirs, published in 1978, Colby recorded his feelings about meeting the Olsons. "I made a particular point of contacting the family and extending the CIA's sincere apologies," he wrote. "But one of the most difficult assignments I ever had was to meet with [Olson's] wife and now-grown children to discuss how to give them the CIA records and thus open up and overcome a twenty-year secret that had had such an impact on their lives."

In fact, contrary to Colby's seemingly earnest words, Alice Olson did not attend the meeting. She was undergoing radiation treatments for her cancer and was too ill to make the trip. She also was not inclined to meet Colby for other reasons. David Kairys said that regardless of her treatments:

> Alice refused to see Colby or to go to the CIA. I remember her saying that Colby was there all through these events and he said nothing and did nothing. She was pretty angry with any of them who were there back then.

According to Eric and Nils Olson, their mother never spoke with or met separately with Colby. Equally odd is that, according to Nils Olson, "Colby himself never contacted our family to extend any sentiment prior to our visit to the CIA."

Additionally, Eric recalls, there were never any discussions between his family and the CIA concerning "how the Agency was going to give us copies of any of its documents about my father." Eric says, "They gave them to us, as far as I know, because Ford told them to do it."

David Kairys says that prior to meeting with Colby, he, his partner David Rudovsky, and the three Olsons met with Mitchell Rogovin. Just a few days earlier, Rogovin had been appointed special counsel for the beleaguered CIA director Colby. Rogovin was a highly regarded civil liberties attorney who, as noted earlier, had once served as general counsel for the leftist Institute for Policy Studies. Prior to that, in 1963, Rogovin had caused a minor national stir when, as advisor to the Internal Revenue Service, he helped draw up a target list of tax-exempt "right wing groups" for investigation at the request of Attorney General Robert Kennedy. Rogovin, perhaps unknown to Kennedy at the time, was the CIA's secret liaison to the IRS. During the first quarter of 1964, Rogovin, as a special assistant to the IRS Commissioner, also handled numerous administrative matters related to the Warren Commission's investigation of JFK's assassination.

"We raised two matters with Rogovin," Kairys recalls. "Press coverage of our meeting with Colby and surveillance of us while at the CIA." According to Kairys, Rogovin told the group that Colby "intended to apologize, but that no statement or publicity was intended, and that we would not be surveilled, recorded, photographed, or monitored in any way while at the CIA." Satisfied, the group moved on to Colby's office.

Asked to recall the meeting, Eric Olson said:

> Colby was cordial, reserved, but somewhat nervous. My sister said after the meeting that she thought he was cold and distant. Colby apologized to us for what had happened to our father. He said, 'This is a terrible thing. It never should have happened. Some of our people were out of control in those days, they went too far. There were problems of supervision and administration.'

David Rudovsky recalled in a 1999 interview that the meeting was much like going to "the enemy's fortress," with Colby "kind of fumbling around to apologize to the family." David Kairys offered similar observations:

> Colby was very cold, with an awkward, pro forma apology. He apologized on behalf of himself and everyone at the CIA. He said that he had no explanation for the failure of the CIA to tell the Olsons the true circumstances of Frank's death. He said the CIA is changing and that he had issued a directive in 1973 that prohibits the kind of experiment that killed Frank Olson.

Kairys asked Colby if the new directive prohibited experiments only in the United States or did it include all areas of the world. Colby said that it applied to people everywhere. Somewhat surprisingly, said Kairys:

> He also indicated that the CIA's activities against Allende in Chile constituted an abuse, although it was initiated and ordered from the White House. I asked if there was any executive branch directive on undermining noncapitalist regimes and the right of self-determination, and he said there was not.

Eric Olson recounts that Colby then handed Kairys a thick folder of documents and that Colby stated, "This is everything the CIA has concerning Frank Olson's death."

"We gathered every document we could find," Kairys recalls Colby saying.

Kairys wanted to be sure. "Do these documents include all of the information and materials available to the CIA concerning Frank's death and the events leading up to it and following its occurrence?" he asked.

Colby and Rogovin both responded that the documents did. "They should clear up any questions that you have," Rogovin added.

"We appreciate your giving us these," said Kairys, accepting the file.

At this point, Kairys says that Colby thanked them all for coming and excused himself, saying that he had other business to attend to. Rogovin then asked everyone to follow him to another room down the hall where, Kairys recounts, "we were going to go through the documents with him." Once there, Kairys says, "Rogovin showed us some of the excised portions, which we were to skim to see that they contained nothing on Frank Olson, but which they would not give us copies of." After completing this task, which Kairys says made him quite uneasy, Rogovin invited the group to have lunch with him in an adjoining private dining room.

As soon as the group was seated, Kairys says, "Colby unexpectedly came in and joined us. It really took me by surprise. I felt very uneasy about the idea of eating with Colby. I wanted to leave, but I knew I could not since this was the Olson's visit, not mine. If we had known this would happen and could have talked it out, we may all have wanted to leave, but I didn't feel I could do it on my own."

Eric agrees, saying, "I was surprised when Colby returned to join us. It was completely unexpected. I know that everyone felt uncomfortable with his coming back.... Lunch was served to us on china bearing the CIA crest. We sat at a round table. Colby and Rogovin sat to my right. My brother and sister were to my left, and to their left were Kairys and Rudovsky"

Eric recounts that Colby stiffly tried to make conversation by asking him and Nils what they did for a living. Nils told Colby he was attending college to become a dentist. Eric told Colby he was a graduate student at Harvard.

"I expect to receive my Ph.D. in clinical psychology next year," Eric added.

"Oh, really," said Colby. "I'm very interested in psychology. Exactly what are you doing in your studies?"

"I'm trying to develop a new form of psychology based on collage," Eric explained. "It combines elements of psychodiagnostic testing with the process of treatment itself."

"I'm also very interested in psychological testing," Colby said.

"What sort of tests are you interested in?" Eric asked.

"I'm mostly interested in the polygraph," Colby replied.

Eric said that he was momentarily speechless. "I didn't quite know how to respond to that, given the reasons we were there," he said. Kairys remembers feeling awkward that Colby had not asked Lisa about her profession (she worked as a speech therapist at the Maryland State School for the Deaf).

Recovering his composure, Eric asked Colby, "Does the CIA polygraph its own employees?"

"Everyone is polygraphed before hiring," Colby answered, "and periodically thereafter."

Kairys and Rudovsky asked Colby about what types of information the CIA wanted to know about prospective employees. "What types of political criteria are there?" Kairys asked.

Kairys says that Colby responded, "We don't have political criteria, as long as you can do the job."

Eric then asked, "So you have socialists as employees, people who are against the war [in Vietnam]."

Kairys says that Colby responded that there was "considerable discontent at the CIA with the Cambodian invasion, particularly among the younger people," but Colby said, "these employees are still here."

At this, Kairys quipped, "You mean you haven't let them leave the building."

Years later, Kairys told the author, "I was joking, of course. At the moment, I was drawing a line in my mind between the case and an informal lunch with Colby, and my comment probably also reflected my wish to do so since I viewed him as instrumental to governmental policies and actions that I abhor." Kairys chuckles, recalling, "When I made the comment Rogovin dropped his spoon into some very good soup. Colby kind of smiled and nodded at me. I took it as meaning 'good one,' or something like that."

Eric says that the discussion then turned toward Vietnam. "During our earlier introductions," Eric explains, "I provocatively mentioned that before starting graduate school I had been teaching in public schools to avoid being drafted and sent to Vietnam."

Eric told Colby, "Prior to these revelations of CIA drugging and the mishandling of my father, the thing that most upset me about the United States had been the involvement in this immoral and unwinnable war."

Kairys says that "Colby kind of bristled at Eric's comment" and that the ensuing Vietnam discussion "lasted for some time." He recalls that Colby "criticized the presidents and the army for failing to see the political nature of the war."

Colby said, "The CIA was more realistic in its intelligence concerning the strength of the enemy and saw the struggle as political."

Kairys remembers that Colby referred "to numerous memos where the CIA set this out in opening paragraphs but failed to say or do anything concrete about it, getting into the military situation and strategy." In notes recorded shortly after the meeting, Kairys wrote:

> When we questioned [Colby] on what he meant by 'political' and why he thought the war was lost (and whether it was lost— or won by the

side that should win) HE DID exactly what he was condemning: he put the whole thing in military terms. He said the war was lost because the U.S. stopped giving necessary military aid. Soldiers were limited to a set number of shots fired per day. The people had swung over to the side of the Theiu regime, he said. The evidence of this was, first, that although the Tet offensive of 1968 was conducted by 'guerrillas,' the offensives of the 1970s were carried out by North Vietnamese regular units. The guerrillas, he said, had all come over to the side of the Theiu regime. The further evidence to him was that he rode around freely and was not shot, he gave 'half a million guns to the people' and they didn't use them on us, and he had talked to a lot of people and he knew they were for the Theiu regime.

Kairys also asked Colby how he could imagine that the Vietnamese people would tell him what they really think. Wrote Kairys in his notes: "If the people were on the side of Theiu, how did the S.V. army fold in two weeks? Weren't there good political reasons why the people would be for the NLF and against the Theiu regime, and wasn't that the essence of the struggle and the outcome?" Concluded Kairys:

> To Colby, the [Vietnamese] people were essentially mindless pawns— it depended on who got to them first with the most guns. He saw no political content to the struggle or the people; it was all a question of guns, aid, propaganda, military strategy.

As the lunch discussion was drawing to a close, Kairys observed that:

> Colby was obviously uncomfortable with the discussion. He was trying throughout to be as warm as he could, which is not very warm. The press was waiting at the gate, and, given the president's statements and the publicity, he had to try to satisfy the Olsons. He is also obviously not used to being questioned or asked his basis for what he says. Sometimes he had a vicious tone, particularly when he discussed the Phoenix program and the half-a-million guns.

David Kairys also recalls that Colby asked Eric about *Living and Dying*, the book he had written with Robert Jay Lifton. Kairys said, "Colby seemed genuinely curious about its subject matter."

Unknown to the Olsons and their attorneys at the time was that Colby had recently become deeply interested in the psychology of death, after having lost his twenty-four year old daughter to the combined effects of depression, epilepsy, and anorexia nervosa. Catherine Colby, a student at Johns Hopkins University, had died in April 1973 after a decade long struggle. Her death, according to people close to Colby, strongly affected him, with some officials claiming that Colby "experienced a real epiphany that produced a sharp philosophical turn in his life."

The Olsons left CIA headquarters feeling confident that they were finally nearing the end of years of confusion, thinking that soon they would have all the answers to the questions that had plagued them for so long.

But it was not to be.

The Colby Documents

"The Colby documents." Within a few short days, this is how the Olsons' attorneys began referring to the thick packet of documents handed to them. David Kairys read through all 153 pages the evening following the meeting at CIA headquarters. As he described it:

> I carefully read through them once and then again. When I set them down that night I was more convinced then ever that there was far more to Frank Olson's story than what was being said. I read them through again early the next morning and felt the same way, even more so.

Kairys also realized with his third reading that the bulk of the documents had been assembled in December 1953 and January 1954 as part of CIA Inspector General Lyman B. Kirkpatrick's review of the Olson incident.

"It wasn't clear at first because of the order of the papers given us," Kairys explained. "To make sure, I read them carefully through again, this time making longer notes and listing questions that arose. By the time I was done several hours had passed and I had nearly filled a legal pad."

Just hours after the Olsons' CIA meeting concluded, Rogovin had written Kairys a brief letter telling the attorney that any questions about the documents would be welcomed. Rogovin specified:

> I have assured others at the Agency that we have an agreement to the effect that the documents turned over to you are for the sole purpose of prosecuting any claim against the United States Government with respect to the death of Frank R. Olsen [sic]. When you get a moment, I would appreciate it if you would simply send me a note confirming that.

Several hours after leaving the CIA's headquarters, David Kairys had noticed that the documents handed to him included a signed letter from Colby addressed to Alice Olson. In the letter, Colby wrote that he wanted to:

> ... join with President Ford in expressing my deepest personal sympathy and hope you and your family will also accept my sincere apologies on behalf of the Central Intelligence Agency for the suffering you and your family have endured as a result of the untimely loss of your husband in 1953....

The uniform reaction of the employees of the Agency at this disclosure has been dismay and regret that this could have occurred. I can find no explanation for why you were not fully informed of the circumstances at the time and apologize equally for that omission.

Colby then cited Alice's letter of July 17 concerning her suit against the CIA and addressed each of the three areas of reply demanded by the Olsons. He wrote:

With regard to the full and complete disclosure of all of the details surrounding the circumstances which led to the administration of LSD, I have made available to your attorney the information available to the Central Intelligence Agency.

With respect to the second item mentioned in your letter, an Agency directive was issued on 29 August 1973 which expressly prohibits any experiment or use of drugs or other techniques for influencing human behavior to be conducted on unwitting American citizens.

This stems from the Agency's and my reaction to this case and our conviction that such an event should never recur in America.

The August 29, 1973 directive, obtained through the Freedom of Information Act from the CIA, reads:

Any experiment or use of drugs or other techniques for influencing human behavior will be undertaken only with the Director's specific approval and in no case on unwitting American citizens.

Presumably, experiments on foreigners overseas or on non-citizens in the United States, with approval, were allowed.

Colby's letter to Alice Olson continued:

In addition to this Agency's policy, Congress, in passing the National Research Act on July 12, 1974 (PL 93-348), established a National Commission for the Protection of Human Subjects of Biomedical and Behavioral Research. This Commission was established to specifically develop guidelines applicable to all departments and agencies of the Government conducting any biomedical and behavioral research on human subjects. This Agency will adhere to all guidelines suggested by the National Commission.

Lastly Colby stated, "With regard to the third matter raised in your letter, your claim for monetary damages, I am advised that President Ford designated the Attorney General as the appropriate official to discuss your claim."

After reading the documents one more time, Kairys made copies and forwarded the original set to the Olsons. In his brief cover letter, he suggested, "As you go through the CIA documents, it would be helpful to start thinking about follow-up questions, which I would like to send in one letter from all of us."

In his package to the Olsons, Kairys also enclosed a copy of the July 24 letter he had received from Mitchell Rogovin. "The letter indicates that he has gotten some flack for giving us the documents without an agreement concerning public disclosure," Kairys wrote. Years later he explained to the author:

> Before we went to meet with Colby and Rogovin, we all discussed the possible issues that could arise around the documents. At the top of the list was disclosure. What I recommended was that we shouldn't raise the issue at all during the meeting and assume that we were free to use the documents however we wanted so long as they didn't raise the issue and place any limits on their use prior to handing them over.
>
> When they said nothing at the meeting, when they raised no issues at all, and I saw that the documents were declassified, I also saw no legal problems with public disclosure. Even then we didn't share the documents with anyone; it would still be months before we did that. We spent a lot of time considering whether, in the event that we did make them public, how we would want to do so.

That same day, July 29, Kairys and Rudovsky also sent a letter to DCI William Colby about another issue related to the documents. This issue concerned the completeness of the documents. The attorneys explained in their letter that after closely studying the file and reading all the documents, they had concluded that the documents did not represent the entire file on Olson's death because numerous key matters and subjects were not even touched upon.

In support of this contention, the attorneys told Colby that the Olsons, on the day after their meeting at the CIA, had met with Attorney General Edward Levi at the Justice Department to initiate discussions concerning their pending lawsuit. During the course of that meeting Kairys and Rudovsky had been surprised to discover that the Justice Department had some additional documents in their CIA files on Frank Olson's death that had not been given to the Olsons.

In their letter to Colby, the attorneys said they had immediately asked for copies of the additional pages. Attorney General Levi told them that he could not give them copies without the approval of the CIA, but he had indicated that he thought such approval would be easy to obtain in light of statements made by Colby and President Ford.

But, Levi was wrong.

Two days later, as the attorneys explained to Colby, they had received a call from the Justice Department informing them that the CIA was refusing to give them two of the documents. According to the official who called them, the reasons for the refusal were that the CIA didn't think the documents would be "useful" because "one was handwritten and unsigned" and the other "only concerned LSD experimentation in general." Wrote the attorneys to Colby:

> We were not told we were getting the 'useful file.' Nor were we told that the CIA would determine what was useful for us and withhold the rest. Based on a brief reading, we found both of these documents important to an understanding of what happened, whether or not we could or would want to introduce them into evidence in a court of law. Obviously, the CIA also thought they were useful—to our adversaries at the Justice Department.

As Kairys recalled to the author, "We were fairly perturbed about the whole issue. Coming on top of reading the documents it was especially bothersome. The obvious question was what other materials was the CIA withholding and for what reasons? At that juncture it seemed clear that there were two or more Olson files. We operated in good faith, took the President at his word, Colby and Rogovin at their words, and accepted what we thought was the entire CIA file." Kairys elaborated on the importance of this communication to Colby:

> We had to have assurances that we had everything that anyone else had. So we formally requested in our letter to Colby that we wanted the entire CIA file and all reports, materials, and information, everything, about Olson's death and the related events leading up to it. To drive the request home we also asked Colby to give us his written assurance in the form of a sworn affidavit stating that we had received the entire file. At that point, we didn't want to take any chances with anything or anybody.

Two days later, Mitchell Rogovin called Kairys in response to his letter to Colby. Rogovin said that copies of the two additional documents were in the mail (they had arrived earlier that day) and apologized for what he said was the Agency's "mistake" in not giving them to Kairys in the original file.

Said Rogovin, "David, I assure you that you now have everything."

"I hope so," replied Kairys.

"I understand why you wrote to Colby like you did, but," asked Rogovin, "could you send a note to everyone who was copied on the letter saying that you are now satisfied that you have everything?" (Copies of the letter to Colby had been sent to Roderick Hills at the White House and Attorney General Edward Levi.)

"The first step in that direction," Kairys said, "is our receipt of the sworn affidavit that we requested."

Rogovin said, "I'll see to it that you get it."

"Mitch," Kairys said changing the subject, "one of the new documents, the handwritten list of steps to take following Olson's death, it's unsigned and undated, but do you know who may have written it?"

"Yes," said Rogovin, "Allen Dulles, but please keep that under your hat."

"We'll see," said Kairys.

True to his word, twenty-eight days later, Rogovin sent Kairys a sworn and notarized affidavit carefully stating what Kairys had requested, only the affidavit was signed by Donald F. Chamberlain, Inspector General of the CIA, not Colby. Rogovin explained that Colby was away from the office and that Chamberlain, as Inspector General, had closer personal knowledge of the agency's search for documents.

These would not be the last documents "discovered" by the CIA.

On August 29, Rogovin notified Kairys by letter that additional documents had been found. These were two pages of diary entries made in late-1953 and early-1954 by Lyman B. Kirkpatrick, the CIA's Inspector General. Rogovin, who enclosed the pages with his letter, wrote that they had been "recently discovered in connection with a records search, unrelated to the Olson case, undertaken for the Senate Select Committee on Intelligence Activities." (See next chapter for more on the Select Committee.)

In the same letter, Rogovin also enclosed two pages from a 1953 memo provided to the Olsons at the June 24 CIA meeting. These new pages had somehow been separated from the rest of the document. This document was a "Memorandum for the Record" from Office of Security chief Sheffield Edwards dated November 28, 1953 bearing the subject line, "Suicide of Frank OLSEN [sic], Army Civilian Employee, Camp Dietrich [sic]."

On August 8, Kairys and Rudovsky wrote a strongly worded letter to Rogovin about the Olsons' reactions to the Colby documents:

> The Olson family and we, as their counsel, are not satisfied that the documents provided adequately describe or explain the death of Frank Olson or constitute the entire CIA file on this matter.
>
> Obvious areas of vital concern are not even touched upon. Inconsistencies abound; secrecy and ambiguity are rampant, while attempts to arrive at the truth, and the persons responsible for this atrocity, seem only incidental.

Kairys and Rudovsky went on to list four-pages of "major areas where we find the documents wholly inadequate." First on their list was that nowhere was there a "complete discussion of whether or not the application of LSD to Olson was involuntary." The attorneys pointed out that the documents contained vague references to a meeting where "experts" agreed in principle "to an experiment involving unwitting application," but with no indication who these experts were or "if the group included Olson." How could the experiment at Deep Creek Lake be considered a scientifically valuable test of an unwitting application of a drug, the attorneys asked, if the subjects had known and agreed to it in advance?

"Where are interviews with the other seven subjects of the experiment concerning, at least, whether they knew in advance or agreed 'in principle'?" the attorneys asked. "In this regard," they pointed out, "Vincent Ruwet, who was drugged at the same time Frank Olson was, has told us that his participation was wholly unwitting, involving no agreement 'in principle' or in any other way."

Next, the attorneys complained that, "there is nothing that describes or explains this 'experiment.'" Was there a written proposal or statement setting out the objectives of the experiment? They asked. Who proposed it to begin with? Did Dr. Harold Abramson participate from the start? How and by whom were the subjects chosen? How and by whom was the dosage determined? If indeed it was an experiment, why was there no report on its results? Why were there no medical personnel present for the test? If knowledge was to be gained, why were the subjects sent home so soon, which meant they would not be observed? What happened with the other subjects who were dosed with LSD? Concerning Frank Olson's treatment in New York by Dr. Harold Abramson, the attorneys asked, where was there an independent psychiatric report on Olson?

Dr. Abramson, who is not a psychiatrist, gave three inconsistent statements. Robert Lashbrook apparently dictated the final statement to Abramson. How could the investigators and the Director fail to obtain independent psychiatric and medical opinions and evaluations?

Next Kairys and Rudovsky wrote that from reading the documents, "It was not completely clear that the death of Frank Olson was an accidental suicide." By this, they explained, "We do not mean to suggest that we believe he was intentionally killed," but primarily that they did not know from the documents "exactly what happened." But, they wrote, "in light of what we do know about the matter and other CIA activities, we are not prepared to dismiss this possibility." Bluntly, the attorneys summarized their findings:

> The documents indicate that the overriding concern of CIA personnel throughout this matter was secrecy and security, not the health or well-being of Frank Olson. We know that Dr. Olson had thought of resigning before this experiment and had told at least one person at Detrick about the possibility of his resigning. Once he was drugged, he was delusional and out-of-control, even throwing away his wallet and secret identification papers. He did not trust the CIA or Army personnel charged with his care and perceived a plot against him (understandably, as a usual reaction to LSD, and as a reality—they had plotted against him).

Did CIA and Army personnel perceive Frank Olson as a security risk? the attorneys asked. And why was he taken to Dr. Abramson, a cleared CIA consultant, rather than to a qualified psychiatrist? Were there not cleared physicians stationed at Camp Detrick's hospital, at Edgewood Arsenal, or at Walter Reed Hospital? What about the CIA's own medical staff, which consisted of at least four highly trained psychologists at the time? Why did Abramson wait so long before he decided to institutionalize Olson? Why did he allow Olson to be housed on the tenth floor of a hotel if Olson were so sick? Why didn't Ruwet stay the full time in New York with Olson? Why did Lashbrook have to tell Abramson what to write in his report?

Why, why, why? The documents raised far more questions than they answered or clarified. As Kairys put it, "The documents were just so vague, so carefully written as if to avoid certain mysterious things, so seemingly contrived in places... it was as if each sentence had been gone over and over by several sets of eyes and hands before they were finalized. They were absolutely frustrating in what they didn't say, in what they didn't reveal."

The attorneys concluded their letter to Rogovin by stating:

> We realize that some documents may have been destroyed by Sidney Gottlieb in 1973 or may be otherwise unavailable. However, our discovery of two quite important documents provided to the Justice Department that were not provided to us (which is discussed in our letter of July 29, 1975), leads us to believe that the CIA may have additional materials and information.
>
> Furthermore, the documents provided indicate that there were several separate files, some of which would not seem to be available to Sidney Gottlieb. The General Counsel apparently had a complete file, based upon which he reached the conclusion that there was 'culpable negligence' by CIA personnel.
>
> The Inspector General and Division of Security also had files and conducted investigations that would not seem to be available for destruction by Sidney Gottlieb.

Because of their concerns and suspicions, Kairys and Rudovsky now requested, in addition to the affidavit they had asked for in their July 29 letter, that the CIA conduct not only another, thorough search for materials and information, but also make available to them, for sworn depositions, people who could answer their questions.

"We know who some of these people are," wrote the attorneys. "Many of them have been mentioned in this letter and our discussions. But we are not limiting our request to persons who we can identify; we are asking you to make available people who can answer our questions."

The Olsons' attorneys knew they would need access to CIA personnel in order to build their case. As Kairys said in an interview with the author:

> It was obvious that the one way to throw light on all the issues we had identified was to get the people who had been there, people directly involved in what had happened, to go on record. We wanted to speak with Gottlieb, of course, but we also wanted to be allowed to question other key people. People like Lashbrook, who was in the room, like Sheffield Edwards, Kirkpatrick, Houston, George White, and Dr. Abramson, as well as all the people who had attended the Deep Creek Lake meeting. These were the people that held the answers and the truth.

THE SETTLEMENT

Having concluded their meetings with President Ford at the White House, and William Colby at the CIA, the Olson family continued to answer nonstop questions, at all hours of the day and night, from the ever-inquisitive press. Their attorneys, meanwhile, were still doing everything possible to move ahead with the family's lawsuit against the CIA. Kairys was conducting almost daily telephone conferences with White House Counsel Roderick Hills, and also with the Department of Justice.

In his July 16, 1975 memorandum to President Ford, Hills had written: "We recommend that the Attorney General be authorized now to seek to negotiate a settlement with the Olson's lawyer." Hills stated:

> The Civil Division [of the Department of Justice] has advised us preliminarily that the case has a settlement value of between $500,000 and $1 million. I have asked for a final recommendation....
>
> The Civil Division also has stated that any settlement may require a private bill [in Congress] to approve the settlement, but they are reconsidering this decision....
>
> A private bill in the House would be introduced in Congressman Walter Flowers' subcommittee [Subcommittee on Administrative Law and Governmental Relations, House Judiciary Committee], which probably would not encourage any in depth hearings about Dr. Olson's job. In the Senate, the Judiciary Committee assigns private bills to the staff for recommendation back to the full committee. Again, we would expect that there would be only a small chance of extensive hearings on the underlying facts.

In conclusion, stated Hills: "Depending upon the exact amount of the settlement and a final decision from the Department of Justice, it may be possible for the Attorney General to approve a settlement and pay it without a private bill."

On September 24, Special Counsel Hills, following several meetings with Kairys and Department of Justice attorneys, received a letter from Attorney General Edward H. Levi, informing Hills that:

> An amicable disposition of the Olson family claim for damages can be accomplished without litigation either by settlement or private bill. In this regard, the Justice Department has determined that the reasonable settlement value of the Olson family claim is $500,000. We have also determined that a private bill would reasonably provide compensation in the range $1 million to $1.25 million.

In reaching these figures, Levi explained:

> ...We have appreciated fully the emotional appeal of the unique circumstances of the Olson claim and its likely impact on any court's

interpretation of applicable legal principles. On the other hand, we have not ignored the fact that damages in Federal Tort Claims Act suits are established by a judge and not a jury; punitive damages are not permitted; and no action is available for misrepresentation or deceit.

Concluded Levi's letter, "I assume that if the Olsons are to seek a private bill, the agency which would express its views, if asked, as to the amount, would be the [Department of Defense] or the CIA."

On September 30, Hills advised Richard Cheney that the Olsons' pending lawsuit "threatens to be a reality this week if no new effort to settle the case is made." Hills explained that Attorney General Levi has made a final offer of $500,000, which had been promptly rejected by the Olsons and their attorneys. Said Hills, "The Olson family has countered with a request for $3 million but [have] indicated a willingness to settle for less." Hills told Cheney that in Levi's opinion, the Olsons' claim "is worth $1 million, but must be discounted by $500,000 by reason of the possibility that the government will ultimately succeed in the case on the grounds that exclusive remedy for the Olson family comes from the benefits provided by the Federal Employees Compensation Act."

Summarized Hills, "In short, the Justice Department argues that there is a substantial possibility that a court will find that Dr. Olson <u>died in the course of his employment.</u>" [Underlining original.]

However, Hills told Cheney:

I fully disagree with this analysis and believe that there is a real probability that an appellate court would decide that as a matter of law when one dies under the circumstances such as those causing Dr. Olson's death, he cannot be said to have died 'in the course of his employment.'

Hills therefore recommended that Cheney immediately advise President Ford to authorize Special Counsel to the CIA, Mitchell Rogovin, to attempt a settlement with the Olsons "at a sum not to exceed $1,250,000 plus a waiver of an offset of the monies received to date by the Olson family [through Federal Bureau of Employee's Compensation benefits, which totaled about $143,583.]

Reasoned Hills, at length:

In the event a settlement can be reached within these guidelines, the CIA and the Olson family can jointly petition the Department of Labor to re-consider its 22 year old decision that Dr. Olson did die in the course of his employment. Should the Labor Department so rule, the Justice Department is on record as supporting a settlement of $1 million without an offset.

The CIA could agree in a settlement with the Olson family that any excess amount would be made the subject of a private bill and supported by the Administration. Alternatively, if the Labor Department does waive the FECA decision, we could ask the Justice Department to re-consider its settlement limitation. In the event that the Labor Department should reaffirm the 22-year-old decision that Dr. Olson did die in the course of his employment, we would agree that the private bill would be in the amount of $750,000.

The next day, October 1, Alice Olson sent a Western Union Mailgram to President Gerald Ford at the White House. Alice wrote that she had been informed that her family's financial claim had been referred to the White House.

"In light of what we feel to have been a very satisfactory meeting with you this summer," wrote Alice, "we would like again to convey directly to you our thoughts on this matter."

According to David Kairys, Alice had written the note on her own, without much input from her attorneys. In her letter, she stated:

> There is no doubt as to the egregiousness of the American government wrongdoing both in the original conduct of the LSD experiment on Frank Olson and the concealment of the truth for twenty-two years. This incident must constitute one of the most flagrant violations of the rights of American citizens in recent history, and we believe we are entitled to substantial compensation for our suffering.
>
> But beyond our own recompense for this incident it is our strong wish that the meaning of Frank Olson's life may be extended through good work undertaken in his name. When our case is resolved we hope to be in a position to make a very substantial contribution to the establishment of a center for the treatment of alcoholics in our community. The struggle against alcoholism was one of the battles our family had to wage in the aftermath of Frank Olson's death. It is our wish that an alcohol treatment center may be endowed in Frank Olson's name so that the increasingly vital work of alcohol rehabilitation may be carried on as an extension of our father and husband's tragically shortened life. We believe that there is justice in our seeking to be in a position to make a major charitable contribution in Frank Olson's memory.

On October 21, Olson family attorney David Rudovsky wrote to Special Counsel Rogovin at the CIA, outlining his understanding of the government's present offer to the Olsons: "that by October 31, 1975, we will be in receipt of a formal offer, approved in writing by the Attorney General of the United States of $1,250,000 for settlement of the Olson claim." Added Rudovsky: "please notify us immediately if this statement does not conform to our conversations of October 20 and 21."

Eight days later, CIA director William Colby wrote to President Ford stating: "pursuant to your instructions, efforts were made to negotiate a settlement of the claim of the family of Mr. Frank R. Olson against the Government based on the circumstances of his untimely death."

Colby noted that Attorney General Levi was not prepared to approve a settlement of $1,250,000, and that the Olsons' attorneys were prepared to formally file suit. Stated Colby, "Such litigation would doubtless be prolonged and in the view of the Department of Justice, it would fail. Under the circumstances this would not appear to be in the best interests of the nation or the Olson family. I believe in good conscience that the circumstances of this case require an equitable response from the Government."

Concluded Colby: "I recommend that you forward a request to Congress for passage of a private bill in the sum of $1,250,000."

On November 25, President Ford approved drawing up a private bill for the amount recommended by Colby, and the Olsons agreed. Richard Cheney informed Ford the same day "the CIA is currently drafting this bill and it will soon be ready for submission to Congress." Included in the bill was preamble language common to lawsuit settlements:

> ...the Secretary of the Treasury is authorized and directed to pay, out of any money in the Treasury not otherwise appropriated, the sum of $187,500 each to Alice W. Olson, Lisa Olson Hayward, Eric Olson, and Nils Olson, in full settlement of all of their claims against the United States arising out of the death of Doctor Frank R. Olson in November 1953, if all of them waive any and all rights arising out of such death. The payment of such sums shall be in full satisfaction of all claims of Alice W. Olson, Eric Olson, Lisa Olson Hayward, and Nils Olson of any nature whatsoever against the United States, or against any past or present employee or agent of, or persons associated with, the United States, his estate or personal representative, in connection with the circumstances surrounding such death and such payments shall be in lieu of further compensation otherwise due under chapter 81 of title 5, United States Code, or any award thereunder.

Years later this language would come back to haunt Eric Olson.

Nearly nine months later, David Kairys telephoned Alice Olson to tell her that, finally, it appeared as if Congress was ready to take action on the Olsons' bill.

Earlier in the summer of 1976, Senate Bill 3035, a "private relief bill for the Olson family," had gone before the House Judiciary Committee, where it had been approved, but in September, when the bill came before the full House of Representatives for a vote, remarkably, three members stood in opposition to it. The Olsons were shocked to learn that nearly all private bills failed and that under House voting tradition, a few opposing members could easily kill a private bill. The Olsons also quickly learned that the three congressman who opposed the Olson bill were led by John H. Rousselot of California, a tough, arch-conservative and longtime member of the ultra-right wing John Birch Society.

David Kairys rushed from Philadelphia to Washington to meet with the White House and Department of Justice attorneys and favorable House members, many of whom had already unsuccessfully attempted to get Rousselot to support the bill. When one House member offered to have Ford call him personally, Rousselot shot back, "Fuck the president. I'm not changing my mind on this." Other House members tried to sway Rousselot by telling him that the newly appointed director of the CIA, George H.W. Bush, who had replaced William Colby on January 30, 1976, was completely supportive of the bill. But, Rousselot only scoffed at this, and said, "That's not what he told me. He told me he didn't give a damn one way or another."

Several House members advised the Olsons to quickly settle for $500,000, before even that amount might be lost. Kairys told the Olsons that he wanted to meet with Rousselot before any such decision was considered.

Kairys recounts that he met with the California congressman in the Republican cloakroom on the floor of the House.

"We don't have much time," Rousselot said brusquely. "I'm opposed to the bill. I'm opposed to private bills in principle."

"I've heard that," said Kairys, "and I can understand it, but surely none is more compelling than this bill."

Rousselot waved the remark off, and said, "The government shouldn't be handing out money to individual people."

Kairys persisted, explaining, "This is a man whose work was dedicated to his nation and his military, who was drugged and struck down by that military and the CIA. We wouldn't be here except the same government officials who did this covered it up by giving the widow paltry employee compensation benefits. That's a legal barrier to the usual sort of legal claim. This is a legitimate, compelling use of a private bill. The CIA and the military fully support it."

Rousselot seemed affected by the attorney's words. "It's extremely large for a private bill," he said. "I don't think the CIA or military really want it. They're only bowing to media pressure. This family should take $500,000. They've got Ford on his knees apologizing. Isn't that enough?"

"Sir, with all due respect," Kairys replied, "that would barely cover the lost income of this well-educated scientist. The family has lived close to the edge of poverty all this time and had to deal with all the lies about some inexplicable suicide."

"There are always sacrifices to be made," Rousselot said.

"You're absolutely correct," said Kairys, "and this family has made more than any can be expected to bear."

After a moment, Rousselot said, "You get me a letter, exclusively to me, from CIA director Bush saying unequivocally that he wants this, and I'll go for a bill even a little higher, maybe $600,000."

Kairys held his ground, and said, "We'll get the letter for you, but I can't in all conscience recommend that figure to the Olsons. But, if we take our chances with a lawsuit this story will be all over the media and will be an embarrassment to many people for years to come."

Rousselot thought a moment, and replied, "Seven hundred and fifty thousand, and you get me that letter. That's as far as I'll go."

Kairys left the House cloakroom and drove to meet the Olsons at Alice's home in Frederick. After a long discussion, the family decided to accept the $750,000. Eric recounts that he argued that the offered figure was not a fair offer and that the family should hold out for more money or file their lawsuit, but he explained, "My mother had had enough at this point. She wanted everything to be over. She stood firm and fast, and eventually everyone else, except me, agreed with her."

A few days later, after John Rousselot had received his letter from DCI Bush, President Ford signed the private bill into law. Said Ford, in a statement prepared and redrafted several times by Donald Rumsfeld and Richard Cheney:

> The approval of this bill underscores the basic principle that an individual citizen of this nation should be protected from unreasonable transgressions into his personal activities. There should be no doubt that my Administration is opposed to the use of drugs, chemicals or other substances without the prior knowledge and consent of the individual affected. At the request of the family of Dr. Olson, I take this opportunity to highlight this continuing policy.

Not long after the Olsons' private bill was passed, John Rousselot was accused by an alleged "former FBI and CIA employee" named Harry Dean of conspiring, along with former Army General Edwin Walker, to have President John F. Kennedy killed. Dean claimed he had "an avalanche of evidence" implicating Rousselot, who at the time of the alleged conspiracy was the western region director of the John Birch Society. The evidence included tape recordings of Rousselot making threats against Kennedy's life.

"I know that John Rousselot organized the murder plot and with other right-wingers financed it," stated Dean. "General Walker ramrodded and trained the hired guns." When he first made his controversial statements, many observers seriously questioned why Dean waited nearly twelve years to reveal his claims, which eventually did draw the interest of a Congressional committee looking into Kennedy's assassination.

Countered Dean, "The truth of the matter is, I told my superiors about this plot when I first learned of the details, but they ignored it." Dean added that he was in constant fear for his life and those of his family.

"I was with a man in September 1963 when he picked up $10,000 from Rousselot," said Dean. "The money was taken to Mexico City to help finance the murder of Mr. Kennedy. The assassination planning team operated out of Mexico City for several weeks before the president was shot in Dallas."

John Rousselot passed away in 2003 at the age of 75.

5

August 12, 1975
Harold Blauer Redux

On August 12, 1975, following several news accounts about Army-sponsored experiments similar to those of the CIA, a Pentagon spokesman disclosed that Harold Blauer, a 42-year old patient at the New York State Psychiatric Institute, had died the same year as Frank Olson after Blauer had unwittingly been given a massive amount of synthetic mescaline during a secret Army experiment. Like the Olsons, the Blauer family had been kept in the dark about the death for over twenty-two years.

Several days before the disclosure, the Army had officially stated that there had been "no deaths or any serious reactions" to any of the drug experiments it had conducted. There was no mention of the CIA in any of the stories concerning Harold Blauer. Nobody drew a nexus between Frank Olson and the Army's experiments at the New York Institute. Nobody raised the possibility of other strange deaths.

These new Army revelations added startling complexities to the Olson story, but at the same time served to reduce it to a mere sidebar in an ever growing litany of shocking stories. Reporters had all they could handle in chasing down new leads, having little time to step back, connect the myriad dots, and examine the big picture.

On August 13, 1975, CIA Inspector General Donald F. Chamberlain sent a memorandum to the Agency's legislative counsel; the subject was "Drug-Related Death of Harold Blauer." Wrote Chamberlain:

> The Offices of the General Counsel, Inspector General, Security [Office] and Technical Services Division have searched their files for any evidence of a CIA association with the death on 8 January 1953 of Harold Blauer, while a patient at the New York State Psychiatric Institute. The results of the search were negative except for the attached Memorandum for the Record, dated 29 January 1954.
>
> The Army Inspector General informed me that the Army's Special Operations Division, Fort Detrick, the unit that Frank Olson was in, had a contract for two years with the Psychiatric Institute (1952-53) to test

various mescaline-related and other drugs that the Army was interested in. Blauer died 2 1/2 hours after an injection of an apparent overdose of 450 milligrams of EA-1298.

[The "attached Memorandum" referred to is the memo concerning Robert Lashbrook's call from the Pentagon that readers have already learned about. See Book One Chapter 15.]

Chamberlain's memo had been written in response to an urgent verbal instruction from CIA director William Colby to several Agency branches "to conduct immediate and thorough file and records searches for any information pertaining to private U.S. citizen Harold Blauer." Colby's directive had been generated by a surprise public announcement by the Army the day before, on August 12. During the previous two weeks, questions had persisted from the media about rumored drug-related deaths. Following a series of emphatic, but inadequate, denials, Pentagon spokesman Joseph Laitin appeared at a hastily called news conference to say that the Army had found "a file disclosing the death of a 42-year old man and civilian patient, in the course of a drug test program administered by the New York State Psychiatric Institute under an Army contract."

Asked by reporters who the man was, Laitin replied, "The name of the victim is being withheld while the Pentagon tries to locate surviving relatives." Laitin explained that a representative of the Army Inspector General's office had come across "a file disclosing the death while examining records discovered in a safe at the Edgewood Arsenal in Maryland." [The records were found in the office safe of Dr. Van Sim, successor to Dr. Amedeo Marrazzi. The bound files bore instructions not to open them without Dr. Sim's authorization.] Reporters asked Laitin if the victim in question had signed any waivers regarding the drug tested, and Laitin responded, "I don't recall seeing any signed waivers." Anticipating further questions, he added, "The file has raised a lot more questions than it answers."

Before concluding the press conference, Laitin said that the Army experiments with mescaline, LSD and other drugs had been halted only three weeks earlier, as a result of the revelations about Frank Olson, and that the Army's experiments had involved altogether "about four thousand soldiers and civilians." Stunned, reporters at the press conference peppered Laitin with questions about the large number of experimental subjects, but he declined to provide additional details or to say anything about where the experiments had been conducted, except for his mention of NYSPI. Laitin said nothing to reporters about CIA-funded experiments at NYSPI before or after Blauer's death, or about the CIA having funded a large portion of the experiments that had involved thousands of other subjects used by the Army over the previous twenty-four years.

The following day, the *New York Times* reported that the unnamed NYSPI victim had been identified as Harold Blauer. The Army had identified him after one of Blauer's two daughters, Elizabeth Barrett, had been contacted. Barrett, a young widow and former model who lived in Manhattan, told *Times* reporter Joseph B. Treaster that although she had been only thirteen years old at the time, she recalled her mother telling her at the time that her father had "reacted badly [and] been very upset" by drugs he had been given at NYSPI.

Barrett also revealed to Treaster that she had met the day before "with three Army officers in civilian clothes" who told her that her father had been "given the drug for a diagnostic purpose," which, she said, she did not believe. Barrett told Treaster that her father had "absolutely not" volunteered to participate in an Army drug experiment, and that he had told her mother, Amy, that "he didn't like" the drugs he had been given at the Psychiatric Institute.

The *Times* contacted Dr. Sidney Malitz, acting NYSPI director, who had not been employed by the facility at the time of Blauer's death. Malitz said, "As far as we know, permission was obtained voluntarily [from Blauer]." But, he said, "I'm sure he was not told all the ramifications of the drug. There was a feeling in those days if a patient was told too much about a drug it might influence the experiment. Today, that couldn't happen. There would be much greater discourse of all the pros and cons of the medication."

At the time of Malitz's interview, it was unclear if he was aware of the actual nature of the experiments performed on Blauer or if he was simply attempting to gloss over the fact that the drugs had had no diagnostic purpose whatsoever. Dr. Malitz told the *Times* that NYSPI on its own had begun experiments with mescaline, LSD, and "various depressants" in 1946 and that these experiments "continued at least until the early 1960s." He erroneously stated that he was "inclined to think that" the Army-funded tests stopped after Blauer's death.

In early September 1975, Elizabeth Barrett, distressed and angered about revelations concerning her father's treatment and death, filed an $8.5 million claim against the Army. Barrett was especially angry about details she learned concerning the involvement of the State of New York and U.S. Justice Department in the cover-up of the facts surrounding the Army's tests at NYSPI. She was also outraged by a statement made by Dr. James Cattell who had assisted in the experiments on her father and who had commented that the drug injected into Blauer "could have been dog piss for all anyone knew."

General William Creasy, commander of the Army Chemical Corps in 1953, also angered Barrett when he denied any knowledge of her father's death. Creasy even denied the Army's participation in any settlement with the Blauer's in the 1950s, despite the existence of numerous records documenting that Creasy was well aware of all aspects of the case.

In September 1975, Elizabeth Barrett, testifying about her father's death, told the Senate Committee investigating CIA activities, "It's an outrage that this type of experiment has been permitted." Before testifying, Barrett had spoken stronger words to Senate investigators who had invited her to the nation's capital. She also handed the investigators copies of a report written by Dr. Amedeo

Marrazzi in 1954. The report revealed that, after her father's death, Marrazzi had blamed the fatality on a mistake Dr. Paul Hoch had made "with the toxicity" of the drug administered to Harold Blauer. Hoch had objected to Marrazzi blaming him and after considerable discussion, according to the report, Marrazzi claimed that tests of mescaline (referred to as "EA-1298") conducted on animals by SOD scientists at Camp Detrick had not been thorough enough. Former Camp Detrick researchers interviewed for this book say that the tests with EA-1298, and related drugs, conducted both by SOD scientists at Camp Detrick and Edgewood Arsenal, "used up about one hundred to two hundred dogs and monkeys. We went through what could have been a year's supply. We thought that was really enough of a track record before moving on to humans. When Dr. Marrazzi had completed his final report on Blauer's death, he handed a copy to an Army attorney working on the suit against the NYSPI by Blauer's survivors, who in turn delivered a copy to the newly appointed U.S. Assistant Attorney General heading the Civil Rights Division at the Department of Justice. This was Warren Burger, who would become Chief Justice of the U.S. Supreme Court in 1969.

Early in Marrazzi's twenty-five page report, the doctor clearly admits that had it not been for the Army's secret experiments, which obviously were not necessary to the patient's health, Blauer would have been discharged from the NYSPI and sent home. Instead, states Marrazzi, Blauer died under conditions that were not "in accord with good medical practice and free from negligence."

The same week that Burger was given a copy of Marrazzi's report, two of his Civil Rights division attorneys alerted him that there were real problems with the Blauer case. The attorneys told Burger bluntly that Dr. Paul Hoch, if called in to court by Blauer's family as a witness against the NYSPI, that he should not testify about certain issues, including the tests performed on animals at Camp Detrick and Edgewood Arsenal. Additionally, the attorneys wrote: "We have been advised that neither the patient nor his family were advised of the proposed [Army] therapy, or gave permission."

At the same time that Justice Department attorneys in Burger's office were beginning to worry about containing the case and minimizing damages done to the Government, Army attorneys and officials were growing increasingly worried that undue exposure of the physicians at NYSPI might harm the Army's ongoing experiments with psychochemicals, which involved numerous—"over seventy-five universities and private organizations, at last count"—non-military researchers.

In July 1954, Army attorneys met with attorneys in Burger's office and decided they would ask David Marcus, the New York assistant attorney general in charge of defending the NYSPI against the Blauers, to offer Blauer's wife, Amy, $15,000 to settle the case. The Army agreed to pay $7,250 of the settlement as long as the Army's role in Blauer's death was kept secret from Blauer's family, the Blauer's attorneys, the judge hearing the case, and, of course, the media.

Amy Blauer refused the settlement offer for several months, but her own poor health and the needs of her daughters forced her to reconsider. After a few days of negotiations, and threats that doctors at the NYSPI could reveal "very embarrassing details" of her marriage if the case went to court, Amy settled for $18,000, only because the judge in the case objected to $15,000 as an appropriate amount. The only thing remaining to be done, after the Army had agreed to the amount, was for Warren Burger to approve the settlement.

On April 27, 1955, Burger wrote a letter of approval to David Marcus, and suggested: "New York might obtain an assignment from the Blauer estate of all claims arising from the same event." After Marcus sent the suggested signed release, Burger wrote a letter on May 23 requesting that the Army send its secret check for $9,000 "to me as soon as possible for delivery to Mr. Marcus."

In 1977, two *Rolling Stone* reporters came across the details of the Blauer case and of Burger's role in the secret Army settlement given to Amy Blauer. In the process of writing their story, reporters Howard Kohn and Martin Power questioned Congressional representatives about Burger's possible criminal actions. They were told: "You're not going to find too many people in Congress willing to investigate Burger for something that happened twenty years ago."

In 1987, ten years after Elizabeth Barrett filed her $8.5 million suit against the United States Government, she was awarded a little over $700,000. Defending against Barrett's claims for justice was then-United States Attorney Rudolph W. Giuliani. Giuliani argued strongly that the government was not responsible for Harold Blauer's death, but the court found otherwise. After thirty-four years of deception and lies, federal judge Constance Baker Motley concluded:

> This court [was] faced with assessing a sad episode in the conduct of the United States Government and a personal tragedy for an unsuspecting victim and his family. The case arises from the death of Harold Blauer, a mental patient who died in 1953 as a guinea pig in an experiment to test potential chemical warfare agents for the United States Army.
>
> Rather than admit its role in Blauer's death, the Government covered up its involvement in the affair, thus this opinion is issued today rather than in the early 1950's when the death occurred....
>
> [This court finds that] the United States negligently caused the death of Harold Blauer in 1953 and therefore is liable to his Estate for his wrongful death.

Because the evidentiary files showing the CIA's involvement in the experiments that killed Blauer — as well as the CIA's funding of tests conducted at Camp Detrick and Edgewood Arsenal related to those experiments — were never revealed from 1953 through to 1987, the Agency's role was never considered in any phase of the Blauer case.

A month after the Army's 1975 revelations about Harold Blauer's death, Dr. Amedeo S. Marrazzi was again in the national news, and not in a flattering light. U.S. Air Force spokespeople, taking their lead from the Army, reported on July 30 that, between the years 1958 and 1969, the Air Force's Office of Scientific Research had funded a series of LSD experiments at the University of Minnesota, New York University, Duke University, University of Missouri and Baylor University in Texas. What the Air Force failed to reveal, however, was that all of these experiments, and additional experiments at another five state universities, had been funded covertly by the CIA's TSS Chemical Branch.

At the University of Minnesota, Dr. Marrazzi, who had left his post at the Army Chemical Corps in 1956, directed the LSD experiments himself. A research assistant with the tests, Mary Ray, told reporters that in her two years working with Marrazzi she never saw a consent form for any of the psychiatric patients involved. Said Ms. Ray, "Even if they were signed they would seem to have been meaningless in some of the cases." As an example, Ms. Ray recalled,

> They used one 17-year old mental patient whose mother was also a mental patient and whose father was an alcoholic. The girl came in acting more or less normal. After they gave her LSD she was devastated. I saw her as they were taking her in to administer LSD and she definitely didn't want to be part of that experiment.

A *Washington Post* story on July 31, cited a 1967 article co-authored by Dr. Marrazzi and published in the medical journal *Recent Advances in Biological Psychiatry*. In it, he described a young female patient who had been admitted into the LSD experiment with a diagnosis of "personality disorder." Four days after LSD was administered to her, Marrazzi wrote, the woman's diagnosis was changed to "psychosis of an acute schizophrenic variety."

Research Assistant Mary Ray testified in 1975 before the 1975 Congressional subcommittee investigating CIA drug testing. She said that she herself had volunteered at Minnesota in 1966 to take a series of LSD injections in return for $30 and that she had experienced "terrifying hallucinations of iridescent rats and a fanged monster" and had become so frightened she had tried to jump out a third-floor window.

Additional reports about the CIA-funded Air Force experiments revealed that Dr. Marrazzi, after leaving his post at the University of Minnesota in 1969, moved his LSD work to St. Louis, where declassified documents reveal that he was awarded at least two more CIA-funded contracts. The St. Louis experiments were conducted at the Missouri Institute of Psychiatry, which was then part of St. Louis State Hospital. Former employees of the Institute testified in 1975 that the experiments "used patients who were homeless and had no relatives in the area." One employee recalled a laboratory used for the tests that had "walls lined with raw fiberglass insulation and had the sort of wooden booth that you'd see at a carnival." The employee recalled, "A doctor told me they used to wire the patients to EEGs, administer the LSD, and then start a sort of light show in the booth."

At one point in Dr. Marrazzi's work in Missouri, another psychologist, Dr. Hugh Angle, had released an affidavit highly critical of Marrazzi's LSD and mescaline experiments. The affidavit charged that Dr. Marrazzi gave LSD to numerous people "without their consent." Shortly after this, the U.S. Drug Enforcement Administration asked Dr. Marrazzi to surrender his license to administer LSD, which he did. For unexplained reasons, however, he was able to regain his license within weeks.

In a 1975 interview, Marrazzi told a *St. Louis Dispatch* reporter: "We were using LSD to test performance of individuals to determine their ability to perform tasks under stress." Marrazzi claimed that the LSD doses he administered in St. Louis were relatively small—less than 65 micrograms orally—and "produced none of the typical symptoms of a larger dose, such as hallucinations." Other persons associated with Dr. Marrazzi's St. Louis experiments said, however, that LSD amounts "ranged from 65 micrograms to 250 micrograms, and sometimes larger amounts."

—6—

July 22, 1975
Capitol Hill, Washington, D.C.

I daresay the Central Intelligence Agency has done as much or more to protect the freedoms and rights you are talking about as any other agency over the course of the last 27 years.
— CIA General Counsel Lawrence Houston, 1975

Twenty-two years after Frank Olson's death, CIA General Counsel Lawrence Houston was called to testify before a Congressional subcommittee hearing chaired by the late Rep. Bella S. Abzug, a Democrat representing New York. The hearing had been convened to investigate the Department of Justice's handling of criminal cases involving the CIA, and its findings have been largely overlooked in histories of the period. During the proceedings, Abzug questioned CIA lawyer Houston extensively. As the record makes clear, she was quite concerned about the implications of the 1954 secret agreement between the CIA and Justice Department regarding Frank Olson's death. [See Book One, chapter 14.]

At one point in her grilling of Houston, Abzug asked, "Was [the Frank Olson case] ever referred to the Department of Justice?"

Houston answered, "I do not recall that it was referred to the Department of Justice." Houston then added, "My only dealings with the case were with the Bureau of Employees' Compensation.

Abzug pressed, "It may well have been a State offense if there was foul play. Was it ever referred to the New York Police Department or State authorities for consideration?"

"Not that I recall," said Houston.

According to the official government account of the hearing, the following remarkable exchange then occurred.

Abzug: *In other words, this [1954 agreement] in your judgment gave authority to the CIA to make decisions, to give immunity to individuals who happened to work for the CIA for all kinds of crimes, including possible murder.*

Houston: It was not designed to give immunity to individuals. It was designed to protect operations or information of the Agency, which was highly [sic] sensitive.
Abzug: *Was that not the effect of the actual interpretation made by CIA and their advisors?*
Houston: It could have that effect, yes.
Abzug: *Did it not have that effect?*
Houston: In certain cases it did.

General Counsel Houston was being less than forthcoming with the members of the Congressional subcommittee. As readers have learned in Book One, Chapter 14, his handling of the Olson case in 1953 and 1954 entailed much more than merely dealing with employee compensation matters.

Later, during the same session, Congresswoman Abzug continued her questioning of Houston.

Abzug: *Is it your testimony that there was no other example of possible criminal activity on the part of individuals employed by the CIA except those contained in the Inspector General's report?*
Houston: I'm sorry, I did not hear the question.
Abzug: *I am talking about the whole course of your tenure as counsel to the CIA over a period of 20 years.*
Houston: Yes.
Abzug: *We all have the benefit of hindsight. We have the benefit of knowledge. There are any number of things that took place, including a large number of illegalities described in the Inspector General's report. There are further illegalities in Watergate. There were further illegalities described in the Houston report. You even testified here today that no authority was notified as to the death and cause of death of Mr. Olson who was a person who received unknowingly, unknown to him, various forms of drugs, including LSD, which raised some question as to the suicide death of Mr. Olson in New York.*

You testified throughout the day that you never referred any of these possible criminal violations to the Justice Department. You and I even had colloquy in which I said to you, and you agreed, that if there were even allegations of murder, if it meant revealing sources and methods, you did not believe they ought to be referred to the Attorney General.

I ask you by what authority, given that there was a statute on the books which specifically said that you could not do it, and that there were two communications from two Attorneys General whom you admit were not notified by you of this memorandum of understanding, which directed your Agency as well as other agencies to report all criminal violations, and there was a very specific way in title 28 in which to be exempted from the statute but that procedure was not followed by you.

What you have been testifying to all day is that the CIA determined itself what had to be prosecuted, who was to be prosecuted, who was not to be prosecuted to be more apt. CIA by itself elected to set itself up as a body unto itself, as a court, as a judge, as a prosecutor without regard to the laws that every other single citizen of this country, every other employee of this Government, was subjected to.

On what basis did you justify this?

Houston: As I testified on several occasions here, there was a balancing of interest between the statutory responsibility of the [CIA] Director and the statutory requirements of the Department of Justice. That is what the agreement was directed at, to try and reach that balance.

If a crime or evidence of a crime was produced it was our desire to carry out the prosecution, if it in any way could be done without doing serious damage to the national interest.

Abzug: *You mean the commission of illegal activity, as long as it was committed by the CIA, supersedes every other national interest?*

Houston: No, ma'am. Evidence of a crime which arose under circumstances which necessarily involved serious sensitive information required a balancing of the interest between the protection of the sensitive information and the prosecution of the crime.

Abzug: *You testified just a moment ago in connection with some papers which were in the custody of the CIA that you never had files destroyed in connection with criminal investigations. Is that right?*

Houston: To my knowledge.

Abzug: *What happened to the files and the CIA search of the Olson case?*

Houston: I don't know. I don't know what search has been made or what has been found.

[This Congressional hearing took place at about the same time the Olson family was meeting with DCI William Colby. Abzug and Houston most likely were unaware of the documents that were handed over to the Olson family at this point in time.]

Abzug: *There has been testimony that the files in that case have been destroyed.*

Houston: If so, I am not aware of it.

Abzug: *What administrative and legal action would you recommend against the CIA in regard to this Olson matter?*

Houston: I am told they have located a memorandum of mine in which I was seriously perturbed about the case, but I do not know what specific recommendation, if any, I made at the time.

Abzug: *Was the question of legal violation explored?*

Houston: I don't know.

Abzug: *Do you have records to refresh your recollection?*

Houston: No, ma'am, I took no records with me when I left the Agency.

Abzug: *You mean to tell me a dramatic event like that took place; namely, a CIA drug researcher died under peculiar circumstances, and you as counsel of this Agency never inquired as to what the facts and circumstances were?*

Houston: We inquired into the episode at the time. My main interest at the time was to see what we could do to provide some pay for the family. I dealt with the Bureau of Employees Compensation on that. What specific other internal recommendations I made I do not recall at this time.

Abzug: *And there is nothing to refresh your recollection?*

Houston: I understand they have located a memorandum of mine, which I assume they would make available to you if you wish it.

Abzug: *Would you be good enough to request present counsel to make that available to us? We will request it directly ourselves.*

Houston: Yes, ma'am.

Abzug: *Let the record so show.*

Well worth noting is another section of the same hearing session involving questions to Houston from Rep. Andrew Maguire, a Democrat from New Jersey.

Maguire: *Did you know of CIA infiltration of the Bureau of Narcotics and Dangerous Drugs [Federal Bureau of Narcotics renamed]?*

Houston: Infiltration? No, sir. I know of cooperation with them.

Maguire: *You didn't have agents who were on a mission there surreptitiously?*

Houston: Not that I know of. All our arrangements with the Bureau of Narcotics were carried on with the agreement of the top officials of that department.

Maguire: There are some newspaper reports to the contrary.

Following this exchange, Rep. Abzug once again questioned Houston:

Abzug: *How does the average citizen feel about the fact that the Agency operated without regard to the law, totally without regard to the law? Give me your judgment about this. I would like to have your judgment as to this kind of behavior. This is the greatest democracy in the world. What does this mean? How does this fit into our concept of equal justice? How does this fit into the question of our being guided by a rule of law? How does this fit into these philosophical issues? Are there any greater national interests than the rules of law? Would not a democracy fall if there is no rule of law? You talked about the balancing of interest. What is a greater interest in this great country?*

Houston: I daresay the Central Intelligence Agency has done as much or more to protect the freedoms and rights you are talking about as any other agency over the course of the last 27 years.

Abzug: *I would suggest to you that that is very debatable at this moment in history.*

Houston: Obviously it is debatable but I maintain they have done more to protect those freedoms than almost any other single agency.

Abzug: *Violating freedoms of the Americans here in this country?*

Houston:Individual...

Abzug: *You cannot be strong outside if you are weak inside. You have to defend your own principles in order to be able to fight for acceptance of your principles in other places in the world. That is not the role of the CIA, anyhow.*

The question of the protection of our liberties and our freedom is the basis upon which this country remains strong. This was totally violated by every bit of the evidence which has been presented here today by you and previous witnesses. Certainly your statement with respect to the violations of law which were not reported to the Attorney General, going so far as to say even murder could be condoned if sources might be revealed. I think these are highly questionable concepts of justice and democracy.

Houston: Is that a question?

Abzug: *I would like you to respond to that. I would be happy for you to respond to it because I don't understand any attorney testifying that these violations of the law are not reported to the Justice Department and can be sustained and condoned. There is no evidence there is a legal basis for it.*

Houston: Your characterization ignores the argument I made that there was also a statutory duty to protect sensitive intelligence sources and methods. You are reading into a practical arrangement, looking back at it with the advantage of present day, and reading into it motives and practices which did not exist. I maintain that this arrangement was a practical solution to a practical problem which served its purposes well.

Abzug: *By every bit of evidence, both in writing and otherwise, we have a letter which we will discuss with Mr. Warner which states that the intention of the memorandum was to deal with matters which affected employees in the nature of violations for personal gain. Yet you testify today that anything which might involve possible revelation of sources, including murder, could be determined by the CIA, so obviously there is a scope which went beyond what was originally contemplated. Nor is there justification for that being conducted in the manner it was since a statute intervened which stated specifically how you can be exempt; namely, by determining what the process should be with the Attorney General. Clearly we are all aware of the fact that certain sources and methods have to be protected. You have not produced a scintilla of evidence to indicate anybody was prosecuted because there was a need to protect sources and methods. There is no evidence of that in this record.*

Houston: There is evidence in the sense that I testified, that we looked at each case very carefully with the intent to find some way to prosecute, and only when we came to a determination that the information involved could not be released did we make the determination not to prosecute.

Abzug: *Yes, but under the law which superceded the memorandum of understanding, title 28, section 535, and the directive of both Attorneys General Brownell and Mitchell, that was not the process that I believe was authorized. I think if there was to be some exemption in terms of a prosecution or investigation it had to have been discussed with the Attorney General, and that is what the statute says and that is what the two Attorneys General said. By your own evidence and statements today you testified the Attorneys General never were even informed of the existence of this understanding.*

Maguire: I have a brief comment.

Abzug: Very well.

Maguire: *I wanted to say before we concluded with this witness that I think— I appreciate the gentlewoman's comments at this point because I think they are very, very germane. I think the problem here is essentially this: That legality was one of the last considerations that decision-makers in the CIA addressed themselves to if they were trying to figure out what course of action they would pursue. In effect, the memorandum of 1954 gave the CIA a blank check to cover its tracks wherever it felt it was important that those tracks be covered. The regular processes of Government were put into suspension and what we had was an irregular process.*

I thought the comment by the witness that well, perhaps Mr. [Allen] Dulles and Mr. Brownell discussed this among themselves was very revealing because I suspect that is the way most of the business was conducted for an extended period of time, and it was not done with an eye toward legality or having it be on the record or toward having it be processed through memorandums, or formalized discussions. It was an irregular process.

It was the old boy's club where decisions were made without regard to questions of legality or illegality. The rule of law was put into suspension. This is precisely why it is so essential that this Congress develop some guidelines for the future activities of the CIA and other investigatory agencies, so that we will not have recurrences in the future of these illegal activities which are a threat to the very core of our constitutional system.

Houston: Sir, you asked me whether it was possible that Mr. Dulles spoke to Mr. Brownell. I said it was possible but I did not know. I do not think you can build that possibility into the thesis you just set forth.

Maguire: *I did not mean to suggest you said anything other than that there was a possibility. What I said was that I felt everything we know indicates there was a pattern which was irregular rather than regular to the way decisions were made and as to whether or not the law was followed.*

Houston: On the whole, sir, I disagree with you as to that conclusion.

Abzug: *Thank you very much, Mr. Houston. The witness is excused.*

7

September 10, 1975,* Capitol Hill, Washington, D.C., Senate Hearing,

Senator Edward Kennedy: *Final comments will now be made by the Olson family and Colonel [Vincent] Ruwet.*

We welcome you here. I think the story is probably well known by the American public. It has been written about extensively. I would appreciate it if you would just briefly tell us how your husband came to take LSD, and was he aware that he was going to get it, and then perhaps Mr. Ruwet can tell us a little bit about the follow-up.

Alice Olson: I knew nothing about the LSD until June of this year when I read it in the Washington Post, that he had been administered LSD and that as a result he had gone out the window. This whole twenty-two years, I had thought that somehow or other he had had a breakdown, and whether he jumped or fell from the window I don't know, but I knew nothing about any LSD experiments.

Senator Kennedy: Perhaps Colonel Ruwet could tell us a little bit about the circumstances.

Vincent Ruwet: Shall I start from the beginning, Senator?

Kennedy: *Summarize it, yes.*

Ruwet: To summarize it very briefly, the incident occurred at a meeting in the vicinity of Deep Creek Lake in western Maryland. The purpose of the meeting was completely disassociated with the incident. The attendees at the meeting, aside from two CIA representatives [sic] of whom I am aware and myself, there were five people [sic] in my division, which included Dr. Olson. After dinner that night we were offered liqueur, four of us were, one of whom was myself.

After the drug took effect— it later proved that the liqueur was laced with LSD—they did notify us that we had been drugged.

Kennedy: *After you had taken it?*

Ruwet: That is correct.

Senator Charles Mathias: *While you were under the influence?*

Ruwet: While I was under the influence, correct; while we were, excuse me. Attempts were made to continue the discussion in a logical fashion, and to make a long story short, that was a disaster. I would guess I can only state that my reaction was pretty well described by Mrs. Ray and Colonel Jordon. [Two witnesses who testified before Ruwet and Mrs. Olson about the effects of LSD.]

To me, it was the most frightening experience I ever had or hope to have. Perhaps this was complicated by the fact that I did not know what was wrong with me. I suspect that Dr. Olson had the same feeling, although I do not want to put myself into his mind, and I suspect the other two gentlemen did also.

As best I can recall, this took place Wednesday evening [sic], a week before Thanksgiving 1953. We went home to Frederick, Maryland, Friday afternoon. I suspect we all had a bad weekend. I did.

On Monday, Dr. Olson, who was also a personal friend of mine, came into work. He was quite agitated. We sat down in my office, and he informed me that he had decided to resign from his position with the Civil Service, and he seemed to be quite concerned about committing a security break, and he felt that his performance at the meeting was not very good. I suggested to Frank that he go home and rest and we could talk again the following day.

My own condition at that point, I guess, was you might call marginal, but I did have control. The following morning he came in, and he was disoriented and it was pretty obvious to me that he needed help. I got in touch with the Agency, and they asked me to have him at the...

Kennedy: *Is this the CIA?*

Ruwet: CIA. They asked me to have him at the airport as soon as possible [sic]. Frank asked me to go with him. We were going to New York. I was told that we were going there because that was the place where they could get the best treatment for him, and in an atmosphere where he need have no fear of security breaks; that he would be completely free to say anything he chose.

Kennedy: *Is it your impression that one of the factors that was distressing to him was this, that evidently he was under this kind of cloud that he may have said something?*

Ruwet: He appeared to be quite concerned over a possible security break at this time.

Mathias: *At that time at Fort Detrick security was a very major preoccupation?*

Ruwet: Certainly it was, and certainly in the particular division we were in, it was more sensitive in some respects; yes, sir.

Kennedy: *He had never been bothered by this before, had he?*

Ruwet: Not that I can recall, sir. We went to New York, and as best as I can recall, we were accompanied by representatives of the Agency, and we went directly to the office of Dr. [Harold] Abramson. I just met him, that is all, and he talked to Frank, and this was on a Tuesday.

On Wednesday afternoon at their suggestion I returned home for Thanksgiving with the understanding that I would return on Friday morning.

Frank and the man who was with him called me Friday morning to tell me that they did not feel it was necessary for me to go back.

That evening Dr, Olson called me. I guess it was about 10 or 10:30. He appeared to be in very good spirits and indicated to me that he would be seeing me the following day, which was Saturday; that they were coming down home, and that they had arranged—and I believe it was Dr. Abramson who had arranged—for him to receive treatment at an installation, what I understand to be a mental institution, on the outskirts of Rockville.

He told me the name of it, and the best I can recall it was Chestnut Lodge or something similar to that. I repeat, he seemed to be in the best of spirits and saying he looked forward to seeing me. The next word I had was about, I would guess, 3 or 3:30 in the morning when a CIA representative—not the one who was with him—phoned me to tell me what had happened and asked me to inform the family. I did it—at dawn.

Kennedy: *Would members of the family like to add anything?*

Mathias: *Before they do that, Mr. Chairman, let me just ask Colonel Ruwet two things. One, Colonel, you say you didn't get—you weren't advised that you had this drug until after you had already swallowed it.*

Ruwet: That is right. After it had taken effect.

Mathias: *You were really under the influence.*

Ruwet: The best I can recall, that is correct. I was wondering what was wrong with me.

Mathias: *That is about the same as telling you you are on the way to the Moon when you see Cape Kennedy disappearing in the other direction, isn't that right?*

Ruwet: Not having been to the Moon, I can't say for sure, sir.

Mathias: *But there is no more chance of getting back or getting out.*

Ruwet: You are beyond the point of no return.

Mathias: *How long did you continue your association at Fort Detrick after this event?*

Ruwet: This was November of 1953 and I was transferred to Washington here in August of 1954.

Mathias: *And later you returned to Fort Detrick.*

Ruwet: I returned to Fort Detrick to be its commander in late 1963. I took command in...

Mathias: *And you were commanding officer here for what period of time?*

Ruwet: April 1964 until I retired in September of 1966.

Kennedy: *Let me just ask you—did the group that took the drug understand that at some time in a given time frame that they were going to be administered some drug?*

Ruwet: To the best of my knowledge, Senator—as far as I am concerned, the answer to that question is "No."

Kennedy: *Well, you are just invited down to somebody's house to get together with a group of friends and the next thing you know, you...*

543

Ruwet: This was a meeting that took place approximately quarterly. It was a skull session type of thing—to review progress and plan research.

Kennedy: *But you had no awareness or understanding, you yourself had no awareness or understanding that this meeting was going to be any different from any other that you had been to?*

Ruwet: That is absolutely correct.

Kennedy: *And at none of the other meetings, when you drank after dinner—it was just a normal...*

Ruwet: Social drink.

Kennedy: *Social drink.*

Ruwet: Yes, sir.

Mathias: *Mr. Chairman, it might also be useful to set this thing in context, to describe the actual location at Deep Creek Lake, at that period of time a fairly remote and isolated area, not as accessible as it is today. Medical facilities in the area were very much limited, is that right, Colonel?*

Ruwet: That is absolutely correct, Senator. As far as I know, there was no medical person present.

Mathias: *The small hospital in Oakland [nearest town] really is the only fall-back medical facility that was available at that time.*

Ruwet: I didn't even know that there was a hospital in Oakland at that time.

Mathias: *So there was no provision made for any kind of adverse reaction to this administration?*

Ruwet: Not to my knowledge.

Kennedy: *Do you have any idea why you people were chosen to be given the drug?*

Ruwet: No, sir.

Kennedy: *Do you know who gave you the drug?*

Ruwet: I presume it was the CIA people who gave me the drink.

Kennedy: *Would the members of the family like to make a brief remark? You understand what our particular interests are in terms of notification and other factors. If there is anything else any of you would like to say, we would be glad to hear you.*

Eric Olson: I think we want to emphasize that there are many areas involved in this whole incident about which we know little or nothing. One area is the whole trip to New York, what exactly the purpose of that trip was, the kind of treatment he received, if it was treatment, what the purpose of the consultation was with Dr. Abramson, who we now know from the CIA documents was a psychiatrist [sic] and had been practicing in that specialty.

The concern that we have had has been that apparently my father did pose some kind of security risk after he was given the drug, and, given that, what kind of precautions were going to be taken for his well being. We know very little about that. We do know that there was no medical professional available at the meeting where the drug itself was administered.

Kennedy: *Senator Schweiker?*

Senator Richard Schweiker: *No questions.*

Mathias: *Could you supplement Colonel Ruwet's testimony in any way with respect to Dr. Olson's behavior when he came back from Deep Creek Lake?*

Alice Olson: When he came back from Deep Creek, he had been gone for three days and he came in very depressed, very quiet. And I sat at the table and I said it was a shame that the adults in this family don't communicate any more, because it was totally unlike him. On the weekend he spoke very little, but he was concerned about a bad mistake—he had not done well at the meetings, people had laughed at him, and it was totally unlike the kind of person that he was.

There was no way to reason with him, which is what I was trying to do. Of course, I had no idea that this was not a normal depression. It wasn't a normal kind of concern which he had—but it was not like him. It was the most unreal weekend I could ever remember.

Mathias: *The most unreal weekend?*

Alice Olson: Unreal. When he left on Monday morning to resign, because he had done so badly at the meetings—and, of course, I accepted this as fact. He walked out of the house and then called me about 10 o'clock in the morning and said he had talked to Colonel Ruwet and everything was fine. And that night his mood was ever so much better. So the next day, when he walked into the house about 10 o'clock in the morning and told me that he had consented to have psychiatric care and that someone had wanted to accompany him home because they were afraid he might do me bodily harm, I suddenly had to sit down. I could not comprehend what was happening.

Mathias: *Had he ever considered the possibility of psychiatric care before this weekend at Deep Creek Lake?*

Alice Olson: No. I assumed, of course, I was talking to a rational person, and that was the first time—when he said they felt that I might be harmed—the first time it dawned on me that this man was not rational.

Then I asked if I could go to Washington and drove down with him and Colonel Ruwet, and took him to a building, which I could not identify, which I assumed was the CIA building. That was the last I ever saw him.

I talked to him on Friday night just after Colonel Ruwet had talked to him, and it was a fine discussion—everything was, we will see you tomorrow—it was not a goodbye. That was the one thing that consoled me, was that I knew that this could not have been an intentional act, because he did not call up to say goodbye—it was, I will see you tomorrow.

Mathias: *Forward looking.*

Alice Olson: Yes.

Mathias: *Now, when did you know that he was going to New York?*

Alice Olson: When he came home on Tuesday morning, he said he had consented to have psychiatric treatment and he was going to New York to receive it.

Mathias: *He knew then it would be in New York?*

Alice Olson: Yes. They had apparently discussed that at work before he came home. And this was about the middle of the morning on Tuesday.

Mathias: *But you did not know the name of the doctor?*

Alice Olson: No, I had no idea. I later was told that the reason they had taken him to Dr. Abramson was because he knew him slightly from a tour at Edgewood, and also the doctor had high security clearance so Frank would be able to talk with him freely, which was necessary. I assumed he was going to be getting psychiatric care from him, or treatment.

Mathias: *Colonel Jordon, I can't help but observe that once again you are nodding in a reminiscent way as if these experiences are being relived, is that right?*

Colonel William Jordon: [Jordon was present at the hearing to testify about his own experience with LSD tests given by the Army.] That is right.

Ruwet: Mr. Chairman, could I say one thing?

Kennedy: *Certainly.*

Ruwet: Something that has troubled me for twenty-two years is the fact that, while I never recall having told Mrs. Olson anything that was flatly untrue, I did allow her to think things that were not true. I would like to have that put on the record that I do regret it.

Kennedy: *That is a very honorable gesture.*

Mathias: *Colonel Ruwet is a very honorable man.*

Kennedy: *It points up even more dramatically, I think, that we are talking about some of the most loyal and committed and dedicated and patriotic Americans who have been included in this kind of testing procedure, and whose lives have been obviously, in terms of the direct testimony we have heard today, altered and changed in the most significant and dramatic way, and tragic way, including death, contemplation of death, disruption of lives. Certainly, no one would question the need for drug experimentation if there is to be progress in this field, but no one should experience what we have heard here today, in terms of the gross misrepresentation about potential side effects of any of these drugs, the complete failure of notification in terms of some of those that participated, so they are completely unprepared to cope or deal with these tragic after effects.*

---

*"Joint Hearings Before the Subcommittee on Health of the Committee on Labor and Public Welfare and the Subcommittee on Administrative Practice and Procedure," Committee on the Judiciary, United States Senate, 94th Congress, First Session on Human-Use Experimentation Programs of the CIA, September 10, 12; and November 7, 1975, p.138-145.

8

November 1975, Frederick, Maryland

*B*lood money. It would be nothing more than dirty money soaked in blood, Agnes Tanner thinks. Agnes had been surprised about the article in the *Washington Post* that morning. Just a few weeks ago the Olson family had announced they were going to sue the CIA, the government, and anybody else that had a hand in Frank Olson's dosing with LSD and his subsequent death. Now, here was yet another man dead, leaving behind an angry family threatening to sue, because of this insane drug.

Blood money, Agnes thinks. *It would be like receiving blood money. Money, no matter how much there is, can't replace a life.* Less than two weeks after the shocking revelations about Frank Olson, Alice had told Agnes she was going to sue. She and Alice had discussed it during lunch one afternoon, and then several of their closest friends in the Women's Club had urged her to join in Alice's suit. Alice had not said much about it to Agnes, but Agnes had already made her position clear to everyone.

"What could I get now that would make Herbert's suffering go away?" Agnes argued. "Herbert's gone now. What difference would the money make? It won't bring him back, it won't erase what has happened; it won't make all the suffering go away."

"But you'd have the money," said her friends.

"No," said Agnes. "I don't want that kind of money. It would be like receiving blood money— dirty money to make you shut up and go away."

With the additional revelations about more men being given this horrible drug by their government, Agnes no longer knew what to think. This was the same government that Herbert gave his best years to; the same government that put an end to his life, and now apparently put an end to the lives of other good and loyal men. Agnes gazed down at the newspaper containing the latest article and asked herself what was happening to the country that she and Herbert, and so many others, loved.

The article was about a forty-eight year old man named James Christensen. Col. James Christensen of the United States Marine Corps. In 1966, Christensen, disappointed that he had not been promoted to the rank of General, decided to join the CIA. He realized he was older than most new recruits, but friends with the Agency told him not to be concerned about his age because his superior skills in other areas far outweighed any minor disadvantage.

His friends had been right. Christensen was almost immediately offered a job in Southeast Asia. He was pleased with the offer but had to turn it down. Months earlier, while still serving with the Marine Corps, he had been deeply enmeshed in strategic wartime planning and had made an official promise not to leave the United States for at least one year. The CIA still wanted him and was willing to wait, assigning him to a domestic post, which he was pleased with. Meanwhile, he needed to complete his security clearance process and so Christensen flew from his home in Virginia to Washington, D.C. where he stayed for a few days. When he returned home from what was supposedly a few days of filling out forms and taking a routine polygraph test, his wife immediately noticed that something was wrong. James was acting strange and seemed extremely nervous. He paced back and forth in the house, day and night, and he talked out loud to himself.

When Agnes Tanner read about James Christensen's behavior she couldn't help but recall Herbert's odd behavior in the days following his visit to Deep Creek Lake. Agnes, who did not even like the effect of caffeine on her, thought, *Lord, what were these crazy drugs the government was giving to people and why?*

When Christensen's wife asked him what was wrong, he told her the CIA had given him some sort of "truth drug." Christensen's wife thought the effects of whatever he had been given would wear off quickly, but his condition worsened. He was having hallucinations and, at times, appeared completely out of touch with reality. Other times he appeared normal, but would become terribly paranoid. He claimed he was being secretly observed no matter where he was, and that people were following him. Like Frank Olson before him, he thought the CIA had poisoned his food and drinks. His nights were disrupted by vivid apocalyptic dreams and violent hallucinations. His body's temperature veered up and down sharply. Christensen's wife sought to have him hospitalized at the Portsmouth Naval Hospital, but doctors there advised her to wait and to come back in a week.

Christensen stopped eating because he claimed his food tasted odd. He told his wife that they should not have any serious conversations in their home because the government had bugged their house. When James drove his car with his wife as a passenger he told her the CIA was following them. He was afraid to leave the house because he was convinced the CIA would send people into his home while he was away.

Ten days after he had returned from his Washington meetings with the Agency, Christensen got in his car alone and drove aimlessly for about an hour. He parked in the driveway of an Army general's house and, after a few minutes, picked up his service revolver from the seat next to him and blew his brains out.

Agnes Tanner cried when she thought about Christensen's final moments in his car. She wondered if Herbert had ever considered ending his life in such a terrible way. She knew he would never have told her about any such thoughts if he had had them.

Agnes shuddered when she thought about the frightful experience of yet another service man, William Chaffin. But Chaffin had been more fortunate than James Christensen. He had come close to ending his life, but in the end he had not done so. Chaffin and his wife had appeared before a Congressional joint committee hearing chaired by Senator Edward Kennedy two months earlier in September 1975. (See Chapter 7 of this book.) The committee had been convened to investigate the CIA's MKULTRA and MKNAOMI programs.

Dorothy Chaffin, choking back tears, had told the assembled senators and representatives that in 1958, after her husband, an Air Force sergeant, had returned home from a temporary assignment to the Chemical Corps' Edgewood Arsenal she had "almost immediately" noticed "basic changes in his personality." The changes, she explained, ranged from mild to deep depression "for no apparent or explainable reason," and often her husband would become "withdrawn and non-responsive." William's altered behavior went on for months and slowly worsened, Dorothy recounted, until one night, he got up out of bed, dressed, and took his gun from a drawer. Alarmed, she asked him what he was doing. Dorothy said William had replied that he "was going out for a ride and then stated that he was going to kill himself." Shocked, Dorothy tried to reason with her husband by asking him to explain what was wrong and what he was feeling. After considerable effort, Dorothy stated, she convinced William "to put the gun up, which he did, and he returned to bed." The next day William recalled nothing about the previous night.

In late 1958, Dorothy told the subcommittee, she had suffered a miscarriage and was "informed by the doctor that the fetus was probably malformed or deformed." Additionally, she said, "One of my children [born after 1958] suffers from cystic fibrosis, a genetically inherent disease." Fighting back tears, Dorothy stated, "Since we have learned for sure that my husband was administered LSD, our situation has been very difficult. We are a rather normal and private family and it is difficult to talk openly about our problems."

William Chaffin then testified to the subcommittee that at Edgewood Arsenal, where he believed he had gone to participate in gas mask training, he and five other enlisted men had been asked to go to the base hospital to meet with a psychologist from the University of Maryland. The psychologist had informed the men "that we would be administered a drug or substance in distilled water. We were further informed that this substance would be odorless, tasteless, and colorless. We were asked to perform certain tests prior to the ingestion of the substance." Chaffin stated he was never informed "of the nature or qualities of the substance" and said, "Certainly, no reference was made to any possibility of detrimental, psychological or physical effects on myself, or my future family, by taking the substance." The three days following ingestion of the substance were a hallucinogenic blur for Chaffin. Days later, after he began to feel somewhat normal, a feeling of "utter and total depression" took hold of him.

Chaffin said he had never had any confirmation that the substance he had been given was LSD or a stronger drug, until he had read a newspaper article in the summer of 1975 about Frank Olson. He had immediately contacted officials at the Pentagon, who informed him that he had been given LSD.

Will this be the end of it? Agnes Tanner wonders. *Or will there be more? Will there be more horror stories about men whose lives have been ruined by the government's insane actions? I hope not,* Agnes thinks, knowing almost instinctively that in the days to come, her hopes would be repeatedly dashed.

9

August 8, 1977
Department of Defense, Washington, D.C.

arold Brown, Secretary of Defense in the Carter Administration, was irritated to the point of anger. He snatched up the phone receiver and asked his administrative assistant to get the department's general counsel for him.

"I need to speak to her right away," Brown said. "It doesn't matter what she's in the middle of."

Brown, who succeeded Donald Rumsfeld as Defense Secretary in January 1977, was a brilliant scientist who had been a protégé of theoretical physicist and hydrogen bomb designer Edward Teller. Nicknamed "Childe Harold" and holding a doctorate in physics from Columbia University, Brown was highly regarded by most officials at the Pentagon and was considered a "suspicious pragmatist."

About two minutes after Brown's urgent request to his administrative assistant, a voice on the intercom informed him that general counsel Deanne Siemer was on the line. Seconds later, Brown told Siemer that he wanted a search undertaken as quickly as possible of all military files. Brown explained that he wanted "to determine the extent of the Department's participation" in three CIA drug projects identified that week by newspapers nationwide, following CIA director Stanfield Turner's public release of details about the programs. Turner had testified before a joint session of the Senate Select Committee on Intelligence and the Senate Subcommittee on Health and Scientific Research. On August 3, he informed the committee members that the CIA had just recently located a number of boxes of financial records from human subject experiments involving drugs for "mind control" and "behavior modification" purposes. He explained that the Agency was able to glean from the records that three of the projects -- MKULTRA, MKDELTA, and MKNAOMI -- had also involved the Department of Defense.

"I want everything we have on these three programs and any other projects involving the CIA," Brown snapped. "And I want background, deep background, information on all of them." Brown paused, and then explained that he did not want to get blindsided again by the press or any other federal agency.

"Damn," he added, "there may be a book coming out any day now on these programs and I'm not going to be caught in a position where I can't answer for things I should know about."

The book Brown had referred to was the now widely read title by John Marks, *The Search for the Manchurian Candidate*. The story of how Marks' book came to be published deserves attention here. Marks, a writer and former State Department Foreign Service officer, had worked in Vietnam on the pacification program, and had also served as a staff assistant to the State Department's director of Intelligence and Research. In the spring of 1977, Marks was informed by the CIA, in response to a Freedom of Information request he had filed over a year earlier, that several boxes of files — or about 16,000 MKULTRA documents — had been located. Marks had filed his initial FOI request based on his belief that the CIA held many secrets about "mind control" and other drug projects that had barely been hinted at in the Rockefeller Commission's report. Initially the CIA had informed Marks that it had destroyed all of its drug testing and behavior manipulation documents on orders from DCI Richard Helms in 1973. Subsequently, however, so the explanation went, six boxes of mostly "financial records" had turned up in storage.

According to Thomas Powers, who wrote the Introduction to the 1988 edition of Marks' book, which first appeared in 1979, "To help go through the huge mass of material turned over by the CIA and to organize it by subject matter and chronology, Marks hired four researchers" [and Taylor Branch as his editor]. Almost every document turned over had names of individuals blacked out, with the exception of Sidney Gottlieb's. "Why the Agency made an exception for Gottlieb, Marks never learned," Powers wrote.

Marks' book was shocking to many readers; few people in America had any idea that their government was conducting such experiments. Many Washington insiders felt that the CIA would have a difficult time surviving the fury and outrage caused by the book's contents.

On September 20, about six weeks after Secretary Brown made his request, the Defense Department's General Counsel, Deanne P. Siemer, handed Brown a single-spaced, twelve page report detailing her findings about the CIA's programs conducted in partnership with the DOD. Siemer told Brown that her "search was conducted during the period August 15, 1977 through September 15, 1977 and covered the records of the Military Departments [including Camp Detrick's SOD and the Chemical Corps] from 1950 to the present [September 1977]." Continued Siemer:

> The results of the search indicate that there were three such programs in which the Army participated over the period 1969 to 1973; five such programs in which the Navy participated over the period 1947 to 1973; and no such programs in which the Air Force participated. In four of these

eight programs the Department of Defense participation was limited to channeling funds to outside contractors in order that the sponsorship of the Central Intelligence Agency be covered. In two of the remaining four programs there was no testing on human subjects. Four of the programs were terminated in the 1950's or early 1960's and the remainder were terminated in 1973.

All of the projects identified by Siemer were described as "primarily CIA projects." MKDELTA, Siemer reported, was the first project established by the CIA that involved Department of Defense participation. [Apparently, Siemer either overlooked or did not have the opportunity to review the CIA's BLUEBIRD and ARTICHIOKE projects, which without doubt involved extensive Army and Navy participation.] MKULTRA, described by Siemer as the successor project to MKDELTA, had been established in April 1953. "Drugs," she wrote, "were only one aspect of this activity." Project MKNAOMI, Siemer wrote, "began in the 1950's" and was intended "to stockpile severely incapacitating and lethal materials, and to develop gadgetry for the dissemination of these materials." MKSEARCH was described as a successor to MKULTRA, sharing the same objectives. MKCHICKWIT (also called CHICKWIT) was an adjunct project to MKSEARCH. Its purpose was to identify new drug developments in Europe and Asia and to obtain samples. MKOFTEN had followed MKSEARCH, and its objective was to test mind control and toxicological effects of certain drugs on humans.

Other projects discovered in the search included one which Siemer could not definitely identify by codename but involved "identification of non-addictive substitutes for codeine." Wrote Siemer:

> This project began in 1954 and was continued at least until 1964. It was performed at the facilities of another government agency, located in Kentucky. The involvement of the Navy was only as a conduit for funds between the CIA and a researcher who was associated with a federal government agency. One of the funding documents identifies this as part of [the CIA's] project MKPILOT.
>
> The CIA transferred at least $282,215 to the Office of Naval Research for this program, with instructions to make the funds available to the researcher at the U.S. Public Health Service Hospital. The project costs appear to have been between $34,000 and $45,000 per year. [Project] documents specify that 'the interest of CIA in this project is classified Secret and is not to be revealed.'

A second project tested the "effects of blast concussion." This project, according to Siemer's report, "began in October, 1954 and was terminated, at least with respect to the Navy, in December, 1955. It was performed by a contractor located in California. The involvement of the Navy was primarily as a conduit of funds from the CIA to the contractor. A small amount of Navy funds may also have been used for this contract. In December, 1955 this project was terminated as far as the Navy involvement was concerned, and it thereafter apparently became subproject 54 of the MKULTRA project."

Third was an LSD experiment involving human subjects which "began in 1952 and apparently completed by 1956." It was performed by "a researcher located in New York. {This was Dr. Harold A. Abramson.] Navy [was] listed as a sponsor in only one CIA document prepared at a later date, and not otherwise corroborated. If Navy was involved, it was solely as a conduit for funds between the CIA and the researcher. This project has been identified as subprojects 7, 27 and 40 of the MKULTRA project."

The Fourth set of projects was aimed at the "development and administration of speech-inducing drugs." Siemer wrote that the projects "apparently began in 1947," but only provided details of the years 1950 forward. According to Siemer's report:

> The Navy arranged in 1950 to obtain marijuana and heroin from the FBI; for the use in experiments and entered a contract with a researcher in New York to develop drugs and instrumentation for use in interrogation of prisoners of war, defectors and similar persons. The security cover for the project was a study of motion sickness. The study began with six of the researcher's staff as knowing volunteers. The project was expanded to cover barbiturates and Benzedrine. Other substances were evaluated.
>
> In August, 1952 the Office of Naval Intelligence informed the CIA that it had developed drugs that might have the desired characteristics and was about to test them on human subjects who would be unaware of the test. The drugs were administered to about eight subjects, each of whom was a Soviet defector, and each test was done in Europe in September 1952. The tests were apparently not satisfactory because the drugs used had such a bitter taste that it was not possible to keep the human subjects from knowing about the test.

Siemer's report made only brief mention of joint CIA-Army experiments conducted in Philadelphia at Holmesburg State Prison. The report read: "Edgewood [Arsenal] also engaged in clinical testing on humans [subjects at the prison].... It appears that all of the test subjects were volunteers and that stringent medical safeguards and followup procedures were used." In reality, these experiments were quite harmful, despite safeguards.

Details of the Holmesburg experiments would be slow to emerge. In 1979, the *Philadelphia Inquirer* newspaper revealed that the CIA, in partnership with the Army's Edgewood Arsenal Research Laboratories, had secretly experimented with LSD at the prison using human subjects. The experiments took place as late as 1971, and perhaps earlier. Relying almost completely on CIA documents obtained by a non-profit research organization affiliated with the Church of Scientology, the *Inquirer* reported that the experiments involved 20 human subjects, 15 from the military services and 5 Holmesburg inmates. "The CIA transferred $37,000 to the Edgewood researchers," read an article, "to finance the experiment, part of a larger drug project with the codename OFTEN." The project was so secret, according to a 1975 [CIA] memo, that "most results had been conveyed verbally, leaving only a sparse written record."

The article continued, "Edmund H. Lyons, superintendent of the Philadelphia prisons, said in a telephone interview that he did not remember Project OFTEN. But he said Holmesburg Prison volunteers had been used for several drug experiments before 1973. He said all of them were cleared through a biology advisor from the University of Pennsylvania." A follow-up *Inquirer* article revealed that from 1964 to 1968, the CIA, Army, and the University of Pennsylvania "were turning 320 prisoners into human guinea pigs" under a $386,486 grant with the university.

The *Inquirer* story identified the physicians overseeing the experiments as Drs. Albert M. Klingman and Herbert W. Copelan. Other newspaper accounts reported that in addition to having done experiments at the University of Pennsylvania, the Army and CIA also carried out human subject experiments at Philadelphia's Hahnemann Medical College and the Bordentown Reformatory in New Jersey. In 1977, Dr. Robert Cooke, president of the Medical College of Pennsylvania, said, "My guess is that experiments approved in the past wouldn't be approved now." Dr. Klingman, however, when asked about the human experiments he had conducted said, "I'd do it all again." Despite evidence to the contrary, Klingman claimed that his work "had nothing to do with the CIA" and that his tests focused on trying "to determine whether agricultural contaminants possessed by the United States could be used without detection."

In 1977, after the media's revelations about CIA involvement with Holmesburg, Donald Langenberg, vice provost for graduate studies and research at the University of Pennsylvania, said that university officials were studying newly proposed restrictions on CIA-sponsored research drawn up by Harvard University. Said Langenberg:

> We've all gotten used to looking under the table. We've been lied to, we've been deceived, we've been snookered. None of us is as innocent as we used to be.

In 1981, it was revealed that experiments at Holmesburg had begun in April 1951 and had continued until at least December 1968. Klingman's private company, Ivy Research Laboratory, received over $750,000 from the CIA, in addition to funds from the Army Medical Corps, Medical Research Laboratory. Six separate CIA and Army contracts were awarded to the University of Pennsylvania, starting in 1951 with a "study of chemical warfare casualties in man." Two studies involved the "evaluation in animals and man, of drug and drug mixture intended for use in prevention or treating chemical casualties." According to the *Philadelphia Tribune*, the fifth and sixth contracts, awarded in the mid-1960s, were to test the "threshold dosage in humans and evaluation of drugs in man." Approximately 320 inmates were dosed "with 16 different chemical agents including Diton, Atropine, scopolamine and various experimental glycolote agents." The newspaper stated that, according to a report by the U.S. Inspector General, "the chemical agents [used] were choking, nerve, blood, blister, vomiting, incapacitating and toxin agents."

Also in the mid-1960s, according to other news reports, about 70 Holmesburg inmates were experimentally dosed with herbicides, primarily dioxin, a highly poisonous component of Agent Orange, the defoliant used in Vietnam. These tests were conducted under a contract with Dow Chemical (the manufacturer of Agent Orange) and the Army. Most chemistry experts consider dioxin to be one of the most powerful carcinogens known. Dow Chemical scientists told the *New York Times* in 1983 that they had initially tested dioxin on the ears of rabbits, but then they had "wanted to find out how the sensitivity of a rabbit's ears compared with human ears."

During several years when the experiments were underway at Holmesburg, the Army's Chemical Corps set up and manned work trailers on the prison's grounds. Three former civilian Army scientists have stated that the Corps' experiments may have also included other populations in other areas of Pennsylvania. Two of these scientists pointed out a "somewhat mysterious and perhaps suspicious" outbreak of Hong Kong flu at a Philadelphia home for the indigent in 1969. More than 266 of the 830 Riverview Home residents fell gravely ill. Within weeks, sixteen residents had died of the disease. Around the time of the tenth death, a joint study of Riverview was undertaken by city of Philadelphia, state, and federal officials with the object of "charting the path of the outbreak." At the same time, Riverview began receiving shipments of Hong Kong flu vaccine from Merck, Sharp & Dohme. Former Camp Detrick researchers say that Detrick's SOD and other divisions had maintained "a high level of interest in various Asian flu's for a good number of years in the 1960s and beyond."

On December 8, 1969, about a month into the Riverview flu outbreak, a committee of the Philadelphia County Medical Society recommended that "guidelines for protection of patient-subjects in research projects at Riverview" be adopted. Apparently, Riverview had been used in the past as a research site because a newspaper article the next day stated, "The ad hoc committee named in 1968 to review the matter of research at Riverside recommended that all human subjects in non-therapeutic research at the home be paid a participation fee." By way of background, the article pointed out:

> The [committee's] report related that 25 years ago in the aftermath of international revulsion over Nazi 'medical experiments,' the Nuremberg Code was drafted and more recently national agencies added more refined and detailed guidelines for research involving human subjects.

In 1984, a group of former Holmesburg prisoners sued the University of Pennsylvania and the city of Philadelphia. Nearly all of the men were African Americans, as were most of the inmates used in all the experiments at the prison. The men who brought the suit had cancer, severe lung problems, and a slew of other maladies that they claimed were caused by their exposure to the highly toxic chemicals in the experiments. Eventually, the men settled for sums in the $20,000 to $40,000 range. Edward Anthony, one of the former inmates, said, "They have destroyed my life. My hand swelled up. My hands were as big as boxing gloves. My fingers were fat, my fingernails, as you can see, are deformed, and this is after 34 years."

Holmesburg Prison was closed in 1995.

General Counsel Siemer concluded her report by stating: "There are no programs currently maintained by any Department of Defense component or contractor involving drug testing on human subjects in which the CIA is in any way involved. All current Department of Defense programs involving the use of investigational drugs on humans, including its contractor programs, have been approved by the Food and Drug Administration." Siemer did not list or detail the approved FDA programs.

Declassified Top Secret documents reveal that the Army, at the same time that its CIA sponsored programs were underway, conducted a number of human subject experiments on its own. These were not detailed in Siemer's report, nor were they uncovered by the media in the 1970s. Chief among these were contracts running from May 1950 to June 1954 for "psychological studies on the effects of CW agents" on humans. These contracts amounted to $63,178. From March 1957 to August 1960, the Army spent $89,897 studying the "effects of LSD on intellectual functions" of human subjects, although it is not clear who these subjects were.

Despite earlier denials, the Army spent $32,444 from 1952 to 1956 on "studies and experimental investigations into the effects of certain psychochemical agents on human subjects" at New York State Psychiatric Institute. For a two-year period from 1957 to 1959, it spent $164,000 on similar studies with the Research Foundation for Mental Health, Inc., a veiled incarnation of the NYSPI program.

At Tulane University and the University of Washington, the Army spent $53,000 and $40,000 respectively studying the effects of LSD on human subjects. The Washington experiments were also aimed at identifying "riot control agents," "lethal chemical agents" and "incapacitating compounds." At prestigious Johns Hopkins University, $492,000 was expended on "chemical warfare agent and toxic compound studies" using human subjects. Other schools conducting experiments that exposed human subjects to biological and chemical warfare agents were Louisiana State University, University of Utah, and Baylor University. The company North American Aviation spent $52,000 to study the effects of the powerful hallucinogen BZ on "aircraft crew performance."

Additional evidence of CIA/DOD collaboration in drug experiments can be found in yet another source that is, curiously, not mentioned in General Counsel Siemer's report to Defense Secretary Brown. Specifically, in 1958, a meeting took place at Fort Detrick that produced a 118-page report detailing highly classified projects involving drug experiments on human subjects. The report also mentions drug-related incidents that took place at NIKE missile sites – incidents that are not mentioned in Siemer's report.

The 1958 meeting at Fort Detrick was attended by over thirty high-level biological warfare officials, both enlisted and civilian. Among the officials were the heads of Detrick's Dissemination and Field Testing Division, its Engineering and Production Laboratories Branch, and several representatives from its SOD. Dr. Van Sim, chief of Edgewood Arsenal's Chemical Research Division, thoroughly briefed the gathering about ongoing human experiments with a compound called EA-1729, the Army's codename for LSD. Dr. Sim informed attendees, who were obviously familiar with the Army's use of LSD from previous briefings, that the Army's interest in LSD centered on the drug's "ability to produce psychotic effects," in connection with "a depression or a stimulation to the central nervous system." Sim explained that in the Army's "K Program," as he said it was called, drugs that caused "psychic changes" were "apt to be referred to as incapacitating agents." Sim then showed two films to the gathering.

The first film featured an experiment carried out on a cat. Sim explained that the cat "was one of the regular laboratory group of animals, and was known to have an aggressive nature." Said Sim, "He was an animal more or less in command of any situation in the various cages he occupied." To demonstrate this, Sim pointed to a portion of the film that depicted the cat toying with and then killing a mouse placed in its cage, not an unusual act for a normal feline.

After the cat was injected with "400 micrograms of LSD" (a very large amount for a small animal, by any standard), the cat displayed remarkably different behavior. Sim's film showed the cat cowering in fear of the mouse and showing "actual terror" as it clawed frantically at its cage attempting to get away from the meandering, and much smaller, rodent.

Sim's second film depicted a small cadre of enlisted men undergoing routine training exercises. In the first segment, each of the men in the squad – but not the squad's leader – had been given LSD. The men were obviously paying little attention to their leader's commands. In the next segment of the film, the squad leader, as well as the men, had been given the drug. Narrated Dr. Sim, "When an officer told the squad leader to put the men through the routine drill, the leader refused and told the officer to do it himself.... There was no discipline."

Dr. Sim told the attendees that an additional series of eight tests had been conducted on human subjects six months earlier at Aberdeen Proving Ground in Maryland. Objectives of these tests included trying to ascertain if "a man under the influence of LSD" could operate a radarscope or "drive a tank." Sim also explained that upcoming experiments possibly included one at a NIKE missile installation, and another experiment in Maryland, where the Army's Counter Intelligence Corps would test LSD for use in "various interrogation procedures."

According to the report of this meeting, one of the physicians listening to Sim's presentation, Dr. Herbert E. Longnecker, expressed his concern about "a very unhappy thought that had gone through his mind." He asked Dr. Sim, "Suppose permission is granted to go ahead with the tests and suddenly there is an occurrence at a NIKE installation similar to the episode experienced a few weeks ago?"

Longenecker was referring to an accident that had taken place at a NIKE missile base in Middletown, New Jersey on May 22, 1958. Several missiles had exploded, killing ten men — six Army enlisted personnel and four civilian technicians. Debris and body parts were found over three miles away. The explosion had been massive, involving at least twelve warheads. Sim, according to the 1958 document, "responded that only simulated [missile] firing is proposed; the firing of a missile is not contemplated."

Defense Department's General Counsel Siemer's report to Secretary Brown made no mention of this 1958 incident or of the experiment that had actually prompted the 1958 Fort Detrick gathering. This is a very controversial but little-known incident that had taken place the year before in August and September 1957 in Manchester, New Hampshire at the now-defunct Arms Textile Mill. As we already know, Frank Olson and several other SOD scientists had traveled in 1953 to an unidentified woolen mill in New Hampshire for reasons unknown. However, subsequent events at the Arms Mill certainly did involve other scientists from Fort Detrick. Here we shall examine the strange events that occurred at the Arms Mill in 1957.

SEPTEMBER 5, 1957, MANCHESTER, NEW HAMPSHIRE

One day in early September 1957, Antonio Jette came home from his job at the Arms Textile Mill in Manchester, New Hampshire and uncharacteristically went to bed early. He told his wife, Anna, that he was tired, wasn't in the least hungry and felt like he was coming down with a cold.

The next morning, Antonio said he was feeling better. It was Saturday and he and Anna drove to Vermont, four hours away, to attend the Rutland State Fair. It was an event they had been looking forward to for months. But as they were entering the fairgrounds, Antonio turned to Anna and said they had to go back home. "I'm sorry," he told her. "I feel really sick." On the way home, Antonio experienced several fits of dry coughing and he said that his chest hurt.

The following day, Sunday, Antonio and Anna went to church. Upon returning home, Antonio again felt tired. He told Anna he was going to lie down for a couple hours. An hour later Anna checked on her husband and found him soaked with perspiration and mumbling incoherently. She took his temperature, saw that it was 103 degrees Fahrenheit and called the family's doctor. The doctor gave Antonio a shot of penicillin for what he thought was a bronchial infection. He told Anna to keep Antonio in bed for the next few days.

Two hours later, Anna found Antonio still feverish and, even more alarming, she was unable to wake him up. With the help of neighbors, Anna took her unconscious husband to a nearby hospital. Doctors at St. Joseph's Hospital in Nashua, New Hampshire found Antonio's temperature to be 105 degrees. His breathing was rapid and shallow. Rales, small clicking sounds, were audible in both his lungs. Tests revealed blood in his lumbar region. Doctors told Anna that they thought her husband had suffered a cerebral hemorrhage. His chances for recovery did not look good, they said.

Antonio never regained consciousness. He died the next morning, September 6, 1957 at 6 A.M.

Anna was grief stricken by her husband's sudden death. He was only forty-nine years old. She had never seen him sick before. She didn't know how she would manage alone with seven children. Anna had Antonio buried three days later. The church was full of Antonio's friends and relatives, but nobody from management at the Arms Mill attended the funeral. Nobody, at the time, told Anna that the Arms Textile Mill was the site of tests being conducted by the Biological Warfare Laboratories at Fort Detrick. It would be another forty-five years before Anna heard about these tests.

Albert Langlois, sixteen years younger than his co-worker Antonio Jette, had been employed at the Arms Mill for only nine weeks when he became sick one day while on the job. It was October 30, a little over seven weeks after Antonio had died. Albert tried to keep working, but the next day he could hardly stand up. He was so thirsty and drank so much water that he vomited. "I've just got the flu," he told his wife Stella. "It'll go away soon."

Albert's doctor visited him at home on October 31 and diagnosed his ailment as Asian influenza. The doctor gave Stella eight tablets of oral penicillin for her husband. Two days later, Albert seemed better, but the following day he complained of trouble breathing. He was unable to keep down any liquids and his jaw clamped tightly closed. He thrashed about in bed and began frantically rubbing his legs.

Albert was rushed to the Manchester Veteran's Administration Hospital. Doctors there thought that he possibly was suffering a laryngeal obstruction. Albert died less than an hour later. Like Anna Jette, Stella Langlois was shocked by the suddenness and violence of her husband's death. And like Anna, Stella had been told nothing about Army biowarfare tests underway at the Arms Mill.

Following the tragic events of September 11, 2001, five people in the United States died as a result of a series of still mysterious, lethal anthrax-laden letters sent through the mail. Nearly fifty three years earlier, four other people, all workers at the Arms Mill, including Antonio Jette and Albert Langlois, had died in what the U.S. Centers for Disease Control still calls "America's only anthrax epidemic."

Throughout the 1950s, a central activity at the Arms Textile Mill was the processing of goat hair imported from Pakistan, Iraq, and Iran. The refined hair was used in the lining of expensive men's suits and overcoats manufactured at the mill. The Arms Mill, in 1957, had employed 632 workers spread throughout its complex of large red brick buildings located on the banks of the Merrimack River and near the edge of downtown Manchester.

At the time of the deadly anthrax outbreak at Arms Mill, the manufacturing plant was the site for tests of an experimental anthrax vaccine. Tests on the mill's workers— who were considered at risk for anthrax due to handling animal products such as goat and sheep hair -- had begun quietly in May 1955 and were sponsored by the Biological Warfare Laboratories of the U.S. Chemical Corps at Fort Detrick. The prototype vaccine tested at the mill had been developed by Detrick scientist Dr. George G. Wright. The pharmaceutical company Merck, Sharp & Dohme, today Merck and Co., Inc, briefly produced the vaccine a few years later. Company head George Wilhelm Merck, readers will recall, had been a principle advocate for biological warfare in the 1940s and 1950s and was a founder of Camp Detrick. Dr. Wright's vaccine is essentially the same serum administered today to American troops and others at risk of anthrax.

Over a half-century after the Arms Mill outbreak, no definitive scientific explanation or cause of the epidemic has been discovered. Scientists at UCLA's Department of Epidemiology and other research centers have speculated, "the circumstantial evidence suggested a relationship to a particular batch of goat hair." However, because no samples of that animal hair exist today, no up-to-date testing can be accomplished, and therefore results from tests conducted in 1957 and 1958 remain inconclusive. Further compounding matters is that, despite the vast distances from the original source of the animal hair in question, there were no cases of any type of anthrax ever reported or recorded along the extremely lengthy transit routes from their distant source into New Hampshire.

Equally perplexing to many who have studied the outbreak is that, despite the severity of the epidemic — not only did four workers die, but an additional 21 workers came down with cutaneous anthrax — the Arms Mill never ceased operations, even temporally, during the outbreak and it continued operating uninterrupted until 1968, when it went out of business for financial reasons. In grim testimony to the virulent nature of the anthrax that infected the mill, in 1966, nine years after the original outbreak, a man working in the machinery shop across from the mill suddenly died of inhalation anthrax. New Hampshire health officials speculated at the time that lethal spores remaining from 1957 had migrated from the Arms buildings through a ventilation system shared by the two businesses.

Following this additional death nine years after the epidemic, State health officials sealed the mill while trying to decide how to make the site environmentally safe. Despite an expensive decontamination process in 1971, the buildings still tested positive for anthrax, so the entire complex was demolished. The

561

remaining, colossal pile of rubble was then systematically soaked in chorine and other chemicals for additional decontamination. Astonishingly, even that proved ineffective for the mill's huge hickory beams, so incinerators were erected on the site and all the wood was burned to fine ash. The remaining bricks and stones were carted away for burial. Today, the Arms Mill site is a parking lot for a riverside park and an upscale shopping area.

Speculation that the Arms anthrax epidemic may not have been a coincidental occurrence has been ongoing among scientists for years. In 1999, former United Nations official and BBC correspondent Edward Hooper published a book entitled, *The River: A Journey to the Source of HIV and AIDS*. Buried deep within Hooper's 1,070-page book is a brief section that concerns the Arms Mill outbreak. Hooper's research inadvertently led him to the incident through his unrelated interviews with Dr. Stanley A. Plotkin. At the time of the Arms Mill experiments, Dr. Plotkin worked for the CDC's Epidemic Intelligence Service, the Wistar Institute in Philadelphia, and was assigned the task of medically evaluating the outbreak.

In 1960, Dr. Plotkin's analysis of the New Hampshire incident, which is still widely circulated and studied by anthrax experts today, was published in the *American Journal of Medicine*. Entitled, "An Epidemic of Inhalation Anthrax, the First in the 20th Century," the paper was co-authored with Dr. Philip S. Brachman. Brachman was Plotkin's supervisor in 1957 and the outbreak's chief investigator employed by the Anthrax Investigations Unit, CDC, and the Wistar Institute. The paper, which meticulously details the facts of the outbreak, makes no mention of the fact that Army scientists from Fort Detrick were involved in the events surrounding the epidemic or that the mill was the site of anthrax vaccine experiments being conducted by the Army at the time of the outbreak.

In his book, *The River*, Hooper recounts the basic facts of the Arms Mill incident and writes:

> It may of course be that [Fort Detrick] scientists were simply lucky from a research perspective, and that Mother Nature started an epidemic of inhalation anthrax at just the right moment to test their vaccine under field conditions. And yet, of course, there is another, more ominous possibility. That is that, unbeknownst to the Wistar team of Plotkin and Brachman, humans played a conscious role, and that a decision was made by the Chemical Corps [or Detrick's SOD] to subject the vaccine to the ultimate field test– that of challenge with virulent anthrax organisms.

Hooper writes that although this "appalling" possibility "may sound far-fetched:

> ... the hypothesis is supported by internal Army reports from the period. The 1959/60 annual report for the Commission on Epidemiological Survey, part of the Armed Forces Epidemiological Board, contains the minutes of a meeting held on march 23, 1960, which was largely devoted to

anthrax. Dr. Harold Glassman of Fort Detrick (whose assistance had been acknowledged at the end of the Plotkin/Brachman paper) was the main speaker, and he opened his address with a review of the anthrax organism, including 'ease of preparation and stability in storage and as an aerosol.' He was especially interested in air-sampling studies at the Manchester mill and with the case of a young military volunteer who had died of inhalation anthrax at Fort Detrick in 1958, after receiving a series of inoculations of killed and live vaccines, including one against anthrax.

... [Glassman] stressed the fact that the Soviets appeared to have recently developed an attenuated anthrax vaccine for humans, and said that there was an urgent need on the U.S. side for 'an examination of the protective properties of various vaccine preparations.' Clearly, the Manchester [Arms Mill] vaccine trial had not provided all the answers. After this, Hooper added that a portion of Dr. Glassman's presentation was omitted from the minutes, presumably for security reasons.

Other Army documents obtained by the author, not cited in Hooper's book, reveal that the censored portion of Dr. Glassman's report may have concerned a top-secret project called the St. Jo Program. That program predated the Arms Mill outbreak by at least two years. Additional documents obtained by this author bear the signature of Dr. Glassman and speak of human subject studies under consideration at the University of Chicago, "using human volunteers" who were "inmates at the State Penitentiary." Further documents hint at the possibility that the Arms Mill and Chicago tests involved the CIA through the direct participation of Detrick's SOD. Indeed, it may well be that Frank Olson's travel to New Hampshire in 1953 was for advance preparatory work involving the Arms Mill. Former SOD scientist Yonetz said, "It was not unusual to make advance trips to get ready for formal [project] launching. You could say it was standard practice."

The Arms Mill debate flared up yet again at a November 2000 Institute of Medicine, National Academy of Sciences meeting in Washington, D.C. Attending the meeting as separate expert witnesses were Dr. Meryl Nass, a biologist and medical doctor, and Dr. Stanley Plotkin. The meeting centered on the Defense Department's anthrax vaccine program, and Dr. Nass raised a number of cogent concerns about the vaccine's safety, which Dr. Plotkin strongly rejected. When the subject of the Arms Mill study came up, Dr. Nass remarked that the outbreak occurred "serendipitously at the same time" that Army scientists were on the site. Plotkin heatedly responded, "I reject any implied or stated accusation that this was a biological warfare experiment."

In a September 2002 interview with this author, Plotkin, who today is a respected AIDS researcher and emeritus professor of immunology at the University of Pennsylvania, said he did not "think much of conspiracy theories and theorists" and that author Hooper's "innuendo that we purposely launched the outbreak is false and vicious."

Plotkin explained that he "came to the Anthrax Investigation Unit in August 1957, fresh from a training course." He said, "My supervisor, Dr. Philip Brachman, was in Europe. He had launched a study of anthrax vaccine in May 1957. I had never been to the mill in question when I received a telephone call early in September to tell me that anthrax had been diagnosed in a mill worker in Manchester, New Hampshire. I went up to investigate, and the results have been published in the medical literature."

Asked why Fort Detrick was involved in the tests, Plotkin said, "I think the answer is obvious. The vaccine had been developed at Fort Detrick, and the purpose of our study, aside from protecting the mill workers, was to find out what value the vaccine could have against an anthrax attack."

It may be relevant that Dr. Plotkin's article provides historical background on anthrax. He points out the fact that between 1900 and 1957, there had been only 21 random cases of anthrax in the world, and "no epidemics have been reported in the world literature." Suddenly, within a 10-week period, however, in a single woolen mill, 9 cases of anthrax are reported, 5 of them the rarest form of all — "inhalation anthrax." It is difficult to ignore the fact that the site of this outbreak is one of four mills under experimental "study" by Fort Detrick in the context of biowarfare research. There were no reported clusters (epidemics) of anthrax in any other mills in the United States during this period.

On the issue of why the mill was never closed, even temporarily, Plotkin said, "The outbreak appeared to be over before the issue of what to do came up. Closing the mill would have been an economic hardship for the workers. Instead, all workers were offered the vaccine in November [1957], ending their utility for the study, but protecting everybody." Asked if follow-up studies had been conducted on the Arms Mill workers after the outbreak, Plotkin answered, "Not to my knowledge."

(The question arises about how it would be determined that the outbreak was "over" and no further risks were present when anthrax spores are known to be among the hardiest of micro-organisms in existence, capable of surviving for decades without a host. Moreover, given the fact that no similar outbreaks had occurred anywhere in more than 50 years, the lack of standard, precautionary public health procedures is puzzling.)

Previously top-secret documents, obtained by the author under the Freedom of Information Act, reveal that Fort Detrick's interest in the New Hampshire epidemic, even months after it had ended, was ongoing and intense, and that numerous scientists at the installation were assigned to study its various aspects. At the time, Fort Detrick was deeply involved in developing anthrax as an offensive weapon of war. According to the former chief of Detrick's anthrax production plant, Orley R. Bourland, Jr., throughout the 1950s deadly anthrax spores were manufactured "24 hours a day, seven days a week." Detrick's massive anthrax fermenters, housed in Building 470, held 1,800 gallons of wet anthrax solution and pumped out about 7,000 grams of refined anthrax a week. During the post-9/11 anthrax mailings to Washington, D.C.'s Capitol Hill, about two grams of anthrax caused the evacuation of several federal buildings and the expenditure of millions of dollars for clean up. CDC officials said at the time that, "under the right conditions," an attack involving "several grams could result in the deaths of thousands of people."

The meeting at Fort Detrick in 1958 (discussed above) that resulted in the 118-page Army report had included several SOD scientists and at least one official from Britain's Porton Down Biological Warfare Center. Also in attendance were Dr. Stanley Plotkin and Dr. Philip Brachman, representing the U.S. Public Health Service, and the authors of the two journal articles about the Arms Mill outbreak. The 118-page report includes a review provided by Dr. Brachman of the "follow-up studies resulting from the New Hampshire outbreak."

Brachman explained that "during a 10-week period" from August to November 1957 there had been nine cases of anthrax at the Arms Mill, five of inhalation anthrax and four of cutaneous. Reads the report: "Four of the five inhalation cases were fatal. In three of the four cases, autopsies were performed, proving the diagnosis; in the instance of the woman who was buried without an autopsy, it had been impossible to get permission to exhume the body." (This was a 65-year old woman who had worked at the mill for nearly twelve years. She died on September 8, 1957, two days after Antonio Jette's death.)

The document continues by describing how Brachman separated the mill's workers into two categories for purposes of the tests, which began approximately 12 weeks before the first reported case of anthrax in 1957. Workers were deemed either "susceptible" or "immune." Simply put, "susceptibles" were those employees who were either not given the vaccine or those who were instead given the "control material" or placebo. "Immunes" were those workers who had "the full course of the antigenic material," or those "who had had the disease at some time in the past and were therefore assumed to be immune."

During the Arms outbreak, 313 of the mill's 632, or about half of the employees received the experimental anthrax vaccine. None of the five Arms employees who contracted inhalation anthrax (one did not die) had been vaccinated as part of the tests; two received the placebo instead and the remaining three, for reasons not clearly stated, had not participated in the tests.

Not explained in the course of the meeting, or in the articles authored by Drs. Brachman and Plotkin, is why the employees had been divided into the two groups unless an exposure to anthrax had been anticipated within the time frame allotted for the study. As Brachman himself pointed out in a 1966 article, "Since 1900, there have been fewer than 20 cases of inhalation anthrax reported in the United States." The coincidence of 5 cases in one mill during a 10-week period within the time frame of the Army's experimental vaccine study at that mill is noteworthy.

Midway through his 1958 review, according to the 118-page report, Dr. Brachman was asked if the Arms Mill was still open, to which he replied that it was "operating full force." However, he explained, alterations had been made in the mill's operations and that, following the outbreak, the experiment had been terminated and all employees "had been offered the vaccine."

This question was followed by another concerning "whether the viable spores," which were assumed to be still present in the mill's buildings, ever got "through the fabric to infect customers" who purchased the products produced at the mill. The document reads: "The response was that this is a touchy question," and that "some products" did test positive for anthrax, but that after further treatment they tested negative. Yet, the document goes on to state that an unidentified "grocery clerk in Philadelphia" came down with cutaneous anthrax after purchasing "a new woolen coat four weeks before his illness."

Later in the document, it is noted that Fort Detrick pathologist Dr. Edwin V. Hill reported that autopsies had been performed "on monkeys which died following a respiratory exposure to the anthrax organisms isolated in the New Hampshire outbreak." The document states: "These animals died very suddenly without premonitory symptoms. The gross and microscopic findings in the autopsies were similar to those observed in the work with the strain which has been under study in the past."

The 1958 document, despite all its detail, is noticeably silent on the subject of when, if ever, the Arms Mill employees had been informed that there was an anthrax outbreak of any sort in their workplace. Surviving families of the workers who died told this author that they "knew nothing about the Army's tests" in 1957 or later. At least one family said that they "knew nothing about the Army's involvement" and "nothing about any vaccine tests conducted by anyone until after the 9/11 attacks." Another family told the author, "We were unaware that anyone at all had died of anthrax" until after September 11, 2001, "when a reporter called to ask some questions about the mill."

Also not explained in the 1958 document is why the local medical community and hospitals in the Manchester area were never informed about the anthrax outbreak. Local doctors treated at least three of the Arms Mill employees who died, and the others were treated at nearby hospitals, yet it appears that none of those doctors had any idea that there was an epidemic underway. Even allowing for unsophisticated disease reporting and surveillance systems — making it difficult for cases treated in different hospitals to have been quickly identified as an epidemic — every case was made known to the Army and the Army's physicians had quickly identified the cluster as an epidemic. Yet, apparently, this was not communicated to local health authorities or even to the workers at the Arms Mill.

Antonio Jette's daughter, Anita Simonds, now 80 years old, told the author that her mother, Anna Pratte, "never found out that my father died of anthrax until about seven to eight months later when her insurance man told her something." Simonds said, "My father never mentioned anything about any tests or shots being given at the mill. He never got any shots. Nobody ever said a thing to anybody about anthrax back then. We'd never heard of it."

Simonds added, "My father worked hard every day of his life for his family. He took good care of his children and wife. He didn't have time to think about what the Army or anybody else was doing."

10

September 20, 1977*
Capitol Hill, Washington, D.C.

My name is Sidney Gottlieb and I reside in California. I am appearing at this hearing as I have appeared in others in the past, voluntarily and prepared to offer whatever constructive testimony made possible by my background and remembrance of things past.

I would like to first comment on project MKULTRA.

To the best of my recollection, several research inquiries— which much later came to be organized under the cryptonym MKULTRA— were begun in about 1952. Their purpose was to investigate whether and how it was possible to modify an individual's behavior by covert means. The context in which this investigation was started was that of the height of the Cold War, with the Korean War just winding down; with the CIA organizing its resources to liberate Eastern Europe by paramilitary means; and with the threat of Soviet aggression very real and tangible, as exemplified by the recent Berlin airlift.

In the judgement [sic] of the CIA, there was tangible evidence that both the Soviets and the Red Chinese might be using techniques of altering human behavior which were not understood by the USA and which would have implications of national survival in the context of national security concerns at that time. It was felt to be mandatory and of the utmost urgency for our intelligence organization to establish what was possible in this field on a high priority basis.

To mention just a few examples, there was a concern about the apparent manipulated conversions of Americans interned in Red China for a very short time; there was also a concern about apparently irrational remarks made by a senior American diplomat returning from the Soviet Union; perhaps most immediate and urgent in our minds was the apparent buying up of the world supply of at-that-time-little-known new psychogenic material LSD; lastly, there was a growing library of documented instances of routine use by the Soviet Security Services of covertly-administered drugs. This last, by the way, has grown and been added to, up to the time I left the Agency (CIA).

I accept full responsibility for my own role in these activities, in relation to what my position in the CIA implied, as to my level of responsibility as it changed over the years. At the outset, in the period 1951-1957, I was head of a branch of a division charged with the responsibility of looking into the matters, which I described above. I set up and handled some projects myself, and supervised and administered other CIA employees monitoring other projects. As the years went on and I assumed broader responsibilities, my personal involvement in the projects lessened. Thus, my involvement was most direct in the period 1951-1957. From 1957 to the end of 1960, I was not directly involved at all, being assigned to other matters. I was stationed overseas 1957-1959 and was assigned to another unit in headquarters in the period 1959 to the end of 1960. Late in 1960, I returned to TSD [Technical Services Division] to become Chief of the Research and Development component; in 1962, I became Deputy Chief of TSD; and from 1966 to 1973, I was Chief of TSD. I retired from the CIA on June 30, 1973. I want to stress, however, that a policy review of project MKULTRA and all of the projects I was connected with took place at least once a year during MKULTRA active period, which I remember as 1952-1965. In addition, as each project was funded, approval in writing at least two levels above mine was required in all research and development activities.

Project names like ARTICHOKE and Bluebird have been mentioned in the press, associated with my name. My remembrance is that project ARTICHOKE was managed by the Office of Security and that I had no direct or indirect responsibility for it, although I became aware of its existence and general nature over the years. Project Bluebird, as I remember it, was also an Office of Security concept, possibly never actually realized, which later evolved into a TSS-sponsored activity looking into brainwashing, and ultimately included the Society for the Investigation of Human Ecology.

One unusual project, started in 1952, and continued until about 1965, was an arrangement originally set up by me with the Federal Bureau of Narcotics. In this regard, I have previously furnished my recollections of this matter during my 40 odd hours of testimony to the Senate Select Committee on Intelligence, but I am glad to discuss these matters again with this Committee. The origin of the Bureau of Narcotics activity rested in my becoming aware through reading OSS research files of an investigation into the behavior-altering possibilities of Tetrahydrocannabinol, a synthetic material related to the naturally active constituent of marijuana. I was able to contact an officer of the Bureau of Narcotics who had participated first-hand in the OSS investigations. With him, I made an arrangement, funded by the CIA, whereby he would covertly administer chemical materials to unwitting people. The Bureau of Narcotics, through this individual, had their own interest in determining whether chemical materials could be used to elicit or validate information obtained from drug informants. The arrangement would benefit the CIA's program in that information would be obtained, unobtainable in any other way, on the effects of these materials used in situations closely resembling those in actual operations. I have no personal awareness of specific individuals to whom these materials were administered. To the best of my knowledge and remembrance, the materials administered in the

569

great majority of cases under the Bureau of Narcotics project were LSD and Meretran. I do not have detailed information on the exact number of individuals involved, but the impression I have is that the number involved was between 20 and 50 individuals over the years of the project. I would like to add that the Bureau of Narcotics project was the only one of its kind in the sense of trying to gain urgently needed information in the administration of materials in an operational context. Although it has drawn considerable attention in the news media, because of its unusual nature, it was a very small part of an overall program, which took place in a more conventional project, in the more normal setting of universities and laboratories, as born out by the records shown to me by the Committee staff. This Committee might be interested to know that the total amount of money spent on everything related to MKULTRA was limited to 10% of the total research done by TSD. To my remembrance, at the height of the spending on MKULTRA related activities, it never even reached this percentage.

The great bulk of the research done under the general umbrella of Project MKULTRA took place in academic and other research settings. These projects almost always represented work that the individual investigators would have been doing in any case. The Agency's role was to provide the funds and, in many cases, provide access to the investigator if specific interpretation of his results in terms of our interests were needed. To my recollection, in every case, the results of the related research were published.

The degree of wittingness of the principal investigator on these projects varied depending on whether we judged his knowledge of our specific interests to be necessary in providing useful results to us. Thus, many projects were established in which the principal investigator was fully knowledgeable of who we were and exactly what our interests in the research were. Others were simply provided funds through a covert organization and had no idea of ultimate CIA sponsorship.

The degree to which individuals other than the principal investigator needed to be witting of the Agency's connection to the research varied. It was generally left to the principal investigator to advise us as to whether anyone else in either his research team or in the administrative part of the university or research organization needed to be made witting of the Agency's relationship. To the best of my remembrance, although for general security reasons we were eager to keep this kind of information to a minimum, we went along with the principal investigator's desires and cleared and briefed whomever he felt was necessary.

The general subject of why we felt it necessary to use funding mechanisms like the Society for the Investigation of Human Ecology or the Geschickter Fund for Medical Research needs some comment. This involves the more general question of why we felt all of this research needed to be kept secret insofar as Agency sponsorship was concerned. The reason, however it may seem with the benefit of hindsight, was that we felt any potential enemies of this country would be greatly benefited in their own possible future aggressive acts against the USA if they were forewarned as to what the nature and progress of our research in this field was.

The largest overall picture that can be given of this group of academic and other formal research undertakings is that they were an attempt to harness the academic and research community of the United States to provide badly-needed answers to some pressing national security problems, in the shortest possible time, without alerting potential enemies to the United States Government's interest in these matters.

In all cases, research results were published through the normal overt channels for publication of medical and physiological research. I would like to remind the members of the Committee that at this point in history the amount of available reliable data on LSD and similar materials was essentially nil.

I understand from reading newspaper accounts that one of the principal interests of the Committee in this kind of research is the degree of protection that was afforded to the subjects used in those experiments where human subjects were used. As far as the Bureau of Narcotics project is concerned, my impression was there was no advance knowledge or protection of the individual concerned. The only comment I would like to make on this is that, harsh as it may seem in retrospect, it was felt that in an issue where national security might be concerned, such a procedure and such a risk was a reasonable one to take. I would like again to remind the Committee that, as far as those of us who participated in this work were concerned, this country was involved in a real covert war in the sense that the Cold War spilled over into intelligence activities.

Insofar as protection of individuals in the bulk of this work, as represented by formal research projects, is concerned, the matter of informed consent and protection to the volunteers participating was left to each investigator according to the standards that either he or his institution felt were appropriate to the situation. Our general feeling was that if we chose reputable and responsible investigators, appropriate standards in this area would be used. I think, in general, the procedures actually used in these experiments were representative of what was considered to be adequate safeguards at the time.

A comment should be made on the kind of interest that the Agency had in these matters and how it may have changed over the years. The original impetus for this work, as mentioned above, was the concern about aggressive use of behavior-altering techniques against this country by its enemies. Although this remained a continuing and probably primary focus in the history of these projects, the Agency did become interested in the potential use of behavior modification techniques in unforeseen circumstances that might occur in the future.

It is undoubtedly true that some of these research activities were continued into the middle or late 1960's, when in looking backward now the real possibility of their successful and effective use either against us or by us was very low. In fact, I remember writing a report when I was on detached assignment with another unit in the clandestine services in about 1961, which concluded that the potential effectiveness of these techniques and the inclination of American intelligence officers to use them were limited.

The only reasons I can provide now for the continuance of a small number of these activities was that it was felt we needed to be more certain than we were of these negative results and also that we felt a need to maintain contact with individuals knowledgeable in the fields to keep ourselves abreast of what was happening.

In conclusion, I would like to comment on three things which trouble me very much about the situation I find myself in.

First, there have been many references in the press to attempts by me to avoid testifying. These allegations are without any basis in fact, either in terms of "hiding" or making myself unavailable to congressional committees. In the case of my testimony before the Church Committee in 1975, I voluntarily and immediately returned from India as soon as I was made aware at the Missionary Hospital, where I was performing voluntary services, that I might be needed. I have been available for all legitimate inquiries at all times through my counsel.

Second, I feel victimized and I am appalled at the CIA's policy, wherein someone or some group selectively pinpoints my name by failing to delete it from documents released under the Freedom of Information Act without any permission from me. That is, my name is selectively left on released documents where all or most others are deleted. I have great concern for past, present and future employees of the Agency involved in sensitive, difficult, and potentially misunderstood work, as this policy of selective disclosure of individuals names gets applied to them. I am sincerely concerned that the CIA's ability to recruit clandestine assets in the future could be severely impaired.

Thirdly, my concern is for the reputations of the many individuals not employees of the Agency, in the academic and professional life who, for the most patriotic and constructive of reasons, and guaranteed both by myself and the Agency of confidentiality and non-disclosure, chose to assist the Agency in its research efforts over the past years. By now, the association in the news media of any name in the academic or professional work with CIA brings immediate and automatic negative connotations, and irreparably damages their reputations. With regard to my testimony, I hope this Committee will understand my reluctance, except when absolutely essential, to mention other names. I am desirous and willing to share any knowledge of matters of interest to the Committee that I have in my memory but, whatever the CIA's policies may be on this matter, I feel it is a point of personal responsibility to honor the commitment of confidentiality that I feel towards these individuals and not to be a party to further damage their reputations.

In summary, I would like this Committee to know that I considered all this work—at the time it was done and in the context of circumstances that were extant in that period— to be extremely unpleasant, extremely difficult, extremely sensitive, but above all, to be extremely urgent and important. I realize that it is difficult to reconstruct those times and that atmosphere today in this room.

Another thought that I would like to leave you with is that should the course of recent history have been slightly different from what it was, I can easily imagine a congressional committee being extremely critical of the Agency for not having done investigations of this nature.

In any event, it is my simple wish to be as helpful as possible to this Committee in obtaining its appropriate legislative goals, and I am prepared to be as helpful and forthcoming as possible in the areas in which you are interested.

*Verbatim Statement of Sidney Gottlieb before U.S. Senate Select Committee on Intelligence and Subcommittee on Health and Scientific Research of the Committee on Human Resources, MKULTRA Programs, Joint Hearing, August 3, 1977, 95th Congress, 1st session, Washington, D.C.

11

The Victims Task Force: 1978-1979

Part of our problem is not knowing what we don't know.
                                            — CIA official Frank Laubinger, 1978

U nknown to many people interested in the CIA's mind control programs is that the Agency, in 1978, formed what it called the Victims Task Force. It was formed primarily as a result of the publicity surrounding exposure of the deaths of Frank Olson and Harold Blauer, as well as the testimony of then CIA director Stansfield Turner before the Senate Select Committee on Intelligence. The Task Force's stated objective was "to attempt to identify and inform MKULTRA experiment subjects who may have been given drugs without their permission between the years 1952 and 1963."

Just two employees — CIA officer Frank Laubinger and former Federal Bureau of Narcotics agent Richard Salmi — staffed the Victims Task Force (VTF), a misnomer of sorts. The CIA had hired Laubinger in February 1952 as an analytical chemist. He had worked for the Agency's Technical Services Division under chief Culver Ladd, then Willis Gibbons, and after Sidney Gottlieb became head of TSS, he was supervised by Chemical Branch chief Linwood Murray. Salmi had become a well-respected and highly experienced narcotics agent who had worked many high-profile cases involving French, Corsican, and Turkish drug traffickers.

Early on in their brief investigation, which lasted only from March 1979 through late September 1979, Laubinger and Salmi decided to limit their investigation to six MKULTRA subprojects, one MKSEARCH subproject, and "the independent activities" of CIA Technical Services "scientists which involved giving drugs to Americans." Each of these subprojects had entailed a CIA relationship with only the Federal Bureau of Narcotics, and therefore did not touch the various other networks spawned over the years of the CIA's drug experiments. Laubinger and Salmi limited their inquiry, in effect, to the drug experiments that were connected to the 5 CIA-funded safe houses, beginning with the one in New York located at 81 Bedford Street. Stated a VTF report: "These were the only activities believed to have involved unwitting human testing." However, the two investigators also determined that "Mr. George White, alias Morgan Hall, is believed to have been the key figure in the unwitting testing efforts."

Clearly, as readers have learned through the proceeding pages of this book, there were numerous, perhaps countless, other unwitting victims of MKULTRA activities, but nobody challenged Laubinger or Salmi on their limited investigation or its findings. From the standpoint of a journalist intensely interested in gaining more information and insight into the particulars of MKULTRA and the CIA's other behavior modification programs, the VTF investigation was sadly disappointing. Indeed, in this author's opinion the investigation was deliberately less than thorough and a sham. Despite the fact that the Task Force had full and complete access to all CIA and FBN files, it made no effort whatsoever to find any of the many unwitting victims of those MKULTRA experiments conducted by Drs. Harold Abramson, Harris Isbell, Robert Hyde, Carl Pieffer or any of the other MKULTRA physicians. For that matter, the Task Force found that no other FBN agents besides George White participated in safe house drug activities despite the fact that White's date book identifies numerous instances when other agents, who are named, were present during experiments. Careful study of the VTF files, however, does reveal a few items of particular interest. These items are detailed below.

INVESTIGATING IRA "IKE" FELDMAN

Salmi and Laubinger interviewed Ira Feldman on April 26, 1979. Since White had passed away four years earlier, they felt that Feldman could be a major source for information about the San Francisco safe house activities. Contrary to many recently published reports, Feldman never worked directly for the CIA. Indeed, as the Task Force's interview with Feldman revealed, the Agency knew very little about Feldman's role with White, and it had had its own serious concerns about him.

Feldman told the two investigators he had been hired by White on June 10, 1955 after being interviewed by FBN officials in Washington, D.C. Feldman's job with White was "special employee." His work primarily involved tailing narcotics suspects and, on occasion, luring them into the San Francisco safe houses with the assistance of several prostitutes he and White hired "as needed."

Feldman said he had met Sidney Gottlieb once but that he had never had a conversation with him. He called TSS Chemical Branch employee Ray Treichler, who often visited the safe houses in San Francisco, "a milktoast" who "expressed no interest in women." Salmi, on the other hand, noted in his subsequent report that Treichler "liked Feldman" and sometimes "was protective of him." Feldman recalled that Treichler on one occasion brought "gas cartridges to test." Feldman explained, "The cartridges put out an incapacitating material which was worse than tear gas." The shells were "tested at Stinson Beach and Feldman, White, and Treichler would take turns running through the cloud." Feldman also recounted that they had tested "a defoliant at Stinson Beach by injecting it into trees," using it "on eucalyptus trees believing them to be the toughest." The trees died.

Feldman also told Laubinger and Salmi that about three weeks after he reported to work in 1955, he had gone to White's San Francisco office and found

DCI Allen Dulles and FBN Commissioner Harry Anslinger there. He said the three men were discussing "various means of assassination" and that later White told him "that the assassination of Castro was being considered." (Given that it was 1955, this seems highly dubious.)

Laubinger asked Feldman about a little known safe house in New York City located in apartment 1B at 212 East 18th Street. Feldman said he knew the apartment had been paid for by White, but denied that he had any other information about the location. Feldman also told the two investigators that "if they really wanted to know details of what happened they would call him, and other involved people, grant them total immunity, and ask them to tell everything they know."

When Laubinger asked Feldman what he now did for work, he replied, "Investments." He said he traveled often to places in South America and Europe.

"What type of investments?" asked Laubinger.

"Let's just say investments in lives," replied Feldman.

Laubinger's conclusion from his encounter with Feldman was: "Feldman knows more that he is admitting and even infers as much. His testimony is full of inferences that he knows much more including his statement that if they really want to know, etc. I believe he agreed to meet with us just to learn what we were up to."

The subject of Frank Olson never came up in the interview with Feldman. Nobody appeared to ask Feldman about the identities of other CIA and FBN officials who had visited the safe houses, but Laubinger did ask about Pierre Lafitte.

> Did Feldman know where Lafitte was? It appears that the CIA and FBN had lost track of him.

Questions for Sidney Gottlieb

In April 1979, Laubinger wrote a letter on CIA stationary to Sidney Gottlieb informing him of the Task Force's investigation and posing 8 questions to the former CIA official. Laubinger asked Gottlieb to clarify or identify 1) what drugs and dosages White and Feldman used in CIA safe houses; 2) what, if any, follow-up was done on unwitting victims; 3) how White submitted his reports; 4) what was the primary purpose of the unwitting experiments; 5) how many safe houses were there; 6) where did White's code name for the San Francisco safe houses, "Midnight Climax," come from; 7) how many experiments were run, in total, in the five safe houses operated by the CIA and White; and 8) was there a second safe house in New York?

Wrote Laubinger to Gottlieb:

> It now appears that all of the Agency's files have been searched and that all drug related material which is subject to release has been released. The

investigation into the Agency's drug research is now targeted for completion in June. Hopefully, this entire subject will soon be relegated to history. If I don't hear from you within a couple weeks, I will give you a call.

Amazingly, Laubinger and Salmi asked Gottlieb no more than these questions. They asked Gottlieb nothing about Frank Olson or Harold Blauer.

Gottlieb called Laubinger 10 days later. Laubinger's one-page written account of the call states Gottlieb's 8 answers, as follows:

1. The LSD used by White was packaged as a solution in approximately 80 microgram units in plastic ampoules. The LSD was sometimes packaged in combination with meratran.

2. Follow-up was conducted when practical—there was no set practice.

3. White's reports on drug tests were submitted in his own handwriting.

The identity of the subject [victim] was not mentioned. Dr. Gottlieb does not believe that any tests were conducted in the 60s. The New York safe house, Greenwich Towers, [opened in the 1960's at 105 West 13th Street] was obtained by new people brought in to take over management of the program. The new project officers felt we needed a facility on each coast for contingency purposes. He does not believe any unwitting testing was performed in New York after White's departure from New York in 1955.

4. Unwitting testing was performed to explore the full range of the operational use of LSD. Both interrogation and provoking erratic behavior were of interest.

5. There were no other safe houses involved in the Program [besides the five that the Task Force had identified].

6. White had a fertile imagination and a literary mind, which conjured up [two lines redacted]. He has no other explanation for it. {Midnight Climax code name.]

7. He remembers no breakdown of tests and no accurate count of tests. As he recalls, the number was probably about 40. He recalls nothing which would identify any specific tests or test sites.

8. He knows nothing of a second apartment inNew York during the 60's. TSD has nothing to do with any apartment, which may have been procured by Ira Feldman.

WHEN WERE THE MKULTRA DOCUMENTS ACTUALLY DESTROYED?

One document found in the Task Force papers is quite interesting because it appears to contradict the controversial 1973 account concerning the destruction of MKULTRA files. The one-page CIA memorandum dated October 17, 1978 from the Agency's Executive Secretary to its Deputy Director of Administration bears the Subject heading, "Review of Records about Drug Experimentation" and it reads:

Furthermore, a review of what might be squirreled away in Records Center has revealed the attached memorandum dated 15 April 1960, wherein the Chief/Executive Registry/DCI instructed that materials related to MKULTRA and ARTICHOKE be destroyed. An examination of the Job number suggests that the materials had to do with authorizing expenditure of funds for specific operations 1951-55.

Psychopaths & MKULTRA Subproject 39

The files of the VTF reveal that in December 1978 Laubinger and Salmi investigated MKULTRA Subproject 39. This subproject, according to CIA documents, was created in late 1954 and was operated for about 2 years. Its stated objective was "to exploit the research potential that is represented by a group of 142 criminal-sexual psychopaths confined in the Ionia State Hospital for the Criminally Insane as well as at the Psychopathic Clinic in Detroit, Michigan. Several materials and techniques will be assessed for their information-eliciting properties... It is thought that these individuals have the kind of motivation for withholding certain information that is comparable to operational interrogation situations in the field."

A Glimpse of Dr. Harold Abramson

Salmi and Laubinger also briefly examined the work of Dr. Harold Abramson, communicating by written letters with the New York-based physician. Abramson told the two investigators that he "never used unwitting subjects" in his experiments and that there had "never been any reported problems with any of my subjects." Abramson also told the two that he knew nothing about Project MKULTRA.

In their examination of CIA files pertaining to Abramson's work for the Agency, Laubinger wrote that the physician's 1953-1954 request for MKULTRA funding "says that a psychiatrist will 'analyze the verbatim recordings in over 100 experiments in which LSD has already been given.'"

There is no indication in any of the released VTF files that Abramson was asked anything about his treatment of Frank Olson. Other CIA files have clearly indicated that Abramson recorded his sessions with Olson. In 1999, this author filed a FOI request for those recordings. The CIA, to date, has never responded in any way to that request.

The Victims of George White

By searching the contents of George White's date books, the VTF stated in its 1979 final report, it had actually identified 8 people whom George White had dosed unwittingly with LSD. All 8 of these individuals were friends of White and his wife, however, and held absolutely no interest or importance to the FBN, CIA, or any other Governmental agency. Why they were dosed at all is unclear.

Laubinger and Salmi managed to locate, after "considerable effort," the husband of one of the victims, a woman who had died of cancer in 1978. Her husband agreed to be interviewed and, according to the VTF report: "He said their marriage had broken up in 1959 [six years after the date indicated for the experiment]. Shortly after the separation, his wife became severely paranoid, requiring hospitalization. Subsequent treatment included electroshock regression therapy. The treatment reportedly cured her paranoia but destroyed her personality."

Another victim who had been surreptitiously dosed with LSD told the investigators that White, obviously using his training from Mulholland, had poured drinks from 2 pitchers when entertaining.

The VTF's final report describes, somewhat incoherently, an account of a third victim who was dosed with LSD: "Two dinner guests [of the White's at the time of the dosing] remember a 'weird' female guest...[or]...a female becoming ill and leaving with Mrs. White. Mrs. White returned shortly thereafter and abruptly terminated the party.... [The victim's name] has admission records for 1953 but no admission record for [redacted hospital name] near the date indicated [for the experiment]."

Another intriguing "possible victim," according to the VTF report, was an unnamed person who visited the safe house at 81 Bedford Street. The man was contacted by Laubinger but declined to submit to an interview, and refused to have his name revealed or to say why he had visited the safe house. "I'd rather not say," he said. Laubinger noted that this possible experiment took place very close to "the significant event" of Frank Olson's suicide.

On the issue of prostitutes employed by White and Feldman, the report attempts to seriously downplay the use of prostitutes, but then states: "One prostitute, alias [redacted], resided at 225 Chestnut Street [one of the San Francisco safe houses] for a few days with Ike Feldman as part of a cover arrangement while Feldman, White, and others were investigating the Red Ferrari case [a narcotics investigation]."

On the question of safehouses used by White and the CIA, the report reads: "A total of five CIA provided safe houses were used in the CIA/FBN projects." These were located at 81 Bedford Street, New York City; 225 Chestnut Street, San Francisco; 261 Green Street, Mill Valley, Marin County, California; Room 49 in the Plantation Inn at Lombard and Webster Streets, San Francisco; and apartments 5A and 5B in the Greenwich Towers at 105 West 13th Street, New York City. All of the safe houses were equipped with sophisticated sound recording and motion picture equipment, as well as two-way mirrors.

"SUICIDE" IN HOUSTON

In 1978, the VTF produced an intriguing document pertaining to Frank Olson's death. The document concerned the 1954 shooting death of a Houston, Texas detective. The death was ruled a "suicide" despite the fact that the detective was shot twice in the heart. The document, resulting from an interview with a former FBN agent, George Gaffney, reads:

> [redacted name] remembered the LSD provoked suicide by [Frank] Olson and after the recent revelations put 2 and 2 together and suggested the possibility that White had used a drug (possibly LSD) on [the Houston detective] which had similarly provoked his suicide.

Besides the above two seemingly significant mentions of Frank Olson's suicide in the VTF's investigation, Olson's name was not mentioned again in Salmi and Laubinger's reports. However, in a 1983 deposition, Laubinger was questioned about Frank Olson's death. He was asked if Olson's death had occurred as a result of a CIA Technical Services branch project. He answered, "Olson was part of a TSD activity, not a project." [A verbatim transcript of the questioning, not always easy to comprehend, follows below.]

Question: *It wasn't a part of MKULTRA or anything like that?*
Laubinger: I don't know that you could say it was or was not part of MKULTRA. Olson was one of a group of military people who were interested in the same sort of thing. This is my interpretation of it now. I'm part of the tribal knowledge coming out that Gottlieb met with about every six months and occasionally others at Fort Detrick and at one of the meetings of this Fort Detrick group with CIA representatives, LSD was administered in a liquor. So it was, in essence, the experimenters experimenting on themselves. There's a difference. The record is not consistent in terms of whether it was witting or not. There are two points of view on that.
Question: *Is it your opinion from the Olson affair, then, that the Army did have some interest in experimentation with LSD research?*
Laubinger: I think the group that was involved in the Olson incident had very little interest in LSD. I don't think you can—*It's hard for me to really understand why they were involved in this particular experiment at all.* [Italics added.]

They produced hardware-type items for us that were used for any one of a number of things, and the experiment participated in some other experimentation, essentially, subcontractors of ours. What else they did with any of the information, in terms of supporting Army units, I have no idea. I don't think the people at Detrick that we dealt with were primarily interested in LSD.
Question: *Do you think that there was some interest as reflected in the history of the Olson case, as you know it?*
Laubinger: Repeat that, please?
Question: *Do you think, is it your opinion now, that there was some military interest in LSD as reflected by the knowledge you have gained from the Olson case?*

Laubinger: I would be hard-pressed, really, from the Olson case or any of the associations we had with it to try to document or illustrate any real military interest. It could have been. I just don't—

Question: *You never saw, from anything that you saw, a clear military program, project, interest, in LSD that involved the Olson affair?*

Laubinger: As a result of the Olson affair—The Olson affair to me did not indicate any real military interest or involvement in LSD. At any point in time, there were a lot of documents that would circulate on LSD, I mean, put out by USI, whatever; that Army generate one; maybe Navy generate one; these information bulletins that circulate perpetually in the federal government, so that everybody had some interest in it.

Question: *I think you testified earlier, and I just wanted to be sure that it was that you hadn't thought of something else that would change your opinion, that you were really unaware of any military interest or involvement in the experimentation research with LSD?*

Laubinger: That's correct.

Question: *That remains your opinion based on your knowledge?*

Laubinger: Well, in the context that we have been talking about LSD. At one point it was a proposed, the military proposed it as this marvelously humane battlefield weapon. They were going to fill shells with LSD and lob it over and drop it all over the battlefield and everybody would inhale it and troops would come in and you could grab them by the scruff of the neck and take them up to the local detox center and, you know, the war is over. So there was a lot of military involvement in LSD, but in terms of, and obviously from this fellow that took place in Paris or in France somewhere, the, I think, Army Corporal that was subjected to considerable abuse, there was some intelligence in LSD.

In terms of my involvement with any of this, I came across, well, let's see, early on, in the very first part of the exploration [the VTF investigation], the decision to explore drugs in various ways, there was not only, there was a lot; there was foreign interest and there was a military interest. So yes. I can't say they didn't have any interest, but in terms of our programs and the way we were doing it, there was very little in the way of liaison activity with the military.

THE CASE OF JAMES R. THORNWELL: TORTURE AND LSD

The "Army Corporal" in France that Laubinger was referring to is a prime example of the Army's deep interest in LSD and of its use of the drug. In March 1961, James Thornwell, a 22 year-old African American soldier serving as an administrative clerk in France, was accused of stealing two folders containing highly classified documents from an Army communications center. At least one of the folders, according to one former high-ranking Army officer who declined to be named for this book, contained "details and data specific to a certain joint [CIA and Army] project that took place in summer 1951 in Pont-St.-Esprit, France."

Following a brief and disorganized investigation by Army Counter-Intelligence Corps (CIC) agents, Thornwell was singled out as the primary suspect. Thornwell protested and said that he was innocent. He further told CIC investigators that file folders "routinely went missing" and that "eventually lost or misplaced folders showed up on some officer's desk."

Explained Thornwell, provoking anger and disbelief from the CIA agents, "The folders were lost while in the possession of two officers who were notorious for losing or misplacing things."

Thornwell later said that he initially did not take the investigation seriously because he believed that he had been targeted because he was African American and a scapegoat was needed in the interim "until the folders were found." But, days went by and the folders were still missing, and Thornwell was placed into a small cell and held in solitary confinement. Thornwell continued to say that he was innocent. "It didn't help that the two officers I had last seen with the folders didn't care for me at all," he later said.

In a 1981 interview, Thornwell explained, "It's no secret the Army was a really racist place back then. But I didn't think that they would go after me and treat me the way they did. I never thought it would get that bad. Never in a million years. I was wrong."

Within days, Thornwell began receiving beatings from CIC agents. Over time, the beatings became severe. Between the beatings, teams of three CIC interrogators questioned Thornwell for hours on end. Some sessions lasted over ten hours. Thornwell was given no food or water for several days, and then handed only a stale piece of bread and a cup of water.

When he did not respond to his interrogator's questions with the answers they wanted, Thornwell was told that it was only a matter of time before he would be killed.

"One day they told me that French intelligence agents had put a bounty on my head," he said. "They said they [the French] would torture me until I told them where the documents were, and then they'd cut me up into a pile of pieces and feed me to a pack of wild dogs. When I laughed at that, not a really bright thing to do, one of the Army [CIC] guys kicked me in the testicles and said 'Laugh at that, asshole.'"

Thornwell recounted, "On another day they came in and told me that my life was in danger, that my friends wanted to kill me. After that they hypnotized me and were angry about what I had supposedly said while under. They gave me sodium pentothal by needle once to check the results of the hypnosis. Then they told me the French agents were nearby and ready to kill me."

CIC interrogators told Thornwell that French intelligence agents would torture him before they killed him. "They're going to pull your fingernails out," a CIC agent told him.

"Why would they want to do that?" Thornwell asked.

"They want the same documents we want," shouted the CIC agent. "They're going to put you on a rack and cut your penis off."

After about six weeks of this treatment, Thornwell was handed a glass of water to drink. The water contained about 150 micrograms of LSD. After he drank the water, Thornwell thought his head was on fire.

"It felt like my head was growing larger and larger and then exploding. I thought they could see into my head and see all my thoughts."

"Where are the documents? Where are the documents?" his interrogators shouted at him, over and over.

"I don't know," he screamed back. "You have to believe me, I don't know." And then, "I'm dying, my head is on fire. I'm dying, please, please, I don't know, please."

After about seven weeks, Thornwell had "confessed" to whatever his interrogators put before him. He was released, a broken man. A few months later, he was informed that he would be subject to a general court martial, but before that occurred he was discharged from the Army because he was no longer considered fit for duty. Thornwell spent the next few years drifting around the United States, suffering periodic psychological breakdowns and blackouts. In 1981, he said, "I had no life after they gave me that LSD. I had nothing. I lived in a twilight world where nothing was real or important."

James Thornwell did not learn of his being drugged with LSD until 16 years later. When he did, in 1978, he filed a $10 million lawsuit against the Government. By then, Thornwell had been plagued with severe psychiatric disorders and physical pain for years. Congress settled his suit by placing $625,000 in a trust fund for his benefit and providing ongoing medical and psychiatric care.

In 1984, a few years after this author interviewed him for an article then unrelated to this book, Thornwell died of an apparent epileptic seizure while swimming in a pool. He was 46 years old.

Unfortunately, in 1984, this author was unaware of the possible connections between Thornwell's experiences and the Pont-St.-Esprit incident, but Thornwell had said at one point in his interview that he "thought the information [in the folders] had something to do with a special project that took place in France in the early 1950s or around there."

The Army has consistently claimed that James Thornwell was the "only U.S. soldier" ever given LSD. Many individuals from the military, however, including several former Army and Navy officers, disagree with this. "It has happened a lot more times than anybody would like to think or imagine," said one former Army officer.

At the same time that Thornwell had been confined in France, the Army was conducting Operation THIRD CHANCE, an intensive enhanced interrogation project that targeted at least nine foreign nationals who were drugged with LSD during the course of their interrogations. Operation THIRD CHANCE had been developed after extensive consultation with

CIA ARTICHOKE team members, SOD scientists, and Agency Security Office officials.

Laubinger Questioned on the CIA and France

In the same 1983 deposition quoted above, Laubinger was questioned in detail about the CIA's activities in France during the 1950s. Much of this line of questioning concerned the case of a young American artist who had been drugged with LSD in Paris in 1952, but the information that emerged about the Agency and France is, as readers shall see, pertinent to this book's overall investigation and to Frank Olson's death. Readers will also see from this exchange of questions and answers the extreme lengths to which the CIA went in order to obscure information about Agency activities in France.

> Question: *Did the office cover, within its functions, activities in France?*
> [Laubinger had just stated that he had been assigned to Western Europe as a CIA employee in the Technical Service Section (TSS) from about 1958 to about 1959.]
> Laubinger: Yes.
> Question: *How long were you assigned there?*
> Laubinger: That time, two years.
> Question: *Did you have occasion to travel to France?*
> Laubinger: I'm sure I did. I don't recall any details of it or precisely when, but yes.
> Question: *On company business, so to speak?*
> Laubinger: Yes.
> Question: *Did that include Paris?*
> Laubinger: Yes.
> Question: *I will just call it TSD if that seems—*
> Laubinger: That's fine.
> Question: *If we understand each other. Did TSD have an office in Paris at that time?*
> Laubinger: No. Excuse me?
> CIA Attorney: We would object to that question on the grounds of privilege on behalf of the Central Intelligence Agency and would ask that the answer be stricken from the record.
> Question: *Do you know whether TSD had an office in Paris in 1952?*
> CIA Attorney: Again, same objection. I direct the witness not to answer.
> Question: *Without asking you whether the answer is affirmative or negative, do you know whether TSD had an office in Paris—*
> CIA Attorney: You can answer that.
> Laubinger: Yes.
> Question: *—in 1952? Do you know the answer to the question?*

Laubinger: Yes, I do. At least I think I do.

Question: *Do you know whether the office to which you were assigned in this Western European country that you were instructed not to identify had personnel that traveled to France and Paris in 1952, assigned there?*

CIA Attorney: Now, you can say whether or not you know the answer, but do not give the answer itself.

Laubinger: I know the answer to that question.

Question: *Well, you have already told us that while you were stationed in West Europe, 1958-59; is that roughly when it was?*

Laubinger: Yes.

Question: *That you, on occasion, on company business did travel to Paris or France?*

Laubinger: Correct.

Question: *I now ask you whether you know whether people assigned to TSD stationed where you were stationed in 1958-59 made similar trips to Paris and to France in 1952, 1953?*

Laubinger: Yes, I know that.

Question: *And I will ask you whether the answer is they did or they did not.*

CIA Attorney: Again, I have to interpose an objection on behalf of the Central Intelligence Agency and direct the witness not to answer the question.

Question: *Can you tell us why—*

CIA Attorney: Can you excuse me a minute?

(*Whereupon, a discussion ensued off the record.*)

CIA Attorney: Sorry. Was there a question pending or not?

Question: *You still object?*

CIA Attorney: Yes, I do.

Question: *Realizing that you are denying us information from him as to whether TSD had people in Paris in October-November 1952?*

CIA Attorney: Yes. I understand what the question was.

Laubinger: Let me just add to my last question in the sense that you sharpened the question to October-November '52, I have no idea. I don't know the answer to that question.

Question: *Sure.*

Question: *You don't know when they may have traveled, if they did?*

Laubinger: That's correct.

Question: *But in a way, your answer has made us assume that they did travel there, because if you didn't know what months, you must have assumed they were traveling at some time, but that is just logic. Let me ask you whether TSD personnel—*

CIA Attorney: Can we break a moment, please? I want to speak to Mr. Laubinger for a second.

(*Whereupon, a discussion ensued off the record.*)

CIA Attorney: Can we go back on the record? I was just querying Mr. Laubinger about whether, if fact, to make sure that he understood the time frame of your last series of questions, about whether or not he knew people had traveled to France from somewhere else in Western Europe in 1952 and '53. My understanding from my conversation with him outside was I believe he misunderstood your question. I will ask Mr. Laubinger to explain.

Laubinger: I thought you were referring to during my tour in Europe, if I knew anybody had traveled there, and I explained that I did. I had the answer to that question, but I certainly do not have the answer to that question in terms of the time frame 1953 or during time I was in the Far East. [Laubinger had been in the Far East prior to going to Europe.] So I had assumed, since we were talking about my tour in Europe and then had I traveled to Paris and had anyone else, that I know the answer to, but in terms of '53 to '56, I do not.

Question: *Well, let me ask you whether you presently have knowledge from any source, whenever you may have acquired it, as to whether TSD had personnel traveling to Paris and France in 1952 and 1953 on company business.*

Laubinger: We have done a lot of research for this case and I know, checking people's travel records and this sort of thing, so that I think we have documented some travel to Paris. I don't recall that I know any TSD people traveling to Paris. If you ask me do I know they did, no, I do not know they did.

Question: *From any point, Washington or any city in West Europe or anywhere?*

Laubinger: That's correct.

Question: *Are you saying, then, that you have never seen any financial or other records that reflect TSD personnel travel to or through Paris in 1952-1953?*

Laubinger: *To the best of my recollection, I cannot say I have never seen anything like that. I do not recall seeing anything like that.*

Question: *In 1958 and 1959, the office in West Europe to which you were assigned did have TSD personal who traveled to –*

Laubinger: Right.

Question: *– Paris, during that period.*

CIA Attorney: I think the question was asked earlier, and we –

Question: It was asked and answered.

CIA Attorney: – we objected. Well, no, what his answer was that Mr. Laubinger knows whether or not people in '58 and '59 traveled to Paris.

Question: *He testified that he himself traveled.*

CIA Attorney: I understand that. We are talking aside from himself. We objected to that question and directed the witness not to answer, and I will do so again.

Question: *Have you withdrawn your objection to knowledge he might have of travel in 1952 and 1953?*

CIA Attorney: No, I haven't, but I wanted to make it clear for the record that he had misunderstood your earlier question and doesn't have that knowledge. I mean, I don't object to him telling you whether or not he knows, and I believe he told you that he doesn't know as to '52 and '53. But if he did know, I would object to him telling you what the answer is, but I don't think we get to that second step for '52 and '53.

Question: [To Laubinger.] *Do you know whether there was travel from the office in West Europe to which you were assigned to Paris in addition to your own travel to Paris during the period that you were assigned there, 1958 and 1959?*

CIA Attorney: You can answer whether or not you know.

Laubinger: *I'm just trying to think how best to answer it. I'm afraid it would, any answer I have in the affirmative, would be presumptive. I do not know for an absolute fact in the sense that I cannot, in my own mind, decide, you know, a name or a person or a subject matter that they might have gone to Paris on.*

Question: *How many times did you go there?*

Laubinger: I have no idea.

Question: *Would it be —*

Laubinger: Not many.

Question: *— half a dozen?*

Laubinger: Not that many.

Question: *Three or four?*

Laubinger: That sounds likely.

Question: *How long did you stay there on those trips?*

Laubinger: *A question of meeting people; whether they were on time for appointments or late; if they were there. I went there to consult, usually for three days.*

12

Fall 1984

I am so relieved to see that you don't have a gun.
— Sidney Gottlieb, 1984

In the late fall of 1984, Alice, Eric and Nils Olson decided to visit both Sidney Gottlieb and Robert Lashbrook. Says Eric, "They were two of the very last people to see my father alive and the feeling was that their recollections, if they were willing to share them with us, would make the story of what had happened to my father easier to reckon with, to possibly accept." The Olsons met first with Lashbrook at his home in Ojai, California, where he had been teaching chemistry in a local high school. Ojai is a small, upscale community east of Santa Barbara that has been home to many celebrities, including Anthony Hopkins, Johnny Cash, and Jerry Bruckheimer, and served as the setting for the hit television show, *The Six Million Dollar Man*.

Eric Olson recalls, "The thing that struck us all the most powerfully was Lashbrook's incredible nervousness." Eric described the former CIA officer as a "nervous wreck" for the entire two hours they spent with him.

> He sat in a rocking chair and bobbed up and down like a jack-in-the-box, pushing himself up on his forearms, and then down again. He spoke in a jerky, unconnected manner, seeming to hold much back and then suddenly spitting things out as if they were being pushed from behind by a damned up reservoir of enormous volume.

In the course of Lashbrook's nervous blurting to the Olson's, some odd and contradictory information emerged. Whether or not this was the result of a faulty or lapsed memory, old age, guilt, or extreme nervousness is anyone's guess.

Eric recounted that he, Nils and Alice were stunned when Lashbrook said a number of times that Sidney Gottlieb had been present in New York with him, Ruwet, and Olson. Reflected Eric, Lashbrook was:

> Apparently forgetting the cover story, but he said repeatedly that Gottlieb had been there. He said he couldn't remember exactly how long Gottlieb had been there, but he thought it was most if not all of the time. He said that he and Gottlieb and my father had had dinner at the Statler on the night my father died.

On the face of it, it does seem to contradict numerous, formerly classified documents never intended for public viewing, and several dozen pages of testimony given by Lashbrook in civil suit depositions. There is also the fact that at least six CIA officials met with Gottlieb in Washington, D.C. about four hours after Olson's death. With Lashbrook and Gottlieb now dead we will never know for sure, and had it been the case, in the author's view, it does not seem to add anything significant to the overall story.

Eric Olson's opinion, however, is different. In his view, the presence of Gottlieb "obviously contradicted a key part of the story." Explained Eric, "It made immediate sense to me, as I had been totally unconvinced when Gottlieb himself [two weeks later] told me that he had been in Washington all that week, basically going about business as usual, having only occasional phone contact with Lashbrook. It also made sense that Gottlieb would want first-hand contact with a situation of such sensitivity as that unfolding in New York."

Far more intriguing, in this author's view, is Lashbrook's account of how Frank Olson was acting after he returned to Washington for the aborted Thanksgiving dinner with his family. According to Eric, Lashbrook said that while Frank Olson was in his (Lashbrook's) apartment waiting to return to New York, he "was acting very bizarrely."

Lashbrook recalled that Olson was "standing on his head" in the corner of his living room and "then doing somersaults on the living room carpet." Eric said, "Lashbrook explained this with such candor that I am very nearly persuaded that it was true, perhaps the consequence of whatever drugging my father was receiving in New York."

Added Eric, "How a man who was making somersaults on the carpet on Thursday could possibly have made the calm, reassuring call to my mother that Frank made on Friday is, of course, a problem in this story, one that I wish my mother would have had the presence of mind to ask."

That Alice had even accompanied Eric and Nils to this interview with Lashbrook was, in itself, a tribute to her fortitude. Eric recalled that "she was really a wreck during this whole experience herself, and after we left Lashbrook's house, and the next morning as well, she was vomiting violently. The whole experience made her sick."

In a 1986 civil suit deposition, plaintiff's attorney Joseph Rauh asked Lashbrook about the Olson's visit to his home in Ojai, California:

Question: *When did you talk to Mrs. Olson?*
Lashbrook: Couple years ago.
Question: *What do you remember about your conversation with Mrs. Olson?*
Lashbrook: Just talk. She was interested in what I remembered, and I told her what I remembered.
Question: *You told her about the LSD then?*

Lashbrook: Sure.

Question: *Can you remember exactly when this was?*

Lashbrook: Exactly when?

Question: *Yes.*

Lashbrook: No. A couple years ago.

Question: *Where was it?*

Lashbrook: My home. She visited me. She and her two sons.

Question: *What did she say was her reason for visiting you?*

Lashbrook: General interest, I think. A number of points that had been bothering her which she was hoping to clear up.

Question: *What were the points that had been bothering her which she was hoping to clear up?*

Lashbrook: I don't recall.

Question: *You can't recall it two years ago?*

Lashbrook: I think that would be personal, and anyway, I don't recall specifically. We talked a long time.

Question: *Are you refusing to tell me? There is no privilege that could possibly– are you refusing?*

Lashbrook: I'm saying I can't think of an answer to your question, no.

Question: *You won't say one word about that question?*

Lashbrook: I already said it was a general conversation. I don't know that she told me specific things one, two, three, but there were general things that had been bothering her.

Question: *Could you tell me what those general things that bothered her were?*

Lashbrook: I don't know that she ever told me.

Question: *You had a long conversation, and all you can remember is there were general things that bothered her, but she didn't tell you what they were; is that right?*

Lashbrook: I recounted everything that I recalled to her and answered questions she might have, yes.

Question: *Answered what?*

Lashbrook: And answered questions that she might have, or her sons.

Question: *What were the questions?*

Lashbrook: Many of them, millions.

Question: *Well, state one. We'll start with any one.*

Lashbrook: I think you're being ridiculous.

Question: *That is not the point. You have to answer the questions.*

Lashbrook: Look, I had a conversation with the woman. So what?

Mr. Kragie [CIA attorney]: Mr. Lashbrook, to the best of your recollection, do you recall any specific questions that she asked you? Obviously they dealt with the death of her husband. Do you recall anything more specific about her questions?

Lashbrook: Okay. Maybe one question was did I feel Dr. Abramson was a competent doctor?

Question [by Rauh]: *What did you say to that?*

Lashbrook: And I said, to the best of my knowledge, yes, he was. She said that she tried to get in touch with Dr. Abramson many times—several times, anyway, and she had been very put out with Dr. Abramson.

I don't know why he should have been rude to her, but apparently he was, and apparently that bothered her a great deal. She had the idea that he wasn't very competent. I've heard that idea before. I suspect that the idea originated with her and it has been repeated from there.

Question: *That's one question. You said there was a number of questions Can you remember another question?*

Lashbrook: No. That came to mind, and that's the type of thing that she explained, that she and her sons had been bothered for many years with things like that.

Question: *But at this moment you cannot remember any questions except whether Dr. Abramson was competent?*

Lashbrook: Yes.

Question: *Is that right?*

Lashbrook: Yes.

In a 1988 civil suit deposition, Alice Olson briefly recalled the visit to Lashbrook's home, as well as the visit to Gottlieb, in a line of questioning by a government defense attorney:

Question: *I understand you went to see or saw Mr. Lashbrook some time in the last ten years, is that correct?*

Alice Olson: Um-hum.

Question: *When was that?*

Alice Olson: I think it was fall of '85, excuse me, around Christmas time.

Question: *Why did you go to see him?*

Alice Olson: Wanted to talk to him, find out what had happened, confront him. This thing has haunted my children for 20 years, 25, 30 years.

Question: *What did Dr. Lashbrook tell you?*

Alice Olson: Not anything new. He was very, very nervous, very apprehensive seeing us. He was very polite. He was very gracious. He was very uncomfortable. We had reason to suspect that somebody had shoved Frank out the window, and that has always been a suspicion and we confronted him with it. And he gave us assurances that this had not happened, that he knew nothing about such a thing. I don't know that we learned any more than we knew before, but at least we had eyeballed him and told him what we had suspected.

Question: *Anything else discussed during that conversation?*

Alice Olson: It was a conversation that went on for four or five hours, and we told him about a telephone call which we had received from a man who had been with Frank on the ground when he landed.

He ran out. He was the night clerk at the hotel. [This was Armond Pastore.] He had called me to tell me he had called a priest and that Frank had mumbled some unintelligible things. This was the first time that I had even thought that he was alive when he hit the ground, and we gave him that kind of information, talked about that. But I don't believe he gave us— we asked him questions.

Question: *Why did he tell you he had not told you about the LSD when he came to see you after your husband's death?*

Alice Olson: We didn't ask him why he hadn't told us. Everybody was under orders not to tell the family anything. It was an unnecessary question.

Question: *When did you see Dr. Gottlieb in the last ten years?*

Alice Olson: A couple of weeks after we saw Lashbrook. As soon as we called Lashbrook to tell him we were coming, he called Gottlieb and said that we were coming, and they had conversations about what we were going to do and what we were like and what kind of agenda we had.

So when I called Dr. Gottlieb and said I would like to talk to you, he said, well, he was anticipating a phone call.

Question: *Was that also out in California?*

Alice Olson: No, we went down to Virginia where he lives now.

Question: *What did Dr. Gottlieb tell you?*

Alice Olson: We told him our same suspicion. Talked to him a little bit about his background, how he had gotten into the CIA, what kind of thoughts he had experimenting on people, talked about his previous experiences with LSD, he told us about some students he had given LSD to, and there was some kind of remuneration, I don't know exactly what it was. And he said they all laughed and carried on while they were receiving LSD, but nobody ever volunteered to come back for another trip, which he noted. I was particularly— he told us what had happened to him after he burned the files and left the country.

The Olsons had met with Sidney Gottlieb, about two weeks after their visit with Lashbrook, at his home in Boston, Virginia, situated in the foothills of the Blue Ridge Mountains. Gottlieb and his wife lived in a 6,000 square-foot modern, solar-heated house with a swimming pool, designed by the couple and situated on about fifty-acres at the end of a long dirt lane called Turkey Ridge Road. The Gottlieb's were well liked by everyone in Boston, and Sidney was respected as a highly skilled speech therapist who had helped many young people overcome serious impediments.

Eric recalls that after they knocked on Gottlieb's door, Gottlieb answered almost immediately. "He stood there, lean, wiry, reminding me very much of Paul Newman," Eric says.

Gottlieb stood silently for a moment looking at the Olsons, and then he said, "I am so relieved to see that you don't have a gun."

Eric says he, Nils and his mother were speechless. Gottlieb explained, "I had a dream last night in which I opened this same door and you pulled a gun and shot me."

The Olsons were flabbergasted. Eric fumbled for a reply, saying, "We didn't come here to harm you or anyone. We only want to talk with you and to ask you a few questions about my father." Eric says he looked at his mother and saw that she had turned ghostly pale.

Later he told this author, "So the master of mind control had done it again. Before we were even in the door he had disarmed us and taken control— we were already apologizing to him for any suspicions he might have."

Some of Gottlieb's friends and neighbors take exception to this view. It has been reported that locals in the town of Boston thought of the former CIA official as nothing more than an "aging hippie," but this is far from the truth, according to those who knew the Gottliebs well. Said one of their closest neighbors, "This entire area, for several towns all around us, is comprised of a lot of former intelligence people, retirees who knew each other well when they were all in the game together. Sidney was an eclectic character in some ways, but hippie? No way."

Others say, "It was Sid's way to be honest about his feelings and thoughts. He was a compassionate, introspective man; he cared a lot about the important things in life. He's never been the monster he's painted out to be. The media always needs a bad guy, somebody to demonize regardless the real truth. Sid was it when all the turmoil in the mid-Seventies arrived."

Perhaps nobody knew this better than Gottlieb's old boss, Richard Helms. Said Helms, before his recent death, "Sidney was treated very unfairly. He's not the only one, but he's at the top of the list."

After Gottlieb invited the Olsons into his house, his wife, Margaret, made a brief appearance for a few minutes, quickly establishing a rapport with Alice Olson. Both their fathers had been Congregational ministers and missionaries in Asia, at different times and places, but the coincidence provided for friendly small talk. Eric recalls that Mrs. Gottlieb "seemed a little stressed by the whole occasion," but was very friendly, and her brief presence seemed to put his mother somewhat at ease.

After Margaret Gottlieb excused herself, her husband asked the Olsons to join him in the living room.

Eric recounts that, "After we were all seated, Gottlieb proceeded to tell us his version of what had happened at Deep Creek Lake.

"We wanted to know what would happen if a scientist were taken prisoner and drugged," explained Gottlieb. "Would he divulge secret research and information? And, if so, would he speak coherently enough that the valuable scientific information would come through intact."

Eric and Nils were not satisfied with Gottlieb's answers and explanations. Alice listened with little reaction. She had called Gottlieb to arrange the meeting two weeks beforehand and found it extremely difficult to talk to and be in the presence of the man she had come to blame mostly for her husband's death.

Eric says he "pressed Gottlieb in many different ways, trying to point out some of the ways in which the overall story of my father's death did not make sense, but every time I took that tact he went immediately on the offense."

"Look," said Gottlieb to Eric, "if you don't believe me, there is no reason for you to be here. There is no reason for me to tell you anything. I agreed to meet with you to tell you what I know."

When Eric continued to press, Gottlieb said, "Your father and I went into this type of work because we were patriotic. We cared about our country and its survival in the face of aggressive Communism." Eric recalls that Gottlieb was both skillful and charming in the way "he tried to paint himself as exactly like my father."

Gottlieb paused, and then added, "Maybe we both went too far."

Eric remained dissatisfied with Gottlieb's explanations, which tracked the vague story laid out in the Colby documents. Eric was unable to get Gottlieb to say anything he considered significant.

At the end of their meeting with the former TSS chief, Gottlieb walked them to the door, and, looking at Eric said, "Look, you are obviously very troubled by your father's suicide. Have you ever considered getting into a therapy group for people whose parents have committed suicide?"

Says Eric decades after the meeting,

> I didn't have the confidence then in my skepticism to ignore his ploys, but when he made the therapy group suggestion— that was the moment in which he overplayed his hand. Whatever my father's death was, it was certainly no ordinary suicide. Gottlieb's effort to put me out of the play became fully transparent at that point. I didn't realize it until later, but I eventually knew that it had been exactly at that moment that I understood how much Gottlieb had at stake in defusing me. And it was also at that moment that the determination to show that he had played a hand in murdering my father was born.

BOOK FIVE
1994-2005

1

September 28, 1994*
United States House of Representatives,

This Bill represents an apology from the American people for what our family has suffered. If you compromise an apology, you don't have an apology.
— Alice Wicks Olson, 1977

M r. Chairman, members of the Committee, my name is Eric W. Olson, and I want to begin by thanking you for inviting me to come here and speak about my family's experience with U.S. government testing on unwitting subjects, which begins more than forty years ago.

In November 1953, my father, Dr. Frank Olson, was given a dose of LSD, without his knowledge and without his consent in an after-dinner drink. This bizarre incident occurred during a meeting of Camp Detrick scientists, organized by Dr. Sidney Gottlieb, who at that time was in the early stages of what became a very long program of mind-manipulation research at the CIA.

At the time of that strange meeting, which one hesitates to call "scientific" even though it was organized by and for a small group of scientists, my mother was still a young woman. She was thirty-eight years old. I was nine, my sister was seven, and my brother was five.

Nine days after that meeting at Deep Creek Lake, in the pre-dawn morning hours of November 28, 1953, which was the Saturday after Thanksgiving, I was awakened to be told that my father was dead. I was told that he died from a fall out of the window of a New York hotel room.

For me, on that pre-dawn morning it was as if the lights went out. I could not understand what I had been told. I remember seeing my mother sitting on the sofa across from me, motionless, with a frozen expression on her face. I remember an overwhelming feeling of isolation, a crushing sensation that the world in which I had been living was suddenly gone forever.

Our family did not know what hit us. We did not know that my father had been the subject of an experiment. We did not know why he had been suddenly whisked away to New York to get some kind of psychiatric help—if that was indeed the purpose of his visits to a CIA consultant named Harold Abramson.

We did not learn these things for twenty-two years, until 1975; and even then we learned them by accident. On June 11 of 1975—one day after my mother was told by her doctor that she had cancer—the *Washington Post* reported that an unnamed scientist had plunged to his death in 1953 after being drugged with LSD by the CIA. We deduced that this unnamed scientist must be my father. Eventually Vincent Ruwet, one of my father's colleagues, confirmed for us that this was in fact the case. But we were never officially notified by either the Rockefeller Commission, in whose report this story first appeared, or by the CIA, whose failure to contact us rendered that agency's subsequent apology rather empty in our ears. It was as if a body long missing in action had at last been found, but the family was not notified.

Later that summer we were invited to the White House to receive a formal apology from President Gerald Ford. And we received from William Colby a set of heavily censored documents, which he assured us contained everything the CIA had on this case.

White House attorneys helped our lawyers draft a bill that would compensate our family financially for my father's death and for the twenty-two year cover-up that followed it. After months of discussion, with participation by the White House, the CIA, the Justice Department, the Treasury Department, and the Labor Department, we arrived at an agreement, supported by all these agencies, with which we were satisfied. White House attorneys assured us that Congress was overwhelmingly in favor of the bill, and that it would face no serious opposition.

On the day of the vote, however, we discovered that a single congressman opposed the bill. We were also informed that private bills require unanimous support, and that due to the opposition of this congressman, the bill could not pass. This individual later agreed to support the bill only if the proposed financial amount, carefully negotiated over many months, were cut by forty percent.

We had no choice but to accept the terms dictated by this individual, even though the makeshift quality of this emergency compromise deprived us of a feeling of integrity in the settlement process. I remember my mother's comment to this congressman, who had refused even to meet with us. My mother said, "This bill represents an apology from the American people for what our family has suffered. If you compromise an apology you don't have an apology." And I remember too this congressman's response to my mother: "Oh, Mrs. Olson, I would never want to compromise your pain or suffering."

No one ever did compromise my mother's pain or suffering: she had it full measure. She bore her burdens with great dignity, but she paid a heavy price. She never remarried. After my father died my mother maintained her public stance in the community as a woman of great, almost incredible, strength. But privately she began a twenty-year descent into alcoholism from which, after repeated hospitalizations, she only narrowly escaped with her life.

My mother's serious drinking began shortly after my father's death. At the time of day when my father would normally have been returning home from work, one of my father's colleagues began coming to our house, to have a drink with my mother. In 1975, we learned from the documents we received from William Colby that this colleague had been directed by the CIA to "keep track of the wife." Unfortunately, "keeping track" did not include telling my mother the truth.

My brother, sister, and I grew up in a home from which our father had inexplicably vanished, and in which our mother was gradually becoming severely alcoholic. On the surface, we lived a remarkably normal life; most of the pain was hidden from those who knew us and from ourselves.

My father's death affected each of the members of my family differently. For all of us, though, there was a feeling of shame—shame not only that out father had vanished, had perhaps committed some inexplicable kind of suicide, but shame especially because we didn't know how to speak about his death; that we had no idea what to say to our friends. My brother, sister, and I used to dread the moment when anyone would ask us how our father died. We eventually learned to reply to such questions by saying that out father had died of a nervous breakdown—though we had no idea what that might mean.

It is easier for me to speak about my own reactions than about those of my brother and sister. I was nine years old when my father vanished—a delicate age when interruptions to the logic of cause and effect can have a crushing impact on one's confidence that the world is a reasonable place, and that one can trust people and events.

My son, who is here with me today, will never know his grandfather. I have to try to explain to him why, just as my brother has to explain this to his children. My sister, her husband and their two-year old child were all killed in an airplane crash in 1978, while flying to upstate New York to consider an investment of their share of the money we received in the settlement of my father's case.

The best way in which I can convey the depth of impact which the revelations of 1975, and the settlement we made with the government, made upon me is that, beginning in the late 1970's, after finishing my Ph.D. at Harvard, I spent nearly a decade and a half living outside the United States. I moved to Sweden to live in the country from which my father's parents had emigrated as optimistic immigrants to the United States in the 1890's. I relate these things to stress the way in which an incident like this reverberates for decades through the generations of a family and its close friends.

During the last year of his life, my father spoke of wanting to leave his job in bacteriological warfare research, and reeducate himself as a dentist. Dentistry is, in fact, the profession my brother has taken up. I suspect that the atmosphere of eerie silence in our family around my father's death strongly influenced my sister's decision to become a speech therapist, and to teach deaf children to speak. I know that it determined my decision to become a psychologist, as well as the particular path I followed within that discipline.

When I started graduate school in psychology in the early 1970's, I was still strongly motivated by the need to understand what had happened to my father and the consequences of this loss for the history of my family. I chose to work with the well-known psychiatrist Robert Jay Lifton at Yale, the sequence of whose research comprised a virtual curriculum in the issues raised by my father's death. Lifton's early work concerned the psychology of brainwashing. Later, he studied the psychology of survivors of massive trauma, identity-formation without the father, and the psychology of weapons scientists. In more recent work he has concentrated on the motivations of Nazi doctors who performed immoral experiments on human subjects in the Nazi death camps.

After World War II, in a project known as "Operation Paperclip," many of those Nazi scientists were in fact recruited by the American military to work side-by-side with American scientists preparing the experiments whose effects we are considering today. This fact helps us to understand that, in other circumstances, the perpetrators of these acts would not be enjoying their retirements: *they would be prosecuted as war criminals*.

How did my father die? Sadly, I believe that we still don't know for sure.

For a brief moment in 1975 I thought the lights had been turned on again. Unfortunately, the feeling of illumination did not endure. In the years after 1975, my brother and I became increasingly convinced that we still did not know the truth about what had happened to my father.

In fact, I believe we cannot be certain about anything concerning my father's death, except that he died just outside the Statler Hotel in New York City (or was it in the hotel room itself?), after falling some thirteen stories from the room he shared with Dr. Robert Lashbrook, who was Sidney Gottlieb's associate at the CIA.

The documents we received from the CIA in 1975 are so riddled with contradictions, omissions, and outright lies that it is difficult to have any confidence in them at all. The documents that would have been really informative were almost certainly shredded by Sidney Gottlieb when he retired from the CIA in 1975 [sic: it was 1973]. What we have are remains of the cover-up within the CIA itself, that began immediately after my father's death. *Over the past two decades my brother and I have become increasingly convinced that, in fact, my father was murdered.*

In June of this year we had his body exhumed so that a full-scale autopsy—blocked by the CIA in 1953—could now be performed. For the first time in forty-one years my brother and I saw my father's body, which was remarkably intact. No one in my family had ever seen my father's body after he died. At the funeral, the casket was closed, because my mother had been told that my father's body was so maimed that we would not want to see it. Now, in its mummified state, we discovered that this had not been true. Even that bit of consolation had been denied us.

Professor James Starrs of the George Washington University National Law Center is now overseeing an exhaustive investigation of my father's remains.

600

Professor Starrs' findings will be reported in a press conference to be held in late November, on the anniversary of my father's death. Professor Starrs' forensic investigation is not yet complete, but its preliminary results, which increasingly point toward the likelihood of homicide, are tending to confirm our most dire suspicions.

Meanwhile, I have managed to locate a former CIA employee who worked in Gottlieb's small group during the years after my father's death. This source has confirmed that the members of that small group all believed that my father was murdered.

My father's case—still unresolved after four decades—illustrates what can happen when civil liberties are violated in the name of national security research. Once one starts on the dangerous path of poisoning one's own citizens in order to protect them, one enters a zone of lunacy, where anything is possible, where sadists can disguise their maliciousness as patriotic duty.

In such a situation, any experiment, if it goes awry, can quickly become a risk to the careers of the experimenters themselves. The path from experimental mind-manipulation to murder may then be a short one, for how else can one guarantee the security of an immoral research program in which one's fellow citizens are used as guinea pigs?

My brother and I can only hope that our father's case, and our family's experience, remain a lesson in the risks posed to a free society by pretentious pseudo-science, self-serving secrecy, and bureaucratic arrogance. Thank you.

*Testimony of Eric Wicks Olson before the Committee on Government Operations, Oversight Hearing on Cold War Era Human Subject Experimentation, Legislative and National Security Subcommittee, U.S. House of Representatives, John Conyers, Chairman, September 28, 1994.

2

The Starrs Investigation

In the years following Frank Olson's death, the small town of Frederick was transformed into Maryland's second largest city. By the mid-1950s, a little over a decade after the establishment of Camp Detrick, nearly half the large farms that surrounded Frederick had been swallowed up by developers eager to erect bedroom communities for the seemingly endless number of families wanting to move to the area. The Interstate road system, begun in 1956, greatly accelerated residential and commercial growth over the next twenty years.

At the same time, Fort Detrick (the installation had been designated a "fort" in 1956) was significantly expanding its programs. Beginning in 1958, the Army undertook several huge construction projects on the 1,300-acre Fort Detrick site. Chief among them was a sprawling multi-million dollar laboratory complex that focused exclusively on genetics research, or what insiders called "Special Operations X." By the mid-1960s, Fort Detrick had solidly established itself as the region's largest employer, with nearly 3,000 civilian workers and hundreds more enlisted personnel. In all, the installation pumped about $30 million a year into Frederick's economy. Life was good in the bustling city that managed to maintain all the finer amenities of urban living without many of its ills.

Beginning in 1959 and the early 1960s, Fort Detrick became the target of intense demonstrations against biological warfare. The first demonstration, a wholly new phenomenon to Frederick, was held by a group of peace activists led by Larry Scott, a well-known and respected pacifist who later helped found the Washington Peace Center. Another protest, organized by a Quaker group, lasted almost two years and involved over 1,000 picketers, none of whom lived in Frederick. The demonstration was so well organized that fresh teams of picketers were trucked in daily with signs and box lunches in hand. Beginning in 1961 and for about a year, a group of about sixty protestors, seeking an "end to biological warfare research," maintained a twenty-four hour vigil at the fort's front gates. By the mid-1960s, the tableau of picketers at the gates had become so calcified that when Detrick's guards changed, if no protestors were in sight, security became even tighter than before. Demonstrations calling for an end to chemical and biological warfare research continued well into 1968 at Fort Detrick, and after many years, they began at last to receive some very serious attention.

In 1969, U.S. Representative Richard D. McCarthy, a Democrat and former newspaper reporter from Buffalo, New York, mounted a congressional investigation into the nation's chemical and biological warfare (CBW) programs. McCarthy was especially critical of Fort Detrick's operations, claiming that between 1954 and 1962 there had been over 3,000 accidents, some fatal, at the Frederick complex. Remarkably, almost none of these accidents were common knowledge in the Frederick area. For years there had been an unspoken, unwritten bond that prevented Fort Detrick employees and their families from discussing anything that occurred behind the facility's fences. Alice Olson, as well as other "Detrick wives," sensed that there had been serious accidents over the years. In 1987, she said, "The men were always getting shots. I knew about one death. Frank went to the funeral." Alice said she had asked Frank, "What did he die of?" Frank had told her pneumonia. "I said, you liar," Alice recalled. "I knew if he hadn't died of a classified disease Frank would not have gone."

Ironically, Congressman McCarthy had first become interested in the Army's CBW program after watching an NBC television program one evening in February 1969. The one-hour special featured vivid segments on animal testing, including the horrific results of one Army aerosol experiment gone awry. This incident had taken place about a year earlier, at the Army's massive Dugway, Utah testing site. There, winds had carried over 300 gallons of lethal nerve gas high into the atmosphere during secret tests. Heavy rains fell shortly thereafter, bringing the gases down twenty-seven miles away into Skull Valley, a high desert area where thousands of sheep grazed. Within hours, the sheep were staggering about in a dazed, painful agony. Soon, the bodies of nearly 7,000 dead sheep were scattered across the desert. At first, the Army told ranchers, state health officials, and Utah's governor that no lethal weapons had been tested. After reluctantly admitting that tests had been performed, the Army still gave Utah officials fake and misleading information about the gas tested.

McCarthy's wife was so shocked by what she saw on the program that, even before it was over, she turned to him and said, "You're a Congressman. What do you know about this?"

"Nothing," McCarthy answered.

But, later, wrote McCarthy, "my interest and indignation climbed as I continued to watch the story unfold; indignation because I realized that I had undoubtedly voted funds for this kind of activity but which, apparently, were buried in other appropriation bills." McCarthy quickly learned that he wasn't the only member of the House or Senate who was not knowledgeable about what was going on with CBW programs. Only five House Appropriations Committee members were cleared to know "top secret" information, McCarthy discovered. They were the same five members who dealt with CIA funding and programs and, as McCarthy was amazed to learn, even House Majority leader Carl Albert didn't know their identities.

In the fall of 1969, having established himself as a leading critic of CBW, Congressman McCarthy enlisted nearly one hundred House members as cosponsors of legislation that required President Richard Nixon to resubmit the

Geneva Protocol to the Senate for ratification. The Protocol bans its signatories from "the first use of chemical and biological methods of warfare." As a result of McCarthy's actions, the Subcommittee on National Security and Scientific Developments of the House Committee on Foreign Affairs undertook a series of hearings on chemical and biological warfare programs. The hearings ran through November and December 1969, generating thousands of pages of testimony and background materials. In the course of its hearings, the subcommittee unearthed a considerable amount of information about Fort Detrick, including the fact that at least 31 employees at the Frederick site had contracted anthrax, resulting in at least two deaths.

Nothing surfaced about Frank Olson's death, or about Fort Detrick's work with LSD, or the SOD's relationship with the CIA. However, McCarthy did stumble across the fact that the military was manufacturing large quantities of BZ, the powerful hallucinogen which, he was informed, produced "symptoms very much like those of a person after a dose of LSD." A former employee of the Army's Pine Bluff Arsenal in Arkansas, where large amounts of BZ were manufactured, told McCarthy that when production workers and engineers would accidentally get a whiff of BZ, they would sometimes be "placed in a padded cell with their hands manacled," until the effects wore off.

In a 1999 interview with Dr. Sidney Gottlieb, the author asked if Congressman McCarthy's activities or those of the subcommittee had been of any concern to the CIA. "Of course, there was some consternation about the hearings uncovering certain things," Gottlieb said, "but, if I recall correctly, the investigation was more contemporaneously focused."

McCarthy's activities quickly gained the serious attention of high-ranking officials in the Nixon administration. On April 30, 1969, Secretary of Defense Melvin Laird wrote Nixon a brief memo stating that it "is clear the Administration is going to be under increasing fire as a result of numerous inquiries [into CBW programs], the more notable being Congressman McCarthy's and Senator Fulbright's."

On Veteran's Day, November 11, 1969, Richard Nixon announced that he was about to submit to Congress legislation banning the offensive use of chemical and biological weapons. On November 25, Nixon told a congressional leadership group that he would submit the Geneva Protocol of 1925 to the Senate "for its advice and consent to ratification." In addition, Nixon renounced the use of lethal and incapacitating biological warfare weapons. Nixon said that the United States would confine itself only to defensive measures such as immunization programs. Declassified "talking points" for Nixon's congressional meeting reveal that the decision-making process leading to Nixon's announcements had included detailed briefings from CIA director Richard Helms. Helms reportedly did not support the ban on the use of incapacitating CBW agents, but did not speak against it.

Frederick, Maryland was jolted by Nixon's announcements. Immediately, predictions of massive layoffs spread throughout the community. Elected officials worried that the President's actions would decimate the local economy. Alice Olson, at the time, told a friend, "I'm afraid that a lot of families might get hurt, but maybe it's all for the best."

The panic in Frederick proved to be overblown. There were no massive lay-offs, and the President's decision ultimately had little impact on the city. On October 19, 1971, Nixon visited Fort Detrick. Flown in by helicopter, with several grinning congressmen, Nixon announced to a selected audience that he was authorizing construction of the Frederick Cancer Research Facility of the National Cancer Institute on the grounds of Fort Detrick. The new facility would take up nearly seventy acres and seventy-five buildings of the compound. By the end of 1975, ownership of the acreage and buildings was transferred from the Army to the U.S. Department of Health and Human Services' National Institutes of Health. By the early 1990s, the facility had been renamed the National Cancer Institute at Frederick and employed nearly three thousand scientists.

JUNE 2, 1994, FREDERICK MEMORIAL PARK CEMETERY, MARYLAND

June 2, 1994 was a picture perfect day in Frederick, Maryland. The sky was gloriously blue, the sun shining brightly with promises of a warm summer. In Frederick Memorial Park Cemetery, the sounds of picks and shovels shattered the normal calm of the graveyard. Nearby, hovering expectantly under tall shade trees, were photographers, television cameramen and reporters, all waiting for the exhumation of the vault containing Frank Olson's body.

Alice Olson had died less than a year before, on August 19, 1993. Her cancer, beaten into remission in 1976, had returned with a vengeance. The second time around she had not had the strength to fight as before. Observed one of her closest friends, "She had used up every reserve she had. Alice was strong beyond belief, but not strong enough to beat her disease yet again." Shortly after the Olsons had received their government settlement, Lisa and Greg Hayward had also died. The Hayward's, along with their two-year old son, Jonathan, were killed on March 19, 1978, when a small private airplane they were traveling in encountered a blinding snowstorm and flew into the dense and rocky Adirondack Mountains outside Lake Placid, New York. Lisa was four months pregnant when she died. Once again, Alice had stood stiffly in a Frederick church for a family funeral. Cruelly reminiscent of Frank's service, caskets were closed due to massive injuries. Friends worried that the deaths of the Hayward family would push Alice back toward her dependence on alcohol, but she stayed resolute and sober.

Several months after Alice's death, Eric and Nils Olson had contacted James E. Starrs, a professor of law and forensic science at George Washington University in Washington, D.C. Their late brother-in-law Greg Hayward had been a student of Starrs and the two had developed a close friendship based on their shared fondness for bicycling and rock climbing. Hayward had been a rugged outdoorsman and had served in Viet Nam as an Army Ranger. Both Starrs and

605

Eric Olson say that Hayward had been preparing to run for one of Maryland's Congressional seats after establishing himself as a lawyer. Starrs' close friendship with Hayward eventually extended to the rest of the Olson family.

The grandson of a mortician, Starrs, whose business card features a Sherlock Holmes-style cap perched atop a microscope, is widely known for his forensic investigations into some of America's most notorious murder cases. Over the years, he participated in or directed investigations into the Lindbergh kidnapping, the Sacco and Vanzetti robbery-murder, the Alfred Packer cannibalism controversy, and the assassination of Senator Huey "Kingfish" Long. In 1995, Starrs exhumed the body of legendary desperado Jesse James to run DNA tests that put to rest lingering doubts about the cause of James' death. In October 2000, Starrs instituted a reinvestigation into whether convicted Boston Strangler, Albert H. DeSalvo, had actually murdered his last victim. In August 2002, Starrs briefly entered the fray over the issue of what to do with the remains of the 9/11 hijackers, by advocating that there be public oversight of what the government did with the remains. Said Starrs, "Good persons or bad persons, you can't assume that the relatives are going to come to the fore and try to reclaim their remains." (Given that any such "remains" were crushed to dust when the towers came down, blown to bits over Pennsylvania, and completely absent from the scene at the Pentagon, Starrs' concerns were odd.)

Starrs is no stranger to controversy, and as one of his close associates has pointed out, "He hasn't always been received well by his colleagues." Some forensic scientists have complained that Starrs "tends to relish the spotlight more than he does details," and "sometimes he overlooks, or tends to brush aside, pertinent facts, or evidence, in favor of his opinions or theories." Other forensic authorities also quietly criticize Starrs because "his advanced degrees do not include medical or forensic studies," and because "he 'cherry picks' cases that are sure to be controversial and sensational."

Professor Starrs enjoys being referred to as "the father of Indiana Jones," due to his resemblance to actor Sean Connery. The distinguished looking, gray-bearded professor has a flair for waxing poetic and is quite adept at dealing with the media. He says he "became involved in the academic side of forensic science when I was invited by the FBI to be the law school's representative to a fledgling program in the forensic sciences at George Washington University."

Following their mother's death, Eric and Nils Olson explained to Starrs that their mother had been buried in Frederick's Mount Olivet Cemetery, and that they had decided to disinter their father's body from its Memorial Park grave and move it to their mother's plot. At the same time, Eric and Nils asked Starrs if he would be willing to oversee a scientific examination of Frank Olson's remains to see what, if any, tangible evidence there was of the cause of his death. Said Eric later, "I had been thinking about the possibility for years. I knew that my mother would never allow it, but after she passed away, the time seemed appropriate, and I thought the opportunity had arrived to put all my questions, suspicions, and doubts to the test and possibly to rest."

Starrs was already quite familiar with the many puzzling and unanswered questions surrounding Frank Olson's death, and he promptly agreed to the Olson's request. But, said Starrs, "I'll coordinate the project only if my exacting criteria for an exhumation are fulfilled." Starrs summarized his criteria, which had previously been published in *Scientific Sleuthing Review*, for the Olsons, emphasizing "the imperative of establishing that there was a substantial controversy over the cause of the death of the person to be exhumed, that there was a genuine belief that current scientific technologies could shed light on the dispute over the person's death or otherwise assist in the examination and, last but not least, that all family members support such a scientific reexamination." Starrs' criteria seemed tailor made for the case of Frank Olson; Eric and Nils readily agreed.

Starrs' first step in investigating Olson's death was to secure a copy of the Manhattan Medical Examiner's report from 1953. If there had been any doubt at all in Starrs' mind about taking the case, it must have been quickly erased by what he found, or, perhaps more to the point, what he did not find in the document.

Expecting a detailed report, Starrs was startled to receive a document that was, as he put it, "brief and to the point," consisting of only a few paragraphs on two pages. The report, written by Manhattan assistant medical examiner Dr. Dominick DiMaio, concerned only an external examination of Olson's body performed the same night that he died. Dr. DiMaio noted numerous external wounds on Olson's body, as well as fractures, including a large chest wound that contained slivers of green plywood, and multiple cuts and gashes around Olson's face and neck — injuries wholly consistent with the impact of a crash through a closed window and a fall nearly fifty-three meters, or one-hundred-and-seventy feet, to the pavement, striking a plywood barrier in the process. However, there had been no internal examination of the body; no thoroughgoing autopsy had been performed. Moreover, as Starrs noted in his preliminary findings:

> Indeed, the accompanying toxicological report only assayed the presence of methyl and ethyl alcohol [with negative results], including no drug scan of any kind. So far there was potentially more that could be accomplished by an exhumation and a full autopsy.

Starrs telephoned Dr. DiMaio who, remarkably, was still working in the Manhattan medical examiner's office. DiMaio confirmed that there had been no autopsy and that he had not taken any X-rays. In his defense, he explained to Starrs he had been "taken in" by the reports from the police, as well as by Lashbrook's statement to his fellow officers. As we have seen, beginning in the mid-1970s, DiMaio had followed the Olson case closely through the newspapers and televised reports. DiMaio told Starrs, "I was so mad when I read the stories that came out in 1975 that I considered reopening the case." Wrote Starrs in his report:

> Straight from the shoulder, true to the style of a New Yorker, Dr. DiMaio asserted his belief that the remains of Dr. Olson would be in suitable condition for an autopsy in 1994. He based this conviction on the embalming that would have occurred prior to the remains having been transported from New York to Maryland for burial.

At this point in his investigation, Professor Starrs said, given his discussions with Dr. DiMaio, as well as the record of congressional investigations into Olson's death, he was convinced "that my bedrock rubrics to protect the dead from specious and otherwise unwarranted disturbance of their graves were amply fulfilled." Starrs notified the Olsons of this and told them what the primary objectives of his impending forensic examination would be:

> (1) To give the Olson family confidence that all available scientific and investigative measures had been employed to bring the truth of Frank Olson's death to light;
> (2) To provide a forum for the utilization of new scientific technologies and experience, such as the bio-engineering aspects of falls from heights, the analysis of the causal features in fractures resulting from such falls, the toxicological analysis of bodily tissues and hair for therapeutic and abused drugs, and the use of the computer to simulate a reenactment scenario of the event and to provide an identification of the remains by a computerized skull superimposition, and
> (3) To examine and to provide whether the tragedy of scientific experimentation with the lives and well-being of unwitting persons which marred and stigmatized this CIA research enterprise could be replicated in today's society.

After obtaining the required local and state permits to disinter human remains, Starrs' next step was to assemble a team of "qualified and eminent specialists" in the multiple scientific disciplines required to perform a comprehensive forensic investigation. Recounted Starrs in 2002, "All the members of my team jumped at my invitation, even after hearing the many and varied complexities and uncertainties that were involved." In earlier statements, Starrs had said that putting together a team for the Olson case had been harder than any other he had assembled. In 1994 he told writer Nina Burleigh, "I tried to get people to work with me who'd worked with me before, but they said no because the CIA was involved."

On June 2, 1994, at 9:00 o'clock in the morning, Frank Olson's concrete burial vault was hoisted from its grave. Attendants removed Olson's wooden coffin from its asphalt-sealed vault and carefully wrapped it in black vinyl. It was then carried to a waiting van marked Kerfoot Livery Service, and transported to the Hagerstown Police Department Crime Laboratory, twenty-five miles from Frederick. Starrs' plan called for performing initial x-rays and evaluations in Hagerstown, and then transporting the remains to the Biology Laboratory at Hagerstown Junior College. There, Olson's body would be prepared for "skeletal features analysis." At that stage, specimens for toxicological tests would be taken, as well. After that, the remains were to be transported to York College, in Pennsylvania, for intensive examination by forensic anthropologists. Starrs' rigid schedule called for reburial of the body alongside Alice and Lisa Olson in late-July. At the time, nobody even remotely suspected that Frank Olson's body would remain disinterred for another eight years.

In his preliminary report, Starrs commented, "It may seem almost insanely superfluous for us to have labored to identify the remains from the grave marked as that of Frank Olson as those of the Frank Olson whom we set out to examine. But such are the intrusive necessities of such a scientific investigation."

When Olson's body was removed from its coffin in Hagerstown it was found, as Dr. DiMaio predicted, to be remarkably well preserved. Starrs would later say that he "was very surprised" at the condition of the body, which appeared incredibly mummy-like, with its skin blackened with age and shrunken tight to its bones. Still tied to one of its toes was the New York coroner's identification tag from 1953.

Starrs' team member, Jeffrey C. Kercheval, a forensic chemist with the Hagerstown Police Department, rolled the palmar surface of Frank Olson's fingers with ink, and Starrs cast them in Mikrosil, a specialized putty-like substance favored by forensic and fingerprint experts because of its excellent rendering of the smallest details. The expectation was that the results, when compared to Olson's ante-mortem fingerprints, would produce definitive identification. But, said Starrs, "We were not blessed by such good fortune."

Army officials at Fort Detrick informed the professor that no files containing Frank Olson's fingerprints existed at the installation. Further, officials at the National Military Personnel Records Center, in St. Louis, Missouri, reported that they, too, were unable to locate any files on Olson. They expressed fears that his records may have been destroyed in a massive 1973 fire that had burned to ash over 18,000,000 files covering the years 1912 through 1960.

Starrs had also requested Olson's Fort Detrick dental records, but quickly received the same response — no records were available. Undeterred, Starrs assembled a number of photographs of Olson taken in the late 1940s and early 1950s. In each, the biochemist could be seen smiling broadly from different angles. These photographs, along with Olson's actual skull, were forwarded to the team's forensic odontologist at the University of Colorado, Dr. John McDowell, a former president of the American Academy of Forensic Scientists. Forensic odontolgy is a relatively new branch of dental science that involves not only identification through photographs and image analysis, but also bite mark analysis.

609

McDowell's report promptly came back stating strong support that the skull was that of Frank Olson. "At that point," Starrs recalls, "it was safe to say that there was no reasonable doubt of the identity of the remains, but we decided to go one long stride forward to attempt a computerized superimposition of the skull to other photographs of Olson's face." To accomplish that, Dr. McDowell forwarded Olson's skull to Dr. Victor Spitzer, an anatomist and Associate Professor of Radiology and Cellular and Structural Biology, also located at the University of Colorado. Spitzer combined expertise with Michael Sellbert, a computer expert with Engineering Animation, Inc., a company based in Ames, Iowa. Through the use of what Starrs called a "break-through, cutting edge of science process," which combined computed tomography scans of Olson's skull with computer-enhanced facial photographs, they were able to determine with "a high degree of confidence" that the skull in hand was Frank Olson's.

Next in Starrs' investigation was a trip to New York to examine and recreate the scene of Olson's fall and death at the Statler Hotel. Five team members accompanied Starrs on the trip. Armond Pastore, the hotel's former night manager, joined the group in downtown Manhattan, at Starrs' request.

At mid-morning on the appointed day, team investigators worked with Pastore to position and chalk line the body of a volunteer sprawled on the Seventh Avenue sidewalk. A crowd of curious gawkers, many drawn from Penn Station and Madison Square Garden across the street from the hotel's entrance, gathered on the busy avenue. Starrs, wearing his trademark Indiana Jones-style hat, reviewed with Pastore what he had observed on the night of November 28, 1953. Starrs was able to determine that Olson had landed 2.8 meters from the base of the hotel, after striking a green-painted wooden barricade that had blocked off a section of the hotel's exterior for the purpose of steam-cleaning.

Pastore enjoyed bantering with the several reporters who covered the event. One journalist asked him if he thought Olson had jumped.

"No," said Pastore emphatically. "I never thought even for a minute that he jumped." Pastore pointed to the hotel's windows above and added, "I think he had a lot of help going through the window, if you know what I mean. I worked for over thirty years in the business and never once heard of anyone else jumping through a closed window."

Starrs' had Pastore recount how he entered Olson's room behind the police. Starrs noted in his report, without comment, Pastore's suspicions about the condition of Olson's empty bed, with its sheets and blankets on the floor, which Pastore said, "Looked pretty much like someone had thrown or ripped them from the bed." Starrs concluded his report's section on Pastore's recollections by stating, "the priest who came to the site for the purpose of giving Dr. Olson the Last Rites was quickly moved aside." This statement is at odds with Pastore's account. According to Pastore's memory, the priest did indeed give Olson the rites before his body was removed from the sidewalk.

While Pastore was available, investigators explored his memory about where Olson's body had landed on the sidewalk in front of the hotel. Pastore later said, "I knew the exact spot. How could I ever forget it? That I could see, not a thing had changed there since that night." Pastore also told the team about the wooden barrier that had been in place that night, describing how it had been set up around the Little Penn Bar (now relocated) near the spot where he had found Olson's body. He explained that the barrier had been placed there about a week before Olson's fall, for the purposes of steam cleaning the façade of the hotel.

Starrs described the process of determining the location of Olson's body: "Having in mind that the distance from the sidewalk to the window sill of Room 1018A was about 175 feet, it was calculated by the engineers at Engineering Animation, Inc. that Olson's exit velocity would have had to be no more than 1.5 miles per hour for him to have struck the barrier at the sidewalk level. A speed of more than 1.5 miles per hour would have propelled his body beyond striking range of the barrier. 1.5 miles per hour is about half the speed of a normal walker's pace. Such an estimated horizontal velocity does not shed light on whether Olson went through an open window or a closed one, with or without a drawn shade." Starrs then posed the issue of the window exit, as follows:

> Among the few matters on which we dare only to speculate is the likelihood that the traditional view of Olson's exiting the window—glass, shade, and all—is scientifically plausible. This is a matter which is just not scientifically testable in view of our not knowing and not being able to reconstruct, if we did know, the state of mind of Olson as he hurtled through the window of his own misbegotten choice, if such was indeed the case. For myself, I am solidly skeptical of anyone in what has been said to be Olson's distraught state of mind, or even one of sound mind and memory, clearing a 31-inch high window sill fronted by a radiator and passing through a three-foot by five-foot window opening obscured by a drawn shade and all in the darkness of a hotel room at night without having his line of travel so obstructed as to cause the venture to misfire.

Team members working inside the hotel — which is today known by its original name, the Pennsylvania Hotel — diligently recreated the layout and measurements of Room 1018A, overlooking Seventh Avenue, with special attention to the room's window. Of perplexing interest to the team was that the autopsy performed by team member Dr. James Frost, Deputy Chief Medical Examiner for the State of West Virginia, had found no lacerations on Olson's face, head, or neck. Further, close examination had revealed no lacerations at all on the body's mid-section and legs, except for the wounds caused by multiple, compound fractures produced by the fall. Dr. Frost discovered an appendectomy scar on Olson's abdomen, which he called "unremarkable, except that it was not mentioned in Dr. DiMaio's 1953 report."

Starrs' report does not state whether the appendectomy was, in fact, confirmed. More importantly, Starrs also does not mention any puncture wounds to Olson's body caused by wood splinters from the temporary plywood barricade outside the Statler hotel on the night of November 28, 1953. Armond Pastore had commented on this barricade several times and had stated that he had witnessed "a large piece of tan wood protruding from Olson's chest." However, Starrs offered the following observations:

> The significance of this absence of lacerations is less a criticism of Dr. DiMaio than it is a commentary on the way Dr. Olson exited through the window. Certainly exiting through an open window would be one feasible explanation for the lack of lacerations. And that can be said with assurance without even testing the hypothesis.
>
> If, on the other hand, the window was closed when Dr. Olson crashed through it, it is reasonable to hypothesize that the glass would have cut his skin at some place or other. But if the glass were separated from Olson's body by a drawn shade, then it can be reasoned that the buffering by the shade blocked the glass from piercing Dr. Olson's skin. The lack of cuts on the front of the lower extremities from dragging across glass shards on the bottom edge of the window is nevertheless quite inexplicable.

Starrs does not say anything about the condition of the shade or how it might have been slashed by glass. Pastore told this author that he recalled "the shade to be fully intact and not slashed or cut at all." Unfortunately, Starrs did not act to test either hypothesis because such tests, he explained, were "beyond the financial and other realistic limits of this project." Starrs report concludes:

> For now we can only say that it is most probable either that Dr. Olson went to his death through an open window or that he went through a closed window with a shade drawn in front of it. The lack of lacerations gives only an immeasurable edge to the open window hypothesis.

Starrs' report does not mention Armond Pastore's consistent recollections in other interviews of seeing broken glass on the sidewalk around Olson's body, or his observation that the window shade had been intact.

Toxicological tests performed on Olson's remains proved far more complicated than anticipated. Starrs posed the question to team toxicologists, "What drugs, or their metabolites, should we seek to discover?" Obviously, LSD was of primary interest, but Starrs suggested that other drugs be placed on the list as well. Said Starrs, "With all the outrage over the CIA's LSD experimentation, little attention had been paid to the government's testing other drugs, many of which have hallucinogenic effects, some like benztropine, or BZ, even more potent in even smaller doses than LSD." Following discussions with team members, Starrs said, "I narrowed the field of candidates for our drug testing to tetrahydrocannabinol, the active ingredient of marijuana, mescaline, morning glory, LSD, including radioactive LSD, and benztropine." Next, Starrs "personally delivered a variety of well-preserved, carefully logged and continuously refrigerated bodily tissues" to Dr. Yale Caplan, a forensic toxicologist with the National Center for Forensic Science in Baltimore, Maryland. In addition to the tissue samples, Starrs also delivered a number of carefully selected hairs, some with a root structure intact, that had been taken from Olson's head and body.

Dr. Caplan's eagerly anticipated toxicology report came back in two parts. Because of the unusual and mystifying role of LSD in Olson's death, the drug was considered separately from other substances. Said Starrs, "The testing of bodily tissues for substances other than LSD was negative." While the Colby documents had appeared rather definitive about Dr. Abramson having given Olson "Nembutal," a strong sedative, four days prior to his death, no traces of the drug revealed themselves through Caplan's arduous testing. More surprising was that LSD testing of Olson's tissues through radioimmunoassay (RIA) proved inconclusive. The tests had been run by Dr. Bruce Goldberger, a widely respected toxicologist at the University of Florida College of Medicine in Gainesville and a colleague of Caplan's. When Starrs phoned for the results, Goldberger explained the special problems encountered in analyzing biological samples obtained from embalmed and exhumed bodies. He said that the RIA tests had "all given positive results for the presence of LSD in the tissues." However, cautioned Goldberger, "The results were so unusually uniform as to be unworthy of being considered as reliable." According to Starrs, Dr. Goldberger had concluded that something "about the RIA kits was out of whack in the testing of the preserved tissues." Goldberger recommended that further testing be conducted by Dr. Rodger Foltz, a research professor of pharmacology and toxicology at the University of Utah Health Sciences Center in Salt Lake City.

Dr. Foltz's testing found no traces of LSD at all. Stated Starrs' report, "The determination limits set by Dr. Foltz for his analysis were so low that it can be said with not even a hint of uncertainty that those tissues were, at the time of testing, without any evidence of LSD." However, Starrs later points out that Foltz's finding was not a definitive affirmation of the absence of LSD in Olson's body at the time of his death, or any time prior to it, when one considered the relatively low dosage (70 micrograms) of LSD allegedly given to Olson, as well as the "low determination limits" used in Foltz's tests. In addition, the lability of LSD in embalmed tissues over a long period of time — in Olson's case nearly forty years — is "so unknown," as Starrs put it, "that one not finding LSD is no proof, nor even suggestion, that Dr. Olson had not ingested LSD in 1953."

This left Olson's hair samples still to be tested for LSD. Dr. Goldberger told Starrs that the best facility for such testing was at the Japanese National Institutes of Health Sciences in Tokyo. Subsequently, samples of Olson's hair were sent to Dr. Yuji Nakahara, director of the Institute's Narcotics Section. Weeks later, the results from this round of testing also came back negative, but with the same cautionary caveats as the results from the Utah tests.

In summary, there was no definitive proof that Olson was dosed with LSD days before his death. In 2002, the author asked Dr. Goldberger if tests had been conducted on Olson's body for the drug Meretran, a drug that Sidney Gottlieb had consistently said had been mixed with much of the LSD used by the CIA in the 1950s and had been present in the LSD used at the Deep Creek Lake gathering. Goldberger replied that there had been no testing for Meretran, nor had he been asked to test for the drug. Goldberger also told this author that he had assumed that Nembutal "had already been cleared from Olson's body long before testing." When the author queried Dr. Foltz about tests, he replied, "I don't recall receiving or attempting to analyze forensic tissue samples for LSD. The chances of detecting LSD in an embalmed body that was exhumed after 40 years is extremely unlikely."

Explained Dr. Foltz, however, on negative test results: "A negative test result normally means that the analytical data did not meet established criteria for a positive result. Often this means that the measured concentration was below an established cutoff concentration. Tests for LSD are normally performed on either urine or blood. LSD is normally only detectable in blood or urine for a few days following ingestion. I am aware of only two published reports on detection of LSD in human hair samples. I don't recall any attempts in our laboratory to detect and measure LSD in forensic samples consisting of human tissue."

While the drug results were intriguing, but inconclusive, Starrs thought his investigation might have better luck in examining Olson's bones, and the remains were sent to Dr. John Levisky, Professor of Behavioral Science, at York College in Pennsylvania. Levisky meticulously removed Olson's mummified skin and soft tissue to expose his broken skeleton. Then, with the precision of a cartographer, Levisky charted each and every broken and cracked bone. When he was finished, he found that there were three distinctive groupings, each providing horrific evidence of the details of Olson's fall.

Levisky first identified a group of fractures in Olson's left arm, shoulder, and ribs. All of these were found to be consistent with Olson having struck the plywood barrier shielding the hotel's facade. The second group included the fractures in Olson's feet, legs, and pelvic region. Levisky found that these breaks were consistent with Dr. Frost's speculation that, after hitting the barricade, Olson had hit the ground feet first. Olson's lower right leg bones had actually penetrated his skin in the region of his heel. Levisky's third group consisted of the fractures in Olson's skull. There were several breaks in different regions of the skull.

Professor Starrs turned his attention next to analysis of trauma to Olson's head and skull. "If an hypothesis of homicide in the death of Dr, Olson were to have any factual foundation discoverable by post-mortem scientific means," stated Starrs, "that foundation was most probably to be found in an examination of the flesh of his head or in cephalic insults resulting in skull fracture."

Employing scanning electron microscopy, Dr. Frost, according to Starrs, had elucidated an external examination of Olson's skull that revealed "a linear laceration running mainly horizontally in the right parietal region." Stated Starrs, "Underlying this laceration was a massive hinge fracture transecting the lower half of the skull, as described by Dr. Levisky. Whether the blow causing these traumatic events was inflicted in Room 1018A or by something at the street level were the two most likely causative events to be weighed."

Intensive study of this laceration microscopically, using a stereo light microscope and scanning electron microscopy, revealed that the laceration "was a unit and not the sum of more than one blow at the same site inflicted at different times and, possibly, at different places." The scanning study of the laceration, along with energy dispersive X-ray, revealed "the presence of a number of elements, one of which in high concentration was silicon...a principle component of glass."

Where did this micron size piece of glass come from? Surmised Starrs, either from the window of Room 1018A or from broken window glass of Room 1018A "already lying on the sidewalk of 7th Avenue when Dr. Olson's head hit there." Reasoned Starrs:

> The laceration in question and its subsequent skull fracture plainly seem to be linked to one impact. In addition, that impact would have had to have been a blow well beyond the capacity of a window or it's housing to inflict. Consequently, the glass in that laceration must have originated from a particle of glass picked up at the street level. But whether that glass was the window glass of Room 1018A or some foreign piece of glass infinitesimally minute size that had been lying about on the 7th Avenue sidewalk of the Statler Hotel are equally possible and irreconcilable by scientific means. We can infer that the laceration had glass in it and that it came from glass from the sidewalk. Further than this we cannot even hazard a guess.

(Again, apparently, Professor Starrs seemed unaware of Armond Pastore's statements about seeing glass on the sidewalk around Olson's head.)

Of particular interest to Starrs' team was an autopsy-revealed hematoma over Olson's left eye imbedded in the galeal sheath. Wrote Starrs:

> This sub-galeal hematoma necessarily resulted from the hemorrhage of a blood vessel over the left eye. The flesh in that area of [Olson's scalp] was intact, having experienced neither a laceration nor an incised wound... Once again we were confronted with the elusiveness of a triad of possibilities as to the cause of the hematoma. A third person, the window of the room, or the sidewalk, which of the three was the originator?

Starrs felt that the possibility of Olson striking his head on the window "stood on uncertain footing mainly because of the site of the hematoma and its relation to the most likely trajectory of Dr. Olson's body if he exited the window on his own motion. Reasoned the professor, "We know that the horizontal divider on this double-hung window was five-feet-ten-inches from the floor of Room 1018A. We accept also as a fact that Dr. Olson himself was five feet ten inches tall, necessitating his bending over to some degree to clear the horizontal bar of the window."

The team's forensic analysis of the hotel room in Manhattan had also revealed the following:

> The lower window ledge of the window was thirty-one inches from the floor, requiring a person bent on throwing himself head first through the window to elevate himself and be airborne to clear the ledge. The combination of these two gymnastic feats leaves it highly problematic that striking the window glass or the window's housing can realistically be said to have been the cause of a hematoma situated just over and traveling to the orbit of the left eye.

Starrs continued, "The third possibility is that this hematoma occurred at the street level" when Olson's body, moving at a speed in excess of sixty miles per hour, "struck one or more hard and unresisting objects."

Starrs consulted with Dr. Steven C. Batterman, the team's bioengineer, who, according to Starrs, "left me with the distinct understanding that if this part of Dr. Olson's frontal bone had come into direct contact with an object at ground level at any speed above eleven miles per hour the frontal bone would have suffered a fracture. There being none, that possibility seems to be excluded."

On the existence of the hematoma, Starrs eventually concluded:

> In the present state of our factual knowledge about the death of Dr. Olson, I would venture to say that this hematoma is singular evidence of the possibility that Dr. Olson was struck a stunning blow to the head by some person or instrument prior to his exiting through the window of Room 1018A.
>
> I would say further that the convergence of this physical evidence from our scientific investigations with the results of our non-scientific inquiries raises this possibility from the merely possible to the realm of a real possibility.

Unfortunately, Starrs does not provide in his written report any details or explanations of what the "non-scientific" evidence was that prompted him to conclude that Olson was "struck a stunning blow" to the head. Also, in none of his reports that this author obtained, did Starrs mention that he and team member Dr. James Frost seriously disagreed on the possible nature of Olson's hematoma.

Once he was satisfied that his forensic efforts had gleaned everything possible from Olson's remains, Professor Starrs turned his attention to what he deemed the "non-scientific evidence." Much of this evidence, of course, came from the various Colby documents, and the statements of individuals interviewed during the numerous investigations into Olson's death. In his preliminary report, Starrs was quick to state that the non-scientific evidence "considered in combination" with his forensic findings "are rankly and starkly suggestive of homicide." However, Starrs seemed somewhat, perhaps inadvertently, to hedge this conclusion when he also wrote in the same report:

> It is well-nigh impossible to separate the truth from the fabrications in the documentary evidence we have exhaustingly and exhaustively reviewed. In 1953 the lies outpaced the truth by a mile. Not only were these lies told patently to conceal the full nature of the CIA's involvement in behavioral modification experiments through the use of drugs, only one of which was LSD, but the lies were also motivated by a calculated effort to keep the Olson family in the dark and from becoming suspicious, by providing the necessary foundation for an award of a Federal employee death benefit to Dr. Olson's survivors.
>
> The extent to which this manhandling of the truth also evolved from a desperate concern lest a homicide by the CIA be revealed is beyond the ability of anyone but the possible malefactors to say.

At the top of his list of "outpacing lies," Starrs placed the issue of Frank Olson's state of mind, or mental stability, "prior to the Deep Creek experiment on November 19, 1953." Somewhat paradoxically, Starrs, who concluded that Olson was a "well balanced individual" prior to Deep Creek, based this conclusion on the same "documentary evidence" that he called into question in his statement quoted above. Specifically, that evidence consisted of statements from Lt. Col. Vincent Ruwet and Dr. John L. Schwab, given on December 7, 1953 in the course of CIA Inspector General Lyman B. Kirkpatrick's investigation. Stated Ruwet:

> During the period prior to the experiment, my opinion of his state of mind was that I noticed nothing which would lead me to believe that he was of unsound mind. He had normal family worries, (worries that I consider to be normal). Occasionally he had trouble with his ulcers but was always reluctant to discuss personal trouble with anyone.

Stated Schwab:

> [Olson] was always extremely cheerful, more than willing to help anyone in distress, often times making it a point to cheer not only his friends but others who were in a depressed mood. Dr. Olson enjoyed an occasional alcoholic drink but did not indulge excessively. His general state of mind and outlook on life was always that of extreme optimism. Never was there any indication of pessimism.

617

But, as Starrs pointed out, CIA Technical Services chief Dr. Willis Gibbons, Lashbrook's and Gottlieb's superior, had stated otherwise. According to a December 1, 1953 memo written by Kirkpatrick, Gibbons had told the Inspector General "Olson has a history of mental disturbances. Last summer he apparently told his wife that he was upset and she suggested he see a doctor." The memo contains no explanation of what Olson's "history" of disturbances consisted of, what he was "upset" about, or whether he actually saw a doctor.

Next on Starrs' list of non-scientific evidence was a review of what was known at the time about the effects of LSD. As Starrs pointed out, "one of the well-documented effects, in some few persons, of LSD use is the occurrence of flashbacks, days and even months after the LSD has been taken." Starrs had waded through hundreds of medical journals and other papers concerning flashbacks – the alleged phenomenon by which LSD users experience the effects of the drug days, weeks, or months after its ingestion. He had concluded that "during flashbacks LSD users do not commit violent acts such as throwing themselves through a closed window." Added Starrs, "Even a Government study commissioned on account of Dr. Olson's death and published by the Government Printing Office makes a telling point that LSD flashbacks are a rarity and that during such flashbacks violence is all but non-existent." (This author was unable to locate any government study commissioned because of Frank Olson's death and printed by the GPO. The subject of flashbacks remains controversial. Some Army studies done in the 1970s claim that flashbacks do occur commonly in some subjects and that violence is sometimes associated with them.)

Continuing along these lines, Starrs emphasized, "Of course violent, even self-destructive, acts are not uncommon concomitants in the immediate aftermath of LSD use.... The death of Diane Linkletter, daughter of celebrity Art Linkletter, is said to have occurred while she was in the grip of LSD and not during a flashback, although it is difficult to say which is which in the case of an LSD habitué." (Again, Starrs seemed to be unaware of the CIA's own studies on LSD in relation to suicide, including the suicide death reported by Dr. Henry K. Beecher in the mid-1950s and referenced several times before various Congressional committees that looked into the Olson case and related matters in the 1970s.)

Starrs then raised an intriguing prospect: "Is it possible, then, that in the early morning hours of Saturday, November 28, 1953, in Room 1018A of the Statler Hotel that Frank Olson's body and mind were possessed by a dose of LSD that he had been given that night and which precipitated his going out the window to his death?" Added Starrs dramatically and without explanation, "That possibility is not as fantastical as it might at first blush appear to be."

Starrs next turned his attention to what he called, "the enigma of Dr. Harold Abramson's involvement." Members of Starrs' team were surprised to read in Vincent Ruwet's December 7, 1953 statement that Abramson had visited Olson's Statler Hotel room on the evening of Tuesday, November 24, bringing with him "a bottle of bourbon and some 'Nembutal' for Dr. Olson."

According to Ruwet, Olson had "a couple of 'high-balls'" and then Abramson had told Olson to take a "Nembutol," (what Ruwet meant was Nembutal) which Olson did. Abramson also left more of the pills with Olson, said Ruwet, telling him "to take another should he have difficulty sleeping."

Said Starrs, "Medicating Dr. Olson with two interacting central nervous system depressants had the real potential of killing him, as columnist Dorothy Killgallen learned." Killgallen, a well-known reporter, columnist, and television celebrity, was found dead in her New York apartment on November 8, 1965. Dr. James Luke of the Manhattan Medical Examiner's Office reported at the time that she had died of a "lethal combination of alcohol and barbiturates [later reported to be Nembutal]." Asked Starrs, "What sort of medical practitioner would so prescribe with such reckless abandon?"

In researching Dr. Abramson, Starrs said that he discovered that the doctor "was a true believer... in the value of LSD in psychotherapy for disturbed persons." Abramson had died in September 1980, at the age of eighty, but Starrs learned that Dr. Margaret W. Ferguson — identified in a December 4, 1953 CIA memo as "a psychiatrist...hired by Dr. Abramson"— was still living.

Starrs attempted to speak with Dr. Ferguson by telephone, but, he said, the doctor "abruptly terminated" the call by saying that she was not interested in discussing Olson's treatment by Abramson or Abramson's experiments with LSD. Dr. Ferguson would later tell this author, "I didn't at all care for the ways [Starrs] posed his questions, or for the manner with which he seemed to direct our brief conversation." Nonetheless, regarding Harold Abramson, Starrs speculated:

> The extant record of Dr. Abramson's commitment to LSD in psycho-therapy and his ministrations to Dr. Olson trembles with the disquieting possibility that it might have been another, a second, dose of LSD given to Dr. Olson under Dr. Abramson's misguided belief that it would relieve his symptoms of depression that eventuated in his death while under the influence of that dose of LSD.

Yet, Starrs agilely distanced himself from the extant record (and even from his own theory) by concluding:

> For myself, however, the likelihood of Dr. Abramson's direct involvement in the death of Dr. Olson is less plausible than that it was the outcome of the CIA's own calculated misdeeds. Not only does the paper record do more than whisper of this possibility, but the statements and the silence of persons privy to insider information on the matter who were interviewed or sought [after] to be interviewed by me reinforce that conviction.

619

To underscore this, Starrs said pointedly:

> Notwithstanding...purported justifications for silence, there are those whose intimate knowledge of critical factual details imposes upon them a singular duty to speak, the refusal of which can legitimately be read as evidence of concealment and, conceivably, even more incriminatory motives.

After Dr. Ferguson had rejected his attempts to inquire about Abramson, Starrs tried to contact Col. Vincent Ruwet, Olson's former superior at Camp Detrick, who had accompanied Olson and Robert Lashbrook to Manhattan to visit Dr. Harold Abramson. Starrs telephoned Ruwet at his home in Frederick. Ruwet listened quietly as Starrs introduced himself and told the former officer why he was calling. When the professor paused, Ruwet said, "I have no interest in discussing the matter," and hung up. Ruwet would later tell his wife and friends that he felt badly about Olson's body having been exhumed, and that he felt it would never have happened if Alice Olson had still been alive. Hazel Ruwet told friends, "Vince knew that Alice was content with what she knew and that she wanted Frank to rest in peace. My husband did more than anyone knows about for that family. Alice would have been very unhappy about what is happening."

Starrs also attempted to interview retired New York City policeman Joseph Guastefeste by paying an unannounced visit to Guastefeste's Florida home. Guastefeste had identified himself as the lead uniformed investigator of Olson's death by signing the 1953 police report released to the Olson's by the CIA. Apparently, the former police officer was less than pleased that Starrs had tracked him down. Starrs reported that their brief, but "amiable tête-à-tête" took place "on [Guastefeste's] lighted front porch." Starrs later said, "Guastefeste took a different tack but his uncommunicativeness was just as indefatigable as that of Ruwet." The retired officer told Starrs he remembered very little about the Olson case, but did confirm Armond Pastore's account of Olson lying on the sidewalk, still breathing when uniformed officers arrived at the Statler Hotel. Starrs wrote: "He also recalled that Olson was in a supine position on the sidewalk when he came upon him." On the subject of Robert Lashbrook, the former police officer's memory "went blank," said Starrs.

"Look," said Guastefeste, "I'm just a dumb cop. I can't help with this stuff after so many years. That's a long time ago. You know how many bodies I've seen since that time?"

Starrs concluded that Guastefeste's memory was "very selective, sometimes showing crystal clarity and sometimes mired in opacity." Concluded the professor poetically, "Silence comes in many shapes and sizes; a failure to recall is but one kind."

Surprisingly, according to Starrs' report, former TSS Chemical Branch deputy Robert Lashbrook discussed the case with one of Starrs' team members. Why

Starrs himself did not choose to speak to the only living witness to Olson's state of mind and body immediately before his death is not explained.

Starrs was surprised when he learned from his team member (whose name is not known) that Lashbrook had provided a "most important new revelation," as he termed it, "that contradicted all of the previous reports of what had caused him to awaken when Olson plummeted to his death." The "revelation" was Lashbrook's statement to the interviewer that "the noise of the window shade spinning in its upper housing" had wakened him that night – a statement and recollection that Lashbrook had indeed made at least twice before in the summer of 1975, and subsequently.

"As to whether the glass had been broken at all," Starrs said, "he asserted he had no recollection even though the New York City Police report had simply repeated his own recitations that he had heard 'a crash of glass.'"

Asked Starrs rhetorically, "Was Lashbrook's memory playing tricks on him or was he playing hob with the truth of the matter?" Why Lashbrook, who was extremely reluctant to make himself available for questioning about the Olson case, was not asked more pertinent questions about the events of the fateful night is a question for the ages, now that he too is dead.

Starrs considered his interview with Dr. Sidney Gottlieb to be "the most perplexing of all the personal interviews I conducted." The professor met with the retired CIA officer in Gottlieb's home in Virginia, but Starrs is quick to point out that the encounter "had almost been foiled by my initial attempt to engage him in conversation unannounced, with CBS cameramen in the background." That initial encounter, said Starrs, "came to naught because of {Gottlieb's} distress over the presence of the media." Starrs does not explain why he attempted this seemingly self-sabotaging act, but fortunately for him, Gottlieb followed up after the CBS encounter, telephoning Starrs at his office. Gottlieb agreed to allow the professor to interview him for one hour, if Starrs returned the courtesy. Said Starrs, "A most uncommon request, but one to which I acceded."

Starrs met with Gottlieb on a Sunday morning, and concluded, "My over-all assessment of this interview was not at all favorable to Dr. Gottlieb or to his lack of complicity in Olson's death." Starrs based his reaction on Gottlieb's "undue concerns over my investigation and its findings, evidenced [through] more than idle curiosity," and that Gottlieb's "actions both before and after Olson's death were at least unsatisfactory and at most incredible."

Unfortunately, Starrs, who had a small tape recorder in his pocket during the meeting, decided to take only a few pages of handwritten notes, so we do not have a verbatim record of the dialogue between the two men.

Starrs led off his questions by asking Gottlieb "whether any of the eight unwitting [sic] participants in the LSD experiment [at Deep Creek Lake] had been pre-screened for any medical disabilities that might put them at risk in such an endeavor?" Starrs says, "Gottlieb unhesitatingly said, 'No.'" (This is odd, given that not only Gottlieb and Lashbrook, but also Vincent Ruwet, are all on record saying, on several occasions, that not everyone at Deep Creek Lake received LSD. They had earlier explained that those who were not given the drug had been specifically ruled out because of health problems or, in one case, because the man did not drink alcohol. At any rate, the record is quite clear that not all present at the Deep Creek Lake meeting were given LSD.)

Continued Starrs, "other questions gave rise to answers sufficient to stand plausibility on its head."

Starrs asked Gottlieb if he had destroyed documents "relevant to this matter?"

"Sure," Gottlieb replied.

"But why?" Starrs asked.

"So that they wouldn't be misunderstood," said Gottlieb.

"Was it rather necessary to destroy them so that they would not be understood?" rejoined Starrs.

Starrs then asked Gottlieb, "What action did you take upon being apprized by Robert Lashbrook of Olson's death?"

Replied Gottlieb. "I called my superior, Dr. Willis Gibbons, and arranged a meeting immediately."

Starrs says that in reply to "my raised eyebrows and my inquiry as to the purpose of such a meeting with such urgency," Gottlieb had stated that the purpose of the meeting was "informational."

Asked Starrs, "Informational and not to plot to cover the tracks of persons responsible for Dr. Olson's death. If informational only, why the rush to have an immediate meeting? If not a deliberate effort to present a united front in the event of a skeptical and official inquiry, why not wait until regular business hours for the informational meeting?"

Starrs' questions seem odd for a man so seemingly outraged by Olson's death; why an *immediate* meeting would be requested and expected does not seem at all out of the ordinary to a reasonable person. After all, a man had just died. One can only guess what Starrs' reaction would have been if Gottlieb and his CIA superiors had waited until normal operating hours to meet and discuss Olson's death. Even more importantly is that Starrs' questions to Gottlieb seemed to fall very short of composing any actual comprehensive inquiry into Olson's death. Why did he not ask what Frank Olson's reaction to the LSD had been? How had Olson acted under the influence? Was there a specific reason Olson had been given LSD laced with Meretran? What happened the remainder of the night after the LSD was administered? What happened the following day? Who were the people actually present for the Deep Creek Lake meeting? What was the actual purpose of the meeting?

Starrs' report on his interview with Gottlieb concluded without sharing with us what, if any, questions Dr. Gottlieb had had for the professor. Wrote Starrs:

> Probably the most unsettling, even unnerving moment in my conversation with Dr. Gottlieb occurred toward its close when he spontaneously

sought to enlighten me on a matter of which I might not take due notice, so he thought. He pointedly explained that in 1953 the Russian menace was quite palpable and that it was potentially worsened by the Russian's having cached many kilograms of LSD from the Sandoz laboratory in Switzerland. 'Professor,' he said, 'the national security of this country was on the line.' He did not say more nor need he have done so. The means-end message was pellucidly clear. Risking the lives of the unwitting victims of the Deep Creek Lake experiment was simply the necessary means to a greater good, the protection of national security.

More than a year later, this author would briefly discuss with Gottlieb Starrs' meeting with him on that Sunday morning. Said Gottlieb, after some hesitancy to discuss the subject:

> He was an interesting man, so properly poised, yet rigid, in the style of some English manor lord or such... his discomfort was infectious. I was surprised later to note that his questions were so reflective of what I had already been asked many times over. I assume he hadn't looked at the extant records before we met. Had I been in his place, I would have taken another course of inquiry, but that is the way I reacted to nearly all these situations over the years... Ideology and conditioned thinking, assumptions always...prevented any objective analysis and thoughtful questions.

Thus ended Starrs' investigation into the death of Frank Olson. Weeks after he had written up his findings, and on the anniversary of Olson's death, Starrs held a press conference, during which he issued his conclusion:

> [The] documentary evidence from 1953 demonstrates a concerted pattern of concealment and deception on the part of those persons and agencies most closely associated with—and most likely to be accountable for—a homicide most foul in the death of Dr. Olson. And the steeled reluctance to be honest, forthright and candid by persons with knowledge of the occurrence on matters pivotal to the question of homicide or suicide bespeaks an involvement more sinister than mere unconcern, arrogance or even negligence. The confluence of scientific fact and investigative fact points unerringly to the death of Frank Olson as being a homicide, deft, deliberate and diabolical.

In 2005 professor Starrs released his book, *A Voice For the Dead*. Co-authored with Dr. Katherine Ramsland, a highly respected forensic scientist and writer who teaches forensic psychology at De Sales University in Pennsylvania, the book includes a long chapter on Frank Olson's death. Unfortunately, the chapter contains many unsubstantiated claims and factual errors that serve to cloud Starrs' findings and in some ways, perhaps his credibility. Those mistakes, too numerous to cover completely herein, include mistakenly identifying CIA

Inspector General Lyman Kirkpatrick as a hotel "window shade manufacturer"; asserting that George Hunter White operated "massage parlors" in Manhattan at the direction of the CIA's "Operation Realism"; alleging that Frank Olson spent an entire night wandering the streets of New York after he fled his Statler Hotel room; claiming that Frank Olson began to wildly hallucinate twenty minutes after he was dosed with LSD at Deep Creek Lake; and that Frank Olson was "a full-fledged CIA employee."

I attempted on a number of occasions to discuss with Starrs not only these errors, but his other findings, as well. Initially, I received no response to my four written requests for an interview, and then, after several months, Starrs hurriedly wrote: "I was thunder-struck by your email and its lack of specifics. Obviously I believe firmly in giving credit where credit is due and also in avoiding factual mistakes. I take it your criticisms are directed to the latter, to which I cannot respond without more detail." Starrs had misplaced the list of mistakes initially forwarded by this author to Dr. Ramsland, so I sent the list again to both Starrs and Ramsland. About a month later, Starrs wrote again: "Sorry about the delay in responding to your e-mail...I thought you might understand... that nothing can be done at this time to remedy any of your points that Katherine and I agree need remedying. The paperback is the next best place to take your criticisms into account."

3

District Attorney Robert Morgenthau's Investigation

I would turn our gaze from the past, it is dangerous, frankly, to keep looking over our shoulders.
— CIA director George Tenet, 1998

If this story turns out the way we are being told, it will be as big a story as stories come: that the government killed one of its own citizens and got away with it.
— Assistant Manhattan DA Steven Saracco, 2000

Is this case convoluted? You bet it's convoluted. More so than any case I can recall.
— Assistant Manhattan DA Daniel Bibb, 2001

Jesus, it's like a nightmare that never ends, that is replayed constantly on all channels.
— Eric Olson, 2001

On May 16, 1995, New York District Attorney Robert Morgenthau received a brown manila envelope postmarked New York City. The envelope contained a thick memorandum stamped, "CONFIDENTIAL." Morgenthau had been the District Attorney for the borough of Manhattan since 1975, the year he was first asked to look into Frank Olson's death. Prior to that, he was United States Attorney for the Southern District of New York, appointed in 1961 by President John F. Kennedy.

The May 16 memorandum had been sent to Morgenthau by Eric Olson and his attorney, Harry Huge through a close friend of Morgenthau's named Mary Perot Nichols, a New York University professor and a Village Voice editor. The title of the document was: "Memorandum in Support of a Criminal Investigation into the Death of Dr. Frank Olson." The document opened with the following statement:

Based upon the factual information as now known, the need for a criminal investigation into Dr. Olson's death is necessary to ascertain the truth of what happened to Dr. Olson and who should be held personally responsible for his death.

The memorandum then emphasized that one of the key prospective witnesses in Olson's death, former CIA Inspector General Lyman Kirkpatrick, had died recently, and that the remaining witnesses — former DCI William Colby, Robert Lashbrook, Sidney Gottlieb, Vincent Ruwet, Ike Feldman and Armond Pastore — were all "elderly, and it is uncertain how long any of them will live." Not included in the list were any of the other Deep Creek Lake participants, any former CIA Security Office staff, or other individuals who had been cited in the Colby documents.

Subpoena power, Huge noted, is essential to a renewed investigation because it will "be able to force these witnesses to testify and to obtain all documents which are still in existence."

Huge then pointed out one of his client's biggest concerns: "no civil action is available" as a means to investigate Frank Olson's death:

> [The] humanitarian relief bill for the Olson family passed by the United States Congress in 1975 was conditioned on broad general releases from future civil action. To try and overcome these general releases now would take years of litigation, even if successful. By then, the witnesses will likely be gone or their memory severely impaired. Also, the Olson brothers do not have the funds for lengthy protracted litigation of this type.

Huge argued for reopening the investigation based on the combined results of Professor James Starrs' forensic investigation. "[H]is team's scientific and non-scientific" findings, wrote Huge, were "rankly and starkly suggestive of homicide."

Huge's memo recounted the basic "facts" leading up to Olson's "suicide," but then seems to make a quantum leap in offering a motive for Olson's murder:

> If Dr. Olson blew the whistle on the top-secret mind-control research, much more than the MKULTRA program was at risk. During the previous year Dr. Olson had already talked with his wife about wanting to leave his bacteriological research job at Camp Detrick. After he was unwittingly drugged these feelings intensified. The CIA experimenters worried that, had Dr. Olson left his job after they drugged him, and had he then divulged bacteriological secrets, the responsibility would have been theirs. These experimenters would certainly have realized how reckless their drug experiments would appear if Dr. Olson's subsequent behavior became impossible to predict or control. Hence, they could well have decided that not only the future of their mind control research, but the security of the

country's chemical-bacteriological research program as well, depended on eliminating Dr. Olson, and doing so quickly. The opportunity presented itself during the period suddenly created [in New York City after Ruwet had returned to Maryland] and before Olson could rejoin his family. In the aftermath of their reckless experiment [at Deep Creek Lake], and in the context of the bizarre corner into which they had painted themselves, it is hard not to imagine how these CIA agents could have perceived that they had no choice.

For reasons unknown, the memorandum from Eric Olson's attorney sat on Morgenthau's desk for about nine months without action or decision. Finally, in April 1996, after extensive consultation with his chief assistant James Kindler, Morgenthau decided to open a criminal investigation into the death of Frank Olson. Contrary to many accounts, Morgenthau never actually convened a grand jury to hear the case, however. Instead, he assigned it to his newly formed Cold Case Unit, headed by seasoned assistant district attorney Steve Saracco.

A tough, 56-year old, no nonsense, former Marine Corps officer with a law degree from Villanova University, Saracco is an avid reader of enigmatic author Thomas Pynchon and frequently quotes obscure lines from Pynchon's books, recited off the top of his head. Assisting Saracco, and comprising the other half of the cold case unit, was Daniel Bibb, a rugged, six-foot-five, former college football player and graduate of Seton Hall University and Villanova University. Both Saracco and Bibb are well experienced in interrogating crime suspects, including the high profile Central Park "Preppy" Murder Case. At the time their fledgling Cold Case Unit was assigned the Olson re-investigation, they had already chalked up a few successful cases, including one that had gone unsolved for over fifty years.

On September 21, 1997, the New York Post published the first news report of Morgenthau's reopened investigation under the sensational headline, "CIA Under Suspicion." Reporter John O'Mahony wrote that Morgenthau's office had reopened the "44-year old probe" and quoted Eric Olson: "We have had extremely good and close communication with the D.A.'s office for a year and a half, and they're working very hard on [the case]." CIA spokeswoman Carolyn Osborn told O'Mahony that the agency "is cooperating with the D.A.'s inquiry" and that "she thought there was little likelihood probers would find CIA wrongdoing."

Later, the Sunday supplement to the London Mail published an article by Kevin Dowling and Phillip Knightly, stating that Saracco had "requested [the grand jury to] hand down indictments for murder and conspiracy to murder" if it found the evidence he had uncovered compelling. The article stated:

[Saracco] says that the men he wants named in the indictments will include some of America's most respected CIA veterans and, if the grand

627

jury agrees to his request to widen his investigation, former officers of the British Secret Intelligence and Security as well.

Although the report was sensational and intriguing, Saracco denied ever saying anything of the sort to the two writers.

When Saracco and Bibb's had their first meeting with Morgenthau's chief assistant, James Kindler to review the Olson case, Kindler handed the two prosecutors a copy of Huge's 14-page memorandum, along with several thick attachments. Kindler also handed over a bound copy of the Colby documents. "This may also help," he said. "The story is fairly complicated with lots of holes in it." The Colby documents, reader may recall, were the CIA's files on various aspects of the death of Frank Olson. They had been released to the Olson family by DCI William Colby in 1975.

Saracco was excited about being given the Olson case. He later remarked, "It was a real departure from what I normally did, the type of cases we routinely handled, and the story was fascinating, filled with mystery." Several aspects of the case immediately drew Saracco's attention particularly the alleged "cause of death." Like the detectives who had first investigated the case in 1953, he had never encountered a report saying that death resulted from jumping through a closed, shaded window. "I don't recall even hearing about such a case," he said. "It was out of the ordinary and outlandish."

Saracco's partner, Dan Bibb, who was skeptical from the start about reopening the case, said, "There's a first time for everything."

But there was much more that provoked Saracco's interest, including the CIA's assassination manual, which recommended throwing someone from a high place as an ideal method of disguising murder as an accident or a suicide. While it did not prove that the CIA had done so in the case of Frank Olson, the manual certainly revealed that the Agency was willing to assassinate anyone, and had devised methods and means to do so.

Saracco was also drawn to the results of James Starrs' forensic autopsy. He had been surprised to learn that Starrs had been unable to obtain copies of Olson's fingerprints, dental records, or any personnel records from the Army or CIA. Saracco also noted with interest that Starrs had interviewed Dr. Sidney Gottlieb at length. The details caught Saracco's eye, particularly Professor Starrs' conclusion that Gottlieb was an "unreliable witness" and "was concealing information on many critical points." Why? Saracco wondered. Gottlieb's parting comment to Starrs had been cryptic: "Professor, the national security of this country was on the line." What exactly did that mean? What did the CIA want concealed because of national security?

Security or no security, Saracco thought, Starrs' interview with Gottlieb was some forty years after the fact. What possible defensible reason could there be for Gottlieb to withhold information, particularly since the CIA claimed Olson had simply fallen or jumped? Moreover, Saracco wondered, why had Gottlieb requested and received immunity from prosecution from Congress in 1977, and had it been related to Olson's death? And why did the Colby documents, given to the Olson family, still contain numerous deletions? Were these deletions hiding names and facts that could lead to indictments? Saracco also thought it odd that William Colby had produced the documents so quickly in 1975, especially since Gottlieb had testified to Congress that he had destroyed all of the MKULTRA operational files in 1973.

Despite their many deletions, Saracco was drawn to several perplexing, but seemingly portentous, passages in the Colby documents. These passages described the activities and observations of the CIA security officers who had been dispatched to Manhattan immediately following Olson's death. If Olson had simply fallen or jumped, why was there all of this skullduggery? One of the CIA security officers reported that he had secretly eavesdropped on a conversation between Robert Lashbrook and Dr. Harold A. Abramson the day after Olson's death. As readers have seen in Book One, during that conversation, Lashbrook and Abramson had listened to a tape recorded "interview" with Olson and then conspired to portray the dead biochemist as a "psychotic person" prone to suicide and suffering "from guilt and persecution complexes." In their background review of Abramson, Saracco and Bibb had learned that in the popular literature on the history of LSD in the United States, Abramson was widely known for having turned on anthropologist Margaret Mead and her husband Gregory Bateson to the drug, and that Bateson in turn had a hand in introducing writer Ken Kesey to LSD. Well before Kesey and Dr. Timothy Leary became notorious for their "trips," Abramson, throughout the 1950s, was well known in select circles for staging almost weekly LSD sorties at his Long Island estate. The gatherings were said to be so popular that guests had to be turned away.

Then there was the issue of Frank Olson's image. Saracco knew from interviews with Olson's family, friends, and former colleagues that there was considerable disagreement on this subject. Don Falconer, who had befriended Olson in 1943 when the two men had been recruited to work at Camp Detrick, described Olson as a "good-humored man," even a bit of a "practical joker." Gerald Yonetz, who also worked at Camp Detrick, said that Olson was a "happy-go-lucky guy" whose favorite drink was "Maalox and vodka." Even Lashbrook, in a 1975 interview with a reporter, said that prior to the Deep Creek Lake meeting, Olson had been "perfectly normal." But, as Saracco would soon learn, some of Olson's colleagues had been less kind about him and had remarked that he was "arrogant and egotistical," a man who "often refused to listen to reason" and who "did things only his way." Others, including Frank Olson's brother in law, Arthur Vidich, a highly respected sociologist, would tell this author that Frank was a notorious anti-Semite and bigot.

"I didn't like to be around him when Jewish people were present," said Vidich. "I'd leave the room. He could be awful. It was embarrassing."

"He was that bad?"

"Oh, you can't know how bad he was. I really would leave the room."

Vidich paused a moment, and added, "I always wondered how he was around Gottlieb and Harold Abramson. Abramson was a Norwegian Jew, I think, and I couldn't imagine Frank not saying something to him."

"This was after Frank's death that you thought about this?"

"Yes, quite a while after, in the mid-1970s, when it all became news. That final summer that Frank was alive, I saw him for the last time. He and Alice and the children, while on vacation in New York. I was surprised to see Frank reading from a Bible. I'd never known him to read anything. I had the impression he was doing some soul searching."

"About what?"

"That I was aware of, nothing specific. He just seemed more introspective — which was unusual for him."

"Frank wasn't much of a reader?"

"No, he wasn't. He was pretty superficial. Everything was black or white to him. He hadn't been exposed to much of the world or anything in it. He never went overseas during the war. What he saw in Europe after the war was a shock. Alice was far more thoughtful, open minded, and curious about life."

About six months into his investigation, Saracco discovered that James Starrs had been wrong to conclude that there were no existing military files on Frank Olson. Some of Olson's files had survived. The two prosecutors reviewed their contents and found that several of Frank Olson's Camp Detrick superiors, prior to his joining SOD, had had problems with his performance and attitude. Comments were wide ranging:

> [Olson] had expressed sympathies toward Germany in preference to England prior to the time that the United States entered the war.
>
> [Olson] thought Russia had the lowest way of life and hated Communists.
>
> The applicant [Olson] drinks to excess occasionally and is inclined to be quick tempered.
>
> In [my] opinion [Olson] is conceited, talks too much, and is not particularly reliable from a technical standpoint.
>
> Olson is violently opposed to control of scientific research, either military or otherwise, and opposes supervision of his work. He does not follow orders and has had numerous altercations with the military guards at the gates.

Wrote another of Olson's superior's in 1947:

> I must admit, however, that he is extremely tactless and has made many enemies which will probably in later life affect his career. I have seen

[OLSON] under the influence of alcohol to the extent of mild exhilaration on occasion. He has made no breeches of security to my knowledge
but is violently opposed to control of scientific research, either military or
otherwise, and opposes supervision of his work in any form. He is not the
type of individual who follows orders and rules easily; as a result he had
numerous altercations with the MP[military police] on the post, refusing
to show his pass while entering or leaving the installation and for exceeding the speed limit. I do not believe that [OLSON] is engaged in any
military activity against military supervision of research at Detrick, but
like other professional research men on the post, he opposes it, and does
not hesitate to so state anyone's presence regardless of their authority.

Despite the foregoing information, I believe [OLSON] is satisfactory
from a standpoint of honesty and loyalty and therefore recommend him
for continued work in scientific research. However, I do not believe [OL-
SON] intends to remain in this work very long as he has stated to me in
confidence that he wishes to engage in business for himself, manufacturing
chemicals for use in scientific research. He has had this ambition for many
years and undoubtedly will be discontented until he attains this goal.

Saracco wondered why it had been necessary to project a false picture of Olson - as deeply depressed, unstable, even psychotic — in the Colby documents.
Was it merely to provide a psychological basis for his supposed suicide? Was it
to substantiate the idea that the LSD had pushed him to places in his psyche
that he could not handle?

Such a strategy did not appear to be the wisest choice. But Saracco was
more curious about one of Abramson's final remarks to Lashbrook during the
overheard conversation. According to the eavesdropping CIA officer, Abramson
had said that he was "worried as to whether or not the deal was in jeopardy"
and that he thought "that the operation was dangerous and that the whole deal
should be reanalyzed." What 'deal'? What 'operation'? Clearly, there was more
here than met the eye and even Bibb, the quintessential cynic, shared Saracco's
suspicion.

Another source of suspicion for Saracco was a CIA memo reporting a secret
conversation among CIA officials on December 14, 1953. The memo read:

> Lovell reported that Quarles and George Merck were about to kill the
> Schwab activity at Detrick as 'un-American.' Is it necessary to take action
> at a higher place? Lovell knew of Frank R. Olson. No inhibitions. Baring
> of inner man. Suicidal tendencies. Offensive usefulness?

Saracco and Bibb quickly figured out that "Lovell" was Dr. Stanley Platt
Lovell, a high level consultant emeritus to the CIA and Detrick's Special Operations Division. As readers have seen, his specialties were biological warfare and
assassination techniques. Described once as "a sunny little nihilist" who took
great delight in inventing "diabolic devices" of destruction and death, Lovell

appeared to be a foreboding figure, a constant presence lurking in the shadows surrounding Olson's death. Once, during World War II, in his capacity as director of OSS Division of Research and Development, Lovell had ordered large nets erected on the roof of the Statler Hotel (then called the Pennsylvania Hotel), so that hundreds of bats could be captured. The nocturnal creatures were to be used to carry small, incendiary bombs. Later, in his role as CIA consultant, Lovell assisted Gottlieb, Lashbrook, and Army officials with two secret projects, Operation Big City and Project Mad Hatter, conducted in New York City in the 1950s. These two covert operations used Detrick-designed aerosol devises to spray LSD into a Manhattan street and inside the city's subway system.

The identity of "Quarles" was puzzling, but upon consultation with this author, the prosecutors learned that he was Donald Aubrey Quarles, Deputy Secretary of Defense under Eisenhower and a former official of Sandia Corporation, a subsidiary of Western Electric. Quarles oversaw the Sandia Laboratory, a weapons development and testing facility in New Mexico, for the Atomic Energy Commission. In 1956, Quarles would be selected by President Eisenhower to become Secretary of Defense, but he died of a massive heart attack days before taking office. Saracco later commented, "I knew that if someone at Quarles' level was concerned with any "activity," it had to be something that undoubtedly would be taken very seriously."

George Merck, named in the CIA memo along with Quarles and reportedly "about to kill the Schwab activity," was George Wilhelm Merck, president of the giant New Jersey-based Merck pharmaceutical company. Merck had formerly overseen the government's initial foray into chemical warfare when he headed the War Research Service. Merck essentially founded the Camp Detrick biological warfare center.

"Schwab" was, of course, Dr. John L. Schwab, director of Camp Detrick's Biological Laboratories and Frank Olson's ultimate division superior. Schwab was quite familiar with Olson, having worked closely with him in 1943 and 1944 on a "classified research project."

Further strengthening Saracco's and Bibb's perceptions of the seriousness of the "Schwab activity" memorandum, the prosecutors learned that the document had been authored by Dr. H. Marshall Chadwell after consultation with Sheffield Edwards, CIA Security Office chief. Chadwell, as readers have seen, was director of the CIA's Office of Scientific Intelligence. Fifty-five years old in 1953, Chadwell, who held a degree in physical chemistry from Harvard, came to the Agency from the New York office of the Atomic Energy Commission. Prior to that, he had been employed at the Rockefeller Foundation in Manhattan.

The prosecutors sensed they would ultimately have to unravel the meaning of this brief and intriguing memo. What was the so-called "Schwab activity"? And what was so unacceptable about it that even hardened Cold War operatives dubbed it "un-American" and called for its termination? How did Olson fit into this and why was he mentioned in this context? Why was he labeled a man who had "no inhibitions" and who was "baring" his inner self? To whom and about what was Olson "baring"?

Saracco also wondered if this memo was related to a cryptic note discovered in a Fort Detrick file in 1994 by an AP reporter researching a story about Olson's exhumation. The note read:

Trip to Paris and Norway in 1953 and possible fear of security violation. After death—apparently large number of government checks left uncashed in personnel file.

Why were Olson's trips to France and Norway of significance? What were the trips about? And what was the feared "security" violation? And why did Olson have a "large number" of uncashed checks remaining after his death? Checks from whom? How many? How large?

And then, high on the prosecutor's list, were two telling sections from the Colby papers given to the Olson family in 1975. These were Dr. Harold Abramson's December 4, 1953 statement:

I attempted to confirm what I had heard, that an experiment had been performed especially to trap him. [Italics added.]

And Olson's superior's John Schwab's statement in 1953:

I had first learned on Monday, November 23rd, 1953 From Lt. Col. Vincent Ruwet that Dr. Olson had been Exposed and was showing symptoms of reaction. [Italics added.]

Huge's memorandum to Morgenthau had seemingly overlooked these two sections. What did they mean? Certainly the words "trap" and "exposed" bore a significance that nobody yet understood. Why was it necessary to trap Olson? Trap him into what? Exposed him how? And why?

Intrigued by the complexities of the case, the two prosecutors decided to move quickly to interview the key individuals identified in Huge's memorandum: William Colby, Vincent Ruwet, Robert Lashbrook, and Sidney Gottlieb. According to the Colby documents, as readers have seen, both Ruwet and Lashbrook had been with Olson at the Deep Creek Lake meeting and in New York with him the week of his death. Clearly, Saracco thought, both these men would be able to explain a great deal about Olson's state of mind.

Both prosecutors had noticed from their review of the Colby documents that very little had been reported about what had actually happened at the Deep Creek Lake meeting. The lack of specifics on the meeting seemed to be deliberate, as if people had been instructed not to discuss the gathering. Curiously, despite the decades of stories alleging that Olson was psychotic after

633

being unwittingly dosed with LSD, Saracco and Bibb could find nothing to support this in any of the documents. Indeed, there was no mention whatsoever of Olson's behavior following his being dosed with the drug.

Saracco drafted letters requesting interviews with the four men. He mailed the letter to William Colby first. Several days later, on April 28, 1996, Saracco was stunned to learn from the televised evening news that former DCI William Colby was reported missing. He had disappeared from his weekend home on Rock Point Road in Cobb Island, Maryland.

"It was surreal," says Saracco. "I had just mailed a letter to a man who had vanished. I was really stunned. I mean, who wouldn't stop and think, 'What the hell is going on here?'"

THE STRANGE DEATH OF WILLIAM COLBY

According to initial news reports, neighbors had reported Colby missing on April 28, after they noticed that his sports utility vehicle was still parked in his driveway on that Sunday evening, long after Colby would normally have departed for his Washington, D.C. home. One of Colby's closest neighbors, also a former CIA official on his way to D.C. at the end of the weekend, had decided at the last minute to pull into Colby's driveway to see if everything was alright. Colby's vehicle was empty, no overnight bags inside, so the man approached the home's side door. He could hear voices inside, so he knocked and called out, "Bill? Are you there?" There was no answer and he realized the voices he heard were coming from either a radio or television. The door was unlocked, so he knocked again, and then opened it and stepped inside. The radio resting on the kitchen countertop was broadcasting local news. Nearby, on the same countertop, was an opened laptop computer, its screen lit. On the kitchen table was a glass of white wine and the remnants of a meal of black mussels and pasta.

The overhead light was still on, but nobody was in the house.

Outside, the neighbor noticed that Colby's green fiberglass canoe was not in its usual spot. He had no way of knowing yet that Colby's canoe had already been found a couple hours before by a caretaker and his wife and daughter, out boating on the Wicomico River. The canoe was overturned, floating on its side, empty. The neighbor knew that Colby was not the type of person who left his doors unlocked, not to mention an unkempt kitchen, and an open, on computer, so he had called the police

One of the first officers on the scene remarked, "There were still dinner items on the table, lights and radio on... it was like he'd gotten up to answer the phone or the door and then just vanished." But the missing canoe was a major clue.

It was odd, agreed Charles County Sheriff Fred Davis, but no foul play was suspected. "For now he's a missing person," said Davis. "We are currently canvassing everybody along the shoreline and anybody who might have seen anything." Davis also told reporters that State Police divers were assisting the search for Colby. Helping with the shoreline and water search were twelve additional divers and several Coast Guard crews.

"There's no visibility in any of the waters," said one diver, "so it's all done by feel."

Within hours, CNN reported that several helicopters had joined the search, as well as a team of dogs. Meanwhile, light aircraft were flying low over Chesapeake Bay, scanning the waters for any unusual objects. Colby's son Paul rushed to the scene with his own diving gear to join the search. Complicating matters was that searchers were soon informed that, besides Colby, they should be on the lookout for another man, Wolfgang Siebeck. A lifelong boater, Siebeck had fallen out of a sailboat and presumably drowned. Colby's wife, Sally Shelton-Colby, an official with the U.S. Agency for International Development, was contacted in Texas where she was attending meetings. She was shocked and immediately made arrangements to return home. The next day an Associated Press report misquoted Mrs. Colby, stating that she had spoken to her husband the day he disappeared and that he had told her he "hadn't been feeling well, but was going canoeing anyway." She corrected the report, saying that Colby had telephoned her in Texas and said he planned on eating dinner and then taking a shower and going to bed. He had said nothing about not feeling well. He had been feeling fine and had no health problems of any significance.

Later, questions about where the AP report had originated would be raised. Some observers pointed out that it conveniently laid the subtle groundwork for an accidental death caused by illness and drowning. Once home, Mrs. Colby remained upbeat, telling reporters that her husband had faced adversity all his life, including parachuting behind enemy lines during World War II and experiencing a "terrible mugging" on the streets of Washington, D.C. several years beforehand.

The search for the missing, former DCI continued for a week, and then searchers discovered his decomposed, waterlogged body on the beach of an uninhabited Chesapeake Bay island. (The same day they also found the body of Siebeck who had drowned.) Maryland's medical examiner, John Smialek, found that Colby had "likely collapsed..."either from a heart attack or a stroke" before falling out of his canoe, into the water where he "suffered hypothermia and drowned." No drugs were found in Colby's body, said Smialek, except for small traces of the wine he had consumed just before his death.

At the time of his death, William Colby, who had left employment with the CIA in January 1976, had been a highly active attorney, representing a number of financial investment funds, and sitting on a number of prestigious boards of directors. Nobody seemed to notice that Colby, according to several financial reporting sources, was on the board of American Equity Investors, or AEI, a firm founded by Prescott Bush, former CIA director George Herbert Walker Bush's father, which included several other former CIA officials, George

Clairmont, Howard Hebert, and, of Iran-Contra fame, Robert McFarlane, as well as attorney Harry Huge, of the law firm Rogovin, Huge, and Schiller, as president.

Just before Colby's body was found, Saracco's office received an anonymous telephone call from a person who stated that it would be wise for the Assistant District Attorneys on the Olson case to look into the death of another CIA employee who had also died in the waters of Maryland's Chesapeake Bay. This was John Arthur Paisley.

"I had never heard of him," Saracco later said, "and besides, Maryland isn't my jurisdiction. People do die regardless who they are, but..." Saracco left his last word hanging and did not finish. He sighed, and said, "I went ahead and looked into it anyway. I didn't see many similarities. I didn't see any connections to Olson, more to the point."

The CIA had hired John Paisley at the end of 1953, two weeks after Frank Olson's death. After twenty-five years with the Agency, working mainly in the Office of Strategic Research, Paisley vanished one day in September 1978 while sailing in a boat he had owned for years. The spot where he vanished was about thirty-seven miles from where Colby had disappeared. Days after Paisley went missing, his body was pulled from the Chesapeake Bay. There was a bullet hole in his head and weighted divers' belts were strapped to his body. His death was ruled a suicide. Rumors were strong that he had been a Soviet spy, and some of his friends and family expressed real problems with the ruling of suicide.

In the days after Colby was buried, Saracco and Bibb heard all sorts of rumors about the former DCI having been assassinated. Saracco resorted to quoting his favorite author, Thomas Pynchon and chose this line from the novel *V*: "Events seem to be ordered into an ominous logic." Nonetheless, Saracco chalked Colby's death up to coincidence and huddled with partner Bibb to decide their next move.

Also at this time, Saracco was urged by some of his colleagues to look into the "suicide" of the nation's first Secretary of Defense James Forrestal, because of similarities with Olson's death. Forrestal had been a strong advocate for biological warfare. In March 1948, fourteen months before his shocking death, he had written a letter to President Truman that many biological warfare historians feel was the first giant step toward the creation of Camp Detrick's Special Operations Division. Forrestal had told Truman there "is a real need for a thorough study and review of national policy on biological warfare." The chief factors to be considered in formulating the policy, wrote Forrestal, were "public reaction in this country, our relationships in the United Nations, our international relationships, [the] future security of the country, [and] the probable value of biological warfare." The probable value as a military weapon, said Forrestal, included "whether biological warfare comes within the scope of the language 'weapons of mass destruction.'"

A little over a year after writing this letter, Forrestal was no longer Secretary of Defense, having been forced to resign in March 1949 due to political reasons by President Truman. He was, in fact, confined to a guarded room in the Bethesda Naval Hospital on the edge of Washington, D.C. His physician hospitalized him for treatment of exhaustion and stress. On May 22, 1949, Forrestal, according to Bethesda Naval Hospital officials, "jumped or fell" to his death from the window of his hospital room. Prior to his resignation, Forrestal had knocked heads hard with White House and Congressional officials over the post-World War II "Morgenthau Plan," which was devised by Henry Morgenthau Jr., Robert Morgenthau's father. (The Plan was the proposal for the postwar partition and demilitarization of Germany. It was designed to eliminate Germany's military power, but also to transfer its industrial and mining capacity to the control of the United States. Henry Morgenthau Jr. was Secretary of the Treasury at the time.) Forrestal's death remains mysterious and controversial to this day. Forrestal's brother claimed that he had been murdered.

George White's close friend and political ally Rudolph Halley also died suddenly on November 19, 1956. Halley had been privy to many of the details of White's work with the CIA, including Frank Olson's death. White's date books for the years 1952 and 1953 are replete with references to Halley, including several meetings with the attorney-politician at the Bedford Street safe house. Halley was only 43 years old at the time of his death. He had left New York to live in Puerto Rico where he became an unlikely investor in a jai alai project. The official cause of his death was listed as "pneumonia" but many close to him seriously questioned this. They reported that Halley had been in excellent health at the time of his passing. Given Halley's large number of enemies in the underworld, his death is likely to remain a mystery for years to come.

Digging a bit deeper, Saracco was astounded to discover the number of odd deaths that befell people who were on the periphery of the Olson case or intersected with it in some way. Former OSS director William Donovan, who spurred the "truth drug" experiments into reality, had acted bizarrely before his death in 1957, frantically reporting that he had spotted a battalion of Russian troops marching into Manhattan across the Fifty-Ninth Street Bridge, and telling anyone who would listen that there were "Commies" deeply embedded in the ranks of the CIA and that they "knew everything worth knowing well before the president himself knew it." Donovan reportedly died from a rare brain condition.

And CIA founder and Director of Plans, Frank Wisner in 1965 had blown his head off with a shotgun at his farmhouse on Maryland's Eastern Shore. He had been forced to undergo a long series of shock 'therapy' and psychoactive drug treatments at Sheppard Pratt Hospital in Baltimore for severe depression. Before he committed suicide, Wisner had developed an obsession with notorious Nazi Martin Bormann, who had escaped apprehension after World War II.

Closer to Olson, there was the reported suicide, sometime in the early 1960s, of Everett Champlin who had attended the Deep Creek Lake meeting. Moreover, rumors had circulated that at least two other people who had been in attendance at the Deep Creek meeting had died mysteriously. Saracco and Bibb told this author in 2000 that they intended to look into some of the possibly related deaths, but the results, if any, of their inquiry are unknown. In a conversation with this author, however, Saracco had prophetically remarked:

> There's bodies all around this case that have mysteries all their own. I imagine it's only a matter of time before [the Olson] case bumps into the JFK assassination.

This author had suggested to Saracco that, to assist his inquiries about William Colby's background, he might want to pick up a copy of Colby's book, *Honorable Men*, published in 1978.

"You're not going to believe this," I said, "but take a close look at the two pages where Colby writes about Frank Olson."

"What's it say?" Saracco asked.

"Let me read it to you," I said. "Colby is writing about the Rockefeller Commission's report and he states: *'Indeed, even the CIA professionals, myself included, were shocked and shamed to learn of the true circumstances around this CIA officer's suicide, as revealed in the report, following his being administered LSD without his knowledge in 1953 in a joint CIA-Army test program.'*"

"You're kidding?" said Saracco. "All these years and nobody noticed that?"

"It just goes to show that it's like people say today, nobody reads carefully, if at all," I replied.

"So what does it mean if he had been a CIA employee?"

I hesitated to answer. Eric Olson had asked me the very same question when I had pointed out the passage to him. Remarkably, Colby's words had also escaped Eric's attention.

"At the very least, if it's true that Olson was an Agency employee, it's another dimension to the cover-up, but still it could be a mistake, however, there are Lashbrook's words also to consider in the Colby documents," I said.

"What does he say?"

"In his statement given to a CIA security agent the morning after Olson's death, which the agent wrote in his report: 'Mr. Lashbrook advised that the SUBJECT [Olson] was a biochemist and Agency employee assigned to a project at Camp Detrick.'"

"That's Lashbrook's statement?"

"As taken by the CIA security officer in New York. And there's a little more," I said.

"What's that?"

"The July 1975 document that Eric calls 'the mysterious document.'"

"The one the AP reporter found?" Saracco asked.

"Yes. One of the listed items of that document reads: 'After [Olson's] death—apparently large number of government checks left uncashed in personal file. Sources— Mrs. Haller Best and Col. Ruwet.'"

"Were these Camp Detrick checks?" asked Saracco.

"We don't know," I said. "I would guess they were government pay checks for either Detrick or CIA work. One possibility is that Olson was being paid by both the CIA and Camp Detrick and that he decided not to cash certain checks so that he would not be double dipping, so to speak. Or they could have been the disability checks that he supposedly felt guilty about."

"So, Olson was actually an Agency employee," Saracco ventured.

"It certainly could be argued that he was, but maybe you could do something to confirm that. I'm not ready to assume anything."

That I know of, nobody in the district attorney's office made any moves to confirm Olson's possible CIA employment. In 2001, I wrote a letter to the CIA's Public Information office requesting verification, but I never received an answer. In follow-up months later, I requested that the CIA send me any files pertaining to Frank Olson's employment. The reply I received was that there were no additional files on Frank Olson other than those given to the Olson family in 1975.

The "mysterious document" cited above – actually a facsimile of a document given on July 24, 1975 to an unknown recipient at Fort Detrick – contains a number of interesting items. It was found in 1994, around the time that Olson's body was exhumed. The person who discovered the document was Associated Press reporter Deb Riechmann who had gone to Fort Detrick to interview scientists there. Before she departed the installation, she discovered a one-page, typed document in a file pertaining to Frank Olson.

The document is headed: "Re - Dr. F. W. Olson." [The middle initial "W" is an obvious mistake, but reveals that the unidentified author of the document was aware of the middle initial – and perhaps name, Wicks – of Olson's wife, Alice, and his three children.] The document reads: "Suggest review of following items," and then lists six items to be looked into regarding Olson's death. Two of these, items 3 and 4, are most germane to Olson's death. They are:

> 3. Reason for request to be released as Chief, S.O. Division in Spring 1953. Source—Dr. J.L. Schwab.
> 4. Trip to Paris and Norway in 1953 (?) and possible fear of security violation. Sources—F.W. Wagner, H.T. Eigelsbach, Robert Lashbrook, and Dr. Harold Abramson.

As cryptic as these items were, Saracco would soon learn what they meant.

During the same week as the conversation with Saracco about Frank Olson's possible CIA employment, Saracco and Bibb queried this author about the completeness of the Colby documents.

Said Saracco, "I know there's a lot in the pages given to the Olson's, but do you think there's more?"

"More pertaining to Olson's death?" I asked.

"His death and his work."

"I'm certain there is," I said.

"Why?"

"Well, initially my gut told me there was, but then the CIA confirmed it."

"Confirmed it recently?"

"Yes," I said. "In one of my recent FOIA [Freedom of Information Act] requests there was a document included that confirmed it."

"What'd it say?"

I put the phone down while I pulled the document from a file. "It's a memorandum for the record, dated 30 July 1975, with the top and bottom headings: 'KEEP ON TOP OF FILE,'" I explained to Saracco. "Its subject is: 'Frank Olson Suicide' followed by three short, numbered paragraphs. The last two paragraphs are the most important." I read them to Saracco verbatim:

> 2. *Considerable information concerning Mr. Frank Olson, as well as the ARTICHOKE/BLUEBIRD drug experiments, is contained in the* [several words redacted], *which is maintained in the office of* [several words redacted].
> 3. *It should further be noted that on 24 July 1975, the Director of Central Intelligence* <u>declassified</u> *much of the material relating to Frank Olson.* [Italics added; underlining original.]

"Is it possible that the memo is referring to the files that were destroyed by Helms and Gottlieb?" asked Saracco.

"No," I said. "Those files were destroyed in 1973. The date on this memo is 1975. It also states 'much of the material' which clearly says to me there's more material that wasn't released."

ATTEMPTING TO INTERVIEW RUWET AND LASHBROOK

In August 1996, the prosecutors met with Vincent Ruwet, Olson's former SOD superior, at his Frederick, Maryland home. They sat on his back porch drinking iced tea as the sky darkened and a thunderstorm rolled off the Cacoctin Mountains. Despite his Southern hospitality, Ruwet was evasive. His answers were mechanical and seemed rehearsed. He said that he, too, had been dosed with LSD at the Deep Creek Lake meeting and that he had hallucinated wildly and "experienced the direct and indirect effects of the drug for weeks after."

But, when Saracco asked why, then, had he been entrusted to escort Frank Olson to New York just days later, Ruwet's explanation was less than satisfactory. He seemed thrown off balance by the question and fumbled about for an adequate answer that never came. Saracco and Bibb decided to re-interview him, but by the time they could re-schedule, it was too late. Ruwet dropped dead from a heart attack while at church on November 16, 1996.

Colleagues kidded Saracco that he had become the "kiss of death," but Saracco ignored this and proceeded with efforts to interview Lashbrook and Gottlieb, convinced that the odd chain of events had played itself out. After several letters to Lashbrook went unanswered, Saracco issued the first subpoena of the case. On September 2, 1997, when the sheriff in Ojai, California knocked on Lashbrook's door to serve him, the retired CIA officer told him that he had the wrong address and that he "did not know anyone by the name of Robert Lashbrook."

On October 24, Lashbrook's attorney filed a motion in the District Court of Los Angeles to quash any request to depose his client. Six months later an appeals court ruled to enforce the subpoena. Saracco and Bibb booked flights to California, but at the last minute they were blocked by CIA and DOJ attorneys, demanding to know in writing what questions the prosecutors intended to ask Lashbrook. Only after the CIA and DOJ had reviewed and approved the questions would they agree to make Lashbrook available, and then only if he would be guaranteed immunity under New York law.

The CIA's attorneys told Saracco that the Agency had serious concerns that deposing Lashbrook might expose matters "still held top secret," thus "posing a risk to national security." Bibb quipped to Saracco that by the time they sat down with Lashbrook, they would be in their retirement years.

Finally, a year later, in October 1998, following months of missed deadlines, delays, and broken commitments by CIA and Department of Justice attorneys, Saracco and Bibb flew to California to depose Lashbrook. The event, not wholly unexpectedly, was anticlimactic, though useful. Despite his advanced age of 80 and his chronic health problems, the former CIA official was lucid and characteristically caustic. Bibb later characterized Lashbrook's attitude as "confident and cavalier." The two prosecutors questioned Lashbrook for nearly seven hours. CIA attorneys who were present for the session berated the prosecutors for "taking advantage of an old man."

As agreed, as a result of Lashbrook being subpoenaed and formally questioned by prosecutors for grand jury testimony, as opposed to being deposed, under New York law he was granted immunity from prosecution in the case.

I asked Eric Olson about this and he said, "That would have been a fair trade if Saracco and Bibb had gotten something which they could have used to carry the investigation further. For reasons that you can speculate upon as well as I can, that did not happen."

Unfortunately, Lashbrook's testimony is considered secret and not available to anyone outside the District Attorney's office. When this author asked Saracco and Bibb over lunch about Lashbrook's testimony I received expressionless, silent stares in reply. "Well, fine," I pressed, "if you can't share anything, at least tell me whether or not you believed what he testified about." The two of them feigned exasperation.

"So you believed everything he told you?" I asked.

Bibb shook his head and said, "Not everything, no." Saracco looked down at the table and said nothing.

Eric had also attempted to discover what Lashbrook had told the prosecutors. He described his efforts to me:

> Saracco and Bibb told me that Lashbrook did not confess, that he stuck to the 'conventional story.' I asked them, 'Which version of the conventional story?' but I never got a clear answer to that. After a few months, I again tried to probe about this. I said to Bibb, 'Well, you said that Lashbrook stuck to the conventional story. If that is so, and if you believed what he said, you would have closed the investigation down. As you have not done that I can only conclude that you didn't believe what Lashbrook told you.' To which Bibb said, 'We believed some of it, some of it we didn't believe, and some of it was simply absurd.'

THE UNEXPECTED REVELATIONS OF BILL HAYWARD

About the same time that Saracco and Bibb were attempting to interview Lashbrook, this author was contacted by Bill Hayward, a former Hollywood producer. As a young boy, Hayward had been treated by Dr. Lawrence Kubie. Kubie was a psychologist who had been deeply involved in the early OSS truth drug experiments and later, following World War II, had been a consultant for the Army and CIA. Hayward had read one of this author's articles about Frank Olson in which Kubie was mentioned. Hayward had been unaware of Kubie's relationship with the American intelligence community and was curious to learn more. After several lengthy conversations with this author, Hayward began to suspect that perhaps he had been used as some sort of guinea pig.

"I'm amazed at Kubie's connections to the OSS and CIA," Hayward said. "Do these guys have no shame? People trust them with their lives and sanity."

Hayward had been a rebellious and adventurous youth causing his father to think that he needed special attention psychologically; he was sent to Kubie for treatment and also to the Menninger Clinic, where he spent four years. At that time, Kubie and Karl and William Menninger, close friends with DCI Allen Dulles, were all professional consultants with the CIA. (Bill's sister, Bridget Hayward, also was sent to Kubie and the Menninger Clinic. Bill produced a movie in 1980 based on the book, *Haywire*, written by his other sister, Brooke, about their family and his sister's experience.)

"I didn't really understand what Kubie or the Menninger Clinic were trying to do with me," Hayward said. "I knew it didn't make much sense and it sure as hell didn't make me feel any better about myself or the world. In a lot of ways it confused the hell out of me. I found life to be pretty exciting and it seemed to me they wanted to suck the passion and excitement for life right out of me. The drugs I was given made me feel like I was half-dead, emotionless, robotic."

Said Hayward, "I don't know if I was used in any experiment sponsored by the government or not. And at this point in my life it doesn't really matter. I'd just hate to see anyone else go through what I did."

Hayward, whose mother died from a drug overdose in 1960, really brought to life for me a lot of the pain and anguish felt by victims of misguided psychiatry. Reading about mind control and behavior modification victims was one thing, but to hear about it from someone firsthand was nothing less than terrifying. In short, it really brought home the chamber of endless horrors that the CIA had created for so many unwitting and innocent people.

Hayward told me several times that he loved riding motorcycles and that he found "true freedom" while riding. (Among other movies, Hayward had produced the classic, *Easy Rider*.) Hayward's friends often feared that his passion for riding would result in his death. And it almost did. About two years after we had begun talking, Hayward had a bad accident on his bike in 2003 that left him severely disabled and depressed. He killed himself in March 2008.

THE STRANGE CASE OF STANLEY GLICKMAN

Two weeks before they traveled to California, Saracco and Bibb had learned that Lashbrook's former CIA superior, Dr. Sidney Gottlieb, was the subject of a civil lawsuit for the alleged LSD dosing of an American citizen in Paris in 1952. The case was of obvious interest to the two prosecutors because of Gottlieb's involvement in Olson's dosing a year later. Saracco was informed that the attorney bringing the suit against Gottlieb was Sidney Bender of the New York firm Leventritt, Lewittes, & Bender. Saracco called Bender who told him the fascinating story behind the case.

In 1952, a twenty-four year old American named Stanley Milton Glickman was pursuing a promising career as an artist in France. Glickman, the son of a successful New York furrier, had moved to Paris in the summer of 1951 to study painting at the Academie de la Grande Chaumiere, and about seven months later, as an apprentice in the studio of renowned French modernist Fernand Leger. (In the 1940s, Leger had decorated the New York City apartment of Nelson A. Rockefeller.) By early autumn 1952, Glickman had his own studio on the outskirts of Paris and already had one of his paintings displayed in New York's Metropolitan Museum of Art.

One evening in mid-October, about thirteen months after the peculiar outbreak at Pont-St.-Esprit, the young artist went into Paris to meet a friend at the Café Select. They were soon joined by two American men who Glickman did not know. After some casual conversation and several glasses of wine, the two strangers fell into a heated debate with Glickman about politics, power, and patriotism. The debate went on for hours. The men told Glickman that he was a naïve bohemian unmindful of the real ways of the world. Glickman told

643

the two conservatively dressed men that their attitudes of political superiority were offensive to all that he felt was right with the world. When it grew late and Glickman was preparing to leave, one of the men offered him a drink as a conciliatory gesture. Glickman had been drinking only coffee, but reluctantly accepted. The man got up from the table and went to the bar, returning with a glass of Chartreuse for the artist. As the man moved back to the table, Glickman noticed that he walked with a pronounced limp.

Glickman sipped the drink slowly, and the conversation turned to other subjects. One of the men remarked that France was fascinating for its many sites of religious miracles. Midway through his liqueur, Glickman began to feel strange. A tremendous feeling of anxiety filled his chest. The anxiety quickly gave way to the sensation that he was floating above the table. His perception of objects and their dimensions became distorted. Sounds took on an odd resonance, some painful to his ears. The two men watched him intently. One of them leaned toward him and said, "Surely a man of your many talents can perform your own miracles. Can't you?"

Believing that he had been poisoned, Glickman fled into the street, leaving his friend behind. When he woke up the next morning he realized he had lost several hours of time. He was also hallucinating wildly. For two weeks he wandered about Paris "in the pain of madness, delusion, and terror." He returned to the Café Select, went to the same table as before, and sat with his eyes closed, irrationally waiting "for someone to come and tell me what had happened." When he refused to leave, he was taken away to the American Hospital of Paris and given electroshock treatment. After his release, he lived in a state of "stress, terror, and hallucination" for eight months, until his family learned of his condition and brought him back to the United States in July 1953.

A psychiatrist treated Glickman for the next twenty-five years. He lived in New York's East Village, never again painted, and ran a small antiques shop. His closest friends were his three dogs, Charlie, Gent, and Kuma. Sometimes he told people his name was Paul Galen.

But that was only the beginning of the story Bender revealed to Saracco.

One day in late September 1977, Stanley Glickman's sister, Gloria Kronisch, was watching the televised U.S. Senate hearings about CIA abuses, chaired by Sen. Ted Kennedy. A witness was describing an experimental CIA drug program called MKULTRA, which had used hundreds of unwitting American citizens as guinea pigs.

The witness, former CIA official Dr. Sidney Gottlieb, informed the Senate committee that he justified the CIA experiments on the basis of national security. The U.S. was essentially at war with the Soviets, Gottlieb said, and if using drugs like LSD on unsuspecting people was necessary, then so be it. Said witness Gottlieb: "Harsh as it may sound in retrospect, it was felt that in an issue where national survival might be concerned, such a procedure and such a risk was a reasonable one to take."

Gloria had heard enough. She went straight to the telephone and called her brother Stanley.

"Are you watching television?" Gloria asked.

"No, there's never anything on," said Stanley.

"There's something on right now that you have to see," Gloria said.

Glickman was shocked at what he saw and heard. Never in his wildest imagination had he thought that he might have been the subject of a CIA experiment with mind-expanding drugs. He was stunned. He recognized the man from the Paris café. After several days, sitting in his small apartment, watching the hearings, Glickman talked to some of his neighbors who had also been watching the Kennedy committee hearings. They told him about the death of a man named Frank Olson and the ordeal his family had gone through just prior to the hearings, trying to find out what happened. Indeed, Glickman learned that Alice Olson had appeared earlier as a witness before the Kennedy committee. Glickman's neighbors also told him that Dr. Sidney Gottlieb walked with a limp because he had been born with a clubfoot. They weren't sure, his neighbor's said, but they had heard somewhere that Gottlieb was involved somehow in Frank Olson's death.

Stanley nervously tried to telephone Sen. Kennedy's Washington, D.C. office and the office of the U.S. Attorney General. He had something to tell them that they might be interested in, he told the people that answered his calls. But nobody wanted to listen to what he had to say. A sympathetic secretary at the Department of Justice finally told Glickman that he needed to get a lawyer. But he had no money. His sister, Gloria, told him that she would pay the costs of hiring an attorney. Stanley Glickman died on December 11, 1992. Following his death, Gloria, with Sidney Bender as her attorney, pushed her brother's case forward.

Bender concluded his story by telling Saracco that the case, following many delays and appeals, was now finally due to be heard in court within months. Saracco was momentarily speechless after hearing about Glickman's saga. Later he would say that he felt that he "had become an involuntary participant in an X-Files episode." He reasoned that the Glickman case could be wholly unrelated to Olson's and just coincidental, but his instincts said otherwise.

Again, Saracco thought of a line from one of Pynchon's books, *The Crying of Lot 49*: "There are some irregularities, Miz Maas."

GOTTLIEB AND LASHBROOK: IN THEIR OWN WORDS...

As a result of their exposure to the Glickman case, Saracco and Bibb became aware of a number of depositions that had been taken from Gottlieb and

Lashbrook not only in the Glickman case but in past civil court actions. A number of sections from those depositions were intriguing and illuminating.

> Question: *Were you present after Dr. Olson consumed his drink that contained LSD?*
> Gottlieb: Yes.
> Question: *Did he say anything to you?*
> Gottlieb: Not to me.
> Question: *How long were you in his presence?*
> Gottlieb: For the next three, four hours.
> Question: *And did he say anything to anybody in the room?*
> Gottlieb: I don't know.
> Question: *What was his reaction after drinking that, in your words? You were there, and you saw him consume it and he was in your presence for three or four hours. How did he react?*
> Gottlieb: I don't remember any particular way that he reacted.
> Question: *Was he just silent?*
> Gottlieb: I just... he said or did nothing that is rememberable by me.
> Question: *Did you see him on the same day?*
> Gottlieb: No.
> Question: *On the next morning?*
> Gottlieb: The answer is no to that.

In 1986 Robert Lashbrook was questioned extensively about the events of Deep Creek Lake. He testified, as follows:

> Question: *Who made the decision to do LSD that night? You or Gottlieb?*
> Lashbrook: I think Gottlieb probably thought of it. He suggested it to me.
> Question: *You concurred in it?*
> Lashbrook: Yes. I felt that it was nothing really more drastic than what we had already done in our little coffee classes, yes. [Earlier in the questioning, Lashbrook had stated that CIA-TSS personnel took LSD during "coffee classes."]
> Question: *Could you go through now the evening, exactly what happened? You had dinner, and then you were standing around the fireplace. Could you give me the details?*
> Lashbrook: I assume so. Sitting at dinner, and after-dinner drinks, and in some of the after-dinner drinks, there was LSD.
> Question: *How was that administered?*
> Lashbrook: In an after-dinner drink.
> Question: *Well, how?*
> Lashbrook: In an after-dinner drink.
> Question: *Well, did you put it into the Cointreau bottle, or did you put it into each of the glasses?*
> Lashbrook: In the bottle.
> Question: *You put into a Cointreau bottle LSD?*

Lashbrook: Right.

Question: *And then that bottle was poured to these various people?*

Lashbrook: Yes.

Question: *Now, it is your testimony, and you are under oath,* that Olson knew this was coming?

Lashbrook: That Olson knew it was coming?

Question: *Yes.*

Lashbrook: It was my understanding that this had been discussed with the people at Detrick, yes.

Question: *From whom did you get that understanding?*

Lashbrook: Sid Gottlieb.

Question: *Well, if Gottlieb had testified the other way, would that affect your testimony any? Gottlieb never suggested that Olson knew this was coming.*

Lashbrook: Are you sure?

Question: *Yes.*

Lashbrook: Okay. He definitely told me this before the meeting.

Question: *What did he tell you exactly?*

Lashbrook: That he discussed it with, and I think specifically, Vincent Ruwet. I'm surprised that he would say the opposite at the present time.

Question: *This is not the answer. You changed your testimony.*

Lashbrook: I did not.

Mr. Kragie [CIA attorney]: He's entitled to finish his answer.

Question: *Please finish your answer.*

Lashbrook: I've discussed this with Sidney Gottlieb when all this business broke and all the publicity on this occurred, and at that point Sidney said, yes, I recalled correctly that he had discussed with people at Detrick and that he was very surprised that at this point apparently Vincent Ruwet was saying the opposite.

Question: *Did Sidney Gottlieb tell you he had mentioned this to Ruwet or he had mentioned this to Olson, question mark?*

Lashbrook: If I remember right, it was Ruwet.

Question: *Told you he...*

Lashbrook: But specifically... well, it would be the people at Detrick. And I think a specific name which was mentioned was Ruwet.

Question: *Did he tell you he had told Olson that they were going to get LSD that night?*

Lashbrook: I don't recall that he specifically mentioned Olson.

Question: *Well, Olson was the important one because he's the dead one.*

Lashbrook: Right.

Question: *And he never mentioned Olson, did he, as knowing?*

Lashbrook: The only name specifically I recall was Vincent Ruwet.

Question: *And Mr. Ruwet has died?*

Lashbrook: He died?

Question: *Yes.* [Not true.]

Lashbrook: I don't know.

Question: *You don't know?*

Lashbrook: I don't know that he's dead, no.

Question: *I see.*

Lashbrook: Apparently he lived long enough to say that isn't true.

Question: *Lived long enough to say what isn't true?*

Lashbrook: That Sidney talked with him.

Question: *Sidney never told you he talked with any of the others, did he?*

Lashbrook: I don't really recall. I mean I recall that one name as being specifically mentioned. Now, Vincent Ruwet was in charge of the unit, and so it would primarily... and this is not part of the CIA... so it would be primarily up to Vincent Ruwet to discuss this with the other people in the particular unit. We dealt primarily with Vincent Ruwet as being chief of the group.

Question: *Now, if Vincent Ruwet and the others knew LSD was coming, why did you sneak it into a Cointreau bottle?*

Lashbrook: Sneak it in? My understanding was that what the agreement was that they were willing to have it... to take it sometime, not that specific time. The agreement was not that particular night, that a night or a time. I'm not sure I know what you mean by sneak it into a bottle.

Question: *Well, you didn't tell anybody you were putting it into the bottle, did you?*

Lashbrook: The people there?

Question: *Yes.*

Lashbrook: No, not for that specific time. That's what I'm trying to say. The semi-not-knowing-about—it was not knowing specifically when this would occur, and if they were to know specifically when it was to occur, then I guess something would have to be sneaked into something at a particular time, yes.

Question: *But this isn't like the coffee item, is it? Here you gave it to all of them, didn't you?*

Lashbrook: No.

Question: *Well, you put it in a Cointreau bottle. Did they all take the Cointreau?*

Lashbrook: No, not everyone had... it was not given to everyone.

Question: *How were the people chosen to whom it was given?*

Lashbrook: Okay. There was one of the people at Detrick that was specifically excluded because of a medical problem. And I do not know about the medical problem and information on the medical problem. I think it would have had to have come from Ruwet. I did not take it. I do not believe Sidney took it, because we felt that there must be people on hand who would be able to do something if anything was required to be done. So not everyone took it, no.

Question: *Well, if the man with the medical problem reached for the Cointreau bottle, what would you do, pull it away? You knew that there was LSD in the Cointreau bottle.*

Lashbrook: There were two Cointreau bottles.

Question: *You shifted then around so only the people—*

Lashbrook: Sure.

Question: *—who you wanted to have it, had it?*

Lashbrook: (Nods head up and down.)

Question: *Is that right?*

Lashbrook: "One in your left lapel, one in your right lapel." Yes, of course. [Here Lashbrook is referring to Mulholland's past training.]

Question: *Was that meant as a joke?*

Lashbrook: Okay.

Question: *I don't think it's very funny when somebody dies as a result of something you did. You may think it's funny, but I don't. Now, what do you mean in your lapels? Where were these two bottles you are talking about?*

Lashbrook: Okay. As I recall, the after-dinner drink was served to the individuals. There was no provision made for anyone to go back for a second portion of the after-dinner drink, which contained LSD, because the amount in each dose was... yeah... in each drink was purposely small, and there was certainly concern... or wanted to make sure that no one got an excessive amount. So the bottle which contained LSD was very carefully controlled.

Question: *Who controlled it?*

Lashbrook: As I recall, I did. And it was very careful how much was taken out of that particular bottle, yes.

Question: *How did you choose Olson to receive the bottle?*

Lashbrook: I guess because he was there.

Question: *Did everybody get it? I thought you said everybody didn't get it.*

Lashbrook: Except those who were specifically excluded for some specific reason.

Question: *How many were specifically excluded for some specific reason?*

Lashbrook: At least one person from Detrick, and I don't recall how many, but I think at least two people from our group.

Question: *Who were the two from your group? There were only three of you there, you, Gottlieb and Hamilton.* [Oddly, plaintiff's attorney Joe Rauh confuses Hughes with Dr. James Hamilton, an OSS associate of George White's.]

Lashbrook: Who?

Question: *I think the name in the report was Hamilton, but if it's somebody else, I don't know it.*

Lashbrook: I don't know. So at least two.

Question: *Who were the two excluded?*

Lashbrook: Me and Gottlieb.

Question: *Now, what happened after that night?*

Lashbrook: As far as I know?

Question: *Yes.*

Lashbrook: Well, I guess first thing I knew after everyone had left the next morning, left and went home, and I guess it was several days later... I think probably the following week... and I received a phone call from Vince Ruwet. And he said that Frank had been acting strangely and we should do something immediately, and he and Frank Olson were getting in the car and coming to Washington, D.C.

In the same 1986 deposition quoted above, Robert Lashbrook was questioned about the events of November 28, 1953 and Frank Olson's final hours alive.

Lashbrook: When we were through [our last meeting with Dr. Abramson], we were ready to come back to Washington, D.C., only we couldn't get a reservation on the airplane. And so there was a question whether we'd go to the airport and just wait and see if we could get on standby or stay in New York until the following morning when we could get a reservation. And I think I was reluctant to go to the airport on standby. I wasn't... I was sure Frank would be all right, but it would be very crowded, very boring. I was a little hesitant. So we decided to stay overnight in New York.

Question: *Where did you stay?*

Lashbrook: I think it was the Statler Hotel.

Question: *What happened that night?*

Lashbrook: Well, he jumped out the window.

Question: *Where were you when he jumped out the window?*

Lashbrook: In bed.

Question: *Did you know he had gotten out of bed?*

Lashbrook: No.

Question: *You didn't hear him get out of bed?*

Lashbrook: No.

Question: *What did you do when he jumped out the window? What floor were you on?*

Lashbrook: I think it was the thirteenth floor, although I don't know they had a thirteenth floor. It was very high.

Question: *What did you do when he jumped out the window?*

Lashbrook: Ran to the window and looked out the window.

Question: *Then what did you do?*

Lashbrook: Well, what did I do? Well, I could see that Frank was out the window on the sidewalk and people rushing over to him. What did I do? I got on the phone and I called, as I recall, I called down to the desk. I called Sid Gottlieb, and I called Dr. Abramson.

Question: *And then what happened?*

Lashbrook: I figured I better wait in the room, wait for the police.

Question: *Police come to the room?*

Lashbrook: Yes.

Question: *What did you tell them?*

Lashbrook: What could I tell them?

Question: *What did you tell them?*

Lashbrook: He jumped out the window.

Question: *Did you tell them he was an Army man that had taken LSD?*

Lashbrook: I'm sure I told them he was an Army man.

Question: *Isn't it a fact that a cover story was made up for the police, that everybody lied, you and the others, lied to the police and made up a cover story that wasn't true at all?*

Lashbrook: That's not quite correct.

Question: *What exactly happened?*

Lashbrook: I did not... wasn't... I did not tell the police that he had taken LSD. That would have been very stupid to have done so. To begin with, no one knew the name LSD at that time. Beyond that, it didn't really matter. He had jumped out the window.

Question: *Well, didn't the CIA want to cover up the fact that he had jumped out the window?*

Lashbrook: No. It was public knowledge. It was in the newspaper.

Question: *But wasn't it covered up that that resulted from the LSD he had been given? Wasn't that covered up until it came out about 22 years later in the President's Commission report?*

Lashbrook: It was not revealed for the simple reason that the CIA did not wish to indicate an interest in LSD, yes. This does not imply any evil motives whatsoever.

Question: *You said earlier that you couldn't understand why Sandoz would have wanted to cover up the same thing.*

Lashbrook: Right.

Question: *Why did you want to cover this up?*

Lashbrook: It was defined as being classified, if you can understand that.

Question: *Do you remember what the cover story was that was given the police and the papers?*

Lashbrook: That Frank jumped out the window, period.

Question: *Well, usually the question is asked why a man jumps out the window. Wasn't the cover story worked out on a telephone call between you and Gottlieb and the Security Office?*

Lashbrook: No. I think the only thing that I indicated as far as a reason was that it was my understanding he had been having some emotional problems of some type, perhaps he was depressed or whatever.

Question: *Had he been having any emotional problems?*

Lashbrook: I think at that time that was my understanding. I'm fuzzy on that, whether he really did or not. And I believe... I'm sure that at the time I had been told, you know... after Frank started having problems, the question arose why should he have, you know, had problems, or what role, if any, the LSD had played in the problems that he obviously had developed. And I'm sure it was indicated at that time somehow that Frank had some preexisting problems.

Getting Sidney Gottlieb to Testify

The "irregularities" continued. Following Lashbrook's deposition taken by Saracco and Bibb, the prosecutors concluded that it was time to sit down with Dr. Sidney Gottlieb. Saracco knew it would be difficult because Gottlieb was in the middle of the Glickman trial, underway in the U.S. Southern District Court in New York. After a long delay, a three-judge panel of the Second Circuit Court of Appeals had ruled that Glickman's suit could go forward against Gottlieb. The jury trial began in April 1999.

Saracco and Bibb were intrigued with Gottlieb, having read all that they could find on the elusive CIA official. They were well aware that, besides Lashbrook, he was perhaps one of the only people alive who could unlock the mysteries of Frank Olson's death. Saracco began to painstakingly assemble a profile of the enigmatic Gottlieb in preparation of their anticipated meeting. (This author supplied a number of biographical sources and relevant subject memoranda on Gottlieb to Saracco and Bibb in response to their requests.)

As Saracco and Bibb learned, Gottlieb had admitted to "self-administering" LSD on "at least thirty or forty separate occasions" during his career as a CIA official. Gottlieb was also known to have participated in at least five assassination plots against various world leaders, including Cuba's Fidel Castro and the Congo's Patrice Lumumba. After retiring from the CIA in 1973, he worked briefly as a "special consultant" for the Drug Enforcement Administration, successor agency to the Federal Narcotics Bureau, and then left the country for India.

In New Delhi, he and his wife worked in a hospital for lepers for nearly two years. He returned to the U.S. in the early 1980s and, after going back to college and receiving a degree in speech therapy, he and his wife took up residence on another old farm situated on fifty acres of land in Washington, Virginia, a small village in the Blue Ridge Mountains. The farm was acquired with the idea of establishing a "communal home" that would include several other families. In 1993, Gottlieb told a reporter who made an uninvited J.D. Salinger-like excursion to his residence, that he was "on the side of the angels now" and that he had no interest in talking about his past.

"What can you say about Frank Olson's death?" asked the reporter.

"I don't want to talk about it," said Gottlieb.

"Really? Why not?"

"I just don't want to talk about it," insisted Gottlieb. "It's in my past, and that is where it is going to stay."

Assistant District Attorney Steve Saracco thought he might have better luck asking Gottlieb for an interview. On Monday, March 8, 1999 just moments after he sat down to draft his request to Gottlieb, he received a telephone call from Eric Olson informing him that Sidney Gottlieb had unexpectedly died the day before. According to his attorney, Tom Wilson, Gottlieb had become "dispirited" because of the Glickman litigation, realizing that "he might never find any sense of peace in life."

Said Wilson, "He'd had heart problems for about ten years and then just a few days ago he came down with a severe pneumonia. He was eighty-three and just didn't have enough fight left."

Days after Gottlieb's death, Saracco told the author: "It was uncanny. It took me by complete surprise, I didn't know what to think." When Bibb heard the news his only remark was, "This thing is cursed, and I don't even believe in curses." Within weeks, Saracco officially requested a copy of Gottlieb's death certificate "just to be sure," as he put it.

Several days later, Saracco received an unexpected call from attorney Sidney Bender. Bender told Saracco that during a short break just after the Glickman trial testimony had concluded, and before the jury had begun their deliberations, the judge, Dominick DiCarlo, had dropped dead while exercising in the federal court gym.

"There are some irregularities, Miz Maas."

THE STRANGE AND UNTIMELY DEATH OF DAVID BELIN

David W. Belin would also die on January 17, 1999, just days before Saracco planned to contact him. Belin, 70 at the time of his death, had been a lawyer for the Warren Commission, which investigated the JFK assassination, and at the time of his death was a co-owner of the *Tribune*, a newspaper in Ames, Iowa, and a senior partner in the Des Moines law firm Belin, Lamson, McCormick, Zumbach, Flynn. Belin specialized in corporate law, litigation, and estate law, and in New York was a close advisor to a number of very wealthy families. In 1964, Belin had been appointed by U.S. Supreme Court Chief Justice Earl Warren to be assistant counsel to the President's Commission to Report Upon the Assassination of President Kennedy, commonly called the Warren Commission. Belin's views on the assassination were decidedly controversial: he concluded that Lee Harvey Oswald had acted entirely alone as Kennedy's killer, and that all speculation about conspirators or Government agencies such as the CIA being involved was totally false. Throughout his life, Belin stuck to these beliefs and he wrote two books upholding them. At the time of his death, a *Tribune* editorial stated:

> He was sure—more sure than he was of anything else—that Lee Harvey Oswald acted alone when he killed John F. Kennedy on that awful day in Dallas in 1963. He would argue the minutest detail with anyone who challenged him, and he would excoriate Oliver Stone and others who advanced what he considered conspiracy theories. That issue could make his blood boil.

Critics of Belin's stance on the assassination, especially noted University of Wisconsin history professor and Kennedy assassination expert David W. Wrone, have strong feelings about Belin's honesty and integrity. Professor Wrone pulls no punches and claims that Belin, while on the Commission, "suborned perjury" and "corrupted" witness testimony. Moreover, Wrone writes:

> [Belin] began his work at the Warren Commission with the unforgivable and political premise of Oswald's lone guilt in the assassination and developed 'evidence' to fit that thesis. The supporting documentation to sustain that statement is of the best and unquestionable.

Belin had also been appointed executive director of the Rockefeller Commission that had investigated the CIA in 1974-75 and first revealed that Frank Olson had been dosed with LSD days before his fatal fall. President Gerald Ford, who had also been a member of the Warren Commission, appointed Belin to the Rockefeller Commission.

Saracco realized, in reviewing the Rockefeller Commission's findings, that it had never been adequately explained exactly how the Commission's investigators had discovered the details of Olson's drug dosing. Nor had it been explained how the Commission had acquired specific details about the Deep Creek Lake meeting. Saracco thought that an informal discussion with Belin could possibly be revealing and helpful. But the discussion would never happen. On January 17, 1999, Belin died of head injuries suffered in a fall in a hotel room. The details of his fall are vague; sources within his office said that he had taken a freak fall in the shower of a hotel room in Rochester, Minnesota, where he had gone for his annual physical at the Mayo Clinic. Three days before Belin's death, Eric Olson had contacted this author with the suggestion that Belin be interviewed about several of the mysteries that still surrounded Frank Olson's death and that he might be able to shed some light on. A few weeks earlier I had contacted two of the lead investigators for the Rockefeller Commission, both of whom refused to be interviewed. The day I telephoned Belin's office in Iowa, his administrative assistant informed me that he was hospitalized and in a coma. He died two days later. His *New York Times* obituary read:

> While Mr. Belin lay in a coma in his last days, a friend, visiting him, sought to appraise how ill he really was. He held Mr. Belin's hand, watched his face hopefully and, after a preliminary remark, said, 'David, I think there was a conspiracy to kill John F. Kennedy.' The friend was grieved when, for once, Mr. Belin gave no rebuttal.

THE NEW YORK INVESTIGATIONS CONTINUE

With Colby's, Gottlieb's and Belin's deaths, Saracco and Bibb felt that their case had hit a brick wall. What witnesses remained to speak with? Who remained that could say what had actually happened to Frank Olson? Was the sketchy account laid out in the Colby documents an accurate explanation for why Olson had gone through a hotel window? Saracco turned to the secondary list of witnesses he and Bibb had drawn up. First on the list was Dr. Margaret Ferguson who had worked closely with Dr. Harold Abramson in 1953. (See Book One)

The two prosecutors contacted the elderly psychiatrist in New York, where she was bedridden, but quite lucid, with a recent illness. Saracco said she was most cordial to him but was reluctant to answer many questions about Abramson or Frank Olson. When pressed, she told the prosecutor that he should locate and talk to Dr. Edward Pelikan, stating explicitly that Pelikan would have the answers Saracco wanted. At Saracco's request, this author located Dr. Pelikan but it is unknown if Saracco or Bibb ever spoke with him. Research into Pelikan revealed that the CIA considered him to be an expert in "truth dugs" used for interrogation. (As noted earlier in this book, Pelikan, who is affilitated with the Boston University School of Medicine, declined to answer any of this author's questions.)

At about the same time, the author also located Robert Lashbrook's former Washington, D.C. roommate, Edwin Henry Spoehel. Spoehel also declined to be interviewed by the author; it is not known if the New York Districty Attorny's spoke with Spoehel, who possibly could have been present when Frank Olson was taken to Lashbrook's apartment prior to the last trip to New York.

Meanwhile, friction was developing between Eric Olson and one of his attorneys. Eric contacted me in late January 1999 to say that his legal team was struggling to identify what admissible evidence they had for filing a lawsuit. Eric was especially irked by one of Huge's associates who "never misses a chance to harp on our lack of evidence in a most irritating way." Said Eric, "The most irritating thing is that he never comes up with any creative ideas about what to do with what we have, or how to get more."

I asked Eric what hard evidence his team had acquired thus far and his answer surprised me: "We have the forensic investigation."

"You mean Starrs' findings?" I asked.

"Yes," said Eric.

"But is that enough to make any sort of case?" I asked. I knew the details of Starrs' findings and thought them to be extremely weak and limited in scope, but I did not say this. I had also just learned days before that one of Starrs' key findings — that no military records existed for Frank Olson — was not accurate. Army officials had informed me that such records did exist. I wondered what else Starrs had determined that might be incorrect?

Eric said, "Well, we have the hematoma."

"Anything else?"

"That's really about it, and the problem there is that Frost [Dr. Jack Frost, a Starrs team member] is in disagreement with Starrs about the significance of that. I link the hematoma to the CIA's assassination manual and the recommendation that a blow to the head is advisable in such situations but is that 'evidence' in a legal sense?"

I shook my head. I felt that the hematoma was not really evidence of anything other than that Olson might have struck his head in the course of his fall, especially since the window was reportedly closed.

ARMOND PASTORE'S REVELATIONS

Several potential witnesses that Saracco contacted went out of their way to avoid interviews. Some refused to talk without clearance from the CIA. One witness who did cooperate, however, was Armond Pastore, the assistant manager at the Statler Hotel the night Olson died. Pastore had comforted Olson and also had summoned a priest from a nearby church to administer the last rites. The bloody and broken scientist had desperately attempted to speak to Pastore, but the sounds from Olson had not been coherent. Pastore was also the one who discovered that CIA official Robert Lashbrook was still in the hotel room he had shared with Olson at the time of his fall.

"He was just calmly sitting there waiting for the police to arrive," Pastore said.

"Had he called down to the desk?" asked Saracco.

"He didn't call down to the desk to report anything," said Pastore. "He didn't even go down to the street to see if Olson was still alive. He told the police he didn't see any reason to go down. No reason? I mean, what kind of animal reacts like that?"

According to Pastore, Lashbrook did make one phone call, however, and it was of considerable interest to Saracco. Pastore explained, as follows:

> After the police took him [Lashbrook] down to the 14th Precinct for questioning, I asked the hotel operators if any of them had placed a call from room 1018A, the room that Olson and Lashbrook shared. One of the operators had. And you know how it was back then. The operator placed the call for you and then stayed on the line to make sure it went through. She told me that Lashbrook had her place a call to a number out on Long Island. When a man answered, Lashbrook said, 'Well, he's gone.' And the man on the other end said, 'Well, that's too bad,' and hung up. That was it in its entirety.

But like the countless media people who questioned Pastore since 1975, Saracco made the mistake of not asking the former hotel night manager about events well before Olson's trip to New York and his death.

It was only by chance that this author, during a break halfway through a five hour interview with Pastore in 2000 at his Florida home, that the subject of Pastore's wartime experiences in the Army came up. Pastore revealed that while stationed in Europe he had met "an absolutely beautiful French woman from a small town outside of Paris." (At the end of the war, Pastore had returned to New York where he met and married another woman with whom he had lived happily until her death, shortly before he and I first met.)

While telling me about the French woman he had met during the war, Armond remarked, "After I came back to New York and found a job at the Statler Hotel, I met a guy from France who came in one night after he'd been hired as a night porter. I remember it pretty well because I was worried about the French woman's family. Her father had come to see me after I was back in New York. He was really upset about things... Anyway, this Frenchman who'd been hired [at the Statler Hotel] came in and we got to talking and he thought he remembered the woman I had known in France. He said he'd been in the town she was from a few times."

"Do you remember the Frenchman's name?" I asked.

"Yeah, sure. It was Martin, his last name. Jean Martin. But a lot of us called him 'Pierre,' you know, because he was French."

"How long did he work at the Statler?"

"Not that long, as I remember. He sort of came and went. A lot of guys did back then. I remember that his English was unbelievably good."

"Was he there at the Statler for months?"

"Yeah, I guess it would have been at least a few months, around that. I don't really remember."

"Was he there when Olson died?"

"Yes. I remember that because a few hours after it happened, he asked me about it."

"About 'it'?"

"About the Olson thing."

"What did he ask you?"

"I don't remember any of what we said. He was just curious, is all. A lot of the staff came up to me afterwards to see what was going on. Things like that didn't happen all the time."

"So Jean Martin was working the night that Olson died?"

"I'm pretty sure that he was."

"Do you know if he had worked at any other New York hotels?"

"Yeah, I'm sure he did. We didn't hire any people that didn't have some experience. I'm sure he did."

I did not tell Pastore until weeks later that Jean Martin was Pierre Lafitte, one and the same. When I did tell him, Armond said, "Well, doesn't that take the cake."

4

What Did Allan Hughes Know?

CIA's research into the [TSS] meeting with Camp Detrick SO Division employees, including *Frank Olson, shows that besides Drs. Gottlieb and Lashbrook being present and representing [TSS], Allan Hughes was also there. A search is presently being conducted for more information about Hughes.*
        – CIA Memorandum to Rockefeller Commission, 1975

Saracco and Bibb continued to search for witnesses who had attended the Deep Creek Lake meeting. At the urging of this writer they spent close to three weeks trying to locate former CIA official Allan Hughes and SOD scientist Ben Wilson. When I had first read the Colby papers, I felt that in order to understand what happened to Frank Olson, it was essential to understand the reason for Hughes' presence at the Deep Creek Lake meeting, as well as to have first hand knowledge of that meeting. I presented my findings to Morgenthau's office in a lengthy memorandum about Hughes and Wilson, the substance of which follows.

WHO WAS ALLAN F. HUGHES?

Throughout the decades of research, investigations, commissions and litigation into the death of Frank Olson, Allan F. Hughes has been oddly overlooked. An openly acknowledged CIA officer and openly listed as a participant at the Deep Creek Lake meeting where Frank Olson was dosed with LSD, Hughes has been completely ignored. Who was Hughes? Why was he in attendance at the meeting? What was his role with the CIA? What happened to him after November 1953?

During the first several years of research for this book, Hughes's name produced no memories in anyone interviewed. Some of those questioned said the name sounded familiar, but they were not sure; others said they were totally unfamiliar with anyone named "Allan Hughes" who had worked at CIA or SOD. Eventually, a few people were located who did clearly recall Hughes, but they were unwilling to talk about him for a variety of reasons, most related to concerns about secrecy oaths and government pension benefits. Two people said that Hughes had passed away sometime in the late-1970s; others reported different acounts, but no confirmation of this could be found. A few people were under the erroneous impression that Hughes was somehow related to Howard Hughes. He was not, but, as will be explained, Allan Hughes did work for legendary millionaire Howard Hughes at one point, as did at least one other person who was indirectly tied to the Olson story.

Several people whom I interviewed were willing to provide small leads or bits of information about Allan Hughes, and several sources reported that Hughes' work sometimes involved "planned wet jobs" — i.e., assassinations.

Multiple requests to the CIA for information about Hughes brought replies that the Agency had nothing on him in its files. When the CIA was asked if perhaps files on Hughes had been destroyed in 1973 during the infamous document purge ordered by Richard Helms, the Agency declined to reply. Despite these difficulties, over time some details were discovered. Particularly after writer and criminologist Alan A. Block generously provided this writer some solid direction, a number of facts emerged about Hughes that added new dimensions to the story surrounding Frank Olson's death.

In 1999, when former TSS chief Sidney Gottlieb was first queried about Allan Hughes, he remarked he had forgotten about Hughes until he had been questioned during a 1995 deposition about several people who, in the employ of the CIA, had taken LSD on an experimental basis with Gottlieb. Allan Hughes was among these names. When questioned about Hughes for this book, Gottlieb said, "Yes, I now remember him. Not very well, but I do recall him and yes, he was with the group at Deep Creek Lake in 1953."

Hughes was among those people in the early 1950s that took LSD in controlled CIA settings?

"Yes, he was."

Did he work for the CIA?

"He worked for my unit, TSS, but was assigned, or detailed, to CIA from the military."

How long was he assigned to TSS?

"I'm not sure of that. At least several years... from 1953 to 1956 or thereabouts."

What was his job with TSS?

"He performed tasks as directed by myself or sometimes by Bob Lashbrook...he was assigned projects also, as I remember."

Can you be more specific?

"Not really."

Would it be fair to assume his work was connected to MKULTRA?

"In part, yes."

During a deposition taken from you in 1983, you referred to Hughes as a "man from the Air Force who was a meteorology officer detailed to CIA and who worked with us in TSS."

"I don't recall saying that. I may have had him confused with someone else. I'm not sure."

In 1995, you answered in another deposition that Hughes had not been part of your unit.

"Technically, he wasn't, but later on in that questioning I clarified that he had been part of my unit." [This is correct.]

What did Hughes have to do with Camp Detrick's SOD?

"He had a lot to do with liaison between TSS and SOD."

He knew Frank Olson?

"Oh, I'm sure that he knew a good many SOD members."

But he knew Olson?

"Sure."

What part of the military did Hughes come from to CIA?

"Army. He was a CIC [Army Counter Intelligence Corps] officer."

Reportedly, he was expert in electronic surveillance and interrogation.

"Yes."

Was he at Deep Creek Lake for these purposes?

"I'm not sure what you mean."

Was he there to record anything electronically or to film anything?

"Not that I recall."

Was any part of that meeting recorded or filmed?

"I don't recall that."

Did Hughes have anything to do with assassinations?

"Not in my unit, he didn't. No."

Where did Hughes go after he left TSS?

"I don't know."

Did he go back to CIC or, perhaps, to another CIA assignment?

"I have no idea where he went."

Did he officially leave the CIA's payroll in 1956 or 1957, or whenever he left TSS?

"I have no idea... I didn't have anything to do with hiring him or how he was paid."

Was he connected somehow to William Harvey's operations in Germany prior to 1953, or had he been engaged in Artichoke activities in Germany or elsewhere prior to coming to TSS?

"I don't recall what he did before coming to my unit."

While with TSS, did he do anything in Germany or any place else in Europe?

"Maybe, but I don't recall specifics."

France, perhaps?

"I have no idea."

Allan F. Hughes, according to former intelligence sources who refused to go on the record regarding information about him, came to TSS in early 1953 from the Army's Counter Intelligence Corps (CIC), for whom he had worked in Germany and France. While working with TSS under Gottlieb, Hughes occasionally used the aliases "Robert King," "Bob King," and "Bob Fine." FBI files confirm this.

FBI files further reveal that Hughes left TSS sometime in late 1955 and went to work for former FBI agent and CIA contractor Robert Aime Maheu, a private investigator whose firm, Robert A. Maheu Associates, was located near the State Department in Washington. Coincidentally, Robert A. Maheu Associates was also just a block away from the CIA's safe house in D.C. According to these same sources, Hughes and "one or two technicians from TSS" outfitted the CIA's Washington safe house with sound recording and motion picture cameras as well as telephone surveillance equipment.

Maheu, Hughes's employer at this time, is an intriguing character who deserves attention here in order to better understand Hughes' role with the CIA.

Maheu, born in Maine in 1917, was a graduate of Holy Cross College in Massachusetts. He was employed as an FBI Special Agent from 1940 to 1947, frequently coming in contact with James McCord and William Harvey. After leaving the Bureau, he went into the private sector with a business called Dairy Dream Farms that went bankrupt in 1952. From there, he served briefly as director of security for the Small Business Administration, but was forced to resign for political reasons. In February 1954, Maheu opened his own investigation firm, initially sharing space with another former FBI agent, Carmine Bellino. According to CIA files, Maheu "successfully handled" a number of "prestige accounts, including [Greek shipping line] Niarchos [and] Schenley Distillers," and he maintained offices in Washington, D.C., Los Angeles, and Las Vegas. A few weeks after he started his investigation outfit in 1954, the CIA's Office of Security says it "recruited" Maheu. Former Agency officials recall that Maheu received a large amount of contractual support from Paul Gaynor's Agency security section before he was placed on a $500 a month retainer.

George White had dealings with Maheu in 1954 in Las Vegas when FBN-CIA special employee Pierre Lafitte was on an undercover assignment there. Also occasionally working closely with Maheu, during his years with the FBI through to about 1959, was Detective Lt. Arthur E. Schultheiss, commanding officer of the 14th Detective Squad of the New York City Police Department. Schultheiss was boss of the two detectives, Ward and Mullee, who handled the short-lived case involving Frank Olson's death.

The CIA officially granted Maheu a Covert Security Approval on August 30, 1954. Maheu was then assigned to several "highly sensitive projects" and "accepted assignments from elements of the predecessor of the Deputy for Operations." CIA files reveal that Maheu assisted the Agency with the delicate task of "procurement of feminine companionship" for certain foreign dignitaries during their official state visits to the United States. Maheu also recruited, according to former CIA officials, "women of less than upstanding character" for employment in the Washington, D.C. safe house used by TSS and other

Agency branches. Assisting Maheu's firm with its 'human procurement' tasks was notorious, debonair gangster Johnny Rosselli.

CIA Office of Security records state: Maheu met with "various officers of the Clandestine Service...over the years from 1954 to 1970 to determine the feasibility of using his firm for non-official cover purposes." As writers Alan Block and Jim Hougan have underscored, Maheu's business was set up CIA-style in a "severely compartmentalized" fashion "with different employees handling different assignments on a need-to-know basis, providing a magnificent framework for deniability."

In 1975, during a press conference in Washington, D.C., the following exchange took place:

> Newsman Daniel Schorr: Then your business was a proprietary cover for the CIA?
> Maheu: Not necessarily. There were a few instances in which they used my organization; in other words we, the people, were paid through me and I was reimbursed.... [People] needed a cover for certain assignments. I never knew what the assignment was and they just placed [a person] on my payroll so that he could go on and do his work.

From 1954 through to 1970, Maheu worked full time for billionaire Howard Hughes (no relation to Allan Hughes). In 1970, Howard Hughes and Maheu parted company and not long after that, Hughes asserted in a news conference that Maheu "stole me blind." Maheu, in turn, sued for $17 million in defamation damages. In court, Maheu testified that in 1968 billionaire Hughes had asked him if "I would make some arrangement with the CIA whereby some part of the Hughes Tool Company would become a front for the intelligence agency.":

> Quite interesting to note, and perhaps most revealing of the clandestine aspects of Maheu's operations, is that when the CIA seriously dedicated itself to trying to assassinate Fidel Castro, it turned to Maheu. Accounts about how the Agency first approached Maheu for this operation have been repeated widely, but they remain vague on specifics about why the CIA choose Maheu, a private investigator with no known experience in state-sponsored assassination.
>
> The CIA described it this way: "Robert A. Maheu was contacted, briefed generally on the project, and requested to ascertain if he could develop an entrée into gangster elements as the first step toward accomplishing the desired goal." Somehow, Maheu recruited Florida Mafia don Sam Trafficante, Jr., Chicago Mafia head Momo Salvatore Giancana, and mobster Johnny Rosselli. CIA officials were pleased; they were confident – foolishly, it turned out – that Fidel's days were numbered.

Maheu's connection with Allan Hughes, meanwhile, had begun four years before Castro took over Cuba. In early 1956, Maheu hired Allan Hughes. Having left both the Army CIC and CIA, Hughes had been working for an obscure company called Research Products. Little is known about Research Products other than it was supposedly headquartered in Danbury, Connecticut and, according to former intelligence officials, was a CIA cutout in which Maheu may have had a controlling hand. According to an interview with Maheu, Allan Hughes' first job came from Howard Hughes and involved electronic eavesdropping — in New York's Old Manhattan Hotel — on a man who was attempting to blackmail billionaire Hughes.

During the 1950s, Allan Hughes worked on a number of Maheu's CIA projects: the electronic wiring of prostitutes offered to foreign and domestic dignitaries and politicians; overhauling the electronic security system of Dominican Republic dictator Rafael Leonidas Trujillo y Molina; setting up security equipment in the Dominican Republic and training its operators. In the Dominican Republic, Hughes reported directly to the American Embassy. Hughes also traveled on a number of occasions to San Francisco to learn the proper use of X-ray machines and inspector-scopes purchased through a company closely tied to George Hunter White. As readers will learn, White was then stationed in San Francisco, operating more CIA safe houses.

Hughes, still in the employ of Maheu, also arranged the wiretapping of singer Phyllis McGuire, hoodlum Sam Giancana's mistress, to see if she was cuckolding Giancana by bedding Frank Sinatra. Giancana was stunned to learn through the illegal wires that McGuire was instead sleeping with comedian Dan Rowan. When the wiretapping was exposed, Las Vegas and federal law enforcement officials brought criminal charges against Maheu. CIA security chief Sheffield Edwards, with the blessings of Attorney General Bobby Kennedy, worked overtime to quash the charges by telling the FBI the wiretap on McGuire's room was part of a national security operation related to the Mafia.

Allan Hughes was reportedly also involved in a celebrated case in Las Vegas involving local newspaper publisher Hank Greenspun, a close associate of Maheu. In 1954, a few months after Frank Olson's death, Greenspun, at the recommendation of Maheu, hired CIA-FBN "special employee" Pierre Lafitte to entrap and expose a corrupt local sheriff who was suing Greenspun for libel.

Lafitte and Allan Hughes collaborated on another occasion in a very bizarre and revealing episode having to do with accused JFK assassination co-conspirator Clay Shaw. As readers will learn, Hughes, Lafitte and investigative writer James Phelan — who some maintain was in league with both Maheu and the CIA - literally crawled into New Orleans District Attorney Jim Garrison's office to purloin documents having to do with Clay Shaw. Lafitte would later tell George Hunter White that the Garrison office break-in was "maybe one of the only jobs I ever did that made me worry any at all."

Interviews with former intelligence officials turned up information that Allan Hughes also worked with former Washington, D.C. police detective and expert wireman Joe Shimon. Shimon, who was dismissed from the police force for illegal wiretapping activities, maintained very close ties to the mob and media, especially legendary columnist Jack Anderson. Said one source who formerly worked for Anderson:

> Hughes worked at least a couple times with Shimon. . .[mostly] doing secret film jobs on visiting dignitaries staying in either the Madison or Mayflower hotels. For a while Shimon and Hughes could be found hanging out at Duke Zeibert's or late nights at the Old Ebbitt Grill. One night, drunk, the two threatened to toss an FBI agent off the garden roof of the Hotel Washington.

Records discovered among the private papers of George Hunter White reveal that on at least three occasions in 1954 and 1955 and presumably while still in the employ of the CIA, Hughes assisted FBN-CIA special employee Pierre Lafitte with undercover assignments for the CIA and possibly other federal government agencies.

Questioned by the author in 2001, Maheu said he "was sure that Hughes was dead," but he had no recollection of when the former CIC-TSS man had passed away, nor was he able to provide any leads to confirm Hughes' death. FBI files from October 23, 1958 state that Hughes "had left the employ of Maheu" by that date and that his "whereabouts was [sic] unknown." The same files contain an implicit statement that Hughes may have returned to employment with the CIA, but this is unconfirmed. Adding to the confusion about Hughes is another unconfirmed report that he was mysteriously murdered in South America sometime in 1959.

5

What Did Dr. Benjamin Wilson Know?

That I saw nobody become psychotic [at Deep Creek Lake], I'm certain. Nobody even acted strangely.
                                        — Dr. Benjamin Wilson

D r. Benjamin Wilson was another largely overlooked participant in the infamous Deep Creek Lake meeting. At the time of the meeting, Wilson was SOD's [Biological] Agents Branch chief. As we have seen, that branch handled the most lethal of biological agents.

Wilson was born in 1923 in Pennsboro, West Virginia and earned his undergraduate degree and master's degree at West Virginia University. Not long afterwards, he was hired to work as a civilian scientist at Camp Detrick, where he was considered hard working, reserved and serious. He was employed for a little over ten years at Camp Detrick and became SOD's Microbiological Branch chief. While working at Camp Detrick, Wilson earned his doctorate in Medical Sciences from George Washington University. About a year later, he became an associate professor at David Lipscomb College (today Lipscomb University) in Nashville. In 1963, he joined the teaching faculty at Vanderbilt University Medical Center, and also researched naturally occurring toxic compounds from bacteria, fungi and plants. Wilson discovered a number of toxic compounds in food consumed by humans, pets and farm animals— including rubratoxin, which can contaminate cereal grains. He steadfastly established himself as an internationally recognized expert in the toxicology of natural products.

Wilson, who died July 4, 2007, at the age of 84, had been interviewed about Frank Olson and SOD in 1978, but the results of that lengthy interview were never published, except for two incomplete and somewhat misleading paragraphs. At that time, Wilson initially denied he had been at the CIA-SOD meeting, even claiming, "It didn't happen."

Pressed on the subject of Deep Creek Lake, Wilson revealed that he had been advised by none other than James F. Neal, a prominent Nashville attorney who is best known as lead prosecutor in the Watergate trials, "to keep my mouth shut." He then confirmed, out of the blue, that he had been present at Deep Creek Lake. In answer to questions about Frank Olson's reaction to LSD, Wilson said that Olson had not become psychotic, as some were claiming in

1975. Olson, in Wilson's estimation, did become "quite disturbed" by the fact that he had been given LSD but "was better" the next morning.

During the same interview, again without explanation, he said, "It was a bad setting." Observed Wilson cryptically, "Olson was very temperamental, probably because of something in his personal life. He developed some guilt feelings." Wilson's description of the mood at Deep Creek Lake was strikingly bland:

> To me everyone was pretty normal. No one was aware that anything had happened until it [LSD] was mentioned. We were asked by Gottlieb, 'Have you noticed anything wrong?' Everyone was aware once it was brought to their attention, but reaction was not strong until then.

Wilson said he had been included among the SOD scientists who were given the drug and that he experienced "no hallucinations, but was unable to sleep that night." He then recalled, "I saw shooting stars because of pressure on retinal vessels.... It was my first experiment with the drug."

Asked about the reactions of others, however, he contradicted himself:

> ...[Frank Olson] was psychotic. He wanted to go home. He couldn't seem to understand what happened. He thought someone was playing tricks on him... One of his favorite expressions was, 'You guys are a bunch of thespians,' and he said it to them that night... There was a lot of giggling. People had a tendency to overreact with laughter.

According to Wilson, Sidney Gottlieb had conducted this type of surprise experiment at other places. Added Wilson:

> Frank Olson encouraged this sort of experiment. Once he had gotten angry with me for not being willing to participate in a hazardous experiment. I wouldn't do it because it was too dangerous. I said, 'Why don't you do it.' He said he couldn't because he had ulcers... [Olson] was a likeable person, but hyper-excitable. If he liked you, he liked you. Quick tempered.

Wilson then went on to explain he had left employment with the Chemical Corps at Camp Detrick because of "the many inept people in uniform who didn't know what they were doing." He recounted a story about the commander of the Chemical Corps, a general, not being able to get into SOD's buildings because of inoculation requirements.

> That's the way we kept them out. Those types didn't need to know. Only we needed to know. Most of the security violations came from the top level. They were blabbermouths... [The commander of the Chemical Corps] could have come in without the shots if he had insisted. The

safety director would have protested, but he could have. They thought they needed to know but they changed so often... The civilian element was more stable.

Twenty-nine years after his 1978 interview, Wilson was questioned about Olson for this book. It was only the second time anyone had attempted to interview him. After skillfully avoiding a series of phone calls from this author, he reluctantly agreed to talk. He repeated much of what he had said over two decades earlier, but was vague when asked to be more specific on some counts. Asked who besides Olson and himself had been dosed with LSD, he answered he could not recall, but "thought Ruwet and maybe two others" had been. "It's not something I've given much thought to over the years," he said. Why? "It wasn't a high point of my career."

Did you know Frank Olson well?

"Not to the extent that I'd call him a friend, no."

There appears to be some confusion in the interview you granted in 1978 about Olson becoming "psychotic" at Deep Creek Lake.

"That I saw, he wasn't psychotic."

Were you able to observe him the entire night?

"Not that I can... no, I don't think so. We were spread out in the lodge. I think some [people] there had rooms elsewhere, in another nearby lodge. I'm not really sure... That I saw nobody become psychotic, I'm certain. Nobody even acted strangely. What I know, that really is not in the nature of the drug in small... or in reasonable amounts."

Did you speak with Olson that night or the next day?

"Not that I remember."

You knew about Olson's ulcers?

"Everyone did. He complained about them a lot."

You said in 1978 that Olson developed 'some guilt feelings.' How do you know this?

"I don't remember. Most likely it was after the fact; scuttlebutt I heard after he had died."

Was everyone at SOD, prior to the Deep Creek Lake meeting, aware of LSD and its effects?

"I'm sure we were. Some of us were well aware of it."

Was Olson?

"Yes."

Do you recall Alan Hughes being at the Deep Creek Lake meeting?

"Yes. I didn't know him well, but he was there."

Do you know why Hughes was there?

"No. He wasn't with our group, the SO group."

He was with the CIA?

"As far as I know, he was."

Who else was there?

For [SOD]... myself, Olson, Herb Tanner, Ruwet, Schwab, Joe Stubbs, Everett Champlin... Mal...Malinowski... CIA there was Gottlieb, Hughes, Lashbrook, and... maybe one other. I'm not sure now who that was. Maybe there wasn't anyone else. I can't remember. Maybe [Henry] Bortner was there. But we had a lot of these type meetings that lasted a few days. There at the lake and at other places. That wasn't the first time we'd met as a group. It wasn't uncommon."

The experiment part [of the meeting] was uncommon, wasn't it?

"I wouldn't say that."

Why?

"That was the nature of a lot of our meetings, experiments. That's what we discussed most of the time. That and various devices we were working on for them [CIA]."

In your 1978 interview, you didn't put yourself among those given LSD.

"I don't really recall the details of that interview. It was a phone call or two."

Were you dosed at the meeting?

"I really don't want to get into that."

Was Dr. Schwab given LSD at the meeting?

"I don't think he was there for that part of the meeting. That was... It was after normal work hours."

Did you ever hear anything about Olson being a security risk or that he broke security prior to the Deep Creek Lake meeting?

"There were stories... stories, rumors... some from Olson himself. But I don't recall the specifics."

Did you travel outside the United States for SOD?

"No comment."

You knew Sidney Gottlieb?

"We all did... everyone with the SO Division knew him."

And everyone knew Robert Lashbrook?

"We all knew him."

Did you know Stanley Lovell?

"Sure. He was a consultant to [SOD] or to the CIA...maybe both, I'm not sure."

Do you recall anything that happened to Herbert Tanner after the Deep Creek Lake meeting?

"I'm not sure... there was something about possible epilepsy or problems... I'm not sure of that."

Besides Olson and Tanner, did others in attendance have problems after the meeting?

"I really don't care to discuss that or to talk about it."

You said in the 1978 interview that Deep Creek Lake 'was a bad setting.' What did you mean by that?

"I don't remember saying that."

668

Was it a bad setting?

"I guess for some it was. I'm not interested in discussing it any further."

Two more questions?

"Go ahead."

Related to SOD's work: Did SOD scientists ever travel overseas to any country in Europe, besides England and Porton Down, for experimental purposes?

"I don't recall all my travel. That was a long time ago. I can't answer for others."

Did Frank Olson ever travel to Germany or France?

"Probably, but I can't swear to it."

"Were there secret operations in France that you were aware of?"

"No comment."

WHAT DID CIA INSPECTOR GENERAL LYMAN KIRKPATRICK REALLY KNOW?

Apparently IG Kirkpatrick's 1953 investigation into Olson's death had delved into areas that the Colby papers failed to reflect. In 1999 and 2000, additional Kirkpatrick records were uncovered by this author that throw far more light onto Olson's death. Kirkpatrick's records, including several memoranda that were shared with Saracco and Bibb in New York, were all written in December 1953. The first, dated December 3, was a memo for IG Kirkpatrick bearing the subject: "About the police intervidwing [sic] Lashbrook." The memo reads:

> ...Among Lashbrook's papers examined by the detectives ((investigating the Olson "suicide")) was one which contained Dr. Abrahmson's [sic] office and home addresses and telephone numbers. This paper also contained the following:
>
> G.W. 59 West 12th Street, Apt. 6-E Chelsea 3-7176 UNDERNEATH THAT Bedford M.H. 81 Bedford Street, Oregeon [sic] 5-0257 Lashbrook identified G.W. to the reporting agent as George White, chief of the Boston office of the U.S. Bureau of Narcotics.
>
> He (Lashbrook) said that M.H. stood for Morgan Hall an undercover name for George White.

The second memorandum, dated December 4, was also for IG Kirkpatrick and its subject was: "Olson 'suicide.'" It reads:

> Dr. Abrahmson [sic] met re reporting agent (below) the follow up with G.W. (M.H.) with Jean Lafitte (Martin/bellman) and (FNU) Spirito ((?? J.M.)) at Cold Spring Harbor site.... see att.

This memo was carbon copied (cc) to: "Neuman."

The third memorandum was dated "22 December 1953" and appeared to be a CIA-SRS memo bearing the subject: "Olsen [sic], Frank, No. 73317-SI."

It reads:

> McC [redacted] reported that 21 December interview with Col. White was less than satisfactory. White said that he was in Carlsbad and Los Angeles on dates in question.
>
> He maintained that he knows nothing about the whereabouts of [FNU] 'Martin' on same dates. Col. White said that Welch and Eisenberg "could vouch" for his time in California. However, he did confirm that 'Martin' had been an employee (bellman) at both the Roosevelt and Statler hotels in the past.
>
> (McC [redacted] verified.) Records show that 'Martin' was here about a year ago for special sessions at [redacted] Manger Annapolis.
>
> Col. White said he had spoken to Lovell about the incident since his return from Mexico but remarked that he was "confident Lovell is privy to the facts" and that Lovell was also displeased with Rewet's [sic] insistence for recompensation [sic]. Follow-up? [Redacted line.]
>
> Ward's remarks on Gianini [sic] slaying and HDW [Harry Dexter White]–Gottlieb trip to New Haven and meetings with subject (Marresca).

The memo was carbon copied (cc) to a redacted name.

All three of the above memos deserve some explanation and clarity. The first memo is the most straightforward of the three. Its purpose seems to center on concern about the contents of Lashbrook pockets, especially with respect to revealing connections to George White and his CIA alias Morgan Hall. If White had been in Carlsbad, California at the time of Olson's death, as the third memo states, why would there be concern about White?

In 1978, Kirkpatrick gave a self-serving interview in which he tried to distance himself from MKULTRA. Asked what he knew of the program's human experiments, he claimed that he knew nothing at the time that they were being performed and, had he known, he would have protested. However, as the extant, and now publically available MKULTRA files — over 22,000 documents — reveal, Kirkpatrick was on the "approved" list of recipients for all project reports and updates. Kirkpatrick was also approved to receive ARTICHOKE reports from 1952 through to 1956. The claim that he did not know of CIA human experiments appears ludicrous.

THE GORDON THOMAS AFFIDAVIT

On November 30, 1998, an excited Eric Olson telephoned Steve Saracco to tell him that he had just received a copy of an affidavit that he thought "could blow the case wide open." The affidavit was from British writer Gordon Thomas. Thomas was the author of thirty-eight books published worldwide, including the 1989 title *Journey into Madness*, a nonfiction work that details the horrible MKULTRA experiments of Dr. Ewan Cameron in Montreal. Eric faxed a copy of Thomas' 10-page affidavit to Saracco's office.

Thomas' affidavit, addressed to Eric Olson, recounts a series of conversations between Thomas and British psychiatrist William Walters Sargant. Thomas first met Sargant around the "period 1968-1969"when Sargant was Director of Psychological Medicine at St. Thomas' Hospital in London, England. At the time, Sargant was well known and regarded for his work with World War II servicemen who were suffering from shell shock. Thomas says that Sargant was also "a consultant to the British Secret Intelligence Service (MI5/6)" at the time, although some former colleagues of Sargant's dispute this.

In any case, Thomas claimed that after he had gained Sargant's trust, the psychiatrist told him that he "had visited Langley several times and had met with Dr. Sydney [sic] Gottlieb, Richard Helms and other senior CIA officials." During the same visits, Thomas wrote, Sargant "also met with Dr. Ewan Cameron and, on one occasion, he had met Dr. Lashbrook and your father, Frank Olson." The affidavit continues:

> Subsequently Dr. Gottlieb and Frank Olson visited London and, according to Dr. Sargant, he accompanied them to Porton Down, Britain's main research centre for biological/chemical research. Dr. Sargant's interest in the work going on there was to study the psychological implications of mind-blowing drugs such as LSD. He told me that he developed a rapport with Frank Olson during a number of subsequent visits Frank Olson made to Britain. Dr. Sargant remarked that 'he was just like any other CIA spy, using our secret airfields to come and go.'

Thomas states that Sargant told him "that Frank Olson and Cameron knew each other and that Frank Olson also shared his (Sargant's) view that some of the work Dr. Gottlieb was funding Cameron to do through the Human Ecology Foundation was bordering on the criminal."

According to Thomas, Sargant explicitly said that Thomas "could publish what he had said after his death," including the information that "in the summer of 1953 Frank Olson travelled to Britain, once again to visit Porton Down." [The British Army was also conducting its own LSD experiments on English troops at Porton Down, but Thomas does not mention this.] According to the affidavit, Sargant informed Thomas that during Olson's alleged 1953 visit:

> Olson said he was going to Europe to meet with a CIA team led by Dr. Gottlieb.... Sargant was satisfied that the CIA team were [sic] doing similar work that M16 were conducting in Europe—executing without trial known Nazis, especially SS men.... Sargant saw Frank Olson after his brief visit to Norway and West Germany, including Berlin, in the summer of 1953. He said he was concerned about the psychological changes in Frank Olson.

671

In Sargant's view Olson, primarily a research-based scientist, had witnessed in the field how his arsenal of drugs, etc. worked with lethal effect on human beings (the 'expendable' SS men etc.). Sargant believed that for the first time Olson had come face to face with his own reality. Sargant told me he believed Frank Olson had witnessed murder being committed with the various drugs he had prepared. The shock of what he witnessed, Sargant believed, was all the harder to cope with given that Frank Olson was a patriotic man who believed that the United Sates would never sanction such acts....

I remember Sargant telling me that he spoke several times in 1953 with Frank Olson at Sargant's consulting rooms in Harley Street, London. These were not formal patient/doctor consultations but rather Sargant trying to establish what Frank Olson had seen and done in Europe....

[Sargant] decided that Frank Olson could pose a security risk if he continued to speak and behave as he did. He recommended to his own superiors at the SIS that Frank Olson should no longer have access to Porton Down or to any ongoing British research at the various secret establishments Olson had been allowed prior free access to. Sargant told me his recommendation was acted upon by his superiors. He was also certain that his superiors, by the nature of the close ties with the CIA, would have informed Richard Helms and Dr. Gottlieb of the circumstances why Frank Olson would no longer be given access to British research.

Effectively a substantial part of Frank Olson's importance to the CIA had been cut off. When Dr. Sargant learned of Frank Olson's death... Sargant came to the immediate conclusion that Olson could only have been murdered. I recall him telling me that in many ways the staged death was almost classic.

There are many questionable features to Thomas' affidavit in this author's view. Overseas CIA experimental activities were conducted under the auspices of ARTICHOKE and not MKULTRA. Therefore Gottlieb would not have traveled with, or headed up, any "team" to Europe. There is no evidence that Gottlieb and Olson ever traveled together to Europe in the 1950s. Former Camp Detrick SOD scientists say that, to their knowledge, Gottlieb never traveled overseas with any Detrick researchers. [In several depositions taken in the 1980s and 1990s from Gottlieb, he testified that he never traveled to Europe until after 1953.]

Thomas's claim that Sargant visited Gottlieb, Helms, Lashbrook and Olson "several" times "at Langley" during the 1953-1955 period is highly doubtful because the Langley headquarters of the CIA was constructed in 1959 and opened in 1961.

Thomas' allegation that Sargant claimed that a CIA team was "executing without trial known Nazis, especially SS men" appears quite dubious given that both the United States and Britain (and Russia) were doing everything possible to locate and recruit former Nazis and SS officers, particularly those with scientific expertise, for intelligence work in the United States and elsewhere.

Apart from Thomas' assertions, there is no corroborating evidence that Dr. William Sargant ever met with Thomas, Gottlieb, Lashbrook, Richard Helms, or Frank Olson. Thomas himself claims that Sargant handed over all of his records concerning his work with the CIA and Frank Olson to British intelligence.

And lastly, of course, as other astute observers have asked, if Sargant was both an active British intelligence and CIA operative why would he say anything at all to Thomas? If what Thomas is saying is factual, and not deliberate disinformation as some have maintained, clearly Olson knew whom Sargant worked for. Was Olson so naive or stupid that he would risk his job, his life, and his family's future by confiding in someone who had a direct line to Olson's bosses? And there is also the issue of Olson confiding in Sargant, an obvious and severe security breech on Olson's part.

Lastly, there is the issue of Frank Olson's state of mind. Alice Olson and the Olson family have consistently stated that CIA claims that Frank Olson had had psychiatric problems and had consulted a psychologist for help are absolutely false. Coincidentally, Thomas' account of Olson's alleged disclosures to Dr. Sargant lends tremendous credence to the Agency's claim that Olson was unstable.

When this author asked Saracco for his views on the value and credibility of the affidavit, Saracco said, "Number one it's hearsay, and number two, well, there is no number two. What does it really say? That one person told another person that possibly told another person that they thought Olson's death had been murder? You tell me: What do I do with that?"

THOMAS FINGERS GEORGE WHITE FOR MURDER

To continue the examination of Gordon Thomas' contributions to the Olson case, it is necessary here to jump to the year 2007, when Thomas published the aptly titled book, *Secrets and Lies*. In many ways the book is a rehash of his earlier work, *Journey into Madness*, with the exception of its additions about Frank Olson's death. One of Thomas' most sensational assertions is that George Hunter White killed Frank Olson, a claim that he skillfully formats as having come out of the mouth of Eric Olson: "According to Eric Olson's reconstruction, what happened was this: White entered Frank Olson's room in the early hours of that November morning....White delivered his famous blow and then hurled Olson out the window."

According to Thomas, White's "famous blow" was the same that he used in Calcutta "to kill a Chinese spy... with one fist blow of such sufficient force that it made a hole in the man's skull." [As readers have seen in Book Three, White actually shot the spy. Moreover, Eric Olson, having read White's 1953 date book, was well aware that White was not in New York on the night in question.]

In support of his claim that White murdered Olson, Thomas offers no evidence other than statements that he attributes to deceased CIA official William Buckley. Buckley, Thomas claims, was assigned by DCI Dulles in 1953 to look into the death of Frank Olson. However, in 1953 Buckley was still attending college and had not yet been recruited by the CIA. Even after he was employed by the Agency, he was never involved in MKULTRA work and was never assigned to Dr. Gottlieb's TSS branch as Thomas claimed.

Thomas's account of White killing Olson is indeed fascinating and provocative stuff, but one problem with it is that White, at the time of Olson's death, was over 3,000 miles away, having departed New York on November 10, 1953 for California to help his father arrange for the burial of his mother who passed away on November 26, 1953. (See forthcoming section for more details on this.)

Again, there is ample reason to question Thomas's claims. Many of his cited dates and time frames are simply wrong. For example he claims that Sidney Gottlieb traveled to Tokyo in 1950 on orders from DCI Walter Smith, but Gottlieb was not yet recruited or employed by the CIA until the following year.

Another: "By 1953, the year Frank Olson died, there had been nearly 500 other deaths resulting among his fellow workers from being infected by anthrax or Bolivian hemorrhagic fever... Dr. Gottlieb called the dead 'our unsung heroes." This claim is patently absurd. CDC officials say that if this had been true, it would have been America's largest anthrax outbreak and would have been impossible to suppress or hide.

Other claims by Thomas appear to be a bit over the line even to the harshest of CIA and Army critics. But the primary reason for discounting Thomas' assertions about the death of Frank Olson is simply that they do not square with the evidence and, instead, dovetail with official versions that were clearly intended as cover up.

Huge Consults with Former DCI James Woolsey

In January 1999, Eric Olson's attorney Huge initiated discussions with James R. Woolsey, who served briefly as director of the CIA under President Bill Clinton. Woolsey's two-year tenure as DCI was notable because he never had a one-on-one meeting, or any relationship, with the President. When Huge contacted him, Woolsey was an attorney with the high-powered Washington, D.C. law firm Shea & Gardner. According to Eric Olson, Huge had approached Woolsey about joining the Olson legal team. Eric was impressed not only with Woolsey's credentials and credibility, but also because he had "represented some Guatemalan families some years back in a suit against the U.S. government."

Eric once commented that Huge "loves to attack the establishment with one of its own by his side, which I think is risky, to say the least."

On February 10, 1999 Huge held a conference call with Saracco, Bibb, Woolsey, and Woolsey's Shea & Gardner colleague Anthony A. Lapham, a former

CIA general counsel under the Ford and Carter administrations. Lapham, called "Tony" by his friends, had earlier served as an assistant U.S. attorney and had been in Army intelligence. Said an upbeat Eric after the call, "Woolsey and Lapham seem disposed to get involved now, though we're not sure yet in what way or how public a role they could have. In any case, Saracco and Bibb are planning to come down to Washington, possibly as soon as late this week, to meet with Woolsey and Lapham."

About two weeks later, no meetings had taken place and Eric was becoming frustrated with the slow pace and lack of decisiveness on the part of the attorneys. "Harry [Huge] can be as exasperating and as disappointing as all hell, but we have a long history together which goes very deep, and I know he wants to see this thing through."

Eric asked me what I thought about Woolsey and Lapham joining the case and I hesitated before answering. "Sure," I said, less than enthusiastically, "it could help with bringing more visibility and media attention to the case." At the same time, I thought, when one is threatened in the jungle, it isn't always wise to attempt to recruit a lion.

I called Woolsey to verify his possible involvement and to get a comment. He was testy on the phone and seemed irritated that I knew about the talks. "I don't have much to say," he said. I pressed, and he offered, "I have met with Mr. Olson at the request of his current counsel, a longtime friend and colleague of a number of people in this firm, but beyond that I'm not saying anything."

I had not known that Eric had met with Woolsey. Discovering this gave me pause about the other things Eric had said. So, too, did an article published about a year later. On July 23, 2000, a *New York Times Magazine* article by Andrew Cockburn revealed that recent litigation handled by Woolsey had made the former CIA director acutely aware of the government's abilities at duplicity and deception. Would it really require a *New York Times* article to make Woolsey aware of government deception and duplicity?

Presumably, Woolsey and Lapham decided not to assist Huge, because nothing ever came of it. I was, however, informed a few weeks later by a source close to Woolsey's firm, that "Woolsey was concerned about exposure of the long-existing links between reliable gangster types," or those who the CIA and Congress more fashionably dub 'unsavory characters,' and the nation's intelligence community."

At about the same time that Huge was speaking with Woolsey and Lapham, he was also holding discussions with people at the prestigious, Washington, D.C. public relations firm Hill and Knowlton. Eric was excited about the prospect of the firm — which is well known to have worked closely with the CIA over the years — becoming involved in the case. Indeed, the firm has employed a number of former CIA officials over the years. But, like the Woolsey possibility, the Hill and Knowlton talks went nowhere.

The Ignatieff *New York Times* Story

In early February 1999, a writer and Harvard University professor named Michael Ignatieff visited Saracco and Bibb in Manhattan. Ignatieff, the son of a Canadian diplomat and grandson of two former Russian counts and Tsarist ministers, is a noted historian and public policy commentator. He had earned a Ph.D. in history at Harvard University, where he became good friends with Eric Olson, then also a graduate student there. In 2000, Ignatieff was also the director of the Carr Center for Human Rights at Harvard's John F. Kennedy School of Government.

Eric had informed me about four weeks earlier that Ignatieff was writing an article about Olson's father's death for the *New Yorker* magazine, and that I should expect to hear from him. Ignatieff telephoned me about two weeks later. I asked him if we were speaking off-the-record, and he replied that we were.

"Eric tells me you think his father was murdered," he said.

"Well," I said, "With all respect, I don't think it, I know it."

"You're sure?"

"What good would it do to tell you that I am? I'm guessing you'd still have reservations since you don't know me at all. But frankly, at this point in time, it makes little difference to me."

"You have proof?"

"I've seen evidence that leaves me no doubt whatsoever."

"Have you shared anything with Saracco in New York?"

"I think it's best that he answer that."

"Have you ever worked for the CIA?" he asked.

"Not that I'm aware of," I replied. "Have you?"

I thought of a past trip I had made to land-locked Lesotho in the middle of South Africa. The trip had happened during Apartheid and I felt it important to be completely forthright with Ignatieff.

"Once, back in the early Eighties," I told him, "I was in Lesotho and was asked to do something by a State Department official. I suspect he was connected somehow to the CIA, but I'm not sure. He was a really nice guy, and he had helped me out while there. His request was pretty reasonable in my eyes."

"Any chance of talking to your sources about Frank Olson?"

"No. I don't know if Eric told you, but I plan to write a book about Olson's death."

After I had hung up, I realized that Ignatieff had never answered my question back to him about his working for the CIA, not that it made any real difference.

We talked again about a week later. He called from a hotel in New York. I missed the call and when I called him back a couple of hours later, a woman with a heavy Eastern European accent answered and handed the receiver to Ignatieff. I shared a few on-the-record general items with him, nearly all of which ended up somewhat twisted in his subsequent *New York Times* Sunday magazine article that appeared on April 1, 2001. Eric had told me two weeks earlier that Ignatieff had informed him that *New Yorker* editors had decided against publishing the Frank Olson article because the subject of CIA assassination's "were not really anything new" and that "everyone knew the CIA killed people."

Ignatieff's *New York Times* story contributed little to the overall case, other than to draw wider attention to it and, again, highlight its complexities. The article was titled, "What Did the CIA Do to Eric Olson's Father?" but readers were left with no idea who did what to whom, much less why Frank Olson was murdered and by whom. The article focused largely on Eric and made him appear to be some sort of madcap character, a reclusive Syd Barrett type, who lived in a house of ghosts and cackled aloud.

Eric, who had had high hopes regarding the article's impact, was sorely disappointed. Reportedly only one reader wrote a letter to the *New York Times* in response to the piece. It was from someone who had known Dr. Harold Abramson and who objected to the article's treatment of him.

Early on, I had asked Eric if he were sure Ignatieff could provide his father's story the kind of treatment we both felt it deserved. I thought that Ignatieff seemed an odd choice for the piece. Some of his past magazine articles and scholarly journal pieces seemed out of step with the paramount issues that surrounded the Olson case. A few weeks after the 9-11 attacks on America, Ignatieff wrote another *New York Times* Sunday magazine article that cemented my concerns. Despite his image as director of a prestigious "human rights" think tank, Ignatieff strongly argued in the piece that Western democracies had a right to resort to the practice of "lesser evils," meaning they could engage in indefinite detentions and withholding of due process of captured enemy combatants, could practice "coercive interrogations" (a euphemism for torture), targeted assassinations, and pre-emptive wars in order to combat the greater evil of terrorism. Not surprisingly, many human rights advocates did not agree with Ignatieff, and some even questioned his true intentions with the Frank Olson article.

By 2001, according to Eric Olson, Saracco and Bibb were now closing in "on a finding of foul play" in his father's case. In late-January, Harry Huge told the author that he was reasonably certain that District Attorney Robert Morgenthau would soon possibly issue "a definitive finding of murder" in the case of Frank Olson. Huge said that the long-anticipated finding would remove the legal obstacles created by the Olson family's 1976 settlement agreement. Huge then would be free to file a massive lawsuit against the federal government.

At about this same time, I began to question and become concerned about some of Eric Olson's actions and motivations. Briefly, my concerns centered on Eric so easily buying into the claims of people like Gordon Thomas. It appeared to me that Eric wanted confirmation that his father was a potential whistle blower, a man who had serious reservations about his SOD and CIA work and who experienced an epiphany of sorts and became a murdered martyr in the process.

I wrote to Eric, "Truth can be a slippery fish, Eric. You may not always find what you want or what you wish was true. The good comes with the bad."

When I questioned Eric about his father's feelings toward Jews in an email message, he wrote back that his father's bigotry was only a reflection of the conventional thoughts of the times his father lived in.

Once while meeting in Washington, D.C. with Eric and his attorney Harry Huge, Eric lost his temper over something I had said about his father's work with SOD and he screamed across the table at me, "Who do you really work for? Tell us that, huh. Who do you really work for?" I said nothing. I liked Eric, and understood what he was going through, but my concerns continued to grow, and I became more and more worried that Eric was allowing himself to be used as a pawn in the spinning of tales inside tales that were nowhere near the truth.

District Attorney Saracco said it best in November 2000, "This case has been around for a long time, and it may well take some more time to get to the bottom of what actually happened in that hotel room and to determine why it happened." Explained Saracco:

> From hard-earned experience, I know the difficulties of cases like this. Each one comes with its own unique set of complexities. Much of the so-called evidence in the Olson case is, to put it politely, the product of years of supposition, embellishment, manipulation, and sometimes-journalistic liberties. And that's being kind to some people. This is not to say there isn't a case here, not at all. It's only to say, and to emphasize, that one must be extremely careful in assuming anything to be factual.

Eric Visits Norman Cournoyer

On May 19, 2001, Eric traveled to Amherst, Massachusetts to visit one of his father's friends who had contacted him about a week after Ignatieff's New York Times article had appeared. Norman Cournoyer, then 82 years old and in a wheelchair, had been a major in the Army during the early-1940s and, for several years, had worked closely with Frank Olson. In 1946, Cournoyer resigned from the Army and took over the management of Camp Detrick's food service which fed 5,000 people daily. After this, in the early 1950s, Cournoyer bought a local restaurant and ice cream factory in Frederick.

Eric says, "I remember going there with my father as a boy, sitting at the counter eating ice cream sundaes while he and my father talked."

Following his early culinary ventures, Cournoyer had bought more restaurants, ventured into the hotel business, gained a law degree, a Ph.D. in econometrics, became a college professor, and founded a computer software company.

When Cournoyer had first telephoned Eric, he said he had some important information to share about Frank Olson's death and that it would be best if Eric came to meet with him rather than discussing it on the telephone.

Recalls Eric, "Due, no doubt, to his years of university training, my father's old colleague wanted to conduct our conversations in something of the style of a university seminar. I had brought my big (3' X 6') timeline with me. He asked me to remove all the paintings on one wall of his dining room so we could tape it up in front of us. During portions of our talk I took him through the historical sequence to refresh his memory, interrupting constantly by interjections, corrections, and amplifications as the old memories rushed back."

Cournoyer began by explaining that Frank Olson had told him "sometime in 1946-47 that he was on a 'new path.'" The path, according to Cournoyer, concerned "information retrieval" and "it was in this connection that Frank Olson became active in the so-called Bluebird and ARTICHOKE interrogation projects being set up by the CIA." (As readers have seen, the CIA did not formulate Project Bluebird, which came before ARTICHOKE, until early 1950, but "information retrieval" was a term used for "interrogations" which were the primary concern of OSS immediately after the war.)

"Do you know if my father worked for the CIA," Eric asked.

"Yes, your father worked for the CIA," replied Cournoyer, "he told me that directly."

Eric explains that his father's colleague then told him "that the issue I have not understood and emphasized enough is Korea."

Said Cournoyer, "Korea is the key."

In his summary of his two days with Cournoyer, Eric writes that after Cournoyer made his dramatic announcement about Korea, he "told me that the trips to Europe that my father made in the 1950s involved various kinds of de-briefings related to this 'information retrieval' work."

Eric writes that Cournoyer explained "that much of this involved de-briefings of Americans, *and he was not aware of the use of Germans or other nationals, though he did not rule it out.* He said that American intelligence was very keen to have someone like my father involved in this due to his familiarity with biological warfare, which was the focus of the 'information retrieval' activity." [Italics added.]

Eric's summary continued:

> [Cournoyer] said that during the early 1950's, and especially after the trip to Europe in the summer of 1953, my father had become very upset. His agitation seemed to involve several things. He was quite upset, [Cournoyer] said, to learn that, using the methods that had been developed, it was in fact possible to get information from people regardless of their willingness to divulge it. Second, these efforts to retrieve information had apparently involved some deaths, and this had upset my father very much.

Third, from this work and possibly in other ways as well, my father had become aware that the Americans were using biological warfare in Korea. He was horrified to discover this. 'If biological warfare was used in Korea,' [Cournoyer] said, 'your father definitely would have known it. Being in Special Operations at Detrick...oh yes, he would have known it.'

Eric believed that "Korea had to have been a crucial piece of the puzzle" of his father's death, and he recalled that his mother had always said that "my father was very concerned about whether biological was being used in Korea," but that she never knew if it had been or if her husband was in a position to know if it had been.

In his summary of his meeting with Cournoyer, Eric wrote at length about Korea, citing his interest in "the notion of" brainwashing and books by historians on the subject, but his thoughts seemed disorganized, contradictory, and random, finally concluding:

> In fact, the significance of what my father's colleague [Cournoyer] told me, and in reaction to which he has now become ill [see next section], can only be grasped when one realizes that the question of biological warfare in Korea was, from the American side, the biggest state secret of the Cold War. Settling this issue in the affirmative would mean that the U.S. was not only the first nation to employ nuclear weapons, but biological ones as well. According to my father's old colleague and dear friend [Cournoyer], this is quite probably what got my father murdered.

More Tragedy and the Cournoyer Revelations Expand

The day after Eric left Cournoyer's and returned home, he received a telephone call from a friend who left a message on Eric's answering machine that a very close friend of Eric's, New York jazz singer Susannah McCorkle, was dead. She had killed herself a few days earlier by jumping from a window of her 16th floor apartment. Like Frank Olson, she died on the sidewalk. Eric was stunned and crumbled to the floor at the news. He had just spoken with McCorkle about two weeks before, inviting her to accompany him to see the film *Judgment at Nuremberg*. She already had plans but had said that she wanted to see Eric soon. Eric told her, "I'll call you in a week or two,"

McCorkle and Eric had often sat in her apartment talking about his father's alleged suicide by jumping. Eric had taken assistant district attorney Steve Saracco and his wife Donna to one of McCorkle's shows at the Oak Room at the Algonquin. When things had become strained with Saracco's office, Eric had confided his frustrations to McCorkle. He said, "She was always sympathetic and understanding. She was always there to reassure me."

Five days after his visit with Cournoyer, indeed on the same day he wrote his summary, May 24, Eric says he was interrupted from the task by a phone call from Norman Cournoyer's wife. She was calling to tell Eric that "the stress involved" in meeting with Eric had caused her husband to fall quite sick and become hospitalized. He had not slept since Eric departed and "he had begun suffering from intense nausea." Eric said Mrs. Cournoyer speculated, "His anxiety had much to do with concerns about the impact his revelations might have on his children and grandchildren." Said Eric, "At least for now, he would not be willing to tell me more."

Apparently, Norman Cournoyer recovered enough to speak with two German writers and documentary producers, Egmont R. Koch and Michael Wech, months later. Cournoyer, they said, told them that Frank Olson had been murdered by the CIA, but all of Cournoyer's statements to that effect seemed carefully couched in ambiguity. In the German's documentary, *Code Name: Artichoke*, the producers dramatically ask: "So was it in fact murder? But, for what reason? Why did Olson speak of a 'terrible mistake' he had made?" Then Cournoyer says:

> 'There is a piece missing and I am not sure that I am the one to give it to you. What happened was, that he just got involved in it in a way that he was unhappy about it. But there was nothing he could do about it. He was CIA and they took it to the end.'

Cournoyer's next on-camera statement concerns Frank Olson's trip to Europe in July and August of 1953 when he visited London, Paris, Stockholm, and Berlin. The producers speculate that he was perhaps on a "secret Artichoke mission" but offer no evidence of this.

Then Cournoyer, who had just a few weeks earlier told Eric Olson that his father was "not aware of the use of Germans or other nationals," states:

> After he came back from Germany the last time he sounded different. When he talked to me he said, I can probably tell you things that I can't tell other people, because they are still in top secret material. The people he saw in Germany went to the extreme. He said, 'Norm, did you ever see a man die?' I said, 'No.' He said, 'Well, I did.' Yes, they did die. Some of the people they interrogated died. So you can imagine the amount of work they did on these people.

The obvious security violations of Olson's alleged statements to Cournoyer aside, who "these people" were is not stated by Cournoyer, but the documentary gives the impression that they were former Nazis and other foreign nationals.

After his statement about people dying, Cournoyer says, "He [Olson] said that he was going to leave. He told me that. He said, 'I am getting out of that CIA. Period.'"

A segment about the germ warfare confessions of American pilots in Korea shortly follows this. Claim the producers, in a statement that could not be further from the truth solely because the Chinese never employed psychochemicals or any drugs in their so-called brainwashing:

> The American soldiers who claimed to have committed biological warfare were apparently manipulated using Artichoke techniques. This documented in CIA papers [sic]. [Italics added.]

Cournoyer is then asked to comment on camera about this subject. He says:

> "I took an oath when I left the Army that I would not talk about that. I am sorry."

This is peculiar, given the fact that he resigned his army commission several years before the outbreak of the Korean War, and the fact that security oaths are administered when first entering the service.

The documentary then charges that the CIA used "cruel methods" of interrogations on Americans returning from Korea to get them to recant their germ warfare confessions, a charge that has never been formerly made by anyone. The film shows Eric Olson responding to this charge, as follows:

> This fits with what my mother had always said: 'Korea really bothered your father'. Finally when one of my father's colleagues [Cournoyer] within the past year only told me that my father had come to understand that Korea was the key thing and that they were using biological warfare methods in Korea. And then I proceeded to ask him about germ warfare confessions, this was alleged to be by the American government, these confessions made by the American government, these confessions made by the American servicemen were immediately discredited by the U.S. government under the idea that these were manipulated and produced only by the effect of brainwashing.

When the producers, with Eric present, asked Cournoyer to respond to this on camera, he said again: "I took an oath when I left the United States Army that I would never divulge that stuff."

"You divulged it to me," said Eric.

"You cannot prove it, can you?"

"I can assert it. You told me."

"Hearsay," countered Cournoyer.

"So you don't want to say?"

"No.... I don't want to say it. But, there were people who had biological weapons and they used them. I won't say anything more than that. They used them."

The documentary then cuts to Cournoyer saying: *"Was there a reason for your Dad being killed by the CIA? Probably so."* [Italics added.]

Norman Cournoyer's alleged revelations to British writer Jon Ronson were far more sensational. The satirical Ronson revealed them in a 2004 book entitled *The Men Who Stare at Goats*. The book is a half-comical, half-serious, unscientific look at the U.S. military's experiments with psychic warfare and parapsychology.

Ronson briefly recounts Eric's visit to Cournoyer, stating that the visit and dredging of secret revelations was so stressful "for Norman that he repeatedly excused himself so he could go to the toilet to vomit."

As to the Gordon Thomas allegations of Artichoke techniques being used on "expendables, captured Russian agents and ex-Nazis" and Olson witnessing "a terminal experiment" during which "one or more" of the expendables died, Cournoyer, according to Ronson, told Eric "that the Artichoke story was true."

Writes Ronson:

> Frank told Norman that 'they didn't mind if people came out of this or not. They might survive, they might not. They might be put to death.'
>
> Eric said, 'Norman declined to go into detail about what this meant but he said it wasn't nice. Extreme torture, extreme use of drugs, extreme stress.'

Ronson then writes that, "Norman told Eric that his father was in deep and horrified at the way his life had turned. He watched people die in Europe, perhaps he even helped them die, and by the time he returned to America he was determined to reveal what he had seen. There was a twenty-four hour contingent of Quakers down at Fort Detrick gates, peace protesters, and Frank would wander over to chat to them, much to the dismay of his colleagues.

Frank asked Norman one day, 'Do you know a good journalist I can talk to?'"

Ronson then writes, "I drove to Connecticut [sic], to Norman Cournoyer's house." There Cournoyer was cordial, told Ronson that he was sure Olson was murdered, and, after a few minutes, dropped a bombshell on Ronson.

According to Ronson, Norman said, "I saw Frank after he'd been given the LSD. We joked about it."

Ronson asked: "What did he say?"

Replied Cournoyer, "He said, 'They're trying to find out what kind of guy I am. Whether I'm giving away secrets.'"

Ronson's book continues:

"You were joking about it?" I said.

"We joked about it because he didn't react to the LSD."

"He wasn't tripping at all?" I said.

> "Nah," said Norman. "He was laughing about it. He said, 'They're getting very, very uptight now because of what they believe I am capable of.' He really thought they were picking on him because he was the man who might give away the secrets."
>
> "Was he going to talk to a journalist?" I asked.
>
> "He came so close to it wasn't even funny," said Norman.
>
> "Did he come back from Europe looking very upset?" I asked.
>
> "Yeah," said Norman. "We talked about a week, ten days, after he came back. I said, 'What happened to you, Frank? You seem awfully upset.' He said, 'Oh, you know...' I must admit, in all honesty, it's just coming to me now. He said..."
>
> Suddenly, Norman fell silent.
>
> "I don't want to go on further than that," he said. "There are certain things I don't want to talk about." [Italics added.]

Unfortunately, Ronson did not query Cournoyer any further. The fact is, there were no Quaker demonstrations at Camp Detrick in 1953; those demonstrations did not begin until years later, after Olson's death. He did not question Norman about the dates of Olson's alleged remarks about LSD. Perhaps Ronson was unaware of the timing involved in Olson's return from Deep Creek Lake and of Alice Olson having stated in a deposition that Frank stayed home all weekend, except for going to a movie with her, until he went in Monday morning to see Ruwet and attempt to resign. When did Frank have time to speak to Norman about his LSD experience? Did Frank really mock his LSD dosing? Did he really not react at all to the drug? This author believes the answers to all these questions are negative and cannot imagine what Cournoyer was attempting to accomplish by making these statements.

When this author telephoned Cournoyer weeks later, he was neither forthcoming nor certain about anything. Before talking with him, I was told by someone close to the Cournoyer family that they were "really upset" about the way "various people were twisting and manipulating Norman's thoughts and words." I asked if Norman had Alzheimer's, as another source had told me, and the answer was uncertain.

When Norman spoke to me he seemed quite confused and disoriented. When I questioned him about his claims he said that he had been misunderstood and that he was only "supposing stuff like everyone else." He said, "I can't remember if I saw Frank after the Deep Creek Lake thing." When I asked him about Olson's state of mind when he had returned from Europe, he said that Frank was the same "happy-go-lucky guy he always was." Do you know what he witnessed in Europe?" I asked.

"No, how would I know that," he said. "I didn't go with him. I'm not even sure where I was when he came back."

I reminded him that it had been August of 1953. He said, "That was a long time ago...long time. I can't remember that kind of thing right away."

When this author asked prosecutor Steve Saracco about the revelations of Norman Cournoyer, there was a long silence and then a deep sigh. "Again, I'm not sure what I should say," Saracco said. "Some people may think information and statements like his [Cournoyer's] are very helpful in a case like this, but I hate to say it, they're not."

6

A Major Break in the Case

In 2001, Saracco and Bibb got the big break they so desperately needed in the case. After being introduced to the author by Eric Olson about eighteen months earlier, and following at least a dozen telephone conversations, Saracco and I forged a cautious relationship that eventually resulted in Morgenthau approving Saracco's request to bring me to New York. Their objective was for me to assist the District Attorney's office in deciphering the most puzzling aspects of the case. The relationship that ensued eventually led to Saracco and Bibb contacting the two former CIA sources who had provided me with crucial information about events in Manhattan during the week of Olson's death. I was very careful in my dealings with Saracco and Bibb to make it clear that my agreement to assist would be limited. Specifically, that while I would connect the District Attorney's office with those sources, I would also honor my own prior agreement with them to maintain their confidences.

In short, as will be detailed below, Saracco and Bibb learned that Olson had indeed been murdered. In addition, they learned the identities of the two unsavory characters who had committed the act, and they also learned the motive. Below are details of what the two prosecutors were told by the two CIA sources who shall be referred to as "Albert" and "Neal."

According to Albert and Neal, Frank Olson had been brought to remote Deep Creek Lake as part of an informal gathering whose purpose was, among other things, to observe the effects of the potent psychochemical LSD. By late 1953, however, the CIA had dosed hundreds of unwitting subjects with LSD and well understood its effects. Thus, it was not necessary to drug Olson or any of his colleagues in order to learn about the powers of LSD. Nonetheless, the sources recounted to Saracco and Bibb that Olson had been given a small amount of LSD – about 70 micrograms – "mixed with Meretran." As Sidney Gottlieb had previously explained to the author, Meretran was added as a "pressure mechanism in interrogations" to "loosen tongues and persuade subjects to speak freely about matters they otherwise wouldn't share." As noted earlier, the CIA and the Army in the 1950s commonly employed LSD mixed with Meretran to enhance interrogations in what they jointly termed "ARTICHOKE sessions."

Olson had been drugged at Deep Creek Lake not to explore the drugs, but because he had been talking to "the wrong people" about a top-secret SOD experiment that had taken place in France in the summer of 1951. The CIA and Army, deeply concerned about his security violations, wanted to know the full extent of his indiscretions. Frank Olson had been given the drugs at Deep Creek Lake to "enhance" his interrogation.

Saracco and Bibb discovered that the "TOP SECRET" operation Olson had talked about had been the highly sensitive experiment conducted in Pont-St.-Esprit, France under the innocuous code name, Project SPAN ("SPAN" presumably because the French word *pont* means bridge). The experiment had gone awry, killing several people and injuring numerous others. This was the "un-American" activity referred to in the Colby documents; this was Olson's "possible security violation" that was alluded to in the cryptic note found at Fort Detrick. It also explained Lovell's peculiar remarks about Olson having "*No inhibitions. Baring of inner man,*" meaning that Olson had wrongly spoken out about Pont-St.-Esprit, revealing his arrogance and recklessness. For Saracco and Bibb, pieces of the puzzle were falling into place.

It also explained Dr. Harold Abramson's report, written in December 1953, about three weeks after Olson's death, in which he referrred to the Deep Creek Lake meeting and Olson's drugging as having "been performed especially to trap [Olson]."

Supporting Abramson's contention was an internal CIA staff memo written to CIA Inspector General Lyman Kirkpatrick, who had performed a perfunctory investigation of Olson's death in 1953:

> After the incident in [Europe] and subsequent statements made by Olsen [sic] to unauthorized personnel in the field and at his post, Lovell was livid and confronted Schwab.

Saracco learned additional information about Olson's behavior following the Deep Creek Lake incident. Specifically, Olson had been fearful for his safety, extremely nervous and agitated. Eric Olson also told Saracco that he had been informed by one of his father's Camp Detrick colleagues that one day shortly before his death, Frank had been riding to work with a neighbor and Camp Detrick colleague when he had oddly and suddenly blurted out that he was worried that he was telling and giving away secrets. As Olson's superior John Schwab stated in 1953: at Deep Creek Lake, Frank Olson had "been exposed."

Indeed, during Thanksgiving week of 1953, Olson had been behaving like a man scared out of his wits. On his way to the airport to go to New York, he had told his wife Alice that someone was trying to poison him. In Manhattan that last fateful week, Olson had begged Lashbrook and Ruwet, "Let me go. Let me just disappear." He had pleaded with Ruwet, his superior and friend, to tell him, "What's behind all this? What are they trying to do with me; are they checking me for security?" On his second evening in Manhattan he had told Ruwet, he "knew people were waiting to arrest him."

In the early morning hours of Thanksgiving Day, November 26, Olson had reportedly fled the hotel room he shared with Ruwet, only to have what seemed to be a change of heart — but after having disposed of his wallet and credentials. For Saraccoc and Bibb, all the signs seemed to point to the murder of a major security risk who could have thrown a giant spotlight into the CIA's dark chamber of horrors.

This was the basic outline of what Saracco and Bibb initially learned. Now they needed something more definitive, something in writing, something that revealed the identities of Olson's killers. After weeks of haggling back and forth, Albert and Neal reluctantly agreed to furnish Saracco with documentation of their government employment and their connections to the CIA and also to provide a letter outlining exactly what they knew. Following several unexplained delays, they sent the letter to Saracco and Bibb in April 2000. Providing the letter had been a real source of contention for Albert and Neal. They knew that the District Attorney's requests for information would most likely not stop with the letter even though Saracco had promised that it would. After considerable debate between the DA's office and the two CIA sources, they supplied the letter with the explicit stipulation understanding that they, Albert and Neal, would provide nothing further — other than to answer a few follow-up questions for the sake of clarity. A week after Albert and Neal had furnished their letter to the New York prosecutors, I received a faxed copy of it from Morgenthau's office. The letter was written in an odd and perplexing style. It read, in part:

> To the cardinal task at hand- Frank Olson, deceased biochemist, among other things. Without prompting, I appreciate your professional interest in the whole affair. Mine in it, 'interest' I mean, much like that in the elusive scribe above, presently takes a more abstract course, but is equally cradled in professionalism (of a decidedly past tense).
>
> The point being- I, as employee of CIA, along with others, had the luck of the draw to deal directly with Olson's demise. That dealing, as I understand you have already been informed, transpired at a time most allied with the event itself: within hours.
>
> This, in turn, being not that long after the- how do you put it?- caper involving Ray Lemons. (Ask Henry [this author] ask too about tugging the SGO thread and openings the wurms can.)
>
> In short, and more to your objectives, Mr. Olson's fateful flight on the night in question was ventured on wings bestowed by enfants terrible, LaFitte and Le Grande Lydio.

The letter concluded with the Latin phrase: "*Gravior quaedam sunt remedia periculis*. Regards." ('Some remedies are worse than the disease.')

Initially, there was some confusion and irritation about several parts of the strange missive. First, there was the reference to Olson's killers, the "enfants

terrible, LaFitte and Le Grande Lydio." The name "LaFitte" was quickly identified as being FBN and CIA "special employee" Pierre Lafitte. But who or what
was "Le Grande Lydio."

With effort and a fair amount of luck, the prosecutors were able to identify
"Le Grande Lydio" as an alias for heroin trafficker Francois Spirito. Indeed, the
FBI wanted sheets and Narcotics Bureau watch lists from the mid-1950s identi-
fied "Le Grande Lydio" as a well-established nickname for Spirito.

Who was "Ray Lemons?" It was discovered that this was the street name for
a shady businessman named Raymond Maresca (who readers first encountered
in Book Two). Lemons had been involved in a number of illicit endeavors and
George White had been assigned by FBN to his case. Why this person was
mentioned in the letter, however, remains unknown.

The references to "tugging the SGO thread" and "wurms can" were related to
an internal investigation headed by a Federal Bureau of Narcotics official whose
last name was Wurms. The investigation had reportedly involved a number of
Bureau agents, including George White and Garland Williams, and it implicated
the FBN's corrupt narcotics agents. According to informed sources this investigation was connected with Olson's death only in a "very minor sort of way."
However, as this author was informed, the files related to the investigation were
still classified and unavailable.

WHAT REALLY HAPPENED TO FRANK OLSON

Saracco and Bibb were at once intrigued and frustrated by the April 2000 letter from Albert and Neal. Where was any information about the motive for
Olson's death? Their frustration eased substantially after they received a copy
of an undated White House memorandum that bore the heading: "IDENTITY
SHEET." [See copy of this memorandum in this book's Exhibits.]

The memorandum clearly pertained to the Frank Olson case and listed in
numerical order, from numbers 7 through 13, seven names, including Spirito
and Lafitte. Apparently, the list had been generated, or reproduced, either for
or by the Rockefeller Commission or the CIA. Typed at the bottom of the list
was: "Routing: Colby, Belin." This, presumably, referred to CIA director William Colby and Rockefeller Commission head David Belin.

Also listed at number 11 were the words: "Pont Saint Esprit incident (Olsojn)
[sic]."

Saracco and Bibb had no idea what "Pont Saint Esprit" referred to, but
soon these cryptic words were explained to them, along with the truth about
the alleged "ergot outbreak" in France that had been shrouded in mystery for
decades. The explanation was stunning.

As long suspected, Frank Olson had indeed been speaking "out of security
lines," as Neal put it, in violation of his security oath with both the Army and
CIA. Specifically, Olson had spoken about the clandestine, "EYES ONLY"

SOD project called Project SPAN that had taken place in August 1951 in Pont-St.-Esprit, France. This, of course, was the so-called "ergot outbreak" that had caused hundreds of the townspeople, young and old, to become temporarily and terrifyingly insane, causing the deaths of at least four people.

Saracco noted that Eric Olson had told him that among his father's old home movies, there was a brief clip of what appeared to be a military crop duster taking off from an unidentified field. Frank Olson himself had shot the film on one of his trips to Europe in the early 1950s.

According to Albert and Neal, several weeks before the meeting at Deep Creek Lake, Frank Olson had "broken security" and talked about the French experiment on at least two occasions. He had been specifically cautioned by Vincent Ruwet and John Schwab about the "high level of security and sensitivity involving the experiment."

"After being firmly cautioned, Olson had again broken security and "spoken out of line"about Pont-St.-Esprit with several of his colleagues, including "with a neighbor he occasionally car-pooled to work with." The neighbor immediately reported Olson to Camp Detrick security officials. As a result of this last indiscretion, the decision was made to interrogate Olson.

The question was posed to the two sources: "Was this, the incident in France at Pont-St.-Esprit, the 'un-American activity' referred to in the papers given to the Olson's by William Colby?

Not surprisingly, the answer was, "Yes."

Was Pont-St.-Esprit solely a SOD operation?

No. It was a pre-ARTICHOKE joint operation between SOD and CIA's security branch.

Did it involve any other intelligence agency such as the French?

Silence.

This author questioned three of Olson's former colleagues on the subject of Pont-St.-Esprit. What had occurred in the town involving SOD or CIA officials?

Said Gerald Yonetz, "Gee, I don't remember much about activity in France. Were we there, some of us, in the 1950s? Yeah, some of us were, but I don't remember what we were doing. That was a long time ago."

Said Henry Eigelsbach, "France, yes, sure. Some of us went there, at times, for certain work. I'm sure SO Division people did also. But I don't remember the particulars of the work."

Don Falconer, a close friend of Olson's, said, "I don't remember anything about France. Nothing. Not a thing."

"Don't remember or don't want to remember?"

"I have nothing to say about it."

But other former Camp Detrick scientists, speaking on condition of anonymity, recounted that the Pont-St.-Esprit experiment had involved the aerosol spraying of a potent LSD mixture as well as "the contamination of local food products." One scientist claimed that the "spraying had been an all-out failure."

Because Frank Olson had been "exposed," as John Schwab had so succinctly put it in his 1953 statement to CIA Security agents, the decision had been made to interrogate Olson at the upcoming Deep Creek Lake meeting through the use of skilled interrogators, including CIC officer Allan Hughes, and to use LSD mixed with Meretran. The drug had been mixed into the Cointreau bottle earlier, as Lashbrook had described in his 1986 deposition (quoted earlier). As first hinted at by Schwab's remarks to reporters in 1975, Olson's interrogation had taken place in another part of the Deep Creek Lake grounds, away from his colleagues.

As stunning as these revelations were, the story that emerged about what had happened in New York City the week of Olson's death was even more amazing to the two prosecutors.

Olson had been taken to Dr. Harold Abramson for further evaluation of his attitudes and intentions. Because the two men had known each other well during the 1940s and subsequently, it was perhaps believed that Olson would be forthcoming about the reasons for his security breaches. In fact, in the years 1952 and early 1953, Olson and Abramson had encountered one another on "numerous occasions" in connection with CIA projects MKULTRA and MKNAOMI. Noted Albert:

> The two seemed to enjoy each other's company, but there was always the strain and tension of Olson's biases that had to be contended with, but Abramson was pretty adept at avoiding this.

Added Neal:

> This was not always the case with others, notably [Sidney] Gottlieb. There were tensions there also about Olson's leanings, even though Gottlieb had once made it clear to Olson that he was agnostic and didn't subscribe to or practice any religious persuasion.

These were obviously references to Frank Olson's rabid anti-Semitism.

In New York, everything had gone as planned, recounted Albert and Neal, until the morning of November 26 when Olson had left the room he shared with Ruwet and "walked the streets for about an hour or so." Albert explained, "Prior to that Olson had been pleading with Ruwet to let him go, to just let him wander off and do whatever he had in mind, assumely flee to someplace. Of course, that would not be allowed."

This provoked the need for "additional security for Frank," Neal explained, as Lashbrook "was not completely confidant that he could control Olson should anything else go wrong." Neal explained, "Abramson's assessment of Olson had led to his recommendation that Frank be confined to Chestnut Lodge for intensive treatment."

Intensive treatment?

691

"Well, this would have involved the same techniques that [CIA official] Frank Wisner went through later— rounds of shock treatment and chemical therapy. Nobody wanted to take any chances with him [Olson] coming out and continuing to be indiscrete."

Explained Albert, "It was only logical, or so it was thought, to go to [George] White for assistance with Olson. White was expert at this sort of thing... But, nobody counted on White's mother passing away in California."

White's mother had fallen seriously ill a week prior to the Deep Creek Lake meeting. On November 10, White recorded in his date book: "Virginia calls says mother had stroke and can't talk." White left New York City on November 11th for Los Angeles and went straight to Carlsbad, California where his parents lived and where White remained through his mother's death and funeral, which took place on November 30. White did not return to New York City until Tuesday, December 15.

Albert and Neal provided the following details about what then transpired:

> That [White's mother's death] necessitated a changing of the guard, so to speak... And that's where Lafitte and Spirito came in. George asked Pierre to step in, to keep tabs on Olson, while he was away in Carlsbad. It only made sense; Lafitte was still working undercover jobs at the Statler. Everyone knew him there, by a different name, of course, but he could roam the place at will with no problems.

But, said Neal, "Things often go wrong when last minute changes occur in planning," and things did go wrong after Lafitte brought in Spirito to back him up with the Olson assignment. Why or how Lafitte enlisted the assistance of Spirito is unknown. What we do know is that Spirito had been unexpectedly released from federal prison in Atlanta and had journeyed to New York the week before Olson arrived there with Ruwet and Lashbrook. Spirito's long acquaintance with Lafitte is a matter of historical record.

Details of what happened the night that Olson died are still somewhat vague because neither Albert nor Neal would go into specific details.

At some point during Olson's last night in New York, Neal explained, Lashbrook had become concerned that "Olson was once again becoming unhinged." Before Olson and Lashbrook retired for the night, the decision was made that "it would be best" if Olson were transported back to Maryland for confinement at Chestnut Grove, as Abramson had recommended, but by means other than the commercial flight Lashbrook had booked for the next day.

The alternative plan involved Lafitte and Spirito, apparently as personal escorts for Olson. Said one source, "White would have been the ideal alternative, perhaps along with Lafitte, but he was in California." That Spirito had just been released from prison in Atlanta where he had been a subject in Dr. Carl Pfeiffer's "psychotic experiments" was either overlooked or unknown. "I don't think anyone knew where he had come from or where he had been; he was recruited by Lafitte," said Albert.

According to Albert and Neal, when a late night "attempt was made to remove a subdued Olson from the room to transport him by automobile to Maryland" things went drastically wrong. The short and entire explanation is that "[Olson] resisted and in the ensuing struggle he was pitched through the closed window."

Pitched? It seemed an odd word. *Pitched.*

Does that mean thrown or pushed?

"It may not be the correct word, but it will have to suffice. Anyone can imagine that in such situations things can become confusing."

But was the intent to murder Olson?

"The intent initially was to remove him from the hotel without incident and to take him to Maryland where he would be tucked away and further assessment would be allowed so as to decide what to do with him."

When I first heard this account, I could not help but recall a conversation I had had with a CIA official about four months earlier. The official had berated me for pursuing the Olson story as a book, and had told me rather emphatically, "Don't you understand, for Christ's sake, we don't kill our own. CIA simply does not do that. We don't kill our own."

"So, are you saying that Frank Olson did or did not work for the Agency?" I had asked.

The official had hesitated, and then repeated, "I'm saying we *do not* kill our own."

But he did go through the closed window? I now asked Neal.

"Absolutely."

And Lashbrook? Was he awake during it all?

"Yes, awake and out of the way."

But he knew in advance of the attempt to remove Olson?

"He helped arrange it."

Albert and Neal were questioned about their statement about Olson "becoming unhinged."

What was Olson's condition?

"In a nutshell," Neal recounted, "[Olson] was coming apart with fear and confusion. The LSD had left some residue hangover, as had the interrogation, but there was no lasting reaction. He was a frightened man. His arrogance and attitude were gone. He was scared. He had made a bad mistake and he knew he was going to somehow pay for it."

Did he threaten to reveal any CIA operations to the media?

"That's laughable," Neal said. "Who in the media would he go to? This was 1953, not 1975 or 2000. Who did he know? Who would have believed him back then?"

And the claims about Korea?

"Olson was never in Korea," said Neal. "He had little to nothing to do with the war there."

So had he experienced a change of heart, as some claim?

"Not that I'm aware of," said Albert. "However, it was common knowledge that he wanted out since the whole ulcer incident in the late 1940s. He wasn't cut out for the type of work he was doing. He was in way over his head, and he knew it at the last."

When I received that answer I recalled an email exchange I had with Fort Detrick's public relations official and historian, Norman Covert (a surname most appropriate for his duties). I had asked Covert to tell me about Frank Olson and he had commented that, among other things, "Olson was in over his head with his work."

Were others, besides Olson, drugged with LSD at Deep Creek Lake?

"Yes. But only as a cover for what was really taking place with Olson."

Was Schwab drugged?

"No."

Ruwet?

"No."

Was Olson actually a CIA employee?

"He was employed as a civilian employee by the Army at Camp Detrick's Special Operations Division. He was never recruited by the CIA."

How did Lafitte and Spirito get into Olson's and Lashbrook's room?

"Through the adjoining room door. Lafitte worked at the hotel and had ready access. It could not have been easier."

At Saracco's request, I sent him a lengthy narrative concerning Lafitte's background, including sections on his employment in New Orleans and his apparent connections to Lee Harvey Oswald and Clay Shaw around the time of President Kennedy's death. About a week later, Saracco called to say, "Like I said before, I knew it was only going to be a matter of time before this case somehow connected to JFK's assassination." Saracco and Bibb would eventually trace Lafitte's last known whereabouts to a small town in New Hampshire. Briefly, there was some belief that he was still alive in 2000 but further investigation revelaed that he had passed away about ten years earlier. Prosecutors would also learn that after Olson's death, Lafitte traveled to St. Petersburg, Florida, only about 13 miles from Indian Rocks Beach, where he stayed in a small beachside house owned by Mafia kingpin Santo Trafficante, Jr. While it was never confirmed, it is believed that George White had arranged for Lafitte's hideaway in the Sunshine State.

At about the same time as the White House Identity document was sent to Saracco and Bibb, this writer received a carbon copy of an October 23, 1954 letter George White had sent to Garland Williams, White's former Narcotics Bureau supervisor. The letter, apparently sent by White from somewhere other than New York, contained many cryptic and intriguing references and passages.

Dear Garland,

I hope that this letter finds you and Edmere in good spirits and health. I understand from Tine that the two of you have been in Nags Head recently.

You asked in your earlier letter about my trip to Habana and I wanted to tell you that it was enjoyable. Tine came by boat with Dad and they also had a time of it. Dad complained about the heat but it was good for him. Paul Gross was there and we had dinner together. Vance, of course, didn't make it as he still has some mopping up to do with the Smith-Melton-Morrison mess [See previous section on the CIA's Victim's Task Force Book, four, Chapter 13.] *Gross asked about you, as always. We had fun talking about the Houston scandal, which just won't seem to go away. Vance, Fred and I are going to continue to work the Billnitzer murder until something hard and fast gets pinned down....*

When I get back I want to speak with you about Bedford Street and get your advice before I ask Gottlieb about the move to San Francisco. Now with the Olsen [sic] thing and Herlands affairs behind us the time might be right to make the jump from Chicago and Detroit.

The imp Owen Winkle has made another unexpected appearance in NY at the same time that our friend decided that his term at the Statler was overextended. I seriously doubt that he knows anything at all about the Olsen [sic] thing and Lashbrook apparently had no qualms about bouncing right back a month later for Pelican planning with Hawk [sic], Ahbramson [sic], the crews from Lexington and Detrick, and Pieffer [sic].

I received a letter from Edmond Bailleul last week. He's overly worried about everything as usual. He and Marie are doing fine. That's good given the circumstances and Marie's recent illness. Edmond wrote that she can no longer work and that her lung infection will mean more time in the mountains. He's still bragging about that 8 lbs. seizure and proud that he knew about Gene's last ride. Naturally he wrote nothing about that little French village's Stormy epidemic [*"Stormy"* was White's code word for LSD]. I suspect that is in everybody's past where it belongs.

Siragusa told me last week that Dejea and Aranci are still holding the roof up over Edmond. For how long is anyone's guess. Charlie and Blemont possibly has a piece of Drap D'Or in Paris. Maybe after our friend returns from his jaunt out west he can return to France for a few weeks. I suspect his moonlighting work at NYC hotels is over once and for all. Tine loved him in his little bellman's outfit.

As you remarked a few weeks ago, the last year has been a tough one on the emotions. Gene was one thing but then with Croft, Linda, Kate, Olsen [sic] and Billnitzer it was floodgate time. Anyway, here's hoping the piper will play a different tune in San Francisco.

Tine sends her love to Edmere. [Italics added.]

695

To assist the prossecutors in deciphering the letter, this author prepared the following list of identifications:

"Edmere" is the first wife of Garland H. Williams.

"Tine" is White's wife, Albertine.

"Habana" is Havana, Cuba. White went to Havana for work and relaxation in 1954.

"Paul Gross" is another Federal Narcotics agent who sometimes worked closely with White.

"Vance" is Vance Newman, another narcotics agent who worked closely with White, often out of the Bedford Street safe house funded by the CIA.

"Gene" was Eugenio Giannini, who was murdered in New York City.

"Croft" was a FBN agent who allegedly killed himself.

"Linda" and "Kate" were both friends of White, who he dosed with LSD.

"Billnitzer" is Martin A. Billnitzer, a Houston, Texas police department detective, who committed "suicide" on June 3, 1954 by firing two bullets into his heart.

"Sears" is Will Sears, city attorney of Houston in 1953-1954.

"Bedford Street" readers will recall was the two-story, two-unit apartment house on the corner of New York City's Bedford and Barrow Streets, Greenwich Village. The unit fronting Bedford Street was used as a CIA safe house overseen by White.

"Olsen" is Frank R. Olson.

"Owen Winkle" is an alias that was interchangeably used by White for Dr. Hinkle and former OSS officer Alfred Hubbard.

"Statler" is the Hotel Statler in New York City where Frank Olson died on November 28, 1953.

"Our friend" refers to Pierre Lafitte, who worked undercover at a number of NYC hotels, including the Statler, for the FBN and CIA.

"Pelican" was a top-secret code word for a multi-service behavior modification project operated by the CIA, Navy, and U.S. Army. CBS Pentagon reporter David C. Martin revealed its existence years ago in his book *Wilderness of Mirrors.*

"Hawk" is NYSPI physician Dr. Paul Hoch.

"Ahbramson" is a misspelling of Dr. Harold Abramson's name.

"Edmond Bailleul" is a high-ranking French narcotics officer.

"Marie" is Edmond's wife.

"Siragusa" is FBN agent Charles Siragusa.

"Blement" is Robert Blement (aka Robert Banner, Eric Holt), a notorious French contract-assassin and drug trafficker.

"Drap D'Or" was a well-known club in Paris, which served on occasion as a drop point for CIA couriers and FBN agents.

Along with White's letter to Williams, this author also shared with the prosecutors the fact that Alice Olson's telephone number was found in

White's 1954 address book. The reason for this has never been ascertained. It is not known if prosecutors requested any telephone records in the Olson case.

THINGS FALL APART; THE CENTER CANNOT HOLD...

Shortly after the New York prosecutors received the documents from Albert and Neal, including the one indentifying Lafitte and Spirito as the two who had thrown Frank Olson from the hotel window, the case began inexplicably to unravel.

As indicated in this Author's Introduction, Saracco and Bibb, presumably at the direction of Morgenthau, had insisted that the CIA verify the identities of the two sources, Albert and Neal. Indeed, the two had already provided ample documentation of their government employment to the two prosecutors. Moreover, initially Saracco had stipulated that "the only thing they would be required to do" was to identify Olson's killers and to explain why Olson had been murdered. Nonetheless, the deal had suddenly changed. Now the District Attorney's office wanted the CIA to verify Albert and Neal's employment, which, of course, would mean revealing their names to the Agency.

"I need you to ask them to agree to this, Hank," Saracco said to me on the telephone.

"I can't," I said. "I can't do it."

"Why not?"

"Because that wasn't our agreement," I said, "and because nobody in their right mind would agree to such a request."

"It's really important to the case."

They want what you have and they won't stop at anything to get it.

"And if one of these guys happens to have a fatal accident weeks after they agree to it, are you going to explain to his family what happened?" I asked.

"That's not going to happen."

"It's not even worth discussing," I said. "Christ, Steve, they've gotten you this far... how can you ask them to do this? It's insane."

"We need you to do it," Saracco said.

"Absolutely not," I replied. "If I ask them that, I guarantee you that will be the end of any help from them to anyone."

When I hung up moments later with Saracco, I realized that my last remark to the prosecutor was perhaps exactly what was wanted – *an end to any help from them to anyone.*

Dan Bibb called me several days later with the same request. My answer was the same, but Bibb insisted he would send a draft agreement outlining what the District Attorney's office was looking for from the two sources. [See: Exhibit headed "Witness Testimony" marked "Draft" in this book.]

Before Bibb hung up I asked him, "Dan, have you or Steve discussed this with the CIA?"

"Not in any real detail," he said.

"Well, let me ask you this," I said, "was my name mentioned?"

"I'm not sure. Most likely it was."

I received the draft "Witness Testimony" agreement days later, but, after reading it, I never presented it to anyone. Its wording confirmed my worst fears. It read in part: "In exchange for information and/or testimony...[t]he Manhattan District Attorney's Office will recommend to the United States Department of Justice that immunity be granted for any federal violations or contractual violations in connection with the CIA."

A few weeks later, on March 28, 2001, I received a letter from Saracco telling me that unless I was willing "to complete the arrangements for any of the witness interviews by May 31, 2001," the District Attorney's office "would be forced to conclude that these officials do not wish to cooperate with this Office in any manner. Your involvement with the investigation will then be concluded."

It was a relief to receive the letter. I conveyed to Eric Olson what was going on with the District Attorney's office as it occurred. Eric was justifiably disappointed that things had turned out the way they had, but he understood completely. I had kept him informed all along about developments with Saracco and Bibb. I did not tell Eric about my suspicions that perhaps the prosecutors' last request regarding the two sources had been intended to put an end to the case, but I sensed that Eric also understood this.

Once again I reflected on the words of my friend, the criminologist: *They want what you have and they won't stop at anything until they get it.* By becoming involved in the case as a *de facto* investigator, I had acted against my better instincts. I had become a part of the case I was writing about. It had been my 'terrible mistake,' and I had nobody to blame but myself.

The day after the horrible events of 9-11, attorney Harry Huge called Eric Olson and said that he was sorry, but he could no longer handle his case and lawsuit.

"I have to leave the case," Eric recounts Huge saying. "A couple of my other cases have really exploded on me."

Stunned, Eric had replied, "Harry, I'm so far out on a limb I can't even see the tree...And this has nothing to do with the fact that the World Trade Center was bombed yesterday? That's just a coincidence, right?"

"I didn't even think of the timing," Eric says Huge replied.

Eric would note, months later, that Huge "was no longer comfortable serving subpoenas to Cheney and Rumsfeld to grill them over Frank Olson." However, in reality, the case never even remotely came close to this stage of activity.

The 2002 Press Conference and Reburying Frank Olson

By early summer 2002, Eric was feeling more and more pessimistic about the likelihood that Morgenthau's office would issue any conclusive finding about his father's death. The strain from the lack of momentum in the case was showing in Eric's tone of voice and written messages; he was becoming increasingly angry and bitter, and frequently his emotions were aimed at anyone in the way.

Frustrated by his inability to replace Harry Huge, and by the stony silence emanating from the Manhattan District Attorney's office, Eric and Nils Olson decided to rebury their father, whose body had remained in cold storage for eight years since the Starrs' team had completed its investigation.

On August 8, 2002, the remaining members of the Olson family held a press conference in Frederick, Maryland in the backyard of Frank and Alice Olson's home, the same site as the press conference 27 years earlier.

Eric Olson opened the event by announcing to the small group in attendance, "The gist of what we want to say can be compressed into three headlines."

The three statements, none of which appeared in any newspapers the next day, were: "The death of Frank Olson...was a murder not a suicide"; Frank Olson's story was not an LSD drug experiment gone awry, but instead a biological warfare story that had resulted in his death because the United States used germ warfare in Korea; and, lastly, that high level officials in the American government, including members of the George W. Bush administration, had covered up the overall Olson murder.

The three charges were extremely dramatic; the assembled press listened raptly for the anticipated evidence. Days earlier Eric had enticed the media with a preliminary statement:

> My father's coffin has turned out to be a Pandora's box. It's no surprise that the CIA's unethical human experiments would turn out to be linked to assassination. Once the value of human life has been cheapened, then murder lurks just around the corner. The surprising thing is that it's taken so long to make the connection. Even to historians, these two domains appeared to be discreet areas of endeavor. Now that has all changed. [Italics added.]

But the press departed without further evidence for Eric Olson's allegations.

The next day, August 9, 2002, Frank Olson's family — sons Eric and Nils, Eric's son, Stephen, and Nil's two daughters, Lauren and Kristin — once again laid Frank Olson to rest, alongside Alice Olson in Mt. Olivet Cemetery in Frederick, Maryland. No major newspapers or television networks covered the press conference or the re-internment. No one from the New York District Attorney's office attended.

EPILOGUE

And pray to God to have mercy upon us
And I pray that I may forget
These matters that with myself I too much discuss
Too much explain

Because I do not hope to turn again
Let these words answer
For what is done, not to be done again
May the judgment not be too heavy upon us.
                    — T.S. Eliot, "Ash Wednesday," 1930

The last this author knew, Eric Olson still lived in the small, modest home his parents had built in the early 1950s on a hillside overlooking Camp Detrick, the home that Eric's brother Nils calls "the ghost house." When I first visited Eric in 1998, he was living there "temporarily." I remember driving up the winding dirt road and glimpsing the house for the first time. It was set well back from the turn into its driveway. Surrounded by towering trees, the house seemed perpetually in a state of shade and shadow.

I had sat in my car and looked at the house for a while, picturing what it must have looked like decades ago when the trees would have been just small, strong young saplings, some of them probably planted by Frank and Alice Olson. I pictured the couple in their front yard looking proudly at their new home with visions of a bright future in their eyes. I imagined their three children running across the front lawn for the first time, happy and full of life, perhaps still arguing about who was going to get which bedroom.

I thought of Frank Olson stepping through his front door one gray morning in late November 1953 and walking across that lawn to a waiting car that whisked him off to Deep Creek Lake. I thought about Frank coming home a few days later and telling Alice that he had made a "terrible mistake."

Whether Alice knew that Frank's "terrible mistake" was that he had talked about the secret of Pont-St.-Esprit, we do not know for certain. But, like any loving wife, Alice had tried to lessen the impact of that mistake on her husband, even though ultimately, she could not solve his problem. Little did she know that she would carry her husband's burden for the remainder of her life.

Perhaps in his final days, when Frank thought about his terrible mistake and reflected on his life, he may have thought that many of the paths and turns he had chosen were also, in retrospect, mistakes. Perhaps Frank thought, for the first time, that the work he had devoted himself to had all amounted to a big mistake. Perhaps he thought that the nation's entire concentrated effort to devise chemical and biological weapons of mass destruction had been a terrible mistake. Perhaps when he witnessed the effects of testing those weapons — the pained, anguished faces of some of the thousands of defenseless people and helpless animals that Camp Detrick experimented upon — he had seen a look that resembled, however briefly, something he had seen on his children's faces when they had been hurt or injured.

In 1951, Frank Olson was a high ranking Special Operations Division officer; he had responsibility for project planning and intelligence operations; by many accounts, he was an expert in aerosol delivery systems for chemical and biological weapons, many of them highly lethal.

We can't know for sure what Frank Olson witnessed when he was in Pont-St.-Esprit, France in 1951. Was he there for the actual outbreak? Was it his aerosol design that had delivered the terrifying mass psychosis to an entire town? Had he witnessed its effects firsthand, up close and personal? If he had done so, surely he would have seen terrible pain, anguish, terror and confusion on the faces of men, women, and children there. He would have heard their cries and screams; he would have seen them running from and fighting off horrible, unimaginable monsters that they believed were going to harm or consume them. What effect would it have had on Frank Olson to see the frightened, contorted face of a young child in the grip of LSD psychosis? How would it feel to know that you were the cause of that look?

Was Frank Olson haunted to his death by the nightmarish images of Pont-St.-Esprit? Did his guilt feelings for his actions there finally catch up with him, or did his reported arrogance cause him simply to talk too much about the event? Was he remorseful, or was he boastful?

Regardless of the fact that the CIA was virtually in bed with the American media in the 1950s, news stories that the American military, in concert with the CIA, had poisoned an entire French village, causing many of the townspeople to go mad and some to die, would not play out well domestically or internationally — especially coming on the heels of the heinous Nazi crimes and medical atrocities of World War II. The Russians would have had a field day painting the United States as a monstrous nation that had no respect for the rights of others. France might justifiably have raised direct comparisons to the Nazi atrocities they had so recently witnessed and experienced. Make no mistake about it, the Pont-St.-Esprit experiment, by anyone's estimate, was a gross criminal act, a violation of international law and a crime against humanity that might have dwarfed any allegations about the Korean War.

What was Frank Olson's "terrible mistake"?

Was it the "Pont-St.-Esprit secret" as one sly Sandoz company official said to the CIA? Was it that Frank Olson was not willing to play a cooperative role in keeping this secret from the world? Was he racked by his conscience by what had happened in France? Or, as others have suggested, did Olson's arrogance provoke him to use his knowledge to attempt to secure personal gains? Did he threaten to quit his employment at Camp Detrick and go into the private sector where his "skills" might be better appreciated? Could he possibly have been bragging about his aerosol design? Was he seeking not forgiveness, but credit?

Without doubt, the Deep Creek Lake interrogation of Olson was an attempt to discover his true intentions for the future; to get him to reveal his real concerns; to assess his capacity to provoke an international incident.

Regardless of Olson's intentions, the fact that the experiment at Pont-St.-Esprit was ever contemplated, planned, organized and carried out is shocking – so shocking that some hardened CIA and Army Cold Warriors at the time rightfully deemed it "un-American."

So intense was the pressure being applied to silence Frank Olson in 1953 that even he himself, in a moment of sheer desperation and fear, had begged, "Just let me go; just let me disappear."

Dr. Sidney Gottlieb died before this book was completed. Gottlieb strongly believed in what he did for the CIA. While the record indicates quite clearly that the vast majority of the programs he administered did not originate with him, he did his absolute best to carry them out, and there is no escaping the fact that many of the programs resulted in needless and irreparable harm to people.

Dr. Robert Lashbrook, Gottlieb's good friend, died about two years after Gottlieb. Lashbrook carried all his secrets to the grave.

A few years before this book was completed, I received a telephone call from one of Armond Pastore's relatives. Armond, the night manager at the Statler Hotel at the time of Frank Olson's death, had passed away two weeks earlier. The relative had wanted to call me sooner, but had misplaced my phone number. I had not realized how much Armond meant to me until I was told that he was gone. We had become good friends and we would get together every few weeks for dinner. About four months before he died, I had told Armond the details of how Frank Olson had been killed and why. He didn't seem surprised at all.

"I knew it had to be something like that," he had said. "But, now I know, and that feels better than not knowing all these years. I only wish that Alice Olson were still alive to know the truth."

I told Armond that the simple fact of the matter was that the case might never have been solved without him.

"Oh hell, I didn't do anything," Armond said, always true to form.

Not long after Armond's death, I received another sad message – that one of the two sources who had reluctantly assisted the Manhattan District Attorney with the Olson case had drowned while fishing in harsh waters off the Carolina coast. As with the body of William Colby, this man's body had taken days to recover and, inevitably, there was speculation about what had caused his death. I wondered about it myself. My suspicions were laid to rest by his close colleague, the other of the two sources. Sometimes accidents do happen.

Manhattan Assistant District Attorneys Steve Saracco and Dan Bibb put aside the Olson case after the events of 9-11. The attacks on the World Trade Center and Pentagon, the frightening anthrax mailings scare, had the effect of rallying the country and, at the same time, pushing aside, or totally burying, anything that ran counter to, or placed a black mark upon, the nation's intelligence services and military. It would be six to seven years before most Americans realized that the vengeful fervor they had felt over the attacks was not all good and rational, but by that time the Frank Olson case had faded from the media and memory.

Steve Saracco retired a few years after 9-11; reportedly, he was less than pleased to have his name associated with the unresolved Olson case. His cold case partner, Dan Bibb, quit the District Attorney's office in 2006, amid controversy over a case involving two young men convicted of murder in 1992 and then sent to prison. Over the years, and through his own official investigations, Bibb had become convinced they were innocent. In 2005, Bibb tried to convince Manhattan District Attorney Robert Morgenthau that the men had been wrongly convicted, but he was ordered to defend the conviction. Instead, Bibb deliberately lost the case.

"I was angry," he explained, "that I was being put in a position to defend convictions that I didn't believe in."

Disciplinary agencies investigated Bibb's actions for months and, finding that he had acted ethically, they ruled in his favor. Morgenthau told reporters, "Mr. Bibb was never asked to prosecute someone he believed to be innocent."

When I first read about the controversy involving Bibb, I thought back to a lunch I'd had with Saracco and Bibb in an Italian restaurant near their offices. We had spent the entire morning discussing Frank Olson's death, and I could not help but notice that Bibb had been mostly quiet during the session, asking only a few questions. I asked him if he thought the Olson case would go anywhere much less result in the handing down of indictments. He did not answer my question, but gave me a look that spoke volumes.

Long-time Manhattan District Attorney Robert Morgenthau announced his retirement in February 2009. "It took me a while to realize I was getting old," Morgenthau said. On several occasions in 2000 and 2001, I had requested that Saracco or Bibb ask Morgenthau what he recalled about his dealings with Pierre Lafitte in the Joe Valachi affair, but I never received an answer. Eventually, and reluctantly, I came to the conclusion that the Frank Olson case had only been reopened because it had been expected that it would go nowhere. After some "acceptable" interlude, it would once and for all be laid to rest, much like Olson's body had once again been properly reburied.

William Hayward also died the year before this book could be completed. Bill was an American icon, the producer of the seminal films *Easy Rider* and *The Hired Hand*. I had met Bill, an extremely intelligent and artistic man, after I read a magazine article he had written about his boyhood trials and terrors at the hands of a renowned psychiatrist, who had been an OSS and CIA contractor. The experience with this physician, and a subsequent involuntary commitment to the Menninger Clinic, had done irreparable harm to Bill, the true extent of which I did not fully understand until after his death.

Through my conversations with Bill Hayward, I was better able to know the terrible damage that misdirected psychiatry can do to a person. Talking with Bill about my interviews with a number of MKULTRA survivors helped me more fully understand what the CIA's and Army's "behavior modification" experiments had done to the people they selected as their unwitting subjects. Bill was able to confirm and substantiate just how horrific it would have been for them.

Bill died by his own hand. His act was a terrible and tragic response to the pain and the demons he had been fighting all of his adult life as a result of his encounters with CIA-sponsored psychiatry. I know that he sought to drag each and every one of those monsters to their own deaths and I can only hope that he found true peace in the process.

As for me, I had started this project with the best of intentions to write an historical account about a perplexing mystery. Over time, due to circumstances beyond my control, that account also became a tale of tragedy and despair over the evidence of a nation that had lost its way on history's road. It became an account of a nation whose best and brightest scientists and physicians, in their quest to preserve democracy and combat Communism, were willing to sacrifice virtually everything that was good about America, not to mention the lives and well being of innocent people. What was it that made these researchers so uncaring about the enormous amount of pain and suffering they caused? Did the physicians involved even contemplate their oaths to "first, do no harm" as practitioners of medicine? Were they no better than the Nazi doctors who had been tried and convicted at Nuremberg?

While writing this book, I had countless interactions with Eric Olson, with his attorneys in Washington, D.C., with various former and current CIA officials, and with officials in the Manhattan District Attorney's office. Often these contacts were not at my initiative or choosing, and frequently I found myself as a writer in the difficult position of being asked to sacrifice my objectivity and to adopt an advocate's role. Early on in my research, which spanned seven years, I had warned myself not to become part of the story I was writing, not to become a character in its telling, but there came a point when that was inescapable. I became caught in the proverbial middle between my sources and my solemn promise to them of confidentiality, on the one hand, and those who had either personal, financial, or professional responsibilities to uncover the truth, on the other. It was often an extremely uncomfortable and difficult position for me to maintain.

For about three years, hardly a week passed without some important or troublesome issue taking up squatter's rights in my conscience. At times, things became especially difficult for my family and loved ones, especially when I received subtle threats of harm or of being jailed for obstruction. In the end, however, I am proud to say that I never betrayed anyone's confidence, despite these irksome events. Indeed, I never even considered the possibility. I often recalled the words of T.S. Eliot:

> *Your business is not to clear your conscience but to learn how to bear the burdens of your conscience. With the future of the others you are not concerned.*

One night, shortly after I finished this book, I dreamed that I had once again driven up to Frank and Alice Olson's house on Braddock Lane in Frederick, Maryland. It was a cloudy day, and the lawn surrounding the house needed attention and cutting. Large patches of earth showed through the neglected green. The house badly needed painting. In my dream, I knocked on the door and after a moment a young boy opened it. He just stood there, staring up at me. He did not say a word.

I asked, "Is your father home?"

The boy shook his head. "He hasn't been here for a long time. He's gone."

I looked at his sad face and I saw in it the struggle, hurt, confusion, and anger of a young boy who was trying to come to grips with the fact that his father was no longer home and would not ever be home again. The boy opened the door wider and nodded toward a small wooden stool just inside the entrance.

"My father made that," said the boy, who I knew in my dream was young Eric Olson.

"That's very nice," I awkwardly replied.

"Yes," said Eric, "it's the only thing I have in this house that was my father's. He made it with his own hands."

Indian Rocks Beach, 2009

Appendixes, Exhibits, Notes & Index

– Appendix 1 –

Mind Control Victims

On 26 October, [redacted], an employee of the [redacted], contacted the Office of the Inspector General here at the Agency and related the following information. His wife, whose maiden name is {redacted}, was previously married from 1955 until 1960 to [redacted], who was employed by CIA at that time. In the summer of 1956, according to [redacted], she accompanied her husband to the farm of her husband's supervisor for dinner, drinks and wine. She believes her husband worked for Dr. Gottlieb, who was chief of the Technical Services Staff Chemical Division, and heavily involved in MKULTRA activities. Her next recollection is receiving electric shock treatment at George Washington University Hospital for some time...
— Letter from CIA Assistant General Counsel to John Gavin, Esq., Office of Legal Counsel, U.S. Department of Justice, 2 November 1977.

Over the past nine years, while working on *A Terrible Mistake*, about two- dozen people separately contacted me wanting to share experiences that they believed were part of CIA mind control projects. Most of these people seemed quite sincere in their approach and claims. Some had written passionate articles about their experiences; a few had even written books about what had happened to them. Several of the books had been published and their authors were happy to send me copies, hoping that I would read and perhaps review them. Each of these individuals seemed more than convinced that they had fallen under the control of the CIA after being targeted at an early age. A surprising number claimed to have become involved through their fathers, who were somehow connected to the Agency, or were officials who worked for the Agency. Nearly all of these people had also been physically and sexually abused by their fathers. Memories of abuse, as well as feeling controlled by the CIA, were often brought to the surface as a result of working with psychotherapists or psychologists.

One woman told me a cadre of CIA men, including her father and Dr. Sidney Gottlieb — who she said routinely paraded about dressed in a Nazi SS uniform and jackboots — had mercilessly beaten and raped her so as to condition her to be "a programmed assassin." Another individual, who has written a number of articles about various government activities, told me he had been selected years ago as part of a deep-black project that involved being constantly bombarded with electro-waves of some sort. When I asked him specifically why he and others had been targeted by the CIA, he grew angry and said, "The technology I'm being subjected to is much farther advanced than you know. The experiences I mentioned were pretty elementary. If you don't get that, how can you understand what a target of the technology is going through?"

A woman told me the CIA had targeted her for mind control when she worked for the State Department. She claimed she had been transformed into an unwitting, programmed assassin and she was convinced she had actually murdered several foreign diplomats overseas. I asked her for the names of some of these diplomats and she told me that they had been erased from her memory. Could you tell me what countries you worked in? I asked her. "No," she said. "That is a matter of national security." Well then how can I verify your claims? I asked. Can you at least show me proof you work for the government? "No," she said, "you have to trust me. Why would I lie about such a thing?"

The human mind is complex and intriguing. I am not a scientist, psychologist or psychiatrist. I don't know what provokes some people to invent situations that they claim to be true, and that they believe to be true. At the same time, it is possible that people sounded irrational, delusional and paranoid because they had, in fact, been subjected, perhaps repeatedly, to mind altering drugs from which they had not recovered. I came to disbelieve most of the stories I was told, but to believe some of them.

I am an investigative reporter and I am most concerned with objective evidence and facts. I can't settle for the argument, "Trust me, I'm telling the God's honest truth." However, let me be clear here: I am not calling these people liars. I believe that many of them honestly believe their own stories and that some of them may be true.

One story that came my way was clearly different from all the others. This story involved a woman who, in the mid-1950s, had been married to a CIA employee. In fact, the man had worked in the Agency's TSS branch and had answered directly to Drs. Sidney Gottlieb and Robert Lashbrook. The woman also had worked for the federal government, holding a classified position with another intelligence organization. There was no doubt about any of this. Numerous sources, including former CIA and White House officials, verified these facts. I have changed this woman's name and that of her husband in order to protect the woman's privacy and safety.

SALLY'S STORY

It was the summer of 1956. Sally and Jim Hartman had been married for about a year, and it had not been easy thus far. A month earlier, Sally had suffered a miscarriage. It had been her longtime dream to have children but

Jim, despite earlier agreement, now had doubts about starting a family. Their arguments about her pregnancy were greatly upsetting for Sally. Jim had insisted that, if she wanted a baby, she would have to stay at home and not work at all. Sally disagreed, telling her husband that she had not gone to college for four years just to be a housewife. "Times are changing, Jim" Sally says she argued. "I told him women could have careers and also be good mothers." Jim said, "Not my wife." Sally asked Jim to please consider her needs. Jim argued back that Sally should try harder to be "a good Christian" before attempting to become "a good Christian mother." Sally countered that she was a good Christian and that a woman who maintained a professional career could also be a good Christian. "You're wrong," Jim said. "Read your Bible more often."

When Sally lost the baby, it was after weeks of arguing with Jim. She silently and partially blamed Jim for putting so much strain on the both of them. He was sullen for days after their last argument and was hardly speaking to her. Sally recalled that, after this, Jim began to "lecture me on morality, like I was stupid." She said, "He would quote from the Bible to back his lectures, and tell me about the forces of evil in the world guised as Communism."

Jim had been a graduate student at MIT in 1953 when Sally and he had decided to marry. When he was close to completing his studies, the CIA had recruited Jim. The Agency had offered him a good starting salary and the opportunity to travel. His recruiter told him the Agency would help with his remaining tuition costs and hold his position until he received his Masters Degree in chemistry and completed a six-month obligation for active duty with the Army Reserve. About a week before he was to start work, he had been called in to meet his superiors, Drs. Sidney Gottlieb and Bob Lashbrook. He had come home that evening excited and anxious to begin his CIA training.

"Sid and Bob are the nicest guys you can imagine," he told Sally. "And the job sounds really great."

Sally asked what he would be working on, but Jim said he couldn't tell her anything about it other than that it was in his field, chemistry, and that he'd have to travel on a fairly regular basis. Travel where? she asked. Jim said he couldn't tell her that either. Sally said that it would be difficult to raise children if he were to travel a lot and she was working, and Jim said maybe she should listen more to him about when they would start a family. A few days after Jim started work for the Agency, he was required to attend an intensive secret training school that took him out of town for three months. Sally knew that Jim was happy about his Agency job and didn't argue, but Jim could tell she was not happy.

Sally was working at the National Security Agency at Fort Meade, a job she had taken a few months before she and Jim had married. In charge of a classified computer data-storage project, she now threw herself into her work as a way of not dwelling on her miscarriage. Like Jim's job, Sally's required complete secrecy, and a security clearance. She could not speak to anyone, including Jim, about what she was doing. When friends asked about her work, Sally said she would reply that she "was just an administrative assistant to a mid-level government bureaucrat." Usually, this ended the questions. "People asking wouldn't have any more interest in the subject."

One sunny Sunday afternoon in August 1956, Sally and Jim drove from their apartment just outside Washington, D.C. to the home of Jim's boss in rural Vienna, Virginia, about forty miles away. Jim had come home from a weeklong trip the day before and told Sally that they had been invited to go to Sidney Gottlieb's house for dinner the next day. "We don't have to dress up or anything," Jim had told her. "Sid lives on a small working farm."

It was a gorgeous day and Sally recalled that the ride out of town almost immediately worked wonders at relaxing the two of them. "It was like we were dating again and we didn't have a care in the world," Sally recalled. " Jim was unusually talkative, smiling, laughing... he even pulled me over close to him in the front seat like we were a couple of school kids. It was great." At Gottlieb's house, Sidney and his wife, Margaret, warmly greeted the couple. "Margaret introduced me to her three or four children. I got the impression that Jim had already met the children. They were really nice kids, and the family seemed very happy. I remember wondering why, if Jim's boss could have such a large family, we couldn't have a small one. I don't recall now if Margaret had a job outside the home, but she surely had her hands full with the farm."

Sally recalls that the Gottliebs raised goats. Sidney had told her that he tested and drank the milk the animals produced. "I learned right away that he was a chemist, like Jim, because he said he tested the milk himself, because, as he said, 'I'm a chemist and enjoy doing things like that.'" Sally remembers that Sidney also said he had worked at the Department of Agriculture before joining the Agency.

"I asked him if he had worked with animals at the department and he said, 'Oh goodness, no. I never had the opportunity to leave Washington while there.'"

After taking a tour of the Gottliebs' farm, Sally says everyone, including the children, sat down to dinner. "We had a wonderful home cooked meal and some wine. After I had a glass full, I don't remember anything else about being there," Sally recounts. "I drank socially. I never drank a lot, but on weekends two or three drinks wasn't out of the question. But something happened that night, something really strange."

Sally has no recollection of the drive home other than a vague image of asking Jim to stop the car once because, "I felt like I was going to be very sick." Thinking back, she says, "I also remember having to urinate badly, and thinking, my God, did one glass of wine make me feel like this?" At home, she recalls sitting up all night and "reading the Bible's Book of Apocalypse [also called the Book of Revelations]. I don't remember what Jim was doing or saying."

Sally recalls experiencing dark visions of ancient, crumbling cities and death and mayhem. She becomes visibly shaken when she tries to recount what she saw and felt:

I was like in a dream state. Or perhaps more like a nightmare state. I was frightened, but at what I can't remember. I think I remember Jim laughing at something or maybe smiling or... I'm really not sure what it was. I was scared, really scared, but I don't know why.

Even today, over thirty-five years after the incident, Sally becomes very upset and nervous when she tries to recall that night. Her hands tremble and she looks about, as if expecting some dark shape to form in front of her.

The morning following their (1956) visit to the Gottliebs' farm, Sally had gone into work exhausted. From that day forward, Sally found it almost impossible to concentrate on anything. She began to experience episodes of lost time, periods where she would function normally but not be aware of where she was or what she was doing.

After about six weeks, the episodes became even more frequent. At home one evening, Sally told Jim that she was concerned that she didn't always feel she was in control of her actions or thoughts. Jim said he thought she was overworked and needed a break. He tried to cheer her up, once playfully suggesting that he hypnotize her as a way of relieving her stress. Sally said he had never been interested in matters esoteric, and when she asked him what had provoked his interest in mesmerism, he had just shrugged and said, "Sometimes it's wise to keep an open mind about certain things." A few days later, Sally says, she remembers receiving electric-shock treatment. "I know it sounds crazy," she says. "I have no idea where I was or how it happened, but I know that it did."

One day not long after, Sally was at work at the NSA when she became confused and then hysterical, for reasons unknown to her. She ran from her office and out of the building, across an expansive grassy field, and tried to climb the eight-foot security fence surrounding the area. NSA guards struggled to pull her from the fence. On the ground she fought to get away, screaming at the guards, "You don't understand, let me go, let me go."

Sally was hospitalized at George Washington Hospital in Washington, D.C. At Jim's insistence, she stayed there for a little over a month. Besides being assigned a psychiatrist, she received 14 electric shock sessions as part of treatment for diagnosed schizophrenia.

During one of Jim's visits, he tells her that his boss, Dr. Gottlieb, whom he sometimes calls "Uncle Sid," is very good friends with the superintendent of a well respected mental health hospital in Boston. Since her family still lives in the Boston area and he is frequently required to travel for the CIA, Jim suggests that Sally transfer to the Massachusetts facility. Sally agrees, and she and Jim travel to Boston, where her father greets the couple, and the three go to the admission's desk of the hospital. Sally says at this time she had begun to experience "laughing jags, followed by periods of rapidly evolving thoughts and deep depression."

Sally remained in the Boston facility for a number of weeks. In addition to visits from her family, she was visited a few times by Jim's boss, Sidney Gottlieb, because Jim was often away on travel assignments. She remembers very little about Gottlieb's visits other than going outside for a walk with him sometimes, at Gottlieb's suggestion. Sally recounts one such walk when it was "very cold with lots of snow on the ground." They went outside, but Sally remembers nothing more about the visit, other than that she was wearing hospital slippers and a bathrobe, and yet, "I was not cold." On another one of Gottlieb's visits, they again went outside and Sally remembers that he mentioned something about Jim not being able to come, but she remembers nothing more.

Sally also recalls being visited by a physician whose last name she thinks was Goodnow. This was most likely Dr. Robert E. Goodnow, a contractor with the CIA's TSS and with the Human Ecology Fund. Goodnow was associated with the Anesthesiology Department at Harvard Medical School and Massachusetts General Hospital. Sally says, "I can't remember anything about Goodnow except that he was there in my room sometimes. Maybe once with Gottlieb or someone."

In February 1957, Sally is still in the Boston hospital when she is informed that she may be released soon but she first needs to "undergo one more test." She is taken from her room to another room where she is shown what she recalls "as cards similar to Rorschach cards." The technician showing her the cards has "very intense eyes," Sally recalls, and she has never seen him before at the hospital. After being shown a few cards, Sally thinks she blacked out because she remembers nothing more until "waking up about two days later back in my room" with "an intravenous line and needle in my arm." A nurse enters Sally's room and tells her she hasn't eaten for two days.

Sally's mother also recalls this incident because it occurred the same week that her daughter was to be discharged. She says when Sally was discharged, she walked through the main doors and, after standing outside for a few moments, turned around and went back inside and asked to be readmitted.

A month later she was discharged again and she went to her parent's house. A few days prior to her release, Jim had visited her. He announced that the CIA had agreed to pay for his return to MIT for his PhD in chemistry. Sally wants to return to work at NSA, but she discovers that she has forgotten nearly everything she had learned while working there for nearly two years. She retrains herself as a computer programmer while staying with her parents.

Jim soon arrives in Boston to resume his studies; he and Sally rent a "very nice apartment near the MIT campus." Over the next few months, Sally begins to feel quite happy. She also feels that her relationship with Jim is becoming better and closer. However, within a year, the tensions return when she tells Jim she would like to try to become pregnant again and begin a family. Jim does not share her feelings and by the summer of 1960, Sally decides to leave Jim.

During this time, Sally has continued to experience episodes of lost time and depression. Sally wants to reconcile with Jim, but he seems quite pleased with their living apart. They see each other a few times, but Sally can't remember anything about these dates. They decide to divorce within a few months. Sally is distressed that her marriage has ended this way. When she meets another man who seems to share her desire to have a family, she hastily marries him, but this marriage goes bad within months.

Nonetheless, by this time, Sally has resumed her work in the computer field, and she is again in line for a position that requires a Top Secret clearance. Sally is concerned that "my mental breakdown and hospitalization will hinder a clearance" but she encounters no problems at all. She has no recollection of how her high-level NSA security clearance was handled. Despite her second divorce Sally is extremely happy with her work and excels in her field, making several significant advancements. She does not recall how her employment with NSA officially ended, but in 1966, she decides to start her own company and within months of doing so, she has developed an international reputation for her creative approaches to the computer industry.

By this time, Sally had lost all contact with Jim, and no longer knew if he was still employed with the CIA. Occasionally, her old symptoms returned, but she was able to put them off by taking medication. On one or two occasions she felt herself fall into a "strange state, like sleepwalking while awake" and once, while on the West Coast, she woke up in a hotel room "unsure of where I'd been for the last twenty-four hours. I recalled getting unto a hotel elevator and there was a group of people already in it, and someone nodded and said something and that was it. Later, I thought I remembered waking up in my room and finding someone standing there looking at me, telling me everything was just fine, not to worry about a thing. I don't remember any more than that."

Sally's business continued to be very successful and time consuming. She fell in love with one of her closest associates, a former investigative reporter. They were married in 1969. Two years later, Sally and her new husband, Fred, sold her computer company for a lot of money. All of Sally's hard work had paid off, and the couple was happy with their life together. They started a small consulting firm that also became quite successful. Months later, one of their accounts resulted in Sally being hired to oversee a large data system for the U.S. Congress. The work was stressful, and some of Sally's old symptoms began to reappear. She had trouble sleeping and began to have strange dreams. At times, she found herself wondering what she had done or where she had been for the past few hours. Her doctor prescribed tranquilizers, and she began to feel better. Fred had also taken a demanding job with Congress, and the two remained happy together.

At the beginning of 1977, Sally went to work for the Carter White House on a special project. In August of that year, while working in the White House, Sally picked up a copy of the *Washington Post* and read an article about a CIA project called MKULTRA. The story mentioned that the Massachusetts hospital where she had been a patient was part of the MKULTRA project.

Sally went home that night and told Fred about the article, and also told him about Jim's peculiar interest in hypnotism and that he had once tried to

715

hypnotize her. She recalled later that this was the first time she had told Fred about her seven months' hospitalization in Massachusetts, and about her "inexplicable recollections about her visits to the Gottlieb's farm."

The next month, Fred obtains the complete transcripts of the Congressional hearings investigating Project MKULTRA. He takes detailed notes, including the fact that Sidney Gottlieb and Robert Lashbrook were directors of the project. Having heard Sally talk about her strange experiences with Gottlieb, Fred tells Sally what he has discovered in the transcripts. Sally tells him that Jim used to call Lashbrook Bob or "Lash" and that sometimes she heard Jim on the phone referring to Gottlieb as "Uncle Sid."

Fred asks Sally how her Massachusetts hospital bills were paid. She tells him that she has no recollection of ever paying any bills. She recalls seeing one bill, but has no idea what became of it. Fred asks if her parents might have paid the bills. She calls them, and they tell her they have never seen any bills or paid anything related to her illness. Fred asks Sally if she was in the hospital for the entire seven months, or if she was released and readmitted at any time. Sally seems to recall being released at times and going somewhere, but she can't recall when or where. Did you travel anywhere? Fred asks. Sally seems to remember going somewhere on an airplane once, but the more she struggles to recall, the more distant the memory becomes. She tries to think harder, and she becomes overwhelmed with inexplicable sensations of swirling colors and flashes of light. Sometimes she imagines she hears a voice in her head telling her, "Relax, just relax. Everything is fine. Now relax."

Shortly after these conversations, Fred consulted several physicians and was told by one, "Perhaps Sally is an unwitting victim of some sort of mind control effort." The physician advised Fred that, given the dimensions of the MKULTRA project as reported in the newspapers, anything would be possible if Sally had somehow become a test subject.

Fred began to develop a theory about what had happened to his wife. Based on public revelations about Frank Olson, Fred thought Sally had been given LSD by her husband Jim or by Sidney Gottlieb, or both. Once she was placed in a secure hospital, he speculated, Sally became an ideal, unwitting test subject. Fred thought, "What better cover can there be, or greater achievement, than to control the mind of a person who is a patient in a mental hospital without detection?" Sally's sudden "breakdown" and electric shock treatments seem to be connected to her having been given some sort of drug that triggered her radical change in behavior.

Fred called the Massachusetts hospital and requested his wife's medical records. After a few days, the hospital returned his call, but told him there was no record of Sally having been a patient. Fred told the caller there had to be some sort of mistake. Please recheck your records, Fred asked. The hospital told Fred someone would call him back within a day or two. Two days later, the hospital told Fred that Sally's records had been located. Fred asked that they be copied and sent to him and Sally.

The same week, Fred consulted a noted psychologist about Sally. The psychologist confirmed that the CIA had experimented extensively with "hypnosis and post-hypnotic suggestion used in combination with certain drugs." The psychologist also told Fred the Agency had experimented with a variety of surreptitious methods for delivering drugs to unwitting subjects. These methods included "techniques for penetrating clothing with drugs" and "treating paper in books and magazines with certain drugs."

At that point, Fred asked Sally if Jim had ever sent or brought books or magazines to her when she was in the hospital. Sally said Jim had not, but she did recall that someone else had brought her books while she was in the hospital, but she could not recall who it was. Where are the books now? Fred asked. Sally could not recall bringing any books home with her.

Meanwhile, additional articles appeared in Boston newspapers about the Massachusetts hospital where Sally had been committed. Some articles revealed that doctors there had surreptitiously tested LSD, mescaline and other powerful drugs on patients. Many of these experiments had taken place during the time when Sally was a patient in the same hospital.

Based on these revelations, Fred's concerns intensified about what may have happened to Sally. They significantly deepened after he read a July 1952 CIA document citing the "narco-hypnotic control" of subjects placed under what the Agency dubbed "psychiatric-medical control." For such control, hospitalization was required. "In each case," the memo stated, "a psychiatric-medical cover was used to bring ARTICHOKE techniques into action."

After thinking long and hard about it, Fred decided to pay a visit to Sally's former husband, Jim. Within about a week, Fred located Jim, who was then running his own consulting firm outside Washington, D.C. Jim agreed to talk with Fred, provided Fred came alone.

Jim confirmed that he had been a CIA employee assigned to Gottlieb's Chemical Division. He also confirmed that he and Sally had gone to the Gottliebs' home for dinner in the summer of 1956. Jim described the visit much the same way Sally had recalled it, but denies that Sally was dosed with any drug while there. He told Fred that Sally's mental problems were a result of other factors, and of her having had a miscarriage. Jim said he had obtained a "good Catholic" psychiatrist for Sally to help her while she was hospitalized. He also said he had been unable to visit Sally as often as he would have liked because he was often traveling for TSS overseas, spending a fair amount of time in Greece.

Fred asked Jim for the name of the "good Catholic" psychiatrist. Jim said it was Dr. John Cavanagh. Fred did not know it at the time, but Cavanagh reportedly was a covert contractor for the Agency. Very reliable sources told this author that Cavanagh had made over fifty trips overseas related to CIA Project ARTICHOKE. Cavanagh also consulted closely with Drs. Harold Abramson, Harris Isbell, and Robert Hyde. Jim cut short his visit with Fred, saying he had "a family affair to attend."

In 1977, after the initial revelations about Frank Olson's death and Project MKULTRA, the Department of Justice was notified by confidential sources about what had happened to Sally Hartman. The Department contacted the CIA with its concerns. A November 2, 1977 letter from the CIA's Assistant General Counsel to the Justice Department's Office of Legal Counsel reads:

> She [Sally] recalls being referred by her husband's supervisor [Gottlieb] to a friend of the supervisor's at the "Boston Psychiatric Hospital." She and her husband, [redacted name and TSS title], went to Boston where she entered that Hospital. Both her husband and his supervisor visited her there and she recalls a strange walk out of doors with the latter. She also remembers taking various tests at the Hospital. [Sally] suffered a "relapse" and required psychiatric care two years ago, but apparently has since "come out of it." The recent Senate hearings and attendant publicity concerning Project MKULTRA prompted [Sally's husband] to review the Senate transcripts which he found contained information supportive of his wife's recollections. [Sally's husband] did not ask for any specific action or relief. He has been advised and voiced no objection regarding our opinion that this matter should not be investigated directly by CIA at this time but should be referred to Justice for consideration....
>
> This matter obviously deserves further investigation to clarify, by confirming her suspicions or allaying her fears, the basis for whatever emotional distress [Sally] may continue to suffer. Of course, it may not be possible at this date to gather sufficient evidence to accomplish either result. In any event, however, it does not appear appropriate for CIA to conduct this investigation, even insofar as questioning [Sally's husband] who has already contacted an Agency official on 31 October to inform CIA of the fact that his wife had related these allegations to him. Since it might appear to some that CIA has an interest in not confirming that individuals were in fact "victimized" by MKULTRA-type activities, the Agency could be accused at some point, in this or any other investigation of the same general nature, of having not conducted the investigation in a proper manner. Should these matters proceed to litigation, this perceived conflict of interest on the part of CIA or its employees could become particularly damaging.
>
> The Agency continues to be anxious to do everything possible to assist those who may have been adversely affected by MKULTRA-type activities. However, the complications surrounding any action contemplated by CIA itself continue to plague us, as the above-described case again illustrates. We shall be happy to assist you further, in any way you may deem necessary, in achieving a satisfactory resolution to these difficult problems.

After learning about Sally's story and her real name, I was stunned to realize that I knew her from my own work with the Carter Administration. I called her on June 1, 2000 and asked if she would tell me about her recollections of what had happened in 1956 during her visit to the Gottliebs' farm. She agreed but almost immediately became extremely upset and began to cry.

"I'm sorry," she says, "I can't seem to talk about it without becoming upset."

She tells me that she found the Gottliebs to be "very nice." She says, "We had a wonderful visit and dinner. Everything was fine, and then I remember riding home with Jim feeling really strange and becoming very upset about something. I had to urinate and asked Jim to pull the car over on the side of the road. After that I can't remember anything else until later, when I was put in the hospital."

Do you recall the incident at NSA with climbing the fence?

"Vaguely," she says. "I have no idea what I was doing or where I was going."

"How are you today?" I ask Sally.

"Not good," she says. "I feel like my life has been taken away from me. I'm never sure of anything. Most of the time I feel like I'm only half here."

"Half here?"

"Like part of me is always somewhere else. Somewhere where I'm not."

Author's Note:

In 1999, I had a long conversation with a CIA official about Sally, during which the official asked me, "Are you familiar with the Bible's Book of Genesis?" I answered that I had read it, but was not well versed in it. "Well," he said, "you should read it again. Read it in light of what is occurring in today's world."

"Meaning what?" I asked.

"Read the Book of Genesis. Read it completely through. Focus on the serpent in the garden, on how that serpent came to the woman, made from the rib of a man fashioned in God's image and likeness, and convinced her to ignore the warning of God and eat the forbidden fruit of the tree of knowledge of good and evil. The woman told the serpent, 'We may eat of the fruit of the trees of the garden,' but God said, 'You shall not eat of the fruit of the tree which is in the midst of the garden, neither shall you touch it, lest you die.' The serpent mocked God's words to the woman, saying, 'You will not die. For God knows that when you eat of it your eyes will be opened, and you will be like God, knowing of good and evil.' So the woman ate from the tree and then had her husband eat from the tree, and the rest is history."

"I'm not sure I understand what you're saying," I said, amazed the official could quote so readily from the Book of Genesis.

"The point is that the serpent is still the representation of evil in the world today. The serpent is best exemplified by the forces of terrorism, and God remains with us in order to guide us away from the evil that wants to dominate the world and destroy the representatives of God."

A Study of Assassinations*

DEFINITION

Assassination is a term thought to be derived from "Hashish," a drug similar to marijuana, said to have been used by Hasan-Dan-Sabah to induce motivation in his followers, who were assigned to carry out political and other murders, usually at the cost of their lives.

It is here used to describe the planned killing of a person who is not under the legal jurisdiction of the killer, who is not physically in the hands of the killer, who has been selected by a resistance organization for death, and whose death provides positive advantages to that organization.

EMPLOYMENT

Assassination is an extreme measure not normally used in clandestine operations.

It should be assumed that it will never be ordered or authorized by any U.S. Headquarters, though the latter may in rare instances agree to its execution by members of an associated foreign service. This reticence is partly due to the necessity for committing communications to paper. No assassination instructions should ever be written or recorded. Consequently, the decision to employ this technique must nearly always be reached in the field, at the area where the act will take place. Decision and instructions should be confined to an absolute minimum of persons. Ideally, only one person will be involved. No report may be made, but usually the act will be properly covered by normal news services, whose output is available to all concerned.

JUSTIFICATION

Murder is not morally justifiable. Self-defense may be argued if the victim has knowledge which may destroy the resistance organization if divulged. Assassination of persons responsible for atrocities or reprisals may be regarded as just punishment. Killing a political leader whose burgeoning career is a clear and present danger to the cause of freedom may be held necessary.

But assassination can seldom be employed with a clear conscious. Persons who are morally squeamish should not attempt it.

CLASSIFICATION

The techniques employed will vary according to whether the subject is unaware of his danger, aware but unguarded, or guarded. They will also be affected by whether or not the assassin is to be killed with the subject. Hereafter; assassinations in which the subject is unaware will be termed "simple"; those where the subject is aware but unguarded will be termed "chase"; those which the victim is guarded will be termed "guarded."

If the assassin is to die with the subject, the act will be called "lost." If the assassin is to escape, the adjective will be "safe." It should be noted that no compromises should exist here. The assassin must not fall alive into enemy hands.

A further type division is caused by the need to conceal the fact that the subject was actually the victim of assassination, rather than an accident or natural causes. If such concealment is desirable the operation will be called "secret"; if concealment is immaterial, the act will be called "open"; while if the assassination requires publicity to be effective it will be termed "terroristic."

Following these definitions, the assassination of Julius Caesar was safe, simple, and terroristic, while Huey Long was lost, guarded, and open. Obviously, successful secret assassinations are not recorded as assassinations at all. Ananda Mahidol of Thailand and Augustus Caesar may have been the victims of safe, guarded and secret assassination. Chase assassinations usually involve clandestine agents or members of criminal organizations.

THE ASSASSIN

In safe assassinations, the assassin needs the usual qualities of a clandestine agent. He should be determined, courageous, intelligent, resourceful, and physically active. If special equipment is to be used, such as firearms or drugs, it is clear that he must have outstanding skill with such equipment.

Except in terroristic assassinations, it is desirable that the assassin be transient in the area. He should have an absolute minimum of contact with the rest of the organization and his instructions should be given orally by one person only. His safe evacuation after the act is absolutely essential, but here again contact should be as limited as possible. It is preferable that the person issuing instructions also conduct any withdrawal or covering action, which may be necessary.

In lost assassination, the assassin must be a fanatic of some sort. Politics, religion, and revenge are about the only feasible motives. Since a fanatic is unstable psychologically, he must be handled with extreme care. He must not know the identities of the other members of the organization, for although it is intended that he die in the act, something may go wrong. While the assassin of Trotsky has never revealed any significant information, it was unsound to depend on this when the act was planned.

Planning

When the decision to assassinate has been reached, the tactics of the operation must be planned, based upon an estimate of the situation similar to that used in military operations. The preliminary estimate will reveal gaps in information and possibly indicate a need for special equipment, which must be procured or constructed. When all necessary data has been collected, an effective tactical plan can be prepared. All planning must be mental; no papers should ever contain evidence of the operation.

In resistance situations, assassination may be used as a counter-reprisal. Since this requires advertising to be effective, the resistance organization must be in a position to warn high officials publicly that there lives will be the price of reprisal action against innocent people. Such a threat is of no value unless it can be carried out, so it may be necessary to plan the assassination of various responsible officers of the oppressive regime and hold such plans in readiness to be used only if provoked by excessive brutality. Such plans must be modified frequently to meet changes in the tactical situation.

Techniques

The essential point of assassination is the death of the subject. A human being may be killed in many ways but sureness is often overlooked by those who may be emotionally unstrung by the seriousness of this act they intend to commit. The specific technique employed will depend upon a large number of variables, but should be constant in one point: Death must be absolutely certain. The attempt on Hitler's life failed because the conspiracy did not give this matter proper attention.

Techniques may be considered as follows:

1. Manual.
It is possible to kill a man with the bare hands, but very few are skillful enough to do it well. Even a highly trained Judo expert will hesitate to risk killing by hand unless he has absolutely no alternative. However, the simplest local tools are often much the most efficient means of assassination. A hammer, axe, wrench, screwdriver, fire poker, kitchen knife, lamp stand, or anything hard, heavy and handy will suffice. A length of rope or wire or a belt will do if the assassin is strong and agile. All such improvised weapons have the important advantage of availability and apparent innocence. The obviously lethal machine gun failed to kill Trotsky where an item of sporting goods succeeded.

In all safe cases where the assassin may be subject to search, either before or after the act, specialized weapons should not be used. Even in the lost case, the assassin may accidentally be searched before the act and should not carry an incriminating device if any sort of lethal weapon can be improvised at or near the site. If the assassin normally carries weapons because of the nature of his job, it may still be desirable to improvise and implement at the scene to avoid disclosure of his identity.

2. Accidents.

For secret assassination, either simple or chase, the contrived accident is the most effective technique. When successfully executed, it causes little excitement and is only casually investigated.

The most efficient accident, in simple assassination, is a fall of 75 feet or more onto a hard surface. Elevator shafts, stairwells, unscreened windows and bridges will serve. Bridge falls into water are not reliable. In simple cases a private meeting with the subject may be arranged at a properly cased location. The act may be executed by the sudden, vigorous seizing of the ankles, tipping the subject over the edge. If the assassin immediately sets up an outcry, playing the "horrified witness," no alibi or surreptitious withdrawal is necessary. In chase cases it will usually be necessary to stun or drug the subject before dropping him. Care is required to insure that no wound or condition not attributable to the fall is discernable after death.

Falls into the sea or swiftly flowing rivers may suffice if the subject cannot swim. It will be more reliable if the assassin can arrange to attempt rescue, as he can thus be sure of the subject's death and at the same time establish a workable alibi. [Italics added.]

Falls before trains or subway cars are usually effective, but require exact timing and can seldom be free from unexpected observation.

Automobile accidents are a less satisfactory means of assassination. If the subject is deliberately run down, very exact timing is necessary and investigation is likely to be thorough. If the subject's car is tampered with, reliability is very low. The subject may be stunned or drugged and then placed in the car, but this is only reliable when the car can be run off a high cliff or into deep water without observation.

Arson can cause accidental death if the subject is drugged and left in a burning building. Reliability is not satisfactory unless the building is isolated and highly combustible.

3. Drugs.

In all types of assassination except terroristic, drugs can be very effective. If the assassin is trained as a doctor or nurse and the subject is under medical care, this is an easy and rare method. An overdose of morphine administered as a sedative will cause death without disturbance and is difficult to detect. The size of the dose will depend upon whether the subject has been using narcotics regularly. If not, two grains will suffice.

If the subject drinks heavily, morphine or a similar narcotic can be injected at the passing out stage, and the cause of death will often be held to be acute alcoholism.

Specific poisons, such as arsenic or strychnine, are effective but their possession or procurement is incriminating, and accurate dosage is problematical. Poison was used unsuccessfully in the assassination of Rasputin and Kolohan, though the latter case is more accurately described as a murder.

4. Edge Weapons.
Any locally obtained edge device may be successfully employed. A minimum of anatomical knowledge is needed for reliability.

Puncture wounds of the body cavity may not be reliable unless the heart is reached. The heart is protected by the rib cage and is not always easy to locate.

Abdominal wounds were once nearly always mortal, but modern medical treatment has made this no longer true.

Absolute reliability is obtained by severing the spinal cord in the cervical region. This can be done with the point of a knife or a light blow of an axe or hatchet.

Another reliable method is the severing of both jugular and carotid blood vessels on both sides of the windpipe.

If the subject has been rendered unconscious by other wounds or drugs, either of the above methods can be used to ensure death.

5. Blunt Weapons
As with edge weapons, blunt weapons require some anatomical knowledge for effective use. Their main advantage is their universal availability. A hammer may be picked up almost anywhere in the world. Baseball and [illegible] bats are very widely distributed. Even a rock or a heavy stick will do, and nothing resembling a weapon need be procured, carried or subsequently disposed of.

Blows should be directed to the temple, the area just below and behind the ear, and the lower, rear portion of the skull. Of course, if the blow is very heavy, any portion of the upper skull will do. The lower frontal portion of the head, from the eyes to the throat, can withstand enormous blows without fatal consequences.

6. Firearms
Firearms are often used in assassination, often very ineffectively. The assassin usually has insufficient technical knowledge of the limitations of weapons, and expects more range, accuracy and killing power than can be provided with reliability. Since certainty of death is the major requirement, firearms should be used which can provide destructive power at least 100% in excess of that thought to be necessary, and ranges should be half that considered practical for the weapon.

Firearms have other drawbacks. Their possession is often incriminating. They may be difficult to obtain. They require a degree of experience from the user. They are [illegible]. Their [illegible] is consistently over-rated.

However, there are many cases in which firearms are probably more efficient than any other means. These cases usually involve distance between the assassin and the subject, or comparative physical weakness of the assassin, as with a woman.

(a) The precision rifle.
In guarded assassination, a good hunting or target rifle should always be considered as a possibility. Absolute reliability can nearly always be achieved at a distance of one hundred yards. In ideal circumstances, the range may be extended to 250 yards. The rifle should be a well made bolt or falling block action type, handling a powerful long-range cartridge. The .300 F.A.B. Magnum is probably the best cartridge readily available. Other excellent calibers are . 375 M.[illegible]. Magnum, .270 Winchester, .30 - 106 p.s., 8 x 60 MM Magnum, 9.3 x 62 kk and others of this type. These are preferable to ordinary military calibers, since ammunition available for them is usually of the expanding bullet type, whereas most ammunition for military rifles is full jacketed and hence not sufficiently lethal. Military ammunition should not be altered by filing or drilling bullets, as this will adversely affect accuracy.

The rifle may be of the "bull gun" variety, with extra heavy barrel and set triggers, but in any case should be capable of maximum precision. Ideally, the weapon should be able to group in one inch at one hundred yards, but 2 1/2" groups are adequate. The sight should be telescopic, not only for accuracy, but because such a sight is much better in dim light or near darkness. As long as the bare outline of the target is discernable, a telescope sight will work, even if the rifle and shooter are in total darkness.

An expanding, hunting bullet of such calibers as described above will produce extravagant laceration and shock at short or mid-range. If a man is struck just once in the body cavity, his death is almost entirely certain.

Public figures or guarded officials may be killed with great reliability and some safety if a firing point can be established prior to an official occasion. The propaganda value of this system may be very high.

(b) The machine gun.
Machine guns may be used in most cases where the precision rifle is applicable. Usually, this will require the subversion of a unit of an official guard at a ceremony, though a skillful and determined team might conceivably dispose of a loyal gun crew without commotion and take over the gun at the critical time.

The area fire capacity of the machine gun should not be used to search out a concealed subject. This was tried with predictable lack of success on Trotsky. The automatic feature of the machine gun should rather be used to increase reliability by placing a 5 second burst on the subject. Even with full jacket ammunition, this will be absolute lethal if the burst pattern is no larger than a man. This can be accomplished at about 150 yards. In ideal circumstances, a properly padded and targeted machine gun can do it at 850 yards. The major difficulty is placing the first burst exactly on the target, as most machine gunners are trained to spot their fire on target by observation of strike. This will not do in assassination, as the subject will not wait.

(c) The Submachine Gun.

This weapon, known as the "machine-pistol" by the Russians and Germans and "machine-carbine" by the British, is occasionally useful in assassination. Unlike the rifle and machine gun, this is a short-range weapon and since it fires pistol ammunition, much less powerful. To be reliable, it should deliver at least 5 rounds into the subject's chest, though the .45 caliber U.S. weapons have a much larger margin of killing efficiency than the 9 mm European arms.

The assassination range of the sub-machine gun is pointblank. While accurate single rounds can be delivered by sub-machine gunners at 50 yards or more, this is not certain enough for assassination. Under ordinary circumstances, the 5MG should be used as a fully automatic weapon. In the hands of a capable gunner, a high cyclic rate is a distinct advantage, as speed of execution is most desirable, particularly in the case of multiple subjects.

The sub-machine gun is especially adapted to indoor work when more than one subject is to be assassinated. An effective technique has been devised for the use of a pair of sub-machine gunners, by which a room containing as many as a dozen subjects can be "purifico" in about twenty seconds with little or no risk to the gunners. It is illustrated below.

While the U.S. sub-machine guns fire the most lethal cartridges, the higher cyclic rate of some foreign weapons enable the gunner to cover a target quicker with acceptable pattern density. The Bergmann Model 1934 is particularly good in this way. The Danish Madman SMG has a moderately good cyclic rate and is admirably compact and concealable. The Russian SHG's have a good cyclic rate, but are handicapped by a small, light protective which requires more hits for equivalent killing effect.

(d) The Shotgun.

A large bore shotgun is a most effective killing instrument as long as the range is kept under ten yards. It should normally be used only on single targets as it cannot sustain fire successfully. The barrel may be "sawed" off for convenience, but this is not a significant factor in its killing performance. Its optimum range is just out of reach of the subject. 00 buckshot is considered the best shot size for a twelve gauge gun, but anything from single balls to bird shot will do if the range is right. The assassin should aim for the solar plexus as the shot pattern is small at close range and can easily [illegible] the head.

(e) The Pistol.

While the handgun is quite inefficient as a weapon of assassination, it is often used, partly because it is readily available and can be concealed on the person, and partly because its limitations are not widely appreciated.

While many well known assassinations have been carried out with pistols (Lincoln, Harding, Ghandi), such attempts fail as often as they succeed, (Truman, Roosevelt, Churchill).

If a pistol is used, it should be as powerful as possible and fired from just beyond reach. The pistol and the shotgun are used in similar tactical situations, except that the shotgun is much more lethal and the pistol is much more easily concealed.

In the hands of an expert, a powerful pistol is quite deadly, but such experts are rare and not usually available for assassination missions.

.45 Colt, .44 Special, .455 Kly, .45 A.S. [illegible] (U.S. Service) and .357 Magnums are all efficient calibers. Less powerful rounds can suffice but are less reliable. Sub-power cartridges such as the .32s and .25s should be avoided.

In all cases, the subject should be hit solidly at least three times for complete reliability.

(f) Silent Firearms

The sound of the explosion of the propellant in a firearm can be effectively silenced by appropriate attachments. However, the sound of the projective passing through the air cannot, since this sound is generated outside the weapon. In cases where the velocity of the bullet greatly exceeds that of sound, the noise so generated is much louder than that of the explosion. Since all-powerful rifles have muzzle velocities of over 2000 feet per second, they cannot be silenced.

Pistol bullets, on the other hand, usually travel slower than sound and the sound of their flight is negligible. Therefore, pistols, submachine guns and any sort of improvised carbine or rifle which will take a low velocity cartridge can be silenced. The user should not forget that the sound of the operation of a repeating action is considerable, and that the sound of bullet strike, particularly in bone, is quite loud.

Silent firearms are only occasionally useful to the assassin, though they have been widely publicized in this connection. Because permissible velocity is low, effective precision range is held to about 100 yards with rifle or carbine type weapons, while with pistols, silent or otherwise, are most efficient just beyond arms length. The silent feature attempts to provide a degree of safety to the assassin, but mere possession of a silent firearm is likely to create enough hazard to counter the advantage of its silence. The silent pistol combines the disadvantages of any pistol with the added one of its obviously clandestine purpose.

A telescopically sighted, closed-action carbine shooting a low velocity bullet of great weight, and built for accuracy, could be very useful to an assassin in certain situations. At the time of writing, no such weapon is known to exist.

7. Explosives.

Bombs and demolition charges of various sorts have been used frequently in assassination. Such devices, in terroristic and open assassination, can provide safety and overcome guard barriers, but it is curious that bombs have often been the implement of lost assassinations.

The major factor, which affects reliability, is the use of explosives for assassination. The charge must be very large and the detonation must be controlled exactly as to time by the assassin who can observe the subject. A small or moderate explosive charge is highly unreliable as a cause of death, and time delay or booby-trap devices are extremely prone to kill the wrong man. In addition to the moral aspects of indiscriminate killing, the death of casual bystanders can often produce public reactions unfavorable to the cause for which the assassination is carried out.

Bombs or grenades should never be thrown at a subject. While this will always cause a commotion and may even result in the subject's death, it is sloppy, unreliable, and bad propaganda. The charge must be too small and the assassin is never sure of: (1) reaching his attack position, (2) placing the charge close enough to the target and (3) firing the charge at the right time.

Placing the charge surreptitiously in advance permits a charge of proper size to be employed but requires accurate prediction of the subject's movements.

Ten pounds of high explosive should normally be regarded as a minimum, and this is exclusive of fragmentation material. The latter can consist of any hard, [illegible] material as long as the fragments are large enough. Metal or rock fragments should be walnut-size rather than pea-size. If solid plates are used, to be ruptured by the explosion, cast iron, 1" thick, gives excellent fragmentation. Military or commercial high explosives are practical for use in assassination. Homemade or improvised explosives should be avoided. While possibly powerful, they tend to be dangerous and unreliable. Anti-personnel explosive missiles are excellent, provided the assassin has sufficient technical knowledge to fuse them properly. 81 or 82 mm mortar shells, or the 120 mm mortar shell, are particularly good. Anti-personnel shells for 85, 88, 90, 100 and 105 mm guns and howitzers are both large enough to be completely reliable and small enough to be carried by one man.

The charge should be so placed that the subject is not over six feet from it at the moment of detonation.

A large, shaped charge with the [illegible] filled with iron fragments (such as 1" nuts and bolts) will fire a highly lethal shotgun-type [illegible] to 50 yards. This reaction has not been thoroughly tested, however, and an exact replica of the proposed device should be fired in advance to determine exact range, pattern-size, and penetration of fragments. Fragments should penetrate at least 1" of seasoned pine or equivalent for minimum reliability. Any firing device may be used which permits exact control by the assassin. An ordinary commercial or military exploder is efficient, as long as it is rigged for instantaneous action with no time fuse in the system. The wise [illegible] electric target can serve as the triggering device and provide exact timing from as far away as the assassin can reliably hit the target. This will avoid the disadvantages of stringing wire between the proposed positions of the assassin and the subject, and also permit the assassin to fire the charge from a variety of possible positions. The radio switch can be [illegible] to fire [illegible], though its reliability is somewhat lower and its procurement may not be easy.

EXAMPLES

([Illegible] may be presented brief outlines, with critical evaluations of the following assassinations and attempts:

Marat
Hedrich
Lincoln
Hitler
Harding
Roosevelt
Grand Duke Sergei
Truman
Pirhivie
Mussolini
Archduke Francis Ferdinand
Benes
Rasputin
Aung Sang
Madero
[illeg]
Kirov
Abdullah
Huey Long
Ghandi
Alexander of Yugoslavia
Trotsky

*CIA Assassination Manual: The manual was first drafted in early 1952 as part of the CIA's plan, Operation PBSUCCESS, to overthrow the freely-elected President of Guatemala, Jacobo Arbenz Guzman. Along with its manual, the Agency also drew up a "disposal list" of at least 58 local Guatemalan leaders to be targeted by "K-teams" ['K' for kill] to be assassinated.

Nuremberg Code — 1947

The decisions of the Nuremberg Military War Crimes Tribunal in the case of the *United States v. Karl Brandt et. al.* includes what is now called the Nuremberg Code, a ten-point statement of ethical principles delineating permissible medical experimentation on human subjects. According to the Code, human experimentation is justified only if its results benefit society and it is carried out in accord with basic principles that "satisfy moral, ethical, and legal concepts."

Among other principles, the Code enunciates the requirement of *voluntary informed consent* of the human subject, protecting the right of the individual to control his or her own body. It also states that any unnecessary pain and suffering must be avoided and that doctors should avoid actions that may cause harm, and not conduct any experiments that may cause disabling injuries, or death.

To some extent, the Nuremberg Code has been superseded by the Declaration of Helsinki as a guide for human experimentation because The Code does not address Clinical Research in patients with illnesses.

1. The voluntary consent of the human subject is absolutely essential.

This means that the person involved should have legal capacity to give consent; should be so situated as to be able to exercise free power of choice, without the intervention of any element of force, fraud, deceit, duress, overreaching, or other ulterior form of constraint or coercion; and should have sufficient knowledge and comprehension of the elements of the subject matter involved as to enable him to make an understanding and enlightened decision. This latter element requires that before the acceptance of an affirmative decision by the experimental subject there should be made known to him the nature, duration, and purpose of the experiment; the method and means by which it is to be conducted; all inconveniences and hazards reasonably to be expected; and the effects upon his health or person which may possibly come from his participation in the experiment.

The duty and responsibility for ascertaining the quality of the consent rests upon each individual who initiates, directs or engages in the experiment. It is a personal duty and responsibility which may not be delegated to another with impunity.

2. The experiment should be such as to yield fruitful results for the good of society, unprocurable by other methods or means of study, and not random and unnecessary in nature.

3. The experiment should be so designed and based on the results of animal experimentation and a knowledge of the natural history of the disease or other problem under study that the anticipated results will justify the performance of the experiment.

4. The experiment should be so conducted as to avoid all unnecessary physical and mental suffering and injury.

5. No experiment should be conducted where there is an a priori reason to believe that death or disabling injury will occur; except, perhaps, in those experiments where the experimental physicians also serve as subjects.

6. The degree of risk to be taken should never exceed that determined by the humanitarian importance of the problem to be solved by the experiment.

7. Proper preparations should be made and adequate facilities provided to protect the experimental subject against even remote possibilities of injury, disability, or death.

8. The experiment should be conducted only by scientifically qualified persons. The highest degree of skill and care should be required through all stages of the experiment of those who conduct or engage in the experiment.

9. During the course of the experiment the human subject should be at liberty to bring the experiment to an end if he has reached the physical or mental state where continuation of the experiment seems to him to be impossible.

10. During the course of the experiment the scientist in charge must be prepared to terminate the experiment at any stage, if he has probable cause to believe, in the exercise of the good faith, superior skill and careful judgment required of him that a continuation of the experiment is likely to result in injury, disability, or death to the experimental subject.

"Permissible Medical Experiments." Trials of War Criminals before the Nuremberg Military Tribunals under Control Council Law No. 10: Nuremberg, October 1946-April 1949. Washington: U.S. Government Printing Office (n.d.), vol. 2, pp. 181-182.

731

Photographs & Documents

Late 1940s photo of Frank and Alice Olson with children Eric and Lisa.

Frank and Alice Olson and children (left to right) Eric, Lisa, and Nils.

735

1953 photo of Frank Olson (left) with SOD colleague.

Frank Olson with cigar, 1952.

ARMY SERVICE FORCES
HEADQUARTERS CAMP DETRICK
FREDERICK, MARYLAND

31 October 1947

GARDED

SUBJECT: OLSON, Frank Rudolph   182492

TO   : Commanding General, Headquarters Second Army, Baltimore 2, Md.
           ATTN: A C of S, G-2.

                         complete background
        1. It is requested that a loyalty investigation be made of the
above named subject who is being considered for a position as _____
 Bio-Chemist   at this station. Proposed duties involve
habitual access to   TOP SECRET   information and materials
and afford a   ready   opportunity to compromise the
national security. PLEASE EXPEDITE.

        2. The investigation requested is deemed necessary to the military
service, and the proper safeguarding of military information.

           For the Commanding Officer:

                                      PHILLIPS D. THAYER
                                      Maj, Cml C, Chief
                                      Intelligence & Security Div.

Incl:
     Personal History Statement (in triplicate)

CD 7-9L (REV)
24 July 1946

October 31, 1947 Army Intelligence Division request that Frank Olson be the
subject of a "complete background investigation" for a TOP SECRET clearance.

OLSON, Frank Rudolph
AIABB-Z 182402

neighborhood. To my knowledge OLSON had no bad habits and they seemed
to lead a quiet home life. Both he and his wife attended the Central
Presbyterian Church in Lafayette, Indiana. I considered them to be good
neighbors and was sorry when it became necessary for them to move away.
I know of nothing derogatory concerning OLSON's honesty, loyalty,
integrity or character and would recommend him for a position of trust
and confidence.

AGENT'S NOTE: Mrs. Lupton, paragraph 10, is a substitute character
reference for persons not in this area.

11. Dr. Ralph Caldwell, Head of the Department of Botany, Agricultural
Experimental Station, Purdue University, West Lafayette, Indiana, character reference, and former associate, was interviewed on 13 January 1948
and stated in substance:

OLSON was employed in the Botany Department as a biochemist from
approximately 1938 until 1942 at which time he went into the Army. I
considered his work to be satisfactory and would be happy having him
again on the staff at Purdue University. He was reliable, cooperative,
dependable and seemed well liked by his associates. He possessed a wonderful personality and was, to some extent, the "happy-go-lucky" type of
person. SUBJECT married a very fine woman who, I believe, was from his
home state of Wisconsin. He enjoyed a good reputation at the University
and as I know of nothing derogatory concerning his honesty, integrity,
loyalty or character, I would recommend him for a position of trust and
confidence.

12. Dr. J. L. Roberts, bacteriologist and character reference, Camp
Detrick, Frederick, Maryland, was interviewed on 2 December 1947 and
stated in substance:

I first met SUBJECT in 1934 at the University of Wisconsin in
Madison when we were taking graduate work together. We shared an apartment, the address of which I do not recall, and during one period SUBJECT
also lived at his fraternity house, which I believe, was Sigma Xi.
SUBJECT's habits were temperate and he worked extremely hard having
little time for relaxation. Later we worked together at Purdue University where SUBJECT was employed as a chemist at the Agricultural Experimental Station, Lafayette, Indiana. He resigned to take a commission in
the U. S. Army. SUBJECT was separated from service while at Camp Detrick
and accepted an appointment in a similar capacity as a civilian. I have
found SUBJECT's work to be exceptional in all ways and cannot recommend

Gregg S. Bertram, Special Agent, 109th CIC Detachment, Second Army
Leslie R. Harrison, Special Agent, 109th CIC Detachment, Second Army

4

Two pages from a 1949 Report by Army Counterintelligence agent Gregg
Bertram that in part is highly critical of Olson.

OLSON, Frank Rudolph
AIABB-Z 182402

him too highly from that standpoint. I must admit, however, that he is extremely tactless and has made many enemies which will probably in later life affect his career. I have seen SUBJECT under the influence of alcohol to the extent of mild exhilaration on occasion. He has made no breaches of security to my knowledge but is violently opposed to control of scientific research, either military or otherwise, and opposes supervision of his work in any form. He is not the type individual who follows orders and rules easily; as a result he had numerous altercations with the MP on the post, refusing to show his pass while entering or leaving the installation and for exceeding the speed limit. I do not believe that SUBJECT is engaged in any militant activity against military supervision of research at Detrick, but like other professional research men on the post, he opposes it, and does not hesitate to so state to anyone's presence regardless of their authority. Despite the foregoing information, I believe SUBJECT is satisfactory from a standpoint of honesty and loyalty and therefore recommend him for continued work in scientific research. However, I do not believe SUBJECT intends to remain in this work very long as he has stated to me in confidence that he wishes to engage in business for himself, manufacturing chemicals for use in scientific research. He has had this ambition for many years and undoubtedly will be discontented until he attains this goal.

13. The records of the Lafayette Credit Bureau, Lafayette, Indiana, were examined on 30 December 1947 and revealed that OLSON had maintained accounts with two department stores in Lafayette from 1939 until 1941, with an approximate high credit of \$35. All payments were promptly made as agreed.

14. Citizens National Bank, credit reference, Frederick, Maryland, records were checked on 3 December 1947 and revealed that SUBJECT has maintained a satisfactory checking account in the low four-figures since 1944. His account has been satisfactory and although he has made no claim for credit, would be favorably considered for such.

15. A. E. Fisher, plumbing supply house, credit reference, 13 East Patrick Street, Frederick, Maryland, records were checked on 3 December 1947 and revealed that SUBJECT purchased one Bendix washer for cash.

AGENT'S NOTE: No other information was available.

Gregg S. Bertram, Special Agent, 109th CIC Detachment, Second Army
Leslie R. Harrison, Special Agent, 109th CIC Detachment, Second Army

5

739

DIRECCION GENERAL DE TRANSITO

El Sr. White George H.

está autorizado por la Dirección General de Tránsito, para practicar el manejo de automotores, por dentro y fuera de la ciudad, *sin* profesional a su lado y *sin* pasajeros por el término de 30 días, contados desde esta fecha.

Quito, a 9 de Marzo de 1953

(f.) _____
Director General de Tránsito

CLASE

1953 travel document for George Hunter White

A. M. G.   F. T. T.

ALLIED FORCE PERMIT

The bearer of this permit is authorised to enter Br/US Zone of Free Territory of Trieste. This permit must be produced on request together with the holder's passport or other identity document.

Il titolare di questo permesso è autorizzato a entrare nella Zona Anglo-Americana del Territorio Libero di Trieste. Questo permesso deve essere presentato su richiesta insieme al passaporto o ad altro documento d'identità del titolare.

Nº 02196

PERMIT TO BOARD.

Permanent Pass No AO.45.436

Name GEORGE HUNTER WHITE

The above is permitted to board the vessels endorsed below for legitimate purposes ONLY.

All Merchant Vessels including Hired Transports.

Valid from 22-3-45 to 21-3-46.

Signed _____

1946 Allied Force Permit for George Hunter White.

Note in French from Pierre Lafitte (aka "the Pirate") to Federal Bureau of Narcotics Commissioner Harry Anslinger.

Francois Spirito (left) with partner-in-crime Paul Carbone.

Statler Hotel, showing window where Olson fell from.

741

(273)

AGENDA – ARTICHOKE MEETING
19 November 1953

1. Discussion of LSD.

2. Discussion of restatement of aims and functions of ARTICHOKE Project papers recently circulated.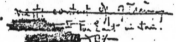

3. Status of ARTICHOKE teams.

4. TSS comments.

5. OSI comments.

6. Medical Division comments.

7. DD/P comments.

8. Director of Security comments.

ARTICHOKE meeting agenda dated November 19, 1953. This was the same day that Frank Olson was drugged with LSD at Deep Creek Lake, Maryland meeting.

MEMORANDUM FOR: Inspector General   De . 3 , 1953

SUBJECT: About the police intervidwing Lashbrook.

"...Among Lashbrook's papers examined by the detectives
((investigating the Olson 'suicide')) was one which contained
Dr. Abrahmson's office and home addresses and telephone numbers.
This paper also contained the following:

    G. W. 59 West 12th Street, Apt. 6-E CHelsea 3-7176

    UNDERNEATH THAT
          Bedford
    M.H. 81 ~~Bedford~~Street, ORegeon 5-0257

Lashbrook identified G.W. to the reporting agent as
George White, cheif of the Boston office of the US Bureau
of Narcotics. He (Lashbrook) said that M.H. stood for Morgan
Hall, an undercover name for George White.

CIA Security Office memorandum to CIA Inspector
General Lyman B. Kirkpatrick regarding Olson's death.

HAROLD A. ABRAMSON, M. D.
133 EAST 58th STREET
NEW YORK 22, NEW YORK

February 9, 1954

Mr. Sherman C. Grifford
Chemrophyl Associates
P. O. Box 8176
Southwest Station
Washington 24, D. C.

Dear Mr. Grifford:

For your information and files I am enclosing a case report which might be of interest.

Yours sincerely,

Harold A. Abramson, M. D.

HAA/nb

February 9, 1954 letter and report on Frank Olson (aka "John Q. Smith") from Dr. Harold Abramson to Dr. Sidney Gottlieb. Note letter is addressed to a CIA-TSS front organization.

CASE REPORT ON PATIENT JOHN Q. SMITH

I was called in consultation to see Mr. John Q. Smith
about ten days after Mr. Smith had received 70 micrograms by
mouth in a highly protected situation. Mr. Smith, although
agitated and concerned over his relationships in work situations
related very well to his friends, to me, and to community proble
in general. It appeared that Mr. Smith had profound guilt feelings because he had been retired as an officer during the last
war and was drawing a pension. His intense feelings of guilt
resulted from receiving government money to which he felt that h
was not entitled. These feelings were not eliminated by his
realistic understanding that he had appeared before a retirement
board. A strong feeling of inadequacy dominated his present wor
He felt that he was not doing as good a job as he thought he
should even though he was thought well of by his colleagues and
promotions had come readily. In several hours of interviewing
for a period of two days his agitation could not be directly
linked with a psychotic state until he said that his sleeplessness had been caused by the FBI who had surreptitiously been
placing amphetamine or caffeine in his food at night to keep
him awake. These feelings of having drugs being placed in his
food had been present for at least five months before he had
received his therapeutic dose of 70 micrograms. He also disclosed that he had shown bizarre behavior for nine months before
so that his wife thought he needed medical attention. This led
to an outpouring of an intense desire on his part to be punished
by the authorities for his past conduct of taking money fraudulently from the government following his retirement by an Army
board.

Subsequent discussion with the patient and an accompanying friend led to his agreeing to entering a mental institution. Different hospitals were discussed. He chose one near
his home and appeared to be relieved that some decision had
been made to take care of his problems. Accompanied by his
friend who shared the same room with him he went to a hotel for
the night because the hospital chosen was distant and he could
not be accepted at once. In the middle of the night without
any warning he plunged head-first through a heavy glass window
shattering it and fell to his death on the pavement below.

Information subsequently received revealed that he
had discussed suicide frequently during the previous year and
to the best of my information had been talked out of suicide
twice. In my opinion Mr. Smith had been suffering for some
time with a paranoid type of depressive psychosis which,
although reluctantly recognized by his family and friends, had
not received adequate medical care. It is my opinion, also,
in view of my experience with various ambulatory types of
subjects. that this dosage could hardly have had any significant role in the course of events which followed.

One of several reports to the CIA from Dr. Harold Abramson's on Frank
Olson's (John Q. Smith) alleged mental state.

MEMORANDUM FOR:

Heims —

10 Feb.

Done 11 Feb. '54

Mt

*Please hand carry
to Gibbons
Drum
Gottlieb.
Have them note having
read + return to Kirk
for Eyes Only file. These are
not reprimands + no personnel
file notation being made.*

CPC

FORM NO. 10.101 JAN 1952

(47)

Handwritten February 10, 1954 memorandum from CIA Director Allen Dulles to his assistant requesting that letters concerning Olson's death be hand-carried to Willis Gibbons, James Drum, and Sidney Gottlied. Memorandum partially reads: "These are not reprimands and no personnel file notations being made."

CENTRAL INTELLIGENCE AGENCY

WASHINGTON 25, D. C.

OFFICE OF THE DIRECTOR

Allen Dulles

91

/\   FEB 10 1954

"EYES ONLY"

MEMORANDUM FOR: Chief, Technical Services Staff

SUBJECT   :   Unwitting Application of LSD

        1. This is to advise you that I consider the unwitting application of LSD in an experiment with which you are familiar to be an indication of bad judgment on the part of two members of your staff: James H. Drum and Dr. Sidney Gottlieb.

        2. The purpose of this memorandum is to inform you officially of this conclusion and to advise you to take all appropriate steps to insure a thorough and careful review within TSS of all experiments. The Deputy Director (Plans) has been instructed to constitute a review board composed of the appropriate officials from within the Agency periodically to review TSS research and experiments.

ALLEN W. DULLES
Director

11-2-54.

February 10, 1954 letter concerning Olson's death from DCI Dulles to TSS chief Dr. Willis Gibbons.

CENTRAL INTELLIGENCE AGENCY *From Allen Dulles*

WASHINGTON 25, D. C.

To James Drum

OFFICE OF THE DIRECTOR

(92)

FEB 10 1954

PERSONAL

Colonel James H. Drum
Chief, Technical Operations
Technical Services Staff

Dear Colonel Drum:

I have personally reviewed the case in which
your staff employed the use of a drug on a group of
subjects not entirely witting that such an experiment
was to be made on themselves. It is my view that poor
judgment was demonstrated by you in authorizing the use
of this drug on such an unwitting basis and without
proximate medical safeguards.

This is to advise you that in the position of
responsibility which you hold you are expected to
exercise greater judgment than was indicated in this
case.

Sincerely,

Allen W. Dulles
Director

February 10, 1954 letter concerning Olson's death from DCI Allen Dulles
to Col. James Drum.

CENTRAL INTELLIGENCE AGENCY
WASHINGTON 25, D. C.

OFFICE OF THE DIRECTOR

Allen Dulles
To: Gottlieb

FEB 10 1954   93

PERSONAL

Dr. Sidney Gottlieb
Chief, Chemical Division
Technical Services Staff

Dear Dr. Gottlieb:

    I have personally reviewed the files from your
office concerning the use of a drug on an unwitting group
of individuals. In recommending the unwitting application
of the drug to your superior, you apparently did not give
sufficient emphasis to the necessity for medical collaboration and for proper consideration of the rights of the
individual to whom it was being administered. This is to
inform you that it is my opinion that you exercised poor
judgment in this case.

                              Sincerely,

                              Allen W. Dulles
                              Director

February 10, 1954 letter concerning Olson's death from DCI Dulles to Dr.
Sidney Gottlieb.

CMLCD-7IO

APR 30 1954
C.W. Ritenour/jlc

SUBJECT: Personnel Clearances for Access to RESTRICTED
DATA of the U.S. Atomic Energy Commission

TO: Office of the Chief Chemical Officer
Department of the Army
Gravelly Point
Washington 25, D. C.
ATTN: Chief, Intelligence Branch

This is to advise that Frank R. OLSON, who was granted access
to RESTRICTED DATA of the Atomic Energy Commission, File No. WA-11568,
granted 13 April 1950, is now deceased.

FOR THE COMMANDING OFFICER:

MAX ETKIN
Major, Cml C
Intelligence Officer

F R OLSON

April 30, 1954 Army Intelligence document officially noting that Frank Olson, who had Atomic Energy Commission (AEC) access to restricted data,
"is now deceased."

18 June 1962

If you recall, this is the case that we discussed some time ago concerning the successful use of the drug on a subject. ████████, according to this has found out that the drug is LSD. Please return the cable after you have noted it.

Appreciated sincerely,

6/18/62

June 18, 1962 CIA document regarding LSD drugging of Frank Olson.

MEMORANDUM FOR : Director of Central Intelligence

VIA   : Deputy Director of Central Intelligence

SUBJECT   : Unwitting Testing

1. This memorandum contains a recommendation for the approval of the Director of Central Intelligence. Such recommendation is contained in paragraph 5.

2. ▓▓▓▓▓▓▓▓▓▓▓▓▓▓▓▓▓▓▓▓▓▓▓▓ I am sure you are also aware of several other indications during the past year of an apparent Soviet aggressiveness in the field of covertly administered chemicals which are, to say the least, inexplicable and disturbing.

3. I wish to remind you that our testing program which deals with unwitting persons has been in a stand down stage for over one year. Two points concern me regarding this stand down:

   a. Our positive operational capability to use drugs is diminishing, owing to a lack of realistic testing. We are approaching the point where the operational target itself becomes the test subject.

APPROVED FOR RELEASE
DATE 17 *January 1981*

December 1963 letter from CIA Deputy Director of Plans Richard Helms to CIA Director John McCone regarding MKULTRA unwitting LSD and other drug experiments.

b. With decreasing knowledge of the state of the art, we are less capable of staying up with Soviet advances in this field. This in turn results in a waning capability on our part to restrain others in the intelligence community (such as the Department of Defense) from pursuing operations in this area.

4. As we understand it, our testing of unwitting persons was halted on the grounds that in spite of the cut out mechanism (Narcotics Bureau), the risks of embarrassment to the Agency, coupled with the moral problem were too great to permit continuation of the program. We have been unable to devise a better method of pursuing such a program than the one we have with the Narcotics Bureau which has been completely secure for over eight years and we have no answer to the moral issue.

5. While I personally believe we should continue our testing program, I can well understand the apprehension and concern expressed by others. I feel, however, that either continuation of the program or a definitive cancellation of it are better solutions than the status quo. As matters now stand, we are living with the illusion of a capability which is becoming minimal and furthermore is expensive. If we are to terminate this capability (which includes a certain amount of research and development, procurement of items, etc.) we could probably save about $500,000 annually. Since we strongly believe that without testing of unwitting persons, the program tends to lose its meaning, I recommend that:

a. We resume the testing program immediately, or

b. We withdraw from the field of manipulation of human behavior by covertly administered chemicals.

2

Your approval of either of the alternatives cited above is requested.

Richard Helms
Deputy Director for Plans

753

31 JAN 1975

MEMORANDUM FOR THE RECORD

SUBJECT: Project ARTICHOKE

    ARTICHOKE is the Agency cryptonym for the study
and/or use of "special" interrogation methods and techniques.
These "special" interrogation methods have been known to
include the use of drugs and chemicals, hypnosis, and
"total isolation," a form of psychological harassment.

    A review of available file information obtained from
Office of Security resources failed to reflect a comprehensive
or complete picture of the ARTICHOKE program as participated
in by the Office of Security. Fragmentary information
contained in a variety of files previously maintained by the
Security Research Staff (SRS) reflected several basic papers
which described, in general terms, the program known as
ARTICHOKE. Information contained therein indicated that
prior to 1952, the Office of Security had studied the use
of drugs and chemicals in "unconventional interrogation."
These studies were evidently coordinated with the Agency
unit which was then called OSI. OSI at that time apparently
was the coordinating unit within CIA.

    One paper reflected that an Office of Security team
as early as 1949-50 experimented with drugs and hypnosis
under a project called BLUEBIRD. This paper also reflected
that by 1951 actual interrogations utilizing drugs were
conducted by a combined team of Office of Security and Office
of Medical Services personnel, but few details were available.

    File information indicated that in 1952, overall respon-
sibility for Project ARTICHOKE passed from OSI to the Office
of Security. References to operational use of drugs as an
aid to interrogation since that time were found in various
files, but few details concerning these experiments were
reflected. A memorandum, subject title: Project ARTICHOKE,
dated 21 November 1952, by Mr. Sheffield EDWARDS, reflected

75-42

January 31, 1975 five-page CIA memorandum providing partial overview
of Project ARTICHOKE for Rockefeller Commission investigators.

transfer of control of Project ARTICHOKE from OSI to the
Office of Security. The memorandum indicated that I&SO
(Office of Security) should call upon the research and
support facilities of the CIA Medical Staff and the Office
of Technical Services as required. Responsibility for the
evaluation of foreign intelligence aspects of the project
were to remain with OSI.

The unit within the Office of Security which apparently
coordinated Project ARTICHOKE activities was SRS, with
Mr. ▓▓▓▓▓▓▓▓ for many years the focal point. Details
of Office of Security involvement in individual Project
ARTICHOKE operational utilizations were found in very few
instances. A reference in an SRS log (1951-67) reflected,
however, that SRS had been involved in the experimentation
and use of hypnosis "from the start." In the same reference,
it was stated that "SRS has examined and investigated numerous
unusual techniques of interrogation including psychological
harassment and such matters as 'total isolation!'" The SRS
log referred to above, which covered a period from 1951 to
1967, indicated that, as of 1967, 'the term ARTICHOKE is not
in general use now, and drug interrogation is conducted from
the recommendation of an Agency committee of which the Chief,
SRS, is the Office of Security representative." No record
was found which reflected when or if overall responsibility
for Project ARTICHOKE was transferred from the Office of
Security to any other Agency component.

One of the few areas where detailed information was
available was concerned with hypnotic experimentations. A
log of hypnotic experiments conducted by Office of Security
personnel was reviewed. The log reflected that numerous
(probably several hundred) experiments with hypnotism were
conducted in Agency buildings, apparently utilizing the staff
employee volunteers as subjects. In some instances, representatives from Agency components other than the Office of
Security were present. The log reflected hypnotic experimentations during 1951, 1952, and 1953. It could not be
determined from available file information when the hypnotic
experiments actually began or were caused to be ceased. No
record was located which reflected hypnosis utilized as an
actual operational tool in the field. In connection with hypnotism, it appears that SRS utilized an Agency employee, one
▓▓▓▓▓▓▓▓▓▓▓▓▓▓▓▓▓, as an informant in various societies
dealing with hypnotism to keep abreast of current developments
in the field.

- 2 -

75-43

Few references were found pertaining to the area of "total isolation" as an interrogation aid. A memorandum pertaining to this subject, dated 21 March 1955, was written by Mr. ███████████ of SRS to the Director of Security. The paper discussed "total isolation" techniques as an operational tool of potential. Another paper (a sterilized version, probably written by an element of the Department of Defense) dated 16 March 1955, reflected the results of "total isolation" experiments on six volunteers, all members of the U.S. military. No reference was found to any additional experiments in this field, nor was any reference found which reflected actual use of this technique in an operational situation.

As far as the experimentation and/or utilization of various drugs is concerned, references to a few instances were located, but little detail was available, and it was clear from the files that much of the detailed information probably was maintained by Agency units other than the Office of Security, i.e., the Office of Medical Services and the Office of Technical Services.

Among the instances where details were located in which drugs were used in an operational environment under the auspices of Project ARTICHOKE, were the following:

(a) In 1954 three subjects were interrogated by a Project ARTICHOKE team utilizing drugs of an unspecified nature. The three subjects were identified as ████████████████, ████████████████, and ████████████████ in a memorandum dated 13 January 1955, with a cover sheet signed by Mr. ████████. The interrogations took place in ████████, and the memorandum mentioned injections of "solution #1" and "solution #2," but these drugs were not further identified. It was noted in the memorandum that the cases were handled "under straight drug techniques -- hypnosis or narco-hypnosis was not attempted."

(b) A memorandum dated 20 January 1959 to Mr. ████████████ from ████████████████ indicated that a field request had been made for a "P-1 interrogation." The writer ████████ identified a "P-1 interrogation" as one using LSD. Approval was granted on 27 January 1959 by the initials ████████," presumably Mr. ████████████████. No further reference to the case could be found, thus no details were available.

- 3 -

75-44

756

(c) A series of cables between ▓▓▓▓ and Headquarters in 1955 requested ARTICHOKE interrogations for nine persons. No disposition in this instance was found, however, a transmittal slip affixed to the materials dated in 1960 indicated that the ARTICHOKE interrogations probably did not actually take place in ▓▓▓▓ at that time.

(d) A memo contained in the security file of ▓▓▓▓▓▓▓▓▓▓▓ reflected that an ARTICHOKE team was dispatched to ▓▓▓▓▓▓ in June 1952 to conduct ARTICHOKE interrogations on ▓▓▓▓▓. No further reference to this operation was noted, and no disposition could be found.

(e) In the case of ▓▓▓▓▓, ▓▓▓▓▓ operation in ▓▓▓▓▓▓ drugs were utilized in the interrogation which took place i▓▓▓▓▓ Again, details of the operation were not available. However, an interview with the Office of Security representative who participated in the interrogation revealed that a form of LSD was used in this instance. In this case, approval was granted by Headquarters for the ARTICHOKE interrogation. A memorandum dated 6 July 1960, signed by Mr. ▓▓▓▓▓▓▓ Deputy Director of Security, reflected that approval for use of drugs in this case was granted at a meeting of the Drug Committee on 1 July 1960 and cabled to ▓▓▓▓▓

As stated earlier, little detail was available in file information concerning the conduct of actual cases utilizing Project ARTICHOKE techniques: It appears obvious, however, that the few cases noted above were only a small part of the actual utilization of ARTICHOKE techniques in the field. For one thing, almost no information was available for the period prior to 1952, so that Project BLUEBIRD experiments and operations were not noted specifically. In addition, annual reports of accomplishments found in SRS log materials reflected a substantial amount of activity in the Project ARTICHOKE area. The review for 1953-1954 stated in part that SRS had "dispatched an ARTICHOKE team for permanent location in an overseas area." The review for 1954-1955 stated in part that SRS conducted numerous ARTICHOKE experiments and "prepared and dispatched an ARTICHOKE team to an overseas area to handle a number of sensitive cases."

- 4 -

75-45

Review of file materials consistently reflected that the Office of Security exercised caution in the utilization of drugs under the ARTICHOKE Program. Although it is apparent that SRS for a number of years was engaged with certain other Agency components in research and operational work with hallucinogenic drugs, the work was apparently conducted under strict controls. As previously stated, no information pertaining to when or if control of Project ARTICHOKE was transferred from the Office of Security to another Agency component was located. Apparently, SRS at one time maintained an inventory of ARTICHOKE materials which contained numerous drugs of all types including LSD-25. A memorandum dated 14 October 1957 requested authorization for SRS to transfer ARTICHOKE materials and apparatus to Dr. ████████████ of Medical Services. The memorandum was written by Mr. ████████████ and approval to transfer the materials was granted by Mr.████████████ on 17 October 1957.

In the review of file information contained in SRS materials, one incident which occurred in November 1953 appears worthy of note. Although it was not clear from file information whether or not the incident occurred under the auspices of Project ARTICHOKE, the incident did involve use of LSD in an experimental exercise. One Frank OLSON, a civilian employee of the Department of the Army, committed suicide a week or so after having been administered LSD by an Agency representative. Details concerning this incident apparently will be reported in a separate memorandum, but it appears that the drug was administered to several unwitting subjects by a Dr. GOTTLIEB, at that time a branch chief in TSS (now OTS). A short time after the LSD was administered, the subjects were told that they had been given LSD. On the day following the experiment, OLSON began to behave in a peculiar and erratic manner and was later placed under the care of a psychiatrist. A few days later, OLSON crashed through a window in a New York hotel in an apparent suicide.

A memorandum dated 1 December 1953 from the IG Staff caused the impoundment of all LSD materials. Information contained in the above mentioned files reflected that the drug had been administered without the prior knowledge or approval of the Office of Security or the Office of Medical Services.

MEMORANDUM

THE WHITE HOUSE
WASHINGTON

```
                    IDENITY SHEET
                     (partial)


    Frank R.Olson
    Identity 17: see att.



    7. Pierre (Jean) LaFitte (bellmAN?FBN)'

    8. FNU Spiritto (a/k/a/s)

    9. George H. White

    10. French embaSSY"
         JM

    11. Pont Saint Esprit incident (Olsojn)

    12. Lovell-Detrick

    13. Ruwet, V.



    Routing: Colby, Belin.
```

Undated White House draft memorandum and Identity Sheet citing "Pont Saint Esprit incident."

-9-

Security Consultants International, Inc. Furniture for the apartmen
was leased by Muldoon, as a representative for Central Investigation
Agency. Conein described the use of Muldoon as a technique to conce
the fact of DEA's involvement. Conein described Muldoon as an
individual whom he knew from Vietnam. He said that Muldoon was
not an employee of CIA, but was non-committal as to whether or not
Muldoon had contact with CIA.

Conein said that the CIA did not have access to or use of
the apartment. He also said that there were no electronic devices
installed in the apartment. There was access to the apartment from
Muldoon's office located on the floor below. However, locks were
changed to prevent such access.

C. B.R. FOX LABORATORIES

Conein, on behalf of DEA, has purchased a total of $4,760.
worth of surveillance equipment from B.R. Fox Laboratories of
Alexandria, Virginia. The purchases involved surveillance cameras,
recording and transmitting equipment. The agent for B.R. Fox was th
same James P. Muldoon mentioned above. Conein used B.R. Fox because
his "bona fides" were established with that company and they could
obtain sanitized equipment quickly. Conein indicated that sanitized
equipment is the kind that cannot be traced to ████████████
████████and that this is necessary because the Government must ha
deniability.

During the course of his dealings with B. R. Fox, Conein
was shown certain explosive devices, which he described as the kind
of equipment used in insurgency operations. These were booby-trap
type explosive equipment, which could be characterized as assassinat:
devices. Conein described this demonstration as an unsolicited side
show. He said that Fox was trying to sell the devices, but he had n
interest in them. (See testimony of Lucien E. Conein before Senate
Permanent Subcommittee on Investigations, January 28, 1975. Testimo:
of George Belk before Senate Permanent Subcommittee on Investigation:
January 31, 1975).

D. CIA TRAINING OF DEA PERSONNEL

News media reports of the summary of findings of the
Commission on CIA Activities within the United States refer to an
Inspection related matter as follows:

"B. Narcotics Law Enforcement Agencies"

Beginning in late 1970, the CIA assisted the
Bureau of Narcotics and Dangerous Drugs to uncover possib:
corruption within that organization. The CIA used one of
proprietary companies to recruit agents for BNDD and gave
them short instructional courses. Over 2½ years, the CIA
recruited 19 agents for the BNDD. The project was termin:
in 1973."

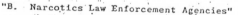

Section of a 1970s CIA report that bears handwritten note: "This is example
of type of material that will prove embarrassing if things like Olson files are
probed."

Flash

THE WHITE HOUSE

WASHINGTON

Secret

July 11, 1975

SECRET

MEMORANDUM FOR:	DON RUMSFELD
FROM:	DICK CHENEY
SUBJECT:	The Olson Matter / CIA Suicide

Attached is a proposed brief statement for the President to use at his Press Conference. It would be best for him to use it in response to a question, although if he wished, he can use it as an opening statement.

There is also attached a four page memo prepared by the Civil Division, the Department of Justice, based upon information obtained from the CIA regarding the events surrounding Mr. Olson's death.

Rod Hills has questions concerning the last paragraph of the Justice Department memo which expresses the Justice Department opinion that court action against the U.S. would be barred. He will pursue the matter with the Attorney General.

At this point, we do not have enough information to be certain we know all of the details of this incident. Furthermore, there are serious legal questions that will have to be resolved concerning the Government's responsibility, the possibility of additional compensation, and the possibility that it might be necessary to disclose highly classified national security information in connection with any court suit, or legislative hearings on a private bill intended to provide additional compensation to the family.

o be an administrative marking
r E.O. 12356, Sec. 1.3 and

July 11, 1975 "secret" memorandum from Dick Cheney, White House deputy chief of staff to White House chief of staff Donald Rumsfeld regarding the "CIA suicide" of Frank Olson.

-2-

Therefore, Marsh, Hills and Cheney strongly recommend that the President limit his remarks to an expression of regret over this tragic event and a willingness to meet personally with Mrs. Olson and her children to offer an apology on behalf of the Government. Any discussion that goes beyond those issues raises questions which we are not yet in a position to answer.

In response to any questions which go beyond the above, we would recommend that the President indicate that the entire matter, both with regard to the adequacy of compensation and circumstances surrounding Mr. Olson's death, are under review by the Justice Department.

Attachments

cc: Jerry Jones

As An Answer To A Question or An Opening Statement

The recent disclosure of the facts concerning the death of

Dr. Frank Olson are of great concern to me. I am equally

distressed by the fact that the full details of Dr. Olson's

death were not made known to Mrs. Olson and other members

of his family.

Mrs. Olson and her family deserve our deepest sympathy.

I hope to meet with the family at the earliest opportunity to

personally extend an apology on behalf of the United States

Government.

> Richard Cheney's draft answers/remarks on Olson's death for President Gerald Ford.

Alice Olson meets President Gerald Ford, July 21, 1975.

CENTRAL INTELLIGENCE AGENCY

WASHINGTON, D. C. 20505

OFFICE OF THE DIRECTOR

July 24, 1975

David Kairys
Kairys and Rudovsky
1427 Walnut Street
Philadelphia, Pennsylvania 19102

Dear David:

I hope the meeting and turnover of documents was to
your satisfaction. I enjoyed your spirited questioning
of Bill Colby at lunch.

I have assured others at the Agency that we have an
agreement to the effect that the documents turned over
to you are for the sole purpose of prosecuting any claim
against the United States Government with respect to
the death of Frank R. Olsen. When you get a moment,
I would appreciate it if you would simply send me a
note confirming that.

As I indicated, you doubtless will have questions
growing out of the documents. Feel free to contact me
directly and I will get you answers.

Cheers,

Mitchell Rogovin
Special Counsel to the Director

July 24 1975 letter to Olson family attorney David Kairys from Mitchell Rogovin, Special Counsel to CIA Director William Colby. Note misspelling of Frank Olson's name.

At about 1520 hours, Thursday, 24 July 1975, a plain white, 3-5/8" by 6" envelope was handed to me by the person (retired Army and retired DAC) who addressed the envelope and wrote the contents. The envelope was hand-addressed to me, "Mr. (last name)," and marked "Personal." The envelope contained one sheet of 8" by 10½", white, blue-lined, 5-hole-punched, loose-leaf paper. One side of the sheet of paper was blank, and the other side contained the following hand-written in pencil:

¶Re - Dr. F. W. Olson

"Suggest review of following items.

"1. Medical record of Army Lt Olson prior to transfer to Edgewood Arsenal/;_/ ulcers?

"2. Medical record of Capt Olson in regard to loss of commission for reason of health and subsequent successful appeal before Medical Review Board for disability pay status. Was he a retired Army officer at time of death?

"3. Reason for request to be relieved as Chief, S. O. Division in Spring 1953. Source - Dr. J. L. Schwab.

"4. Trip to Paris and Norway in 1953(?) and possible fear of security violation. Sources - F. W. Wagner, H. T. Eigelsbach, Robert Lashbrook, and Dr. _____.*

"5. After death - apparently large number of government checks left uncashed in personal file. Sources - Mrs. Hallar Best and Col Ruwet.

"6. Possible lapse of V. A. Life Insurance payments prior to death. Sources - Mrs. Hallar Best and Col Ruwet."

* The doctor's name was left blank because he couldn't remember how to spell it; however, he meant it to be Dr. Harold Abramson, the New York psychiatrist, who examined Olson. When the man handed me the envelope, he said, "I hate to do this. The man /Olson/ was one of my best friends, but I think the things in here /the envelope/ ought to be checked."

> July 1975 "mysterious document" about Frank Olson. The document, written by an unidentified Fort Detrick employee, was discovered by an Associated Press reporter investigating Frank Olson's death.

KAIRYS & RUDOVSKY
ATTORNEYS AT LAW
1427 WALNUT STREET
PHILADELPHIA, PENNSYLVANIA 19102

)AVID KAIRYS
)AVID RUDOVSKY
IOLLY MAGUIGAN
AYMA ABDOO, Legal Worker

(215) LO 3-8312

29 July 1975

William E. Colby
Director
Central Intelligence Agency
Washington, D.C.   20505

Dear Mr. Colby:

On July 24, 1975, you and Mitchell Rogovin, Special Counsel to the Director, told Eric Olson, Lisa Olson Hayward, Nils Olson, and us that you were providing us with all of the materials available to the CIA concerning the death of Frank R. Olson and the related events leading thereto and following thereafter. David Kairys specifically asked you if we were getting "all" of the materials available to the CIA, and you said we were. You also pointed to the materials provided to us and said they constitute the "entire file."

We studied the materials you provided that night. It seemed clear to us that what you provided could not be the entire file, since obvious areas of concern, to anyone investigating the matter and the Director as well as to us, are not even touched upon.

The next day, we met with Attorney General Edward Levi and other officials of the Justice Department, and we discovered that the materials you provided to them include documents that were not provided to us. We asked them for copies of these additional documents. They indicated that they could not provide us with copies of any CIA documents without the approval of the CIA, although they thought CIA approval would be easy to obtain given the statements by you, Mr. Rogovin, and President Ford.

We received a call yesterday from a Justice Department official who indicated that the CIA refuses to give us two of these docu-

---

July 29, 1975 3-page letter from Olson family attorneys David Kairys and David Rudovsky to CIA Director William Colby expressing concern about the completeness of the "Colby papers" given to the family on July 24, 1975.

page 2

ments. He said the CIA does not think they are "useful" since one is handwritten and unsigned and the other concerns LSD and LSD experimentation generally.

We were not told we were getting the "useful file." Nor were we told that the CIA would determine what was useful for us and withhold the rest. Based on a brief reading, we found both of these documents important to an understanding of what happened, whether or not we could or would want to introduce them into evidence in a court of law. Obviously, the CIA also thought they were useful--to our adversaries at the Justice Department. We would like to receive copies of these two additional documents.

This whole course of events raises an obvious question: what other materials have been withheld, and on what basis? We now know there are at least two versions of the Olson file-- the "useful" file given to us and the more useful file given to the Justice Department. What we want, and what we thought you were going to give us, is the entire CIA file.

Accordingly, we are hereby requesting, on behalf of the Olson family, and pursuant to the President's statement and assurances of July 21, 1975 and the Freedom of Information Act, 5 U.S.C. §552, et seq.:

    1. The entire CIA file and all reports, statements, materials, and information (hereinafter referred to as "materials and information") in the possession of or available to the CIA concerning the death of Dr. Olson and the related events leading thereto and following thereafter. This includes materials and information concerning LSD and LSD experimentation generally. If there are any materials or information of any type or kind that you do not believe we should receive, let us know their nature and the reasons why you believe you should not provide them.

    2. Your written assurance, in the form of a sworn affidavit, that we have received all such materials and information.

    3. Appropriate precautionary actions to guarantee that these materials and information, and any further materials and information the CIA may receive in the future, remain

page 3

available and intact.

Sincerely,

David Kairys   David Rudovsky

767

<u>KEEP ON TOP OF FILE</u>

30 July 1975

MEMORANDUM FOR THE RECORD

SUBJECT: Frank Olson Suicide

1. Any inquiries concerning the suicide of Mr. Frank Olson, as a result of his participation in experiments with LSD by the CIA in the early 1950's, should be referred to Chief, Security Analysis Group. The Subject has recently been of considerable interest to the Presidential Commission to Investigate the CIA, as well as the Senate Select Committee on Intelligence Operations.

2. Considerable information concerning Mr. Frank Olson, as well as the ARTICHOKE/BLUEBIRD drug experiments, is contained i████████████████████████ which is maintained in the office of ████████████████████ Inquiries concerning ██████████ should be directed to ████████████

3. It should further be noted that on 24 July 1975, the Director of Central Intelligence declassified much of the material relating to Frank Olson. A copy of the declassified material is contained in a soft file entitled "LSD Material," which is contained within the above mentioned ████████
████████

s Group

b (1) b (3)

<u>KEEP ON TOP OF FILE</u>

Approved for Release
Date ___FEB___ 200█

(1)

July 30, 1975 CIA memorandum indicating that "Colby papers" did not contain the entire record of Olson's death.

18 JAN 1979

The Honorable Edward M. Kennedy
Chairman, Subcommittee on Health and
    Scientific Research
Committee on Human Resources
United States Senate
Washington, D.C. 20510

Dear Mr. Chairman:

The Washington Post issue of Friday, 5 January 1979, carried a
report under the by-line of Bill Richards that recently released CIA
documents contradict my testimony and the testimony of another CIA officer before the Senate Subcommittee on Health and Scientific Research
in September 1977. I have reviewed that testimony in relation to the
documents cited in the Richards' article and I want to assure you that
I find no such contradiction. Taken out of the context of the total
record on Project OFTEN it is possible to attribute to the documents
cited by Mr. Richards the interpretation he has given them. Other documents that are a part of the total record, however, support the testimony as given.

I am reminded by this incident of the commitment I made to you in
September of 1977 to make every effort to seek out and notify individuals who may have suffered some harm as a result of having been used as
unwitting subjects of drug experimentation sponsored by CIA. While I
am not in a position to report to you finally on the outcome of this effort, I feel, nevertheless, that it is appropriate to bring you up to
date on actions that have been taken and where we stand generally with
our progress in the notification program.

In my letter of 14 September 1978 I advised you that I had directed
a thorough review of the information available to the Agency to determine the most efficient and appropriate means of implementing the opinion of the Attorney General, a copy of which I furnished to you at the
time. That opinion reached the conclusion that the Agency may be under
an obligation to identify, locate and notify any unwitting subjects of
MKULTRA drug testing activities where it can reasonably be determined
that their health may continue to be adversely affected by their involvement in that program. Since early September 1978 a senior officer

---

January 18, 1979 two-page letter from CIA director Stansfield Turner to
Sen. Edward Kennedy regarding CIA Victim's Task Force.

769

of the Agency has devoted his full time to that effort and I am pleased
to report his very preliminary findings encourage us to believe that
there were very few, if any, individuals who may have been used by CIA
as subjects of drug research without their knowledge or consent. Moreover, there appear to be very few, if any, substances used that might
have had a potential for causing harmful long term aftereffects.

Despite the encouragement we derive from our progress thus far
there remains a nagging uncertainty growing out of the fact that all of
the returns are not yet in. I regret that I am not able to state unequivocally that we have all the facts. Of course, we recognize the
reality that documents can and will continue to be selected out of the
voluminous materials released to members of the public under the Freedom
of Information Act which could reflect adversely on the Agency. We realize this can occur if individuals do not have the benefit of all relevant information; it can occur out of careless research; and it can occur out of deliberate, malicious intent to cause damage to the national
intelligence effort. Nevertheless, you continue to have my assurances
that I will report all relevant facts as objectively as possible. I
look forward to the time when I can submit to you my final report on
this phase of the CIA history. Meanwhile, an interim report is enclosed.

Yours sincerely,

/s/ Stansfield Turner

STANSFIELD TURNER

Distribution:
Orig - DCI
1 - DDCI w/att
1 - ER w/att
1 - OLC w/att
1 - OLGC w/att
1 - DD/PA w/att
1 - DDA Sbj w/att
1 - DDA Chrono w/att
1 - JFB Chrono w/att
1 - SA/DDA Sbj file w/att
███████:SA/DDA:███(11 Jan 79)

CENTRAL INTELLIGENCE AGENCY
WASHINGTON, D.C. 20505

30 April 1979

Dear Dr. Gottlieb,

You are aware of the Agency's efforts to investigate its past involvement with drugs, with emphasis on the use of drugs on unwitting subjects. The Director of CIA made a commitment to Congress to attempt to identify unwitting subjects and, if there was a possibility they had been harmed by the experience, to inform them of CIA's involvement.

Your oral offer to help in this effort is appreciated. Now that our investigation is nearly completed we have formulated a few questions answers to which may help fill voids in the final report. You were not sent a letter earlier as the only questions we then knew to ask, you had already addressed in Congressional testimony.

Although the primary thrust of the investigation is to identify test subjects, per the Director's commitment, secondary efforts are to assess the possibility of harm by the specific drugs in the quantities used, and to flesh out the report with enough details of the safehouse operations to lend credence to the report which is emerging. Any help you can offer on the following is welcome.

1. What "drugs" were used/tested by White/Feldman and in what dosages? In view of the tiny amounts required of a substance like LSD, how was the drug packaged such that the amount delivered was known with any degree of certainty?

2. What, if any, test follow-up was practiced? Was there an effort to determine the effect, if any, on the health of the subjects? Was there an effort to determine to what the test subjects attributed their peculiar symptoms?

April 30, 1979 CIA Victim's Task Force two-page letter to Dr. Sidney Gottlieb asking among other questions what the purpose of MKULTRA unwitting experiments was. CIA official Frank Laubinger signed the letter.

3. How did White transmit the results of the tests to you? Were they typed or handwritten? Did they contain names of subjects? Did all reports come through White or did Feldman report directly? Did anyone else report on drug tests? How were tests in N.Y., 1960's (if any) reported? Who in CIA had access to those reports? If unwitting testing was not intended as the purpose of procuring the safehouses through the auspices of the FBN, what was the rationale for obtaining the safehouses?

4. What was the primary purpose of the "unwitting" testing: to see if someone's behavior could be subtley sabotaged; as an aid to interrogation a la White's OSS/N.Y. experience?

5. White, in his diary (1960) occasionally refers to ▓▓▓ or ▓▓▓▓▓▓ as well as to ▓▓▓▓▓▓ ▓▓, as though he were attempting to distinguish between two coexisting installations. Did ▓ support a safehouse which was separate and distinct from ▓▓▓▓▓▓ ▓▓▓▓▓▓▓▓▓▓

6. The term, "Midnight Climax" is largely responsible for the brothel image of the safehouses. Can you shed any light on its origin? Quite frankly, to date we have no evidence to support the brothel image.

7. Could you hazard an estimate of the number of the tests performed by FBN in the safehouses and the number conducted in bars/nightclubs, etc.? If the absolute numbers are a problem can you estimate a percentage breakdown between the two groups? In what cities did the tests in bars and nightclubs take place?

8. Dr. Treichler procured a safesite (1961) ▓▓▓▓▓▓ ▓▓▓▓▓▓▓▓▓ through the FBN, Charles Siragusa. It appears that Feldman was denied the use of that apartment. He procured an apartment, ▓▓▓▓▓▓▓▓▓▓▓▓▓ in 1962. Was the latter apartment provided (financed) by CIA?

I realize that some of these questions deal with details of little significance and are very possibly not remembered after 20 plus years. Whatever you do will be appreciated.

It now appears that all of the Agency's files have been searched and that all drug related material which is subject to release has

been released. The investigation into the Agency's drug research is now targeted for completion in June. Hopefully, this entire subject will soon be relegated to history. If I don't hear from you within a couple of weeks, I will give you a call.

Yours truly,

MAR-16-1999 15:06   D A OFFICE   212 335 9109   P.02/02

DISTRICT ATTORNEY
OF THE
COUNTY OF NEW YORK
ONE HOGAN PLACE
NEW YORK, N.Y. 10013
(212) 335-9000

ROBERT M. MORGENTHAU
District Attorney

Hank Albarelli
Indian Rocks Beach, Florida 33785-2705

                                    March 16, 1999

Mr. Albarelli:

        I agree to the terms set forth in your FAX dated March 12,
1999.

        Any information you provide will only be used by persons
investigating the Olson matter for the District Attorney's Office
or the Grand Jury.

        If further information is needed, please contact my paralegal,
David Landsberg at (212) 335-9297.

                              Sincerely,

                              Stephen Saracco
                              Assistant District Attorney
                              (212) 335-9162

March 16, 1999 letter to author H.P. Albarelli Jr., from Stephen Saracco,
New York District Attorney.

PERSONAL and CONFIDENTIAL

FAX TO: Stephen Saracco

1 April 1999

TO: S. Saracco

FR: Hank Albarelli, Journalist

Re: Frank Olson Information

I have requested that the remainder of the attached federal government memorandum be forwarded to you from another source. Please let me know if you haven't received it by the end of next week.

The handwritten notation at the bottom left hand corner of this page reads:

"This is example of [type] material that will prove very embarrassing if things [like] Olson files are probed."

Hank Albarelli

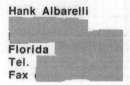

Florida
Tel.
Fax

Author's April 1, 1999 memorandum to District Attorney Saracco.

April 17, 2000

...aracco,

...ry informs me that you are a devotee of the works of Pynchon. Frankly, I n...
...countered difficulty with his works. Regardless, some years back, for reasons
now lost, I was given a short piece of his to read that bore a singular inscription on
its rear page. I pass it on verbatim in hopes that you find it of greater worth than I.
It reads:-

" OF pincon, pinson. Norman-Picard pinchon, 'finch', used as a symbol of gaiety
("gai comme un pinson"); nickname from OF pincon, pinchon, 'pincers', 'forceps'.
Ecilop tales of Nipmetight remembered by the honest pirate. [!] "I took you for a
spy. Yet saw me not no more than a Molewarp." "They begin their work with a
mine underground." "Take heed that the moldywarp hills be spread." "I cannot
choose: sometime he angers me with telling of the moldwarp and the ant, of the
dreamer Merlin and his prophecies... and such a deal of skible-skable as puts me
from my faith.

"Can you keep a secret? If you can you must not laugh, You must smile, And you
must not cry."

To the cardinal task at hand- Frank Olson, deceased biochemist, among other
things. Without prompting, I appreciate your professional interest in the whole
affair. Mine in it, 'interest' I mean, much like that in the elusive scribe above,
presently takes a more abstract course, but is equally cradled in professionalism (of
a decidedly past tense). The point being- I, as employee of CIA, along with others,
had the luck of the draw to deal directly with Olson's demise. That dealing, as I
understand you have already been informed, transpired at a time most allied with
the event itself: within hours. This, in turn, being not that long after the- how do
you put it? - caper involving Ray Lemons. (Ask Henry- ask too about tugging the SGO
thread and opening the wurms can.)

In short, and more to your objectives, Mr. Olson's fateful flight on the night in
question was ventured on wings bestowed by enfants terrible, LaFitte and Le
Grande Lydio.

Graviora quaedam sunt remedia periculis. Regards.

A cryptic April 17, 2000 letter to New York Assistant District Attorneys
Steve Saracco and Dan Bibb from former CIA employees identifying Frank
Olson's killers.

DRAFT

Witness Testimony

In exchange for the information and/or testimony set forth below, which will be submitted to a Grand Jury, by operation of New York law, the witness will receive immunity from prosecution by the State of New York. The Manhattan District Attorneys' Office will recommend to the Untied States Department of Justice that immunity be granted for any federal violations or contractual violations in connection with the CIA, and will recommend to the Department of Justice and the CIA that the witness not be held any further to any confidentiality agreement which the witness has signed and is currently binding on the witness. Further, with respect to the Manhattan District Attorneys' Office, the witness is not a target of this Grand Jury investigation

If called to testify, I would state as follows:

1. My name is _____.

2. The following is based upon my personal knowledge.

3. I was an employee of the Central Intelligence Agency ("CIA") in the office of _____ from ____ to _____.

4. During my employment at the CIA, I had responsibilities for _____

5. In my capacity as a _____, I became familiar with the circumstances surrounding the death of Dr. Frank Olson.

6. With regard to Dr. Olson's death, I know _____

    A   Who was in the room the night Dr. Olson was murdered.
    B.   The circumstances of his death.
    C.   Who ordered his murder.
    D.   Who ordered the cover up.
    E.   Did the Director have knowledge of the murder
    F   Other individuals with knowledge regarding the murder.

7. I have personal knowledge that Dr. Olson was murdered based upon:

    A   Discussions with other individuals/CIA employees,
    B.   Documents

8. Based upon my discussions with other CIA personnel, the cover up of Dr Olson's murder by the CIA was for the following reasons:

_____ **DRAFT**
[WITNESS]

March 2001, New York District Attorney's Office draft of "Witness Testimony" agreement for former CIA officials and sources on Frank Olson's murder.

Frank Olson's gravesite, Frederick, Maryland.

Notes

Notes on Book One, Chapter 1:

[Author's interviews with Armond Pastore in Sun City, Florida, 1998, 1999, 2000; author's interview with Pastore in Sand Key, Florida, 1999; Eddie Becker's and author's videotaped interview with Pastore in Sun City, Florida, 2000.

Notes on Book One, Chapter 2:

This chapter is drawn from the document: *CIA Office of Security Report on Frank Olson's Death*, November 29, 1953.

Bluebird Project details are drawn from numerous declassified CIA Project Bluebird documents received by the author through the Freedom of Information Act.

The CIA's Technical Services Staff (TSS) was officially created in September 1951, following consultation between then-CIA Deputy Director for Plans, Allen Dulles, and Stanley Platt Lovell, the former director of war time research and development for the Office of Strategic Services (OSS), the CIA's predecessor. Lovell recommended that the new CIA create a well-staffed technical division tasked with designing and producing specialized tools and weapons for field and operational staff. Lovell's recommendation resulted in a detailed report on the CIA's specific technical needs drafted by Col. James H. Drum, called "Trapper" by his friends. Drum, at the time, headed the Agency's fledgling Operational Aids Division (OAD). On September 7, 1951, Agency Deputy Director of Plans, Frank G. Wisner, ordered that OAD become the Technical Services Staff (TSS) and asked Col. Drum to become its first director. Gibbons succeeded Col. Drum a year later and served as TSS chief until April 1959. Dr. Robert V. Lashbrook was Gottlieb's deputy chief of the TSS Chemical Branch. The name of the Technical Services Staff was changed to the "Technical Services Division" (TSD) in the late 1950s, but for the sake of continuity, and to create less confusion, the initials TSS shall be used throughout this book.

Sheffield Edwards, CIA Office of Security Chief: Edwards was the son of Muriel and J.C. Hiden Edwards, an attorney who died in 1916 when Sheffield was 14 years old. He was then raised by his mother Muriel Edwards, a schoolteacher and real estate and insurance salesperson, who oversaw an 18,000-acre community farm in Ynez, California. Sheffield was accepted to West Point, graduated in 1923 and commissioned in the Field Artillery. He served as Chief of Staff, 8th Air Support Command, and Chief of Staff, 9th Fighter Command in the European Theater, 1942-1943. He was G-3 Section, 12th Air Group, 1944-1945, receiving the Legion of Merit and the Bronze Star medal during those assignments. After the war, the Army outsourced him to the CIA. He retired from the Army in 1953 at the rank of colonel and stayed with the CIA until the early 1970s. For a brief period of time he ran a private investigation company in Washington, D.C. Some say the company was a front for the Agency. Edwards died on July 15, 1975.

Notes on Book One, Chapter 3

This chapter was drawn from a July 10, 1975 Olson Family Statement made by Alice W. Olson and her children; from the Affidavit of Mrs. Alice W. Olson, County of Frederick, State of Maryland, October 6, 1986; electronic interviews with Eric Olson, 1999, 2000, 2001; an interview with Vincent Ruwet in 1997; and the Deposition of Alice W. Olson, United States District Court for the District of Columbia, Civil Action, No. 80-3163 (JGP), Mrs. David Orlikow, et al. v. United States of America, Defendant, September 16, 1988.

Notes on Book One, Chapter 4

Fritz Haber: Haber was a Jew who tried to conceal it, and converted to Protestantism; he died in 1934, never learning that many members of his family would be gassed in concentration camps through the use of Zylon B, the deadly cyanide-based gas he helped develop.

The Josiah Macy, Jr. Foundation 1930-1955, A Review of Activities, New York, 1955, pp. 32-34.

McDermott, Jeanne, *The Killing Winds: The Menace of Biological Warfare*, Arbor House, New York, 1978, p.139.

Consent For Medical Treatment and Hospitalization and for Burial in Event of Death "A" form signed by Frank R. Olson on 5 August 1945 and witnessed by Capt. Francis Richards.

Values & Visions: A Merck Century, Merck & Co., Inc., 1991. See also: Harris, Robert and Paxman, Jeremy, *A Higher Form of Killing*, Hill and Wang, NY, 1982; Brophy, Leo P. and Cochrane, Rexmond C., *The Chemical Warfare Service: From Laboratory to Field*, Office of the Chief of Military History, Department of the Army, Washington, D.C., 1959.

Richard M. Clendenin, Science and Technology at Fort Detrick, 1943-68, Fort Detrick Technology Information Division, Frederick, Maryland, 1968, p.5.

Peter Williams and David Wallace, *Unit 731: Japan's Secret Biological Warfare in World War II*, The Free Press, New York, 1989 pp. 91-93; see also McDermott, *The Killing Winds*.

Leo P. Brophy, Wyndham D. Miles and Rexmond C. Cochrane, *The Chemical Warfare Service: From Laboratory to Field*, Office of the Chief of Military History, Department of the Army, Washington, D.C., 1959, pp. 103-106.

Letter to Stanley P. Lovell, OSS, from Brig. Gen. Alden H. Waitt, War Dept., Office of Chief, Chemical Warfare Service, March 24, 1943, author's files.

Deposition of Alice Olson, September 16, 1988, Civil Action No. 80-3163 (JGP), Mrs. David Orlikow, et al. V. United States of America.

Agent Report on Olson, Frank Rudolph to Assistant Chief of Staff, G-2, HQ Fifth Army, 19 March 1948, David E. Kelly, 113th CIC Det., 5th Army; Agent Report, 19 March 1948, Wm. H. Johnston, 113th, CIC Det., 5th Army.

Confidential FBI Report by Guy Hottel, SAG, Washington, D.C., December 22, 1949; Veterans Administration Award of Disability Compensation to Frank R. Olson, File No. 3,435,465, June 21, 1944.

CIC Security Agent's Report by Fred P. Berry, 503d CIC Detachment, 18 October 1949, AIAHB-Z-226066 marked Top Secret; FBI Report on Olson, Frank Rudolph, 12 December 1949, by Special Agent John J. Grogan, Baltimore, Maryland.

Memorandum for the Officer in Charge, Subject: OLSON, Frank Rudolph, AIABB-Z 182402, 19 January 1948, from Gregg S. Bertram and Leslie R. Harrison, Special Agents, 109th CIC Detachment, Second Army.

J.W. Corey, Report on OLSON, Frank Rudolph, Biochemist, 2 December 1953. For unexplained reasons this report was marked with the handwritten: "#181."

Author's interview with Uri Geller, 2001. Puharich, Andrija, *The Sacred Mushroom: Key to the Door of Eternity*, Doubleday & Company, New York, 1959, p. 13. See also: Puharich, Andrija, *Beyond Telepathy*, Anchor Books, New York, 1973, and Picknett, Lynn & Prince, Clive, *The Stargate Conspiracy*, Time Warner Paperbacks, 2003. Readers may be interested in knowing that notorious hippie guru and convicted murderer Ira Einhorn wrote the introduction to Puharich's book, *Beyond Telepathy*.

"Memorandum on the Use of Volunteers in Research," to Commanding General, Chemical Corps Research and Engineering Command, Army Chemical Corps, Maryland from Col. Norman W. Elton, Medical Corps, Commander.

"On Select Soldiers of the Future, Presentation" by Dr. Henry Puharich to U.S. Army Psychological Warfare Assembly, Manger-Annapolis Hotel, 22 December 1953, Washington, D.C.

Army Intelligence report on interview with Vincent Ruwet, June 1975; Letter from George Hunter White to FBN agent Vance Newman, May 8, 1953.

Rosebury, Theodor, *Experimental Air-Borne Infection, Microbiological Monographs*, Society of American Bacteriologists, Williams & Wilkins, Baltimore, 1947.

Article entitled, Kepnuk v. Eek, *Time* magazine, December 19, 1938.

Memorandum from John Edgar Hoover, Director FBI to Director of

Intelligence, Dept. of Army, Pentagon, 16 September 1949; Memorandum from [redacted] to H.B. Fletcher, Subject: Biological Warfare, 8 July 1949; in 1950 the FBI was also shown a fountain pen from Poland and a cigarette lighter from Czechoslovakia used for covert biological attacks that SOD scientists had obtained through the CIA.

Unpublished interview with Dr. John Schwab, Ohio, October 14, 1975.

Notes on Book One, Chapter 5:

Contrary to published reports, Olson and Sidney Gottlieb never traveled overseas in 1950 or 1951. Gottlieb did not join the CIA's staff until July 1951.

Author's interviews with former CIA-TSS Chemical Division chief, Dr. Sidney Gottlieb, January-March 1999.

CIA Memorandum for the Record, Subject: Discussions Regarding MKNAOMI, June 29, 1975. According to this once Top Secret document the relationship between SOD and CIA contained "some well established guidelines for the management of work" and "no written records were kept; verbal communications, close associations among the people involved, and human continuity kept the program together." This same document states that there were "swarms of project requests" and a number of examples are provided. These included "suicide agents for the U-2 pilots, L-pills, means for incapacitating guards or guard dogs, material to anesthetize the inhabitants of a building so as to allow its entry, material to dissolve the Berlin Wall, aphrodisiacs for operational use, etc." Also, according to the document, "some requests for support approved by the [CIA] had apparently involved assassination." Lastly, the document stated: "It was clear that—to some extent—MKNAOMI was wrapped up with the drug activities of MKULTRA."

Milan, Michael, *The Squad, The U.S. Government's Secret Alliance With Organized Crime*, Shapolsky Publishers, Inc., New York, 1989.

"Psychochemical Warfare: A New Concept of War, A Preliminary Report," by L. Wilson Greene, Scientific Director, Chemical Corps Technical Command, Army Chemical Center, Maryland, 17 August 1949.

New York *Newsday* article by David Wise, "No License to Kill," October 22, 1989; Congressional Record, CIA, Senate, January 23, 1990. Contrary to some reports, Pash and TSS Chemical Division chief Sidney Gottlieb did not direct the Health Alteration Committee.

AG to Chief, CWS, 12 February 1945, Sub: Possible Introduction of Disease Producing Agents by Japanese Balloons; CCI/AG to Chief, CWS, 24 May 1945, Report on Japanese Balloons.

A Review of German Activities in the Field of Biological Warfare, MIS, Alsos Mission, 12 September 1945; Cochrane, Rexford, Biological Warfare Research in the United States, Plans, Training and Intelligence Division, Office of the Chief, Chemical Corps, November 1947, unpublished draft report. Cochrane's 600-page draft was never released because Pentagon officials felt it revealed far too much information; Pash, Boris T., *The Alsos Mission*, Charter Books, N.Y., 1980; Bar-Zohar, Michel, *The Hunt for German Scientists, 1944-60*, Arthur Baker Ltd., Liverpool, 1967; Goudsmit, Samuel A., *Alsos,* American Institute of Physics, Woodbury, N.Y., 1996; Williams, Peter and Wallace, David, *Unit 731: Japan's Secret Biological Warfare in World War II,* Free Press, NY, 1989; Harris, Sheldon H., *Factories of Death*, Routledge, London, 1997; Regis, Ed, *The Biology of Doom,* Henry Holt & Co., NY, 1999; and McDermott, Jeanne, *The Killing Winds,* Arbor House, NY, 1987. The horrific Unit 731 experiments list is from McDermott's book, on pages 128-129. The 1987 Sanders statement about Ishii lecturing at Camp Detrick appears on page 138 of McDermott's book. Ishii also proposed the use of biological weapons against American troops on Saipan and Iwo Jima.

Biological Weapons Tests: Operation Harness, *The New West Indian,* 20 November 2002, p. 1.

U.S. Naval Radiological Defense Laboratory Memorandum Reports, Technical Objective AW-5c, September-October 1950.

Security Disposition Form, File No. CMLWO I.4, Cancellation of AEC "Q" Personnel Clearance—OLSON, Frank Rudolph by Maj. Joseph C. Hiett, Cm1C for Col. R.B. Strader, Cm1C, Chief, Plans, Tng. and Intel. Div, 1 December 1953; Security Disposition Form, File No. P&O 313.5, AEC to Chief, Chemical Corps, from Col. J.K. Wilson, Jr., GSC. That the author is aware of, only investigative writer John Kelly has carefully researched the CIA's radiological warfare work and experiments.

Author's interviews with former Camp Detrick scientists, Dr. Gerald Yonetz and Dr. Henry Eigelsbach, 1999, 2000, and 2001; Carroll, Michael Christopher, *Lab 257,* Harper Collins Books, New York, 2004.

Hunt, Linda, *Secret Agenda*, St. Martin's Press, New York, 1991.

Author's interview with Dr. Henry Eigelsbach, August 7-8, 2002, Florida.

Interview with William Harvey's biographer, and former CIA official and Newsweek reporter, Bayard Stockton; CIA Memorandum headed: Unknown Soviet Drug, 5 May 1953; Memorandum for the Record,

Artichoke Committee Meetings, Berlin and Frankfurt, August 1953; several secret CIA cables from May-June 1953 concerning the Berlin Poison case; the "Berlin Poison Case" is mentioned in a number of top secret CIA documents turned over to the Rockefeller Commission in 1975 and later to the Church Committee in 1976. Several of these documents were marked "Olson case," indicating that perhaps they had once been part of CIA Inspector General Lyman Kirkpatrick's investigatory files on Olson's death. Also see: Scheflin, Alan W. and Opton, Edward M., *The Mind Manipulators,* Paddington press, Ltd., New York, 1978. Scheflin and Opton, who first raised curiosity about the Berlin poison incident, wrote about a December 27, 1952 article in the *Saturday Evening Post* by Marguerite Higgins that described the incident "as an attempt by enemy agents to poison a group of Russian deserters living in Germany in 1948 under American protection."

Koch, Egmont R. and Wech, Michael, *Deckname Artischoke: Die geheimen Menschenversuche der CIA*, C. Bertelsmann, Germany 2002.

In 2001, the author was cryptically told by a former Edgewood Arsenal employee, "Take a look at Project Strange Man, if you can. You'll find some interesting stuff there about what happened at Pascagoula and other places." Initially, the author thought the project was merely a misunderstood allusion to a graphic novel or science fiction film, but nonetheless, after months of effort, the author was able to verify that there had indeed been a Project Strange Man conducted by the Army at Edgewood Arsenal in the 1950s, but officials there steadfastly refused to provide any information about the project. Residents of Edgewood, Maryland and nearby Aberdeen have in the past thirty-five years reported seeing a strange manlike creature that appears on occasion in suburban backyards and wooded areas. Local law enforcement officials verified the sightings, and one former Edgewood civilian scientist intriguingly warned, "It's my sincere suggestion that these sightings be marked up to fantasy."

Unpublished interviews with former Camp Detrick SOD researcher Dr. Benjamin Wilson, Louisiana and North Carolina, 1976-1977.

Notes on Book One, Chapter 6:

Greenspun: Denton, Sally and Morris, Roger, *The Money and the Power,* Vintage Books, New York, 2002.

Dulles and McCarthy: Kirkpatrick, Lyman, B., *The Real CIA,* The Macmillan Company, New York, 1968.

Paul Gaynor and McCord: Shachtman, Robert K. and Lamphere, Thomas, *The FBI-KGB War,* W.H. Allen, New York, 1986.

Paul Gaynor's secret "fag file": Hougan, Jim, *Secret Agenda: Watergate, Deep Throat and the CIA*, Random House, New York, 1984.

Lashbrook's D.C. roommate, Edwin Henry Spoehel: Spoehel died Sept. 25, 2006 at the age of 80 in Las Cruces, New Mexico. He joined the Army Air Corps in WWII and became a navigator on B-17's. Spoehel was President of the MIT Rocket Research Society. His passion for aerospace engineering was evident throughout his career as he worked on pioneering technologies for satellites, rocket propulsion systems, and the Space Shuttle flight and satellite payload integration systems. After college, Spoehel joined the CIA in Washington, D.C., where he met and married a co-worker, Geraldine (Jerri) Hoskins. Before his marriage, he had shared an apartment with Lashbrook for about eighteen months in 1953-54. His work later took him and his wife to Los Angeles, due to its active aerospace defense industry, and he lived there until retiring in 1990 to Las Cruces. The author interviewed Spoehel briefly in 2000. Spoehel confirmed that he had roomed with Lashbrook, but refused to say what his job was with the CIA. He also refused to say whether or not he was in his apartment on the day Frank Olson was taken there. He was polite and expressed no curiosity or confusion about any of the author's questions regarding Olson or the use of his apartment. Asked specifically if he recalled ever meeting Olson, he said, "I wish you the best of luck with your book, but I really have no interest in answering that question, nor any others about [Olson] or Bob Lashbrook."

Walter P.T., Jr.: CIA Office of Security Report, Agent WALTER P.T., Jr., Case No. 73317, 3 December 1953.

Notes on Book One, Chapter 7:

Edwards was referring to the 90-page study: *An OSI Study of the Medical Significance of LSD*, 30 August 1955. The study was first undertaken in early November 1953 and involved over fifty-five consulting physicians.

George Kennan: In a 1969 interview conducted by Paige Mulhollan, Richard Helms said: "Coincidently, I think that it was in 1952, Ambassador Kennan came out of Moscow and made a speech in Berlin that the Soviets regarded as so egregious that they declared him *persona non grata*. We wondered whether he'd been administered some drug that caused him to act in such an aberrant fashion. There were a number of things going on that puzzled us." Helms would later say in a 1983 deposition that when the Kennan episode occurred, Allen Dulles became upset and ordered his operational directors to instruct Agency scientists to investigate what might have happened to the ambassador. In the same deposition, when Helms was asked about Projects Bluebird and Artichoke and MKDELTA, he responded by saying he did not remember any such projects. Interestingly, when asked if he had ever "taken LSD or any other hallucinogenic in connection with any experiment," he replied, "No, I have never knowingly participated in any experiment." Asked about his use of the word "knowingly," and if perhaps he had participated unknowingly, he said, "I don't know." During the Mulhollan interview, in response to a comment that the Rockefeller Commission "said it is clearly illegal to test potentially dangerous drugs on unsuspecting U.S. citizens," Helms remarked: "There was one instance in which that was the case, and in retrospect I agree, we should not have done it." Presumably Helms was referring to Olson, but it was the only comment he made about possible illegal CIA experiments.

Smith's promise to Kirkpatrick: Hoopes, Townsend, *The Devil and John Foster Dulles*, Little Brown, New York, 1973, p. 82; Powers, Thomas, *The Man Who Kept the Secrets*, Alfred A. Knopf, New York, 1979, p. 57.

Riebling, Mark, *Wedge*, Alfred A. Knopf, 1994; Hersh, Burton, *The Old Boys*, Tree Farm Books, Florida, 2001; Hersh, Burton, *Bobby and J. Edgar*, Basic Books, New York, 2008.

Declassified CIA documents commonly referred to as "the Colby Documents;" other internal memoranda, and reports and notes written by CIA Inspector General Lyman B. Kirkpatrick, Jr. in November-December 1953 and January-February 1954 regarding the case of Frank Olson, Library of Congress, Washington, D.C., and National Security Archives, George Washington University, Washington, D.C.; Kirkpatrick, Lyman B. Jr., *The Real CIA*, (Macmillan Co., New York, 1968); declassified CIA Office of Security files on the case of Frank Olson from November and December 1953, January and February 1954; U.S. Senate Hearings Before the Subcommittee on Health & Scientific Research, September 20 and 21, 1977; and transcripts of unpublished interviews conducted with Kirkpatrick at Brown University in February and March 1978; and unpublished interview with Lyman B. Kirkpatrick conducted in August 1979.

Interviews with former SOD scientists; and Regis, Ed, *The Biology Of Doom*, Henry Holt, New York, 1999, p. 197-198.

Alice Olson 1988 deposition: Deposition of Alice Olson, United States District Court for the District of Columbia, Civil Action No. 80-3163 (JGP), *Mrs. David Orlikow, et al. V. United States of America*, Defendant, September 16, 1988, p.13-16. Questioning Alice was Kathleen A. McGinn, Assistant U.S. Attorney, Washington, D.C. Alice Olson also testified in the same deposition, that Frank told her that Stubbs came home with him because "they were afraid he might do me some harm." She did not explain why Frank said this, and that she thought it sounded "absolutely incomprehensible."

Despite later reports to the contrary, Kirkpatrick gave no indication in his report that he ever impounded Gottlieb's file or any other files as a result of his investigation.

Hughes (OP), Ulmer (OSI) and Cooper (PP) were all CIA employees. Hughes was on assignment to TSS from the military.

Dr. Willis Gibbons & Stevenson Committee: This Committee's report stated: "Biological warfare is a weapon which may become exceedingly important. Present evidence indicates that it could be an effective weapon of war, but the degree of its effectiveness is unknown because it has never been used on a large scale or subjected to adequate field tests." See: Report of the Secretary of Defense's Ad Hoc Committee on Chemical, Biological and Radiological Warfare, 30 June 1950.

Schwab Pentagon experiment: Regis, Ed, *Biology Of Doom*, p. 117.

CIA Office of Security files on Robert Vern Lashbrook, 1951-1953; Lashbrook, Robert V., Civil Action Deposition, May 1986, Ventura, California.

Eric Olson has written in several places that Robert Lashbrook and Frank Olson had Thanksgiving dinner in a Horn & Hardart automat in downtown Manhattan. This obviously contradicts Lashbrook's account, and Eric's alternate setting appears based on no reliable or independent information.

Notes on Book One, Chapter 8:

Author's interview with Dr. Margaret Ferguson, May 17, 2000, New York City, with the assistance of Manhattan assistant district attorney Steve Saracco. Dr. Ferguson's "Dr. Pelican" is Dr. Edward Pelikan. Dr. Ferguson also told the author that she understood Dr. Abramson conducted LSD and mescaline experiments "under agreement with the Army's Chemical Corps" using subjects at Columbia University in New York. Dr. Ferguson recalled that there had been a dispute about contractual language concerning the human subjects used. "The university wanted strong wording saying they would not be responsible for anything that happened to any of the human subjects. I'm not sure how it came out in the end, but the experiments never ceased," recalled Dr. Ferguson. The author's research revealed a Chemical Corps document dated 4 June 1953 concerning Columbia's request that a "hold harmless" clause be inserted into its contract with the Corps. The remarkable, once-classified Army document read in part: "The administration of chemical agents or drugs to human beings involves risk and unusual hazards since it is impossible to foretell with complete accuracy whether one particular subject may deviate from the average or normal in response to a chemical. This is the same kind of risk that is taken daily by many practicing physicians and by all hospitals. The unusual responses result ordinarily in mild discomfort, but may be more alarming, and occasionally may result in unavoidable fatality."

Dr. Murray E. Jarvik: Jarvik, a psychopharmacologist, who died in May 2008, may be a familiar name with readers. He was internationally known for developing the nicotine patch. (His nephew, Dr. Robert Jarvik, developed the first artificial heart to be transplanted in a human being.) During the 1950s, Murray Jarvik worked closely with Dr. Harold Abramson on CIA-funded LSD experiments. After speaking with Dr. Ferguson, the author contacted Dr. Jarvik, who was very cordial. He said that he was aware that the CIA financed much of his early work, and that he "very much enjoyed working with LSD." Many of his test subjects, Jarvik recalled, were college students and his experiments with them were conducted at Mt. Sinai Hospital in New York. He said that he "did not recall ever meeting Frank Olson," but that he did, on occasion, "meet officers from [Camp] Detrick and Edgewood Arsenal, as well as the [Federal] Narcotics Bureau, while working with LSD." He recalled, when questioned, that Dr. Edward Pelikan was working closely with Dr. Abramson and the CIA at the time of Frank Olson's death. "I'd never heard Olson's name until all the revelations of the 1970s," Jarvik said, however he did recall that there had been "one or two, maybe more, deaths by suicide" as a result of the work of physicians with LSD. He emphatically stated, "Harold Abramson was a top-notch researcher and a very honorable man. He would have never been involved in anything dishonest or having to do with murder."

Notes on Book One, Chapter 9

Grose, Peter, *Gentleman Spy, The Life of Allen Dulles*, University of Massachusetts Press, Amherst, 1994.

Dulles' handwritten list, originally turned over to the Olson family in 1975, contained several misspellings, including Abramson's name and Ruwet's. Today Charles Pearre Cabell has mostly become a minor, fleeting footnote in any full account of the CIA. Peter Grose's biography of Dulles only contains two very brief mentions of Cabell in over 600 pages. JFK fired Cabell as deputy director after the Bay of Pigs fiasco.

Toddy's seduction: Srodes, James, *Allen Dulles: Master of Spies*, Regnegry Publishing, Inc., Washington, D.C., 1999, p. 193.

Author's 1997 interview with Albert Haney; and unpublished 1974 interview with George H. White, author unknown.

Dulles and Guatemala: Eveland, W.C., *Ropes of Sand*, 1980, p. 29-31; Immerman, R., *The CIA in Guatemala*, 1982, p. 139-40; *New Republic* magazine, March 7, 1995, p. 35-36.

Request for Program MKULTRA approval: Memorandum from Richard Helms to DCI Allen Dulles, 3 April 1953.

Richard Helms on brainwashing and LSD: Interview with Helms by Paige Mulhollan in Washington, D.C., April 4, 1969. Oral History Interview, LBJ Library, Austin, Texas.

Kinzer, Stephen, *All the Shah's Men*, John Wiley & Sons, Inc., New Jersey.

James Kronthal, U.S. Civil Service Commission Federal Employee Application, 19 September 1946, CIA file copy; James Kronthal, CIA Status and Efficiency Report, May 1947. One of Kronthal's closest administrative assistants in Bern, Switzerland was Dorothy Louise Wetzel who later married CIA operative E. Howard Hunt.

Sheffield Edwards, CIA Memorandum for the Record, Subject: James Kronthal, 31 March 1953; various CIA Office of Security files on the death of James Kronthal, 1953, author's files.

"CIA Officer Found Dead, Vial Nearby," *Washington Post*, Tues., April 1, 1953, page 1A.

Trento, Joe, *The Secret History of the CIA*, Carroll & Graf Publishers, New York, 2004.

Notes on Book One, Chapter 10:

Statement by Dr. Harold A. Abramson made Saturday, November 29, 1953. This statement was made at the request of the CIA Security Agent who visited New York following Olson's death.

Memorandum for CIA General Counsel, Observations on Mr. Frank Olson from 24 November through 27 November 1953 made by Dr. Harold A. Abramson M.D., 4 December 1953.

"Case Report on Patient John Q. Smith" by Dr. Harold A. Abramson, New York. The report was sent on February 9, 1954 with a brief cover letter signed by Abramson reading: "For your information and files I am enclosing a case report which might be of interest." This partially redacted letter was given by the CIA in 1975 to the Olson family, but was not included in those documents given to the 1975 Congressional Subcommittee headed by Sen. Edward Kennedy.

Memorandum to Chief, Investigation Division, Subject: OLSON, Frank, No. 73317-S.I., 4 December 1953; Memorandum to Col. Sheffield Edwards, SO Chief, from Chief, SSD, Subject: Abramson, Harold A., 2 December 1953.

Notes on Book One, Chapter 11:
Kirkpatrick's Final Report: Memorandum to the Director of Central Intelligence from Lyman B. Kirkpatrick, IG, Subject: The Suicide of Frank Olson, 18 December 1953. Allen Dulles' file copy of Kirkpatrick's memo bears a handwritten note on its second page that reads: "We concur generally in the above recommendations." The word "generally" is underlined. The note bears the initials of Richard Helms and Frank Wisner. It is difficult to overlook Kirkpatrick's sloppiness on the Olson case. He consistently misspells Olson's name and those of other involved individuals, as well as locations (e.g. "Camp Dietrich.") Decades later, it would be revealed that Kirkpatrick's investigation may not have ended with the conclusions and recommendations he issued at this time.

Admiral deFlorez letter to Dulles: Typed at the bottom of the copy of the deFlorez letter to Dulles is: "Memo for Record: Original returned to Adm. deFlorez on 10 Feb., with note from Gen. Cabell (on the cover sheet) as follows: 'Your request acceded to.'" This may partially explain why the letters of "reprimand" to Gottlieb, Drum, and Gibbons were redrafted so many times by Dulles.

Eyes Only memoranda from DCI Allen W. Dulles to Dr. Willis Gibbons, Chief, Technical Services Staff; Colonel James H. Drum, Chief, Technical Operations, TSS; and Dr. Sidney Gottlieb, Chemical Division Chief, TSS, February 10, 1954. Dulles' memos to the three TSS men were revised several times before being delivered.

Kirkpatrick would also state, decades later, that Gottlieb's taking Olson to New York to see Dr. Abramson, rather than taking him to a Washington, D.C.-based or CIA physician, was an "attempt to keep the whole affair in house." Kirkpatrick would also claim years later that he knew nothing about the CIA administering drugs to other unwitting persons through MKULTRA or any other program. This claim seems highly unlikely due to the fact that in 1951 and 1952 Kirkpatrick had been cleared to receive copies of Project Bluebird and Artichoke's reports and briefings. His remarks about Gottlieb also seem dubious, because there were several psychologists in the Washington, D.C. area and within the CIA who were familiar with LSD and would be considered "in-house" by TSS employees.

Kirkpatrick on the report that angered Dulles and Cabell: Lyman B. Kirkpatrick Jr. interview by Joseph E. O'Connor in Providence, RI, on April 26, 1967. Oral History Interview, JFK Library, Boston, Massachusetts.

General Counsel Lawrence Houston's December 9, 1953 memorandum for the record: It appears as if this memo was written at the request of and exclusively for use by those government agencies that were handling Alice Olson's request for death benefits. That Houston did not refer to Olson's death as a suicide seems deliberate.

Houston's final comments on the case: Memorandum for: Inspector General, Subject: Frank R. Olson, 4 January 1954.

Notes on Book One, Chapter 12:
Memorandum for the Record on Backstopping Robert V. Lashbrook, from Robert H. Cunningham to Sheffield Edwards, 28 December 1953.

Notes on Book One, Chapter 13:
Memorandum concerning "Discussion with Sandoz Company Officials," September 4, 1953, files of Dr. H. Marshall Chadwell, CIA OSI chief.

Chemical Corps visit to Eli Lilly: formerly declassified, and then once again classified in 2002, Memorandum to Commanding Officer, Chemical Corps, Subject: Eli Lilly Research Laboratories Visit by Capt. Maas and E.A. Metcalf, Chemical Corps Command Historical Office, Maryland, Row 2, File 78.

CIA Information Report, Subject: Meeting with U.S. Sandoz Representative, Report No. B-72015, December 8, 1953.

Notes on Book One, Chapter 14

Memorandum for Director of Central Intelligence from General Counsel Houston, Report of Criminal Violations to the Department of Justice, February 23, 1954; and Memorandum for Deputy Attorney General, Department of Justice from CIA General Counsel Houston, Washington, D.C., March 1, 1954.

Albarelli, H.P. Jr. and Kelly, John, "Evidence Builds in CIA-Related Death," World Net Daily, WND.com, July 19, 2001.

Notes on Book One, Chapter 15:

Memorandum for the Record, by CIA Security Office chief Sheffield Edwards, January 29, 1954. In 2000, the author asked the CIA to comment on this memorandum. CIA public affairs official Tom Crispwell responded by telephone requesting that a copy be sent to him by fax. This was promptly done, but no comments were ever received.

Blauer Lawsuit Papers, compliments of Belinda Blauer.

Dill, D.B., "Physiologists at Med Labs," *American Physiological Society Journal*, Historical Articles Section, 1999, pp. 474-477.

Diary notations of George Hunter White, April 15-16, 1954, Perham Foundation, Sunnyvale, California.

Notes on Book One, Chapter 16:

Interview with Ruth Norris, Largo, Florida, 1998; interviews with Eric Olson, 1998 and 1999; interview with Arthur Vidich, 1999; Alice W. Olson Deposition, Civil Action No. 80-3163 (JGP), Washington, D.C., September 16, 1988.

Camp Detrick Security Memorandum, Subject: Olson, Dr. Frank Rudolph by J.W. Corey, 1 December 1953, author's files.

Hunt, Linda, *Secret Agenda*, St. Martin's Press, New York, 1991; Federal Narcotics Bureau documents, Special Collections, Penn State University; letters from Garland Williams to George Hunter White, author's files; interview with Dr. Sidney Gottlieb, 1998

Notes on Book One, Chapter 17

PROJECT MKULTRA, Morse Allen, 9 June 1954, Library of Congress, Manuscript Division, Washington, D.C. Copy given to author by a CIA attorney in 2000. Allen was reporting these events to his superior, Security Research Service chief Paul Gaynor, and most likely keeping a written record for his own files. This is a peculiar document in that it seems to offer information that Allen should have been in a position to know in far greater detail as director of Projects Bluebird and Artichoke. Allen's motivation for writing this memo may have been that he had liability concerns about Gottlieb's actions overseas and/or the "suicide" of the Army officer in New York City, or it could have been that due to frictions between Gottlieb and Allen, that Allen's unit, SRS, was spying on TSS. In the early 1950s the Agency was heavily compartmentalized, with little to no exchange of information between or among units or divisions. Former CIA officials say that it was not at all uncommon for one division to know nothing about what another division was doing, regardless that the two could be working on projects in the same country or subject matter. Allen is reported to have died in the late-1980s, but the author was unable to confirm this with the CIA, which declined to supply any information about Allen. In January 2008, journalist Wayne Madsen reported that a member of the family of Martin Luther King, Jr. had given him a copy of a CIA memorandum dated May 11, 1965 which detailed a conversation Morse Allen had with an unnamed individual about Martin Luther King, Jr. in which Morse and the unnamed individual expressed concerns about King's movement being infiltrated by Communists and left-leaning people. Madsen wrote that the memo stated: "It is [redacted]'s belief that somehow or other Martin Luther King must be removed from the leadership of the Negro movement, and his removal must come from within and not from without. {Redacted] feels that somehow in the Negro movement, at the top, there must be a Negro leader who is 'clean' [free from Communist infiltration and influences] who could step into the vacuum and chaos if Martin Luther King were exposed or assassinated." Madsen's article appears on numerous sites on the Internet. Readers may also want to note that Morse Allen's name appears in CIA records concerning the JFK assassination and Lee Harvey Oswald: In October 1960, CIA-OS deputy chief Robert L. Bannerman requested that Morse Allen, Bruce Solie, and Paul Gaynor research American defectors to Russia. See: Armstrong, John, *Harvey and Lee: How the CIA Framed Oswald,* Quasar, Ltd., Texas, 2003, p. 306; and Newman, John, *Oswald and the CIA*, Carroll & Graf, New York, 1995, p. 171.

Notes on Book One, Chapter 18

Interviews with Dr. Herbert G. Tanner's wife Agnes Tanner, Maryland, 1976, 1977; interview with Agnes Tanner, 1978, compliments of John F. Kelly, also on file at Kings College, Liddell Hart Centre for Military Affairs, London; interviews with former Camp Detrick scientists and public affairs officials, 1999, 2000; interviews with Dr. Benjamin Wilson, and Dr. Donald Falconer, 1999; interviews with Dr. Henry Eigelsbach, 2000, 2001.

Notes on Book Two, Chapter 1:

Interviews with Robert Hunter, November 1977; December 1977; January 1978,

National Security Archives, Washington, D.C.

Hunter, Edward, *Brainwashing in Red China: The Calculated Destruction of Men's Minds*, Vanguard Press, New York, 1951.

Seed, David, *Brainwashing: The Fictions of Mind Control, A Study of Novels and Films,* Kent State University Press, Ohio, 2004.

The issue of biological weapon use in Korea was recently raised again with the release of a documentary broadcast by the German state television channel, ARD, in August 2002. Entitled *Codename Artichoke*, the documentary, produced by two German TV journalists, Edmond R. Koch and Michael Wech, focused on the case of Frank Olson and the Korean War. Koch and Wech advanced the shaky theory that Olson had "probably" witnessed experiments in Germany involving former Nazi physicians working alongside Camp Detrick scientists that resulted in the deaths of human subjects and that Olson experienced pangs of conscience that caused him to question his position with the military and in life. Further, the two German producers attempted to draw a direct nexus between Olson and the alleged use of biological weapons in Korea by the Americans by quoting a former Camp Detrick colleague and friend of Olson's, who had left his employment at Camp Detrick prior to the outbreak of the Korean War and the creation of SOD's MKNAOMI relationship with the CIA. According to Koch and Wech, Olson's former colleague told them, "Korea is the key to Frank Olson's death." The two producers then claimed that the American Air Force had used biological weapons in Korea, and that this was "probably" the reason Olson was killed, as opposed to committing suicide; meaning that Olson's troubled conscience created undefined problems with the Army and CIA. Koch and Wech offered no evidence to substantiate the more-than-vague claims of Olson's former colleague and failed to include in their documentary that other people had interviewed the same man and that he had retracted some of his statements, and that his own family raised serious doubts about his statements and stability. To make matters worse, Koch and Wech attempted to draw a connection between Frank Olson and the unsolved anthrax attacks of October 2001, following the 9/11 attacks on America, and posed a question that many observers found unfathomable: "Is it conceivable that the U.S. army carried out further research on biological weapons in spite of binding international treaties, even after the official termination of offensive projects involving biological weaponry in 1969?" The two then partially answered their question, without offering any evidence, by charging that there are "very concrete indications that the Pentagon does not give a damn about international agreements on biological warfare." Readers will learn far more about the German documentary, and a subsequent book released in Germany under the same title, in the final chapters of this book.

Interviews with Albert Biderman, October 1977; November 9, 1977; July 13, 1978; August 1978, National Security Archives, Washington, D.C.

Biderman, Albert and Zimmer, Herbert, *The Manipulation of Human Behavior*, John Wiley & Sons, Inc., New York, 1961.

Lech, Raymond B., *Broken Soldiers*, University of Illinois Press, Urbana and Chicago, 2000.

U.S. Department of the Army, *Communist Interrogation, Indoctrination and Exploitation of Prisoners of War,* Washington, D.C.: U.S. GPO, 1956. Army Pamphlet No. 30-101.

Biderman, Albert, *March to Calumny: The Story of American POW's in the Korean War,* The Macmillan Company, New York, 1963.

"Collaboration in Korea," review of Albert D. Biderman's *March to Calumny, Time* magazine, Friday, January 18, 1963.

Communist Control Techniques, An Analysis of the Methods Used by Communist State Police in the Arrest,

Interrogation, and Indoctrination of Persons Regarded as "Enemies of the State." 2 April 1956. Declassified

September 2000. The author's name is not on the 121-page document, but is known to be Dr. Harold G. Wolff.

Contrary to published reports over the past four decades, Dr. D. Ewen Cameron was not "ordered" or "directed" by Allen Dulles to go to Germany in 1945 to interview Nazi Rudolph Hess and other Nazi war criminals. Dulles had nothing to do with Cameron's trip.

Nuremberg Trial Transcripts, Court Transcripts of Trials of War Criminals Under Control Council Law, November 30, 1945; and Medical/Psychiatric Reports from British psychiatrist, American psychiatrists, Russian psychiatrists, and Dr. Jean Delay, November 19, 20, 17, 16, 1945 respectively, War Crimes Group, WO files, National Archives, Washington, D.C.

Deposition of John W. Gittinger, U.S. Court for the Western District of Okalahoma, January 19, 1983, Case D.D.C. Civil Action No. 80-3163, *Mrs. David Orlikov, et al vs. United States of America*, Defendant.

Regis, Ed, *The Biology of Doom*, Henry Holt and Company, LLC, New York, 1999. Regis's book contains an excellent overview of the charges against the United States regarding the use of biological weapons in Korea. Another excellent book is: Bruning, John R., *Crimson Sky: The Air Battle for Korea*, Brassey's, Dulles, Virginia, 2000.

CIA Memorandum for the Record by E. Howard Hunt, February 27, 1950.

CIA Memorandum to Chief, Security Branch, from Interrogation Research Branch, Subject: *Over-All Report on Two Month Machle Trip*. Dated 26 September 1949.

In 1986, Robert Jay Lifton published the groundbreaking book, *The Nazi Doctors*, which detailed many of the horrific experiments of the Nazi's Ahnenerbe, including those of SS Captain Dr. Helmuth Vetter, who tested a wide array of drugs for German pharmaceutical companies, including Bayer, on Auschwitz and Mauthausen inmates. Lifton, Robert J., *The Nazi Doctors, Medical Killing and the Psychology of Genocide*, Basic Books, 1986.

Vogeler, Robert, *I Was Stalin's Prisoner*, Harcourt, Bruce and Company, New York, 1951. Without identifying them as such, Vogeler thanks a number of CIA officials in his book's acknowledgements.

CIA draft memorandum, *Truth Drug Report*, 1950, no month or names given.

CIA *"EYES ONLY"* Memorandum on Russian Interrogation Methods to DCI, October 7, 1951; CIA Special Report, *Soviet Interrogation Techniques*, Security Research Staff, November 28, 1951.

Notes on Book Two, Chapter Two:

Typed verbal message to DCI Dulles from Chadwell given to "A.T." and hand-dated 18 August 1951.

CIA Memorandum to Chief, Inspection & Security Section from Chief, Staff D/OSO, Subject: BLUEBIRD Project, 4 November 1950.

Memorandum For the Files dated 25 July 1950 from Dr. H. Marshall Chadwell to Project BLUEBIRD Cleared Personnel.

OSO SI Planning Committee, BLUEBIRD Project Proposal, November 9, 1950.

Memorandum to Chief, Security Branch from Interrogation Research Section co-coordinator Morse Allen, Over-All Report on Two-Month Trip, 26 September 1949. The number of personnel in Allen's overseas trip is unknown; however, it is known that the group did contain at least three hypnotists and four detailed Army CIC interrogators. Given Allen's claim that "several hundred POWs" were interrogated, his group may have been larger in number.

Memorandum to Security Branch Chief Sheffield Edwards from Morse Allen, Establishing of Validation Teams, 27 September 1949.

Memorandum to DCI on Project BLUEBIRD from Frank G. Wisner, Assistant Director, OPC, 6 April 1950.

Memorandum for the Record, OSI and I&SS, Project BLUEBIRD, May 9; May 11; and May 12, 1950.

Medical Report, BLUEBIRD interrogation session held in January 1951, undated, unsigned.

Lovell on White: Lovell, Stanley, *Of Spies and Stratagems*, Prentice-Hall, Inc., New Jersey, 1963, p.57.

OSS Truth Drug. Investigation of the Use of TD in Interrogations, OSS Report by Allen Abrams, undated. Abrams's 26-page report states that in all about fifty subjects were subjected to TD experiments. Memorandum Relative to the use of TD in Interrogation, OSS, undated; Memorandum to General William Donovan on Development of Truth Drug, 21 June 1943; several undated draft reports by Allen Abrams and George

White, thought to have been written in 1943. See also: Brown, Anthony Cave, *The Last Hero: Wild Bill Donovan*, Times Books, New York, 1982, p. 746-747.

Drs. Adams and Loewe: FBN Research Bulletin 51, 1941. In 1970, after the Army's marihuana experiments at Edgewood and Detrick were revealed at a 1969 National Institute of Mental health conference, Dr. Van Sim, head of the Army's Edgewood laboratory, reported that Dr. Loewe's studies in the 1940s (which, after public exposure, were stopped by the government "because of political pressure" and "fears of addictive powers of marihuana") essentially proved that certain types of THC were "very effective" in preventing epileptic seizures. Sims also later reported that his laboratory "turned up more evidence of marihuana's positive effects besides its useful medical characteristics."

Memorandum to Sidney Gottlieb from George White, New York City, April 4, 1954.

Ulias Amoss: Amoss, after his time with the OSS, founded the anti-Communist organization, International Services of Information, Inc. headquartered in Baltimore, Maryland. Amoss' involvement in the truth drug experiments is notable because he is claimed to have fathered a concept known as "leaderless resistance." The concept is best described as a leaderless alternative for underground groups under which group activity is autonomous and shared among a small, tight knit band of individuals that operate without any deemed leader or point of central control. Today, the model is favored worldwide by countless terrorist cells, as well as extremist groups in the United States.

White's self-dubbed "Mafia Plan" has often been misconstrued and misidentified by other writers as being Operation Underworld, or the plan to free Lucky Luciano from prison. The "Mafia Plan" was White's first less-than-crafty code name for the assassination program run jointly by CIA and FBN that was just then coming into existence. The record appears quite clear that White had nothing to do with Luciano's release and deportation other than what he claims was a brief conversation in 1943 with August Del Grazio, who approached White for possible assistance on behalf of Meyer Lansky's attorneys. Publicly, White consistently said that he flatly turned Del Grazio down and subsequently reported the approach to his superior OSS chief Wild Bill Donovan, who also refused to have anything to do with Luciano's release.

New York Times articles from 1915 and 1920 refer to August Del Grazio as "Augie the Wop." George White and August Del Grazio, as the record clearly reveals, were close friends. For a variety of reasons, the OSS truth drug records concerning Del Grazio being a subject in an experiment were greatly exaggerated. White did test the truth drug on a "criminal-type," but it was not Del Grazio. Readers having any doubts about this should consult the William B. Herlands Collection at the University of Rochester Archives. See especially: Witness Appearance Transcript, George H. White, April 1, 1954, William J. Grafenecker, Chief Investigator, Office of the Commissioner of Investigations, State of New York, Executive Department.

Edward Lansdale's role in the OSS truth drug experiments has long been rumored to have been far more involved, but the only evidence this author was able to unearth about Lansdale's role were brief September 1943 mentions in White's correspondence noting Lansdale's assistance to Abrams, White, Hamilton, and Siragusa with the experiments.

Meyer Lansky: Siegel quote from the masterful book, *The Money and the Power: The Making of Las Vegas and Its Hold on America, 1947-2000* by Morris, Roger and Denton, Sally, Knopf, New York, 2001. Morris and Denton's book factually lays out the secret alliance between organized crime and government better than any other book.

EYES ONLY AD/SO Memorandum to: Assistant Director/OSO, from Chief, I&SS, Subject: Priority Requirement for BLUEBIRD Team in the Field, 23 June 1950; EYES ONLY AD/SO Memorandum for Assistant Director/OSO, Subject: Priority Requirement for BLUEBIRD Team, 21 June 1950 inclusive of handwritten notes of AD/SO; Memorandum to the File, AD/SO, BLUEBIRD Project, 4 May 1951.

According to White's date book, he met with Allen Dulles and George Wadsworth in New York City on March 20, 1950.

A July 7, 1951 Memorandum for the Record to DCI Smith contains a list of 82 names (with over sixty blacked out) of people cleared for Project BLUEBIRD. The names include: James Angleton, H. Marshall Chadwell, Gen. Cuyler Clark, Harold H. Cooper, Robert Cunningham, Dr. E.H. Cushing, Col. James Drum, Allen Dulles, John Earman, Sheffield Edwards, William K. Harvey, Richard Helms, Frank Wisner, and Lyman B. Kirkpatrick. It is interesting to note Kirkpatrick's name because in 1975 when the so-called facts behind Frank Olson's death became public, Kirkpatrick maintained that he knew nothing about the CIA's mind control programs or use of LSD. Kirkpatrick's name also appears throughout the 1950s on lists of cleared personnel for Project Artichoke and MKULTRA.

Hypnosis and suicide: BLUEBIRD Project Report by Morse Allen, SRS, on February 5-8, 1951 Training Sessions.

Notes on Book Two, Chapter 3:

Albertine White: "[George] drank sometimes to relieve the stress from too much work, travel, and tension," as she later explained it. Said Albertine: "I was constantly worried about the wear and tear he put himself through. I suppose some people would call it reckless but George was dedicated to his job, and most people can't understand that kind of dedication...devotion, and the kind of terrible stress his job brought."

Memorandum on Secured Personnel for Special Artichoke Project to Acting Deputy Director, Scientific Intelligence from Chief, Medicine Division, SI, 7 April 1953.

Report of Intra-Agency fighting over ARTICHOKE: Marks, John, *The Search for the Manchurian Candidate, The CIA and Mind Control,* W.W. Norton & Co., New York, 1979, p. 32.

Memorandum for OS/OSI, Disposal of Maximum Custody Type Defectors of all Categories, 7 March 1951.

LSD with Angleton: White letter to Irwin Eisenberg, December 12, 1952 regarding LSD usage and his jailing for contempt of court.

White's jailing: Gottlieb interview 1999. See also: Columnist Victor Riesel's *Inside Labor,* New York Daily Mirror, December 8, 1952, and Abrams, Norma and Patterson, Neal, *Fed Is Jailed for Hiding Name of Luchese Accuser,* New York Daily News, Saturday, December 6, 1952.

Gottlieb's 1954 verbal report to Morse Allen: Memorandum for the Record by Allen, Subject: OTS (Gottlieb) Statement of Activities of Interest to QKHILLTOP and ARTICHOKE, 26 October 1954; Memorandum to Files by Morse Allen, SRS, on Conference with Sidney Gottlieb, 3 February 1953.

James Jesus Angleton: Angleton was an OSS officer during World War II, serving as chief of the Italian Desk for the European Theatre of Operations and as commanding officer of Special Counterintelligence Unit Z, a group of American and British personnel who at the end of the war worked to apprehend "stay-behind" enemy agents; See: Mangold, Tom, *Cold Warrior: James Jesus Angleton: The CIA's Master Spy Hunter,* Simon & Schuster, New York, 1991, p. 40-43.

Dr. Willard Machle: Machle was instrumental in the creation of the CIA's Office of Scientific Intelligence. He was a hard working, strong willed, forceful man who maintained an unwavering bias that only scientists conduct scientific research as opposed to "ill-trained, ignorant spooks." Chadwell replaced Machle as OSI chief on March 6, 1950, however, Machle stayed on with the Agency for a number of years and also performed extensive outside consulting work. Readers can only imagine what Machle's impression of George White could have been.

Alfred Hubbard: Hubbard became the "Johnny Appleseed of LSD." Contrary to what has been written by several authors, Hubbard, whom George White despised, was never an employee or consultant for CIA, nor was he ever an informer for the Federal Narcotics Bureau, as some have claimed. Hubbard's extensive FBI file, released recently, reveals no formal or covert links to any federal agency.

Reid on Giannini: Reid, Ed, *The Shame of New York,* Random House, New York, 1953, p.83-84.

According to White's 1951 date book, he was married to Albertine Calef on August 18, 1951. This was White's second marriage.

"Explosive": Artichoke Conference Minutes, 9 April 1953; 16 April 1953; 19 April 1953. Interesting to note, even Frank Olson's close friends interviewed for this book at times referred to him as being "explosive" at times, or having the capacity to "easily explode in certain situations."

Disposal problem: Memorandum for the Record, Informal Discussion with Chief, OS, Regarding "Disposal," 7 March 1951.

George White's datebook for 1952 shows that on Friday, June 13, 1952 he met with a CIA representative named "McCleary" to discuss Lafitte's travel to Washington, D.C. to meet with OSO.

Gottlieb telephone interviews, 1998; interviews with other former intelligence agency employees, 1999-2002.

Gottlieb's LSD experience: Authors telephone interview with Gottlieb (see above). This author was struck by Gottlieb's description of how LSD made him feel. See also: Deposition of Sidney Gottlieb, Kronisch v. U.S., September 19, 1995, Cr62448.0, p.28-29.

Other SOD and Camp Detrick scientists whose names arose on occasion in various reports related to Project ARTICHOKE work were: Drs. Calderone Howell; Capt. Henry Bookman; Arnold Wedum; Grayson Hoffman; Jeanne Whallon; and Werner Braun.

ARTICHOKE Assassination Problem Report, Concerning Germany visit January 8 to January 15, 1954. Report not dated; believed to have been authored by ARTICHOKE Project director, Morse Allen in late January 1954.

Author's interviews with Gottlieb; 1995 deposition of Gottlieb in civil litigation, Kronisch v. U.S., September, 1995. Gottlieb told the author he had no recollection of Project BLUEBIRD until he was shown CIA documents concerning the project and even then he barely recalled the project. "I know it started before I was there, but I don't know when. It may have ended or had its name altered before I came to the Agency," he said.

MKULTRA Subproject Three and Dr. James A. Hamilton: Ross, Colin A. Dr., *BLUEBIRD: Deliberate Creation of Multiple Personality by Psychiatrists,* Manitou Communications, Texas, 2000, p. 318; draft copy of *CIA MKULTRA Briefing Book,* 1976.

Notes on Book Two, Chapter 4:
Interview with Sidney Gottlieb, 1997; Gottlieb Deposition, 1996, ibid; interview with Uri Geller, 1999-2000.

Ray Treichler: Other books claim that TSS chemist Treichler took over liaison with SOD after Olson's death, but this is wrong. He first assumed those duties at the start of 1953, and they continued for at least eighteen months after Olson's death. Gottlieb first met Treichler, before either man worked for the CIA, when they both worked for other government agencies in Washington, D.C. At the time, Gottlieb and Treichler were working on a project involving the vitamin content of milk. Lashbrook first met Treichler at Stanford University, as did Bortner.

Robert S. Goodenow: Deposition of John W. Gittinger, *Mrs. David Orlikov, et al v. U.S.A.,* U.S. District Court for the Western District of Oklahoma, Case No.

D.D.C. Civil, Action No. 80-3163. Gittinger identified Goodenow as a "paid CIA consultant."

Dr. S.L. Quimby: MKULTRA files reveal a number of references to Dr. S.L. Quimby, Columbia University. Letters from Dr. Harris Isbell to Sidney Gottlieb at TSS refer to Dr. Quimby as being involved in an undefined project, perhaps an MKULTRA subproject formerly known as HKDECOY, along with Isbell, Dr. Harold Abramson, and Dr. E.W. Pelikan, who at the time was conducting research for the Agency on curare and other toxic drugs; CIA Memorandum for the Record, from Henry Bortner to Sidney Gottlieb, Subject: The Conversion of HKDECOY from ONR Cover to MKULTRA, 10 January 1956; Draft Memorandum for the Record, from Sidney Gottlieb to S.L. Quimby, Subject: ONR Cover of DECOY Project and Related Developments, 8 January 1956; interviews with former SOD Camp Detrick researchers about precursor program to DECOY, Project Ram, 1999-2001; *Merlins,* article in TIME magazine, June 10, 1929, p. 23.

John Mulholland: Price, David, *MAGIC, A Pictorial History of Conjurers in the Theater,* Cornwall Books, New York, 1985, p. 316-318; Edwards, Michael, *The Sphinx & the Spy,* Genii, The Conjurers' Magazine, Vol. 64, No. 4, April 2, 2001, p. 23-39. Edwards' article presents a good overview of Mulholland's CIA work as well as Frank Olson's death. However, his article states factually that Olson was taken to see Mulholland the week of his death, an event that turns on other published accounts that are wholly erroneous and based upon the highly circumstantial evidence of a mere receipt bearing John Mulholland's name found by the New York City police in the pocket of Robert Lashbrook on the night of Olson's death. The alleged Olson visit to Mulholland's New York office was first reported in John Marks' book *The Search for the Manchurian Candidate: The CIA and Mind Control.* In his chapter on Olson's death, Marks wrote: "[Olson] and Ruwet accompanied Lashbrook on a visit to a famous magician named John Mulholland.... Lashbrook thought that the magician might amuse Olson, but Olson became 'highly suspicious'. The group tactfully cut their visit short..." In 1998, when writer John Kelly asked Marks how he knew Olson had visited Mulholland, Marks answered he had only "surmised" it from the receipt police found in Lashbrook's pocket. Marks said he "did not know for sure" if the visit had happened. Shortly after Marks' book was published, British writer Gordon Thomas published his book *Journey Into Madness.* In that book, Thomas creatively builds upon Marks' book and writes: "The biochemist [Olson] became agitated when he thought Mulholland was going to make him vanish like one of the magician's rabbits." Since the publication of these two books, numerous other books, and articles, have treated the alleged Mulholland visit as a matter-of-fact. One book even has Olson attempting to run out of Mulholland's office. Indeed, many alleged "facts" about the Olson case also fall into this same ambiguous category. A recently discovered 1954 interview with Vincent Ruwet by Pentagon intelligence officers contains nothing about a visit to Mulholland. A later interview with Ruwet by Army Intelligence officers also contains no mention of Mulholland. Robert Lashbrook, interviewed by another writer about the alleged visit, said there had been "no visit to Mulholland with Olson in tow," but he refused to answer any other questions about the magician or about Frank Olson. Asked where the visit was to, Lashbrook only said: "Not to Mulholland." Edwards also maintains in the same article that Mulholland was not interested in hypnotism, despite that CIA files indicate otherwise. Mulholland never incorporated hypnosis into his stage act, but, as CIA files demonstrate, he was very much interested in the practice and history of mesmerism, and he served as a consultant to the Agency, and most likely the Army, on the use of a number of other stage magicians and hypnotists. Author Ben Robinson reveals in his book (see below) that Mulholland, initially a skeptic about hypnotism, gradually became more accepting of its effectiveness.

John Mulholland's Manual for the CIA: *Some Operational Applications of the Art of Deception*, 71 pages, 1953 (TSS Copy #3, and sections of Copy #7), author's files.

George Hunter White's 1952,1953,1954,1955 date books, with selected papers, letters, memorandum, and notations. Copies provided by CIA Public Affairs Division as assembled for the CIA Victims Task Force.

Robert Lashbrook deposition: Mrs. David Orlikow, et al., vs. the United States of America, Civil Action No. 80-3163, Ventura, California, May 14, 1986, p. 40-41, author's files; Paul Avery interview with Robert Vern Lashbrook, 1976.

Robert Lashbrook's letter on the Faraday Cage: Robinson, Ben, *The Magician: John Mulholland's Secret Life*, Library Books, New York, 2009. Page 170 of the book contains a facsimile of the letter. Robinson, a magician himself, provides some very intriguing documentation, and conjecture, about Mulholland's work with Gottlieb and Lashbrook, and Mulholland's connections to the death of Frank Olson. Clearly there is far more research to be accomplished to understand the full extent of Mulholland's work for the CIA, as well as the CIA's venture into the paranormal realm. Robinson's book is a bit overly dramatic in places. For example, Robinson writes that on the day he met with New York assistant district attorney Steve Saracco to assist with the Olson case, a man, who he claims was Sidney Gottlieb, encountered him on the sidewalk outside the DA's office, this despite that Gottlieb was on his deathbed at the time and died about two weeks later. Of course, this does not rule out the possibility of astral projection.

Puharich and Faraday Cage: Puharich, Andrija, *Beyond Telepathy*, Anchor Books, New York, 1973; Geller, Uri, *My Story*, Warner Books, New York, 1976; Puharich, Andrija, *The Sacred Mushroom: Key to the Door of Eternity*, Doubleday & Co., New York, 1959; *The Iceland Papers: Select Papers on Experimental and Theoretical Research on the Physics of Conscious*, edited by Andrija Puharich, M.D., LL.D., Essentia Research Associates, Amherst, Wisconsin, 1979. Martin Ebon also edited a book on Geller entitled, *The Amazing Uri Geller*, New American Library, Signet Books, 1975.

Thomas, Evan, *The Very Best Men*, Touchstone Book, Simon & Schuster, New York, 1995.

CIA's esoteric pursuits: Readers familiar with Freemasonry will recognize that many of these esoteric subjects are related to that secret society. Some readers may also know that many of the CIA's subcontractors under MKULTRA and ARTICHOKE, as well as other programs, throughout the 1950s and 1960s, were Masons, some of the 33rd degree. For decades there has been rampant speculation about Freemasonry and MKULTRA. Nowhere is this best witnessed than on the Internet. Some of this speculation has been fueled by the documented activities of the Scottish Rite of Freemasonry as related to behavior modification programs. The possible connections are intriguing but not a primary subject for this book. When this book was close to completion, in yet another of numerous coincidences that occurred over the course of its writing, author Peter Levenda had just completed a book on Freemasons and America. I asked Peter about the CIA's pursuits of such matters, and he said: "CIA's interest in matters esoteric was prompted by several concerns. In the first place, esoteric organizations – secret societies, cults, etc. – run parallel to intelligence agencies in terms of the culture of secrecy and deception. A secret society operates below the radar of social and governmental oversight and control; their membership lists are secret; their members use pseudonyms; and they believe that they have secret power to control the outcome of world events. Members of secret societies are often intelligent, are familiar with foreign languages and cultures, and travel incognito across national borders. Thus, purely as a security matter, CIA would be interested in these groups and would be tempted to infiltrate them or otherwise keep an eye on them. The SS and Gestapo did the same in Germany in the 1930s and 1940s, when it was understood that secret societies – like the Masons, but also the Golden Dawn and other groups – provided a covert network of potential anti-government operatives that had to be suppressed. In the second place, the very arcane pursuits of the secret societies hinted at avenues of knowledge, power and control that were not available to the government. CIA would have wanted to know how cults were so successful in 'brainwashing' their members, convincing them of the truth of the most unbelievable ideas and concepts. Was the Korean War era method of brainwashing captured American soldiers equivalent to the approach used by cults and occult groups on their own members? What was the effect of these methods on memory, perception, volition? Did the cults know something about the functioning of the human brain that the government scientists did not?

Thirdly, the interest of CIA in such matters paralleled that of the Nazis and their SS-Ahnenerbe. Himmler's desire to find ancient artifacts – including the Holy Grail, the Ark of the Covenant, etc – was motivated not by a sincere religious sentiment but by the naked pursuit of the power they represent. This is an astonishing development, for it indicates that somewhere within CIA's labyrinthine bureaucracy there were (and are) individuals who were able to get funding to search the world for these artifacts. For instance, Robert K. Temple in the new preface to his much-acclaimed The Sirius Mystery tells of how CIA approached him as he was researching the religion of the African Dogon tribe. What possible reason could CIA have for keeping tabs on such an arcane, academic study involving ancient astronomy? If we realize that such practices as remote viewing, hallucinogenic drug research, and the investigation of cults, ESP, hypnosis and other factors were taking place all at the same time within America's intelligence establishment – involving not only CIA but also the Army and the Navy – then we are forced to consider that CIA had a reason for all of this that transcends mere curiosity. It was the era of the weaponization of esoterica, something that had not been seen in the western world since the Middle Ages."

"CIA's Role in the Study of UFO's, 1947-1990," paper by Gerald K. Hines, CIA Center for the Study of Intelligence, 1997. Throughout the past ten years, this author [Albarelli] was contacted by people who shared theories that Frank Olson was killed because he had knowledge about UFO's and aliens, and that the government did not want that knowledge revealed. One person, who seemed quite knowledgeable about Camp Detrick, claimed that "definitive evidence proving alien contact with Earth" had been removed from UFO crash or landing sites by the government. This evidence was allegedly transported for study to Camp Detrick and other military installations. That several of the key CIA and Army participants in Olson's death were involved in the governments UFO research in the 1950s is certainly interesting. Had this writer not known that Olson was murdered for other reasons some of these theories may have been much more provocative.

Lockridge, Richard and Estabrooks, G.H., *Death In The Mind*, The World Publishing Company, Cleveland and New York, 1945; Estabrooks, G.H., *Hypnotism*, E.P. Dutton & Co., Inc., 1959 edition.

"Hypnosis in Interrogation" by Edward F. Deshere, CIA-CSI Historical Review Program, 22 September 1993.

"Hypnosis Comes of Age" by George H. Estabrooks, Ph.D., *Science Digest*, April, 1971, p.44-50.

CIA Memorandum for the Record, to Chief SRS from Chief, Technical Branch, Subject: Terminal Experiments and Hypnosis/Estabrooks, July 12, 14, 15, and 16, 1954.

Notes on Book Two, Chapter 5:

Summary of Remarks by Mr. Allen Dulles at the National Alumni Conference of the Graduate Council of Princeton University, Hot Springs, Virginia, April 10, 1953, National Security Archive, Washington, D.C.; File: Artichoke Docs. 362-388, Box 5, CIA Behavior Control Experiments Collection, National Security Archive, Washington.

Notes on Book Two, Chapter 6:

Author's interviews with Sidney Gottlieb, 1997-1998. George Hunter White's date books and letters, Perham Foundation, Sunnyvale, California; Deposition of Dr. Sidney Gottlieb, U.S. District Court for the Northern District of Georgia, Atlanta Division, Civil Action 81-291, Don Roderick Scott, et al vs. William Casey and CIA, et al, December 8, 1981, author's files.

Herlands Commission: Confidential Memorandum from George White to Sidney Gottlieb, New York City, April 4, 1954; Transcript of George White's Testimony, State of New York, Executive Department, Office of the Commissioner of Investigation, April 1, 1954, author's files.

Memorandum for the Record from Sidney Gottlieb to Dr. Willis Gibbons, 20 July 1953.

Chemrophyl Associates: various letters from George White and Dr. Harold Abramson were sent to Chemrophyl Associates, P.O. Box 8176, Southwest Station, Washington 24, D.C., a front corporation established by the CIA for TSS programs.

Jekyll-Hyde letter: George White to Sidney Gottlieb, May 26, 1953.

Treasury Department, Bureau of Narcotics, Washington receipt for 330 ounces of marijuana for National naval Medical Research Institute, May 16, 1951; Memorandum from Commanding Officer, Naval Medical Research Institute to Commissioner of Narcotics requesting 25 grams of heroin, 9 February 1951.

Dr. James A. Hamilton: Mauch, Christof, *The Shadow Against Hitler*, Columbia University Press, New York, 2005, p. 138-139; O'Donnell, Patrick K., *Operatives, Spies, and Saboteurs: The Unknown Story of the Men and Women of World War II's OSS*, Free Press, New York, 2004, p.21-22.

Abramson, Harold A., M.D., *The Use of LSD in Psychotherapy and Alcoholism*, Bobbs Merrill Co., Inc., New York, 1967.

CIA Memorandum for Anthony A. Lapham and Ernest Mayerfeld from A.R. Cinquegrana, CIA Office of General Counsel, Subject: "MKULTRA: Extent and Nature of Institutional Involvement," 28 July 1976.

Letter from attorney James C. Turner to Adele Lerner, Cornell Medical Center, January 24, 1983; deposition of John W. Gittinger, U.S. Court for the Western District of Oklahoma, January 19, 1983, Case D.D.C. Civil Action No. 80-3163, Mrs. David Orlikov, et al vs. United States of America, Defendant; deposition of Frank Herbert Laubinger, CIA employee, Washington, D.C., July 20, 1983. Laubinger testified that in 1952-1960 he worked in TSS under chiefs Culver C. Ladd, George Grudenfelder, and Colin C. Reid. He also testified that in 1960 he worked in the TSS Chemical Division under chief Linwood A. Murray. (Gottlieb was then overall TSS chief.) Laubinger also stated that John McMahon headed TSS in the early 1970s.

Noll, Richard, *The Jung Cult*, Free Press Books, New York, 1994. Dr. Noll's book is an excellent account of Jung's early years and the origins of his beliefs. Noll's footnotes on the swastika and its use "as the alternative to the cross" are enlightening.

Graham, Bill and Greenfield, Robert, *Bill Graham Presents*, Delta Book, Dell Publishing, New York, 1992.

Alston Chase, *A Mind for Murder: The Education of the Unabomber and the Origins of Modern Terrorism*, W.W. Norton & Company, New York, 2004.

Evidence Suggests CIA Funded Experiments at State Hospital, article by reported Louis Porter, Rutland Herald newspaper, November 30, 2008; interviews with former Vermont State Hospital employees, December-January 2008-2009. In the late 1960s, various experiments were conducted using LSD and isolation tanks at the University of Vermont. Former UVM professor Dr. Ronald Steffenhagen oversaw some of this work, but no CIA documents could be found that support any direct Agency involvement with UVM.

There are several excellent books available about the experiments of Dr. D. Ewen Cameron. The best is Don Gillmor's *I Swear by Apollo*, Eden Press, Montreal, 1987. Also very good is *In the Sleep Room* by Anne Collins, Key Porter Books, 1998; and Dr. Harvey M. Weinstein's *Psychiatry and the CIA*, American Psychiatric Press, Washington, D.C., 1990.

CIA and Radiation Experiments: untitled manuscript by John Kelly, 1995, author's files; Memorandum for CS III, Subject: [Redacted], Boris T. Pash, 23 January 1950; Memorandum from Assistant Director for Scientific Intelligence to OPC, Frank Wisner/AD/OPC, 20 November 1950; CIA Memorandum for the Record for DD/P through C/SE, Subject: Radiological Warfare, 28 October 1954; letter from Dr. James Alexander Hamilton, San Francisco to CIA cut-out organization the Geschickter Fund for Medical Research, Washington, D.C. concerning Hamilton's request for a grant to continue research project: "Measurement of Thyroid Function in the Puerperium," March 30, 1965. The letter reads in part: "The availability of subjects and inmate-technicians which we have trained, has made it possible to extend our investigations into certain areas involving relations between psychological states and organic and toxic conditions. These ancillary studies are done without interference with the thyroid project, which proceeds along a rigid schedule set up months in advance."

Interviews with Sidney Gottlieb 1997-1998, and NBC Nightly News report, NBC TV, September 21, 1977, "Nixon Staff Drugged Abroad."

Memorandum for the U.S. Secretary of Defense Robert S. McNamara, Subject: Special Prisoner Interrogation, from V.H. Krulak, Major General, USMC, Joint Chiefs of Staff, Office of Counterinsurgency and Special Activities, SACCA-M 59-63, 31 JANUARY 1963.

Notes on Book 2, Chapter 7:

For more information on the Lexington, Kentucky Narcotics Farm and ARC see the excellent article *Narco Brat* by Marjorie Senechal, in the journal *Of Human Bondage, Historical Perspectives on Addiction*, Douglas Lane Patey, Editor, Smith College Studies in History, Volume LII, Northampton, Mass., 2003, p.171-200. Also see the book, *The Narcotic Farm* by Nancy D. Campbell, J.P. Olsen, and Luke Walden, Abrams, New York, 2008. The author sincerely thanks Dr. Daniel Winkler and his sister, Marjorie Senechal, for providing him with an advance copy of *Narco Brat*. Dan and Marjorie's father, Dr. Abraham Wikler, worked closely with Dr. Isbell. He is referred to in at least four CIA documents concerning Dr. Isbell's work for the CIA, and it is the author's belief that Wikler was probably aware of the CIA's involvement in ARC experiments.

Memorandum for Liaison and Security Office/TSS by Sidney Gottlieb, Chemical Division Chief, Subject: An Account of the Chemical Division's Contacts in the National Institutes of Health, July 24, 1953.

Readers may be interested to learn that Robert Hanna Felix, a psychiatrist who was the first director of the National Institute of Mental Health, NIH, a position that required oversight of Isbell's experiments, is often referred to by some writers for his MKULTRA connections because he was a 33rd degree Freemason. Before World War II, Felix was the clinical director at the Lexington Narcotics Farm; from 1975 to 1983, he was research director of the Scottish Rite Psychophrenic Research program in Lexington, Mass.

Robert C. Tryon: Tryon, OSS Psychology Division, worked closely with hypnotist George Estabrooks, and often touted the U.S. Army's use of propaganda and rumors to induce African Americans to reject induction into the Confederate army and to rebel against the Confederacy and join Northern troops in the Civil War.

Letter to Willis Gibbons, CIA-TSS Chief from Dr. Harris Isbell, Director of Research, NIMH Addiction Research Center, 9 April 1953; and letter to Sandoz Chemical Company, New Jersey from Dr. Harris Isbell, 30 April 1953.

Letter from Dr. Harris Isbell, Director NIMH-ARC, to Dr. Sidney Gottlieb, c/o Chemrophyl Associates, Washington, D.C., 3 August 1953.

Letter to Dr. Harris Isbell from Dr. Henry Bortner, CIA-TSS, March 5, 1954. Bortner's letter was typed by "mk," initials for the administrative secretary for TSS at the time and the source of the randomly selected designation MK for TSS projects.

CIA Memorandum for the Record by Robert V. Lashbrook, Subject: Trip to Lexington, Kentucky on 15 July 1954.

LSD Research Report by Harris Isbell, M.D., NIMH Addiction Research Center, to Dr. Sidney Gottlieb, CIA-TSS Chemical Division, September 15, 1954.

CIA Memorandum for the Record by Robert V. Lashbrook, Deputy Director, TSS Chemical Division, Subject: Trip to Lexington, Kentucky Narcotics Farm, 29 December 1955.

Memorandum for the Record by Sidney Gottlieb, Chief, Branch II, TSS/Chemical Division, Subject: Trip to Lexington, Kentucky, 21-23 August 1956, 24 August 1956.

See also: Ott, Jonathan, *Pharmacotheon: Enthnogenic Drugs, Their Plant Sources and History*, Natural Products Co., Kennewick, WA, 1993; and Stafford, Peter, *Psychedelic Encyclopedia*, Third Edition, Ronin Publishing, Inc., Berkeley, Calif., 1992.

Isbell Ibogaine letter: see the fascinating book, *The Ibogaine Story* by Paul De Rienzo and Dana Beal, Autonomedia Books, Brooklyn, New York, 1997.

Notes on Book Two, Chapter 8:
MKNAOMI and SOD financial documents submitted with supportive documentation to CIA-TSS for spending approval, Camp Detrick, Frederick, Maryland, 1952-1956, author's files.

Author's interview with Dr. Gerald Yonetz, Frederick, Maryland; March 5, 2000; e-mail message from Ed Regis regarding his interviews with Yonetz. Yonetz told this author, and Regis, that the dart gun was "noisy" but quite lethal when fired at the "proper range," which he recalled to be "no more than about forty or fifty feet, give or take some."

Hart, Gary, and Cohen, William, *The Double Man*, Avon Books, New York, 1985. On January 18, 2002 Senator Hart, in response to questions from the author, wrote: "I wanted to talk to QJ/WIN [in 1975] about his involvement in the Castro plots. Someone in the Agency asked him to help on the matter. He briefly appeared, then disappeared. When we [Senate investigative committee] discovered the CIA/Mafia connection on the Castro plots, it opened up a variety of new possibilities in connection with the Kennedy assassination, which committee member Richard Schweiker and I pursued for the full committee. Our report is contained in the full committee report. I don't believe QJ/WIN was originally trained by the Agency. He got his start as a contract agent for a number of European security services and was a ubiquitous contract hit-man whom we recruited in the late 50s because we didn't have experience in those matters." Hart also wrote: "The late CIA director, William Colby, undertook in 1975 to put me (as a member of the Senate Select Committee to Investigate the Intelligence Agencies of the US Government) together with the man codenamed QJ/WIN in Amsterdam. The meeting never took place, although Mr. Colby's agent for this purpose alleged that QJ/WIN had been in the location where we met earlier in the evening before I arrived. I know nothing further about QJ/WIN but have seen speculation that he was a Belgian and had died some years ago."

QJ/WIN: File and notes on QJ/WIN, National Security Archives, Washington, D.C.; William King Harvey handwritten notes on QJ/WIN, CIA documents requested under the freedom of Information Act; interviews with Phen Lafitte, 2001-2003, and Pierre Lafitte's journal/letter notes 1954-1963; unpublished 1987 article by

Stephen J. Rivele entitled "Three Contracts; Who Is QJ/WIN?" By Stephen J. Rivele, *The National Reporter,* Vol. 10, No. 3, Spring 1987; "The Plot to Kill Lumumba: The Corsican Connection" by Stephen J. Rivele, *The National Reporter,* Vol. 10-11, No. 4-1, Fall 1987.

Letter to William Donovan, November 29, 1949, and follow-up letter, author unknown, author's files; In 1979, the author had the occasion, unrelated to the subject of Frank Olson, to ask Ambassador Richard M. Helms what his views were on the letter to Donovan.

Brown, Anthony Cave, *The Last Hero: Wild Bill Donovan,* Times Books, New York, 1982, p. 269-270.

"A Modern Marriage of Convenience: A Collaboration Between organized Crime and U.S. Intelligence" by Alan A. Block, found in Kelly, Robert, J., editor, *Organized Crime: A Global Perspective,* Rowan and Little-field Publishers, New Jersey, 1986.

McCoy, Alfred W., *The Politics of Heroin: CIA Complicity in the Global Drug Trade,* Lawrence Hill Books, Chicago, Illinois, 1991.

Scott, Peter Dale, *Deep Politics and the Death of JFK,* University of California Press, Berkeley, 1993.

CIA Assassination Manual, 1952: this manual has since its earliest days of "discovery" been controversial and the object of many erroneous claims. Perhaps the most outrageous is one made in 1999 by British writer Gordon Thomas, who claimed that the manual had been authored by Dr. Sidney Gottlieb and had been "dis-covered" in Gottlieb's home shortly after he had passed away as a result of a drug overdose. A spokesperson for Gottlieb's survivors and family said they were "shocked and outraged at the continued indignities and untruths heaped upon Dr. Gottlieb that are continuing even now after his death."

John F. Kelly, *The Cave of Bugs,* draft of unpublished article, 1998-1999.

Waldron, Lamar with Hartman, Thom, *Ultimate Sacrifice: John and Robert Kennedy, the Plan for a Coup in Cuba, and the Murder of JFK,* Carroll & Graf Publishers, New York, 2005.

Stockton, Bayard, *Flawed Patriot: The Rise and Fall of CIA Legend Bill Harvey,* Potomac Books, Virginia, 2006.

H.P. Albarelli Jr., "William Morgan: Patriot or Traitor?" World Net Daily article, April 21, 2002, worldnetdaily. com; Federal Bureau of Narcotics Special Report on Paul Mondolini, "Cuba Activities," 1959-1961, Pilot Project drafts.

FBI files and dossier on Sam "Momo" Giancana, 1936-1975; FBI files and dossier on Santo Trafficante, Jr. 1950-1973; FBI files on Jean-Pierre Lafitte; FBI and FBN files on John Maples Spiritto, 1958-1961.

U.S. Senate Select Committee to Study Governmental Operations with Respect to Intelligence Activities: *Sup-plementary Detailed Staff Reports on Foreign and Military Intelligence,* Book IV, 94th Congress, 2nd Session, Report No. 94-755, Washington, D.C., 1976, p.128-133. Pash, Oppenheimer, and Jean Tatlock: For decades it has been speculated in some quarters that Pash and narcotics agent George White may have had their hands in Tatlock's death, however, a thorough investigation in the 1970s, involving private investigators, yielded no evidence of this. Also, published reports that Pash and White worked together, and that Pash supervised White on his "truth drug" experiments, are false. There is no evidence that Pash supervised White or col-laborated in any way on his experiments. The extensive OSS files available on the truth drug project make no mention whatsoever of Boris Pash, nor do any of White's many letters and date book notations made at the time of these tests. In 1978, British writer Leonard Mosley wrote in his book *Dulles,* a biography of Eleanor, John Foster, and Allen Dulles, that Boris Pash and Sidney Gottlieb "directed" a "noxious enterprise" called "the Health Alteration Committee," implying in his source notes that this information came from Richard Bissell, Jr. This author could locate no evidence apart from Mosley's report that Pash and Gottlieb ever worked together. When Gottlieb was queried about Pash, he said, "That's not a name I recall." See: Mosley, Leonard, *Dulles,* The Dial Press, New York, 1978, p. 459.

Lucian Conein: files of Intelligence Division, U.S. Department of Justice, Washington, D.C.; Conein files, Center for National Security Studies, Washington, D.C.; *Washington Post* article by George Crile, June 13, 1976; interview notes with George Crile, Center for National Security Studies, Washington, D.C.; interviews in North Carolina with Gerry Patrick Hemming, 1998-2001; interviews in Florida with former soldiers-of-fortune in Cuba during 1958-1960; FBI files on Gerald Patrick Hemming; National Archives files on Hemming, 180-1001 through 180-10105; Twyman, Noel, *Bloody Treason,* Laurel Publishing, California, 1997; Hurt, Henry, *Reasonable Doubt,* Holt, Rinehart, & Winston, New York, 1985; Rappleye, Charles and Becker, Ed, *All American Mafioso,* Doubleday, New York, 1991; Church Committee investigation notes, files, and reports, 1976; O'Leary, Bradley S. and Lee, Edward, *The Deaths of the Cold War Kings,* Cemetery Dance Publications,

Maryland, 2000; Fonzi, Gaeton, *The Last Investigation*, Thunder Mouth Press, New York, 1994. In 1988, an expansive federal government investigation, Operation Cobra, involving the illegal import of exotic snakes, drugs, money, murder, and corruption, resulted in a mistrial for one of those arrested, Guillermo Tabraue, "after the shocking revelation that he had secretly worked as a high-level informant for a covert DEA-CIA narcotics operation run by Lt. Col. Lucien Conein." See: Christy, Bryan, *The Lizard King*, Twelve, Hachette Book Group, New York, 2008.

For information on the Martin/Mitchell defection case see: "The Worst Internal Scandal in NSA History Was Blamed on Cold War Defectors' Homosexuality" by Rick Anderson, *Seattle Times*, July 18, 2007.

Watson, Peter, *War on the Mind: The Military Uses and Abuses of Psychology*, Basic Books, Inc., Publishers, New York, 1978.

CIA Memorandum for the Record, Subject: *Report on the Plots to Assassinate Fidel Castro*, by J.S. Earman, Inspector General, 23 May 1967.

CIA Assassination Manual: *A Study of Assassinations*, Job-79-01025A, Box 73. Note on cover sheet: "Training File for PB/Success, Early 1950's." Approved for release July 1995; actually released Spring 1997, National Archives, Washington, D.C. A National Archives News Release issued on May 22, 1997 states: "The majority of the documents [released with the Assassination Study] relate to three covert actions in Guatemala that resulted in the collapse of the government of President Jacobo Arbenz Guzman. The three phases of the covert actions were known by their code-words: PBFORTUNE, PBSUCCESS, AND PBHISTORY." Former intelligence officials report that the Assassination Study was written in part by Idries Abutahir Shah, aka Arkon Daraul, an Indian of Afghan descent, who wrote several books and had intelligence ties worldwide. Here it should be noted that the CIA presence in Latin America produced yet another manual, this one in 1983 on the subject of torture and coercion. In October 1984, the Agency was embarrassed by public disclosure of another training manual that was intended for Nicaraguan contras. This manual aimed to teach "how to kidnap and kill public officials, and to blackmail citizens and destroy entire villages."

Notes on Book Two, Chapter 8:

Ott, Jonathan, *Pharmacotheon*, Natural Products, Inc., Kennewick, WA., 1993.

Stafford, Peter, *Psychedelics Encyclopedia*, Third Edition, Ronin Publishing, Inc., Berkeley, CA., 1992.

Rinkel, Max, editor, *Biological Treatment of Mental Illness*, L.C. Page & Co., New York, 1966.

Cohen, Sidney, *Drugs of Hallucination*, Paladin, Granada Publishing, Limited, London, 1970. Cohen dedicated this book to Dr. Albert Hofmann.

Newland, Constance A., *Myself and I: The Explosive Experiences of Constance A. Newland Who Took Twenty-Three Doses of the Dangerous New Mind Drug LSD*, Third Printing, Signet Books, New York, 1962.

Stolaroff, Myron J., *Thanatos to Eros, 35 Years of Psychedelic Exploration*, VWB Publisher, Berlin, Germany, 1994.

Perrine, Daniel M., *The Chemistry of Mind-Altering Drugs*, The American Chemical Society, Washington, D.C., 1996.

Wasson, Gordon R., Hofmann, Albert, Ruck, Carl A.P., *The Road to Eleusis: Unveiling the Secret of the Mysteries*, A Harvest/HBJ Book, New York, 1978.

Telephone interview with Faye and Ken Kesey, June 1975, compliments of J.P. Mahoney, Burlington, Vermont. Mahoney also provided the author with details of LSD, mescaline, and isolation tank experiments conducted at the University of Vermont in the early 1970s. The CIA through front groups, the National Institutes of Health, and the National Institute of Drug Abuse, funded these experiments, which resulted in a fair amount of Sandoz and Lilly LSD finding its way into the local community.

Dr. John P. Clay passed away in Florida in February 1991. He had retired years earlier as chairman of the chemistry department at Lehman College, part of the City University of New York, and was widely recognized as a superb chemist. He served for six years in the Army during and after World War II, rising to the rank of colonel. In 1949 and 1950, he studied Germany's technology and experimental record in chemical warfare as an adviser to the European Command. From 1952 to 1954 he was the first scientific director of the Dugway Proving Ground in Utah. Asked about Frank Olson's death in the early 1980s, Clay said, "I view it as a matter better left alone. I don't care to discuss it. Those that should know what happened know; those that are unaware have little business asking or knowing."

The "Wilson Memorandum": Top Secret Memorandum from the Secretary of Defense for the Secretary of the Army, Secretary of the Navy, and Secretary of the Air Force, Subject: Use of Human Volunteers in Experimental Research, 26 February 1953. Copies of the memorandum were also given to the Joint Chiefs of Staff and the Research and Development Board.

Fuller, John G., *The Day of Saint Anthony's Fire*, The Macmillan Company, New York, 1968. Fuller and Puharich wrote a book together: *Arigo: Surgeon of the Rusty Knife*, Crowell Publishers, New York, 1974. A November 10, 1951 article by Janet Flanner on the Pont-St.-Esprit outbreak in *The New Yorker* stated: "The Pont-Saint-Esprit mystery has grown murkier. There is still talk of crime. There is a new theory that polluted water was really responsible."

Johnson, Dr. Donald McIntosh, *Indian Hemp: A Social Menace*, Christopher Johnson, London, England, 1952.

United States Passport, No. 15403, SP-14592, of Frank Rudolph Olson, issued on April 26th, 1950 by the U.S. Department of State. Olson's passport reads: "The bearer is proceeding to the British Isles on Official Business for the Department of the Army." On another page, Olson's passport reads: "Extended July 14, 1953 to April 25, 1954. The bearer will also travel in France." [Signed]: R.B. Shipley, Director, Passport Office.

British Medical Journal, Book Reviews, *Poison in Pont-St.-Esprit* by Griffith Edwards, 3 May 1969, p. 302.

British Medical Journal, *Ergot Poisoning at Pont-St.-Esprit*, Drs. Gabbai, Lisbonne, and Pourquier, September 15, 1951, p. 650-651.

Dr. Albert Hofmann, *LSD: My Problem Child*, McGraw-Hill, New York, 1980. Hofmann's book can also be found on numerous web sites on the Internet.

Dr. Henry Beecher, Select Committee Report, U.S. Congress, August 3, 1977.

CIA, Office of Scientific Intelligence, *Study on the Strategic Medical Significance of LSD-25*, 30 August 1955, p. 27; and draft copy of same report, August 12, 1955, author's files.

Fuller, John G., *The Interrupted Journey*, Dell Books, New York, 1987. On the same subject, Fuller also wrote: *Incident at Exeter*, Berkley Medallion, 1968.

Healy, David, *The Creation of Psychopharmacology*, Harvard University Press, Cambridge, Massachusetts, 2002.

Thuillier, Jean, *Ten Years That Changed the Face of Mental Illness*, English edition approved by David Healy, Martin Dunitz, Ltd., 1981, 1999.

"An OSI Study on the Strategic Medical Significance of Lysergic Acid Diethylamide (LSD-25)," CIA, OSI, 30 August 1955, Limited Release, Copy 14, author's files. Oddly, the OSI report mentions Dr. Albert Hofmann only once briefly. Before his recent death, and for many decades, Hofmann, as readers may be aware, was often overly prone to discuss LSD. By the mid-1980s, he had become a sort of patron saint of LSD, yet uncharacteristically he never publicly spoke of the incident at Pont-St.-Esprit or of his involvement in the outbreak there.

The Church Committee report on the suicide read: "In one long memorandum on current research with LSD which was supplied to TSD, Henry Beecher described the dangers involved with such research in a prophetic manner. 'The second reason to doubt Professor Rothlin came when I raised the question as to any accidents which had arisen from the use of LSD-25. He said in a very positive way, 'none.' As it turned out this answer could be called overly positive, for later on in the evening when I was discussing the matter with Dr. W. A. Stohl, Jr., a psychiatrist in Bleulera's Clinic in Zurich where I had gone at Rothlin's insistence, Stohl when asked the same question, replied, 'yes' and added spontaneously 'there is a case Professor Rothlin knows about. In Geneva a woman physician who had been subject to depression to some extent took LSD-25 in an experiment and became severely and suddenly depressed and committed suicide three weeks later. While the connection is not definite, common knowledge of this could hardly have allowed the positive statement Rothlin permitted himself. This case is a warning to us to avoid engaging subjects who are depressed, or who have been subject to depression.'"

"Report on Ego-Depressants" by Dr. Henry K. Beecher, Consultant to CIA, *Information From Europe Related To The Ego-Depressants, 6 August to 29 August 1952*, September 4, 1952. Dr. Beecher wrote over one-hundred reports to the CIA and more to the Army. He categorized his CIA reports as "Summation Report" or "Daily Report." In summer 1952 alone, he sent over twenty reports to the Agency; Letter concerning Dachau concentration camp to Dr. Beecher from Dr. Arthur R. Turner, Chief, Medical Intelligence branch, War Department, Washington, D.C., February 7, 1947; letter to Dr. Beecher from Maj. Arthur R. Lund,

Security Officer, War Department, May 20, 1952; letter concerning report on the Mauthausen concentration camp to Dr. Beecher from Dr. Arthur R. Turner, March 24, 1947; letter from Dr. Beecher regarding Bedford "pharmacological lobotomies" to Dr. Stanley Cobb, March 15, 1952. A recently produced German documentary makes the claim that Dr. Beecher was also involved in the experiment that killed tennis pro Harold Blauer and that he even ordered the experiment, but this author has seen no evidence whatsoever revealing that Beecher had any involvement in Blauer's death or in any of the experiments conducted at the NYSPI; Heather Munro Prescott, "Using the Student Body: College and University Students as Research Subjects in the United States during the Twentieth Century," Journal of the History of Medicine, Vol. 57, January 2002, Oxford University, p.3-38; Dr. Beecher changed his name when he was in his early twenties. He had been born Harry Unangst in Kansas but changed it to Henry Beecher to capitalize on his family's relation to author Harriet Beecher Stowe.

Haiti experiments: Other former CIA consultants told the author that some of the secret test programs and pharmaceutical house experiments run in Haiti were "facilitated by the close relationship between [U.S. Congressman Daniel J.] Flood and Haitian president for Life Jean-Claude Duvalier." Said one source: "Flood promised and delivered a lot of loot, foreign aide, to Duvalier. There was a lot of tit-for-tat and stink in those deals. I'm sure 'Papa Doc' green lighted anything the American companies wanted down there. It was like one open pit cesspool where anything went as long as you had the funds and lack of compassion to do it."

Partial draft of Edgewood Arsenal "Oral History Project" interview with Dr. L. Wilson Greene, Maryland, Constance Newman, 1954-55, Edgewood Arsenal Archives/Library, Maryland; author interviews with Norman Covert, Fort Detrick historian and public relations official, Frederick, Maryland, 2000-2001.

Whitmer, Peter O., with Van Wyngarden, Bruce, *Aquarius Revisited*, Citadel Press Books, New York, 1991.

Greenfield, Robert, *Timothy Leary, A Biography*, A James H. Solberman Book, Harcourt, Inc., New York, 2006.

Lixfeld, Hannjost, *Folklore & Fascism, The Reich Institute for German Volkskunde,* Indiana University press, Bloomington & Indianapolis, 1994.

Hale, Christopher, *Himmler's Crusade: The Nazi Expedition to Find the Origins of the Aryan Race*, John Wiley & Sons, Inc., New Jersey, 2003.

Pringle, Heather, *The Master Plan: Himmler's Scholars and the Holocaust*, Hyperion, New York, 2006; author's interview with Dr. Michael Kater, York College, Canada, 1999.

Bernadac, Christian, *Devil's Doctors: Medical Experiments on Human Subjects in the Concentration Camps*, Ferni Publishing House, Geneva, 1978

Notes on Book Two, Chapter 10:
"An OSI Study on the Strategic Medical Significance of Lysergic Acid Diethylamide (LSD-25)," 30 August 1955, CIA, Office of Scientific Intelligence, author's files.

Kornfeld, Fornefeld, Kline, Mann, Morrison, Jones, and R.B. Woodward, "The Total Synthesis of Lysergic Acid," Journal of the American Chemical Society, Volume 78, p. 3087-3114, 1956.

Notes on Book Two, Chapter 11:
Transcripts and decisions of United States District Court, Northern District of California, and United States Court of Appeals for the Ninth Circuit, *Wayne A. Ritchie v. United States of America and DEA and CIA*, No. C00-03940 MHP.

Besides its safe house at 225 Chestnut Street, San Francisco, the CIA operated at least two additional safe houses in the Bay area, both overseen by White with Feldman assisting. One was located in the city's Tenderloin district; the other was situated in Marin County at 261 Green Street.

Ketchum, James S., Dr., *Chemical Warfare: Secrets Almost Forgotten*, Chembooks, 2006; interview of Dr. James Ketchum by R.U. Sirius, Ten Zen Monkeys web site, January 13, 2007.

Notes: Book Three, Chapter 1:
Operation Bloodstone: see the excellent book, *Blowback* by Christopher Simpson, Collier/Macmillian, 1988.

Report of Inspection of MKULTRA/TSD, Inspector General John S. Earman, 14 August 1963.

MKULTRA Program, Meeting Report, 29 November 1963, J.S. Earman, CIA IG.

Worth noting is another section of Earman's MKULTRA report, which reads: "As of 1960 no effective pill, truth serum, aphrodisiac, or recruitment pill was known to exist. MKDELTA was described as inherently a high-risk, low-yield field of operations. Three years later the situation remains substantially unchanged, with the exception that real progress has been made in the use of drugs in support of interrogation. Ironically, however, the progress here has occurred in the development of a total psychological theory of interrogation, in which the use of drugs has been relegated to a support role. Today, only two of the MKDELTA materials— P-1 [LSD], which lowers psychological defenses and induces psychotic conditions, and A-2 [Meretran], a Benzedrine-like stimulant which induces euphoria and insomnia— are now being used with great caution but with success. This total interrogation theory has been applied in five operations involving 30 individuals during the past three years. The results have been significant and it would now appear that TSD has achieved a potent, if exacting and time-consuming, approach to effective interrogation of hostile subjects. [New section.] The problem of testing in realistic pilot operations: This subject has been discussed above... It should be noted that testing on operational targets overseas is considered by some operations officers to be quite impracticable. Unilateral operations are imperative which substantially complicates the delivery problem. The possibilities of unexpected or critical reactions in test subjects and of ensuing compromise of the activity make most senior command personnel unwilling to take the risks involved."

Helms' memorandum to McCone and Carter recommending that testing begin again clearly states that experiments had ceased during the time DCI McCone was considering a decision on MKULTRA's unwitting experiments in FBN safe houses, but there is evidence in George White's files that experiments involving CIA personnel continued through this so-called "stand down" phase.

TSS Memorandum for the Record, MKULTRA Safe House, 15 July 1954.

Notes on Book Three, Chapter 2:

George Hunter White: Diaries, date books, letters, and numerous documents concerning White held in the archives of the Perham Foundation, Sunnyvale, California. Interviews with White's wife, Albertine, 1998; Federal Bureau of Narcotics files, Record Group 170, National Archives, Washington, D.C.; Harry Anslinger Papers, Pennsylvania State University. Much of the chapter on George Hunter White is drawn from the forthcoming book by this author: *Operation Midnight Climax: The Life and Times of George Hunter White, Federal Narcotics Agent and CIA Operative Extraordinaire.*

William Gibbs McAdoo: McAdoo was also a New York City Police Commissioner in the early 1900s, and ran twice, unsuccessfully, for the Democratic nomination for U.S. President, in 1920 and 1924.

Dr. Henry Murray: In 1943, Murray, who, according to at least one biography, engaged in some less-then-common sexual practices, authored an OSS report that maintained Adolph Hitler had participated in homosexual activity because of his "feminine characteristics" and because many members of his political party were homosexuals. In the 1950s, Murray conducted experiments at Harvard University that involved 'Unabomber' Ted Kaczynski as a subject. Coincidentally, this author would learn in 2007 that a Vermont-based friend, Tim Murphy, is the "unknown" young boy in the widely published photo of youngster Ted and his brother.

Moon, Tom, *This Grim and Savage Game: The OSS and U.S. Covert Operations in World War II*, Da Capo Press, Cambridge, Massachusetts, 2000.

Illegal drugs from established European pharmaceutical factories: Block, Alan A., *Space, Time & Organized Crime*, Second Edition, Transaction Publishers, New Jersey, 19994.

In 1965, the CIA created the Amazon Natural Drug Company (ANDCO) with Garland Williams and J.C. King at the controls. King, the CIA's former Western Hemisphere chief, was fond of life south of the border, having spent considerable time in Argentina and Guatemala. ANDCO was an offshoot of former Nazi scientist Dr. Friedrich Hoffman's exotic drug collection project in South and Latin America, a project first undertaken in 1951 for Camp Detrick's SO Division.

Clark, Donald, *Billie Holiday: Wishing on the Moon*, Da Capo Press, Cambridge, Massachusetts, 2000.

Noble, John Wesley and Bernard Averbuch, *Never Plead Guilty*, Bantam Books, New York, 1958 edition.

Jack Ruby/Chicago: article in Mob Magazine, "The Lost Boy," by John William Tuohy, April 3, 2001; George White's diary and date book entries contain at least three references to Ruby.

Valentine, Douglas, *The Strength of the Wolf: The Secret History of America's War on Drugs*, Verso Books, London, 2004.

White and leather hobby: Douglas Valentine writes in his 2004 book, *The Strength of the Wolf*, an excellent history of the Federal Bureau of Narcotics, that White departed New York in late 1954 for his new assignment in San Francisco, "the new MKULTRA Leather Project." Valentine also writes in the same book that "White's first MKULTRA briefing at the Bedford [Street] pad [safe house] occurred on 23 June 1953 and included James Angleton, Dr. James Hamilton, and Gregory Bateson, a former OSS officer with radical ideas about political and psychological warfare." Apart from the fact that White was never aware of the MKULTRA cryptogram, and that he had his own label for his New York-based subproject, "Operation Stormy," White never briefed Angleton, Hamilton, or Bateson on his New York subproject. White's diary and date book for June 23, 1953 reveals that he attended the "signing of a protocol" at the UN that day, worked on a "reply to a Rufus King article in the Yale Law Review, and "met Ina Telberg, a UN interpreter" and "a friend of Gregory Bateson and Jim Hamilton." There are no meetings with Angleton or Bateson noted in White's 1953 date book. This would not be worth pointing out or correcting, except that Valentine goes on to draw Bateson, a highly respected anthropologist and philosopher, into a ludicrous scheme to assist White and the CIA in using "LSD and narcotics" to "reconstruct American society." Perhaps Valentine confused Bateson with Timothy Leary, but neither Bateson nor the CIA had any intention of employing LSD to "reconstruct" anything. To actually believe that the CIA would entrust a mid-level narcotics agent to oversee the alteration of American society is far-fetched. To set the record straight, Bateson did meet several times with White, whom he knew from his OSS days, in the years immediately following World War II. The two met for dinner in New York a couple of times a few years before White met Sidney Gottlieb. It is a matter of record that Bateson ingested LSD on at least two occasions. First, in 1956, under the guidance of Dr. Harold Abramson, and second, in 1958, under the guidance of Dr. Joe K. Adams at the Palo Alto Mental Research Institute in California. Dr. Adams, a psychologist, also administered LSD to poet Allen Ginsburg, and took LSD himself several times, suffering two psychotic episodes and once having to be confined in a mental ward. This author has seen no evidence that Gregory Bateson was closely aligned with MKULTRA, other than working under a CIA grant in California and knowing that the CIA was funding additional LSD research nationwide, a fact that nearly every LSD researcher in the United States knew in the mid-to-late 1950s. In his book, Valentine states that Angleton attended the fictional meeting because "he was curious to know" how LSD could be used to uncover moles within the CIA. This claim is absurd in light of the fact that Angleton had been very privy to Projects BLUEBIRD, ARTICHOKE and MKULTRA from their inceptions. He did not need White to show him anything. He was well acquainted with the powers of LSD and other drugs. He, like Bateson, knew White from his OSS days, and he had met with White several times after the war on a social basis, and had once ingested LSD with White, in 1952.

Other excellent books helpful in this chapter: McWilliams, John, *The Protectors*, Associated University Presses, Inc., New Jersey, 1990; Marshall, John, Drug Wars, Cohan & Cohen Publishers, Forestville, California, 1991; Block, Alan A., *Perspectives on Organizing Crime*, Kluwer Academic Publishers, The Netherlands, 1991; *The Best of BIZARRE*, A John Willie Magazine 1946-1956, Glittering Images, Italy, 1989, 1994; Willie, John, *The Adventures of Sweet Gwendoline*, Belier Press, Inc., new York, 1974.

In 1965, the CIA created the Amazon Natural Drug Company (ANDCO) with Garland Williams and J.C. King at the controls. King, the CIA's former Western Hemisphere chief, was fond of life south of the border, having spent considerable time in Argentina and Guatemala. ANDCO was an offshoot of former Nazi scientist Dr. Friedrich Hoffman's exotic drug collection project in South and Latin America, a project first undertaken in 1951 for Camp Detrick's SO Division.

Notes on Book Three, Chapter 3:
James Phelan quote: from his article "Too Hot to Handle," *True, The Man's Magazine,* March 1956, p.14; articles in newspaper the *Kentucky Standard*, Bardstown, Nelson County, Kentucky, section 1, page 1, November 20, 1952, and section 2, page 1, October 8, 1953 courtesy of Kathleen R. McDonald.

Information on Jean-Pierre Lafitte came primarily from interviews with his daughter and other family members; from the interviews of others with Henri Delaconte, a former associate of Lafitte's; Dr. Amalie Phelan and Janet Phelan, James Phelan's wife and daughter; Dr. Sidney Gottlieb; Isabelle Voigener; and with several retired CIA and FBI officials who asked to be unnamed. Dr. Amalie Phelan, now deceased, was instrumental in helping the author locate Lafitte's last place of residence and members of his family. Information on Lafitte's 1969 New Orleans arrest is from "The Gourmet Pirate," *TIME* magazine, December 19, 1969. Specifics on Lafitte's work for the government, Cuba, and other matters, came from his notes for an unpublished book, tentatively titled, *The Many Lives of Pierre Lafitte*, believed to have been partially edited by George White, Ed Reid, and James Phelan. Other published sources, include: Busch, Francis X., *Casebook of the Curious and True*, Charter Books, NY, 1957; McLeave, Hugh, *Rogues in the Gallery*, David R. Godine, Publishers, Boston, 1981; and Phelan, James, *Scandals, Scamps and Scoundrels, The Casebook of an Investigative Reporter*, Random House, NY, 1982; and Denton, Sally and Morris, Roger, *The Money and the Power: The*

Making of Las Vegas and Its Hold on America 1947-2000, Alfred A. Knopf, NY, 2001, an important and excellent book.

George White on Lafitte: White letter to Garland Williams, July 6, 1972.

Joseph Orsini: Pierre Lafitte's book notes on Orsini and the "Joe Casabianca case" (also referred to as the "Joe Casablanca case"); 206 F.2d 86, *United States v. Sansone*, No. 279, Docket 22725, United States Court of Appeals, Second Circuit, Argued June 3, 1953;article in True, the Man's Magazine, June 1957, p. 19-20, 26-33, *Tight Trap for a Top Dealer*, by Pierre Lafitte as told to James Phelan; Wighton, Charles, *Dope International*, Frederick Muller Limited, London, 1960; Kruger, Henrik, *The Great Heroin Coup*, South End Press, Boston, 1980; Galante, Pierre and Sapin, Louis, *The Marseilles Mafia*, W. H. Allen, London, 1979; Goodman, Derick, *Villainy Unlimited*, Elek Books, London, 1957; Staff and Editors of Newsday, *The Heroin Trail*, Holt, Rinehart and Winston, NY, 1973, 1974; Jonnes, Jill, *Hep-Cats, Narcs, and Pipe Dreams, A History of America's Romance with Illegal Drugs*, Johns Hopkins University Press, Baltimore, Maryland, 1999; Federal Bureau of Narcotics files, 1953-1956; Drug Enforcement Agency, Confidential Pilot Project File draft documents 1953-1964, courtesy of John Kelly and Jill Jonnes.

Joe Valachi: E-mail messages to the author from Dr. Alan Block, June 6, 1999; Peterson, Virgil W., *The Mob: 200 Years of Organized Crime in New York*, Green Hill Publishers, Inc., Illinois, 1983, p.379-386; Maas, Peter, *The Valachi Papers*, Bantam Books, New York, 1969.

Henri Déricourt and Air Opium: Marshall, Robert, *All the King's Men*, William Collins Sons & Co. Ltd., Great Britain, 1988, p. 275-276.

Over the past several decades rumors have persisted that White had first encountered Lafitte earlier, in New Orleans, during the early war years when White was there as part of the OSS truth drug experiments. White, indeed, was in that city for experiments, accompanied by OSS officer and future U.S. Supreme Court Justice Arthur Goldberg, but the reports concerning their encounter with Lafitte remain unconfirmed. Source: White's date books for 1941-1942, Perham Foundation, Sunnyvale, California.

Las Vegas and the Clippinger's: the taped conversations between Roxie Clippinger and Lafitte and Sheriff Jones and Lafitte were published in part in Reid, Ed and Demaris, Ovid, *The Green Felt Jungle*, Pocket Books, New York, 1963; the FBI raided and closed Roxie's shortly after Lafitte left town. The Clippinger's were indicted and imprisoned on charges of violation of the federal Mann Act, which concerns transporting women across state lines for immoral purposes.

Howard Hughes: Denton and Morris, p. 289; see also Bartlett, Donald L. and Steele, James B., *Howard Hughes: His Life and Madness*, W.W. Norton & Company, Inc., NY, 1979.

James Phelan and FBI and CIA: DiEugenio, James and Pease, Lisa, editors, *The Assassinations*, Feral House, California, 2003, p. 188-189, 313-318.

Malachi Harney on Lafitte: Harney, Malachi L. and Cross, John C., *The Informer in Law Enforcement*, Charles C. Thomas Publishers, Springfield, Illinois, 1960, p. 47-48. Harney's information on Lafitte appears to have come mainly from his dealings with Lafitte in 1953 and from accounts provided by George White, who was Harney's close friend.

Sen. Hennings (Democrat-Missouri): citation for Nichols' response: FBI file re: Hennings request to Bureau: Lafitte file section number 66-18621-269.

Lafitte and Cuba: Cirules, Enrique, *The Mafia in Havana*, Ocean Press, New York, 2004, p.111-118; Eisenberg, Dennis, Dan, Uri, and Landau, Eli, *Meyer Lansky, Mogul of the Mob*, Paddington Press, United States, 1979.

U.S. Treasury on Battisti: Report of W.W. Johnston, U.S. Treasury Department Representative in Charge, Havana, Cuba, to the Commissioner of Customs, Division of Investigations, March 27, 1958.

Cuba and Kirkpatrick: Kirkpatrick, Lyman B., *The Real CIA*, Macmillan Company, NY, 1968, p.156 & 169; Kirkpatrick quote: Thomas, Evan, *The Very Best Men*, Touchstone Books, NY, 1995, p. 181. Long before Castro was any threat, or even known, to the intelligence community, or America, the CIA viewed Cuba as a strategic and important country for a variety of reasons, not the least of which were its convenient use as a one-stop shop money laundering site, a covert operations launching pad, and an attractive rest-and-relaxation spot.

Lansky and French connection: Denton and Morris, p. 103-104; Lansky and J.C. King: Lafitte's handwritten notations contain only the last names, "Lansky" and "J.C. King" and a Washington, D.C. telephone number.

Martino/Lafitte/White: George Hunter White Papers, Perham Electronics Foundation, Sunnyvale, California. The author, courtesy of foundation manager Ms. Rachael Wager, spent three days reviewing and studying

White's papers in 1999.The papers have subsequently been reorganized and transferred to Stanford University, California.

CIA Memorandum for the Record, Subject: Meltzer, Harold, January 19, 1961.

Notes on Book Three, Chapter 4:

Borsalino: the 1970 film, based on the lives of Spirito and Carbone, was drawn from a novel by Eugene Saccomano. The working title of the film had been *Carbone and Spirito*, but was changed to *Borsalino*, the name of a hat favored by gangsters in the 1940s and 1950s, after the film's producers became concerned about reprisals from family and criminal descendants of the two men. In the film, Belmondo, named Francois Capella, plays Spirito; Delon, named Roch Siffredi, plays Carbone. The movie was filmed on the streets of Marseilles, and upon release was seen by over five million filmgoers. A 1974 sequel, *Borsalino & Co.,* did not do as well.

Francois Spirito: information on Spirito's life and exploits comes from many sources, including Pierre Lafitte's case notes; Federal Bureau of Narcotics files; DEA Pilot Projects II & III files; interviews in 2002 and 2004 with former French intelligence operative Roger Charbonneau; and 2000 Spirito/Orsini/Martin Briefing Memorandum to New York Assistant District Attorney Steve Saracco; and Illicit Narcotics Traffic: Hearings Before the Subcommittee on Improvements in the Federal Criminal Code of the Committee on the Judiciary, United States Senate, Eighty-fourth Congress, First Session By United States, United States Congress. Published by U.S. Govt. Printing Office, 1955.

McCoy, Alfred W., *The Politics of Heroin: CIA Complicity in the Global Drug Trade,* Lawrence Hill Books, New York, 1991.

Morain on white slavery and drugs: Morain, Alfred, *The Underworld of Paris,* Blue Ribbon Books, New York, 1931, fourth edition, p. 255-262.

"Top-hat overlord": Oursler, Will and Smith, Laurence Dwight, *Narcotics: America's Peril*, Doubleday & Company, New York, 1952, p. 113-129.

Manouche: Peyrefitte, Roger, *Manouche,* Grove Press, New York, 1974.

Kid Francis: His chaotic fight with Al Brown, boxing's first Hispanic world champion, took place on July 10, 1932 in Marseilles. His actual name was Francesco Buonagurio, and he was born in Naples, Italy. In 1940, perhaps unknown to Spirito and Carbone, Francesco was arrested by the Gestapo and sent to Auschwitz concentration camp. There he was forced to box in the many shows put on by Nazi officers, who bet on the fighters. His opponents were Jews and Gypsies. Francesco won over 300 straight knockout fights in the camp. It is said that he would tell many of his weaker opponents he to fake their knockouts so he could avoid actually injuring them. The reward for winning a fight was continued life; the penalty for losing was death by execution. Sometime in 1943 Francesco was murdered by his Nazi guards. The Kid was five feet four inches tall and weighed 130 pounds. He was 35 years old when he died.]

Blacklisted Stories, Secret Histories from Chicago to 1984, Youth International Party News Service, Berkeley, California, 1970-1982.

OSS European Crime Investigation files, Record Group 226, National Archives, Washington, D.C.

"Spirito and Carbone, Fathers of Modern Prostitution," undated *Tableau* magazine article found in George Hunter White's Perham Foundation files.

Block on Eliopoulos: *Space, Time, & Organized Crime*, second edition, Transaction Publishers, New Brunswick, N.J., 1994, p. 110-111.

Block on drug stocks diverted to illegal markets: *Space, Time, & Organized Crime*, p. 99-102.

Goodman, Derrick, *Villainy Unlimited,* Elek Books, London, 1957, p. 75, 130, 118-143.

Ryan, Donna F., *The Holocaust & the Jews of Marseille: The Enforcement of Anti-Semitic Policies in Vichy France*, University of Illinois Press, 1996, p. 18-20.

Sarazin, James, *Dossier M: Comme Milieu*, Alain Moreau, Paris, 1977; Pierre LaFontain interview in 1969 with Francois Spirito Translation courtesy of Kathleen R. McDonald.

McCoy on Carbone/Spirito collaboration with Gestapo: p. 51.

Anslinger to Sicot: letters from Harry Anslinger, U.S. Commission on Narcotics to Monsieur M. Sicot, Security General, International Criminal Police Commission, Paris, France, August 28, 1951 and October 3, 1951, author's files.

Article by Carlo Tresca in the *World* newspaper, "Atlanta Prison Thriving Market for Drug Traffic," April 14, 1929, p. 1.

MKULTRA Subprojects 9, 28, and 47: Besides Spirito it is also known that notorious gangster James J. "Whitey" Bulger took part in the Atlanta CIA experiments. Some writers have claimed that murderer Charles Manson was a victim in later CIA experiments in a California prison, but this has never been proven, and Manson has never mentioned it in any of his many rants.

Notes on Book Three, Chapter 5:

CIA Reports and Memoranda on 1973 Destruction of MKULTRA and MKNAOMI Files; FBI File, including AIRTEL messages, on "Sidney Gottlieb and Destruction of Government Records," August-September 1975. Transcript of Dr. Sidney Gottlieb's Church Committee statement and testimony, held in closed-secret session, October, 1975, author's files; deposition of Richard McGarrah Helms, Civil Action No. D.D.C. 80-3163, Washington, D.C., March 14, 1983.

Notes on Book Four, Chapter 1:

Norman Dorsen and Stephen Gillers, ed., *None of Your Business: Government Secrecy in America*, Viking Press, New York, 1974.

Thomas, Evan, *The Very Best Men*, Touchstone, Simon and Schuster, Inc., New York, 1996.

Johnson, Loch K., *A Season of Inquiry: Congress and Intelligence*, The Dorsey press, Chicago, Ill., 1988.

Wise, David and Ross, Thomas, B., *The Invisible Government*, Random House, New York, 1964.

Colby, William and Forbath, Peter, *Honorable Men: My Life in the CIA*, Simon and Schuster, New York, 1978.

Rockefeller Commission, CIA, and U.S. Department of Justice files and letters sent to the Commission: files of the United States President's Commission on CIA Activities within the United States, Files: [1947-1974]; 1975, Gerald R. Ford Library, Ann Arbor, Michigan.

Notes on Book Four, Chapter 2:

Lifton, Robert Jay and Olson, Eric W., *Living and Dying*, Praeger Publishers, Inc., New York, 1974; Praeger as a CIA conduit: see Saunders, Frances Stonor, *The Cultural Cold War*, New Press, New York, 2001.

"FBI Is Accused of Aiding A Crime" by Donald Janson, *New York Times,* March 16, 1972, p1 and p. 42.

The Philadelphia Office of the NECLC, Report 1971-1978, p.5; Donner, Frank J., *The Age of Surveillance*, Alfred A. Knopf, Inc., New York, 1980; author's interviews and correspondence with David Kairys, 2001-2003.

Roach v. Klingman, Civil Action No. 73-2428, April 30, 1976; Rudovsky, David, *The Rights of Prisoners*, Avon Books, New York, 1977; also see Hornblum, Allen M., *Acres of Skin: Human Experiments at Holmesburg Prison*, Routledge, New York, 1998. Hornblum's book is an excellent account of those experiments conducted at Holmesburg Prison from the early 1950s through the mid-1970s.

Fuller, John, *The Day of St. Anthony's Fire*, The Macmillian Company, New York, 1968.

Wolfram, Neil S., *Psychiatric Research and the Politics of Law*, Exposition Press, New York, 1981.

Olson Family Letter to William E. Colby, Director CIA, dated July 17, 1975, delivered by hand, author's files.

The White House, Memorandum for the President from Roderick Hills, July 16, 1975, Gerald R. Ford Presidential Library, Ann Arbor, Michigan.

The White House, Memorandum for Donald Rumsfeld from Richard Cheney, Subject: Frank Olson, Gerald R. Ford Presidential Library, Ann Arbor, Michigan.

Notes on Book Four, Chapters 3 and 4

Author's interviews with David Kairys, 2002; Letter from David Kairys to Olson family, July 29, 1975; author's interviews with David Kairys, October, 2002 and April-July, 2003; Letter to William Colby, Director CIA from Kairys and Rudovsky, 29 July 1975, author's files; Kairys' personal notes, August 1975; David Kairys, "Some Recollections of Meeting With CIA Director Colby on July 24, 1975," unpublished notes, author's files; and letter to David Kairys from Mitchell Rogovin, August 29, 1975, author's files; letter from David Kairys and David Rudovsky to Mitchell Rogovin, Special Counsel to the Director of the CIA, August 8, 1975, author's files.

Notes on Book Four, Chapter 5:

Memorandum to the CIA Legislative Counsel from Donald F. Chamberlain, CIA Inspector General, Subject: The Death of Harold Blauer, August 13, 1975; Blauer Family Papers, compliments of Belinda Bluer; interview with Belinda Blauer, June 1998; article in *Rolling Stone* magazine, *The Secret Army Drug Experiment: What Did Warren Burger Know?* By Howard Kohn and Martin Porter, April 21, 1977; Memorandum from H.P. Albarelli, Jr. to Steve Saracco, ADA-NYC, Subject: Frank Olson Case Information, 21 December 1998; Pentagon Press Release on Drug Experiments, August 12, 1975.

Notes on Book 4, Chapter 6:

"Justice Department Treatment of Criminal Cases Involving CIA Personnel and Claims of National Security," Hearings Before A Subcommittee of the Committee On Government Operations, House of Representatives, Ninety-Fourth Congress, First Session, July 22, 23, 29, 31, and August 1, 1975.

Notes on Book Four, Chapter 8:

Interview with Agnes Tanner, 1978, on file at King's College, London, England; Author's copy compliments of John F. Kelly; and private letters of Agnes Tanner.

James Christensen: Information provided by attorney David Kairys, 2001-2002.

Statements of Mrs. Dorothy Chaffin and William Chaffin before a Joint Session of the Senate Subcommittee on Health and the Senate Subcommittee on Administrative Practice and Procedures, September 10, 1975.

Notes on Book Four, Chapter Nine:

Harold Brown as "suspicious pragmatist": *TIME* magazine, Monday, January 3, 1977.

Memorandum for the Secretary of Defense from Deanne P. Siemer, General Counsel of the Department of Defense, Subject: "Experimentation Programs Conducted by the Department of Defense That Had CIA Sponsorship or Participation and that Involved the Administration to Human Subjects of Drugs Intended for Mind-Control or Behavioral Modification," September 20, 1977.

The full title of Marks' book is: *The Search for the Manchurian Candidate: The CIA and Mind Control, The Story of the Agency's Efforts to Control Human Behavior*. In addition to the John Marks' book, two other books appeared at roughly the same time. These were the excellent *The Mind Manipulators* by Alan Scheflin and Edward M. Opton, and Walter Bowart's difficult to find and provocative *Operation Mind Control*. The author strongly recommends all of these books to anyone interested in knowing more about the subject of the CIA's mind control programs.

Sidney Gottlieb's name in documents: Gottlieb told this author he was "greatly disappointed" that the CIA had released his name in such a manner without any advance notice or warning. "I was as surprised as anyone would be," he said. He explained, "Perhaps I made an enemy somewhere along the way, or maybe it was convenient to put my name out there in order to create another target besides CIA." Others, including former CIA officials, have suggested more devious reasons on the part of the CIA, suggesting that by releasing Gottlieb's name, attention would be drawn away from the redacted names of many others, and allow people to demonize Gottlieb more than the Agency itself. One former Agency official said, "CIA spends a tremendous amount of money and time on studying the public's reactions and thinking about various media stories. It would be an understatement to say that the Agency is very adept at exploiting and manipulating the press and its stories and in knowing and understanding the various ways in which people will react to media generated stories, or to stories surreptitiously fed to the media by Agency sources. I believe what happened to Sid Gottlieb is but one very good example of this." Another official, speaking on conditions of anonymity, told the author that the CIA had for several decades conducted a program called Project Apate. The program is aimed at devising ways to better manipulate the American and foreign media. The official explained, "The Agency, over the past several decades, has done a large amount of work at creating, fostering, and adding to a lot of selected conspiracy theories with the object of what it terms 'off-balancing' the public's mind set toward these theories.... Put succinctly, it's in the Agency's best interest to have as many so-called kooks as possible out there raising dust and appearing as deranged or semi-sane as possible. That so many intelligent and sincere theorists have been pigeonholed as 'fruit loops' is an intended byproduct of Apate. The more the general public discounts serious speculation and fact finding on certain matters the better off the intelligence community is and will remain."

"CIA Drug Tests Conducted in '71 at Holmesburg," article by Aaron Epstein, *Philadelphia Inquirer*, March 4, 1979.

"Dioxin Tests Conducted in 60's on 70 Inmates, Now Unknown," article by William Robbins, *New York Times*, July 17, 1983, p. A16.

Rules Urged For Research at Riverview, Philadelphia Bulletin, December 9, 1969.

For a comprehensive and excellent study of the Holmesburg Prison experiments see the excellent book: *Acres of Skin* by Allen Hornblum, Routledge, New York, 1998.

Report on Fort Detrick Meeting, Chaired by Dr. Riley D. Housewright, Fort Detrick Scientific Research Director, summer 1958. Housewright opened the meeting by informing attendees that the gathering was a continuation of Fort Detrick's commitment to "give maximum support to BWL (Biological Warfare Laboratories) program of follow-up investigation on 'N' (Army codename for weapons grade anthrax) resulting from the New Hampshire outbreak of anthrax."

The section on the Arms Mill anthrax outbreak drew heavily from the author's October 7, 2002 article, *Did the Army Cause Anthrax Outbreak in Mill?* It can be found on the World Net Daily web site.

Hooper, Edward, *The River: A Journey to the Source of HIV and AIDS*, Little Brown and Company, New York, 1999.

Former Army as well as Fort Detrick researchers have reported to the author that the Arms Mill was not the only textile operation involved in anthrax experiments conducted by Fort Detrick in the 1950s. They say that "at least four other mills" were involved in tests. A 1960 medical paper authored by Dr. Philip Brachman and Dr. Stanley Plotkin verifies this. The paper, entitled, "Field Evaluations of a Human Anthrax Vaccine," states that "epidemiological studies" were conducted in "four mills located in the northeastern United States" where "Bacillus anthracis contaminated raw materials were handled and clinical infections occurred." The paper identifies the mills only as code letters" "A, M, P, and S." The Army refused to identify any of these test sites, but other sources said that two of the mills were "in the Philadelphia area" and that another was "the Arel Textile Mill located near Charlotte, North Carolina." In 1995, documents related to the Arms Mill outbreak were turned over, without explanation, to the National Committee on Human Radiation Experimentation in response to the committee's request to the Department of Defense for records related "to human experimentation" of any type conducted by the Army. The National Committee was created in January 1994 by President Bill Clinton to "investigate reports of possibly unethical experiments funded by the U.S. government decades ago." The Committee's Final Report makes no mention of the Arms Mill incident or any of the Army's anthrax tests. Following the 9/11 attacks nearly all of the declassified records assembled by the Committee were once again classified and the public was denied access to them. FOI requests for some of these documents were denied on the grounds of "national security."

In April 2004, a copy of the paper *On the Trail of the Goat Hair Mills That Participated in Anthrax Vaccine Evaluations, 1955-1959* was sent to the author. Written by Walter R. Schumm, Robert P. Brenneman, and Bracha Arieli, Kansas State University, the paper identifies all the mills used by the Army as: Arms Mill, Manchester, N.H.; the A.Y. Michie Mill of Philadelphia; the Puritan Looms Mill or the Philip Sheerr Mill of Philadelphia; and the Sackville Mill of Wallingford, Pennsylvania. The paper sates: "The location of these mills is of interest because they not only were associated with anthrax infection with respect to their employees but nearby residents, including children, also became victims of anthrax infection."

Also see: LSD Follow-up Study, U.S. Army Health Services Command (HSC), Walter Reed Army Medical Center, Washington, D.C., 1980; BZ, Quinuclidinyl benzilate, or what the Army sometimes called EA-2277: In 2001, months before the 9/11 attacks on the World Trade Center and Pentagon, this author found that over 500 barrels of BZ were still stored outside in Maryland. A simple Internet search turned this information up. There were even photographs of the piled barrels, which were surrounded by an 8-foot chain-link fence. Following the 9/11 attacks, the government web site that contained this information and photographs was removed from the web. There are many detailed reports that the U.S. Army used BZ against the Viet Cong in the 1970s. The Army has refused to confirm these reports. The popular 1990 film *Jacob's Ladder* starring Tim Robbins vividly portrays the effects of BZ on humans: DAIG-IN 21-75, Report on the Use of Volunteers in Chemical Agent Research, The Inspector General, Department of Army, 10 March 1978; Chief of Staff Memorandum for AC-723 Chemical Corps Advisory Council, Medical and Related Problems Committee Meeting, 20-21 March 1953; Army Chemical Corps Memorandum Number 11, Military Volunteers, 25 January 1955; AC 727-729 Chemical Corps Advisory Council Meeting, 23-25 April 1953; 13 May 1953.

Notes on Book Four, Chapter 11
Files of the CIA's Victims Task Force, 1978-1979 received from the CIA Public Information office through a Freedom of Information request; deposition of Frank Hubert Laubinger, *Mrs. David Orlikow, et al. v. United States of America and CIA*, District Court for the District of Columbia, Case 80-3163, Washington, D.C.,

Wednesday, July 20, 1983, author's files; Billnitzer "suicide": readers interested in learning more about this intriguing episode in George White's story should read: H.P. Albarelli's September 8, 2002 article, "Government-linked 'Suicide' Probed," at the World Net Daily website.

James Thornwell case: see Scheflin, Alan W. and Opton, Edward M. Jr., *The Mind Manipulators*, Paddington press, Ltd., New York and London, 1978; *New York Times* article by Tom Buckley, "TV: A Soldier's Ordeal in 'Thornwell'" January 28, 1981; "James R. Thornwell, 46, Dies; Sued Army Over Test of LSD," AP report, June 29, 1984; author's 1981 interview with James Thornwell, for an article unrelated to this book.

Notes on Book Four, Chapter 12:

Author's interviews with Eric Olson, December 7-8, 2000; Eric recalled that, "Somewhere in the course of the meeting with Gottlieb we asked him if he could help set up a meeting with Lashbrook." Alice Olson recalled that the family met first with Lashbrook and then Gottlieb, and that Lashbrook called Gottlieb to tell him to expect the Olsons. Gottlieb also has stated that the Olsons met with him after their visit to Lashbrook.

Deposition of Robert Vern Lashbrook, U.S. District Court for the District of Columbia, Civil Action No. 80-3163, Wednesday, May 14, 1986, p67-71.

Deposition of Alice Wicks Olson, U.S. District Court for the District of Columbia,

Civil Action No. 80-3163 (JGP), Friday, September 16, 1988. Alice Olson was questioned by Assistant U. S. Attorney, Kathleen A. McGinn, Counsel for Defendant, United States of America. The suit concerned a number of Canadian citizens who had been used as experimental subjects in the work of Dr. Ewen Cameron, McGill University, Montreal, Canada.

At least one author has written that Gottlieb took LSD "200 times," claiming that Gottlieb provided this number in a deposition. This does not appear to be true. The largest number of times Gottlieb said he took LSD in any deposition was "about 40." The author did not directly query Dr. Gottlieb on the subject.

Notes on Book Five, Chapter 2:

Congressman Richard D. McCarthy's work on CBW is often mistakenly credited to U.S. Senator Eugene J. McCarthy. Indeed, Fort Detrick's official history, *Cutting Edge*, wrongly credits the senator from Minnesota with most of Rep. Richard McCarthy's accomplishments.

McCarthy, Richard D., *The Ultimate Folly: War By Pestilence, Asphyxiation, and Defoliation*, Alfred A. Knopf, Publisher, New York, 1969.

Hersh, Seymour M., *Chemical & Biological Warfare: America's Hidden Arsenal*, Anchor Books, Garden City, New York, 1969.

McDermott, Jeanne, *The Killing Winds: The Menace of Biological Warfare*, Arbor House Publishing Company, New York, 1987.

Cookson, John and Nottingham, Judith, *A Survey of Chemical and Biological Warfare*, Monthly Review Press, New York & London, 1969.

The President's [Richard Nixon] Talking Points, Congressional Leadership Meeting, Tuesday, November 25, 1969, Top Secret. NODIS.

National Security Study Memorandum Number 59, to the Secretary of State, Secretary of Defense, & CIA, from National Security Council, Subject: U.S. Policy on CBW and Agents, May 28, 1969.

Secret Memorandum to Secretary of Defense, from Ronald I. Spiers, Department of State: Subject: U.S. Policy on Chemical and Biological Warfare, November 17, 1969.

Confidential White House Memorandum for the Secretary of Defense, from Henry A. Kissinger, Subject: CBW Study, May 9, 1969; and Confidential Memorandum for Assistant to the President for National Security Affairs, from the Secretary of Defense, 30 April 1969.

"The Man Who Knew Too Much," article by Mary A. Fischer, *GQ* magazine, January 2000.

Starrs, James E., *An Information Packet on a Scientific Investigation into the CIA-Influenced Death of Frank R. Olson, Ph.D.* (1910-1953), 1994.

Starrs, James E. and Ramsland, Katherine M., *A Voice For The Dead: A Forensic Investigator's Pursuit of the Truth in the Grave*, Putnam Publishers Group, New York, 2005.

Starrs' Project Team included: Dr. James Frost; Dr. Steven C. Batterman; Dr. John S. Levisky; George C. Stephens, Ph.D.; Yale H. Caplan, Ph.D.; Jeffery C. Kercheval; Mike Calhoun; Jean A. Garner, Esq.; Gerald B.

Richards; James P. Kendrick; Patrick D. Zickler; David Benjamin, Ph.D.; Wendy Harris, Esq.; Kendra Styers, M.S.; Tom Wetzel; and Rick Graf.]

Fall Guy, article by Nina Burleigh, *Regardie's* magazine, September-October, 1994.

E-mail correspondence and information sent to the author from Dr. Bruce Goldberger, October 22-24, 2002.

Numerous interviews in Washington, D.C. and Frederick, Maryland with Eric Wicks Olson, 1998-2000; and email messages to author from Eric Wicks Olson 1999-2001.]

E-mail correspondence and information sent to the author from Dr. Rodger Foltz, October 12, 2002. Dr. Foltz's noted citations were: Rohrich, J., *Forensic Science Int.*, 2000, Vol. 107, 181-90; and Nakahana, Y.; Kikura, R.; Takahashi, K.; Foltz, R.L.; Mieczkowski, T.J., *Anal. Toxicology*, 1996, Vol. 20, pp. 323-9.

Reportedly, Dr. James Frost frequently disagreed with some of Starrs' methods and central findings. Frost was also the medical examiner on the controversial "suicide" death of investigative writer Danny Casalaro.

Dorothy Kilgallen: Kilgallen died in her New York City apartment on November 8, 1965, reportedly from a lethal mix of alcohol and drugs: Nembutal, Secobarbitol, Amobarbital, and Pentobarbital. According to some reports, she was murdered because of her knowledge about secret details involving the assassination of JFK and the CIA's mind control experiments.

Covert, Norman, *Cutting Edge: The History of Fort Detrick*, Chapter 8, End of an Era, U.S. Army Chemical Corps, Fort Detrick.

CNN News Transcript on Frank Olson Case, March 1999, General Media, New York.

Transcript of Dr. James Starrs' interview with Dr. Robert Gibson, December 21, 1994, Sheppard Pratt Institute, Baltimore, Maryland.

Email correspondence and information sent to the author from Harry Huge, Esq., Washington, D.C., 1999-2001.

Prepared Testimony of Eric Wicks Olson, Ph.D. before the House Committee on Government Operations, Federal Information Systems Corp., Federal News Service, September 28, 1994.

"Who Killed Frank Olson?" Article by Stephanie Pain, *New Scientist* magazine, July 1997, p. 35-37.

"Digging for New Evidence," article by Brian Mooar, *Washington Post*, June 3, 1994, p. A1-D6.

Reexamining a Body of Evidence: Frank Olson Exhumed, article by John Kelly, *Unclassified* magazine, June-July-August 1994, p. 8.

"Frank Olson File: The CIA's Bad Trip," article by Melissa Roth, *George* magazine, October 1997, p. 44.

"Early Tests Contradict '53 Claim of Researcher Suicide," article by Brian Mooar, *Washington Post*, July 12, 1994, p. A1, B8.

Starrs did not explain during the course of his investigation why he did not seek to interview other persons in his overall inquiry, especially those who were still alive and had attended the gathering at Deep Creek Lake, an event central to any complete investigation of the Olson case. When this author posed the question to Starrs, he did not respond.

Notes on Book Five, Chapter 6

Author's chronological file of written, telephone, and e-mail correspondence with Eric Olson, Steve Saracco, Daniel Bibb, Harry Huge, Esq., Allison Scaloppini, Esq., and Rich Medway, Esq. 1997-2006.

Privileged and Confidential Work Product Memorandum to Robert M. Morgenthau, Esq., New York District Attorney, from Harry Huge, Esq., Powell, Goldstein, Frazer & Murphy, Washington, D.C., May 12, 1995.

FBI Security Report, file no. 116-10740, Baltimore, Maryland office, Subject: Frank Rudolph Olson, WA-11568, December 12, 1949; Department of Army, Security Report on Frank R. Olson, by Special Agent David E. Kelly, 113th CIC Det. Army, March 19, 1948; U.S. Army Dossier No. X-866030, 3 July 1975, Frank R. Olson.

Rudolph Halley: Special thanks to *New York Daily News* writer Owen Moritz for details about Halley's life and death.

Deposition of Robert Vern Lashbrook, United States District Court for the District of Columbia, *Mrs. David Orlikow, et al vs. United States of America*, Civil Action No. 80-3163, Ventura, California, Wednesday, May 14, 1986.

Harry Huge's office queried the CIA in November 1998 about Dr. Sargant, asking for "all information at the CIA related to Dr. William Sargant [sic] from January 1, 1953 to the date of this FOIA request." The CIA responded in writing that by law it could not release information or documents concerning foreign nationals.

Woolsey and Lapham: Anthony Lapham died at age 70 in November 2006. He suffered a heart attack while fishing, his son reported. Lapham played a major role for the CIA, beginning in June 1976, by apologizing for the Agency's mind control research on campuses across the nation. The *New York Times* has reported that in March 1977, Lapham sent a memorandum to members of Congress and policy makers "urging care in rewriting laws governing intelligence leaks." He pointed out that the phrase 'information relating to national intelligence' could mean vital military secrets or something as simple as daily stock market reports. He also argued for precision in defining who and what the law should cover, and for "prompt and independent review of any questions raised." Lapham, as a private attorney, represented Adolfo Calero, leader of the Nicaraguan Democratic Force, a contra group, and the chief paymaster for the brutal government of Charles Taylor, past Liberian president. James Woolsey, Jr. reportedly was to be John McCain's Secretary of Energy, had McCain been elected. Woolsey once joked, "Remember the guy who in 1994 crashed his plane onto the White House lawn? That was me trying to get an appointment to see President Clinton." There is little known about his tenure as DCI from 1993 to 1995, but within hours of the September 11, 2001 attacks, Woolsey appeared on television suggesting that Iraq was involved. Woolsey also later claimed, without offering any evidence, that Iraq was involved in the bombing of the Oklahoma Federal Building, a crime for which Timothy McVeigh was executed.

David Belin's death: "David W. Belin, Warren Commission Lawyer, Dies at 70" by Eric Pace, *New York Times*, January 18, 1999.

James Forrestal letter to President Harry Truman, March 16, 1948, Eisenhower Papers, 1916-52, Box 113, Folder: War Council.

Colby, William and Forbath, Peter, *Honorable Men: My Life in the CIA*, Simon and Schuster, New York, 1978.

Eric Olson, email message to Courtney Bullock, ABC Television, New York, May 24, 2001, with attached: "CIA Diary: Sighting the Loch Ness Monster (Notes on meeting with my father's old colleague," Eric Olson, May 16-19, 2001; Susannah McCorkle's death: *New York Times*, article by Stephen Holden, May 20, 2001; and *Washington Post* obituary, May 19, 2001.

Ronson, Jon, *The Men Who Stare at Goats,* Simon and Schuster, New York, 2004.

Thomas, Gordon, *Secrets and Lies*, Octavo Editions, Connecticut, 2007. Many of Thomas's claims in this book seriously challenge the credulity of his loyal readers. Additionally, many of his claims, besides being wrong in this author's view, are unsupported by any documentation or cited sources.

Sargant, William, *Battle for the Mind*, Malor Books, ISHK, Cambridge, Mass., 1997; and Sargant, William, *The Unquiet Mind*, Pan Books Ltd., London, UK, 1967.

Letter from George Hunter White to Garland Williams, October 23, 1954, Perham Foundation, Sunnyvale, California. The letter to Williams was one of 14 copies of letters to Williams from White. This was the only one of the 14 that mentioned Frank "Olsen" [sic]. Alice Olson's telephone number was in White's date book for 1954, author's files.

CIA review of Gordon Thomas's book *Secrets & Lies*: CIA's official website: https:// www.cia.gov/library/ center-for-the-styudy-of-intelligence/csi-publications/csi-studies.

Michael Ignatieff: A few weeks after Ignatieff wrote his *New York Times* article advocating torture, the Abu Ghraib photos were published. Ignatieff, presumably shocked into reality by the starkness of the photos, reversed himself and criticized American lawyers (an indirect reference to torture advocate Alan Dershowitz) saying, rather disingenuously: "Enthralled by narcissism and deluded by servility, American lawyers forgot their own Constitution and its preemptory prohibition of cruel and unusual punishment."

In June 2002, a woman I did not know wrote to me, saying, "You probably never would think how much Eric Olson, a Harvard trained psychologist, hates you for withholding the 'smoking gun' from him for years." The email message, addressed to "Mr. Albarelli," continued: "Eric knows how crucial what you have is to his potential millions of dollars lawsuit against the U.S. government, though his attorney has been presently quitting his case after being fed up with him. To Eric, suing the CIA to get another big payoff from the government is the only way for him to get rich in addition to paying off all his big debt so he can always lie on the beach year after year, stay in hotels all the time, take vacation after vacation, buy all kinds of luxury cars." The woman, I soon learned, had been romantically involved with Eric for about a year. She was a Chinese citizen, who was working in the Washington, D.C. area as a schoolteacher, who remarkably had my nephew as one of her students. Perhaps coincidentally, when I first met Eric in person, he was dating another teacher from the same school, who had worked in Japan for the nephew of a very good friend of mine. The Chinese woman continued her communication a few days later: "Eric relies his whole life on his father's case.... He wants the hardworking tax dollars of others to support the luxury he's been longing for... he hates you, hates Mr. Huge, hates Steve Saracco. He thinks all you people didn't help him and all have your motivations and agenda. He suspects Steve Saracco works for the CIA; Mr. Huge would not do the case since it's just like suing his own friends... He called you a jerk, a psychotic, a CIA man pretending to write a book." The message went on at length revealing a deep understanding of the case and many of its primary players, including several developments never before publicly revealed. The information could have come only from Eric, and I was at once hurt and angered by the disclosure. I asked Eric about the woman. He replied that neither she nor her message were worth talking about. I forwarded the woman's message to Eric (I asked her first if she had any problem with my doing so), asking him about it, and his only reply was: "Not worth comment on." The brusque message was one of the very last I was to receive from Eric. The incident altered our relationship, which had become increasingly tenuous as a result of all the pressure Eric was under.

Robert A. Maheu: Interviews with Maheu by investigative writer John Kelly, 1999-2000; author's interview with former intelligence official H. F. O'Neill; Memorandum for Director of Central Intelligence on Rosselli, Johnny, 19 November 1970; CIA-OS File #111540 on Robert Maheu, 3 June 1971; CIA EYES ONLY, Subject: Robert Maheu, Oct. 4, 1973; FBI Files on Robert A. Maheu, 1957-58; Bryan Smith, How the CIA Enlisted the Chicago Mob to Put a Hit on Castro, Chicago Magazine, November 2007. Also see: Denton, Sally and Morris, Roger. The Money and the Power: The Making of Las Vegas and Its Hold on America, 1947-2000. New York: Alfred A. Knopf, 2001.

Maheu suit and Howard Hughes: The New York Times, Thursday, May 16, 1974.

Det. Lt. Arthur E. Schultheiss: Interesting to note is that Schultheiss served as a "technical advisor" on two Frank Sinatra films, 1968's The Detective and 1980's The First Deadly Sin.

A cutout company is generally created—or purchased—at the direction of the Agency so as to appear privately owned and controlled by someone or something other than the CIA. There are an estimated 8,000 CIA front or cutout companies, small and large, based in the United States alone.

Allan Hughes: Hughes' first name has been either mistakenly or intentionally misspelled in several government documents; Deposition of Sidney Gottlieb, Orlikow v USA, Civil Action No. 80-3163, Tuesday, April 19, 1983, Culpepper, Virginia; Block, Alan A., Perspectives on Organizing Crime: Essays In Opposition, Kluwer Academic Publishers, The Netherlands, 1991, pp. 150-169; Hougan, Jim, Spooks, The Haunting of America-The Private Use of Secret Agents, William Morrow & Co., NY, 1978, p. 350; FBI reports on Hughes: FBI Interview Report on Robert A. Maheu, 1957, WFO-PJM: KAM p. 40-48, courtesy of Alan A. Block.

Dr. Benjamin Wilson: On February 6 and 21, 1978, Wilson was interviewed for John Marks' book, The Search for the Manchurian Candidate: The CIA and Mind Control. Investigative writer John Kelly provided copies of the interviews to this author after Kelly's interview with Marks in 1999. The author interviewed Wilson in 1999-2000. Wilson initially refused several times to be interviewed, but after the author emailed his former attorney, James Neal, to which Neal never replied, Wilson relented, agreeing to "answer a few questions."

SOD-CIA compound: Memorandum dated May 29, 1957, from University of Maryland to J. Edgar Hoover, Director FBI; Letter dated June 4, 1957 from J. Edgar Hoover, Director FBI to Department of Pharmacology, University of Maryland; Letter dated July 6, 1957, from SAC Baltimore to Director FBI; Letter dated July 23, 1957 to J. Edgar Hoover from Ohio Chemical & Surgical Equipment Co.; Letter dated July 29, 1957 to Ohio Chemical & Surgical Equipment Co. from J. Edgar Hoover, FBI Director; interview with Dr. Benjamin Wilson, 2000; confidential interviews with former Chemical Corps scientists, Baltimore, Maryland and Seattle, Washington.

Coen, Bob and Nadler, Eric, Dead Silence: Fear and Terror on the Anthrax Trail, Counterpoint Books, Berkeley, CA, 2009

Notes on Appendix One:

Letter dated November 2, 1977 from CIA Assistant General Counsel to John Gavin, Esq., Office of Legal Counsel, U.S. Department of Justice, Washington, D.C. Approved for release by the CIA in October 1991, author's files.

Author's interviews with "Sally Hartman," June 2000, Florida.

Index

T

825

Since 1954, the world's most powerful people have met in secret once a year ... until now!

The True Story of THE **Bilderberg Group**

DANIEL ESTULIN

UPDATED, REVISED AND EXPANDED
NORTH AMERICAN UNION EDITION

The True Story of the Bilderberg Group
BY DANIEL ESTULIN

More than a center of influence, the Bilderberg Group is a shadow world government, hatching plans of domination at annual meetings ... and under a cone of media silence.

THE TRUE STORY OF THE BILDERBERG GROUP goes inside the secret meetings and sheds light on why a group of politicians, businessmen, bankers and other mighty individuals formed the world's most powerful society. As Benjamin Disraeli, one of England's greatest Prime Ministers, noted, "The world is governed by very different personages from what is imagined by those who are not behind the scenes."

Included are unpublished and never-before-seen photographs and other documentation of meetings, as this riveting account exposes the past, present and future plans of the Bilderberg elite.

Softcover: **$24.95** (ISBN: 9780979988622) • 432 pages • Size: 6 x 9

Dr. Mary's Monkey
How the Unsolved Murder of a Doctor, a Secret Laboratory in New Orleans and Cancer-Causing Monkey Viruses are Linked to Lee Harvey Oswald, the JFK Assassination and Emerging Global Epidemics
BY EDWARD T. HASLAM, FOREWORD BY JIM MARRS

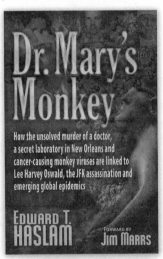

Dr. Mary's Monkey

How the unsolved murder of a doctor, a secret laboratory in New Orleans and cancer-causing monkey viruses are linked to Lee Harvey Oswald, the JFK assassination and emerging global epidemics

EDWARD T. HASLAM   FORWARD BY JIM MARRS

Evidence of top-secret medical experiments and cover-ups of clinical blunders
The 1964 murder of a nationally known cancer researcher sets the stage for this gripping exposé of medical professionals enmeshed in covert government operations over the course of three decades. Following a trail of police records, FBI files, cancer statistics, and medical journals, this revealing book presents evidence of a web of medical secret-keeping that began with the handling of evidence in the JFK assassination and continued apace, sweeping doctors into cover-ups of cancer outbreaks, contaminated polio vaccine, the genesis of the AIDS virus, and biological weapon research using infected monkeys.

Softcover: **$19.95** (ISBN: 0977795306) • 320 pages • Size: 5 1/2 x 8 1/2

The Oil Card
Global Economic Warfare in the 21st Century
BY JAMES NORMAN

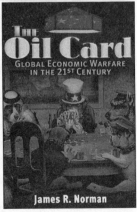

The **Oil Card**
GLOBAL ECONOMIC WARFARE IN THE 21ST CENTURY

James R. Norman

Challenging the conventional wisdom surrounding high oil prices, this compelling argument sheds an entirely new light on free-market industry fundamentals.
By deciphering past, present, and future geopolitical events, it makes the case that oil pricing and availability have a long history of being employed as economic weapons by the United States. Despite ample world supplies and reserves, high prices are now being used to try to rein in China—a reverse of the low-price strategy used in the 1980s to deprive the Soviets of hard currency. Far from conspiracy theory, the debate notes how the US has previously used the oil majors, the Saudis, and market intervention to move markets—and shows how this is happening again.

Softcover **$14.95** (ISBN 0977795390) • 288 PAGES • Size: 5.5 x 8.5

The Franklin Scandal
A Story of Powerbrokers, Child Abuse & Betrayal
BY NICK BRYANT

A chilling exposé of corporate corruption and government cover-ups, this account of a nationwide child-trafficking and pedophilia ring tells a sordid tale of corruption in high places. The scandal originally surfaced during an investigation into Omaha, Nebraska's failed Franklin Federal Credit Union and took the author beyond the Midwest and ultimately to Washington, DC. Implicating businessmen, senators, major media corporations, the CIA, and even the venerable Boys Town organization, this extensively researched report includes firsthand interviews with key witnesses and explores a controversy that has received scant media attention.

The Franklin Scandal is the story of a underground ring that pandered children to a cabal of the rich and powerful. The ring's pimps were a pair of Republican powerbrokers who used Boys Town as a pedophiliac reservoir, and had access to the highest levels of our government and connections to the CIA.

Nick Bryant is a journalist whose work largely focuses on the plight of disadvantaged children in the United States. His mainstream and investigative journalism has been featured in *Gear, Playboy, The Reader*, and on Salon.com. He is the coauthor of *America's Children: Triumph of Tragedy*. He lives in New York City.

Hardcover: **$24.95** (ISBN:0977795357)•676pages•Size:6x9

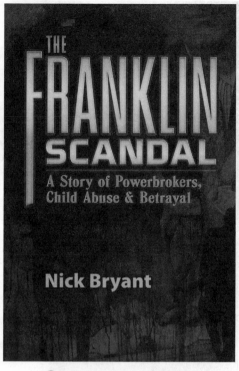

The Strength of the Pack
The Personalities, Politics and Espionage Intrigues that Shaped the DEA
BY DOUG VALENTINE

Through interviews with former narcotics agents, politicians, and bureaucrats, this exposé documents previously unknown aspects of the history of federal drug law enforcement from the formation of the Bureau of Narcotics and Dangerous Drugs and the creation of the Drug Enforcement Administration (DEA) up until the present day. Written in an easily accessible style, the narrative examines how successive administrations expanded federal drug law enforcement operations at home and abroad; investigates how the CIA comprised the war on drugs; analyzes the Reagan, Bush, and Clinton administrations' failed attempts to alter the DEA's course; and traces the agency's evolution into its final and current stage of "narco-terrorism."

Douglas Valentine is a former private investigator and consultant and the author of *The Hotel Tacloban, The Phoenix Program, The Strength of the Wolf*, and *TDY*.

Softcover: **$24.95** (ISBN:9780979988653)•480pages•Size:6x9

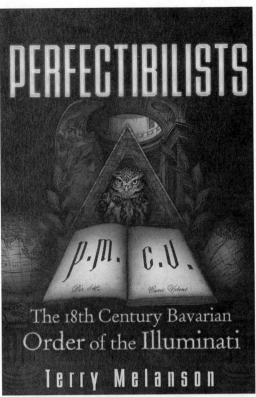

PERFECTIBILISTS
The 18th Century Bavarian Illuminati
BY TERRY MELANSON

The shadowy Illuminati grace many pages of fiction as the sinister all-powerful group pulling the strings behind the scenes, but very little has been printed in English about the actual Enlightenment-era secret society, its activities, its members, and its legacy ... until now.

First choosing the name Perfectibilists, their enigmatic leader Adam Weishaupt soon thought that sounded too bizarre and changed it to the Order of the Illuminati.

Presenting an authoritative perspective, this definitive study chronicles the rise and fall of the fabled Illuminati, revealing their methods of infiltrating governments and education systems, and their blueprint for a successful cabal, which echoes directly forward through groups like the Order of Skull & Bones to our own era.

Featuring biographies of more than 400 confirmed members and copiously illustrated, this book brings light to a 200-year-old mystery.

Softcover: **$19.95** (ISBN: 9780977795381) • 530 pages • Size: 6 x 9

PARADISE LOST?
HIGH-SPEED TRAINS GET WAYLAID, SHADY POLITICIANS GET BILLIONS AND TAXPAYERS GET THE SHAFT!

BY RICHARD TRAINOR.

Reminiscent of a detective novel, this political exposé explores the corruption of some of the richest and most powerful political figures in California. From Mayor Willie Brown, Senator Dianne Feinstein, and a 50-billion-dollar insider-trading scandal to whistle blowers, phantom high-speed trains, and unbridled greed, this investigation details the complex history of California's public works projects that were promised and commissioned, but never built. From a Bay Bridge addition that never materialized to the San Francisco airport expansion that disappeared, this hard-hitting look at the Golden State's political shenanigans outlines the slimy details behind massive pump-and-dump schemes that have plagued progress in the state. With direct parallels to the corruption that inspired the films *Chinatown* and *The Two Jakes*, this investigation reveals how money and relationships have played into a slick political game in recent California history.

Richard Trainor is the author of *Sacramento: The Heart of California: A Contemporary Portrait*. He has contributed to *Elle*, the *Los Angeles Times*, the *Sacramento Bee*, *The Saturday Review*, *Sight & Sound*, and the *Vancouver Sun*. He is a former capitol bureau correspondent for *California* magazine and a former managing editor of *France Today* magazine.

Softcover • $24.95 • ISBN 978-0-9799886-4-6 • 384 pages

Expendable Elite
One Soldier's Journey into Covert Warfare
BY DANIEL MARVIN , FOREWORD BY MARTHA RAYE

A special operations perspective on the Viet Nam War and the truth about a White House concerned with popular opinion

This true story of a special forces officer in Viet Nam in the mid-1960s exposes the unique nature of the elite fighting force and how covert operations are developed and often masked to permit—and even sponsor—assassination, outright purposeful killing of innocents, illegal use of force, and bizarre methods in combat operations. *Expendable Elite* reveals the fear that these warriors share with no other military person: not fear of the enemy they have been trained to fight in battle, but fear of the wrath of the US government should they find themselves classified as "expendable." This book centers on the CIA mission to assassinate Cambodian Crown Prince Nordum Sihanouk, the author's unilateral aborting of the mission, the CIA's dispatch of an ARVN regiment to attack and destroy the camp and kill every person in it as retribution for defying the agency, and the dramatic rescue of eight American Green Berets and hundreds of South Viet Namese.

—NEW SPECIAL VICTORY EDITION— Commemorating our Free Speech Federal Court triumph that allows you to read this book exposing the true ways of war!

—READ THE BOOK,"THEY" DON'T WANT YOU TO!—

DANIEL MARVIN is a retired Lieutenant Colonel in the US Army Special Forces and former Green Beret.
Softcover: **$19.95** (ISBN 0977795314) • 420 pages • 150+ photos & maps

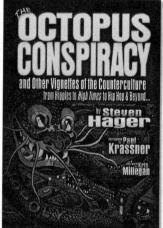

The Octopus Conspiracy
and Other Vignettes of the Counterculture from Hippies to High Times to Hip Hop and Beyond ...
BY STEVEN HAGER

Insightful essays on the genesis of subcultures from new wave and yuppies to graffiti and rap.

From the birth of hip-hop culture in the South Bronx to the influence of nightclubs in shaping the modern art world in New York, a generation of countercultural events and icons are brought to life in this personal account of the life and experiences of a former investigative reporter and editor of High Times. Evidence from cutting-edge conspiracy research including the real story behind the JFK assassination and the Franklin Savings and Loan cover-up is presented. Quirky personalities and compelling snapshots of life in the 1980s and 1990s emerge in this collection of vignettes from a landmark figure in journalism.

STEVEN HAGER is the author of *Adventures in Counterculture, Art After Midnight,* and *Hip Hop.* He is a former reporter for the New York Daily News and an editor of *High Times.*

Hardcover: **$19.95** (ISBN 0975290614) • 320 pages • Size: 6 x 9

Fixing America
Breaking the Stranglehold of Corporate Rule, Big Media, and the Religious Right
BY JOHN BUCHANAN, FOREWORD BY JOHN MCCONNELL

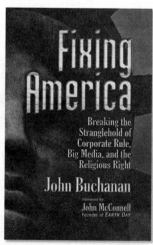

An explosive analysis of what ails the United States

An award-winning investigative reporter provides a clear, honest diagnosis of corporate rule, big media, and the religious right in this damning analysis. Exposing the darker side of capitalism, this critique raises alarms about the security of democracy in today's society, including the rise of the corporate state, the insidious role of professional lobbyists, the emergence of religion and theocracy as a right-wing political tactic, the failure of the mass media, and the sinister presence of an Orwellian neo-fascism.
Softcover: **$19.95**, (ISBN 0-975290681) 216 Pages, 5.5 x 8.5

ORDER BY ONLINE OR BY PHONE:
TrineDay.com
1-800-556-2012

THE 9/11 MYSTERY PLANE
AND THE VANISHING OF AMERICA

BY MARK GAFFNEY

FOREWORD BY

DR. DAVID RAY GRIFFIN

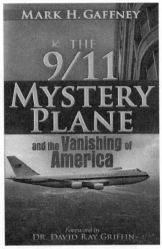

Unlike other accounts of the historic attacks on 9/11, this discussion surveys the role of the world's most advanced military command and control plane, the E-4B, in the day's events and proposes that the horrific incidents were the work of a covert operation staged within elements of the US military and the intelligence community. Presenting hard evidence, the account places the world's most advanced electronics platform circling over the White House at approximately the time of the Pentagon attack. The argument offers an analysis of the new evidence within the context of the events and shows that it is irreconcilable with the official 9/11 narrative.

Mark H. Gaffney is an environmentalist, a peace activist, a researcher, and the author of *Dimona, the Third Temple?*; and *Gnostic Secrets of the Naassenes*. He lives in Chiloquin, Oregon. Dr. David Ray Griffin is a professor emeritus at the Claremont School of Theology, and the author of *The 9/11 Commission Report: Omissions and Distortions*, and *The New Pearl Harbor*. He lives in Santa Barbara, California.

Softcover • $19.95 • ISBN 9780979988608 • 336 Pages

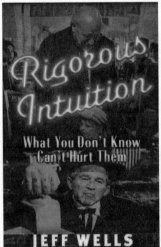

Rigorous Intuition
What You Don't Know, Can't Hurt Them
BY JEFF WELLS

"In Jeff's hands, tinfoil hats become crowns and helmets of the purest gold. I strongly suggest that you all pay attention to what he has to say."
—Arthur Gilroy, Booman Tribune

A welcome source of analysis and commentary for those prepared to go deeper—and darker—than even most alternative media permit, this collection from one of the most popular conspiracy theory arguments on the internet will assist readers in clarifying their own arguments and recognizing disinformation. Tackling many of the most difficult subjects that define our time—including 9/11, the JonBenet Ramsey case, and "High Weirdness"—these studies, containing the best of the Rigorous Intuition blog as well as original content, make connections that both describe the current, alarming predicament and suggest a strategy for taking back the world. Following the maxim "What you don't know can't hurt them," this assortment of essays and tools, including the updated and expanded "Coincidence Theorists' Guide to 9/11," guides the intellectually curious down further avenues of study and scrutiny and helps readers feel empowered rather than vulnerable.

Jeff Wells is the author of the novel *Anxious Gravity*. He lives in Toronto, Ontario.

Softcover • $19.95 • 978-0-9777953-2-1 • 505 Pages

Fighting For G.O.D.
(Gold, Oil, Drugs)
BY JEREMY BEGIN, ART BY LAUREEN SALK

This racehorse tour of American history and current affairs scrutinizes key events transcending the commonly accepted liberal/conservative political ideologies — in a large-size comic-book format.

This analysis delves into aspects of the larger framework into which 9/11 fits and scrutinizes the ancestry of the players who transcend commonly accepted liberal/conservative political ideologies. This comic-book format analysis examines the Neo Con agenda and its relationship to "The New World Order. This book discusses key issues confronting America's citizenry and steps the populace can take to not only halt but reverse the march towards totalitarianism.

Jeremy Begin is a long-time activist/organizer currently residing in California's Bay Area. Lauren Salk is an illustrator living in Boston.

Softcover: **$9.95**, (ISBN 0977795330) 64 Pages, 8.5 x 11

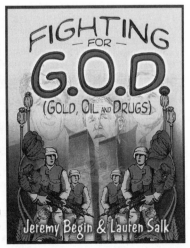

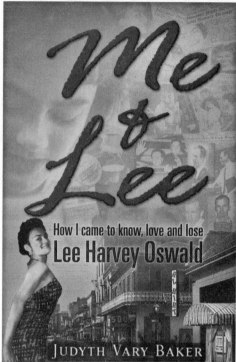

Me & Lee
HOW I CAME TO KNOW, LOVE AND LOSE LEE HARVEY OSWALD
BY JUDYTH VARY BAKER

FOREWORD BY

EDWARD T. HASLAM

JUDYTH VARY WAS ONCE A PROMISING science student who dreamed of finding a cure for cancer; this exposé is her account of how she strayed from a path of mainstream scholarship at the University of Florida to a life of espionage in New Orleans with Lee Harvey Oswald. In her narrative she offers extensive documentation on how she came to be a cancer expert at such a young age, the personalities who urged her to relocate to New Orleans, and what lead to her involvement in the development of a biological weapon that Oswald was to smuggle into Cuba to eliminate Fidel Castro. Details on what she knew of Kennedy's impending assassination, her conversations with Oswald as late as two days before the killing, and her belief that Oswald was a deep-cover intelligence agent who was framed for an assassination he was actually trying to prevent, are also revealed.

JUDYTH VARY BAKER is a former secretary, teacher, and artist. Edward T. Haslam is the author of *Dr. Mary's Monkey*. He lives in Florida.

Hardcover • $24.95 • ISBN 9780979988677 • 480 Pages

ORDER BY ONLINE OR BY PHONE:
TrineDay.com

Mary's Mosaic
MARY PINCHOT MEYER & JOHN F. KENNEDY AND THEIR VISION FOR WORLD PEACE
BY PETER JANNEY

FOREWORD BY DICK RUSSELL

CHALLENGING THE CONVENTIONAL WISDOM surrounding the murder of Mary Pinchot Meyer, this exposé offers new information and evidence that individuals within the upper echelons of the CIA were not only involved in the assassination of President John F. Kennedy, but her demise as well. Written by the son of a CIA lifer and a college classmate of Mary Pinchot Meyer, this insider's story examines how Mary used events and circumstances in her personal life to become an acolyte for world peace. The most famous convert to her philosophy was reportedly President John F. Kennedy, with whom she was said to have begun a serious love relationship in January 1962. Offering an insightful look into the era and its culture, the narrative sheds light on how in the wake of the Cuban Missile Crisis, she helped the president realize that a Cold War mentality was of no use and that the province of world peace was the only worthwhile calling. Details on her experiences with LSD, its influences on her and Kennedy's thinking, his attempts to negotiate a limited nuclear test ban treaty with Soviet Premier Nikita Khrushchev, and to find lasting peace with Fidel Castro are also included.

—Available 2010—

Peter Janney is a former psychologist and naturopathic healer and a cofounder of the American Mental Health Alliance. He was one of the first graduates of the MIT Sloan School of Management's Entrepreneurship Skills Transfer Program. He lives in Beverly, Massachusetts. Dick Russell is the author of *Black Genius: And the American Experience*, *Eye of the Whale*, *The Man Who Knew Too Much*, and *Striper Wars: An American Fish Story*. He is a former staff writer for *TV Guide* magazine, a staff reporter for *Sports Illustrated*, and has contributed numerous articles to publications ranging from *Family Health* to the *Village Voice*. He lives in Boston, Massachusetts and Los Angeles.

Hardcover • $24.95 • ISBN 978-0-9799886-3-9 • 480 Pages

ShadowMasters

BY DANIEL ESTULIN

AN INTERNATIONAL NETWORK OF GOVERNMENTS AND SECRET-SERVICE AGENCIES WORKING TOGETHER WITH DRUGS DEALERS AND TERRORISTS FOR MUTUAL BENEFIT AND PROFIT

THIS INVESTIGATION EXAMINES HOW behind-the-scenes collaboration between government, intelligence services, and drug traffickers has lined the pockets of big business and Western banks. Among the examples cited are the cozy relationship between Victor Bout, the largest weaponry dealer in the world, and George Bush's administration; the NGOs who are plundering Darfur with the help of big multinationals seeking to take over the oilfields around the country; the ties that the Muslim Brotherhood maintains with the White House despite their involvement with the March 11th attacks in Madrid; and the embezzlement of more than $2.8 million from the International Monetary Fund by Roman Abramovich, the biggest oligarch in Russia.

DANIEL ESTULIN is an award-winning investigative journalist and author of *The True Story of the Bilderberg Group*.

Softcover: **$24.95** (ISBN: 9780979988615) • 432 pages • Size: 6 x 9

Radical Peace

BY WILLIAM HATHAWAY

REFUSING WAR

THIS SYMPHONY OF VOICES—a loosely united network of war resisters, deserters, and peace activists in Afghanistan, Europe, Iraq, and North America—vividly recounts the actions they have personally taken to end war and create a peaceful society. Frustrated, angered, and even saddened by the juggernaut of aggression that creates more counter-violence at every turn, this assortment of contributors has moved beyond demonstrations and petitions into direct, often radical actions in defiance of the government's laws to impede its capacity to wage war. Among the stories cited are those of a European peace group that assisted a soldier in escaping from military detention and then deserting; a U.S.-educated Iraqi who now works in Iran developing cheaper and smaller heat-seeking missiles to shoot down U.S. aircraft after U.S. soldiers brutalized his family; a granny for peace who found young allies in her struggle against military recruiting; a seminary student who, having been roughed up by U.S. military at a peace demonstration, became a military chaplain and subverts from within; and a man who expresses his resistance through the destruction of government property—most often by burning military vehicles.

WILLIAM T. HATHAWAY is a political journalist and a former Special Forces soldier turned peace activist whose articles have appeared in more than 40 publications, including *Humanist*, the *Los Angeles Times*, *Midstream Magazine*, and *Synthesis/Regeneration*. He is an adjunct professor of American studies at the University of Oldenburg in Germany, and the author of *A World of Hurt, CD-Ring*, and *Summer Snow*.

Softcover: **$14.95** (ISBN: 9780979988691) •240 pages • Size: 5.5 x 8.5

America's Secret Establishment
An Introduction to the Order of Skull & Bones
BY ANTONY C. SUTTON

The book that first exposed the story behind America's most powerful secret society
For 170 years they have met in secret. From out of their initiates come presidents, senators, judges, cabinet secretaries, and plenty of spooks. This intriguing behind-the-scenes look documents Yale's secretive society, the Order of the Skull and Bones, and its prominent members, numbering among them Tafts, Rockefellers, Pillsburys, and Bushes. Far from being a campus fraternity, the society is more concerned with the success of its members in the post-collegiate world.

Softcover: **$19.95** (ISBN 0972020748) 335 pages

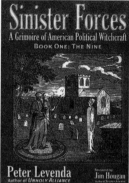

Sinister Forces
A Grimoire of American Political Witchcraft
Book One: The Nine
BY PETER LEVENDA, FOREWORD BY JIM HOUGAN

A shocking alternative to the conventional views of American history.
The roots of coincidence and conspiracy in American politics, crime, and culture are examined in this book, exposing new connections between religion, political conspiracy, and occultism. Readers are taken from ancient American civilization and the mysterious mound builder culture to the Salem witch trials, the birth of Mormonism during a ritual of ceremonial magic by Joseph Smith, Jr., and Operations Paperclip and Bluebird. Not a work of speculative history, this exposé is founded on primary source material and historical documents. Fascinating details are revealed, including the bizarre world of "wandering bishops" who appear throughout the Kennedy assassinations; a CIA mind control program run amok in the United States and Canada; a famous American spiritual leader who had ties to Lee Harvey Oswald in the weeks and months leading up to the assassination of President Kennedy; and the "Manson secret."

Hardcover: **$29.95** (ISBN 0975290622) • 396 pages • Size: 6 x 9

Book Two: A Warm Gun
The roots of coincidence and conspiracy in American politics, crime, and culture are investigated in this analysis that exposes new connections between religion, political conspiracy, terrorism, and occultism. Readers are provided with strange parallels between supernatural forces such as shamanism, ritual magic, and cult practices, and contemporary interrogation techniques such as those used by the CIA under the general rubric of MK-ULTRA. Not a work of speculative history, this exposé is founded on primary source material and historical documents. Fascinating details on Nixon and the "Dark Tower," the Assassin cult and more recent Islamic terrorism, and the bizarre themes that run through American history from its discovery by Columbus to the political assassinations of the 1960s are revealed.

Hardcover: **$29.95** (ISBN 0975290630) • 392 pages • Size: 6 x 9

Book Three: The Manson Secret
The Stanislavski Method as mind control and initiation. Filmmaker Kenneth Anger and Aleister Crowley, Marianne Faithfull, Anita Pallenberg, and the Rolling Stones. Filmmaker Donald Cammell (Performance) and his father, CJ Cammell (the first biographer of Aleister Crowley), and his suicide. Jane Fonda and Bluebird. The assassination of Marilyn Monroe. Fidel Castro's Hollywood career. Jim Morrison and witchcraft. David Lynch and spiritual transformation. The technology of sociopaths. How to create an assassin. The CIA, MK-ULTRA and programmed killers.

Hardcover: **$29.95** (ISBN 0975290649) • 422 pages • Size: 6 x 9